ANTIQUE MAP PRICE RECORD & HANDBOOK

FOR 1993

AMERICAE SIVE NOVI ORBIS, NOVA DESCRIPTIO.
ANIAN.
SEPTENTRIO.
QVIVIRA.
TOLM.
TOTO
TEAC.
MARATA.
CULIACAN.
CHILAGA.
SAGVENAI.
CANADA.
NOVA FRANCIA.
NORVMBEGA
ESTOTILANT
TERRA CORTEREALIS
CALICVAS.
CAPASCHI.
TERLICHICHIMECHI.
HISPANIA NOVA.
CVBA
HISPANIOLA
Las Açores
ARCHIPELAGO DI SAN LAZARO.
OCCIDENS.
MAR DEL SVR, quod
Circulus Æquinoctialis
et PACIFICVM
ORIENS.
Insulæ Salomonis.
NOVA GVINEA.
TERRA AVSTRALIS, SIVE MAGELLANICA HACTENVS INCOGNITA.
PERV.
Caribana
Amazones
Picora
BRESILIA
PARANA
CHARCAS
CHILI.
PATAGONES.
REGIO GIGANTVM
Rio de la Plata
Archipelago del C. desseado.
Golfo de S. Sebastiano
TERRA DEL FVEGO.
MERIDIES.

ANTIQUE MAP PRICE RECORD & HANDBOOK FOR 1993

Including SEA CHARTS, CITY VIEWS, CELESTIAL CHARTS and BATTLE PLANS

Compiled and edited
by
Jon K. Rosenthal

Amherst, Massachusetts
Kimmel Publications
1993

ISBN 0-9638100-0-6 ISSN 1070-8421

Library of Congress Catalog Card Number 83-139904

Printed in the United States of America

Volume 11

Volumes 1 and 2 appeared as *Antique Maps, Sea Charts, City Views, Celestial Charts & Battle Plans: Price Guide and Collectors' Handbook* (ISSN 0747-7597).

Volumes 3 through 10 appeared as *Antique Maps, Sea Charts, City Views, Celestial Charts & Battle Plans: Price Record & Handbook* (ISSN 0749-4971)

See advertisement at the end of this volume for ordering information. Orders, requests for information, communications to the editor and all other correspondence should be sent to:

Jon K. Rosenthal
Kimmel Publications
P.O. Box 12
Amherst, Massachusetts 01004, USA

WARNING!

Users of this work are warned that typographical errors may be present, and that prices for some items may not reflect the price that would be set by a majority of dealers. The publisher disclaims responsibility for any consequences of such errors and anomalies. Price information is given as an approximate guide to market values, and should be used with caution. An expert should always be consulted before making purchases or sales.

To David C. Jolly

His vision and his will

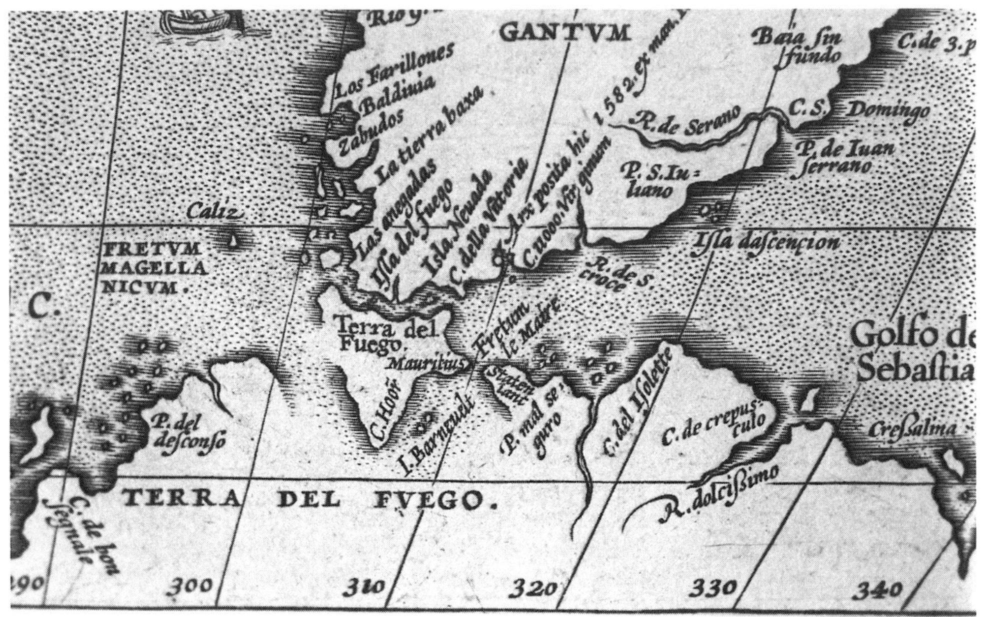

The frontispiece is a photograph of an Abraham Ortelius' map of *America* (circa 1628).

The illustration above is of a detail of the same map showing the island "Tierra del Fuego" and "Fretum le Maire". What is pictured is a rare variant of Ortelius' *America* showing Cape Horn and the Straits of Le Maire which were discovered by Schouten and Le Maire in their circumnavigation (1615-1617). Previous states of the map had Tierra Del Fuego unambiguously as part of a vast meridional continent. What appears as "Staten lant", a peninsula on the southern continent, is the modern "Staten Island", separated from larger Tierra del Fuego by the same Strait of Le Maire.

It was thought that the publication of Ortelius' contemporary maps ceased after 1612. (The final edition of the classical Perergon was issued in 1624.) However, according to the records in the Plantin Museum, in 1628 the engravers Ferdinand Arsenius and Arnold Floris van Langren were paid to update Ortelius' maps. Apparently, this major revision of the atlas never reached fruition, and only a few examples of these later maps are known. Schilder reports three copies of the variant *America*, plus recently another was found in a Spanish text edition of Ortelius' *Theatrum* at the Newberry Library, Chicago. Thus the photographs of the variant, which has a Spanish text verso, are of one of four recorded copies -- a rare map indeed!

References: Denuce, *Oud-Nederlandsche Kaartmakers in Betrekking met Plantin* (1912-13), II, 90, 244; Keuning, "The Van Langren Family" in *Imago Mundi* XIII (1956), 107; MCCS No. 34 (1967), 20 & Pl. XII (Ortelius' world map only); Schilder, *Monumenta Cartographica Neerlandica* (1993), III, 256-8; Weinreb + Douwma Ltd., *Catalog 7* (1971), # 2 (world map only).

Illustrations, discussion and references through the courtesy of George Ritzlin, Maps & Books, Highland Park, Illinois.

CONTENTS

PREFACE

Map collecting is a fascinating but little known avocation. The market is fragmented among specialists, rare book establishments, antique dealers and print sellers. The beginner is often at a loss as to where to turn for useful advice. Ten years ago, David C. Jolly stepped into the void and began publishing the annual which became *Antique Map Price Record & Handbook.*

Information on prices of old maps and charts is not easily obtained without maintaining an extensive file of dealer catalogues. This is seldom practical for the beginner or casual collector. Assembling and using such a file can be tedious. With this volume, over 52,000 entries have appeared since 1983. For the first time, the frequency of the appearance of maps by a particular map-maker has been tabulated so that entries are easy to find in back issues. Although primarily intended for map dealers and collectors, this book is also useful to those who encounter old maps occasionally in their business or as a collector. Institutions may find this work useful in making acquisitions, suggesting approximate valuations for donors and evaluating holdings. *Antique Map Price Record & Handbook* is a needed supplement to *American Book Prices Current* and *Bookman's Price Index* on the reference shelf.

With this volume, responsibility for publication of the annual edition passes to Kimmel Publications. We expect to maintain the high standards established by David Jolly. When improvements can be made, they will be undertaken cautiously and deliberately. In this regard, suggestions are always welcome.

ACKNOWLEDGMENTS

I could not have undertaken the task of producing the *Price Record* without a great deal of help and encouragement from many people. First and foremost I must acknowledge the contribution and assistance of David Jolly who has watched his baby grow up and leave home. As if it were a house warming present, George and Mary Ritzlin have graciously provided the frontispiece with the explanation and supplementary illustration, to say nothing of continuing reassurance. I am indebted to Thomas Aalund, of Trade Winds Gallery in Mystic, Connecticut for guiding me through catalogues in German. Ed Ayres of Cambridge, Massachusetts has helped wrestle with the essential and omnipresent computer programs. Thanks are due the dealers whose catalogues made this book possible. On each and every occasion in which I have been in contact with one or another of them, to check on a matter or just to chat, they have invariably been helpful and supportive. I can think of no finer group of people with whom to be associated professionally. Finally, I must express especial gratitude to my son, Alexander, for his patience and his optimism, and my beloved wife, Bernice Massé Rosenthal, who gave freely of her time and talent on every occasion to push this enterprise to completion.

Jon K. Rosenthal

On the occasion of the transition to a new compiler and publisher, I have been asked to contribute a few biographical remarks. After graduating from college, I began a career in scientific research, eventually rising to become one of the world's foremost authorities on bird droppings (see *Discover* magazine, May 1986, p.8-10). Unfortunately, the market for that type of expertise is quite limited. Casting about for something to do for a living that was more dependable and not too onerous, a map price record suggested itself, and with the help of a Radio Shack Model I computer, the *Price Record* was born.

I have found book publishing to be quite rewarding, and would like to take the opportunity to thank all those who have written with words of praise and encouragement. It is always gratifying when one's books are actually used and not left to gather dust on some bookshelf. My favorite example occurred when a library had been victimized by a stack thief who had cut maps from their British periodicals. He was apprehended, along with a stack of loose maps. The librarian thanked me for *Maps of America in Periodicals before 1800,* which had proven useful in returning maps to their rightful volumes. I later checked my records and found that the thief had ordered a copy of the *Price Record,* presumably to pick which maps to steal. I was quite pleased that my books were useful at both ends of this affair, and even considered advertising the *Price Record* as "the first choice of thieves," but decided not to push my luck. As a word to the wise, I have received several requests for free copies of the *Price Record* over the years from inmates in state penitentiaries who said that they planned to go into "the antique business" when released.

Having published the *Price Record* for ten years, it is time for me to step aside and let a fresher mind take up the task. It was not easy to find a successor with both map and computer expertise, but I have succeeded. I am confident that Jon Rosenthal will continue the *Price Record* with distinction.

David C. Jolly, July 1993

NEWS and COMMENT

The *Antique Map Price Record & Handbook* is alive and well. The major event of 1993 was the transfer of operations from David Jolly to Kimmel Publications, with Jon K. Rosenthal continuing as compiler and editor. We are gratified by the confidence in the new organization which David has expressed.

David Jolly *was* the *Price Record*. It was his concept. He drove it through from the idea to reality. He did it by himself for ten years. David set the standards. His discipline and rigor were uncompromising. It gives pause to a successor, at times bringing doubts as to whether the enterprise demands a mind set of a rare sort. Fortunately, his procedures and patterns have become sufficiently well established to be capable of emulation. The *Price Record* became an institution in David's hands.

David Jolly initiated the *Price Record* in the Dark Ages of personal computing. The first three editions were the product of a Tandy Radio Shack Model I running at 1.774 megahertz decked out with 48K of memory and no hard disk. From 1986 to 1991 he used another Tandy, the *2000* with a 80186 chip which came and went with a legacy similar to that of the 1936 Chrysler Air-Flow. Clearly, David Jolly went modern with his 386/25 Northgate for the '92 edition. But that's only part of the story. In the old days, software was primitive. His answer was to write his own. Some of it came with the transfer; we've adapted it to off-the-shelf software with which we are familiar. With the advent of the laser printer, the clickety-clack of the old dot-matrix was replaced with the 1985 edition.

Lest one misunderstand David's persona, it is only necessary to look over his own *News and Comment* sections over the years. Along with his dry, incisive wit, there is always an impatience with foolishness, whether the source were a certain bureaucratic establishment on which we all depend for delivery of the *Price Record* or the demoralizing and debilitating consequences of totalitarianism. We can confirm David's expertise on bird droppings and place his contribution into the context of ornithologically induced electrical outages. At last report he was headed back into the library, pushing forward on another of the cartobibliographies for which he is justly famous.

Changes This Year

The form of the *Price Record* has changed somewhat; the substance is unaltered. The title has been streamlined to *Antique Map Price Record & Handbook*. Nevertheless, it still includes *sea charts*, *city views*, *celestial charts* and *battle plans*. In fact, it now includes *globes* as well.

The sequence of sections has been changed, some have been consolidated, some have new titles and a couple have been omitted. For example, "News and Comments" has been moved forward. Since most of the "References Cited" are also *recommended*, they have been grouped together under "Recommended References". For the new arrangement, see "Contents".

A few thematic categories have been established in the "Price Listing." One is *Railroad Company Maps,* a new heading for maps showing the routes or proposed plans of particular railways. The reason for the change is to halt the proliferation of listings under individual lines and bring such comparable items under a single umbrella. *Local and State Government Maps* is another category intended to collect items published for governmental units below the national level, and infrequently offered for the same jurisdiction. A third new heading is *Real Estate and Promotional Maps,* a catch-all for an increasing number of like items seldom offered by the same enterprise or publisher. Finally, there has been a slight break with the past in providing first names or initials for some map-makers with the same surname, say, *Morse*, if it is helpful to make a distinction.

Dimensions in the "Price Listing" are now rounded to the nearest centimeter and the nearest half-inch. This degree of significance brings metric and English units into comparable levels of precision and avoids the illusion of greater accuracy which cannot be confirmed with confidence.

Statements of condition, previously limited to a summary of reported flaws, have been enlarged to include a brief positive word, if provided. It is done with some trepidation, however, since the buyer must determine for himself the meaning that each dealer gives to words such as *excellent*, *fine*, *very good*, *good*, *fair* and so forth. Even then, the term "excellent map" is fraught with ambiguity; does it mean "significant map" or "excellent condition". The time has probably arrived to establish some conventions about the condition of antique maps which can be widely underwritten.

Provision of a "Cumulative Frequency Distribution of Map-Makers" is an entirely new feature which will make it easy to find where particular map-makers appear in the "Price Listings" of all eleven volumes. Look for a name in the table and it will tell how many entries appeared in each year. Its a cinch!

United States dealers are cross-referenced by city and state. The itinerant dealer or collector can plan a rational trip, hopping from source to source. Best to phone ahead.

"Frequent Questions About This Book" may remain, even though the section has been eliminated to economize on space. We still make an effort to sample a wide range by including North American and European dealers, expensive and inexpensive maps, and well-known and smaller dealers so that the reader may draw his own conclusions. The *Price Record* is not advertising in disguise; instead, dealers whose catalogues are used receive a free copy of the book. Slightly different titles may still appear because the editor can not be certain that the dealer is not offering a little known variant. David Jolly's protocol of including initial fragments of names, such as *de*, *van* or *von*, has been continued. The customer list is confidential and is not divulged to any third part. Purchasers of the book from the publisher may expect to receive announcements of future editions of the price record.

Catalogues are rolling in for inclusion in Volume 12 in 1994. We are aiming for a publication date in late Spring. Dealers should submit their catalogues by December 31, 1993. In the preparation of catalogues, we suggest referral to "Dealers' Concerns" (Page 47). In the next volume we will make a special effort to include reference citations when provided by the dealer or if we can be certain of them ourselves.

Name Change News

Intra-national realignments continue to plague the "Geographical Index". David Jolly never did recognize the *U.S.S.R.* as a category for antique maps, so we were spared the need to include the *C.I.S.* (*Commonwealth of Independent States*, was it?) for even a year. But can we be sure where *Russia* ends and *Ukraine* begins. Should we use *Kazakhstan* or *Uzbekistan* or is it best to stick with *Tartary*? Fortunately, relative peace has prevailed in the former Soviet Union. Not so with Yugoslavia. We are horrified by the inhumanity which is exhibited! The world has barely had time to recall in Yugoslavia the names of *Serbia*, *Croatia* and *Bosnia* before beginning to worry about borders that will probably change within a year. Give Peace a Chance!

HOW TO USE THIS BOOK

This book is divided into six parts:

1. **Reference material.**
2. **Cumulative Frequency Distribution of Map-Makers**
3. **Main PRICE LISTING.**
4. **Title index to main price listing.**
5. **Geographical index to main price listing.**
6. **Currency conversion table and catalogue codes.**

Beginners might want to skim the reference material, reading any portions of interest. Others might want to glance at the book reviews to see if any new publications might be of interest. The core of the information is in the main Price Listing.

To look up an item, first see if any names appear on the map or view. If so, then try under that name in the main **Price Listing**. If not found there, then try the **Title Index**. If still not found, and if there were no entries in the main listing under the names on the map or view, then try the indexed **Cumulative Frequency Distribution** of Map-Makers to see if there were any entries under those names in past years.

There are a number of special categories for maps not involving personal names or names of private companies. These include: *Admiralty* [British]; *Anonymous*; *Depôt de la Marine* [French Admiralty]; *Dirreción Hidrografica* [Spanish Admiralty]; *Ordnance Survey*; *U.S.*; *U.S. Coast Survey*; *U.S. Exploring Expedition*; *U.S. Pacific R.R. Survey*; *U.S. State Surveys* [Surveyor General; General Land Office]. Maps from the various editions of Ptolemy's Geography are listed under Ptolemy, except for those by Sebastian Münster, which are listed under Münster.

Several categories have been established for maps printed in non-Roman letters, including: *Armenian Cartography, Chinese Cartography* and *Japanese Cartography*. Maps in Cyrillic characters are normally listed under their transliterated author and titles.

Beginning in 1993, some thematic categories have been initiated, such as *Railroad Company Maps*, *Local and State Government Maps* and *Real Estate and Promotional Maps*. Previously, "Railroad Maps" were listed under the individual rail line. Now, they have been collected into a single category of comparable items. Similarly, a scattering of maps by local governments and their officials, such as engineers and assessors, have been listed together. Maps with a local, commercial, land use purpose have been consolidated under the "Real Estate and Promotional" heading.

Entries in the main Price Listing appear in the following standard form:

CLUVER

SICILIAE ANTIQUAE DESCRIPTIO [1729] 26x32cm (10x13") Minor staining [99] £44 $60

The name in boldfaced type is the **MAP-MAKER**. Assigning an item to a particular name is somewhat arbitrary. For example, a map may have been surveyed by Smith, drawn by Jones, engraved by Black, published by White in an atlas edited by Brown, and then reissued in another atlas published by Green. There is no consistent standard for assigning a map to one of these names. The name assignments in this book generally follow custom. For example, maps from atlases published by Ortelius, the Blaeu family or Mathew Carey are usually assigned to Ortelius, Blaeu and Carey rather than to the name of a cartographer that might appear on the map itself. Cross references are provided to help locate maps that might appear under different names. Where more than one map is listed under the same name, the name is not repeated. Often first initials are omitted since in some cases they are not known, but when it is helpful to distinguish between different map-makers, they are provided when possible.

Next is the **TITLE**, given in upper-case letters. This is not as straightforward as it might seem. Some maps have two titles, frequently one in the top margin and the other in a cartouche. Others have two separate title cartouches, while others have the same title in several languages. Some maps have no titles at all, in which case a title is supplied in square brackets **[ ]**. Others have a jumble of words scattered about, from which some attempt may be made to extract a coherent title. In other cases a dealer might have paraphrased or abbreviated the title. Diacritical marks such as umlauts and accents are omitted here. Where appropriate, **U** and **V** are given in their intended form, for example, *NOUA* is transcribed as *NOVA*.

Next, in square brackets, is the **DATE**, which is usually the date given in the catalogue. This may be either the date of first appearance, or the date of actual publication of the map. A "c" (for *circa*) before the date indicates that the date is approximate. It is safest to regard most dates as approximate.

The **DIMENSIONS** are rounded to the nearest centimeter -- height first and width second -- followed, in parentheses, by dimensions to the closest half-inch. Dimensions are usually for the outer neat line, but in some cases may represent the plate mark size, or the paper size. A "c" before the dimensions indicates that the dimensions are approximate.

After the dimensions, in lower case, are any **COMMENTS**. These are usually condensed from the catalogue, and may include the source of the map, its condition, and other information. If provided, flaws and an indication of condition -- usually ranging from "mint" or "pristine" to "fair" and rarely "poor" -- are reported, with the caveat that in the antiquarian map trade there is little agreement as to the meaning of the terms. One dealer's "good" may be another dealer's "excellent", while the second dealer's "good" may actually mean "just good enough". Some dealers say nothing of condition; others issue a blanket statement covering an entire catalogue except as noted. In general, expansive laudatory comments are omitted.

Next, in square brackets, is the **CATALOGUE CODE** indicating where the map was offered for sale. The catalogue corresponding to the code number can be found at the end of the book.

Last is the **PRICE**, given in both pounds and dollars. The conversion rates at mid-year, used in computing the prices, are given at the end of the book. Note, however, that the volatility of relative currency values in the course of a year may significantly affect prices across borders. Although the same item may appear at different prices, it cannot be inferred that one is overpriced, or the other underpriced. Condition is extremely important and may not be adequately described in but a few words. For these reasons, prices should be regarded as an approximate guide. See the section, "Factors Affecting Value" (Page 8).

COLLECTORS' CONSIDERATIONS

It is easy to start collecting. One's interest may be piqued by a connection between an old map and the experience of a particular place through personal experience or study. The artistry of period cartography may arouse one's appreciation. A good starting point is with some of the more general books listed under "Recommended References" (Page 13) which provide a good overview of early cartography. Many of them can be found in the larger public libraries. Some of these are still in print or can be obtained from those map dealers who sell reference books.

In the meantime, write for a few catalogues. They can be quite educational, since many dealers present the context and detailed descriptions of the items offered for sale. Some dealers may charge a nominal fee for their catalogues to defray the printing and mailing costs. If you live near a dealer, you may wish to visit the establishment. An extensive listing appears in the "Directory of Dealers" (Page 50) which is cross-referenced by city and state for those in the United States. Most dealers will be happy to discuss maps with you and show you their stock. Some may require an advance appointment. It is generally advisable to call ahead anyway, since the dealer may be busy with a multitude of tasks or may not have the type of material in which you are interested.

Most beginners have some sort of idea of what types of maps they wish to collect. In reading books and looking through catalogues, your interests should become clearer. Some collectors choose to concentrate on a geographical area, for example, New England, Holy Land, Africa, Japan, Australia, the Arctic, and so on. Others collect world maps, celestial charts, decorative maps, very early maps, miniature maps, battle plans, or maps and charts showing early exploration. Others prefer to concentrate on a particular map-maker. Some enjoy tracing the evolution of cities through city plans and views. Some collect oddities, such as maps showing California as an island, or countries represented as allegorical figures. Places of ancestry, or where one has lived or traveled can be another focus. The possibilities are limited only by one's imagination. When corresponding with dealers, it is best to give them as clear an idea of your interests as possible. They are then able to keep your name and your wishes on file and quote prices to you on items that may not appear in their catalogues.

The collector should avoid initial over-enthusiasm. When buying a map, ask yourself if you really want to keep it for the next few decades. If the answer is yes, and the price reasonable, definitely buy it. A map that might not be especially rare may suddenly become scarce when you are looking for it. If you are unsure about the map, it is better to do some further research and think it over for a few days.

Acquiring an interesting collection need not require emptying the bank account, but money is a factor in the acquisition of the more celebrated and rare maps. While the prices of antiquarian maps have appreciated rapidly in recent years, there is no guarantee that the trend will continue. Compared to other art forms and antiquarian objects, old maps are reasonably priced. But buying an antique map as an investment map solely because it is expected to increase in value is risky. Further, the market is relatively illiquid because of the need to match a buyer with a defined and perhaps narrow objective with a particular map. Making this match is the function of a dealer;

it takes time and presence of mind; it is definitely not "commodity trading". While antique maps will probably continue to increase in value in the long run due to the law of supply and demand, it is probably safer, and definitely more fun, to concentrate on maps of special interest to you.

Maps can be bought by mail or in person. Buying maps in person is perhaps most satisfactory, since the map can be discussed with the dealer. A substantial portion of the antiquarian map trade is by mail, however. Usually new mail customers will be required to send payment with their order. Most dealers will let you return merchandise within a few days for a full refund, except possibly for the shipping charge. The return policy and shipping charges can be found in the dealer's catalogue. Maps can also be bought at auction, either in person or sometimes by mail. This can be risky for the beginner since sales are usually final unless the item was mis-described. However, if you know what you are doing, auctions can often be the source of some real bargains. Sometimes old maps are to be found in establishments that sell mainly other items. Art galleries, antique stores, and used book stores often have a map or two.

If you plan to buy just a few maps, you may wish to frame them. This protects them from wear and soiling due to handling, enhances their beauty and enlarges the opportunities for appreciation. However, any dealer can tell you about framed maps that have been brought to the shop that were damaged by improper framing and care. One-hundred-percent acid-free rag matting material should be used to avoid harming the map, which may be in contact with the matting for 50 years or more. Philistine framers occasionally want to dry mount the map or paste it to cardboard or even trim it to fit the frame. Go elsewhere. In hanging framed maps, direct sunlight or constant fluorescent light should be avoided because the ultraviolet component causes the paper to deteriorate. Note that antiquarian maps are almost unique among wall objects insofar as they require reading up close as well as viewing from afar.

If you plan to assemble a larger collection, you should refrain from framing all of your initial purchases. Victims of map-collecting fever, a chronic, incurable, but rarely fatal malady, may wish to purchase a blueprint file. These are available from office equipment suppliers. The maps can be kept flat in the drawers in acid-free, archival-quality folders or plastic sleeves (not all plastic is inert) which can be purchased at art supply houses. Maps may be stored rolled, but the paper has a memory and may not easily uncurl and lay flat; accidental rips can occur if they are inspected frequently or without great care. Maps backed with cloth or paper should be kept flat, if possible, to prevent peeling of the paper from the backing. Maps that are brittle or otherwise fragile should be kept in individual clear, archival-quality plastic protectors. Maps that fold down to a smaller size should be folded and unfolded as little as possible to avoid separations along the folds. Temperature and humidity should be kept as near to museum standards as possible, that is, room temperature, with humidity in the mid-range, without a great deal of variation.

Be cautious when contemplating repairs or restoration. *Never, never* repair tears with self-adhesive tapes, especially transparent tape or masking tape. The adhesive on some brands causes the paper to brown, and some tapes are difficult to remove, even for a professional. While some collectors may be quite capable of making routine repairs with archival materials, it may be well to consult a professional conservator. Often a small outlay, even for such procedures as deacidification, can protect a substantially larger investment. The American Institute for Conservation of Historic & Artistic Works (1717 K Street, N.W., Suite 301, Washington, D.C. 20006; Tel: (202)-452 9545, Fax. (202) 452-9328) maintains a *Referral System* and a directory of members by professional specialties, including "Books and Paper".

Periodicals of Interest

Mapline. A quarterly newsletter with brief articles, news of the map world, and reviews of books. Mapline, The Newberry Library, 60 W. Walton Street, Chicago, IL 60610; $8 per year.

The Map Collector. Published quarterly, with articles on early maps and map collecting, with dealer advertisements and classifieds. Map Collector Publications, Ltd. 48 High Street, Tring, Hertfordshire HP23 5BH, England; £29 per year, $51 in the U.S.

Factors Affecting Value

Over time, value is determined by supply and demand. The attribution of value is based on reports of transactions between willing buyers and willing sellers who are appropriately informed about the object in question. There are some general factors that can be taken into account. These can be placed in three categories: those related to the identity, condition and color.

Identity

HISTORICAL IMPORTANCE. Maps which are pivotal in the history of exploration and cartography tend to be in great demand. Particularly sought after are maps that are the first to show some discovery or event. Examples might be maps initially revealing features of the New World or with the first depiction of an important battle. A derivative map of similar appearance, published a few years later, might be worth considerably less. The relative importance of a particular map is usually difficult to judge until it is placed in an historical context. It is thus vital to be as well informed as possible through reading and observation in an area of interest.

REGION DEPICTED. This factor is probably most important in explaining the wide range in the price of maps from a given source, say an atlas by Ortelius, Blaeu, or Sanson. "World" maps are of global interest; demand is high and prices follow. Collectors in certain countries have developed a particular fondness for maps of their own regions: Americans, Australians, Canadians, the Dutch, the English, Germans, Scandinavians and others have a long tradition of collecting, with the result that maps of these areas tend to be more expensive. Other regions in demand include Bermuda, some of the West Indian islands and Greece. Maps of Eastern Europe, some Mediterranean countries and parts of Asia, Africa and Latin America, which may be remote, less affluent or with alternative cultural interests, tend to be less expensive. Reduced demand may be the result of adverse currency exchange rates and inconvertibility. Nevertheless, a market does exist among emigrés and travelers. And since maps of some remote regions can be artistically attractive, those seeking decorative maps can often find bargains in the Africa and Asia bins of dealers.

THE MAP-MAKER. For similar maps, the maker can strongly influence the price. To take one example, Ortelius and de Jode both produced similar maps at about the same time. However, Ortelius produced far more editions of his atlas, making de Jode maps relatively scarce by comparison. Thus, de Jode maps appear far less frequently on the market; that is, the supply is less. The result is that maps of comparable areas from de Jode's atlas are considerably more expensive than those of Ortelius.

AGE. For similar maps, the older map is generally the more valuable. Using age as the sole basis of evaluation is risky, since some maps from the 1500s can be bought for under $100, while some maps of the 1800s are worth thousands.

SIZE. For maps of about equal age and subject matter, larger maps tend to be more valuable. Folio maps of an area will bring considerably more than miniature or pocket versions by the same map-maker. Larger maps allow for more detail and decoration, and make a more impressive display.

ÆSTHETIC QUALITIES. Many buyers intend to frame their maps for display. Naturally a map with sea monsters, scrollwork, decorative borders, sailing ships, gargoyles, putti, and the like are much more tempting to such buyers, and consequently decorative maps sell for a premium.

Condition

Condition plays a major role in pricing. When a map is extremely rare, condition may be relatively unimportant, since choice may be simply "to have or to have not." Another offering may not be forthcoming in a lifetime. With maps in greater supply, condition becomes a discriminating factor. Problems affecting appearance are more serious for a decorative map than for an item primarily of historical value. While very minor flaws, such as tiny spot stains or a slight crease, generally have only a minimal effect on value, more serious problems can cause a substantial disparity in price between copies of the same item.

STAINS. Several types of stains plague maps. Foreign matter such as ink or coffee can be spilled on a map. Water spills, even of clean water, leave stains by redistributing soluble material in the paper. Browning, caused by oxidation, tends to occur at the centerfold, where paste contacts the paper. It also tends to occur at the edges of atlas maps, where the paper was more exposed to airborne pollutants. Sometimes the entire map browns. Mildew spots, called foxing, also occurs. Stains in the printed area are more serious than stains in the blank margin.

TEARS. From handling and use, many maps eventually develop rips and tears. Certain maps, especially large folding maps such as those from Moll's *The World Described ...*, tend to develop weakness and tears along the fold lines. Maps folding into books tend to rip at the corner of the guard holding them into the book. Maps in atlases often develop tears or separations at the centerfold. Tears affecting only the blank margin are considered less serious than tears entering the printed area. If the map is to be handled, tears should be repaired to prevent them from lengthening.

Professional restorers can make reversible repairs which are almost invisible. Under no circumstance should repairs be made with non-archival self-adhesive tapes.

MARGINS. The blank margins of maps may get trimmed over the years. It may be the work of the original binder, a recent framer, or it may be a means of removing flaws from a chipped or torn margin. Trimming reduces value, especially if the margin is less than about one-quarter inch (5 mm.), making it difficult to mat for display. A few maps normally have narrow margins, among them the larger Dutch sea charts.

CREASES. This is a minor fault. Folding maps, or maps with centerfolds, will always show traces of the folds, and this does not affect the value. Unintended minor creases can usually be flattened out pretty well and are considered unimportant. Multiple and repeated hard creasing from mis-folding can be visually intrusive and detracts from value.

BACKING. Sometimes maps are pasted or glued to cheap backing, such as cardboard, pressboard, or brown paper. This can substantially reduce value. Paper conservators can often reverse this form of abuse with a minimum of side effects if modern mounting material has not been used. In other cases, maps are professionally backed, with thin tissue or rice paper. This is acceptable when done to reinforce a weak or brittle item, but should not be done on a sound copy.

Color

Antique maps come in a variety of color styles. They may be in full color (also called wash color); full color to the primary subject; outline color of the political subdivisions; highlight color for features such as cities; map border color; cartouche color; any combination of the above heightened with gold, and not least -- uncolored. Prior to the printed color of the mid to late 19th-century, all coloring was by hand.

Since most decorative maps look better colored, these are the maps in highest demand. Coloring may be original (also called *contemporary*, i.e., contemporary with the time of original publication) or modern (i.e., recent). The original color on some maps may be carried further with modern color, as with later color to a cartouche or the map border. Further, color from any period can be tastefully and skillfully applied or less so. Modern color can be historically "correct" or, by contrast, clearly inappropriate.

Collectors seem to agree that original color commands a premium, but this is where agreement ends. Some prefer the original condition whether with color or without. Others may choose good modern color instead of an uncolored original. Most agree that no coloring is preferable to bad, unskilled application of modern color, if for no other reason than that the option remains to have color skillfully applied by a knowledgeable artisan in a way that is historically plausible. Some maps were almost never colored, such as Dudley's sea charts and U.S. Coast Survey maps. Knowledgeable collectors might refuse to buy such items if colored. A few collectors even prefer uncolored examples under any circumstances to better appreciate the engraving. Collectors should inquire as to the period of the color. While sometimes it may be difficult to guarantee original color, it may be easier to confirm a suspicion of modern color.

How To Detect Reproductions

An *original* generally refers to a copy printed more or less at the time the map or view first appeared. In some cases, maps were printed for a century or more from the same copperplate or woodblock, occasionally with updating to include newer information. In such cases, as long as the plate or block was being employed commercially, impressions from it are considered to be "originals." Sometimes the block or plate survived to a later time, and was used to print restrikes. These are often identified by special watermarks or stamps. In any event, restrikes of old maps are almost unheard of on the market.

Reproductions are a different matter. They can be defined as impressions made by some process, nowadays usually photographic, based on an original impression. Reproductions are not necessarily printed recently. Some 19th-century reproductions exist, many of excellent quality, but most reproductions encountered will have been done in the last few decades. After a degree of exposure to antique maps, one gets to sense the presence of a reproduction. Some can only be distinguished with certainty by experts. Many can be detected by those with less experience by applying the following tests:

SIZE. Reproductions *not intended to deceive* are often produced somewhat larger or smaller than the original. Of course, one must know the size of the original. The *Price Record* and many cartographic reference books give dimensions which can be helpful in this regard. The dimensions given here may not be definitive, however, since they are the result of different methods or standards of measurement by the contributing dealers. Further, variation in humidity can cause changes of a few percent in the dimensions of a sheet of paper. The measurements in the *Price Record* are rounded off to the nearest centimeter and half-inch to remove any suggestion of greater accuracy, but they should be sufficient to detect a reproduction intentionally differentiated from the original by size.

COLORING. Colored reproductions often employ halftone colors. These consist of patterns of small dots, geometrically arranged, which can be seen quite readily with a magnifying glass. A few reproductions, however, are colored by hand, just like the originals.

PRINTING QUALITY. Sometimes reproductions have a slightly blurred appearance. The black lines do not have the fine, dense quality of a true engraving. This can show up especially in cross-hatched areas, where the lines may fuse together.

PLATE MARK. When an engraved map is printed, the impression of the metal plate crushes the paper, resulting in a depressed area. The depressed area is usually rectangular, and extends slightly beyond the printed area. This can often be seen, or felt, as a slight step or ridge. In a few cases, where the paper is thin, or where the map has been trimmed to the border, the plate mark may not be visible. On a very few reproductions, plate marks have been added to enhance realism. While visible on steel and copper engravings, a plate mark is normally not found on woodcuts, since much less pressure is used in printing from a wooden block. It is absent from lithographically produced maps dating from the mid-19th century or later.

LEGENDS. On most reproductions, there is a legend, usually in fine print, saying something like "Copyright 1968" or "From an original in the Library of Congress." The legend can be hard to find; some tiny legends have been embedded in the borders of woodcut maps. If outside the border, the legend might have been trimmed off or there may have been an attempt to erase the legend, although this should leave a thin-spot or scuff marks.

PAPER. Probably the best method of distinguishing is to study the paper. Chain marks (see Glossary) are visible on paper made before about 1800. Some reproductions are printed on modern paper having chain marks, but the markings tend to be more regular on the modern paper. Watermarks can also be an important clue, but some expertise may be needed in interpreting them. Many of the folio-sized maps have watermarks, but smaller maps often do not. Folio atlas maps, and many of smaller size, have a centerfold crease with only the occasional exception of proof copies. The paper on originals tends to have an aged appearance, perhaps being browned, or even brittle, and sometimes having foxing or spotting. Often originals show signs of use, such as stains, soiling, wear, and tears. Originals often show slight offsetting, either of color, or printer's ink, depending on how they were originally bound or folded. If colored, the pigments sometimes oxidize the paper, which can be seen by looking for browning or even corrosion on the reverse corresponding to the colors on the map.

The above advice will help, but there is no substitute for long-term experience. Before making a commitment to purchase, it is best to consult an experienced dealer. Some may charge a small amount for authenticating an item. Local libraries, art galleries, or museums may also be able to help in some cases.

RECOMMENDED REFERENCES

Books that were listed in this section and "References Cited" in previous editions of the *Price Record* have been consolidated here. The list of books is necessarily scattered and brief, for there are scores, even hundreds, of fine books dealing with antiquarian maps in general or focusing on limited geographical regions, individual map-makers or maps with a special purpose. Many of the books listed are still in print or are available as used books from map dealers. For additional recently published books, see the "Cumulative Index of Books Reviewed".

Books on this list which have been reviewed in the *Price Record* are indicated by the date of the review in square brackets. When an author's name is in **boldface**, the citation appears in this year's "Price Listing".

Bagrow, Leo, *The History of Cartography,* Chicago: Precedent Publishing, Inc., 1985. R.A. Skelton, ed. This is perhaps the most highly regarded book on old maps, although not specifically about collecting. The text is definitive, and the numerous plates, some in color, are of the highest quality.

Baynton-Williams, Roger, *Investing in Maps,* New York: Clarkson N. Potter, Inc., 1969. Despite the title, the major emphasis is on how maps were produced and who made them. There are many fine illustrations in this good book for beginners.

Brown, Lloyd A., *The Story of Maps,* Boston: Little, Brown & Co., 1949. Reprinted by Dover Books, New York. A readable and scholarly history of map-making.

Faupel, W. John, *A Brief and True Report of the New Found Land of Virginia: A study of the de Bry Engravings*. East Grinstead: Antique Atlas Publications, 1989. [1990]

George, Wilma, *Animals & Maps,* Berkeley: University of California Press, 1969. A zoologist finds that the animals decorating old maps are not mythical beasts located at random. On the contrary, old maps turn out to be an interesting source of zoological data. This is not an essential book, but it is fun to read.

Haskell, Daniel C., "Manhattan Maps - A Co-operative List," in *Bulletin of the New York Public Library*, April - October 1930.

Howes, Wright, *U.S.iana (1650-1950) A selective bibliography in which are described 11,620 uncommon and significant books relating to the continental portion of the United States*, revised and enlarged edition, New York: R.R. Bowker, 1962.

Jolly, David C., *Maps in British Periodicals: Part I, major monthlies before 1800* Brookline: David C. Jolly, 1989. [1990]

Jolly, David C., *Maps in British Periodicals: Part II, annuals, scientific periodicals & miscellaneous magazines, mostly before 1800,* Brookline: David C. Jolly, 1990. [1991]

Lister, Raymond, *Antique Maps & their Cartographers* London: G. Bell & Sons Ltd., 1970. This is a very fine introductory book for collectors.

Lister, Raymond, *Old Maps & Globes,* London: Bell & Hyman, 1979. An exceptionally fine introductory book. Ample material on early cartography, map-making techniques, and early globes is supplemented with a lengthy dictionary of map-makers and illustrations of about 200 watermarks.

Koeman, I.C., *Atlantes Neerlandici: Bibliography of terrestrial, Maritime and celestial atlases and pilot books, published in the Netherlands up to 1880*, 5 vols. Amsterdam: Theatrum Orbis Terrarum, 1967-71.

Laor, Eran, *Maps of the Holy Land: Cartobibliography of Printed Maps, 1475-1900*, New York: Alan R. Liss, 1986. [1988]

Map Collectors' Series, London: The Map Collectors' Circle. 110 numbered issues in 11 volumes, 1964-1974.

Modelski, Andrew M., *Railroad Maps of the United States: A selective annotated bibliography of original 19th-century maps in the Geography and Map Division of the Library of Congress*, Washington: Library of Congress, 1975.

Moreland, C. & D. Bannister, *Antique Maps: A Collector's Handbook,* Oxford: Phaidon/Christies, 1986. A superior reference, with many illustrations and much useful information. [1987]

Nordenskiöld, A.E., *Facsimile-Atlas to the Early History of Cartography,* Stockholm, 1889. Reprinted by Dover Publications, New York. Although somewhat out of date, a useful reference work for those interested in maps of the 15th and 16th centuries. There are almost 200 illustrations of old maps.

Norwich, Oscar I., *Maps of Africa: An illustrated and annotated carto-bibliography,* Johannesburg: A.D. Doncker, 1983. [1986]

Phillips, Philip L., *A List of Geographical Atlases in the Library of Congress*, Vols. I-IV, continued by Clara Egli LeGear, Vols. 5-8. Washington: Government Printing Office, 1909 through 1974. Volumes I through IV reprinted in two volumes at Amsterdam: Theatrum Orbis Terrarum, 1971. An exhaustive listing of the Library's extensive collection of atlases. Many are collated or with a list of maps pertaining to America. May be difficult to use due to complicated indexing, but becomes easier with familiarity.

Phillips, Philip L., *A List of Maps of America in the Library of Congress Preceded by a List of Works Relating to Cartography*, Washington: Government Printing Office, 1901. This is the starting point in looking up any American map, and is normally found at the right hand of all dealers in American maps.

Potter, Jonathan, *Country Life Book of Antique Maps: An introduction to the history of maps and how to appreciate them*, Seacaucus: Chartwell Books, 1989. Similar in concept to Tooley and Moreland & Bannister, this well-illustrated, interesting, and informative work is ideal for collectors. [1990]

Reps, John W., *Views and Viewmakers of Urban America: Lithographs of towns and cities in the United States and Canada, notes on the artists and publishers, and a union catalog of their work, 1825-1925*, Columbia: University of Missouri Press, 1984. [1985]

Ristow, Walter W., *American Maps and Mapmakers: Commercial Cartography in the nineteenth century*, Detroit: Wayne State University Press, 1985. A scholarly treatment of this period. [1986]

Schwartz, Seymour I., & Ralph E. Ehrenberg, *The Mapping of America*, New York: Harry N. Abrams, Inc., 1980. A detailed, informative, and well-illustrated work of great value to collectors and dealers.

Sellers, John R. **&** Patricia M. **van Ee**, *Maps and Charts of North America and the West Indies 1750-1789: A guide to the collections in the Library of Congress*, Washington: Library of Congress, 1981. An excellent compilation of maps just before, during and right after the American Revolution.

Shirley, Rodney W., *The Mapping of the World: Early printed world maps 1472-1700*, London: Holland Press Cartographica, 1983. The definitive listing of early world maps.

Skelton, R.A., *Decorative Printed Maps of the 15th to 18th Centuries,* London: Spring Books, 1965. A good reference for collectors of decorative maps. There are 84 plates, some in color.

Stevens, Henry & Roland Tree, *Comparative Cartography Exemplified in an Analytical & Bibliographical Description of Nearly One Hundred Maps and Charts of the American Continent Published in Great Britain during the Years 1600 to 1850,* London: Map Collectors' Circle, No.39, 1967 (Revised 2nd ed.). Revised 3rd ed. appears as Chapter 2 of R.V. Tooley, The Mapping of America, London: Holland Press Cartographica, 1980.

Tooley, R.V., *Maps and Map-Makers,* New York: Crown Publishers, 1982, revised ed. Perhaps the most useful general purpose book for map collectors. It is always reasonably priced and usually in print. *Buy it!*

Tooley, R.V., *Tooley's Dictionary of Mapmakers* 1979, and *Tooley's Dictionary of Mapmakers, Supplement* 1985, New York: Alan R. Liss, Inc., & Amsterdam: Meridian Publishing Co. These books give information about almost any cartographer likely to be encountered. Recommended for *all* dealers. [1987]

Tooley, R.V., C. Bricker, & G.R. Crone, *Landmarks of Mapmaking,* New York: Thomas Y. Crowell, 1976. Numerous illustrations, including folding color plates, and an informative text make this an excellent book for the collector.

Wallis, H.M. & A.H. Robinson, eds., *Cartographical Innovations: An international handbook of mapping terms to 1900,* Tring: Map Collector Publications, Ltd., 1987. Contains a wealth of information on early mapping, with numerous references for further reading. [1988]

Warner, D., *The Sky Explored: Celestial Cartography 1500-1800,* New York: Alan R. Liss, Inc. & Amsterdam: Theatrum Orbis Terrarum, 1979. This is the definitive work on early celestial charts and should be obtained by anyone interested in that area of collecting. [1986]

Wheat, Carl I., *Mapping the Transmississippi West 1540-1861*, Vols. 1-5. San Francisco: Institute of Historical Cartography, 1958-63. The definitive work on maps of the American West.

Wheat, James C. **&** Christian F. **Brun**, *Maps and Charts Published in America before 1800: A bibliography*, London: Holland Press Ltd., 1985 (Revised 2nd ed.). Lists the 919 maps known in 1978.

Wilford, J.N., *The Mapmakers,* New York: Alfred A. Knopf, 1981. Very similar to Brown's book, this is essentially a history of cartography, and good background reading for the collector.

BOOK REVIEWS

In this transition year of *Antique Map Price Record & Handbook*, guest contributors have assisted in the review of books received. The commentary remains the full responsibility of the editor, however. In 1994, we expect to return to the review of a full complement of books in Voume 12. Books for review should be sent to Kimmel Publications, P.O. Box 12, Amherst, MA 01004, USA.

The following reviews are arranged alphabetically by author. The trim dimensions give width first. Bindings are characterized as cloth, hard cover (i.e., non-cloth), and paper. Most books can be ordered directly from the publisher. If available, addresses and prices are given. Since prices may change, and there may be shipping charges, it is wise to write or call the publisher for precise ordering information. In North America, most books by North American publishers can be ordered through book stores. Some map dealers also stock reference books as a helpful complement to their trade in antiquarian maps.

The Atlas of Atlases: The map maker's vision of the world, Phillip Allen, N.Y., Harry N. Abrams, Inc., 1992, ISBN-0-8109-3918-5, 12 x 10½ inches, 160 pp., 300+ full color illustrations, leatherette (Harry N. Abrams, 100 Fifth Avenue, New York, N.Y. 10011, $49.50)

The atlases described in this lavishly illustrated book were donated to the Birmingham (England) Public Library by William Cadbury of the famous confectionery firm. The collection is indeed toothsome, ranging from a beautifully colored copy of the 1482 Ulm Ptolemy through more obscure works such as those of Bacler Dalbe, and ending with the 1897 Times Atlas. In all, more than 40 atlases are described, grouped around five general topics (Classical and Medieval Tradition, the Era of Exploration, Dominance of the Dutch, the Age of Empire, and the Modern Age). Commentary is by Phillip Allen, special collections officer at the Birmingham. His prose is concise and clearly written; the only lapse noticed by this reader was attributing Blaeu's map of Virginia to William, not John, Smith.

The quality of the photography is a particular pleasure. Even black and white maps are illustrated in color, allowing the reader to appreciate nuances of paper and ink tone. Equally pleasing is the choice of subject matter: while many individual maps are reproduced, attention is also given to title pages, vignettes, bindings, and non-cartographic illustrations found in atlases.

Many travellers to the U.K. never make it to the "provinces." This book provides a tantalizing glimpse of a lesser-known, but clearly important collection, and a good reason for visiting Birmingham. It is highly recommended.

Early Maps of South-East Asia, R.T. Fell, Singapore, Oxford & NY,, Oxford University Press, 1991, ISBN 0-19-588972-X, 7¾ x 5¼ inches, xii, 122 pp., 21 uncolored + 13 colored illustrations, paper covered boards (Oxford University Press, Unit 221, Ubi Avenue 4, Singapore 1440)

There is surprisingly little English-language literature on maps of Asia. R.T. Fell, a "keen amateur collector," has set out to improve the situation with this small book aimed at the collector of maps of South-East Asia. The first three chapters cover early exploration of the region, European map publishers of the time, and general observations on collecting maps. The last chapter offers sound advice on caring for a collection. The short bibliography is composed mainly of general map collecting books and histories of South-East Asia.

This information can readily be obtained elsewhere, and merely acts as wrapping for the meat of the book which is in the middle. There are eight chapters on mapping of different areas within South-East Asia, including discussion of individual maps. Historic events and their impact on maps are noted. This central section is useful, and the book is recommended to collectors of maps of Asia.

The History of Cartography Volume Two, Book One: Cartography in the Traditional Islamic and South Asian Societies, J.B. Harley and David Woodward, Chicago & London, University of Chicago Press, 1992, ISBN 0-226-31635-1, 11 x 8 inches, xxiv, 579 pp., illustrated, cloth ($125.00)

The monumental task of producing a general history of cartography continues. The extent and complexity of non-western mapping has led the editors to divide Volume Two of this series into two large books. Book One contains two parts, "Islamic Cartography" and "South Asian Cartography." (The forthcoming Book Two will be on "Cartography in the Traditional East and Southeast Asian Societies.") As noted in the review of Fell's *Early Maps of South-East Asia*, there is a dearth of English-language literature on mapping outside the European tradition. This volume is a major effort to redress the situation.

Because the editors employed, correctly in this reviewer's opinion, a broad definition of cartography, both cosmography and nautical charts are dealt with in each section. As much of the material is unfamiliar to Western readers, the text can be slow going. However, it is a worthwhile effort as there is much to be learned. The numerous illustrations, including 40 color plates, not only illuminate the text, but are an education in themselves, since many are not easily recognizable as maps to Western eyes. As one would expect in a work of this nature, there are extensive footnotes and a lengthy bibliography, plus a thorough index. This book is recommended not only as an integral part of a major historical survey, but to readers wishing to broaden their knowledge of cartography.

Cosmography: Maps from Ptolemy's Geography Introduction by Lelio Pagani, Leicester, Magna Books, 1990, ISBN 1-85422-103-5, 14½ x 10 inches, xv [text], 27 double-page color plates, laminated covers (Magna Books, Magna Road, Wigston, Leicester, LC8 2ZH, England)

Originally published in Italian under the title *Claudii Ptolemaei Cosmographia*, this volume contains facsimiles of the maps (but not the accompanying text) from a 15th century manuscript, now in the National Library collection in Naples. The manuscript is unsigned, but attributed to Nicolaus Germanus, chiefly on stylistic grounds. That some, including Pagani, believe Germanus prepared the printed 1482 Ulm edition, lends further interest to these maps.

In his introduction, Pagani reviews theories of Ptolemy and other geographers from the classical period. He emphasizes the impact that reintroduction of Ptolemy's works had on the rise of humanist thought in western Europe, and gives detailed descriptions of the physical aspects of the manuscript.

The color plates are handsomely printed on matte paper which gives depth to the colors, particularly the lapis lazuli blue. This reader was not able to examine all 27 plates, as the copy inspected suffered from binding errors (one signature dropped, another repeated). However, the quality of the photography and the informative commentary make this a welcome addition to any cartophile's library.

BEL ET UTILE: The Work of The Robert De Vaugondy Family of Mapmakers, Mary Sponberg Pedley, Tring: Map Collector Publications, 1992, ISBN-0-906430-12-7, 12 x 9¼ inches, 251pp, illustrated, cloth (Map Collector Publications Ltd., 48 High Street, Tring, Herts. HP23 5BH, England, £85)

While focusing on the prolific output of Gilles and Robert De Vaugondy, this book casts a strong -- and welcome -- light on the publishing and allied trades in 18th century Paris, filling a large gap in English-language literature on the subject. There are numerous illustrations (eight in color), a selected bibliography, a short-title index and separate, well-organized catalogs for maps, atlases and globes produced by the Vaugondys, as well as a general index. Though the map catalog alone runs to 500 entries, Dr. Pedley is already compiling an appendix, and welcomes additions from readers.

Like its title, this book is both "beautiful and useful." However, the high price for this limited edition (750 copies) may keep it from the audience it deserves. A puzzling detail is the illustration of a handsomely colored title page for the *Atlas Universel* (also used for the dust jacket) which is from a 1776 edition published by Santini in Venice. Yet there is no mention of this Italian edition in the text or indices.

Maps, Charts, Globes: Five centuries of exploration an exhibition in commemoration of the Columbus Quincentenary, Sandra Sider with Anita Andreasian and Mitchell Codding, New York: The Hispanic Society of America, 1992, ISBN 87535-145-X, Cloth, 12¼ x 9½ inches, xvi, 128 pp, 73 full page illustrations,46 in color, ($35.00)

The Hispanic Society, founded in 1904, houses a treasure-trove of cartographic manuscript material. It is amazing to realize the bulk of its collection was acquired in a few brief years prior to the First World War. The book succeeds on two levels -- as an exhibition catalog its high quality plates illustrate many rarities, some never before published. It also updates and expands E.L. Stevenson's 1911 *Brief History of Portolan Charts*, a scarce and important reference work. Research conducted since Stevenson's time has shed new light on some of the Society's holdings, and recent cleaning and restoration of some charts and globes revealed new information, which has been documented in this volume. Material acquired since Stevenson's book was published is included. Each plate is described in detail; a helpful feature in each caption is a notation which cites the page number for the descriptive text. There is an index and a room-by-room listing of material on display at the Society. The works of dozens of early cartographers are arranged chronologically, ranging from a chart of the Mediterranean by Jacobus de Giroldis in 1447, to an anonymous Spanish chart of the Caribbean dated circa 1750. There is a separate section devoted to globes, including a rare model by Herman Moll of circa 1711. This volume does justice to the Society's collection, and to the memory of E.L. Stevenson.

Cumulative Index of Books Reviewed

All books reviewed are listed below, including the current year. Review copies have been requested of any book recently published that has come to our attention. The number in parentheses after the title is the year of review.

Akerman, J.R. & D. Buisseret, *Monarchs, Ministers & Maps: A cartographic exhibit at the Newberry Library* (1988)

Allen, P., *The Atlas of Atlases: The map maker's vision of the world* (1993)

Bagrow, L., *A history of cartography of Russia up to 1600* and *A history of Russian cartography up to 1800* (1990)

Bagrow, L. & R.A. Skelton, *History of cartography, 2nd ed.* (1987)

Bellec, F., *Océan des Hommes* (1989)

Beresiner, Y., *British County Maps: Reference and price guide* (1985)

Brandão, A.F., *Dialogues of the Great Things of Brazil* (1988)

Buczek, K., *The History of Polish Cartography from the 15th to the 18th Century* (1985)

Buisseret, D., *Tools of Empire: Ships and maps in the process of westward expansion* (1988)

Cajori, F., *The Chequered Career of Ferdinand Rudolph Hassler* (1989)

Calissano, M, et al., *Architettura Rurale In Valle Stura: Il paesagio agricolo nel Cabreo Spinola di Campofreddo* (1988)

Campbell, T., *The Earliest Printed maps 1472-1500* (1989)

Campbell, T., *Early Maps* (1989)

Cobb, D. & N. Vick, eds., *Early Maps of Terra Sancta: Maps of the Holy Land* (1989)

Cobb, D., *New Hampshire Maps to 1900: An annotated checklist* (1989)

Conzen, M.P., ed., *Chicago Mapmakers: Essays on the rise of the city's map trade* (1986)

Cook, T., *Archival Citations* (1985)

Coppo, P., *Il Portolano* (1988)

Cotter, C., *A History of the Navigator's Sextant* (1989)

Dawson, J., *The Mapmaker's Eye: Nova Scotia through early maps* (1992)

Delpar, H., ed., *The Discoverers: An encyclopedia of explorers and exploration* (1989)

Dilke, O.A.W., *Greek and Roman Maps* (1987)

Dörflinger, J., *Österreichische Karten des 18. und zu Beginn des 19. Jahrhunderts unter besonderer Berücksichtigung der Privatkartographie zwischen 1780 und 1820* (1991)

Dreyer-Eimbcke, O., *Die Entdeckung der Erde: Geschichte und Geschichten des kartographischen Abenteuers* (1991)

Dreyer-Eimbcke, O., *Island, Grönland und das nördlich Eismeer im Bild der Kartographie seit dem 10 Jahrhundert* (1990)

Dubreuil, L., *Early Canadian Topographic Map Series: The Geological Survey of Canada 1842-1949* (1992)

Dubreuil, L., *Sectional Maps of Western Canada, 1871-1955: An early Canadian topographic map series* (1992)

Dubreuil, L., *Standard Topographical Maps of Canada, 1904-1908* (1992)

Edwards, A.C. & K.C. Newton, *The Walkers of Hanningfield: Surveyors and mapmakers extraordinary* (1987)

Emlen, R.P., *Shaker Village Views: Illustrated maps and landscape drawings by Shaker artists of the nineteenth century* (1990)

Falk, M.W., *Alaskan Maps: A cartobibliography of Alaska to 1900* (1987)

Farrell, B. & A. Desbarats, *Explorations in the History of Canadian Mapping: A collection of essays* (1992)

Faupel, W.J., *A Brief and True Report of the New Found Land of Virginia: A study of the de Bry engravings* (1990)

Fell, R. T., *Early Maps of South-East Asia* (1993)

Gasset, J., ed., *Cartografia de Catalunya Dels Segles XVII i XVIII* (1989)

Globe, A., *Peter Stent, London Printseller, Circa 1642-1665: Being a catalog raisonné of his engraved prints and books with an historical and bibliographical introduction* (1987)

Goss, J., *Blaeu's The Grand Atlas of the 17th-Century World* (1992)

Graffagnino, J.K., *The Shaping of Vermont from the Wilderness to the Centennial 1749-1877* (1986)

Hadjipaschalis, A., *Cyprus: 2500 years of cartography* (1989)

Hale, E., *The Discovery of the World: Maps of the earth and the cosmos. From the David M. Stewart Collection* (1988)

Harley, J.B. & D. Woodward, *The History of Cartography Volume Two, Book One: Cartography in the Traditional Islamic and South Asian Societies* (1993)

Harris, H.M., *The Asiatic Fathers of America: Book one, The Chinese discovery and colonization of ancient America (2640 B.C. to 2200 B.C.)*; *Book two, the Asiatic kingdoms of America (458 A.D. to 1000 A.D.)* (1988)

Heijden, H.A.M. van der, *The Oldest Maps of the Netherlands: An illustrated and annotated carto-bibliography of the 16th century maps of the XVII provinces* (1988)

Higman, B.W., *Jamaica Surveyed: Plantation maps and plans of the eighteenth and nineteenth centuries* (1990)

Holton, M., *The James W. Macnutt Collection of maps of the Gulf of St. Lawrence with Particular Emphasis on Prince Edward Island* (1991)

Jackson, J., R. Weedle & W. de Ville, *Mapping Texas and the Gulf Coast: The contributions of Saint-Denis, Oliván, and Le Maire* (1991)

Javorski, M., *The Canadian West Discovered: An exhibition of printed maps from the 16th to early 20th centuries* (1985)

Johnson, P., *Celestial Images: Astronomical charts from 1500 to 1900* (1986)

Jolly, D.C., *Maps in British Periodicals: Part I, major monthlies before 1800* (1990)

Jolly, D.C., *Maps in British Periodicals: Part II, annuals, scientific periodicals & miscellaneous magazines mostly before 1800* (1991)

Jolly, D.C., *Maps of America in Periodicals before 1800* (1989)

Jourdin, M.M. du, & M. de la Roncière, *Sea Charts of the Early Explorers, 13th to 17th Century* (1987)

Karamitsanis, A., ed., *From Terra Incognita to the Prairie West: A map exhibit* (1990)

King, G.L., *The Printed Maps of Staffordshire 1577-1850* (1990)

Klein, C., *Maps in Eighteenth-Century British Magazines: A checklist* (1990)

Koepp, D.P., ed., *Exploration and Mapping of the American West: Selected essays* (1988)

Konvitz, J., *Cartography in France, 1660-1848: Science, engineering, and statecraft* (1988)

Kroessler, J., *A Guide to Historical Map Resources for Greater New York* (1989)

Krogt, P.C.J. van der, *Advertenties Voor Kaarten, Atlassen, Globes e.d. in Amsterdamse Kranten 1621-1811* (1989)

Krogt, P.C.J. van der, *Old globes in the Netherlands: A catalogue of terrestrial and celestial globes made prior to 1850 and preserved in Dutch collections* (1986)

Lago, L. & C. Rossit, *Pietro Coppo Le "Tabulae" (1524-1526): Una preziosa raccolta cartografica custodita a Pirano. Note e documenti per la storia della cartografia* (1988)

Lanman, J., *Glimpses of History from Old Maps: A collector's view* (1991)

Lanman, J., *On the Origin of Portolan Charts* (1989)

Laor, E., *Maps of the Holy Land: Cartobibliography of printed maps, 1475-1900* (1988)

Larsgaard, M.L., *Map Librarianship: An introduction* (1990)

Lemon, D.P., *Theatre of Empire* (1990)

Lépine, P. & J. Berthelette, *Documents Cartographiques Depuis la Découverte de l'Amérique jusqu'à 1820: Inventaire sommaire* (1989)

Luebke, F, F. Kaye & G. Moulton, eds., *Mapping the North American Plains: Essays in the history of cartography* (1989)

Lyons, R., *The Conquest of Mexico by Hernan Cortez 1518-1521* (1988)

Mackal, R.P., *A Living Dinosaur? In search of Mokele-Mbembe* (1991)

Mackower, J., ed., *The Map Catalogue: Every kind of map and chart on earth and even some above it, 2nd ed.* (1991)

Martin, J.C. & R.S. Martin, *Maps of Texas and the Southwest, 1513-1900* (1987)

Martin-Merás, L. & B. Rivera, *Catologo de Cartografía Historica de España del Museo Naval* (1992)

Meinig, D.W., *The Shaping of America, Volume 1: Atlantic America, 1492-1800* (1987)

The Mercator Society, *English Mapping of America 1675-1715* (1989)

Mertz, H., *Pale Ink: Two ancient records of Chinese exploration in America, 2nd ed.* (1988)

Meurer, P.H., *Atlantes Colonienses: Die Kölner Schule der Atlaskartographie 1570-1610* (1990)

Michael, D.M.M., *The Mapping of Monmouthshire: A descriptive catalogue of pre-Victorian maps of the county (now Gwent) from Saxton in 1577 with details of British atlases published during that period* (1991)

Mickwitz, A.M., ed., *The A.E. Nordenskiöld Collection: Annotated catalogue of maps made up to 1800, vol. 3, Books containing maps, loose maps, addenda to vols. 1-2* (1986)

Monmonier, M., *Maps with the News: The development of American journalistic cartography* (1992)

Mooney, J., *Maps, Globes, Atlases and Geographies through the Year 1800: The Eleanor Houston and Lawrence M.C. Smith Cartographic Collection at the Smith Cartographic Center, University of Southern Maine* (1992)

Moore, J.N., *The Mapping of Scotland: A guide to the literature of Scottish cartography prior to the Ordnance Survey* (1986)

Moreland, C. & D. Bannister, *Antique Maps: A collector's handbook, 1983 ed.* (1985)

Moreland, C. & D. Bannister, *Antique Maps: A collector's handbook, 1986 ed.* (1987)

Moulton, G.E., ed., *Atlas of the Lewis & Clark Expedition: The journals of the Lewis and Clark Expedition, Volume 1* (1987)

Mueller, G.F., *Bering's Voyages: The reports from Russia* (1988)

National Library of Ireland, *Ireland from Maps* (1985)

Nebenzahl, K., *Atlas of Columbus and the Great Discoverers* (1992)

Nebenzahl, K., *Maps of the Holy Land: Images of Terra Sancta through two millennia* (1988)

Norwich, O.I., *Maps of Africa: An illustrated carto-bibliography* (1986)

Pagani, L., (Introduction), *Cosmography: Maps from Ptolemy's Geography* (1993)

Pedley, M. S., *BEL ET UTILE: The work of the Robert De Vaugondy Family of mapmakers* (1993)

Pennick, N., *Lost Lands and Sunken Cities* (1989)

Popescu-Spineni, Marin, *Rumänien in seinen Geographischen und Kartographischen Quellen* (1992)

Portinaro, P. & F. Knirsch, *The Cartography of North America 1500-1800* (1990)

Potter, J., *Country Life Book of Antique Maps: An introduction to the history of maps and how to appreciate them* (1990)

Public Archives of Canada, *National Map Collection* (1989)

Quaini, M., ed., *Carte e Cartografi in Liguria* (1988)

Quaini, M., *Piante delle Due Riviere della Serenissima Repubblica di Genova Divise ne' Commissariati di Sanita* (1987)

Reinhartz, D. & C.C. Colley, *The Mapping of the American Southwest* (1990)

Reps, J.W., *Views & Viewmakers of Urban America: Lithographs of towns and cities in the United States and Canada, notes on the artists and publishers, and a union catalog of their work, 1825-1925* (1985)

Rey, L., ed., *Unveiling the Arctic* (1987)

Ristow, W., *American Maps & Mapmakers: Commercial cartography in the nineteenth century* (1986)

Schulz, Juergen, *La Cartografia Tra Scienza e Arte: Carte e cartografi nel Rinascimento italiano* (1992)

Sertima, I. van, ed., *African Presence in Early America* (1989)

Shirley, R., *The Mapping of the World: Early printed world maps 1472-1700* (1985)

Sider, S., A. Andreasian & M. Codding, *Maps, Charts, Globes: Five Centuries of Exploration An Exhibition in Commemoration of the Columbus Quincentenary* (1993)

Simpson, A., *The Mysteries of the "Frenchman's Map" of Williamsburg, Virginia* (1987)

Society for the History of Discoveries, *Terrae Incognitae: The journal of the history of discoveries*, v.18 (1989)

Snyder, G., *Maps of the Heavens* (1985)

Stevens, A.R. & W.M. Holmes, *Historical Atlas of Texas* (1991)

Stommel, H., *Lost Islands: The story of islands that have vanished from nautical charts* (1987)

Suarez, T., *Shedding the Veil: Mapping the European discovery of America and the world based on selected works from the Sidney R. Knafel collection of early maps, atlases, and globes, 1434-1865* (1992)

Taliaferro, H.G., comp., *Cartographic Sources in the Rosenberg Library* (1991)

Tompkins, E., *Newfoundland's Interior Explored* (1990)

Tooley, R.V., *Dictionary of Mapmakers: Supplement* (1987)

Tooley, R.V., *Tooley's Handbook for Map Collectors: The map collector's vade mecum arranged by subjects and personalities alphabetically* (1988)

Van Ermen, E., *The United States in Old maps and Prints* (1992)

Wallis, H.M. & A.H. Robinson, *Cartographical Innovations: An international handbook of mapping terms to 1900* (1988)

Walsh, J., *Maps Contained in the Publications of the American Bibliography, 1639-1819: An index and checklist* (1990)

Walsperger, A., *Untitled World Map of 1448* (1988)

Warner, D.J., *The Sky Explored: Celestial cartography, 1500-1800* (1986)

Williams, G. & A. Frost, eds., *Terra Australis to Australia* (1990)

Wolter, J.A., ed., *World Directory of Map Collections, 2nd ed.* (1988)

Woodward, D., ed., *Art and Cartography: Six historical essays* (1988)

Zögner, L., ed., *Bibliographia Cartographia: International documentation of cartographical literature*, vol. 11 (1986)

Zögner, L., *Von Ptolemaeus bis Humbolt. Kartenschätze der Staatsbibliotek Preußischer Kulterbesitz: Ausstellung zum 125jährigen Jubiläum der Kartenabteilung* (1986)

GLOSSARY OF TERMS

AGE TONING. A pleasant-sounding synonym for browning. See *browning*.

AQUATINT. A type of etching in which rosin is dusted onto a copper plate. Upon heating, the particles fuse and merge, leaving small portions of the copper still exposed. When treated with acid, a speckled pattern of pits results. Impressions from the plate will approximate a gray tone. Aquatint was occasionally used for maps in the late 18th and early 19th centuries. Henry Pelham's beautiful 1777 map of Boston is perhaps the most noted example.

BACKED. Sometimes a map is pasted or glued onto another material, such as cloth, to make the map more rugged and durable. Many folding maps and many wall maps were backed with cloth when issued. Maps are sometimes backed for conservation purposes, usually with thin tissue. Archival quality paste and backing material should be employed to prevent chemical deterioration of the paper. This protects fragile maps from further damage from handling. Maps should not be backed when there is no good reason to do so.

BAROQUE. A style of decoration developed in late 16th-century Italy characterized by exaggerated form and extravagant ornamentation. Cartouches on maps from this period were often in a baroque style.

BIRD'S-EYE VIEW. A realistic view of a city or village drawn from a usually hypothetical aerial vantage point.

BLEACHING. This is sometimes done to remove stains, or lighten browning. Bleaching almost inevitably weakens paper, and should not be done casually, nor should it be done without regard to modern conservation practices. Excessive bleaching gives the paper a ghostly white appearance that experienced collectors avoid.

BORDER. The printed area toward the edges of a map constitutes the border. In some cases, the border may consist of a simple neat line. In other cases the border may be scrollwork, geometrical designs, or even decorative panels with costumed figures or town views. Occasionally, a map may have no border at all. Do not confuse border with margin. See *margin* and *neat lines*.

BROWNING. As the organic material in paper ages, it undergoes a chemical transformation that causes the paper to darken. The early stages of browning may produce a pleasing tone. Extreme browning is often accompanied by embrittlement of the paper. To retard aging, maps should be protected from atmospheric pollutants, contact with cheap paper or cardboard, and from exposure to too much ultraviolet light from sunlight or fluorescent lamps.

CARTA MARINA. A term applied to 16th-century rectangular world maps, usually with rhumb lines.

CARTE à BORDURES, CARTE à FIGURES. A map having decorative panels of costumed figures, views, and the like, at the borders.

CARTOUCH, CARTOUCHE. Information surrounded by a border. Cartouches typically enclose the title, the scale, or the imprint. The cartouche may be a simple rectangle or oval, or may incorporate decorative elements such as scrollwork, botanical elements, gargoyles, costumed figures, appropriate scenery, and so on.

CENTERFOLD. Many old maps have been removed from atlases. Often such maps have a vertical fold down the center. Opening and closing the atlas often results in a weakening of the paper at the centerfold, frequently necessitating repair. Browning tends to occur at the centerfold because the paste used to hold the map in the atlas attacks the paper.

CHAIN MARKS, CHAIN LINES. Part of the visible impression left by the wire grid used in the fabrication of laid paper. The chain marks are the coarsely spaced lines running parallel to the short dimension of the original sheet. They are typically about 1 inch (25 mm.) apart. See also *laid lines* and *laid paper*.

COLORING. Color applied to the map, usually watercolor applied by brush. Coloring generally greatly enhances the appearance of decorative maps, but not all maps were intended to be colored.

COMPASS ROSE. A small starlike device used to indicate direction, often found in combination with radiating rhumb lines. North is usually indicated by a pointer on the compass rose.

COMPOSITE ATLAS. An atlas compiled, often to order, by a mapseller from maps on hand. Maps by different map-makers are often bound together in such atlases.

CONTEMPORARY. Indicates something done at about the time the map was published, for example, contemporary coloring.

DECKLE-EDGED. Used to characterize hand-made paper retaining the original rough edges as produced by the papermaker. Most maps have the deckled edge trimmed off during binding, and deckle-edged maps are considered quite desirable.

DECORATIVE. Having definite aesthetic appeal. Decorative elements can include animals, sea monsters, mermaids, scrollwork, costumed figures, putti, and so on. Many consider the first half of the 17th-century to be the pinnacle of decorative map-making, though many beautiful maps were produced before and after that time.

DISSECTED. Cut into sections. This is often done with large maps, which are cut into rectangles and pasted to cloth so that they can easily be folded down to the size of a single section for easy carrying and storage.

EDITION. See discussion at the end of this section.

ENGRAVING. A printing process employing a metal plate on which has been scratched a design. When ink is applied to the plate, and the plate wiped, ink remains behind in the grooves. A dampened sheet of paper is laid onto the plate and under pressure the inked design is transferred.

ETCHING. A printing process similar to engraving, except that the plate is produced by coating it with an acid resistant material upon which the design is scratched. Acid is used to eat away at the scratched areas, creating the grooves to hold the ink for printing.

FOLIO. A folio book is bound from sheets of paper folded one time. A map from such a book is sometimes said to be folio-sized. Typically, the vertical paper dimension of a folio map is greater than about 11 inches (24 cm.). Large folio maps would be about 17 to 22 inches (45 to 55 cm.), and imperial folio greater than about 22 inches (55 cm.)

FOXING. Small, usually brown, spots on the paper caused by mold. Foxing ofte results from storage in damp conditions.

GORE. A section of a globe printed on paper, intended to be cut out and pasted to the surface of a sphere. Gores are usually shaped like an American football.

IMPRESSION. See discussion at the end of this section.

IMPRINT. Information printed on a map giving some combination of the publisher, place of publication, or date of publication.

INCUNABULA, INCUNABLE. Terms used to describe books printed prior to 1500 A.D., and also to maps printed before that time.

INSET MAP. A smaller map within the border of a larger map.

ISSUE. See discussion at the end of this section.

LAFRERI ATLAS. A term used to describe 16th-century Italian composite atlases of printed maps. These were apparently often made to order, and contents vary from atlas to atlas.

LAFRERI MAP, MAP OF THE LAFRERI SCHOOL. Terms often applied to Italian maps of the 16th-century, particularly those issued separately or in composite atlases.

LAID DOWN. See *backed*.

LAID LINES. Part of the visible impression left by the wire grid used in the fabrication of laid paper. The laid lines are the finely spaced lines running parallel to the long dimension of the original sheet. There are typically 25 lines per inch (10 lines per cm.). See also *chain marks* and *laid paper*.

LAID PAPER. Handmade paper made by depositing cloth fibers suspended in water onto a wire grid. The grid leaves an impression on the paper, which may be seen when looking though the paper at a bright light. Most maps before about 1800 are printed on laid paper. See also *chain marks*, *laid lines*, and *wove paper*.

LEO BELGICUS. A species of map depicting the low countries in the form of a lion.

LINED. See *backed*.

LITHOGRAPHY. A form of printing first used for maps early in the 19th-century. The image is printed from a stone or other material on which ink adheres only to specially treated areas.

LOSS OF (PRINTED) SURFACE. A cataloger's term to describe a map in which a portion of the paper is missing. Sometimes maps lacking printed surface are restored by pasting paper at the missing area on which the design is reproduced in facsimile.

LOXODROMIC LINES. See *rhumb lines*.

MANUSCRIPT. Handwriting. A manuscript map is one drawn by hand. Manuscript notations are handwritten notes on a map.

MARGIN. The blank area outside the border of a map. Do not confuse margin with border.

MEDALLION. A circular or oval region, usually containing a portrait, sometimes used to embellish maps.

MOUNTED. See *backed*.

NEAT LINES. The straight, printed lines bounding the map.

OCTAVO. An octavo book is bound from sheets of paper folded in half three times. A map from such a book is sometimes said to be octavo-sized. Typically the vertical paper dimension of such a map is about 8 to 9 inches (20 to 23 cm.). Abbreviated 8vo.

OFFSETTING. When the surface of a map contacts another surface for many years, as in an atlas, there may be a transfer of printer's ink or color, or a chemical reaction, which faintly reproduces a mirror image of the other surface. Offsetting can even occur from one part of a map to another if the map is folded on itself.

ORIGINAL. An original is a map or view printed from the original plate, block, or stone before it has been retired from commercial use. Sometimes the last user does not destroy the plate or block, and it is later used to make restrikes.

OUTLINE COLOR. Coloring of only the boundaries, borders, or coastlines.

PANELS. Usually rectangular frames around the outside of a map enclosing views, scenes, or figures.

PANORAMIC VIEW. A realistic depiction of a city or village from a point on the ground, often covering a wide horizontal angle.

PERIPLUS. A text of sailing directions used in classical times.

PLATE. See discussion at the end of this section.

PLATE MARK. Impressions made from metal plates often show an indentation of the paper extending to just outside the printed area, made when the paper was crushed by the plate during printing.

PORTOLANO, PORTOLAN CHART. A manuscript sea chart prepared for the use of mariners from about the 14th through the 16th-centuries.

PUTTO. Cupid-like child used to decorate maps. The plural is *putti*.

PRINTER'S CREASE. When a map is printed, a small wrinkle in the paper may be compressed to form a permanent crease.

QUARTO. A quarto book is bound from sheets of paper folded in half twice. A map from such a book is sometimes said to be quarto-sized. Typically the vertical paper dimension of such a map is about 9 to 11 inches (23 to 28 cm.). Abbreviated 4to.

RAG PAPER. Paper made from cloth fibers.

RECTO. The side of the paper on which the image of interest appears. Also, the right-hand page of an open book.

REMARGINED. A remargined print has had paper added to the edges to extend them, protecting the original edges, and improving the appearance.

REPRODUCTION. A copy, usually photographically produced, of an original print. The reproduction may in some cases be difficult to distinguish from the original. See the section on "How To Detect Reproductions."

RESTRIKE. A map or view printed from the original plate, block, or stone, after the plate, block, or stone had fallen into disuse. The collector of maps will seldom, if ever, encounter restrikes since few plates or blocks have survived.

RHUMB LINES. Lines criss-crossing old charts at various angles, usually along the directions of the compass points, to help plot courses.

ROCOCO. A style of ornamentation evolving from the baroque in early 18th-century France distinguished by refined use of scrollwork, seashells, foliage and so on. Rococo-style cartouches are often found on maps of the 18th- century.

SEPARATELY PUBLISHED, SEPARATELY ISSUED. A separately published map is one not issued as part of a book or atlas. Sometimes maps usually found in atlases were also separately sold to customers who did not need an entire atlas. Separately issued maps tend to be in poor condition since they were not protected inside a book.

STATE. See discussion at the end of this section.

VERSO. The reverse or opposite side of the sheet from the image of interest. Many maps from atlases have text on the verso. Also the left-hand page of an open book.

VOLVELLE. A contrivance with moving parts for making certain astronomical calculations, sometimes made of paper and found in old geographical works.

WALL MAP. A large map, typically four or five feet (1.5 m.) on a side, with a top rail and a roller, designed to be displayed on a wall. Many are very decorative. Because wall maps are easily soiled and damaged, many were discarded, and examples of early wall maps are quite scarce and often in bad condition.

WATERMARK. A design in the paper visible by transmitted light. For handmade paper, the watermark is made with bent wires placed on the rack on which the fibers are deposited to make the paper. Designs vary from simple initials to intricate coats of arms. Watermarks are often helpful in identifying the age of the paper. See *chain marks*.

WIND ROSE. See *compass rose*.

WOODCUT. An image made by printing from a wooden block on which a mirror image of the design has been carved. Woodcut maps are most often associated with the earliest days of map-making, up to about 1600, but many examples are found well into the 18th-century and later, often as text illustrations.

WOOD ENGRAVING. Similar to a woodcut, but the design is engraved on the end grain, resulting in better detail and a somewhat more uniform appearance. Since the size of exposed end grain is limited by the diameter of the tree trunk, it was usually more economical to cut the design on small squares, which can be glued together for final printing. The joint lines are often visible, for example on the views in *Harper's Weekly*.

WORMING, WORMHOLES, WORM TRACKS. Damage to paper by hungry insect larvae that eat the paper, leaving small holes or tracks.

WOVE PAPER. Machine-made paper deposited during manufacture on a fine wire screen having about the same mesh size as gauze. The impression left by the screen can often be seen by holding the paper to the light. Wove paper came into use around 1800, and is often watermarked with the maker's name.

Terms That Distinguish a Printing or Publication

From a bibliographical standpoint, maps can be difficult to classify because they combine elements of both books and prints. There is particular confusion about the terms *impression*, *plate*, *state*, *issue*, and *edition*. The definitions here follow Lloyd Brown's *Notes on the Care & Cataloging of Old Maps* as closely as possible. Any confusion in the explanation is the fault of the editor, not his. The term *plate* is used below generically as shorthand for *plate, block,* or *stone*.

IMPRESSION. A single copy of a map. For example, if 1,000 copies of a map are printed, there will be, at that time, 1,000 impressions. By this definition, expressions like "second impression" are meaningless, since at this late date, one cannot know the order in which copies were printed. Occasionally, however, it is possible to distinguish between early and late impressions of copper engravings. Copper is soft, and tends to wear. Therefore early impressions tend to be darker, and sometimes faint lettering guidelines used by the engraver are visible on impressions made early in the plate's life.

PLATE. Strictly speaking, the plate is the object from which impressions are made. Sometimes the plate becomes worn or damaged, and is replaced with a second plate. Impressions from the second plate are sometimes referred to as something like "2nd Plate."

STATE. All impressions printed from a given plate, without deliberate alteration of that plate, belong to the same state. If the plate is altered, for example, by adding a new place name or changing the date, impressions from that plate constitute a new state. Some maps have a dozen or more states. States are usually numbered serially. However, "intermediate" states often turn up later. When giving a state number, one should specify who numbered the states, since different authorities often have different numbering. If a new plate was cut, the state numbering may start anew, as in "first state of the second plate."

ISSUE. All impressions printed at one time without alteration of the plate belong to the same issue. Thus, if two impressions are different states, the plate has been altered and they cannot belong to the same issue. However, an unaltered plate might have been used several times over a period years. In that case, the several issues would all be of the same state. Issues can sometimes be distinguished by the watermark, since different paper might have been used for each issue. For maps from atlases, different issues can often be distinguished by the text on the verso.

EDITION. Following Brown, an edition of a map is determined only by the imprint. If the imprint is changed, then there is a new edition. Obviously, since the plate has been changed, a new edition means a new state. However, a new state is not necessarily a new edition, since the imprint may not have been changed.

FOREIGN LANGUAGE DICTIONARIES

Dutch-English

Dutch resembles a cross between English and German. Many variant spellings are found in old Dutch. For example, France has appeared on maps as *Francrijck, Francryck, Frankrijk, Frankryk, Vranckrijck, Vranckryck, Vrancrijck, Vrancryck, Vrankrijk, Vrankryck,* and *Vrankryk,* to mention a few. In some cases, variant spellings are given below. However, users should be aware that many other variants exist. The following letters are often used interchangeably: **(c-ck-k), (d-dt-t), (f-v), (i-ij-y),** and **(s-z).**

aan *adj* on, at
aangrenzend *adj* adjacent
aardbodem *n* earth, earth's surface
aarde *n* earth
aardkloot *n* earth-sphere
acht *card num* eight
achter *prep* behind
Achter Indie *n* Further India
achtste *ord num* eighth
afbeelding *n* depiction, picture
afteekening *n* depiction
al, alle *adj* all
algemeen *adj* general
als mede as well as
anders *adv* otherwise
Antwerpen *n* Antwerp
baai, bay *n* bay
beginnende, beghijnnende *pres part* beginning
begrepen *adj* included
behalve *prep* except, besides
bekend *adj* known
belegering *n* siege
Beloofde Landt *n* Promised Land
bemagtigd *adj* captured
berg *n* mountain
beschrijving *n* description
bij *prep* by (location)
bocht *n* gulf, bight, bend
boeckverkooper, boekverkoper *n* bookseller
Bretagne *n* Brittany
canaal *n* channel
clippen, klippen *n* rocks, reefs
cust *n* coast
d' *art* the
de *art* the
deel *n* part
derde *adj* third
diepte *n* depth
Donau *n* Danube
door *prep* by (authorship), through
dorp *n* village
drie *card num* three
droogte *n* dryness
Duitsland *n* Germany
duizend *card num* thousand
een *art* an, one
eerst *adj* first
eiland *n* island; also *eijland, eijlandt, eylant*
elf *card num* eleven
elfde *ord num* eleventh
en, ende *conj* and
gaet, gat *n* entrance
gebetert *adj* improved
gebiedt *n* region
gecorrigeert *adj* corrected
gedeelte *n* portion
gedruckt *adj* printed
geheel *adj* whole, entire
gelegen *adj* situated
gelegenheid *n* situation; also *gelegentheijt, gelegentheyt, ghelegentheyt*
gelijk gradige zee kaart plane chart
getrokken *adj* extracted
gezigt, gezicht *n* view
Goud Kust *n* Gold Coast
graadboogh *n* quadrant
graade *n* compass
graafschap *n* county, earldom
's-Gravenhage *n* The Hague
Groenlandt *n* Greenland
groot *adj* great
Groot-Brittannie *n* Great Britain
haar *pron* their; also *hare, heure*
half eilandt *n* peninsula
halfrond *n* hemisphere
haven *n* harbor
heerlijkheid *n* manor, district
heilig *adj* holy
Heilige Land *n* Holy Land
het *art* the
Heylighe Landt *n* Heligoland
Hispangien *n* Spain
hoek *n* angle, corner
honderd *card num* hundred
hoofdstad *n* capital
Ierland(t) *n* Ireland
in *prep* in
in sig begrypende containing; also *in zig begrypende*
inde in the
ingang *n* entrance
inhoudende *adj* containing
inkomen, inkoomen *n* entrance
Ioodtsche Landt *n* Holy (i.e., Jewish) Land
jaar *n* year
kaap *n* cape
kaart *n* map; also *caart, caert, kaert*
kaartje *n* maplet, small map
kaartverkoper *n* mapseller
keizerrijk, keyzerryk *n* empire
klein *adj* small
koningrijk *n* kingdom
kust *n* coast
laatste *adj* latest

landengte *n* isthmus
landschap *n* landscape
landstreek *n* region
langs *prep* along
meer *n* lake
met *prep* with
Middellandsche Meer *n* Mediterranean Sea
mitsgaders *prep* together with
mond, mont *n* mouth
na *prep* after
naar *prep* to, towards
naaukeurige, nauwkeurig *adj* accurate
nabijgelegen, nabygelegen *adj* adjacent
neder, neer *adj* lower
Nederland *n* The Netherlands
negen *card num* nine
negende *ord num* ninth
nieuwe *adj* new
noord *adj* north; also *noord, nort*
noordelijk *adj* northern
noordelijkste *adj* northernmost
Noorwegen *n* Norway
oceaan *n* ocean
of, ofte *conj* or
om *prep* round, round about, about
omleggende *adj* surrounding
onder *prep* under
onderkoningschap *n* viceroyalty
ondiepte *n* shoal
ontdekking *n* discovery
ook *adv* also, likewise
oost *adj* east
oostelijcke *adj* eastern
oostelijkste *adj* easternmost
Oostenrijk *n* Austria
op *prep* on, upon, at
opdoeningh *n* discovery
opper *adj* upper
oud *adj* old
over *prep* over, across, beyond
pascaart *n* sea chart; also found with hyphen or space, as *pas-caart* or *pas caart;* also *pascaert, paskaart, paskaert*
plaatsnijder *n* engraver
plaeten, platen *n* banks
platte zee kaart plane chart
plattegrond *n* ground plan, map
Polen *n* Poland
Pruisen *n* Prussia
reede *n* roadstead
reize *n* journey
rievier, rivier *n* river
rijk, ryk *n* kingdom
Rusland *n* Russia
sande plaeten *n* sand banks
schets *n* sketch, outline
schipvaert *n* navigation, seafaring
slick, slijk *n* mire
Soute Eijlanden *n* Cape Verde Islands
Spanje *n* Spain
stad *n* city, town
steeg, steegh *n* alley, lane
straet *n* strait
strekkende *adj* stretching
strom, stroem *n* stream
stuck, stuk *n* part
stuurman *n* helmsman
t' *prep* at, in
't *art* the
Tandt Kust *n* Ivory Coast
te *prep* at, in
tegenvoeters *n* antipodes
tegenwoordig *adv* nowadays
tekening *n* sketch, drawing
tien *card num* ten
tiende *ord num* tenth
tocht, togt *n* journey, expedition
toneel *n* theater, scene
tot *prep* until, to, as far as
tot aan as far as, up to
tusschen, tussen *prep* between, 'twixt
twaalf *card num* twelve
twee *card num* two
tweede *adj* second
uit, uyt *prep* out
uitgegeven *adj* published
van *prep* from, of
vande of the
verbeetert *adj* improved
verdeelt *adj* divided
verdeling *n* division
verdrag *n* treaty, pact
vereenigd, verenegd *adj* united
Verenigde Staten *n* United States
vermaard, vermaerde *adj* famous
vermeerdert *past part* augmented
verthoonende, vertonende *pres part* showing
vertooninghe *n* appearance
vier *card num* four
vierde *adj* fourth
vijf *card num* five
vijfde *ord num* fifth
Vlaanderen *n* Flanders
Vlaemsche *adj* Flemish
Vlaemsche Eijlanden *n* The Azores
vliet *n* brook
vlijt *n* diligence
voerbij *prep* before
volgens *prep* according to
volksplanting *n* colony
voor *prep* for
voornaamste *adj* principal
waar *adj* true
waar *adv* where
waarneming *n* observation
waerachtig *adj* true, accurate
wassende *pres part* increasing
wassende gradige pascaart increasing degree chart, i.e., a Mercator chart
wereld *n* world; also *waereld, wareld, weereld, werreld, werelt*
west *n* west
westelijcke *adj* western
westelijkste *adj* westernmost
wijk *n* district

Dutch-English

woestyne, woestijn *n* desert
Yerlandt, Yrlandt *n* Ireland
Ysland, Ijsland *n* Iceland
zee *n* sea, ocean
zee kaart sea chart
zeer *adv* very
zes *card num* six
zeste, seste *ord num* seventh
zeven *card num* seven
zevende *ord num* seventh
zijne *pron* its
zuid *n* south; also *zuijd, zuyd, zuyt, zur, suyt*
zuidelijk *adj* southern
zuidelijkste *adj* southernmost
Zwarte Zee *n* Black Sea

French-English

French nouns and adjectives have two genders, masculine and feminine. Adjectives and articles agree in gender with the nouns they modify. Plurals are formed as in English by adding **s**, except for words ending in **-au** or **-eu** which add **x**. Adverbs are usually formed from adjectives by adding *-ment* as in *exactement* (exactly). Verbs are conjugated in a somewhat complex manner. Generally the infinitive ends in **-er -ir -oir** or **-re**. The third person singular present indicative often ends in **-t** (*il peut*, he can), while the third person plural ends in **-nt** (*ils peuvent*, they can). In the definitions below, adjectives are given in their masculine and feminine forms.

a *v* (he, she, it) has
à *prep* at, in, to
abrégé, -ée *adj* shortened, condensed
académie *n* academy
Acadie *n* Nova Scotia
actuel, -elle *adj* present, current
adjacent, -ente *adj* adjoining, contiguous
aiguille aimantée *n* compass needle
Allemagne *n* Germany
alors *adv* then
Américain, -aine *adj* American
Amérique *n* America
ancien, -enne *adj* ancient, previous
Anglais, -aise *adj* English
Angleterre *n* England
année *n* year
anse *n* cove
Anvers *n* Antwerp
appellé, -ée *adj* called
après *prep* after
aquatique *adj* aquatic
archiduché *n* archduchy
archevesché, archevêché *n* archbishopric, archdiocese
archipel, archipelague *n* archipelago
armée *n* army
arpent *n* land measure of about an acre
Asie *n* asia
assujetti, -ie *adj* attached, subject
au at the, in the, to the, contraction of *à le*
augmenté, -ée *adj* enlarged, augmented
auspices *n* patronage
aujourd'hui *adv* today
aussi *adv* also, likewise
auteur *n* author
autres *adj* other
autrefois *adv* formerly
Autriche *n* Austria
Autrichien, -ienne *adj* Austrian
aux at the, in the, to the, contraction of *à les*
avec *prep* with
baie, baye *n* bay
banc *n* bank
bas, basse *adj* low
blanc, blanche *adj* white, empty
Bohême *n* Bohemia
bois *n* forest
bouche *n* mouth
bourg *n* borough, market town
boussole *n* compass
Brésil *n* Brazil
Bretagne *n* Brittany
Britannique *adj* British
campement *n* encampment
canal *n* channel, canal
cap *n* cape, headland
capitaine *n* captain
carénage *n* careenage
carte *n* map
Catalogne *n* Catalonia
catholique *adj* catholic
ce *pron* this, that
ceci *pron* this
cela *pron* that
célèbre *adj* celebrated
celles *pron* these, those
celui, celle *pron* this, that
cent *card num* hundred
cet, cette *pron* this, that
cercle *n* circle
ces *adj* these
ceux *pron* these, those
chemin *n* path, track, route
chez *prep* at the place of
Chine *n* China
chinois, -oise *adj* Chinese

chrétien, -enne *adj* Christian
cinq *card num* five
cinquième *ord num* fifth
circonvoisin, -e *adj* surrounding
cité *n* city
Cochinchine *n* Cochin China
colonie *n* colony
comme *conj, adv* like, as
composé, -ée *adj* composed, constituted
comprenant *pres part* comprising, covering
comprend *v* comprises, includes, covers
compris *past part* comprised, included
comte *n* count
comté, comtez *n* county
confins *n* confines, borders
connaissance *n* understanding, knowledge
connu, -ue *adj* known
contenant *pres part* containing
contre *prep* against
copié, -ée *adj* copied
Corée *n* Korea
corrigé ée *adj* corrected
cosmographe *n* cosmographer
cosmographie *n* cosmography
cosmographique *adj* cosmographic
côte, coste *n* coast
couronne *n* crown
cours *n* course
croquis *n* sketch
curieux, -euse *adj* curious, strange
dans *prep* in
dauphin, -ine *n* prince(ss)
de *prep* of
débouquement *n* where a river or strait disembogues, or enters, the sea
déclinaisons *n* magnetic variations
découverte *n* discovery
décrit, -te *past part* described
dédié, -ée *adj* dedicated, inscribed
degré *n* degree
dépost, dépôt *n* depository
depuis *prep* from
dernier, -ère *adj* past, latest
des of the, contraction of *de les*
description *n* description
dessinateur *n* draftsman
dessiné, -ée *adj* drawn, laid out, designed
dessus *prep* upon
destroit, détroit *n* straits
détaillé, -ée *adj* detailed, itemized
deux *card num* two
deuxième *ord num* second
devant *prep* before
dire *v* to say
distinctement *adv* distinctly
distingué, -ée *adj* distinguished
divers *adj* diverse, different, varying
divisé, -ée *adj* divided
dix *card num* ten
dixième *ord num* tenth
Dominique *n* Dominica
dont *rel pron* of which
douze *adj* twelve
douze *card num* twelve
douzième *ord num* twelfth
dressé, -ée *adj* drawn, laid down
du of the, contraction of *de le*
duc *n* duke
duché, duchez *n* duchy
echelle *n* scale
Écosse *n* Scotland
église *n* church
électorat, eslectorat *n* electorate
elle *pron* it, she
elles *pron* they
embouchure *n* river mouth
empereur *n* emperor
empire *n* empire
en *prep* in, at, to
encore *adv* again, more
entier, -ère *adj* entire
entre *prep* between
environs *n* environs
équateur *n* equator
Escosse *n* Scotland
Espagne *n* Spain
espagnol, -ole *adj* Spanish
Espagnols *n* the Spanish
Espérance, Cap de Bonne *n* Cape of Good Hope
esquisse *n* sketch
essai, essay *n* trial, first attempt
est *n* east
est *v* (he, she, it) is
et *conj* and
établissement *n* settlement, establishment
état, estat *n* state
été *past part* been
étendu, -ue, estendu *adj* lying, stretched
étude *n* study, early draft
évangile *n* the Gospel
évêché, éveschez *n* bishopric, see
exactement *adv* exactly
extrait *n* extract
extrémite *n* extrémity, end of the earth
faisant *pres part* making
fait, faite *adj* made, done
faubourg *n* suburbs, outskirts
feu *n* fire
feuille *n* leaf, sheet
fils *n* son
fleuve *n* river
flibustier *n* buccaneer
Floride *n* Florida
fond *n* depth, bottom
fort *n* fort
fort, forte *adj* strong, large
Français, -aise *adj* French
françaises *n* the French
frégate *n* frigate
frère *n* brother
général, -ale *adj* general, universal
Gênes *n* Genoa
Genève *n* Geneva
géographe *n* geographer
géographie *n* geography

géographique *adj* geographical
Georgie *n* Georgia
globe *n* Globe
golfe, golphe *n* gulf, bay
gouvernement *n* government, governance
grand, grande *adj* large, great
gravé, -ée *adj* engraved
Grèce *n* Greece
Grenade *n* Grenada
Groenland *n* Greenland
Gueldre *n* Gelderland
guerre *n* war
habit *n* dress, attire
haut, haute *adj* high
havre *n* harbor
héritier *n* heir
histoire *n* history
historique *adj* historical
horloge *n* clock
huit *card num* eight
huitième *ord num* eighth
hydrographe *n* hydrographer
hydrographie *n* hydrography
hydrographique *adj* hydrographic
illustré, -ée *adj* illustrated
il *pron* he, it
ils *pron* they
impératrice *n* empress
important, -ante *adj* important
imprimé, -ée *adj* printed
inclinaison magnétique *n* magnetic dip
les Indes *n* the Indies
Indien *n* Indian
indiquant *pres part* indicating
inférieur, -ieure *adj* lower
ingénieur *n* engineer
intelligence *n* intelligence, understanding
intérieur, -ieure *adj* interior, inland
intitulé, -ée *adj* entitled
isle, île *n* island
isthme *n* isthmus
itinéraire *n* route
Jamaique *n* Jamaica
Japon *n* Japan
journal *n* journal, logbook, pl. *journaux*
jusque *prep* up to, as far as
l' *art* the (singular)
la *art* the (singular)
lac *n* lake
laquelle *rel pron* who, which
le *art* the (singular)
lequel *rel pron* who, which
les *art* the (plural)
lesquels, lesquelles *rel pron* who, which
leur *pron* their, them
levé, -ée *adj* raised, levied
libraire *n* bookseller
lieu *n* place, pl. *lieux*
lieue *n* league, pl. *lieues*
ligne *n* line, one-twelfth inch
limite *n* limit, boundary
limitrophe *adj* adjoining, bordering
Londres *n* London
lors *adv* then
Louisiane *n* Louisiana
lui *pron* him, her
lunaire *adj* lunar
luy *pron* he
maison *n* house
Malouines *n* Falkland Islands
La Manche *n* English Channel
manière *n* manner, behaviour
manuscrit *n* manuscript
mappe *n* map
mappemonde *n* world map
Maragnon *n* Amazon
marine *adj* marine
marine *n* navy
marqué, -ée *adj* marked
marquisat *n* marquisate
meilleur, -eure *adj* better
même *adj* same
mémoire *n* memoire, report
mer *n* sea
Mer Glaciale *n* Arctic Ocean
Mer du Nord *n* Atlantic Ocean
Mer du Sud *n* Pacific Ocean
méridional, -ale *adj* southern
Mexique *n* Mexico
mieux *adv* better
mille *card num* thousand
ministre *n* minister
moderne *adj* modern
moin *adv* less; least (with *definite article)*
monde *n* world, earth, universe
monseigneur *n* title of respect
mont *n* mountain
montagne *n* mountain
montrant *pres part* showing
mouillage *n* anchorage
mouvement *n* movement, motion
navigateur *n* navigator, sailor
neuf *card num* nine
neuf, neuve *adj* new
neuvième *ord num* ninth
nom *n* name
nord *n* north
nouveau, -el, -elle *adj* new
nouvellement *adv* recently
nouvelles *n* news
observations *n* observations
occident *n* west
occidental, -ale *adj* western
océan *n* ocean
océanique *adj* oceanic
on *pron* someone, one, he
ont *v* (they) have
onze *card num* eleven
onzième *ord num* eleventh
opération *n* operation
ordinaire *adj* ordinary, usual
ordre *n* order
oriental, -ale *adj* eastern
ou *conj* or
où *adv, pron* where
ouest *n* west
ouvrage *n* work
païs, pays *n* land, country, nation
palais *n* palace
palatinat *n* palatinate
par *prep* by, at
particulier, -ière *adj* particular, detailed, special
particulièrement *adv* particularly

partie *n* part
pas *adv* not
pas *n* strait
passage *n* passage
Perse *n* Persia
petit, petite *adj* small
peuples *n* peoples
plan *n* plan, draft, urban map
planisphere *n* planisphere
plus *adv* more; most (with definite article)
plusieurs *adj, pron* several
point *n* point
politique *adj* political
Pologne *n* Poland
port *n* harbor, seaport
portugais, -aise *adj* Portuguese
possédé, -ée *adj* possessed
possédent *pres part* possessing
possessions *n* possessions
pouce *n* inch
pour *prep* for
premier, -ière *adj* first, foremost
près de near
presenté, -ée *adj* presented, offered
preséntement *adv* for the time being, presently
presque *adv* almost, nearly
presqu'île *n* peninsula
principal, -ale *adj* principal, leading, main
principalement *adv* principally, mainly
principauté *n* principality
pris, prise *adj* taken
privilège *n* permission, copyright
province *n* province, country
publié, -iée *adj* published
quatre *card num* four
quatrième *ord num* fourth
quay *n* quay, wharf
que *conj* that
quelque *adj* some
qui *rel pron* who, which, that
rade *n* roadstead, anchorage
recent, -ente *adj* recent, new
récif *n* reef
reconnu, -ue *adj* recognized
rectifié, -iée *adj* corrected
recueil *n* collection, compendium
redigé, -ée *adj* composed, drafted, edited
reduite *adj* reduced, scaled down
reine *n* queen
relation *n* narrative, account
remarque *n* sailor's landmark, comment
remarqué, -ée *adj* remarked, observed
renommé, -ée *adj* well-known
retour *n* return
revu ue *n* revised
riviere *n* river
rocher *n* rock
roi, roy *n* king
route *n* course, road
royaume *n* kingdom
rue *n* street
Russe *n* Russian
Russie *n* Russia
sa *pron* his, her, its
saint, sainte *adj* holy
sauvage *n* savage
se, s' *reflex pron* himself, herself, themselves
seigneurie *n* manor, domain
selon *prep* according to
sept *card num* seven
septentrional, -ale *adj* northern
septième *ord num* seventh
service *n* assistance, service
servir *v* to assist, to serve
ses *pron* his, her, its
siège *n* siege, seat
situé, -ée *adj* located, situated
six *card num* six
sixième *ord num* sixth
son *pron* his, her, its
sonde *n* sounding
sont *v* (they) are
sortie *n* going out, exit
sous *prep* under
statistique *adj* statistical
successeur *n* successor
sud *n* south
Suède *n* Sweden
Suisse *n* Switzerland
suite *n* continuation
suivant *prep* according to, following
supérieur, -ieure *adj* upper, higher
sur *prep* on, upon, above
tableau *n* picture, view
Tamise *n* Thames
terre *n* land, earth, world
Terre Neuve *n* Newfoundland
terrestre *adj* terrestrial
territoire *n* territory, district
tiré, -ée *adj* extracted, derived
titre *n* title
toise *n* fathom
topographique *adj* topographical
tout, toute *adj* all, whole; pl. *tous, toutes*
traduit, -e *adj* translated
treize *card num* thirteen
très *adv* very
tributaire *n* tributary
trois *card num* three
troisième *ord num* third
trouvé, -ée *adj* found
un, une *card num* one
uni, -ie *adj* united
universel, -elle *adj* universal
usage *n* use, *à la usage de* for the use of
vaisseau *n* vessel, pl. *vaisseaux*
vent *n* wind
vierge *n* virgin
vieux, vieil, vieille *adj* old
ville *n* city, town
Virginie *n* Virginia
voir *v* to see
voisin, -ine *adj* neighboring, nearby
voyage *n* voyage
voyageur *n* traveller
vue *n* view

German-English

This list of words most commonly found on German maps should help decipher most titles and legends. Plurals of nouns usually form by adding **-en**, **-e**, **-er**, or **-eln**, and practically never by adding **-s**. Nouns, pronouns, adjectives, and articles have four cases, these also being indicated by endings. It is usually not necessary to know these endings to get the meaning of a short title or phrase. Vowels with umlauts are sometimes written without umlauts followed by an **e**. Thus **ä** becomes **ae**, **ö** becomes **oe**, **ü** becomes **ue**. Sometimes **ss** is writtin as **ß**. German spelling has mutated over the centuries. Sometimes interchanged are: **(c-z)**, **(ch-k)**, **(dt-t)**, **(f-v)**, and **(i-y)**.

Abbildung *n* illustration
Abriß *n* summary, plan, outline
acht *card num* eight
achte *ord num* eighth
all *adj* all
allgemeine *adj* general
alt *adj* old
am at the (*an dem*)
Amt *n* office
an *prep* at, on, by
ander *adj* other
angrenzend *adj* bordering
ans to the (*an das*)
Armee *n* army
auch *conj* also
auf *prep* on, at, by
aus *prep* from, out of, by
ausführlich *adj* detailed, complete
außer *adj* exterior, outer
Aussicht *n* view, prospect
Bach *n* brook, stream
Bad *n* bath
Bahn *n* road, path
Bai, Bay *n* bay
Bayern *n* Bavari
begreifend *pres part* comprising, containing
Begriff *n* concept, idea
bei, bey *prep* at, with, by
Belagerung *n* siege
Belgien *n* Belgium
benachbart *adj* adjoining, neighboring
Berg *n* mountain, hill
berühmt *adj* famous
Beschreibung *n* description
bis *prep* as far as (spatial), till (temporal)
Bisthum, Bistum *n* bishopric, diocese
Blatt *n* sheet
Böhmen *n* Bohemia
Brasilien *n* Brazil
Bruch *n* swamp
Bucht *n* bay, inlet, creek
Charte *n* chart
Churfürstenthum *n* electorate
das *art* the
den *art* the
der *art* the
des *art* the
deutsch *adj* German
Deutschland *n* Germany
die *art* the
Dorf *n* village
drei *card num* three
dritte *ord num* third
durch *prep* through, by means of
eigentlich *adj* true, proper
ein *card num* one
ein, eine *art* a, an
Eismeer *n* Polar Sea
elf *card num* eleven
elfte *ord num* eleventh
Elsaß *n* Alsace
Entdeckung *n* discovery
enthaltend *pres part* containing
Entwurf *n* sketch, draft, plan
Erbe *n* heir
Erde *n* earth, world
Eroberung *n* conquest, acquisition
erst *ord num* first
Erzbisthum *n* archbishopric, archdiocese
Erzherzogthum *n* archduchy
Erzstift *n* archbishopric, archdiocese
Etlich *adj* some, several
Eyland, Eiland *n* island
Fluß *n* river, flow
Fortsetzung *n* continuation
Frankreich *n* France
französisch *adj* French
frey, frei *adj* free
fünf *card num* five
fünfte *ord num* fifth
Fürstenthum *n* principality
gantz, ganz *adj* entire
Gasse *n* street, alley
Gebiet *n* district, region
Gebirge *n* mountain range
gegen *prep* towards, opposite to
Gegend *n* region, district
gehörig *prep* belonging to
Gelobte Land *n* Promised Land
gennant *adj* called, named
Geschichte *n* history
Gestalt *n* shape, form, figure
gezeichnet *past part* signed, drawn, designed
Grafschaft *n* count's domain, county
Griechenland *n* Greece
Grönland *n* Greenland
groß *adj* large
Grundriß *n* ground plan, sketch
Guten Hoffnung, das Kap der *n* Cape of Good Hope
Hafen *n* harbor
Haff *n* lagoon
Halbkugel *n* hemisphere
Halbinsel *n* peninsula

German-English

Haupt *n* principal; *Haupt-* main
Hauptmannschaft *n* captaincy
Hauptstatt, Hauptstadt *n* capital
heilig *adj* holy
Herrschaft *n* manor, estate, dominion
Herzogthum, Herzogtum *n* dukedom, duchy
heutig *adv* nowadays
Hinterindien *n* Indochina
Hochstift *n* bishopric
hundert *card num* hundred
ihr *pron* its, their
im in the (*in dem*)
in *prep* in
Indien *n* India
ins in the (*in das*)
Insel *n* island
Island *n* Iceland
Jahr *n* year
jenseits *prep* beyond
Kap *n* cape
Karte *n* map, chart
Kaspische Meer *n* Caspian Sea
Keyser *n* emperor
klein *adj* small
Kloster *n* monastery, nunnery
Köln *n* Cologne
König *n* king
Königriech *n* kingdom
Kreis *n* circle, district
Kriegsshauplatz *n* theater of war
Kriegstheater *n* theater of war
Krim, der *n* the Crimea
Kurfürstentum *n* electorate
Küste *n* coast
Lager *n* camp
Land *n* land, country
Landgrafschaft *n* landgraviate
Landkreis *n* district, hinterland
Landschaft *n* landscape, estate, district
Lauf *n* course, route
Litauen *n* Lithuania
Livland *n* Livonia
Lothringen *n* Lorraine
Magalhãesstraße *n* Straits of Magellan
Mähren *n* Moravia
Markgrafschaft *n* margraviate
Markt *n* market, market-town
Maßstab *n* scale
Meer *n* sea, ocean
Meerbusen *n* bay, gulf
Meerenge *n* strait, channel
Meile *n* mile, league
mit *prep* with
Mittag *n* south, noon
Mittelländische Meer *n* Mediterranean Sea
Mitternacht *n* north, midnight
Moldau *n* Moldavia
München *n* Munich
nach *prep* after, according to
Neapel *n* Naples
nebst *prep* besides
neu *adj* new
neuest *adj* newest
neun *card num* nine
neunte *ord num* ninth
nieder *adj* low
die Niederlande *n* the Netherlands
Nörd *n* north
nördlich *adj* northern
Nördlicher Polarkreis *n* Arctic Circle
Norwegen *n* Norway
ober *adj* upper, higher
oder *conj* or
Ort, Ohrt *n* place, region
Ost *n* east
Österreich *n* Austria
Ostindien *n* East Indies
östlich *adj* eastern
Ostsee *n* Baltic Sea
die Pfalz *n* the Palatinate
Plan *n* plan, map, chart
Platz *n* place
Preußen *n* Prussia
Provinz *n* province
Quell *n* source
Reich *n* empire. kingdom
Reichsstadt *n* imperial city
Reise *n* voyage
richtig *adj* correct
Russland *n* Russia
sampt, samt *prep* together with
Schlesien *n* Silesia
Schloß *n* castle
die Schweiz *n* Switzerland
sechs *card num* six
sechste *ord num* sixth
See *n* lake, sea, ocean
sehr *adv* very
sein *its* its
sieben *card num* seven
siebente *ord num* seventh
so *adv* so, thus
solch *adj* such
sowohl *conj* as well as
Staat *n* state, country
Stadt, Statt *n* city
Stift *n* bishopric
Stille Meer *n* Pacific Ocean
Straße *n* street, strait
Stück *n* part
Süd *n* south
südlich *adj* southern
Südlicher Polarkreis *n* Antarctic Circle
Südsee *n* South Sea
Sund *n* sound, strait
Tafel *n* table, chart
Tag *n* day
tausend *card num* thousand
Theil, Teil *n* part
Tote Meer *n* Dead Sea
Treffen *n* encounter, battle
über *prep* over, above
übrig *adj* remaining
um *prep* about, around
und *conj* and
Ungarn *n* Hungary
Venedig *n* Venice
verbessert *adj* improved
vereinigt *adj* united
Vereinigten Staaten *n* United States
Vestung *n* fortress
vier *card num* four
vierte *ord num* fourth

German-English

vom from the, of the (*von dem*)
von prep from, of
vor *prep* before, in front of
Vorgebirge *n* promontory, cape, headland, foothills
Vorstellung *n* conception, representation
wahr *adj* true, correct
wahrhaftig *adj* true, genuine
Wald *n* forest
Wasser *n* water
welch *rel pron* which, what, who
Welt *n* world
weltberühmt *adj* world-famous
Welttheil, Weltteil *n* part of the world
Wendekreis des Krebses *n* Tropic of Cancer
Wendekreis des Steinbocks *n* Tropic of Capricorn
Westindien *n* West Indies
wie *adv* how
Wiek *n* bay, cove
Wien *n* Vienna
zehn *card num* ten
zehnte *ord num* tenth
zu *prep* to
zum to the (*zu dem*)
zur to the (*zu der*)
zwei *card num* two
zweite *ord num* second
zwischen *prep* between, among
zwölf *card num* twelve
zwölfte *ord num* twelfth
Zypern *n* Cyprus

Italian-English

A number of early maps have titles in Italian, among them maps by Coronelli, Dudley, Zatta, and publishers of the Lafreri School. Most titles are fairly easy to guess, but the following list of terms may be helpful. Italian nouns and adjectives have two genders, masculine and feminine. Many masculine words end in **-o**, which changes to **-i** in the plural. Many feminine words end in **-a**, which changes to **-e** in the plural. However, there are exceptions. Nouns ending in **-e** in the singular become **-i** in the plural.

For the articles and article-preposition combinations, several forms are given. The form used depends on the gender and starting letter of the following word, but the rules need not be known to translate into English. Occasionally, when a word ends in a vowel, and the following word begins with a vowel, the terminal vowel is often replaced by an apostrophe, as in *dell'America*..

a *prep* to
adiacente *adj* adjacent
ai, agli, alle *prep* to the (pl.)
al, allo, alla *prep* to the (sing.)
alto *adj* high, upper
altrementi *adv* otherwise
altro *adj* other
anticamente *adv* anciently
appresso *prep* near
arcano *n* mystery
atlante *n* atlas
australe *adj* southern
baia *n* bay
banco di sabbia sandbank
basso *adj* low, lower
Belgio *n* Belgium
bocca *n* mouth
boreale *adj* northern
caduta *n* waterfall
canale *n* channel
capitale *n* capital
capo *n* cape
carta *n* map, chart
cento *card num* hundred
che *conj* that
chi *rel pron* who, whom, whose
chiamato *adj* named
Cina *n* China
cinque *card num* five
citta, civita *n* city
coi, cogli, colle *prep* with the, by the (pl.)
col, collo, con lo, colla *prep* with the, by the (sing.)
cominciare *v* to begin
con *prep* with
conosciuto *adj* known
contea *n* county, earldom
contenere *v* to contain
corretto *adj* correct
corso *n* course
cosmografo *n* cosmographer
costa *n* coast
da *prep* from
dai, dagli, dalle *prep* from the, by the (pl.)
dal, dallo, dalla *prep* from the, by the (sing.)
Danimarca *n* Denmark
decimo *ord num* tenth
dei, degli, delle *prep* of the (pl.)
del *prep* of

del, dello, della *prep* of the (sing.)
delineato *adj* drawn
della *prep* of
descritta *adj* described
descrittione, descrizione *n* description
detto *adj* said, called
di *prep* of
dieci *card num* ten
disegno *n* plan, drawing
dodicesimo *ord num* twelfth
dodici *card num* twelve
ducato *n* duchy
due *card num* two
e, ed *conj* and
Egitto *n* Egypt
emisfero *n* hemisphere
entrata *n* entrance
esatto *adj* exact
est *n* east
fatto *adj* done
finire *v* to finish, to end
fino *prep* as far as, until
fiume *n* river
foce *n* mouth
foglio *n* sheet
fortezza *n* fortress
fra *prep* in, between, among
Francia *n* France
Galles *n* Wales
geografia *n* geography
geografico *adj* geographical
geografo *n* geographer
gia *adv* formerly
Giappone *n* Japan
gli *art* the
golfo *n* gulf
grado *n* degree
grande, gran *adj* large
Grecia *n* Greece
hoggidi *adv* nowadays
i *art* the
il *art* the
impero *n* empire
in *prep* in
Inghilterra *n* England
Inglesi *n* Englishmen
intagliata *adj* engraved
intagliatore *n* engraver
intorno *prep* around
Irlanda *n* Ireland
isola *n* island
isoletta *n* islet
istmo *n* isthmus
la *art* the
lago *n* lake
le *art* the
levante *n* east
lo *art* the
Luigiana *n* Louisiana
maestro *adj* main
maestro *n* master
maggiore *adj* greater, major
mappa *n* map
mare *n* sea
meridionale *adj* southern
Messico *n* Mexico
meta *n* half
miglio *n* mile
mille *card num* thousand
minore *adj* lesser, minor
molto *adj* much
mondo *n* world
montagna *n* mountain
monte *n* mount
navigare *v* to navigate, to sail
nei, negli, nelle *prep* in the (pl.)
nel, nello, nella *prep* in the (sing.)
nono *ord num* ninth
nord *n* north
nove *card num* nine
Nuova Zelanda *n* New Zealand
nuovamente *adv* again, newly
nuovo *adj* new
o *conj* or
occidentale *adj* western
Olanda *n* Holland
Olandesi *n* the Dutch
orientale *adj* eastern
osservazione *n* observation, comment
ostro *n* south
ottavo *ord num* eighth
otto *card num* eight
ovest *n* west
ovvero *conj* or
paese *n* country, village
parte *n* part
particolare *adj* particular
penisola *n* peninsula
pianta *n* map
piu *adj* most
polo *n* pole
ponente *n* west
porto *n* harbor, port
Portogallo *n* Portugal
presso *prep* at, by, near, in
primo *ord num* first
principale *adj* principal
privilegio *n* copyright
projezione *n* projection
provincia *n* province, pl. *-cie*
quarto *ord num* fourth
quattro *card num* four
questo, questa *adj* this
qui *adv* here
quinto *ord num* fifth
rada *n* roadstead
rappresentante *pres part* representing
redatto *adj* written, drawn up
regno *n* kingdom
ridotto *adj* reduced
ritratto *n* image
riviera *n* coast
scoperta *n* discovery, pl. *scoperte*
scoperto *adj* discovered
Scozia *n* Scotland
secca *n* shoal
secondo *ord num* second
secondo *prep* according to
sei *card num* six
selvaggio *n* savage, native
sesto *ord num* sixth
sette *card num* seven
settentrionale *adj* northern
settimo *ord num* seventh
sia *conj* else; *sia...sia,* both...and; *o sia,* or else
sino *prep* as far as, until
sobborgo *n* suburb
sonda *n* sound

Italian-English

Soria *n* Syria
sotto *prep* under
Spagna *n* Spain
Spagnuola *n* Hispaniola
specchio *n* mirror
spiaggia *n* shore, beach
stabilimento *n* establishment
stampa *n* printing press, print
stamperia *n* printing establishment
Stati Uniti United States
stretto *n* straits
su *prep* on
sud *n* south
sui, sugli, sulle *prep* on the (pl.)
sul, sullo, sulla *prep* on the (sing.)
suo *adj* his, her, its
superiore *adj* upper
Svezia *n* Sweden
Svizzera *n* Switzerland
tavola *n* map
terra *n* earth
terzo *ord num* third
tramontana *n* north
tre *card num* three
Turchia *n* Turkey
tutto *adj* all
ultimo *adj* latest
un, uno, una *art* a
undicesimo *ord num* eleventh
undici *card num* eleven
Ungheria *n* Hungary
universale *adj* universal
uno *card num* one
vecchio *adj* old
veduta *n* view
vero *adj* true

Latin-English

The following list of words may help beginners translate Latin titles and legends appearing on maps. The Renaissance Latin used on maps is very similar to classical Latin, although there are vocabulary differences.

One cannot teach Latin in a paragraph. However, as a reminder, Latin is an inflected language. Word endings change to reflect usage. Nouns are declined, and entries below give the nominative (subject) case, followed by the genitive (possessive) ending. Plurals and other cases exist, but are not given here. Adjective entries give the three endings for the masculine, feminine, and neuter nominative case. Verbs appear in the third person singular. The vocabulary below should be sufficient to extract the essence of simple phrases. Bear in mind that adjectives may appear before or after the nouns they modify. Also, the letters **i** and **j** are often used interchangeably. In addition, words such as *sculpsit* and *scripsit* were often used loosely, and may merely indicate some unspecified connection between the person named and the map. Some examples may be helpful:

W. Marshall sculpsit. Literally, W[illiam]. Marshall engraved, or more loosely, engraved by William Marshall.

Americae Nova Tabula. Here *America* has been inflected, and appears in the genitive (possessive) singular. Thus the title is New Map of America.

Hispaniae Novae Descriptio. This is very similar to the above example, but now *Novae* agrees with, and thus modifies, *Hispaniae.* Therefore, the translation is Map of New Spain, and not New Map of Spain, which would have been written as *Hispaniae Nova Descriptio.*

a, ab *prep* from, by
Aberdonia *n* Aberdeen
ac *conj* and, and also
accuratissimus, -a, -um *adj* most accurate
adjacens *pres part* adjoining, connecting
Aestivarum Insulae *n* Bermuda, lit. Islands of Summers, i.e., Sommer's Islands
Africus *n* southwest wind
Albion *n* Britain
Albis Fluvius *n* Elbe River
aliquot *indecl num* some, several
Alostum *n* Aalst
Alsatia *n* Alsace
alter, -era, -erum *adj* other

Latin-English

amplissimus, -a, -um *adj* most glorious, splendid, or esteemed
Amstelodamum, -i *n* Amsterdam
Andegavensis Ducatus *n* Anjou
Andegavum *n* Angers
Andreapolis *n* St. Andrews
Anglia, -ae *n* England
annus, -i *n* year
anthropophagi *n* cannibals
Antverpia *n* Antwerp
Aparctias *n* northwind
Apelliotes *n* eastwind
apud *prep* at the establishment of; usually indicates publisher or printer
aqua, -ae *n* water
Aquilo *n* north by northeast wind
Aquisgranum *n* Aachen
archiducatus, -us *n* archduchy
archiepiscopatus, -us *n* archipiscopate
Archipelagus Meridionalis *n* Cyclades Islands
Archipelagus Septentrionalis *n* Aegean Sea
Argentina *n* Strassburg
Argentoratum *n* Strassburg
Argestes *n* northwest wind
Artesia *n* Artois
atque *conj* and, and also
auctor, -is *n* author, creator; *auctore* usually indicates cartographer or draftsman
Augusta *n* Augsburg
Augusta Perusia *n* Perugia
Augusta Trebocorum *n* Strassburg
Augusta Treverorum *n* Treves
Augusta Trinobantum *n* London
Augusta Vangionum *n* Worms
Augusta Vindelicorum *n* Augsburg
Augustodunum *n* Autun
Aurea Chersonesus *n* Malay Peninsula
Aurelia *n* Orleans
Aurelia Allobrogum *n* Geneva
Auster *n* southwind
australis, -e *adj* southern
Babenberga *n* Bamberg
Barchino *n* Barcelona
Bardum *n* Barth
Batavia *n* Djakarta
Bellovacum *n* Beauvais
Bercheria *n* Berkshire
Biturigum *n* Berry
Bononia *n* Bologna
borealis, -e *adj* northern
Borbetomagus *n* Worms
Boreas *n* north by northeast wind
Borussia *n* Prussia
Borysthenis *n* Dniepr River
Brechiniae Comitatus *n* Brecknockshire
Brema *n* Bremen
Breslanus *n* Breslau, Wroclaw
Britannia *n* Britain, Brittany
Brixia *n* Breschia
Brugae *n* Bruges
Brunopolis *n* Braunschweig
Bruxellae *n* Brussels
Byzantium *n* Istanbul
Cadomum *n* Caen
caelavit *v* (he) engraved
caelestis, -e *adj* celestial
Caesar Augusta *n* Saragossa
Caesarea Insula *n* Jersey
Caesarodunum Turonum *n* Tours
Calatia *n* Ciazzo
Caletensium *n* Calais
Caletum *n* Calais
Cambria *n* Wales
Candia, -ae *n* Crete
Cantabrigiensis Comitatus *n* Cambridge
Cantium *n* Kent
Carinthia *n* Karnten
Cecias *n* northeast wind
centum *card num* hundred
Ceretica *n* Cardigan
Cestria *n* Chester
chalcographus, -i *n* engraver
chersonesus, -i *n* peninsula
chorographica, -ae *n* geography
Cimbrica Chersonesus *n* Jutland
Circius *n* north by northwest wind
cis *prep* on this side of
citra *prep* on this side of
Claudiopolis *n* Cluj
Clivia *n* Cleve
cognitus, -a, -um *adj* known, reconnoitered
Colonia *n* Cologne
Colonia Agrippina *n* Cologne
Colonia Allobrogum *n* Geneva
Colonia Claudia *n* Cologne
Colonia Munatiana *n* Basle
Colonia Ubiorum *n* Cologne
Comensis Lacus *n* Lake Como
comitatus, -us *n* county
compendiosus, -a, -um *adj* abridged
complectens *pres part* embracing, comprising
comprehendens *pres part* including
Conatia *n* Connacht
conatus, -us *n* effort, endeavor; *ex conatibus,* by the efforts of
Condivincum Nannetum *n* Nantes
confinis, -e *adj* adjacent
confinis, -is *n* neighboring region
Constantia *n* Constance
Constantinopolis *n* Istanbul
continens, -entis *adj* adjacent, neighboring
conventus, -us *n* district assigned to a city, association
Corcagia *n* Cork
Cornubia *n* Cornwall
Corus *n* northwest wind
Cracovia *n* Cracow
cum *prep* with

Cumbria *n* Cumberland
Dania *n* Denmark
Darbiensis Comitatus *n* Derbyshire
Daventria *n* Deventer
decem *card num* ten
decimus, -a, -um *ord num* tenth
delineavit *v* (he) sketched; usually indicates cartographer or draftsman
Delphi *n* Delft
Denbigiensis Comitatus *n* Denbigh Shire
descripsit *v* (he) drew, indicates cartographer or draftsman
descriptio, -ionis *n* map, representation, description
Devonia *n* Devonshire
dicio, -ionis *n* dominion, sovereignty; also *ditio, -ionis*
dioecesis, -is *n* district, governor's jurisdiction, diocese
Divio *n* Dijon
divisus, -a, -um *adj* divided, separate
dominium, -ii *n* ownership, property, rule
Dorcestria Comitatus *n* Dorsetshire
Dordracum *n* Dordrecht
Duacum *n* Douay
ducatus, -us *n* duchy, dukedom
Dunelmensis Episcopatus *n* Durham
duo, duae, duo *card num* two
duodecim *card num* twelve
Eblana *n* Dublin
Eboracensis Ducatus *n* Yorkshire
editus, -a, -um *adj* published, produced
Elvetiorum Argentina *n* Strassburg
emendatus, -a, -um *adj* corrected, improved, amended
Enipontius *n* Innsbruck
episcopatus, -us *n* episcopate, bishopric
Erfordia *n* Erfurt
et *conj* and
Euroafricus *n* south by southwest wind
Euroauster *n* south by southeast wind
Euronotus *n* south by southeast wind
Euros *n* southeast wind
Eustadium *n* Eichstadt
ex *prep* from, out of
exactissime *adv* most exactly
exactissimus, -a, -um *adj* most exact
excudebat, excudit, excud., exc. *v* (he) made or struck; usually indicates printer or publisher
exhibens *pres part* displaying
Exonia *n* Exeter
facies *n* shape, appearance, face
Faventia *n* Faenza
Favonius *n* westwind
fecit *v* (he) made, produced, created, or prepared; usually indicates engraver
fere *adv* approximately
finitimus, -a, -um *adj* neighboring
Fionia *n* Funen Island
Firenze *n* Florence
Florentia *n* Florence
florentissimus, -a, -um *adj* most flourishing, prosperous, or eminent
flumen, -inis *n* river
fluvius, -ii *n* river
forma, -ae *n* figure, design, sketch, plan
formis indicates publisher
Forum Iulii *n* Friuli
Forum Livii *n* Forli
fretum, -i *n* strait, channel
Frisia *n* Friesland
Fulgineum *n* Foligno
Gades *n* Cadiz
Gallia, -ae *n* France
Gallovidia *n* Galway
Ganabum *n* Orleans
Gand, Gandavum *n* Ghent
Gebenna *n* Geneva
Geldria *n* Gelderland
Genabum *n* Orleans
geographicus, -a, -um *adj* geographical
Germania Inferior *n* Netherlands
Glascua *n* Glasgow
Glotta *n* Clyde
Graecia *n* Greece
Gratianopolis *n* Grenoble
Gravionarium *n* Bamberg
Hafnia *n* Copenhagen
Haga Comitis *n* The Hague
Hammona *n* Hamburg
Hannonia *n* Hainaut
Hanovia *n* Hanau
Hantonia Comitatus *n* Hampshire
Hassia *n* Hesse
Helenopolis *n* Frankfort on Main
Hellas *n* Greece
Hellespontius *n* northeast wind
Helvetia *n* Switzerland
Herbipolis *n* Wurtzburg
heres, heredis *n* heir, successor
Hibernia, -ae *n* Ireland
Hierosolyma *n* Jerusalem
Hispalis *n* Seville
Hispania *n* Spain
hodie *adv* today, nowadays
hodiernus, -a, -um *adj* present, modern
Holmia *n* Stockholm
Holsatia *n* Holstein
Huntingdonensis Comitatus *n* Huntingdonshire
Illyricum *n* Dalmatia
imago, -inis *n* image, likeness, copy
Imaus Mons *n* Himalayas

impensa, -ae *n* cost, expense; *impensis* usually indicates publisher
impensus, -a, -um *adj* expensive
imperium, -ii *n* empire, dominion
in *prep* in, on, at
incidit, incidebat *v* (he) cut; usually indicates engraver
incola, -ae *n* inhabitant
inferior, -ius *adj* lower
instruavit *v* usually indicates engraver
insula, -ae *n* island
integro, -a, -um *adj* whole, entire
invenit *v* (he) devised; usually indicates cartographer or draftsman
inventor *n* usually indicates cartographer
Islandia *n* Iceland
item *adv* likewise, also, in the same manner
Iuliacensis Ducatus *n* Julich
Iutia *n* Jutland
iuxta, juxta *prep* near
lacus, -us *n* lake
Lancastria Palatinatus *n* Lancashire
Larius Lacus *n* Lake Como
Latium *n* Lazio
Legio *n* Leon
Leida *n* Leyden
Leicestrensis Comitatus *n* Leicestershire
Lemovicense Castrum *n* Limoges
Lemovicum *n* Limousin
Leodium *n* Liege
Leucorea *n* Wittemburg
Libonotus *n* south by southwest wind
Libs, Lips *n* southwest wind
limes, limitis *n* boundary, route
Lipsia *n* Leipzig
litus, litoris *n* coast, beach
locus, -i *n* place, district
Londinum *n* London
Lotharingia *n* Lorraine
Lovanium *n* Louvain
Ludoviciana *n* Louisiana
Lugdunum *n* Lyons
Lugdunum Batavorum *n* Leiden
Lusatia *n* Lausitz
Lusitania *n* Portugal
Lutetia *n* Paris
Lutzenburgum *n* Luxembourg
Mantua Carpetanorum *n* Madrid
mappa, -ae *n* map
marchionatus, -us *n* marquisate
Mare Hyrcanum *n* Caspian Sea
Mare Rubrum *n* Red Sea
mare, -is *n* sea, ocean
Matritum *n* Madrid
Mediolanum *n* Milan
meridionalis, -e *adj* southern
Mervinia Comitatus *n* Merionethshire
milia, -ium *card num* thousand
mille *adj* a thousand
Misnia *n* Meissen
Moguntia *n* Mainz
Moguntiacum *n* Mainz
Momonia *n* Munster
Mona *n* Isle of Man
Monachium *n* Munich
Monasterium *n* Munster
Montensis Ducatus *n* Bergh
Montisferratus *n* Monferrato (Italy)
Monumenthis Ducatus *n* Monmouthshire
mundus, -i *n* the world, the universe, the earth
Mutina *n* Modena
Namurcum *n* Namur
Nannetum *n* Nantes
Nassovia *n* Nassau
Natolia *n* Asia Minor
nec non besides, and also
nec, neque *conj* and besides, and also
Neocomum *n* Neuchatel
neotericus, -a, -um *adj* modern
Nicsia *n* Naxos
nonus, -a, -um *ord num* ninth
Nordovicum *n* Norwich
Norimberga *n* Nuremberg
Northantonensis Comitatus *n* Northamptonshire
Notus *n* southwind
novem *card num* nine
Novesium *n* Neuss
Noviodunum *n* Nevers
Noviomagum *n* Nijmegen
novissimus, -a, -um *adj* newest, most recent
noviter *adv* newly
novus, -a, -um *adj* new
nunc *adv* now, nowadays
ob *prep* because of, against
occidentalis, -e *adj* western
oceanus, -i *n* ocean
octavus, -a, -um *ord num* eighth
octo *card num* eight
officina, -ae *n* workshop, factory, *ex officina --,* from the workshop of, i.e., published or printed by
olim *adv* once, at that time, formerly
oppidum, -i *n* town
ora *n* border, coast
ora maritima *n* seacoast
orbis, -is *n* globe, circle, world, earth, orbit
Orcades *n* Orkneys
orientalis, -e *adj* eastern
Oxonium Comitatus *n* Oxfordshire
pagus *n* village, province
Palatinatus Bavariae *n* Oberpfalz
Palatinatus Rheni *n* Rheinland-Pfalz
Panormum *n* Palermo
Papia *n* Pavia
pars, partis *n* part, region
Parthenope *n* Naples
Parthenopolis *n* Magdeburg

passim *adv* here and there, all over
Patavium *n* Padua
Pedemontana *n* Piedmont
per *prep* through, by
Perusia *n* Perugia
Pictavium *n* Poitiers
pictor, -oris *n* painter
pinxit *v* (he) drew, painted, or decorated
plus, pluris *adj* more
Polonia *n* Poland
Pontus Euxinus *n* Black Sea
praecipuus, -a, -um *adj* excellent, extraordinary, special
praesertim *adv* especially
praeter *conj* besides
praeter *prep* past, beyond
presbiter *n* elder, priest
Presbiter Ioannis *n* Prester John
pretiosus, -a, -um *adj* expensive, valuable, precious
primus, -a, -um *ord num* first
privilegium, -ii *n* private law; *cum privilegio* usually indicates copyright
promissionis *n* promise
proprius, -a, -um *adj* special, individual, particular
prout *conj* as, just as
Provincia *n* Provence
quartus, -a, -um *ord num* fourth
quattuor *card num* four
-que *conj* and, used as a suffix
qui, quae, quod *rel pron* who, which, what, that
quinque *card num* five
quintus, -a, -um *ord num* fifth
Ratisbona *n* Regensburg
recens, -entis *adj* recent
recens, recenter *adv* recently, newly
regio, -ionis *v* line, boundary, region
Regiomontium *n* Konigsberg
regnum, -i *n* kingdom, dominion
retectus, -a, -um *adj* discovered, opened, made accessible
Rhedones *n* Rennes
Rhenolandia *n* Rheinland
Rhenus Fluvius *n* Rhine River
Ripen *n* Ribe
Rothomagum *n* Rouen
Rugia *n* Rugen Island
Rupella *n* La Rochelle
Sabaudia *n* Savoy
Sacra Insula, Insula Sacra *n* Holy Island
Salmantica *n* Salamanca
Salopia *n* Shrewsbury
Salopiae Comitatus *n* Shropshire
sanctus, -a, -um *adj* holy
Sarnia Insula *n* Guernsey
Saxonia Inferior *n* Lower Saxony
Saxonia Superior *n* Upper Saxony
Scania *n* Zealand Island
Schedamum *n* Scheidam
scilicet *adv* certainly, naturally
Scio *n* Chios
Sclavonia *n* Slavonia
Scotia, -ae *n* Scotland
scripsit *v* (he) wrote or drew; sometimes indicates lettering engraver
sculpsit, sculp., sc. *v* (he) carved; usually indicates engraver
secundum *prep* according to
secundus, -a, -um *ord num* second
sedes belli *n* seat of war
Senae *n* Siena
septem *card num* seven
Septentrio *n* northwind
septentrionalis, -e *adj* northern
septimus, -a, -um *ord num* seventh
Servia *n* Serbia
seu *conj* or
sex *card num* six
sextus, -a, -um *ord num* sixth
Sinarum Regio *n* China
Sinus Gangeticus *n* Bay of Bengal
situs, -a, -um *adj* situated
situs, -us *n* position, situation, site
sive *conj* or
Somersettensis Comitatus *n* Somersetshire
sophus, -a, -um *adj* wise
Soria *n* Syria
Sorlinges *n* Scillies
stellatus, -a, -um *adj* starry
Stiria *n* Steiermark
subjacens, -entis *adj* near
Subsolanus *n* eastwind
Suecia *n* Sweden
Suevia *n* Sweden
sumptus, -us *n* cost; *sumptibus,* at the cost of; usually indicates publisher
superior, -is *adj* upper, higher
Sylva Ducis *n* Bois-Le-Duc
tabula, -ae *n* map
tam *adv* so, so much, to such an extent
tam ... quam... both ... and ...
Taprobana *n* Ceylon
Taraco *n* Tarragona
Tarvisium *n* Treviso
Taurica Chersonesus *n* Crimea
Taurinum *n* Turin
Terra Sancta *n* Holy Land
terra, -ae *n* the earth, land
terrestris, -e *adj* earthly, terrestrial
tertius, -a, -um *ord num* third
theatrum belli *n* theater of war
Tholosa *n* Toulouse
Thrascias *n* north by northwest wind
Ticinum *n* Pavia
Tigurum *n* Zurich
Toletum *n* Toledo
Tornacum *n* Tournai

totus, -a, -um *adj* all, entire, total; gen. *totius*
tractus, -us *n* district, region
Trajectum *n* Utrecht
Trajectum ad Mosam *n* Utrecht
Trajectum ad Viadrum *n* Frankfort on Oder
trans *prep* across, beyond
Transisulana *n* Overijssel
Trebia *n* Trevi
Trecae *n* Troyes
tres, tria *card num* three
Treveris *n* Treves (Trier)
tribus, -us *n* tribe
Tricasses *n* Troyes
Tridentum *n* Trent
Turcicum Imperium *n* Ottoman Empire
Turonum *n* Tours
Tuscia *n* Tuscany
typus, -i *n* image, figure
Ultonia *n* Ulster
Ultrajectum *n* Utrecht
Ulyssipo *n* Lisbon
undecim *card num* eleven
universalis, -e *adj* universal
unus, -a, -um *card num* one
urbs, urbis *n* city
Ursina *n* Bern
uterque, utraque, utrumque *adj or pron* each, both; gen. *utriusque*
Utinum n Udina
Valesium *n* Valois
Vallisoletum *n* Valladolid
Vectis Insula *n* Isle of Wight
vel *conj* or
Venetia *n* Venice
Venetum *n* Veneto
ventus, -i *n* wind; *ventorum,* of the winds
verissimus, -a, -um *adj* truest
vernacule *adv* in the vernacular
Veromandua *n* Vermandois
Verona *n* Bonn, Verona
verus, -a, -um *adj* true, actual
vetus, -eris *adj* old
Vicentia *n* Vicenza
vicinus, -a, -um *adj* nearby
Vienna *n* Vienne
Vindobona *n* Vienna
Vitemberga *n* Wittemburg
Vormatia *n* Worms
vulgo *adv* commonly, generally, in the vernacular
Vulturnus *n* southeast wind
Wallia *n* Wales
Wetteravia *n* Wetterau
Wigorniensis Comitatus *n* Worcestershire
Wiltonia, Wiltoniensis Comitatus *n* Wiltshire
Zephyrus *n* westwind
Zerbi *n* Djerba Island

DEALERS' CONCERNS: Organizing a Catalogue

At the outset, one must decide how to organize the catalog. There are several systems in common use:

1. Chronologically, beginning with the earliest item.
2. Alphabetically by author.
3. Geographically, and chronologically within each region.
4. Geographically, and alphabetically by author within each region.

All of these systems are used. The drawbacks of 2 and 4 are that the 'author' can sometimes be one of several names, perhaps misleading someone trying to find a particular item. For example, should Crepy's version of the Popple map of North America be listed under Crepy or Popple? The most popular arrangements are 3 and 4, but any sensible arrangement that suits the material is fine.

In describing each item, the following information should be given:

MAP-MAKER. There is some ambiguity in map authorship. One might cite the engraver, publisher, cartographer, or others associated with the map production. Custom generally dictates the choice. For example, maps in Blaeu's atlases are generally attributed to Blaeu, regardless of engraver or cartographer.

TITLE. The title should be given as fully as possible. Strict bibliographical standards dictate copying the exact spelling and punctuation. Some titles are very long, and it is customary in such cases to omit some of the unnecessary verbiage. Ellipses (". . .") should be used to indicate portions omitted. However, it is best to retain places, dates, and personal names, since these are of most value in identifying the item. For example, a title might be:

> **A New & Accurate Chart of the World. Drawn from Authentic Surveys, Assisted by the Most Approved Modern Maps & Charts & Regulated by Astronl. Observations.**

A barely acceptable abbreviation might be:

> **A New & Accurate Chart of the World . . .**

Some confusing abbreviations would be:

> **A New and Accurate Chart of the World . . .** (& replaced by *and*)
>
> **A New & Accurate Chart of the World Etc.** (*Etc.* not really part of title)
>
> **The World** (Much too vague to identify)
>
> **Chart of the World** (Too vague, and no ellipses)
>
> **. . . Chart of the World . .** (Better, but still too vague)

For purposes of the *Price Record*, it is well to have the exact beginning of the title, since that makes the alphabetical "Title Index" more useful. It is also helpful to have the title set off by quotes, underlining, boldface type, or some other method, since it is sometimes hard to tell where the title stops and the description begins. Common problems in title transcription include interchanging 'and' and '&,' or 'etc.' and '&c.,' or substituting 'U.S.' for 'United States'. Map titles can be a confusing mix of lettering styles, with upper and lower case letters. Most dealers just use normal capitalization, or give the title in all capitals. Sometimes there is an engraver's signature or publisher's imprint on the maps. Strictly speaking, these should be described separately, but are sometimes strung at the end of the title, as in *A New Map of America. J. Gibson Sc*. When a map has no title, a descriptive title can be supplied in brackets [ ].

DATE. The date can be somewhat confusing. For example, a map from a 1587 edition of Ortelius could be dated as **1587**. However, the map may have first appeared in the 1570 edition, and last appeared in the 1612 edition. Ideally, one could explicitly state something like **1570 (1587)**. However, it is sometimes not possible for the dealer to determine the exact edition. In such cases, the date of first publication is often used. If one knows the range, but not the exact date, one might give **1570-1612**. Sometimes it is easier to just explain what is known about the date.

DIMENSIONS. The dimensions should be given accurately. Height first, and width second, is the most common system. Dimensions are usually measured to the outside of the border. Sometimes a title or signature appears outside the border. It is preferable to exclude this from the dimensions, but there is no standard system. Dimensions can, of course, be given in inches or metric units (either cm. or mm.). Dimensions in the *Price Record* are rounded to the nearest centimeter and half-inch. To be on the safe side and because some customers may want more accurate measurements, it is well to measure small maps to the nearest eighth-inch or millimeter. On larger maps this precision can be difficult, and the nearest quarter-inch or half-centimeter is usually adequate. On huge wall maps, or folding maps, the nearest half-inch or nearest centimeter is about the best attainable.

CONDITION. If the map is in reasonably typical condition for its age, condition is sometimes omitted. It is advisable to mention noticeable flaws. Long tears into the margins, separations at the centerfold, spotting (foxing), offsetting, stains, narrow margins, and other flaws should be mentioned. Any repairs should be noted.

COLORING. This should be noted. Outline coloring usually means that just the boundaries or coastlines are colored. When the land areas are wash colored, this is sometimes referred to as *fully colored* or *body color*. Sometimes the land area is fully colored, but the cartouche has been left uncolored. This can be specifically mentioned.

PRICE. Do not forget this! It can (and does) get omitted from time to time. Some dealers provide a separate sheet listing the prices for the items in their catalogue.

Items which are helpful, but not necessary, include an illustration of the map, the publisher and place of publication, the work (if any) from which the map was removed, comments about the significance of the map, reference books mentioning the map, and a number for customer reference when ordering. The arrangement of each entry should be as pleasing to the eye, and as easy to read, as possible. Different type styles and indentation can be used to separate the various types of information.

There are a few terminology problems, including confusing margin and border. The border is the printed line or design surrounding the map. The margin is the blank area outside the border. The term *marginal* should be avoided, since *marginal staining* could mean either staining in the margins, or minor staining. *Mounted* is also ambiguous, since it often means backed, but could also mean matted.

Lloyd Brown's *Notes on the Care & Cataloguing of Old Maps*, is a good source of information for preparing a catalogue.

Map Dealer Questionnaire

Note to Map Dealers: We urge you to return a photocopy of this form annually so that our records and the information about your firm is certain to be current and correct. You may make any modifications you wish or simply indicate that there is no change. We have provided a line for FAX numbers which are increasingly widespread. Dealers world-wide may now supply information about their mode of business and specialties.

If you were omitted and wish to appear in the "Directory of Dealers" next year, please complete a photocopy of this form and return it to us by our year end deadline, December 31. Thank you for your cooperation.

1. Your business name: ______________________________

2. Your personal name: *(optional)* ______________________________

3. Your preferred address: ______________________________

____

____

4. Telephone number: ________________________

5. FAX number: ________________________

6. Check any that apply:

(a) ______ Do you maintain regular shop hours?

(b) ______ Do you see customers by appointment only?

(c) ______ Do you sell by mail?

(d) ______ Do you exhibit at fairs?

(e) ______ Do you issue catalogs or price lists?

(f) ______ Is your establishment an auction house?

7. If you have a specialty (i.e., Americana, sea charts, maps of the Holy Land, decorative maps, etc.), please indicate it briefly. Be careful in answering. Users may assume your stock is restricted to the area you specify. If your stock is reasonably general, leave blank.

____

8. If you are *no longer in business*, check here. ______

Please return a photocopy of this form to:

Kimmel Publications, P.O. Box 12, Amherst, MA 01004, USA. Fax (413) 256-6291

DIRECTORY OF DEALERS

The following list of dealers has been compiled from various sources. Originally, questionnaires were sent to over 200 dealers when Volume 1 was in preparation, and the information received in reply was incorporated in the 1983 edition. Since then, the number has grown to about 700 dealers globally as current information is added. The list is also used for sending announcements of each new volume. While every attempt is made to keep it reasonably current, there may be some inappropriate entries. Some dealers may be retired, no longer active or may have moved. Others may be book, print, or antique dealers who deal only occasionally in maps. One or two dealers in modern maps have been included. Since no questionnaires were sent outside North America, the international dealer lists include only addresses and telephone numbers.

With Volume 12, in 1994, we will be expanding the scope of information supplied for international dealers to match that given for North America. Many have added fax machines to assist in communications. We will need the cooperation of dealers world wide in assembling the data. We urge all dealers in antique maps to take a moment to return a copy of the ***Map Dealer Questionnaire*** (on Page 49) to us by December 31, 1993, for inclusion in the next edition of the *Antique Map Price Record & Handbook.* This way we can update information or confirm that which is presently in our records. For your convenience, you may use the publisher's Fax Number on the questionnaire.

Apologies are extended to any dealers inadvertently omitted or mistakenly included. Again, dealers who are not yet listed should use the questionnaire. And any errors should be called to the attention of the publisher so that corrections can be made in future editions.

Inclusion of a name should not be regarded as an endorsement by the publisher, nor should omission be regarded as a lack of such endorsement.

Finally, when writing to dealers for catalogs or quotes, please remember that it is far more efficient to give a detailed description of the material you desire, and that some dealers charge a small fee for their catalogues.

IMPORTANT!

Even though some entries do not indicate that an appointment is required, the information is not always complete, and even dealers with shop hours can be preoccupied with some activity such as preparation for a book fair. Therefore it is suggested that you either write or telephone before visiting.

United States Dealers in Alphabetical Order

H. Abrams, P.O. Box 13673, Atlanta, GA 30324.

Acquitania Gallery, 158 Carl St., San Francisco, CA 94117. (415) 664-2707, Fax same. By appt..

Richard H. Adelson, North Pomfret, VT 05023.

Alaskana Book Shop, 4617 Arctic Blvd., Anchorage, AK 99503. (907) 561-1340. Alaska, mountain climbing, hunting, U.S.G.S. Shop hours, by mail.

Alaskan Heritage Bookshop, P.O. Box 22165, Juneau, AK 99802. (907) 586-6748.

Americana Mail Auction, George M. Rinsiland, 4015 Kilmer Ave., Allentown, PA 18104.

Amherst Antiquarian Maps, P.O. Box 12, Amherst, MA 01004. (413) 256-8900. By appt., by mail, shows & fairs, catalogues/lists.

Joyce Amkraut, 35 Winding Wood Rd. N., Port Chester, NY 10573. (914) 939-1509. By appt., by mai auction.

Andover Antiquarian Books / Gallery, 68 Park St., Andover, MA 01810. (617) 475-1645. Shop hours.

Anian Ltd., James V. Walker, 4450 Pinecrest Dr., Eugene, OR 97405. (503) 485-8727.

Antipodean Books, D. & C. Lilburne, P.O. Box 189, Cold Spring, NY 10516. (914) 424-3867. Australia.

Antiquarian Map & Book Den, James E. Hess, 217 E. New St.; P.O.Box 412, Lititz, PA 17543. (717) 626-5002, Fax same (push #6). By appt., by mail, shows & fairs, auction.

The Antiquarian Old Book Store, 1070 Lafayette Rd., Portsmouth, NH 03801. (603) 436-7250.

The Antiquarian Shop, 4246 N. Scottsdale Rd., Scottsdale, AZ 85251. (602) 947-0535.

Antique Brokers, 1716 Westheimer, Houston, TX 77098.

Antique Maps & Prints, 3583 Cosmos St., Palm Beach, FL 33410.

Antique Prints Ltd., Robert & Marth Seamans, Central Ave #42; Rt. 1, Box 156, Ocean View, DE 19970. (302) 539-6702. Topographical views, 17th-19th century maps. By appt., by mail, shows & fairs, auction.

Antiquities, Ltd., Rhodes T. Rumsey, P.O. Box 18659, Atlanta, GA 30326.

W. Graham Arader III, 1000 Boxwood Court, King of Prussia, PA 19406. (215) 825-6570. Shop hours, by mail, shows & fairs, catalogues/lists.

W. Graham Arader III, 29 E. 72nd St., New York, NY 10021. (212) 628-3668, Fax (212) 879-8714.

W. Graham Arader III, 1835 County Line Rd., Villanova, PA 19085. (215) 527-7950.

W. Graham Arader III, 620 N. Michigan Ave., #470, Chicago, IL 60611. (312) 337-6033.

W. Graham Arader III, 2800 Virginia St., Houston, TX 77098. (713) 527-8055.

W. Graham Arader III, 435 Jackson St., San Francisco, CA 94111.

Argonaut Book Shop, 792 Sutter St., San Francisco, CA 94109. (415) 474-9067.

Argosy Gallery, 116 E. 59th St., New York, NY 10022. (212) 753-4455.

Ark-La-Tex Book Company, L.S. Hooper, P.O. Box 564, Shreveport, LA 71102.

Arkadyan Books & Prints, Gerald Webb, 926 Irving St., San Francisco, CA 94122. (415) 664-6212. California as an island. Shop hours, by mail, shows & fairs, catalogues/lists.

Richard B. Arkway, 538 Madison Ave., New York, NY 10022. (800) 453-0045, (212) 751-8135, Fax (212) 832-5389. Shop hours, by mail, shows & fairs, catalogues/lists.

Art Source International, 1237 Pearl, Boulder, CO 80302. (303) 444-4080, Fax (303) 444-4298. Shop hours, by mail, catalogues/lists.

Asian Rare Books, Inc., 234 5th Ave., 3rd floor, New York, NY 10001.

The Atlas, Thomas E. Greene, 119 Olney Ave., P.O. Box 3822, North Providence, RI 02911. (401) 353-1161. By appt., by mail.

Authentic Antique Maps, Stuart Kaminsky, 3101 State Rd., 580, Safety Harbor, FL 33572.

Barrister's Gallery, (At Nearing's Antiques), 526 Royal, New Orleans, LA 70130. (504) 525-2767. 19th century, search service for finer items. Shop hours, by mail.

Donald M. Barton, 2336 Magnolia Blvd. West, Seattle, WA 98199. (206) 285-4500. General, north Pacific & northwest America. By appt., by mail, catalogues/lists, auction.

Bay Books, David N. Harbaugh, P.O. Box 40306, Bay Village, OH 44140. (216) 835-5444. Atlases & maps,pre-1915. By appt., by mail, shows & fairs, catalogues/lists.

Bayou Books, 1005 Monroe St., Gretna, LA 70053. (504) 368-1171.

Mary Beth Beal, 3913 N. Claremont Ave., Chicago, IL 60618. (312) 539-0105.

James K. Beier, Maps, Atlases, Prints, Newspapers, 2432 Springdale Rd. #16, Waukesha, WI 53186. (414) 549-5985. Maps & prints of all areas, specializing in early European, Colonial, Civil War, and Old West newspapers. Shop hours, by mail, catalogues/list.

Susan Benjamin, 13721 W. Telegraph Rd., Santa Paula, CA 93060. (805) 933-3193.

Bickerstaff's, Stephen P. Hanly, 3 Ellery Road, Waltham, MA 02154. (617) 899-5504. 18th & 19th-century American maps with emphasis on New England. By mail, shows & fairs, catalogues/lists.

United States Dealers

Bill George International, William G. Smith, 200 E. 66th St. #C1702, New York, NY 10021. (212) 688-2693.
Book & Record Land, 708 W. Wisconsin Ave, Milwaukee, WI 53233.
The Book Cellar Ltd., 8227 Woodmont Ave., Bethesda, MD 20814.
Booked Up, 1214 31st St. NW, Washington, DC 20007. (202) 965-3244.
The Bookpress, P.O. Box KP, Williamsburg, VA 23187. (804) 229-1260. Located at 420 Prince George St. Shop hours, by mail, shows & fairs, catalogues/lists.
The Bookstall, 570 Sutter St., San Francisco, CA 94102.
Boxwood Farm, Antique Prints, Richard Procopio & Diane Ihrig, P.O. Box 422, Rockport, ME 04856. (207) 236-8233.
Branford Rare Books, P.O. Box 2088, Branford, CT 06405.
Phyllis Y. Brown, Antique Prints & Maps, 736 De Mun, St. Louis, MO 63105. (314) 725-1023. Shop hours.
Buxbaum Geographics, P.O. Box 465, Wilmington, DE 19899.
California Book Auction, Butterfield & Butterfield Div., 220 San Bruno Ave., San Francisco, CA 94103. (415) 861-7500, ext 204, Fax (415) 861 8951. Auctions.
California Land & Exploration Co., Scott Brake, 358 East Yale Loop, Irvine, CA 92714. (714) 857-2392, Fax (714) 559-1854. California coastal & "island" maps. By appt., by mail.
Camelot Books, James A. Kissko, 2403 Hillhouse Rd., Baltimore, MD 21207. America. By appt., by mail, catalogues/lists, auction.
Lawson J. Cantrell, Maps, Books & Prints, Shadow Hill, P.O. Box 576, Accomac, VA 23301. (804) 787-1285.
Caravan Book Store, Lillian Bernstein, 550 S. Grand Ave., Los Angeles, CA 90071. (213) 626-9944.
Bernard Conwell Carlitz, 1970 New Rodgers Rd., #C-36, Levittown, PA 19056.
Thomas Edward Carroll, Antiques - Maps, P.O. Box 323, Montague, MA 01351. (413) 367-9753. Early maps to 1800. By mail, shows & fairs.
Cartographic Arts, Patricia & Luke Vavra, P.O. Box 2202, Petersburg, VA 23804. (804) 861-6770. By appt., by mail, shows & fairs, catalogues/lists.
Cartographics of Vermont, P.O. Box 145, East Middlebury, VT 05740. (802) 388-6488, Shop (802) 388-6229. Atlases, school geogs., pocket/wall maps of N. Amer., Vt., Lake Champlain & New England; Shop at Middlebury Antique Ctr. Shop hours, by mail, catalogues/list.
The Cartophile, William T. Clinton, 934 Bridle Lane, West Chester, PA 19382. (215) 692-7697. By mail.
El Cascajero, The Old Spanish Book Mine, 506 W. Broadway, New York, NY 10012. (212) 254-0905. Shop hours, by mail, shows & fairs, catalogues/lists.
Jo-Ann & Richard Casten, Ltd., 4 Dodge Lane, Old Field, NY 11733. (516) 689-3018, Fax (516-689-8909). World, America, Holy Land, Asia. Also at 101 W. 81st St. #207, New York, NY 10024; (212) 496-5483. By appt., by mail, shows & fairs, catalogues/lists.
The Centuries, 517 St. Louis, New Orleans, LA 70130.
Chafey's Books & Prints, 3511 Sunnyside Ave., Philadelphia, PA 19129. (215) 843-2499.
Chartifacts, Walter J.Auburn, P.O. Box 8954, Richmond, VA 23225. (804) 272-7120. U.S. Coast Survey charts & reprints, 1840s to 1900s. By appt., by mail, shows & fairs, catalogues/lists.
Chartwell Mapsellers, S.I. Miller, P.O. Box 1207, Huntsville, AL 35807. (205) 536-1521. Alabama, Southeast U.S. By mail.
Chesapeake Galleries, Ridgely Bldg. #103, 205 E. Joppa Rd., Towson, MD 21204.
Chilton's Inc., 4404 Old Shell Rd., Mobile, AL 36604. (205) 343-1736.
Dennis Clare, 818 Duboce Ave., San Francisco, CA 94117. (415) 552-0437. Western U.S.
Taylor Clark Gallery, 2623 Government St., Baton Rouge, LA 70806. (504) 383-4929.
The Clipper, R. Antonation, 4911 S. Genesee St., Seattle, WA 98118.
John P. Coll, 2944 Pine Ave., Berkeley, CA 94705. (415) 845-8475.
Collectors Circle Ltd., Lili Ramonis, P.O. Box 225, Lemont, IL 60439. (312) 257-5958.
Colony Auction Gallery, Joseph J. Einhorn, 141 State St., New London, CT 06320. (203) 444-1415, Fax (203) 447-3800. Shop hours, by mail, catalogues/lists, auction.
Condy House, 1893, Antiquarian Maps & Prints, 820 N. Madison, Stockton, CA 95202. (209) 465-9951. Americas, U.S. West, all pre-1850. By appt., by mail, shows & fairs, catalogues/lists.
Country Lane Books, P.O. Box 47, Collinsville, CT 06022.
Darvills Rare Print Shop, P.O. Box 47, Eastsound, WA 98245. (206) 376-2351.
Dawson's Book Shop, 535 N. Larchmont Blvd., Los Angeles, CA 90004. (213) 469-2186.

United States Dealers

C. Dickens Books, Mel Rechtman, Lenox Sq., 3393 Peachtree Rd., N.E., Atlanta, GA 30326. (800) 548-0376, (404) 231-3825, Fax (404) 364-0713. Shop hours, by mail, shows & fairs, catalogues/lists.

Frank Draskovic, P.O. Box 803, Monterey Park, CA 91754. (818) 281-9281.

Drew's Bookshop, P.O. Box 163, Santa Barbara, CA 93102. (805) 966-3311. Shop hours, by mail, catalogues/lists.

Drumbeat Americana Books, 2169 Silverwood Ln., Chesterfield, MO 63017.

Andre Dumont, Maps & Books, P.O. Box 10117, Santa Fe, NM 87504. (505) 986-9603. Western Americana. By appt., by mail, shows & fairs, catalogues/lists.

V. & J. Duncan, Antique Maps, Prints & Photos, 12 E. Taylor St., Savannah, GA 31401. (912) 232-0338. Open 10 a.m. to 5 p.m., Monday-Saturday. By appt., by mail, shows & fairs.

Elizabeth F. Dunlap, Books & Maps, 6063 Westminster Pl., St. Louis, MO 63112. (314) 863-5068. By appt., by mail, catalogues/lists.

Emery's Book Auctions, Duston Rd., Contoocook, NH 03229.

The Erie Book Store, 717 French St., Erie, PA 16501. (814) 452-3354.

Eugene Galleries, 76 Charles St., Boston, MA 02114. (617) 227-3062. Shop hours.

Exnowski Enterprises, Eugene Exnowski, 31512 Reid, Warren, MI 48092. (313) 264-1686. By mail, shows & fairs, catalogues/lists.

F & I Books, P.O. Box 1900, Santa Monica, CA 90406.

Joseph J. Felcone Inc., Rare Books, P.O. Box 366, Princeton, NJ 08540. (609) 924-0539.

Clifton F. Ferguson, Antique Maps & Atlases, 4999 Meandering Creek Dr., Belmont, MI 49306. (616) 874-9297. By appt., by mail, catalogues/lists.

First of Florida Maps, Ashby Moody, 4305 El Prado, Tampa, FL 33629. (813) 839-7098.

Richard Fitch, Old Maps, Prints & Books, 2324 Calle Halcon, Santa Fe, NM 87505. (505) 982-2939. North America. By appt., by mail, shows & fairs, catalogues/lists.

Fleetstreet Appraisals, Harold Square, 153 Madrone Lane North, Winslow, WA 98110. (206) 842-7488, Fax (206) 842-7489. Shop hours.

Craig Flinner Gallery, 505 N. Charles St., Baltimore, MD 21201. (301) 727-1863. Shop hours, by mail.

Freeman Fine Arts, 1808 Chestnut St., Philadelphia, PA 19103. (215) 563-9275.

Daphne Frost, Antique Maps, Books & Prints, P.O. Box 57, Rancho Palos Verdes, CA 90274.

Gallery 515, M. Sisk & D. McAfee, 515 E. Paces Ferry Rd., N.E, Atlanta, GA 30305. (404) 233-2911.

GA Maps & Books, Randall A. Detro, 202 Windsor East, Thibodaux, LA 70301. (504) 446-1726. North America, Mississippi Valley, Southeast U.S., general worldwide travel books & maps. By appt., by mail, catalogues/lists.

David L. Gibson, Rare Prints & Maps, 6431 Lake Circle Cr., Dallas, TX 75214.

Michael Ginsburg Books, Inc., P.O. Box 402, Sharon, MA 02067. (617) 784-8181.

Goodspeed's Book Shop, Antique Map & Print Dept., 7 Beacon St., Boston, MA 02108. (617) 523-5970. Shop hours, by mail, shows & fairs.

Goreham Collectibles, Dennis B. Goreham, 1539 East, 4070 South, Salt Lake City, UT 84124. By appt., by mail, shows & fairs.

Grace Galleries, Inc., Jacqueline Grace, Box 2488, R.R.5, Brunswick, ME 04011. (207) 729-1329. By appt., by mail, shows & fairs, catalogues/lists.

Graton & Graton, 100 Ocean Terr., P.O. Box 889, Islamovada, FL 33036. (305) 644-9419.

C.E. Guarino,Americana, P.O. Box 49, Berry Rd., Denmark, ME 04022. (207) 452-2123. By appt., by mail, catalogues/lists, auction.

William F. Hale Books, 1222 31st St. NW, Washington, DC 20007. (202) 546-2293.

Milton Hammer, Books, 789 N. Ontare Rd., Santa Barbara, CA 93105.

Wendell P. Hammon, 1115 Front, Sacramento, CA 95814. (916) 446-1782.

Hanzel Galleries, 1120 S. Michigan, Chicago, IL 60605. (312) 922-6234.

Douglas N.Harding, P.O. Box 184, Rt. 1, Webhannet Farm, Wells, ME 04090. (207) 646-8785.

Michael D. Heaston Co., P.O. Box 91147, Austin, TX 78709.

Heinoldt Books, T.H. Heinoldt, Central & Buffalo Aves., South Egg Harbor, NJ 08215. (609) 965-2284.

Here Be Dragons, Ed Curley, P.O. Box 57520, Tucson, AZ 85732. (602) 326-3132.

Heritage Antique Maps, William L. Cawood, 551 Christopher Lane, Doylestown, PA 18901. (215) 340-9662 [eves.]. By appt., by mail, shows & fairs, catalogues/lists, auction.

Robert M. Hicklin Jr.,Inc., 509 E. St. John St., Spartanburg, SC 29302. (803) 583-9847. Southeastern North America. Shop hours, by mail, catalogues/lists.

United States Dealers

High Latitude, P.O. Box 11254, Bainbridge Island, WA 98110. (206) 842-0202. Voyages & maritime books, seldom individual maps.
High Ridge Books Inc., P. O. Box 286, Rye, NY 10580. (914) 967-3332, Fax (914) 976-6056.
Jonathan A. Hill, 470 West End Ave., New York, NY 10024.
Historical Technology, 6 Mugford St., Marblehead, MA 01945. (617) 631-2275. Antique instruments, charts, books, globes, orreries. By appt., by mail, catalogues/lists.
Historical Americana, 3405 Woodley Rd. N.W., Washington, DC 20016.
Historic Urban Plans, John W. Reps, P.O. Box 276, Ithaca, NY 14851. (607) 273-4695. Reproductions.
Hobbit Shop, 305 W. South Ave., Westfield, NJ 07090. (201) 654-4115.
The Holmes Book Co., 274 14th St., Oakland, CA 94612. (415) 893-6860.
The Holy Land, Dr. Samuel Halperin, 3041 Normanstone Terr. N.W., Washington, DC 20008. (202) 965-4831.
Holy Land Treasures, 1200 Edgehill Dr., Burlingame, CA 94010. (415) 343-9578. Holy Land maps, views, prints. By appt., by mail, shows & fairs, catalogues/lists.
Houle Rare Books & Autographs, 7260 Beverley Blvd., Los Angeles, CA 90036. (213) 937-5858.
Murray Hudson, Books & Maps, 109 S. Church St., P.O. Box 163, Halls, TN 38040. (800)-748-9946 [USA], (901) 836-9057. Books with maps, atlases, geographies, southeast & southwest U.S. By appt., by mail, shows & fairs, catalogues/lists.
The Impecunious Collector, Harlan H. Hutchins, P.O. Box 4156, Christiansted, St. Croix, VI 00822. (809) 773-7171; after 5 pm, 778-3352. U.S. & British Virgin Is., Puerto Rico, English speaking West indies. By appt., by mail, shows & fairs.
Jeltrup's Books, Thomas & Dorothy Jeltrup, King Cross St., Christiansted, St. Croix, VI 00820.
The Jenkins Company, P.O. Box 2085, Austin, TX 78768. (512) 444-1616. Maps & books on America. Shop hours, by mail, shows & fairs, catalogues/lists.
David Jolly Antique Maps, P.O. Box 1003, Brookline, MA 02146. (617) 232-6222. By appt., by mail, catalogues/lists.
Capt. Kit S. Kapp, Antiquarian Maps, P.O. Box 64, Osprey, FL 34229. (813) 966-4181. Maps & prints of the Americas. By appt., by mail, shows & fairs, catalogues/lists.
Kauai Fine Arts, Paul & Mona Nicholas, P.O. Box 1079, Lawai, Kauai, HI 96765. (808) 335-3778 [bus.], (808) 332-8508, Fax (808) 332-9808. By mail, catalogues/lists.
Keith Library & Gallery, 217 W. Front St., Red Bank, NJ 07701. (201) 842-7377.
Robert P. Kipp, 16 Wedgemere Rd., Beverly, MA 01915. (508) 922-6852.
H.P. Kraus, 16 E. 46th St., New York, NY 10017. (212) 687-4808.
Lahaina Printsellers Ltd., 636 Luakini St., Lahaina, Maui, HI 96761.
Maggie Lambeth-Books, Star Rte. 4, P.O. Box 361, Blanco, TX 78606. (512) 833-5252.
The Lamp, Wr. G. Mayer, Jr., P.O Box 11302, Pittsburgh, PA 15238. (412) 963-0663. Atlases & maps of all U.S. states. By appt., by mail, shows & fairs, catalogues/lists.
Latitudes Inc., Tom Lazor, P.O. Box 66, Essex, CT 06426. (203) 767-3001. Americana, sea charts, wall maps, atlases of the Northeast. Shop hours, by mail, shows & fairs, catalogues/lists.
Don Leeper, 3645 N.W. Glenridge Drive, Corvallis, OR. (503) 758-3242.
Edward J. Lefkowicz, 43 Fort St., P.O. Box 630, Fairhaven, MA 02719. (617) 997-6839. Nautical books, sea charts Catalogues/lists.
Harry A. Levinson, Rare Books, P.O. Box 534, Beverly Hills, CA 90213. (213) 276-9311. By appt., by mail, shows & fairs, catalogues/lists.
Librairie Bookshop, 823 Chartres St., New Orleans, LA 70116.
Lincoln Rare Books & Globes, P.O. Box 85, Lincoln, MA 01773. (617) 259-8496. By mail, catalogues/lists.
Linlo House Inc., 403 E. 75th St., New York, NY 10021.
Little Hundred Gallery, Paul L. Whitfield, 6028 Bentway Dr., Charlotte, NC 28226. (704) 372-8322. By mail, catalogues/lists.
Lombard Antiquarian Maps / Prints, P.O. Box 281, Cape Elizabeth, ME 04107. (207) 799-1889. By appt., by mail.
Lorson's Books & Prints, James Lorson, 116 W. Wilshire Ave., Fullerton, CA 92632. (714) 526-2523.
Phyllis Lucas Gallery, 981 2nd Ave., New York, NY 10022. (212) 755-1516.
Lyons Ltd., 2700 Hyde, San Francisco, CA 94109. (415) 441-2282.
George S. MacManus Co., 1317 Irving St., Philadelphia, PA 19107. (215) 735-4465.
Thomas D. Mahoney, 513 Virginia St., Buffalo, NY 14202. (716) 856-6024.

United States Dealers

G.B. Manasek, Inc., Rare Books, Maps & Prints, P.O. Box 1204, Norwich, VT 05055. (802) 649-1722, Fax (802) 649-2256. General early maps, Japanese woodblock maps, cartography reference books. By appt., by mail, shows & fairs, catalogues/lists.

Manning's Antiquarian Books & Prints, Kathleen Manning, 209 Corbett St., San Francisco, CA 94114. (415) 621-3565. By appt., by mail, catalogues/lists.

The Map Bin, 109 39th St., Sea Isle City, NJ 08243.

Map Centre, 2611 University Ave., San Diego, CA 92104. (619) 219-3830.

Map Land, Robert Caruthers, P.O. Box 358, Nevada City, CA 95959. By appt., by mail, catalogues/lists.

Mapquest, J. Scott Smith, P.O. Box 14211, Atlanta, GA 30324.

Maps of Antiquity, Lynn Vigeant, P.O. Box 569, Montclair, NJ 07042. (201) 744-4364. By appt., by mail, shows & fairs, catalogues/lists.

Maps of the Holy Land, Howard I. Golden, 360 Lexington Ave., 20th Floor, New York, NY 10017. (212) 682-2300. Holy Land. By appt., by mail, catalogues/lists.

The Map Store, Mike McGuire, 5821 Karric Sq. Dr., Dublin, OH 43017. (800) 848-0304, (614) 792-6277, Fax (614) 848-5045. Shop hours, by mail, shows & fairs, catalogues/lists.

Map World, 112 S. El Camino Real, Encinitas, CA 92024. (619) 942-9642, in Calif (800) 246-MAPS. Shop hours, by mail.

Margolis & Moss, P.O. Box 2042, Santa Fe, NM 87504. (505) 982-1028.

Douglas W. Marshall & Co., 545 University Pl., Grosse Pointe, MI 48230. (313) 882-9590. North America. By appt..

Martayan Lan Inc., Rare Books, Maps & Prints, 48 E. 57th St., New York, NY 10022. (800) 423-3741, (212) 308-0018, Fax (212) 308-0074. By appt..

Melvyn Mason, Historical Maps, 4728 Rosita Place, Tarzana, CA 91356.

McClendon's Trash & Treasure, 1714-16 Westheimer Rd., Houston, TX 77098. (713) 522-7415. Shop hours.

Metsker Maps, P.O. Box 110669, Tacoma, WA 98411.

Mickler's Floridiana, P.O. Box 38, Chulota, FL 32766. (305) 365-3636. Florida material only. By appt., by mail, shows & fairs, catalogues/lists.

J.T. Monckton Ltd., 1050 Gage St., Winnetka, IL 60093. (708) 446-1106, Fax (708) 446-1103. Catalogues/lists.

Moon Marine Inc., Martin M. Cassidy, 12926 Bowing Oaks, Cypress, TX 77429.

Musgrave Antique Prints/Maps, Mrs. Helen Musgrave, P.O. Box 4895, Cave Creek, AZ 85331.

Kenneth Nebenzahl, Inc., P.O. Box 370, Glencoe, IL 60022. (708) 835-0515, Fax (708) 835-0519. America, world, Great Lakes, early maps & portolans. Shop hours, by mail, shows & fairs, catalogues/lists.

Ken Nesheim, 881 Indian Hill Rd, Orange, CT 06477.

Walter Neuman, F.R.G.S., 10500 Wyton Dr., Westwood, CA 90024.

New Albion Island Classics, Louis Lewis, P.O. Box 10517, Oakland, CA 94610. (415) 893-7543.

Cheryl M. Newby Inc., 5001 N. Kings Hwy., #106, Myrtle Beach, SC 29577. (803) 449-4157.

Newman's Books & Maps, 1414 Mariposa St., Vallejo, CA 94590. (707) 642-9091.

New York Bound Bookshop, Barbara Cohen, 29 E. 11th St. #1, New York, NY 10003.

Nineteenth Century Prints, E. Burdon, 2732 S.E. Woodward St., Portland, OR 97202. (503) 234-3538.

Jeremy Norman & Co. Inc., 720 Market St., San Francisco, CA 94102.

Northern Map Co., Victoria Bates, 103 Cherokee Circle, Dunnellon, FL 32630. (904) 489-3967.

North Shore Antique Maps & Prints, Bob & Marian Teplin, 339 Woodlyn Dr., Mequon, WI 53092. (414) 241-5704.

Oak Dale Maps & Prints, W. R. Landefeld, 268 Lenape Rd., Kennett Square, PA 19348. (215) 347-2423.

The Observatory, Dee Longenbaugh, 235 Second Street, Juneau, AK 99801. (907) 586-9679, 586-1631.

Oinonen Book Auctions, Richard E. Oinonen, P.O. Box 470, Sunderland, MA 01375. (413) 665-3253. Auction.

Old Ink, Mr. Jan L. Hanna, 4016 Woodland Rd., Annandale, VA 22003. (703) 941-8256. By appt., by mail, shows & fairs, catalogues/lists.

The Old Map Gallery, Paul F.Mahoney, 1746 Blake St., Denver, CO 80202. (303) 296-7725, Fax (303) 296-7936. Shop hours, by mail, catalogues/lists.

Old Maps & Prints, Preston Figley, P.O. Box 2234, Fort Worth, TX 76113. (817) 923-4535. America. By appt., by mail, catalogues/lists.

The Old Print Gallery, 1220 31st St. NW, Washington, DC 20007. (202) 965-1818. Shop hours, by mail, shows & fairs, catalogues/lists.

The Old Print Shop, 150 Lexington Ave., New York, NY 10016. (212) 683-3950.

United States Dealers

Old World Mail Auctions, Tim Coss, 5614 Northfield Rd., Bethesda, MD 20817. (301) 657-9074 [eves.], Fax (301) 652-0418.

Orientalism, Joseph Snyder, P.O. Box 540, Sharpsburg, MD 21782.

Overlee Farm Books, Box 1155, Stockbridge, MA 01262. (413) 637 2277.

K.C. Owings, Jr., Historical Americana, P.O. Box 19, North Abington, MA 02351. (617) 587-6441. By appt., by mail, catalogues/lists.

Pacific Book House, 435 Atkinson Dr., Honolulu, HI 96814.

Pacific Shore Maps, Richard S. Cloward, 5664 Menorca Dr., San Diego, CA 92124. (619) 571-7487. By mail, catalogues/lists.

Pageant Book & Print Shop, Shirley Solomon, 109 E. 9th St., New York, NY 10003. (212) 674-5296.

John G. Panacy, 196 Walnut St., Stoughton, MA 02072. (617) 344-5043.

N. & N. Pavlov, 37 Oakdale Dr., Dobbs Ferry, NY 10522. (914) 693-1776. By appt.

Scott Petersen, P.O. Box 384, Kenilworth, IL 60043.

The Philadelphia Print Shop, 8441 Germantown Ave., Philadelphia, PA 19118. (215) 242-4750, Fax (215) 242-6977. Shop hours, by mail, shows & fairs, catalogues/lists.

Philips, Son & Neale, Inc., 406 E. 79th St., New York, NY 10021. (212) 570-4851. Auction.

Donald T. Pitcher, P.O. Box 64, North Haven, CT 06473. (203) 239-2660.

Gary Pletcher, 410 Surrey Ln., Bloomsburg, PA 17815. (717) 784-7892. By mail, shows & fairs, auction.

Princeton Rare Maps, Richard Gafgen, Jr., 9 Sherman Place, Lawrenceville, NJ 08648. (609) 396-2239. Maps of America, prints, Braun & Hogenberg. By appt., by mail, shows & fairs, catalogues/lists.

The Print Mint Gallery, Betty D. Sobel, 1147 Greenleaf Ave., Wilmette, IL 60091. (312) 256-4140.

Ptolemaeus, Bruce F. DeVine, 1243 Rossmoyne Ave., Glendale, CA 91207. (818) 507-1201. By appt..

Charles Edwin Puckett, 3767 Forest Lane, Suite 116-445, Dallas, TX 75244. (214) 351-3242, Fax (214) 351-3018. By appt., by mail, shows & fairs. General; 16-18th century America, Texas, Southwest.

William Reese Co., 409 Temple St., New Haven, CT 06511. (203) 789-8081, Fax (203) 865-7653.

Regency Gallery, Derek Nicholls, 750 N. LaCienega Blvd., Los Angeles, CA 90069. (310) 659-3616, Fax (310) 659-3614. Shop hours, by mail, catalogues/lists.

Royd L. Riddell, Rare Maps & Prints, 2607 Routh Street, Dallas, TX 75201. (214) 953-0601.

Warren H. Ringer, 55 Gay Street, Needham, MA 02192. (617) 444-9430.

George Ritzlin, Maps & Books, 469 Roger Williams Ave., Highland Park, IL 60035. (708) 433-2627, Fax (708) 433-6389. Shop hours, by mail, shows & fairs, catalogues/lists.

Cedric L. Robinson, Bookseller, 597 Palisado Ave., Windsor, CT 06095. (203) 688-2582. By appt., by mail, catalogues/lists.

Charles Robinson Rare Books, P.O. Box 57, Pond Rd., Manchester, ME 04351. (207) 622-1885. By appt., by mail, shows & fairs, catalogues/lists, auction.

George Robinson, Old Prints & Maps, 124-D Bent St., Taos, NM 87571. (505) 758-2278, Fax (505) 758-1606. Shop hours, by mail, catalogues/lists.

Robert Ross & Co., Antiquarian Maps, Prints & Related Books, P.O. Box 8362, Calabasas, CA 91372. (818) 348-7867, Fax same. By appt., by mail, shows & fairs, catalogues/lists, auction.

Rouse's Bookhouse, Rte. 2, Eaton Rapids, MI 48827.

Rudisill's Alt Print Haus, J.& B. Rudisill, P.O. Box 199, Worton, MD 21678-0199.

Robert Ellis Rudolph Corp., 1119 S.W. Park Ave., Portland, OR 97205. (503) 223-7518.

Barry Ruderman, 2648 Montclair, San Diego, CA 92104. (619) 282-4945, Fax (619) 238-0257. By appt., by mail.

Rulon-Miller Books, Red Hook, P.O. Box 41, St. Thomas, VI 00802.

Russell Books & Bindery, P.O. Box 686, Spokane, WA 99210. (509) 534-1959.

Sadlon's Ltd., Fine Print Gallery, 1207 Fox River Dr., De Pere, WI 54115.

John Scopazzi, 278 Post St., #305, Union Sq., San Francisco, CA 94108. (415) 362-5708.

The Scriptorium, 427 N. Canon Dr., Beverly Hills, CA 90213. (213) 275-6060.

Charles Sessler, Inc., 1308 Walnut St., Philadelphia, PA 19107. (215) 735-8811. Shop hours, by mail, catalogues/lists.

John Sharp, P.O. Box 163, Sebastopol, MS 39359. (601) 625-8162. Maps of Mississippi, U.S., world.

Sherwood's Gallery, Sherwood P. McCall III, 2618 Briar Ridge, Houston, TX 77057. (713) 974-7780. Early maps, Americana, Texana. Catalogues/lists.

The Shorey Bookstore, 1411 1st Ave. #200, Seattle, WA 98101.

Sign of the Lion Antique Maps, George Preston, 4226 Reaumur, Dallas, TX 75229. (214) 350-3030.

Dorothy Sloan, Books, P.O. Box 49670, Austin, TX 78765. (512) 477-8442.

E. Forbes Smiley III, 954 Lexington Ave, #186, New York, NY 10021.

United States Dealers

Walter W. Smith & Son Inc., 51 Pondfield Rd., P.O. Box 66, Bronxville, NY 10708. (914) 337-2794.

Solomon's Antique Maps, 371 Hollis St., Framingham, MA 01701. (617) 877-6940. Catalogues/lists.

Sotheby Parke-Bernet, Inc., 980 Madison Ave., New York, NY 10021. (212) 472-3400.

The Jean Spedden Gallery, Ltd., 73 Broad St., Charleston, SC 29401.

David R. Spivey, Books, Old Maps, Fine Arts, 825 Westport Road, Kansas City, MO 64111. (816) 753-0520.

Carolyn Staley, Fine Prints, 313 First Ave. S., Seattle, WA 98104. (206) 621-1888. Shop hours, by mail, shows & fairs, catalogues/lists.

Harry L. Stern Ltd., 29 N. Wacker, Chicago, IL 60606.

Paul Roberts Stoney, Print & Mapseller, P.O. Box F, Williamsburg, VA 23187. (800) 732-4923, (804) 220-3346 [10-6 EST]. America, colonial North America By mail, shows & fairs, catalogues/lists.

Richard D. Stout, P.O. Box 1274, Fort Payne, AL 35967. (205) 845-5171.

Thomas & Ahngsana Suarez, Rare Maps & Prints, 1146 Irving St., Valley Stream, NY 11580. (516) 285-7419, Fax same. Early world, America, curiosa (Temporary address) By appt., by mail, shows & fairs, catalogues/lists.

Bernard Sussman, Antique Maps, 565 Sanctuary Dr, #B104, Longboat Key, FL 34228. (813) 383-5823. By appt., by mail, auction.

Swann Galleries, Inc., 104 E. 25th St., New York, NY 10010. (212) 254-4710, Fax (212) 979-1017.

Sykes & Flanders, P.O. Box 86, Weare, NH 03281.

1023 Booksellers, P.O. Box 3668, Omaha, NE 68103.

Terramedia Books, 19 Homestead Road, Wellesley, MA 02181. (617) 237 6485.

Jeffery Thomas, Fine & Rare Books, 49 Geary St. #230, San Francisco, CA 94108. (415) 956-3272. Maps only sold peripherally. Shop hours, by mail, shows & fairs, catalogues/lists.

Tombstone & Western Americana, P.O. Box 7, Tombstone, AZ 85638.

Tradewinds Gallery, Thomas K. Aalund, 20 W. Main St., Mystic, CT 06355. (203) 536-0119. Shop hours, by mail, shows & fairs, catalogues/lists.

Tuttle Antiquarian Books, Inc., P.O. Box 541, Rutland, VT 05701.

G. H. Tweney, Antiquarian Bookseller, 16660 Marine View Dr., S.W., Seattle, WA 98166. (206) 243-8243. By appt., by mail, shows & fairs, catalogues/lists.

Unicorn Bookshop, James Dawson, Route 50; P.O. Box 154, Trappe, MD 21673. (301) 476-3838. Maryland & Chesapeake Bay. Shop hours, by mail.

Paul Victorius Framing Shop, Inc., 1413 University Ave., Charlottesville, VA 22903. (804) 296-3456, (804) 293-3342. Shop hours.

Village Bookship, Inc., Rt. 130, P.O. Box 169, New Harbor, ME 04554. (207) 677-3720.

Adelhe von Hohenlohe, 1696 Nordentoft Way, Solvang, CA 93463.

Von Maritime, Inc., Fred von Wiegen, 4928 Kuhio Hwy., Kapaa, Kauai, HI 96746. (808) 822-4999.

Washington Square Gallery Ltd., Denise DeLaurentis, 229 S. 9th St., Philadelphia, PA 19107. (215) 923-8873. Shop hours, by mail, shows & fairs, catalogues/lists.

Waverly Auctions Inc., Dale A. Sorenson, President, 4931 Cordell Ave, Suite AA, Bethesda, MD 20814. (301) 951-8883. Shop hours, catalogues/lists, auction.

R. M. Weatherford,Inc., Booksellers, P.O. Box 5, Southworth, WA 98386. (206) 871-3617. 6 catalogs/yr. By appt., by mail, shows & fairs, catalogues/lists.

Ann H. Wells, Rare Tennessee Maps, 117 Prospect Hill, Nashville, TN 37205. (615) 383-2767. Maps of Tennessee. By appt., by mail.

Wildwood Books & Prints, 1972 Wildwood Lane, Anchorage, AK 99503.

A. A. Wills & Sons Inc., P.O. Box 148, Marshfield Hills, MA 02051.

Yellowhouse Galleries & Annex, Jack Sandberg, P.O Box 554, Nags Head, NC 27959. (919) 441-6928.

Yesterday's Gallery, Earl M. Manz, P.O. Box 154, East Woodstock, CT 06244. (203) 928-5409. By mail, shows & fairs, catalogues/lists.

Yesteryear Book Shop, 3201 Maple Drive, N.E., Atlanta, GA 30305. (404) 237-0163.

Yu Heng Art Co., Tina Li, 303 East 57th St., New York, NY 10022. (212) 838-2126. China maps & atlases. By appt..

Samuel Yudkin & Associates, 2109 Popkins Ln., Alexandria, VA 22307. (703) 768-1858. Bimonthly book, print & map auctions, none solely cartographic.

United States Dealers by State and City

For complete information, see United States dealers in Alphabetical Order above.

ALABAMA

Fort Payne Richard D. Stout
Huntsville Chartwell Mapsellers
Mobile Chilton's Inc.

ALASKA

Anchorage Alaskana Book Shop
Anchorage Wildwood Books & Prints
Juneau Alaskan Heritage Bookshop
Juneau The Observatory

ARIZONA

Cave Creek Musgrave Antique Prints/Maps
Scottsdale The Antiquarian Shop
Tombstone Tombstone & Western Americana
Tucson Here Be Dragons

CALIFORNIA

Berkeley John P. Coll
Beverly Hills Harry A. Levinson, Rare Books
Beverly Hills The Scriptorium
Burlingame Holy Land Treasures
Calabasas Robert Ross & Co.
Encinitas Map World
Fullerton Lorson's Books & Prints
Glendale Ptolemaeus
Irvine Calif. Land & Exploration Co.
Los Angeles Caravan Book Store
Los Angeles Dawson's Book Shop
Los Angeles Houle Rare Books & Autographs
Los Angeles Regency Gallery
Monterey Park Frank Draskovic
Nevada City Map Land
Oakland The Holmes Book Co.
Oakland New Albion Island Classics
Rancho Palos Verdes Daphne Frost
Sacramento Wendell P. Hammon
San Diego Map Centre
San Diego Pacific Shore Maps
San Diego Barry Ruderman
San Francisco Acquitania Gallery
San Francisco W. Graham Arader III
San Francisco Argonaut Book Shop
San Francisco Arkadyan Books & Prints
San Francisco The Bookstall
San Francisco California Book Auction, Butterfield & Butterfield
San Francisco Dennis Clare
San Francisco Lyons Ltd.
San Francisco Manning's Antiquarian Books & Prints
San Francisco Jeremy Norman & Co. Inc.
San Francisco John Scopazzi
San Francisco Jeffery Thomas
Santa Barbara Drew's Bookshop
Santa Barbara Milton Hammer, Books
Santa Monica F & I Books
Santa Paula Susan Benjamin
Solvang Adelhe von Hohenlohe
Stockton Condy House, 1893
Tarzana Melvyn Mason
Vallejo Newman's Books & Maps
Westwood Walter Neuman, F.R.G.S.

COLORADO

Boulder Art Source International
Denver The Old Map Gallery

CONNECTICUT

Branford Branford Rare Books
Collinsville Country Lane Books
East Woodstock Yesterday's Gallery
Essex Latitudes Inc.
Mystic Tradewinds Gallery
New Haven William Reese Co.
New London Colony Auction Gallery
North Haven Donald T. Pitcher
Orange Ken Nesheim
Windsor Cedric L. Robinson, Bookseller

DISTRICT OF COLUMBIA

Washington Booked Up
Washington William F. Hale Books
Washington Historical Americana
Washington The Holy Land
Washington The Old Print Gallery

DELAWARE

Ocean View Antique Prints Ltd.
Wilmington Buxbaum Geographics

FLORIDA

Chulota Mickler's Floridiana
Dunnellon Northern Map Co.
Islamovada Graton & Graton
Longboat Key Bernard Sussman, Antique Maps
Osprey Capt. Kit S. Kapp
Palm Beach Antique Maps & Prints
Safety Harbor Authentic Antique Maps
Tampa First of Florida Maps

GEORGIA

Atlanta H. Abrams
Atlanta Antiquities, Ltd.
Atlanta C. Dickens Books
Atlanta Gallery 515
Atlanta Mapquest
Atlanta Yesteryear Book Shop
Savannah V. & J. Duncan

HAWAII

Honolulu Pacific Book House
Kapaa, Kauai Von Maritime, Inc.
Lahaina, Maui Lahaina Printsellers Ltd.
Lawai, Kauai Kauai Fine Arts

ILLINOIS

Chicago W. Graham Arader III
Chicago Mary Beth Beal
Chicago Hanzel Galleries
Chicago Harry L. Stern Ltd.
Glencoe Kenneth Nebenzahl, Inc.
Highland Park George Ritzlin
Kenilworth Scott Petersen
Lemont Collectors Circle Ltd.
Wilmette The Print Mint Gallery
Winnetka J.T. Monckton Ltd.

LOUISIANA

Baton Rouge Taylor Clark Gallery
Gretna Bayou Books
New Orleans Barrister's Gallery
New Orleans The Centuries
New Orleans Librairie Bookshop
Shreveport Ark-La-Tex Book Company
Thibodaux GA Maps & Books

MAINE

Brunswick Grace Galleries, Inc.
Cape Elizabeth Lombard Antiquarian Maps / Prints
Denmark C.E. Guarino,Americana
Manchester Charles Robinson Rare Books
New Harbor Village Bookship, Inc.
Rockport Boxwood Farm, Antique Prints
Wells Douglas N. Harding

MARYLAND

Baltimore Camelot Books
Baltimore Craig Flinner Gallery
Bethesda The Book Cellar Ltd.
Bethesda Old World Mail Auctions
Bethesda Waverly Auctions Inc.
Sharpsburg Orientalism
Towson Chesapeake Galleries
Trappe Unicorn Bookshop
Worton Rudisill's Alt Print Haus

MASSACHUSETTS

Amherst Amherst Antiquarian Maps
Andover Andover Antiquarian Books / Gallery
Beverly Robert P. Kipp
Boston Eugene Galleries
Boston Goodspeed's Book Shop
Brookline David Jolly Antique Maps
Fairhaven Edward J. Lefkowicz
Framingham Solomon's Antique Maps
Lincoln Lincoln Rare Books & Globes
Marblehead Historical Technology
Marshfield Hills A. A. Wills & Sons Inc.
Montague Thomas Edward Carroll
Needham Warren H. Ringer
North Abington K.C. Owings, Jr.
Sharon Michael Ginsburg Books, Inc.
Stockbridge Overlee Farm Books
Stoughton John G. Panacy
Sunderland Oinonen Book Auctions
Waltham Bickerstaff's
Wellesley Terramedia Books

MICHIGAN

Belmont Clifton F. Ferguson
Eaton Rapids Rouse's Bookhouse
Grosse Pointe Douglas W. Marshall & Co.
Warren Exnowski Enterprises

MISSOURI

Chesterfield Drumbeat Americana Books
Kansas City David R. Spivey
St. Louis Phyllis Y. Brown
St. Louis Elizabeth F. Dunlap

MISSISSIPPI

Sebastopol John Sharp

NORTH CAROLINA

Charlotte Little Hundred Gallery
Nags Head Yellowhouse Galleries & Annex

NEBRASKA

Omaha 1023 Booksellers

NEW HAMPSHIRE

Contoocook Emery's Book Auctions
Portsmouth The Antiquarian Old Book Store
Weare Sykes & Flanders

NEW JERSEY

Lawrenceville Princeton Rare Maps
Montclair Maps of Antiquity
Princeton Joseph J. Felcone Inc.
Red Bank Keith Library & Gallery
Sea Isle City The Map Bin
South Egg Harb. Heinoldt Books
Westfield Hobbit Shop

NEW MEXICO

Santa Fe Andre Dumont
Santa Fe Richard Fitch
Santa Fe Margolis & Moss
Taos George Robinson

NEW YORK

Bronxville Walter W. Smith & Son Inc.
Buffalo Thomas D. Mahoney
Cold Spring Antipodean Books
Dobbs Ferry N. & N. Pavlov
Ithaca Historic Urban Plans
New York W. Graham Arader III
New York Argosy Gallery
New York Richard B. Arkway
New York Asian Rare Books, Inc.
New York Bill George International

New York	El Cascajero
New York	Jonathan A. Hill
New York	H.P. Kraus
New York	Linlo House Inc.
New York	Phyllis Lucas Gallery
New York	Maps of the Holy Land
New York	Martayan Lan Inc.
New York	New York Bound Bookshop
New York	The Old Print Shop
New York	Pageant Book & Print Shop
New York	Philips, Son & Neale, Inc.
New York	E. Forbes Smiley III
New York	Sotheby Parke-Bernet, Inc.
New York	Swann Galleries, Inc.
New York	Yu Heng Art Co.
Old Field	Jo-Ann & Richard Casten, Ltd.
Port Chester	Joyce Amkraut
Rye	High Ridge Books Inc.
Valley Stream	Thomas & Ahngsana Suarez

OHIO

Bay Village	Bay Books
Dublin	The Map Store

OREGON

Corvallis	Don Leeper
Eugene	Anian Ltd.
Portland	Nineteenth Century Prints
Portland	Robert Ellis Rudolph Corp.

PENNSYLVANIA

Allentown	Americana Mail Auction
Bloomsburg	Gary Pletcher
Doylestown	Heritage Antique Maps
Erie	The Erie Book Store
Kennett Square	Oak Dale Maps & Prints
King of Prussia	W. Graham Arader III
Levittown	Bernard Conwell Carlitz
Lititz	Antiquarian Map & Book Den
Philadelphia	Chafey's Books & Prints
Philadelphia	Freeman Fine Arts
Philadelphia	George S. MacManus Co.
Philadelphia	The Philadelphia Print Shop
Philadelphia	Charles Sessler, Inc.
Philadelphia	Washington Square Gallery
Pittsburgh	The Lamp
Villanova	W. Graham Arader III
West Chester	The Cartophile

RHODE ISLAND

No. Providence	The Atlas, Thomas E. Greene

SOUTH CAROLINA

Charleston	The Jean Spedden Gallery
Myrtle Beach	Cheryl M. Newby Inc.
Spartanburg	Robert M. Hicklin Jr.,Inc.

TENNESSEE

Halls	Murray Hudson, Books & Maps
Nashville	Ann H. Wells

TEXAS

Austin	Michael D. Heaston Co.
Austin	The Jenkins Company
Austin	Dorothy Sloan, Books
Blanco	Maggie Lambeth-Books
Cypress	Moon Marine Inc.
Dallas	David L. Gibson
Dallas	Charles Edwin Puckett
Dallas	Royd L. Riddell
Dallas	Sign of the Lion Antique Maps
Fort Worth	Old Maps & Prints
Houston	Antique Brokers
Houston	W. Graham Arader III
Houston	McClendon's Trash & Treasure
Houston	Sherwood's Gallery

UTAH

Salt Lake City	Goreham Collectibles

VIRGINIA

Accomac	Lawson J. Cantrell
Alexandria	Samuel Yudkin & Assoc.
Annandale	Old Ink
Charlottesville	Paul Victorius Framing Shop
Petersburg	Cartographic Arts
Richmond	Chartifacts
Williamsburg	The Bookpress
Williamsburg	Paul Roberts Stoney

VIRGIN ISLANDS

Christiansted	The Impecunious Collector
Christiansted	Jeltrup's Books
St. Thomas	Rulon-Miller Books

VERMONT

East Middlebury	Cartographics of Vermont
North Pomfret	Richard H. Adelson
Norwich	G.B. Manasek, Inc.
Rutland	Tuttle Antiquarian Books, Inc.

WASHINGTON

Bainbridge Is.	High Latitude
Eastsound	Darvills Rare Print Shop
Seattle	Donald M. Barton
Seattle	The Clipper
Seattle	The Shorey Bookstore
Seattle	Carolyn Staley, Fine Prints
Seattle	G. H. Tweney
Southworth	R. M. Weatherford,Inc.
Spokane	Russell Books & Bindery
Tacoma	Metsker Maps
Winslow	Fleetstreet Appraisals

WISCONSIN

De Pere	Sadlon's Ltd., Fine Print Gallery
Mequon	North Shore Antique Maps & Prints
Milwaukee	Book & Record Land
Waukesha	James K. Beier

Canadian Dealers in Alphabetical Order

The Allery, 322 1/2 Queen Street West, Toronto, Ontario M5V 2A2. (416) 593-0853.

Hugh Anson-Cartwright Books, 229 College Street, Totonto, Ontario M5T 1R4.

The Astrolabe Gallery, John W. Coles, 91 Sparks Street, Ottawa, Ontario K1P 5A5. (613) 234-2348. Shop hours, shows & fairs, catalogues/lists.

Isadore Baum, C.P. 276, succ. Youville, Montréal, P.Q. H2P 2VS. (514) 687-0632.

Beach Antique Maps & Prints, A.B. & C.R. Parley, 3 Firstbrooke Road, Toronto, Ontario M4E 2L2. (416) 694-8119. Retail, Tue-Sun, Harbour Front Antique Market, Queens Quay.

John Channell Berry, Rare Books, Maps & Prints, 112 Montréal St., Kingston, Ontario K7K 3E8. (613) 549-6652.

Canadiana Fine Arts Ltd., 1208 Belavista Crescent S.W., Calgary, Alberta T2V 2B1. (403) 252-3421. Canadian maps, pre-confederation. Shop hours, by mail.

Fulford Gallery, Daniel Fulford, 75 Hinton Avenue North, Ottawa, Ontario K1Y 0Z7. (613) 722-0440, Fax (613) 722-4528. Decorative maps & prints, Canadiana. Shop hours, by mail.

Galerie Mazarine, Librairie Ancienne et Moderne, 1524 Sherbrook W., Montréal, P.Q. H3G 1L3. (514) 931-8182.

Helen R. Kahn, Antiquarian Books, P.O. Box 323, Victoria Station, Montréal, P.Q. H3Z 2V8. (514) 844-5344. By appt., by mail, shows & fairs, catalogues/lists, auction.

Kershaw Old Maps & Prints, P.O. Box 7113, 442 Wilson Street E., Ancaster, Ontario L9G 3J3.

D. & E. Lake Ltd., 239 King Street E., Toronto, Ontario M5A 1J9. (416) 863-9930. Shop hours, by mail, shows & fairs, catalogues/lists.

The Loose Page, Joachim M. Waibel, P.O. Box 91158, West Vancouver, B.C. V7V 3N6. (604) 926-1010.

The Map Room, Neil H. & Liana Sneyd, 18 Birch Avenue, Toronto, Ontario M4V 1C8. (416) 922-5153, (416) 923-2580. Shop hours, by mail, shows & fairs, catalogues/lists.

Brendan M. Moss, 5637 Wallace Street, Vancouver,, B.C. V6N 2A1. (604) 662-8171 [Bus.], (604) 261-7108 [Home]. At "Lemagazin," 110-332 Water St. General, emphasis on Pacific NW, voyage/travel, mountaineering. By appt., by mail, shows & fairs, catalogues/lists.

North by West, P.O. Box 11538, Edmonton, Alberta T5J 3K7. (403) 429-2226. North America, Canada, Arctic, books on travel & exploration. By appt., by mail, shows & fairs, catalogues/lists.

North by West, 1016 Fort Street, Victoria, B.C. V8V 3K4. (604) 383-3442.

Pagurian Gallery, 13 Hazelton Avenue, Toronto, Ontario M5R 2E1. 968-0255.

Ptolémée Plus, David Chandler, C.P. 344, succ. Cartierville, Montréal, P.Q. H4K 2J6. (514) 334-7418. North America & general. By appt., by mail, shows & fairs, catalogues/lists.

Russborough, P.O. Box 422, Station R, Toronto, Ontario M4G 4C3. (416) 425-2457. Emphasis on North America, Canada, Arctic, British Isles. By appt., by mail, shows & fairs, catalogues/lists.

Schooner Books, 5378 Inglis Street, Halifax, Nova Scotia B3H 1J5. (902) 423-8419. Shop hours, by mail, shows & fairs, catalogues/lists.

Vauxhall Antiques Ltd., 1023 Fort Street, Victoria, B.C. .

Ronald Whistance-Smith, Antique Maps & Prints, 14520 - 84 Avenue, Edmonton, Alberta T5R 3X2. (403) 483-5858. By appt.

Joyce Williams, Antique Prints & Maps, 346 West Pender Street, Vancouver, B.C. V6B 1T1. (604) 688-7434.

William P. Wolfe Inc., P.O. Box 1190, Pointe Claire, P.Q. H9S 5K7.

Thomas N. Yarmon, 8 King Street East, Toronto, Ontario M5C 1B5. (416) 363-5086. By appt., by mail.

International Dealers Alphabetically Within Country

ARGENTINA

Liberia l'Amateur, Esmeralda 882, Buenos Aires 1007. (312-7635).
Libreria de Antano, P.O. Box 1425, Sanchez de Bustamente 1876, Buenos Aires. (83-7178).
Magallanes Books, Virginia Guller de Santiago, 25 de Mayo 158 Of. 114, Buenos Aires 1002. (54-331102).

AUSTRALIA

Antiquarian Maps & Prints Pty Ltd., Brian Chester, 247 Victoria St., Darlinghurst, Sydney NSW 2010. (331-2745).
Antique Print Room, L. & S. Kissajukian, 130 King William Rd., Goodwood 5034, SA. (08-272-3506).
Bibliophile, Susan Tompkins, 24 Glenmore Rd., Paddington NSW 2021, Sydney. (02-331-3411).
The Map & Print Collector, Jackie MacDougall, P.O. Box N130, Sydney, NSW 2000. (02-969-7953).
Tim McCormick, 53 Queen St., Woollahra, Sydney NSW 2025. (02-325383).
Robert Muir, Old & Rare Books, P.O. Box 364, Nedlands 6009 WA. (09-3865842).
Read's Rare Bookshop, Harri Peltola, 62 Charlotte St., Brisbane 4000. (07-2293278).
Gaston Renard Fine & Rare Books, Julien Renard, 51 Sackville St., Collingwood, Victoria 3066. (613-417-1044).
Rex Map Centres, Jim Bowden, 413 Pacific Highway, Artarmon NSW 2064. (428-3566).
Salamanca Place Gallery, Dick & Carol Bett, 65 Salamanca Pl., Hobart TAS 7000. (002-233320).
Spencer Scott Sandilands, 546 High St., East Prahran 3181, Victoria. (03-51-5709).
Terra Australis Maps & Prints Pty, Nigel Tully, 2/10 Hazelbank Rd., Wollstonecraft NSW 2065. (02-929-6510).
Trowbridge Prints, S. Marcuson & M. Trowbridge, Old Theatre Ln., Bayview Terr., Claremont, Perth WA 6010. (09-384-4814).
Ulimaroa Fine Maps & Prints, Robert & Christine Clancy, P.O. Box 48, New Lambton, NSW 2305. (02-9297074; 049-527348).
Irene Veasey, 19 Swansea St., Swanbourne, Perth WA 6010. (09-384-5403).
Weekend Gallery Books Pty, Barbara & Sally Burdon, 5 Birdwood St., Hughes, ACT 2605. (062-515191).

BAHAMAS

Balmain Antiques, Johathan C.B. Ramsay, Charlotte St., Box N9562, Nassau. (809-323-7421).

BARBADOS

Antiquaria, David Collins, St. Michaels Row, Bridgetown. (809-426-0635).

BELGIUM

Le Cadre d'Art, Evelyne & Stephane Uhoda, 33 rue St. Paul, 4000 Liege. (041-223817).
Antiquariaat Garcia, Jacques & Anne Marie Garcia, Sankt Kathelynestraat 1 & 10, 2800 Mechelen. (015-290985).
Greenhill, L.F.J. Hoppenbrouwers, Wielewaalstraat 7, 2350 Vosselaar. (014-422723).
Elisabeth Hermans, Guffenslaan 50 B10, 3500 Hasselt. (011-22-74-45).
Antiquariaat Logenhaghen, Philippe Swolfs, Nieuwe Steenweg 31, 2698 Elversele (Temse). (052-462119).
Librairie van Loock, 51 rue St. Jean, 1000 Brussels. (02-512-74-65).
Librairie Louis Moorthamers, rue Lesbroussart 124, Brussels 1050.
Micheline van der Perre, rue van Moer 6, 1000 Bruxelles. (02-512-1433).
De Renaissance van het Boek, Mme. Moreau-Derryx, Walpoorstraat 7, 9000 Gent. (091-254808).
Antiquariat Sanderus, F. Devroe, Brugsestraat 88, B-8500 Kortrijk. (056-35-25-41).
Antiquariaat H. van Veldeke, Elisabeth Hermans, Guffenslaan 50, Bus 10, 3500 Hasselt. (011-227445).
Librairie au Vieux Quartier, Adrienne Goffin, 11 ruedes Fripiers, 5000 Namur. (081-221994).
Antiquariaat Marc van de Wiele, Sankt Salvatorkoorstraat 3, 8000 Brugge,. (050-3366317).

BERMUDA

Nicholas Lusher Art & Antiques, Apartment 11, 8 Mount Wyndham Drive, Hamilton Parish CRO 4. Bermuda & American East Coast antiquarian maps. Shop hours, by mail, catalogues/lists.
Pegasus Print & Map Shop, Robert F.Lee, P.O. Box 1551, Hamilton 5. (809-29-5-2900).
Anthony Pettit, P.O. Box 318, Flatts Village FL. BX.. (809-29-22482, Fax 809-295-5416).

International Dealers

CYPRUS

Antonios Hadjipanayi, P.O. Box 27, Larnaca. (041-52782).
Andreas G. Pitsillides, Collectors' Centre, 10 Pythonos St., Nicosia-101. (02-444316).

DENMARK

Boghallens Antikvariat, Old Dam, Raadhuspladsen 37, 1585 Kobenhavn-V. (01-118511 ext. 763).
Branners Bibliofile Antikvariat, Maria Bloch, Bredgade 10, Kobenhavn DK-1260. (10-15-91-87).
Harcks Antikvariat, GEC Gad-Norreport, Fiolstraede 34, 1171 Kobenhavn. (01-121344).
Kaabers Antikvariat, Alette & Henning Kaaber, Skindergade 34, 1159 Kobenhavn-K. (01-154177).
Rosenkilde & Bagger A/S, Kron-Prinsens-Gade 3-5, Postboks 2184, DK 1017 Kobenhavn K. (01-15-70-44).

ENGLAND

W.F. & V. Ainsworth, Springfield Cottage, The Green, Skelton, York YO3 6XX. (0904-470339).
Angel Antiques, Nigel & Anne Harding, 50 High St., Tring, Herts HP23 5A9. (0296-688424).
Antique Map & Book Shop, H.M. & C.D. Proctor, 32 High St., Puddletown, Dorset DT2 8RU. (030-584-633).
Antique Maps & Prints, 30 St. Mary's St., Stamford, Lincolnshire PE9 2DL.
Anything Illustrated, Louis F. Leopold, 134 WisbechRd., March, Cambridgeshire PE15 8EU. (0354-54735).
Arundel Prints, 59 High St., Arundel, West Sussex. (0903-882522).
Ascotiques, Gether Cottage, King's Ride, Ascot, Berkshire SL5 7JW. (0990-28124).
J. Ash Rare Books, Laurence Worms, 25 Royal Exchange, London EC3V 3LP. (071-626-2665, Fax 071-623-9052).
Ashworth Maps, Mrs. M. Ashworth, Hazelwood, Holtye, Cowden, Kent TN8 7EC. (034-286710).
David Bannister F.R.G.S., 26 Kings Rd., Cheltenham GL5 26BG. (0242-514287).
Barnsbury Gallery, Judith Lassalle, 24 Thornhill Rd., London N1 1HW. (01-607-7121).
Roderick M. Barron, 21 Bayham Road, Sevenoaks, Kent TN13 3PQ. (0732-742558, Fax same).
Roger Baynton-Williams, 37a High Street, Arundel, W. Sussex BN18 9AG. (0903-882898).
Beaches of Salisbury, D.M. Beach, 52 High St., Salisbury, Wilts. SP1 2PG. (0722-333801).
Benet Gallery, G.H. Criddle, 19 Kings Parade, Cambridge CB2 1SP. (0223-353783).
Paul Bentley, 8 Baxendale, London N20 0EG. (01-445-9791).
Bernard Gallery, F.B. Poynter, Grange Farm, Brewery Ln., Everton, Doncaster. (0777-817324).
Andrew Block Ltd., J. Martin, 20 Barter St., London WC1A 2AB. (01-405-9660).
Bloomsbury Rare Books, Arthur Page, 29 Museum St., London WC1A 1LH. (02-636-8206).
Books from India, S. Vidyarthi, 45 Museum St., London WC1A 1LR. (01-405-7226).
Thomas J. Booth, Antique Maps & Prints, 33 Beaconsfield Rd., Claygate, Esher, Surrey. (0372-62764).
Bow Windows Bookshop, 128 High St., Lewes, E. Sussex BN7 1XL. (0273-472839).
Les Briggs, 174 Ashbrow Rd., Fartown, Huddersfield, W. Yorkshire HD2 1DU. (0484-546883).
Brobury House Gallery, Eugene Okarma, Brobury, Herefordshire HR3 6BS. (09817-229).
Brown Jack Bookshop, Reg Leete, 78 Main St., Lubenham, Leicestershire. (0858-65787).
Burgess Browning, 25 Blue Ball Yard, St. James St., London SW1A 1ND. (01-491-1811).
Clive A. Burden Ltd., 46 Talbot Rd., Rickmansworth, Herts WD3 1HE. (0923-778097).
Gabriel Byrne, 29 Museum St., London WC1 A1LH. (01-636-8206).
Cartographia Ltd., Pied Bull Yard, Bury Place, Bloomsbury, London WC1A 2JR. (01-404-4050).
Channel Bookshop, David Dawson, 5 Russell St., Dover, Kent CT16 1PX. (0304-213016).
Channel Islands Galleries Ltd., Les Clospains, Rue de l'Ecole, Vale, Guernsey. (0481-47337).
Chantry Bookshop, M.P. Merkel, 11 Higher St., Dartmouth.
Chelsea Rare Books, Leo Bernard, 313 King's Rd., London SW3 5EP. (01-351-0950).
Christie's, 8 King St., London SW1Y 3JS.
Christie's South Kensington, 85 Old Brompton Rd, London SW7 3JS.
Clevedon Fine Arts Ltd., The Gallery, Cinema Bldg., Old Church Rd., Clevedon, Avon BS21 7JY. (0272-875862).
Coach House Books, M.K. & J.S. Ellingsworth, 31 Broad St., Pershore, Worcestershire WR10 1AV. (0386-556100).
Coltsfoot Gallery, Edwin Collins, Hatfield, Leominster, Herefordshire HR6 0SF. (056-882-277).
Connoisseur Gallery, Makram Irani, 14/15 Halkin Arcade, Belgravia, London SW1X 8JT. (01-245-6431).
A.J. Coombes, 24 Horsham Rd., Dorking, Suffolk RH4 2JA. (0306-880736).
Michael & Verna Cox, 139 Norwich Rd., Wymondham, Norfolk NR18 0SJ. (0953-605948).

International Dealers

Peter Crowe, 77 Upper St. Giles St., Norwich NR2 1AB. (0603-624800).
Davies Antiques, 40a Kensington Church St., London W8 4BX. (01-937-3379).
Deighton Bell & Co., 13 Trinity St., Cambridge CB4 4LZ. (0223-353939).
Ivan R. Deverall, Duval House, The Glen, Cambridge Way, Uckfield, Sussex TN22 2AB. (0825-762474).
Richard Doughty, Wessington Gardens, Woolhope, Herefordshire HR1 4QN. (043-277-292).
Robert Douwma Ltd., 173 New Bond St., 2nd Floor, London W1Y 9PB. (071-495-4001, Fax 071-495-4002).
Francis Edwards, The Old Cinema, Castle Street, Hay-on-Wye HR3 5DF. (0497-820071).
Egee Art Consultancy, 9 Chelsea Manor Studio, Flood St., London SW3 5SR. (01-351-6818).
W.J. Faupel, 3 Halsford Lane, East Grinstead, W. Sussex RH19 1NY. (0342-315813, Fax 0342-318058).
Susanna Fisher, Spencer, Upham, Southampton SO3 1JD. (0489-860-291, Fax same).
Foss Street Galleries, Bryan Trevorrow, 17 Foss St., Dartmouth, Devon TQ6 9DR. (080-43-4311).
Fox-Smith Gallery, 11 Alfred St., The Hoe, Plymouth, Devon. (0752-221843).
J.A.L. Franks, Ltd., 7 New Oxford St., London WC1A 1BA. (071-405-0274, Fax 071-430-1259).
The Gallery, The Square, Yarmouth, Isle of Wight PO41 0NS. (0983-760784).
The Gallery, J. Alan Hulme, 54 Lower Bridge St., Chester. (0244-44006).
John Garner Fine Arts, 51 High St. E., Uppingham, Leicestershire LE15 9PY. (0572-823607).
Garwood & Voigt, 15 Devonshire Buildings, Bath BA2 4SP. (0225-24074).
J.R. Geldart, Antique Maps & Engravings, 13 Oakwood Rd., Wetherby, W. Yorkshire LS22 4QY. (0937-63385).
George & Dragon Gallery, Denis King, Reepham, Norwich, Norfolk NR10 4JN. (0603-870360).
H.G. Girou, 92 Sterndale Rd., London W14. (01-602-4169).
Great Ayton Bookshop, Madalyn Jones, 47 High St., Great Ayton, Cleveland. (0642-723358).
Great Russell St. Books, Denise Altman, 44 Great Russell St., London WC1B 3PA. (01-637-7635).
Mrs. D.M. Green, 7 Tower Grove, Weybridge, Surrey KT13 9LX. (0932-241105).
Grosvenor Prints, Nigel Talbot, 28 Shelton St., Covent Garden London WC1. (01-836-1979).
Anne Hall Prints, 19 Dam St., Lichfield, Staffordshire WS13 6AE. (0543-263263).
J. Clarke Hall Ltd., S.M. Edgecombe, 22 Bride Ln., London EC4Y 8DU. (01-353-5483).
Harrod's, Old Map & Print Dept., Brompton Rd., Knightsbridge, London SW1. (01-730-1234).
Helgato, 2 The Broadway, Friern Barnet Rd., London N11 3DU. (01-361-8326).
Heritage Maps, Apsley House, 39 Wellington Rd., Edgbaston, Birm. B15 2ES. (021-440-2734).
F. & J. Hogan, 31 Tranmere Rd., Edmonton, London N9 9EJ. (01-360-6146).
R.F.G. Hollett & Son, 6 Finkle St., Sedbergh, Cumbria LA10 5BZ. (0587-20298).
Hollyman & Treacher, M.G. Kadwell, 22 Duke St., Brighton, E. Sussex BN1 1AH. (0273-28007).
Mrs. Julia Holmes, Antique Maps & Prints, Muirfield Pl., Bunch Ln., Haslemere, Surrey GU27 1AE. (0428-2153).
Stephanie Hoppen Ltd., 17 Walton St., London SW3. (01-589-3678).
A. Howard, 26 Brunswick Sq., Hove, E. Sussex BN3 1EJ. (0273-738812).
Hughes & Smeeth Ltd., 1 Gosport St., Lymington, Hampshire SO41 9BG. (0590-76324).
Simon Hunter Antique Maps, Prinny's Antiques Gallery, 3 Meeting House Lane, Brighton, Sussex BN1 1HB. (0273-746983, Fax same).
Ingol Maps & Prints, Valerie Kidd, Cantsfield House, 206 Tag Lane, Ingol, Preston PR2 3TX. (0772-724769).
InterCol London, Yasha Beresiner, 43 Templars Crescent, London N3 3QR. (081-349-2207, Fax 081-346-9539). And 11 Camden Passage, Islington, London N1. (071-354-2599) [Wed & Sat].
Jarndyce Antiquarian Books, Brian Lake, 46 Great Russell St., Bloomsbury, London WC1. (01-631-4220).
Kamiliya Books, Prints & Maps, Box 395, London W23HF. (01-262-6317).
Barry M. Keene, 12 Thameside, Henly on Thames, Oxfordshire. (0491-577119).
Peter Kennedy, Antiquarian Maps, Books & Prints, 1 Langford Close, Fivehead, Taunton, Somerset TA3 6QE. (046-08-479).
King's Court Galleries, Olde King's Head Ct., High St., Dorking, Surrey RH4 1AR. (0306-881757).
Laura's Bookshop, Laura Crooks, 58 Osmaston Rd., Derby DE1 2HZ. (0332-47094).
J. Lawton Ltd., 1 Boundstone Rd., Wrecclesham, Farnham, Surrey GU10 4TH. (025-125-3615).
Leadenhall Gallery, A. & D.L. Greenaway, 12 Palace St., Canterbury CT1 2D2. (0227-457339).
Leafield Maps & Prints, Tony Croft, Cotswald View, Leafield, Oxford OX8 5NY. (099387-357).
G. & R. Leapman, Hollycroft, Common Road, Stanmore, Middlesex HA7 3HX. (01-950-2995).
Andrew Leverton, 19 Barrydene, Oakleigh Rd. North, London N20 9HG. (01-445-2203).

International Dealers

Michael Lewis Gallery, 17 High St., Bruton, Somerset BA10 0AB. (074-981-3557).
Leycester Map Galleries Ltd., Tony Forster, Well House, Arnesby, Leicester LE8 3WJ. (053-758-462).
Kitty Liebreich, 5 Monk's Dr., London W3 0EG. (01-992-5104).
Lion Gallery, R.P. Hepner, 15a Minshull St., Knutsford, Cheshire WA16 6HG. (0565-52915).
London Art, Jane Yule, 127 Portobello Rd., London W11. (01-235-4198).
Norman Lord, Antique City Market, 98 Wood St., London E17 3HX. (01-520-8300).
The Lyver & Boydell Galleries, Paul Breen, 15 Castle Street, Liverpool, Merseyside L2 4SX. (051-236-7524).
Anne Campbell MacInnes, Lantern Gallery, 9 George St., Bath BA1 2EH. (0225-63727).
Maggs Brothers, 50 Berkeley Sq., London W1X 6EL. (01-493-7160).
Magna Gallery, B. Kentish & M.J. Blant, 41 High St., Oxford OX1 4AP. (0865-245805).
The Map House, Sifton, Praed & Co. Ltd., 54 Beauchamp Pl., Knightsbridge, London SW3 1NY. (071-589-4325, 071-584-8559, Fax 071-589-1041).
G. & D. Marrin & Sons, 149 Sandgate Rd., Folkestone, Kent CT20 2DA. (0303-53016).
Peter M. Martin, Antique Maps & Prints, 12 Beech Ave., Radlett WD7 7DE. (09276-7653).
Richard Martin, 23 Stoke Rd., Gosport, Hampshire PO12 1LS. (0705-520642).
Roger Mason, 86A, Banbury Rd., Oxford. (0865-59380).
Maynard & Bradley, 1 Royal Arcade, Silver St., Leicester LE1 5YW. (0533-532712).
W.B. McCormack Books, 6 Rosemary Ln., Lancaster LA1 1NR. (0524-36405).
David Mizon, Yew Tree Cottage, Little Strickland, Penrith, Cumbria CA10 3EG. (093-16-763).
P.J. Morris, 11 the Orchard, Marston Green, W. Midlands B37 7DH. (021-779-3718).
Patrick & Mary Mullen, Stablings Cottage, Goodwin Rd., Ramsgate, Kent CT11 0JJ. (0843-587283).
Richard Nicholson of Chester, 25 Watergate St., Chester CH1 2LB. (0244-26818).
A. Nicolas, 57 Fallow Court Ave., Finchley, London N12 0BE. (01-445-9835).
Avril Noble, 2 Southampton St., Covent Garden, London WC2E 7HA. (071-240-1970).
Northwood Maps Ltd., 71 Nightingale Rd., Rickmansworth, Herts WD3 2BU. (0923-772258).
James of Norwich, Auctions, Lt. Col.D.W. James, 33 Timberhill, Norwich, Norfolk NR1 3LA. (0603-624817).
O'Flynn Antiquarian Booksellers, 35 Micklegate, York YO1 1JH. (0904-641404).
Oldfield Antiquarian Maps/Prints, Anne Downes, 34 Northam Rd., Southampton SO3 0PA. (0703-38916).
Old Hall Bookshop & Gallery, A. Proud, Shutta Rd., E. Looe, Cornwall PL13 1BJ. (050-36-3700).
Old Soke Books, Peter Clay, 68 Burghley Rd., Peterborough PE1 2QE. (0733-64147).
Orbis Terrarum, Christine Faupel, 3 Parkvedras Terrace, Truro, Cornwall TR1 3DF. (0872-77928).
Paul Orssich, 117 Munster Road, London SW6 6DH. (071-736-3869, Fax 071-371-9886).
O'Shea Gallery, 89 Lower Sloane St., London SW1W 8DA. (01-730-0081, Fax 071-730-1386).
Jean Pain Gallery, 7 King's Parade, Cambridge CB2 1SJ. (0223-313970).
Patterson & Liddle, 2c Chandos Rd., Redland, Bristol BS6 6PE. (0272-731205).
Penn Barn, Paul Hunnings, By the Pond, Elm Road, Penn, Nr. High Wycombe, Buckinghamshire HP10 8LU. (0494-81-5691).
Pennymead Auctions, David Druett, Scotton, Knaresborough, North Yorkshire HG5 9HN. (0423-865962, Fax 0423-869614).
Periwinkle Press, Anthony Swain, 23 East St., Sittingbourne, Kent. (0795-26242).
Phillips Fine Art Auctioneers, 7 Blenheim St., New Bond St., London W1Y 0AS. (01-629-6602).
Pierpoint Gallery, A.G. Beaver, 10 Church St., Hereford HR1 2LR. (0432-267002).
Rex Poland, 25 South End, Corydon, Surrey. (01-680-5311).
Porter Prints, A.J. Sedgwick, 205 Whitham Rd., Broomhill, Sheffield S10 2SP. (0742-685751).
Postaprint, Taidswood, Iver Heath SL0 0PQ. (0895-833720).
Jonathan Potter Ltd., 125 New Bond St., London W1Y 9AF. (071-491-3520, Fax 071-491-9754).
Premier Print Collections, Grays Antique Market, 58 Davies St., London W1. (01-409-1498).
The Print Cellar, Elizabeth Tremlett, 35 Church St., Ashbourne, Derbyshire DE6 1AE. (0335-42933).
Printed Page, Christopher & Jean Wright, 2-3 Bridge St., Winchester SO23 9BH. (0962-54072).
The Print Room, John Cumming, 37 Museum St., London WC1A 1LP. (01-420-0159).
Bernard Quaritch Ltd., 5-8 Lower John St., Golden Square, London W1R 4AU. (01-734-2983).
P.J. Radford, Twytton House, Alfriston, Polegate, E. Sussex BN26 5TD. (0323-870440).
T.G. Ramsell, Elm Farm, Burton, S. Wirral, Cheshire L64 5TQ. (051-336-6655).
Reg & Philip Remington, 14 Cecil Court, London WC2N 4HE. (01-836-9771).
Pat Richardson, G12/13 Grays Mews Antiques, 1-7 Davies Mews, London W1. (01-629-1533).

Stanley V. Riddell, Old Down House, Swelling Hill, Ropley, Alresford, Hamp. SO24 0DA.
John Roberts Books, 43 Triangle W., Clifton, Bristol BS8 1ES. (0272-28568).
Louise Ross & Co., Mulberry House, 8 Mount Rd., Landsdown, Bath BA15 5PW. (0225-448786).
C. Samuels & Sons Ltd., 17-18 Waterbeer St., Guildhall Shopping Centre, Exeter EX4 3EH. (0392-73219).
Sanders of Oxford Ltd., 104 High St., Oxford OX1 4BW. (0865-242590).
G.J. Saville, Foster Clough, Heights Rd., Hebden Bridge, West Yorkshire HX7 5QZ. (0442-882808).
Chas. J. Sawyer, Bookseller, The Bees, Camden Rd., Sevenoaks, Kent TN13 3LZ. (0732-457262).
Thomas E. Schuster, 14 Maddox St., London W1R 9PL. (01-491-2208).
2nd Reading Books & Prints, N.H. Anderson, 7 Nightingale Ct. East St., Blandford Forum, Dorset. (0258-850050).
The Selective Eye Gallery, John Blench & Son, 50 Don St., Saint Helier, Jersey. (0534-25281).
Albert F. Sephton, 16 Bloemfontein Ave., Shepherds Bush, London W12 7BL. (01-749-1454).
Settings, Ruth Bowdage, 5 Titchwell Rd., London SW18 3LW. (01-870-2402).
Shropshire Map Exchange, Ian M. Guild, 12 Nantwich Road, Woore, Crewe, Cheshire CW3 95A. (063081-274).
Sotheby's Book Dept., Bloomfield Place, New Bond St., London W1A 2AA. (01-493-8080).
Henry Sotheran, 2 Sackville St., Piccadilly, London W1X 2DP. (071-439-6151, Fax 071-434-2019).
Ken Spelman, B. Miller & T. Fothergill, 70 Micklegate, York YO1 1LF. (0904-24414).
Stage Door Prints, Tony Reynold, 1 Cecil Ct., London WC2N 4HB. (01-240-1683).
Stanton Engravings, J. Trivess & W.H.D. Kennedy, 24 Trenchard Rd., Swindon, Wiltshire SN6 7RZ. (0793-764911).
J.T. Stirling, 33, Clent Rd., Rubery, Rednal, Birmingham B45 9UY. (021-453-2238).
Harold T. Storey, E.J. Kingswood, 3 Cecil Ct., Charing Cross, London WC2N 4EZ. (01-836-3777).
Stratford Trevers, The Long Room, 45 High St., Broadway, Worcestershire WR12 7DP. (0386-853668).
Studio Bookshop & Gallery, Laurence Oxley, 17 Broad St., Alresford SO24 9AW. (096-273-2188).
Studio 18 Ltd, 23a Beresford St., St. Helier, Jersey. (0534-34920).
Surrey Maps & Prints, Little Gables, StokeClose, Stoke d'Abernon, Cobham, Surrey. (0932-62511).
The Swan Gallery, S. Lamb, 51 Cheap St., Sherborne, Dorset DT9 3AX. (0935-814465).
K.W.Swift, 3 The Turl, Oxford OX1 3DQ. (0865-240241).
Taviner's, Auctioneers, Prewett St., Redcliffe, Bristol BS1 6PB. (0272-25996).
Peter Taylor, Antiquarian Booksellers, 1, Ganders Ash, Watford, Hertfordshire WD2 7HE. (0923-663325).
Thomas Rare Books, Lanchester Bookshop, 8/9 Station Road, Lanchester, Co. Durham DH7 0EX. (0207-529066 [bus.], 091-373-3526).
Nicola Thomson, Green Hedges Farm, Mark Cross, E. Sussex TN6 3PA. (089-275-325).
Thornborourgh Gallery, L. Turner, 17 Nicholas St., York YO1 3EQ. (0904-413000).
Tooley, Adams & Co. Ltd., 13 Cecil Court, Charing Cross Rd., London WC2N 4EZ. (071-240-4406, Fax 071-240-8058).
Charles W. Traylen, Castle House, 49/50 Quarry St., Guildford, Surrey GU1 3UA. (0483-572424).
W.D. Trivess, Heathfield House, Meonstoke, Southampton SO3 1ND. (0489-877326).
John Trotter, 11 Laurel Way, London N20. (01-445-4293).
Vandeleur Antiquarian Books, 69 Sheen Lane, London SW14. (01-878-6837).
Robert Vaughan Rare Books, 20 Chapel St, Stratford on Avon, Warwickshire CV37 6EP. (0789-205312).
Vecta Insula, 62 High St., Ryde PO33 3HJ, Isle of Wight. (0983-64362).
L. Walton, 41 WoodlandRd., Levenshulme, Manchester M19 2GW. (061-224-6630).
Warwick Leadlay Gallery, 5 Nelson Road, Greenwich, London SE10 9JB. (081-858-0317, Fax 081-853-1773).
R.G. Watkins, 9 North Street, Stoke Sub Hamdon, Somerset TA14 6QR. (0935-822891, Fax 0935-825485).
Ian Watson, 31 Dene Ave., Rowland's Gill, Tyne & Wear NE39 1DY. (0207-542883).
Leonora Weaver, 6 Aylestone Dr., Aylestone Hill, Hereford HR1 1HT. (0432-267816).
The Welbeck Gallery, Doreen Spellman, 18 Thayer St., London W1M 5LD. (01-935-4825).
Wendover Enterprises Ltd., G.F.C.Sampson, 34A Chiltern Rd., Wendover, Bucks. HP22 6DA. (0296-624368).
David Weston Ltd., 44 Duke St., Saint James's, London SW1. (01-839-1051).
Weston Antique Gallery, Boat Lane, Weston, Nr. Stafford ST18 0HU. (0889-270450).
Edna Whiteson Ltd., 66 Belmont Ave., Cockfosters, Herts. EN4 9LA. (01-449-8860).
Willcocks Antiques, E3 Chenil Galleries, 183 Kings Road, Chelsea, London SW3. (01-352-8653).
M.& B.E. Wilmington, Gilling Garth Cottage, Harmby, Leyburn, N. Yorkshire. (0969-23502).

Winton Publications Ltd., 17 Branksome Towers, Westminster Road, Poole, Dorset BH13 6JJ. (0202-764638).

Witch Ball Prints & Maps, Gina Daniels, 48 Meeting House Ln., Brighton, E. Sussex BN2 1HB. (0273-26618).

Charles Woodruff, Rare Books & Prints, 26 Yeoman's Row, London SW3 2AH. (01-584-0370).

Vivian Wright, Fennelsyke, Raughton Head, Carlisle, Cumbria CA57DU. (069-96-431).

Zeno Booksellers, M.P. Zographos, 6 Denmark St., London WC2H 8LP. (01-836-2522).

FINLAND

Antikki-Kirja, Jan Strang, Kalevankatu 25, Helsingfors SF-100. (90-611775).

Classic Antique Shop Ltd., Christer Pettersson, Kefattie 2c, 02200 Espoo. (3580-0-8038373).

C. Hagelstams Antiquarian Bookshop, Cecil Hagelstram, Frederikinkatu 35, Helsingfors 120. (90-649291).

NordiskaAntikvariska Bokhandeln, Tove Olsoni-Nilsson, N. Magasinsgatan 6, 00130 Helsingfors 13. (62-63-52).

FRANCE

Librairie Ancienne - Curiosites, Pierre Sieur, 3 rue de l'Universite, 75007 Paris. (42607594).

Librairie Bellanger, M. France Maramraud, 6 Passage Pommeraye, 44000 Nantes. (40890608).

Odile Bienvault, 3 rue Corneille, 37000 Tours. (47610071).

Librairie Brocante du Palais, Foucald Bachelier, 28 rue Jean Jaures, 44000 Nantes. (40484364).

Librairie Dudragne, Patrick Dudragne, 86 rue de Maubeuge, 75010 Paris. (878-50-95).

Librairie Elbe, Jean-Louis Bonvallet, 213 bis boulevard St. Germain, 75007 Paris. (45487797).

La Galerie du Bastion, D.R. Lyon, 2 rue du Bastion, 65000 Menton. (93-358632).

Edwouard Lagnel-Tastemain, 25 boulevard Marechal Leclerc, 14300 Caen. (31861335).

Louis Loeb-Larocque, 36, Rue Le Peletier, 75009 Paris. (878-11-18).

R. Musson, 10 bis quai Cypierre, 45000 Orleans. (38535434).

Librairie des Pyrenees, Jacques Saint-Hilaire, 21 rue Vieille Boucherie, 64100 Bayonne. (59597874).

G. Raffy, Stand 83, Marche Biron, 85rue des Rosiers, 93400 Saint Ouen. (47703651).

Friedrich Weissert, 22 rue de Savoie, 75006 Paris. (43-29-72-59, Fax 46-34-60-63).

GERMANY

Antiquariat Peter Babendererde, Jurgen Babendererde, Grosse Burgstrasse 35, D-2400 Lübeck 1. (0451-70776).

Galerie Boisserée, Walter Schilling, Drususgasse 7-11, D-5000 Köln 1. (0221-237733).

F. Dorling, Neuer Wall 40-2, D-2000 Hamburg 36. (040-36-46-70). Auctions.

Hans G. Fay Antiquariat, Postfach 1108, D-8907 Thannhausen. (08281-3712).

Jochen Granier, Buch- und Kunstauktionen, Postfach 1640, D-4800 Bielefeld, Welle 9. (0521-67148).

Die Gravüre, Elisabeth Keller, Rüttenscheiderstrasse 56, D-4300 Essen 1. (0201-793182).

Hartung & Karl, Karolinenplatz 5a, D-8000 München 2. Auctions.

Peter Hattesen, 239 Flensburg, Holm 76. (25077).

Antiquariat & Kunsthandlung Huste, Buch-und Kunstauktionen, Liebigstrasse 46-48, D-4600 Dortmund 1. (0231-122638).

Ruthild Jager, Steinweg 17, D-2120 Luneburg. (04131-42797).

E. & R. Kistner, Rolf Kistner, Weinmarkt 6, D-8500 Nürnberg. (0911-203482).

Hans Horst Koch, Buch- und Kunstantiquariat, Ku'damm 216, D-1000 Berlin 15. (030-882-63-60).

Antiquariat Köhl, Peter H. Köhl, St. Johanner Markt 20, D-6600 Saarbrücken. (0681-399667).

Kunstantiquariat Hans Marcus, Ritterstrasse 10, D-4000 Düsseldorf 1. (0221-325940).

Lüder H. Niemeyer, Simrockallee 34, D-5300 Bonn 2. (0228-351277).

Reiss & Auvermann, Antiquariat, Adelheidstrasse 2, D-6240 Königstein. (49-6174-1017, Fax 49-6174-1602). Auctions.

Ruffs Bücher & Graphik Etage, Edgar A. Ruff, Rheinstrasse 45/46 (Aufg. 1), Berlin. (030-859-1050).

Monika Schmidt, Turkenstrasse 48, D-8000 München 40. (089-284223).

Monika Schmidt, Galerie am Hausder Kunst, Karl-Scharnagl-Ring 60, D-8000 München 22. (089-222315).

Antiquariat Hanno Schreyer, Georg Schreyer, Euskirchenerstrasse 57-59, D-5300 Bonn 1. (0228-621059).

Das Bücherkabinett A. & C. Simon, Carlota Simon u. Dr. Maria Conradt, Poststrasse 14-16, D-2000 Hamburg 36. (040-34-32-36-38).

Antiquariat Wolfgang Staschen, Potsdammerstr. 138, D-1000 Berlin 30. (030-262-2075).

Antiquariat Stenderhoff, Theo Hobbeling, Alter Fischmarkt 21, D-4400 Munster. (0251-44749).

Kunstantiquariat Valentien, Heinrich Valentien, Niederwall 14, D-4800 Bielefeld 1. (0521-64420).
Venator KG, Cacilienstrasse 48, D-500 Köln 1.
Rainer G. Voigt, Langerstr 2, D-8000 München 80. (089-470-3066).
H. Th. Wenner Antiquariat, Heger Str. 2-3, D-4500 Osnabrück. (0541-3310366).
Zisska & Kistner, Buch-und Kunstauktionhaus, Unterer Anger 15, D-8000 München 2. (089-263855, Fax 089-269088). Auctions.

GREECE

Les Amis du Livre, Julia & Augusto Spandonaro, 9 Valaoritou St., GR-106 71 Athens. (361-5562).
Vanghelis Dimakarakos, 6 Normanou St., GR-105 55 Athens. (324-5241).
K.E.B.E., Andreas Nicolas, Odos Sina 44, 10672 Athens. (21-3615548).
George Patriarcheas, 6 Solonos St., GR-106 73 Athens. (361-5320).
Aglaia Sambos, 32 Ploutarchou St., GR-106 76 Athens. (721-6578).
Stavros Stavridis, 18 Panagitsas St., Kifisia, 14562 Athens. (801-7079).

GUADELOUPE

A la Reserche du Passe, Laurent Chassaniol, BP 668, 97169 Pointe-a-Pitre. (908415).

GUATEMALA

Paul F. Glynn, Casa el Carmen, 3A Avenida Norte 8, Antigua. (032-0207).

HONG KONG

The Asian Collector Gallery, Frank Castle, Wilson House, G/F, 19-27 Wyndham St. Central. (5-232181).

ICELAND

Bokavardan, Bragi Kristjonsson, Vatnsstigur 4, Reykjavik. (29720).

INDIA

Maria Brothers Antiquarians, O.C. Sud & Sons, 78 The Mall, Simla HP 171001. (5388).
Phillips Antiques, Habib & Farooq Issa, Indian Mercantile Mansions, Madame Cama Rd., Bombay 400039. (2020564).

IRELAND

Kenny's Bookshop & Gallery, Desmond Kenny, High St., Galway, County Galway. (091-62739).
Neptune Gallery, A. Bonar Law, 41 S. William St., Dublin 2. (01-715021).
James H. White, 43 Monkstown Rd., Monkstown, Dublin. (01-809-127).

ISRAEL

The Collector, Jerusalem Hilton Hotel, P.O. Box 4075, Jerusalem 91040. (972-02-53-38-90).
Larry Freifeld, Books, Prints & Maps, Rehov Bialik 9, Tel Aviv 65241. (03-658497).
M. Pollak Antiquariat, 36 & 42 King George St., Tel Aviv 65298. (03-288613).
Terra Sancta Arts, P.O. Box 10009, Tel Aviv 61100. (02-289630).
Z. Wiluzanski, P.O. Box 3183, Tel Aviv 61031. (03-297073).

ITALY

L'Arca, Roberto Fontanella, Via Mazzini 11, Brescia. (030-295740).
Antiquariato Librario, Bado & Mart, Stefania Bado, Via Tadi 21, Padova. (049-586098).
Uberto Bowinkel, Via Santa Lucia 25, Napoli 80132. (081-417-739).
Giampaolo Buzzanca, Via S. Andrea 5, Padova. (049-651831).
L'Antiquario del Garda, Maruizio Campisi, Via Dal Molin4, 25015 Desenzano BS. (030-9142582).
Garisenda Libri E Stampe, Maria Fiammenghi, Strada Maggiore 14/A, Bologna 40125. (23-18-93).
Libreria Kairos, Dott. Edoardo Rozza, Via Baldinucci 6, Milano 20158. (02-603-066).
Libreria Antiquaria Mediolanum, Luca Pozzi, Via Montebello 30, Milano. (02-653-637).
Armando Morbiato, Via Liguria 68, 35020 Camin, Padova. (059-219-452).
Plinio Nardecchia, Piazza Navona 25, Rome. (06-6569318).
Old Times, Le Stampe Antiche, Cesare Giannelli, Via Campo di Marte, 26, 06100 Perugia. (075/7520 18).
Libreria Antiquaria Perini, Ruth Perini, Via Amatore Sciesa 11, 37122 Verona. (045-30073).
Libreria Antiquaria Pregliasco, Arturo Pregliasco, Via Accademia Albertina 3 bis, Torino. (011-877-114).
Libreria Antiquaria Rappaport, E.S. Rappaport Seacombe, Via Sistina 23, Rome 187. (06-483-826).

Libreria Antiquaria Soave, V. & E. Soave, Via Po 48, 10123 Torino. (011-878957).
Valeria Bella Stampe, Via S. Cecilia 2, 20122 Milano. (02-782009).
Vecchia Liberia Modenese, Marcello Broseghini, Viale Storchi 26, Modena 41100. (059-219-452).

JAMAICA

Bolivar Bookshop & Gallery, P.O. Box 413, Kingston 10. (926-8799).

JAPAN

Yushodo Booksellers Ltd., 29 San-ei-cho, Shinijuku-ku, Tokyo 160. (357-1411).

LICHTENSTEIN

Antiquariat Gallus, E. Adelsberger, Postfach 298, FL-9485 Nendeln. (075-3-17-44).

MALTA

Paul Bezzina, 114 St. Lawrence St., Vittoriosa. (785812).
Emmanuel L. Muscat, 161 Congress Rd., Mosta. (448791).

The NETHERLANDS

J.L. Beijers B.V., Achter Sint Pieter 140, Utrecht 3512 HT. (030-310958).
Antiquariaat C. Broekema, Postbus 75880, 1007 AW Amsterdam. (020-62-95-10).
Cartographica Neerlandica, Dr. M.P.R. van den Broeche, Soestdijkseweg 101, 3721 AA Bilthoven. (31-30-202396, Fax same).
Kunsthadel Drie Kronen BV, Pep Mensink, Luttik Oudorp 114, 1811 MZ Alkmaar. (072-116311).
S. Emmerling, Nieuwe Zijds Voorburgwal 304, Amsterdam 1012 RV. (020-231476).
Van Gendt Book Auctions BV, 96-8 Keizersgracht, Amsterdam 1015CV.
Greenhill BV, L.F.J. Hoppenbrouwers, Torenwijck V, Ruimzicht 137, 1068 CS Amsterdam. (020-198960).
Gysbers & van Loon, F.R. van Loon, Postbus 396, 6800 AJ Arnhem. (085-424421).
B.M. Israel BV, Boekhandel en Antiquariaat, NZ Voorburgwal 264, 1012 RS Amsterdam. (020-247040).
Nico Israel, 489 Keizersgracht, Amsterdam 1017 DM. (020-22-22-55).
Firma Loose, R. Loose, Papestraat 3, 2513 AV den Haag. (070-64-49-99).
Werner Lowenhardt, DeLairessestraat 40-1, Amsterdam 1071 PB. (020-62-00-89).
Marcus v/h Sothmann, Johannes Marcus, Nieuwezijosvoorburgwal 284, 1012 RT Amsterdam. (020-236920).
A. van der Meer, P.C. Hoofstraat 112, 1071 CD Amsterdam. (020-621936).
Pampiere Wereld Antiquariaat, S.S. Meyer, Keizersgracht 428-432, 1016 GD Amsterdam. (020-252069).
't Prentenkabinet, E.M. Hauch, Oostzeedijk 350, 3063 CD Rotterdam. (010-4111193).
Boekhandel J. de Slegte, 48-52 Kalverstraat, 1012 PE Amsterdam. (020-225933).
Speculum Orbis Terrarum, Robert Putman, Postbus 70084, 1007 KB Amsterdam. (020-64-47-95).
Paulus Swaen Old Maps & Prints, Hofstraat 19, P.O. Box 317, 5664 HS Geldrop. (+31-40-853571, Fax +31-40-854075).
Antiquariaat Vorkink-Heeneman, D.J. Vorkink, Beeklaan 327-329, 2562 AJ den Haag. (070-634428).
Jan J. van Waning Galerie, Westersingel 35, 3014 GS Rotterdam. (010-4360198).

NEW CALEDONIA

Galerie Ad Lib, Max Shekleton, BP 362, Noumea. (284040).

NEW ZEALAND

Anah Dunsheath, Antiquarian Booksellers, P.O. Box 4181, Auckland 1. (09-790379).
Neil McKinnon Ltd., P.O. Box 847, Timaru. (056-81-931).

NORTHERN IRELAND

Phyllis Arnold Gallery, 24 Dufferin Ave., Bangor, County Down BT20 3AA. (0847-469899).
Emerald Isle Books, J.A. & J.E. Gamble, 539 Antrim Rd., Belfast BT15 3BU. (0232-771798).
Ultonia Maps, David Hogg, Doorus, Liggartown, Strabane, Tyrone. (06626-58515).

NORWAY

Damms Antiqvariat A/S, Claes Nyegaard, Tollbodgaten 25, 157 Oslo 1. (02-410402).

PORTUGAL

R.W. Bremner, Chao dos Arcos, Linho, 2710 Sintra.
Antonio Capucho, Viv. Naria Amelia, Av. Marques Leal, S. Joao do Estoril 2765.

Livraria Historica & Ultramarina, J.C. Silva, Travessa da Queimada, 28 Lisboa 2. (36-85-89).

SCOTLAND

Aberdeen Rare Books, A.J. & P.M. Campbell, Slains House, Collieston, Ellon, Aberdeenshire AB4 9RT. (035-887-275).
Billson of St. Andrews, 15 Greyfriars Garden, St. Andrews, Fife KY16 9HG. (0334-75063).
The Carson Clark Gallery, Scotia Maps-Mapsellers, 173 Canongate, Edinburgh EH8 8BN. (031-556-4710).
Corn Exchange Bookshop, B.R. & E.M.B. Young, 55 King St., Stirling FK8 1DR. (0786-73112).
Benny Gillies, 31 Victoria St., Kirkpatrick Durham, Kirkcudbrightshire DG7 3HQ. (055-665-412).
The Inverness Bookshop, Charles Leakey, 10 Bank St., Inverness IV1 1QY. (0463-239947).
John Mathieson Gallery, 48A Frederick St., Edinburgh EH2 1HG. (031-225-6798).
Colin Murdoch, 56 High St., Kingussie, Inverness Shire. (05402-552300).
John Nelson, 22 Victoria St., Edinburgh. (031-225-4413).
The Ship's Wheel, A.H. & H.E. Munro, 2 Traill St., Thurso, Caithness. (0847-62485).

SINGAPORE

Antiques of the Orient Ltd., Michael J. Sweet, 21 Cuscaden Road #01-02, Ming Arcade, Singapore 1024. (7330830).

SOUTH AFRICA

Clarke's Bookshop, P.V. Mills & H. Dax, 211 Long St., Capetown 8001. (021-235739).
Gail & Jonathan Schrire, P.O. Box 241, Rondebosch 7700, Capetown.
Jeffrey Sharpe, Rare Books & Maps, Box 32342, Camps Bay 8040. (337-8138).
Peter Visser Antiques, 117 Long St, Cape Town 8001. (021-237870).

SPAIN

El Asilo del Libro, Antonio Lorenzo, c/. Corretgeria 34, 46001 Valencia. (96-3310060).
Llibreria Antiquaria Catedral, Jose del Rio & Teresa Mercade, Cos del Bou 14-16, 43003 Tarragona. (977-232451).
Frame, Grabados y Mapas Antiguas, General Pardinas, 69, Madrid 28006. (91-411-3362, Fax 91-564-1520).

SWEDEN

Aspingtons Antikvariat, Mat Aspington, V„sterl†nggatan 54, 111 29 Stockholm. (08-201100).
Era Antikvariat, Francesco Bacoccoli, Box 45511, 10430 Stockholm. (08-7581412).
K.M. Flodin & Co., S. Flodin, V„sterl†nggatan 37, 11129 Stockholm. (08-204881).
Lundquist & Ohman, Kristinelundsgaten 7, Goteborg S-41137.
Medaco, Rolf Ottoson, Verkstadsvagen 21, 5-14170 Huddinge. (08-468918).
Ronnells Antikvariat AB, Birger Jarlsgaten 32, Stockholm. (08-115411).

SWITZERLAND

Asia House Museum, T.P. Nguyen, 16 Hotel-de-Ville, 1204 Geneve. (022-297190).
Buchantiquariat Benz, Aathalstrasse, 8607 Seegraben. (01-9323022).
La Fiera del Libro, Via Marconi 2, 6900 Lugano. (091-227649).
Finden S.A., Via Volta 1, Chiasso 6830. (091-445687).
Germann, Zeltweg 67, Zurich CH-8032.
Haus der Bücher AG, Baumleingasse 18, Basel CH-4051.
Galerie Kempf, Johannes Kempf, Strehlgasse 19, 8001 Zurich. (01-2213830).
August Laube, Trittligasse 19, 8001 Zurich. (01-2518550).
Karl Mohler, Buch- u. Kunstantiquariat, Rheinsprung 7, Basel 4001. (061-25-98-82).
Antik-Pfister Antiquariat, Postfach 784, 8025 Zurich 1. (01-47-62-32).
Rene Simmermacher AG, Postfach 215, 8024 Zurich. (01-2525512).

TAIWAN

Bipolar International Corp., Oliver Yeh, No.9, Alley 10, Lane 237, Wan Ta Road, Taipei. (2-3011000, Fax 2-3077777).

THAILAND

White Lotus Co. Ltd., Diethard Ande, G.O.P. Box 1141, Bangkok 10501. (662-2861100, Fax 662-2131175).

International Dealers

TRINIDAD

McLeod's Antiques, Julian Bruce & Odette McLeod, La Seiva & Saddle Road, Maraval, Port of Spain. (629-2224).

TURKEY

F. Muhtar Katircioglu, Karanfil Araligi No.14, Levent, 80620 Istanbul. (1641786).

WALES

Antiques of Newport, J.M. Duggan, 82 Chepstow Rd., Maindee, Newport, Gwent. (0633-59935).
David Archer, The Pentre, Kerry, Newtown, Powys SY16 4PD. (068-688-382).
The Corner Shop, E.B. Okarma, 5 St. John's Place, Hay on Wye, Hereford. (0497-820045).
Country Antiques, Richard Bebb, Castle Mill, Kidwelly, Dyfed. (0554-890534).
Olwen Caradoc Evans, Bodvor, The Esplanade, Penmaenmawr, Gwynedd LL34 6LY. (0492-623955).
D.G. & A.S. Evans, 7 the Struet, Brecon, Powys LQ3 7LL. (2714).
Sue Lloyd-Davies, Castle House, 12 Picton Terrace, Carmarthen, Dyfed. (0267-235462).
Mona Antiqua, Karel Lek, 31 Castle St., Beaumaris, Anglesey, Gwynedd. (0248-810203).
David Windsor Gallery, E. Creathorne, 201 High St., Bangor, Gwynedd LL57 1NU. (0248-364639).
E. Wyn-Thomas, Old Quarry, Miners' Lane, Old Colwyn, Clwyd LL29 9HG. (0492-515336).

THE GEOGRAPHY OF CLAUDIUS PTOLEMY

The maps of Claudius Ptolemy are among the earliest and most interesting that are available to the collector. Ptolemy, not to be confused with the Egyptian kings of that name, lived from about 90 to 168 A.D., and probably worked in Alexandria. He produced a number of scholarly works on astronomy, astrology, music, optics, history, and geography. Ptolemy compiled his *Geographia* from the works of Marinus of Tyre and other geographers. Aside from the lost works of Marinus, it is the only ancient atlas that we know about. Fortunately, copies survived into the Middle Ages, perhaps in Constantinople, apparently passing into Europe around 1400 A.D. as the Eastern Roman Empire disintegrated. Handmade copies circulated until the advent of engraving and printing made mass production possible. The 27 maps are believed to date back to ancient times, providing a valuable record of early geography. The classical Ptolemaic maps usually consist of the World, 10 maps of Europe, 4 of Africa, and 12 of Asia. The maps for each continent are numbered, and maps from Ptolemy are usually recognizable by a legend such as *Tabula Europae VII*, i.e., the seventh map of Europe.

The earliest printed editions of Ptolemy adhered closely to the original maps. As geographers became more confident, so-called 'modern' maps were added. So great was respect for ancient wisdom, that the first standardized atlas to break with Ptolemy was not printed until 1570, although specially assembled sets of maps could be purchased before that date. The debt of cartography to Ptolemy is not widely known. Features now taken for granted stem directly from his maps, including north being at the top, a labeled grid of latitude and longitude, the conventions depicting land and sea areas, and the use of mathematical projections. Lest these seem obvious, one need only look at medieval European maps of non-Ptolemaic origin. Even locating the continents or determining the orientation on such maps often takes the beginner some time. Some maps by non-European cultures, such as Pacific Islanders, do not even look like maps to nonspecialists. In contrast, maps printed over 500 years ago for the Florence edition of Ptolemy are instantly recognizable for what they are.

During the 16th and 17th centuries, some of Ptolemy's practices were abandoned. Elaborate decorations were added to maps, and the top of the map was often east, west, or even south. Towns were depicted as small castles, rather than dots or circles. Gradually cartographers returned to Ptolemy's way of doing things. It is a measure of his genius that, with little apparent tradition to rely on, his maps so closely resemble the form finally adopted by cartographers 1800 years later.

The collector will often encounter loose maps from the various editions of Ptolemy in catalogs or showrooms. To help identify these maps, the early editions of Ptolemy's Geography and closely related works are listed at the end of this section. The list is believed to be complete and accurate, but additions or corrections will be appreciated. For further information, consult the references on the next page.

The Regional Maps of Ptolemy's *Geographia*

The 26 ancient Ptolemaic regional maps are usually designated by continent and number. Thus *Tabula Europae III* would indicate the third map of Europe. To assist in cases where the map is not further described, the area shown by each map is given here:

Europe

I	The British Isles (Scotland, Ireland, England & Wales)
II	Spain & Portugal
III	France & the Low Countries
IV	Germany
V	The Dalmatian Coast (present-day Yugoslavia)
VI	Italy & Corsica
VII	Sardinia & Sicily
VIII	Eastern Europe from the Vistula to the Sea of Azov
IX	Ancient Dace & Thrace (present-day Balkans north of Greece)
X	Greece & Crete

Africa

I	Mauritania (present-day Morocco & Algeria)
II	Present-day Libya
III	Egypt
IV	North Africa

Asia

I	Asia Minor (present-day Turkey)
II	Sarmatia (present-day Crimea, Sea of Azov & northern Caucasus)
III	Armenia
IV	Holy Land, Cyprus & Mesopotamia
V	Persia (present-day Iran)
VI	Arabia
VII	Scythia (present-day Caspian Sea with land to north & east)
VIII	Central Asia, Tartary
IX	Present-day Pakistan
X	Southern Asia, including India
XI	Present-day Burma & Malaya
XII	Ceylon

References:

A.E. Nordenskiöld, *Facsimile-Atlas to the Early History of Cartography*, Stockholm, 1889. Reprinted by Dover Publications, Inc., New York, 1973.

Harold L. Ruland, "A Survey of the Double-page Maps in Thirty-five Editions of the Cosmographia Universalis 1544-1628 of Sebastian Münster and in His Editions of Ptolemy's Geographia 1540-1552," *Imago Mundi* **XVI** 84-87 (1962).

Henry N. Stevens, *Ptolemy's Geography, A Brief Account of All the Printed Editions down to 1730*, London: Henry Stevens, Son & Stiles, 1908.

Justin Winsor, *A Bibliography of Ptolemy's Geography*, Cambridge (Massachusetts): University Press, Henry Wilson & Son, 1884.

List of the Editions of Ptolemy's *Geographia*

1475	Vincenza	folio	No Maps. Latin text.
1477(?)	Bologna	folio	24 crudely executed copperplate maps, usually colored: 1 world, 10 Europe, 4 Africa, 11 Asia. Latin text. The colophon is misdated 1462.
1478	Rome	folio	27 copperplate maps: 1 world, 10 Europe, 4 Africa, 12 Asia. Latin text. Later editions: 1490, 1507, 1508.
1482(?)	Florence	folio	31 crude copperplate maps, including 4 'modern' maps of Italy, Spain, France, and Palestine. Italian text. This is the only edition to use the original equidistant projection. It could have been published as early as 1478.
1482	Ulm	folio	32 colored woodcut maps: 1 world, 14 Europe, 4 Africa, 13 Asia, including 5 'modern' maps. All maps are double page except for Taprobane. Latin text. Later edition: 1486.
1486	Ulm	folio	32 woodcut maps same as the 1482 Ulm edition. Latin text.
1490	Rome	folio	27 copperplate maps from the same plates as the 1478 edition. Latin text.
1507	Rome	folio	33 copperplate maps, 27 the same as the 1478 edition with minor alterations, plus 'modern' maps of Northern Europe, Spain, France, Central Europe, Italy, and Judaea. Latin Text.
1508	Rome	folio	34 copperplate maps, the same as the 1507 edition, plus the world map of Ruysch, the first map in an edition of Ptolemy to show the New World. Latin text.
1511	Venice	folio	28 woodcut maps: 2 world, 10 Europe, 4 Africa, 12 Asia. The heart-shaped map is the first in an edition of Ptolemy to show part of North America, called "Regalis Domus." Latin Text.
1512*	Cracow	quarto	An introduction to Ptolemy's Geography edited by Stobnicza, with 2 rare woodcut maps, one of the Old World, the other of east Asia and North America. Latin text. Later edition: 1520.
1513	Strassburg	folio	47 woodcut maps: 27 Ptolemaic and 20 new. Includes one map devoted to the discoveries in the New World. Latin text. Later edition: 1520.
1514	Nuremberg	folio	No maps. Latin text.
1519*	Cracow	quarto	2nd edition of 1512 Cracow introduction. There were apparently no maps in the 2nd edition.
1520	Strassburg	folio	47 woodcut maps, the same as the 1513 edition, except for the map of Switzerland. Latin text.
1522	Strassburg	folio	50 woodcut maps similar to the 1513 edition but smaller. Latin text. Later editions: 1525, 1535, 1541.
1525	Strassburg	folio	50 woodcut maps printed from the same blocks as the 1522 edition except for Asia V. Latin text.
1532*	Strassburg	folio	8 double page woodcut maps. Latin text.
1533	Basle	quarto	No maps. Greek text. Later edition: 1546.
1533	Ingolstadt	quarto	No maps. Latin text.
1535	Lyons	folio	50 woodcut maps from the same blocks as the 1522 edition. Latin text.
1540	Basle	folio	48 woodcut maps: 27 Ptolemaic, 21 new. Edited by Sebastian Münster. Later editions: 1541, 1542, 1545, 1551, 1552.
1540	Cologne	sm. octavo	No maps. Latin text.
1541	Basle	folio	48 woodcut maps, same as 1540 edition. Latin text.
1541	Vienne	folio	50 woodcut maps from the same blocks as the 1522 edition. Latin text.
1542	Basle	folio	48 woodcut maps, same as 1540 edition. Latin text.
1545	Basle	folio	54 woodcut maps, 42 from 1540 edition, 12 new. Latin text.
1546	Paris	quarto	No maps. Greek text. Reissue of 1533 Basle edition.
1548	Venice	sm. octavo	60 copperplate maps by Gastaldi: 26 Ptolemaic, 34 new. Italian text.

1551	Basle	folio	54 woodcut maps same as 1545 edition. Latin text.
1552	Basle	folio	54 woodcut maps same as 1545 edition except "Lacus Constan" replaced with "Pomerania." Latin text.
1561	Venice	quarto	64 copperplate maps: 27 Ptolemaic, 37 new, mostly enlarged copies of the 1548 edition with Toscany, northern regions, Brazil, and the Ptolemaic world added. Italian text. Later eds. in 1562, 1564(2), 1574, 1598, 1599.
1562	Venice	quarto	64 copperplate maps from the same plates as the 1561 edition. Latin text.
1564	Venice	quarto	64 maps from same plates as 1561 edition. Italian text.
1564	Venice	quarto	Same maps as Italian edition. Latin text.
1571*	Basle	folio	An edition of Strabo with 27 woodcut maps from Münster's Ptolemy including 3 duplicates. Latin text.
1574	Venice	quarto	65 copperplate maps, the same as the 1561 edition, except that the Ptolemaic world has been engraved on a conic projection and a map of Rome added. Italian text.
1578	Cologne	folio	28 copperplate maps by Mercator. No text. Later editions: 1584, 1605(2), 1618-19, 1624, 1695, 1698, 1704, 1730.
1584	Cologne	folio	28 copperplate maps from the same plates as the 1578 edition. Latin text.
1596	Venice	quarto	64 copperplate maps, newly engraved by Porro. All maps but the world are single page. Edited by Magini. Latin text. Later editions: 1597(2), 1597-98, 1608, 1617, 1621.
1597	Cologne	quarto	64 copperplate maps. Latin text. Second edition of 1596 edition.
1597	Cologne & Arnhem	quarto	64 copperplate maps. Latin text. Variant of above.
1597-98	Venice	sm. folio	64 copperplate maps same as 1596 edition. Italian text.
1597*	Louvain	quarto	19 copperplate maps of America. Latin text. Wytfliet's Supplement to Ptolemy. Later editions: 1598, 1603, 1605, 1607, 1611, 1615.
1598*	Louvain	quarto	19 copperplate maps. Latin text. Wytfliet's Supplement.
1598	Venice	quarto	69 copperplate maps, similar to 1561 edition, but with decorations added. Italian text.
1599	Venice	quarto	69 maps same as the 1598 Venice edition. Italian text.
1603*	Douay	quarto	19 copperplate maps. Latin text. Wytfliet's Supplement.
1605*	Douay	quarto	19 copperplate maps. Latin text. Wytfliet's Supplement.
1605	Amsterdam	folio	28 copperplate maps by Mercator. Greek and Latin text.
1605	Frankfort	folio	Variant of above.
1607*	Douay	quarto	23 copperplate maps. Latin text. Enlarged version of Wytfliet's Supplement.
1608	Cologne	quarto	64 copperplate maps. Latin text. Reissue of 1596 Magini.
1611*	Douay	quarto	23 copperplate maps same as 1607 edition. Wytfliet's Supplement.
1615	Arnhem	folio	19 copperplate maps. Jansson's reissue of Wytfliet.
1617	Arnhem	quarto	64 copperplate maps same as 1596 Magini edition. Latin text.
1618-19	Amsterdam	folio	47 copperplate maps by Mercator. Greek and Latin text.
1621	Padua	folio	64 copperplate maps. Italian text. Reissue of 1596 Magini edition.
1624	Frankfort	folio	28 copperplate maps by Mercator. Greek and Latin text.
1695	Franeker & Utrecht	folio	28 copperplate maps by Mercator with ornamentation added. No text.
1698	Franeker & Utrecht	folio	28 copperplate maps by Mercator. Latin text. Reissue of 1695 edition.
1704	Amsterdam & Utrecht	folio	Same as above.
1730	Amsterdam	folio	Same as above with added index.

* Not a formal edition of Ptolemy's Geography.

SKETCHES OF MAP-MAKERS

This dictionary is intended for quick reference when more extensive reference material is not available. For each entry, only the place or places where the individual's work was published, and the approximate date of publication are given. Since the dates are approximate, "late 1600s" might also include a little of the early 1700s.

For more detailed information, readers are referred to Tooley's *Dictionary of Map-makers*. That work often lists some of the maker's major works. A debt is owed to that work for first names of some of the more obscure persons listed here.

Ackermann Lith.; New York, mid 1800s
Adrichom; see Van Adrichem
Albrizzi, Giambatista; Venice, mid 1700s
Allard (Family); Amsterdam, late 1600s
Allen, William and Co.; London, mid 1800s
Almon, John; London, late 1700s
Alting, Menso (the younger); Amsterdam, early 1700s
American Litho. Co.; New York, mid 1800s
American Publishing Co.; Milwaukee, late 1800s
Anbury, Thomas; London, late 1700s
Andreas, Alfred T.; Chicago, late 1800s
Andriveau-Goujon (Family); Paris, mid 1800s
Angelo, Theodore G.N.; Danish, early 1800s
Anson, George; London, mid 1700s
Antoine, Louis; Paris, mid 1800s
Apianus, Peter; German, early 1500s
Apianus, Philip; German, mid 1500s
Appleton, D. & Co.; New York, late 1800s
Aquila, Prospero dell'; Venice, late 1700s
Archer, Joshua; London, mid 1800s
Arrowsmith, Aaron (Jr.); London, early 1800s
Arrowsmith, Aaron (Sr.); London, early 1800s
Arrowsmith, John; London, early 1800s
Arrowsmith, Samuel; London, early 1800s
Ashby, H.; London, late 1700s
Asher & Adams; New York, late 1800s
Aspin, Jehoshaphat; London, early 1800s
Atwater, Caleb; American, early 1800s
Atwood, J.M.; Philadelphia, late 1800s

Bachiene, Willem Albert; Amsterdam, late 1700s
Baedeker (Company); Leipzig, late 1800s
Bailey, H.H., & J.C. Hazen; New York, late 1800s
Baldwin & Cradock; London, early 1800s
Baldwin, Richard (Jr.); London, mid 1700s
Bankes, Thomas; London, late 1700s
Barclay, T.; London, late 1800s
Barfield, J.; London, early 1800s
Barker, William; Philadelphia, late 1700s
Barnes & Burr; New York, mid 1800s
Barrow, Sir John; London, late 1700s
Bartholomew, John (II); London, mid 1800s
Bartlett, W.H.; London, mid 1800s
Basire, James (no.1); English, mid 1700s
Basire, James (no.2); English, early 1800s
Basire, James (no.3); English, mid 1800s
Baudin, Admiral; Paris, early 1800s
Baumgarten, Siegmund Jakob; Halle, mid 1700s
Beautemps-Beaupre, Charles Francois; Paris, late 1700s
Beers (Company); New York, late 1800s
Bell, A.; Edinburgh, late 1700s
Bell, James; Glasgow, early 1800s
Bell, Peter; London, late 1700s
Bellere, Jean; Antwerp, late 1500s
Bellin, Jacques Nicolas; Paris, mid 1700s
Benard, Jacques Francois; Paris, early 1700s
Bernard, Jean Frederic; Amsterdam, mid 1700s
Berry, William; London, late 1600s
Bertelli, Fernando; Venice, mid 1500s
Bertius, Pieter; Amsterdam, early 1600s
Betts, John; London, mid 1800s
Bickham, George Jr.; London, mid 1700s
Bien, Julius; New York, mid 1800s
Bion, Nicolas; Paris, mid 1700s
Black, Adam & Charles; Edinburgh, mid 1800s
Blackie & Son; Glasgow, Edinburgh, London, late 1800s
Blaeu (Family); Amsterdam, mid 1600s
Blanchard, Rufus; Chicago, mid 1800s
Blankaart, Nicolas; Leyden, mid 1600s
Blome, Richard; London, late 1600s
Blondeau, Alexandre; Paris, early 1800s
Blundell, J.; London(?), early 1700s
Blunt, Edmund; Newburyport, Massachusetts, early 1800s
Bodenehr (Family); Augsburg, early 1700s
Bohn, Carl Ernst; Hamburg, late 1700s
Bolton, Solomon; London, late 1700s
Bonne, Rigobert; Paris, late 1700s
Bonner, John; Boston, early 1700s
Bordiga, F.; Venice, early 1800s
Borthwick, J.; London, mid 1800s
Botero, Giovanni; Italian, late 1500s
Bouchette, Joseph; London, early 1800s
Bowen, Emanuel; London, mid 1700s
Bowen, Thomas; London, late 1700s

Bowles, Carington; London, late 1700s
Bowles, John; London, mid 1700s
Bowles, Thomas; London, early 1700s
Boynton, George W.; Boston, mid 1800s
Bradford, Thomas Gamaliel; Boston, New York, early 1800s
Bradley, Wm. & Co.; Philadelphia, late 1800s
Braun, Georg & Remigius Hogenberg; Cologne, late 1500s
Brightly, C. & E. Kinnersley; Bungay, Suffolk, early 1800s
Brion de la Tour, Louis; Paris, late 1700s
Brooke, W.H.; American, mid 1800s
Browne, Christopher; London, late 1600s
Brue, Adrien Hubert; Paris, early 1800s
Bryant, A.; London, early 1800s
Buache, Phillipe; Paris, mid 1700s
Buchon, Jean Alexandre; Paris, early 1800s
Bufford, J.H.; Boston, mid 1800s
Buisson; Paris, late 1700s
Bunting, Heinrich; Hanover, late 1500s
Burgess, D.; New York, mid 1800s
Burgis, William; Boston, early 1700s
Burney, J.; London, early 1800s
Burr, David H.; New York, early 1800s
Burriel, Father Andres Marcos; Madrid, mid 1700s
Butler, Samuel; English, early 1800s

Cadell, Thomas; London, late 1700s
Callot, Jacques; Nancy, early 1600s
Camden, William; English, early 1600s
Camocio, Giovanni Francesco; Venice, mid 1500s
Campanius Holm, Tomas; Stockholm, late 1600s
Cantelli da Vignola, Giacomo; Modena, late 1600s
Capper, Benjamin Pitts; London, early 1800s
Carey, Henry Charles, & Isaac Lea; Philadelphia, early 1800s
Carey, Mathew; Philadelphia, early 1800s
Carez, J.; Paris, early 1800s
Carleton, Osgood; Boston, late 1700s
Carolus, Frans; Amsterdam, early 1700s
Carver, Capt. Jonathan; London, late 1700s
Cary, John; London, early 1800s
Case, O.D.; Hartford, Connecticut, mid 1800s
Cassini, Giovanni Maria; Rome, late 1700s
Castilla, A. de; Madrid, early 1800s
Catesby, Mark; English, mid 1700s
Catlin, George; American, early 1800s
Cellarius, Andreas; Amsterdam, mid 1600s
Chambers, William & Robert; Edinburgh, late 1800s
Chamouin, Jean-Baptiste-Marie; Paris, early 1800s
Chanlaire & Mentelle; Paris, early 1800s
Chanlaire, Pierre Gregoire; Paris, early 1800s
Chapin, William; New York, mid 1800s
Chapman & Hall; London, mid 1800s
Chapman, John; London, late 1700s
Chastenet-Puisegur, Jacques Comte de; Paris, late 1700s
Chatelain, Henry Abraham; Amsterdam, early 1700s
Child, G.; London, mid 1700s
Chiquet, Jacques; French, early 1700s
Citti, Louis F.; Richmond, mid 1800s
Claesz, Nicolas; Amsterdam, early 1600s
Clark, M. Lewis; American, mid 1800s
Clouet, Jean Baptiste Louis, L'Abbe; Paris, late 1700s
Cluver, Philip; Leyden, early 1600s
Cochin, Nicolas; Paris, mid 1600s
Colburn, H.; London, mid 1800s
Colden, Cadwallader; London, mid 1700s
Cole, Benjamin; London, early 1700s
Coleti, Sebastiano; Venice, mid 1700s
Collins, Greenville; London, late 1600s
Colnett, Capt. James; London, late 1700s
Colton, George Woolworth; New York, mid 1800s
Conant, A.; New York, mid 1800s
Conder, Thomas; London, late 1700s
Conservancy, Thomas; English, late 1700s
Cook, Capt. James; London, late 1700s
Cornelis, Lambert; Dutch, early 1600s
Coronelli, Vicenzo Maria; Venice, late 1600s
Cotovicus, J. (also Kootwyck); Dutch, early 1600s
Count & Hammond; New York, mid 1800s
Covens & Mortier; Amsterdam, early 1700s
Cowley, John; English, mid 1700s
Cowley, R.; London, late 1700s
Cowperthwait, H.; Philadelphia, mid 1800s
Cox, G.; London, mid 1800s
Coxe, Rev. William; English, late 1700s
Cram, George; Chicago, late 1800s
Crantz, David; London, late 1700s
Crawford, C.G.; New York, late 1800s
Crepy (Chez); Paris, mid 1700s
Cross, Joseph; London, mid 1800s
Cross, Thomas; London, mid 1600s
Cruchley, George Frederick; London, mid 1800s
Cummings, Jacob Abbot; Boston, early 1800s
Cutler, Nathaniel; London, early 1700s

D'Anville, Jean B.B.; Philadelphia, mid 1700s
D'Apres de Mannevillette, J.B.; Paris, late 1700s
Dal Re, Marc Antonio; Milan, early 1700s
Dalrymple, Alexander; London, late 1700s
Dampier, William; London, early 1700s
Danckerts (Family); Amsterdam, mid 1600s
Danet, Guillaume; Paris, early 1700s
Dapper, Olivier; Amsterdam, late 1600s
Darton, William; London, early 1800s
Davenport, S.; London, mid 1800s
Davies, Benjamin Rees; London, early 1800s
Dawson Bros.; Montreal, late 1800s
Day & Sons; English, mid 1800s
De Bar, Alexandre; London, late 1800s
De Beaurain, Jean Chev.; Paris, mid 1700s
De Belle Forest, Francois; Paris, late 1500s
De Berey, Nicolas; Paris, mid 1600s

De Bouge, Jean Baptiste; Brussels, late 1700s
De Bruyn, Cornelis; Delft, early 1700s
De Bry, Theordore; Frankfort, late 1500s
De Chabert, Joseph Bernard Marquis; Paris, late 1700s
De Charlevoix, P.F. Xavier; Paris, mid 1700s
De Crevecoeur, Michel Guillaume St. Jean; London, late 1700s
De Fer, Nicolas; Paris, early 1700s
De Fleurieu, Claret; Paris, late 1700s
De Grado, Philip; Spanish, early 1700s
De Hooghe, Romain; Amsterdam, late 1600s
De Jode, Cornelis; Antwerp, late 1500s
De Jode, Gerard; Antwerp, late 1500s
De L'Isle, Guillaume; Paris, early 1700s
De La Potherie, B.; Paris, early 1700s
De La Rue, Phillipe; French, mid 1600s
De Laet, Joannes; Leyden, early 1600s
De Lat, Jan; Deventer, mid 1700s
De Leth, Hendrik (the younger); Amsterdam, mid 1700s
De Rienzi; Paris, mid 1800s
De Rossi, Giovanni Battista; Rome, mid 1600s
De Stobnicza, Johannes; Cracow, early 1500s
De Vaugondy, Didier Robert; Paris, late 1700s
De Vaugondy, Gilles Robert; Paris, mid 1700s
De Wit, Frederick; Amsterdam, late 1600s
De la Feuille (Family); Amsterdam, early 1700s
Dean & Munday; London, mid 1800s
Dearborn, Benjamin; Boston, early 1800s
Delamarche, Charles Francois; Paris, late 1700s
Den Schryver; Dutch(?), early 1700s
Denis, Louis; Paris, late 1700s
Denison, J.; Boston, late 1700s
Des Barres, Joseph F.W.; London, late 1800s
Desilver, C.; Philadelphia, mid 1800s
Desnos, Louis Charles; Paris, late 1700s
Dewing, Thomas; London, Providence, Boston, early 1700s
Dezauche, J.A.; Paris, early 1800s
Dezoteux; French, late 1700s
Dicey, William & Cluer; London, mid 1700s
Didot, Firmin; Paris, early 1800s
Dilly, Charles; London, late 1700s
Dixon, George; London, late 1700s
Dolendo, Bartholomew; Leyden, early 1600s
Doncker, Hendrik; Amsterdam, late 1600s
Doolittle, Amos; Philadelphia, late 1700s
Doppelmayr, Johann Gabriel; Nuremberg, early 1700s
Dorr, Howland & Co.; Worcester, Massachusetts, mid 1800s
Dou, Jan Jansz; Dutch, late 1600s
Dower, John; London, mid 1800s
Drayton, Michael; London, early 1600s
Drinkwater, John; London, early 1800s
Dripps, Matthew; New York, late 1800s
Du Sauzet, Henri; Amsterdam, early 1700s
Du Val, Pierre; Paris, mid 1600s
Du Vivier, F.; Paris, late 1600s
Duchetti, Claudio; Rome, late 1500s
Dudley, Robert; Florence, mid 1600s
Dufour, Adolphe Hippolyte; Paris, mid 1800s
Duncan, E.; London, mid 1800s
Dunn, Samuel; London, late 1700s
Dupuis; French(?), late 1700s
Dwight, T.; London, early 1800s

Edwards, Bryan; London, late 1700s
Ehrmann, Theodor Friedrich; Weimar, early 1800s
Elliott Publishing Co.; San Francisco, late 1800s
Ellis, John; London, late 1700s
Elwe, Jan Barend; Amsterdam, late 1700s
Emory, Major W.H.; Amsterdam, mid 1800s
Entick, John; London, mid 1700s
Ertl, Anton Wilhelm; Munich, early 1700s
Esquemeling, Alexandre Oliver; English, late 1600s
Ettling, Theodore; London, mid 1800s
Euler, Leonhard; Berlin, mid 1700s
Evans, John; London, late 1700s
Exshaw, John; Dublin, mid 1700s

Faden, William; London, late 1700s
Fairburn, John; London, late 1700s
Farnham, Thomas; New York, mid 1800s
Fenner, Sears & Co.; London, early 1800s
Ferrer, Juan; M, early 1800s
Fidalgo, Joaquin Francisco; Madrid, early 1800s
Fielding, John; London, late 1700s
Findlay, Alexander; London, mid 1800s
Finley, Anthony; Philadelphia, early 1800s
Fisher, H.; London, early 1800s
Fisk & Russell; New York, mid 1800s
Fisk & See; New York, late 1800s
Flemming, Carl; Glogau, mid 1800s
Florimi, Matteo; Siena, early 1600s
Foot, Thomas; London, late 1700s
Forlani, Paolo de; Venice, mid 1500s
Forster, J.R.; London, late 1700s
Foster, G.G.; London, mid 1800s
Franklin, Sir John; English, early 1800s
Fremin, A.R.; Paris, mid 1800s
Frezier, Amedee Francois; Paris, early 1700s
Fricx, Eugene Henri; Brussels, early 1700s
Fullarton, Archibald; Glasgow, Edinburgh, London, mid 1800s
Fuller, Thomas; English, mid 1600s

Gall & Inglis; Edinburgh, London, late 1800s
Galle, Philippe; Antwerp, late 1500s
Galt & Hoy; New York, late 1800s
Gardner, James Sr.; London, mid 1800s
Garnier, F.; Paris, mid 1800s
Gaskell, C.A.; Chicago, late 1800s
Gastaldi, Giacomo; Venice, mid 1500s
Gaston, Samuel N.; New York, mid 1800s
Gebauer, J.J.; Halle, mid 1700s
Geddes, James; Albany, New York, early 1800s
Gemma Frisius; Louvain, early 1500s

Gerritsz, Hessel; Amsterdam, early 1600s
Gerstmayr; German(?), late 1700s
Gibson, John; London, mid 1700s
Gilliam; Philadelphia, mid 1800s
Gilman, E.; Philadelphia, mid 1800s
Gilpin, William; Philadelphia, mid 1800s
Glazier, Willard; Philadelphia, late 1800s
Goddard, John; London, mid 1600s
Goeree, Jan; Amsterdam, early 1700s
Goering, A.; Leipzig, late 1800s
Gold, Joyce; London, early 1800s
Goodrich, Samuel Griswold; Boston, mid 1800s
Goos (Family); Amsterdam, mid 1600s
Gordon, P.; Dublin, late 1700s
Graf, Adolf; Weimar, mid 1800s
Graf, C.; Weimar, mid 1800s
Gratton & Gilbert; London, mid 1800s
Gravius, N.T.; Amsterdam, mid 1700s
Gray, O.W.; Philadelphia, late 1800s
Greenleaf, Jeremiah; Boston, mid 1800s
Greenleaf, Moses; Portland, Maine, early 1800s
Greenwood (Co.); London, early 1800s
Gridley, Richard; London, mid 1700s
Grierson, George; Dublin, mid 1700s
Griswold; New Orleans, mid 1800s
Guicciardini, Luigi; Antwerp, late 1500s
Guilquin & Dupain; Paris, mid 1800s
Gussefeld, Franz Ludwig; Nuremberg, late 1700s
Guthrie, William; London, late 1700s

Habermann, F.X.; Augsburg, late 1700s
Hachette, Louis Christophe Francois; Paris, mid 1800s
Hadfield, W.; London, mid 1800s
Haliburton, T.C.; Halifax, early 1800s
Hall, Sidney; London, early 1800s
Halma, Francois; Amsterdam, Leeuwarden, early 1700s
Hardesty, H.H.; Richmond, Virginia, late 1800s
Harper & Bros.; New York, mid 1800s
Harper, J.J.; New York, early 1800s
Harrewyn (Family); Brussels, early 1700s
Harris, John; English, early 1700s
Harrison, John E.; London, late 1700s
Hasebroek, Jochem; Amsterdam, late 1600s
Hayden, Ferdinand Vandeveer; American, late 1800s
Hayward, John; Hartford, Connecticut, mid 1800s
Hearne, Samuel; London, late 1700s
Heather, William; London, early 1800s
Hennepin, Louis de; Amsterdam, late 1600s
Henriol, J.N.; Paris, mid 1800s
Herbert, William; London, mid 1700s
Herisson, Eustache; Paris, early 1800s
De Herrera, Antonio; Madrid, early 1600s
Heylin, Peter; London, late 1600s
Hildburg Institut; German, mid 1800s
Hill, H.H., & Co.; Decatur, Illinois, late 1800s
Hill, J.W.; Cincinnati, mid 1800s
Hill, Samuel; b, early 1800s
Hinshelwood, R.; New York, mid 1800s
Hinton & Simpkins; London, early 1800s
Hinton, John; London, mid 1700s
Hinton, Simpkin & Marshall; London, early 1800s
Hodges, J.; London, mid 1700s
Hogenberg, Frans; Cologne, late 1500s
Hogg, Alexander; London, late 1700s
Hole, William; London, early 1600s
Hollar, Wenceslaus; London, mid 1600s
Holme, Thomas; London, late 1600s
Homann, Johann Baptist; Nuremberg, early 1700s
Hondius (Family); Amsterdam, London, early 1600s
Honter, Jan; Kronstadt, Zurich, mid 1500s
Horatius, Andreas Antonius; Rome, early 1700s
Hornius, Georg; Dutch, late 1600s
Houze, Antoine Philippe; Paris, mid 1800s
Howen, A.; Baltimore, mid 1800s
Hughes, William; London, mid 1800s
Hulett, J.; London(?), mid 1700s
Hulsius, Levinus; Frankfort, late 1500s
Hume & Smollett; London, mid 1800s
Huntington, F.J.; New York, mid 1800s
Huot, Jean Jacques Nicolas; French, mid 1800s
Hurd, D.H.; Boston, late 1800s
Hutchins, Thomas; London, late 1700s
Hutchinson, Thomas; London, mid 1700s

Illman Bros.; New York, mid 1800s
Illman, T. & Sons; English, mid 1800s
Imbert, J. Leopold; Paris, late 1700s
Imray, James; English, mid 1800s
Ivison & Blakeman; Chicago, late 1800s

Jackson, P.; London, early 1800s
Jacobz (Family); Amsterdam, mid 1600s
Jaillot, Hubert; Paris, late 1700s
Jansson, Jan; Amsterdam, early 1600s
Janvier, Jean; Paris, late 1700s
Jefferys, Thomas; London, mid 1700s
Johnson & Browning; New York, mid 1800s
Johnson & Ward; New York, mid 1800s
Johnson, A.J.; New York, mid 1800s
Johnston, Thomas; Boston, mid 1700s
Johnston, W. & A.K.; Edinburgh, mid 1800s
Jones, Benjamin; Philadelphia, early 1800s
Judd, James; English, mid 1800s

Kaempfer, Engelbert; German(?), early 1700s
Kaerius; see Van den Keere
Kane, Elisha Kent; Philadelphia, mid 1800s
Keller, A.; Dutch(?), late 1800s
Kelly, Thomas; London, mid 1800s
Kepohoni; Hawaii, mid 1800s
Keur, Jacob & Hendrik; Dutch, mid 1700s
Key, John R.; New York, mid 1800s
Keyser, Jacob; Amsterdam, early 1700s
Keystone Publishing Co.; Chicago, late 1800s
Kiepert, Heinrich; Weimar, mid 1800s

Kilbourne, John; Columbus, Ohio, early 1800s
Kilburn; Boston, mid 1800s
King, Daniel; London, mid 1600s
Kingman Bros.; Chicago, late 1800s
Kino, Eusebio Francisco; Spanish, late 1600s
Kip, William; English, early 1600s
Kircher, Athanasius; Amsterdam, mid 1600s
Kitchin, Thomas; London, mid 1700s
Knight, Charles; London, mid 1800s
Kootwyck; see Cotovicus
Krayenhoff, Baron C.T.R. van; French, early 1800s
Kreffeldt, Mart. Karol; Dutch(?), mid 1500s
Kruikius, Nicolas Samuelsz; Delft, early 1700s

La Hontan, Baron Louis de; The Hague, London, early 1700s
La Perouse, Comte Jean de; Paris, late 1700s
Labat, J.B.; The Hague, early 1700s
Lacoste, Charles; Paris, late 1800s
Lafreri, Antonio; Rome, mid 1500s
Lambert, J.; London, early 1800s
Lane, W.; London, late 1700s
Langenes, Barent; Amsterdam, late 1500s
Langley, Edward; London, early 1800s
Langsdorff, G.; Frankfort, early 1800s
Lapie, Alexandre Emile; Paris, early 1800s
Lapointe, D.; Paris, mid 1600s
Lasor a Varea, Alphonsus; Padua, early 1700s
Lattre, Jean; Paris, late 1700s
Lauremberg, Johannes Wilhelm; Amsterdam, mid 1600s
Laurie & Whittle; London, late 1700s
Laurie, Robert; London, late 1700s
Lavoisne, C.V.; London, early 1800s
Lawson, John; London, early 1700s
Le Beau, Claude; Amsterdam, mid 1700s
Le Bruyn, Cornelis; early 1700s
Le Clerc, Sebastian; Paris, late 1600s
Le Page du Pratz; Paris, mid 1700s
Le Rouge, George Louis; Paris, mid 1700s
Lea, Isaac; Philadelphia, early 1800s
Lea, Philip; London, late 1600s
Leigh, Samuel; London, early 1800s
Lemercier; French, late 1800s
Leval, P.; Paris, early 1700s
Levanto, Francesco Maria; Genoa, mid 1600s
Levasseur, Victor; Paris, mid 1800s
Lewis & Arrowsmith; Boston, Philadelphia, early 1800s
Lewis, Samuel; Philadelphia, late 1700s
Liebaux, Jean Baptiste; Paris, late 1600s
Liefrinck, Mynken; Antwerp, late 1500s
Lizars (Family); Edinburgh, early 1800s
Lloyd, H.H.; New York, mid 1800s
Lodge, John; London, late 1700s
Longman (Co.); London, mid 1800s
Lootsman; see Jacobsz
Lopez de Vargas Machuca, Tomas; Madrid, mid 1700s
Lotter (Family); Augsburg, late 1700s
Lowizio, George Moritz; Nuremberg, mid 1700s
Lucas, Fielding; Baltimore, early 1800s
Luffman, John; London, early 1800s
Lufft, Hans; Wittenberg, early 1500s
Lyell, Charles; English, mid 1800s

MacGregor, M.; London, mid 1800s
MacKenzie, Alexander; London, early 1800s
MacKenzie, William; London, Edinburgh, Glasgow, Dublin, late 1800s
MacKinlay, A.; London, late 1800s
MacLure & MacDonald; Glasgow, mid 1800s
MacPherson, D.; Philadelphia, early 1800s
Mackenzie, Murdoch; English, late 1700s
Macpherson, A.; London, early 1800s
Maffeius, Peter; Venice, Cologne, late 1500s
Maggi, C.; Turin, mid 1800s
Magini, Giovanni Antonio; Venice, late 1500s
Magnus, Charles; New York, Liverpool, mid 1800s
Mallet, Alain Manesson; Paris, late 1600s
Malte-Brun (Family); Paris, mid 1800s
Mante, T.; London, late 1700s
Marcy, Capt. R.B.; New York, mid 1800s
Mariette, Pierre (the elder); Paris, mid 1600s
Marshall, William; London, mid 1600s
Martin, Benjamin; English, mid 1700s
Marzolla, Benedetto; Naples, mid 1800s
Maspero, M.; Turin, early 1800s
Mast, Crowell & Kirkpatrick; Philadelphia, late 1800s
Matthews, Northrup Co.; Buffalo, late 1800s
Mawman, J.; London, early 1800s
Mayer, Johann Tobias; German, mid 1700s
McGregor, J.; London, early 1800s
McIntyre, A.; Edinburgh, late 1700s
McNally, F.; New York, mid 1800s
Mears, J.; London, late 1700s
Megarey, Henry I.; New York, early 1800s
Meijer, Peter; Amsterdam, late 1700s
Meisner, Daniel; Frankfort, Nurmeberg, mid 1600s
Meissas, Achille Pr. de; Paris, mid 1800s
Melish, John; Philadelphia, early 1800s
Mentelle, Edme; French, early 1800s
Mercator, Gerhard; Duisburg, late 1500s
Merian, Matthaus; Frankfort, mid 1600s
Metellus, Natalius Sequanus; Cologne, late 1500s
Meyer, H.; New York, mid 1800s
Meyer, Joseph; Hildburg, mid 1800s
Michault, R.; Paris, late 1600s
Middleton, C.T.; London, late 1700s
Migeon, J.; Paris, late 1800s
Millar, Andrew; London, mid 1700s
Millar, George H.; London, late 1700s
Miller, William; London, early 1800s
Mitchell, Samuel Augustus; Philadelphia, mid 1800s
Moffat, J.; Edinburgh, early 1800s
Moll, Herman; London, early 1700s

Mollhausen, Baldwin; London, mid 1800s
Monin & Fremin; Paris, mid 1800s
Monk, Jacob; Baltimore, Philadelphia, mid 1800s
Montanus, Arnoldus; Amsterdam, late 1600s
Moore, John Hamilton; London, late 1700s
Morden, Robert; London, late 1600s
Morgan, T.J.; American, late 1800s
Morrison & West; London(?), early 1800s
Morse & Breese; New York, mid 1800s
Morse, Jedediah; Boston, early 1800s
Mortier, Pierre; Amsterdam, late 1600s
Moule, Thomas; London, mid 1800s
Mount & Page; London, mid 1700s
Moxon, Joseph; London, late 1600s
Mudie, Robert; London, early 1800s
Muller, Johann Ulrich; Ulm, late 1600s
Munster, Sebastian; Basle, mid 1500s
Murphy & Co.; Baltimore, late 1800s
Murray, John; London, early 1800s
Mutlow, I.; London, early 1800s
Myers, J.F.; Halifax, mid 1800s

Neele (Family); London, early 1800s
Nelli, Nicolo; Venice, mid 1500s
Newbery, Francis John; London, late 1700s
Nicholls, Sutton; London, early 1700s
Nicol, G.; London, late 1700s
Nicolosi, Giovanni Battista; Rome, mid 1600s
Nolin, Jean Baptiste (the elder); Paris, late 1600s
Norden, John; English, early 1600s
Norie, John William; London, early 1800s
Nuttall, Fisher & Dixon; Liverpool, early 1800s

Ogilby, John; London, late 1600s
Olney, Jesse; New York, mid 1800s
Ortelius, Abraham; Antwerp, mid 1500s
Ottens (Family); Amsterdam, early 1700s
Overton, Henry; London, early 1700s
Overton, John; London, late 1600s
Owen & Bowen; London, mid 1700s
Owen, David Dale; Washington, mid 1800s

Padley, James Sanby; English, mid 1800s
Palfrey, John Gorham; Boston, mid 1800s
Paoli, Sebastiano; Rome, early 1700s
Papen, Augustus; Hannover, mid 1800s
Parke, Lieut. J.G.; American, mid 1800s
Parker, Rev. Samuel; Utica, mid 1800s
Parr, Richard; London, mid 1700s
Parry, William Edward; London, early 1800s
Payne, John; New York, late 1700s
Peabody & Co.; New York, mid 1800s
Pease (R.H.) Lith.; New York, mid 1800s
Peeters, Jacques; Antwerp, late 1600s
Pelham, C.; London(?), early 1800s
Pendleton (John B.) Lith.; Boston, mid 1800s
Perelle; Paris, late 1600s
Perkins, G.; London, mid 1800s
Perthes, Justus; Gotha, mid 1800s

Petermann, Augustus Herman; Germany, mid 1800s
Petri, Heinrich; Basle, mid 1500s
Petrini, Paolo; Naples, late 1600s
Petroschi, Giovanni; Rome, early 1700s
Philip, George; Liverpool, London, mid 1800s
Philippe de Pretot, Etienne Andre; Paris, late 1700s
Phillips, Richard; London, early 1800s
Picquet, Charles; Paris, early 1800s
Pigafetta, Filippo; Rome, late 1500s
Pigot (James) & Co.; Liverpool, London, early 1800s
Pine, John; London, early 1700s
Pinkerton, John; Edinburgh, early 1800s
Pitt, Moses; London, late 1600s
Plancius, Petrus; Amsterdam, late 1500s
Playfair, James; Edinburgh, early 1800s
Pluche; Paris, late 1700s
Poirson, Jean Baptiste; Paris, early 1800s
Popple, Henry; London, early 1700s
Porcacchi, Tomaso; Venice, late 1500s
Porro, Girolamo; Venice, late 1500s
Portlock, Nathaniel; London, late 1700s
Prevost d'Exiles, A.; Paris, mid 1700s
Price, Charles; London, early 1700s
Price, William; Boston, mid 1700s
Probst, Johann Michael; Augsburg, late 1700s
Proud; London, mid 1700s
Purchas, Samuel; London, early 1600s

Quad, Matthias; Cologne, late 1500s

Radefeld, Carl Christian Franz; German, mid 1800s
Raignauld, H.; French, early 1600s
Ramsay, D.; Charleston, early 1800s
Ramusio, Giovanni Battista; Venice, mid 1500s
Rand, Avery & Co.; Boston, late 1800s
Raspe, Gabriel Nikolaus; Nuremberg, late 1700s
Ratelband, Johannes; Amsterdam, mid 1700s
Rau, Jacob; New York, late 1800s
Rawlings, T.; London, mid 1800s
Reed, John A.; Philadelphia, late 1700s
Reichard, Christian Gottlieb Theophil; Weimar, early 1800s
Reland, Adrien; Amsterdam, early 1700s
Renard, Louis; Amsterdam, early 1700s
Renner; German, mid 1800s
Revere, Paul; Boston, late 1700s
Robertson, G.J.; Cincinnati, mid 1800s
Robinson, G.G.; London, late 1700s
Robson, T.; Newcastle, late 1700s
Rocque, Jean; London, mid 1700s
Rollos, G.; London, late 1700s
Romans, Bernard; London, late 1700s
Rossi, Giacomo Giovanni; Rome, late 1600s
Rossi, Luigi; Milan, early 1800s
Rouargue, F.; Paris, early 1800s

Roux, Joseph; Marseilles, late 1700s
Ruscelli, Girolamo; Venice, mid 1500s
Russell, John; London, late 1700s

Sanson, Nicolas; Paris, mid 1600s
Santini, P.; Venice, late 1700s
Saxton, Christopher; London, late 1500s
Sayer & Bennett; London, late 1700s
Sayer, Robert; London, late 1700s
Schedel, Hartmann; Nuremberg, late 1400s
Schenk (Family); Amsterdam, early 1700s
Scherer, Heinrich; Munich, early 1700s
Schmidt, M.F.; Berlin, early 1800s
Schomburgk, R.; Leipzig, mid 1800s
Schonberg; New York, mid 1800s
Schouten, Willem Cornelisz; Amsterdam, early 1600s
Schrader, Th.; St. Louis, mid 1800s
Schraembl, Franz Anton; Vienna, late 1700s
Scott, Joseph; Philadelphia, late 1700s
Seale, Richard William; London, mid 1700s
Seile, Anne; London, mid 1600s
Seile, Henry; London, mid 1600s
Seller, John; London, late 1600s
Senex, John; London, early 1700s
Serres, D.; London, early 1800s
Seutter (Family); Augsburg, mid 1700s
Seymour, J.H.; Philadelphia, early 1800s
Shallus, Francis; Philadelphia, early 1800s
Silver, Thos.; London, mid 1700s
Silvestre, Israel; Paris(?), late 1600s
Simons, Mathew; English, mid 1600s
Slatter, H.; Oxford, early 1800s
Smith, Charles; London, early 1800s
Smyth, W.; London, mid 1800s
Soules, Francois; Paris, late 1700s
Southack, Capt. Cyprian; Boston, early 1700s
Speed, John; London, early 1600s
Speer, Capt. Joseph Smith; London, late 1700s
Spilbergen, Joris van; Leiden, early 1600s
Stackhouse, Thomas; London, late 1700s
Stampioen, J.; Amsterdam, late 1600s
Stanford, Edward; London, mid 1800s
Starling, Thomas; London, early 1800s
Staveley, E., & H.M. Wood; English, early 1800s
Stedman, Charles; London, late 1700s
Stedman, John Gabriel; London, late 1700s
Stent, Peter; London, mid 1600s
Steudner, Johann Philip; Augsburg, late 1600s
Stevens, I.I.; American, mid 1800s
Stockdale, John; London, late 1700s
Stocklein, Joseph; Augsburg, mid 1700s
Stoopendaal, Daniel; Amsterdam, early 1700s
Stopius, Nicolaus; Dutch(?), mid 1500s
Striedbeck, Johann; Strassburg, mid 1700s
Strobridge & Co.; Cincinnati, late 1800s
Stuart, Oliver J.; New York, late 1800s
Sudlow, E.; London, late 1700s
Tallis, John; Lond., Glasgow, Edinb., Dublin, NY, mid 1800s
Tanner, Henry Schenck; Philadelphia, New York, early 1800s
Tardieu (Family); Paris, early 1800s
Tarleton, B.; London, late 1700s
Tassin, Nicolas; Paris(?), early 1600s
Tavernier (Family); Antwerp, mid 1600s
Teesdale, Henry; London, mid 1800s
Tegg, T.; London, mid 1800s
Thackera, James; Philadelphia, early 1800s
Thaxter, S., & Son; Boston, late 1800s
Thevenot, Melchisedech; Paris, late 1600s
Thierry; Paris, early 1800s
Thomas, Cowperthwait & Co.; Philadelphia, mid 1800s
Thompson Bros. & Burr; American(?), late 1800s
Thomson, John & Co.; Edinburgh, early 1800s
Thornton, John; London, late 1600s
Tindal, Nicolas; London, mid 1700s
Tirion, Isaak; Amsterdam, mid 1700s
Tombleson; London, mid 1800s
Toms, William Henry; London, mid 1700s
Topham; London, early 1800s
Torbett, C.W.; London, early 1800s
Torniello, Augustine; Milan, late 1500s
Torrente, M.; Madrid, early 1800s
Toudy, H.J.; Philadelphia, late 1800s
Tramezini, Michaelo; Rome, Venice, mid 1500s
Tremaine, George C.; Toronto, mid 1800s
Trusler, John; English, late 1700s
Trutch, J.W.; Ottawa, late 1800s
Tunison; Jacksonville, Illinois, late 1800s
Turner, Charles; London, early 1800s
Turner, James; Boston, mid 1700s
Tyson, Philip; Washington, mid 1800s

Valdor, Joannes; Liege(?), early 1600s
Valentyn, Francois; Amsterdam, Dordrecht, early 1700s
Valk & Schenk; Amsterdam, early 1700s
Valk (Family); Amsterdam, early 1700s
Vallance, J.; Philadelphia, early 1800s
Van Adrichem, Christian; Cologne, late 1500s
Van Doetecum (Family); Deventer, Haarlem, late 1500s
Van Jagen, Jan; Amsterdam, mid 1700s
Van Keulen (Family); Amsterdam, late 1600s
Van Linschoten, Jan Huygen; Amsterdam, late 1500s
Van Lochom, Michael; Paris, early 1600s
Van Loon, Johannes; Amsterdam, mid 1600s
Van den Keere, Pieter; Amsterdam, early 1600s
Van der Aa, Pieter; Leiden, early 1700s
Van der Schley, Jacob; German, mid 1700s
Vancouver, Capt. George; English, late 1700s
Vandermaelen, Philippe Marie Guillaume; Brussels, mid 1800s
Varela y Ulloa, J.; Madrid, late 1700s
Varle, P.C.; French(?), early 1800s
Varte, P.C.; Philadelphia(?), late 1800s
Vascellini, G.; Milan, late 1700s

Vaughan, Robert; London, mid 1600s
Verbiest, Pieter; Antwerp, mid 1600s
Virtue, George; London, mid 1800s
Visscher (Family); Amsterdam, mid 1600s
Vivien, L.; Paris, early 1800s
Von Humboldt, Alexander; German, early 1800s
Von Reilly, Franz Johann Joseph; Vienna, late 1700s
Von Stahlin, Jacob; German, late 1700s
Von de Sandrart, Jacob; German, late 1600s
Vooght, Claes Jansz; Amsterdam, late 1600s
Vrients, Jan Baptista; Antwerp, late 1500s
Vuillemin, Alexandre A.; Paris, mid 1800s

Waghenaer, Lucas Janszoon; Leiden, Antwerp, Amsterdam, late 1500s
Wagner & McGuigan; Philadelphia, mid 1800s
Waldseemuller, Martin; Lorraine, early 1500s
Walker, J. & C.; London, mid 1800s
Walker, Samuel Jr.; Boston, mid 1800s
Wall, J. Sutton; Harrisburg, Pennsylvania, late 1800s
Walling & Gray; Boston, late 1800s
Walling, Tackabury & Co.; Boston, late 1800s
Wallis (James) & Reid (W.H.); London, early 1800s
Walther, Johann Georg; Frankfort, late 1600s
Walton, Robert; London, mid 1600s
Warburton, John; English, early 1700s
Ward, H.; London, early 1800s
Ward, J.; London, mid 1800s
Warden, D.; Edinburgh, early 1800s
Watson, Gaylord; New York, late 1800s
Wayne, C.P.; Philadelphia, early 1800s
Weber, P.; Karlsruhe, mid 1800s
Weigel, Christopher (the elder); Nuremberg, early 1700s
Weld, Isaac; London, late 1700s
Weller, Edward; London, late 1800s
Wells, Edward; London, Oxford, early 1700s
Werner; Leipzig, early 1800s
Whymper, F.; London, late 1800s
Wilcocke, S.H.; London, early 1800s
Wilkes, J.; London, early 1800s
Wilkinson, Robert; London, early 1800s
Willdey, George; London, early 1700s
Willmann, Edward; Karlsruhe, mid 1800s
Wilson, Charles; London, mid 1800s
Winslow, E.N.; Boston, late 1800s
Witsen, Nicolaas; Amsterdam, early 1700s
Wolff, Jeremias; Augsburg, early 1700s
Woodbridge, William Channing; Hartford, Connecticut, mid 1800s
Wright, Benjamin; English, late 1500s
Wyld (Family); London, mid 1800s
Wytfliet, Cornelis; Louvain, late 1500s

Young, J.; Washington, mid 1800s

Zaltieri, Bolognini; Venice, mid 1500s
Zatta, Antonio; Venice, late 1700s
Ziegler, Jacob; Vienna, early 1500s
Zurner, Adam Friedrich; Amsterdam, early 1700s

CUMULATIVE FREQUENCY DISTRIBUTION OF MAP-MAKERS

The cumulative frequency table which appeared through 1992, Volume 10, has been augmented to include a tabular distribution of frequency on an annual basis. This addition greatly simplifies a search through all volumes in quest of entries for a particular map maker and helps to direct one toward the greatest concentration of entries.

Total Entries for 1993: 4,354 — Different Map-Makers in 1993: 616

Cumulative Entries since 1983: 52,037 — Different Map-Makers since 1983: 2,127

	Total	'83	'84	'85	'86	'87	'88	'89	'90	'91	'92	'93
Abert	**1**	.	1	.	.	.	.	.	.	.	.	.
Ackermann Lith.	**7**	.	1	.	2	1	3	.	.	.	.	.
Adams & Son	**1**	.	.	.	.	.	.	.	.	1	.	.
Admiralty	**551**	17	7	37	64	62	56	87	51	48	56	66
Adrichom; see Van Adrichem.		.	.	.	.	.	.	.	.	.	.	.
Ainslie	**4**	.	.	1	.	.	.	.	2	1	.	.
Ainsworth	**1**	.	.	.	.	.	.	1	.	.	.	.
Alabern	**1**	.	.	.	1	.	.	.	.	.	.	.
Alaska	**1**	.	.	.	.	.	.	1	.	.	.	.
Albrizzi	**137**	25	9	13	4	24	38	8	7	4	3	2
Alden	**2**	.	.	.	.	1	1	.	.	.	.	.
Alexander	**1**	.	.	.	.	.	1	.	.	.	.	.
Allard	**44**	4	1	8	5	7	4	2	1	4	2	6
Allardt	**1**	.	.	.	.	.	.	.	1	.	.	.
Allen	**7**	.	.	.	.	.	.	.	1	.	6	.
Allen & Co.	**1**	1	.	.	.	.	.	.	.	.	.	.
Almon	**2**	.	1	.	1	.	.	.	.	.	.	.
Alting	**1**	1	.	.	.	.	.	.	.	.	.	.
Amer. Antiquarian Soc.	**4**	.	.	.	.	.	.	.	2	1	1	.
Amer. Bank Note Co.	**2**	.	.	.	.	1	.	.	1	.	.	.
Amer. Ethnological Soc.	**1**	.	.	.	.	.	.	.	.	1	.	.
Amer. Jour. of Science	**3**	.	.	.	.	.	.	.	1	.	2	.
American Litho. Co.	**3**	1	.	.	1	.	.	.	1	.	.	.
American Publishing Co.	**4**	.	1	.	.	.	.	1	1	.	1	.
Amman	**1**	.	.	.	.	.	.	.	.	.	1	.
Analectic Magazine	**2**	.	.	.	.	.	.	.	.	2	.	.
Anburey	**3**	.	1	.	.	.	2	.	.	.	.	.
Anderson	**7**	.	.	.	.	1	1	1	.	.	4	.
Andreas	**18**	2	2	2	3	2	1	3	1	.	1	1
Andrews	**12**	.	5	1	.	.	2	.	1	.	3	.
Andrews & Dury	**2**	1	.	1	.	.	.	.	.	.	.	.
Andriveau-Goujon	**16**	2	2	1	.	.	2	1	3	.	2	3
Andrus & Judd	**3**	.	.	.	.	1	.	.	1	.	.	1
Angelo	**1**	1	.	.	.	.	.	.	.	.	.	.
Angelocrator	**2**	.	.	.	1	.	1	.	.	.	.	.
Annales des Mines	**1**	.	.	.	.	1	.	.	.	.	.	.
Annin & Smith	**2**	.	.	.	.	1	.	.	1	.	.	.
Anonymous	**466**	77	59	54	49	69	28	29	37	29	13	22
Ansart	**3**	.	.	1	.	2	.	.	.	.	.	.
Anson	**25**	3	4	3	1	2	1	3	2	2	1	3
Anthony	**1**	.	.	.	.	.	1	.	.	.	.	.
Antoine	**3**	.	2	.	.	1	.	.	.	.	.	.
Anton	**1**	.	.	.	1	.	.	.	.	.	.	.
Apianus	**30**	4	2	2	1	8	3	3	.	5	1	1
Appleton	**36**	8	6	9	2	4	.	.	2	3	.	2
Appleton's Journal	**2**	.	.	.	.	.	1	.	.	1	.	.
Apthorp	**1**	.	.	.	.	.	.	.	.	.	1	.
Aquila	**2**	1	.	1	.	.	.	.	.	.	.	.
Aragon	**1**	.	.	.	.	.	.	.	.	.	1	.
Arbuckle Bros.	**2**	.	.	.	.	.	.	.	.	2	.	.
Archaeological Americana	**1**	.	.	.	.	.	.	1	.	.	.	.
Archer	**25**	.	5	.	.	10	5	1	2	1	.	1
Arias Montanus	**7**	.	.	.	.	.	2	2	.	1	2	.
Armenian Cartography	**1**	.	.	.	.	.	.	1	.	.	.	.
Armstrong	**3**	.	.	3	.	.	.	.	.	.	.	.
Arrowsmith	**342**	48	33	45	19	15	41	23	35	17	39	27
Arrowsmith & Lewis; see Lewis & Arrowsmith		.	.	.	.	.	.	.	.	.	.	.
Artaria & Co.	**3**	.	.	.	.	.	.	.	.	.	2	1
Aschbach	**1**	.	.	.	.	.	.	1	.	.	.	.
Ashby	**1**	.	1	.	.	.	.	.	.	.	.	.
Asher	**1**	.	.	.	.	1	.	.	.	.	.	.
Asher & Adams	**100**	2	11	4	5	7	3	12	6	30	5	15
Asher & Co.	**6**	.	.	.	.	2	.	1	1	1	1	.
Aspin	**2**	2	.	.	.	.	.	.	.	.	.	.
Astley Magazine	**1**	.	.	.	.	.	.	.	.	.	.	1
Atcheson	**2**	.	.	.	.	.	1	.	.	1	.	.
Atchison, Topeka & Santa Fe R.R.	**1**	.	.	.	.	1	.	.	.	.	.	.
Atlantic Neptune; see Des Barres		.	.	.	.	.	.	.	.	.	.	.
Atlas Maritimus & Commercialis; see Cutler		.	.	.	.	.	.	.	.	.	.	.
Atwater	**1**	.	1	.	.	.	.	.	.	.	.	.
Atwood	**8**	2	1	.	.	1	.	2	1	.	1	.
Aveline	**1**	.	.	1	.	.	.	.	.	.	.	.
Avery	**1**	.	.	.	1	.	.	.	.	.	.	.
Bachiene	**41**	.	2	8	.	22	3	1	1	1	1	2
Bachmann	**6**	.	.	1	.	.	.	2	3	.	.	.
Bacon	**24**	.	.	.	.	2	.	2	3	3	8	6
Baeck	**1**	.	.	.	1	.	.	.	.	.	.	.
Baedeker	**14**	.	14	.	.	.	.	.	.	.	.	.
Baffin	**1**	.	.	.	.	.	.	1	.	.	.	.
Bailey	**1**	.	.	.	.	.	.	.	1	.	.	.
Bailey & Co.	**6**	.	.	.	1	1	.	2	.	.	.	2
Bailey & Hazen	**1**	.	1	.	.	.	.	.	.	.	.	.
Bailleul	**1**	.	.	.	.	1	.	.	.	.	.	.
Baillie	**1**	.	.	1	.	.	.	.	.	.	.	.
Baines	**1**	.	.	1	.	.	.	.	.	.	.	.
Baker	**4**	.	.	.	.	.	2	1	.	1	.	.
Baker & Harper	**1**	.	.	.	.	.	.	.	.	1	.	.
Baldwin	**17**	2	5	2	2	4	2	.	.	.	.	.
Baldwin & Cradock; see S.D.U.K.	**35**	3	7	5	5	4	2	2	4	2	.	1

	Total	'83	'84	'85	'86	'87	'88	'89	'90	'91	'92	'93
Baldwin & Thomas	**1**	.	.	.	.	.	.	.	.	.	1	.
Ballino	**1**	.	.	.	.	.	.	.	.	.	1	.
Ballou	**5**	.	.	.	3	.	.	1	1	.	.	.
Bancroft	**3**	.	.	.	1	.	1	.	.	1	.	.
Bancroft & Knight	**2**	.	.	.	1	1	.	.	.	.	.	.
Bankes	**5**	.	2	.	.	.	.	.	.	2	1	.
Banvard	**1**	.	.	.	1	.	.	.	.	.	.	.
Barclay	**6**	1	1	.	1	1	.	1	.	.	.	1
Barcleus	**1**	.	.	.	1	.	.	.	.	.	.	.
Bardin	**1**	.	.	.	.	.	.	.	.	.	.	1
Barfield	**1**	1	.	.	.	.	.	.	.	.	.	.
Barker	**1**	1	.	.	.	.	.	.	.	.	.	.
Barlaeus	**1**	.	.	.	.	1	.	.	.	.	.	.
Barlow	**7**	.	.	.	1	1	2	1	.	.	1	1
Barnes	**6**	.	.	.	1	1	1	.	.	.	1	2
Barnes & Burr	**9**	.	8	.	.	.	.	.	.	1	.	.
Barrow	**10**	.	2	1	1	.	.	2	.	4	.	.
Bartholomew	**53**	.	8	.	4	4	1	23	1	5	3	4
Bartlett, J.R	**18**	2	2	4	4	2	2	1	.	.	.	1
Barton	**2**	.	.	.	.	.	.	.	1	.	1	.
Basire	**7**	1	1	3	1	.	.	.	1	.	.	.
Batelli & Fanfani	**3**	.	.	1	.	1	.	.	.	1	.	.
Baudartius	**12**	12	.	.	.	.	.	.	.	.	.	.
Baudin	**1**	1	.	.	.	.	.	.	.	.	.	.
Bauerkeller	**1**	.	.	.	.	.	.	.	.	.	.	1
Baumgarten	**5**	.	5	.	.	.	.	.	.	.	.	.
Bauza	**1**	.	.	.	.	1	.	.	.	.	.	.
Bayly	**1**	.	.	.	.	1	.	.	.	.	.	.
Beadle	**1**	.	.	.	.	.	1	.	.	.	.	.
Beaulieu	**2**	.	.	1	.	.	.	1	.	.	.	.
Beautemps-Beaupre	**7**	.	1	.	.	1	.	.	.	2	2	1
Beck & Pauli	**2**	.	.	.	.	.	.	1	1	.	.	.
Beechey	**3**	.	.	.	1	.	.	2	.	.	.	.
Beer	**1**	.	.	.	.	.	1	.	.	.	.	.
Beers	**26**	1	.	.	1	1	.	1	1	1	20	.
Beers & Lake	**1**	.	.	.	.	.	.	.	.	.	1	.
Beers, Comstock & Cline	**4**	.	.	.	1	1	1	1	.	.	.	.
Beers, Ellis & Soule	**8**	.	.	.	1	.	.	.	2	1	.	4
Beischlag	**1**	.	.	.	.	.	.	.	.	.	1	.
Belcher	**1**	.	.	.	.	.	.	.	.	.	1	.
Belden	**2**	.	.	.	.	.	1	.	.	.	.	1
Beldin	**5**	1	2	.	1	1	.	.	.	.	.	.
Bell; see Scot's Magazine	**14**	1	11	.	.	1	.	.	1	.	.	.
Bellairs	**1**	.	.	.	.	1	.	.	.	.	.	.
Bellere	**1**	1	.	.	.	.	.	.	.	.	.	.
Bellin:	**1515**	220	105	157	.	.	.	.	.	.	.	.
(large); see Depot de la Marine	.	.	.	.	33	23	35	18	24	15	17	22
(small); see De Charlevoix, Prevost d'Exiles	.	.	.	.	178	149	72	58	62	103	101	123
Benard	**48**	13	.	9	.	1	8	3	2	4	7	1
Benton	**2**	.	.	.	.	.	.	.	1	.	.	1
Berard	**1**	.	.	1	.	.	.	.	.	.	.	.
Berey	**1**	.	.	.	.	1	.	.	.	.	.	.
Bergen, Daniel & Gracey	**1**	.	.	.	.	.	.	1	.	.	.	.
Berghaus, H.	**2**	.	.	.	.	.	.	.	.	1	.	1
Bernard	**4**	1	1	.	.	.	1	.	.	.	1	.
Bernhardt	**1**	.	.	.	.	.	.	.	1	.	.	.
Bero, D.	**1**	.	.	.	.	.	.	.	.	.	.	1
Berry	**8**	1	2	.	.	1	1	.	.	2	1	.
Bertelli	**9**	.	2	2	.	3	.	1	.	.	.	1
Bertholon	**3**	.	.	.	.	.	.	.	.	.	3	.
Bertius	**177**	38	9	29	5	6	48	10	11	9	5	7
Betts	**12**	1	.	.	.	.	1	1	2	2	.	5
Bew; see Political Mag.	**8**	.	.	1	1	6	.	.	.	.	.	.
Bezzera	**1**	.	.	.	.	1	.	.	.	.	.	.
Bickham	**3**	.	2	.	.	.	.	.	1	.	.	.
Biddle	**1**	.	.	.	.	.	.	.	.	.	1	.
Bien	**13**	1	1	1	1	.	4	1	1	1	2	.
Bill	**1**	.	.	.	.	.	.	.	.	.	1	.
Bineteau	**1**	.	.	.	.	.	1	.	.	.	.	.
Bingham	**1**	.	.	.	1	.	.	.	.	.	.	.
Bion	**2**	1	.	.	.	.	.	.	.	.	.	1
Birkbeck	**1**	.	.	.	.	.	.	.	1	.	.	.
Blachford	**1**	.	.	.	.	.	.	1	.	.	.	.
Black	**130**	19	14	10	13	10	11	17	9	6	12	9
Blackie & Son	**27**	10	3	2	.	4	4	1	.	.	2	1
Blackmore	**1**	.	.	.	.	.	.	.	1	.	.	.
Blackwood	**1**	.	.	.	.	.	.	.	.	.	1	.
Blaeu	**1189**	171	104	188	158	204	119	52	66	47	28	52
Blair	**14**	.	.	1	1	1	1	2	2	5	1	.
Blanchard	**7**	.	1	3	.	.	.	.	3	.	.	.
Blankaart	**3**	3	.	.	.	.	.	.	.	.	.	.
Blankman	**1**	.	.	.	.	.	.	.	.	1	.	.
Blatchford	**3**	.	.	.	.	.	1	.	.	2	.	.
Blau	**1**	.	.	.	.	.	.	1	.	.	.	.
Blodget	**1**	.	.	.	.	1	.	.	.	.	.	.
Blome	**80**	9	11	6	11	2	5	1	3	9	4	19
Blondeau	**4**	.	1	.	.	2	.	.	.	.	.	1
Bluhme	**1**	.	1	.	.	.	.	.	.	.	.	.
Blundell	**7**	3	.	1	.	1	.	.	1	.	.	1
Blunt	**106**	.	13	5	10	13	19	19	11	10	2	4
Boardman	**2**	.	.	.	.	1	1	.	.	.	.	.
Bocharti	**1**	.	.	.	.	.	.	.	.	.	.	1
Bock	**1**	.	.	.	.	.	.	1	.	.	.	.
Bodenehr	**113**	26	.	.	6	.	1	1	10	.	69	.
Bogart & Andrews	**1**	.	.	.	.	1	.	.	.	.	.	.
Bohn	**8**	1	.	.	.	.	3	1	1	.	2	.
Boileau de Bouillon	**1**	.	.	.	.	1	.	.	.	.	.	.
Boisseau	**8**	.	.	1	2	2	1	.	.	.	1	1
Bolton	**5**	1	.	.	1	.	.	.	.	.	.	3
Bond	**1**	.	.	.	.	.	.	.	.	.	1	.
Bonne	**483**	44	48	35	38	103	56	21	22	50	38	28
Bonner	**1**	.	.	.	.	.	1	.	.	.	.	.
Bonneville	**1**	.	1	.	.	.	.	.	.	.	.	.
Booth & Hulbert	**1**	.	.	.	.	1	.	.	.	.	.	.
Borden	**1**	.	.	.	.	.	.	.	.	.	1	.
Bordiga	**2**	.	1	.	.	.	.	.	1	.	.	.
Bordone	**76**	.	.	53	2	5	3	4	1	1	5	2
Borghi	**7**	.	.	1	.	.	5	.	.	.	1	.
Bormeester	**1**	.	.	.	.	.	.	.	.	1	.	.
Borthwick	**1**	.	1	.	.	.	.	.	.	.	.	.
Boschini	**1**	.	.	.	.	.	.	.	1	.	.	.
Bossi	**1**	.	.	.	1	.	.	.	.	.	.	.
Bossuet	**7**	.	.	.	5	2	.	.	.	.	.	.
Botero	**9**	1	.	1	.	.	.	2	1	3	.	1
Bouchette	**38**	4	1	16	1	4	.	2	1	.	7	2
Boulton	**1**	.	.	1	.	.	.	.	.	.	.	.
Bourgoin	**4**	.	.	1	1	1	.	1	.	.	.	.
Bourrelier	**1**	.	.	.	.	.	.	.	.	1	.	.
Boutatts	**1**	.	.	1	.	.	.	.	.	.	.	.
Bowen	**461**	98	68	89	22	41	42	29	13	34	25	.
Bowen & Gibson	**7**	.	.	.	6	.	.	.	1	.	.	.
Bowen & Kitchin	**2**	.	.	.	2	.	.	.	.	.	.	.
Bowen, E.	**31**	.	.	.	.	.	.	.	.	.	.	31
Bowen, M.	**1**	.	.	.	.	.	.	.	.	.	1	.
Bowen, T.	**5**	.	.	.	.	.	.	.	.	.	.	5
Bowles	**79**	14	15	10	7	2	4	2	9	3	6	7
Bowles, S.	**1**	.	.	.	1	.	.	.	.	.	.	.
Boydell	**1**	.	.	1	.	.	.	.	.	.	.	.
Boynton	**9**	.	4	1	.	.	.	.	.	2	.	2
Bradford	**346**	19	71	20	23	10	28	35	11	75	22	32
Bradford & Goodrich	**52**	.	.	.	.	.	.	.	1	40	9	2
Bradley	**77**	14	7	1	3	4	9	5	6	7	14	7

	Total	'83	'84	'85	'86	'87	'88	'89	'90	'91	'92	'93
Bradshaw	**1**	.	.	.	.	.	.	.	.	.	1	.
Brandard	**1**	.	.	1	.	.	.	.	.	.	.	.
Braun & Hogenberg	**545**	69	69	34	8	11	87	36	25	34	148	24
Bretez	**1**	.	.	.	.	.	1	.	.	.	.	.
Briet	**3**	.	.	.	2	1	.	.	.	.	.	.
Brightly	**2**	.	1	.	.	1	.	.	.	.	.	.
Brightly & Kinnersley	**5**	2	.	2	.	.	.	.	1	.	.	.
Brion	**3**	.	.	.	.	.	1	.	1	.	1	.
Brion de la Tour	**32**	3	4	1	3	6	2	.	5	3	1	4
British Amer. and Co.	**1**	.	.	.	.	.	.	1	.	.	.	.
British Government	**1**	.	.	.	.	.	.	.	.	.	.	1
British Magazine	**1**	.	.	.	.	.	.	.	1	.	.	.
Britton & Rey	**2**	.	.	.	.	.	1	1	.	.	.	.
Britton Lith.	**1**	.	.	.	.	.	.	.	1	.	.	.
Bromfield	**1**	.	.	.	.	.	1	.	.	.	.	.
Bromley	**1**	.	.	.	1	.	.	.	.	.	.	.
Brooke	**2**	1	.	.	.	.	1	.	.	.	.	.
Brookes	**5**	.	.	.	.	5	.	.	.	.	.	.
Broughton	**1**	.	.	.	.	.	.	.	.	.	1	.
Brown	**2**	1	.	.	.	.	.	.	.	1	.	.
Brown & Parsons	**3**	.	.	.	.	2	.	.	1	.	.	.
Brown, T.	**5**	.	.	.	.	2	.	1	.	1	.	1
Browne	**8**	.	1	3	.	4	.	.	.	.	.	.
Browne, E.	**1**	.	.	.	1	.	.	.	.	.	.	.
Browne, H.	**1**	.	.	1	.	.	.	.	.	.	.	.
Bruce, J.	**2**	.	.	.	.	.	.	.	.	.	.	2
Brue	**81**	7	5	5	3	18	2	4	14	12	5	6
Brunacci	**1**	.	.	.	.	.	.	.	1	.	.	.
Brunton	**1**	.	.	.	.	.	1	.	.	.	.	.
Bryan	**1**	.	.	.	.	.	.	.	.	.	1	.
Bryant	**7**	3	1	1	.	.	1	.	.	.	1	.
Bryant Union	**1**	.	.	.	.	.	.	.	.	.	.	1
Buache	**39**	1	8	1	5	2	5	4	2	4	3	4
Buchanan	**1**	.	.	.	.	.	.	.	.	.	1	.
Buchon	**140**	13	5	9	17	18	16	15	16	9	13	9
Buffier	**5**	.	.	3	1	.	.	.	1	.	.	.
Bufford	**8**	1	1	.	.	1	1	1	1	2	.	.
Buisson	**1**	1	.	.	.	.	.	.	.	.	.	.
Bullock	**2**	.	.	.	2	.	.	.	.	.	.	.
Bunney & Gold	**2**	.	.	.	1	1	.	.	.	.	.	.
Bunting	**33**	2	.	5	5	2	2	4	.	4	.	9
Burchell	**1**	.	.	.	.	.	.	.	.	1	.	.
Burgess	**18**	2	7	.	1	3	.	1	.	.	3	1
Burleigh & Thomson	**1**	.	.	1	.	.	.	.	.	.	.	.
Burleigh Lith.	**2**	.	.	.	.	.	.	.	.	.	1	1
Burney	**5**	1	.	1	1	.	1	.	.	1	.	.
Burr	**197**	5	12	12	5	53	10	6	13	7	28	46
Burriel	**1**	1	.	.	.	.	.	.	.	.	.	.
Burritt	**6**	.	.	.	3	.	.	.	.	1	2	.
Buschbeck	**1**	.	.	.	.	.	.	.	.	1	.	.
Bushman	**3**	.	.	.	.	1	.	.	.	2	.	.
Bussemacher; see Quad	.	.	.	.	.	.	.	.	.	.	.	.
Butler	**9**	1	.	1	4	.	.	2	.	.	1	.
Butterfield	**1**	.	.	.	.	1	.	.	.	.	.	.
Byrne, P.	**1**	.	.	.	.	.	.	.	.	.	.	1
Byron	**1**	.	.	1	.	.	.	.	.	.	.	.
Cadell	**4**	1	1	.	.	1	1	.	.	.	.	.
Cadell & Davies	**6**	2	.	2	.	1	1	.	.	.	.	.
Cady & Burgess	**1**	.	.	.	.	1	.	.	.	.	.	.
Caillet	**1**	.	.	.	.	1	.	.	.	.	.	.
California	**2**	.	.	1	.	.	1	.	.	.	.	.
Callot	**2**	.	2	.	.	.	.	.	.	.	.	.
Calmet	**6**	.	.	3	.	.	.	1	.	.	1	1
Calvert	**1**	1	.	.	.	.	.	.	.	.	.	.
Camden; see Hole, Kip	**55**	2	16	20	5	.	6	1	.	.	4	1
Cammermeyer	**1**	.	.	.	.	.	.	.	.	.	1	.

	Total	'83	'84	'85	'86	'87	'88	'89	'90	'91	'92	'93
Cammeyer	**1**	.	.	.	.	.	.	.	.	1	.	.
Camocio	**43**	24	4	11	.	.	.	1	1	1	1	.
Campanius Holm; see Holme, 1983	**12**	1	3	6	1	.	.	.	1	.	.	.
Canada	**11**	3	4	1	1	.	.	.	.	1	1	.
Canada Southern Rwy.	**1**	.	.	.	.	.	1	.	.	.	.	.
Cantelli da Vignola	**6**	.	1	1	.	1	.	1	.	.	.	2
Canzler	**1**	.	.	.	.	.	.	.	1	.	.	.
Capewell & Kimmel	**1**	.	.	.	.	.	.	.	.	.	1	.
Cappelen	**1**	.	.	.	.	.	.	.	1	.	.	.
Capper	**10**	.	10	.	.	.	.	.	.	.	.	.
Carey & Lea	**245**	13	26	9	10	33	61	20	10	29	16	18
Carey & Warner	**2**	.	2	.	.	.	.	.	.	.	.	.
Carey; see Lewis	**363**	17	50	25	39	11	31	17	43	36	54	40
Carez	**1**	1	.	.	.	.	.	.	.	.	.	.
Carleton	**8**	1	.	.	1	.	1	1	1	.	3	.
Carli	**3**	.	.	.	.	1	1	.	.	1	.	.
Carolus	**1**	1	.	.	.	.	.	.	.	.	.	.
Caron	**1**	.	.	.	.	.	.	.	.	.	1	.
Carpelan	**1**	.	.	.	.	.	.	.	.	.	.	1
Carr	**1**	.	.	.	.	.	.	.	.	.	1	.
Carter	**3**	.	.	.	.	.	.	.	.	1	2	.
Carteret	**1**	.	.	.	.	.	.	.	.	1	.	.
Cartwright	**2**	.	.	.	.	.	.	.	.	.	2	.
Carver	**2**	.	2	.	.	.	.	.	.	.	.	.
Cary	**219**	30	42	22	59	6	4	12	6	11	18	9
Case	**3**	.	1	.	.	.	.	1	1	.	.	.
Case, Tiffany & Co.	**3**	.	.	.	.	1	.	.	1	.	1	.
Cassell	**4**	.	.	2	.	1	1	.	.	.	.	.
Cassell & Galpin	**2**	.	.	.	1	.	1	.	.	.	.	.
Cassell, Peter & Galpin	**3**	.	.	.	.	.	.	2	1	.	.	.
Cassini	**62**	2	2	12	4	1	6	4	13	8	5	5
Castelli	**1**	.	.	.	.	.	.	.	1	.	.	.
Castilla	**2**	2	.	.	.	.	.	.	.	.	.	.
Catesby	**4**	.	1	.	.	.	.	1	1	.	.	1
Catlin	**4**	1	2	.	1	.	.	.	.	.	.	.
Cavazza	**4**	.	.	.	.	.	1	.	.	.	2	1
Cave	**2**	.	.	.	.	1	1	.	.	.	.	.
Cellarius	**71**	.	14	10	.	29	1	.	.	1	14	2
Central Pacific R.R.	**2**	.	.	.	.	1	1	.	.	.	.	.
Century Atlas	**22**	.	.	.	1	2	.	2	1	4	.	12
Chabert; see De Chabert, 1988.	.	.	.	.	.	.	.	.	.	.	.	.
Chain & Hardy	**1**	.	.	.	.	.	.	.	1	.	.	.
Chambers	**13**	.	2	.	2	2	3	1	1	2	.	.
Chamouin	**2**	.	1	.	.	1	.	.	.	.	.	.
Champlain	**1**	.	.	.	.	.	.	.	.	1	.	.
Chanlaire	**4**	.	3	.	.	.	.	.	.	1	.	.
Chanlaire & Mentelle	**11**	2	.	1	.	.	2	3	.	2	1	.
Chapin	**3**	1	.	.	.	1	.	.	1	.	.	.
Chapin & Taylor	**2**	.	.	.	.	1	.	.	.	1	.	.
Chapman	**17**	2	.	.	2	1	6	.	.	1	3	2
Chapman & Hall; see S.D.U.K.	**18**	2	4	.	.	8	.	.	.	2	1	1
Chapman & Silas	**9**	.	.	.	3	.	1	.	4	1	.	.
Chardin	**5**	.	.	.	.	5	.	.	.	.	.	.
Chardon	**1**	.	.	.	.	.	1	.	.	.	.	.
Charles	**2**	.	.	.	1	1	.	.	.	.	.	.
Charlevoix; + see De Charlevoix, 1987	.	.	.	.	.	.	.	.	.	.	.	.
Chase	**2**	.	.	.	.	.	1	.	.	.	1	.
Chastenet-Puisegur	**2**	.	1	.	.	.	1	.	.	.	.	.
Chatelain	**172**	14	13	34	11	7	13	23	10	14	23	10
Chetwind	**14**	.	.	1	3	1	3	1	1	2	2	.
Chevalier	**1**	.	.	.	.	.	.	.	.	.	.	1
Chic. & Northwestern Rwy	**2**	.	.	.	2	.	.	.	.	.	.	.
Chic. Burlington & Quincy	**2**	.	.	.	2	.	.	.	.	.	.	.
Chic. Rock Island & Pac.	**2**	.	.	.	1	.	.	.	.	.	1	.

	Total	'83	'84	'85	'86	'87	'88	'89	'90	'91	'92	'93
Child	**10**	3	2	.	.	.	.	.	1	.	4	.
Childs	**1**	.	.	.	.	.	.	.	.	.	1	.
Chinese Cartography	**1**	.	.	.	.	.	.	.	.	1	.	.
Chiquet	**24**	.	11	.	3	8	.	.	.	1	.	1
Choris	**1**	.	.	.	.	.	.	.	.	.	1	.
Church	**2**	.	.	.	.	.	.	1	.	.	1	.
Churchill	**3**	.	.	.	.	1	.	.	2	.	.	.
Citti	**1**	.	1	.	.	.	.	.	.	.	.	.
Claesz	**1**	.	1	.	.	.	.	.	.	.	.	.
Clarendon	**16**	.	.	.	.	16	.	.	.	.	.	.
Claret de Fleurieu	**1**	.	.	.	.	.	.	.	.	.	.	1
Clark	**7**	.	1	.	.	.	2	2	.	.	1	1
Clark & Tackabury	**1**	.	.	.	.	.	.	.	.	.	1	.
Clark & Wagner	**1**	.	.	.	.	.	.	.	.	.	1	.
Clarke & Stephenson	**1**	.	.	.	.	.	1	.	.	.	.	.
Clarke Lith.	**1**	.	.	.	.	.	1	.	.	.	.	.
Clason Map Co.	**1**	.	.	.	.	.	.	.	.	.	.	1
Clayton Lith.	**1**	.	.	.	.	.	1	.	.	.	.	.
Clemens	**1**	.	.	.	.	.	.	.	.	1	.	.
Clerk	**1**	.	.	.	.	.	.	.	1	.	.	.
Cloppenburgh	**8**	.	.	4	.	2	.	.	.	1	.	1
Clouet	**17**	.	3	1	1	4	1	.	2	3	.	2
Cluny	**2**	1	.	1	.	.	.	.	.	.	.	.
Cluver	**133**	16	4	41	26	17	5	2	4	8	5	5
Cobbett	**2**	.	.	.	.	1	.	1	.	.	.	.
Coccetus, J.	**1**	.	.	.	.	.	.	.	.	.	.	1
Cochin	**7**	.	6	1	.	.	.	.	.	.	.	.
Cochrane Co.	**1**	.	.	.	1	.	.	.	.	.	.	.
Coello	**5**	.	.	.	.	1	.	1	.	2	.	1
Coggins	**1**	.	.	.	.	.	.	.	.	1	.	.
Coghlan	**1**	.	.	.	.	1	.	.	.	.	.	.
Colburn	**6**	.	4	1	.	.	.	.	1	.	.	.
Colby	**8**	.	.	.	.	.	.	.	.	1	6	1
Colden	**1**	1	.	.	.	.	.	.	.	.	.	.
Cole	**18**	.	.	13	.	3	.	.	1	.	.	1
Collin	**1**	.	.	.	.	1	.	.	.	.	.	.
Collins & Clark	**1**	.	.	.	.	.	.	.	1	.	.	.
Collins & Son	**1**	.	.	.	.	1	.	.	.	.	.	.
Collins, G.	**193**	19	9	26	24	13	12	15	49	9	9	8
Collins, H.G.	**8**	.	.	.	1	3	1	.	2	1	.	.
Collins, William	**5**	.	.	1	3	.	.	.	1	.	.	.
Collot	**11**	.	.	.	.	1	.	3	.	4	2	1
Colnett	**2**	.	1	.	.	.	.	.	.	.	.	1
Colom	**32**	.	.	5	6	8	1	3	3	1	3	2
Colo. & Red Riv. Land Co.	**1**	.	.	.	.	.	.	1	.	.	.	.
Colton	**1014**	35	43	35	135	79	154	78	120	104	134	97
Columbian Magazine	**4**	.	.	.	1	.	2	1	.	.	.	.
Comettant	**3**	.	.	1	.	.	.	.	1	1	.	.
Comite Geologique	**1**	.	.	.	.	.	.	1	.	.	.	.
Company Maps	**1**	.	.	.	.	.	.	.	.	.	.	1
Comstock & Cassidy	**1**	.	.	.	.	.	.	.	.	1	.	.
Conant	**1**	.	1	.	.	.	.	.	.	.	.	.
Condamine; see De La Condamine		.	.	.	.	.	.	.	.	.	.	.
Conder	**27**	3	5	1	2	10	2	.	.	1	.	3
Connecticut	**1**	.	.	.	.	.	1	.	.	.	.	.
Conover	**1**	.	.	.	.	.	.	.	.	1	.	.
Conradi & van der Plaats	**1**	.	.	.	1	.	.	.	.	.	.	.
Conservancy	**1**	1	.	.	.	.	.	.	.	.	.	.
Constable	**5**	.	.	.	.	1	3	.	1	.	.	.
Cook; see Hogg	**165**	4	8	21	25	12	16	13	20	23	5	18
Cooke	**11**	.	.	2	2	1	3	.	.	1	1	1
Cooper, H.	**3**	.	.	.	.	.	.	.	1	1	.	1
Cooper, J.	**2**	.	.	.	.	.	.	.	.	1	.	1
Cooper, T.	**1**	.	.	1	.	.	.	.	.	.	.	.
Copley	**3**	.	.	.	.	.	.	2	.	1	.	.
Coreal	**1**	.	.	.	.	.	1	.	.	.	.	.
Cornelis	**1**	.	1	.	.	.	.	.	.	.	.	.
Cornell	**7**	.	.	.	.	2	.	2	2	.	.	1
Coronelli	**322**	26	42	54	28	33	29	25	21	27	16	21
Cotovicus	**12**	.	5	7	.	.	.	.	.	.	.	.
Count & Hammond	**1**	.	1	.	.	.	.	.	.	.	.	.
Cousen	**1**	1	.	.	.	.	.	.	.	.	.	.
Cousin	**1**	.	.	.	1	.	.	.	.	.	.	.
Covens & Mortier	**232**	14	17	45	35	39	17	15	30	8	8	4
Cowles (Union & Confed.)	**27.**	.	.	.	.	.	.	.	.	21	6	.
Cowley	**25**	2	7	11	.	2	2	.	.	.	.	1
Cowperthwait	**8**	1	1	2	.	2	2	.	.	.	.	.
Cowperthwait, Desilver & Butler	**3**	.	.	.	.	.	.	.	1	2	.	.
Cox; see S.D.U.K.	**7**	.	2	1	.	.	.	1	1	.	1	1
Coxe	**3**	.	1	.	.	.	.	.	1	1	.	.
Craddock & Joy	**2**	.	.	.	.	1	.	.	.	1	.	.
Crafts, H.	**3**	.	.	1	.	.	.	1	.	.	.	1
Cram	**403**	9	22	15	27	21	32	68	31	43	74	61
Cramer, J.A.	**1**	.	.	.	.	.	.	.	.	.	.	1
Crantz	**6**	.	4	.	.	1	.	.	1	.	.	.
Craskell & Simpson	**1**	.	.	1	.	.	.	.	.	.	.	.
Crawford	**5**	1	2	.	.	1	.	.	1	.	.	.
Crepy	**6**	1	.	.	.	.	1	1	3	.	.	.
Crevecoeur; see De Crevecoeur, 1987+	.	.	.	.	.	.	.	.	.	.	.	.
Crocker	**3**	.	.	.	.	.	1	.	1	1	.	.
Crocker & Brewster	**1**	.	.	.	.	.	.	.	.	.	1	.
Crofutt	**1**	.	.	.	.	1	.	.	.	.	.	.
Croix	**1**	.	.	.	.	.	.	.	.	1	.	.
Crosman & Mallory	**1**	.	.	.	.	.	.	.	.	.	.	1
Cross, J.	**5**	1	1	1	.	.	1	.	.	.	.	1
Cruchley	**30**	2	6	4	2	2	1	1	3	1	1	7
Cruikshanks	**1**	.	.	.	.	.	.	.	.	1	.	.
Cruttwell	**1**	.	.	.	.	.	.	.	.	.	1	.
Cuccioni	**1**	.	.	.	.	.	.	.	.	.	.	1
Cullen	**1**	.	.	.	.	1	.	.	.	.	.	.
Cummings	**1**	.	1	.	.	.	.	.	.	.	.	.
Cummings & Hilliard	**3**	.	.	.	.	.	.	1	1	.	.	1
Currier, N.	**3**	.	.	.	.	.	1	.	1	.	.	1
Curtice & Stateler	**1**	.	.	.	.	.	.	.	1	.	.	.
Custodis	**2**	.	.	1	.	1	.	.	.	.	.	.
Cutler	**12**	1	.	2	1	1	1	3	2	.	.	1
D'Anville	**97**	13	15	5	9	5	3	15	8	5	4	15
D'Apres de Mannevillette	**136**	24	2	2	6	4	31	6	14	13	23	11
D'Expilly	**14**	.	.	7	.	4	1	.	1	.	.	1
Dablon	**1**	.	.	.	.	.	1	.	.	.	.	.
Dahlberg	**1**	.	.	.	.	.	.	.	.	.	.	1
Daily Graphic	**3**	.	.	.	.	.	1	.	1	.	1	.
Dal Re	**1**	1	.	.	.	.	.	.	.	.	.	.
Dalrymple	**17**	1	3	.	2	.	2	.	1	2	4	2
Dampier	**14**	1	3	1	.	2	1	.	1	1	2	2
Dana	**9**	.	.	.	2	.	.	.	.	3	4	.
Danby, T.	**1**	.	.	.	.	.	.	.	.	.	.	1
Danckerts	**134**	14	9	64	9	15	9	2	3	1	2	6
Danckwerth	**3**	.	.	.	.	.	.	.	1	1	1	.
Danckwerth & Meyer	**2**	.	.	.	.	.	.	.	1	.	1	.
Danet	**4**	.	2	.	1	.	.	.	.	1	.	.
Dapper; see Montanus	**42**	7	14	10	1	1	4	.	2	.	3	.
Darton	**18**	1	4	3	.	1	.	.	3	1	.	5
Darton & Clark	**2**	.	.	.	.	.	.	.	1	.	.	1
Darton & Harvey	**1**	.	.	.	.	1	.	.	.	.	.	.
Dashiell	**1**	.	.	.	.	.	1	.	.	.	.	.
Daumont	**3**	.	.	.	.	1	.	.	1	.	.	1
Davenport	**7**	3	.	2	.	.	.	1	1	.	.	.
Davies	**2**	.	1	1	.	.	.	.	.	.	.	.
Davison	**3**	.	.	.	.	1	1	.	1	.	.	.

	Total	'83	'84	'85	'86	'87	'88	'89	'90	'91	'92	'93
Dawson Bros.	5	.	1	.	.	.	1	.	2	1	.	.
Day	1	.	.	.	1	.	.	.	.	.	.	.
Day & Haghe	3	.	.	1	.	.	1	.	.	1	.	.
Day & Sons	5	1	.	4	.	.	.	.	.	.	.	.
De Aefferden	4	.	.	.	.	.	.	.	.	1	2	1
De Azara	7	.	.	.	.	.	6	.	.	1	.	.
De Bar	1	.	1	.	.	.	.	.	.	.	.	.
De Beaurain	4	.	1	1	.	2	.	.	.	.	.	.
De Belleforest	16	2	6	3	1	.	1	.	.	.	2	1
De Belleyme	1	.	.	.	.	1	.	.	.	.	.	.
De Berey	3	1	.	1	.	.	.	.	.	.	1	.
De Bougainville	1	.	.	.	.	.	.	.	1	.	.	.
De Bouge	1	.	1	.	.	.	.	.	.	.	.	.
De Brahm	1	.	.	.	1	.	.	.	.	.	.	.
De Bruyn	73	.	58	.	10	2	.	2	.	.	.	1
De Bry	292	38	28	34	41	14	11	18	48	10	20	30
De Chabert;	16	.	3	4	.	1	2	2	1	2	1	.
see Chabert, to 1986												
De Charlevoix;	24	5	2	3	3	1	.	1	3	4	2	.
see Charlevoix to 1986												
De Chastellux	4	.	.	.	.	.	.	.	2	.	1	1
De Crevecoeur	12	.	1	.	.	1	1	2	2	.	.	5
De Fer:	214	18	19	43	9	11	14	.	.	.	.	.
De Fer (large)	.	.	.	.	.	.	.	10	.	5	3	6
De Fer (small)	.	.	.	.	.	.	.	15	17	8	8	28
De Freycinet;	7	.	.	1	.	6	.	.	.	.	.	.
see Freycinet, 1985												
De Grado	1	1	.	.	.	.	.	.	.	.	.	.
De Herrera,	52	6	2	5	7	3	2	6	4	6	5	6
see Herrera, to 1987												
De Hondt	2	.	.	1	.	.	1	.	.	.	.	.
De Hooghe	1	1	.	.	.	.	.	.	.	.	.	.
De Jode	71	14	13	11	9	12	1	3	6	.	.	2
De l'Isle	183	31	14	21	9	16	15	17	25	7	10	18
De la Bastide	1	.	.	.	.	.	1	.	.	.	.	.
De la Condamine;	8	.	.	1	.	4	.	.	2	.	1	.
see Condamine, 1985												
De la Croix	2	.	.	.	.	.	.	.	.	2	.	.
De la Feuille;	21	.	2	1	7	9	.	.	1	.	.	1
see La Feuille, 1984												
De la Haye	1	.	.	.	.	.	.	1	.	.	.	.
De la Hire	1	.	.	.	.	.	.	.	.	.	1	.
De la Potherie	7	4	.	3	.	.	.	.	.	.	.	.
De la Rue	8	1	.	2	1	.	1	.	1	.	.	2
De Laborde	5	.	.	.	.	.	2	2	.	1	.	.
De Laet	57	2	17	4	1	2	2	8	5	5	6	5
De Laporte	6	.	.	.	.	.	.	2	2	1	1	.
De Lat	8	2	.	2	2	1	.	.	1	.	.	.
De Leth	8	.	2	.	2	.	.	1	.	.	2	1
De Monthuchon	1	.	.	.	.	1	.	.	.	.	.	.
De Nicolay	2	.	.	.	.	1	.	1	.	.	.	.
De Pages	1	.	.	.	1	.	.	.	.	.	.	.
De Pretot	2	.	.	.	.	1	.	.	.	.	.	1
De Ram	1	.	.	.	.	.	.	.	.	1	.	.
De Rienzi	1	.	1	.	.	.	.	.	.	.	.	.
De Rossi	3	.	.	2	1	.	.	.	.	.	.	.
De Solis	1	.	.	.	.	.	.	1	.	.	.	.
De Stobnicza	.	.	.	.	.	.	.	.	.	.	.	.
De Ulloa	2	.	.	1	.	.	.	.	1	.	.	.
De Vaugondy;	598	43	78	54	135	50	89	19	51	31	21	27
see Delamarche, Diderot												
De Vou	1	.	.	.	.	.	.	.	.	1	.	.
De Wit	312	30	30	63	36	51	28	9	21	20	8	16
De Witt	2	.	.	1	.	.	.	.	.	.	1	.
Dean & Munday	1	.	1	.	.	.	.	.	.	.	.	.
Dearborn	5	2	.	2	.	1	.	.	.	.	.	.
Decker	1	.	.	.	.	.	.	.	1	.	.	.

	Total	'83	'84	'85	'86	'87	'88	'89	'90	'91	'92	'93
Deffenbaugh & Burroughs	1	.	.	.	.	.	.	.	.	.	1	.
Delahaye	1	.	.	.	.	.	1	.	.	.	.	.
Delamarche;	66	3	4	4	5	23	5	7	4	3	6	2
Della Gatta	2	.	.	.	.	.	1	.	.	.	1	.
Demarest	1	.	.	.	.	.	.	.	.	1	.	.
Dember	1	.	.	.	.	.	.	.	.	1	.	.
Den Schryver	1	1	.	.	.	.	.	.	.	.	.	.
Denis	3	1	.	2	.	.	.	.	.	.	.	.
Denison	1	1	.	.	.	.	.	.	.	.	.	.
Denver & Rio Grande RR	1	.	.	.	.	.	1	.	.	.	.	.
Deposito Hidrografico	1	.	1	.	.	.	.	.	.	.	.	.
Depot de la Marine; see	254	16	41	17	21	16	15	13	30	19	51	15
Bellin, Vincendon-Dumoulin												
Depot General de la Guerre	2	.	.	1	.	.	.	.	.	.	.	1
Derfelden van Hinderstein	1	.	.	.	.	.	.	1	.	.	.	.
Deroy	1	.	.	.	.	.	.	.	.	.	.	1
Des Barres	139	29	6	3	3	1	3	46	6	20	5	17
Desbordes	1	.	.	.	.	.	.	.	1	.	.	.
Desbruslins	2	.	.	1	.	.	.	.	.	.	.	1
Desgranges	2	.	.	.	.	.	.	.	2	.	.	.
Desilver	145	5	24	9	9	8	16	16	9	9	4	36
Desnos	33	1	2	2	2	6	5	5	4	2	3	1
Desobry	1	.	.	.	.	.	1	.	.	.	.	.
Desoer	1	.	.	.	.	.	1	.	.	.	.	.
Dessing	1	.	.	1	.	.	.	.	.	.	.	.
Dezauche	33	2	3	1	3	1	5	4	7	5	2	.
Dezoteux	5	.	2	.	1	2	.	.	.	.	.	.
Dheulland	1	.	.	.	.	.	.	.	.	.	.	1
Di Arnoldi	2	.	.	.	.	.	2	.	.	.	.	.
Diamond Atlas	3	.	.	.	.	.	.	3	.	.	.	.
Dicey	1	1	.	.	.	.	.	.	.	.	.	.
Diderot; see De Vaugondy	67	.	.	.	1	3	2	13	18	10	20	.
Didot	7	.	1	.	.	2	.	.	3	.	1	.
Dien	1	.	.	.	.	.	.	.	1	.	.	.
Dilly	3	1	.	.	1	.	.	.	.	1	.	.
Dinsmore	4	.	.	.	1	.	2	.	1	.	.	.
Direccion de Hidrografia	70	2	1	13	10	15	6	6	3	1	2	11
Disturnell	12	.	.	1	1	2	3	.	1	1	2	1
Dixon	12	2	5	1	1	.	.	1	.	.	.	2
Dixson	1	.	.	.	1	.	.	.	.	.	.	.
Dobson	1	.	.	.	1	.	.	.	.	.	.	.
Dobson & Cobbett	1	.	.	.	.	.	.	1	.	.	.	.
Dockam	1	.	.	.	.	1	.	.	.	.	.	.
Dodd, Mead	1	.	.	.	.	.	.	.	.	1	.	.
Dodge	2	.	.	.	.	.	1	.	1	.	.	.
Dodsley	2	.	.	1	.	.	.	.	.	.	.	1
Dolendo	1	1	.	.	.	.	.	.	.	.	.	.
Dollar Weekly Tribune	1	.	.	.	.	.	.	.	1	.	.	.
Donaldson, T.	2	.	1	.	.	.	.	.	.	.	.	1
Doncker	39	1	.	2	8	3	3	4	10	4	2	2
Doppelmayr	7	3	.	.	1	.	.	.	.	.	.	3
Dorr, Howland & Co.	1	.	1	.	.	.	.	.	.	.	.	.
Dou	1	.	1	.	.	.	.	.	.	.	.	.
Doughty	1	.	.	.	.	.	.	.	.	1	.	.
Douglas	1	.	.	.	.	.	.	1	.	.	.	.
Dower	47	7	7	3	9	3	2	1	7	4	1	3
Drake	1	.	.	.	.	1	.	.	.	.	.	.
Drayton	55	29	.	12	5	.	8	1	.	.	.	.
Drew	2	.	.	.	.	.	.	.	1	.	.	1
Drinkwater	1	1	.	.	.	.	.	.	.	.	.	.
Drioux	1	.	.	.	.	.	1	.	.	.	.	.
Drioux & Leroy	1	.	.	.	.	.	.	1	.	.	.	.
Dripps	9	.	1	.	2	1	.	.	2	2	1	.
Drummond	1	.	.	.	.	.	1	.	.	.	.	.
Du Bocage	4	.	.	.	.	1	1	.	2	.	.	.
Du Bosc	2	1	.	.	.	.	.	.	.	1	.	.
Du Four	1	.	.	.	.	.	.	.	.	1	.	.

	Total	'83	'84	'85	'86	'87	'88	'89	'90	'91	'92	'93
Du Pinet	**1**	.	.	.	.	.	.	1	.	.	.	.
Du Sauzet; see De Sauzet, 1985	**7**	2	2	2	.	1	.	.	.	.	.	.
Du Val:	**103**	9	4	10	2	11	18	.	.	.	.	.
Du Val (large)	.	.	.	.	.	.	.	7	3	3	5	2
Du Val (small)	.	.	.	.	.	.	.	12	.	8	4	5
Du Vivier	**1**	.	1	.	.	.	.	.	.	.	.	.
Duchetti	**4**	.	.	2	.	.	.	1	.	.	1	.
Dudley	**234**	10	1	15	132	4	9	14	16	20	2	11
Dufertre	**1**	.	.	.	.	.	.	1	.	.	.	.
Duflot de Mofras; see DeMofras to 1988	**24**	.	.	12	.	4	3	4	1	.	.	.
Dufour	**55**	4	3	5	2	12	5	6	3	10	2	3
Duluth News Co.	**1**	.	.	.	.	.	.	.	.	1	.	.
Dumont d'Urville; see D'Urville, 1985	**6**	.	.	2	.	.	.	.	.	2	2	.
Duncan	**2**	.	1	1	.	.	.	.	.	.	.	.
Dunn; see Laurie & Whittle, Sayer	**30**	1	.	1	2	.	5	2	3	8	5	3
Duperrey	**12**	.	.	6	1	3	2	.	.	.	.	.
Dupont-Buisson	**1**	.	.	.	1	.	.	.	.	.	.	.
Dupuis	**1**	.	1	.	.	.	.	.	.	.	.	.
Durell	**3**	.	.	.	1	1	.	.	.	.	.	1
Durocher	**1**	.	.	.	.	.	.	.	.	1	.	.
Dury	**10**	.	2	2	2	.	1	1	1	.	1	.
Dury & Bell	**1**	.	.	1	.	.	.	.	.	.	.	.
Dusacq & Cie.	**1**	.	.	.	.	.	.	.	1	.	.	.
Dussieux	**3**	.	.	.	.	1	1	.	.	.	.	1
Dutton	**8**	.	.	.	.	4	1	.	1	1	.	1
Duval	**9**	.	.	.	6	.	.	.	1	.	.	2
Duvotenay	**8**	.	.	.	1	2	2	1	.	.	.	2
Dwight	**2**	1	.	1	.	.	.	.	.	.	.	.
Eastman	**10**	.	.	.	.	3	2	.	3	.	.	2
Ecker	**1**	.	.	.	.	.	.	.	.	.	1	.
Eckhoff & Riecker	**1**	.	.	.	.	.	.	.	.	1	.	.
Eddy	**4**	.	.	.	1	.	1	1	.	.	1	.
Edgar	**1**	.	.	1	.	.	.	.	.	.	.	.
Edinburgh Magazine	**1**	.	.	.	.	.	.	.	.	.	1	.
Edsall	**3**	.	.	.	1	1	.	.	.	1	.	.
Edwards	**86**	9	5	6	5	7	11	10	9	3	19	2
Ehrenberg	**1**	.	.	.	.	.	.	.	.	1	.	.
Ehrmann	**4**	1	.	.	.	1	.	.	1	.	.	1
Eldridge	**1**	.	.	.	.	.	.	.	.	.	1	.
Ellicott	**1**	.	.	.	.	.	.	.	.	.	.	1
Elliot	**1**	.	.	.	.	1	.	.	.	.	.	.
Elliott Publishing Co.	**3**	.	1	.	.	.	.	1	.	1	.	.
Ellis	**16**	1	12	2	.	.	.	1	.	.	.	.
Elwe	**37**	1	2	4	18	5	3	1	.	1	.	2
Ely	**1**	1	.	.	.	.	.	.	.	.	.	.
Emery	**1**	.	.	.	.	.	.	.	.	.	.	1
Emmerlich	**1**	.	.	.	1	.	.	.	.	.	.	.
Emmons	**1**	.	.	.	1	.	.	.	.	.	.	.
Emory	**2**	.	1	.	.	.	.	.	.	.	.	1
Encyclopaedia Britannica	**2**	.	.	1	.	.	.	.	.	.	1	.
Endicott & Co.	**2**	.	.	1	.	.	.	.	.	1	.	.
Endicott Lith.	**3**	.	.	.	1	.	.	1	1	.	.	.
Engelmann Lith.	**1**	.	.	.	.	.	1	.	.	.	.	.
Engelmann, Graf, Coindet	**1**	.	.	1	.	.	.	.	.	.	.	.
English Pilot; see Mount & Page	.	.	.	.	.	.	.	.	.	.	.	.
Enouy, J.	**1**	.	.	.	.	.	.	.	.	.	.	1
Ensign	**7**	.	.	.	.	.	1	.	2	1	1	2
Ensign & Bridgman	**1**	.	.	.	.	1	.	.	.	.	.	.
Ensign & Thayer	**21**	.	.	.	6	3	8	.	.	1	2	1
Ensign, Bridgman & Fanning	**13**	.	.	.	4	1	5	.	1	1	1	.

	Total	'83	'84	'85	'86	'87	'88	'89	'90	'91	'92	'93
Entick	**11**	1	3	1	2	1	.	2	.	.	.	1
Eriksson	**1**	.	.	.	.	.	.	.	.	.	1	.
Ertl	**24**	24	.	.	.	.	.	.	.	.	.	.
Espinosa y Tello	**1**	.	.	.	.	.	.	.	.	1	.	.
Esquemeling	**20**	.	3	5	4	1	1	1	4	.	.	1
Etablissement Geographique de Bruxelles	1	.	.	.	.	.	.	.	.	.	.	1
Ettling; see Weekly Dispatch	**22**	.	4	5	.	3	3	3	1	.	1	2
Euler	**2**	1	.	.	.	1	.	.	.	.	.	.
Euling	**1**	.	.	.	.	1	.	.	.	.	.	.
European Magazine	**1**	.	.	.	.	.	.	.	1	.	.	.
Evans	**9**	2	.	1	.	.	.	1	.	3	2	.
Everts	**6**	.	.	3	.	.	1	1	.	1	.	.
Everts & Richards	**1**	.	.	.	.	.	.	.	.	.	.	1
Everts & Stewart	**4**	.	.	.	.	.	.	.	.	.	4	.
Every Saturday	**2**	.	1	.	.	.	.	.	.	.	1	.
Ewen	**1**	.	.	.	.	.	.	.	.	1	.	.
Ewings	**1**	.	.	.	.	1	.	.	.	.	.	.
Exshaw	**3**	1	.	.	.	1	.	1	.	.	.	.
Faden	**261**	36	27	24	29	23	25	27	23	17	10	20
Fairbanks	**1**	.	.	.	.	.	.	.	1	.	.	.
Fairburn	**2**	1	.	1	.	.	.	.	.	.	.	.
Family Times	**2**	.	.	.	.	.	.	.	1	.	.	1
Fanning	**1**	.	.	.	.	1	.	.	.	.	.	.
Farmer	**3**	.	.	.	.	.	.	1	.	1	1	.
Farmer, Silas & Co.	**4**	.	.	.	1	2	1	.	.	.	.	.
Farnham	**2**	1	.	.	.	1	.	.	.	.	.	.
Fassmann	**1**	1	.	.	.	.	.	.	.	.	.	.
Faulkner	**15**	.	.	.	.	15	.	.	.	.	.	.
Faure	**1**	.	1	.	.	.	.	.	.	.	.	.
Featherstonhaugh	**1**	.	.	.	.	.	.	.	.	1	.	.
Felton, Parker & Barker	**1**	.	.	.	.	1	.	.	.	.	.	.
Fenner	**2**	.	.	1	1	.	.	.	.	.	.	.
Fenner, Sears & Co.; see Hinton *et al*	**43**	2	4	.	2	14	5	.	4	7	5	.
Ferraris	**1**	.	.	.	.	.	1	.	.	.	.	.
Fidalgo	**8**	.	7	.	.	.	1	.	.	.	.	.
Fielding	**11**	4	1	.	1	.	2	.	2	.	.	1
Fielding & Walker	**1**	.	.	.	1	.	.	.	.	.	.	.
Filloeul	**1**	.	.	.	.	.	.	.	.	.	.	1
Filson	**1**	.	.	.	.	.	.	.	.	1	.	.
Finaeus, Orontius	**2**	.	.	.	.	1	.	1	.	.	.	.
Findlay	**16**	4	1	1	1	1	1	2	1	1	1	2
Finley	**214**	22	4	23	10	41	21	11	22	17	16	27
Finn	**1**	.	.	.	.	.	.	.	.	.	.	1
Fisher	**2**	1	.	.	.	.	.	.	.	1	.	.
Fisher & Son	**2**	.	.	.	.	1	1	.	.	.	.	.
Fisher, H.	**6**	.	.	.	1	1	1	.	1	1	.	1
Fisk	**1**	.	.	.	.	.	.	.	.	1	.	.
Fisk & Co.	**1**	.	.	.	.	.	.	.	1	.	.	.
Fisk & Russell	**3**	1	.	.	.	.	2	.	.	.	.	.
Fisk & See	**1**	1	.	.	.	.	.	.	.	.	.	.
Fitch	**1**	.	.	.	1	.	.	.	.	.	.	.
Flamm	**2**	.	.	.	.	.	.	.	.	.	.	2
Flamsteed	**7**	.	.	4	.	.	.	.	3	.	.	.
Fleming	**1**	.	.	.	1	.	.	.	.	.	.	.
Flemming	**19**	.	.	.	1	7	1	3	4	3	.	.
Fleurieu	**2**	.	1	.	.	.	1	.	.	.	.	.
Flinders	**1**	.	.	.	1	.	.	.	.	.	.	.
Florianus	**2**	.	.	.	.	.	1	1	.	.	.	.
Florimi	**2**	.	.	1	.	.	.	.	.	1	.	.
Flushing & North Side RR	**1**	.	.	.	.	.	1	.	.	.	.	.
Foot	**2**	.	1	1	.	.	.	.	.	.	.	.
Foppen	**1**	.	.	.	.	.	.	.	.	.	.	1
Forbes	**1**	.	.	.	.	.	.	.	.	.	1	.
Forbes & Russell	**1**	.	.	.	.	.	.	1	.	.	.	.

	Total	'83	'84	'85	'86	'87	'88	'89	'90	'91	'92	'93
Forlani	4	.	.	1	1	1	.	.	.	1	.	.
Forster	3	.	1	.	.	.	.	.	.	1	.	1
Forster & Maurice	1	.	.	.	1	.	.	.	.	.	.	.
Foster	3	.	1	.	.	.	1	1	.	.	.	.
Foster Groom	1	.	.	.	.	.	.	.	.	.	.	1
Fostes	1	.	.	.	.	.	.	.	1	.	.	.
Fourdrinier	1	.	.	1	.	.	.	.	.	.	.	.
Fowler	1	.	.	.	.	.	1	.	.	.	.	.
Fowler & Moyer	5	.	.	.	.	2	1	1	.	.	1	.
Fox	1	.	.	.	.	.	.	.	1	.	.	.
Frank Leslie's Illustrated Newspaper	16	.	1	2	3	.	1	4	3	1	1	.
Franklin	25	5	5	5	.	.	1	.	5	.	2	2
Franklin Mint	1	.	.	.	.	.	.	.	.	.	1	.
Fraser	2	.	.	.	1	.	.	.	.	.	1	.
Frazier	1	.	.	1	.	.	.	.	.	.	.	.
Fremin	5	1	.	1	.	1	.	.	.	2	.	.
Fremont	8	.	.	.	.	.	4	1	.	1	.	2
French	2	.	.	.	.	.	.	.	.	.	2	.
French & Smith	1	.	.	.	.	.	.	.	1	.	.	.
French Admiralty; see Depot de la Marine	.	.	.	.	.	.	.	.	.	.	.	.
French, Wood & Smith	1	.	.	.	.	.	.	.	1	.	.	.
Freycinet, see De Freycinet	.	.	.	.	.	.	.	.	.	.	.	.
Frezier	5	.	4	.	.	1	.	.	.	.	.	.
Fricx	5	.	1	2	2	.	.	.	.	.	.	.
Fried	1	1	.	.	.	.	.	.	.	.	.	.
Friedenreich	1	.	.	.	.	.	1	.	.	.	.	.
Friederichs, J.	1	.	.	.	.	.	.	.	.	.	.	1
Fries	5	.	.	.	.	.	.	.	.	.	.	5
Fritz	1	.	.	.	.	1	.	.	.	.	.	.
Froiseth	1	.	.	.	.	.	.	.	.	1	.	.
Fullarton	237	48	33	29	15	18	26	13	20	7	16	12
Fuller	79	20	.	40	7	1	.	3	2	.	.	6
Funcke	1	.	.	.	.	.	.	.	.	1	.	.
Furne	4	.	.	.	.	.	1	1	.	1	1	.
Gage	1	.	.	.	.	.	.	.	.	.	1	.
Galiani	1	.	.	1	.	.	.	.	.	.	.	.
Galiano & Valdes	2	.	.	.	.	.	.	.	1	.	1	.
Galignani	2	.	.	.	.	.	.	.	.	.	1	1
Gall & Inglis	21	1	2	.	.	5	1	3	3	2	1	3
Galle	12	.	3	1	.	.	.	.	2	5	.	1
Galluci	1	.	.	1	.	.	.	.	.	.	.	.
Galt & Hoy	3	1	.	.	.	.	.	.	.	1	.	1
Gamble	4	.	.	1	.	2	.	1	.	.	.	.
Gardiner	1	.	.	.	1	.	.	.	.	.	.	.
Gardner	7	6	.	1	.	.	.	.	.	.	.	.
Garneray	2	.	.	.	.	.	.	.	.	.	.	2
Garnier	9	1	.	1	.	4	.	.	1	1	.	1
Garran	7	.	.	.	.	7	.	.	.	.	.	.
Gaskell	8	.	1	.	1	1	.	1	1	1	.	2
Gast & Co.	1	.	.	.	.	.	.	.	1	.	.	.
Gastaldi; see Ptolemy (1548)	5	.	1	.	.	.	.	.	.	.	.	4
Gaston	7	6	.	.	.	1	.	.	.	.	.	.
Gaston & Johnson	1	.	.	.	.	.	.	.	.	.	1	.
Gaubil	2	.	.	.	.	.	.	.	.	1	1	.
Gaudy	1	.	.	1	.	.	.	.	.	.	.	.
Gaultier	1	.	.	.	.	.	.	.	.	.	.	1
Gavarrete	1	.	.	.	.	.	1	.	.	.	.	.
Gavin	1	.	.	.	.	.	1	.	.	.	.	.
Gavit	2	.	.	.	2	.	.	.	.	.	.	.
Gavit & Duthie	2	.	.	.	.	1	.	.	.	.	.	1
Gazzettiere Americano	101	31	5	18	5	4	9	4	14	6	2	3
Gebauers, J.	1	.	.	.	.	.	.	.	.	.	.	1
Geddes	2	1	1	.	.	.	.	.	.	.	.	.
Geil & Jones	1	.	.	.	.	.	.	.	.	1	.	.

	Total	'83	'84	'85	'86	'87	'88	'89	'90	'91	'92	'93
Geil, Leamings & Cathcart	1	.	.	1	.	.	.	.	.	.	.	.
Gell, W.	1	.	.	.	.	.	.	.	.	.	.	1
Gemellis	1	.	.	.	1	.	.	.	.	.	.	.
Gemma Frisius; see Apianus	1	.	.	1	.	.	.	.	.	.	.	.
Gendron	6	.	.	.	5	.	.	.	.	1	.	.
General Magazine of Arts & Sciences	10	.	.	.	.	1	.	1	3	2	2	1
Gensoul	3	.	.	.	.	1	1	.	1	.	.	.
Gentleman's & Lond. Mag.	2	.	.	.	.	.	.	.	.	.	1	1
Gentleman's Magazine	390	28	27	16	19	31	28	20	136	36	18	31
Genty	1	.	.	.	.	.	1	.	.	.	.	.
Gerritz	2	1	.	.	1	.	.	.	.	.	.	.
Gerstmayr	3	.	2	.	.	1	.	.	.	.	.	.
Gibbes	1	.	.	.	.	1	.	.	.	.	.	.
Gibson; see . Gentlemen's Magazine	82	5	6	13	8	13	8	8	8	5	4	4
Gilbert	4	.	.	.	.	.	2	1	1	.	.	.
Gill	5	.	.	.	.	.	.	2	1	2	.	.
Gillet	1	.	.	.	1	.	.	.	.	.	.	.
Gilliam	1	.	1	.	.	.	.	.	.	.	.	.
Gilman	4	.	1	.	.	2	1	.	.	.	.	.
Gilpin	7	.	1	.	.	.	.	1	2	.	3	.
Gilquin & Dupain	2	.	.	.	1	1	.	.	.	.	.	.
Giustiniano	4	3	.	.	.	1	.	.	.	.	.	.
Glazier	1	.	1	.	.	.	.	.	.	.	.	.
Gleason	6	.	.	.	2	1	.	1	2	.	.	.
Gleason's Pictorial	4	1	.	.	.	.	2	.	.	.	1	.
Goad	25	.	.	14	1	.	1	.	.	.	9	.
Goeree	5	3	.	2	.	.	.	.	.	.	.	.
Goering	3	.	3	.	.	.	.	.	.	.	.	.
Goggins	1	.	.	1	.	.	.	.	.	.	.	.
Gold; see Naval Chronicle	20	4	5	2	2	6	.	1	.	.	.	.
Goldthwait	8	.	.	.	2	1	2	.	1	.	.	2
Goodrich	50	6	.	.	2	1	2	.	3	34	2	.
Goodwin	1	.	.	.	.	.	.	.	1	.	.	.
Goos	153	6	13	15	4	11	58	5	7	13	7	14
Gordon	21	1	3	.	2	.	1	.	3	1	10	.
Goschen	1	.	.	.	.	.	1	.	.	.	.	.
Gosse & Pinet	7	.	.	.	7	.	.	.	.	.	.	.
Gottfried	2	.	.	.	1	.	.	.	1	.	.	.
Gould	2	.	.	.	.	.	1	.	.	.	1	.
Gourlay	1	.	.	1	.	.	.	.	.	.	.	.
Graham's Magazine	1	.	.	.	.	.	.	.	.	.	1	.
Grand Magazine	2	.	.	1	.	1	.	.	.	.	.	.
Grand Mag. of Magazines	6	.	.	.	.	.	.	2	.	.	.	4
Grand Magazine of Universal Intelligence	2	.	.	.	.	.	.	.	2	.	.	.
Grant, A.	5	.	.	.	.	1	.	.	.	.	.	4
Graphic, The	2	.	.	.	2	.	.	.	.	.	.	.
Grattan & Gilbert	4	.	1	.	2	.	.	.	.	.	1	.
Gratz	3	.	.	.	3	.	.	.	.	.	.	.
Gravius	4	.	3	.	.	.	.	.	.	.	.	1
Gray	192	7	6	5	9	29	19	25	24	16	25	27
Gray & Johns	1	.	.	.	.	.	.	1	.	.	.	.
Great Britain	4	.	1	.	.	.	.	.	1	1	1	.
Greenebaum & Sampson	1	.	.	.	.	1	.	.	.	.	.	.
Greenhow	1	.	.	.	.	.	.	1	.	.	.	.
Greenleaf	109	3	2	4	4	1	3	16	7	46	15	8
Greenwood	28	5	20	3	.	.	.	.	.	.	.	.
Gregory	2	.	.	.	.	.	.	.	1	.	.	1
Grenier	1	.	.	.	1	.	.	.	.	.	.	.
Gridley	4	1	1	.	.	2	.	.	.	.	.	.
Grierson	11	.	3	3	2	.	.	.	2	.	.	1
Grigg	1	.	.	.	1	.	.	.	.	.	.	.
Griswold	6	.	6	.	.	.	.	.	.	.	.	.
Grose	5	.	.	.	5	.	.	.	.	.	.	.
Gross, R.	1	.	.	.	.	.	.	.	.	.	.	1

	Total	'83	'84	'85	'86	'87	'88	'89	'90	'91	'92	'93
Grosse	2	.	.	.	.	.	.	2	.	.	.	.
Grundy	1	.	.	1	.	.	.	.	.	.	.	.
Grynaeus	6	.	.	.	2	1	2	.	.	1	.	.
Gugler Lith.	1	.	.	.	1	.	.	.	.	.	.	.
Guicciardini	37	.	1	1	.	24	1	8	.	.	.	2
Guilquin & Dupain	1	1	.	.	.	.	.	.	.	.	.	.
Gurney Cab Service	1	.	.	.	1	.	.	.	.	.	.	.
Gussefeld; see Homann	14	1	4	.	2	.	1	1	3	1	1	.
Gussfield	1	.	.	.	.	.	.	.	.	.	.	1
Guthrie	28	1	4	1	2	5	5	1	3	2	4	.
Haasis & Lubrecht	3	.	.	.	.	1	1	.	.	.	.	1
Habermann	7	.	3	1	.	3	.	.	.	.	.	.
Hachette	3	.	1	.	.	.	.	.	1	.	1	.
Hack	1	.	.	.	.	.	.	.	1	.	.	.
Hadfield	1	.	1	.	.	.	.	.	.	.	.	.
Haffner, J.C.	1	.	.	.	.	.	.	.	.	.	.	1
Hagaman & Markham	1	.	.	.	.	.	.	.	.	1	.	.
Haines, D.	1	.	.	.	.	.	.	.	.	.	1	.
Haines, W.	1	.	.	.	.	.	.	.	.	.	.	1
Hale	1	.	.	.	.	.	.	.	.	.	1	.
Hales	1	.	.	.	.	1	.	.	.	.	.	.
Haliburton	11	2	1	2	.	.	.	.	.	.	6	.
Hall	83	7	18	13	9	11	4	9	4	2	1	5
Halley	1	.	.	.	.	.	.	.	.	.	.	1
Halma	2	.	1	1	.	.	.	.	.	.	.	.
Hals & Rydstrom	1	.	.	.	.	.	.	1	.	.	.	.
Hamelmann	1	.	.	.	1	.	.	.	.	.	.	.
Hamilton, Adams & Co.	2	.	.	.	.	1	.	.	.	.	.	1
Hammond	2	.	.	.	.	.	.	.	.	.	1	1
Handtke	3	.	.	.	1	1	.	.	.	.	.	1
Hanna	1	.	.	1	.	.	.	.	.	.	.	.
Hannibal & St. Joseph Short Line	1	.	.	.	.	.	1	.	.	.	.	.
Hansard & Sons	1	.	.	.	.	.	1	.	.	.	.	.
Happel	1	.	.	.	.	.	.	.	.	.	.	1
Hardesty	15	.	4	.	.	1	2	.	1	2	.	5
Hardy	2	.	.	.	1	.	1	.	.	.	.	.
Harmon	1	.	.	.	.	.	.	.	.	.	1	.
Harper	15	.	1	.	.	.	.	.	14	.	.	.
Harper & Bros.	5	.	1	1	.	.	2	.	1	.	.	.
Harper Bros.	6	.	.	.	.	.	.	1	.	4	.	1
Harper's Weekly	64	.	5	6	4	1	7	16	4	2	8	11
Harrewyn	1	.	1	.	.	.	.	.	.	.	.	.
Harris; see Bowen, E.	53	5	3	2	4	1	7	5	3	13	4	6
Harrison	30	3	6	5	2	5	2	.	4	3	.	.
Harrison & Sons	1	.	.	.	.	.	.	.	.	1	.	.
Harrison & Warner	2	.	.	.	1	.	.	.	.	.	.	1
Hart	2	.	.	.	.	.	.	.	.	.	2	.
Hassenstein	1	.	.	.	.	.	1	.	.	.	.	.
Hassler	1	.	.	.	.	.	.	.	.	.	1	.
Haszard	1	.	.	.	.	.	.	.	.	.	1	.
Hatch	1	.	.	.	.	1	.	.	.	.	.	.
Hauducoeur	1	.	.	.	.	.	.	.	.	1	.	.
Haven	2	.	.	.	.	.	2	.	.	.	.	.
Hawkes	2	.	.	.	.	.	.	1	1	.	.	.
Hawkins	2	.	.	.	.	.	1	.	1	.	.	.
Hayden, F.	5	.	1	.	.	.	.	.	.	.	.	4
Hayward	5	1	1	.	1	1	.	.	1	.	.	.
Hazard	1	.	.	.	.	.	.	.	1	.	.	.
Heaphy	3	.	.	.	3	.	.	.	.	.	.	.
Hearne	12	5	.	.	3	1	.	.	1	2	.	.
Heather	19	1	.	2	2	8	.	1	1	.	2	2
Hebner	1	.	.	.	1	.	.	.	.	.	.	.
Heck	11	.	.	.	.	1	.	.	.	.	10	.
Heliotype Printing Co.	1	.	.	.	.	.	1	.	.	.	.	.
Heller, C.	1	.	.	.	.	.	.	.	.	.	.	1

	Total	'83	'84	'85	'86	'87	'88	'89	'90	'91	'92	'93
Hemback	1	.	.	.	.	.	1	.	.	.	.	.
Henderson	2	.	.	.	.	.	.	1	1	.	.	.
Henn, Williams & Co.	2	.	.	.	.	.	2	.	.	.	.	.
Hennepin	13	.	3	1	1	1	2	2	2	.	.	1
Henriol	1	1	.	.	.	.	.	.	.	.	.	.
Henry	1	.	.	.	.	.	1	.	.	.	.	.
Hentschell	1	.	.	.	.	.	.	1	.	.	.	.
Herberstein	1	.	1	.	.	.	.	.	.	.	.	.
Herbert	73	1	.	3	1	2	1	2	.	50	1	12
Herder	1	.	.	.	.	1	.	.	.	.	.	.
Heriot	8	.	.	8	.	.	.	.	.	.	.	.
Herisson	12	1	2	1	1	2	.	1	1	1	.	2
Hermann Bros.	1	.	.	.	.	.	.	.	.	1	.	.
Hermannides	1	.	.	1	.	.	.	.	.	.	.	.
Hermet	1	.	.	.	.	.	.	.	.	.	1	.
Herrera; see De Herrera, 1988+	.	.	.	.	.	.	.	.	.	.	.	.
Herrman	1	.	.	1	.	.	.	.	.	.	.	.
Hesse, J.	1	.	.	.	.	.	.	.	.	.	.	1
Heubache	1	.	.	.	.	1	.	.	.	.	.	.
Hewitt	1	.	.	.	.	.	.	.	1	.	.	.
Heydt	1	.	.	1	.	.	.	.	.	.	.	.
Heylin	7	.	1	.	.	1	.	.	2	1	1	1
Hickling	1	.	.	.	.	.	1	.	.	.	.	.
Higginson	1	.	.	.	.	.	.	.	1	.	.	.
Hildburg Institut	22	2	2	2	4	4	5	.	2	1	.	.
Hildebrandt	2	.	1	1	.	.	.	.	.	.	.	.
Hill	2	1	.	.	.	1	.	.	.	.	.	.
Hill, A.J.	2	.	.	.	1	.	.	.	.	.	.	1
Hill, H.W. & Co.	1	.	1	.	.	.	.	.	.	.	.	.
Hill, N.	1	.	.	.	.	.	.	.	.	.	.	1
Hilliard d'Auberteuil	1	.	.	.	.	.	.	.	.	.	1	.
Hilliard, Gray & Co.	1	.	.	1	.	.	.	.	.	.	.	.
Hills	2	.	.	.	.	2	.	.	.	.	.	.
Hilton	1	.	.	1	.	.	.	.	.	.	.	.
Hind	3	.	.	.	.	.	.	1	.	1	1	.
Hinrichs	1	.	.	.	.	.	1	.	.	.	.	.
Hinshelwood	3	1	.	.	1	.	1	.	.	.	.	.
Hinton	51	4	4	5	8	18	6	2	.	.	.	4
Hinton & Simpkin	1	1	.	.	.	.	.	.	.	.	.	.
Hinton, Simpkin & Marshall; see Fenner, Sears	9	1	6	1	.	.	.	.	.	.	1	.
Hitchcock	4	.	.	.	.	1	.	.	.	3	.	.
Hobbs	2	.	.	.	.	.	1	.	.	1	.	.
Hobbs & Wilson	2	.	.	.	2	.	.	.	.	.	.	.
Hodges	1	1	.	.	.	.	.	.	.	.	.	.
Hodges & Smith	1	.	.	.	.	.	.	.	.	.	.	1
Hoen & Co.	5	.	.	1	.	.	3	.	.	.	1	.
Hoffman	1	.	.	.	.	.	1	.	.	.	.	.
Hogenberg	4	1	2	.	.	.	.	.	.	1	.	.
Hogg; see Cook	66	12	6	7	14	8	2	1	2	4	3	7
Holden's Dollar Magazin	1	.	.	.	.	.	.	.	.	1	.	.
Hole; see Camden	30	15	4	3	.	1	3	1	2	.	.	1
Hollar	7	3	.	3	.	.	.	.	.	.	.	1
Holman	1	.	.	.	.	.	.	.	.	1	.	.
Holmes	5	.	.	.	4	.	1	.	.	.	.	.
Holt	6	.	.	.	1	.	1	.	2	1	1	.
Holtrop	6	.	.	.	.	5	.	.	1	.	.	.
Homann & Homann Heirs	935	216	31	74	111	37	31	31	111	92	32	169
Home Insurance Co.	5	.	.	.	.	.	.	2	3	.	.	.
Hondius; see Jansson, Mercator	499	47	76	78	48	44	76	29	18	14	24	45
Honter	38	1	2	31	1	.	1	.	.	.	1	1
Hood	3	.	.	.	2	.	.	.	.	1	.	.
Hooker	2	.	.	.	.	.	.	.	2	.	.	.
Hooper	2	.	.	.	.	.	.	1	.	.	1	.
Hooper & Berner	2	.	.	.	.	.	.	1	1	.	.	.

	Total	'83	'84	'85	'86	'87	'88	'89	'90	'91	'92	'93
Hopkins	**4**	.	.	.	.	.	.	.	1	2	1	.
Horatius	**1**	1	.	.	.	.	.	.	.	.	.	.
Hornius	**3**	1	1	.	.	.	.	1	.	.	.	.
Horsburgh	**14**	.	.	1	2	3	5	1	1	1	.	.
Horwood	**1**	.	.	1	.	.	.	.	.	.	.	.
Hough	**1**	.	.	.	.	.	.	.	1	.	.	.
Houze	**6**	3	.	2	1	.	.	.	.	.	.	.
Howell	**4**	.	.	1	.	.	.	1	.	.	1	1
Howells	**1**	.	.	.	.	1	.	.	.	.	.	.
Howen	**1**	.	1	.	.	.	.	.	.	.	.	.
Hoxford & Co.	**1**	.	.	.	.	1	.	.	.	.	.	.
Hubbs	**1**	.	.	.	.	.	1	.	.	.	.	.
Huber	**1**	.	.	.	.	.	.	.	1	.	.	.
Huberti	**4**	.	4	.	.	.	.	.	.	.	.	.
Hughes	**6**	.	1	1	.	.	3	.	.	.	1	.
Hulett	**2**	.	.	2	.	.	.	.	.	.	.	.
Hulsius	**13**	4	4	1	.	1	.	.	1	1	1	.
Humboldt; See Von Humboldt, 1987+	.	.	.	.	.	.	.	.	.	.	.	.
Hume & Smollett	**1**	1	.	.	.	.	.	.	.	.	.	.
Hunt & Eaton	**10**	.	.	.	.	.	.	6	.	3	1	.
Hunter	**1**	.	.	.	1	.	.	.	.	.	.	.
Huntington	**3**	.	2	.	.	.	.	1	.	.	.	.
Huntington & Willard	**1**	.	.	.	.	.	.	.	.	.	1	.
Huot	**2**	1	.	1	.	.	.	.	.	.	.	.
Huquier	**1**	.	.	.	.	1	.	.	.	.	.	.
Hurd	**1**	.	1	.	.	.	.	.	.	.	.	.
Husson	**6**	.	.	4	1	.	.	.	.	.	.	1
Hutawa	**1**	.	.	.	.	.	.	.	1	.	.	.
Hutchings	**1**	.	.	.	.	.	.	.	.	1	.	.
Hutchins	**4**	2	.	.	.	.	.	1	.	.	.	1
Hutchinson	**2**	1	.	.	.	1	.	.	.	.	.	.
Hyde & Co.	**6**	.	.	.	1	.	2	.	1	.	2	.
Hydrographical Office; see Admiralty	.	.	.	.	.	.	.	.	.	.	.	.
I.C.M.R.	**1**	.	.	.	1	.	.	.	.	.	.	.
Iliff	**1**	.	.	.	.	.	.	1	.	.	.	.
Illman	**5**	4	.	.	.	1	.	.	.	.	.	.
Illustrated London News	**65**	2	1	12	2	11	14	9	2	5	5	2
Illustrated News	**6**	1	.	.	5	.	.	.	.	.	.	.
Imbert	**3**	.	1	.	.	2	.	.	.	.	.	.
Imray	**92**	5	.	3	3	13	8	25	3	16	7	9
Ingersoll	**1**	.	.	.	.	.	.	.	.	.	1	.
Irving	**2**	.	.	.	.	.	.	1	.	.	1	.
Ivison & Blakeman	**2**	.	2	.	.	.	.	.	.	.	.	.
Jackson	**6**	.	1	1	1	.	1	1	.	.	1	.
Jacobsz	**34**	2	5	4	7	3	5	3	3	.	1	1
Jacottet	**1**	.	.	.	.	.	.	.	.	1	.	.
Jaeger	**3**	.	.	.	1	.	.	.	2	.	.	.
Jaillot; see Mortier	**205**	19	31	36	25	12	28	15	10	8	9	12
James, J.A. & U.P.	**1**	.	.	.	.	.	.	.	.	.	.	1
James, W.	**4**	.	1	.	.	.	1	.	.	.	.	2
Jamieson, A.	**1**	.	.	.	.	.	.	.	.	.	.	1
Jansson; see Hondius, Mercator	**922**	237	50	97	57	100	88	31	43	30	72	117
Janvier	**34**	3	5	4	2	2	7	1	3	2	4	1
Japanese Cartography	**13**	.	.	4	.	.	.	4	.	3	2	.
Jarves	**1**	.	.	.	1	.	.	.	.	.	.	.
Jean	**2**	.	.	.	.	.	.	.	1	.	.	1
Jefferys & Faden	**1**	.	.	.	.	.	1	.	.	.	.	.
Jefferys; see Laurie & Whittle, Sayer *et al*	**336**	59	26	32	32	22	48	29	22	32	14	20
Jeppe	**1**	.	.	.	.	.	.	.	.	1	.	.
Jewett, Thomas & Co.	**1**	.	.	.	.	.	1	.	.	.	.	.
Jewett & CO.	**1**	.	.	.	.	.	.	.	.	.	.	1

	Total	'83	'84	'85	'86	'87	'88	'89	'90	'91	'92	'93
Johnson; see variants	**583**	14	23	10	11	22	49	31	41	72	78	49
Johnson & Browning	.	4	2	.	26	2	13	8	.	.	.	.
Johnson & Ward	.	26	28	20	8	15	12	19	.	.	.	.
Johnston	**245**	25	33	18	23	19	17	17	39	6	33	15
Johnstone	**1**	.	.	.	.	.	.	.	1	.	.	.
Joly, J.	**1**	.	.	.	.	.	.	.	.	.	.	1
Jourdan & Defrenoy	**1**	.	.	.	.	.	.	.	.	.	1	.
Journeaux L'Aine	**1**	.	.	.	.	.	.	.	.	.	.	1
Jouvet	**1**	.	.	.	.	.	1	.	.	.	.	.
Judd	**1**	1	.	.	.	.	.	.	.	.	.	.
Kaempfer	**2**	1	.	.	.	.	.	.	.	.	.	1
Kaerius; see Van den Keere	.	.	.	.	.	.	.	.	.	.	.	.
Kane	**2**	.	1	.	.	.	.	1	.	.	.	.
Kearfott	**3**	.	.	.	.	.	1	.	1	.	1	.
Kearsley	**2**	.	.	.	2	.	.	.	.	.	.	.
Keefer	**3**	.	.	.	1	.	.	.	2	.	.	.
Keeler	**1**	.	.	.	.	.	.	.	.	.	1	.
Keere; see Van den Keere	.	.	.	.	.	.	.	.	.	.	.	.
Keller	**2**	1	.	.	.	.	.	.	.	.	.	1
Kellogg	**2**	.	.	.	.	.	1	.	1	.	.	.
Kelly	**28**	2	4	2	1	7	3	2	3	1	.	3
Kemble	**2**	.	.	.	.	.	.	.	.	2	.	.
Kennard	**1**	.	.	1	.	.	.	.	.	.	.	.
Kensett	**3**	.	.	.	1	.	1	.	.	.	.	1
Kepler	**1**	.	.	.	.	.	.	.	1	.	.	.
Kepohoni	**1**	.	1	.	.	.	.	.	.	.	.	.
Keur	**7**	.	.	.	.	1	.	.	2	2	1	1
Key	**1**	1	.	.	.	.	.	.	.	.	.	.
Keyser	**6**	2	1	1	.	1	.	.	.	1	.	.
Keystone Publishing Co.	**1**	.	1	.	.	.	.	.	.	.	.	.
Kiepert	**7**	2	.	.	.	.	.	.	1	.	.	4
Kilbourn	**1**	.	1	.	.	.	.	.	.	.	.	.
Kilburn	**1**	1	.	.	.	.	.	.	.	.	.	.
Kimmel & Foster	**1**	.	.	.	.	.	.	.	.	.	1	.
Kincaid, A.	**2**	.	.	.	.	.	.	1	.	.	.	1
King	**1**	1	.	.	.	.	.	.	.	.	.	.
Kingman Bros.	**6**	.	6	.	.	.	.	.	.	.	.	.
Kingsbury	**2**	.	1	.	.	.	.	.	.	.	.	1
Kinnersley	**2**	.	.	.	.	.	1	.	.	1	.	.
Kino	**3**	1	.	1	.	.	.	1	.	.	.	.
Kip; see Camden	**31**	10	17	2	.	1	.	1	.	.	.	.
Kircher	**37**	3	7	4	6	2	2	2	3	5	2	1
Kirkwood	**2**	.	.	1	.	1	.	.	.	.	.	.
Kitchin	**247**	35	41	59	24	27	15	15	9	5	9	8
Klaproth	**1**	.	.	.	.	.	.	.	.	.	1	.
Klauprech & Menzel	**1**	.	.	.	.	.	.	.	.	1	.	.
Kleinknecht	**2**	.	.	.	.	.	.	.	2	.	.	.
Klinckowstrom	**1**	.	.	.	.	1	.	.	.	.	.	.
Klockhoff	**2**	.	.	.	.	1	.	1	.	.	.	.
Knapton	**1**	.	.	.	.	.	1	.	.	.	.	.
Knight; see S.D.U.K.	**14**	3	.	2	2	1	1	.	3	2	.	.
Knipe	**1**	.	.	1	.	.	.	.	.	.	.	.
Knox	**1**	.	.	.	.	.	.	.	.	.	1	.
Koch	**1**	.	.	.	.	.	.	.	1	.	.	.
Kohl	**1**	.	.	.	1	.	.	.	.	.	.	.
Kok	**3**	.	.	.	2	1	.	.	.	.	.	.
Kolb	**3**	.	.	3	.	.	.	.	.	.	.	.
Kolben	**3**	.	.	.	.	.	.	3	.	.	.	.
Koller	**2**	.	.	.	.	1	.	1	.	.	.	.
Kootwyck, see Cotovicus	.	.	.	.	.	.	.	.	.	.	.	.
Kotzebue; see Von Kotzebue	.	.	.	.	.	.	.	.	.	.	.	.
Krayenhoff	**2**	.	2	.	.	.	.	.	.	.	.	.
Kreffeldt	**1**	.	1	.	.	.	.	.	.	.	.	.
Krevelt	**3**	.	.	.	.	.	.	1	.	.	2	.
Kruikius	**11**	.	1	.	.	.	.	.	.	.	10	.
Kuchel	**1**	.	.	.	1	.	.	.	.	.	.	.

	Total	'83	'84	'85	'86	'87	'88	'89	'90	'91	'92	'93
Kutrz & Allison	1	.	.	.	.	.	.	1	.	.	.	.
La Harpe	3	.	.	.	.	.	.	.	.	.	.	3
La Hontan;	47	3	6	8	4	5	6	4	7	.	1	3
see Lahonton, 1989												
La Perouse; see Robinson	105	11	4	3	5	3	8	13	8	14	12	24
La Pointe	1	.	.	1	.	.	.	.	.	.	.	.
La Rochefoucault-Liancourt	1	.	.	.	.	.	.	.	.	1	.	.
Labat	7	.	1	2	.	.	.	1	1	1	.	1
Labelye	1	.	.	1	.	.	.	.	.	.	.	.
Lacoste	3	1	.	.	.	1	.	.	.	1	.	.
Ladies Repository	21	.	6	.	1	.	.	3	3	3	1	4
Lafreri School	9	1	3	1	.	.	.	.	.	.	1	3
Lake Shore & Michigan	2	.	.	.	1	1	.	.	.	.	.	.
Southern Rwy.												
Lallemand	2	.	.	.	.	.	.	.	.	.	.	2
Lambert, J.	5	1	.	3	.	.	.	.	.	.	.	1
Lancelot	1	.	.	.	.	1	.	.	.	.	.	.
Lane	3	2	.	.	.	.	.	.	1	.	.	.
Lange	5	.	.	1	.	.	.	.	2	.	.	2
Lange & Kronfeld	1	.	.	.	.	.	.	.	.	.	.	1
Langenes	10	.	1	1	1	.	1	.	1	1	1	3
Langhans	1	.	.	.	1	.	.	.	.	.	.	.
Langley	12	12	.	.	.	.	.	.	.	.	.	.
Langlois	2	.	1	.	1	.	.	.	.	.	.	.
Langsdorff	2	1	.	1	.	.	.	.	.	.	.	.
Lapie	50	9	.	2	.	6	7	4	5	4	7	6
Lapointe	1	1	.	.	.	.	.	.	.	.	.	.
Laporte	1	.	.	1	.	.	.	.	.	.	.	.
Las Cases	2	.	.	.	.	2	.	.	.	.	.	.
Lasor a Varea	76	.	4	1	2	1	.	3	22	1	42	.
Lathrop	3	.	.	.	.	2	.	1	.	.	.	.
Latrobe	1	.	.	.	.	1	.	.	.	.	.	.
Lattre	27	.	2	4	.	2	1	2	1	2	9	4
Lauremberg	8	7	.	.	.	.	.	.	.	.	1	.
Laurent	3	.	1	.	.	1	1	.	.	.	.	.
Laurie	17	2	.	.	1	2	3	2	.	3	4	.
Laurie & Whittle;	261	24	15	26	11	47	27	18	17	17	22	37
see Dunn, Jefferys												
Lavoisne	7	2	.	1	.	.	.	2	.	.	.	2
Law	5	.	1	.	.	1	.	.	.	.	2	1
Lawrence	1	.	.	.	1	.	.	.	.	.	.	.
Lawson	3	.	1	.	.	.	1	.	1	.	.	.
Lay	4	.	.	.	.	.	2	1	.	.	1	.
Lazius	1	.	.	.	.	.	.	.	1	.	.	.
Le Beau	1	1	.	.	.	.	.	.	.	.	.	.
Le Bruyn	15	15	.	.	.	.	.	.	.	.	.	.
Le Clerc	17	.	9	2	.	1	.	2	1	1	1	.
Le Gentil	1	.	.	.	.	.	.	.	1	.	.	.
Le Maire	1	.	.	.	.	.	.	.	.	.	.	1
Le Maitre	1	.	.	.	.	.	1	.	.	.	.	.
Le Page du Pratz	3	1	.	.	1	.	.	.	.	.	.	1
Le Rouge	182	15	22	11	12	38	10	8	13	18	24	11
Le Sage	5	.	.	.	.	.	3	.	.	1	.	1
Le Temps	1	.	.	.	.	.	1	.	.	.	.	.
Le Vasseur de Beauplan	1	.	.	1	.	.	.	.	.	.	.	.
Lea	23	2	.	7	8	1	1	2	.	.	.	2
Lea & Blanchard	1	.	.	.	.	.	.	.	1	.	.	.
Lea & Overton	4	.	.	4	.	.	.	.	.	.	.	.
Leadville Daily Herald	1	.	.	1	.	.	.	.	.	.	.	.
Legrand	2	.	.	.	.	.	.	.	2	.	.	.
Leigh	10	.	10	.	.	.	.	.	.	.	.	.
Leitch	4	.	.	3	.	.	1	.	.	.	.	.
Leitch & Co.	1	.	.	.	.	.	.	.	1	.	.	.
Lejeune	1	.	.	.	.	.	.	.	.	.	1	.
Lemercier	2	1	.	.	.	.	.	.	.	1	.	.
Lester	1	.	.	.	.	.	.	.	1	.	.	.

	Total	'83	'84	'85	'86	'87	'88	'89	'90	'91	'92	'93
Letts	9	.	.	1	.	2	.	2	1	1	2	.
Leval	1	1	.	.	.	.	.	.	.	.	.	.
Levanto	3	1	1	1	.	.	.	.	.	.	.	.
Levasseur	73	8	5	4	6	11	8	8	3	6	10	4
Levi	1	.	.	.	.	.	.	.	.	.	.	1
Lewis & Arrowsmith	83	2	2	7	9	6	4	7	4	7	9	26
Lewis & Clark	2	.	.	.	.	.	1	.	.	1	.	.
Lewis & Co.	2	.	.	.	.	.	2	.	.	.	.	.
Lewis, Samuel & Co.	7	.	.	.	5	.	.	.	.	.	.	2
Lewis; see Carey	26	7	5	2	3	5	.	.	3	.	1	.
Liebaux	1	1	.	.	.	.	.	.	.	.	.	.
Liefrinck	1	.	1	.	.	.	.	.	.	.	.	.
Ligon	8	.	.	1	.	.	.	3	3	.	1	.
Lincoln & Edmands	1	.	.	.	.	.	.	.	.	.	.	1
Lindeman	1	.	.	1	.	.	.	.	.	.	.	.
Lindner	1	.	.	.	.	.	.	.	.	.	1	.
Lindsay & Blakiston	1	.	.	.	.	.	.	.	.	.	1	.
Lindstrom	1	.	.	.	.	.	.	.	1	.	.	.
Linforth	2	.	.	1	1	.	.	.	.	.	.	.
Linschoten; see	.	.	.	.	.	.	.	.	.	.	.	.
Van Linschoten, 1986+												
Linton	4	.	.	1	.	1	.	.	1	1	.	.
Lippincott	5	.	.	.	.	.	.	4	1	.	.	.
Lippincott & Grambo	2	.	.	.	.	1	.	.	.	1	.	.
Lirelli	1	.	.	.	.	.	.	.	.	1	.	.
Literary Magazine	1	.	.	.	.	.	.	.	1	.	.	.
Lizars	45	2	6	3	1	2	5	12	4	3	3	4
Lloyd	53	1	.	1	5	10	9	5	6	7	2	7
Lloyd Bros.	1	.	.	.	.	.	.	.	1	.	.	.
Lobeck	29	.	.	.	.	.	.	.	.	.	29	.
Local & State Gov't Maps	4	.	.	.	.	.	.	.	.	.	.	4
Lockman	1	.	.	.	.	.	1	.	.	.	.	.
Lockwood	1	.	.	.	.	.	.	.	.	.	.	1
Lodge	43	1	6	8	6	9	8	2	.	2	.	1
Logan & Hartley	1	.	.	.	.	1	.	.	.	.	.	.
Logerot	5	.	.	.	.	.	.	.	.	.	2	3
Loggan	2	.	.	2	.	.	.	.	.	.	.	.
London Benevolent	1	.	.	.	.	.	.	.	.	1	.	.
Repository												
London Gazette	5	2	.	.	.	2	1	.	.	.	.	.
London Illustrated News	2	.	.	.	2	.	.	.	.	.	.	.
London Journal	4	.	.	.	.	.	4	.	.	.	.	.
London Magazine	232	13	18	28	16	21	17	11	37	24	28	19
London News	21	5	4	10	2	.	.	.	.	.	.	.
London Printing & Pub.	1	.	.	.	.	.	.	.	.	.	.	1
London Steam Boat Co.	1	.	.	.	.	.	.	.	.	.	1	.
London Times	6	.	.	.	6	.	.	.	.	.	.	.
Long	3	.	.	.	.	.	2	.	.	1	.	.
Longchamps	1	.	.	.	.	.	1	.	.	.	.	.
Longman	16	2	4	5	1	1	.	1	2	.	.	.
Longman & Rees	1	.	.	.	.	.	1	.	.	.	.	.
Longworth, D.	1	.	.	.	.	.	.	.	.	.	.	1
Lootsman; see Jacobsz	0	.	.	.	.	.	.	.	.	.	.	.
Lopez	15	2	.	1	.	1	.	4	1	1	2	3
Lorrain	4	.	.	.	1	.	.	.	.	1	1	1
Lothian	5	.	.	.	.	1	.	2	.	2	.	.
Lotter	240	14	16	29	14	17	10	9	50	8	60	13
Lottery Magazine	2	.	.	.	.	.	.	.	.	.	1	1
Lottin	1	.	.	.	.	.	.	.	.	1	.	.
Loveringh	1	.	.	.	.	.	.	.	1	.	.	.
Lowden & Johnson	1	.	.	.	.	.	1	.	.	.	.	.
Lowizio	1	.	1	.	.	.	.	.	.	.	.	.
Lowry	4	.	.	1	2	1	.	.	.	.	.	.
Lubrecht	1	.	.	.	.	.	.	.	.	1	.	.
Lucas	165	6	50	5	4	2	7	19	15	5	32	20
Luffman	30	4	.	17	.	6	.	1	1	.	.	1
Lufft	3	1	.	1	.	1	.	.	.	.	.	.

	Total	'83	'84	'85	'86	'87	'88	'89	'90	'91	'92	'93
Lumsden	**1**	.	.	.	.	.	.	.	.	.	.	1
Luther	**1**	1	.	.	.	.	.	.	.	.	.	.
Lyell	**1**	.	1	.	.	.	.	.	.	.	.	.
MacDonald	**2**	.	.	2	.	.	.	.	.	.	.	.
MacDougall & Southwick	**1**	.	.	.	.	.	1	.	.	.	.	.
MacGregor	**2**	.	1	.	.	1	.	.	.	.	.	.
MacKenzie	**42**	6	3	5	1	4	7	.	4	3	2	7
MacKinlay	**7**	.	1	.	.	.	1	.	1	.	3	1
MacLure & MacDonald	**5**	.	1	1	1	.	1	1	.	.	.	.
MacPherson	**4**	.	1	.	2	1	.	.	.	.	.	.
Madison	**1**	.	.	.	.	.	.	1	.	.	.	.
Maescamp	**1**	.	.	1	.	.	.	.	.	.	.	.
Maffeius	**2**	.	1	.	.	.	.	1	.	.	.	.
Maggi	**2**	.	1	.	.	1	.	.	.	.	.	.
Magini; see Ptolemy(1596-1621)	**2**	.	.	.	.	.	.	2	.	.	.	.
Magnus	**29**	.	1	4	1	2	3	6	6	3	3	.
Maire, N.	**1**	.	.	.	.	.	.	.	.	.	.	1
Maitland	**1**	.	.	1	.	.	.	.	.	.	.	.
Malby, T.	**1**	.	.	.	.	.	.	.	.	.	.	1
Malham	**14**	.	.	.	.	14	.	.	.	.	.	.
Mallery & Ward	**1**	.	.	.	.	.	.	.	1	.	.	.
Mallet	**462**	14	45	83	27	25	72	51	49	18	26	52
Malte-Brun	**65**	7	4	2	18	3	5	.	23	1	1	1
Mandrillon	**1**	.	.	.	1	.	.	.	.	.	.	.
Manouvier	**1**	.	.	.	.	.	.	.	.	.	1	.
Mansell, F.	**1**	.	.	.	.	.	.	.	.	.	.	1
Mante	**5**	1	1	1	.	.	.	.	.	2	.	.
Marchand	**1**	.	.	.	.	.	.	.	.	.	1	.
Marchetti	**3**	.	.	.	.	.	.	.	.	.	3	.
Marcy	**2**	.	2	.	.	.	.	.	.	.	.	.
Mariette	**4**	.	1	.	.	.	1	1	.	.	.	1
Marks	**1**	.	.	.	.	1	.	.	.	.	.	.
Marlin	**1**	.	.	.	.	1	.	.	.	.	.	.
Marryat	**1**	.	.	1	.	.	.	.	.	.	.	.
Marsh, W. S.	**1**	.	.	.	.	.	.	.	.	.	.	1
Marshall	**83**	.	2	13	20	14	3	3	6	7	13	2
Martell	**1**	.	.	1	.	.	.	.	.	.	.	.
Martenet	**2**	.	.	.	.	.	.	.	2	.	.	.
Martin	**4**	.	1	.	.	.	2	.	1	.	.	.
Martin & Smith	**1**	.	.	.	.	.	.	.	.	1	.	.
Marzolla	**8**	.	1	.	.	.	.	.	.	3	2	2
Mason	**2**	.	.	.	.	.	.	1	.	1	.	.
Mason & Dixon	**1**	.	.	.	.	.	1	.	.	.	.	.
Maspero	**3**	1	.	.	1	.	.	.	1	.	.	.
Mast	**1**	.	.	.	.	.	.	.	.	1	.	.
Mast, Crowell	**3**	.	.	.	.	.	2	.	.	.	.	1
Mast, Crowell & Kirkpatrick	**11**	.	2	.	3	3	.	2	.	1	.	.
Mather	**2**	.	1	.	.	.	.	.	1	.	.	.
Mathews	**3**	.	.	2	.	.	.	1	.	.	.	.
Matthews, Northrup	**29**	.	3	4	5	1	8	5	1	.	2	.
Maundressi	**2**	1	.	1	.	.	.	.	.	.	.	.
Maurepas	**1**	.	.	.	.	.	.	1	.	.	.	.
Mauritius	**1**	.	.	.	.	1	.	.	.	.	.	.
Mawman	**10**	3	.	1	2	.	.	2	.	2	.	.
Maximilian of Wied	**1**	.	.	.	.	.	1	.	.	.	.	.
Maxwell Land Grant Co.	**1**	.	.	.	.	.	.	1	.	.	.	.
May	**1**	.	.	.	.	.	.	.	.	1	.	.
Mayer	**3**	1	.	1	.	.	.	.	1	.	.	.
Maynard	**1**	.	.	1	.	.	.	.	.	.	.	.
McConnell	**1**	.	.	.	.	.	1	.	.	.	.	.
McElroy, Son & Brown	**1**	.	.	.	.	.	.	.	1	.	.	.
McGregor	**37**	.	16	1	.	3	.	14	.	.	3	.
McIntyre	**5**	2	1	.	.	.	1	.	1	.	.	.
McLoughlin Bros.	**1**	.	.	.	.	.	.	.	1	.	.	.
McMillan	**2**	.	.	.	.	.	.	.	.	.	2	.
McNally	**15**	10	.	.	.	.	.	3	1	1	.	.
Meares	**26**	2	9	4	1	3	2	.	4	.	.	1
Megarey	**1**	.	1	.	.	.	.	.	.	.	.	.
Meierus	**1**	.	.	.	.	.	.	.	.	1	.	.
Meijer	**4**	1	.	.	.	.	1	.	1	.	.	1
Meisner	**30**	27	2	.	.	1	.	.	.	.	.	.
Meissas	**2**	1	.	.	.	1	.	.	.	.	.	.
Mela	**1**	.	.	1	.	.	.	.	.	.	.	.
Melish	**60**	2	14	1	1	4	6	2	8	7	10	5
Melling	**3**	.	.	.	.	.	.	.	3	.	.	.
Mendel Lith.	**1**	.	.	.	.	.	.	.	.	1	.	.
Mendenhall	**4**	.	.	.	2	.	2	.	.	.	.	.
Mentelle	**6**	.	.	.	.	1	.	.	.	.	4	1
Menzies	**1**	.	.	.	.	.	.	.	.	.	.	1
Mercator:	**808**	.	.	.	.	.	.	.	.	.	.	.
(folio) see Hondius; Jansson; Ptolemy	.	41	33	26	81	36	45	74	54	9	17	57
(small) see Purchas	.	60	11	15	44	18	18	69	40	20	22	18
Mercurio Peruano	**1**	.	.	.	.	.	.	.	.	.	1	.
Merian	**436**	250	18	11	56	14	3	9	22	6	45	2
Merritt & Co.	**1**	.	.	.	.	.	.	.	.	1	.	.
Merula	**6**	.	.	1	.	.	1	1	1	.	1	1
Metellus	**3**	1	1	.	.	.	.	.	.	.	.	1
Meyer	**129**	7	6	4	1	14	17	13	12	7	10	38
Mialhe	**1**	.	.	.	.	.	.	.	.	.	.	1
Michault	**3**	1	1	.	.	.	.	.	.	.	.	1
Michaux	**1**	.	.	.	.	.	1	.	.	.	.	.
Michelin	**1**	.	.	.	.	.	.	1	.	.	.	.
Michigan Central R.R.	**2**	.	.	.	1	.	1	.	.	.	.	.
Middleton	**16**	.	1	1	2	2	3	.	1	4	.	2
Migeon	**10**	.	1	1	.	3	1	2	.	2	.	.
Milbert	**2**	.	.	.	1	1	.	.	.	.	.	.
Miles	**9**	.	.	9	.	.	.	.	.	.	.	.
Millar	**20**	2	1	5	1	2	2	3	.	3	1	.
Miller	**4**	1	.	2	.	.	.	.	1	.	.	.
Mills	**1**	.	.	.	.	.	1	.	.	.	.	.
Mills & Co.	**2**	.	.	.	.	1	.	.	1	.	.	.
Milne	**2**	.	.	1	.	.	.	.	.	.	.	1
Milton & Cheadle	**1**	.	1	.	.	.	.	.	.	.	.	.
Missouri	**1**	.	.	1	.	.	.	.	.	.	.	.
Missouri River, Ft. Scott . & Gulf R.R	**1**	.	.	.	.	.	1	.	.	.	.	.
Mitchell, George	**1**	.	.	.	.	.	.	.	.	.	1	.
Mitchell, John	**10**	.	1	.	1	.	1	1	3	1	1	1
Mitchell, S.A.	**1122**	67	89	80	66	82	127	176	92	127	113	5
(Atlas Maps to.1859)	.	.	.	.	.	.	.	.	.	.	.	42
(Atlas Maps 1860+)	.	.	.	.	.	.	.	.	.	.	.	56
Moffat	**4**	1	2	1	.	.	.	.	.	.	.	.
Mogg	**9**	.	.	1	.	1	.	.	2	1	.	4
Moithey	**4**	.	.	.	1	1	2	.	.	.	.	.
Molini	**1**	.	.	.	.	.	.	.	.	.	1	.
Moll:	**572**	74	92	83	.	.	.	.	.	.	.	.
(large)	.	.	.	.	2	7	5	17	7	8	2	9
(small)	.	.	.	.	39	53	38	24	33	23	28	28
Mollhausen	**2**	1	.	.	.	.	.	.	1	.	.	.
Molyneux	**1**	.	.	.	.	1	.	.	.	.	.	.
Monaldini	**3**	.	.	.	.	1	.	.	1	1	.	.
Monarch Co.	**19**	.	.	15	.	1	2	1	.	.	.	.
Monath	**3**	.	.	.	.	.	.	.	.	1	2	.
Mondhare	**1**	.	.	.	.	.	.	.	.	1	.	.
Monin	**13**	.	.	1	1	4	1	1	1	2	1	1
Monin & Fremin	**4**	.	3	.	.	.	.	.	1	.	.	.
Monin & Vuillemin	**1**	.	.	.	.	.	.	.	1	.	.	.
Monk	**13**	.	2	.	.	3	3	.	3	.	.	2
Montanus; see Dapper, Ogilby	**76**	7	.	4	2	23	22	5	1	8	.	4

	Total	'83	'84	'85	'86	'87	'88	'89	'90	'91	'92	'93
Monthly Chronologer	**2**	1	.	.	.	.	1	.	.	.	.	.
see London Magazine												
Monthly Intelligencer	**3**	.	.	1	1	.	1	.	.	.	.	.
see London Magazine												
Montresor	**5**	.	.	.	.	2	.	2	.	.	.	1
Moon	**1**	1	.	.	.	.	.	.	.	.	.	.
Moore	**7**	2	.	.	.	3	.	1	1	.	.	.
Morales	**2**	.	.	.	.	1	1	.	.	.	.	.
Morden	**344**	28	31	58	57	45	8	7	10	42	32	26
Morden & Berry	**2**	.	1	1	.	.	.	.	.	.	.	.
Morden & Lea	**1**	.	.	1	.	.	.	.	.	.	.	.
Morgan	**2**	.	1	.	.	.	.	1	.	.	.	.
Morrill	**1**	.	.	.	.	.	.	.	.	1	.	.
Morris	**50**	.	.	3	2	9	.	8	.	.	.	28
Morrison	**7**	.	.	.	.	.	3	1	2	1	.	.
Morrison & West	**2**	1	1	.	.	.	.	.	.	.	.	.
Morse	**210**	24	37	29	22	20	17	19	11	19	12	.
Morse & Breese	**109**	4	12	3	7	10	4	5	9	39	5	11
Morse & Gaston	**12**	.	.	.	.	1	6	.	1	1	1	2
Morse, J.; see Stockdale	**26**	.	.	.	.	.	.	.	.	.	.	26
Morse, S.	**3**	.	.	.	.	.	.	.	.	.	.	3
Mortier; see Jaillot	**260**	17	104	51	19	14	13	10	10	8	7	7
Mortimer & Co.	**1**	.	.	1	.	.	.	.	.	.	.	.
Mosting	**1**	.	.	.	.	.	.	.	1	.	.	.
Mottram	**1**	.	.	.	.	.	.	.	.	1	.	.
Moule	**7**	.	5	.	.	.	1	1	.	.	.	.
Mount & Page	**261**	28	16	41	35	50	13	29	15	16	10	8
Mouzon	**2**	.	.	.	.	.	1	.	.	.	.	1
Moxon	**15**	2	.	3	.	2	3	1	.	2	1	1
Mudie	**1**	1	.	.	.	.	.	.	.	.	.	.
Mueller	**10**	.	.	10	.	.	.	.	.	.	.	.
Muller	**27**	6	10	.	.	3	2	1	.	3	.	2
Munson	**1**	.	.	.	.	.	1	.	.	.	.	.
Munster	**579**	83	28	74	86	65	81	48	24	20	23	47
Murphy & Co.	**1**	.	1	.	.	.	.	.	.	.	.	.
Murray	**13**	3	3	3	.	.	2	.	.	2	.	.
Murray, Heiss & McLaughlin	**1**	.	.	.	.	.	.	.	.	.	1	.
Murray, J.	**8**	.	1	.	.	.	1	1	1	.	.	4
Mutlow	**1**	1	.	.	.	.	.	.	.	.	.	.
Myers	**1**	1	.	.	.	.	.	.	.	.	.	.
Myritius	**2**	.	.	.	.	.	.	.	.	1	.	1
Nagel & Weingartner	**1**	.	.	.	1	.	.	.	.	.	.	.
Narborough	**1**	.	.	.	.	1	.	.	.	.	.	.
National Geographic Soc.	**2**	.	1	.	.	.	.	.	.	.	.	1
Nat'l Soc. for Promoting	**2**	.	.	.	.	.	.	.	.	.	2	.
Education of the Poor												
Nat'l Union Executive Comm.	**1**	.	.	.	.	.	.	1	.	.	.	.
Nautical Magazine	**2**	.	.	.	.	.	.	.	2	.	.	.
Naval Chronicle; see Gold	**16**	.	.	1	.	1	6	.	4	1	1	2
Neele	**19**	1	5	1	2	2	.	2	4	2	.	.
Nell	**5**	.	.	.	.	.	3	.	1	1	.	.
Neptune Francois; see	.	.	.	.	.	.	.	.	.	.	.	.
Depot de la Marine												
Nevers	**1**	.	.	.	.	.	.	.	.	.	1	.
New England Lith. Co.	**1**	.	.	.	.	1	.	.	.	.	.	.
New York	**1**	.	.	.	.	.	.	.	.	1	.	.
New York Herald	**25**	.	.	.	6	.	.	17	.	.	2	.
New York Illustrated News	**1**	.	.	.	.	.	.	.	.	1	.	.
New York Manual	**2**	1	.	.	.	.	.	.	.	.	1	.
New York State	**2**	.	.	.	2	.	.	.	.	.	.	.
NY State Documentary Hist.	**5**	.	.	.	.	.	.	.	.	.	.	5
New York Sun	**1**	.	.	.	.	.	.	.	.	.	1	.
New York Tribune	**1**	.	.	.	1	.	.	.	.	.	.	.
Newbery	**1**	.	1	.	.	.	.	.	.	.	.	.
Newton	**1**	.	.	.	1	.	.	.	.	.	.	.
Newton & Berry	**2**	.	.	.	.	.	.	.	.	.	.	2

	Total	'83	'84	'85	'86	'87	'88	'89	'90	'91	'92	'93
Nicholls	**1**	1	.	.	.	.	.	.	.	.	.	.
Nicholson	**5**	.	.	.	.	.	.	.	.	.	5	.
Nicol	**8**	3	.	1	1	1	.	.	.	.	.	2
Nicolosi	**7**	1	4	.	.	.	1	.	.	1	.	.
Nieuhoff	**2**	.	.	.	.	.	.	.	.	1	1	.
Nolin	**51**	4	4	10	2	5	2	5	4	4	4	7
Noll	**1**	.	.	1	.	.	.	.	.	.	.	.
Norden	**1**	.	1	.	.	.	.	.	.	.	.	.
Nordenankar	**1**	.	.	.	.	.	.	.	1	.	.	.
Norie	**27**	2	.	4	2	5	2	2	2	5	1	2
Norman	**2**	.	.	.	.	.	.	1	.	.	.	1
Norris	**1**	.	.	1	.	.	.	.	.	.	.	.
Norris Peters Co.	**1**	.	.	.	.	.	.	.	.	.	.	1
Norris, Wellge & Co.	**1**	.	.	.	1	.	.	.	.	.	.	.
Northern Pacific R.R.	**3**	.	.	.	.	1	1	.	.	1	.	.
Norwood	**1**	.	1	.	.	.	.	.	.	.	.	.
Nuremberg Chronicle;	**0**	.	.	.	.	.	.	.	.	.	.	.
see Schedel												
Nuttall & Dixon	**2**	.	.	.	.	.	.	2	.	.	.	.
Nuttall, Fisher & Dixon	**4**	1	1	1	.	1	.	.	.	.	.	.
Nutzhorn	**1**	1	.	.	.	.	.	.	.	.	.	.
Oakland Land, Loan & Trust	**1**	.	.	.	.	.	.	1	.	.	.	.
Oesfeld	**1**	.	.	.	1	.	.	.	.	.	.	.
Ogilby; see Montanus	**177**	35	23	30	20	8	16	6	10	13	5	11
Olaus Magnus	**1**	.	.	.	.	.	.	.	.	1	.	.
Oldmixon	**1**	.	.	.	.	.	.	.	.	.	1	.
Olearius	**1**	.	.	1	.	.	.	.	.	.	.	.
Oliver	**1**	.	.	1	.	.	.	.	.	.	.	.
Oliver & Boyd	**2**	.	.	.	.	.	.	1	.	.	.	1
Olmsted	**1**	.	.	.	.	.	.	.	1	.	.	.
Olney	**14**	1	2	1	1	.	.	4	.	2	.	3
Ordnance Survey	**7**	.	.	1	.	.	.	.	.	.	6	.
Orr	**1**	.	.	.	.	.	.	.	1	.	.	.
Ortelius	**1071**	.	.	.	.	.	.	.	.	.	.	.
Ortelius (folio)	.	143	99	113	91	122	110	45	26	47	34	44
Ortelius (miniature)	.	76	16	13	10	19	18	7	9	6	8	15
Osborne	**1**	.	.	1	.	.	.	.	.	.	.	.
Ottens	**88**	14	8	8	9	10	17	4	5	.	4	9
Overton	**12**	1	.	3	1	.	2	2	.	.	.	3
Overton & Bowles	**1**	.	.	1	.	.	.	.	.	.	.	.
Overton & Morden	**1**	.	.	1	.	.	.	.	.	.	.	.
Owen	**8**	1	1	3	1	1	.	.	1	.	.	.
Owen & Bowen	**17**	.	9	2	5	.	1	.	.	.	.	.
Owen's Magazine	**1**	.	.	.	1	.	.	.	.	.	.	.
Oxford Magazine	**1**	.	.	1	.	.	.	.	.	.	.	.
Pacific Coast Atlas	**9**	.	.	.	.	2	.	3	2	2	.	.
Packard & Bros.	**2**	.	.	.	1	.	.	.	.	.	1	.
Padley	**1**	1	.	.	.	.	.	.	.	.	.	.
Page	**6**	.	.	.	.	.	1	.	4	1	.	.
Palairet	**3**	.	.	.	.	.	1	1	.	.	.	1
Palfrey	**2**	1	.	1	.	.	.	.	.	.	.	.
Panter-Downes	**1**	.	.	1	.	.	.	.	.	.	.	.
Paoli	**1**	1	.	.	.	.	.	.	.	.	.	.
Papen	**2**	2	.	.	.	.	.	.	.	.	.	.
Parke	**1**	.	1	.	.	.	.	.	.	.	.	.
Parker	**9**	.	2	2	.	.	2	1	.	.	2	.
Parker, N.H.	**1**	.	.	.	.	.	.	.	.	.	.	1
Parley	**1**	.	.	.	.	.	.	.	1	.	.	.
Parr	**1**	1	.	.	.	.	.	.	.	.	.	.
Parry	**19**	6	3	7	.	1	1	.	1	.	.	.
Pate	**1**	.	.	.	.	.	.	.	.	.	1	.
Paulin & Chevalier	**1**	.	.	.	.	1	.	.	.	.	.	.
Pawley	**3**	.	.	.	2	.	.	1	.	.	.	.
Payne	**60**	.	2	4	2	.	12	5	3	14	8	10
Payot, Upham & Co.	**1**	.	.	.	1	.	.	.	.	.	.	.

	Total	'83	'84	'85	'86	'87	'88	'89	'90	'91	'92	'93
Peabody & Co.	**1**	.	1	.	.	.	.	.	.	.	.	.
Pease	**10**	1	.	1	.	3	3	2	.	.	.	.
Pease & Niles	**1**	.	.	.	.	.	.	.	.	.	1	.
Pease Lith.	**2**	.	.	.	.	.	.	.	.	2	.	.
Peck, J.	**2**	.	.	.	.	.	.	.	1	.	.	1
Pedemonte	**1**	.	.	.	.	1	.	.	.	.	.	.
Peeters	**28**	.	.	.	3	23	2	.	.	.	.	.
Pelham	**1**	.	1	.	.	.	.	.	.	.	.	.
Pelton	**2**	.	.	.	.	.	.	.	.	.	1	1
Pendleton	**2**	.	1	.	.	.	.	1	.	.	.	.
Pennsylvania	**2**	.	.	.	1	.	.	1	.	.	.	.
Penn. Historical Society	**1**	.	.	.	.	.	.	.	.	.	1	.
Pennsylvania Magazine	**7**	1	.	1	.	.	.	.	1	.	1	3
Penny Magazine	**1**	.	.	.	.	1	.	.	.	.	.	.
Penny National Atlas	**1**	.	.	.	.	.	.	.	.	.	1	.
People's Atlas	**37**	.	.	1	4	3	8	4	4	8	1	4
Perelle	**3**	.	2	.	.	.	.	.	.	.	.	1
Perkins	**1**	1	.	.	.	.	.	.	.	.	.	.
Perrine	**2**	.	.	.	.	.	.	.	1	.	1	.
Perrot	**3**	.	.	3	.	.	.	.	.	.	.	.
Perry & Spaulding	**2**	.	.	.	.	1	.	.	.	1	.	.
Perthes	**32**	1	2	.	2	2	6	7	9	3	.	.
Petavius	**1**	.	.	.	.	.	.	1	.	.	.	.
Petermann	**22**	1	.	1	1	.	6	3	2	4	.	4
Petri; try Munster	**1**	1	.	.	.	.	.	.	.	.	.	.
Petrini	**45**	1	.	6	17	9	10	1	.	.	1	.
Petroschi	**1**	.	.	1	.	.	.	.	.	.	.	.
Pharus-Verlag	**1**	.	.	.	.	.	.	.	.	.	.	1
Phelan	**1**	.	.	.	.	.	.	.	.	.	1	.
Phelipeau	**7**	.	.	.	.	2	.	1	2	1	1	.
Phelps	**13**	.	.	.	2	1	4	1	2	1	2	.
Phelps & Ensign	**9**	.	.	.	1	.	2	.	5	.	1	.
Phelps & Watson	**7**	.	.	.	1	.	2	.	.	3	.	1
Philip	**124**	3	4	3	54	8	29	9	6	2	6	.
Philip, G.	**16**	.	.	.	.	.	.	.	.	.	.	16
Philippe	**1**	1	.	.	.	.	.	.	.	.	.	.
Phillips	**22**	14	2	.	.	2	1	.	1	.	1	1
Phinn	**1**	.	.	.	1	.	.	.	.	.	.	.
Piale	**1**	.	.	.	.	.	.	.	.	.	1	.
Picart	**1**	.	.	.	.	.	.	.	.	1	.	.
Picquet	**4**	.	2	.	.	2	.	.	.	.	.	.
Pictorial Times	**1**	.	.	.	.	.	.	.	.	.	1	.
Pietro	**1**	.	.	.	.	.	1	.	.	.	.	.
Pigafetta	**2**	1	.	.	1	.	.	.	.	.	.	.
Pigot	**15**	.	1	11	.	.	.	.	.	.	3	.
Pine	**2**	2	.	.	.	.	.	.	.	.	.	.
Pingeling	**2**	1	.	.	1	.	.	.	.	.	.	.
Pinkerton	**61**	6	10	9	3	3	7	3	6	4	10	.
Pinnock	**1**	.	.	1	.	.	.	.	.	.	.	.
Pinnock & Maunder	**2**	.	.	.	.	1	.	.	1	.	.	.
Piquet	**2**	.	.	.	.	.	.	.	.	.	1	1
Pitt	**35**	3	1	8	3	4	3	.	4	2	5	2
Plancius	**19**	2	2	4	1	2	2	1	2	.	1	2
Platen	**1**	.	.	.	.	.	.	.	.	1	.	.
Playfair	**4**	1	.	.	.	1	1	1	.	.	.	.
Plot	**1**	.	.	1	.	.	.	.	.	.	.	.
Pluche	**1**	.	1	.	.	.	.	.	.	.	.	.
Pluth	**2**	.	.	.	1	.	.	.	1	.	.	.
Poirson	**19**	2	4	.	.	2	2	2	2	2	.	3
Political Magazine	**77**	4	32	5	1	1	.	.	7	2	17	8
Pomarede	**1**	.	.	1	.	.	.	.	.	.	.	.
Pomba	**1**	.	.	.	.	1	.	.	.	.	.	.
Pont	**1**	1	.	.	.	.	.	.	.	.	.	.
Pontanus	**1**	.	.	.	.	1	.	.	.	.	.	.
Poole Bros.	**1**	.	.	.	.	.	.	1	.	.	.	.
Poor	**1**	.	.	.	.	.	1	.	.	.	.	.
Popple	**37**	5	4	1	5	5	2	3	4	2	2	4
Porcacchi	**116**	9	14	27	11	8	11	12	6	7	8	3
Porro	**3**	1	.	.	.	.	.	.	.	.	.	2
Port Folio	**1**	.	.	.	.	1	.	.	.	.	.	.
Porter, D.	**1**	.	.	.	.	.	.	.	1	.	.	.
Porter, T.	**1**	.	.	.	.	.	.	.	.	.	.	1
Portlock	**3**	.	2	.	.	.	.	.	1	.	.	.
Postlethwait	**3**	.	.	.	.	.	1	.	2	.	.	.
Pouchot	**2**	.	.	1	.	.	.	.	.	.	1	.
Poussin	**1**	.	.	.	.	.	.	.	.	1	.	.
Powell	**1**	.	.	.	.	1	.	.	.	.	.	.
Pozzi	**1**	.	.	.	.	.	.	.	.	.	1	.
Prang	**8**	.	.	.	.	1	1	5	1	.	.	.
Presdee & Edwards	**2**	.	.	.	.	.	.	.	2	.	.	.
Preuss	**2**	.	.	.	1	1	.	.	.	.	.	.
Prevost d'Exiles; see Bellin	**34**	5	2	4	3	1	2	1	5	5	5	1
Price	**2**	.	1	.	.	.	1	.	.	.	.	.
Price & Senex	**1**	.	.	.	1	.	.	.	.	.	.	.
Price, Senex & Maxwell	**1**	.	.	1	.	.	.	.	.	.	.	.
Prinald	**1**	.	.	.	.	.	.	.	1	.	.	.
Prior	**1**	.	.	1	.	.	.	.	.	.	.	.
Probst	**9**	1	.	.	1	1	.	.	.	4	1	1
Propper	**1**	.	.	.	.	.	.	.	1	.	.	.
Proud	**1**	1	.	.	.	.	.	.	.	.	.	.
Ptolemy; see Munster		.	.	.	.	.	.	.	.	.	.	.
Ptolemy (1478-1508 Rome)	**3**	.	.	.	.	.	2	1	.	.	.	.
Ptolemy (1482 Florence)	**3**	3	.	.	.	.	.	.	.	.	.	.
Ptolemy (1482-86 Ulm)	**17**	2	4	3	2	2	1	2	.	.	1	.
Ptolemy (1511 Venice)	**8**	.	1	3	2	.	.	1	.	1	.	.
Ptolemy (1513-20 Strassburg)	**53**	2	19	4	7	6	3	6	2	.	4	.
Ptolemy (1522-41 Strassburg)	**154**	11	16	18	30	19	24	19	4	6	6	1
Ptolemy (1548 Venice)	**85**	2	27	21	3	7	3	7	2	1	5	7
Ptolemy (1561-99 Venice)	**333**	23	29	69	13	26	17	19	18	16	15	88
Ptolemy (1578-1730 Mercator)	**18**	.	2	2	.	.	1	3	.	7	2	1
Ptolemy (1596-1621 Magini)	**132**	30	37	2	.	16	16	4	3	9	4	11
Purcell	**1**	.	.	.	.	.	.	.	.	.	.	1
Purchas; see Mercator	**16**	1	4	3	2	.	1	1	1	1	1	1
Purdy	**2**	.	.	.	.	1	1	.	.	.	.	.
Quad	**203**	48	6	5	20	12	48	8	27	13	7	9
Quick	**1**	.	.	.	.	.	1	.	.	.	.	.
Radefeld	**29**	6	1	.	5	3	.	1	10	1	1	1
Raignauld	**5**	.	2	1	.	1	.	1	.	.	.	.
Railroad Company Maps; see individual RRs to 1992	**15**	.	.	.	.	.	.	.	.	.	.	15
Railway News	**4**	1	.	.	2	.	1	.	.	.	.	.
Rainaldi	**1**	.	.	1	.	.	.	.	.	.	.	.
Ramble	**27**	.	.	13	5	.	9	.	.	.	.	.
Ramsay	**10**	2	1	3	2	.	.	.	2	.	.	.
Ramsey	**1**	.	.	.	.	.	.	.	.	.	1	.
Ramsey, Milleet & Hudson	**2**	.	.	.	.	.	2	.	.	.	.	.
Ramusio	**100**	9	11	17	6	10	10	8	9	5	9	6
Rand, Avery & Co.	**2**	1	.	.	.	1	.	.	.	.	.	.
Rand, McNally & Co.	**399**	15	7	44	32	30	51	62	42	48	22	46
Ranney	**2**	.	.	.	.	.	.	.	.	2	.	.
Ransom & Doolittle	**2**	.	.	.	.	1	.	.	1	.	.	.
Rapin; see Tindal	**3**	.	.	.	.	.	.	.	.	.	3	.
Rapkin; see Tallis	**2**	.	.	.	.	1	.	.	.	.	.	1
Rasciotti	**1**	.	.	.	1	.	.	.	.	.	.	.
Raspe	**5**	1	.	.	.	.	.	.	1	2	.	1
Ratcliff	**1**	.	.	.	.	.	.	.	.	1	.	.
Ratelband	**10**	.	1	1	.	.	.	.	7	1	.	.
Ratino	**1**	.	.	1	.	.	.	.	.	.	.	.

	Total	'83	'84	'85	'86	'87	'88	'89	'90	'91	'92	'93
Rau	1	.	1	.	.	.	.	.	.	.	.	.
Ravenstein	2	.	.	.	.	.	.	1	.	.	.	1
Rawlings	2	.	1	.	.	.	1	.	.	.	.	.
Raymond	1	.	.	1	.	.	.	.	.	.	.	.
Raynal	13	.	.	.	9	.	.	1	.	2	1	.
Real Estate & Promotional	4	.	.	.	.	.	.	.	.	.	.	4
Ream	1	.	.	.	.	.	.	.	1	.	.	.
Reclus	1	.	.	.	.	.	.	.	.	.	.	1
Rector	3	.	.	2	.	.	1	.	.	.	.	.
Reed	2	1	.	.	.	.	1	.	.	.	.	.
Reed & Barber	3	.	.	.	.	.	.	2	.	.	1	.
Reed Parsons Co.	2	.	.	.	.	.	.	.	.	2	.	.
Reese	1	.	.	.	1	.	.	.	.	.	.	.
Regnier & Cie.	1	.	.	.	.	.	.	1	.	.	.	.
Reichard	12	.	3	1	.	2	2	3	.	.	.	1
Reid	50	.	.	1	8	16	5	2	2	2	7	7
Reilly; see Von Reilly, 1984+.	.	.	.	.	.	.	.	.	.	.	.	.
Reisch	4	.	.	.	.	.	3	1	.	.	.	.
Reland	4	1	.	.	.	1	1	.	.	.	.	1
Remond	1	.	.	.	1	.	.	.	.	.	.	.
Remquet	1	.	.	.	.	1	.	.	.	.	.	.
Remy	1	.	.	.	.	.	.	1	.	.	.	.
Renard	42	7	.	11	1	8	4	1	3	1	3	3
Rennel	1	.	.	.	.	.	.	.	.	.	1	.
Rennell	3	.	.	.	.	.	.	.	.	.	1	2
Renner	20	8	1	.	2	.	1	.	8	.	.	.
Renouard	8	.	.	.	.	.	.	1	6	1	.	.
Retnolds, J.	6	.	.	.	.	.	.	.	.	.	.	6
Reyland	1	.	.	1	.	.	.	.	.	.	.	.
Reynolds	4	.	.	.	.	1	.	1	.	1	.	1
Rhode	1	.	.	.	.	1	.	.	.	.	.	.
Rice	2	.	.	.	.	.	.	.	.	.	1	1
Richardson	3	.	.	.	.	.	.	1	.	.	.	2
Ridge	4	.	.	.	.	1	1	1	1	.	.	.
Riedel	1	1	.	.	.	.	.	.	.	.	.	.
Riegel	40	.	.	.	.	.	.	.	.	40	.	.
Ringgold	2	.	.	.	.	.	.	1	1	.	.	.
Risdon	2	.	.	.	2	.	.	.	.	.	.	.
Ritch	1	.	.	.	1	.	.	.	.	.	.	.
Rizzi-Zannoni	4	.	.	.	.	.	.	1	.	.	2	1
Robbins	1	.	.	.	.	.	.	.	.	1	.	.
Robert de Vaugondy, see De Vaugondy	.	.	.	.	.	.	.	.	.	.	.	.
Robert, A.G.	1	.	.	.	.	.	.	.	1	.	.	.
Roberts	8	1	1	1	.	1	4	.	.	.	.	.
Roberts, H.	1	.	.	.	.	.	.	.	.	.	.	1
Robertson	4	1	.	1	.	.	2	.	.	.	.	.
Robijn	3	.	.	3	.	.	.	.	.	.	.	.
Robinson	126	7	30	10	17	13	11	3	5	17	9	4
Robiquet	2	.	.	.	1	.	.	1	.	.	.	.
Robson	1	1	.	.	.	.	.	.	.	.	.	.
Robyn	2	.	.	.	.	.	.	.	.	.	1	1
Rocky Mountain News Co.	1	.	.	.	.	1	.	.	.	.	.	.
Rocque	45	2	6	15	.	1	16	1	1	1	1	1
Roe Bros.	29	.	.	.	.	.	.	.	.	.	29	.
Rogers	6	.	1	1	.	.	2	.	.	2	.	.
Rogers & Johnston	16	.	.	6	.	1	1	3	3	.	2	.
Rogers, Peet & Co.	2	1	.	.	.	.	1	.	.	.	.	.
Rollandet	2	.	.	.	.	.	.	.	.	2	.	.
Rollinson	2	1	.	1	.	.	.	.	.	.	.	.
Rollos	33	3	5	10	2	2	2	.	1	5	2	1
Romans	1	1	.	.	.	.	.	.	.	.	.	.
Romolo Bulla	1	.	.	.	.	.	.	.	.	.	.	1
Root	1	.	.	.	.	.	.	.	.	1	.	.
Root & Tinker	1	.	.	.	.	.	.	.	.	.	1	.
Rosaccio	14	.	.	9	.	2	1	2	.	.	.	.
Rose & Woolman	10	.	.	.	.	.	.	.	.	.	10	.

	Total	'83	'84	'85	'86	'87	'88	'89	'90	'91	'92	'93
Ross	8	.	1	5	.	.	1	.	.	.	1	.
Rosselin	1	.	.	.	.	.	.	.	.	.	1	.
Rossi	33	3	4	2	3	3	2	1	7	6	.	2
Rossi, L.	1	.	.	.	.	.	.	.	.	.	.	1
Rota	2	.	.	2	.	.	.	.	.	.	.	.
Rouargue	1	1	.	.	.	.	.	.	.	.	.	.
Roussin	2	.	.	.	.	.	1	.	.	.	.	1
Roux	34	2	.	22	1	3	.	2	2	1	1	.
Rowe	1	.	.	.	.	.	.	.	.	.	.	1
Royal Geographic Journal	3	.	.	.	.	.	.	.	.	3	.	.
Royal Geographical Soc.	8	1	1	1	.	.	.	.	1	2	.	2
Royal Magazine	8	.	.	.	4	3	1	.	.	.	.	.
Royce	1	.	.	1	.	.	.	.	.	.	.	.
Rudolphi	5	5	.	.	.	.	.	.	.	.	.	.
Ruggles	2	.	.	.	.	.	.	.	1	.	.	1
Rughesi	1	.	.	.	.	.	.	.	.	1	.	.
Ruscelli; see Ptolemy (1561-1599)	.	.	.	.	.	.	.	.	.	.	.	.
Russel	1	1	.	.	.	.	.	.	.	.	.	.
Russell	115	10	9	15	15	7	21	5	12	11	3	7
Russo	3	.	.	.	.	.	2	.	1	.	.	.
Ruysch	1	.	.	.	.	.	.	1	.	.	.	.
S.D.U.K.; see Society for the Diffusion of Useful Knowledge	.	.	.	.	.	.	.	.	.	.	.	.
Sachse & Co.	1	.	.	.	.	1	.	.	.	.	.	.
Sackersdorff	1	.	.	.	.	.	.	.	.	1	.	.
Sacrobosco	2	.	.	.	.	.	.	.	.	2	.	.
Salamanca	1	.	.	.	.	1	.	.	.	.	.	.
Salmon	3	.	.	.	.	.	1	.	1	1	.	.
Sampson, Davenport & Co.	1	.	.	.	.	.	.	.	1	.	.	.
Sanderus	7	.	.	.	.	.	7	.	.	.	.	.
Sands	24	.	.	.	.	.	.	.	24	.	.	.
Sandys	1	.	.	1	.	.	.	.	.	.	.	.
Sanford & Everts	3	.	.	.	.	.	.	.	2	.	1	.
Sanford & Goodhue	1	.	.	.	.	.	.	.	1	.	.	.
Sanson:	610	57	38	43	.	.	.	.	.	.	.	.
(folio) see Mortier	.	.	.	.	22	23	21	31	13	21	55	12
(small)	.	.	.	.	106	75	38	11	6	7	7	24
Santini	83	21	12	11	4	8	4	6	1	10	3	3
Sanuto	1	.	.	.	.	.	.	.	.	.	1	.
Sarony & Major	2	.	.	.	.	.	.	.	2	.	.	.
Sarony Lith.	2	.	.	.	1	1	.	.	.	.	.	.
Sarony, Major & Knapp	2	.	.	.	.	.	1	.	.	1	.	.
Sartine	8	.	.	.	.	2	1	3	.	1	.	1
Saunders	1	.	.	.	.	.	.	.	1	.	.	.
Sauthier	2	.	.	.	.	.	1	.	.	.	.	1
Saxton	87	9	.	27	16	5	3	.	27	.	.	.
Sayer & Bennett	221	13	8	15	15	65	19	16	12	22	12	24
Sayer & Jefferys	1	.	.	.	.	.	.	.	.	1	.	.
Sayer; see Jefferys	85	9	3	8	8	6	11	16	3	8	5	8
Schaus	1	.	.	.	.	.	.	.	.	.	1	.
Schedel	46	6	3	8	4	5	4	6	3	2	3	2
Schenk	139	12	42	19	10	17	2	8	15	2	9	3
Scherer	102	7	22	39	2	1	4	.	1	9	2	15
Schleuen	1	.	.	1	.	.	.	.	.	.	.	.
Schley; see Van der Schley	.	.	.	.	.	.	.	.	.	.	.	.
Schlieben	3	.	.	.	.	.	1	2	.	.	.	.
Schmidt	4	2	.	.	1	.	1	.	.	.	.	.
Schomburgk	5	.	2	1	.	.	.	1	.	.	1	.
Schonberg	5	.	1	.	.	.	2	.	.	2	.	.
Schoolcraft	19	.	1	.	6	1	2	5	1	.	1	2
Schott	1	.	.	.	.	1	.	.	.	.	.	.
Schouten	6	2	1	.	1	1	.	.	1	.	.	.
Schrader	1	.	1	.	.	.	.	.	.	.	.	.
Schraembl	11	.	1	.	3	.	1	.	.	1	4	1
Schreiber	8	1	.	1	.	.	.	1	3	.	1	1

	Total	'83	'84	'85	'86	'87	'88	'89	'90	'91	'92	'93
Schropp & Co.	**1**	.	.	.	.	.	.	.	.	.	.	1
Schroter	**2**	.	.	.	.	.	.	.	1	.	.	1
Schwabe	**1**	.	.	.	1	.	.	.	.	.	.	.
Science	**1**	.	.	.	.	1	.	.	.	.	.	.
Scobie	**1**	.	.	1	.	.	.	.	.	.	.	.
Scots Magazine	**14**	1	3	.	.	.	3	1	4	1	1	.
Scott	**64**	2	13	1	23	1	6	2	1	1	.	14
Scott, E.	**1**	.	.	.	1	.	.	.	.	.	.	.
Scull & Heap	**4**	.	.	1	1	.	1	1	.	.	.	.
Seale	**34**	5	6	2	3	3	3	3	2	4	1	2
Seaton	**1**	.	.	.	.	.	.	.	.	.	1	.
Seile	**5**	2	.	1	.	.	.	.	.	1	1	.
Selden & Johnson	**1**	.	.	.	.	1	.	.	.	.	.	.
Seligman	**1**	.	.	.	.	.	.	1	.	.	.	.
Seligmann	**4**	.	1	.	.	2	.	.	.	.	1	.
Seller	**106**	3	61	8	3	4	10	10	.	3	2	2
Sellwood Real Estate Co.	**1**	.	.	.	.	.	.	1	.	.	.	.
Senex	**173**	4	13	11	45	30	26	16	8	6	4	10
Serres	**1**	1	.	.	.	.	.	.	.	.	.	.
Seutter	**278**	.	.	.	.	.	.	.	.	.	.	.
Seutter (large)	.	34	16	16	16	41	15	52	24	19	1	12
Seutter (small)	.	.	.	.	.	.	.	.	.	.	31	1
Shaffner	**2**	.	.	.	.	.	.	.	2	.	.	.
Shannon	**4**	.	.	.	.	.	1	3	.	.	.	.
Sharp	**1**	.	.	.	.	.	.	.	.	.	1	.
Sharpe	**2**	.	.	.	.	.	.	.	1	.	.	1
Shattuck	**1**	.	.	.	.	1	.	.	.	.	.	.
Shaw	**1**	.	.	.	.	.	.	1	.	.	.	.
Sheafer	**2**	.	.	.	.	.	1	.	1	.	.	.
Shearer	**1**	.	.	.	.	.	.	.	.	.	1	.
Shelton & Kensett	**2**	.	.	.	.	.	1	.	.	.	1	.
Sherman & Smith	**5**	.	.	2	.	.	1	1	.	.	1	.
Sherwood & Jones	**2**	.	.	.	.	.	.	2	.	.	.	.
Sherwood, Neely & Jones	**1**	.	.	.	.	.	.	.	1	.	.	.
Shober	**1**	.	.	.	.	1	.	.	.	.	.	.
Shober & Carqueville Lith.	**2**	.	.	.	.	.	1	.	.	.	1	.
Shobere	**1**	.	.	1	.	.	.	.	.	.	.	.
Sidman	**1**	.	.	.	1	.	.	.	.	.	.	.
Sifton, Praed	**1**	.	.	.	.	.	.	.	1	.	.	.
Silver	**3**	.	1	.	.	.	1	.	.	.	1	.
Silvestre	**1**	.	1	.	.	.	.	.	.	.	.	.
Simonin & Hansen	**1**	.	.	.	.	.	.	.	.	.	1	.
Simons	**1**	.	1	.	.	.	.	.	.	.	.	.
Simplot	**1**	.	.	.	.	.	.	.	.	1	.	.
Sinclair Lith.	**2**	.	.	.	2	.	.	.	.	.	.	.
Skelton	**1**	.	.	1	.	.	.	.	.	.	.	.
Skinner	**1**	.	.	.	.	.	.	.	1	.	.	.
Slator	**1**	.	.	.	.	.	.	.	.	1	.	.
Slatter	**1**	1	.	.	.	.	.	.	.	.	.	.
Smillie	**2**	1	.	.	.	.	1	.	.	.	.	.
Smith	**93**	12	13	6	5	9	5	8	21	4	10	.
Smith & Jones	**1**	.	.	.	.	.	.	1	.	.	.	.
Smith, Asa	**5**	.	.	.	5	.	.	.	.	.	.	.
Smith, C.	**11**	.	.	.	.	.	.	.	.	1	.	10
Smith, Fern & Co.	**1**	.	.	.	.	.	.	.	.	1	.	.
Smith, J.	**1**	.	.	.	.	.	.	.	.	.	.	1
Smith, John	**4**	.	.	.	.	1	.	2	.	.	.	1
Smith, Mason & Co.	**1**	.	.	.	.	.	1	.	.	.	.	.
Smith, Roswell C.	**2**	.	.	.	.	.	.	.	.	1	.	1
Smith, W. H.	**2**	.	.	.	.	.	.	.	.	.	.	2
Smollett	**2**	.	1	.	.	.	1	.	.	.	.	.
Smyth	**4**	.	3	.	.	1	.	.	.	.	.	.
Snow & Co.	**1**	.	.	1	.	.	.	.	.	.	.	.
Snyder & Black Lith.	**1**	.	.	.	1	.	.	.	.	.	.	.
Snyder, Van Vechten & Co.	**1**	.	.	.	.	.	.	.	.	.	1	.
Society for Anti-Gallicians	**1**	.	.	.	.	.	.	.	.	.	.	1

	Total	'83	'84	'85	'86	'87	'88	'89	'90	'91	'92	'93
Society for the Diffusion of Useful Knowledge	**650**	45	25	44	39	34	120	62	41	64	92	84
Society for the Promotion of Christian Knowledge	**2**	.	.	1	.	.	.	.	.	1	.	.
Society for the Propagation of the Gospel	**2**	.	.	.	2	.	.	.	.	.	.	.
Solinus	**7**	1	1	.	1	.	1	.	.	.	2	1
Sotzmann, D.H.	**1**	.	.	.	.	.	.	.	.	.	.	1
Soulavie	**1**	.	.	.	.	1	.	.	.	.	.	.
Soules	**1**	1	.	.	.	.	.	.	.	.	.	.
Southern Pacific Co.	**3**	.	.	.	1	1	1	.	.	.	.	.
Spanish Admiralty, see Direccion de Hidrografia	.	.	.	.	.	.	.	.	.	.	.	.
Spaulding	**1**	.	.	.	.	1	.	.	.	.	.	.
Specht	**1**	.	.	1	.	.	.	.	.	.	.	.
Speed	**843**	70	202	103	166	119	29	9	14	94	15	22
Speer	**3**	.	1	.	.	.	.	1	.	.	1	.
Spilsbury	**1**	.	.	.	.	.	.	.	.	1	.	.
Spirinx	**1**	.	.	1	.	.	.	.	.	.	.	.
Sprange	**1**	.	.	1	.	.	.	.	.	.	.	.
Sproule	**1**	.	.	.	.	.	.	.	.	.	.	1
St. Aubin Lith.	**1**	.	.	.	.	.	.	1	.	.	.	.
St. Louis Republican	**1**	.	.	.	.	.	.	.	.	.	.	1
St. Louis, Iron Mountain & Southern R.R.	**1**	.	.	.	.	.	.	.	.	1	.	.
Stackhouse	**15**	4	.	1	1	3	.	1	1	2	.	2
Staelin	**1**	1	.	.	.	.	.	.	.	.	.	.
Stalker	**1**	.	.	.	1	.	.	.	.	.	.	.
Standard Atlas	**16**	.	.	.	.	.	.	.	.	11	.	5
Stanford; see S.D.U.K.	**108**	3	4	10	3	5	10	6	4	9	11	43
Stannard & Son	**1**	.	.	.	.	.	.	.	.	.	1	.
Stansbury	**1**	.	.	.	1	.	.	.	.	.	.	.
Stansby, Keily & Rea	**1**	.	.	.	.	.	.	.	.	.	1	.
Starckman	**2**	.	.	2	.	.	.	.	.	.	.	.
Starling	**21**	3	.	9	1	.	.	2	1	.	4	1
Staveley	**1**	.	.	.	.	.	.	.	.	.	1	.
Staveley & Wood	**1**	1	.	.	.	.	.	.	.	.	.	.
Stearns & Hitchcock	**1**	.	.	.	.	.	.	1	.	.	.	.
Stebbins, H.	**6**	.	.	.	.	.	1	.	.	.	1	4
Stedman	**70**	4	11	2	7	5	6	.	3	3	14	15
Stennett	**1**	.	.	.	.	.	1	.	.	.	.	.
Stent	**2**	.	.	1	.	.	.	1	.	.	.	.
Stetter	**1**	.	.	.	.	.	.	.	1	.	.	.
Steudner	**1**	.	1	.	.	.	.	.	.	.	.	.
Stevens	**3**	.	3	.	.	.	.	.	.	.	.	.
Stewart	**1**	.	.	.	1	.	.	.	.	.	.	.
Stieler	**61**	.	.	.	8	6	7	7	18	7	3	5
Stiger & Co.	**1**	.	.	.	.	.	.	.	.	.	.	1
Stockdale; see Morse	**53**	7	9	6	6	3	3	2	3	7	1	6
Stocklein	**1**	1	.	.	.	.	.	.	.	.	.	.
Stoddard	**2**	.	.	.	.	.	.	.	1	.	1	.
Stone & Pomeroy	**1**	.	.	.	.	.	.	.	.	.	1	.
Stoner	**4**	.	.	.	.	.	.	1	.	1	2	.
Stoopendaal	**16**	3	.	4	1	1	1	.	2	1	2	1
Stopius	**1**	.	1	.	.	.	.	.	.	.	.	.
Stouf	**1**	.	.	.	.	.	.	1	.	.	.	.
Stow	**23**	.	.	23	.	.	.	.	.	.	.	.
Strabo	**1**	.	.	.	.	.	.	.	.	.	.	1
Strada	**6**	.	.	1	2	2	.	.	.	.	.	1
Strahan & Cadell	**1**	.	.	.	.	1	.	.	.	.	.	.
Stratford	**2**	.	.	2	.	.	.	.	.	.	.	.
Streit	**2**	.	.	.	.	1	.	.	1	.	.	.
Striedbeck	**1**	.	.	1	.	.	.	.	.	.	.	.
Strobridge & Co.	**1**	.	1	.	.	.	.	.	.	.	.	.
Strong	**1**	.	.	.	.	.	.	.	1	.	.	.
Strype	**11**	.	.	6	.	.	.	.	.	.	.	5

	Total	'83	'84	'85	'86	'87	'88	'89	'90	'91	'92	'93
Stuart	**2**	.	1	.	.	.	.	1	.	.	.	.
Stucchi	**1**	.	.	.	.	.	.	.	.	.	.	1
Studer	**1**	.	.	.	.	.	.	1	.	.	.	.
Studley	**1**	.	.	.	.	.	.	1	.	.	.	.
Stukeley	**1**	.	.	1	.	.	.	.	.	.	.	.
Stukely	**1**	.	.	.	.	.	1	.	.	.	.	.
Stulpnagel; see+	.	.	.	.	.	.	.	.	.	.	.	.
Von Stulpnagel, 1987												
Stumpf	**7**	.	.	.	.	.	1	.	.	5	.	1
Sudlow	**4**	.	2	1	.	1	.	.	.	.	.	.
Suhr	**2**	1	.	.	1	.	.	.	.	.	.	.
Sumner	**5**	.	.	.	.	1	1	1	.	2	.	.
Sumner & Co.	**1**	.	.	.	1	.	.	.	.	.	.	.
Swallow	**1**	.	.	.	.	.	.	1	.	.	.	.
Swanston	**17**	.	.	.	.	5	2	1	1	1	1	6
Sweden	**1**	.	.	.	.	.	.	.	.	1	.	.
Sweet	**1**	.	.	.	.	.	1	.	.	.	.	.
Sweny, M.A.	**2**	.	.	.	.	.	.	1	.	.	.	1
Swinton	**43**	13	8	8	2	.	5	3	1	3	.	.
Synd	**1**	.	.	1	.	.	.	.	.	.	.	.
Tackabury	**5**	.	.	5	.	.	.	.	.	.	.	.
Taintor	**1**	.	.	.	.	.	.	.	1	.	.	.
Taintor & Merrill	**9**	.	.	.	3	3	1	1	.	1	.	.
Taintor Bros.	**2**	.	.	.	.	.	1	.	.	.	1	.
Taintor Bros. & Merrill	**1**	.	.	.	.	.	.	.	.	.	1	.
Talbot	**4**	.	.	.	1	.	.	.	2	.	.	1
Tallis	**687**	47	155	61	65	64	80	18	11	66	105	15
Tanner	**284**	11	25	13	6	24	27	42	30	29	44	33
Tardieu	**71**	9	2	4	6	4	9	12	5	8	6	6
Tarleton	**5**	.	1	.	.	.	.	2	1	.	1	.
Tassin	**1**	.	1	.	.	.	.	.	.	.	.	.
Taunton	**2**	.	.	.	.	.	.	1	.	.	.	1
Tavernier	**10**	.	2	1	2	1	1	.	.	1	1	1
Taylor	**14**	.	.	8	6	.	.	.	.	.	.	.
Taylor, D.	**1**	.	.	.	.	1	.	.	.	.	.	.
Taylor, T.	**2**	.	.	.	1	.	.	.	.	.	.	1
Teesdale; see Dower	**62**	10	13	11	3	10	5	2	3	2	2	1
Tegg	**11**	.	5	.	.	1	1	1	2	.	1	.
Teubet & Burty	**1**	.	.	.	.	1	.	.	.	.	.	.
Texas	**2**	.	.	.	.	.	.	2	.	.	.	.
Texas & Pacific Rwy.	**2**	.	.	.	.	.	.	1	.	1	.	.
Thackara & Vallance	**1**	.	.	.	.	.	1	.	.	.	.	.
Thacker	**1**	.	.	.	.	.	.	.	.	.	1	.
Thaxter	**2**	.	.	.	.	.	1	.	.	1	.	.
Thayer	**9**	.	.	.	.	1	2	.	3	3	.	.
Thayer, Bridgman	**2**	.	.	.	.	.	1	.	.	.	1	.
& Fanning												
Thayer, Horace & Co.	**1**	.	.	.	1	.	.	.	.	.	.	.
Theakston	**1**	.	.	.	.	1	.	.	.	.	.	.
Thesaurus Geographicus;	**9**	.	.	.	5	4	.	.	.	.	.	.
see Moll												
Thevenot	**12**	1	.	.	2	1	3	2	.	2	1	.
Thevet	**4**	.	.	1	1	.	.	1	.	1	.	.
Thierry	**4**	1	.	.	.	.	3	.	.	.	.	.
Thissel	**1**	.	.	.	.	.	.	.	.	1	.	.
Thomas & Andrews	**2**	.	.	.	.	.	.	1	.	.	1	.
Thomas, Cowperthwait	**380**	10	51	25	14	5	16	66	71	69	34	19
Thompson	**5**	.	.	1	.	.	2	2	.	.	.	.
Thompson & Everts	**1**	.	.	.	.	.	.	.	.	.	1	.
Thompson Bros. & Burr	**1**	1	.	.	.	.	.	.	.	.	.	.
Thomson	**407**	56	30	71	26	29	23	19	62	22	54	15
Thornton	**18**	1	3	3	1	1	1	1	1	3	2	1
Thrall	**2**	.	.	.	.	.	.	1	.	1	.	.
Throop	**3**	.	.	.	.	.	.	.	1	1	.	1
Tilden	**1**	.	.	.	.	1	.	.	.	.	.	.
Tilgmann, F.	**1**	.	.	.	.	.	.	.	.	.	.	1

	Total	'83	'84	'85	'86	'87	'88	'89	'90	'91	'92	'93
Tindal	**43**	7	16	5	2	.	9	4	.	.	.	.
Tirinus	**3**	.	.	1	1	.	.	.	.	.	.	1
Tirion; see Albrizzi	**236**	21	13	14	38	64	11	6	32	11	14	12
Titsingh	**1**	.	.	.	.	.	.	.	.	1	.	.
Tombleson	**1**	1	.	.	.	.	.	.	.	.	.	.
Toms	**8**	.	1	1	1	2	1	.	.	.	1	1
Topham	**1**	1	.	.	.	.	.	.	.	.	.	.
Torbett	**2**	.	2	.	.	.	.	.	.	.	.	.
Torniello	**9**	1	1	1	1	1	3	.	.	.	.	1
Torrente	**1**	.	1	.	.	.	.	.	.	.	.	.
Toudy	**1**	1	.	.	.	.	.	.	.	.	.	.
Toussaint	**1**	.	.	.	.	.	.	.	.	.	.	1
Town & Country Mag.	**1**	.	.	.	.	.	.	.	1	.	.	.
Tramezini	**3**	.	2	1	.	.	.	.	.	.	.	.
Tremaine	**2**	.	1	.	1	.	.	.	.	.	.	.
Treuttel	**1**	.	.	.	.	.	.	.	1	.	.	.
Trine & Hills	**1**	.	.	.	.	.	.	.	.	1	.	.
Troncoso	**1**	.	.	.	.	.	.	.	.	1	.	.
Trusler	**7**	1	.	1	3	.	.	1	1	.	.	.
Trutch	**1**	.	1	.	.	.	.	.	.	.	.	.
Truxton	**1**	.	.	.	.	.	.	.	.	.	1	.
Tschesky	**2**	.	.	.	.	2	.	.	.	.	.	.
Tunison	**14**	.	1	1	.	1	.	.	1	4	3	3
Turner	**1**	1	.	.	.	.	.	.	.	.	.	.
Tyson	**2**	.	1	.	.	.	.	.	.	.	1	.
US	**1103**	1	90	36	59	152	130	168	147	138	95	87
US Coast & Geodetic Survey	**9**	.	.	.	.	.	.	.	.	.	9	.
US Coast Survey	**712**	19	37	14	76	145	60	142	29	116	43	31
US Exploring Expedition	**24**	.	1	4	2	1	2	6	2	2	1	3
US Geological Survey	**13**	2	.	.	.	.	.	2	.	.	2	7
US Pacific RR Survey	**105**	.	.	.	.	.	66	6	10	6	5	12
US State Surveys;	**252**	11	.	.	.	.	64	68	32	18	18	41
see U.S. D.O.I., 1983												
U.S. War Department	**73**	2	.	.	.	.	.	.	.	.	.	71
Ulloa	**2**	.	.	.	.	.	.	.	.	1	.	1
Union Pacific R.R.	**1**	.	.	.	.	.	.	1	.	.	.	.
Universal Magazine	**80**	2	17	10	3	10	8	6	12	4	1	7
Universal Museum Mag.	**4**	.	.	1	1	.	1	1	.	.	.	.
Universal Traveller	**1**	.	.	1	.	.	.	.	.	.	.	.
Valdes	**1**	.	.	.	.	.	1	.	.	.	.	.
Valdor	**1**	.	1	.	.	.	.	.	.	.	.	.
Valegio & Diono	**1**	.	.	1	.	.	.	.	.	.	.	.
Valentine's Manual	**5**	1	1	.	1	.	.	.	.	1	1	.
Valentyn	**19**	1	2	2	1	2	1	1	5	.	1	3
Valeso	**3**	.	.	3	.	.	.	.	.	.	.	.
Valk	**54**	14	2	21	3	2	1	2	2	2	.	5
Valk & Schenk	**44**	9	10	11	3	1	1	3	.	1	3	2
Vallance	**1**	.	.	.	1	.	.	.	.	.	.	.
Van Adrichem	**3**	.	1	1	.	.	.	.	1	.	.	.
Van Alphen	**1**	.	.	.	.	1	.	.	.	.	.	.
Van Baarsel	**5**	.	.	.	.	.	2	.	1	1	1	.
Van Call	**1**	.	.	.	1	.	.	.	.	.	.	.
Van den Hoeye	**1**	.	1	.	.	.	.	.	.	.	.	.
Van den Keere	**122**	15	32	51	3	1	3	4	.	1	7	5
Van der Aa	**208**	17	13	24	26	24	20	22	10	13	18	21
Van der Hagen	**1**	.	1	.	.	.	.	.	.	.	.	.
Van der Schley;	**11**	6	.	.	.	1	.	.	2	1	.	1
see Schley, 1983												
Van Doetecum	**2**	1	1	.	.	.	.	.	.	.	.	.
Van Geelkerken	**7**	.	.	.	.	2	1	1	1	1	.	1
Van Harreveldt & Changuion	**2**	.	.	2	.	.	.	.	.	.	.	.
Van Jagen	**2**	.	.	1	.	1	.	.	.	.	.	.
Van Keulen	**251**	10	12	21	14	43	33	22	8	17	40	31
Van Linschoten;	**65**	7	4	10	8	2	3	3	6	9	7	6
see Linschoten, to 1985												

	Total	'83	'84	'85	'86	'87	'88	'89	'90	'91	'92	'93
Van Lochom	**13**	3	1	6	.	.	.	.	.	.	.	3
Van Loon	**7**	.	3	.	.	1	.	.	.	.	1	2
Van Meurs	**7**	.	.	2	.	.	1	1	1	1	1	.
Van Schagen	**1**	.	.	.	.	.	.	1	.	.	.	.
Van Schoel	**3**	.	.	.	.	.	.	1	.	1	1	.
Van Spilbergen; see Spilbergen, 1984	**3**	.	1	.	.	.	.	.	2	.	.	.
Van Zouteveen	**1**	.	.	.	.	.	.	.	.	.	.	1
Vancouver	**33**	.	3	4	7	3	4	4	2	.	.	6
Vandermaelen	**258**	10	8	7	98	15	27	16	5	54	4	14
Varela y Ulloa	**2**	.	1	.	.	.	.	.	1	.	.	.
Varle	**3**	.	1	.	1	.	1	.	.	.	.	.
Varte	**1**	1	.	.	.	.	.	.	.	.	.	.
Vascellini	**1**	1	.	.	.	.	.	.	.	.	.	.
Vaughan	**1**	.	.	.	.	.	.	.	.	.	1	.
Vaugondy; see De Vaugondy	.	.	.	.	.	.	.	.	.	.	.	.
Velten	**5**	.	.	.	.	2	2	.	.	.	.	1
Venegas	**1**	.	.	.	.	.	.	.	.	1	.	.
Verbiest	**1**	.	1	.	.	.	.	.	.	.	.	.
Verdun de la Crenne, Borda & Pingre	**1**	.	.	.	1	.	.	.	.	.	.	.
Verleger	**2**	.	.	.	.	.	2	.	.	.	.	.
Vertue	**2**	.	.	.	.	1	.	1	.	.	.	.
Villalpando	**4**	.	.	.	.	.	.	2	.	1	1	.
Villamena	**1**	.	.	1	.	.	.	.	.	.	.	.
Villedieu	**1**	.	.	.	.	.	.	.	.	.	.	1
Vincendon-Dumoulin; see Depot de la Marine	**6**	.	.	.	.	.	.	.	2	2	2	.
Vincent	**3**	.	.	.	2	1	.	.	.	.	.	.
Vincent, Brooks, Day & Son	**11**	.	.	.	.	.	.	.	11	.	.	.
Virtue	**24**	.	4	4	2	4	3	2	3	1	1	.
Virtue, Yorston & Co.	**11**	.	.	.	.	.	11	.	.	.	.	.
Visscher; see Schenk *et al*	**348**	61	38	42	54	59	33	7	11	12	11	20
Vivien	**23**	1	1	.	.	1	.	1	15	2	1	1
Vliet	**1**	.	.	.	.	.	.	.	.	1	.	.
Von Breydenbach	**2**	.	.	.	.	.	.	.	.	.	2	.
Von de Sandrart	**1**	.	.	1	.	.	.	.	.	.	.	.
Von der Hayden	**1**	.	.	.	.	.	1	.	.	.	.	.
Von Euler	**13**	.	.	.	.	.	.	4	.	.	7	2
Von Humboldt; see Humboldt, 1984	**14**	.	3	.	.	1	4	.	2	3	1	.
Von Kotzebue	**2**	.	.	.	.	.	1	.	.	.	.	1
Von Mechel	**1**	.	.	.	.	.	1	.	.	.	.	.
Von Pufendorf	**5**	.	.	.	.	1	1	2	.	1	.	.
Von Reilly; see Reillly, 1983	**57**	34	1	3	10	.	.	.	7	.	.	2
Von Schlieben	**2**	.	.	.	.	.	.	.	.	1	.	1
Von Spener	**1**	.	.	.	.	.	.	1	.	.	.	.
Von Staehlin; see Staelin, 1983	.	.	.	.	.	.	.	.	.	.	.	.
Von Stulpnagel; see Stulpnagel, to 1986	**11**	1	.	1	2	.	3	.	.	1	.	3
Vose	**2**	.	.	.	.	.	.	.	1	1	.	.
Vouillemont	**2**	.	.	.	.	.	.	.	1	.	1	.
Vrients	**5**	.	3	.	.	.	1	.	.	.	.	1
Vuillemin	**16**	1	.	.	.	.	.	1	1	5	4	4
Wade	**1**	.	.	1	.	.	.	.	.	.	.	.
Wadsworth, Unwin & Browne	**2**	.	.	.	.	.	.	.	2	.	.	.
Waghenaer	**59**	24	4	6	6	3	2	2	3	1	4	4
Wagner & McGuigan	**1**	.	1	.	.	.	.	.	.	.	.	.
Wahl	**2**	.	.	.	.	.	.	2	.	.	.	.
Waite	**37**	.	.	.	3	3	9	6	7	2	.	7
Wakefield	**1**	1	.	.	.	.	.	.	.	.	.	.
Walch	**3**	1	1	.	.	.	.	.	.	.	.	1
Waldseemuller	**1**	.	.	.	.	.	.	.	.	.	.	1
Wales	**2**	1	.	.	.	.	.	.	.	.	.	1
Walker	**57**	6	6	6	12	6	3	4	1	3	10	.

	Total	'83	'84	'85	'86	'87	'88	'89	'90	'91	'92	'93
Walker & Miles	**33**	.	.	.	3	2	7	13	4	1	1	2
Walker, G.	**3**	.	.	.	.	.	.	.	.	.	.	3
Walker, J. & C.	**1**	.	.	.	.	.	.	.	.	.	.	1
Wall	**1**	1	.	.	.	.	.	.	.	.	.	.
Walling	**37**	.	.	.	1	.	19	.	3	.	6	8
Walling & Gray	**14**	.	1	2	.	1	1	1	3	.	1	4
Walling, Tackabury & Co.	**3**	.	1	.	.	.	.	2	.	.	.	.
Wallis	**14**	.	.	.	7	2	.	1	1	.	1	2
Wallis & Reid	**17**	.	17	.	.	.	.	.	.	.	.	.
Walsh	**2**	.	.	.	.	.	1	.	.	1	.	.
Walter	**3**	.	.	.	.	.	3	.	.	.	.	.
Walther	**1**	1	.	.	.	.	.	.	.	.	.	.
Walton	**6**	.	.	1	1	1	.	.	1	.	.	2
Wangersheim	**6**	.	.	2	2	1	.	.	.	1	.	.
Warburton	**4**	1	.	3	.	.	.	.	.	.	.	.
Ward	**5**	3	.	1	.	.	.	.	.	.	1	.
Warden	**2**	1	.	.	.	.	.	.	.	1	.	.
Ware	**3**	.	.	.	1	.	1	.	.	1	.	.
Warner & Beers	**10**	.	.	1	1	1	2	2	.	1	1	1
Warner & Hanna	**1**	.	.	.	.	.	.	1	.	.	.	.
Warner & Higgins	**1**	.	.	.	.	.	.	.	.	1	.	.
Warner, B.	**2**	.	.	.	.	.	.	.	.	.	1	1
Warner, Higgins & Beers	**2**	.	.	.	2	.	.	.	.	.	.	.
Warren	**1**	.	.	.	.	.	.	.	.	1	.	.
Waterlow	**1**	.	.	.	.	1	.	.	.	.	.	.
Watson	**35**	.	1	.	6	5	5	5	3	4	3	3
Watts	**1**	.	.	1	.	.	.	.	.	.	.	.
Waud	**3**	.	.	.	.	1	.	.	1	1	.	.
Weale	**2**	.	.	.	.	.	.	.	1	.	.	1
Weaver, H.	**1**	.	.	.	.	.	.	.	.	.	.	1
Weber	**4**	1	.	.	.	.	1	.	1	.	1	.
Weed	**2**	.	.	.	.	2	.	.	.	.	.	.
Weekly Dispatch; see Dower, Ettling, Lowry, Weller	**40**	.	.	7	1	2	9	3	8	5	2	3
Weekly Herald	**1**	.	.	.	.	.	.	.	.	.	1	.
Weigel	**29**	4	4	.	.	6	1	2	8	1	2	1
Weiland	**5**	.	.	.	1	.	.	1	2	.	1	.
Weimar Geographisches Institut	**41**	.	5	3	3	.	1	2	3	2	.	22
Weis	**1**	.	.	.	.	.	.	.	1	.	.	.
Weiss	**1**	.	.	.	.	.	.	.	.	.	1	.
Weld, I.	**11**	.	1	4	1	1	1	.	.	2	.	1
Weller; see Weekly Dispatch	**57**	7	11	14	4	4	3	4	1	2	3	4
Wellge	**1**	.	.	.	.	.	.	1	.	.	.	.
Wells	**114**	22	4	14	25	9	6	9	4	8	7	6
Wells & Rowley	**1**	.	.	.	.	1	.	.	.	.	.	.
Wells, J.	**6**	.	.	.	1	.	4	.	1	.	.	.
Wells, J.G.	**1**	.	.	.	.	.	.	.	1	.	.	.
Werner	**8**	.	2	1	.	1	1	2	1	.	.	.
Wescoatt	**1**	.	.	.	.	1	.	.	.	.	.	.
West Shore	**7**	.	1	5	.	.	.	1	.	.	.	.
Wetstein	**2**	.	.	.	.	.	.	.	1	.	.	1
Weygand	**2**	.	.	.	.	.	2	.	.	.	.	.
Whitchurch, W.	**1**	.	.	.	.	.	.	.	.	.	.	1
White	**3**	.	.	1	.	.	.	.	.	.	2	.
Whitefield	**1**	.	.	.	.	.	.	.	.	.	1	.
Whitney	**6**	.	.	.	.	.	1	3	.	1	1	.
Whitney & Standish	**1**	.	.	.	.	.	.	.	1	.	.	.
Whittaker	**1**	.	.	1	.	.	.	.	.	.	.	.
Whymper	**4**	.	2	1	.	1	.	.	.	.	.	.
Wiggin	**2**	.	.	.	.	.	1	.	1	.	.	.
Wight	**1**	.	.	.	.	.	1	.	.	.	.	.
Wightman, T.	**1**	.	.	.	.	.	.	.	.	.	.	1
Wilcocke	**2**	.	1	.	.	1	.	.	.	.	.	.
Wild	**1**	.	1	.	.	.	.	.	.	.	.	.
Wilgus	**1**	.	.	.	.	.	.	.	.	1	.	.
Wilkes	**15**	1	8	.	1	1	.	.	1	1	1	1

	Total	'83	'84	'85	'86	'87	'88	'89	'90	'91	'92	'93
Wilkie	5	.	.	.	.	4	1	.	.	.	.	.
Wilkinson	83	6	1	4	2	3	4	5	10	34	9	5
Willard	2	.	.	.	.	.	1	.	.	.	1	.
Willdey	16	4	1	5	1	.	1	2	.	.	.	2
Willemsz	1	.	.	1	.	.	.	.	.	.	.	.
Williams	21	.	2	4	1	4	4	.	2	3	1	.
Williams, C.S.	9	.	.	.	.	.	3	1	3	1	.	1
Williams, W.	9	.	.	.	1	1	2	.	2	.	1	2
Williamson	2	.	2	.	.	.	.	.	.	.	.	.
Willis	1	1	.	.	.	.	.	.	.	.	.	.
Willmann	3	1	.	.	.	1	.	.	.	1	.	.
Willyams, C.	1	.	.	.	.	.	.	.	.	.	.	1
Wilmore	2	.	.	.	.	.	.	.	.	.	1	1
Wilson	20	2	.	2	1	1	1	4	2	.	3	4
Wilson, James	6	.	.	6	.	.	.	.	.	.	.	.
Winchell	1	.	.	.	.	.	.	.	.	1	.	.
Winkelmanns Chronik	2	1	.	.	1	.	.	.	.	.	.	.
Winslow	1	1	.	.	.	.	.	.	.	.	.	.
Winterbotham	8	.	.	2	.	.	1	.	1	1	1	2
Wislizenus, A.	1	.	.	.	.	.	.	.	.	.	.	1
Witsen	1	1	.	.	.	.	.	.	.	.	.	.
Witter	1	.	.	1	.	.	.	.	.	.	.	.
Wolff	2	.	1	1	.	.	.	.	.	.	.	.
Wood	1	.	.	.	.	.	.	.	.	.	1	.
Wood, William	1	.	.	.	.	.	.	1	.	.	.	.
Woodbridge	8	.	5	.	.	.	.	.	2	.	.	1

	Total	'83	'84	'85	'86	'87	'88	'89	'90	'91	'92	'93
Woodford	3	.	.	.	.	1	.	.	2	.	.	.
Woodruff Mining Co.	1	.	.	.	.	.	.	.	1	.	.	.
Woodruff, C.P.	1	.	.	.	1	.	.	.	.	.	.	.
Woodward, Tiernan & Hale	1	.	.	.	.	.	.	.	.	1	.	.
Wooten	1	.	.	.	.	.	.	.	.	.	1	.
Wright	6	1	.	.	1	.	1	.	1	1	1	.
Wyatt	1	1	.	.	.	.	.	.	.	.	.	.
Wyld	269	19	14	26	21	36	32	21	19	22	28	31
Wytfliet	57	6	1	2	9	9	.	3	2	8	10	7
Yeager	4	.	.	.	.	.	.	2	1	.	.	1
Young	4	.	1	.	1	2	.	.	.	.	.	.
Young & Brownlee	1	.	.	.	.	.	.	.	.	.	1	.
Young & Williams	1	.	.	.	.	.	1	.	.	.	.	.
Young, J.H.	8	1	.	.	1	.	2	1	.	.	.	3
Zahn	4	1	.	1	.	.	.	1	.	1	.	.
Zakreski	1	.	.	.	1	.	.	.	.	.	.	.
Zaltieri	1	.	.	.	.	1	.	.	.	.	.	.
Zannoni	1	.	.	.	.	1	.	.	.	.	.	.
Zatta	371	18	44	35	50	62	31	22	41	30	23	15
Zeese & Co.	3	.	.	.	1	.	.	.	.	2	.	.
Zell	2	.	.	.	1	.	1	.	.	.	.	.
Ziegler	7	1	2	1	.	.	.	.	1	2	.	.
Zimmerman	1	.	.	.	.	.	.	.	1	.	.	.
Zurner	3	.	.	1	.	.	1	.	1	.	.	.

PRICE LISTING

ADMIRALTY

A SURVEY OF THE COASTS OF CORNWALL AND DEVONSHIRE...FROM ST. AGNES HEAD TO HARTLAND POINT [1810, c. 1854] 95x62cm. (37½x24½") By Murdoch Mackenzie, Jr. Margins slightly reduced, o/w excellent. [11] £200 $381

A SURVEY OF THE SOUTH COAST OF ENGLAND FROM PLYMOUTH TO THE LIZARD [1809, c.1847] 64x95cm. (25x37½") Deckle-edged. Small, brown spots upper corners; light offsetting; o/w excellent. [11] £250 $476

A TRIGONOMETRICAL SURVEY OF THE BAY OF CORINGA [c. 1840] 36x60cm. (14x23½") Topping, Dalrymple, 1791. [11] £100 $190

ADEN AND ADJACENT BAYS [1865] 64x89cm. (24½x34½") By Haines *et al*, 1836; then Walker for East India Co. Light soiling; one repair to margin edge tear. [11] £90 $171

ALGOA BAY [1856 (1877)] 61x97cm. (24½x38") By Dayman, 1855. Minor edge damage repaired; o/w good. [11] £80 $152

API POINT TO THE RIVER SARAWAK [1846 (1850)] 46x64cm. (18x24½") By Belcher, 1844; Hydrographic Office. Excellent. [11] £160 $304

APPROACHES TO STORNOWAY [1895] 50x65cm. (19½x25½") [11] £35 $67

AZORES OR WESTERN ISLES [1849 (1867)] 48x64cm. (18½x25") By Vidal, 1843-4; Hydrographic Office. Linen backed. Slight dust soiling left edge; a damp mark. [11] £60 $114

BASS STRAIT [1868 (1890)] 97x66cm. (38x25½") Dimensions for each of two sheets. By Stokes *et al*, 1839-87. Pencil navigation marks. Edges slightly chipped and creased; o/w VG. [11] £200 $381

BONACCA ISLAND [Honduras] [1845] 46x64cm. (18½x25") By Smith, 1840; Hydrographic Office. Excellent. [11] £170 $324

BROAD HAVEN BAY [1853 (1895)] 61x97cm. (24x37½") By R. Beechley. Very light printer's smear; o/w very good. [11] £30 $57

CAPE OF GOOD HOPE AND ADJACENT COASTS FROM HONDEKLIP BAY TO PORT NATAL WITH THE AGULHAS BANK [1867 (1872)] 64x97cm. (25x38") Fine. [11] £90 $171

CHILE, MAITENCILLO TO HERRADURA [1841 (1884)] 62x47cm. (24½x18½") By Fitzroy, 1836; Hydrographic Office. Navigation pencil marks. [11] £50 $95

CHINA ... HIESHAN ISLES TO THE YANG-TSE-KIANG INCLUDING THE CHUSAN ISLANDS [1849] 97x64cm. (38x25") Kellett & Collinson, 1843. Linen-backed, with 11 x 8" extension piece. Slight dust soiling; o/w excellent. [11] £90 $171

CHIRIQUI LAGOON [1847] 64x94cm. (25x37") By Barnett, 1839. Sl. offsetting; Good. [11] £100 $190

COQUET ROAD AND CHANNEL [1847 (1891)] 94x61cm. (37x24") By Slater. [11] £60 $114

EAST COAST OF SOUTH AMERICA SHEET VI FROM THE RIO DE LA PLATA TO THE RIO NEGRO ... [1840] 47x62cm. (18½x24½") By Fitzroy *et al.* Hydrographic Office. Numerous ex lib stamps. [16] £131 $250

EAST LOCH TARBERT [1857 (1876)] 66x94cm. (26x37") Repaired edge damage. [11] £25 $48

ENGLAND WEST COAST SHEET II PADSTOW TO THE BRISTOL CHANNEL [1839 (1855)] 64x46cm. (24½x18½") By Sheringham, Denham & Robinson. [11] £85 $162

ENGLAND WEST COAST SHEET VI WALES NEW QUAY TO BARDSEY [1842] 64x46cm. (24½x18½") By Sheringham, H.O. Some brown spotting; o/w good. 11] £80 $152

ENGLAND WEST COAST SHEET VII WALES BARDSEY ISLAND TO POINT LYNUS [1842 (1846)] 64x46cm. (24½x18") By W.L Sheringham Margins reduced; a few small edge tears repaired; two placenames marked with ink. [11] £80 $152

ENTRANCE TO THE RIVER HUMBER [1878 (1899)] 66x94cm. (26x37") [11] £55 $105

FALMOUTH & ENGLISH HARBOURS [Antigua] [1850] 61x46cm. (24½x18") By Barnett, 1847; H.O. Dust marking and brown spotting near left edge; o/w very good. [11] £370 $704

GASPAR STRAIT [1861-62] 99x66cm. (38½x25½") Based on U.S. Navy survey. [11] £45 $86

GORDA SOUND [1850] 48x64cm. (18½x25") By Lawrence, 1848; H.O. Clean; good. [11] £520 $990

GULF OF ST. LAWRENCE, MINGAN ISLANDS. EASTERN SHEET ... [1838] 46x62cm. (18½x24½") First edition. [10] £45 $85

GULF OF ST. LAWRENCE, MINGAN ISLANDS. WESTERN SHEET ... [1838] 46x63cm. (18½x24½") First edition. [10] £45 $85

HARWICH HARBOUR [1873 (1896)] 66x127cm. (26x50") By Tizard. Large scale. [11] £50 $95

MAJICO SIMA GROUP [1852] 48x62cm. (18½x24½") By Belcher; H.O. [11] £90 $171

MILFORD HAVEN [1831 (1852)] 48x61cm. (19x24½") By Denham, Hydrographic Office. With corrections. Deckle-edge. Fine. [11] £90 $171

[same title] [1831, c.1846] 48x61cm. (19x24½") Deckle-edge. Fine. [11] £100 $190

[same title] [1856 (1869)] 64x95cm. (25x37½") By Alldridge. Clean; fine. [11] £75 $143

NEW BRUNSWICK - BAY OF FUNDY - L'ETANG HARBOUR ... [1848-1864] 48x63cm. (19x25") By Kortright under Owen, 1847. Lighthouses colored. Numerous ex lib stamps. [16] £166 $315

NORTH AMERICA EAST COAST SHEET III BANKS OFF NEWFOUNDLAND [1836] 48x62cm. (18½x24½") Numerous ex lib stamps. [16] £159 $302

NORTH AMERICA EAST COAST ... SHEET IV [NOVA SCOTIA AND GULF OF THE ST. LAWRENCE] [1834] 47x62cm. (18½x24½") Numerous ex lib stamps. [16] £159 $302

NORTH AMERICA EAST COAST ... SHEET VII [Ga. to N.C.] [1836] 48x62cm. (18½x24½") After Blunt and others. Numerous ex lib stamps; upper & left margins dusty with tears. [16] £135 $256

PERU CAPE LOBOS TO PESCADORES POINT [1840 (1885)] 48x62cm. (19x24½") By Fitzroy *et al*, 1836; Hydrographic Office. [11] £50 $95

PLANS OF PORTS IN WALES ... [1843 (1859)] 48x61cm. (18½x24") Cardigan and others. By Sheringham, Hydrographic Office. Color. [11] £90 $171

PORT SETUBAL [1860-79] 45x60cm. (18x23½") By Vincendon-Dumoulin, 1852. Two small margin tears repaired. [11] £30 $57

PORTO BELLO AND ADJACENT COAST FROM A SPANISH M.S. COMMUNICATED BY CAPTN. TAITE R.N. [1820, c. 1845] 61x46cm. (24x18") [11] £210 $400

RANGAOUNOU OR AWANUI RIVER [1857] 65x48cm. (25½x19") By Drury, 1852; Hydrographic Office. [11] £120 $228

RIVER HOOGHLY. CALCUTTA TO SAUGOR POINT [1882 (1883)] 97x64cm. (37½x25½") Edge damage and one tear into engraving repaired with no loss. [11] £40 $76

RIVER ST. LAWRENCE, LONG POINT TO LACHINE RAPIDS INCLUDING MONTREAL SURVEYED BY CAPT. H. BAYFIELD 1858 [1860] 97x64cm. (38x25") Montreal street plan. 1st edition. [15] £123 $235

RIVER TAY [1883-1885] 64x99cm. (25½x39") By Cunningham & Tizard. Small damp-mark lower centerfold; o/w very good. [11] £60 $114

RIVER THAMES SHEET 2 N. FORELAND TO THE NORE [1862-3, 1865] 61x69cm. (24x27") By E.K. Calver. Light dust soiling; minor edge damage; o/w good. [11] £100 $190

SEAHAM HARBOUR [1846 (1887)] 61x48cm. (24x18½") With town layout. [11] £70 $133

SHEET 1 POINT DE MONTS TO BERSIMIS RIVER [St. Laurence River] [1837, c. 1845] 46x64cm. (18x25") By Bayfield, 1827-34; H.O. Minor edge tears; generally excellent. [11] £120 $228

SHEET 3 GREEN ISLAND TO THE PILGRIMS [St. Laurence River] [1837, c. 1845] 46x64cm. (18x25") By Bayfield, 1827-34; H.O. Minor edge tears; generally excellent. [11] £120 $228

SKETCH OF NEW SOUTH SHETLAND ... [c.1825] 18x23cm. (7x9") Trimmed to border. [10] £39 $75

SOUTH AMERICA COAST OF CHILE ... [1840] 27x28cm. (10½x11") Herradura or Pichidanque Bay and two insets. By Fitzroy *et al*, 1835. Hydrographic office. A few ex lib stamps. [16] £131 $250

STRAIT OF MALACCA [1860 (1872)] 64x97cm. (25x38") Two sheets; dimensions for each. By Ward *et al*, 1852-69. [11] £340 $647

SUIRAH OR MOGADOR HARBOUR [1844] 46x61cm. (18½x24") By Arlett, 1835; 11] £70 $133

TABLE BAY [1857 (1875)] 94x61cm. (37x24") By Skead, 1858-60. Ink notes, pencil marks, slightly run red ink corrections; minor margin damage and a longer tear into image repaired. [11] £50 $95

TANGIER BAY [1873 (1883)] 48x65cm. (19x25½") By Vincendon-Dumoulin, 1855. Linen-backed. [11] £35 $67

THE CAPE OF GOOD HOPE AND FALSE BAY [1870 (1871)] 99x64cm. (38½x25½") By Archdeacon, 1869. [11] £150 $285

THE ENTRANCE TO THE RIVER TAGUS [1853] 65x94cm. (25½x37") By Richards, 1853; Hydrographic Office. Deckle-edged. Two short edge tears repaired; o/w fine. [11] £90 $171

THE FALKLAND ISLANDS [1841 (1867)] 64x94cm. (25x37") By Fitzroy *et al*, 1838-45; Hydrographic Office. Clean; excellent. [11] £180 $343

THE GRAHAM SHOAL AND OTHER VOLCANIC PATCHES ON THE ADVENTURE BANK [1851] 47x64cm. (18½x25") Between Sicily and Pantellaria. [11] £45 $86

THE ISLAND OF BARBUDA ... [1814, c.1840] 29x20cm. (11½x8") By Deckar; H.O. [11] £190 $362

THE ISLAND OF NAVASSA; BETWEEN ST. DOMINGO & JAMAICA [1862] 28x23cm. (11x8½") By F. Owen. [15] £39 $75

THE PORT OF VERACRUZ, AND ANCHORAGE OF ANTON LIZARDO ... [1825, c. 1845] 60x79cm. (23½x31") Hydrographic Office. Fine. [11] £200 $381

THE WASH SKEGNESS TO BALKENEY [1871 (1890)] 64x97cm. (25x38") By Calver. [11] £90 $171

TOULON AND THE ADJACENT COAST [c. 1845] 46x61cm. (18x23½") By Smyth, 1833; Hydrographic Office. [11] £80 $152

WALES NORTH COAST SHEET VIII POINT LYNUS TO ABERGELE [1839 (1846)] 48x64cm. (18½x25") By Robinson, Hydrographic Office. Right margin shaved to border; three places marked in ink. [11] £55 $105

WEST INDIES BONACCA ISLAND ... [1840] 47x63cm. (18½x24½") Numerous ex lib stamps. [16] £166 $315

WEST INDIES SHEET XI FROM CAYOS RATIONES TO SAN JUAN DE NICARAGUA [1844 (1864)] 48x61cm. (19x24½") By Barnett, 1837; Hydrographic Office. [11] £90 $171

ALBRIZZI

ISOLA CEILON [1742] 28x36cm. (11x14") After Tirion. [10] £79 $150

NUOVA CARTA DEL POLO ARTICO [c. 1740] 28x33cm. (11x13") By G. DeL'Isle. California an island. Color. [15] £97 $185

ALLARD

ACCURATISSIMA EUROPAE TABULA MULTIS LOCIS ... [1697] 51x58cm. (19½x23½") Original color. Excellent. [1] £197 $375

EXACTISSIMA ASIAE DELINEATIO ... [1696] 51x58cm. (19½x23") Based on Witsen. Full original color. Excellent. [2] £499 $950

NOVA TABULA INDIA ORIENTALIS ... [1697] 46x56cm. (18x22") Full color. Lightly toned; marginal repair; o/w very good. [21] £998 $1900

NOVISSIMA ET PERFECTISSIMA AFRICAE ... [1690-1710] 51x58cm. (20x23") By Covens & Mortier. Full original color. Excellent. [2] £657 $1250

PLANISPHAERIUM TERRESTRE, SIVE TERRARUM ORBIS, ... [1696] 51x61cm. (20½x23½") Double hemisphere; 8 smaller hemispheres. Shirley 578. Original color. Fine. [22] £1997 $3800

REGNORUM MAGNAE BRITTANIAE, SIVE ANGLIAE SCOTIAE NEC NON HIBERNIA ... [c. 1690] 51x58cm. (20x23½") Full color. Very good. [21] £289 $550

ANDREAS

PLAN OF COUNCIL BLUFFS [1875] 33x43cm. (13x17") Color. [12] £34 $65

ANDRIVEAU-GOUJON

CARTE DES ETATS-UNIS D'AMERIQUE COMPRENANT UNE PARTIE DES DISTRICTS DE L'OUEST ET DE LA NOUVELLE BRETAGNE [1841] 38x51cm. (15x20") Original outline color. Perfect. [12] £145 $275

CARTE PHYSIQUE ET ROUTIERE DE L'ITALIE INDIQUANT LES DISTANCES D'UN RELAIS A L'AUTRE [mid 19th c.] 121x96cm. (47½x38") Linen-backed folding map in marbled slipcase. Original color. New backing with original label. Very good. [19] £142 $270

ESQUISSE D'UNE CARTE GEOLOGIQUE D'ITALIE [1846] 82x60cm. (32½x23½") Linen-backed folding map. Original color. Very good. [19] £210 $400

ANDRUS & JUDD

AN ANCIENT OR BIBLE MAP, DESIGNED FOR THE USE OF BIBLE CLASSES, SUNDAY SCHOOLS AND PRIVATE FAMILIES [1832] 30x51cm. (12x19½") Pocket map folding into covers. Color. Faint offsetting; fold separations repaired with acid-free tape; small corner piece absent; cover rubbed, corners slightly bent; very good. [8] £76 $145

ANONYMOUS

[MARITIME CANADA AND NEWFOUNDLAND] [c. 1760] 22x35cm. (8½x14") Title in Russian script. After Bellin; probably in Russian edition of Prevost's *Histoire Generale* ... [33] £300 $571

[STANDING GLOBE] [c. 1810] Diameter: 7 cm. (2¾") On 6" orig wooden stand. [2] £1445 $2750

[WORLD & CONTINENTS; 5 MAPS] A' FOLD OT RESZEINEK LER AJZOLASA [with] AMERIKA [and] AFRIKA [and] A'SIA [and] EUROPA [c. 1795] 33x41cm. (12½x16") approx. dimens. for all. Hungarian: engravers include Eras Gabor, Pap Josef & Pethes David. All excellent. [21] £1314 $2500

A MAP OF PARADISE ... [c. 1750] 28x36cm. (10½x14") Scientific approach to Biblical geography. Outline color. Creased, else very good. [34] £79 $150

A NEW MAP OF CANADA, ALSO THE NORTH PARTS OF NEW ENGLAND AND NEW YORK; WITH NOVA SCOTIA AND NEWFOUND LAND [c. 1770] 20x30cm. (8x12") After De Vaugondy. [6] £50 $95

A PLAN OF THE COUNTRY FROM THE LANDING PLACE ... OF THE TROOPS UNDER MAJOR GENERAL ABERCROMBIE TO THE ATTACK OF TICONDEROGA [1758] 11x19cm. (4x7½") Ridge, sc. [10] £50 $95

CARTE DE LA NOUVELLE FRANCE OU SE VOIT LE COURS DES GRANDE RIVIERES ... [c. 1730] 50x55cm. (19½x21½") Enlarged adaption of Chatelain found in Ottens composite atlas. Original wash color. Excellent. [38] £1156 $2200

CARTE DE PHASES DE L'ECLIPSE DU 1 AVRIL 1764 ET DE TOUS LES PAYS DE LA TERRE OU L'ON A PU VOIR CETTE ECLIPSE [1771] 33x33cm. (13x13") Hemisphere with center at Ferro. [12] £92 $175

CITY OF SANTA FE [1885] 13x25cm. (5x10") Bird's-eye view, after Stoner. [12] £37 $70

GRUNDRISS DE STADT JERSALEM [c. 1710] 28x30cm. (10½x12") Engraved by Fehr, based on Van Adrichom's plan. Laor, cf. 93 Fine. [30] £289 $550

GRUNDRISS ... ST. PETERSBURG [c. 1750] 48x69cm. (19x27½") German. Excel. [21] £473 $900

KARTA K' ISTORII NARODOV' OBITAVSHICH' V' SREDNEI AZIL V' DREVNIJA VREMENA [Historical Map of People's Habitation in Central Asia in Ancient Times] [n.d.] 64x145cm. (25x57") All names in Russian. Unbacked folded lithographed map. Good+. [19] £105 $200

KARTE DER QUELLGEBIETE DER FLUSSE WITCHITA, BRAZOS, COLORADO &C IM INNERN VON NORD-AMERIKA [Texas] [1859] 18x20cm. (6½x7½") Pub. Gotha. [12] £71 $135

LA RUSSIE ASIATIQUE TIREE DE LA CARTE DONNEE PAR ORDRE DU FEU CZAR [c. 1750] 41x53cm. (16½x21") [35] £53 $100

LONDON AND WESTMINSTER IN THE REIGN OF QUEEN ELIZABETH, ANNO DOM. 1563 [1791] 20x54cm. (7½x21½") Three folds, one with slight wear; side margins extended. [17] £102 $195

NUOVA CARTA DELL'IMPERIO DEL GIAPPONE [c. 1770] 35x41cm. (14x16") Italian source, after E. Bowen. Color. [5] £750 $1427

PLAN DE LA VILLE DE BOSTON ET SES ENVIRONS [c. 1780] 18x20cm. (6½x8") Based on Bellin's map. Fine. [12] £71 $135

POSTKARTE DES GROSSHERZOGTHUMS BADEN UND DES KONIGREICHS WURTEMBERG NEBST THEILEN DER ANGRENZENDEN LANDER [19th c.] 45x44cm. (17½x17") Linen-backed folding map. Outline color. Very good. [19] £42 $80

THE MIDDLE STATES AND WESTERN TERRITORIES OF THE UNITED STATES INCLUDING THE SEAT OF THE WESTERN WAR [1812-1818] 20x25cm. (7½x9½") From Brooke's *Gazetteer* or Warner's *General Atlas*. Outline color. [12] £84 $160

THE NORTH WEST PROVINCES AND OUDH FOR MURRAY'S HANDBOOK TO BENGAL [n.d] 42x48cm. (16½x19") Linen-backed folding map. Good+. [19] £26 $50

THE WORLD'S INDUSTRIAL AND COTTON CENTENNIAL EXPOSITION, NEW ORLEANS, LA., U.S.A. [c. 1885] 69x94cm. (26½x36½") Folding map; insets & views. Small paper loss at some fold intersections; o/w very good. [36] £53 $100

WAGVISARE I STOCKHOLM. GUIDE ET MANUEL DU VOYAGEUR A STOCKHOLM [c. 1830] 50x45cm. (19½x18") Linen-backed folding plan in original marbled slipcase. Minimal foxing; very good. [19] £105 $200

ANSON

A CHART OF THE PACIFIC OCEAN FROM THE EQUINOCTIAL TO THE LATITUDE OF 39 1/2° NO. [1798] 28x89cm. (11x35") Color. [15] £118 $225

A CHART SHEWING THE TRACK OF THE CENTURIAN ROUND THE WORLD [1748] 23x43cm. (9x16½") Insular California; partial Australia. [26] £95 $180

A PLAN OF JUAN FERNANDES ISLAND IN THE SOUTH SEAS IN LAT. OF 33° 40' S. [1748] 25x51cm. (9½x19½") Color. [15] £45 $85

APIANUS

CARTA COSMOGRAPHICA, CON LOS NOMBRES, PROPRIEDAD, Y VIRTUD DE LOS VIENTOS [(1544)-1575] 19x28cm. (7½x11") Cordiform, after Gemma Frisius. Shirley 96. VG. [31] £946 $1800

APPLETON

A VIEW ON THE HUDSON RIVER [1869] 23x71cm. (8½x28") Excellent. [12] £97 $185

SAVANNAH, GA. [c. 1882] 18x23cm. (7x9") Street plan. NY: Moss Co. Color. [15] £21 $40

ARCHER

MEXICO & TEXAS [1838] 24x28cm. (9½x11") London: Grattan & Gilbert. Color. [15] £76 $145

ARROWSMITH

[MAP OF THE WORLD ON A GLOBULAR PROJECTION] [c. 1794] Diameter: 91 cm. (36") Western Hemisphere only. Original outline color. [10] £499 $950

A CHART OF PART OF NORTH AMERICA, FROM CAPE HATTERAS TO CAPE CANSO ... [1800] 51x79cm. (20x31") By Vinicomb-Penroze, 1795-98. Dimensions for each of two joinable linen-backed sheets. Sea in early wash. Tears repaired with no loss. [11] £600 $1142

AFRICA [1802] 124x146cm. (49x57½") Linen backed folding map. Orig col. VG. [19] £946 $1800

AMERICA [1835] 60x48cm. (24x19") Color. [15] £87 $165

CENTRAL ASIA; COMPRISING BOKHARA, CABOOL, PERSIA. THE RIVER INDUS & COUNTRIES EASTWARD OF IT [1834] 48x72cm. (19x28½") Original outline color. [10] £131 $250

CHART OF THE EAST INDIA ISLANDS, EXHIBITING THE SEVERAL PASSAGES BETWEEN THE INDIA AND PACIFIC OCEANS; ... [1809] 125x188cm. (49x74") Linen-backed folding map. Very good. [19] £1419 $2700

CHART OF THE WEST INDIES AND SPANISH DOMINIONS IN NORTH AMERICA. ... [1803 (1815)] 61x143cm. (24x56½") Printed on 4 sheets; 2 pairs joined, each these dimens. Outline col. Minor damp staining; some marginal chipping; small surface loss restored; folds strengthened. [20] £1997 $3800

CHINA [1842] 52x68cm. (20½x27") Linen backed folding map. Orig col. VG. [19] £79 $150

DARIEN [1825] 23x31cm. (9x12") Color. [15] £50 $95

GREECE AND THE IONIAN ISLANDS [1832] 61x49cm. (24x19") Linen-backed folding map in worn, but whole slipcase. Orig col. Ink & pencil marks; staining at two intersections; o/w VG. [19] £81 $155

LOWER CANADA NEW BRUNSWICK NOVA SCOTIA PRINCE EDWARDS ID. NEWFOUNDLAND ... [1838] 61x48cm. (24x19") Color. [15] £74 $140

MAP OF ASIA MINOR TO ILLUSTRATE THE JOURNEYS OF W. I. HAMILTON ESQ. ... [c. 1837] 48x64cm. (19½x25") Outline color. [36] £42 $80

MAP OF SOUTH ITALY AND ADJACENT COASTS [1807] 131x164cm. (51½x64½") Linen-backed folding map; four sections. Outline color. Very good. [19] £263 $500

MAP OF SYRIA ... 1818, BY CAPTN. ARMAR L. CORRY R.N. ... A. ARROWSMITH. [1823] 83 x 135cm. (32½x53") In two parts, about 66 x 79 cm. Linen-backed folding maps. Color. Some light offset where map folds; very good. [19] £184 $350

MAP OF THE ALPINE COUNTRY IN THE SOUTH OF EUROPE. TO CHARLES VISCOUNT NEWARK ... INSCRIBED [1804] 126x151cm. (49½x59½") Linen-backed folding map. Four sections, each about 63 x 75 cm. Original color. Very good. [19] £263 $500

MAP OF THE ROADS OF PORTUGAL [1811] 58x128cm. (23x50") First edition. Linen-backed folding map. Some color. Very good. [19] £184 $350

MAP OF THE ROADS OF PORTUGAL [1812] 56x130cm. (22x51") Second edition. Linen-backed folding map in original slipcase with label. Original color. Slight foxing; very good+. [19] £184 $350

MEXICO [1825] 23x30cm. (9x12") 1st issue. Color. [15] £74 $140

NORTH AMERICA [1825] 23x30cm. (9½x12") Outline color. [15] £45 $85

OUTLINES OF THE PHYSICAL AND POLITICAL DIVISIONS OF SOUTH AMERICA [1811-1814] 200x240cm. (78½x94½") Six sheets. Orig outline col. Some offsetting; o/w fine. [10] £289 $550

THE INLAND NAVIGATION, RAIL ROADS, GEOLOGY AND MINERALS OF ENGLAND & WALES [1834] 61x49cm. (24x19") Linen-backed folding map. Full orig.color. VG. [19] £210 $400

THE WORLD ON MERCATOR'S PROJECTION [1807] 25x41cm. (9½x15½") London: Longman Hurst. Color. [15] £50 $95

UNITED STATES [1828] 23x30cm. (9x12") To 100 miles west of L. Michigan. Col. [15] £50 $95

UNITED STATES [1834] 61x48cm. (23½x19") Color. [15] £66 $125

W. INDIES [1825] 24x31cm. (9½x12") 1st edition. Color. [15] £50 $95
WEST INDIES [1847] 48x62cm. (19x24½") Color. Minor repair. [15] £50 $95
WORLD ON MERCATOR'S PROJECTION [1825] 25x30cm. (9½x12") Color. [15] £42 $80

ARROWSMITH & LEWIS *Try Lewis & Arrowsmith*

ARTARIA & CO.

NEUESTER PLAN DER HAUPT- UND RESIDENZSTADT WIEN MIT ALLEN VON SEINER MAJESTAT ALLERHOCHST GENEHMIGTEN VERSCHONERUNGEN NEBST DEM GLACIS UND EINGANG IN DIE VORSTADTE, ... [1830] 60x74cm. (23½x29") Vienna. Linen-backed folding plan in orig chemise and slipcase. Pastel col. Some sections detached, but present; o/w VG. [19] £210 $400

ASHER & ADAMS

ARKANSAS AND PORTION OF INDIAN TERRITORY [1872] 41x57cm. (16x22½") Color. [15] £45 $85
ASHER & ADAMS' DAKOTA [1875] 58x41cm. (23x16") Color. Minor edge chipping. [31] £39 $75
ASHER & ADAMS' IDAHO. MONTANA WESTERN PORTION [1875] 58x41cm. (22½x16") Original color. Very good. [31] £58 $110
ASHER & ADAMS' INDIAN TERRITORY AND TEXAS NORTH WEST PORTION [1875] 41x58cm. (16½x23") Orig col. Centerfold separation; small chip just within bottom neat line. [31] £39 $75
ASHER & ADAMS' MONTANA EASTERN PORTION [1875] 41x58cm. (16x22½") Original color. Chip in left margin. [31] £58 $110
ASHER & ADAMS' NEW MEXICO [1875] 43x58cm. (16½x22½") Orig col. VG. [31] £58 $110
ASHER & ADAMS' OREGON [1875] 41x58cm. (16x22½") Orig col. VG. [31] £45 $85
ASHER & ADAMS' UTAH [1875] 41x58cm. (16½x22½") Orig col. VG. [31] £58 $110
ASHER & ADAMS' WASHINGTON [1875] 41x58cm. (16x22½") Orig col. VG. [31] £45 $85
LOUISIANA AND MISSISSIPPI [1871] 58x43cm. (23x16½") Color. [15] £39 $75
MINNESOTA [1874] 56x41cm. (22x16") Color. [15] £32 $60
NEW HAMPSHIRE, VERMONT, MASSACHUSETTS, RHODE IS. & CONN. [1874] 43x58cm. (16½x23") Color. [15] £26 $50
TEXAS EASTERN PORTION [1874] 58x41cm. (22½x16") Color. [15] £42 $80
TEXAS WESTERN PORTION [1874] 56x41cm. (22½x16½") Color. [15] £42 $80
WYOMING [1873] 41x58cm. (16x23") Yellowstone. & Hayden's explorations. Color. [15] £76 $145

ASTLEY MAGAZINE

ISLAND OF MADERA / THE DRAGON TREE [c. 1750] 23x15cm. (9x6") London. Color. Excellent. [37] £45 $85

ATLANTIC NEPTUNE *Try Des Barres*

BACHIENE

AFBEELDINGE DER STAD JERUSALEM [1750] 38x48cm. (15x19½") Full col. VG. [31] £184 $350
KAART VAN HET EILAND JAMAIKA [1785] 23x30cm. (8½x12½") Color. [15] £79 $150

BACON

BACON'S BIRD'S-EYE VIEW OF SOUTH AFRICA [n.d.] 61x96cm. (24x38") Folding map between paper covers. Color. Small tears along folds and at intersections; no loss. [19] £92 $175
BACON'S EXCELSIOR MAP OF WALES AND MONMOUTHSHIRE. ... WITH RAILWAYS, ROADS, AND DISTANCES [n.d.] 120x94cm. (47x37") Linen-backed folding map between orig gilt-stamped boards. Outline & wash col. Wear at fold intersections, one separating; o/w very good. [19] £50 $95
BACON'S LARGE-PRINT MAP OF LONDON AND SUBURBS WITH GUIDE [1882] 69x90cm. (27x35½") Linen-backed city plan; red covers. Color. Very good. [19] £131 $250
BACON'S NEW MAP OF LONDON DIVIDED INTO HALF MILE SQUARES & CIRCLES [c. 1876] 66x97cm. (26x38") With 10 page "Stranger's Guide to London Shopping". Linen-backed folding plan between embossed boards. Pastel color. Minor wear at some folds and intersections. [19] £92 $175
[same title] [1874] 61x82cm. (24x32½") With 45 page illus. "Strangers' Guide ..." Unbacked folding plan between cloth boards. Color. Some tears, age darkening at folds, no paper loss; good+. [19] £66 $125

BACON'S WAR-MAP OF EGYPT INCLUDING SUDAN AND ABYSSINIA [c. 1898] 62x43cm. (24x16½") Folding map, with label. Col. Small holes at fold intersections, no loss; VG. [19] £29 $55

BAILEY & CO.

BIRD'S EYE VIEW OF CLINTON, MASS. [1876] 48x69cm. (18½x27") C. H. Vogt, lith. Reps 1415. Color. Repaired marginal tears, one 1.5" into image; good. [27] £447 $850

VIEW OF GUILFORD, CONNECTICUT [1881] 48x64cm. (19x24½") Reps 549. Color. Several repaired tears just into image, one 3" into it; fair. [27] £447 $850

BALDWIN & CRADOCK *Try Society for the Diffusion of Useful Knowledge*

SOUTH AFRICA COMPILED FROM THE MS MAPS IN THE COLONIAL OFFICE [1834] 33x41cm. (12½x15½") Color. [15] £34 $65

BARCLAY

A PLAN OF EFFINGHAM IN BERKLEY'S SOUND [1787] 20x23cm. (7½x9½") Col.. 15] £45 $85

BARDIN

[STANDING GLOBES: TERRESTRIAL & CELESTIAL] [1807] Globe pair. Diameters: 46 cm. (18") Terrestrial geography by A. Arrowsmith. On original mahogany library stands with calibrated brass horizons. Minor cracks and some small areas of discoloration, o/w excellent. [2] £40,462 $77,000

BARLOW

NORTH AMERICA FROM THE BEST AUTHORITIES [1806] 20x23cm. (7½x8½") Col. [15] £29 $55

BARNES

BARNES DRIVING MAP OF PHILADELPHIA [1867] 76x76cm. (30x30") City and suburbs. Pocket map folded into case. By H.E.B. Tay. Full color. Very good. [3] £223 $425

COUNTY, TOWNSHIP AND RAILROAD MAP OF THE STATE OF PENNSYLVANIA [1857] 84x124cm. (32½x49") Wall map. Color. Minor repair. [15] £236 $450

BARTHOLOMEW

A NEW PLAN OF GLASGOW WITH SUBURBS, FROM ORDNANCE AND ACTUAL SURVEYS, CONSTRUCTED FOR THE POST OFFICE DIRECTORY [1891-92] 77x89cm. (30½x35") Linen-backed folding map, unsectioned, between boards. Slight darkening and wearing at folds; small stains; very good. [19] £66 $125

ALABAMA [c. 1856] 38x28cm. (15x11") Color. [15] £29 $55

BARTHOLOMEW'S REDUCED SURVEY MAP OF SOUTH AFRICA COLOURED TO SHOW HEIGHT OF LAND [n.d.] 59x84cm. (23x33") Linen-backed folding map in original boards with label. Printed color. Boards soiled. [19] £53 $100

PORTS & HARBOURS ON THE SOUTH WEST COAST OF ENGLAND AND WALES [c. 1860] 43x30cm. (17x11½") Seven charts on one sheet. Tinted. [11] £35 $67

BARTLETT, J. R.

TUCSON, SONORA [Arizona] [1854] 13x18cm. (4½x7") Tinted view. Pristine. [12] £58 $110

BAUERKELLER

GEOGRAPHISCH-STATISTISCHE POST UND REISEKARTE ZU DEN BESUCHSTEN RHEIN- UND MAIN-GEGENDEN [19th c.] 50x38cm. (19½x15") Linen-backed folding map in slipcase. Original color. Very good. [19] £26 $50

BEAUTEMPS-BEAUPRE

CARTE HYDROGRAPHIQUE DES PARTIES CONNUES DU GLOBE, ENTRE LE SOIXANTE-DIXIEME PARALLELE AU NORD ET LE SOIXANTIEME AU SUD ... [c. 1796] 38x76cm. (15x29½") Features Marchand's explorations in 1790-92. Col. Minor repair. [15] £171 $325

BEERS, ELLIS & SOULE

PLAN OF STAMFORD [Conn.] [1867] 53x64cm. (21x25½") From *Atlas of New York and Vicinity*. Wash color. A few scattered spots; traces of original folds; fine. [27] £184 $350

TOWN OF DANBURY [Conn.] [1867] 41x33cm. (16x13") From *Atlas of New York and Vicinity*. Color. Good. [27] £66 $125

TOWN OF NORWALK [Conn.] [1867] 43x58cm. (16½x23½") From *Atlas of New York and Vicinity*. Color. Good. [27] £66 $125

TOWN OF WESTPORT [Conn.] [1867] 41x33cm. (16½x13") From *Atlas of New York and Vicinity*. Color. Good. [27] £66 $125

BELDEN

NEW RAILROAD MAP OF THE UNITED STATES AND DOMINION OF CANADA [c. 1871] 43x66cm. (16½x26½") Color. [15] £39 $75

BELLIN (Large) *Try Depot de la Marine*

[TITLE PAGE] L'HYDROGRAPHIE FRANCOIS ... [1756] 39x51cm. (15½x20") From *Maritime Atlas*. Minor marginal damage, especially to right. [5] £85 $162

6ME. CARTE PARTICULIERE DES COSTES DE BRETAGNE ... [c. 1770] 58x81cm. (22½x32") First in Jaillot's 1693 *Neptune Francois*. Light soiling; small repair to lower margin. [11] £110 $209

CARTE DE L'HEMISPHERE AUSTRAL ... [n.d.] 54x54cm. (21½x21½") South Polar projection. Color. Good. [4] £275 $523

CARTE DE L'ISLE DE LA GRENADE ... [1760] 89x56cm. (35x22") Color. [15] £197 $375

CARTE DE L'ISLE DE SAINTE LUCIE ... [1763] 89x57cm. (35x22½") [15] £289 $550

CARTE DES LACS DU CANADA ... SUR LE JOURNAL DU RP. DE CHARLEVOIX [1744] 30x46cm. (11½x17½") Tiny margin wormholes mended; lower left margin extended; else fine. [12] £709 $1350

CARTE DES VARIATIONS DE LA BOUSSOLE ET DES VENTS GENERAUX QUE L'ON TROUVE DANS LES MERS LES PLUS FREQUENTEES ... [1765] 56x86cm. (21½x34") Winds and magnetic variation on Mercator projection. [15] £413 $785

CARTE DU COURS FLEUVE DE SAINT LAURENT... [1761, c. 1780] 57x86cm. (22½x34") A crease near fold; light marginal spotting. [11] £320 $609

CARTE GENERALE DES COSTES D'IRELANDE ET DES COSTES OCCIDENTALES D'ANGLETERRE ... [c. 1770] 61x88cm. (24x34½") [11] £280 $533

CARTE REDUITE D'UNE PARTIE DES COSTES OCCIDENTALES ET MERIDIONALES DE L'AFRIQUE ... [1754, c. 1775] 89x55cm. (35x21½") Fine. [11] £260 $495

CARTE REDUITE DE L'ISLE DE SAINT DOMINGUE ET DE SES DEBOUQUEMENTS... [1754] 56x90cm. (22x35½") Paris: Depot de la Marine. [15] £202 $385

CARTE REDUITE DE L'OCEAN ORIENTAL OU MER DES INDES ... [1740] 61x79cm. (24x31") Early outline color. Early ink track. [11] £350 $666

[same title] [1757] 56x84cm. (21½x33") Depot de la Marine issue. Color. Repaired fold separations; close right margin; else very good. [34] £447 $850

CARTE REDUITE DES COSTES OCCIDENTALES D'AFRIQUE [1754] 89x55cm. (35x21½") Depot de la Marine, pub. [10] £47 $90

CARTE REDUITE DES COSTES ORIENTALES DE L'AMERIQUE SEPTENTRIONALE. 1ST FEUILLE CONTENANT L'ISLE ROYALE, L'ACCADIE, LA BAYE FRANCOISE, LA NOUVELLE ANGLETERRE ET LA NOUVELLE YORC ... [c. 1770] 51x84cm. (20x33") Paris: Depot de la Marine, from *Hydrographie Francoise*. Narrow margins; stain upper left; one inch triangle missing at bottom centerfold inside neat line; laid down. [6] £260 $495

CARTE REDUITE DES DEBOUQUEMENS DE ST. DOMINGUE DRESSEE POUR LE SERVICE DES VAISSEAUX DU ROY PAR ORDRE DE DUC DE CHOISEUL [1768] 58x91cm. (23x36") Paris: Depot de la Marine. [15] £255 $485

CARTE REDUITE DES ISLES ANTILLES ... [1758] 89x57cm. (35x22½") Col. Excel. [1] £197 $375

CARTE REDUITE DES ISLES PHILIPPINES ... [1752] 55x88cm. (21½x34½") Color. Minor staining top & bottom; o/w fine. [5] £475 $904

ESSAY D'UNE CARTE REDUITE CONTENANT LES PARTIES CONNUEES DU GLOBE ... [1748] 50x69cm. (20x27½") Color. Minor fold creases; else very good. [34] £447 $850

PARTIE OCCIDENTALE DE LA NOUVELLE FRANCE ET DU CANADA ... [1755] 48x61cm. (18½x24") [1] £946 $1800

PARTIE ORIENTALE DE LA NOUVELLE FRANCE OU DU CANADA. ... [1755] 47x61cm. (18½x24") [1] £631 $1200

PLAN DE PORT DE MILFORD ... [1757] 51x66cm. (19½x26") After Collins. Color. Margins slightly reduced; o/w good. [11] £140 $266

BELLIN (Small) *Try De Charlevoix, Prevost d'Exiles*

CARTE DE L'ACADIE, ISLE ROYALE ET PAIS VOISINS [1757] 21x33cm. (8x13") Color. Good. [4] £45 $86

CARTE DE L'AMERIQUE ET DES MERS VOISINES ... 1763 [1764] 46x31cm. (18x12") Some color. Narrow right margin; else fine. [12] £202 $385

CARTE DE L'AMERIQUE SEPTENTRIONALE POUR SERVIR A L'HISTOIRE DE LA NOUVELLE FRANCE 1743 [1743-1744] 28x36cm. (11x14") In Charlevoix. [10] £97 $185

CARTE DE L'INDE ... DE SIAM, DE TUNQUIN, PEGU, AVA, ARACAN ETC ... [n.d.] 28x28cm. (11x11") Color. Good. [4] £70 $133

CARTE DE L'ISLE D'ORLEANS ET DU PASSAGE DE LA TRAVERSE DANS LE FLEUVE ST. LAURENT ... [1744] 19x28cm. (7½x11") From Charlevoix's *Histoire* ... Fine. [10] £47 $90

CARTE DE L'ISLE DE CEYLON ... [1750] 26x25cm. (10x9½") Color. Good. [4] £60 $114

CARTE DE L'ISLE DE LA JAMAIQUE [1758] 20x31cm. (8x12") Color. Good. [4] £60 $114

CARTE DE L'ISLE DE PORTSEY, ET HAVRE DE PORTSMOUTH [1764] 21x15cm. (8½x6") From *Petit Atlas Maritime*. [11] £45 $86

CARTE DE L'ISLE DE SAINTE LUCIE ... [1758] 19x30cm. (7½x11½") Color. Good. [4] £75 $143

CARTE DE L'ISLE ST. CHRISTOPHE ... [n.d.] 19x31cm. (7½x12") Color. Good. [4] £70 $133

CARTE DE LA BAIE DE HUDSON [1757] 22x30cm. (8½x12") Color. Good. [4] £45 $86

CARTE DE LA BAYE DE CHESAPEACK; ... [n.d.] 19x29cm. (7½x11½") Col. G. [4] £140 $266

CARTE DE LA BAYE DE CHESAPEAK ET PAYS VOISINS [1757] 28x38cm. (11x15") Later color. Very good. [26] £200 $380

CARTE DE LA BAYE DE HUDSON [1757] 23x30cm. (8½x12") Immaculate. [12] £84 $160

CARTE DE LA BAYE DE MOSAMBIQUE [c. 1752] 21x16cm. (8½x6½") [15] £39 $75

CARTE DE LA CAROLINE ET GEORGIE [1757] 18x29cm. (7x11") Color. Good. [4] £95 $181

[same title] [1757] 25x33cm. (10x13") Modern color. [26] £171 $325

CARTE DE LA CAYQUE DE L'OUEST, ET PARTIE DE CELLE DU NORD [1773] Small format. Repaired worming at margin; some browning. [11] £20 $38

CARTE DE LA COSTE D'ARABIE, MER ROUGE, ET GOLFE DE PERSE [1740] 22x25cm. (8½x10") Color. Good. [4] £50 $95

CARTE DE LA FLORIDE DE LA LOUISIANE [n.d.] 22x30cm. (8½x12") Col. Good. [4] £140 $266

CARTE DE LA FLORIDE, DE LA LOUISIANE, ET PAYS VOISINS. POUR SERVIR A L'HISTOIRE GENERALE DES VOYAGES. ... [1757] 22x30cm. (8½x12") Fine. [28] £171 $325

[same title] 1757 [1757] 25x33cm. (10x13") Modern color. Very good. [26] £223 $425

CARTE DE LA LOUISIANE ET PAYS VOISINS ... [1757] 22x30cm. (8½x12") Color. Good. [4] £140 $266

CARTE DE LA NOUVELLE ANGLETERRE, NOUVELLE YORCK ET PENSILVANIE [1757] 21x30cm. (8x12") Color. Good. [4] £135 $257

[same title, date] 21x30cm. (8x11½") Paris: Prevost d'Exiles. Color. [15] £92 $175

[same title, date] 28x38cm. (11x15") Modern color. Very good, [26] £158 $300

CARTE DE LA NOUVELLE GEORGIE [1764] 21x15cm. (8½x6") Orig col. Excel. [10] £97 $185

CARTE DE LA PARTIE OCCIDENTALE D'INAGUE ... [1773] Bahamas. Small format. Repaired worming at margin; some browning. [11] £25 $48

CARTE DE LA SIBERIE ET DES PAYS VOISINS [c. 1754] 30x46cm. (11½x18") Col. [15] £47 $90

CARTE DE LA VIRGINIE MARI-LAND &A. TIREE DES MEILLEURES CARTES ANGLOISES [1764] 20x30cm. (7½x11½") Full color. Excellent. [21] £184 $350

[same title, date] 20x30cm. (7½x12") [12] £150 $285

[same title] [c. 1764] 18x30cm. (7x12") From *Le Petit Atlas Maritime* ... [6] £208 $395

CARTE DE LAC DE MEXICO ET DE SES ENVIRONS LORS DE LA CONQUETE [1754] 23x15cm. (8½x6") Color. [15] £45 $85

CARTE DES BAYES DU MESLE DES FLAMANDS ET DE CAVAILLON ... [1764] 23x36cm. (9x14") Haiti. [11] £18 $34

CARTE DES BAYES, RADES ET PORT DE PLAISANCE DANS L'ISLE DE TERRE NEUVE ... [1744] 20x29cm. (7½x11½") Fine. [10] £53 $100

CARTE DES COSTES DE LA FLORIDE FRANCOISE ... [1744] 21x14cm. (8x5½") From Charlevoix's *Histoire* ... Fine. [10] £53 $100

CARTE DES DEBOUQUEMENS DE ST. DOMINGUE [1773] Bahamas. Small format. Repaired worming at margin; some browning. [11] £25 $48

CARTE DES EMBOUCHURES DU MISSISSIPI ... PAR N.B. INGR. DE LA MARINE ... [1744] 20x29cm. (8x11") [10] £100 $190

CARTE DES FONDS BLANCS ET RESCIF ENTRE LA PETITE CAYQUE ET FRANC-KEE [1773] Small format. Repaired worming at margin; some browning. [11] £20 $38

CARTE DES ISLES A L'EST DES ISLES TURQUES [1773] Small format. Repaired worming at margin; some browning. [11] £20 $38

CARTE DES ISLES CANARIES [1746] 20x28cm. (8x11") Color. Good. [4] £55 $105

CARTE DES ISLES CAP VERD [1746] 21x28cm. (8½x11") Color. Good. [4] £45 $86

CARTE DES ISLES D'AKLIN DE LA FORTUNE DE KROO-KED [1773] Bahamas. Small format. Repaired worming at margin; some browning. [11] £25 $48

CARTE DES ISLES DE JAVA, SUMATRA, BORNEO &C. ... [n.d.] 25x29cm. (9½x11½") Color. Good. [4] £85 $162

CARTE DES ISLES DU CAP VERD [1756] 21x28cm. (8½x11") Folds, [10] £16 $30

CARTE DES ISLES KOURILES ... [n.d.] 24x26cm. (9½x10½") Color. Good. [4] £65 $124

CARTE DES ISLES PHILIPPINES [1752] 21x30cm. (8x12") Southern Islands. Col. G. 4] £70 $133

CARTE DES ISLES PHILIPPINES [1752] 21x16cm. (8½x6") Northern Islands. Col. G. [4] £45 $86

CARTE DES ISLES TURQUES [1773] (no dimens) Repaired margin worming; browning. [11] £20 $38

CARTE DES LACS DU CANADA... [1757] 20x29cm. (8x11½") Color. Good. [4] £95 $181

CARTE DES OBSERVATIONS ... SUR LA CAYE D'ARGENT [1773] Small format. Repaired worming at margin; some browning. [11] £15 $29

CARTE DES PARTIES DU NORD-OUEST DE L'AMERIQUE SUIVANT LES VOYAGES DE MIDDLETON ET D'ELLIS EN 1742 ET 1746 POUR CHERCHER UN PASSAGE DANS LE MER DU SUD [1753] 21x27cm. (8x10½") Color. Good. [4] £55 $105

CARTE DU BRESIL PREM. PARTIE DEPUIS LA RIVIERE DES AMAZONES JUSQU'A LA BAYE DE TOUS LES SAINTES [c. 1746] 24x32cm. (9½x12½") Paris: Prevost d'Exiles. Color. [15] £39 $75

[same title] [1772] 24x33cm. (9½x13") Dutch edition. Fine. [10] £24 $45

CARTE DU COURS DE FLEUVE DE ST. LAURENT DEPUIS QUEBEC ... LAC ONTARIO ... [1757] 19x28cm. (7½x11") Color. Good. [4] £45 $86

CARTE DU COURS DU FLEUVE DE ST. LAURENT DEPUIS SON EMBOUCHURE JUSQU'AU DESSUS DE QUEBEC...PAR M.B. 1757 [1757] 19x29cm. (7½x11½") Color. [15] £39 $75

CARTE DU DEBOUQUEMENT DE KROO-KED-ISLAND [1773] Bahamas. Small format. Repaired worming at margin; some browning. [11] £25 $48

CARTE DU GOLPHE DE ST. LAURENT ET PAYS VOISINS ... [n.d.] 22x37cm. (8½x14½") Color. Good. [4] £45 $86

CARTE DU GOLPHE DE ST. LAURENT ET PAYS VOISINS. POUR SERVIR A L'HISTOIRE GENERALE DES VOYAGES [1757] 23x36cm. (9x14") Outline & wash color. [36] £66 $125

[same title] [c. 1770] 22x36cm. (8½x14") [10] £47 $90

CARTE DU GOLPHE DU MEXIQUE ET DES ISLES DE L'AMERIQUE [1754] 27x37cm. (10½x14½") Color. Good. [4] £145 $276

CARTE DU MEXIQUE [1754] 20x29cm. (8x11½") Color. Good. [4] £35 $67

CARTE DU PARAGUAY ET DES PAYS VOISINS [1771] 20x31cm. (8x12") Dutch ed. [10] £18 $35

CARTE DU PLACET DES CAYQUES [1773] (no dims) Repaired margin worming; browning. [11] £25 $48

CARTE DU SPITS-BERG [1758] 22x30cm. (8½x12") Color. Good. [4] £40 $76

CARTE HYDROGRAPHIQUE DE LA RIVIERE DE LA PLATA ... [1770] 41x56cm. (15½x22") Clean, good. [11] £90 $171

CARTE REDUITE DES MERS DU NORD [1758] 33x44cm. (13x17½") Col. G. [4] £100 $190

CARTE REDUITE DES PARTIES SEPTENTRIONALES DU GLOBE, SITUEES ENTRE L'ASIE ET L,AMERIQUE ... [1777] 21x34cm. (8x13½") From *L'Histoire Generale ...* [10] £39 $75

CARTE REDUITE DU GOLPHE DU MEXIQUE ET DES ISLES DE L'AMERIQUE [1764] 20x30cm. (8x12") Original outline color. [12] £118 $225

EMBOUCHURES DU FLEUVE ST. LOUIS OU MISSISSIPPI 1763 [1764] 23x18cm. (8½x7") Color. [15] £76 $145

KAART VAN DE LAND-ENGTE VAN PANAMA EN PROVINTIEN VAN VERAGUA, TIERRA FIRMA EN DARIEN [1754] 20x28cm. (8½x11") Also French titles. Color. [15] £66 $125

KARTE VON CAROLINA UND GEORGIEN ZUR ALLGEMEINEN GESCHICHTE DER REISEN ... [c.1757] 18x25cm. (7x10") Color. [15] £84 $160

KARTE VON DEM EYLANDE TERRE-NEUVE ENTWORFEN VON N. B. ... 1744 [1756] 28x36cm. (11½x14½") In Charlevoix. Leipzig: Arkstee & Merkus. Color. [15] £97 $185

KARTE VON DEM MEXICANISHEN MEERBUSEN UND DEM INSELN VON AMERICA [1754] 28x38cm. (10½x15") Outline & wash color. [35] £92 $175

KARTE VON DEN AN DEN MOLUCKEN ... [1748-1753] 20x29cm. (8x11½") [10] £16 $30

KARTE VON DER HUDSONS BAY AND STRASSE ZUR ALLGEMEINEN HISTORIE DER REISEN [c. 1758] 20x30cm. (8½x11½") Differs from 1744 Charlevoix. Color. [15] £47 $90

KARTE VON DER HUDSONS BAY DURCH N. BELLIN 1744 [1756] 23x28cm. (8½x11") By Charlevoix. Leipzig: Arkstee & Merkus. Color. [15] £58 $110

KARTE VON DER INSEL CELEBES ODER MACASSAR [1748-1753] 21x15cm. (8x5½") 10] £26 $50

L'EMPIRE DE LA CHINE [1748] 29x40cm. (11½x15½") Color. Good. [4] £185 $352

LA VERA-CRUZ, VILLE DU MEXIQUE [1764] 22x17cm. (8½x6½") [12] £47 $90

LE PAYS DES HOTTENTOTS AUX ENVIRONS DU CAP DE BONNE ESPERANCE [n.d.] 24x35cm. (9½x13½") Color. Good. [4] £85 $162

[same title] [1754] 25x35cm. (10x14") Cropped to neat line and laid down. [10] £24 $45

LE PORT MARIANNE ... [1764] 23x17cm. (9x6½") [11] £20 $38

PARTIE DE LA COSTE DE LA LOUISIANE ET DE LA FLORIDE DEPUIS LE MISSISSIPI JUSQUA ST. MARC D'APALACHE [1744] 20x44cm. (8x17") From Charlevoix's Histoire. Fine. [12] £197 $375

[same title] [1744] 20x44cm. (8x17") Original green outline color. [10] £137 $260

PLAN DE L'ANCE A L'EAU DANS LA CAYQUE DU NORD [1773] Small format. Repaired worming at margin; some browning. [11] £20 $38

PLAN DE L'ANCE AU CANOT DANS LA CAYQUE DU NORD [1773] Small format. Repaired worming at margin; some browning. [11] £20 $38

PLAN DE L'ISLE D'INAGUE [1773] Bahamas. Small format. Repaired worming at margin; some browning. [11] £25 $48

PLAN DE L'ISLE DE MOGANE [1773] Bahamas. Small format. Repaired worming at margin; some browning. [11] £25 $48

PLAN DE L'ISLE DE SAMANA ... [1773] Bahamas. Small format. Repaired worming at margin; some browning. [11] £25 $48

PLAN DE LA BASSE OU ROCHES DE ST. PHILIPPE ... [1773] Small format. Repaired worming at margin; some browning. [11] £20 $38

PLAN DE LA BAYE DE CHEDABOUCTOU AUJOURD'HUI HAVRE DE MILFORT ... [1744] 20x28cm. (8x11") [10] £97 $185

PLAN DE LA BAYE DE PENSACOLA [1744] 20x28cm. (7½x11") [10] £118 $225

PLAN DE LA BAYE DE PENSACOLA DANS LA FLORIDE [1764] 21x17cm. (8½x6½") A later state on smaller format. Original green outline color. [10] £84 $160

PLAN DE LA BAYE SAINT LOUIS ... [1764] 23x36cm. (9x14") Slight browning. [11] £19 $36

PLAN DE LA CAYQUE DE L'OUEST OU LA PETITE CAYQUE [1773] Small format. Repaired worming at margin; some browning. [11] £20 $38

PLAN DE LA GRANDE SALINE L'UNE DES ISLES TURQUES [1773] Small format. Repaired worming at margin; some browning. [11] £20 $38

PLAN DE LA NOUVELLE ORLEANS [1744] 20x28cm. (8x11") [10] £102 $195

[same title] [1764] 20x29cm. (8x11½") From *Petit Atlas Maritime*. Full col. Excel. [21] £210 $400

[same title] [n.d.] 19x28cm. (7½x11") Color. Good. [4] £135 $257

PLAN DE LA PETITE SALINE LA SECONDE DES ISLES TURQUES [1773] Small format. Repaired worming at margin; some browning. [11] £20 $38

PLAN DE LA RADE ET VILLE DU PETIT GOAVE ... [1764] 23x36cm. (9x14") Haiti. Small margin tear. [11] £18 $34

PLAN DE LA VILLE DE BOSTON ET SES ENVIRONS [n.d.] 16x27cm. (6½x10½") Color. Good. [4] £130 $247

PLAN DE LA VILLE DE DUBLIN [c. 1764] 21x28cm. (8½x11") Color. Very good. [24] £75 $143

PLAN DE LA VILLE DE QUEBEC [n.d.] 20x28cm. (7½x11") Color. Good. [4] £60 $114

PLAN DE MOUILLAGE DE L'ISLE DE KROO-KED [1773] Bahamas. Small format. Repaired worming at margin; some browning. [11] £25 $48

PLAN DE PORT-ROYAL ET DES ENVIRONS DANS LA BAYE DE CAMPECHE [1774] 18x14cm. (7½x5½") Dutch edition. Fine. [10] £18 $35

PLAN DES ISLES PLATES ... [1773] Bahamas. (no dims.) Repaired worming at margin; some browning. [11] £25 $48

PLAN DU BASSIN DE QUEBEC ET DE SES ENVIRONS [1744] 20x28cm. (8x11") [10] £63 $120

PLAN DU CUL DE SAC DES ROSEAUX DANS L'ISLE DE STE. LUCIE 1763 [1764] 23x18cm. (8½x6½") Color. [15] £50 $95

PLAN DU MOUILLAGE DE LA PARTIE DE L'OUEST DE L'ISLE [1773] Bahamas. Small format. Repaired worming at margin; some browning. [11] £25 $48

PLAN DU PORT D'ACAPULCO SUR LA COTE DU MEXIQUE DANS LA MER DU SUD ... [1774] 19x15cm. (7½x6") Minor loss at lower blank corner. [10] £24 $45

PLAN DU PORT DAUPHIN ET DE SA RADE AVEC L'ENTREE DE LABRADOR ... [1744] 20x28cm. (8x11") Fine. [10] £47 $90

PLAN DU PORT DE ST. AUGUSTIN DANS LA FLORIDE [1764] 21x16cm. (8½x6½") Original wash and outline color. [10] £66 $125

PLAN DU PORT ET VILLE DE LOUISBOURG DANS L'ISLE ROYALE [1744] 20x28cm. (8x11") First state. [10] £79 $150

PLAN SCENOGRAPHIQUE DE LA CITE DES ROIS OU LIMA CAPITALE DU ROYAUME DE PEROU [1774] 19x32cm. (7½x12½") Dutch edition. Very fine. [10] £24 $45

SUITE DU BRESIL ... [1774] 23x17cm. (9x6½") Southern part. Dutch edition. Fine. [10] £13 $25

SUITE DU BRESIL, DEPUIS LA BAIE DE TOUS LE SAINTS JUSQU'A ST. PAUL [1774] 23x17cm. (9x6½") Dutch edition. Fine. [10] £18 $35

[same title] [c. 1746] 23x17cm. (9x6½") Paris: Prevost d'Exiles. Color. [15] £34 $65

SUITE DU COURS DE FLEUVE DE ST. LAURENT DEPUIS QUEBEC JUSQU'AU LAC ONTARIO ... [1777-78] 22x34cm. (8½x13½") Fine. [10] £32 $60

SUITE DU PEROU AUDIENCE DE CHARCAS ... [1771] 22x30cm. (8½x12") Southern Peru. Dutch edition. Fine. [10] £13 $25

SUITE DU PEROU AUDIENCE DE LIMA ... [1771] 21x29cm. (8x11½") Northern Peru Dutch edition. Fine. [10] £13 $25

VILLE DE MANATHE OU NOUVELLE-YORC [1764] 23x18cm. (8½x6½") Probably after inset plan by Franquelin, c. 1693. Full color. Excellent. [21] £394 $750

BENARD

CARTE DE LA COTE N.O. DE L'AMERIQUE ET DE LA COTE N.E. DE L'ASIE, RECONNUES EN 1778 ET 1779 [1785] 39x66cm. (15½x26") Cook's 3rd Voyage, French ed. Fold lines. [6] £184 $350

BENTON

THE STATES OF PENNSYLVANIA NEW JERSEY AND DELAWARE FROM THE LATEST AUTHORITIES [1833] 41x53cm. (16x21") Fastened in embossed green folder. Wash color. Some separations & small stains at folds. [6] £158 $300

BERGHAUS, H.

WEST COAST OF SOUTH AMERICA, PERU AND BOLIVIA ... QUILCA TO COBIJA ... [1847] 55x36cm. (21½x14") Potsdam: Geogr. Inst. Marginal tears, wrinkles and dusting. [16] £83 $158

BERO, D.

PLAN DE LA VILLE DE BORDEAUX [1823] 55x72cm. (21½x28½") Pierrugues & Bero; Bordeaux: A. Filliatre et Neveu. Linen-backed city plan in slip-case. Stain on section of plan; VG. [19] £92 $175

BERTELLI *Try Lafrere School*

ISOLA DI CORFU [c. 1570 (1713)] 21x16cm. (8x6") Published by Lasor. Mint. [38] £145 $275

BERTIUS

BRASILIA [1632] 9x13cm. (3½x5") Original outline color. [10] £53 $100

CAMBAIA [1602] 9x13cm. (3½x5") India. [10] £26 $50

DESCRIPTION DE SARDAIGNE [c. 1618] 9x13cm. (3½x5") Color. Very good. [25] £140 $266

FRETUM MAGELLANICUM [1606] 9x13cm. (3½x5") [10] £63 $120

MALACCA [1616] 9x14cm. (3½x5½") Outline color. Excellent. [38] £171 $325
SEPTENTRIONALUM REGIONU DESCRIP. [1602] 8x12cm. (3½x4½") [10] £39 $75
TERRA NOVA [1602] 9x12cm. (3½x5") [10] £223 $425

BETTS

BETTS'S NEW MAP OF ENGLAND AND WALES, ... [1848] 75x64cm. (29½x25") Cover: "Betts's Road & Railroad Map ..." Linen-backed folding map between boards. Color. Top embossed board separated, but present; very good. [19] £97 $185

BETTS'S TOUR THROUGH ENGLAND & WALES [1840's] 66x58cm. (26x23") Map GAME with a numbered interval route. Linen-backed folding map between original blue boards with label. Original color. Very good. [19] £368 $700

.[same title, date] 66x60cm. (26x23½") Map GAME. Linen-backed folding map between original red boards with label. Orig color. Light age darkening and slight soiling at margins; VG. [19] £342 $650

THE WORLD ON MERCATOR'S PROJECTION [c. 1850] 44x76cm. (17½x29½") On cover: "Betts' Voyage Round the World". George Philip & Son. Linen-backed folding map between original, gilt stamped boards. OL & wash col. Light age-soiling and darkening, backstrip worn; VG. [19] £87 $165

UNITED STATES, CANADA & NEW BRUNSWICK [c. 1834] 30x38cm. (12x15") To 101 deg. W. Color. [15] £53 $100

BEW *Try Political Magazine*

BION

PLANISPHERE CELESTE SUR LE QUEL LES ETOILLES SIXE SONT PLACEES COMME ELLES SONT A PRESENT [1720] 15x25cm. (6½x10½") Color. [15] £92 $175

BLACK

AUSTRALIA [1856] 41x55cm. (16½x21½") Original wash color. [10] £21 $40

CHART OF ISOTHERMAL LINES SHEWING THE MEAN ANNUAL TEMPERATURE ... OF THE EARTH'S SURFACE [1854] 28x38cm. (11x15½") By P. Barlow. Color. [15] £18 $35

KENTUCKY AND TENNESSEE [1852] 28x33cm. (10½x12½") Color. [15] £32 $60

NORTH AMERICA [1847] 41x30cm. (15½x11½") Texas as republic. Outline color. [26] £39 $75

NORTH & SOUTH CAROLINA [1856] 28x41cm. (11x15½") By J. Bartholomew. Color. [15] £29 $55

PHYSICAL GEOGRAPHY, HUMBOLDT'S DISTRIBUTION OF PLANTS IN EQUINOCTIAL AMERICA, ACCORDING TO LEVEL ABOVE THE SEA [c. 1830] 28x38cm. (10½x15") Mountain chart. [26] £37 $70

SOUTH AFRICA [c. 1856] 42x56cm. (16½x22") By Bartholomew. Color. [15] £34 $65

WEST INDIES [1851] 26x39cm. (10½x15½") By S. Hall. Color. [15] £32 $60

WESTERN STATES INCLUDING CALIFORNIA, OREGON, UTAH, WASHINGTON, NEW MEXICO, NEBRASKA, ETC. [c. 1861] 43x56cm. (17x22") By J. Bartholomew. Color. [15] £58 $110

BLACKIE & SON

THE UNITED STATES OF NORTH AMERICA. ATLANTIC STATES AND VALLEY OF THE MISSISSIPPI [c. 1850] 51x69cm. (20½x26½") By J. Lowry. 2 sheets: U.S. to 100 deg. West. Color. [15] £45 $85

BLAEU

[TITLE PAGE] NOVUS ATLAS SINENSIS A MARTINO MARTINI [1655] 27x43cm. (10½x17") Original color with gold highlights. [5] £280 $533

[TITLE PAGE] THEATRUM ORBIS TERRARUM SIVE ATLAS NOVUS ... [1644] 25x40cm. (10x15½") From Vol. I. Original color with gold. Some minor verdigris cracking, bottom left; original owner's inscription at bottom. [5] £195 $371

AFRICAE NOVA DESCRIPTIO [1630] 41x55cm. (16x22") Side and top panels. Full original color. Excellent. [2] £1471 $2800

AMERICA NOVA TABULA [c. 1630] 41x53cm. (16x21½") Top and side panels. 3 folds instead of one, no text verso (not from an atlas?) Repaired 2.5" tear & fold breaks. [34] £1576 $3000

[same title, date] 41x55cm. (16x22") Panels at top and sides. Full orig col. Excel. [1] £2365 $4500

[same title] [(1618) c. 1660] 41x57cm. (16x22½") Panels at top and sides. Original color. Minor centerfold creasing. [5] £2750 $5233

[same title] [1633] 36x46cm. (14½x18½") Early variant without panels. Excellent. [1] £2417 $4600

AMERICA NOVA TABULA [1635] 41x55cm. (16x22") "Carte a figures". Orig col.. Exc. [22] £2549 $4850

[same title] [c. 1635] 41x55cm. (16x22") Original color. Excellent. [38] £2838 $5400

AMERICAE NOVA TABULA. AUCT: GUILJELMO BLAEU [1635] 41x55cm. (16x22") Panels at top and sides. Original color. Excellent. [21] £2549 $4850

ANDALUZIA CONTINENS SEVILLAM ET CORDUBAM [1635] 37x50cm. (14½x19½") Outline color. Very good. [34] £158 $300

ANGLIA REGNUM [c. 1635] 38x49cm. (15x19½") Col. Repair at cf margin; o/w VG. [23] £295 $561

ARABIA [1662] 43x53cm. (16½x20½") Original color. Lightly toned, reinforced centerfold split; o/w good. [22] £263 $500

ASIA NOVITER DELINEATA [(1618) c. 1650] 41x56cm. (16x22") "Carte-a-figures". Color. Fine. [5] £1575 $2997

[same title] [1672] 41x55cm. (16x22") Side panels. Full orig color. Excellent. [2] £1471 $2800

BISCAIA ET GUIPUSCOA CANTABRIAE VETERIS PARS [1635] 38x50cm. (15x19½") Outline color. Light text show-through; else very good. [34] £105 $200

BRITANNIA PROUT DIVISA FUIT TEMPORIBUS ANGLO-SAXONUM PRAESERTIM DURANTE ILLORUM HEPTARCHIA [1645] 42x53cm. (16½x21") Seven Saxon kingdoms; 14 side panels. Full color. Excellent. [21] £1156 $2200

[same title, date, dimensions] 14 side panels. Col. Old tape stains at margin; else VG. [34] £1051 $2000

BRITTANIA DUCATUS ... [1635] 33x38cm. (12½x15") Outline color. Very good. [34] £131 $250

CANTABRIGIENSIS COMITATUS; CAMBRIDGE SHIRE [1645-46] 42x53cm. (16½x20½") Original color. Very good. [31] £407 $775

CHINA VETERIBUS SINARUM REGIO [c. 1658] 41x50cm. (16x19½") Color. Near invisible tears just into lower centerfold; o/w fine. [5] £560 $1066

GRAECIA [1640] 41x52cm. (16x20½") Zacharalis 229. Color. Very good. [34] £197 $375

IAPONIA REGNUM [1655] 42x57cm. (16½x22½") From Martini's *Atlas Sinensis*. Original color. Small stain top margin; short split reinforced; o/w fine. [5] £1725 $3283

IMPERII SINARUM NOVA DESCRIPTIO [1655] 47x60cm. (18½x23½") From *Atlas Sinensis*. Color. Short marginal tear at left; minor top centerfold restoration. [5] £680 $1294

INDIA QUAE ORIENTALIS DICITUR, ET INSULAE ADIACENTES [1635] 41x50cm. (16x19½") Original color. Excellent. [22] £788 $1500

[same title] [(1635) c. 1660] 41x50cm. (16x19½") Original color. Fine. [5] £900 $1713

INSULAE AMERICANAE IN OCEANO SEPTENTRIONALI, CUM TERRIS ADIACENTIBUS [1633] 38x53cm. (15x20½") Original color. Excellent. [21] £893 $1700

LACUS LAMANNI ... [c. 1640] 51x41cm. (20x16") OL col. Margins repaired, else VG. [34] £236 $450

MAGNAE BRITTANIAE ET HIBERNIAE TABULA [c. 1631] 38x49cm. (15x19½") Color. Very good. [23] £450 $856

MAPPA AESTIVARUM INSULARUM, ALIAS BARMUDAS DICTARUM ... ACCURATE DESCRIPTA [1630] 40x53cm. (16x21") Original color. Excellent. [21] £946 $1800

MECHLINIA ... [1639] 51x41cm. (20x16") Outline col. Browning at centerfold; else VG. [34] £131 $250

MOLUCCAE INSULAE CELEBERRIMAE [c. 1630] 37x49cm. (14½x19½") OL col. VG. [31] £250 $475

NOVA BELGICA ET ANGLIA NOVA [(1631) c. 1660] 39x50cm. (15x20") Original color. Pristine. [5] £1650 $3140

[same title] [1635] 39x50cm. (15x20") Original color. Excellent. [21] £1314 $2500

[same title, date, dimensions] Orig outline col. Centerfold repair; good. [27] £1182 $2250

[same title] [c. 1635] 39x50cm. (15x19½") Original color. Mint. [37] £1682 $3200

NOVA TOTIUS GERMANIAE DESCRIPTIO [1631 (1643)] 48x38cm. (19½x15½") Outline color. Centerfold creasing; else very good. [34] £236 $450

NOVA TOTIUS TERRARUM ORBIS GEOGRAPHICA AC HYDROGRAPHICA TABULA [1606-1630] 41x54cm. (16x21½") Surround of panels. Shirley 225. Full color. Excellent. [21] £4467 $8500

[same title] [c. 1635] 41x54cm. (16x21½") State 4 of four. Surround of panels. Lower centerfold repaired; good. [30] £3258 $6200

NOVA VIRGINIAE TABULA [1630 / 1642] 37x48cm. (14½x19") Original outline color; engravings in full. Excellent. [1] £788 $1500

[same title] [1634] 37x48cm. (14½x19") Full original color. Excellent. [21] £736 $1400

[same title] [1665] 37x48cm. (14½x19") Full color. Very good. [31] £1051 $2000

NOVUS BRASILIA TYPUS [1642] 38x49cm. (15x19½") Full orig col. Excellent. [21] £289 $550

PARAGUAY, O PROV. DE RIO DE LA PLATA CUM REGIONIBUS ADIACENTIBUS TUCUMAN ET STA CRUZ DE LA SIERRA [c. 1635] 37x48cm. (14½x19") Color. [15] £202 $385

[same title] [1640] 37x48cm. (14½x19") French edition. Original color. Fine. [10] £184 $350

PRAEFECTURAE PARANAMBUCAE PARS BOREALIS [1662 (1680)] 41x53cm. (16½x21") Amsterdam: Covens & Mortier. Outline color. Good. [28] £394 $750

REGNO DI NAPOLI [1635 (1640)] 38x51cm. (15x19½") 12 side panels. Southern Italy. Outline color. Light age-toning; else VG to fine. [34] £342 $650

SUCHUEN IMPERII SINARUM PROVINCIA SEXTA [1655] 40x48cm. (15½x19") Original color. Excellent. [37] £307 $585

TAURICA CHERSONESUS NOSTRA AETATE PRZECOPSCA ET GAZARA DICITUR [1649] 38x50cm. (15x19½") Color. [15] £131 $250

VIRGINIA PARTIS AUSTRALIS, ET FLORIDAE PARTIS ORIENTALIS ... NOVA DESCRIPTIO [1640] 38x51cm. (15x20") Full original color. Excellent. [21] £736 $1400

[same title] [c. 1640] 36x51cm. (14x20") Outline color. Fine. [30] £762 $1450

[same title, date] 39x51cm. (15x20") Original color. Excellent. [37] £631 $1200

BLOME

A GENERAL MAPP OF THE EAST INDIES, COMPREHENDING THE ESTATS OR KINGDOMS OF THE GREAT MOGOL, .. DECAN .. GOLCONDE .. BISNAGAR .. MALABAR .. INDIA WITH OUT THE GANGES .. PEGU .. SIAN .. MALACCA .. COCHINCHINA .. INDIA WITHIN THE GANGES.. MALDIVES [1667] 40x34cm. (15½x13") Minor tear repaired; o/w very fine. [10] £184 $350

A GENERALL MAP OF THE ISLES OF GREAT BRITAINE DESIGNED BY MONSIEUR SANSON [c.1673] 38x50cm. (15x19½") Color. Very good. [23] £250 $476

A GENERALL MAPP OF ARABIA WITH THE RED SEA AND CIRCUMJACENT LANDS [1669] 28x39cm. (11x15½") [10] £145 $275

A GENERALL MAPP OF ASIA ... [1669] 39x55cm. (15½x21½") Trimmed to outer left side border; slight loss of neat line; o/w fine. [10] £92 $175

A GENERALL MAPP OF THE KINGDOM OF TARTARIA ... [1669] 26x39cm. (10x15½") Fine. [10] £32 $60

A MAPP OF THE EMPIRE OF THE SOPHIE OF PERSIA, WITH ITS SEVERAL PROVINCES [1669] 27x39cm. (11x15½") [10] £53 $100

A MAPP OF THE ESTATES OF THE GREAT DUKE OF RUSSIA, BLANCH, OR MOSCOVIA [1669] 28x40cm. (11x16") Fine. [10] £32 $60

[same title] [c. 1680] (no dims.) Outline color. Excellent. [35] £105 $200

A MAPP OF THE HIGHER AND LOWER AETHIOPIA COMPREHENDING YE SEVERAL KINGDOMS &C., IN EACH ... [1669] 30x41cm. (12x16") Side margins trimmed close; o/w fine. [10] £118 $225

A MAPP OF THE KINGDOME OF IRELAND [c. 1673] 37x39cm. (14½x15½") Color. Very good. [24] £250 $476

A MAPP OR GENERALL CARTE OF THE WORLD DESIGNED IN TWO PLAINE HEMISPHERES ... [1670] 39x53cm. (15½x20½") Double hemisphere. Shirley 455. Orig col. VG. [21] £2023 $3850

[same title] [1669] 39x53cm. (15½x20½") Minor splits & fold tears repaired; o/w fine. [10] £920 $1750

A NEW & EXACT MAPP OF YE ISLE OF JAMAICA ... [1671] 29x33cm. (11x13") Probably engraved by Hollar. [33] £400 $761

A NEW MAPP OF AFRICA DESIGNED BY MOUNSIR. SANSON, ... [1669] 39x54cm. (15x21½") Repaired splits and folds; o/w good. [10] £131 $250

A NEW MAPP OF AMERICA SEPTENTRIONALE [1669] 38x54cm. (15x21½") First issue. Insular California after Sanson. Fine. [10] £788 $1500

A NEW MAPP OF YE EMPIRE OF CHINA WITH ITS SEVERALL PROVINCES OR KINGDOMES, TOGETHER WITH THE ADJACENT ISLES OF JAPON OR NIPHON, FORMOSA, HAINAN, &C [1669] 30x39cm. (12x15½") Engraved by Hollar. Color. Excellent. [5] £385 $733

[same title, date, dimensions] Engraved by Hollar. [10] £236 $450

[same title] [1669-1683] 30x39cm. (12x15") Engraved by Hollar. [32] £450 $856

AFRICA OR LIBIA ULTERIOUR WHERE ARE THE COUNTRIES OF SAARA DESERT THE COUNTRIE OF NEGROES AND GUINE ... [1669] 29x40cm. (11x16") Fine. [10] £53 $100

BLONDEAU

ETATS UNIS DE L'AMERIQUE [c. 1798] 18x20cm. (7½x8") Color. [15] £45 $85

BLUNDELL

A PLAN OF JERUSALEM ACCORDING TO JOSEPHUS AND YE RABBIES [c. 1750] 23x18cm. (8½x7") On sheet 23 x 18" with vignettes and text. Some creasing; close margin for binding; else very good. [34] £79 $150

BLUNT

CAPE ANN HARBOUR SURVEYED BY THE REV. C. FETCH & W. MALBONE IN 1819 [1840] 20x20cm. (8x7½") (Gloucester, MA) [15] £29 $55

CHARLESTON HARBOUR [1827] 18x10cm. (7x4") NY: Hooker, sc. [15] £32 $60

ENTRANCE TO THE CHESAPEAKE BAY REDUCED FROM SURVEYS BY D.P. ADAMS BY ORDER OF THE NAVY COMMISSIONERS [1854] 19x21cm. (7½x8½") [26] £32 $60

LITTLE EGG HARBOR [N.J.] [1841] 13x20cm. (5x8½") Color. [15] £42 $80

BOCHARTI

EDENIS SEU PARADISI TERRESTRIS SITUS [1692] 30x20cm. (11½x8") Middle East; Eden is just east of Babylon. Full color. Excellent. [38] £71 $135

BOISSEAU

TYPUS ORBIS TERRARUM DESCRIPTION DE LA TERRE UNIVERSELLE [c. 1686] 13x20cm. (5x8") Double hemispheres. [3] £223 $425

BOLTON

A NEW AND CORRECT MAP OF THE COAST OF AFRICA [1766] 38x48cm. (15x19") From Postlethwayt, after d'Anville. Very good. [31] £197 $375

ASIA, PLATE II, JAPAN, KOREA, THE MOGULS AND PART OF CHINA [1755] 53x36cm. (21x13½") After d'Anville, engraved by Seale. Outline color. [35] £105 $200

ASIA, PLATE III, THE PHILIPPINES, CAROLINES, MOLUCCAS AND SPICE ISLANDS [1755] 48x36cm. (19x13½") After d'Anville, engraved by Seale. Outline color. [35] £92 $175

BONNE

CARTE DE L'ARABIE, DU GOLFE PERSIQUE, ET DE LA MER ROUGE, AVEC L'EGYPTE, LA NUBIE ET L'ABISSINIE [c. 1770] 21x31cm. (8½x12½") [10] £21 $40

CARTE DE L'EMPIRE DE LA CHINE, DE LA TARTARIE CHINOISE, ET DU ROYAUME DE COREE: AVEC LES ISLES DU JAPON [c. 1770] 32x21cm. (12½x8½") [10] £18 $35

CARTE DE L'ISLE DE LA JAMAIQUE [1780] 23x36cm. (9x14") [3] £63 $120

CARTE DE L'ISLE DE LA MARTINIQUE, COLONIE FRANCOISE DANS LES ISLES ANTILLES [c.1780] 36x23cm. (14x9") Minor centerfold soiling. [3] £63 $120

[same title] [1780] 32x21cm. (13x8½") [10] £16 $30

CARTE DE L'ISLE DE ST. DOMINGUE UNE DES GRANDES ANTILLES, COLONIE FRANCOISE ET EXPAGNOLE [c. 1780] 23x36cm. (9x14") [3] £63 $120

CARTE DE LA LOUISIANE ET DE LA FLORIDE [1778] 33x23cm. (13x8½") Col. [15] £79 $150

.[same title] [1780] 41x23cm. (16x9") [3] £79 $150

CARTE DE LA PARTIE INFERIEURE DE L'INDE [c. 1770] 21x32cm. (8x12½") [10] £16 $30

CARTE DE LA PARTIE NORD, DES ETATS UNIS, DE L'AMERIQUE SEPTENTRIONALE [1780] 20x36cm. (8x14") Mild centerfold soiling. [3] £79 $150

CARTE DE LA PARTIE SUD DES ETATS UNIS DE L'AMERIQUE SEPTENTRIONALE [c. 1780] 23x41cm. (9x16") Georgia and Carolinas. [3] £84 $160

CARTE DE LA TARTARIE INDEPENDANTE QUI COMPREND LE PAYS DES CALMUKS, DES USBEKS ET TURKESTAN [c. 1770] 30x46cm. (12½x17½") Color. [15] £66 $125

CARTE DES ISLES ANTILLES ET DU GOLFE DU MEXIQUE; ... [1780-1782] 66x145cm. (26x56½") Probably separately issued. Original wash color. Remargined top and bottom; some loss and mold stain along border; else clean. [21] £1235 $2350

CARTE DES ISLES DE LA SOCIETE [1787] 23x36cm. (9x13½") Color. [35] £39 $75

CARTE GENERALE DE TOUTES LES PARTIES CONNUES DE LA SURFACE DE LA TERRE EN CARTE REDUITE [1782] 25x36cm. (9½x14") With "Sandwich Is." Color. [15] £76 $145

CARTE REDUITE DES TERRES ET DES MERS DU GLOBE TERRESTRE [1782 (1800)] 23x33cm. (8½x13") Mercator projection. Outline color. [12] £66 $125

ISLES MAYORQUE, MINORQUE ET YVICE [1780] 23x36cm. (9½x13½") Outline & wash color. [35] £42 $80

L'ANCIEN ET LE NOUVEAU MEXIQUE, AVEC LA FLORIDE ET LA BASSE LOUSIANE [1787-88] 36x23cm. (13½x9½") From Bonne & Demarest, *Atlas Encyclopedique*. [27] £150 $285

L'ANCIEN MONDE ET LE NOUVEAU EN DEUX HEMISPHERES [1783] 21x41cm. (8½x16") Good. [10] £45 $85

L'ISLE DE TERRE-NEUVE, L'ACADIE, OU LA NOUVELLE ECOSSE, L'ISLE ST JEAN ET LA PARTIE ORIENTALE DU CANADA [1780] 21x32cm. (8½x12½") Color. [15] £71 $135

[same title] [1780] 23x36cm. (9x14") Minor centerfold soiling. [3] £58 $110

LE NOUVEAU MEXIQUE [1780] 21x31cm. (8x12½") [10] £63 $120

LE NOUVEAU MEXIQUE, AVEC LA PARTIE SEPTENTRIONALE DE L'ANCIEN, OU DE LA NOUVELLE ESPAGNE [1780] 21x32cm. (8½x12½") [10] £66 $125

[same title, date, dimensions] Recent outline col. VG. [26] £126 $240

LES ETATS UNIS DE L'AMERIQUE SEPTENTRIONALE, CONTENANT EN OUTRE, LES ISLES ROYALE DE TERRE NEUVE ... DE LA LOUISIANE ET DE LA FLORIDE [1781] 33x23cm. (13x8½") Color. [15] £97 $185

LES ISLES DE LA GUADELOUPE, DE MARIE GALANTE, DE LA DESIRADE, ET CELLES DES SAINTES [1780] 21x32cm. (8½x12½") [10] £16 $30

LES ISLES PHILIPPINES, CELLE DE FORMOSE, LE SUD DE LA CHINE, LES ROYAUMES DE TUNKIN, DE COCHINCHINE, DE CAMBOGE, DE SIAM, DES LAOS; AVEC PARTIE DE CEUX DE PEGU ET D'AVA [c. 1780] 22x32cm. (8½x12½") Wash color. Excellent. [38] £50 $95

PARTIE OCCIDENTALE DU CANADA, CONTENANT LES CINQ GRAND LACS, AVEC LES PAYS CIRCONVOISINS [1780] 21x31cm. (8½x12½") Color. [15] £71 $135

BORDONE

[WEST INDIES, ETC.] [1547] 8x15cm. (3½x5½") [10] £210 $400

[WORLD] [1528] 22x38cm. (8½x15") Shirley 59. Excellent. [38] £1156 $2200

BOTERO

AFRICA [1594] 18x25cm. (7x9½") [36] £105 $200

BOUCHETTE

PLAN OF THE DIFFERENT CHANNELS, LEADING FROM KINGSTON TO LAKE ONTARIO [1815] 22x25cm. (8½x10") [10] £39 $75

PLAN OF THE TOWN OF WILLIAM HENRY [1815] 24x22cm. (9½x8½") Fine. [10] £50 $95

BOWEN, E.

A COMPLETE MAP OF THE SOUTHERN CONTINENT SURVEY'D BY CAPT. ABEL TASMAN [1744] 37x48cm. (14½x19") Minor tears repaired; o/w fine. [10] £972 $1850

A CORRECT DRAUGHT OF THE NORTH POLE AND OF THE COUNTRIES HITHERTO DISCOVERED INTERCEPTED BETWEEN THE POLE AND THE PARALLEL OF 50 DEGREES ... BY EMAN: BOWEN ... [1748] 39x43cm. (15½x17") Fine. [10] £118 $225

A MAP OF INDIA ON THE WEST SIDE OF THE GANGES ... [1740] 32x23cm. (12½x9") 10] £18 $35

A NEW & ACCURATE CHART OF THE WESTERN OR ATLANTIC OCEAN [1748] 37x45cm. (14½x17½") Center split repaired. [10] £92 $175

A NEW & ACCURATE MAP OF CHINA, DRAWN FROM SURVEYS MADE BY THE JESUIT MISSIONARIES ... [1740] 34x42cm. (13½x16½") Harris, pub. Fine. [10] £66 $125

A NEW & ACCURATE MAP OF THE WHOLE RUSSIAN EMPIRE AS CONTAIN'D BOTH IN EUROPE & ASIA [1747] 36x48cm. (14x18½") Color. [15] £66 $125

A NEW AND ACCURATE CHART OF THE WEST INDIES WITH THE ADJACENT COASTS OF NORTH AND SOUTH AMERICA. DRAWN FROM THE BEST AUTHORITIES... [1748] 37x45cm. (14½x17½") [10] £171 $325

A NEW AND ACCURATE MAP OF AMERICA [1748] 35x45cm. (14x17½") Slight offsetting. [10] £184 $350

A NEW AND ACCURATE MAP OF ANATOLIA OR ASIA MINOR WITH SYRIA AND SUCH OTHER PROVINCES OF THE TURKISH EMPIRE ... [1747] 35x43cm. (13½x16½") Color. Excellent. [37] £66 $125

A NEW AND ACCURATE MAP OF FRANCE WITH ITS ACQUISITIONS ... [1747] 36x44cm. (14x17½") With part of Italy. Color. Excellent. [37] £58 $110

A NEW AND ACCURATE MAP OF LOUISIANA, WITH PART OF FLORIDA AND CANADA, AND THE ADJACENT COUNTRIES [1747] 34x42cm. (13½x16½") Outline col. Excel. [35] £210 $400

A NEW AND ACCURATE MAP OF PERSIA WITH THE ADJACENT COUNTRIES ... [1747] 35x42cm. (14x16½") Color. Excellent. [37] £66 $125

A NEW AND ACCURATE MAP OF POLAND, LITHUANIA &C. DIVIDED INTO ITS PALATINATS ... [1747] 35x43cm. (13½x17") Color. Excellent. [37] £66 $125

A NEW AND ACCURATE MAP OF SAVOY, PIEDMONT, AND MONTERRAT, EXHIBITING THE PRESENT SEAT OF WAR ... [1747] 35x43cm. (14x16½") Color. Excellent. [37] £92 $175

A NEW AND ACCURATE MAP OF THE EAST INDIA ISLANDS ... [1747] 34x42cm. (13½x16½") Color. Excellent. [37] £131 $250

A NEW AND ACCURATE MAP OF THE NORTHERN PARTS OF ITALY ... [1747] 32x23cm. (12½x9") With "Road of Leghorn". [37] £39 $75

A NEW AND ACCURATE MAP OF THE WORLD DRAWN FROM THE BEST AUTHORITIES AND REGULATED BY ASTRONOMICAL OBSERVATIONS: DESCRIBING THE COURSE OF THE FOLLOWING CIRCUM-NAVIGATORS VIZ. FERDINAND MAGELLAN, SR. FRANCIS DRAKE AND COMMODORE ANSON[1744] 29x55cm. (11½x21½") Inconspicuous, lengthy tear repaired. [10] £171 $325

A NEW AND ACCURATE MAP OF TURKEY IN ASIA, ARABIA, &C. ... [1747] 35x43cm. (14x16½") Color. Excellent. [37] £66 $125

A NEW AND ACCURATE MAP OF TURKEY IN EUROPE, WITH THE ADJACENT COUNTRIES OF HUNGARY, LITTLE TARTARY &C ... [1747] 35x43cm. (14x16½") Col. Excel. [37] £66 $125

A NEW AND ACCURATE MAP OF VIRGINIA & MARYLAND LAID DOWN FROM SURVEYS AND REGULATED BY ASTRON'L OBSERVAT'NS ... [1752] 33x23cm. (13x9") Second state. Outline color. [6] £313 $595

A NEW AND CORRECT CHART OF ALL THE KNOWN WORLD LAID DOWN ACCORDING TO MERCATOR PROJECTION. EXHIBITING ALL THE LATE DISCOVERIES & IMPROVEMENTS: THE WHOLE BEING COLLECTED FROM THE MOST AUTHENTIC JOURNALS, CHARTS &C [1744] 38x46cm. (15x18½") Fine. [26] £145 $275

[same title, date] 37x45cm. (14½x18") [10] £92 $175

A NEW MAP OF GEORGIA WITH PART OF CAROLINA, FLORIDA, AND LOUISIANA. DRAWN FROM ORIGINAL DRAUGHTS ASSISTED BY THE MOST APPROVED MAPS AND CHARTS [1748] 36x48cm. (14x18½") In Harris. [10] £657 $1250

AN ACCURATE MAP OF IRELAND [c. 1750] 17x22cm. (6½x8½") Color. VG. [24] £75 $143

AN ACCURATE MAP OF NORTH AMERICA DESCRIBING AND DISTINGUISHING THE BRITISH AND SPANISH DOMINIONS ON THIS GREAT CONTINENT ACCORDING TO THE DEFINITIVE TREATY CONCLUDED AT PARIS THE 10TH FEB.Y 1763 ALSO ALL THE WEST INDIA ISLANDS ...[1775] 101x117cm. (40x46") London: Robert Sayer. Gibson, sc. Four sheets joined. Outline color. Lined on tissue; trimmed to neat line. [16] £2347 $4466

[same title] [c. 1772] 51x114cm. (20x45") Upper two of a four sheet map. Engraved by John Gibson. Original outline color. Slight age toning; ragged edges; slight fold separations; VG. [7] £867 $1650

AN ACCURATE MAP OF THE EAST INDIES EXHIBITING THE COURSE OF THE EUROPEAN TRADE BOTH ON THE CONTINENT AND ISLANDS...BY EMAN BOWEN [1744] 37x45cm. (14½x18") [10] £79 $150

AN ACCURATE MAP OF THE WEST INDIES. DRAWN FROM THE BEST AUTHORITIES, ASSISTED BY THE MOST APPROVED MODERN MAPS AND CHARTS... [1747] 35x42cm. (13½x16½") [10] £155 $295

LES PAYS BAS OU SONT REMARQUEES LES AQUISITIONS DE LA FRANCE JUSQUES A LA TREVE DE 1684 [1747] 14x16cm. (5½x6½") Excellent. [37] £34 $65

NUOVA ED ESTATTA CARTA DEL MONDO TRATTA DA AUTHENTICHE INPREZIONE LOCALI E DALLE PUI APPROVATE CARTE MODERNE ET RETTIFICATA DA OBSERVAZIONI ASTRONOMICHE [1744] 38x48cm. (15x18½") Italian ed. Recent outline color. [26] £171 $325

THE GALLAPAGOS ISLANDS DISCOVERED AND DESCRIBED BY CAPT. COWLEY IN 1684 [1744] 32x20cm. (12½x8") Mint. [10] £63 $120

BOWEN, T.

A MAP OF THE ISLAND OF DOMINICA TAKEN FROM AN ACTUAL SURVEY; ALSO PART OF MARTINICO & GUADALUPE ... [1778] 25x20cm. (9½x8") Color. [15] £50 $95

A NEW & ACCURATE MAP OF NORTH AMERICA... [c.1779] 27x44cm. (10½x17") Color. [15] £92 $175

[same title] [1779] 27x44cm. (10½x17") From Middleton's Geography". Fine. [10] £53 $100

A NEW AND ACCURATE MAP OF IRELAND [1780] 29x19cm. (11½x7½") VG+. [18] £58 $110

AN ACCURATE MAP OF THE HOLY LAND WITH ADJACENT COUNTRIES [1750] 28x18cm. (11½x7") Color. [15] £26 $50

BOWLES

A GENERAL MAP OF THE MIDDLE BRITISH COLONIES IN AMERICA ... BY MR. LEWIS EVANS [1771] 49x65cm. (19½x25½") Original outline color. Wear in margins and some at centerfold, with very small hole; expertly repaired; o/w very good. [31] £841 $1600

A NEW AND ACCURATE MAP OF NORTH AMERICA, DRAWN FROM THE FAMOUS MR. D'ANVILLE WITH IMPROVEMENTS FROM THE BEST ENGLISH MAPS; AND ENGRAVED BY R.W. SEALE; ALSO THE NEW DIVISIONS ACCORDING TO THE LATE TREATY OF PEACE, BY PETER BELL, GEO.[1771] 47x51cm. (18½x20") Full original color. Some light staining, o/w very good. [2] £998 $1900

BOWLE'S DRAUGHT OF THE RIVER THAMES, FROM IT'S SPRING IN GLOUCESTER-SHIRE, TO ITS INFLUX INTO THE SEA; WITH A TABLE OF ALL THE LOCKS, WEARS, AND BRIDGES THEREUPON; SHEWING THE TOLLS PAYABLE AT EACH AND THEIR DISTANCE BY WATER FROM ONE ANOTHER [1774 (1793)] 20x88cm. (8x34½") Folding map. Col. Fine. [19] £210 $400

BOWLES' NEW MAP OF NORTH AMERICA AND THE WEST INDIES ... [1763-1780] 101x115cm. (40x45½") Dissected, laid on canvas folding into 19th c. slipcase Orig wash col. [33] £1500 $2855

BOWLES'S NEW ONE-SHEET MAP OF ASIA DIVIDED INTO ITS EMPIRES, KINGDOMS, STATES AND OTHER SUB-DIVISIONS [c. 1760] 48x56cm. (19x22") Bowles & Carver, pub. Full wash and outline color. [10] £63 $120

BOWLES'S NEW POCKET MAP OF THE MOST INHABITED PART OF NEW ENGLAND; ... TOGETHER WITH AN ACCURATE PLAN OF THE TOWN, HARBOUR AND ENVIRONS OF BOSTON ... [1785] 64x51cm. (25x20½") After Jefferys, reduced in scale and updated. Original outline color. Few small repaired tears; else excellent. [22] £1261 $2400

BOWLES'S NEW TRAVELLING MAP OF ENGLAND AND WALES EXHIBITING ALL THE DIRECT AND PRINCIPAL CROSS ROADS; WITH THE DISTANCES IN MEASURED IN MILES [late 18 c.] 59x52cm. (23x20½") 2nd ed. Linen-backed folding map in worn marbled slipcase with original labels. Outline color. Light age-darkening, backing torn at several fold lines with minimal loss. [19] £92 $175

BOYNTON

A MAP OF THE UNITED STATES, FROM THE LATEST SURVEYS, WITH THE HEIGHT OF MOUNTAINS AND LENGTH OF THE PRINCIPAL RIVERS. PATENT. PRINTED BY JOSEPH W. TUTTLE BOSTON ... [1841] 64x61cm. (25½x24") Printed on linen. A few mends, lightly toned; o/w excellent. [22] £631 $1200

[same title, date] 69x61cm. (26½x24½") On linen. Boston: Tremont Print Co. Color. Two small repairs; good. [28] £342 $650

BRADFORD

ALABAMA [1838 (1842)] 36x29cm. (14x11½") Color. Good. [28] £76 $145

ARKANSAS [1838] 29x37cm. (11½x14½") Includes Miller County. Color. [15] £74 $140

BALTIMORE [1838] 28x38cm. (11x14½") Color. [15] £66 $125

[same title] [1842] 29x36cm. (11½x14½") Changes from 1838 issue. Full color. [36] £39 $75

DELAWARE [1838] 36x30cm. (14½x11½") By Lucas. Old color. [15] £71 $135

DISTRICT OF COLUMBIA [1835] 25x19cm. (10x7½") Color. [15] £45 $85

FLORIDA [1842] 36x33cm. (14½x12½") Color. [36] £71 $135

GEORGIA [c. 1839] 25x20cm. (10x8") Color. [15] £45 $85

INDIANA [1838] 36x30cm. (14x12") Full color. Fine. [14] £58 $110

INDIANA [1838] 28x30cm. (11½x11½") Color. Fine. [15] £79 $150

[same title] [1838-1846] 36x28cm. (14x11") "Corrected to 1846". Full col. Fine. [14] £66 $125

[same title] [c. 1839] 36x30cm. (14x11½") 2nd state. Color. [15] £74 $140

INDIANA & OHIO [1835] 20x25cm. (8x10") Outline color. Very good. [14] £45 $85

LOUISIANA AND PART OF ARKANSAS [1838] 25x20cm. (10x8") 2nd ed. Color. [15] £37 $70

LOWER CANADA AND NEW BRUNSWICK [1842] 28x36cm. (11½x14") Inset: Nova Scotia. Full color. [35] £32 $60

MARYLAND [1838] 29x36cm. (11½x14") [36] £47 $90

MEXICO, GUATEMALA AND THE WEST INDIES [1835] 20x28cm. (8x11") Outline color. Minor transference. [26] £66 $125

MISSISSIPPI [c. 1839] 25x20cm. (10x8") Outline color. [15] £45 $85

NEW HAMPSHIRE [1838] 38x28cm. (14½x11") Outline color. Fine. [12] £58 $110

NEW HAMPSHIRE & VERMONT [1835] 25x19cm. (10x7½") Outline color. [9] £66 $125

[same title, date] 25x20cm. (10½x8") [15] £32 $60

NORTH CAROLINA [1838] 29x36cm. (11½x14½") Color. [15] £71 $135

[same title] [1846] 20x28cm. (8x10½") Color. [15] £39 $75

NORTH CAROLINA, SOUTH CAROLINA AND GEORGIA [1835] 20x26cm. (8x10") Outline color. Very good. [13] £39 $75

NORTHERN AFRICA [1835] 20x25cm. (8x10") Color. [15] £16 $30

OCEANICA OR OCEANIA [1835] 20x25cm. (8x10") Color. [15] £21 $40

PENNSYLVANIA [1838] 29x36cm. (11½x14½") Color. [15] £71 $135

SOUTH CAROLINA [1838] 30x38cm. (11½x14½") Color. [15] £71 $135

TENNESSEE [1835] 20x25cm. (7½x10") Color. [15] £42 $80

UPPER CANADA [1838] 29x36cm. (11½x14") Old color. [15] £26 $50

[same title] [1842] 29x36cm. (11½x14") Full color. [35] £32 $60

VERMONT [1843] 36x27cm. (14x10½"). Color. Slight foxing; clean. [9] £87 $165

BRADFORD & GOODRICH

GEORGIA [1841] 36x30cm. (14x11½") With 2 text sheets. Full col. Very good. [13] £87 $165

INDIANA [1841] 36x30cm. (14½x11½") Full color. Very fine. [14] £63 $120

BRADLEY *Try Mitchell, S.A. (Atlas Maps 1860 & Later)*

ARIZONA AND NEW MEXICO [1889] 38x56cm. (15x22") Color. Excellent. [26] £42 $80

COLORADO [1889] 43x56cm. (17x22") Full soft color. [26] £47 $90

COUNTY MAP OF THE STATES OF GEORGIA AND ALABAMA [1887] 30x53cm. (12½x20½") Full color. Fine. [13] £26 $50

INDIAN TERRITORY [1889] 33x43cm. (12½x17") Small Alaska map on page. Full color. [26] £47 $90

INDIANA [1887] 36x30cm. (14x11½") Color. [15] £21 $40

NORTH AND SOUTH DAKOTA [1889] 53x43cm. (21x17") Full soft color. [26] £42 $80

TEXAS [1885] 43x58cm. (16½x22½") Greer Co. contended. Color. [15] £45 $85

BRAUN & HOGENBERG

[TITLE PAGE] DE PRAECIPIUS TOTIUS UNIVERSI URBIBUS LIBER SECUNDUS [1575] 35x22cm. (14x8½") *Civitates Orbis Terrarum*, Vol 2. Original color. Fine. [5] £185 $352

[TITLE PAGE] THEATRI PRAECIPUARUM TOTIUS MUNDI URBIUM LIBER SEXTUS [1618] 36x23cm. (14x8½") *Civitates Orbis Terrarum*, vol. 6. Orig col. Slightly soiled margin; fine. [30] £342 $650

ADEN, ARABIA SOELICIS EMPORIUM CELEBERRIMI NOMINIS, QUO EX INDIA, AETHIOPIA. ER PERSIDE ... [1580] 33x48cm. (13½x18½") Full original color. Excellent. [2] £394 $750

ALEXANDRIA, VETUSTISSUMUM AEGYPTI EMPORIUM ... [1575] 37x49cm. (14½x19") Full color. Excellent. [38] £276 $525

AMSTELREDAMUM, NOBILE INFERIORIS GERMANIAE OPPIDUM ... [1572] 34x48cm. (13½x18½") Original color. [32] £650 $1237

CIVITAS EXONIAE (VULGO EXCESTER) URBS PRIMARIA IN COMITATU DEVONIAE [1617] 33x36cm. (12½x14") Full original color. Excellent. [2] £631 $1200

DAMASCUS [1571-1617] 33x36cm. (13½x14") Repair tears just into lower image. [31] £328 $625

EDENBURGUM, SCOTIAE METROPOLIS [c. 1580] 34x45cm. (13½x18") Full color. Very good. [21] £315 $600

GENUA [1580] 15x48cm. (6½x19") Full original color. Excellent. [2] £355 $675

GRANADA [1563] 33x51cm. (13x20") Full original color. Excellent. [2] £499 $950

HAEC EST NOBILIS, & FLORENS ILLA NEAPOLIS ... [1572] 33x48cm. (13x19") Full original color. Excellent. [2] £499 $950

HIEROSOLYMA CLARISSIMA TOTIUS ORIENTIS CIVITAS IUDAEE METROPOLIS [1572] 33x49cm. (13x19") Pin-holes lower border; upper margin clipped, partial loss of border; else good. [37] £184 $350

[same title] [1582] 34x48cm. (13x19") Full original color. Excellent. [2] £578 $1100

LE BRIXA / SETTENIL [1580] 33x41cm. (13x16½") Full original color. Excellent. [2] £394 $750

LUTETIA, VULGARI NOMINE PARIS, URBS GALLIA MAXIMA ... [1572] 36x48cm. (13½x19") Color. Paper toned; else fine. [1] £525 $1000

OSTIA [c. 1580] 30x48cm. (11½x19½") Ancient port of Rome. Full col. Excellent. [21] £236 $450

PALERMO [1580] 13x48cm. (5½x18½") Full original color. Excellent. [2] £407 $775

ROMA [1575] 33x48cm. (13x19") Outline color. Light age-toning; else fine. [34] £788 $1500

[same title] [c. 1580] 33x48cm. (13x19") Full original color. Excellent. [2] £683 $1300

SEVILLA [1572] 36x48cm. (14x19") Full orig color. Minor staining; else fine. [21] £631 $1200

[same title] [1580] 36x48cm. (14x18½") Full original color. Excellent. [2] £289 $550

TUNETIS URBIS, AC NOVAE EIUS ARCIS, ET GULETAE, QUAE PHILIPPO HISPAN REGI PARENT ... [1575] 33x42cm. (13x16½") Pin-holes lower margin, close top margin; else fine. [37] £131 $250

VILNA LITVANIAE METROPOLIS [1581] 36x51cm. (14½x19½") Full orig col. Excel. [2] £447 $850

ZURYCH [1582] 38x48cm. (14½x19") Original color. Toned; o/w very good. [21] £1051 $2000

BRION DE LA TOUR

AMERIQUE SEPTENTRIONALE, OU SE REMARQUENT LES ETATS UNIS [1783] 51x73cm. (20x29") Original outline color. Considerable repair; no loss. [1] £788 $1500

GUAYANE, TERRE FERME, ISLES ANTILLES, ET NLLE. ESPAGNE [1790] 28x48cm. (11x19") Text at sides. Color. [15] £76 $145

L'IRLANDE DIVISEE PAR PROVINCES CIVILES ET ECCLESIATIQUES [c. 1766] 27x31cm. (10½x12") Color. Very good. [24] £98 $186

NOUVEAU PLAN DE PARIS AVEC SES AUGMENTATIONS TANT FINIES QUE PROJETEES [1786] 57x81cm. (22½x31½") Linen-backed folding plan in original slipcase with label. Backing worn through at junctures, some age darkening; slipcase worn, bottom strip torn. [19] £250 $475

BRITISH GOVERNMENT *Try Admiralty*

PLAN OF MALTA FROM THE SURVEY BY LIEUTT, WORSLEY R.E. MADE IN THE YEAR 1824; PLAN OF GOZO ... ; THE ISLAND OF MALTA FROM VALETTA TO MARSA SCIROCCO ... IN 1854; PLAN OF ST. PAULS'S BAY ...; PLAN OF THE HARBOURS AND FORTIFICATIONS OF VALETTA ...[1824 - 1856] 60x59cm. (23½x23") 5 linen-backed folding maps in original slipcase with label. Some color. Some pencil and ink marks; slight soiling and foxing; all VG. [19] £578 $1100

BROWN, T.

A NEW ACCURATE TRAVELLING MAP OF SCOTLAND WITH THE DISTANCES MARKED BETWEEN EACH STAGE IN MEASURED MILES [1793] 56x47cm. (22x18½") Linen-backed folding map in original slipcase with label. Outline color. Centerfold backing wearing through in places; suggestion of foxing; very good. [19] £105 $200

BRUCE, J.

TO MY WORTHY AND ... THIS PLAN OF TWO ATTEMPTS TO ARRIVE AT THE SOURCE OF THE NILE ... [c. 1790] 51x30cm. (20½x11½") [35] £79 $150

TO THE RIGHT HONORABLE ... THIS MAP SHEWING THE TRACT OF SOLOMAN'S FLEET IN THEIR THREE YEARS VOYAGE FROM ELANITIC GULF TO OPHIR AND TARSHISHI ... [c.1790] 69x30cm. (26½x12½") Full color. [35] £79 $150

BRUE

CARTE DE L'AMERIQUE SEPTENTRIONALE [1821] 36x51cm. (14½x20") Col. [15] £150 $285

CARTE DE LA PALESTINE SOUS LA DOMINATION ROMAINE ... [1828] 51x36cm. (20x14½") Original outline color. [10] £26 $50

CARTE GENERALE D L'ASIE [1820] 36x51cm. (14½x20") Original outline color. [10] £21 $40

CARTE GENERALE DES ILES ANTILLES DES ISLES ET BANCS DE BAHAMA, DES ETATS-UNIS DE L'AMERIQUE-CENTRALE, DE LA MER DU MEXIQUE [1832] 64x94cm. (24½x36½") Paris: C. Picquet. Color. [15] £460 $875

CARTE GENERALE DES INDES EN-DECA ET AU-DELA DE GANGE [1821] 36x51cm. (14½x20") Original color code. [10] £32 $60

NOUVELLE CARTE DU MEXIQUE ET D'UNE PARTIE DES PROVINCES UNIES DE L'AMERIQUE CENTRALE. DEDIEE A L'ACADEMIE ROYALE DES SCIENCES [1837] 94x64cm. (37x25") Paris: C. Picquet. North to 44 deg. Texas as a republic. Wall map. Color. [15] £604 $1150

BRYANT UNION

THE HUDSON BY DAYLIGHT. MAP FROM NEW YORK BAY TO THE HEAD OF TIDE WATER, CONTAINING THE NAMES OF STREAMS, ISLANDS AND HEIGHTS OF MOUNTAINS ... PROMINENT RESIDENCES, HISTORIC LANDMARKS, THE OLD REACHES OF THE HUDSON AND OLD INDIANNAMES [1894] 14x254cm. (5½x100") Unbacked folding map in protective cover. Color. Very good. [19] £29 $55

BUACHE

CARTE D'UNE PARTIE DE L'AMERIQUE POUR LA NAVIGATION DES ISLES ET DU GOLFE DU MEXIQUE [1740] 51x94cm. (19½x36½") Early outline color. Margins repaired; corner replaced just to border. [11] £325 $618

CARTE DE L'ISLE DE LA MARTINIQUE COLONIE FRANCOISE DE L'UNE DES ISLES ANTILLES DE L'AMERIQUE ... [1732] 47x61cm. (18½x24") Brittle outer margins; foxing. [10] £79 $150

CARTE DES LIEUX ON LES DIFFERENT LONGEURS DE PENDULE / CARTE DU GLOBE TERRESTRE ... / CARTE DES TERRES AUSTRALES ... [1740-1746] 51x66cm. (20½x26") 3 maps on one sheet. Color. [15] £236 $450

PLANISPHERE PHYSIQUE OU L'ON VOIT DU POLE SEPTENTRIONALE CE QUE L'ON CONNOIT DE TERRES ET DE MERS ... [1753] 36x46cm. (14x17½") Polar projection with notes at sides. Color. [15] £250 $475

BUCHON *Dimensions sometimes include text around map.*

CARTE DU TERRITOIRE D'ARKANSAS ET DES AUTRES TERRITOIRES DES ETATS-UNIS [1825] 48x61cm. (19x24") dimensions include text at sides. Shows western territories. Col. [15] £181 $345

CARTE GEOGRAPHIQUE, STATISTIQUE ET HISTORIQUE DE L'INDIANA [1825] 28x23cm. (11x8½") Surround of text on double folio sheet. Full color. Very fine. [14] £92 $175

CARTE GEOGRAPHIQUE, STATISTIQUE ET HISTORIQUE DE LA JAMAIQUE [1825] 46x61cm. (18x24") Text at sides. Color. [15] £63 $120

CARTE GEOGRAPHIQUE, STATISTIQUE ET HISTORIQUE DE LA MARTINIQUE [1825] 47x61cm. (18½x24") Text at sides. Color. [15] £63 $120

CARTE GEOGRAPHIQUE, STATISTIQUE ET HISTORIQUE DE L'INDIANA [1825] 46x61cm. (18½x24") Map 15" x 12". Text at sides. Color. [15] £97 $185

CARTE GEOGRAPHIQUE, STATISTIQUE ET HISTORIQUE DE L'AMERIQUE [1825] 48x64cm. (19x25½") dimensions include text. Color. [15] £50 $95

CARTE GEOGRAPHIQUE, STATISTIQUE ET HISTORIQUE DU VERMONT [1825] 46x61cm. (18x24") Dimensions include text. Color. Clean. [9] £110 $210

CARTE GEOGRAPHIQUE, STATISTIQUE ET HISTORIQUE DU KENTUCKY [1825] 28x46cm. (11x18") On sheet with text, 19x24" Color. [15] £79 $150

CARTE GEOGRAPHIQUE, STATISTIQUE ET HISTORIQUE DU NEW-YORK [1825] 47x62cm. (18½x24½") Margin text. [15] £66 $125

BUNTING

AFRICA TERTIA PARS TERRAE [1594] 28x36cm. (11x14½") Two stains; else VG. [22] £342 $650

ASIA SECUNDA PARS TERRAE IN FORMA PEGASI [1594] 28x36cm. (11x14½") Asia as Pegasus. Light toning; o/w excellent. [22] £788 $1500

BESCHREIBUNG DES HEILIGEN LANDES [1581] 27x38cm. (10½x15") Close left margin as usual, else fine. [37] £131 $250

DIE GANTZE WELT IN EIN KLEBERBLAT BELCHES IST DER STADT HANNOVER / MEINES LIEBEN BATERLANDES WAPEN [c. 1581] 25x36cm. (10½x14½") Clover-shaped woodcut map; Jerusalem at center. Margins replaced, no loss of printed surface. [1] £2365 $4500

[same title] [(1581) 1587] 26x36cm. (10½x14") Clover-leaf map from *Itinerarium Sacrae Scriptura.* Shirley 142. Color. Minor centerfold reinforcement. [5] £1850 $3521

EUROPA PRIMA PARS TERRAE IN FORMA VIRGINIS [1581] 24x35cm. (9½x14") Europe as Queen. Repaired worming. [38] £460 $875

[same title] [1594] 25x38cm. (10½x14½") Europe as Queen. Paper toned; o/w excel. [22] £788 $1500

TAFFEL DER LENDER DARIN DER APOSTEL PAULUS GEPREDIGET HAT [1594] 30x38cm. (11½x15") Light staining; o/w very good. [22] £289 $550

TAFFEL DES HEILIGEN LANDES ZU DEM NEWEN TESTAMENT DIENLICH [1594] 28x20cm. (11x7½") Light staining; o/w very good. [22] £236 $450

BURGESS

MAP OF NORTH AMERICA [1839, c. 1850] 27x21cm. (10½x8½") Orig full col. [18] £45 $85

BURLEIGH LITH.

WEST CHAZY, N.Y. [1899] 38x61cm. (15x24") By Fausel. Bird's eye view. Minor repair. [15] £118 $225

BURR

ARKANSAS [1835] 28x30cm. (10½x12") Full color. [3] £84 $160

[same title, date] 28x33cm. (11x13") Color. [15] £118 $225

[same title] [1835 (1836)] 28x32cm. (11x13") Pastel color. [12] £84 $160

DELAWARE AND MARY-LAND [1835] 28x33cm. (10½x12½") Full color. [3] £95 $180

[same title] [1833 (1836)] 28x33cm. (10½x12½") Color. Perfect. [12] £92 $175

ILLINOIS [1835] 33x27cm. (13x11") Full color. [3] £84 $160

INDIANA [1835] 34x27cm. (13x11") Full color. [3] £74 $140

KENTUCKY AND TENNESSEE [1834] 28x36cm. (10½x13½") Color. [15] £92 $175

[same title] [1835] 28x33cm. (10½x12½") Full color. [3] £84 $160

LOUISIANA [1835] 27x32cm. (10½x12½") Full color. [3] £84 $160

LOWER CANADA [1835] 28x33cm. (10½x12½") Full color. [3] £63 $120

MAINE [1835] 32x27cm. (12½x10½") Full color. Very good. [3] £74 $140

[same title, date] 36x25cm. (13½x10½") 10 counties. Color. [15] £87 $165

MAP OF THE CITY AND COUNTY OF NEW YORK WITH THE ADJACENT COUNTRY [1829] 51x127cm. (20x49½") From *Atlas of the State of New York.* Original color. Some light transferring. [31] £447 $850

MAP OF THE STATE OF ALABAMA [1835] 33x28cm. (12½x10½") Full color. [3] £84 $160

[same title] [1834 (1836)] 32x27cm. (12½x10½") Full color. [12] £105 $200

MAP OF THE STATE OF NEW YORK AND THE SURROUNDING COUNTRY [1841] 50x63cm. (19½x24½") Color. [12] £92 $175

MAP OF THE TERRITORY OF FLORIDA [1834 (1836)] 33x28cm. (13x10½") Color. Light stain upper margin; else excellent. [12] £118 $225

MASSACHUSETTS, RHODE ISLAND AND CONNECTICUT [1835] 28x33cm. (10½x12½") Full color. [3] £74 $140

[same title, date, dimensions] NY: Illman. Color. [15] £87 $165

MICHIGAN [1831 (1836)] 30x26cm. (12x10") Full color. Excellent. [12] £197 $375

[same title] [1835] 33x28cm. (13x11") Full color. [3] £171 $325

[same title] [1836] 30x26cm. (12x10") Color. Mint. [12] £197 $375

MISSOURI [1834 (1836)] 28x33cm. (11x12½") Color. Bright & clean. [12] £145 $275

NEW JERSEY [1835] 33x25cm. (12½x10½") Full color. [3] £84 $160

[same title, date] 33x25cm. (13x10½") NY: T. Illman. Color. [15] £87 $165

NEWFOUNDLAND, NOVA SCOTIA AND NEW BRUNSWICK [1835] 28x33cm. (10½x12½") Full rich color. [3] £68 $130

NORTH AMERICA [1835] 33x28cm. (12½x10½") Full color. [3] £84 $160

[same title] [1836] 33x28cm. (12½x11") Color. Fine. [12] £79 $150

NORTH AND SOUTH CAROLINA [1834] 28x33cm. (10½x13") Ilman & Pilbrow. Col. [15] £74 $140

[same title] [1835] 27x32cm. (10½x12½") Full color. [3] £84 $160

OHIO [1831] 27x32cm. (10½x12½") Color. [15] £92 $175
[same title] [1835] 27x31cm. (10½x12½") Full color. [3] £74 $140
OREGON TERRITORY [1833 (1836)] 28x33cm. (10½x12½") Full color. Pristine. [12] £158 $300
[same title] [1836] 28x33cm. (11x13") Full col. Near invisible tears repairs; rebacked. [26] £118 $225
PALESTINE OR THE HOLY LAND OR LAND OF CANAAN [1832] 33x25cm. (13x10½") Color. [15] £45 $85
PENNSYLVANIA BY DAVID H. BURR NEW YORK [1834] 28x33cm. (10½x12½") 51 counties. NY: Illman & Pilbrow. Color. [15] £87 $165
[same title] [1835] 27x31cm. (10½x12½") Full color. [3] £74 $140
[same title] [1836] 27x31cm. (10½x12") Full color. Perfect. [12] £58 $110
THE UNITED STATES OF MEXICO, DRAWN AND PUBLISHED BY DAVID H. BURR NEW YORK [1835] 31x26cm. (12½x10½") Full color. [3] £179 $340
UNITED STATES ... [1835] 27x32cm. (10½x12½") Full color. [3] £126 $240
UPPER CANADA [1833 (1836)] 25x33cm. (10x12½") Full color. Excellent. [12] £71 $135
[same title] [1835] 28x33cm. (10½x12½") Full color. [3] £63 $120
VIRGINIA [1834] 27x34cm. (10½x13½") Color. [15] £71 $135
[same title] [1835] 27x32cm. (10½x12½") Full color. [3] £89 $170
WEST INDIES [1834] 28x33cm. (11x12½") Color. [15] £47 $90

BYRNE, P.

THE WORLD WITH THE LATEST DISCOVERIES [1789] 25x48cm. (10x19") Double hemisphere. Dublin: P. Byrne. Color. Repaired tear 1.5" into map at right; else fine. [35] £92 $175

CALMET

TABULA TERRA PROMISSAE AB AUCTORE COMMENTARII JOSUE DELINEATA ET A LIEBAUX GEOGRAPHO INCISA [1726] 46x23cm. (18x9") Venice: S. Coleti. Laor 153. Color. [15] £97 $185

CAMDEN

[TITLE PAGE] BRITANNIA [1607-1637] 27x17cm. (10½x6½") Wm. Hole, publisher. Slightly faint impression; some soiling; original owner's inscription at top, one erased. [5] £170 $324

CANTELLI DA VIGNOLA

ISOLE DELL' INDIA CIOE LE MOLUCCHE LE FILIPPINE E DELLA SONDA ... [1683] 46x58cm. (17½x23") Some staining; else excellent. [22] £946 $1800
PENINSOLA DELL INDIA DI LA DAL GANGE DIVISA NE I REGNI CHE IN ESSASI CONTENGONO ET ACCRESCIUTTA DI UARIE NOTIZIE ... [1688-1690] 53x41cm. (21x16") Original outline color. Excellent. [37] £736 $1400

CAREY, M.

A CORRECT MAP OF VIRGINIA [1814] 33x48cm. (13x19½") Old color. [15] £171 $325
A MAP OF THE WORLD FROM THE BEST AUTHORITIES [1814] 25x51cm. (10½x19½") Original outline color. Centerfold repair; light marginal stain; o/w good.. [29] £171 $325
CONNECTICUT [1814] 14x20cm. (5½x8") From *American Pocket Atlas*. [6] £66 $125
DELAWARE [1814] 19x14cm. (7½x5½") From *American Pocket Atlas*. [6] £58 $110
DELAWARE, FROM THE BEST AUTHORITIES [1814] 41x23cm. (16x9") Outline color. Narrow upper margin as issued; else fine. [12] £105 $200
GEORGIA [1814] 20x15cm. (7½x6") From Carey's Pocket Atlas. [6] £92 $175
GEORGIA FROM THE LATEST AUTHORITIES [1795] 23x41cm. (9x15½") To Mississippi River. Fine. [13] £355 $675
KENTUCKEY [1814] 15x20cm. (6x8") From *American Pocket Atlas*. [6] £66 $125
LOUISIANA [1814] 15x20cm. (6x8") From *American Pocket Atlas*. [6] £58 $110
LOUISIANA [1818] 41x43cm. (15½x17½") Some light spots. [31] £171 $325
MAINE [1814] 20x15cm. (8x6") From the Pocket Atlas. Tear outside image mended. [6] £53 $100
MASSACHUSETTS [1796] 15x19cm. (5½x7½") W. Barker, sc. Color. [15] £66 $125
MISSISSIPPI TERRITORY [1814] 15x20cm. (6x8") From *American Pocket Atlas*. [6] £92 $175
MISSISSIPPI TERRITORY AND GEORGIA [1805] 15x20cm. (6x8") From *American Pocket Atlas*. Deacidified, brightened; very good. [13] £131 $250
MISSOURI TERRITORY [1814] 30x36cm. (12x14") By S. Lewis. Color. [15] £342 $650

MISSOURI TERRITORY [1818] 30x36cm. (12x14"). Slight discoloration at centerfold. [31] £342 $650

NEW HAMPSHIRE [1814] 20x15cm. (8x6") From *American Pocket Atlas.* [6] £53 $100

NEW YORK [1814] 14x22cm. (5½x8½") From *American Pocket Atlas.* [6] £53 $100

NORTH CAROLINA [1814] 15x20cm. (6x8") From *American Pocket Atlas.* [6] £58 $110

NORTH CAROLINA FROM THE LATEST SURVEYS, BY SAMUEL LEWIS [1814] 28x48cm. (11x19") Color. [15] £202 $385

OHIO [1814] 14x21cm. (5½x8½") From *American Pocket Atlas.* [6] £63 $120

PENNSYLVANIA [1796] 15x20cm. (6x8") Color. [15] £71 $135

[same title] [1814] 15x20cm. (6x8") From *American Pocket Atlas.* [6] £53 $100

PENNSYLVANIA [1814] 30x46cm. (11½x18½") 45 counties. Color. [15] £181 $345

PLAT OF THE SEVEN RANGES OF TOWNSHIPS BEING PART OF THE TERRITORY OF THE UNITED STATES N.W. OF THE RIVER OHIO WHICH BY A LATE ACT OF CONGRESS ARE DIRECTED TO BE SOLD ... [1814] 61x34cm. (24x13") Original outline color. Deacidified; minor stains; top & bottom margins extended. [17] £63 $120

[same title] [1818] 61x34cm. (24x13½") After Hutchins. Very good. [31] £171 $325

RHODE ISLAND [1814] 20x15cm. (8x6") From *American Pocket Atlas.* [6] £63 $120

SOUTH CAROLINA [1814] 15x20cm. (6x8") From *American Pocket Atlas.* [6] £66 $125

THE BRITISH POSSESSIONS IN NORTH AMERICA FROM THE BEST AUTHORITIES ... [1795] 38x44cm. (15x17½") By Lewis. Color. [15] £129 $245

THE STATE OF MARYLAND, FROM THE BEST AUTHORITIES. BY SAMUEL LEWIS [1795] 28x41cm. (11x16") "Engraved for Carey's American Edition of Guthrie's Geography Improved" above top neat line. No page number. [6] £313 $595

THE STATE OF NEW HAMPSHIRE COMPILED CHIEFLY FROM ACTUAL SURVEYS BY SAMUEL LEWIS [1795] 45x28cm. (17½x11") 1st edition. Color. [15] £202 $385

THE STATE OF NEW JERSEY, COMPILED FROM THE MOST AUTHENTIC INFORMATION [c.1795] 47x31cm. (18½x12") Orig outline col. Split at fold repaired; o/w excellent. [2] £171 $325

THE STATE OF RHODE-ISLAND; COMPILED, FROM THE SURVEYS AND OBSERVATIONS OF CALEB HARRIS, BY HARDING HARRIS [1814] 34x24cm. (13½x9½") Color. [15] £123 $235

THE STATE OF VIRGINIA FROM THE BEST AUTHORITIES, BY SAMUEL LEWIS. 1794 [1795] 35x51cm. (14x20") [6] £365 $695

THE UPPER TERRITORIES OF THE UNITED STATES [1818] 43x32cm. (17x13") Small chip at corner; small repaired centerfold hold. [31] £355 $675

UPPER TERRITORIES OF THE UNITED STATES [1814] 20x15cm. (8x6") From *American Pocket Atlas.* [6] £79 $150

VERMONT [1814] 20x15cm. (8x6") From *American Pocket Atlas.* Tear outside image mended. [6] £53 $100

VERMONT FROM ACTUAL SURVEY [1795] 39x31cm. (15x12") By Doolittle. State I. [6] £208 $395

[same title] [1814] 39x31cm. (15x12") Outline col. Restored, deacidified; near fine. [9] £223 $425

VIRGINIA [1814] 15x20cm. (6x8") From *American Pocket Atlas.* [6] £79 $150

CAREY & LEA *Dimensions sometimes includes text around map.*

GEOGRAPHICAL, STATISTICAL, AND HISTORICAL MAP OF ARKANSAS TERRITORY [1822] 37x38cm. (14½x15") On sheet 17 x 22", with text. After Major S.H. Long. Bright color. Very good. [26] £276 $525

GEOGRAPHICAL, STATISTICAL, AND HISTORICAL MAP OF AMERICA [1822] 43x53cm. (16½x20½") dimensions include text. Color. [15] £58 $110

[same title] [1824] 43x53cm. (16½x20½") dimensions include text. 2nd edition. [15] £71 $135

GEOGRAPHICAL, STATISTICAL, AND HISTORICAL MAP OF ALABAMA [1822] 31x23cm. (12x9") Surrounding text. Original color. [12] £171 $325

GEOGRAPHICAL, STATISTICAL, AND HISTORICAL MAP OF GEORGIA [1827] 30x38cm. (11½x15") On folio sheet with surround of text. Color. Very fine. [13] £171 $325

GEOGRAPHICAL, STATISTICAL AND HISTORICAL MAP OF INDIANA [1827] 37x29cm. (14½x11½") Double folio sheet with text. Full col. Marginal chipping; o/w fine. [14] £145 $275

GEOGRAPHICAL, STATISTICAL, AND HISTORICAL MAP OF ILLINOIS [1822] 30x22cm. (12x8½") 16" x 20" sheet with text. Col. Light centerfold glue discoloration; else bright & clean. [12] £184 $350

GEOGRAPHICAL, STATISTICAL AND HISTORICAL MAP OF KENTUCKY [1826] 30x47cm. (12x18½") On sheet with text, 17 x 21" Revised 2nd edition. Color. [15] £97 $185

[same title] [1827] 30x47cm. (12x18½") On sheet 16" x 20" with text. Color. Pristine. [12] £118 $225

GEOGRAPHICAL, STATISTICAL, AND HISTORICAL MAP OF MEXICO [1822 (1827)] 39x37cm. (15½x14½") Side columns of text. Original wash color. Good. [30] £307 $585

GEOGRAPHICAL, STATISTICAL, AND HISTORICAL MAP OF MISSISSIPPI [1827] 32x24cm. (13x9½") On text sheet 16" x 20". Color. Excellent. [12] £158 $300

GEOGRAPHICAL, STATISTICAL, AND HISTORICAL MAP OF NORTH AMERICA [1822] 36x33cm. (14x13") On 17 x 22" sheet with text. Color. [35] £105 $200

GEOGRAPHICAL, STATISTICAL AND HISTORICAL MAP OF NEW JERSEY [1822] 43x53cm. (16½x20½") dimensions include text at sides. 13 counties. Color. [15] £71 $135

GEOGRAPHICAL, STATISTICAL AND HISTORICAL MAP OF RHODE ISLAND [1822] 43x53cm. (17x20½") Map by Lucas, 11 x 8", with surrounding text. Color. [15] £71 $135

[same title] [1827] 29x21cm. (11½x8½") On 17 x 20" sheet with text. Color. Excellent. [35] £84 $160

GEOGRAPHICAL, STATISTICAL AND HISTORICAL MAP OF UPPER AND LOWER CANADA, AND THE OTHER BRITISH POSSESSIONS IN NORTH AMERICA [1822] 43x53cm. (16½x20½") dimensions with text at sides. Color. [15] £39 $75

GEOGRAPHICAL, STATISTICAL AND HISTORICAL MAP OF VERMONT [1823] 31x24cm. (12x9½") On sheet with surround of text on three sides. Color. Age-toned; centerfold separation reattached; clean. [9] £95 $180

UNITED STATES OF AMERICA [1822] 43x54cm. (17x21") Full color. Faint centerfold glue stain; another small stain; else very good. [35] £184 $350

CARPELAN

KARTA OFVER BELAGENHETEN OMKRING STOCKHOLM [1817] 33x55cm. (13x21½") Linen-backed folding map in original marbled slipcase. Some outline color. Small hole with little paper loss; very good. [19] £105 $200

CARY

A MAP OF IRELAND [c. 1805] 51x42cm. (20x16½") Color. Very good. [24] £120 $228

A MAP OF THE PROVINCE OF MEXICO IN NEW SPAIN [c. 1790] 16x23cm. (6x9") After Bellin. [10] £16 $30

A NEW MAP OF EGYPT, FROM THE LATEST AUTHORITIES [1805] 48x53cm. (19x21") Original color. Very good. [31] £118 $225

A NEW MAP OF NOVA SCOTIA, NEWFOUNDLAND ETC. FROM THE LATEST AUTHORITIES BY JOHN CARY, ENGRAVER ... [1807] 46x51cm. (18x20") Color. Crisp; excellent. [15] £97 $185

A NEW MAP OF SCOTLAND [1801] 89x102cm. (35x40") Two sheets: each about 18 x 40". Outline color. Excellent. [36] £131 $250

A NEW MAP OF THE CIRCLE OF FRANCONIA ... [1799] 46x51cm. (18x20") Body color. Small border ink stain; else fine. [34] £53 $100

A NEW MAP OF THE CIRCLE OF UPPER SAXONY WITH THE DUCHY OF SILESIA AND LUSATIA [1801] 46x53cm. (18x20½") Outline and wash color. [36] £47 $90

CARY'S NEW TERRESTRIAL GLOBE, DELINEATED FROM THE BEST AUTHORITIES EXTANT; EXHIBITING THE DIFFERENT TRACKS OF CAPTAIN COOK ... [AND] CARY'S NEW CELESTIAL GLOBE, ON WHICH ARE CORRECTLY LAID UPON UPWARDS OF 3500 STARS ... [1800] Diameters: 30 cm. (12") on 61 cm. (24") high original wooden stands with compasses and horizon and meridian rings. Color. Some minor wear and flaws; celestial globe crack repaired. All components very good or better. [21] £14,714 $28,000

CARY'S REDUCTION OF HIS LARGE MAP OF ENGLAND AND WALES, WITH PART OF SCOTLAND; COMPREHENDING THE WHOLE OF THE TURNPIKE ROADS, WITH THE GREAT RIVERS AND THE COURSE OF THE DIFFERENT NAVIGABLE CANALS ... [(1796) 1805] 75x62cm. (29½x24½") Linen-backed folding map in original marbled slipcase with label.outline color. Age browning and soiling, wear at folds and separating at one edge; slipcase worn at extremities; good. [19] £79 $150

CASSINI

EMISFERO TERRESTRE SETTENTRIONALE [with] EMISFERO TERRESTRE MERIDIONALE [and] L'AFRICA [and] L'AMERICA [and] L'ASIA [and] L'EUROPA [1788-89] 34x46cm. (13½x18") approx. dimensions. Six maps, from *Nuovo Atlante Geografico.* Original outline color. Some foxing on one map; o/w fine. [5] £700 $1332

GLI STATI UNITI DELL'AMERICA ... PRIMO FOGLIO (Great Lakes) [with] SECONDO FOGLIO (East & Maritimes); TERZO FOGLIO (Mississippi & Ohio); QUARTO FOGLIO (East Coast); QUINTA FOGLIO (Florida & Gulf Coast); SESTO FOGLIO (Newfoundland inset) [1797] 35x48cm. (14x19") 6 joinable maps encompassing U.S. east of Mississippi River. From *Nuovo Atlante Geografico.* Original outline color. [5] £885 $1684

LA PARTE ORIENTALE DELL'ANTICO, E NUOVO MESSICO CON LA FLORIDA E LA BASSA LUIGIANA DELLINEATA SULLE ULTIME OSSERVAZIONI [1798] 48x35cm. (19x14") Outline color. Good. [30] £307 $585

LE COSTE NORD OUEST DELL'AMERICA E NORD EST DELL'ASIA [1798] 35x49cm. (14x19½") Original color. Some light browning; small paper fault at cartouche. [5] £240 $457

LE NUOVE EBRIDI Y LA NOUOVA CALEDONIA DELINEATE DEL CAP. COOK [1798] 48x36cm. (19x13½") Color. [15] £223 $425

CATESBY

CAROLINAE FLORIDAE NEC NON INSULARUM BAHAMENSIUM...IOH. MICHAEL SELIGMANN NORIMBERGAE AO, 1755 [1755] (no dims.) Early color. Excellent. [22] £1025 $1950

CAVAZZA

NOVA TOTIUS TERRARUM ORBIS GEOGRAPHICA AC HYDROGRAPHICA TABULA [(1642) 1643] 35x46cm. (14x18") Shirley 357. Color. Fine. [5] £2250 $4282

CELLARIUS

[TITLE PAGE] ATLAS COELESTIS ... [1708] 43x25cm. (17x10½") Amsterdam: Scheck & Valk. Engraved by van Howen. Old color. Small marginal corner repair; good. [30] £394 $750

HEMISPHAERIUM STELLATUM BOREALE ANTIQUUM [1660] 43x51cm. (17x20") Full original color. Excellent. [2] £1156 $2200

CENTURY ATLAS

ARKANSAS [1897] 28x38cm. (10½x15") Color. [15] £13 $25

COLORADO [1897] 28x38cm. (10½x15") 58 counties. Color. [15] £13 $25

LOUISIANA [1897] 28x38cm. (11x15") Color. [15] £13 $25

MANITOBA, BRITISH COLUMBIA AND THE NORTHWEST TERRITORIES [1897] 28x38cm. (10½x15") Color. [15] £13 $25

MARYLAND AND DELAWARE [1897] 28x38cm. (10½x15½") Color. [15] £13 $25

MICHIGAN SOUTHERN PART [1897] 38x28cm. (15x10½") Color. [15] £11 $20

MISSISSIPPI [1897] 38x28cm. (15x10½") Color. [15] £13 $25

MONTANA [1897 (1899)] 28x38cm. (10½x15") Printed color. Pristine. [12] £24 $45

SOUTH CAROLINA [1897] 28x38cm. (10½x15") Color. [15] £13 $25

TENNESSEE, WESTERN PART - EASTERN PART [1897] 20x56cm. (7½x21½") Color. [15] £13 $25

VIRGINIA [1897] 25x41cm. (10x15½") Color. [15] £13 $25

WISCONSIN [1897] 38x28cm. (15x11") Color. [15] £11 $20

CHAPMAN

CHAPMAN'S NEW SECTIONAL MAP OF MINNESOTA [1856] 81x64cm. (32x25") Milwaukee: Dyer and Pasmore. Folding pocket map. Bright color. Fold intact, but not crisp. [3] £84 $160

CHAPMAN'S SECTIONAL MAP OF THE STATE OF IOWA [1857] 69x107cm. (27x42") By Reid. Milwaukee: Dyer and Pasmore. Folding pocket map. Bright full col. Slightly misfolded. [3] £118 $225

CHAPMAN & HALL *Try Society for the Diffusion of Useful Knowledge*

ENGLAND AND WALES RAILWAY MAP [1847] 61x43cm. (24x17") No. 6 of "Sharpe's Corresponding Maps". Linen-backed folding map between original embossed boards with label. Color. Paper slightly detached at center fold intersection; very good. [19] £105 $200

CHATELAIN

CARTE CONTENANT LE ROYAUME DU MEXIQUE ET LA FLORIDE [1710] 40x53cm. (16x21") Color. [15] £244 $465

CARTE DE L'ISLE DE JAVA ... [1719] 38x87cm. (15x34½") Full color. Mint. [38] £394 $750

CARTE DES ANTILLES FRANCOISES ET DES ISLES VOISINES DRESSEE SUR LES MEMOIRES MANUSCRITS [1719] 48x33cm. (19x13") Fine. [10] £118 $225

CARTE DU CANADA OU DE LA NOUVELLE FRANCE, & DES DECOUVERTES QUI Y ONT ETE FAITES [1719] 40x52cm. (16x20½") Color. [15] £229 $435

CARTE DU PLAN DU VENISE, L'ETAT DE SA NOBLESSE, ... [1708] 38x48cm. (15½x19") Amsterdam: Gueudeville. Half bird's-eye view; half text. Full color. Excellent. [22] £578 $1100

CARTE NOUVELLE DE LA GRANDE TARTARIE OU DE L'EMPIRE DU GRAND CHAM [1719] 41x51cm. (16x20") [15] £47 $90

CARTE PARTICULIERE DU FLEUVE SAINT LOUIS ... [1719] 28x33cm. (11x12½") On a 14 x 18" sheet. Very good. [31] £788 $1500

L'EMPIRE DE JAPON TIRE DES CARTES DES JAPONNAIS [1719] 36x44cm. (14x17½") After Reland. Color. [5] £1350 $2569

NOUVAUX MAPPEMONDE OU GLOBE TERRESTRE ... [1732] 46x66cm. (18x26") Hemispheres. Color. Fold break repaired; else very good. [34] £709 $1350

NOUVELLE CARTE D'ANGLETERRE D'ECOSSE ET D'IRLANDE [1719] 47x63cm. (18½x24½") Inset: World in hemispheres. Full color. Mint. [37] £302 $575

CHEVALIER

VOIES DE COMMUNICATION DES ETATS-UNIS - CARTE GENERAL DES ETATS-UNIS 1840 [c.1841] 61x64cm. (24x25") Paris: Gosselin. Minor fold repair. [15] £129 $245

CHIQUET

L'ASIE DRESSEE SELON LES OBSERVATIONS MRS. DE L'ACADEMIE ROYALE DES SCIENCES [1719] 16x22cm. (6½x8½") Spherical projection. Original outline color. [10] £32 $60

CLARET DE FLEURIEU

PLAN DE LA BAIE DE TCHINKITANE (LA BAIA DE GUADALUPA DES ESPAGNOLS EN 1775, ET NORFOLK-BAY DES ANGLAIS EN 1787) A LA COTE N.O. DE L'AMERIQUE. LEVE PAR LE CAP. PROSPER CHANAL 1791 [1798] 22x17cm. (9x6½") [15] £97 $185

CLARK

RUSSIA [1821] 23x18cm. (9x7½") Color. [15] £18 $35

CLASON MAP CO.

CLASON'S GUIDE MAP OF DENVER COLORADO [c.1925] 48x61cm. (19x24") Color. [26] £26 $50

CLOPPENBURGH

VIRGINIA ITEM ET FLORIDAE AMERICAE PROVINCIARUM NOVA DESCRIPTIO [1630] 19x26cm. (7½x10") Full color. Excellent. [38] £255 $485

CLOUET

DES POSSESSIONS FRANCOISES AUJOURD-HUI SOUS LA DOMINATION ANGLOISES ... [1787] 33x56cm. (12½x22") Text at sides. Color. [15] £123 $235

MAPPE MONDE DU GLOBE TERRESTRE [1765] 43x64cm. (17x25½") Paris: Mondhare. Color. Fine. [27] £1471 $2800

CLUVER

AMERICA [1690-1710] 20x26cm. (8x10") Insular California; lacks Great Lakes. Senex, engraver. Top margin extended; very good. [18] £184 $350

[same title, date, dimensions] Reengraved later state; lacks Senex signature as engraver. [18] £184 $350

CHERSONESI QUAE HODIE NATOLIA [c. 1710] 20x26cm. (8x10") Fine. [18] £81 $155

ORBIS TERRARUM TYPUS [c. 1686] 15x23cm. (6x9") Double hemisphere. [3] £223 $425

SARMATIA ET SCYTHIA RUSSIA ET TARTARIA EUROPAEA [1667] 23x25cm. (9x10") [15] £47 $90

COCCETUS, J.

JERUSALEM NIEWLICKS UYTE DE SCHRIFTEN IOSEPHUS AFGEBEELD [1722] 33x41cm. (13x16") Covens & Mortier, pub. Keyed bird's eye plan. Laor 990. Color. [15] £97 $185

COELLO

ISLA DE CUBA ... [and] ... ISLA DE CUBA. MEDIAS HOJAS EXTREMAS ORIENTAL Y OCCIDENTAL O DE DERECHA E IZQUIERDA [1851] 74x102cm. (29½x40") (Two sheets, 74.5 x 197 cm. when joined.) Original outline color. Splits and folds strenthened; o/w fine. [10] £250 $475

COLBY

MAP OF THE STATE OF MAINE [1883] 84x64cm. (32½x25") Colby & Stuart. Color. [15] £97 $185

COLE

A NEW MAP OF THE COUNTIES TEN MILES ROUND THE CITIES OF LONDON WESTMINSTER AND BOROUGH OF SOUTHWARK [c. 1756] 24x29cm. (9½x11½") Color. VG. [23] £75 $143

COLLINS, G.

[ENGLAND: CORNWALL, FOWEY] [1693 (1779)] 46x56cm. (18x22") Polkerris to Pencarrah Head & Wiseman's Point. Small repair, no loss. [11] £160 $304

[ENGLAND: CORNWALL, LAND'S END and THE SCILLIES] [1686 (1693)] 46x58cm. (18x22½") The Lizard & West. Slight offsetting and spotting in margins. [11] £170 $324

[ENGLAND: DEVON] [1693 (1779)] 46x56cm. (17½x22") Bigberry to Exmouth. Faint damp-marking; repair to lower fold split. [11] £160 $304

[ENGLAND: HUMBER] [(1693) 1779] 46x58cm. (18x22½") Withersea to Grimsby; river to Hessle. Lower fold split repaired; o/w clean, good. [11] £150 $285

[IRISH SEA] [1693 (c. 1760)] 46x58cm. (17½x22½") Lizard to Mull of Galloway. Color. Light browning and dust soiling mainly in margins. [11] £170 $324

[ISLE OF MAN] [1693, 1753] 46x56cm. (17½x22") Color. Archival tissue backing to repair tears and weak paper; damp browning, faint spotting. [11] £170 $324

MILFORD HAVEN AND THE ISLANDS ADJACENT [1693, c. 1720] 44x56cm. (17½x22") St. David's Head to Linney Head. Light general browning. [11] £100 $190

YARMOUTH AND THE SANDS ABOUT IT ... [1693, c. 1760] 46x57cm. (18x22½") Color. [11] £130 $247

COLLOT

PLAN OF THE TOWN OF PITTSBOURG [1824-26] 20x28cm. (7½x11") Tardieu, engr. Very good. [31] £736 $1400

COLNETT

VIEW OF ... JAMES' ISLAND ONE OF THE GALAPAGOS - CHATHAM ISLAND IN STEPHENS BAY [1798] 18x28cm. (6½x10½") Bird's eye view. [15] £34 $65

COLOM

DE CUSTE VAN NOORWEGEN TUSSCHEN SCHAERSONDT EN SCHUYTENS ... [1648] 38x53cm. (15x21") [11] £280 $533

DE CUSTE VAN NOORWEGEN VAN BERGEN TOT STEMMESHEST NIEULYX BESCHREVEN [and] HET LIET VAN BERGEN [c. 1660] 38x52cm. (15x20½") Narrow side margins. [11] £280 $533

COLTON

ALABAMA [1855 (c. 1870)] 38x30cm. (14½x12") Color. Stain in outer margin; good. [28] £66 $125

ARKANSAS [1855] 33x41cm. (13x16") 1st edition. 13 counties. Color. [15] £32 $60

[same title] [1856] 41x36cm. (16x13½") Full color. Excellent. [26] £32 $60

CALIFORNIA [1857] 38x31cm. (15x12") Plain border. Full color. [3] £47 $90

[same title] [1860] 33x25cm. (13x10") Shows 39 counties. Color. [15] £45 $85

CANADA EAST OR LOWER CANADA AND NEW BRUNSWICK [1855] 36x43cm. (13½x16½") Color. [15] £21 $40

CANADA WEST OR UPPER CANADA [1855] 33x41cm. (13x16") Color. [15] £21 $40

COLTON'S CALIFORNIA AND NEVADA [1873] 74x43cm. (29x17") Full color. VG. [3] £63 $120

[same title] [1887] 64x43cm. (25x17") [26] £53 $100

COLTON'S DELAWARE AND MARYLAND [1855 (1870)] 33x41cm. (13x16") Original wash and outline color. [10] £16 $30

COLTON'S INDIAN TERRITORY [1887] 33x41cm. (13x16") Full color. [26] £63 $120

COLTON'S INDIANA [1861] 40x33cm. (15½x13") Color. [15] £24 $45

[same title] [1865] 36x28cm. (14x11½") Full color. Margins chipped; o/w VG. [14] £26 $50

COLTON'S KANSAS [1887] 43x61cm. (17x24") Full color. [26] £39 $75

COLTON'S KANSAS AND NEBRASKA [1867] 43x66cm. (16½x25½") Color. [15] £39 $75

COLTON'S KENTUCKY AND TENNESSEE [c. 1855] 36x64cm. (14x25") Color. [6] £26 $50

COLTON'S LAKE SUPERIOR AND UPPER PENINSULA OF MICHIGAN [1881] 43x66cm. (16½x25½") Full color. [35] £39 $75

[same title] [1887] 43x64cm. (17x25") Full color. [26] £37 $70

COLTON'S MAINE [dated 1855] 38x33cm. (15x13") Color. [6] £34 $65

COLTON'S MAP OF LAKE SUPERIOR AND THE UPPER PENINSULA OF MICHIGAN [also titled] MAP SHOWING THE LOCATION OF THE PORTAGE LAKE & LAKE SUPERIOR SHIP CANAL, THE IRON LANDS OF THE COMPANY AND THE RAILROAD TO THEM. [1868] 43x64cm. (16½x24½") Separately published. Old folds; verso repair of minor tears; good. [26] £105 $200

COLTON'S MAP OF NEW YORK [1850] 51x51cm. (20x20") Pocket map. Insets of NYC area and RR routes to Washington. Repair at corners. [3] £118 $225

COLTON'S MAP OF PENNSYLVANIA [1871] 36x46cm. (14x18") Rarely opened pocket map folding into case. Full color. Map crisp and fresh; case very good. [3] £95 $180

COLTON'S MAP OF THE TERRITORY OF ALASKA (RUSSIAN AMERICA) CEDED BY RUSSIA TO THE UNITED STATES [1867] 41x51cm. (16x20") Published in year of purchase. Col. [15] £76 $145

COLTON'S MAP OF THE UNITED STATES OF AMERICA [1876] 38x66cm. (14½x25½") Pocket map on banknote paper with cover. Color. Slight foxing; few fold separations; discoloration at cover attachment. [7] £176 $335

COLTON'S MISSISSIPPI [dated 1855] 40x33cm. (16x13") Color. [6] £34 $65

COLTON'S NEBRASKA [1887] 43x61cm. (17x24") Full color. [26] £39 $75

COLTON'S NEW JERSEY [1868] 51x36cm. (20x14") Originally a pocket map, now flattened. Full color. Repairs. [3] £74 $140

COLTON'S NEW MAP OF THE CITY AND COUNTRY OF NEW YORK INCLUDING THE EXTENSION NORTH OF THE HARLEM RIVER [1887] 69x134cm. (27x53") also 68 x 95 cm. Two maps, north and south of 93rd Street. Folding city plans between boards. Original color. Paper inside backstrip has tear; very good. [19] £129 $245

COLTON'S NEW MEXICO AND ARIZONA [1887] 43x64cm. (17x25") [26] £37 $70

COLTON'S NEW SECTIONAL MAP OF THE STATE OF ILLINOIS, COMPILED FROM UNITED STATES SURVEYS ... [1864] 91x61cm. (36x24") Folding pocket map; by J.M. Peck & John Messinger. Full color. Very good. [3] £147 $280

COLTON'S OREGON, WASHINGTON AND IDAHO [1887] 43x61cm. (17x24") Full col. [26] £53 $100

COLTON'S PENNSYLVANIA [1859] 33x41cm. (13x15½") 69 counties. Color. [15] £26 $50

COLTON'S RAILROAD & TOWNSHIP MAP OF OHIO [1867] 51x61cm. (20x24") Folding packet map. Full color. Lightly foxed; fold tears repaired. [3] £92 $175

COLTON'S TOWNSHIP MAP OF THE STATE OF IOWA [1866] 41x56cm. (16x22") Updated from 1863. Folding pocket map; rarely opened. Bright full color. Map excellent; case VG. [3] £126 $240

COLTON'S VERMONT [1872] 40x33cm. (16x13") Folding pocket map. Full color. One fold needs reinforcement. [3] £118 $225

DAKOTA [1873] 40x32cm. (16x13") Full color. Very good. [3] £42 $80

[same title] [1876] 39x32cm. (15½x12½") Full color. [26] £39 $75

[same title] [1887] 39x32cm. (15½x12½") Full color. [26] £39 $75

DAKOTA AND WYOMING [c. 1868] 34x42cm. (13½x16½") With part of Montana & Nebraska. Color. [12] £79 $150

[same title] [1872] 34x42cm. (13½x16½") Yellowstone N.P is absent. Color. Light marginal dampstainng; else very good. [12] £71 $135

DELAWARE AND MARYLAND [dated 1855] 12x15cm. (4½x6") Wash color. [6] £37 $70

GEORGIA [1855] 36x28cm. (14x11") Color. Fine. [13] £50 $95

GEORGIA, ALABAMA AND FLORIDA [1860] 33x25cm. (12½x10") Color. [15] £29 $55

GUIDE THROUGH OHIO, MICHIGAN, INDIANA, ILLINOIS, MISSOURI, WISCONSIN & IOWA SHOWING TOWNSHIP LINES OF THE UNITES STATES SURVEYS ... [1851] 47x57cm. (18½x22") On cover: "Colton's Western Tourist and Emigrant's Guide". Folding map between original embossed boards with 34 page guide. Color. Some browning at folds; slight paper loss; VG. [19] £116 $220

ILLINOIS [1856] 41x36cm. (16x13½") Full color. Excellent. [26] £39 $75

[same title, date] 36x28cm. (14x11") Full color. Minor foxing and marginal stains; repaired tear, lower left corner; o/w good. [14] £26 $50

INDIANA [1856] 41x33cm. (16x13") Full color. [26] £32 $60

IOWA [1856] 33x41cm. (13x16") Full color. [3] £32 $60

[same title, date, dimensions] Full color. [26] £34 $65

KANSAS [1866 (1872)] 42x61cm. (16½x24") Full col. Marginal dampstaining; o/w fine. [12] £53 $100

LAKE SUPERIOR AND THE NORTHERN PART OF MICHIGAN [1857] 30x38cm. (12x15") Full color. [3] £32 $60

MAP OF GEORGIA CENTRAL R.R. AND CONNECTIONS [c. 1859] 25x36cm. (10x14½") NY: Lang & Liang. Full color. Minor foxing and fold browning; very good. [13] £105 $200

MAP OF ILLINOIS [1854] 36x28cm. (14x11") Folding pocket map. Full col. Close to new. [3] £158 $300

MAP OF IOWA [1854] 33x38cm. (12½x14½") Pocket map on bank note paper folding into covers. Color. Light foxing; folds crisp, some separations; cover lightly soiled and rubbed; VG. [7] £150 $285

MAP OF THE COUNTRY THIRTY THREE MILES AROUND THE CITY OF NEW YORK [1879] 64x61cm. (24½x23½") Circular map. Original color. Excellent. [21] £289 $550

MAP OF THE RICHMOND AND LOUISVILLE R.R. CONNECTING THE RAILROADS OF VIRGINIA WITH THE RAILROADS OF KENTUCKY ON THE SHORTEST ROUTE EAST AND WEST FROM THE MISSISSIPPI VALLEY TO THE ATLANTIC OCEAN [1882] 76x102cm. (30x40") Pocket map folding into octavo case; rarely opened. [3] £158 $300

[same title, date] 64x127cm. (25x50") Folding map in original folder. RR in color. Exc. [6] £131 $250

MAP OF THE TERRITORY OF ALASKA, (RUSSIAN AMERICA) CEDED BY RUSSIA TO THE UNITED STATES [1886] 33x41cm. (13x16") Color. Very good. [3] £39 $75

MAP OF THE UNITED STATES OF AMERICA, THE BRITISH PROVINCES, MEXICO AND THE WEST INDIES AND CENTRAL AMERICA, WITH PART OF NEW GRANADA AND VENEZUELA [1851] 91x117cm. (36x46") Rolled wall map. Col. Repairs on verso; some surface wear. [3] £302 $575

MAP OF VERMONT [1859] 36x28cm. (14x11") Pocket map on bank note paper folding into embossed cover. Color. Soiled, slightly foxed, some separation at fold corners; cover soiled, rubbed, warped, separated along fold; map fair. [9] £66 $125

[same title, date] 36x28cm. (14x10½") Folding pocket with cover. Outline color. Age-toned with some foxing; slight browning along separating folds; covers dirty, warped, separating; good. [7] £79 $150

MICHIGAN [1856] 40x32cm. (16x13") Lower peninsula. Full color. [3] £37 $70

MINNESOTA [1855 (1856)] 33x41cm. (12½x16") Western boundary is Missouri River. Wash color. Fine. [29] £97 $185

[same title] [1857] 33x41cm. (13x16") Last year as a territory. Color. [15] £34 $65

[same title] [1858] 33x41cm. (13x16") 1st statehood year. "Dakotah" is old west part. Col. [15] £34 $65

MISSISSIPPI [1856] 40x33cm. (16x13") Full soft color. [26] £32 $60

MISSOURI [1856] 41x33cm. (16x13") Soft color. [26] £37 $70

MONTANA, IDAHO & WYOMING [1876 (1877)] 46x64cm. (17½x25") Color. [12] £71 $135

[same title] [1887] 43x64cm. (17x25") Full color. [26] £63 $120

NEBRASKA AND KANZAS [dated 1855] 31x39cm. (12x15") Entire high plains; Nebraska extends to Canada and Continental Divide. Wash & outline color. [6] £105 $200

[same title, date] 33x41cm. (12½x15½") Color. [15] £87 $165

[same title] [1856] 33x41cm. (13x16") [26] £92 $175

[same title, date, dimensions] [35] £76 $145

NEW BRUNSWICK, NOVA SCOTIA, NEWFOUNDLAND AND PRINCE EDWARD ID. [1860] 33x41cm. (13x16") Color. [15] £21 $40

NEW RAILROAD MAP OF INDIANA OHIO AND PART OF ILLINOIS [1875] 41x71cm. (16x28") Phila: O.W. Gray. Minor foxing; very good. [14] £39 $75

NEW YORK [1854] 28x36cm. (11x14") Unbacked folding map between embossed boards with label. Color. Light foxing in margins; very good+. [19] £89 $170

NEW YORK AND ADJACENT CITIES [1855] 42x63cm. (16½x25") Color. [12] £66 $125

NORTH AMERICA [1855] 40x33cm. (15½x13") Full color. Fine. [12] £58 $110
NORTH CAROLINA [1856] 33x41cm. (13x16") Full color. [26] £37 $70
NORTHERN AMERICA, BRITISH, RUSSIAN AND DANISH [1856] Full color. VG. [26] £37 $70
NORTHERN REGIONS [1887] 41x33cm. (16x13") Full color. [26] £32 $60
OREGON, WASHINGTON AND IDAHO [1876 (1877)] 43x64cm. (17x25") Color. Pristine. [12] £71 $135
PHILADELPHIA [1855] 41x36cm. (15½x13½") Blank verso. Full color. [12] £32 $60
SOUTH CAROLINA [1861] 33x41cm. (13x16") Color. [15] £29 $55
SOUTHERN REGIONS [1887] 41x33cm. (16x13") Full color. [26] £32 $60
TEXAS [1856] 33x41cm. (13x16") Single page, without truncations. [36] £131 $250
[same title] [1858] 33x28cm. (13x10½") From *Cabinet Atlas*. Color. [15] £66 $125
[same title] [1887] 43x58cm. (17x23") Full color. [26] £63 $120
THE CITY OF SAVANNAH, GEORGIA [and] THE CITY OF CHARLESTON, SOUTH CAROLINA [1855] 28x36cm. (11x14") Two maps on a sheet. Full color. Fine. [13] £39 $75
THE TERRITORIES OF WASHINGTON AND OREGON [1856] 32x41cm. (12½x16") With text sheet. Color. Excellent. [36] £58 $110
THE UNITED STATES OF AMERICA [1857] 38x64cm. (15x25") Color. [15] £66 $125
TOWNSHIP MAP OF THE STATE OF NEW YORK PUBLISHED BY J.H. COLTON [1852] 61x76cm. (24x30") Full color. Some staining at lower edge. [3] £118 $225
TOWNSHIP MAP OF THE STATE OF NEW-YORK WITH PARTS OF THE ADJOINING STATES & CANADA [1853] 56x61cm. (21½x24") Pocket map folding into covers. Color. Crisp bank note paper; occasional separation and foxing; slight discoloration at cover attachment. [7] £150 $285
WISCONSIN [1856] 43x33cm. (17x13") Full color. Very good. [3] £39 $75
[same title, date] 41x33cm. (16x13") 49 counties. Color. [15] £34 $65
[same title, date] 41x36cm. (16x13½") Full color. Excellent. [26] £42 $80
WYOMING, COLORADO AND UTAH [1887] 43x64cm. (17x25") Full color. [26] £63 $120

COMPANY MAPS

GOLD BELT MAP OF COLORADO [c. 1906] 25x36cm. (10x14") East Argentine Mining Co., Denver? Gold color. Very good. [3] £26 $50

CONDER

A MAP OF THE MIDDLE STATES OF AMERICA, ... [1794] 30x46cm. (12x18") Fold lines; mended tears at right border; lower & right margins trimmed, but sufficient. [6] £208 $395
THE NORTHERN HEMISPHERE [1783] 25x25cm. (10x10") Track of Cook's ship "Resolution". By A. Kincaid. Color. [15] £47 $90
[same title, date, dimensions] Track of Cook's ship "Resolution". Color. [15] £50 $95

COOK *Try Benard, Conder, Hogg*

A GENERAL CHART EXHIBITING THE DISCOVERIES MADE BY CAPT. JAMES COOK IN THIS AND HIS TWO PRECEDING VOYAGES WITH THE TRACKS OF THE SHIPS UNDER HIS COMMAND [1782] 58x91cm. (23x36") Minor fold repairs; clean. [15] £202 $385
CARTE DE L'ENTREE DE NORTON ET DU DETROIT DE BHERING OU L'ON VOIT LE CAP [1785] 28x38cm. (10½x15½") Benard, sc. Color. [15] £58 $110
CARTE DE LA RIVIERE DE COOK, DANS LA PARTIE N.O. DE L'AMERIQUE [1785] 23x30cm. (9½x12") Color. [15] £71 $135
CHART OF COOKS RIVER IN THE N.W. PART OF AMERICA [1785] 25x41cm. (9½x16") Minor repair on verso of one fold; o/w excellent. [26] £74 $140
CHART OF NORTON SOUND AND OF BHERINGS STRAIT MADE BY THE EAST CAPE OF ASIA AND THE WEST POINT OF AMERICA [1784] 23x33cm. (8½x13") By Conder. Col. [15] £34 $65
[same title] [1785] 30x41cm. (11½x15½") Vertical folds as issued; clean. [26] £63 $120
CHART OF THE SOCIETY ISLES DISCOVERED BY LIEUT J. COOK 1769 [1777] 30x43cm. (11½x17½") Color. [15] £87 $165
CHART OF VAN DIEMANS LAND [1785] 23x36cm. (9x14") Folds as issued. [26] £32 $60
EASTER ISLAND, LATITUDE 27 Deg. 5' SO. [1777] 23x20cm. (8½x8") Color. [15] £45 $85
KAART VAN DE AWATSKA-BAAI, OP DE OOST KUST VAN KAMTSCHATKA [1784-1795] 25x20cm. (10x8") Allart & Van Cleef, from Dutch ed. of third voyage. Light browning. [11] £18 $34

KAART VAN DE NOORD-WEST KUST VAN AMERIKA EN DE NOORD-OOST KUST VAN ASIA ... [1795] 38x64cm. (15x25½") Allart & Van Cleef. Damp marking; fold repairs. 11] £170 $324

[same title] [1798] 38x65cm. (15x25½") [10] £66 $125

KAART VAN DE ONTDEKKINGEN IN DE STILLE ZUID-ZEE, VAN KAPITEIN COOK JAAR 1774 [1784] 36x46cm. (14x18") By Hawksworth. New Caledonia & New Hebrides. Color. [15] £76 $145

KAART VAN HET Z.O. GEDEELTE VAN HE VUURLAND DE STRAAT LE MAIRE EN EEN GEDEELTE VAN STAATEN-LAND [AND] KAART VAN DE GOOD SUCCESS DAAI IN DE STRAAT VAN LE MAIRE [1795] 30x33cm. (11½x13½") Two plans on one sheet. Allart & Van Cleef; from Dutch edition of first voyage. Light damp-marking. [11] £28 $53

PLAN DE L'ENTREE DE NOOTKA [1784] 28x20cm. (11x8½") Paris. Benard, sc. Color. Minor repair. [15] £45 $85

PLAN OF ADVENTURE BAY ON VAN DIEMANS LAND [1785] 23x15cm. (9x6") [26] £21 $40

SKETCH OF THE HARBOUR OF SAMGANOODA, ON THE ISLAND OF OONALASKA...T. BOWEN, SCT. LONDON PUBLISHED BY ALEXR. HOGG... [1784] 21x33cm. (8x13") Color. [15] £24 $45

SKETCH OF THE MARQUESAS DE MENDOCA [1777] 20x15cm. (7½x6") Color. [15] £39 $75

COOKE

D.B. COOKE & CO.'S RAILWAY MAP OF THE UNITED STATES AND CANADA, SHOWING ALL FINISHED LINES OF RAILWAYS WITH STATIONS AND DISTANCES. [1859] 81x112cm. (32x44") Wall map with rollers. Very good. [3] £263 $500

COOPER, H.

MAP OF THE NORTH PART OF AMERICA ON WHICH IS LAID DOWN MACKENZIE'S TRACK FROM MONTREAL TO THE NORTH SEA [1810] 20x25cm. (7½x10") Color. [15] £34 $65

COOPER, J.

ENGLAND, WALES, AND THE SOUTHERN PART OF SCOTLAND [1849] 78x63cm. (30½x25") London: Metchim, Pope, Reynolds. Folding map between boards. Outline and wash color. Minor age darkening and soiling; good+. [17] £158 $300

CORNELL

UNITED STATES [1855] 32x52cm. (12½x20½") Full color. Small light stains; light scattered foxing; else excellent. [12] £66 $125

CORONELLI *Try Nolin*

[AUSTRALIA, NORTHERN] [1696] 23x28cm. (9x11") With parts of Indonesia Excel. [21] £447 $850

[GLOBE GORE: CHINA / JAPAN] [1693] 46x28cm. (18x10½") For the 42" globe. Excel. [1] £998 $1900

[GLOBE GORE: WEST AFRICA] [1696] 46x28cm. (18x11") Includes Iberian Peninsula [10] £39 $75

[GLOBE GORES: SET OF EIGHT OF THE AMERICAS] [1696] 49x33cm. (19½x13") dimensions for each of 4 sheets, each with two gores. From *Libro dei Globi*, for mounting on 18" (48 cm) globe. Minor stains in blank margins. [33] £2800 $5328

[TITLE PAGE] REGNO DI NEGROPONTE ... [c. 1695] 23x39cm. (9x15½") Sub-title page. No imprint; contemporary manuscript for title panel. [5] £90 $171

CANADA ORIENTALE NELL'AMERICA SETTENTRIONALI DESCRITTA DAL P. MRO. CORONELLI M C COSMOGRAFO DELLA SEREN REPUBLICA DI VENETIA... [c. 1692-94] 45x60cm. (17½x23½") Small stain; else excellent. [21] £447 $850

ISOLA D'ISLAND [c. 1690] 23x31cm. (9x12") Color. Fine. [37] £92 $175

ISOLA DE IAMES, A GIAMAICA, POSSEDUTTA DAL RE BRITANNICO DIVISA IN PARROCCHIE [c. 1690] 22x29cm. (8½x11½") Wash color. Fine. [37] £66 $125

ISOLA DEL GIAPONE E PENISOLA DI COREA...DAL P.M. CORONELLI... [1692] 46x61cm. (18x24") Close top margin, no loss; o/w very good. [22] £1839 $3500

ISOLA DI MARIA GALANTE NELLE ANTILLI POSSEDUTA DA S. M. CRISTIANISSIMA ... [1696] 23x30cm. (8½x12") [15] £129 $245

ISOLE DELL'INDIE, DIVISE IN FILIPPINE, MOLUCCHE, E DELLA SONDA ... [c. 1690] 45x61cm. (17½x24") Color. Fine. [5] £750 $1427

[same title] [1696] 45x61cm. (17½x24") Excellent. [21] £631 $1200

LA SPAGNUOLA DESCRITTA DAL P. COSMOGRAFO CORONELLI, E DEDICATA AD ILLUSTRISE: SIG. GUISTIMIANO LORENZO COCCO [1696] 24x30cm. (9½x12") Color. [15] £97 $185

MARE DEL NORD AUTTORE IL P.M. CORONELLI... [1695-97] 45x60cm. (17½x24") Minor centerfold repair; fine. [30] £736 $1400

MARE DEL SUD, DETTO ALTRIMENTI MARE PACIFICO AUTTORE IL P.M. CORONELLI ... [1691-96] 45x60cm. (18x23½") Color. [5] £1250 $2379

[same title] [1685-97] 44x60cm. (17½x23½") Insular California. Fine. [30] £946 $1800

PARTE OCCIDENTALE DELLA CHINA ... [and] PARTE ORIENTALE DELLA CHINA ... DIVISA NELLE SUE PROVINCIAE ... [c. 1696-98] 61x89cm. (24x35") 4 sheets joined. 1] £1445 $2750

PARTE ORIENTALE DELLA CHINA ... [and] PARTE OCCIDENTALE DELLA CHINA ... [c. 1695] 61x89cm. (24x35") Two folio sheets joined. Color. Excellent. [5] £1300 $2474

PLANISFERO DEL MONDO NUOVO, DESCRITTO DAL P. CORONELLI, COSMOGRAFO PUBLICO DEDICATO ALL'ILLUSTRISSIMO, ET ECCELLENTISSIMO SIGNORE ANDREA MARCELLO [1695] 46x61cm. (18x24") Fine. [10] £1182 $2250

QUANTUNG E FOKIEN ... [c. 1695] 46x61cm. (18x24") With Formosa & Hainan. Col. [5] £950 $1808

TERRE ARTICHE ... [c. 1690] 46x61cm. (18x24") Glacial polar graphics. Color. Some creasing; o/w excellent. [22] £631 $1200

COVENS & MORTIER

[TITLE PAGE] ATLAS NOVUS ... ATLAS FRANCOIS ... [1699-c. 1730] 28x49cm. (11x19½") Romeine de Hooghe, engraver. From Dutch edition of Jaillot. Full original color. [5] £160 $304

ARCHIPELAGUE DU MEXIQUE, OU SONT LES ISLES DE CUBA, ESPAGNOLE, IAMAIQUE, &C ... [1741] 61x99cm. (23½x39") Early col. Minor repair; some folds reinforced; else VG. [21] £1314 $2500

L'HEMISPHERE SEPTENTRIONAL POUR VOIR PLUS DISTINCTEMENT LES TERRES ARCTIQUES PAR GUILLAUME DE LISLE ... [1730] 46x51cm. (18½x20½") Updated edition with Russian discoveries. Color. [15] £181 $345

NOVA ET ACCURATA REGNI HUNGARIAE ... [c. 1730] 46x56cm. (18x22½") Old body color. Minor flaws; o/w very good. [34] £131 $250

COWLEY

A MAP OF THE WORLD FROM THE BEST AUTHORITIES ... [1761] 15x25cm. (6x10") Insular California. Full color. [3] £276 $525

COX *Try Society for the Diffusion of Useful Knowledge*

COX'S TERRESTRIAL GLOBE [and] CELESTIAL GLOBE [1838] Globe pair. Diamters: 6 cm. (2½") on 15 cm. (6") high original wooden stand. London: I. S. Cox. 2nd edition. [2] £2522 $4800

CRAFTS, H.

PLAN OF BOSTON CORRECTED UNDER THE DIRECTION OF COMMITTEE ON PRINTING ... [1864] 71x99cm. (27½x38½") By H. Wightman. Backed. Minor repair. [15] £131 $250

CRAM

ALABAMA [1900] 56x43cm. (22½x16½") Color. 9 index pages. [15] £37 $70

ALASKA [1902] 43x56cm. (17x22") 3 insets. Full color. [26] £32 $60

ARIZONA [c. 1896] 30x23cm. (12x9") Color. [6] £29 $55

[same title] [1888] 30x25cm. (12½x10") Color. [15] £16 $30

ATLANTA [1889] 30x25cm. (12x9½") Rev: New Orleans. Printed color. Fine. [13] £29 $55

BRITISH COLUMBIA [1897] 36x51cm. (13½x20") Color. [15] £21 $40

CALIFORNIA [c. 1875] 48x30cm. (19x12") Color. [15] £24 $45

CALIFORNIA & NEVADA [c. 1896] 28x23cm. (11x9") Color. [6] £29 $55

CITY OF SUPERIOR, WIS. [c. 1892] 33x48cm. (13½x18½") [15] £26 $50

COLORADO [1888] 43x56cm. (17x22") Outline color. [26] £42 $80

[same title] [c. 1896] 23x30cm. (9x12") Color. [6] £24 $45

[same title] [1904] 36x51cm. (14x20") Full color. [26] £32 $60

CRAM'S NEW SECTION MAP OF THE STATE OF MINNESOTA [1872] 97x79cm. (38x31") Pocket map in black cover with gold lettering. On back note paper. Color. Occasional fold separation; cover dirty, rubbed, slight tear on spine; cover G, map VG. [7] £145 $275

FLORIDA [c. 1887] 58x43cm. (22½x16½") Color. [15] £42 $80

GEORGIA [1887] 30x25cm. (12x9½") Reverse: S.C. Printed color. Very good. [13] £16 $30

IDAHO [c. 1896] 30x25cm. (12x10") Color. [6] £24 $45

INDEXED RAILROAD AND TOWNSHIP MAP OF MISSOURI [1878] 64x51cm. (25x20") Folding pocket map. Substantial color. Crisp; very good. [3] £118 $225

INDIANA [1883] 56x38cm. (21½x15½") Printed color. Fine. [14] £21 $40

[same title] [1888] 30x25cm. (12x9½") Color. [15] £13 $25

[same title] [1893] 30x23cm. (11½x9½") From Gaskell's Atlas. Printed color. VG. [14] £13 $25

KENTUCKY - TENNESSEE [1889] 41x56cm. (16x22") Color. [15] £24 $45

LOUISIANA [c. 1896] 30x30cm. (12x12") Color. [6] £24 $45

LOUISVILLE [1892] 25x33cm. (10x13") Color. [15] £16 $30

MAP OF MONTANA [1904] 36x51cm. (14x20") Full color. [26] £32 $60

MAP OF PARKERSBURG WEST VIRGINIA AND VICINITY [1894] 33x25cm. (13x10") By J. Dunbar. Color. [15] £21 $40

MAP OF PORTO RICO [1904] 33x51cm. (13x20") Full color. [26] £24 $45

MAP OF THE CITY OF INDIANAPOLIS [1896] 36x51cm. (13½x20") Color. [15] £21 $40

MAP OF THE CITY OF OAKLAND BERKELEY AND ALAMEDA [c. 1891] 33x51cm. (13½x20½") Color. [15] £39 $75

MAP OF THE HAWAIIAN ISLANDS [1900] 28x43cm. (11x17") Printed color. Fine. [12] £26 $50

MEMPHIS [1892] 33x25cm. (13x10") Color. [15] £18 $35

MINNESOTA [c. 1902] 30x23cm. (12x9") Color. [6] £24 $45

MISSISSIPPI [1892] 30x25cm. (12½x10") Color. [15] £13 $25

MONTREAL [1894] 25x33cm. (9½x13") Color. [15] £16 $30

NASHVILLE [1892] 33x25cm. (13x10") Color. [15] £18 $35

NEBRASKA [c. 1896] 25x33cm. (10x13") Color. [6] £24 $45

NEVADA [1900] 57x42cm. (22½x16½") Printed outline color. Perfect. [12] £39 $75

[same title] [1904] 51x36cm. (20x14") Bright color. [26] £32 $60

NEW MEXICO FROM THE LATEST FEDERAL, STATE AND TRANSPORTATION SURVEYS [1909] 36x28cm. (14x10½") Printed color. [12] £26 $50

NEW RAIL ROAD AND COUNTY MAP OF NEBRASKA [1882] 23x33cm. (8½x13") Full color. [12] £39 $75

NEW SECTIONAL MAP OF IOWA [1878] 61x71cm. (24x28") Pocket map folded into case. Full color. [3] £105 $200

NORTH DAKOTA [1899] 41x56cm. (16x22") Printed color. [12] £39 $75

NOVA SCOTIA AND NEW BRUNSWICK [1885] 23x30cm. (9x12") Color. [15] £8 $15

OFFICIAL MAP OF SACRAMENTO CAL. [1898] 23x33cm. (9x13") Color. [15] £21 $40

OKLAHOMA AND INDIAN TERS. [1904] 36x51cm. (14x20") With index. Color. [26] £32 $60

OREGON [c. 1896] 23x30cm. (9x12") Color. [6] £24 $45

PENNSYLVANIA [1888] 30x41cm. (11½x16") Color. [15] £16 $30

RAILROAD AND COUNTY MAP OF DAKOTA & MANITOBA [1888] 56x43cm. (22x17") Outline color. [26] £39 $75

RAILROAD AND COUNTY MAP OF INDIAN TER. [1888] 43x58cm. (16½x22½") Oklahoma District present. Outline color. [26] £53 $100

RAILROAD AND COUNTY MAP OF MONTANA [1887] 43x58cm. (16½x22½") Banker's and Broker's Atlas. Chicago: A.A. Grant. Some color. [26] £45 $85

RAILROAD AND COUNTY MAP OF NEVADA [1888] 58x43cm. (22½x16½") Soft border color. [26] £45 $85

RAILROAD AND COUNTY MAP OF NEW MEXICO [1889] 57x41cm. (22x16½") Printed outline color. [12] £45 $85

RAILROAD AND COUNTY MAP OF OHIO [1887] 43x58cm. (16½x22½") Banker's and Broker's Atlas. Chicago: A.A. Grant. Color coded railroads. [26] £34 $65

RAILROAD AND COUNTY MAP OF VIRGINIA, WEST VIRGINIA [1887] 43x58cm. (16½x22½") Bankers and Brokers Atlas. Chicago: A. A. Grant. [26] £37 $70

RAILROAD & COUNTY MAP OF TEXAS [1880] 41x56cm. (16½x22½") Greer Co. to Texas. Color. [15] £58 $110

SOUTH DAKOTA [1902] 43x56cm. (17x22") Color. [26] £42 $80

[same title] [1904] 36x51cm. (14x20") With index. Bright color. [26] £32 $60

THE RAILROAD COMMISSIONER'S MAP OF ILLINOIS [1905] 122x71cm. (48x28") Folded into cardboard case. Some color. Wear at folds. [3] £32 $60

WASHINGTON [c. 1896] 25x38cm. (10x15") Color. [6] £24 $45

[same title] [1904] 36x51cm. (14x20") Bright color. [26] £32 $60

WYOMING [1888] 43x58cm. (16½x22½") Border colored. [26] £42 $80

[same title] [1904] 36x51cm. (14x20") Bright color. [26] £32 $60

CRAMER, J.A.

ASIA VULGO MINOR DICTA ANTIQUA ET NOVA CUM INSULIS ADJACENTIBUS [1832] 61x95cm. (24x37½") Oxford: Joseph Parker. Linen-backed folding map, with self-backs and slip case. Original color. Pencil marks; slipcase worn, one corner torn; very good. [19] £155 $295

CROSMAN & MALLORY

PANORAMIC VIEW FROM BUNKER HILL MONUMENT [1848] 17x120cm. (6½x47") With small view: "Perspective View of Bunker Hill Monument". 16 p. text with 160 item reference key; cloth binding with title in gold & embossed front cover. Both plates with orig wash color. Fine. 10] £657 $1250

CROSS, J.

CROSS'S LONDON GUIDE [c. 1837] 43x68cm. (17x27") Linen-backed folding plan in original embossed slipcase with label and green self-backs. Color. Age darkening ; slight soiling of map and case; o/w very good. [19] £197 $375

CRUCHLEY

CRUCHLEY'S ENVIRONS OF LONDON EXTENDING THIRTY MILES FROM THE METROPOLIS [1826] 88x90cm. (34½x35") Linen-backed folding map in original marbled slipcase with label. Partial color. Backing separating at fold; slipcase worn, label legible. [19] £197 $375

CRUCHLEY'S IMPROVED ENVIRONS OF LONDON [1823] 57x57cm. (22½x22½") On cover: "Cruchley's New and Improved Environs of London extending 15 to 18 miles round St. Paul's ..." Linen-backed folding map in original slipcase with label. Outline color. Repair to backing at two folds; slipcase corners bumped; very good. [19] £205 $390

CRUCHLEY'S NEW PLAN OF LONDON SHEWING ALL THE NEW AND INTENDED IMPROVEMENTS TO THE PRESENT TIME [(1832)] 42x60cm. (16½x23½") Linen-backed city plan. Outline and open space color. Slight darkening in margins; very good. [19] £158 $300

[same title] [c. 1847] 42x60cm. (16½x23½") On cover: "Cruchley's New Plan of London Improved to 1847" Linen-backed folding plan between original boards with label. Partial color. Uniform age-browning along fold lines. [19] £105 $200

CRUCHLEY'S NEW TRAVELLING MAP AND ITINERARY COMPRISING THE WHOLE OF ENGLAND, WITH PART OF SCOTLAND AND IRELAND AND A PORTION OF FRANCE AND THE NETHERLANDS, SHEWING THE COMMUNICATION BETWEEN LONDON AND PARIS [1825] 63x50cm. (25x19½") Linen-backed folding map between later boards. Delicate color. Slight age soiling; o/w very good. [19] £87 $165

[same title] [1835] 62x51cm. (24½x20") Linen-backed folding map with self-backs. Original color. Tear at one fold, linen worn through at intersections; map bright and clear. [19] £102 $195

THE WORLD [c. 1830] 53x65cm. (20½x25½") On cover: "Cruchley's New Map of the World (On Mercator's Projection) ..." Linen-backed folding map in original solid but worn slipcase with label. Partial color. Light browning and soiling, ink marks, smudge; some tears at folds; good+. [19] £92 $175

CUCCIONI

PIANTA TOPOGRAFICA DELLA CITTA' DI ROMA COLL' AGGIUNTA DELLE ANTICHITA' RECENTEMENTE SCOPERTE [1848] 54x65cm. (21½x25½") Linen-backed folding plan in two slipcases with index booklet. Index has spine repair. [19] £145 $275

CUMMINGS & HILLIARD

NORTH AMERICA [c. 1825] 23x28cm. (9x10½") Color. [15] £42 $80

CURRIER, N.

[HUDSON RIVER, NY] [1835-46] 41x10cm. (16x4") Unrecorded map. Folds; minor wear. [31] £79 $150

CUTLER

A NEW AND CORRECT CHART OF THE MEDITERRANEAN SEA [c. 1728] 48x120cm. (19x47") Very good. [25] £495 $942

D'ANVILLE

A MAP OF THE GOLD COAST, FROM ISSIMI TO ALAMPI [1852] 20x36cm. (7½x13½") London: G. Child. [15] £45 $85

AMAZONIA TERRA FIRMA, PART BRASIL & PERU, REVISED BY MR. BOLTON [1755] 43x76cm. (16½x30") Pub. London; Kitchin, sc. Color. [15] £87 $165

CANADA, LOUISIANE ET TERRES ANGLOISES [1755] 48x56cm. (19x22") Color. [15] £276 $525

CARTE DE L'INDE DRESSEE POUR LA COMPAGNIE DES INDES PAR LE SR. D'ANVILLE SECRETAIRE DE S.A.S.MGR. LE DUC D'ORLEANS [1752] 89x107cm. (35x42") Linen-backed folding map. Color. Very good. [19] £145 $275

CARTE DU CANADA, DE LA LOUISIANE ... [1776] 48x66cm. (19x25½") Santini's Italian edition. French text & captions. Outline color. Very good. [34] £420 $800

CARTE GENERALE DE LA CHINE [1730] 61x51cm. (23½x20") Vivid body color. Repaired edge tears, creases; else good+. [34] £145 $275

GRAECIAE ANTIQUAE SPECIMEN GEOGRAPHICUM [(1742) 1794] 53x50cm. (20½x19½") Inset: "Graciae (Laxe sumptoe) Partes Borealis". London: Laurie & Whittle. Linen-backed folding map. Original color. Very good. [19] £37 $70

HEMISPHERE OCCIDENTAL OU DU NOUVEAU MONDE ... [1761] 66x61cm. (26x24") Outline color. [15] £171 $325

LES COTES DE LA GRECE ET L'ARCHIPEL [1756] 54x71cm. (21x28") Linen-backed folding map. Some sections detaching, age-staining along folds, but all present and clear. [19] £105 $200

ORBIS ROMANI PARS OCCIDENTALIS ... [1763 (1794)] 69x56cm. (27x22") London: Laurie & Whittle. Linen-backed folding map. Outline color. Very good. [19] £118 $225

ORBIS ROMANI PARS ORIENTALIS AUSPICIIS SERENISSIMI PRINCIPIS LUDOVICI PHILIPPI ... [(1764) 1794] 59x56cm. (23x22") London: Laurie & Whittle. Linen-backed folding map. Outline color. Very good. [19] £74 $140

ORBIS VETERIBUS NOTUS AUSPICIIS SERENISSIMI PRINCIPIS LUDOVICI PHILIPPI AURELIANORUM DUCIS PUBLICI JURIS FACTUS [(1763) 1794] 54x76cm. (21½x30") London: Laurie & Whittle. Linen-backed folding map. Outline color. Very good. [19] £105 $200

PALAESTINA [(1767) 1794] 40x44cm. (15½x17½") London: Laurie & Whittle. Linen-backed folding map. Outline color. Very good. [19] £105 $200

SUITE DE PEROU AUDIENCE DE CHARCAS [1771] 23x30cm. (8½x12") Color. [15] £32 $60

TABULA ITALIAE ANTIQUAE GEOGRAPHICA QUAM EXCELLENTISSIMUS DOMINUS DUX DE LA ROCHEFOUCAULD IN OERE INCIDI CURAVIT [(1764) 1794] 64x50cm. (25x19½") London: Laurie & Whittle. Linen-backed folding map. Original color. Very good. [19] £102 $195

D'APRES DE MANNEVILLETTE

A CHART OF THE CHINA SEA INSCRIBED TO MONSR. D'APRES DE MANNEVILLETTE THE INGENIOUS AUTHOR OF THE NEPTUNE ORIENTAL: AS A TRIBUTE...OF HIS MANY FAVOURS TO A DALRYMPLE [1775] 65x48cm. (26x19") After Dalrymple. In English; only place names in French. Color. [11] £340 $647

CARTE DE L'ENTREE DU GOLFE DE LA MER ROUGE [1781] 34x49cm. (13½x19½") From amended *Neptune Oriental.* [11] £85 $162

CARTE DE LA COTE OCCIDENTALE DE L'ISLE SUMATRA DEPUIS LA LIGNE EQUINOCTIALE JUSQU'AU DETROIT DE LA SONDE [1775 (1781)] 66x48cm. (26½x19") Slight browning in right margin. [11] £35 $67

CARTE DES ISLES ET DANGERS SITUES AU NORD-EST DE L'ISLE MADAGASCAR... [1781] 34x50cm. (13½x19½") Diego Garcia I. Excellent. [11] £75 $143

CARTE DES ISLES NICOBAR ... [1775] 46x30cm. (18x12") Faint browning lower margin. [11] £40 $76

CARTE DU GOLFE PERSIQUE DEPUIS BASSORA JUSQU'AU CAP RASALGATE [1775] 49x67cm. (19½x26½") Slight browning; repaired edge tear just into engraving. [11] £190 $362

CARTE PLATE QUI COMPREND L'ISLE DE CEYLON ET UNE PARTIE DES COTES DE MALABAR ET DE COROMANDEL [1775] 48x67cm. (19x26½") Two small brown marks, two wormholes in lower margin. [11] £90 $171

CARTE POUR ALLER DU DETROIT DE LA SONDE OU DE BATAVIA AU DETROIT DE BANCA [1775] 69x51cm. (26½x19½") Edge tear repair; some damp-marking & browning. [11] £90 $171

COTE ORIENTALE DE MADAGASCAR DEPUIS LA RIVIERE D'IVONDROU JUSQU'A MANANZARI ... [1775] 48x33cm. (19x13½") By Grenier, 1768. Slight marginal browning. [11] £30 $57

PLAN DE L'ARCHIPEL DE MERGUY [and] PLAN DE L'ISLE JUNKSEILON ET DE SON PORT... [1775] 33x48cm. (13x19") Two plans on a sheet. Clean; good. [11] £110 $209

PLAN DU DETROIT DE BANCA ... [n.d] 48x33cm. (19x13") [11] £50 $95

D'EXPILLY

ASIAE [1772] 15x18cm. (6x7") Original outline color. [10] £32 $60

DAHLBERG

OBSIDIUM HAFFNIENSE A. 1658 [c. 1700] 29x105cm. (11½x41½") Panoramic view of Copenhagen under siege. Fine. [38] £289 $550

DALRYMPLE

... CHART OF FELICIA AND PLAN OF THE ISLAND BALAMBANGAN ... [1770 (1775)] 61x48cm. (24x18½") [11] £120 $228

A CHART OF THE ISLANDS TO THE SOUTHWARD OF TCHU-SAN ON THE EASTERN COAST OF CHINA GENERALLY LAID DOWN FROM ONE PUBLISHED BY ALEXANDER DALRYMPLE ESQRE. WITH ADDITIONS AND ALTERATIONS BY J. BARROW [1796] 54x35cm. (21x13½") Narrow upper and lower margins; small edge repairs. [11] £100 $190

DAMPIER

CARTE DE L'ISTHME DE DARIEN ET DU GOLFE DE PANAMA [1715] 18x15cm. (6½x6½") By Lionel Wafer. Kapp (Panama) 39. [15] £139 $265

CARTE DE LA BAYE DE CAMPECHE [1701] 15x27cm. (5½x11") Paris: Marret. Col. [15] £58 $110

DANBY, T.

PLAN OF CINCINATTI [1815] 33x25cm. (12½x10½") From Drake's *Picture of Cincinnati*. Very good. [31] £302 $575

DANCKERTS

ACCURATISSIMA TOTIUS ASIA TABULA RECENS EMENDATA PER I. DANCKERTS. [c. 1680] 48x58cm. (19½x22½") Original color. Repairs to margin; o/w very good. [1] £289 $550

INSULAE AMERICANAE NEMPE: CUBA, HISPANIOLA, IAMAICA, PTO RICO, LUCANIA, ANTILLIAE VULGO CARIBAE BARLO-ET SOTTO-VENTO, &TC. ... [c. 1696] 51x58cm. (19½x22½") Original color. Excellent. [1] £631 $1200

NOVA TOTIUS TERRARUM ORBIS TABULA ... [c. 1680] 48x55cm. (19x21½") Double hemisphere with ornate surround. Shirley 495. Original color. Excellent. [37] £3416 $6500

NOVI BELGII NOVAEQUE ANGLIAE NEC NON PENNSYLVANIAE ET PARTIS VIRGINIAE TABULA [c. 1650] 47x55cm. (18½x21½") With New York City view. Old color. Tissue lined; small area in view lacking, but discretely backed. [16] £1104 $2102

[same title] [1655 (c. 1680)] 47x55cm. (18½x21½") Original color. [38] £2733 $5200

TOTIUS AFRICAE ACCURITISSIMA TABULA [c. 1680] 48x58cm. (19½x22½") Outline color; full color cartouche. Foxing; repaired hole (1/2 x1") in cartouche. [35] £171 $325

DARTON

BROOKE'S TRAVELLING COMPANION THROUGH ENGLAND AND WALES [1819] 56x49cm. (22x19") 2nd edition. Linen-backed folding map in original slipcase with label. Wash and outline color. Uniform age-darkening and slight soiling; slipcase worn but sound. [19] £66 $125

[same title] [1831] 58x49cm. (22½x19½") 2nd edition. Linen-backed folding map in original marbled slipcase with label. Color. Marginal ink marks, linen worn at fold junctures, slipcase worn at edges; very good. [19] £79 $150

THE CIRCUIT OF THE LAKES, IN THE COUNTIES OF CUMBERLAND, WESTMORELAND AND LANCASHIRE [1846] 59x49cm. (23x19") Linen-backed folding map between boards. Original color. Some traveler's inked routes; age-darkening at folds; good+. [19] £126 $240

THE WESTERN HEMISPHERE OR NEW WORLD [1820] 25x23cm. (9½x9") Color. [15] £42 $80

WALKER'S TOUR THROUGH ENGLAND AND WALES, A NEW PASTIME [1809] 51x43cm. (20x17") Map GAME: side text provides rules; counties numbered. Linen-backed folding map in original slipcase with label. Color. Slight foxing on text; very good. [19] £355 $675

DARTON & CLARK

DARBY'S LONDON GUIDE [1843] 42x64cm. (16½x25") Linen backed folding map between original boards with label. Cover title: "Darby's Map of London with all the Railway and Steam-Boat Stations". Color. Covers worn, ties lacking; o/w very good. [19] £205 $390

DAUMONT

VUE DE LA VILLE DU MEXIQUE PRIS DU COTE DU LAC [1754] 25x38cm. (9½x15") Color. [15] £87 $165

DE AEFFERDEN

PLANISPHERIO CELESTE [1695+] 14x27cm. (5½x10½") One tear, two minor splits repaired; o/w fine. [10] £145 $275

DE BELLEFOREST

LONDINUM FERACISSIMI ANGLIAE REGNI METROPOLIS ... [1575] 31x48cm. (12x19") After Braun & Hogenberg. Color. [5] £975 $1855

DE BRUYN

RAMA [1698] 21x62cm. (8½x24½") [Jordan] Panoramic view. [10] £45 $85

DE BRY

[CAPE OF GOOD HOPE] [1601] 14x17cm. (5½x6½") [10] £116 $220

[CHRISTOPHER COLUMBUS DISCOVERING THE NEW WORLD] [c. 1595] 14x20cm. (5½x7½") On sheet with text, 33.5 x 23 cm. [18] £236 $450

[COLUMBO, SRI LANKA(?)] [c. 1605] 15x25cm. (6x10") Bird's-eye, probably Columbo Harbor. [10] £32 $60

[COLUMBUS AND THE EGG] [1594 (c. 1600)] 16x18cm. (6½x7") Dinner with advisors to Spanish crown. Excellent. [37] £92 $175

[COLUMBUS DEPARTS ON HIS FIRST VOYAGE] [1594] 16x20cm. (6½x7½") Col. [10] £92 $175

[COLUMBUS DEPARTS ON HIS FIRST VOYAGE] verso: [COLUMBUS FIRST LANDFALL] [c. 1600] 17x19cm. (6½x7½") Trimmed to side margin; o/w excellent. [5] £180 $343

[COLUMBUS REACHES SAN SALVADOR] [1594] 17x20cm. (6½x7½") German text. Color. [10] £184 $350

[PORT ROYAL] [1591] 15x21cm. (6x8½") View by Le Moyne of French settlement in Carolina. Fine. [37] £118 $225

[SPANISH ARMADA] [c. 1631] 16x18cm. (6x7") 1588 battle. Excellent. [37] £79 $150

AMACAO [1598] 26x33cm. (10x13") Bird's eye view from *Petit Voyages*. [5] £500 $952

ANGLORUM IN VIRGINIAM ADVENTUS [1590] 16x23cm. (6x9") Pictorial map. Cumming 13. Margin added at left. [38] £236 $450

BORNEO INSULA [c.1631] 14x20cm. (5½x7½") Full col. Close side margins; o/w exc. [37] £131 $250

COLUMBUS DER ERSTE ERFINDER DER NEWEN WELT [1594] 15x20cm. (5½x7½") On sheet 34 x 24 cm; 13 x 9". Excellent. [38] £131 $250

DE-SCRIPTIO CHORO-GRAPHICA REG-NI CHI-NE [1628] 29x34cm. (11½x13½") Chinese characters in title. Color. Short tears into engraving; narrow margins as issued reinstated. [5] £600 $1142

DELINEATIO CARTAE TRIUM NAVIGATIONUM PER BATAVOS, AD SEPTENTRIONALEM PLAGEM, NORVEGIA, MOSCOVIA, ET NOVA ZEMBLA ... [1601] 38x28cm. (15x11") Trimmed several mm. left and right. [10] £394 $750

DESCRIPCION DEL DESTIETO DEL AUDIENCA DE LIMA 11 [1617] 15x23cm. (6½x9") By A. de Herrera. [15] £71 $135

DESCRIPTIO CHOROGRAPHICA REFNU CHINAE [c. 1620] 29x34cm. (11½x13½") Trimmed to neat line all around; tears repaired. [10] £197 $375

DESCRIPTION DEL DESTRICTO DEL AUDIENCIA DE NUEVA ESPANA 4 [1623] 18x28cm. (7½x10½") By A. de Herrera. North to 26 degrees. [15] £92 $175

FRANCISCUS DRACO CARTHAGENAM CIVITATEM EXPUGNAT [1590] 15x21cm. (6x8½") Plan of city under attack. Trimmed to right margin; worming above image. [17] £66 $125

HISPANIAE NOVAE SIVE MAGNAE, RECENS ET VERA DESCRIPTIO. 1595 [1595] 33x44cm. (13x17½") [10] £289 $550

I. LADRONES [c. 1610] 14x19cm. (5½x7½") View of shipboard trading near Guam. [38] £66 $125

MAPPE DIESER LANDTSCHAFFT ODER INSEL CELON [c. 1610] 28x19cm. (11x7½") Blank cartouche. [10] £184 $350

MEXICO [CITY] [1631] 15x18cm. (6x7") Text page fragment. Some tiny wormholes. [12] £92 $175

NOVA ALBION [1655] 13x18cm. (5x7") View of Francis Drake in California, with text. [15] £76 $145

OCCIDENTALIS AMERICAE PARTIS, VEL, EARUM REGIONUM QUAS CHISTOPHORUS COLUMBUS PRIMUM DETEXIT ... [1594+] 33x44cm. (13x17") Minor restoration at edges. [10] £2023 $3850

[same title] [1594] 33x43cm. (13x17") Side margins clipped, some border loss; o/w fine. [37] £2207 $4200

RIO JANERO [1631] 15x18cm. (6x7") Color. [15] £76 $145

SUD SEITS DES LANDTS TERSA DEL FUOCO [1630] 15x17cm. (6x7") [10] £50 $95

TABULA GEOGRA. REGNI CONGO [1601] 31x38cm. (12x15") Margins trimmed to neat line. [10] £315 $600

TABULAM HANC AEGYPTI, SI AEQUUS AC DILIGENS LECTOR, CUM ALYS, QUAE HACTENUS PRODICUT ... [1597] 55x40cm. (21½x15½") Two sheets joined. By Pigafetta, 1591. Full color. [38] £1471 $2800

DE CHASTELLUX

CHART FOR THE JOURNAL OF MR. LE MARQUIS DE CHASTELLUX BY MR. DEZOTEUX ... [Virginia] [1787] 18x25cm. (7x10") From *Travels in North America* ..., Dublin: Cole, Moncrieff. [6] £197 $375

DE CREVECOEUR

CARTE DE L'ILE DE MARTHA'S VINEYARD ... [1787] 23x25cm. (8½x10½") Faint offsetting; else very good. [21] £394 $750

CARTE DE L'ILE DE NANTUCKET POUR LES LETTRES D'UN CULTIVATEUR AMERIQUAIN [1787] 20x28cm. (8x11") Engraved by Tardieu. Fold lines. [6] £155 $295

[same title, date, dimensions] Slight offsetting and toning; else very good. [21] £394 $750

CARTE GENERALE DES ETATS DE VIRGINIE, MARYLAND, DELAWARE, PENSILVANIE, NOUVEAU-JERSEY, NEW-YORK, CONNECTICUT ET ISLE DE RHODES ... D'APRES LA CARTE AMERIQUAINE DE LOUIS EVANS ET ... THOMAS-JEFFERYS ... POUR LES LETTRES D'UN CULTIVATEUR AMERIQUAIN [1787] 48x65cm. (19x25½") Color. Faint offsetting; o/w excellent. [21] £788 $1500

ESQUISSE DES RIVIERES MUSKINGHUM ET GRAND CASTOR QUE J'AI TIREE DU JOURNAL DU GENERAL BOUQUET [1787] 25x53cm. (9½x20½") [15] £71 $135

DE FER (Large)

[TITLE PAGE] L'ATLAS CURIEUX OU LE MONDE ... [1705] 23x34cm. (9x13½") [5] £70 $133

L'AMERIQUE MERIDIONALE, ET SEPTENTRIONALE ... [1699 (1717)] 47x60cm. (18½x23½") Blank upper right cartouche. Original outline color. Excellent. [38] £1261 $2400

LA CALIFORNIE OU NOUVELLE CAROLINE, TEATRO DE LOS TRABAJOS, APOSTOLICOS LA DE COMPA. E JESUS EN LA AMERICA SEPT. [1720] 45x65cm. (18x26") Insular California. Original outline color. Early reinforcement on verso; o/w very good. [21] £2890 $5500

MAPPE-MONDE OU CARTE GENERALE DE LA TERRE ... [(1700)-1728] 44x70cm. (17½x27½") Insular California. Shirley 600. Color. Some minor repaired tears. [31] £1787 $3400

MAPPE-MONDE, OU CARTE GENERALE DE LA TERRE, DIVISEE EN DEUX HEMISPHERES SUIVANT LA PROJECTION LA PLUS COMMUNE OU TOUS LES POINTS PRINCIPAUX ... SUR LES OBSERVATIONS DE MRS. DE L'ACADEMIE ROYALE DES SCIENCES ... AVEC PRIVILEGE DU ROY1700 [1705] 44x70cm. (17x27½") Full early color. Excellent. [21] £736 $1400

[same title] [1705-1728] 44x70cm. (17½x27½") Orig outline color. [10] £1182 $2250

DE FER (Small)

ASIE [1746] 13x16cm. (5½x6") [10] £16 $30

ASIE PAR N. DE FER [c. 1700] 14x16cm. (5½x6½") [37] £29 $55

CETTE CARTE DE CALIFORNIE ET DU NOUVEAU MEXIQUE EST TIREE DE CELLE QUI A ETE ENVOYEE PAR UN GRANDE D'ESPAGNE POUR ETRE COMMUNIQUEE A MRS DE L'ACADEMIE ROYALE DES SCIENCES [1700] 23x34cm. (9x13½") First issue. Insular California; with Kino's Sonora travels. Original outline color. Excellent. [38] £736 $1400

EMPIRE D'ALLEMAGNE [c. 1700] 13x16cm. (5x6½") Excellent. [37] £24 $45

ESPAGNE PAR N. DE FER [c. 1700] 14x16cm. (5½x6½") Color. Excellent. [37] £34 $65

ESTATS DE LA COURONNE DE POLOGNE [c. 1700] 14x16cm. (5½x6") Excellent. [37] £24 $45

GLOBE TERRESTRE / GLOBE CELESTE / SPHERE ARTIFICIELLE ... [1717] 23x33cm. (9x13") 3 spheres on stands. Color. [15] £76 $145

GRANDE TARTARIE [c. 1700] 14x16cm. (5½x6½") Color. Excellent. [37] £24 $45

ISLES BRITANIQUES OU SONT LES ROYAUMES D'ANGLETERRE D'ESCOSSE D'IRLANDE [c. 1700] 13x16cm. (5x6") Color. Excellent. [37] £39 $75

L'AMERIQUE MERIDIONALE ET SEPTENTRIONALE DRESSEE SELON LES DERNIERS RELATIONS ET SUIVANT LES NOUVELLES DECOUVERTES ... [1700] 22x33cm. (9x13") [10] £250 $475

[same title, date, dimensions] First issue. Light outline color. Good. [29] £342 $650

L'EUROPE PAR N. DE FER [c. 1700] 13x16cm. (5x6") Excellent. [37] £13 $25

L'ITALIE [c. 1705] 22x33cm. (8½x13") Very good. [25] £75 $143

LA FRANCE ET SES AEQUISITIONS JUSQU'A LA TREVE DE 1684 [c. 1700] 14x16cm. (5½x6½") Color. Excellent. [37] £13 $25

LE CANADA, OU NOUVELLE FRANCE, LA FLORIDE, LA VIRGINIE, PENSILVANIE, CAROLINE, NOUVELLE ANGLETERRE ET NOUVELLE YORCK, L'ISLE DE TERRE NEUVE, LA LOUISIANE ET LE COURS DE LA RIVIERE DE MISISIPI [1705] 24x34cm. (9½x13½") Col. Excel. [38] £394 $750

LE GRAN ROYAUME DE HONGRIE OU PARTIE SEPTENTRIONALE DE LA TURQUIE EN EUROPE, DIVISEE PAR GRANDS GOUVERNEMENTS, SUIVANT RICAUT ANGLOIS [c. 1700] 14x16cm. (5½x6½") Excellent. [37] £34 $65

LE ROYAUME DE NAPLES [c. 1705] 22x33cm. (8½x13") Sardinia inset. VG. [25] £85 $162

LE VIEUX MEXIQUE OU NOUVELLE ESPAGNE AVEC LES COSTES DE LA FLORIDE FAISANT PARTIE DE L'AMERIQUE SEPTENTRIONALE [1705] 23x33cm. (9x13") Outline color. Excellent. [38] £276 $525

LES COSTES AUX ENVIRONS DE LA RIVIERE DE MISISIPI. DECOUVERTES PAR MR. DE LA SALLE EN 1683... [1705] 22x33cm. (8½x13") Fine. [27] £402 $765

LES ISLES DE L'AMERIQUE CONNUES SOUS LE NOM D'ANTILLES, OU SONT LES ISLES DE CUBA ... LES LUCAYES, LES CARIBES ET CELLES DU VENT [1702] 23x33cm. (9x13") 1st edition. H. van Loon, sc. Color. [15] £202 $385

[same title] [1705] 22x33cm. (9x13") Fine. [27] £208 $395

PARTIE MERIDIONALE D'AFRIQUE OU SE TROUVENT LE BASSEE GUINEE ... DE MADAGASCAR [1715] 20x33cm. (8½x12½") Color. [15] £123 $235

PERSE PAR N. DE FER. [c. 1700] 14x16cm. (5½x6½") Color. Excellent. [37] £24 $45

PLAN DES VILLES, FORTS, PORT, RADE ET ENVIRONS DE CARTAGENE... [1705] 23x32cm. (9x12½") Color. [15] £71 $135

PRESQU'ISLE DE L'INDE DE CA LE GOLFE DU GANGE / PRESQU'ISLE DE L'INDE DE LA LE GOLFE DU GANGE [1746] 14x16cm. (5½x6½") Two maps: India; Malay Peninsula. [10] £21 $40

QUEBEC, VILLE DE L'AMERIQUE SEPTENTRIONALE DANS LA NOUVELLE FRANCE ... [1694] 20x30cm. (8x12") 1st edition. Color. [15] £202 $385

RUSSIE BLANCHE OR MOSCOVIE [c. 1700] 14x16cm. (5½x6½") Color. Excellent. [37] £24 $45

TURQUIE EN ASIE [c. 1700] 14x16cm. (5½x6½") Color. Excellent. [37] £24 $45

DE HERRERA

DESCRIPCION DE LAS YNDIAS DE MEDIODIA [1622] 22x29cm. (8½x11½") [17] £150 $285

DESCRIPCION DE LAS YNDIAS OCCIDENTALIS [1622] 23x32cm. (9x12½") [17] £368 $700

DESCRIPCION DEL AUDIENCIA DE LOS CHARCAS [1622] 15x18cm. (5½x6½") [15] £66 $125

DESCRIPCION DEL AUDIENCIA DE PANAMA [1622] 22x29cm. (8½x11½") VG. [17] £131 $250

DESCRIPCION DEL DESTRICTO DE AUDIENCIA DE LA NEUEVA GALICIA [1601+] 20x29cm. (8x11") [10] £63 $120

DESCRIPTION DEL DESTRICTO DEL AUDIENCIA NUEVA ESPANA [1601] 15x28cm. (6½x11") Very good. [31] £92 $175

DE JODE

CHINA REG-NUM [1593] 36x45cm. (14x17½") Color. [5] £3650 $6946

[same title, date] (no dims.) Circular form. Full color. Excellent. [21] £3941 $7500

DE L'ISLE *Try Albrizzi, Covens & Mortier, Buache. Dezauche, Lotter*

CARTE D'AFRIQUE [1722] 53x74cm. (21x29½") Orig outline col. Small spot in center. [31] £499 $950

CARTE D'ASIE [1779] 50x64cm. (19½x25") Original outline color. A little soiled; frayed margins without loss. [10] £97 $185

CARTE DE L'AFRIQUE FRANCOISE OU DU SENEGAL [1726] 48x61cm. (18½x24") Color. [15] £139 $265

CARTE DE LA BARBARIE DE LA NIGRITIE ET DE LA GUINEE [(1707)-1718+] 48x64cm. (19½x24½") Original outline color. Minor centerfold wrinkles. [31] £171 $325

CARTE DE MOSCOVIE... [1780] 99x66cm. (38½x25½") Paris: Chez de Zauche. Two sheets joined. Outline color. Slightly soiled; damp stain along lower margin; very good. [8] £226 $430

CARTE DE TARTARIE DRESSEE SUR LES RELATIONS DE PLUSIERS VOYAGEURS ... [1706] 48x64cm. (19x25") Baltic to Pacific. Outline color. [15] £129 $245

CARTE DU CANADA OU DE LA NOUVELLE FRANCE ET DES DECOUVERTES QUI Y ONT ETE FAITES DRESSEE SUR PLUSIERS OBSERVATIONS ... PAR GUILLAUME DEL'ISLE ... [1703 / 1708] 50x65cm. (19½x25½") Original color. Very good. [1] £1051 $2000

CARTE DU MEXIQUE ET DE LA FLORIDE DES TERRES ANGLOISES ET DES ISLES ANTILLES DU COURS ET DES ENVIRONS DE LA RIVIERE DE MISSISSIPI ... PAR GUILLAUME DEL'ISLE ... [1722] 20x24cm. (8x9½") Amsterdam: Covens & Mortier. Orig outline col. Excel. [26] £709 $1350

CARTE DU PARAGUAY DU CHILI DU DETROIT DE MAGELLAN &C. ... [1703 (1708)] 51x64cm. (19½x25½") Full color. Slight scuffing at lower margin; else excellent. [35] £197 $375

CARTE DU PARAGUAY DU CHILI DU DETROIT DE MAGELLAN &C. DESCRIPTIONS DES ALFONSE D'OVALLE ET NICOLAS TECHO ... [1745] 51x64cm. (19½x25") Paris: P. Buache. Color. [15] £150 $285

HEMISPHERE SEPTENTRIONAL POUR VOIR PLUS DISTINCTEMENT LES TERRES ARCTIQUES [1714] Diameter: 45 cm. (18") Color. Minor spotting; else very good. [34] £184 $350

[same title] [1782] 46x46cm. (18½x18½") Paris: Dezauche. Color. [15] £192 $365

L'AFRIQUE ... [1700] 44x58cm. (17½x22½") 1st edition, "Rue des Canettes" issue. Color. Centerfold split repaired; very good. [34] £525 $1000

L'AMERIQUE MERIDIONALE DRESSEE SUR LES OBSERVATIONS DE MRS. DE L'ACADEMIE DES SCIENCES ... PAR G. DE L'ISLE ... [1700] 46x60cm. (18x23½") 1st edition. "Rue des Canettes" issue. Outline color. Small stains; else very good. [34] £525 $1000

L'AMERIQUE SEPTENTRIONALE. DRESSEE SUR LES OBSERVATIONS ... [1700-1720] 45x58cm. (18x23") Amsterdam: Covens & Mortier. Full original color. Excellent. [2] £631 $1200

L'ASIE ... [1700] 46x58cm. (18x23") "Rue des Canettes" issue. Outline color. Minor flaws, else very good. [34] £525 $1000

L'ITALIE [c. 1755] 49x62cm. (19½x24½") Outline color. Very good. [25] £150 $285

LES ISLES BRITANNIQUES ... [c. 1740] 44x56cm. (17½x22") Outline color. VG. [23] £195 $371

DE LA FEUILLE

L'ASIE [1710] 13x18cm. (5x7") [10] £24 $45

DE LA RUE

REGNUM SALOMONICUM SEU TABULA DIGESTA AD LIBROS JUDICUM REGNUM [1651] 41x53cm. (15½x21") Paris: Mariette. Laor 417. Color. [15] £145 $275

SOURIE OU TERRE SAINCTE MODERNE [1651] 39x53cm. (15½x21") Paris: Mariette. Laor 420. Color. [15] £158 $300

DE LAET

FLORIDA ET REGIONES VICINAE [1630] 28x36cm. (11x14") By H. Gerritsz. Lightly toned; marginal repair; else very good. [21] £946 $1800

NOVA FRANCIA ET REGIONES ADIACENTES [1625] 28x36cm. (11x14") Color. [10] £788 $1500

[same title] [c. 1625] 28x36cm. (11x14") Excellent. [1] £893 $1700

[same title] [1630 (1633)] 28x36cm. (11x14") By Gerritsz. Excellent. [38] £736 $1400

TRUGILLO [1644] 28x36cm. (11x14") Bird's eye of engagement at Truxillo, Honduras. [15] £210 $400

DE LETH

MAPPE MONDE OU DESCRIPTION DU GLOBE TERRESTRE VU EN CONCAVE OU CREUX EN DEUX HEMISPHERES ... [c. 1730] 46x66cm. (17½x26") Surround of six smaller spherical projections. Color. Fine. [15] £815 $1550

DE PRETOT

CHOROGRAPHIE DU CERCLE DE SOUABE [1787] 25x33cm. (10½x13½") Color. [36] £66 $125

DE VAUGONDY *Try Delamarche. Diderot*

[TITLE PAGE] ATLAS UNIVERSEL [1757] 35x48cm. (14x19") [5] £85 $162

AMERIQUE MERIDIONALE, DRESSEE, SUR LES MEMOIRES LES PLUS RECENTS ET ASSUJETIE AUX OBSERVATIONS ASTRONOMIQUE. PAR LE SR. ROBERT DE VAUGONDY, FILS ... [1750] 48x59cm. (19x23") Outline color; cartouche full color. Somewhat weak impression; repaired centerfold split. [16] £83 $158

AMERIQUE SEPTENTRIONALE, DRESSEE, SUR LES RELATIONS LES PLUS MODERNES DES VOYAGEURS ET NAVIGATEURS, ET DIVISEE SUIVANT LES DIFFERENTES POSSESSIONS DES EUROPEANS [1750-1775] 48x59cm. (19x23") Second edition; inset of Northwest at upper left. Original outline color. Good. [2] £499 $950

AMERIQUE SEPTENTRIONALE DRESSEE SUR LES RELATIONS LES PLUS MODERNES DES VOYAGEURS ET NAVIGATEURS OU SE REMARQUENT LES ETATS UNIS [1783] 48x59cm. (19x23½") Color. [15] £342 $650

ANTIQUOR ? IMPERISSUM TABULA ... [1783] 47x62cm. (18½x24½") [Middle East] Original outline color. [10] £39 $75

BAYES D'HUDSON ET DE BAFFINS, ET TERRE DE LABRADOR [1749] 16x16cm. (6½x6½") Color. [15] £47 $90

CARTE DE L'ASIE DRESSE SUR LES RELATIONS LES PLUS NOUVELLES ... [1783] 47x53cm. (18½x20½") Original outline color. [10] £47 $90

CARTE DE L'ITALIE [c. 1770] 47x53cm. (18½x21") Color. Very good. [25] £75 $143

CARTE DE LA CALIFORNIA SUIVANT I. CARTE MANUSCRIT 1604; II. SANSON 1656; III. DE L'ISLE 1700; IV. PERE KINO 1705; V. SOC. DES JESUITS 1767 [1774] 28x38cm. (11x15") From Diderot's Encyclopedie. [6] £223 $425

CARTE DE LA CALIFORNIE ET DES PAYS NORD-OUEST SEPARE'S DE L'ASIE PAR LE DETROIT D'ANIAN ... 1772 [c. 1774] 28x36cm. (11x14") From Diderot's Encyclopedie. Col. [6] £208 $395

CARTE DE LA VIRGINIE ET DU MARYLAND DRESSEE SUR LA GRANDE CARTE ANGLOISE DE MRS. JOSUE FRY ET PIERRE JEFFERSON [c.1752] 49x64cm. (19½x25½") Color. [15] £447 $850

[same title] [1755] 48x64cm. (19x25½") Original outline color. Excellent. [1] £578 $1100

CARTE DES PARTIES NORD ET OUEST DE L'AMERIQUE DRESSE D'APRES LES RELATIONS LES PLUS AUTHENTIQUES PAR M. EN 1764 [1772] 30x38cm. (11½x14½") Col. [15] £139 $265

CARTE DES VOYAGES DE NOTRE SEIGNEUR ET CEUX DES APOSTRES ST. PIERRE ET ST. PAUL DANS L'ASIE ET DANS L'EUROPE [1747] 46x58cm. (18x23") Laor 674. Color. [15] £150 $285

COURS DU MISSISSIPI ET LA LOUISIANE [1749] 22x16cm. (8½x6½") [6] £105 $200

[same title] [c. 1749] 22x16cm. (8½x6½") Original outline color. [12] £118 $225

GOLFE DE ST. LAURENT, ISLE ET BANCS DE TERRE NEUVE [1749] 17x18cm. (6½x7") Color. [15] £53 $100

L'AMERIQUE PAR LE S. ROBERT DE VAUGONDY ... [1762] 25x23cm. (9½x9") Col. [15] £97 $185

L'IRLANDE [c. 1778] 24x22cm. (9½x8½") Color. Very good. [24] £85 $162

L'ISLE ST. DOMINGUE PAR FILS DE MR. ROBERT ... [1749] 15x23cm. (6½x8½") Col. [15] £37 $70

LA FLORIDE DIVISEE EN FLORIDE ET CAROLINE [1749] 17x18cm. (6½x7") [10] £53 $100

NOUVELLE ESPAGNE, NOUVEAU MEXIQUE, ISLES ANTILLES CORRIGES PAR CEN. LAMARCHE, L'AN 3 [1794] 24x31cm. (9½x12") Color. [15] £76 $145

PARTIE DE L'AMERIQUE SEPTENTRIONALE, QUI COMPREND LA NOUVELLE FRANCE OU LA CANADA [1755+] 48x61cm. (18½x23½") Great Lakes inset. Orig outline col. Excel. [22] £394 $750

PARTIE DE LA MER DU NORD, OU SE TROUVENT LES GRANDES ET LES PETITES ISLES ANTILLES, ET LES ISLES LUCAYES. PAR LE SR. ROBERT... [1750] 48x59cm. (19x23") Old color. Cleaned. Wormhole pair in lower margin; upper margin trimmed to neat line. [16] £131 $250

PARTIE DU CANADA OU SE TROUVENT LE FLEUVE ST. LAURENT ET LA NOUVELLE ECOSSE [c. 1749] 17x22cm. (6½x8½") Original outline color. Fine. [12] £58 $110

PARTIE DU MEXIQUE OU DE LA NOUV'LE ESPAGNE OU SE TROUVE L'AUDCE DE GUADALAJARA NOUVEAU MEXIQUE, NOUVELLE NAVARRE, CALIFORNIE &C. [1749] 16x20cm. (6½x7½") [10] £66 $125

[same title, date, dimensions] Original outline color. [12] £150 $285

DE WIT

[TITLE PAGE] [1670-88] 48x25cm. (19½x10") Frontispiece: figure of Atlas on Eastern Hemisphere holding up starry heavens. Color. Repair at top; light marginal soiling; o/w good.. [30] £236 $450

ASIA ... [1661] 44x55cm. (17½x21½") "Carte-a-figures" Original color. Fine. [5] £1200 $2284

DANIAE, FRISIAE, GRONINGAE ET ORIENTALIS FRISIAE LITTORA [1675] 49x57cm. (19½x22") From *Orbis Maritimus*. Bright contemporary color. Repair to 1" hole; tissue backing where color has weakened paper. [11] £400 $761

NIEUWE PASCAERT VAN'T SUYDERLYCKSTEDEEL VAN SUYT AMERICA ... [1675] 48x56cm. (19x22") From *Orbis Maritimus*. Bright early color. Light crease line; faint damp-marking upper margin; tissue backing to repair two small straight tears without loss. [11] £400 $761

NOVA ORBIS TABULA, IN LUCEM EDITA, A. F. DE WIT [with] AFRICA [and] AMERICA [and] ASIA [and] EUROPA [c. 1680] 48x56cm. (19x22") 5 maps. Second state of world map; Shirley 451. Original color. Some minor offsetting; early verdigris cracking repaired and reinforced with no loss. [5] £4995 $9505

NOVA TOTIUS TERRARUM ORBIS TABULA EX OFFICINA F. DE WIT AMSTELODAMI [1668 (1715)] 48x56cm. (19x22") Renard issue. Shirley 444. Full color. Mint. [38] £3783 $7200

NOVISSIMA ET ACCURATISSIMA TOTIUS ITALIAE CORSICAE ET SARDINIAE, DESCRIPTIO CORRECTA MUTIS AUCTA ET IN LUCEM EDITA PER F.D. WITT AMSTELODAMI CUM PRIV... [1680] 49x56cm. (19½x22") Light toning at centerfold. [37] £118 $225

ORIENTALIORA INDIARUM ORIENTALIUM CUM INSULIS ADJACENTIBUS A PROMONTORIO C. COMORIN AD IAPAN / PASCAERT VAN T'OOSTER GEDEELTE VAN OOST INDIEN VAN C. COMORIN TOT IAPAN [c. 1680] 44x54cm. (17½x21½") Color. Excellent. [37] £1629 $3100

REGNUM NEAPOLIS ... [c. 1680] 58x48cm. (23x19½") Original color. Some toning and foxing; else very good. [21] £236 $450

TABULA INDIAE ORIENTALIS [1662] 46x57cm. (18x22½") Color. Minor lower centerfold reinforcement; fine. [5] £625 $1189

TERRA NEUF, EN DE CUSTEN VAN NIEU VRANCKRYCK, NIEU ENGELAND, NIEU NEDERLAND, NIEU ANDALUSIA, GUIANA, EN VENEZUELA [1675] 48x56cm. (19x22") Color. [15] £355 $675

TERRA SANCTA SIVE PROMISSIONIS, OLIM PALESTINA RECENS DELINEATA [c. 1680] 46x56cm. (18x22") Original outline color. Laid down on stiff card; oil stain at one side. [10] £92 $175

[same title, date] 46x55cm. (18x21½") Original color. Excellent. [21] £342 $650

TRACTUS AUSTRALIOR AMERICAE MERIDIONALIS, A RIO DE LA PLATA PER FRETUM MAGELLANICUM AD TORALTUM. NIEUWE PERFECTE PASCAERT VAN 'T SUYDERLYCKSTE DEEL VAN SUYT AMERICA, VAN RIO DE LA PLATA DOOR DE STRAET MAGELLAEN TOT TORAL [1675] 48x55cm. (19x21½") Color. [15] £355 $675

TRACTUS LITTORALES GUINEAE A PROMONTORIO VERDE USQUE AD SINUM CATENBALAE [1675] 49x56cm. (19½x22") From *Orbis Maritimus*. Bright early color. Faint damp-marking in margin edges. [11] £450 $856

ULTRAIECTINI DOMINII TABULA [c. 1680] 46x56cm. (18x22") Centered on Utrecht. Color. Excellent. [35] £105 $200

DELAMARCHE *Try De Vaugondy*

AMERIQUE SEPTENTRIONALE DRESSEE D'APRES LES DECOUVERTES DU CAP. COOK [1782] 20x23cm. (7½x8½") Color. [15] £45 $85

NOUVELLE ESPAGNE NOUVEAU MEXIQUE ISLES ANTILLES ... [1812] 25x38cm. (10x14½") Color. [15] £71 $135

DEPOT DE LA MARINE *Try Bellin*

[TITLE PAGE] NEPTUNE FRANCOIS [c. 1770] 51x36cm. (20x14½") Color. Fine. [27] £289 $550

CARTE DE L'ENTREE DU RIO NUNEZ ... [1848] 89x61cm. (35x24") By de Kerhallet. [11] £45 $86

CARTE DE L'ILE DE LA JAMAIQUE EXTRAITE DES CARTES TOPOGRAPHIQUES ANGLOISES DE THOS. CRASKELL ... 1786 [1799] 58x86cm. (23x34") Minor repair. [15] £223 $425

CARTE DE LA BAIE DE CHESAPEAKE ... [1778] 58x86cm. (23x34½") By Sartine, after Anthony Smith. Fine. [27] £2890 $5500

CARTE GENERALE DE LA MARTINIQUE POUR LA TOPOGRAPHIE ... [1831] 91x64cm. (36x24½") By H. Monnier. [15] £118 $225

CARTE PARTICULIERE DE CANAL DE BRISTOL ... [1797-98] 57x89cm. (22½x35") [11] £180 $343

CARTE REDUITE DE L'OCEAN MERIDIONALE... [1739] 62x78cm. (24½x30½") Early wash color. Upper & lower margins reduced to engraving at corners; o/w excellent. [11] £170 $324

CARTE REDUITE DE L'OCEAN MERIDIONALE CONTENANT TOUTES LES COSTES DE L'AMERIQUE MERIDIONALE DEPUIS L'EQUATEUR JUSQU'AU 57 DEGRE DE LATITUDE ET LES COSTES D'AFRIQUE ... [1753] 55x88cm. (21½x34½") Centerfold repair. [16] £442 $841

CARTE REDUITE DES COTES ET DU GOLFE DE CALIFORNIE DEPUIS LE CAP CORRIENTES JUSQU'AU PORT ST. DIEGO [1826] 84x57cm. (33x22½") After Spanish Government chart, Madrid, 1825. Wash color. Mint. [37] £289 $550

CARTE REDUITE DES COTES ORIENTALES DE L'AMERIQUE SEPTENTRIONALE CONTENANT PARTIE DU NOUVEAU JERSEY, LE PENSYLVANIE ... LA CAROLINE SEPTENTRIONALE, LA CAROLINE MERIDIONALE ET LA GEORGIE [1778] 61x86cm. (23½x34½") [15] £302 $575

COTE ORIENTALE D'ANGLETERRE DEPUIS SOUTH FORELAND, JUSQU'A LOWESTOFT COMPRENANT LES ENTREES DE LA TAMISE... [1797-98] 60x91cm. (23½x36") Margins reduced; small repaired lower fold tear. [11] £180 $343

PLAN D'UNE PARTIE DE L'ILE DE WIGHT ET DE LA COTE DE HAMPSHIRE ... [1823] 94x61cm. (37x24") After Murdoch Mackenzie. [11] £175 $333

PLAN DE LA COTE MERIDIONALE D'ANGLETERRE DEPUIS ST. ALBAN HEAD JUSQU'A ABBOTSBURY [1824] 64x93cm. (25x36½") After Mackenzie's surveys. Fine. [11] £120 $228

PLAN DE LA COTE MERIDIONALE D'ANGLETERRE DEPUIS ABBOTSBURY JUSQU'A SIDMOUTH ... [1824] 62x94cm. (24½x37") After Mackenzie's survey. [11] £120 $228

SUITE DE LA CARTE REDUITE DU GOLPHE DE ST. LAURENT CONTENANT LES COSTES DE LABRADOR ... LE DETROIT DE BELLE-ISLE ET PARTIE DES COSTES DE L'ISLE DE TERRE NEUVE ... [1753] 90x56cm. (35½x22") [15] £171 $325

DEPOT GENERAL DE LA GUERRE

CARTE DE L'EMPIRE FRANCOIS AVEC SES ETABLISSEMENTS POLITIQUES, MILITAIRES, CIVILS, ET RELIGIEUX ... [1807] 65x103cm. (25½x40½") Linen-backed folding map. Some age-soiling at folds; very good. [19] £39 $75

DEROY

VUE DU CANAL DE L'ISTHME DE SUEZ [c. 1861] 30x48cm. (12½x19") NY & Paris: Turgis. Three-color lithograph. Fine. [30] £289 $550

DES BARRES

[CASCO BAY, MAINE] [1776] 74x107cm. (29½x42") From *The Atlantic Neptune*. Full original wash color. Reinforcement of cracking due to color oxidation; o/w very good. [22] £578 $1100

[CHART OF SPRY HARBOR, PORT PALLISSER, PORT NORTH, PORT PARKER, BEAVER HARBOR AND FLEMING RIVER. ...] [1779] 70x99cm. (27½x39") Two sheets joined. Very fine. [10] £394 $750

[FALMOUTH HARBOR, ME] [1776] 76x53cm. (30x21½") From *Atlantic Neptune*. With Portland, ME street plan. [15] £657 $1250

[same title] [1777] 74x53cm. (29½x21") Orig wash color. Offsetting; else excellent. [22] £631 $1200

[MAINE: MUSCONGUS BAY] [1776] 107x76cm. (42x29½") Excellent. [11] £850 $1618

[MARTHA'S VINEYARD, ELIZABETH ISLANDS, BUZZARDS BAY] [1776] 104x74cm. (41½x29") . Full early wash col. Reinforced centerfold split; marginal tears repaired; o/w excel. [21] £2102 $4000

[MARTHA'S VINEYARD, RHODE ISLAND, BLOCK ISLAND COASTAL PROFILES] [c. 1775] 27x78cm. (10½x30½") From *Atlantic Neptune*. Excellent. [37] £1314 $2500

[MASSACHUSETTS COAST: CAPE ANNE TO BOSTON TO PLYMOUTH, WITH OUTER CAPE COD] [1776] 74x104cm. (29x41½") Full original color. Some offsetting; else excellent. [22] £1498 $2850

[same title] [1781] 74x104cm. (29x41½") Minor damage to edge; o/w excellent. [11] £1800 $3425

[PHILADELPHIA AND ENVIRONS] [1776] 76x104cm. (30½x41") From early edition of *The Atlantic Neptune*. Full color. Rice paper reinforcement; small restoration at top centerfold; paper somewhat brittle; else very good. [21] £2365 $4500

[PISCATAQUA HARBOR, NH] [1779] 107x76cm. (41½x30") Portsmouth at center. Minor repair. [15] £657 $1250

[PLYMOUTH, MASSACHUSETTS; BAY & TOWN] [1781] 66x48cm. (26x19") From *The Atlantic Neptune*. Original color. Excellent. [22] £631 $1200

BAY OF CHEDABUCTO - LENOR OR PETIT PASSAGE [Nova Scotia] [1781] 53x64cm. (20½x25") [15] £92 $175

CONWAY HARBOUR - PORT AYLESBURY [Nova Scotia] [1776] 53x69cm. (20½x27½") Fine. [15] £171 $325

EGMONT HARBOR [1779] 81x61cm. (32x23½") [now Jedore Harbor]. Third state. Aquatint. Tears into image expertly repaired; upper right quadrant once separated. [31] £368 $700

PORT MILLS, PORT MANSFIELD, GAMBIER HARBOR [Nova Scotia] [1781] 73x209cm. (28½x82") Four sheets issued as one. Delicate original coloring. [10] £394 $750

THE COAST OF NOVA SCOTIA, NEW ENGLAND - NEW YORK, JERSEY, THE GULF AND RIVER OF ST. LAWRENCE, THE ISLANDS OF NEWFOUNDLAND, CAPE BRETON, ST. JOHN, ANTECOSTI, SABLE &C. ...MDCCLXXVII [1777] 81x119cm. (32x46½") Excel. [15] £1182 $2250

DESBRUSLINS

CARTE DES VOYAGES DE MR. TAVERNIER, DANS LES INDES, ... [c. 1745] 22x30cm. (8½x11½") Full color. Excellent. [37] £131 $250

DESILVER

A NEW MAP OF ALABAMA WITH ITS ROADS AND DISTANCES FROM PLACE TO PLACE ALONG THE STAGE AND STEAM BOAT ROUTES [1856 (1857)] 37x29cm. (14½x11½") Pastel color. Fine. [12] £58 $110

A NEW MAP OF ARKANSAS WITH ITS COUNTIES, TOWNS, POST OFFICES, &C. [1857] 41x36cm. (16x13½") Bright color. [26] £47 $90

A NEW MAP OF CENTRAL AMERICA [1856] 36x41cm. (13½x16") Full color. [26] £34 $65

A NEW MAP OF INDIANA WITH ITS ROADS & DISTANCES [1856] 36x29cm. (14x11½") Color. [15] £45 $85

A NEW MAP OF INDIANA EXHIBITING ITS INTERNAL IMPROVEMENTS ROADS & DISTANCES &C. [1857] 41x36cm. (16x13½") Bright color. Very good. [26] £53 $100

A NEW MAP OF KENTUCKY [1857] 36x41cm. (13½x16") Bright color. Very good. [26] £53 $100

A NEW MAP OF LOUISIANA WITH ITS CANALS, ROADS & DISTANCES ... [1856 (1857)] 30x38cm. (11½x14½") Color. Excellent. [12] £58 $110

A NEW MAP OF MAINE [1856] 38x28cm. (15½x11") Color. [15] £47 $90

[same title] [1856 (1857)] 38x30cm. (15x12") Color. Tiny spots; o/w fine. [12] £39 $75

A NEW MAP OF MARYLAND AND DELAWARE WITH THEIR CANALS, ROADS & DISTANCES [1856] 30x38cm. (11½x15") Color. [15] £42 $80

A NEW MAP OF MICHIGAN WITH ITS CANALS, ROADS & DISTANCES [1856 (1857)] 37x30cm. (14½x11½") Full color. Fine. [12] £53 $100

A NEW MAP OF MISSISSIPPI WITH ITS ROADS AND DISTANCES [1856] 36x30cm. (14x11½") Color. [15] £39 $75

A NEW MAP OF NTH. CAROLINA WITH ITS CANALS, ROADS & DISTANCES FROM PLACE TO PLACE ALONG THE STAGE AND STEAM BOAT ROUTES [1856] 30x38cm. (12x14½") Color. [15] £47 $90

A NEW MAP OF SOUTH CAROLINA WITH ITS CANALS, ROADS & DISTANCES ... [1856 (1857)] 30x36cm. (11½x14") Color. Fine. [12] £47 $90

[same title] ... [c. 1857] 30x36cm. (11½x14½") Color. [15] £47 $90

A NEW MAP OF THE STATE OF CALIFORNIA, THE TERRITORIES OF OREGON, WASHINGTON, UTAH & NEW MEXICO [1856 (1859)] 41x33cm. (15½x12½") Baltimore: Cushings and Bailey. Full color. Immaculate. [12] £202 $385

A NEW MAP OF THE STATE OF GEORGIA EXHIBITING IT'S INTERNAL IMPROVEMENTS, ROADS, DISTANCES &C ... [1856 (1857)] 41x33cm. (16x13") Full color. Fine. [12] £47 $90

A NEW MAP OF THE STATE OF ILLINOIS [1856 (1857)] 41x33cm. (15½x13") Color. [12] £47 $90

[same title] [1857] 41x36cm. (16x13½") Bright color. Very good. [26] £63 $120

A NEW MAP OF THE STATE OF IOWA [1857] 34x41cm. (13½x16") Bright col. VG. [26] £53 $100

A NEW MAP OF THE STATE OF MISSOURI [1856 (1857)] 33x41cm. (13x16") Col. Mint. [12] £58 $110

[same title] [1857] 36x41cm. (13½x16") Bright color. Very good. [26] £53 $100

A NEW MAP OF THE STATE OF OHIO [1856 (1857)] 41x33cm. (16x13") Full col. Fine. [12] £45 $85

A NEW MAP OF THE STATE OF PENNSYLVANIA INCLUDING NEW JERSEY [1860] 41x69cm. (16x26½") Color. [15] £45 $85

A NEW MAP OF THE STATE OF VIRGINIA EXHIBITING ITS INTERNAL IMPROVEMENTS, ROADS, DISTANCES &C. [1856 (1857)] 33x41cm. (12½x15½") Color. Fine. [12] £47 $90

A NEW MAP OF THE STATE OF WISCONSIN [1856] 41x34cm. (16x13½") Color. [15] £50 $95

[same title, date, dimensions] Color. Trimmed close at left; o/w excellent. [26] £63 $120

A NEW MAP OF THE UNITED STATES OF AMERICA [1857] 40x66cm. (15½x26") By J. Young. Color. [15] £123 $235

CANADA EAST FORMERLY LOWER CANADA [1856] 33x41cm. (12½x15½") Color. [15] £21 $40

CHINA [1856] 36x41cm. (14x16") Bright color. [26] £32 $60

MAP OF CONNECTICUT [1856 (1857)] 32x37cm. (12½x14½") Color. [12] £45 $85

MAP OF NEW JERSEY COMPILED FROM THE LATEST AUTHORITIES [1856] 38x33cm. (15½x12½") 20 counties. Color. [15] £45 $85

MAP OF THE STATE OF NEW YORK COMPILED FROM THE LATEST AUTHORITIES [1856 (1857)] 41x66cm. (16x26") Five insets; two columns of data. Color. Mint. [12] £66 $125

MAP OF THE STATE OF TEXAS FROM THE LATEST AUTHORITIES BY J.H. YOUNG [1856 (1857)] 32x40cm. (12½x15½") Full color. Perfect. [12] £250 $475

THE PACIFIC OCEAN INCLUDING OCEANA WITH ITS SEVERAL DIVISIONS, ISLANDS, GROUPS &C. [1856] 36x41cm. (13½x16") Inset: Hawaiian Islands. Some color. [26] £47 $90

WEST INDIES [1856] 28x41cm. (11x16") Color. [15] £24 $45

DESNOS

GLOBE TERRESTRE DRESSEE SUR LES RELATIONS LES PLUS NOUVELLES DE MRS. DE L'ACADEMIE ROYALE DES SCIENCE ... [1760] Globe, mounted on original pedestal. Diameter: 23 cm. (9") Original color evident. Paper mache horizon ring somewhat warped, with one repair; slight rubbing at surface obscures some place names; repaired cracking at top. [22] £6569 $12,500

DHEULLAND

PLAN TOPOGRAPHIQUE DE LA VILLE PORT, ET BAYE DE GIBRALTAR ... [c. 1730] 63x47cm. (25x18½") [33] £200 $381

DIDEROT *Try De Vaugondy*

DIRECCION DE HIDROGRAFIA

BAHIA HONDA. CHART NO. 382 [1882] 18x27cm. (7x10½") Fine. [10] £26 $50

CARTA DE LOS CANALES BAHAMA, PROVIDENCIA Y SANTAREN, COSTA DE LA FLORIDA ... [1838] 56x87cm. (22x34") Light oil stains; hole repaired; small library stamp. [10] £499 $950

CARTA ESFERICA DE LA COSTA ORIENTAL DE CHINA... [1862] 61x94cm. (24x37") After Collinson & Kellett. Two repaired small margin tears; o/w excellent. [11] £65 $124

CARTA ESFERICA DE LA COSTA ORIENTAL DE CHINA DESDE EL RIO NGAU-KEANG HASTA EL WHANG-HO KAU SEGUN LOS TRABAJOS DE LOS CAPITANES KELLETT Y COLLINSON DE LA MARINA REAL INGLESA [1862] 94x61cm. (37x24½") Minor edge tears; o/w good. [11] £60 $114

CARTA ESFERICA QUE COMPRENDE PARTE DE LAS ISLAS DE STO. DOMINGO, JAMAICA, CUBA, LUCAYAS Y GRAN BAHAMAS [1856] 91x61cm. (36½x23½") By de Lersundi. [15] £118 $225

ISLA DE CUBA. COSTA MERIDIONAL. PLANO DEL PUERTO DE CASILDA MASIO, Y DEMAS FONDEADEROS ADYACENTES A LA CIUDAD DE TRINIDAD ... CHART NO. 759 [1882] 31x47cm. (12x18½") Lacks small blank portion at left; o/w fine. [10] £39 $75

ISLA DE CUBA. PLANO DEL PUERTO DE BAITIQUERI LEVANTADO EN 1861 ... CHART NO. 387A [1882] 30x45cm. (11½x17½") [10] £26 $50

ISLA DE CUBA. PLANO DEL PUERTO DE MATA LEVANTADO EN 1860 ... CHART NO. 388A [1882] 30x45cm. (12x17½") [10] £26 $50

PLANO DE LA BOCA DEL PUERTO DE CABANES EN LA COSTA NORTE DE LA ISLA DE CUBA SITUADA LA PUNTA DE LOS CAYOS ... NO. 381 [1882] 22x32cm. (8½x12½") Fine. [10] £21 $40

PUERTO DEL MARIEL. CHART NO. 380 [1882] 18x27cm. (7x10½") Fine. [10] £21 $40

PUERTO ESCONDIDO. CHART NO. 386 [1882] 18x23cm. (7x9") Fine. [10] £24 $45

DISTURNELL

MAP OF THE STATE OF NEW YORK SHOWING THE BOUNDARIES OF COUNTIES & TOWNSHIPS, THE LOCATION OF CITIES, TOWNS AND VILLAGES: AND THE COURSES OF RAIL ROADS, CANALS & STAGE ROADS [1845] 48x61cm. (18½x24½") By J. Calvin Smith. On banknote paper. Color. Some spotting; library mending at two fold separations; cover dirty, rubbed, separating. [7] £171 $325

DIXON

SKETCH BY COMPASS OF PORT MULGRAVE LAT 59^{0} 33'N. [1788] 41x28cm. (16x11") Color. Minor repair. [15] £45 $85

TO THE RIGHT HONORABLE THE LORDS COMMISSIONERS ... CHART OF THE NORTH WEST COAST OF AMERICA, WITH THE TRACKS OF THE KING GEORGE AND QUEEN CHARLOTTE IN 1786-87 [1788] 61x89cm. (23½x35") [15] £197 $375

DODSLEY

A NEW AND CORRECT PLAN OF LONDON, WESTMINSTER AND SOUTHWARK WITH SEVERAL ADDITIONAL IMPROVEMENTS NOT IN ANY FORMER SURVEY [1761] 36x66cm. (13½x26") Color. Creasing at folds; backed; else very good. [34] £236 $450

DONALDSON, T.

MAP SHOWING PRIVATE LAND CLAIMS, PATENTED OR UNPATENTED, OR CONFIRMED, IN NEW MEXICO, COLORADO AND ARIZONA [1883] 33x46cm. (12½x17½") In *The Public Domain,* ... Eight photocopied text pages. Lithographed color. Invisible tear mend through border; else fine. [12] £71 $135

DONCKER

PAS CAERT VAN'T IN KOMEN VAN DE CANAEL ... [c. 1660] 43x53cm. (17x20½") Early color. Slight creasing where two paper layers have separated; o/w good. [11] £240 $457

PASKAART VAN GUINEA VAN C. VERDE TOT R. DE GALION [1665] 43x53cm. (17x21") [15] £223 $425

DOPPELMAYR *Try Homann*

ASTRONOMIA COMPARATIVA [c. 1750] 48x58cm. (19x23") Nuremberg: Homann Heirs. Original color. Very good. [31] £263 $500

HEMISPHAERIUM COELI AUSTRALE IN QUO FIXARUM LOCA SECUNDUM ECLIPTICAE DICTUM AD ANUM 1730 ... [c. 1750] 48x58cm. (19x23") Homann. Orig color. VG. [31] £447 $850

THEORIAN LUNAE [c. 1750] 48x58cm. (19x23") Homann. Original color. VG [31] £263 $500

DOWER

CALIFORNIA, MEXICO, GUATIMALA &C. [1855] 21x26cm. (8x10") Outline color. [6] £79 $150

MAP OF ALABAMA [1866] 36x23cm. (14x9") Color. [15] £26 $50

MEXICO & GUATIMALA [c. 1844] 21x26cm. (8x10") Color. [6] £102 $195

DREW, J.

DREW'S NEW AND CORRECT PLAN OF THE CITIES OF LONDON AND WESTMINSTER, THE BOROUGH OF SOUTHWARK &C, INCLUDING THE LATEST IMPROVEMENTS [1801] 41x53cm. (16x20½") Dissected, mounted on linen, with pocket case. Col. A few stains; else Good. [35] £105 $200

DU VAL (Large)

L'AMERIQUE SUIVANT LES DERNIERS RELATIONS ... AVEC LES ROUTES QUE L'ON TIENT POUR LES INDES OCCIDENTALES. [1679] 41x55cm. (16x21½") dimensions for each of four sheets. Original outline color. Fine. [37] £6043 $11,500

LE CANADA FAICT PAR LE SR. DE CHAMPLAIN, OU SONT LA NOUVELLE FRANCE, LA NOUVELLE ANGLETERRE, LA NOUVELLE HOLLANDE, LA NOUVELLE SUEDE, LA VIRGINIE &C. ... [1664] 35x55cm. (14x21½") Color. Very good. [22] £4099 $7800

DU VAL (Small)

CARTE DE LA VIRGINIE [1660 (1682)] 10x13cm. (4x5") From *Le Monde ou la Geographie Universelle.* Color. Good. [29] £155 $295

IMPERII SINARUM NOVA DESCRIPTIO [c. 1685] 12x12cm. (4½x5") (Attributed to Du Val). Tissue on one margin without loss. [10] £32 $60

INDIA INTRA GANGEM [1678] 10x13cm. (4x5") [10] £34 $65

INSULA MADAGASCAR DICTA ST. LAURENS NUNC INSULA DAUPHINE [c. 1670] 10x13cm. (4x5") Color. [15] £29 $55

ISLES D'AMERIQUE DITES CARIBES OU CANNIBALES ET DE BARLOVENTO [1664] 34x26cm. (13x10") Fine. [10] £302 $575

DUCHETTI *Try Lafrere School*

DUDLEY

CARTA PARTICOLARE CHE MOSTRA IL CAPO BUONA SPERANZA CON IL MARE VERSO PONETE E CON L'ISOLE DI TRISTAN D'ACUNHA E DI MARTN. VAZ [1646] 46x76cm. (18½x29½") [11] £600 $1142

CARTA PARTICOLARE DEL MARE DEL SUR CHE COMINCIA CON L'ISOLE DI SALAMONE E FINISCE CON LA COSTA DI LIMA NEL' PERU [1646] 48x75cm. (19x29½") Slight spotting in margin; a small repair with no loss. [11] £550 $1047

CARTA PARTICOLARE DEL' MARE DEL' ZUR CHE COMINCIA CON IL CAPO S. FRANCESCO NEL' PERU E FINISCE CON IL' CAPO S. LAZARO NELLA NUOVA SPAGNIA. ... D'AMERICA CARTA XXVIIII [c. 1646] 48x76cm. (19x29½") With Galapagos. [15] £512 $975

CARTA PARTICOLARE DELL'ISOLE DI ISLANDIA E FRISLANDIA, CON L'ISOLETTE DI FARE [1646 (1661)] 48x76cm. (19x30") Slight doubling of printing near paper join; repair of some worming near fold; o/w excellent. [11] £1400 $2664

CARTA PARTICOLARE DELLA BRASILIA AUSTRALE CHE COMINCIA DEAL' PORO: DEL' SPIRTO SANTO E FINISCE CON IL CAPO BIANCO ... [1661] 48x38cm. (18½x15") Excellent. [22] £447 $850

CARTA PARTICOLARE DELLA COSTA DEL' PERU PARTE AUSTRALE CON PARTE DI CILI ... [1661] 48x36cm. (19x14½") Excellent. [22] £499 $950

CARTA PARTICOLARE DELLA COSTA DI NUOVA ZEMBLA [1646] 48x74cm. (19x28½") With Barents' discoveries. [11] £275 $523

CARTA PRIMA GENERALE D'AMERICA DELL'INDIA OCCIDENTALE E MARE DEL ZUR [1646] 48x70cm. (19x27½") Inset: "America Maiestale". [38] £1682 $3200

CARTA SECONDA GENERALE DEL'AMERICA [1661] 44x37cm. (17½x14½") Excellent. [22] £2365 $4500

EUROPA. CARTA QUINTA. SECOA [1646 (1661)] 44x72cm. (17½x28½") South coast of France. First edition title, "Carta Particulare del Mare Mediterraneo, che comincia con il capo Dragone, in Ispagna, e finisce con il capo Melle nella Rivera di Genova". Good. [11] £550 $1047

ISOLE NEL MARE DI SUR SCOPERTE NEL 1617 ... [1646] 48x74cm. (19x29") With Tuamotus Archipelago. Printer's crease near centerfold; o/w excellent. [11] £450 $856

DUFOUR

AMERIQUE CENTRALE [c. 1840] 25x33cm. (10x12½") Color. [15] £37 $70

CARTE ADMINISTRATIVE PHYSIQUE ET ROUTIERE DE LA FRANCE INDIQUANT LES CANAUX, LES RIVIERES NAVIGABLES, LES ROUTES DE POSTE AVEC LEURS RELAIS ET DISTANCES &A DEDIEE AU ROI [1832] 53x96cm. (21x37½") Paris: Simmoneau. Two maps: Northern and Southern France. Linen-backed folding maps in original chemise and slipcase. Outline color. Slight age-darkening; o/w very good. [19] £171 $325

CARTE D'AFRIQUE [1841] 56x74cm. (21½x29½") Color. [15] £58 $110

DUNN *Try Laurie & Whittle, Sayer*

A GENERAL MAP OF THE WORLD, OR TERRAQUEOUS GLOBE, WITH ALL THE NEW DISCOVERIES AND MARGINAL DELINEATIONS, CONTAINING THE MOST INTERESTING PARTICULARS IN THE SOLAR, STARRY, AND MUNDANE SYSTEM, ... [1787] 105x123cm.

(41x48½") Full original wash color. Remargined top and bottom; some rubbing, repair and loss; very good. [21] £2890 $5500

A GENERAL MAP OF THE WORLD, OR TERRAQUEOUS GLOBE, WITH ALL THE NEW DISCOVERIES AND MARGINAL DELINEATIONS, CONTAINING THE MOST INTERESTING PARTICULARS IN THE SOLAR, STARRY, AND MUNDANE SYSTEM, ... [1794] 104x123cm. (41x48½") London: Laurie & Whittle. Four sheets joined. Color. Some minor repair and reinforcement. [5] £1200 $2284

SCIENTIA TERRARUM ET COELORUM, OR THE HEAVENS AND EARTH ASTRONOMICALLY AND GEOGRAPHICALLY DELINEATED AND DISPLAYED ... [1772] 103x123cm. (40½x48") Four joined sheets. Original outline color. Some small ink spots and smudges. [31] £946 $1800

DURELL

THIS PLAN OF THE HARBOUR, TOWN AND FORTS OF PORTO BELLO TAKEN BY EDWARD VERNON, ESQR. VICE ADMIRAL OF THE BLUE ON 22ND NOVEMBER 1739 (WITH SIX MEN OF WAR ONLY), ... [1740] 42x58cm. (16½x23") Separately published. Good. [10] £197 $375

DUSSIEUX

CARTES POUR SERVIR A L'HISTOIRE DE LA NOUVELLE FRANCE OU DU CANADA JUSQU'EN 1763 [1851] 20x30cm. (7½x11½") [15] £18 $35

DUTTON & CO.

CHART OF BOSTON HARBOR AND MASSACHUSETTS BAY. WITH MAP OF THE ADJACENT COUNTRY [1865] 63x49cm. (25x19") Unbacked folding map between original embossed boards. Pastel wash and outline color. Some fold intersections worn through; map separating from bottom board; bright and clean; Good+. [19] £58 $110

DUVAL

[UNITED STATES; BOUNDARY MAP] [c. 1848] 33x56cm. (13½x22") Side tables. Color. Folded, stained; edges a bit ragged. [7] £131 $250

NO. 1 INDEX TO RECORDED FIELD NOTES INDIANA [1840] 38x28cm. (15x11") Show's Clark's Grant, etc. Fine. [14] £32 $60

DUVOTENAY

ETATS-UNIS ET MEXIQUE [c. 1850] 36x43cm. (14x17") Outline color. [26] £66 $125

MEXIQUE [1846] 30x23cm. (12x9") Independent Texas. Outline color. Fine. [12] £97 $185

EASTMAN

ETHNOLOGICAL MAP OF THE INDIAN TRIBES OF THE UNITED STATES A.D. 1600 [c. 1853] 23x30cm. (9x12") From Schoolcraft's History of the Indian Tribes. Color coded. Small repairs at edge (2 tears into image area). [26] £47 $90

MAP OF THE SOUTHWESTERN PART OF NEW MEXICO COMPILED FROM THE LATEST EXPLORATIONS ... [1853 (1854)] 20x30cm. (7½x11½") From Schoolcraft. [12] £34 $65

EDWARDS

MAP OF THE ISLAND OF TOBAGO FOR THE HISTORY OF THE WEST INDIES BY BRYAN EDWARDS ESQR. [1799] 18x24cm. (7x9½") Folds. [10] £47 $90

MAP OF THE VIRGIN ISLANDS, FOR THE HISTORY OF THE WEST INDIES BY BRYAN EDWARDS ESQR. [1794] 17x23cm. (7x9") [10] £92 $175

EHRMANN

LOUISIANA [1804] 22x17cm. (8½x6½") Color. [15] £66 $125

ELLICOTT

PLAN OF THE CITY OF WASHINGTON, IN THE TERRITORY OF COLUMBIA, CEDED BY THE STATES OF VIRGINIA AND MARYLAND TO THE UNITED STATES OF AMERICA, AND BY THEM ESTABLISHED AS THE SEAT OF THEIR GOVERNMENT AFTER THE YEAR MDCCC [1792] 53x71cm. (20½x27½") Phila: Thackara & Vallance. Wheat & Brun 531. Excellent. [1] £6569 $12,500

ELWE

NOUVELLE CARTE DE LA PETITE TARTARIE OU TAURIE, MONTRANT LES FONTIERES DE L'IMPERATRICE DE RUSSIA [1787] 51x61cm. (20x23½") Color. [15] £92 $175

UNIVERSELE OF WAERELD KAART VOLGENS DE LAATSTE ONTDEKKINGEN VAN CAPT. COOK [c. 1788] 15x20cm. (6x8½") Hemispheres. Color. [15] £105 $200

EMERY

VIEW OF BUCKSPORT, ME. [1859] 41x74cm. (15½x29½") From Ft. Knox. Meisel Bros., lith. Reps 1193. Color. Repaired tear in title margin; fine. [27] £657 $1250

EMORY

MAP OF THE VALLEYS OF THE RIO GRANDE AND RIO GILA [1854] 20x25cm. (8x10") With Lt. Abert; American Ethnological Society. Mint. [12] £92 $175

ENGLISH PILOT *Try Mount & Page, Thornton*

ENOUY, J.

THE UNITED KINGDOM OF GREAT BRITAIN & IRELAND, WITH THE ADJACENT PARTS OF THE CONTINENT, FROM AMSTERDAM, TO PARIS AND BREST ... [1828] 71x61cm. (28x24") Linen-backed folding map in orig slipcase with label. Orig color. Slipcase worn at extremities. VG. [19] £131 $250

ENSIGN

MAP OF MASSACHUSETTS, RHODE ISLAND AND CONNECICUT ... [1844] 64x86cm. (25x33½") Wall map. Color. Darkened; ragged, chipped edges; brittle, with separations along wrinkles; linen tape reinforcement; good. [7] £87 $165

PHELPS AND ENSIGN'S TRAVEL GUIDE AND MAP OF THE UNITED STATES CONTAINING THE ROADS, DISTANCES, STEAM BOAT AND CANAL ROUTES, ETC. [1845] 43x97cm. (17x38") Wall map. Dull colors. Age-toned; surface loss at upper border; good. [7] £223 $425

ENSIGN & THAYER

MAP OF MASSACHUSETTS, RHODE-ISLAND & CONNECTICUT COMPILED FROM THE LATEST AUTHORITIES ... [1848] 66x84cm. (26x33") On cloth and rolled. Color. Excellent. [6] £155 $295

ENTICK

A PLAN OF THE HARBOUR AND TOWN OF LOUISBOURG IN THE ISLAND OF CAPE BRETON DRAWN ON THE SPOT [1758] 18x25cm. (7x9½") Dublin: Exshaw's Magazine. Color. [15] £39 $75

ESQUEMELIN

A MAP OF THE COUNTREY AND CITTY OF PANAMA [1684] 17x28cm. (6½x11") Color. [15] £192 $365

ETABLISSEMENT GEOGRAPHIQUE DE BRUXELLES

NOUVELLE CARTE DE BELGIQUE, A L'ECHELLE DE 1/300000 ... [n.d.] 75x87cm. (29½x34") Linen-backed folding map between original boards with label. Pastel wash and outline color. Slipcase worn but solid, lacks one tab; very good. [19] £63 $120

ETTLING *Try Weekly Dispatch*

MAP OF THE UNITED STATES OF NORTH AMERICA, UPPER & LOWER CANADA, NEW BRUNSWICK, NOVA SCOTIA & BRITISH COLUMBIA, MEXICO, CUBA, JAMAICA, ST. DOMINGO, AND THE BAHAMA ISLANDS [1861] 66x93cm. (26x36½") Indicative toning. Flawless. [12] £150 $285

[same title, date] 69x94cm. (27x36½") London News Supplement. Color. [15] £66 $125

EVERTS & RICHARDS

STATE OF RHODE ISLAND [1895] 99x76cm. (39x29½") Full color. Fold creases; a fold discoloration and short separations mended with no loss. [12] £66 $125

FADEN

A CHART OF THE ETHIOPIC OR SOUTHERN OCEAN, & PART PACIFIC OCEAN ... [1808] 60x90cm. (23½x35") By J. Foss Dessiou. Features 1806 East Indiaman tracks. [15] £139 $265

A CHOROGRAPHICAL MAP OF THE PROVINCE OF NEW-YORK IN NORTH AMERICA, DIVIDED INTO COUNTIES...BY CLAUDE JOSEPH SAUTHIER ESQR...ENGRAVED AND PUBLISHED BY WILLIAM FADEN (SUCCESSOR TO THE LATE THOS JEFFERYS GEOGR. TO THE KING) CHARING-CROSS.JANUARY 1ST. 1[1779] 122x124cm. (48x48½") Dedication to Gen. Wm. Tryon. Lower 4 sheets of the 6 sheet map. Color. [15] £512 $975

A GENERAL CHART OF THE WEST INDIA ISLANDS WITH THE ADJACENT COASTS OF THE SPANISH CONTINENT ... [1796] 53x75cm. (20½x29½") By De La Rochette. Old color. [15] £236 $450

A MAP OF ENGLAND, WALES & SCOTLAND DESCRIBING ALL THE DIRECT AND PRINCIPAL CROSSROADS IN GREAT BRITAIN WITH THE DISTANCES MEASURED BETWEEN MARKET TOWNS AND FROM LONDON; TO ACCOMPANY PATERSON'S BOOK OF THE ROADS [1801] 74x62cm. (29x24½") Linen-backed folding map in leather and linen slipcase with label. Color. Age darkening, occasional foxing. [19] £92 $175

A MAP OF ENGLAND, WALES & SCOTLAND DESCRIBING ALL THE DIRECT AND PRINCIPAL CROSS ROADS IN GREAT BRITAIN...W. FADEN...AUGUST 12TH 1801 [1819] 73x61cm. (28½x24") Linen-backed folding map in original marbled slip case with label. Wash and outline color. Slight age soiling; slipcase worn and torn at top; map clean and sharp. [19] £145 $275

A MAP OF THE INHABITED PART OF CANADA FROM THE FRENCH SURVEYS; WITH THE FRONTIERS OF NEW YORK AND NEW ENGLAND FROM THE LARGE SURVEY BY CLAUDE JOSEPH SAUTHIER. ENGRAVED BY WM. FADEN, ... [1777] 86x58cm. (33½x22½") Outline color. [15] £499 $950

A NEW MAP OF SPAIN AND PORTUGAL, EXHIBITING THE CHAINS OF MOUNTAINS WITH THEIR PASSES THE PRINCIPAL & CROSS ROADS, WITH OTHER DETAILS REQUISITE FOR THE INTELLEGENCE OF MILITARY OPERATIONS COMPILED BY JASPAR NANTIAT [1810] 116x158cm. (45½x62") Four sections, each about 58 x 79 cm. Linen-backed folding map. Outline color. Very good. [19] £263 $500

A NEW POCKET PLAN OF THE CITIES OF LONDON & WESTMINSTER; WITH THE BOROUGH OF SOUTHWARK: COMPREHENDING THE NEW BUILDINGS AND OTHER ALTERATIONS TO THE YEAR 1790 [(1790)] 45x89cm. (17½x35") Linen-backed folding map with original slipcase with label. Color. Slipcase worn. Very good. [19] £276 $525

A TOPOGRAPHICAL MAP OF THE COUNTRY TWENTY MILES ROUND LONDON, PLANNED FROM A SCALE OF TWO MILES TO AN INCH [1818] Diameter: 58 cm. (23") Second edition. Linen-backed folding map in original slipcase with label. Back label: Sold by Wyld (Faden;s successor). Outline color. Slight darkening at folds; slipcase worn at edges; very good. [19] £155 $295

A TOPOGRAPHICAL MAP OF THE NORTHN. PART OF NEW YORK ISLAND, EXHIBITING THE PLAN OF FORT WASHINGTON, NOW FORT KNYPHAUSEN, WITH THE REBEL LINES TO THE SOUTHWARD WHICH WERE FORCED BY THE TROOPS UNDER THE COMMAND OF THE RT. HONBLE. EARL PERCY... [1777] 47x26cm. (18½x10") Orig outline col. Excellent. [21] £788 $1500

CHART OF THE COAST OF HAMPSHIRE FROM PORTSMOUTH TO SOUTHAMPTON WATER WITH PART OF THE ISLE OF WIGHT FROM CULVER CLIFF TO WEST COWES INCLUDING THE ROADS OF SPITHEAD, ST. HELENS, STOKES BAY &C. ... [1799] 64x54cm. (25x21½") Linen-backed folding chart. Very good. [19] £105 $200

CHART OF THE N.W. COAST OF AMERICA AND THE N.E. COAST OF ASIA, EXPLORED IN THE YEARS 1778 AND 1779. PREPARED BY LIEUT. HENY. ROBERTS...LONDON: PUBLISHED BY WM. FADEN... [1794] 40x68cm. (15½x26½") Original color. Repaired marginal tears; minor wear. [31] £447 $850

[same title, date] 41x69cm. (16x27") Color. [15] £202 $385

[same title] [1821] 38x69cm. (15x27") Cook's Third Voyage, from *The General Atlas ... to show the new Limits as Ratified by the Definitive Treaty of Paris*. Original outline color. [6] £368 $700

GREECE, ARCHIPELAGO AND PART OF ANADOLI [1791] 53x76cm. (21x30") By de la Rochette. Color. [35] £131 $250

PLAN OF THE HARBOUR OF CADIZ SURVEYED BY BRIGADIER DON VINCENT TOFINO DE SAN MIGUEL, ... 1789 [1805] 56x87cm. (22x34") Linen-backed folding plan. Very slight offsetting; very good+. [19] £105 $200

POSITION OF THE DETACHMENT UNDER LIEUT. COL. BAUM, AT WALMSCOCK NEAR BENNINGTON SHEWING THE ATTACKS OFTHE ENEMY ON THE 16TH AUGUST 1777 [1780] 28x36cm. (10½x13½") From Burgoyne, *A State of the Expedition from Canada*. Light wash color. Good. [29] £150 $285

SCANDIA OR SCANDINAVIA COMPREHENDING THE KINGDOM OF SWEDEN INCLUDING NORWAY. WITH THE ADDITION OF DENMARK & FINLAND [1821] 72x50cm. (28½x19½") Second edition: By L.S. Delarochette. Linen-backed folding map. Color. VG. [19] £155 $295

THE PROVINCE OF NEW JERSEY, DIVIDED INTO EAST AND WEST ... [1777] 79x56cm. (30½x22½") Based on Ratzer's 1769 survey. Original outline color. Excellent. [2] £3416 $6500

WESTERN HEMISPHERE - EASTERN HEMISPHERE [1775] 36x71cm. (14x28") First edition. Color. [15] £192 $365

FAMILY TIMES

[LONDON] [1846] 86x93cm. (34x36½") Wood engraved circular plan 12 miles around St. Paul's. Linen-backed folding plan edged with ribbon. Age-darkened, especially backing, some soiling, several worn areas. [19] £197 $375

FENNER, SEARS & CO. *Try Hinton*

FIELDING

PART OF NORTH AMERICA, CONTAINING CANADA, THE NORTH PARTS OF NEW ENGLAND AND NEW YORK; WITH NOVA SCOTIA AND NEWFOUNDLAND [1781] 21x28cm. (8x11") Color. Minor repair. [15] £66 $125

FILLOEUL

AMERIQUE SEPTENTRIONALE [1664] 25x41cm. (9½x15½") Color. Backed. [15] £139 $265

FINDLAY

UNITED STATES [c. 1810] 20x24cm. (8x9½") London: T. Kelly. Color. [15] £24 $45

[same title] [1846] 23x25cm. (9x10½") U.S. to 103° W. London: Tegg. Color. [15] £26 $50

FINLEY

CANADA [1831] 20x28cm. (8x11") Color. [6] £39 $75

CONNECTICUT [1831] 22x28cm. (8½x11") Color. [6] £60 $115

DELAWARE [1824] 30x23cm. (11½x9") Color. [15] £66 $125

[same title] [1831] 29x22cm. (11½x8½") [6] £60 $115

GEORGIA [1829] 29x22cm. (11½x8½") Color. Very fine. [13] £118 $225

ILLINOIS [1831] 29x22cm. (11½x8½") Color. [6] £66 $125

INDIANA [1824] 28x22cm. (11x8½") Full color. Fine. [14] £92 $175

[same title] [1829] 29x22cm. (11½x8½") Full color. Fine. [14] £79 $150

[same title] [1831] 28x23cm. (11x9") Color. [6] £66 $125

KENTUCKY [1831] 22x28cm. (9x11") Color. [6] £66 $125

LOUISIANA [1831] 22x28cm. (9x11") Wash color. [6] £60 $115

MAINE [1831] 28x23cm. (11x9") Color. [6] £60 $115

MAP OF MASSACHUSETTS CONNECTICUT & RHODE ISLAND CONSTRUCTED FROM THE LATEST AUTHORITIES [1826] 43x56cm. (17x21½") By. D. Vance. Color. Minor repair. [15] £129 $245

MAP OF THE STATE OF NEW YORK [1824] 43x53cm. (16½x21") Pocket map on bank note paper with calf cover. Color. Age-toned; a little foxing; covers slightly rubbed and dirty; o/w very good, near fine. [7] £286 $545

MASSACHUSETTS [1831] 23x28cm. (9x11") Wash color. [6] £60 $115

MISSOURI [1831] 28x23cm. (11x9") Color. [6] £66 $125

NEW JERSEY [1825] 30x25cm. (11½x9½") 14 counties. Color. Minor repair. [15] £66 $125

[same title] [1831] 28x22cm. (11x9") Color. [6] £60 $115

NORTH AMERICA [1824] 29x22cm. (11½x8½") Full col. A tiny spot; else bright & clean. [12] £71 $135

NORTH CAROLINA [1831] 22x29cm. (8½x11") Color. [6] £60 $115

OHIO [1831] 29x22cm. (11½x9") Color. Rust spot. [6] £66 $125

PENNSYLVANIA [1831] 23x33cm. (9x13") Wash color. Minor offsetting. [6] £60 $115

RHODE ISLAND [1831] 28x22cm. (11x9") Color. Some stains, not within state. [6] £60 $115

SOUTH CAROLINA [1831] 22x29cm. (9x11½") Wash color. [6] £60 $115

VERMONT [1831] 28x22cm. (11x9") Color. [6] £60 $115

[same title] [1833] 27x22cm. (10½x8½") Color. Clean. [9] £84 $160

WESTERN HEMISPHERE [1824] 23x23cm. (9x8½") Color. [15] £34 $65

FINN

BIRD'S EYE VIEW OF BOSTON HARBOR ALONG THE SOUTH SHORE TO PROVINCETOWN [1917] 51x61cm. (20x24") Printed color. Very good. [26] £47 $90

FISHER, H.

STATES OF AMERICA [1823] 18x22cm. (7x8½") Original full color. [17] £74 $140

FLAMM

NEW WARD AND INDEX MAP OF ST. LOUIS, MISSOURI [1899] 66x89cm. (26x35") Balto: with Joyce Surveying Co. & Globe Map and Atlas Co Pocket map in cardboard case. Some col. VG. [3] £79 $150

TOPOGRAPHICAL MAP FOR COMMERCE OF CHATTANOOGA, TENNESSEE [1891] 64x86cm. (25x34") Give-away map for Chattanooga Land, Coal, Iron & Railway Co. Pocket map, folded as issued into small cardboard case. Folds weak. [3] £92 $175

FOPPEN

RHEIN-PANORAMA COLN BIS MAINZ [1900] 187x18cm. (73½x7") Bonn. Unbacked lithographed map between original boards. Blue on white. Boards separated; previous owner's label; good+. [19] £26 $50

FORSTER, G.

KARTE DES NORDENS VON AMERICA, ZUR BEURTHEILUNG DE WAHRSCHEINLICHKEIT EINER NORD-WESTLICHEN DURCHFAHRT ... [1791] 51x66cm. (20½x26") [15] £255 $485

FOSTER GROOM

GROOM'S POCKET MAP OF LONDON [c. 1900] 47x71cm. (18½x28") Linen-backed folding plan. Color. Some wear of paper at folds; covers soiled; o/w good. [19] £53 $100

FRANKLIN

AN OUTLINE TO SHEW THE CONNECTED DISCOVERIES OF CAPTAINS ROSS, PARRY & FRANKLIN IN THE YEARS 1818 ... [1823] 38x46cm. (14½x18") London: Murray. Color. Minor repair. [15] £76 $145

ROUTE OF THE EXPEDITION FROM ISLE A LA CROSSE TO FORT PROVIDENCE IN 1819 AND 1820 [1823] 51x24cm. (20x9½") [15] £32 $60

FREMONT *Try U.S.*

MAP OF OREGON AND UPPER CALIFORNIA FROM THE SURVEYS OF JOHN CHARLES FREMONT AND OTHER AUTHORITIES [1848] 48x43cm. (19½x16½") By C. Preuss. Color. [15] £150 $285

TOPOGRAPHICAL MAP OF THE ROAD FROM MISSOURI TO OREGON SECTION 2 FROM THE JOURNAL OF CAPT. J. C. FREMONT [c. 1847] 38x61cm. (15x24") U.S.T.E. By C. Preuss. [15] £66 $125

FRENCH ADMIRALTY *Try Bellin, Depot de la Marine*

FRIEDERICHS, J.

THE CIRCUITEER. A SERIES OF DISTANCE MAPS FOR ALL THE PRINCIPAL TOWNS IN THE UNITED KINGDOM. INVENTED BY J. FRIEDERICHS TO SERVE AS A GUIDE FOR ASCERTAINING CAB FARES, PORTERAGE, &C.&C. ... NO. 1 LONDON [1851] 49x69cm. (19½x27") Explanation in English, French and German. Linen-backed plan, folding to 11 x 9.5 cm, between original cloth boards with label. 245 red circles. Wear at folds, some small tears; explanatory booklet lacking; good+. [19] £184 $350

FRIES

DIEFERT SITUS ORBIS HYDROGRAPHORUM AB EO QUEM PTOLOMEUS POSIT [1522 (1535)] 29x46cm. (11x18") Banner title: "Tabu Novi Orbis". Shirley 49. Excellent. [37] £1471 $2800

[same title] [1522 (1541)] 29x46cm. (11x18") Extra title: "Tabula Nova Totius Orbis". Shirley 49. [38] £1682 $3200

TABU. NOVA ORBIS [(1522)-1535] 28x46cm. (11x18") After Walseemuller's 1513 World on reduced scale. Shirley 49 Very good. [31] £1471 $2800

TABULA NOVA INDIAE ORIENTALIS & MERIDIONALIS [1522 (1541)] 28x43cm. (11x17") Very fine. [37] £788 $1500

TABULA TERRAE NOVAE [1522 (1541)] 29x38cm. (11x15") After Waldsemuller's 1513 map. (Suarez; note 153) Excellent. [38] £2733 $5200

FULLARTON

BRITISH POSSESSIONS IN THE INDIAN SEAS [c. 1860] 47x31cm. (18½x12") Ceylon, with smaller panels and vignettes. Original wash color. [10] £39 $75

BRITISH POSSESSIONS ON THE NORTH WEST COAST OF SOUTH AMERICA [1860] 47x31cm. (18½x12") Trinidad and British Guyana. Color. [15] £76 $145

INDIAN ARCHIPELAGO ... [1860] 41x51cm. (16x20") (East Indies.) Orig wash color. [10] £26 $50

ISLAND OF JAMAICA [1860] 15x23cm. (5½x9") By Swanston. Color. [15] £18 $35

NEWFOUNDLAND, NEW BRUNSWICK, NOVA SCOTIA, PRINCE EDWARD ISLAND &C. [c. 1858] 41x53cm. (16x20½") By J.H. Johnson. Color. [15] £24 $45

NORTHERN PORTS & HARBOURS IN THE UNITED STATES [1862] 43x29cm. (17x11½") By Bartholomew. Original outline color. [10] £45 $85

PORTS AND HARBOURS ON THE SOUTH EAST COAST OF ENGLAND [c. 1860] 46x30cm. (18x12") 12 plans on one sheet. Tinted. [11] £35 $67

PORTS & HARBOURS ON THE NORTH WEST COAST OF ENGLAND [c. 1860] 48x30cm. (18½x11½") Liverpool, etc. By Bartholomew. Tinted. [11] £35 $67

SOUTH AFRICA FROM OFFICIAL & OTHER AUTHENTIC AUTHORITIES [c. 1860] 42x53cm. (16½x20½") Original wash color. [10] £18 $35

SOUTH AMERICAN STATES. NEW GRANADA & VENEZUELA ... [1859] 41x53cm. (16x21") By Bartholomew. Color. [15] £32 $60

SOUTHERN PORTS & HARBOURS IN THE UNITED STATES [1862] 41x30cm. (16½x11½") By Bartholomew. Original outline color. [10] £45 $85

THE ARCTIC REGIONS, SHOWING THE NORTH-WEST PASSAGE AS DETERMINED BY CAP. R. MC.CLURE AND OTHER ARCTIC VOYAGERS. COMPILED BY J. HUGH JOHNSON F.R.G.S. [1856] 25x25cm. (10x10") Color. [15] £21 $40

FULLER

DAN [1650] 24x31cm. (9½x12") Laor 289. Very good. [17] £145 $275

EPHRIAM VITULA EST EDOCTA AMANS TRITURARE [1650] 28x34cm. (11x13½") Laor 288. Very good. [17] £145 $275

GAD ... [1650] 28x34cm. (11x13") Laor 281. Very good. [17] £131 $250

LIBANUS ET EJUS VICINIA [1650] 28x33cm. (11x13") Very good. [17] £145 $275

MANASSE TRANS-JORDANICAM [1650] 27x32cm. (10½x13") Laor 282. VG [17] £105 $200

SIMEON [1650] 27x33cm. (10½x13") Laor 290. Very good. [17] £105 $200

GALIGNANI

GALIGNANI'S PLAN OF PARIS [1822] 38x49cm. (15x19½") Linen-backed folding plan in slipcase, with two other smaller plans, "Panorama of the Environs of Paris" and "Panorama of the Curiosities of Paris". Original color. Corners worn on slipcase; o/w very good. [19] £236 $450

GALL & INGLIS

MAP OF NORTH AMERICA [1849] 46x64cm. (18x24½") Color. [15] £66 $125

MAP OF THE UNITED STATES [c.1845] 53x43cm. (21x17½") Edinburgh: Lloyd. Col. [15] £45 $85

MAP OF THE WEST INDIES [c. 1840] 46x58cm. (18½x22½") Color. [15] £45 $85

GALLE

AMERICAE RETECTIO [c. 1585] 22x26cm. (8½x10") Adrien Collaert engraving commemorating discovery of America Various figures, a globe showing America, a stretch of Italian coast from Livorno to Savona. Mint. [38] £1471 $2800

GALT & HOY

THE CITY OF NEW YORK [1879] 188x102cm. (74x39½") Birds-eye view. Restored, rebacked with some loss at previous fold junctions. Excellent. [1] £6569 $12500

GARNERAY

NOUVELLE ORLEANS [1845] 41x51cm. (16½x20½") Aquatint view. Mint. [22] £2890 $5500

VUE DE NEW YORK. PRISE DE WEAHAWK - A VIEW OF NEW YORK, TAKEN FROM VEAHAWK [c. 1834] 38x46cm. (14½x17½") Paris: Chez Basset. 1st state. Portrait on verso. Aquatint. Near invisible repaired tear just into surface; mounted on rice paper; o/w fine. [22] £3416 $6500

GARNIER

GRAND PLAN DE PARIS ILLUSTRE [1860] 60x91cm. (23½x36") Unbacked folding map between original illustrated paper covers. Color. Small holes in corners of margins; VG+. [19] £131 $250

GASKELL

FLORIDA [1887] 33x23cm. (13x9") Color. [15] £18 $35

S. CAROLINA [1887] 25x30cm. (10x12") Color. [15] £13 $25

GASTALDI *Try Lafrere School, Ptolemy (1848, Venice)*

CARTA MARINA NOVA TABULA [1548] 14x17cm. (5½x6½") Shirley 88. Excel. [38] £788 $1500

IL DESSEGNO DELLA TERZA PARTE DELL'ASIA ... [1561] 64x74cm. (25x29") Two joined sheets. [5] £5700 $10,847

UNIVERSALE DELLA PARTE DEL MONDO NUOVAMENTE RITROVATA [1556] State I. Diameter: 27 cm. (10½") on 39 cm. sheet. Excellent. [38] £1997 $3800

[same title] [1556 (1565)] State II. Diameter: 27 cm. (10½") on sheet 32 x 37 cm. Exc. [38] £998 $1900

GAULTIER

AMERIQUE SEPTENTRIONALE ET MERIDIONALE, POUR SERVIR AUX LECONS DE GEOGRAPHIE [c. 1810] 43x36cm. (17x13½") Phillips (atlases) 4127. Color. [15] £87 $165

GAVIT & DUTHIE

MAP OF THE FRONTIERS OF THE NORTHERN COLONIES WITH THE BOUNDARY LINE ESTABLISHED BETWEEN THEM AND THE INDIANS AT THE TREATY HELD BY S. WILL JOHNSON AT FT. STANWIX IN NOV'R 1768. ... [c. 1850] 28x43cm. (11x17") Boundary in color. Six inch tear mended; minor loss at neat line. [6] £39 $75

GAZZETTIERE AMERICANO

CARTA RAPPRESENTANTE I CINQUE LAGHI DEL CANADA [1763] 25x18cm. (10x7") [6] £102 $195

CARTA RAPPRESENTANTE IL GOLFO DEL FIUME S. LORENZO [1763] 25x19cm. (10x7½") Color. [15] £50 $95

PIANO DELLA CITTA DI QUEBEC [1763] 25x23cm. (9½x9½") [15] £71 $135

GEBAUERS, J.

AMERICA DAS SUDLICHE [c. 1750] 33x43cm. (12½x16½") Notes in French. Outline & wash color. [36] £105 $200

GELL, W.

ROME & ITS ENVIRONS, FROM A TRIGONOMETRICAL SURVEY [1834] 72x98cm. (28½x38½") London: Saunders & Otley. Linen-backed folding map. Original color. Some section corners detached, but present; tape marks at margin; very good. [19] £105 $200

GEMMA FRISIUS *Try Apianus*

GENERAL MAGAZINE OF ARTS & SCIENCES

A MAP OF THE BRITISH AND FRENCH SETTLEMENTS IN NORTH AMERICA; (PART THE FIRST) CONTAINING CANADA, ... PART OF NEW YORK, WITH THE LAKES, SIX NATIONS, ... [and] (PART THE SECOND) PART OF NEW YORK, ... COURS OF THE RIVERS OHIO MISSISIPI &C. ... [1755] 41x48cm. (15½x19") Jolly GENMAS-68. Two maps, joined and mounted on linen. Narrow right & lower margin; else excellent. [12] £289 $550

GENTLEMAN'S & LONDON MAGAZINE

A MAP OF THAT PART OF PENSYLVANIA NOW THE PRINCIPLE SEAT OF WAR IN AMERICA WHEREIN MAY BE SEEN THE SITUATION OF PHILADELPHIA, RED BANK, MUD ISLAND, & GERMANTOWN... [1778] 38x29cm. (15x11½") Jolly GAL-116. Repaired folds; some marginal soiling; o/w good. [30] £342 $650

GENTLEMAN'S MAGAZINE

A CHART OF DELAWARE BAY AND RIVER, FROM THE ORIGINAL BY MR. FISHER OF PHILADELPHIA, 1776. [1779] 18x23cm. (7x9") Jolly GENT-268. [12] £53 $100

A GENERAL MAP OF THE DISCOVERIES OF ADMIRAL DE FONTE & OTHERS, BY M. DE L'ISLE. [1754] 20x26cm. (7½x10") Jolly GENT-88. Narrow right margin; else excellent. [12] £97 $185

A MAP OF 100 MILES ROUND BOSTON. [1775] 23x25cm. (9x9½") Jolly GENT-234. Light offsetting; o/w excellent. [12] £92 $175

[same title, date, dimensions] Later pale wash col. Lower left 7 cm of margin replaced. [18] £105 $200

[same title, date, dimensions] Very good. [31] £118 $225

A MAP OF CONNECTICUT AND RHODE ISLAND, WITH LONG ISLAND SOUND, &C. [1776] 17x23cm. (7x9") Jolly GENT-249. Fold lines. [6] £97 $185

A MAP OF PART OF WEST FLORIDA, FROM PENSACOLA TO THE MOUTH OF THE IBERVILLE RIVER, WITH A VIEW TO SHEW THE PROPER SPOT FOR A SETTLEMENT ON THE MISSISSIPI. [1772] 19x34cm. (7½x13½") Jolly GENT-217. Later wash color. Very good. [18] £131 $250

[same title, date, dimensions] Very good. [31] £92 $175

A MAP OF PHILADELPHIA AND PARTS ADJACENT, BY N. SCULL AND G. HEAP. [1777] 34x29cm. (13½x11½") Jolly GENT-256. Fine. [30] £255 $485

A MAP OF THE BRITISH AND FRENCH SETTLEMENTS IN NORTH AMERICA. [1755] 28x39cm. (11x15") Jolly GENT-91. Partly remargined; rice paper backing; o/w fine. [29] £250 $475

A MAP OF THE COUNTRY BETWEEN CROWN POINT AND FORT EDWARD. [1759] 19x12cm. (7½x4½") Jolly GENT-129. Color. [15] £34 $65

A MAP OF THE COUNTRY ROUND PHILADELPHIA INCLUDING PART OF NEW JERSEY NEW YORK STATEN ISLAND & LONG ISLAND. [1776] 18x22cm. (7x8½") Jolly GENT-247. Fine. [12] £105 $200

A MAP OF THE ICY SEA IN WHICH THE SEVERAL COMMUNICATIONS WITH THE LAND WATERS AND OTHER NEW DISCOVERIES ARE EXHIBITED. [1760] 20x20cm. (8x8") Jolly GENT-141. Gibson, sc. Color. [15] £50 $95

[same title, date, dimensions] Polar projection. Jolly GENT-141. Excellent. [12] £71 $135

A MAP OF THE ISLAND OF ORLEANS WITH THE ENVIRONS OF QUEBEC [1759] 11x19cm. (4½x7½") Jolly GENT-136. Slight offsetting. [10] £16 $30

A MAP OF THE ISLAND OF TOBAGO, DRAWN FROM AN ACTUAL SURVEY, BY THOS. BOWEN, 1779. [1778] 19x24cm. (7½x9½") Jolly GENT-262. [10] £102 $195

A NEW PROJECTION OF THE EASTERN HEMISPHERE OF THE EARTH ON A PLANE (SHEWING THE PROPORTIONS OF ITS SEVERAL PARTS NEARLY AS ON A GLOBE) BY J. HARDY, (W.M. & TEACHER OF MATHEMATICS) AT EATON COLLEGE. [1776] 23x21cm. (9x8½") Jolly GENT-242. Short tear neatly repaired. [10] £21 $40

A PLAN OF THE CITY & HARBOUR OF LOUISBURG; SHEWING THAT PART OF GABARUS BAY IN WHICH THE ENGLISH LANDED, ALSO THEIR ENCAMPMENT DURING THE SIEGE IN 1745. [1758] 19x26cm. (7½x10") Jolly GENT-114. [10] £26 $50

AN ACCURATE MAP OF THE BRITISH EMPIRE IN NTH. AMERICA AS SETTLED BY THE PRELIMINARIES IN 1762. [1762] 21x25cm. (8½x9½") Jolly GENT-165. Color. [10] £63 $120

[same title, date, dimensions] Partly remargined on right; good. [29] £139 $265

[same title, date, dimensions] Later outline color. Narrow margins extended. [35] £92 $175

AN ACCURATE MAP OF THE WEST INDIES. EXHIBITING NOT ONLY ALL THE ISLANDS POSSESS'D BY THE ENGLISH, FRENCH, SPANIARDS & DUTCH, BUT ALSO ALL THE TOWNS AND SETTLEMENTS ON THE CONTINENT OF AMERICA ADJACENT THERETO. [1740] 30x39cm. (12x15½") Jolly GENT-6. By Emanuel Bowen. Color. [15] £229 $435

AN EXACT DRAUGHT OF THE CASTLE OF SAN LORENZO YE VILLAGE & RIVER OF CHAGRE WITH THE SITUATION OF ADML VERNON'S SHIPS IN YE ATTACK OF THE FORT MARCH 24. 1740. BY R.T. & SENT OVER IN THE DIAMOND MAN OF WAR... [1740] 14x17cm. (5½x6½") Jolly GENT-11. Color. [15] £29 $55

CHART OF THE TRACK OF THE DOLPHIN, TAMAR, SWALLOW & ENDEAVOR, THROUGH THE SOUTH SEAS; & THE TRACK OF M. BOUGAINVILLE, ROUND THE WORLD. [1773] 26x64cm. (10x25") By T. Bowen. Jolly GENT-227. Color. [15] £145 $275

MAP OF HUDSON'S RIVER, WITH THE ADJACENT COUNTRY. [1778] 29x21cm. (11½x8½") Jolly GENT-257. Pale wash color. [18] £142 $270

PLAN OF ST PETERSBURG; WITH IT'S FORTIFICATIONS, BUILT BY PETER THE GREAT IN 1703. [1749] 19x24cm. (7½x9½") Jolly GENT-65. [15] £45 $85

PLAN OF THE CITY AND HARBOUR OF HAVANNA. [1762] 11x19cm. (4½x7½") Jolly GENT-162. Very good. [18] £66 $125

PLAN OF THE CITY OF HAVANAH. [1740] 10x10cm. (4x4") Jolly GENT-8. Color. [15] £34 $65

PLAN OF THE FORTS ONTARIO AND OSWEGO, WITH PART OF THE RIVER ONONDAGO AND LAKE ONTARIO. [1757] 20x10cm. (7½x4") Jolly GENT-103. [15] £32 $60

SKETCH OF THE COUNTRY ILLUSTRATING THE LATE ENGAGEMENT IN LONG ISLAND. [1776] 20x31cm. (8x12½") Jolly GENT-248. Color. [15] £87 $165

THE SIEGE OF RHODE ISLAND, TAKEN FROM MR. BRINDLEY'S HOUSE, ON THE 25TH AUGUST, 1778. [1779] 13x23cm. (5x8½") [12] £53 $100

GIBSON *Try Gentleman's Magazine*

A PLAIN CHART OF THE CASPIAN SEA [1753] 36x56cm. (14x21½") By Thomas Woodroofe. Split in fold; tear to image; light offsetting. [31] £236 $450

AN AUTHENTIC PLAN OF THE RIVER ST. LAURENCE, FROM SILLERY TO THE FALLS OF MONTMORENCY [1759] 18x18cm. (6½x7½") Color. [15] £32 $60

INDIA ON BOTH SIDES OF THE GANGES [1758] 6x9cm. (2½x3½") [10] £37 $70

NEW YORK AND PENSILVANIA [1758] 8x10cm. (2½x4") London: Newbery. Color. [15] £50 $95

GOLD *Try Naval Chronicle*

GOLDTHWAIT

RAILROAD MAP OF NEW ENGLAND & EASTERN NEW YORK COMPILED FROM THE MOST AUTHENTIC SOURCES. [1849] 64x48cm. (25x19") Some color. Old folds; used; single tear repaired; good. [3] £105 $200

[same title, date] (no dims.) Pocket map. Outline color. Occasional spots; cover rubbed, slight tear at spine ends; very good. [7] £223 $425

GOOS

HET CANAAL TUSSCHEN ENGELAND EN VRANCRIICK ... [1666] 43x55cm. (17x21½") Bright early color. Good. [11] £450 $856

PAS-CAART VAN GUINEA EN DE CUSTEN DAER AER GELEGEN VAN CABO VERDE TOT CABO DE BONA ESPERANCA [1666] 44x54cm. (17½x21½") Margins reduced; lower margin very narrow; lower fold split repaired; o/w good. [11] £340 $647

PAS-CAART VANT CANAAL VERTOONENDE IN 'T GHEHEEL ENGELANDT, SCHOTLANDT, YRLANDT, EN EEN GEDEELTE VAN VRANCRYCK [1669] 45x55cm. (17½x21½") Bright early outline color. Good. [11] £490 $932

PAS CAERTE VAN NIEU NEDERLANDT EN DE ENGELSCHE VIRGINIES VAN CABO COD TOT CABO CANRICK [1666] 44x54cm. (17x21") Framed. Original color, some gold highlight. Some light foxing; else excellent. [21] £2627 $5000

[same title, date, dimensions] Color. Mint. [37] £2365 $4500

PASCAARTE VAN ENGELANT VAN T' VOORLANDT TOT AEN BLAKENEY WAER IN TE SIEN IS DE MONT VANDE TEEMSE [1666] 43x54cm. (17x21½") Early outline col. Good. [11] £375 $714

PASCAERT VANDE CARIBES EYLANDEN [1666] 44x54cm. (17½x21½") Color. Some very light staining; o/w very good. [2] £788 $1500

PASCAERTE VANDE VLAEMSCHE, SOUTE, EN CARIBESCHE EYLANDEN, ALS MEDE TERRA NOVA, EN DE CUSTEN VAN NOVA FRANCIA, NOVA ANGLIA, NIEU NEDERLANDT, VENEZUELA, NUEVA ANDALUSIA, GUIANA, EN EEN GEDEELTE VAN BRAZIL [1666] 45x54cm. (17½x21½") Newfoundland to South America. Old color, time toned. [15] £518 $985

PASCAERTE VANDE ZUYD-ZEE TUSSCHE CALIFORNIA, EN ILHAS DE LADRONES ... [1666] 45x55cm. (17½x21½") Color. Very fine. [37] £1156 $2200

PASKAARTE OM ACHTER YRLANDT OM TE ZEYLEN VAN HITLANT TOT AEN HEYSSAT ... [1669] 44x55cm. (17½x21½") Early color. Fine. [11] £425 $809

PASKAERTE VAN DE ZUYDT EN NOORDT REVIER IN NIEU NEDERLANT STRECKENDE VAN CABO HINLOOPEN TOT RECHKEWACH [1666] 51x60cm. (20x23½") Col. Exc. [37] £4467 $8500

PASKAERTE VAN NOVA GRANADA, EN T'EYLANDT CALIFORNIA [1666] 45x55cm. (17½x21½") Full color. Faint offsetting; o/w very good. [22] £2890 $5500

PASKAERTE VAN'T IN COMEN VAN'T CANAAL ... [1666] 44x53cm. (17½x21") Bright early color. Fine. [11] £325 $618

PASKAERTE ZYNDE T'OOSTERDEEL VAN OOST INDIEN MET ALLES DE EYLANDEN DEER ONTRENDT GELEGEN VAN C. COMORIN TOT AEN JAPAN... [1666] 46x55cm. (18x21½") Orig color; gold highlights. Restoration & verso reinforcement to centerfold & margins. [5] £1670 $3178

GRAND MAGAZINE OF MAGAZINES

A PLAN OF THE SEAT OF WAR AT AND NEAR QUEBEC, WITH THE LINE OF BATTLE. [1759] 11x19cm. (4½x7½") Jolly GMOM-33. Color. [15] £34 $65

MAP OF THE COUNTRY BETWEEN WILLS CREEK AND FORT DU QUESNE. [1758] 19x12cm. (7½x4½") Jolly GMOM-15. Color. [15] £97 $185

PLAN OF FORT DU QUESNE BEFORE IT WAS DESTROY'D, 1758. [1759] 19x11cm. (7½x4") Jolly GMOM-17. [15] £97 $185

THE COUNTRY BETWEEN CROWN POINT AND ALBANY BEING THE GREAT PASS FROM THE ENGLISH TO THE FRENCH SETTLEMENTS IN NORTH AMERICA. [1758] 19x11cm. (7½x4½") Jolly GMOM-7. [15] £45 $85

GRANT, A.

RAILROAD AND COUNTY MAP OF GEORGIA [1885] 58x41cm. (22½x16") Color. [15] £39 $75

RAILROAD AND COUNTY MAP OF LOUISIANA [1885] 58x41cm. (22½x16½") Color. [15] £32 $60

RAILROAD AND COUNTY MAP OF MANITOBA [1885] 41x53cm. (16x21") Color. [15] £26 $50

RAILROAD AND COUNTY MAP OF MISSISSIPPI [1885] 58x41cm. (22½x16") Color. [15] £39 $75

GRAVIUS

KAART VAN DE GEHEELE WERELD NA DE ALDERLACTSTE ONDEKKINGEN VERBETERD [c. 1780] 18x30cm. (7x11½") Color. [15] £123 $235

GRAY

ARKANSAS [1876] 42x62cm. (16½x24½") Color. [15] £34 $65

CALIFORNIA & NEVADA [1876] 66x40cm. (26x15½") Color. [15] £45 $85

CHICAGO [1873] 41x33cm. (15½x12½") First edition, with 7 page directory. Color. [12] £58 $110

CITY OF CINCINNATI [1872] 41x64cm. (16x24½") With 4 page Business Directory. Full color. Scattered light foxing. [12] £79 $150

COLORADO [1877] 33x41cm. (13x16") Full color. Very good. [3] £47 $90

[same title] [1876-77] 31x38cm. (12x15") Color. Fine. [12] £47 $90

DAKOTA [1874] 38x33cm. (15x12½") Original wash color. Fine. [29] £97 $185

FLORIDA [c. 1873] 43x66cm. (16½x26") Color. [15] £42 $80

GRAY'S ATLAS CLIMATOLOGICAL MAP OF THE UNITED STATES SHOWING AVERAGE TEMPERATURE AMOUNT OF RAINFALL &C. [1873] 41x66cm. (16x26½") Color. [15] £32 $60

GRAY'S ATLAS MAP OF INDIANA [1875] 38x30cm. (15x12") Full color. Margins chipped; o/w very good. [14] £24 $45

GRAY'S GEOLOGICAL MAP OF THE UNITED STATES, BY PROFESSOR CHARLES H. HITCHCOCK, PH.D. [1874] 43x69cm. (17x27") Color coded geology. [3] £47 $90

[same title] [1882] 41x64cm. (16x25") Full color as key. Very good. [26] £47 $90

GRAY'S MAP OF THE CITY OF PROVIDENCE [1875] 38x33cm. (15x12½") Col. Excel. [35] £26 $50

GRAY'S NEW MAP OF DAKOTA WITH PART OF MANITOBA, ETC. [1886] 66x43cm. (26x17") Full color. Very good. [3] £47 $90

GRAY'S NEW MAP OF GEORGIA [1881] 64x41cm. (25x15½") Full color. Fine. [13] £29 $55

GRAY'S NEW MAP OF INDIANA [1882] 64x41cm. (24½x16") Full color. Fine. [14] £29 $55

GRAY'S NEW MAP OF KANSAS [1881] 43x69cm. (17x27") Full color. [3] £42 $80

GRAY'S NEW MAP OF NORTH CAROLINA AND SOUTH CAROLINA [1881] 41x69cm. (16½x27½") Color. [15] £24 $45

GRAY'S NEW MAP OF TEXAS AND THE INDIAN TERRITORY [1877] 43x66cm. (17x26") Color. [35] £74 $140

INDIANA [1876] 64x39cm. (25x15½") Full col. Two corners slightly worm eaten; o/w fine. [14] £29 $55

INDIANAPOLIS [and] LOUISVILLE [1878] 38x30cm. (15x12") Two maps one one sheet. Full color. Margins rough; good. [14] £24 $45

MAP OF DAKOTA AND NEBRASKA [c. 1876] 38x30cm. (14½x12") Full color. Very light, scattered foxing; o/w fine. [12] £66 $125

MAP OF INDIAN TERRITORY [1874] 30x38cm. (12x15") G.W. & C.B. Colton, 1872. Wash color. Fine. [29] £87 $165

MAP OF THE CITY OF SACRAMENTO THE CAPITAL OF CALIFORNIA [1873] 30x38cm. (11½x14½") Color. [12] £53 $100

MAP OF THE TERRITORY OF ALASKA (RUSSIAN AMERICA) CEDED BY RUSSIA TO THE UNITED STATES [1884] 30x43cm. (12x16½") Color. [12] £32 $60

NEW RAIL ROAD MAP OF THE STATE OF OHIO [1878] 43x61cm. (16½x24½") Col. [15] £45 $85

NEW RAILROAD AND COUNTY MAP OF THE STATES OF OREGON, CALIFORNIA AND NEVADA [1873] 66x38cm. (25½x14½") First edition. Color. [12] £66 $125

GREENLEAF

ARKANSAS [1842] 30x33cm. (11½x12½") Color. [12] £71 $135

[same title, date] 28x33cm. (11x12½") State in 5 "Districts". Color. [15] £87 $165

INDIANA [1842] 32x27cm. (12½x10½") Full color. Excellent. [14] £66 $125

MISSISSIPPI [1842] 33x28cm. (13x11") Color. [15] £66 $125

MISSOURI [1842] 28x33cm. (11x12½") Color. Fine. [12] £97 $185

NEW YORK [1842] 28x33cm. (10½x12½") Color. [15] £58 $110

UNITED STATES [1842] 29x33cm. (11x13") Color. [15] £50 $95

VERMONT AND NEW HAMPSHIRE [1842] 32x26cm. (12½x10½") Color. Age-toned; clean. [9] £92 $175

GREGORY

CHART OF SOME ISLANDS BETWEEN BORNEO AND BANCA ... [1780] 59x36cm. (23x14½") By J. Powell. Show track of the Osterly in 1758-9. Water stains upper left corner. [10] £79 $150

GRIERSON

A GENERALL CHART FOR THE WEST INDIES [c. 1749] 45x57cm. (17½x22") Similar to Moll; probably in Dublin pirate edition. Barlow, Color. Old folds evident. [33] £350 $666

GROSS, R.

KARTE VON DEUTSCHLAND, HOLLAND, BELGIEN, DER SCHWEIZ, NORD-ITALIEN NEBST THEILEN VON FRANKREICH, UNGARN, POLEN, SLAVONIEN & KROATIEN [1869] 67x87cm. (26½x34") Stuttgart: Nitzschke. Linen-backed folding map between original board with gilt title. Color. Top board separated, but present; very good+. [19] £42 $80

GUICCIARDINI

HOLLANDIAE CATTORUM REGIONIS TYPUS [1590] 24x32cm. (9½x12½") Age toning at margin edges; some show-through; dark bold impression. [18] £131 $250

ZELANDIAE TYPUS [1590] 24x31cm. (9½x12") Deep impression. [18] £131 $250

GUSSEFELD *Try Homann*

GUSSFIELD

[TERRESTRIAL GLOBE] [c. 1830] With J.C. Mather. Shows Cook's voyages. Diameter: 10 cm. (3¾") Wooden box encasement, 5½" wide, 4¾" high. [2] £946 $1800

HAASIS & LUBRECHT

THE EMPIRE CITY. MAP OF NEW YORK CITY AND DIRECTORY [1873] 69x91cm. (27x36") Original color. Slight wear at folds; mounted on rice paper; o/w excellent. [21] £631 $1200

HAFFNER, J.C.

VUE DU ALGERS, EN BARBARIE, SUR LA MER MEDITERRANEE [c. 1720] 32x41cm. (12½x16") Probably a proof version of the plate; with a blank shield, guide lines, and a reversed title. Excellent. [38] £131 $250

HAINES, W.

TRIGONOMETRICAL SURVEY OF THE FALLS OF NIAGARA [c. 1848] 23x41cm. (9x16") Color. [15] £45 $85

HALL

CANADA, NEW BRUNSWICK AND NOVA SCOTIA [c. 1836] 43x51cm. (16½x20½") Color. [15] £34 $65

LEIGH'S NEW ROAD MAP OF ENGLAND, WALES AND SCOTLAND, DRAWN ... BY SIDNEY HALL [19th c.] 100x75cm. (39x29½") Linen-backed folding map in original textured slipcase. Full original color. Slight age soiling at folds; margin damp stain; good+. [19] £87 $165

MEXICO [c. 1840] 26x36cm. (10x14") Independent Texas into Colorado. Outline col. [6] £102 $195

ST. PETERSBURG [1828] 28x38cm. (11x14½") Some wash color. [36] £34 $65

UNITED STATES [1828] 43x53cm. (16½x21") London: Longman, Rees. Color. [15] £74 $140

HALLEY

A CHART OF THE COASTS OF CHINA FROM CAMBODIA TO NAMQUAM WITH PART OF JAPAN [1728] 50x60cm. (19½x23½") Similar to Mount & Page. Color. [5] £375 $714

HAMILTON, ADAMS & CO.

MEXICO [1827] 25x28cm. (9½x11½") North to Santa Fe. Color. [15] £66 $125

HAMMOND

FINAL PLANS OF THE PANAMA CANAL [1907] 25x48cm. (10x19") Color. [15] £18 $35

HANDTKE

VEREINIGTE STAATEN VON NORDAMERIKA [1850] 53x71cm. (21½x27½") Color. Minor repair. [15] £66 $125

HAPPEL

GENERAL-CARTE VON CANADA [1709] 10x15cm. (3½x5½") [12] £84 $160

HARDESTY

MAP OF GEORGIA [1884] 51x36cm. (19½x13½") Rand, McNally. Printed color. VG. [13] £24 $45

MAP OF INDIAN TERRITORY [1882] 33x51cm. (13x20") Printed green outline. [36] £53 $100

MIDDLE BASS ISLAND [Ohio] [1874] 33x43cm. (13x16½") Names land owners. Color. [15] £45 $85

NORTH BASS ISLAND [Ohio] [1874] 41x33cm. (15½x13") Names land owners. Color. [15] £45 $85

OAK HARBOR [Ohio] [1874] 41x33cm. (15½x13") Color. [15] £45 $85

HARPER BROS.

BIRD'S EYE VIEW OF PHILADELPHIA [1872] 53x76cm. (21x30") By T.R. Davis. Exc. [15] £92 $175

HARPER'S WEEKLY

GENERAL VIEW OF THE CITY OF NASHVILLE, TENN. [1862] 23x36cm. (9x14") Color. Fine. [30] £45 $85

MAP OF ALABAMA [1866] 28x23cm. (11x9") Engraved scene above. [6] £24 $45

MAP OF GEORGIA [1866] 28x23cm. (11x9") With vignettes. Very good. [13] £26 $50

MAP OF MISSISSIPPI [1866] 28x23cm. (11x9") Engraved scene above. [6] £24 $45

MOBILE - THE GULF CITY [1884] 23x33cm. (9x13½") View by Davidson. Col. Fine. [30] £45 $85

NEW ORLEANS - THE CRESCENT CITY - LAKE PONTCHARTRAIN IN THE DISTANCE [1884] 51x76cm. (19½x30") Bird's eye view by Graham. Blank verso. Perfect. [12] £236 $450

SALT LAKE CITY [1886] 23x36cm. (9x13½") View after Monsen & Co. photo. Col. Fine. [30] £45 $85

ST. LOUIS, MISSOURI [1876] 23x33cm. (9x13½") View drawn by Schell & Hogan after Vanderhoof. Color. Fine. [30] £45 $85

THE CENTENNIAL NAVAL PARADE IN THE UPPER BAY -- THE U.S.S. 'DESPATCH' AND HER CONVOY PASSING GOVERNOR'S ISLAND, AS SEEN FROM THE WASHINGTON BUILDING [1889] 36x112cm. (13½x43½") Virtually perfect. [12] £158 $300

THE CITY AND HARBOR OF SAVANNAH, GA. [1883] 23x36cm. (9x13½") View by J. O. Davidson. Color. Fine. [30] £45 $85

THE CITY OF CHARLESTON, S.C. [1861] 25x36cm. (9½x14") View. Color. Fine [30] £45 $85

HARRIS *Try Bowen*

A PLAN OF THE CITY OF CANTON ON THE RIVER TA HO [1740] 28x20cm. (11x8") Bird's-eye view. [10] £39 $75

ANTIENT MEXICO [1744] 21x33cm. (8½x13") View. [15] £50 $95

[same title] [1764] 20x33cm. (8x13") View. [10] £45 $85

INDIA, AS DESCRIBED BY ALL AUTHORS BEFORE THE FIFTH CENTURY [1740] 22x31cm. (8½x12") [10] £16 $30

THE GALLAPAGOS ISLANDS DISCOVERED AND DESCRIBED BY CAPT. COWLEY IN 1684 [1744] 32x20cm. (12½x8") Color. [15] £71 $135

VIEW OF THE TOWN AND CASTLE OF MACAO [1740] 20x31cm. (8x12") View. [10] £79 $150

HARRISON & WARNER

RAILROAD & SECTIONAL MAP OF WISCONSIN [1873] 66x64cm. (26½x25") Wall map. Color. Minor repair. [15] £92 $175

HAYDEN, F.

[COLORADO: SOUTHERN] [1882] 28x41cm. (11x16") Topographical map; Trinidad to Conejos. Folds as issued. [26] £21 $40

DIE AMERIKANISCHE STAATS-DOMANE (NATIONAL PARK) IM QUELLGEBIETE DES YELLOWSTONE FLUSSEN ... [1872] 25x43cm. (10x17") Published at Gotha. Color. [15] £50 $95

GEOLOGICAL MAP OF COLORADO [1877] 76x94cm. (30x37") Color coding. [26] £74 $140

MAP OF THE COUNTRY BETWEEN THE YAMPA & WHITE RIVERS [1876] 41x97cm. (16x38") Folds as issued. Very good. [26] £32 $60

HEATHER

... CHART OF THE ENGLISH CHANNEL ... [1801] 81x193cm. (31½x75½") Three sheets joined. Repairs to fold and margin splits without loss; right margin extended where close. [11] £500 $952

TO THE OFFICERS IN THE HONOURABLE EAST INDIA COMPANY'S SERVICE MOST RESPECTFULLY DEDICATED ... [WORLD: Route to the East] [1796] 66x119cm. (25½x47") Two sheets joined; third available after. Light traces of cleaned marks; some weak paper reinforced. [11] £450 $856

HELLER, C.

KARTE VON YUCATAN NACH DER HANDSCHRIFTLICHEN KARTE VON JUAN JOSE DE LEON ... [1847] 48x34cm. (19x13½") Leipzig: Wilhelmi. Old folds; tear lower right margin without image loss; dusty. [16] £83 $158

HENNEPIN

CARTE D'UN TRES GRAND PAIS NOUVELLEMENT DECOUVERT DANS L'AMERIQUE SEPTENTRIONALE ENTRE LE NOUVEAU MEXIQUE ET LA MER GLACIALE AVEC LE COURS DU GRAND FLEUVE MESCHASIPI ... [1704] 38x44cm. (15x17½") Leiden: Vander Aa. Color. Minor repair. [15] £723 $1375

HERBERT

[BAY OF BENGAL] [1780] 60x64cm. (23½x25") Chart: India to northern Sumatra. Centerfold split repaired. [10] £42 $80

[BURMA COAST] [1780] 43x58cm. (17x23") Chart. [10] £79 $150

[GULF OF ADEN] [1779] 42x59cm. (16½x23½") [10] £63 $120

[INDIAN OCEAN] [1779] 59x89cm. (23x35") Chart: Horn of Africa to Indian peninsula. [10] £47 $90

[SRI LANKA AND EXTREME SOUTHERN INDIA] [1779] 58x87cm. (22½x34") Chart, with insets. A little soiled; lower centerfold split. [10] £131 $250

[SUMATRA, WEST COAST] [1780] 44x43cm. (17x17") Chart. Short tear repaired; some browning. [10] £53 $100

A CHART OF THE ISLAND OF BOURBON IN THE INDIAN OCEAN [1779] 55x70cm. (21½x27½") (Reunion Island) [10] £79 $150

A CHART OF THE ISLANDS IN THE MIDDLE PART OF THE INDIAN OCEAN [1780] 50x74cm. (19½x29") [10] £92 $175

A CHART OF THE STREIGHTS OF DRNON, CONTAINING THOSE LANDS ONLY, THAT WERE SEEN ON BOARD THE SHIP BUTE ... 1765 [c. 1768] 45x108cm. (17½x42½") Near Singapore. Two sheets joined. [10] £168 $320

A CORRECT CHART OF THE CHINA SEAS CONTAINING THE COASTS OF TSIOMPA, COCHIN, CHINA, THE GULF OF TONQUIN, PART OF THE COAST OF CHINA AND THE PHILIPPINE ISLANDS [1777] 60x77cm. (23½x30½") Col. Short lower centerfold split reinforced. [5] £250 $476

A PARTICULAR PLAN OF ACHEEN ROAD WITH THE ISLANDS ADJACENT [1780] 50x40cm. (19½x15½") Brown stains in margin. [10] £53 $100

A PLAN OF THE PRINCIPAL HARBOUR AND TOWN OF THE ISL. S. MARIES, ... MADAGASCAR [and] THE BAY OF ANTON GALL ON THE NE PART OF THE ISLAND OF MADAGASCAR. [1779] 44x59cm. (17½x23") (Two charts on one plate.) [10] £63 $120

HERISSON

CARTE DE L'EMPIRE DE TURQUIE EN EUROPE ET EN ASIE [1854] 52x77cm. (20½x30½") Paris: A. Logerot. Linen-backed folding map with original boards with cloth spine. Pastel outline col. Some age-darkening at folds, small ink smudge; extremity of cover backstrips torn; good+. [19] £102 $195

CARTE DE L'OCEANIE COMPRENANT L'AUSTRALIE, LA POLYNESIE ET DU GRAND ARCHIPEL D'ASIE [1836] 53x76cm. (21½x30") Color. [15] £171 $325

HESSE, J.

SACRAMENTO IN CALIFORNIEN [c. 1855] 23x36cm. (9½x14½") After the Endicott lithograph view. Color. Marginal repairs; o/w good. [29] £447 $850

HEYLIN

[TITLE PAGE] COSMOGRAPHIE IN FOURE BOOKES ... [1652] 19x30cm. (7½x12") London: Seile. Color with gold highlights. [5] £100 $190

HILL, A.J.

SECTIONAL MAP OF THE SURVEYED PORTION OF MINNESOTA AND THE NORTH WESTERN PART OF WISCONSIN [1860] 84x64cm. (33x25") St. Paul: Sewell & Iddings. Wear & small holes at folds; backed; o/w good. [31] £250 $475

HILL, N.

A NEW TERRESTRIAL GLOBE ... [1754] Diameter: 6 cm. (2½") In original fish skin case with celestial map lining. [2] £3547 $6750

HINTON

MAP OF MAINE, NEW HAMPSHIRE AND VERMONT [1832] 36x25cm. (14½x10") Modern color. Excellent. [12] £66 $125

MAP OF THE STATES OF INDIANA AND OHIO, WITH PART OF MICHIGAN TERRITORY [1831] 25x40cm. (10x15½") London: Fenner, Sears & Co. Color. Very good. [14] £58 $110

[same title] [1832] 24x40cm. (9½x15½") Modern color. Immaculate. [12] £79 $150

MAP OF THE STATES OF NORTH & SOUTH CAROLINA [1832] 25x41cm. (10x15½") Full modern color. Excellent. [12] £79 $150

HODGES & SMITH

A GENERAL MAP OF IRELAND TO ACCOMPANY THE REPORT OF THE RAILWAY COMMISSIONERS SHEWING THE PRINCIPAL PHYSICAL FEATURES AND GEOLOGICAL STRUCTURE OF THE COUNTRY [c. 1838] 195x162cm. (77x64") Dublin. Linen-backed folding map; six sections, each about 65 x 81 cm. Outline color. Very good. [19] £210 $400

HOGG *Try Cook*

A CHART OF CAPTN. CARTERET'S DISCOVERY AT NEW BRITAIN, WITH PART OF CAPTN. COOK'S PASSAGE THROUGH ENDEAVOR STREIGHTS & CAPTN. DAMPIER'S ... DISCOVERIES IN 1699 [1784] 15x36cm. (6x14") Color. [15] £42 $80

A DRAUGHT OF BONTHAIN BAY ... [1795] 20x33cm. (8x13") After Hawkesworth. [11] £25 $48

A NEW AND CORRECT MAP OF THE PROVINCE OF CONNAUGHT [c. 1784] 29x21cm. (11½x8½") Color. Very good. [24] £60 $114

A NEW AND CORRECT MAP OF THE PROVINCE OF LEINSTER [c. 1784] 30x20cm. (12x8") Color. Very good. [24] £60 $114

A NEW AND CORRECT MAP OF THE PROVINCE OF MUNSTER [c. 1784] 22x32cm. (8½x12½") Color. Very good. [24] £75 $143

A NEW AND CORRECT MAP OF THE PROVINCE OF ULSTER [c. 1784] 20x32cm. (8x12½") Color. Very good. [24] £90 $171

CHART OF NORTON SOUND AND OF BHERINGS STRAIT MADE BY THE EAST CAPE OF ASIA AND THE WEST POINT OF AMERICA. LONDON PUBLISHED BY ALEXR. HOGG... [c. 1784] 20x33cm. (8x13") Conder, sc. Mended tear to right neat line. [6] £79 $150

HOLE *Try Camdem*

HIBERNIAE [c. 1610-37] 26x33cm. (10x13") After Saxton. Color. Very good. [24] £225 $428

HOLLAR

A NEW AND EXACT MAP OF AFRICA AND THE ILANDS ... [1666] 37x48cm. (14½x18½") Separate publication with only centerfold crease. Color. Fine. [32] £1400 $2664

HOMANN *Try Doppelmayr*

[TITLE PAGE] ATLAS NOVUS ... [1737] 48x28cm. (19x11") Orig color. Fine. [30] £255 $485

... CONSISTORII WITTEBERGENSIS [1749] 49x56cm. (19½x22") After Vierenklee. Old color. [39] £97 $184

ABBILDUNG DER KEYSRL. FREYEN- REICHS- WAHL UND-HANDELSTATT FRANCKFURT AM MAYNE MIT IHREM GEBIET UND GRANTZEN [1720] 50x58cm. (19½x23") With views. Old color. [39] £466 $887

ACCURATE VORSTELLUNG DER BERUHMTEN MEER-ENGE ZWISCHEN DER NORD UND OST SEE DER SUND GENANNT, MIT DER HERUMLIGENDEN GEGEND VON SEELAND UND SCHONEN, NEBST DER ... STADT COPENHAGEN [c. 1720] 50x60cm. (19½x23½") With general view and insets. Old color. [39] £483 $919

ACCURATER GRUNDRIS UND PROSPECT DES HOCH-FURSTL. BRANDENB. BAYREUTHISCH. RESIDENZ-SCHLOSS UND LUSTGARTEN IN CHRISTIAN-ERLANG [c. 1720] 50x59cm. (19½x23") Four views. Old color. Short wrinkles, short restored tear at bottom; no centerfold. [39] £1242 $2364

AFRICA SECUNDUM LEGITIMAS PROJECTIONIS STEREOGRAPHICAE REGULAS [c. 1740] 49x58cm. (19½x23") By Haas. Old color. [39] £200 $381

AGRI PARISIENSIS TABULA PARTICULARIS, QUA MAXIMA PARS INSULAE FRANCIAE [c. 1720] 59x49cm. (23x19½") Old color. [39] £76 $144

AMERICA SEPTENTRIONALIS A DOMINO D'ANVILLE IN GALLIIS EDITA NUNC IN ANGLIA COLONIIS IN INTERIOREM VIRGINIAM DEDUCTIS NEC NON FLUVII OHIO CURSU... [1756] 46x51cm. (18x20") Old outline color. [16] £476 $906

AMERICAE MAPPA GENERALIS [1746] 48x55cm. (19x21½") Old col. Some staining. [39] £242 $460

AMERICAE MAPPA GENERALIS SECUNDUM LEGITIMAS PROJECTIONIS STEREOGRAPHICAE... [1746] 46x53cm. (18x21") Color. [15] £394 $750

AMPLISSIMAE REGIONIS MISSISSIPPI SEU PROVINCIAE LUDOVICIANAE A R.P. LUDOVICO HENNEPIN FRANCISC MISS IN AMERICA SEPTENTRIONALI ANNO 1687. DETECTAE, NUNC GALLORUM COLONIIS ET ACTIONUM NEGOTIIS TOTO ORBE CELEBERRIMAE ... [1720] 48x58cm. (19x23") Color, primarily early. Excellent. [22] £631 $1200

[same title] [c. 1735] 49x58cm. (19x23") Original wash and outline color [10] £447 $850

ARCHIDUCATUS AUSTRIAE INFERIORIS [c. 1720] 49x59cm. (19½x23") Color. [39] £76 $144

ARCHIDUCATUS AUSTRIAE SUPERIORIS [c. 1720] 49x59cm. (19½x23") After G.M.Vischer. Color. [39] £190 $361

ARCHIEPISCOPATUS ET ELECTORATUS COLONIENSIS UT ET DUCATUUM JULIACENSIS ET MONTENSIS NEC NON COMITATUS MEURSIAE [c, 1720] 49x58cm. (19½x23") Old color. [39] £380 $722

ASIA SECUNDUM LEGITIMAS PROJECTIONIS STEREOGRAPHICAE [1744] 41x58cm. (16x23") By Haas. Old color. [39] £166 $315

ASIAE MINORIS VETERIS ET NOVAE, ITEMQUE PONTI EUXINI ET PALUDIS MAEOTIDIS [1743] 51x59cm. (20x23") By Haas. 580 [39] £200 $381

AUSFUHRLICHE GEOGRAPHISCHE VORSTELLUNG DER GEGEND UM LONDON ... [1741] 48x57cm. (19x22½") View below. Color. Very good. [23] £650 $1237

[same title, date, dimensions] After T. Bowles. With panoramic view. Old color. [39] £414 $788

BAVARIAE CIRCULUS ET ELECTORAT [1728] 58x49cm. (23x19½") Old color. [39] £166 $315

BAVARIAE PARS INFERIOR [c. 1720] 49x59cm. (19½x23") Old color. [39] £179 $342

BAVARIAE PARS SUPERIOR [c. 1720] 59x50cm. (23x19½") Old color. [39] £200 $381

BELGII PARS SEPTENTRIONALIS VULGO HOLLANDIA [c. 1720] 48x56cm. (19x22") Insets of "New Netherlands" (New York) and East Indies. Original color. Excellent. [21] £499 $950

BESONDERE LAND KARTE DES HERZOGTH. OD CHURKREISES SACHSEN ... [1752] 70x96cm. (27½x38") Four sheets assembled. Old color. Small hole in old fold. [39] £110 $210

BORUSSIAE OCCIDENTALIS TABULA [1775] 58x45cm. (23x17½") By Gussefeld. Old color. [39] £248 $473

CANTON FREIBURG SIVE PAGUS HELVETIA FRIBURGENSIS [1767] 49x58cm. (19½x23") Old color. Narrow margins. [39] £207 $394

CARTE D'ARTOIS ET DES ENVIRONS [c. 1730] 48x56cm. (19x22") After De L'Isle. Old color. [39] £62 $118

CARTE DE L'ISLE DE LA MARTINIQUE DRESSEE PAR MR. BELLIN ... [1762] 48x56cm. (19x22") Old color. [39] £131 $250

CARTE DU GRAND DUCHE DE LITUANIAE ... [1812] 48x53cm. (19x21½") By Jean Nieprecki. Primarily original color. Excellent. [22] £210 $400

CARTE HYDROGRAPHIQUE & CHOROGRAPHIQUE DES ISLES PHILIPPINES [1760] 97x55cm. (38x21½") By Lowitz. Old color. [39] £269 $512

CHARTE VOM HERZOGTHUM CLEVE WORAUF ZUGLEICH DAS FURSTENTHUM MEURS NEBST DEN KONIGL. PREUSSIE. ... [1777] 45x56cm. (17½x22") Old color. Small tear repaired; lined at upper left. [39] £380 $722

CHARTE VON RUSSISCH LITAUEN, WELCHE DIE VON POLEN AN RUSSLAND ABGETRETENE WOIEWODSCHAFTEN, LIEFLAND, WITEPSK, MSCISLAW, UND EINEM THEIL DER WOIEWODSCHAFTEN POLOCK UND MINSK ENTHALT [1775] 56x46cm. (22x18") Old col. [39] £100 $190

CHOROGRAPHIA TERRITORII NAUMBURGOCITIENSIS [1732] 49x58cm. (19½x23") By Schreiber. Old color. Small tear repaired. [39] £69 $131

CIRCULI FRANCONIAE PARS ORIENTALIS ET POTIOR ... [c. 1720] 59x50cm. (23x19½") Pale old color. [39] £166 $315

CIRCULI SUEVIAE [1743] 52x58cm. (20½x23") By Haas. Old col. Narrow top margin. [39] £259 $493

CIRCULI WESTPHALIAE [c. 1720] 59x49cm. (23x19½") Old color. [39] £476 $906

CIRCULUS SAXONIAE INFERIORIS [c. 1720] 49x58cm. (19x22½") Old color. [39] £190 $361

CIRCULUS SAXONIAE SUPERIORIS IN QUO DUCATUS & ELECTORATUS SAXONIAE MARCHIONATUS MISNIAE ET LANGRAVIATUS THURINGIAE [1720] 49x58cm. (19½x22½") Old color. Some place names underlined. [39] £117 $223

COMITATUS FLANDRIAE [c. 1720] 49x59cm. (19½x23") Old color. [39] £207 $394

COMITATUS LIMPURGENSIS [1749] 46x54cm. (18x21½") Old color. [39] £235 $447

COMITATUS MANSFELD [1751] 49x56cm. (19½x22") By Mayer. Old color. [39] £66 $125

COMITATUS NAMUR [1746] 51x58cm. (20x23") Old color. [39] £69 $131

COMITATUS PRINCIPALIS TIROLIS IN QUO EPISC. TRIDENTIN ET BRIXENSIS, COMITATUS BRIGANTINUS, FELDKIRCHIAE SONNEBERGAE ET PLUDENTII [c. 1720] 49x59cm. (19½x23") Old color. [39] £338 $644

COMITATUS SCHOENBURGENSIS [1760] 47x46cm. (18½x18") By Trenckmann. Old col. [39] £173 $328

COMITATUUM OLDENBURG ET DELMENHORST [1761] 50x51cm. (19½x20") By Hunrichs. Old color. Narrow top margin. [39] £449 $854

DANUBII FLUMINIS ... PARS INFIMA IN QUA TRANSYLVANIA, WALACHIA, MOLDAVIA, BULGARIA, SERVIA, ROMANIA ET BESSARABIA [c. 1730] 48x58cm. (18½x22½") Full color. [35] £66 $125

DELINEATIO GEOGRAPHICA GENERALIS, COMPREHENDENS VI. FOLIIS SINGULOS PRINCIPATUS, COMITATUS, DITIONES, DYNASTIAS OMNES, QUOTQUOT IMPERIO SERENISSIMI PRINCIPIS LANDGRAFII HASSO-DARMSTADIENSIS [1754] 45x54cm. (17½x21½") Dimensions for each sheet in a complete set of six. Old color. [39] £621 $1182

DELINEATIO GEOGRAPHICA ... VOGTLANDIAE [c. 1740] 51x58cm. (20x23") Old color. Two worm holes lower margin; small rust spot in cartouche. [39] £155 $296

DER RHEIN DIE MAASS UND MOSEL MIT DEN ANLIEGENDEN LANDERN DES OBER-CHUR-UND NEIDER-RHEINL. WIE AUCH DES BURGUNDISCHEN KREISES INGL. ELSASS UND LOTHRINGEN &. [1783] 62x50cm. (24½x19½") By Gussefeld. Old color. [39] £204 $387

DIE ENGLISCHE COLONIE-LAENDER AUF DEN INSULN VON AMERICA [c. 1740] 50x59cm. (19½x23") 5 maps: Antigua; Bermuda; Barbados; Jamaica; St. Kitts. Outline color. [39] £293 $558

DIE GEGEND UM PRAG ODER DER ALTE PRAGER KREYS, ... [1742] 53x61cm. (21x24") Old color. [39] £110 $210

DIE GRAFSCHAFT PYRMONT MIT DEN UMLIEGENDEN HANOVERISCHEN, BRAUNSCHWEIG, UND LIPPISCHEN AUCH PADERBORNISCHEN GRAENZLAENDERN [1752] 47x57cm. (18½x22½") By Overheide. Old color. [39] £449 $854

DIE GROS-BRITANNISCHE COLONIE-LAENDER, IN NORD-AMERICA [c. 1740] 51x56cm. (20x22") Four maps on one sheet. Old color. [39] £328 $624

DIE STADT U. VESTUNG LUXEMBURG [c. 1735] 52x60cm. (20½x23½") Old color. Small margin tears repaired. [39] £932 $1773

DUCATUS IULIACI & BERGENSIS TABULA GEOGRAPHICA, SIMUL DUCATUM CLIVIAE & MEURSIAE PRINCIPATUM ... DUCAT. LIMBURGENSIS [c. 1750] 57x49cm. (22½x19½") Old color. [39] £345 $657

DUCATUS LUNEBURGICI ET COMITATUS DANNEBERGENSIS [c. 1720] 50x59cm. (19½x23") Strong old color. [39] £290 $552

DUCATUS LUXEMBURGI [c. 1720] 49x59cm. (19x23") Old color. Small rust hole in cartouche. [39] £242 $460

DUCATUS MEKLENBURGICI TABULA GENERALIS CONTINENS DUC. VANDALIAE ET MEKLENBURG COMITATUM ET EPISCOPATUM SWERINENSEM ROSTOCHIENSE ET STARGARDIENSE DOMINIUM [c. 1720] 50x58cm. (19½x23") Old color. [39] £190 $361

DUCATUS SABAUDIAE PRINCIPATUS PEDEMONTIUM ET DUCATUS MONTISFERRATI [c. 1720] 50x58cm. (19½x22½") Old color. [39] £121 $230

DUCATUS SILESIAE TABULA GEOGRAPHICA GENERALIS [(1749)] 48x55cm. (18½x21½") By Mayer. Old color. Restored tears in fold and margins; wrinkles smoothed. [39] £328 $624

DUCATUS STIRIAE [c. 1720] 50x59cm. (19½x23") By G.M. Vischer. Color. [39] £173 $328

DUCATUS WESTPHALIAE [1757] 48x57cm. (19x22") Old color. [39] £283 $539

DUCATUS WURTEMBERGICI CUM ... CIRCULI SUEVICI ... MARCHIONATU BADNSI ET SYLVA VULGO NIGRA [1710] 59x49cm. (23x19½") Dimensions for each of two joinable sheets. By Mayer. Old color. [39] £966 $1839

EPISCOPATUS PADERBORN NEC NON ABBATIAE CORVEI ... COMITATIBUS LIPPE, RAVENSBERG, PYRMONT, RIETBERG [1757] 46x48cm. (18x19") Old color. [39] £414 $788

EUROPA, SECUNDUM LEGITIMAS PROJECTIONIS ... [1743] 49x57cm. (19½x22½") By Johann Matthais Haas. Old color. Small tears repaired. [39] £155 $296

[same title] [1744] 48x53cm. (18½x21") Full color. Bright, clean. [36] £145 $275

EXACTISSIMA PALATINUS AD RHENUM TABULA, IN QUA EPISCOPATUS WORMACIENSIS ET SPIRENSIS DUCATUS BIPONTINUS [c. 1720] 49x58cm. (19½x23") Old color. Four wormholes in margin. [39] £328 $624

GENERAL CHARTE VOM KONIGREICH DAENEMARK NEBST DEM HERZOGTHUM HOLSTEIN [1789] 50x58cm. (19½x23") By Gussefeld. Old color. [39] £169 $322

GEOGRAPHICA DESCRIPTIO MONTANI CUIUSDAM DISTRICTUS IN FRANCONIA IN QUO ILLUSTRISSIMORUM S R I COMITUM A GIECH PARTICULARE TERRITORUM [c. 1720] 50x57cm. (19½x22½") Old full color. [39] £414 $788

GEOGRAPHISCHE LAGE DER SUDLICHEN BRAUNSCHWEIGISCHEN REICHSGEBIETE DARINNEN: ... [1762] 52x57cm. (20½x22½") Old color. [39] £276 $525

HASSIAE SUPERIORIS ET WETTERAU [1746] 48x57cm. (19x22½") Old color. [39] £318 $604

HAUPT UND RESIDENZ STADT LONDON [c. 1720] 48x58cm. (19x23") Col. VG. [23] £450 $856

HELVETIA TREDECIM STATIBUS LIBERIS QUOS CANTONES VOCANT COMPOSITA [1751] 45x57cm. (17½x22") By Mayer. Old color. [39] £228 $433

HIBERNIA REGNUM [c. 1720] 57x48cm. (22½x19") Color. Very good. [24] £180 $343

HUNGARIAE [1744] 51x62cm. (20x24") By Haas. Old color. [39] £93 $177

IMP. CAES. CAROLO VI. ... PROVINCIA BRISGOIA [1718] 59x50cm. (23x19½") Old color. [39] £345 $657

IMPERII RUSSICI ET TATARIAE UNIVERSAE TAM MAJORIS ET ASIATICAE [1730] 47x55cm. (18½x21½") Color. Crease & centerfold discoloration; else very good. [34] £79 $150

IMPERIUM TURCICUM IN EUROPA, ASIA ET AFRICA [c. 1720] 50x58cm. (19½x22½") Old color. Small margin and fold tears repaired; remargined top & left with neat line restoration. [39] £121 $230

INSULA ET PRINCIPATUS RUGIAE [1720] 49x58cm. (19½x23") Old color. [39] £269 $512

INSULAE DANICAE ... ZEELANDIA, FIONIA, LANGELANDIA, LALANDIA FALSTRIA, FEMBRIA MONA [c. 1720] 50x59cm. (20x23") By Hubner. Old color. [39] £169 $322

IUDAEA SEU PALAESTINA ... HODIE DICTA TERRA SANCTA PROUT OLIM IN DUODECIM TRIBUS DIVISA SEPARATIS ... [c. 1707] 51x58cm. (19½x22½") Laor 340. Color. [15] £276 $525

[same title] [1707] 48x56cm. (19x22") Orig wash col. Light waterstain outer margin; fine. [30] £355 $675

[same title] [1720] 50x58cm. (19½x23") Old color. [39] £224 $427

KARTE VON DER GEGEND UM MUNCHEN [1743] 50x59cm. (19½x23") Old color. [39] £318 $604

LANDGRAVIAT THURINGIAE TABULA GENERALIS [1738] 49x57cm. (19½x22½") After Lesser. Old color. [39] £166 $315

LATIUM CUM OMNIBUS SUIS CELEBRIORIBUS UIIS QUOAD ANTIQUUM & NOVUUM STATUM [1745] 51x59cm. (20x23") Old color. Lower left trimmed to neat line. [39] £110 $210

LE COURS DU DANUBE DES SA SOURCE JUSQU'A SES EMBOUCHURES EN 3. FEUILLES [c.1720] 49x56cm. (19½x22") Three sheets. Approx. dimensions for each. Old col. [39] £304 $578

LUSATIAE SUPERIORIS TABULA [1732] 46x57cm. (18x22½") By Schreiber Old color. A few worm holes at sides. [39] £76 $144

MAGN. DUCATUS LITUANIAE [1749] 50x58cm. (19½x23") By Mayer. Old color. [39] £155 $296

MAGNA BRITANNIA COMPLECTENS ANGLIAE, SCOTIAE ET HIBERNIAE REGNA [c. 1740] 48x56cm. (19x22") Also titled, "A General Map of Great Britain and Ireland with Part of Holland, Flanders, France ..." Color. Very good. [23] £225 $428

MAPPA GEOGRAPHICA, COMPLECTENS I. INDIAE OCCIDENTALIS PARTEM MEDIAM CIRCUM ISTHMUM PANAMENSEM II. IPSUMQ. ISTHMUM. III. ICHNOGRAPHIAM PRAECIPUORUM LOCORUM & PORTUUM AD HAS TERRAS PERTINENTIUM [c. 1740] 59x50cm. (23x19½") Outline color. [39] £449 $854

MAPPA GEOGRAPHICA, COMPLECTENS INDIAE OCCIDENTALIS PARTEM MEDIAM CIRCUM ISTHMUM PANAMENSEN [1731] 58x48cm. (23x19") 5 insets. Original outline color; full color view & cartouche. Centerfold reinforcement; else very good. [21] £236 $450

[same title] [1740 (1747)] 61x48cm. (24x19½") 6 insets. Outline color on main map. [35] £210 $400

MAPPA GEOGRAPHICA REGNI POLONIAE [1757] 50x59cm. (19½x23") Old col. [39] £155 $296

MARCHIONATUS MORAVIAE CIRCULI ZNOYMENSIS ET INGLAVIENSIS [c. 1720] 49x59cm. (19½x23") By Muller. Old color. [39] £104 $197

MARCHIONATUS MORAVIAE CIRCULUS BRUNNENSIS... [c. 1720] 51x61cm. (20x24") Dimensions for each of two sheets. Old color. Side margins trimmed to neat line. [39] £110 $210

MARCHIONATUS MORAVIAE CIRCULUS OLOMUCENSIS [c. 1720] 50x58cm. (19½x23") Dimensions for each of a pair of sheets. Old col. Each sheet with two small worm holes [39] £110 $210

MOSELLAE FLUMINIS TABULA SPECIALIS IN QUA ARCHIEPISCOPATUS ET ELECTORATUS TREVIRENSIS ... [c. 1720] 49x58cm. (19½x22½") Published before imperial privilege of 1729. Old color. [39] £338 $644

NEU UND VERBESSERTER PLAN DER ST. U. HAFENS HAVANA AUF DER INS. CUBA MIT DEN WASSER TIEFEN, SANDBAENCKEN UND KLIPPEN ... [AND] NEU UND VERBESSERTER PLAN DES HAFENS VON CARTHAGENA [1740] 49x30cm. (19½x12") Two plans. Old color. [39] £173 $328

NORMANNIA GALLIAE CELEBRIS PROVINCIA [c. 1740] 49x58cm. (19½x23") After De L'Isle. Old color. Three small worm holes in side margins. [39] £131 $250

NOVA ANGLIA SEPTENTRIONALI AMERICAE IMPLANTATA ANGLORUMQUE COLONIIS FLORIENTISSIMA GEOGRAPHICE EXHIBITA... [c. 1714] 49x58cm. (19x23") Original wash color. Excellent. [38] £631 $1200

[same title] [c. 1720] 49x58cm. (19x22½") Old color. [39] £414 $788

NOVA COMITATUS PAPPENHEIMENSIS [c. 1740] 50x59cm. (19½x23") Old color. [39] £414 $788

NOVA ET ACCURATA CARINTHIAE DUCATUS [c. 1720] 50x59cm. (19½x23") Old color. [39] £242 $460

NOVA MARIS CASPII ET REGIONIS USBECK [1735] 50x60cm. (19½x23½") By Maas. Old color. [39] £121 $230

NOVA TABULA SCANIAE, QUAE EST GOTHIA AUSTRALIS PROVINCIAS SCANIAM, HALLANDIAM, ET BLEKINGIAM [c. 1720] 50x59cm. (19½x23") Old color. [39] £318 $604

NOVA TERRITORII ERFORDIEN [1717] 49x59cm. (19½x23") With view. Old color. [39] £148 $282

PALAESTINA IN XII TRIBUS DIVISA, CUM TERRIS ADIACENTIBUS DENUO REVISA & COPIOSIR REDDITA [1750] 48x53cm. (19x21") By J. Harenberg. Laor 325. Color. [15] £236 $450

PARS VEDEROVIAE PLURIMAS DITIONES PRINC. ET COM. NASSOVICOR. IMPRIMIS VERO REGIONEM SCHWALBACENSEM [c. 1720] 49x58cm. (19½x23") Old color. [39] £297 $565

PARTIE OCCIDENTALE DE LA NOUVELLE FRANCE OU DU CANADA ... PAR LES HERITIERS DE HOMANN ... [1755] 44x54cm. (17x21") Modern color. [12] £578 $1100

[same title, date] 48x61cm. (19x24") After Bellin. Color. [15] £486 $925

PARTIE ORIENTALE DE LA NOUVELLE FRANCE OU DU CANADA. PAR MR. BELLIN ... [1755] 43x53cm. (17x21½") Color. Fine. [34] £263 $500

[same title, date] 45x55cm. (17½x21½") Old color. [39] £321 $611

PARTIE ORIENTALE DU GOLFE DE FINNLAND [1751] 50x44cm. (19½x17½") Outline color. Spot in image. [39] £166 $315

PENINSULA INDIAE CITRA GANGEM, HOC EST, ORAE CELEBERRIMAE MALABAR & COROMANDEL CUM ADJACENTE INSULA NON MINUS CELEBRATISSIMA CEYLON [1733] 57x50cm. (22x19½") Old color. Short centerfold tear repaired. [39] £69 $131

PLANIGLOBII TERRESTRIS CUM UTROQ HEMISPHAERIO CAELESTI GENERALIS EXHIBITIO ... [c. 1724] 48x56cm. (19x21½") Old body color; vignettes in pastel. Repaired 1/4" tear at lower border; surface dirt right center; Good+. [34] £946 $1800

[same title] [c. 1744] 48x53cm. (19x21") Hemispheres in original color. Fine. [27] £1498 $2850

PLANIGLOBII TERRESTRIS MAPPA UNIVERSALIS ... [1746] 48x56cm. (18½x22") Double hemisphere with small hemispheres. By Lowitz after Ha Color. [39] £621 $1182

PRINCIPATUS BRANDENBURGICO-CULMBACENSIS VEL BARUTHINUS TABULA GEOGRAPHICA [c. 1740] 50x57cm. (19½x22½") Old color. [39] £276 $525

PRINCIPATUS ISENACENSIS [c. 1720] 50x57cm. (19½x22") Old color. [39] £76 $144

PRINCIPATUS TRANSILVANIAE [c. 1720] 50x59cm. (19½x23") Old color. [39] £173 $328

PROSPECT UND GRUNRIS DER KEISERL. FREYEN REICHS UND ANSEE STADT BREMEN SAMT IHRER GEGEND [c. 1720] 49x58cm. (19½x23") With general view Old color. A few small ink spots. Framed. [39] £897 $1708

PROTOPARCHIAE MINDELHEMENSIS NOVA TABULA GEOGRAPHICA [c. 1720] 49x59cm. (19½x23") Old color. [39] £248 $473

REGNI BOHEMIAE CIRCULUS PILSNENSIS [1769] 49x55cm. (19½x21½") Old col. [39] £104 $197

REGNI GALLIAE SEU FRANCIAE ET NAVARRAE TABULA GEOGRAPHICA [1741] 52x58cm. (20½x23") After De L'Isle. Old color. Centerfold repair. [39] £110 $210

REGNI MEXICANI SEU NOVAE HISPANIAE LUDOVICIANAE, N. ANGLIAE, CAROLINAE, VIRGINIAE, ET PENSYLVANIAE NEC NON INSULARUM ARCHIPELAGI MEXICANI IN AMERICA SEPTENTRIONALI ACCURATA TABULA ... [1714-25] 48x57cm. (19x22½") Original color. Very minor color offsetting; o/w very good+. [20] £525 $1000

[same title] [1720] 48x57cm. (19x22½") Color, primarily early. Excellent. [22] £631 $1200

[same title] [c. 1730] 48x57cm. (19x22½") Original wash color. Excellent. [37] £578 $1100

REGNI NORVEGIAE ACCURATA TABULA IN QUA PRAEFECTURAE QUINQUE GENERALES AGGERHUSIENSIS, BERGENSIS NIDROSIENSIS, WARDHUSIENSIS ET BAHUSIENSIS [c. 1720] 59x50cm. (23x19½") Old color. Two small rust stains; remargined at left. [39] £283 $539

REGNORUM MAGNAE BRITANNIAE ET HIBERNIAE ... [1749] 52x56cm. (20½x22") By Tobias Mayer. Old color. [39] £169 $322

REGNUM ANGLIAE [c. 1715] 56x47cm. (22x18½") Color. Very good. [23] £225 $428

REGNUM BORUSSIAE [c. 1740] 50x59cm. (19½x23") Old color. [39] £442 $841

S.R.I. CIRCULAS RHENANUS INFERIOR SIVE ELECTORATUM RHENI COMPLECTENS TRES ARCHIEPISCOPATUS, MOGUNTINUM COLONIENSEM ET TREVIRENSEM, PALATINATUM RHENI, COMIT. BEILSTEIN NEWENAER, INF. ISENBERG ET REIFERSCHEIT [c. 1720] 60x50cm. (23½x19½") Old color. [39] £169 $322

S.R.I. CIRCULUS RHENANUS SUPERIOR IN QUO SUNT LANDGRAVIATUS HASSO-CASSELENSIS DARMSTADIENSIS ET RHENOFELDENSIS ABBATIA FULDENSIS ... URBES IMPERIALES: FRANCKFURT, FRIDBERG, WETZLAR ET GELENHAUSEN [c. 1720] 50x59cm. (19½x23") Old color. [39] £162 $309

S.R.I. PRINCIPATUS & EPISCOPATUS EISTETTENSIS [1745] 50x59cm. (19½x23") Old color. [39] £338 $644

S. R. I. PRINCIPATUS ET ARCHIEPISCOPATUS SALISBURGENSIS [c. 1720] 49x59cm. (19½x23") Old color. [39] £380 $722

S. R. I. PRINCIPATUS FULDENSIS IN BUCHONIA [c. 1720] 49x58cm. (19½x23") Old color. [39] £304 $578

S.R.IMP. COMITATUS HANAU ... ET COMITATUS SOLMS BUDINGEN ET NIDDA CUMRELIQUA WETTERAVIA [1728] 50x58cm. (19½x23") By Zollmann. With view. Old color. [39] £259 $493

SAC. RO. IMPERII PRINCIPATUS & EPISCOPATUS BAMBERGENSIS NOVA TABULA GEOGRAPHICA [c. 1720] 50x58cm. (19½x23") Old color. [39] £328 $624

SAXONIAE TRACTUS DUCATUM MAGDEBURGENSEM CUM SUO CIRCULO SALICO. PRINC. ANHALTINUM HALBERSTADIENSEM ... BRANDENBERG, SAXONIAE DUCATUS BRUNSUICENSIS ETC. PARTES OSTENDENS [c. 1730] 49x54cm. (19½x21½") With view. Old color. [39] £224 $427

SCENOGRAPHIA PORTUS PULCHRI EX PROTOTYPO LONDINENSI VECUSA [1743] 23x28cm. (9½x11") Bird's eye of assault on Porto Bello Color. [15] £97 $185

SECTIO INFERIOR, DUCATUM VINARIENSEM [c. 1750] 37x48cm. (14½x19") Old color. Wrinkle at centerfold. [39] £221 $420

SEPTEM PROVINCIAE SEU BELGIUM FOEDERATUM QUOD GENERALITER HOLLANDIA AUDIT ... [1748] 47x52cm. (18½x20½") Full color. [36] £118 $225

[same title, date] 48x52cm. (19x20½") By Mayer. Old color. [39] £190 $361

STATUS ECCLESIASTICI NEC NON MAGNI DUCATUS TOSCANAE NOVA TABULA GEOGRAPHICA [1748] 49x57cm. (19½x22½") By Mayer. Old color. [39] £207 $394

TABULA AQUITANIA COMPLECTENS GUBERNATIONEM GUINNAE ET VASCONIAE [c. 1730] 48x58cm. (19x22½") Full color. [35] £97 $185

TABULA FRISIAE ORIENTALIS [1730] 50x59cm. (19½x23") After Coldewey. Old col. [39] £621 $1182

TABULA GENERALIS MARCHIONATUS MORAVIAE [c. 1720] 49x59cm. (19½x23") Color. Remargined at left. [39] £131 $250

TABULA GEOGRAPHICA EXHIBENS REGNUM SCLAVONIAE CUM SYRMII DUCATU [1745] 50x58cm. (19½x23") Old color. [39] £86 $164

TABULA GEOGRAPHICA IN QUA ... PRINCIPATUS GOTHA, COBURG ET ALTERBURG [c. 1720] 49x56cm. (19½x22") Old color. Short wrinkle at left. [39] £152 $289

TABULA MARCHIONATUS BRANDENBURGICI ET DUCATUS POMERANIAE [c. 1720] 49x56cm. (19½x22") Old color. A few ink spots. [39] £269 $512

TERRA SANCTA [c. 1730] 48x56cm. (19x22½") Full color. [35] £223 $425

THEATRUM BELLI INTER IMPERAT. CAROL VI. ET SULT. ACHMET IV. IN PARTIBUS REGNORUM SERVIAE ET BOSNIAE [c. 1740] 54x114cm. (21½x45") Two sheets by Ottinger. Old color. [39] £242 $460

TOTIUS AMERICAE SEPTENTRIONALIS ET MERIDIONALIS NOVISSIMA REPRAESENTATIO ... [1720] 48x57cm. (19x22½") Orig color, but possibly later to cartouche. Excellent. [22] £499 $950

[same title] [c. 1732] 48x57cm. (19x22½") Color. Some surface dirt; else very good. [34] £499 $950

[same title] [c. 1750] 48x57cm. (18½x22½") Full color. Somewhat weak impression; lacking lower left corner without image loss. [16] £407 $775

TOTIUS DANUBII CUM ADJACENTIBUS REGNIS NEC NON TOTIUS GRAECIAE ET ARCHIPELAGI NOVISSIMA TABULA [1766] 47x56cm. (18½x22") Old color. [39] £224 $427

TRACTUS EICHSFELDIAE ... NEC NON TERRITORII MVHLHVSANI CHOROGRAPHIA [1759] 42x52cm. (16½x20½") Old color. [39] £380 $722

TRACTUS NORVEGIAE SUECICUS PRAEFECTURAM BAHUSIAE FINITIMAEQUE DALIAE PROVINCIAE PARTEM [1729] 48x55cm. (19x21½") Old color. Trimmed to neat line; lined. [39] £207 $394

TYPUS GEOGRAPHICUS CHILI PARAGUAY FRETI MAGELLANICI [1733] 49x57cm. (19x22½") Old color. [39] £173 $328

TYPUS GEOGRAPHICUS DUCAT. LAUENBURGICI [1729] 56x48cm. (22x19") Color. [39] £76 $144

VIRGINIA, MARYLANDIA ET CAROLINA IN AMERICA SEPTENTRIONALI ... [c. 1700] 48x58cm. (19x22½") Original color. Excellent. [1] £788 $1500

[same title] [c. 1714] 49x59cm. (19x23") Predates "privilege" notation (c. 1730). Original color. Excellent. [38] £631 $1200

[same title] [c. 1720] 49x59cm. (19x23") Old col. Small repaired tears in lower margin. [39] £338 $644

[same title] [1730] 49x58cm. (19x22½") Original color. Excellent. [22] £631 $1200

[same title] [c. 1730] 51x58cm. (19½x23") Full original color. [15] £499 $950

VIRGINIA UND MARYLAND [c. 1760] 28x20cm. (10½x8") Fragment of "Dominia Anglorum ..." Original color. Remargined; map fine. [12] £145 $275

VORSTELLUNG DER LINIE U. INONDATION VON BRUCHSAHL BIS KETSCH, WOSELBST DIE INONDATION IN RHEIN FLIESET U. FERNER VON DA BIS MANHEIM ... [c. 1735] 34x69cm. (13x27") Old color. [39] £338 $644

VORSTELLUNG DES CAMPEMENTS DER KAYSERL. U. REICHS-ARMEE ZU BRUCHSAL ... 1735 IN DENEN GEGENDEN VON ETTLINGEN BIS LANGENBRUCK [c. 1735] 27x90cm. (10½x35½") From two plates. Old color. [39] £304 $578

HOMANN'S HEIRS *Try Homann*

HONDIUS *Try Jansson, Mercator*

[PORTRAIT] GERARDUS MERCATOR ... IUDOCUS HONDIUS ... [1613] 39x46cm. (15½x18") Double portrait by Coletta Hondius. Color. Slight damage at lower centerfold. [5] £600 $1142

[TITLE PAGE] ATLAS MINOR OU BRIEVE AND VIVE DESCRIPTION DE TOUT LE MONDE [1630] 16x21cm. (6½x8½") Jansson imprint; French title pasted over earlier Latin. [5] £45 $86

A GENERAL PLOTT AND DESCRIPTION OF THE FENNES AND SUROUNDED GROUNDS IN THE SIXE COUNTIES OF NORFOLKE, SUFFOLKE, CAMBRIDGE, WITH IN THE ISLE OF ELY, HUNTINGTON, NORTHAMPTON AND LINCOLNE ETC. [1632] 44x56cm. (17½x22") Color. Trimmed to neat line at sides. [40] £135 $256

AMERICA [1606] 38x51cm. (15x20") Color. Fine. [37] £2365 $4500

[same title] [1606+] 37x50cm. (14½x19½") Color Minor centerfold reinforcement; else excellent. [22] £1839 $3500

AMERICA MERIDIONALIS [1606] 46x56cm. (18x21½") Slight surface loss from oxidation; conservation treatment; o/w very good. [31] £447 $850

AMERICA NOVITER DELINEATA [1631] 38x50cm. (15x19½") Original color, heightened in gold leaf. Excellent. [37] £1471 $2800

ASIA RECENS SUMMA CURA DELINEATA. AUCT: JUD: HONDIO [(1631) c. 1640] 38x50cm. (15x20") Color. Fine. [5] £525 $999

BOLONIA & GUINES COMITATUS [c. 1630] 38x50cm. (15x19½") Old color. [40] £83 $158

BOURBONOIS BORBONIUM DUCATUS [c. 1640] 38x50cm. (15x19½") Strong color. [40] £48 $92

CHAMPAGNE COMITATUS CAMPANIA [c. 1640] 38x50cm. (15x19½") Strong color. [40] £45 $85

CHILI [c. 1630] 37x48cm. (14½x19") Old color. [40] £259 $493

CHINA [1606] 34x46cm. (13½x18") Old color. Some marginal browning; restored minor centerfold worming; dark impression. [5] £995 $1893

[same title, date, dimensions] With Japan & Korea. Original color. Green oxidation reinforced, cartouche area chip replaced; excellent appearance, fair condition. [37] £631 $1200

[same title, date, dimensions] Original color. Lightly toned; fine. [38] £1051 $2000

[same title] [1607] 34x46cm. (13½x18") Orig wash color. Lightly browned paper. [33] £1000 $1903

COMITATUS MANSFELDIA [c. 1630] 39x51cm. (15x20") Color. [40] £117 $223

CYPRUS INS. [1607] 35x49cm. (14x19½") Insets of several islands. Original wash color. Lightly browned paper. [33] £550 $1047

DUCATUS BRUNSUICENSIS [c. 1630] 40x50cm. (15½x19½") Old color. [40] £173 $328

DUCATUS SILESIAE LIGNICIENSIS [c. 1640] 39x49cm. (15½x19") Old color. Lower margin trimmed to neat line; lower centerfold repaired. [40] £145 $276

IAPAN I. [(1607) c. 1620] 13x17cm. (5x6½") Color. [5] £275 $523

IAPONIA [(1606) 1619] 34x45cm. (13½x17½") Color. Fine. [5] £1750 $3330

INDIA QUAE ORIENTALIS DICITUR, ET INSULAE ADIACENTES [c. 1705] 39x49cm. (15½x19") From composite atlas; Amsterdam: Pieter Husson. Original color. Chipping from oxidation of greens; stabilize with rice paper lining. [31] £342 $650

INSULA S. JUAN DE PUERTO RICO CARIBES; VEL CANIBALUM INSULAE [c. 1650] 41x51cm. (16x20½") Original color. Excellent. [21] £788 $1500

INSULAE INDIAE ORIENTALIS ... [1607] 14x20cm. (5½x7½") Orig col. Excellent. [37] £118 $225

INSULAE INDIAE ORIENTALIS PRAECIPUAE, IN QUIBUS MOLUCCAE CELEBERRIMAE SUNT [1606] 35x48cm. (13½x19") Color. Fine. [5] £950 $1808

ITALIA NUOUAMENTE PIU PERFETTA CHE MAI PER INANZI POSTA IN LUCE ... [1631] 38x51cm. (14½x19½") Full orig color. Minor centerfold reinforcement; else excellent. [22] £447 $850
JAPONIA [1606-1607] 34x45cm. (13½x17½") Original color. [32] £2200 $4187
L'ARCHEVESCHE DE CAMBRAY [c. 1640] 37x50cm. (14½x19½") Strong old color. [40] £31 $59
LE DIOCESE DE SARLAT DIOCCESIS SARLATENSIS [1631] 37x48cm. (14½x19") Original color. Fine. [38] £79 $150
MAGNAE BRITANNIAE ET HIBERNIAE TABULA [1631] 38x51cm. (15x20") Old color. Centerfold tears restored; wrinkle at center. [40] £186 $355
MAPPA AESTIVARUM INSULARUM, ALIAS BERMUDAS, DICTARUM... [1633] 39x52cm. (15½x20½") Full color. Light toning; o/w very good. [22] £841 $1600
NOVA AFRICAE TABULA [1606 (1607)] 38x50cm. (15x20") Faint spot; else fine. [34] £709 $1350
NOVA EUROPAE DESCRIPTIO [c. 1620] 38x51cm. (15x20") Color. [40] £1001 $1905
NOVA TOTIUS TERRARUM ORBIS GEOGRAPHICA AC HYDROGRAPHICA TABULA AUCT. HENR. HONDIO [1630] 38x54cm. (15x21½") State I, with date present. Original color. Excellent. [37] £3416 $6500
[same title] [(1633) 1663] 38x54cm. (15x21½") 3rd state by Jansson. Shirley 336. Color. Small repair top centerfold; minor margin reinforcement; o/w fine. [5] £2900 $5519
NOVA VIRGINIAE TABULA [c. 1630] 38x50cm. (15x19½") Old color. [40] £932 $1773
[same title] [c. 1635] 36x47cm. (14x18½") Old color. Slight waterstain lower area. [16] £587 $1116
PROVINCIA. LA PROVENCE [1621] 38x50cm. (15x19½") Color. [40] £207 $394
TERRA SANCTA [1607] 36x49cm. (14x19½") Orig wash col. Lightly browned paper. [33] £350 $666
TURCICI IMPERII IMAGO [1607] 36x48cm. (14x19") Original wash color. Lightly browned paper. [33] £600 $1142
TYPUS ORBIS TERRARUM [c. 1607] 14x20cm. (5½x8") Hemispheres. [15] £158 $300
VIRGINIAE ITEM ET FLORIDAE AMERICAE PROVINCIARUM NOVA DESCRIPTIO [1606] 34x48cm. (13½x19") Cumming 26 Original color. Excellent. [37] £946 $1800
[same title] [1607] 34x48cm. (13½x19") . Orig wash color. Lightly browned paper. [33] £850 $1618
[same title] [1613] 34x48cm. (13½x19") Original color. Very good. [31] £1261 $2400

HONTER

UNIVERSALIS COSMOGRAPHIA. TIGURI IVE MDXLVI [1546 (1548)] 12x16cm. (4½x6½") Cordiform map. Shirley 86. Excellent. [37] £447 $850

HOWELL

A MAP OF THE STATE OF PENNSYLVANIA [1811] 56x86cm. (21½x34") After 1792 edition, by Vallance, sc. Very good. [31] £1261 $2400

HUSSON

CARTE GENERALE DES ROYAUMES D'ESPAGNE & DE PORTUGAL AVEC LEUR DIVISIONS &C. [1705] 48x56cm. (19x22½") Contemporary outline color. Small stain; o/w VG. [21] £355 $675

HUTCHINS

A PLAN OF THE RAPIDS IN THE RIVER OHIO BY THOS. HUTCHINS [1778] 15x18cm. (6x7½") Louisville area. [15] £118 $225

HYDROGRAPHIC OFFICE *Try Admiralty*

ILLUSTRATED LONDON NEWS

MAP OF THE SEAT OF WAR IN VIRGINIA [1863] 35x24cm. (13½x9½") Highlight col. [10] £45 $85
THE GREAT SALT LAKE OF THE MORMONS, LOOKING WEST ... [1858] 23x36cm. (9x13½") Fine. [12] £32 $60

IMRAY

EAST INDIA ARCHIPELAGO [Eastern Passages to China & Japan] [1872] 104x130cm. (41x51") Eight [of nine] blue backed charts; dimensions for each sheet of two joined charts. Northernmost "Yellow Sea" lacking. Good. [11] £500 $952
EAST INDIA ARCHIPELAGO [Western route to China] [1872 (1873)] 104x130cm. (41x51") Six blue backed charts; dimensions for each sheet of two joined charts. Good. [11] £400 $761
HALIFAX HARBOUR [1865] 25x15cm. (10x6½") [15] £16 $30

KATTEGAT [1862 (1869)] 124x102cm. (49x40") Blueback. Surface soiling; some creasing and wear to edges. [11] £60 $114

RICE PORTS OF INDIA [1872] 127x102cm. (50x40") Blueback. Brown mark; o/w good. [11] £55 $105

SOUTH AND EAST COASTS OF AUSTRALIA [IN FOUR CHARTS]. CHART NO.1 AUSTRALIAN BIGHT TO CAPE NORTHUMBERLAND [1867 (1872)] 101x128cm. (39½x50½") Blueback. Clean; good. [11] £200 $381

SOUTH ATLANTIC [1872] 101x158cm. (40x62") Blueback. Extension sheet with information. Some creasing; general surface soiling; o/w very fair. [11] £100 $190

THE IRISH OR ST. GEORGE'S CHANNEL ... [1876] 102x191cm. (40½x75") Many insets. Blue-backed. Surface soiling, particularly left edge; edge tear repaired with no loss; o/w VG. [11] £110 $209

WEST COAST OF NORTH AMERICA FROM SAN BLAS TO SAN FRANCISCO [1885] 130x102cm. (51x40") Blue back with linen bound edges. Many insets. Excellent. [11] £370 $704

JACOBSZ

DE CUSTEN VAN ENGELANT TUSSCHEN DE TWEEN POINTEN VAN POORTLANDT EN LEZARD [c. 1690] 43x53cm. (17x21") [11] £320 $609

JAILLOT *Try Covens & Mortier, Mortier*

[TITLE PAGE] SECOND VOLUME DE L'ATLAS FRANCOIS [1699] 29x45cm. (11½x17½") Color. [5] £100 $190

AMERIQUE SEPTENTRIONALE DIVISEE EN SES PRINCIPALES PARTIES , OU SONT DISTINGUES LES UNS DES AUTRES LES ETATS SUIVANT QU'ILS APPARTIENEMENT PRESENTEMENT AUX FRANCOIS CASTILLANS, ANGLOIS, SVEDOIS, DANOIS, HOLLANDAIS ... PAR SR. SANSON [1685] 56x89cm. (21½x34½") Some light staining lower left, o/w good. [2] £998 $1900

[same title] [1719] 46x64cm. (18x25") Peninsular California. Color. Good. [1] £788 $1500

[same title] [c. 1719] 46x66cm. (18x25½") Peninsular California. Color. [15] £460 $875

CARTE DE L'ENTREE DE LA TAMISE AVEC LES BANCS, PASSES, ISLES ET COSTES COMPRISES ENTRE SANDWICH ET CLAY [1693, c. 1795] 46x91cm. (18x35½") First in *Neptune Francois*; here, "cap of liberty" replaces "fleur de lys" on compass north point. Fine. [11] £150 $285

IUDAEA, SEU TERRA SANCTA QUAE ISRAELITARUM IN SUAS DUODECIM TRIBUS DIVISA ... [1696] 51x81cm. (20½x32½") After Sanson. Original color. Few stains; repair to centerfold bottom; else excellent. [21] £631 $1200

L'AMERIQUE MERIDIONALE [1694] 47x61cm. (18½x24") [10] £210 $400

LA SUISSE DIVISEE EN SES TREZE CANTONS, SES ALLIEZ & SES SUJETS ... [c. 1680] 48x61cm. (19x24") Covens & Mortier. Coats of arms at sides. Full original color. Excellent. [2] £788 $1500

LES ISLES BRITANNIQUES; QUI CONTIENNENT LES ROYAUMES D'ANGLETERRE, ECOSSE, ET IRELANDE ... [c. 1692] 53x85cm. (21x33½") Color. Very good. [23] £240 $457

[same title] [1696] 54x86cm. (21x33½") [21] £631 $1200

MAPPE-MONDE GEO-HYDROGRAPHIQUE, OU DESCRIPTION GENERALE DU GLOBE TERRESTRE ET AQUATIQUE, EN DEUX PLANS-HEMISPHERES... [1719] 46x64cm. (18x25") After Sanson. Color. Minor repair; else excellent. [21] £1156 $2200

ROYAUME D'IRLANDE [c. 1696] 89x62cm. (35x24½") Inset of British Isles, etc. VG. [24] £240 $457

JAMES, J.A. & U.P.

A NEW MAP OF MEXICO, CALIFORNIA & OREGON [1848] 33x25cm. (13x9½") Cincinnati. Wood engraving. [35] £84 $160

JAMES, W.

MAP OF MAJ. GEN. ROSS'S ROUTE, WITH THE BRITISH COLUMN, FROM BENEDICT, ON PATUXENT RIVER, TO THE CITY OF WASHINGTON, AUGUST 1814 [1818] 36x41cm. (13½x15½") Inset: Battle of Bladensburg. From *A Full Account of the Military Occurrences of the Late War* ... Right margin partially extended; rice paper backing; else good. [29] £657 $1250

PLAN OF THE OPERATIONS OF THE BRITISH & AMERICAN FORCES BELOW NEW ORLEANS, ON THE 8TH OF JANUARY 1815 [1818] 51x20cm. (20x8") [15] £87 $165

JAMIESON, A.

[CELESTIAL MAP: AURIGA & TELESCOPIUM HERSCHELII] [1822] 18x23cm. (7x9") Original color to constellations. Fine. [17] £42 $80

JANSSON *Try Hondius, Mercator, Valk & Schenk*

ACCURATISSIMA BRASILIAE TABULA [1639] 38x48cm. (15x19") Orig outline col. VG. [31] £289 $550

AETHIOPIA INFERIOR VEL EXTERIOR [1647] 39x50cm. (15x19½") Old color. [40] £407 $775

AETHIOPIA SUPERIOR VEL INTERIOR; VULGO ABISSINORUM SIVE PRESBITERI IOANNIS IMPERIUM [1647] 39x50cm. (15x19½") Old color. Small rust spot at center. [40] £307 $585

AMERICA NOVITER DELINEATA [1641] 38x50cm. (15x19½") By Hondius. Old col. [40] £1208 $2299

AMERICA SEPTENTRIONALIS [1640] 47x55cm. (18½x21½") Without text on verso. Wash color. Mint. [38] £1997 $3800

[same title, date, dimensions] Outline color. Excellent. [38] £1524 $2900

[same title] [1647] 47x55cm. (18½x22") Insular California. Old color. Fold tear repaired; lower margin replaced. [40] £1035 $1970

AMERICAE PARS MERIDIONALIS [c. 1635] 46x53cm. (18x21½") Old color. [15] £499 $950

ANGLIA REGNUM [c. 1649] 38x49cm. (15x19½") Color. Very good. [23] £225 $428

ARCHIEPISCOPATUS TREVIRENSIS DESCRIPTIO NOVA [1647] 41x48cm. (16½x19") Old color. [40] £380 $722

ARRAGONIA REGNUM [1647] 42x52cm. (16½x20½") Old color. [40] £138 $263

ASIA RECENS SUMMA CURA DELINEATA [(1631) c. 1647] 41x51cm. (16x20") "Carte-a-figures", after Hondius. Color. Small marginal tears; lower centerfold split reinforced; o/w good. [5] £1150 $2188

BELGII NOVI, ANGLIAE NOVAE, ET PARTIS VIRGINIAE NOVISSIMA DELINEATIO [1657] 43x51cm. (17½x20½") First edition. Color. Excellent. [21] £2365 $4500

BISCAIA ET GUIPUSCOA CANTABRIAE VETERIS PARS. AMSTELODAMI APUD IOANNEM IANSSONIUM [1647] 38x50cm. (15x19½") [40] £155 $296

CANDIA OLIM CRETA [1647] 38x53cm. (15x21") Old color. [40] £235 $447

CHILI [1639] 37x48cm. (14½x19") Original outline color. Very good. [31] £236 $450

CHINA VETERIBUS SINARUM REGIO NUNC INCOLIS TAME DICTA [1636] 41x50cm. (16x19½") Full original color. Some faint staining; else excellent. [22] £736 $1400

[same title] [1647] 41x50cm. (16x19½") Old color. [40] £580 $1103

[same title] [c. 1658] 41x50cm. (16x19½") Color. [5] £580 $1104

CIRCULUS WESTPHALICUS, SIVE GERMANIAE INFERIORIS [1647] 41x54cm. (16x21½") Old color. [40] £342 $650

CLIVIA DUCATUS ET RAVESTEIN DOMINIUM [1647] 38x50cm. (15x19½") Old col. [40] £380 $722

COLONIENSIS ARCHIEPISCOPATUS [1647] 38x49cm. (15x19½") Old color. [40] £414 $788

COMITATUS BENTHEIM ET STEINFURT [1647] 38x50cm. (15x19½") Color. [40] £311 $591

COMITATUS LAGENIAE. THE COUNTIE OF LEINSTER [c. 1660] 38x49cm. (15x19½") Color. Very good. [24] £130 $247

COMITATUS WERTHEIMICI FINITIMARUMQUE REGIONUM NOVA ET EXACTA DESCRIPTIO [1647] 38x50cm. (15x19½") Old color. [40] £318 $604

DESCRIPTIO CORSICAE INSULAE [1647] 34x23cm. (13½x9") Old color. [40] £166 $315

DESCRIPTIO SARDINIAE INSULAE [1647] 35x23cm. (13½x9") By Mercator. Old col. [40] £152 $289

DESCRIPTION DU GOUVERNEMENT DE LA CAPPELLE [c. 1630] 37x50cm. (14½x19½") Color. [40] £41 $79

DUCATUS HOLSATIAE NOVA TABULA [1645] 38x51cm. (15x20") Old color. [40] £311 $591

DUCATUS SILESIAE GLOGANI VERA DELINEATIO [1647] 42x53cm. (16½x20½") Old color. [40] £179 $342

DUCATUS SILESIAE GROTGANUS CUM DISTRICTU EPISCOPALI NISSENSI [1647] 40x51cm. (15½x20") Old color. [40] £273 $519

EPISCOPATUS HILDESIENSIS DESCRIPTIO NOVISSIMA AUTHORE IOANNE GIGANTE [1647] 41x45cm. (16x17½") Old color. [40] £224 $427

EPISCOPATUS PADERBORNENSIS DESCRIPTIO NOVA [1647] 38x49cm. (15x19½") Old color. [40] £511 $972

FEZZAE ET MAROCCHI REGNA AFRICAE CELEBERRIMA, DESCRIBEBAT ABRAH ORTELIUS [1647] 39x50cm. (15x19½") Old color. [40] £269 $512

[same title] [1650] 38x50cm. (15x19½") Original color. Excellent. [38] £131 $250

FRANCONIAE NOVA DESCRIPTIO [c. 1645] 42x54cm. (16½x21") Color. [40] £235 $447

FRETI MAGELLANICI AC NOVI FRETI VULGO LE MAIRE EXACTISSIMA DELINEATIO [1647] 38x49cm. (15x19½") Old color. [40] £342 $650

GEOGRAPHIA SACRA [1650] 36x48cm. (14x19") Full color. [38] £202 $385

GERMANIAE NOVA ET ACCURATA DELINEATIO [1647] 35x48cm. (13½x18½") Col. [40] £311 $591

GERMANIAE VETERIS ... [c. 1650] 38x48cm. (18½x15") Color. Repaired cracking at old green; else fine. [34] £158 $300

GERMANIAE VETERIS NOVA DESCRIPTIO [c. 1630] 38x48cm. (15x19") By Kaerius. [40] £238 $453

GOTHIA [1646] 39x49cm. (15½x19") Old color. Lower centerfold restored. [40] £224 $427

GRANATA ET MURCIA REGNA [1647] 38x49cm. (15x19½") Old col. Centerfold wrinkle. [40] £152 $289

GUIANA SIVE AMAZONUM REGIO [1647] 37x49cm. (14½x19") Old color. [40] £328 $624

HASSIA LANDGRAVIATUS [1650] 44x56cm. (17½x22") By Hondius. Old color. [40] £290 $552

HOLY ILAND / GARNSEY / FARNE / JARSEY [1646] 51x41cm. (20x16") Four maps on sheet. Outline color. Centerfold strengthened; else very good. [34] £210 $400

IAPONIA ET TERRA ESONIS [1651] 15x19cm. (6x7½") Japan with islands to north. [5] £300 $571

IAPONIAE NOVA DESCRIPTIO [1647] 34x45cm. (13½x17½") Original color; gold highlights. Minor offset browning. [5] £1750 $3330

[same title] [1647+] 36x46cm. (13½x17½") Full orig col. Centerfold reinforced; else exc. [22] £1445 $2750

INDIAE ORIENTALIS NOVA DESCRIPTIO [(1633) c.1640] 39x50cm. (15½x20") Col. [5] £585 $1113

INSULAE AMERICANAE IN OCEANO SEPTENTRIONALI, CUM TERRIS ADIACENTIBUS AMSTELODAMI, APUD IOANNEM IANSSONIUM [c. 1640] 38x52cm. (15x20½") Wash col. Fine. [38] £447 $850

[same title] [1647] 38x52cm. (15x20½") Old color. [40] £518 $985

[same title] [c. 1647-50] 38x52cm. (15x20½") Color. [10] £289 $550

INSULAE IOHANNIS MAYEN CUM UNIVERSO SITU SINUUM ET PROMONTORIUM NOVA DESCRIPTIO [1650] 41x52cm. (16x20½") Color. Excellent. [37] £192 $365

INSULARUM MOLUCCARUM NOVA DESCRIPTIO. AMSTELOMI APUD IOANNEM IANSSONIUM [1647] 38x50cm. (15x19½") Old color. [40] £273 $519

IULIACENSIS ET MONTENSIS DUCATUS. DE HERTOGHDOMEN GULICK EN BERGHE [1647] 38x50cm. (15x19½") Old color. [40] £518 $985

LALANDIAE ET FALSTRIAE ACCURATA DESCRIPTIO [1646] 41x53cm. (16x21") Old col. [40] £138 $263

LEGIONIS REGNUM ET ASTURIARUM PRINCIPATUS [1647] 38x48cm. (15x19") Old col. [40] £159 $302

LUSATIA SUPERIOR [1647] 38x50cm. (15x19½") Old color. [40] £104 $197

MAGNAE BRITANNIAE ET HIBERNIAE NOVA DESCRIPTIO [c. 1646] 42x53cm. (16½x21") Color. Very good. [23] £450 $856

MAGNI MOGOLIS IMPERIUM [1647] 37x50cm. (14½x19½") Old color. [40] £200 $381

MANTUA DUCATUS [1647] 35x47cm. (13½x18½") Old color. [40] £173 $328

MAPPA AESTIVARUM INSULARUM, ALIAS BARMUDAS DICTARUM...ACCURATE DESCRIPTA [1647] 39x52cm. (15½x20½") Old color. Surface slightly rubbed. [40] £759 $1445

MAR DEL NORT [1657] 43x56cm. (17x22") Outline color. Very good. [31] £946 $1800

MAR DEL ZUR HISPANIS MARE PACIFICUM [c.1650] 44x54cm. (17½x21½") Color. Fine. [5] £1000 $1903

[same title] [1650] 44x54cm. (17x21") Original color. Excellent. [38] £1524 $2900

MAR DI INDIA [c.1650] 44x55cm. (17x22") Color. Short lower centerfold split restored. [5] £800 $1522

MARCHIONATUS BRANDENBURGICUS [1647] 48x55cm. (19x21½") Old color. Remargined at bottom; outer neat line restored. [40] £311 $591

MARCHIONATUS MISNIAE UNA CUM VOITLANDIA [1647] 42x52cm. (16½x20½") Old color. [40] £152 $289

MEKLENBURG DUCATUS [1647] 37x48cm. (14½x19") Old color. [40] £173 $328

MONASTERIENSIS EPISCOPATUS [1647] 37x49cm. (14½x19") Old color. [40] £449 $854

MOSCOVIAE PARS AUSTRALIS AUCTORE ISACCO MASSA [1646] 38x50cm. (15x20") Old color. [40] £148 $282

NASSOVIA COMITATUS [1647] 38x50cm. (15x19½") Old color. [40] £342 $650

NOVA ALEMANNIAE SIVE SUEVIAE SUPERIORIS TABULA [1647] 39x49cm. (15x19½") Old color. [40] £307 $585

NOVA ANGLIA NOVUM BELGIUM ET VIRGINIA [1636] 39x50cm. (15x19½") Full original outline color. Light time-toning, o/w very good. [2] £1156 $2200

NOVA BARBARIAE DESCRIPTIO [1647] 35x52cm. (14x20½") Old color. [40] £235 $447

NOVA BELGICA ET ANGLIA NOVA [1647] 38x50cm. (15x19½") Early color. Toned with light foxing; o/w good. [22] £788 $1500

[same title] [1636 (c. 1694)] 39x50cm. (15x19½") Original wash color. Mint. [38] £1156 $2200

NOVA ET ACCURATA DESCRIPTIO DELPHINATUS VULGO DAUPHINE [c. 1650] 38x51cm. (15x20") Old color. [40] £135 $256

NOVA ET ACCURATA JAPONIAE TERRAE ESONIS AC INSULARUM ADJACENTIUM EX NOVISSIMA DETECTIONE DESCRIPTIO. APUD JOANNEM JANSSONIUM [1652-59] 46x55cm. (18x21½") Color. Slight paper reinforcement at lower corners. [5] £1750 $3330

NOVA ET ACCURATA TABULA EPISCOPATUUM STAVANGRIENSIS, BERGENSIS ET ASLOIENSIS VICINARUMQUE ALIQUOT TERRITORIORUM [1646] 41x50cm. (16x19½") Old color. [40] £338 $644

NOVA HISPANIA, ET NOVA GALICIA [1639] 35x48cm. (13½x19") Original outline color. Crease near centerfold. [31] £263 $500

[same title] [1647] 35x48cm. (13½x19") Old color. Short fold at right. [40] £276 $525

NOVA TOTIUS LIVONIAE ACCURATA DESCRIPTIO [1646] 39x51cm. (15½x20½") Old color. Centerfold and tear repaired; center wrinkles flattened. [40] £269 $512

NOVISSIMA RUSSIAE TABULA [1646] 47x55cm. (18½x21½") Old color. [40] £304 $578

OLDENBURG COMITATUS [1647] 38x49cm. (15x19½") Old color. [40] £255 $486

PALATINATUS BAVARIAE [1647] 37x50cm. (14½x19½") By Mercator. Old col. [40] £169 $322

PARAGUAY [1639] 37x48cm. (14½x19") Original outline color. Very good. [31] £236 $450

PARAGUAY, O PROV. DE RIO DE LA PLATA CUM REGIONIBUS ADIACENTIBUS TUCUMAN ET STA. CRUZ DE LA SIERRA [1647] 37x48cm. (14½x19") Old col. Wrinkles at centerfold. [40] £311 $591

PASCAART VANT CANAAL ... [1650] 43x55cm. (17x21½") British Isles. Color. Fine. [37] £289 $550

PERU [1647] 38x49cm. (15x19") Old color. [40] £276 $525

PORTUGALLIA ET ALGARBIA QUAE OLIM LUSITANIA. AUCTORE VERNADO ALVERO SECCO. AMSTELODAMI APUD JOANNES JANSSONIUM [1647] 38x49cm. (15x19") Old color. Wrinkle at right. [40] £276 $525

PRIMA PARS BRABANTIAE ... [1639] 51x41cm. (20½x16") Outline color. Slight age toning; else very good. [34] £131 $250

PRUSSIA ACCURATE DESCRIPTA [c. 1640] 38x49cm. (15x19½") Old color. [40] £449 $854

RHENUS FLUVIORUM EUROPAE CELEBERRIMUS, CUM MOSA, MOSELLA, ET RELIQUIS, IN ILLUM SE EXONERANTIBUS FLUMINIBUS [1647] 42x94cm. (16½x37") Old col. [40] £1104 $2102

RUSSIAE, VULGO MOSCOVIA DICTAE, PARTES SEPTENTRIONALIS ET ORIENTALIS [1646] 42x54cm. (16½x21½") Old color [40] £100 $190

SAXONIA INFERIOR [1647] 38x46cm. (15x18") Old color. [40] £269 $512

SICILIAE REGNUM [1647] 34x48cm. (13½x19") Old color. [40] £207 $394

SIGNORIA DI VERCELLI [1647] 39x50cm. (15x19½") Old color. [40] £173 $328

SILESIA INFERIOR [1647] 42x52cm. (16½x20½") Old color. [40] £283 $539

STIRIA [1647] 31x42cm. (12x16½") By Mercator. Old col. Centerfold wrinkles smoothed. [40] £204 $387

SUECIAE, NORVEGIAE, ET DANIAE, NOVA TABULA [1646] 48x56cm. (18½x22") Old color. Restoration in margin; lower margin replaced. [40] £338 $644

TABULA ISLANDIAE AUCTORE GEORGIO CAROLO FLANDRO [1638] 38x49cm. (15x19") Color. Very good. [31] £394 $750

TARTARIA SIVE MAGNI CHAMI IMPERIUM [1642] 38x51cm. (15x20") Color. [15] £145 $275

TERRITORII NOVOFORENSIS IN SUPERIORE PALATINATU ACCURATA DESCRIPTIO [1647] 51x52cm. (20x20½") Old color. [40] £273 $519

TERRITORIUM ABBATIAE HERESFELDENSIS. 'T STIFT HIRSSFELD [1647] 38x49cm. (15x19½") Old color. [40] £173 $328

TERRITORIUM NORIMBERGENSE [1647] 36x47cm. (14x18½") Old color. [40] £311 $591

TOTIUS HISPANIAE NOVA DESCRIPTIO. ANNO 1633 [1606-1638] 38x52cm. (15x20½") Reissue of Hondius map. Original outline color. [32] £450 $856

TOTIUS SUEVIAE NOVISSIMA TABULA [1647] 39x49cm. (15½x19½") Old color. [40] £318 $604

TRANSYLVANIA, SIBENBURGEN [1647] 34x43cm. (13½x17") By Mercator. Centerfold wrinkles flattened. [40] £152 $289

UTRIUSQUAE ALSATIAE SUPERIORIS AC INFERIORIS NOVA TABULA [1647] 39x55cm. (15½x21½") Old color. [40] £242 $460

VALENTIA REGNUM. COTESTINI. PTOL. EDENTANI PLIN. [1647] 36x48cm. (14x19") Old color. [40] £204 $387

VENEZUELA, CUM PARTE AUSTRALI NOVAE ANDALUSIAE [1639] 38x49cm. (15x19½") Original outline color. Very good. [31] £276 $525

[same title] [1647] 38x49cm. (15x19½") Old color. [40] £414 $788

WALACHIA SERVIA, BULGARIA, ROMANIA [1647] 34x47cm. (13½x18½") By Mercator. Old color. [40] £100 $190

WALDECK COMITATUS [1647] 38x51cm. (15x20") Old color. [40] £262 $499

WIRTENBERG DUCATUS [1647] 37x45cm. (14½x17½") By Mercator. Old color. [40] £518 $985

JANVIER

L'AMERIQUE SEPTENTRIONALE DIVISEE EN SES PRINCIPAUX ETATS [1762] 31x45cm. (12x17½") 1st state. Original outline color. Centerfold lightly toned; fine. [28] £260 $495

JEAN

PLAN ROUTIER DE LA VILLE ET FAUBOURGS DE PARIS DIVISE EN 12 MAIRIES [1801] 57x85cm. (22½x33½") Linen-backed folding plan in original gilt embossed worn slipcase. Outline color. Very good. [19] £236 $450

JEFFERYS *Try Laurie & Whittle, Sayer, Sayer & Bennett*

A CHART OF THE ENTRANCE INTO ST. MARY'S RIVER TAKEN BY CAPTN. W. FULLER NOV. 1769 [1770] 51x61cm. (20x24") Dedicated to John, Earl of Egmont. Color. [15] £289 $550

A CHART OF THE WORLD UPON MERCATOR'S PROJECTION DESCRIBING THE TRACKS OF CAPT. COOK IN THE YEARS 1768 ... -75 WITH THE NEW DISCOVERIES [1775] 39x46cm. (15½x18") London: Faden. Color. [15] £202 $385

A GENERAL MAP OF THE BRITISH MIDDLE COLONIES IN AMERICA ... [c. 1768] 48x66cm. (19x26") London: R. Sayer. Original outline color. Remargined with early paper; centerfold reinforcement; else good. [21] £2365 $4500

A MAP OF HUDSON'S BAY AND STRAITS [1766] 15x21cm. (6x8½") Color. [15] £34 $65

A MAP OF SOUTH AMERICA CONTAINING TIERRA-FIRMA, GUAYANA, NEW GRENADA, AMAZONIA, BRASIL, PERU, PARAGUAY, CHACO, TUCUMAN, CHILI AND PATAGONIA. FROM MR. D'ANVILLE WITH SEVERAL IMPROVEMENTS AND ADDITIONS, AND THE NEWEST DISCOVERIES [1779] 71x117cm. (27½x46") London: R. Sayer. Color. [15] £192 $365

A MAP OF THE MOST INHABITED PART OF NEW ENGLAND, CONTAINING THE PROVINCES OF MASSACHUSETS BAY AND NEW HAMPSHIRE, WITH THE COLONIES OF CONNECTICUT AND RHODE ISLAND, DIVIDED INTO COUNTIES AND TOWNSHIPS ... [1755 / 1774] 53x99cm. (20½x38½") dimensions for each of two sheets. Orig line color. Somewhat toned;, o/w VG. [1] £1314 $2500

AN AUTHENTIC PLAN OF THE TOWN & HARBOUR OF CAP-FRANCOIS IN THE ISLE OF ST. DOMINGO [1760] 33x48cm. (13x19") [10] £45 $85

AN EXACT CHART OF THE RIVER ST. LAURENCE, FROM FORT FRONTENAC TO THE ISLAND OF ANTICOSTI SHEWING THE SOUNDINGS, ROCKS, SHOALS, &C. WITH VIEWS OF THE LANDS AND ALL NECESSARY INSTRUCTIONS FOR NAVIGATING THAT RIVER TO QUEBEC [1775] 60x94cm. (23½x37") London: Sayer. Outline color. [15] £250 $475

[same title, date, dimensions] 5 insets. Original outline color. Excellent. [22] £473 $900

AN INDEX MAP TO THE FOLLOWING SIXTEEN SHEETS, BEING A COMPLEAT CHART OF THE WEST INDIES [1775] 41x66cm. (15½x25½") London: R. Sayer. Color. [15] £197 $375

DOMINICA FROM AN ACTUAL SURVEY COMPLEATED IN THE YEAR 1773 [1760] 64x48cm. (24½x19") London: R. Sayer. Color. [15] £197 $375

GRENADA DIVIDED INTO ITS PARISHES... [1775] 46x62cm. (18½x24½") R. Sayer. Col. [15] £223 $425

IRELAND [c. 1765] 18x19cm. (7x7½") Color. Very good. [24] £56 $107

NORTH AMERICA [c. 1750] 18x23cm. (7x9") Color. [15] £66 $125

PLAN OF THE HARBOUR OF SAN FERNANDO DE OMOA [17682] 21x28cm. (8x11") London: R. Sayer. [15] £58 $110

PLAN OF THE ROAD AND PORT OF LA VERA CRUZ [1768] 20x31cm. (8x12") London: R. Sayer. Color. [15] £66 $125

PLAN OF THE TOWN AND FORT OF GRENADA BY MR. DE CAYLUS ENGINEER GENERAL OF THE FRENCH ISLANDS [1760] 30x23cm. (12x9") Color. [15] £92 $175

PLAN OF THE TOWN AND FORTIFICATIONS OF MONTREAL OR VILLE MARIE IN CANADA [1758] 33x51cm. (13x20") Two folds, slight offsetting and age-toning, some pinholes; top margin trimmed to neat line as issued; very good. [8] £342 $650

RUATAN OR RATTAN SURVEYED BY ... BARNSLEY WITH IMPROVEMENTS BY T. J. ... [1794] 46x61cm. (18x24") London: Laurie & Whittle. Color. [15] £250 $475

THE ISLAND OF CUBA WITH PART OF THE BAHAMA BANKS & THE MARTYRS [1775] 49x63cm. (19x25") Excellent. [37] £342 $650

JEWETT & CO.

MAP OF THE STATE OF VERMONT [1859] 28x15cm. (11x6") [6] £50 $95

JOHNSON

ILLINOIS [1861] 42x32cm. (16½x12½") Johnson & Browning. Color. [15] £26 $50

IOWA & NEBRASKA [1864] 43x60cm. (17x24") Full color. [3] £32 $60

JOHNSON'S CALIFORNIA, TERRITORIES OF NEW MEXICO, ARIZONA, COLORADO, NEVADA AND UTAH [1863] 43x61cm. (17x24") Johnson & Ward. Full col. Minor spotting near fold. [3] £74 $140

JOHNSON'S CALIFORNIA. TERRITORIES OF NEW MEXICO AND UTAH [1861] 43x62cm. (17x24") Johnson & Browning. Full color. [3] £84 $160

JOHNSON'S CENTRAL AMERICA [1860] 31x40cm. (12x15½") 1st edition. Color. [15] £24 $45

JOHNSON'S DELAWARE AND MARYLAND [dated 1855] 32x41cm. (13x16") Color. [6] £39 $75

JOHNSON'S GEORGIA AND ALABAMA [1861] 43x61cm. (17½x24") Johnson & Ward. Col. [15] £42 $80

[same title] [1863] 36x53cm. (14x20½") NY: A.J. Johnson. Full color. Fine. [13] £39 $75

[same title] [1863] 41x57cm. (16x22½") NY: Johnson & Ward. Full color. Very good. [13] £45 $85

[same title] [c. 1865] 41x57cm. (16x22½") Color. [6] £37 $70

[same title] [1869] 38x56cm. (15½x22") NY: A.J. Johnson. Full color. Fine. [13] £34 $65

JOHNSON'S ILLINOIS [1864] 61x43cm. (24x17") Full color. [3] £37 $70

[same title, date] 58x43cm. (23x17") Johnson & Ward. Color. [15] £32 $60

[same title] [1865] 58x46cm. (23x17½") Full color. [26] £32 $60

JOHNSON'S INDIANA [1864] 56x41cm. (22x15½") NY: A.J. Johnson. Full color. Minor staining; good. [14] £32 $60

JOHNSON'S IOWA AND NEBRASKA [1864] 43x58cm. (17x23") Johnson & Ward. Color. [15] £26 $50

JOHNSON'S LOWER CANADA AND NEW BRUNSWICK [on sheet with] JOHNSON'S UPPER CANADA [c. 1865] 56x36cm. (22x14") Two maps. Wash color. [6] £26 $50

JOHNSON'S MICHIGAN & WISCONSIN [1861] 46x61cm. (17½x24") Johnson & Ward. Mackinaw Strait vignette. Color. [15] £34 $65

JOHNSON'S MINNESOTA [1870] 61x43cm. (24x17") Full color. [3] £32 $60

JOHNSON'S MINNESOTA AND DAKOTA [1864] 33x41cm. (12½x15½") Johnson & Ward. Wash color. Repaired marginal tear; good. [29] £76 $145

JOHNSON'S NEBRASKA, DAKOTA, COLORADO, IDAHO AND KANSAS [1863] 33x41cm. (13x16") Extended Idaho. Full color [3] £34 $65

JOHNSON'S NEBRASKA, DAKOTA, IDAHO AND MONTANA [1865] 48x61cm. (19x24") Johnson & Ward. One Montana county; none in Wyoming. Full color. Very good. [3] £74 $140

[same title] [dated 1865] 43x59cm. (17x23") Wash color. [6] £79 $150

[same title] [1868] 43x59cm. (17x23") Faint stain upper centerfold; else excellent. [36] £58 $110

JOHNSON'S NEW BRUNSWICK, NOVA SCOTIA, NEWFOUNDLAND, AND PRINCE EDWARD ID. [1863] 32x40cm. (12½x15½") Johnson & Ward. Color. [10] £16 $30

JOHNSON'S NEW ILLUSTRATED & EMBELLISHED COUNTY MAP OF THE REPUBLICS OF NORTH AMERICA WITH THE ADJACENT ISLANDS AND COUNTRIES COMPILED, DRAWN & ENGRAVED FROM U. STATES LAND & COAST SURVEYS, BRITISH ADMIRALTY & OTHER RELIABLE SOURCES...[1859] 166x178cm. (65x70") Wall Map. Color. Upper 12" wrinkled and ragged at left with two stains; separations and small hole near top rail; G to VG. [7] £255 $485

JOHNSON'S NEW JERSEY [1860] 38x33cm. (15½x12½") Johnson & Browning; 1st ed. Color. [15] £34 $65

[same title] [c. 1865] 38x33cm. (15x13") Color. [6] £34 $65

JOHNSON'S NEW MAP OF THE STATE OF TEXAS [1863] 43x62cm. (17x24") Johnson & Ward. Full color. [3] £79 $150

JOHNSON'S NEW MILITARY MAP OF THE UNITED STATES SHOWING THE FORTS, MILITARY POSTS &C. WITH ENLARGED PLANS OF THE SOUTHERN HARBORS [1864] 44x59cm. (17½x23") Johnson & Ward. Full color. [3] £47 $90

JOHNSON'S OHIO AND INDIANA [1863] 40x58cm. (15½x22½") NY: Johnson & Ward. Full color. Good. [14] £26 $50

JOHNSON'S OREGON AND WASHINGTON [1866] 46x33cm. (17½x12½") Full color. [3] £37 $70

JOHNSON'S OREGON AND WASHINGTON [on sheet with] JOHNSON'S MINNESOTA [dated 1865] 38x56cm. (15x22") Two maps on one sheet. Color. [6] £32 $60

JOHNSON'S VIRGINIA, DELAWARE, MARYLAND & WEST VIRGINIA [dated 1864] 43x60cm. (17x23½") Several engravings. Color. [6] £53 $100

JOHNSON'S WASHINGTON AND OREGON [1862] 33x41cm. (13x16") Johnson & Ward. WA to South Pass. Full color. [3] £47 $90

JOHNSON'S WASHINGTON, OREGON AND IDAHO [1864] 33x41cm. (13x16") Johnson & Ward. Full color. [3] £47 $90

JOHNSON'S WISCONSIN AND MICHIGAN [1864] 43x59cm. (17x23") Johnson & Ward. Col. [15] £29 $55

JOHNSON'S WORLD ON MERCATOR'S PROJECTION [1865] 42x58cm. (16½x23") Johnson & Ward. Color. Age-toned; foxing in border and at centerfold; marginal tears; very good. [8] £66 $125

MICHIGAN AND WISCONSIN [1863] 43x61cm. (17x24") Full color. [3] £37 $70

MINNESOTA [1869 (1877)] 58x43cm. (23x17") Original wash color. Fine. [29] £87 $165

MISSOURI AND KANSAS [1861] 44x60cm. (17x23½") Johnson & Browning. 3 vignettes. Col.. [12] £47 $90

[same title] [1864] 44x60cm. (17x24") Johnson & Ward. Full color. [3] £34 $65

NEBRASKA, DAKOTA, IDAHO AND MONTANA [1865] 43x59cm. (17x23") 1st issue; few counties. Full color. [26] £47 $90

[same title] [1866] 43x59cm. (17x23") 2nd issue; more counties. Full color. [26] £47 $90

NEBRASKA, DAKOTA, IDAHO, MONTANA AND WYOMING [1870] 43x59cm. (17x23") Full color. [26] £47 $90

NORTH AMERICA [1861] 56x43cm. (22x17") Johnson & Browning. Color. Small brown spits; invisible centerfold mend; o/w excellent. [12] £53 $100

[same title] [1864] 56x43cm. (22x17") Johnson & Ward. Color. [15] £42 $80

NORTH AND SOUTH CAROLINA [1860] 42x59cm. (16½x23½") Johnson & Browning. Color. [15] £39 $75

RUSSIA [1864] 41x33cm. (16x13") Johnson & Ward. Color. [15] £16 $30

JOHNSON & BROWNING *Try Johnson*

JOHNSON & WARD *Try Johnson*

JOHNSTON

AUSTRALIA [1851] 51x61cm. (19½x23½") Outline color. [36] £87 $165

COLONY OF NEW SOUTH WALES AND AUSTRALIA FELIX [1851] 51x64cm. (20x24½") Color. [36] £84 $160

IRELAND [c. 1843] 60x49cm. (23½x19½") From *The National Atlas*. Color. VG. [24] £29 $55

JOHNSTONS' PLAN OF THE SEIGE OF SEVASTOPOL SHOWING THE POSITIONS OF THE ALLIED & RUSSIAN ARMIES ... [1855] 48x63cm. (18½x25") Folding map. Color. partial separation along fold with minute paper loss; very good. [19] £29 $55

MAP OF THE CLANS OF SCOTLAND WITH THE POSSESSIONS OF THE HIGHLAND PROPRIETORS ACCORDING TO THE ACTS OF PARLIAMENT OF 1587 & 1594 ... BY T. B. JOHNSTON ... AND COLONEL JAMES A ROBERTSON ... [1873] 75x57cm. (29½x22½") Second edition. Linen-backed folding map. Color. Slight darkening along folds; good+. [19] £89 $170

NORTH AMERICA [1844] 61x51cm. (23½x19½") Outline color. Pristine. [12] £145 $275

[same title] [1854] 61x51cm. (24½x19½") Color. [15] £58 $110

NUBIA AND ABYSSINIA [c. 1846] 48x61cm. (19½x23½") Color. [15] £34 $65

PALEONTOLOGICAL MAP OF THE BRITISH ISLANDS [1850] 46x28cm. (18x10½") Johnston & E. Forbes; Wm. Blackwood, pub. Color keyed. [36] £66 $125

PALESTINE [1850] 60x50cm. (23½x19½") Outline color. Fine. [34] £45 $85

PHENOMENA OF VOLCANIC ACTION SHOWING THE REGION VISITED BY EARTHQUAKES & THE DISTRIBUTION OF VOLCANOES OVER THE GLOBE [1850] 20x28cm. (8x10½") Insets and key. Color. [36] £26 $50

THE ALPINE CLUB MAP OF SWITZERLAND WITH PARTS OF THE NEIGHBORING COUNTRIES. ... [1876] 104x146cm. (41x57½") London: Stanford. Linen-backed folding map in original slipcase with label of "C. Smith & Son". Some color. Very good. [19] £210 $400

THE WORLD IN HEMISPHERES, WITH COMPARATIVE VIEWS OF THE HEIGHTS OF THE PRINCIPAL MOUNTAINS AND LENGTHS OF THE PRINCIPAL RIVERS ON THE GLOBE [c.1850] 51x64cm. (20x25") Texas as Republic. Color. [26] £92 $175

[same title] [1851] 53x61cm. (20½x24") Outline & wash color. [36] £105 $200

UNITED STATES AND TEXAS [c. 1850] 51x61cm. (20x24") Color. [26] £200 $380

JOLY, J.

DESCRIPTIO SEU ICHNOGRAPHIA VETERIS URBIS HIERUSALEM ET LOCORUM ADJACENTIUM [c. 1798] 36x46cm. (13½x17½") Laor 1057. Color. [15] £87 $165

JOURNEAUX L'AINE

NOUVEAU PLAN ROUTIER DE LA VILLE ET FAUBOURGS DE PARIS DIVISE EN DOUZE MAIRIES ... [1814] 55x77cm. (21½x30½") Linen-backed folding plan between original boards, faded and worn, with label. Outline color. Small intersection holes, two tears at margin on fold, no loss; good+. [19] £158 $300

KAEMPFER

IMPERIUM JAPONICUM [1727] 46x53cm. (18x21") By Scheuchzer, in *History of Japan* after Kaempfer's manuscript map with provinces denoted in Kanji. Color. Good. [5] £2250 $4282

KAERIUS *Try Van den Keere*

KELLER

KELLER'S LITHOGRAPHIERTE REISEKARTE DER SCHWEIZ [c. 1860] 45x65cm. (17½x25½") Linen-backed folding map in original slipcase with label. Some color. Browning at folds, some wear at intersections; extremities of slipcase damaged; o/w very good. [19] £76 $145

KELLY

MEXICO & GUATEMALA [1842] 20x25cm. (8x10") Full color. [26] £53 $100

POST OFFICE LONDON DIRECTORY [1857] 68x90cm. (26½x35½") Linen-backed folding plan. Some soiling and age-darkening; tears in backing at some fold intersections. [19] £181 $345

UNITED STATES [c. 1808] 19x24cm. (7½x9½") Color. [15] £34 $65

KENSETT

A PLAN OF THE TOWN OF NEW HAVEN WITH ALL THE BUILDINGS IN 1748 TAKEN BY THE HON GEN. WADSWORTH OF DURHAM ... JANY. 1806 ... [1806] 69x48cm. (27x19½") Browned; one restored area, a few other repairs; but good. [22] £2365 $4500

KEUR

PEREGRINATIE OFTE VEERTICH-IARIGE REYSE DER KINDEREN ISRAELS UYT EGYPTEN DOOR DE ROOSE ZEE ... [1748] 30x46cm. (12x17½") By J. van Jagen. Color. [15] £202 $385

KIEPERT *Try Weimar Geographisches Institute*

NORD-AMERICA [1867] 42x54cm. (16½x21") From *Neuer Handatlas*. Outline color. [16] £97 $184

OSTLICHES NORDAMERICA [1867] 51x44cm. (20x17½") Outline color. [16] £97 $184

WESTINDIEN CENTRAL-AMERICA UND DAS NORDLICHE UND NORDWESTLICHE SUD AMERICA [c. 1854] 53x64cm. (21x25") Weimar: A. Graf. Color. [15] £71 $135

WESTLICHES - NORDAMERICA [1867] 55x44cm. (21½x17½") From *Neuer Handatlas*. Outline color. [16] £97 $184

KINCAID, A.

PALESTINE OF THE HOLY LAND [1791] 20x15cm. (8½x5½") Color. [15] £24 $45

KINGSBURY

[WESTERN TERRITORY] [1836] 51x89cm. (19½x35") Region of Kansas, Nebraska and Colorado. From *Journal of the Expedition of Dragoons, Under ... Henry P. Dodge, to the Rocky Mountains*. Original outline color. Fold intersection pinholes; else near flawless. [12] £289 $550

KIP *Try Camden*

KIRCHER

MAPPA FLUXUS ET REFLUXUS RATIONES IN ISTHMO AMERICAE ... [1678] 34x41cm. (13½x16") [10] £145 $275

KITCHIN *Try London Magazine*

A MAP OF THE WORLD, FROM THE LATEST AUTHORITIES [1771] 25x51cm. (10x20") Hemispheres. Color. [15] £202 $385

A NEW AND ACCURATE MAP OF ITALY [c. 1750] 43x39cm. (17x15½") VG. [25] £75 $143

A NEW MAP OF IRELAND [c. 1777] 63x56cm. (25x22") Color. Very good. [24] £120 $228

A NEW MAP OF THE PHILIPPINE ISLANDS, ... [1769] 23x13cm. (9x5") Outline col. Excel. [37] £71 $135

ASIA AND ITS SEVERAL ISLANDS AND REGIONS ... [1793] 43x56cm. (17½x22") Dublin: Jackson, for Payne's *Universal Geography*. Outline col. A little wear and creasing; else VG. [34] £66 $125

BRITISH DOMINIONS IN AMERICA AGREEABLE TO THE TREATY OF 1763; ... [1777] 43x53cm. (17x21") Original outline color. Excellent. [1] £893 $1700

MAP OF THE EUROPEAN SETTLEMENTS IN SOUTH AMERICA AND ON THE WESTERN COAST OF AFRICA [c. 1785] 33x45cm. (13x17½") Excellent. [37] £45 $85

NORTH AMERICA DRAWN FROM THE LATEST AND BEST AUTHORITIES [1787] 36x41cm. (13½x15½") London: J. Harrison. Color. [15] £150 $285

KNIGHT *Try Society for the Diffusion of Useful Knowledge*

LA HARPE

CARTE DE L'HEMISPHERE AUSTRALE MONTRANT LES ROUTES DES NAVIGATEURS ... PAR LE CAPITAINE JACQUES COOK [1780] 53x53cm. (21x21") Color. Very good. [34] £131 $250

CARTE DES DECOUVERTES ... LA MER PACIFIQUE ... PAR LE CAPTAINE COOK EN 1774 [1780] 36x46cm. (14½x18½") Pale color. Creasing; else very good. [34] £53 $100

CARTE DES ISLES KOURILES D'APRES LA CARTE RUSSE [1780] 24x27cm. (9½x10½") By J. Laurent. Color. Fine. [37] £50 $95

LA HONTAN

A GENERAL MAP OF NEW FRANCE COM, CALL'D CANADA [1703] 34x22cm. (13½x8½") 2" portion of blank margin added. [10] £221 $420

ATAQUE DE QUEBEC [1705] 10x18cm. (4½x6½") Bird's-eye plan of 1690 attack. La Haye, pub. Color. [15] £50 $95

CARTE GENERALE DU CANADA EN PETIT POINT [c. 1705] 10x15cm. (3½x5½") [15] £66 $125

LA PEROUSE *Try Robinson*

[PORTRAIT] JEAN FRANCOIS GALAUP DE LA PEROUSE [c. 1795] 20x14cm. (8x5½") Portrait after A. Tardieu. [5] £80 $152

CARTE PARTICULIERE DE LA COTE DU NORD-OUEST DE L'AMERIQUE RECONNUE PAR LES FREGATES FRANCAISES LA BOUSSOLE ET L'ASTROLABE EN 1786. 1 FEUILLE [1797] 51x69cm. (19½x27") Mt. St. Elias to Clonard Bay. [15] £118 $225

[same title, but 2E FEUILLE] [1797] 49x69cm. (19½x27") [15] £123 $235

CHART OF NECKER ISLAND [1798] 39x50cm. (15x19½") [10] £26 $50

CHART OF PART OF THE NORTH WEST COAST OF AMERICA EXPLORED BY THE BOUSSOLE AND ASTROLABE [1798] 49x38cm. (19x15") Monterey to St. Elias Mountains [10] £79 $150

[same title, date] 51x38cm. (19½x15") [same coverage]. Color. [15] £97 $185

CHART OF THE ARCHIPELAGO OF NAVIGATORS DISCOVERED BY MR. DE BOUGAINVILLE ... [1798] 39x49cm. (15x19½") Samoa. [10] £45 $85

CHART OF THE COASTS OF AMERICA & ASIA FROM CALIFORNIA TO MACAO ACCORDING TO THE DISCOVERIES MADE IN 1786 & 1787...NOVR. 1ST. 1798, BY G.G. & J. ROBINSON PATERNOSTER ROW [1798] 38x49cm. (15x19½") [10] £92 $175

CHART OF THE DISCOVERIES MADE IN 1787 IN THE SEAS OF CHINA AND TARTARY BY THE BOUSSOLE AND ASTROLABE ... [1798] 36x49cm. (14x19½") Two sheets: Philippines to Korea, China and Japan. [10] £105 $200

CHART OF THE DISCOVERIES MADE IN 1787 IN THE SEAS OF CHINA AND TARTARY BETWEEN MANILLA AND AVATCHA ... [1798] 49x38cm. (19½x15") [10] £66 $125

CHART OF THE GREAT PACIFIC OCEAN OR SOUTH SEA, TO ILLUSTRATE THE VOYAGE OF DISCOVERY MADE BY THE BOUSSOLE AND ASTROLABE ... [1798] 35x49cm. (14x19") Good. [10] £118 $225

CHART OF THE NORTH WEST COAST OF AMERICA EXPLORED BY THE BOUSSOLE AND ASTROLABE [1798] 38x49cm. (15x19½") dimensions for each of three sheets. [10] £184 $350

PART OF THE GREAT PACIFIC OCEAN SHEWING THE ROUTE OF THE SPANISH FRIGATE LA PRINCESA ... [1798] 24x38cm. (9½x15") [10] £47 $90

PART OF THE PACIFIC OCEAN BETWEEN CALIFORNIA AND THE PHILIPPINE ISLANDS ... [1798] 35x48cm. (13½x19") [10] £39 $75

PLAN DE LA PARTIE DES ILES OU ARCHIPEL DE COREE [1798] 50x69cm. (19½x27") [10] £39 $75

PLAN DU PORT DE ST. DIEGO EN CALIFORNIE ... LEVE EN 1782 [and] PLAN DU PORT ... DE SAN BLAS [1797] 51x33cm. (19½x13½") Two plans on one sheet. Outline color. [15] £118 $225

PLAN OF EASTER ISLAND TAKEN IN APRIL 1786 / PLAN OF COOK'S BAY [1798] 37x49cm. (14½x19½") In three panels, with a view. [10] £39 $75

PLAN OF KURILE ISLANDS AND LANDS LITTLE KNOWN ... [1798] 49x38cm. (19x15") [10] £39 $75

PLAN OF PART OF THE ISLANDS OF MAOUNA / PLAN OF MASSACRE COVE [1798] 37x24cm. (14½x9½") Samoa. Two charts on one plate. [10] £26 $50

PLAN OF PART OF THE ISLANDS OR ARCHIPELLAGO OF COREA [1798] 38x49cm. (15x19½") [10] £45 $85

PLAN OF PORT DES FRANCAIS ON THE NORTH WEST COAST OF AMERICA [1798] 57x49cm. (22½x19½") [10] £39 $75

PLAN OF THE BAY OF CONCEPTION IN CHILI [1798] 25x37cm. (9½x14½") [10] £21 $40

PLAN OF THE ENTRANCE OF THE PORT OF BUCARELLI ON THE NORTH WEST COAST OF AMERICA [1798] 38x49cm. (15x19") [10] £45 $85

VIEW OF THE ISLAND OF ST. CATHERINE [1798] 20x30cm. (8x12") With view of Florianopolis. [10] £32 $60

LABAT

ISLE DE LA GUADELOUPE SCITUEE A 16 DEGRES DE LAT. SEPTENTRIONALE [1772] 13x20cm. (5x7½") [15] £58 $110

LADIES REPOSITORY

BUFFALO [1855] (no dims.) View; by Hill. [35] £32 $60

CHARLESTON [1855] 13x20cm. (5x8") View; by Hill. [35] £34 $65

CHICAGO [1856] 15x20cm. (5½x8") View; by Robertson. [35] £34 $65

ST. LOUIS [1855] 15x20cm. (5½x8") View; by Hill. [35] £34 $65

LAFRERI SCHOOL *Try Bertelli, Gastaldi*

AL MOLTO MAGCO SIGOR MARCO DEL SOLE SIGOR MIO OSSER.MO ... D. V. SERVITORE, FERRANDO BERTELLI [c. 1565] 25x36cm. (9½x14") Atlantic and America. On contemporary mounting to achieve full folio size. Light centerfold staining, o/w excellent. [2] £7,882 $15,000

HIERUSALEM [1570] 30x43cm. (11½x16½") By. C. Duchetti. Slight surface abrasion, o/w excellent. [2] £3416 $6500

IL DISEGNO DELLA TERZA PARTE DELL' ASIA. DI GIACOPO DI GASTALDI ... GIROLAMO OLGIATO, SCULPT. [1561-1570] 41x36cm. (16x14") dimensions for each of 4 sheets. Two lower sheets joined. Excellent. [2] £12,086 $23,000

LALLEMAND

NOUVEAU PARIS OU GUIDE DES ETRANGERS DANS LES 20 ARRONDISSEMENTS [1879] 46x62cm. (18x24") Paris: Bernardin Bechet. Folding plan between original boards, worn at extremities, with label. Outline col. Darkening along folds, some small intersection holes, no loss; VG. [19] £66 $125

PLAN PANORAMA DE PARIS FORTIFIE AVEC ILLUSTRATION. PLAN GARANTI OU LE GUIDE DANS PARIS [1855] 59x86cm. (23x34") Folding map between original boards with label. Original wash color. Small holes at some fold intersections, no loss; very good. [19] £92 $175

LAMBERT, J.

MAP OF THE BRITISH SETTLEMENTS, AND THE UNITED STATES OF NORTH AMERICA, FROM THE COAST OF LABRADOR TO FLORIDA [1813] 38x38cm. (15x15") From 2nd edition of *Travels through the United States* ... Color. Narrow right margin and mended 1" tear through border; else excellent. [12] £131 $250

LANGE

ALABAMA, GEORGIA, SUD CAROLINA UND FLORIDA [1854] 33x28cm. (13x10½") By G. Westermann. Color. [15] £29 $55

MICHIGAN [1854] 23x28cm. (9x11") Braunschweig: G. Westerman. Color. [15] £21 $40

LANGE & KRONFELD

BIRDS-EYE VIEW OF THE CITY AND COUNTY OF NEW-YORK WITH ENVIRONS. [c. 1860] 13x20cm. (4½x7½") Fine. [12] £71 $135

LANGENES

INSULAE PHILIPPINAE [1598] 9x13cm. (3½x5") 1st separate map of Philippines. Excel. [38] £118 $225

MALACCA [1598 (1610)] 9x13cm. (3½x5") Outline color. Excellent. [38] £171 $325

TYPUS ORBIS TERRARUM [1599] 9x13cm. (3½x5") Shirley 211. [26] £223 $425

LAPIE

[WESTERN PACIFIC] [1829] 41x56cm. (15½x21½") Philippines to Australia to Marquesas Islands. Outline color. [36] £63 $120

CARTE DE L'EMPIRE CHINOIS ET DU JAPON [1832] 41x53cm. (15½x21") Outline col. 36] £53 $100

CARTE DES ETATS-UNIS D'AMERIQUE ... [1832] 41x53cm. (15½x21") Outline col.. [35] £118 $225

[same title] [1842] 51x76cm. (20x30") Shows trail of the Astorians (?) Outline color. [3] £197 $375

CARTE DES ETATS-UNIS DU MEXIQUE [1842] 55x40cm. (22x16") Outline color. [3] £223 $425

ETATS-UNIS DE L'AMERIQUE SEPTENTRIONALE ... [1816] 23x30cm. (9x11½") Col. [15] £76 $145

LAPORTE

L'AMERIQUE SEPTENTRIONALE DIVISEE EN SES PRINCIPAUX ETATS [1781] 18x23cm. (7x9") Color. [15] £76 $145

LATTRE

CARTE DES GOUVERNMENTS D'ANJOU ET DE SAUMUROIS, DE LA TOURRAINE, DU POITOU, DE PAYS D'AUNIS, SAINTONGE-ANGOUMOIS [1771] 41x30cm. (16x12") By Bonne. Full col. [35] £42 $80

CARTE DES GOUVERNMENTS DE BOURGOGNE, DE FRANCHE COMTE ET DE LYONNOIS [1771] 41x30cm. (16½x11½") By Bonne. Full color. [35] £42 $80

L'ISLE DE LA DOMINIQUE PAR M. J. M. ANGLOIS ... CHEZ LATTRE [1779] 61x48cm. (24½x19") Color. [15] £460 $875

PARTIE OCCIDENTAL DE L'EMPIRE DE RUSSIE ... PARTIE ORIENTALE DE L'EMPIRE DE RUSSIE ... [1785] 43x61cm. (17x24½") Outline color. Light centerfold stain; marginal wormholes; else very good. [34] £79 $150

LAURIE & WHITTLE *Try D'Anville, Dunn, Jefferys*

A CHART OF THE COAST OF DEVONSHIRE FROM EXMOUTH TO RAME HEAD; CONTAINING TOR BAY, START BAY, PLYMOUTH SOUND, &CA. [1799] 64x79cm. (25x31") Light offsetting; narrow top and bottom margins; o/w very good. [11] £420 $799

A CHART OF THE DOWNS ... [1800] 53x71cm. (20½x27½") Offsetting; small edge tears repaired. [11] £200 $381

A CHART OF THE ENTRANCE OF THE RED SEA ... [1802] 58x66cm. (23x25½") By Moffatt, 1801. Additional sailing direction pasted on. Light offsetting; o/w good. [11] £210 $400

A CHART OF THE MADERAS AND CANARY ISLANDS [1794] 61x48cm. (23½x18½") By Lopes. A light crease; o/w excellent. [11] £120 $228

A CHART OF THE MAHE AND ADMIRANTES ISLANDS WITH THEIR SHOALS ... [1803] 43x58cm. (17x23") By Grenier, 1776. Narrow left margin; o/w very good. [11] £160 $304

A CHART OF THE SANDS AND CHANNELS FROM THE NORE TO MARGATE ROAD ... [1794] 46x61cm. (18x24½") By James Grosvenor. [11] £120 $228

A NAUTIC SURVEY OF MOUNTS BAY IN CORNWALL, WITH THE ADJACENT COAST FROM CAPE LIZARD TO CAPE CORNWALL ... [1794] 48x69cm. (19x27½") By John Thomas & William Denys. Two short repaired margin tears. [11] £170 $324

A NEW AND ACCURATE CHART (FROM CAPTAIN HOLLAND'S SURVEYS) OF THE NORTH AMERICAN COAST, FOR NAVIGATION BETWEEN PHILADELPHIA AND FLORIDA RESPECTFULLY INSCRIBED TO HIS EXCELLENCY THOMAS JEFFERSON, PRESIDENT ... [1808] 79x249cm. (31½x98½") Separately published blueback chart for use. Lighthouses in yellow. Some staining and wear; o/w excellent. [22] £3416 $6500

A NEW AND ACCURATE CHART OF THE MOUTH OF THE THAMES AND ITS ENTRANCES, VIZ: THE KINGS THE QUEENS AND SOUTH CHANNELS &CC FROM THE NORE TO ORFORD NESS AND THE NORTH FORELAND ... [1794] 69x102cm. (26½x39½") By Grosvenor & Bean. Dissected and laid down on linen in contemporary marbled paper slip case. [11] £270 $514

A NEW AND COMPLETE MAP OF THE WEST INDIES COMPREHENDING ALL THE COASTS AND ISLANDS KNOWN BY THAT NAME ... [1794] 46x59cm. (18x23½") By D'Anville. Old col. [15] £255 $485

A NEW AND CORRECT CHART EXTENDING FROM LONDON BRIDGE TO ORFORD NESS ON THE ESSEX AND SUFFOLK COAST; & FROM THE NORE TO THE NORTH FORELAND, THE DOWNS, AND SOUTH FORELAND ON THE KENTISH COAST ... [1800] 89x97cm. (35x37½") By George Burn, *et al.* In Sayer & Bennett's *Channel Pilot.* Fold split repaired; a clean tear entering engraved area. [11] £300 $571

A NEW AND CORRECT MAP OF THE BRITISH COLONIES IN NORTH AMERICA COMPREHENDING EASTERN CANADA ... QUEBEC, NEW BRUNSWICK, NOVA SCOTIA, AND ... NEWFOUNDLAND: WITH THE ADJACENT STATES OF NEW ENGLAND, VERMONT, NEW YORK, PENNSYLVANIA AND NEW JERSEY [1794] 48x67cm. (19x26½") Beaver and scroll cartouche. Color. Excellent. [15] £402 $765

A NEW CHART OF THE ISLAND OF GUERNSEY WITH THOSE OF SARK, HERM AND JETHOU ... [1794] 51x71cm. (20x28") First published by Sayer & Bennett in *Channel Pilot.* Slight offsetting; small area of thin paper; generally excellent. [11] £375 $714

A NEW CHART OF THE ISLE OF WIGHT WITH THE ADJACENT COAST OF HAMPSHIRE, WHEREIN ARE PARTICULARLY DESCRIBED THE ROADS OF ST. HELEN'S, SPITHEAD, &C. ... [1800] 64x79cm. (25x31½") Some offsetting; trimmed upper margin just shaves neat line. [11] £380 $723

A NEW CHART OF THE SOUTHERN COAST OF AFRICA FROM THE CAPE OF GOOD HOPE TO DALAGOA BAY ... [1794] 61x74cm. (23½x29") With view of Cape and Capetown. By De Ruyter. Some browning and offsetting. [11] £380 $723

A NEW MAP OF NORTH AMERICA WITH THE WEST INDIA ISLANDS ... [1794] 100x116cm. (39½x45½") By E. Bowen and Gibson. Four sheets, joined to form two, each about 20 x 45.5 inches. Original color. Excellent. [22] £1314 $2500

A NEW MAP OF SCOTLAND COMPILED FROM ACTUAL SURVEYS & REGULATED BY THE LATEST ASTRONOMICAL OBSERVATIONS [1803] 63x49cm. (24½x19½") By Joseph Enouy. Linen-backed folding map. Outline color. Some age soiling; light pencil marks in margin and one place in map. [19] £105 $200

A NEW MAP OF THE SEAT OF WAR, COMPREHENDING GERMANY; POLAND, WITH ITS DISMEMBERMENTS, PRUSSIA; TURKEY IN EUROPE, ITALY &C. ... [1813] 74x81cm. (29x32") Linen-backed folding map. Original color. Age-darkening, some sections corners lifting, small ink marks; self-backs worn and torn. [19] £63 $120

A NEW SURVEY OF THE COAST OF AFRICA FROM SENEGAL AND CAPE VERDE TO CAPE ST. ANN ... [1797] 99x66cm. (38½x26") By Wm. Woodville. [11] £200 $381

A PLAN OF ENGLISH ROAD IN THE ISLAND OF ASCENSION ... [1795] 28x43cm. (10½x17½") By Maxwell, 1793. Offsetting in lower margin; o/w excellent. [11] £180 $343

A PLAN OF MILFORD HAVEN IN PEMBROKE SHIRE, WITH THE FORTIFICATIONS INTENDED [1794] 51x69cm. (20½x27½") Crease lines; two repaired edge tears into engraving. [11] £90 $171

A PLAN OF TABLE BAY, WITH THE ROAD OF THE CAPE OF GOOD HOPE ... [1794] 48x56cm. (19x21½") After Van Keulen. Slight browning at edges; generally good. [11] £260 $495

A PLAN OF THE HARBOUR OF RYE IN SUSSEX [1794] 43x30cm. (17x11½") A small edge tear; o/w good. [11] £120 $228

AN EYE SKETCH OF THE ENTRANCE OF YEALME RIVER WITH THE DEPTHS OF WATER &C. &C. [1795] 48x36cm. (18½x14½") [11] £100 $190

BEQUIA OR BECOUYA, THE NORTHERNMOST OF THE GRANADILLES [1810] 33x46cm. (13x18½") Color. [15] £150 $285

COLUMBIA, OR THE WESTERN HEMISPHERE [1813] Diameter: 60 cm. (24") Orig color. [33] £320 $609

LAURIE & WHITTLE'S NEW MAP OF LONDON WITH ITS ENVIRONS [1809-10] 59x78cm. (23x30½") Linen-backed folding plan in original marbled slipcase with label. Col. VG. [19] £276 $525

PARTICULAR PLANS OF ISLANDS, ROCKS AND SHOALS IN THE INDIAN OCEAN [1794] 53x53cm. (21½x20½") [11] £75 $143

PLAN OF MATHURIN BAY, ON THE NORTH SIDE OF THE ISLAND OF DIEGO RAYS ... [1794] 51x64cm. (19½x25") By Nichelson. Slight offsetting; o/w excellent. [11] £110 $209

PLAN OF THE BAY AND HARBOUR OF RIO-JANEIRO ... [1794] 48x30cm. (19½x12½") After D'Apres de Mannevillette. Excellent. [11] £180 $343

PLYMOUTH SOUND, HAMOAZE AND CATWATER WITH THE LEADING MARKS AND VIEWS OF LAND [1800] 94x66cm. (37x26") Blue-backed. Ex lib stamp; fold splits repaired; damage and damp-stain just entering image at two places. [11] £160 $304

SKETCH OF THE STRAITS OF GASPAR ... [1794] 64x48cm. (25x18½") By Huddart. Clean; good. [11] £140 $266

THE BAY OF ALGOA ... [and] PLAN OF MOSSEL BAY ... [and] PLAN OF FLESH BAY ... [1794] 58x25cm. (23x10½") Three plans on one sheet; after Van Keulen. [11] £180 $343

THE CAPE VERD ISLANDS ... [1794] 53x28cm. (21x11½") By D'Apres de Mannevillette. Good. [11] £40 $76

THE EMPIRE OF JAPAN [1794] 46x64cm. (18½x25") First published by Sayer. Outline color. [5] £425 $809

THE EUROPEAN PART OF THE RUSSIAN [EMPIRE] & THE ASIATIC PARTS ... [1794] 48x127cm. (19x50") With part of Japan. Color. [15] £97 $185

THE ROAD OF PALLEACATE ... [and] THE ROAD OF TENGEPATNAM ... [1794] 53x23cm. (20½x9") Two plans on one sheet. After Van Keulen. [11] £35 $67

LAVOISNE

GEOGRAPHICAL AND STATISTICAL MAP OF ENGLAND [1821] 38x33cm. (15x12½") Old body color. A few fox marks; else very good. [34] £53 $100

GEOGRAPHICAL, HISTORICAL AND STATISTICAL MAP OF AMERICA [1813] 41x51cm. (16x20") dimensions include text. Color [15] £84 $160

LAW *Try Nolin*

LOUISIANA BY DE RIVER MISSISIPPI [c. 1720] 19x16cm. (7½x6") Accompanied *Het Groote Tafereel de Dwassheid*. Mint. [38] £223 $425

LE MAIRE

DESCRIPTION DE LA COSTE SETENTRIONALE DE NOVA GUINEA NOUVELLEMENT DECOUVERT PAR GUILLAUME SCHOUTEN DE HOORN [1619] 15x27cm. (6x10½") Close side margins; o/w fine. [37] £118 $225

LE PAGE DU PRATZ

[LOUISIANA] [c. 1763] 15x18cm. (6x7") Mobile Bay to Trinity River, Texas. From *Histoire de la Louisiane* ... Howes L-226; Storm 2463. Fine. [12] £66 $125

LE ROUGE

[GREAT LAKES SHEET] [c. 1776] 66x48cm. (25½x18½") Part of "Map of the British and French Dominions in North America"; Paris: French edition. Color. [15] £394 $750

AMERIQUE SUIVANT LE R. P. CHARLEVOIX J. TE MR. DE LA CONDAMINE ET PLUSIEURS AUTRES NOUV LE OBSERVATIONS [1746] 48x64cm. (19½x25") Outline color. Repaired tears; good. [1] £946 $1800

CARTE DES TROUBLES DE L'AMERIQUE LEVEE PAR ORDRE DU CHEVALIER TRYON...PAR SAUTHIER ET RATZER. TRADUIT DE ANGLAISES ... [1778] 71x51cm. (27½x20½") Original outline color. Good. [1] £499 $950

[same title] [c. 1778] 71x53cm. (28x20½") Color. Margin repair. [15] £499 $950

CARTE DU JAPON ET DE LA COREE [1748] 20x28cm. (8x11") Orig outline col. Excel. [5] £285 $542

ENTREE DE LA RIVIERE D'HUDSON ... [1778] 66x51cm. (26½x19½") Col. Excel. [22] £1051 $2000

ISLE DE ST. DOMINGUE ... [1748] 20x28cm. (8x11") Color. [15] £45 $85

L'ASIE AVEC LES NOUVELLES DECOUVERTES [1748] 22x27cm. (8½x11") Original outline color. [10] £26 $50

LA GUADELOUPE DEDIEE A MGR. CHARLES PHILIPPE D'ALBERT DUC DE LUYNES ... 1753 [1753] 48x55cm. (19x21½") Color. Minor repair. [15] £236 $450

VIRGINIE, MARYLAND EN 2 FEUILLES PAR FRY ET JEFFERSON TRADUIT, CORRIGE, AUGMENTE... [1751-1778] 67x98cm. (26½x39") 2 sheets. Orig outline col. Excel. [21] £2233 $4250

[same title] [1777] 67x98cm. (26x38½") 2 sheets joined. Outline color. Some repair at fold; o/w good. [29] £2522 $4800

LE SAGE

ARCIPELAGO COLOMBIANO CIOE LE ISOLE LUCAJE LE GRANDE E PICCOLE ANTILLE [1834] 36x48cm. (13½x19") Venice: G. Tasso. Text at sides. Color. [15] £66 $125

LEA

A NEW MAPP OF THE WORLD BY PHIL. LEA. [c. 1687] 43x53cm. (17x20½") Double hemisphere; unusual decoration. Shirley 535. Full col. Repaired tear near centerfold; else excel. [21] £1839 $3500

THE KINGDOME OF POLAND WITH ITS SEVERAL DUKEDOMS & PROVINCES ... [c. 1695] 42x54cm. (16½x21½") Separately published. Original outline color. [33] £260 $495

LEVASSEUR

AMERIQUE MERIDIONALE [1850] 28x32cm. (11x12½") Paris: Combette. Decorative surround. [16] £90 $171

AMERIQUE SEPTENTRIONALE [c. 1840] 28x44cm. (11x17") Pictorial surround. Texas as Republic. Original outline color. Excellent. [37] £92 $175

[same title] [1842] 30x43cm. (12x17") Independent Texas. Full color. [15] £71 $135

PLANISPHERE [1856] 30x41cm. (11½x16") Outline color. Fine. [12] £79 $150

LEVI

AMERIQUE DU NORD [c. 1838] 23x30cm. (9x11½") Paris: Letronne. Color. [15] £66 $125

LEWIS & ARROWSMITH

AUSTRALASIA [1819] 20x25cm. (7½x9½") Very good. [17] £92 $175

CONNECTICUT [1819] 20x25cm. (8x10") Very good. [17] £79 $150

DELAWARE [1819] 25x20cm. (10x8") Very good. [17] £84 $160

GEORGIA [1819] 20x25cm. (8x10") Cleaned; fine. [13] £105 $200

[same title, date, dimensions] Very good. [17] £79 $150

JAPAN [1819] 20x25cm. (8x9½") Very good. [17] £84 $160

KENTUCKY [1819] 20x25cm. (8x10") Very good. [17] £76 $145

LOUISIANA DRAWN BY S. LEWIS [1804] 25x20cm. (10x8") Phila; Conrad. Color. [15] £197 $375

MAINE [1805] 20x25cm. (8x10") [12] £47 $90

[same title] [1819] 20x25cm. (8x10") Very good. [17] £50 $95

MASSACHUSETTS [1819] 20x25cm. (8x9½") Very good. [17] £92 $175

MISSISSIPPI TERRITORY [c. 1804] 20x25cm. (8x9½") From *Maps to Accompany Pinkerton's Modern Geography*. [6] £79 $150

[same title] [1819] 20x24cm. (8x9½") Very good. [17] £76 $145

NEW JERSEY [1819] 25x20cm. (10x8") Very good. [17] £89 $170

NEW YORK [1819] 20x25cm. (8x10") Very good. [17] £74 $140

NORTH AMERICA [1804] 25x20cm. (9½x8") [15] £42 $80

[same title] [1805] 25x20cm. (10x8") Tiny spot; else mint. [12] £71 $135

NORTH CAROLINA [1805] 20x25cm. (8x10") [12] £66 $125

[same title] [1819] 20x25cm. (8x10") Very good. [17] £76 $145

OHIO [1805] 25x20cm. (10x8") Excellent. [12] £123 $235

[same title] [1819] 25x20cm. (10x8") Very good. [17] £105 $200

PENNSYLVANIA [1804] 18x20cm. (7x8") 34 counties Color. [15] £58 $110

TENNESSEE [1819] 20x25cm. (8x10") Very good. [17] £84 $160

UNITED STATES [1819] 20x25cm. (8x10") Small age spots at neat line; VG. [17] £102 $195

VERMONT [1804] 24x20cm. (9½x8") Slightly mottled; good. [9] £84 $160

VIRGINIA [1819] 20x25cm. (8x10") Very good. [17] £68 $130

LEWIS, S. *See Carey*

LEWIS, SAMUEL & CO.

A MAP OF SCOTLAND DIVIDED INTO COUNTIES SHEWING THE PRINCIPAL ROADS, RAILWAYS, RIVERS, CANALS, LOCHS, MOUNTAINS, ISLANDS, &C. [1889] 63x131cm. (25x51½") 3 Maps, each about with these dimensions. Linen-backed folding maps between original covers with gilt borders. Outline color. Covers scuffed on spines and corners. Maps very good. [19] £210 $400

A PLAN OF LONDON AND ITS ENVIRONS [c. 1850] (no dims.) Large folding map. Color. Very good. [23] £150 $285

LINCOLN & EDMANDS

WESTERN STATES [1832] 15x18cm. (6x7") H. Morse, engr. Original pale colors. [6] £39 $75

LIZARS

MAP OF THE UNITED STATES AND CANADA SHEWING CAPT. HALL'S ROUTE THROUGH THOSE COUNTRIES IN 1827 & 1828 [1829] 33x28cm. (13x11") Color. [15] £50 $95

POLAR REGIONS [1822] 41x38cm. (16x15") Edinburgh: Constable. Pole to 58° N. Col. [15] £50 $95

SPANISH NORTH AMERICA [c. 1815] 23x28cm. (9x11") Color. [6] £79 $150

UNITED STATES [c. 1820] 18x23cm. (7½x8½") Color. [15] £37 $70

LLOYD

CLIMATOLOGICAL MAP OF OHIO SHOWING THE MEAN ANNUAL TEMPERATURE AND FALL OF RAIN [1868] 36x30cm. (13½x12½") By L. Blodget. Color. [15] £21 $40

COUNTY MAP OF COLORADO, UTAH, NEW MEXICO, AND ARIZONA [1876] 41x36cm. (16x14") Full color. [12] £84 $160

COUNTY MAP OF KANSAS, NEBRASKA, DAKOTA, AND MINNESOTA [1876] 43x36cm. (16½x13½") Full color. Fine. [12] £47 $90

LLOYD'S NEW MAP OF THE UNITED STATES, THE CANADAS AND NEW BRUNSWICK ... SHOWING EVERY RAILROAD AND STATION FINISHED TO JUNE 1862 ... [1863] 96x127cm. (38x50") Linen-backed folding map. Outline and wash color. Very fragile; some sections torn along folds, but all present. [19] £525 $1000

LLOYD'S RAILROAD, TELEGRAPH & EXPRESS MAP OF THE EASTERN STATES ... [1863] 97x66cm. (38x26") [6] £131 $250

MICHIGAN, WISCONSIN AND MINNESOTA [1868] 30x41cm. (12x15½") Full color. [12] £39 $75

TOLEDO, LUCAS CO. [1868] 38x30cm. (14½x11½") By J. Marston. Color. [15] £47 $90

LOCAL AND STATE GOVERNMENT MAPS

GEOLOGICAL CHART OF MISSISSIPPI [1857] 36x25cm. (14x9½") By I. Harper, State Geologist, Color keyed. Excellent. [36] £39 $75

MAP OF CANON CITY COLORADO [1896] 71x51cm. (28x20") By Henry Lloyd, Assessor; issued by F.A. Reynolds, Canon Cit Folds. [3] £74 $140

RAILROAD MAP OF OHIO [1892] 74x81cm. (29x32") By Kirby, for State of Ohio. Linen backed pocket map folding into case. Some color. [3] £66 $125

VICTORIA [Australia] [1875] 56x84cm. (22½x32½") By A.J. Skene; Melborne: Dept. of Lands & Survey. Chips in top margin. [31] £79 $150

LOCKWOOD

MAP OF RHODE ISLAND AND PROVIDENCE PLANTATIONS; CORRECTED AND ENLARGED WITH MANY ADDITIONS, BY BENONI LOCKWOOD [1819] 25x18cm. (10x7") Hartford: William S. Marsh. [6] £92 $175

LODGE

AN EXACT MAP OF THE FIVE GREAT LAKES WITH PART OF PENSILVANIA, NEW YORK & HUDSONS BAY TERRS. [1778] 23x25cm. (8½x10½") London: J. Russell. Color. [15] £87 $165

LOGEROT

NOUVEAU PLAN DE PARIS DIVISE EN 20 ARRONDISSEMENTS [1860] 69x102cm. (26½x39½") By Ch. Smith. Original color. Small repaired tears in folds. [31] £276 $525

PARIS ILLUSTRE ET SES FORTIFICATIONS [1850] 52x72cm. (20½x28") Linen-backed folding plan with back label of seller, in original marbled slipcase with label, worn at extremities but sound. Some color. Some foxing; very good. [19] £223 $425

[same title] [1862] 52x72cm. (20½x28") Linen-backed folding plan with back label of seller, in original slipcase with torn label. Pastel color. Very good+. [19] £105 $200

LONDON MAGAZINE

A MAP OF THE BRITISH & FRENCH PLANTATIONS IN NORTH AMERICA [1755] 21x26cm. (8½x10½") Jolly LOND-96. Cut to outer neat line; o/w good. [10] £66 $125

[same title, date, dimensions] Color. [15] £97 $185

A MAP OF THE FIVE GREAT LAKES WITH PART OF PENSILVANIA, NEW YORK, CANADA AND HUDSONS BAY TERRITORIES &C. [1755] 21x26cm. (8½x10½") Jolly LOND-97. Good. [10] £131 $250

[same title, date, dimensions] Color. [15] £92 $175

A MAP OF THE FRENCH SETTLEMENTS IN NORTH AMERICA BY THOS. KITCHIN GEOGRR. [1747] 17x18cm. (6½x7") Jolly LOND-28. Color. [15] £97 $185

A MAP OF THE PROVINCE OF PENSILVANIA DRAWN FROM THE BEST AUTHORITIES BY T. KITCHIN GR. [1756] 17x22cm. (6½x8½") Jolly LOND-112. Cut to neat line. [10] £92 $175

A MAP OF VIRGINIA, NORTH AND SOUTH CAROLINA, GEORGIA, MARYLAND WITH PART OF NEW JERSEY, &C. [1755] 22x26cm. (8½x10") Jolly LOND-95. [6] £155 $295

[same title, date, dimensions] Cut close to neat line and outside title. [10] £100 $190

A NEW AND ACCURATE MAP OF EAST AND WEST FLORIDA, DRAWN FROM THE BEST AUTHORITIES. [1765] 18x20cm. (7x8") Engraved by Prokter. Sellers & Van Ee 1619. [6] £155 $295

A NEW MAP, OF THE ONLY USEFUL AND FREQUENTED PART OF NEW FOUND LAND. BY THOS. KITCHIN GEOGR. [1762] 18x24cm. (7x9½") Jolly LOND-215. Color. [15] £53 $100

[same title, date, dimensions] Cut close to border; o/w fine. [10] £50 $95

A NEW MAP OF THE PROVINCE OF QUEBEC IN NORTH AMERICA; DRAWN FROM THE BEST AUTHORITIES: BY THOS. KITCHIN, GEOGR. [1764] 18x23cm. (7x8½") Jolly LOND-241. Color. [15] £66 $125

A NEW MAP OF VIRGINIA, FROM THE BEST AUTHORITIES: BY T. KITCHIN, GEOG'R. [1761] 18x23cm. (7x9") Jolly LOND-205. Fold lines; offsetting at right. [6] £171 $325

A PLAN OF THE STRAITS OF ST. MARY, AND MICHILIMAKINAC, TO SHEW THE SITUATION & IMPORTANCE OF THE TWO WESTERNMOST SETTLEMENTS OF CANADA FOR THE FUR TRADE. [1761] 24x33cm. (9½x13") Jolly LOND-197. Minor repair. [15] £129 $245

LOUISIANA, AS FORMERLY CLAIMED BY FRANCE, NOW CONTAINING PART OF BRITISH AMERICA TO THE EAST & SPANISH AMERICA TO THE WEST OF THE MISSISSIPI. FROM THE BEST AUTHORITIES BY T. KITCHIN GEOGR. [1765] 18x23cm. (7x9") Jolly LOND-245. Col. [15] £145 $275

[same title, date, dimensions] Outline color. Excellent. [38] £118 $225

NOVA SCOTIA, DRAWN FROM SURVEYS BY T KITCHIN GR. [1749] 11x17cm. (4x6½") Jolly LOND-45. Cut close to border; o/w fine. [10] £26 $50

[same title, date, dimensions] Color. [15] £39 $75

PLAN OF NEW ORLEANS THE CAPITAL OF LOUISIANA. [1761] 17x23cm. (6½x9") Jolly LOND-199. Marginal repairs; good. [28] £131 $250

LONDON PRINTING AND PUBLISHING

UNITED STATES [c. 1860] 25x43cm. (10½x17") Civil War state alignments color coded. Traces of original folds; rice paper backing; good. [30] £129 $245

LONGWORTH, D.

PLAN OF THE CITY OF NEW YORK. [1804 / 1807] 38x53cm. (15x21") Third state. Backed on linen with original ribbon. Tears repaired. [1] £946 $1800

LOOTSMAN *Try Jacobsz*

LOPEZ

AMERICA SEPTENTRIONAL [1792] 18x32cm. (7x12½") Orig wash & outline col. VF. [10] £102 $195

CARTA DE LA ISLA DE SAN CHRISTOVAL REDUCIDA Y GRAVADA POR D. JUAN LOPEZ, PENSIONISTA DE S.M. [1780] 37x39cm. (14½x15½") Color. Minor repair. [15] £255 $485

ESTADOS UNIDOS D'AMERICA, TERRA NOVA, CANADA, LUIZIANA E FLORIDA [1792] 24x21cm. (9½x8½") Wash & outline color. Fine. [10] £102 $195

LORRAIN

AMERIQUE SEPTENTRIONALE [c. 1827] 28x38cm. (11x15") Outline color. [26] £42 $80

LOTTER

A MAP OF THE MOST INHABITED PART OF NEW ENGLAND, CONTAINING THE PROVINCES OF MASSACHUSETS BAY AND NEW HAMPSHIRE, WITH THE COLONIES OF CONNECTICUT AND RHODE ISLAND, DIVIDED INTO COUNTIES AND TOWNSHIPS... [1755-1776] 102x97cm. (40x38") German edition of Jefferys. Full orig color. Repairs on verso. Very good. [2] £1025 $1950

A MAP OF THE PROVINCES OF NEW-YORK AND NEW-JERSEY, WITH A PART OF PENNSYLVANIA AND THE PROVINCE OF QUEBEC. FROM THE TOPOGRAPHICAL OBSERVATIONS OF C.J. SAUTHIER [1777] 38x57cm. (15x22") Two sheets; dimensions for each. Original color. Fine. [38] £946 $1800

A PLAN OF THE CITY AND ENVIRONS OF PHILADELPHIA [1777] 58x46cm. (23½x18") Original color. An area rubbed; o/w very good. [21] £1051 $2000

AFRICA ... [c. 1760] 46x58cm. (17½x23") After de L'Isle. Original color. Light hand underlining of names. [31] £236 $450

AFRICAE PARS MERIDIONALIS CUM PROMONTORIO BONAE SPEI... [1778] 46x56cm. (18x22") Original color. Surface smudges; few old ink underlines. [31] £236 $450

AMERICA MERIDIONALIS CONCINNATA JUXTA OBSERVATIONES ... REGALIS SCIENTIARUM ... [1772] 46x57cm. (18x22½") Color. [15] £171 $325

AMERICA SEPTENTRIONALIS, CONCINNATA JUXTA OBSERVATIONES ... [c. 1760] 18x23cm. (7x9") Color. [15] £328 $625

CARTE DE L'OCEAN PACIFIQUE AU NORD DE L'EQUATEUR, ET DES COTES QUI LE BORNENT DES DEUX COTES: D'APRES LES DERNIERES DECOUVERTES FAITES PAR LES ESPAGNOLS, LES RUSSES ET LES ANGLOIS, JUSQU'EN 1780. PUBLIEE PAR TOBIE CONRAD LOTTER AUGSBOURG [1781] 46x51cm. (18½x20") Show Cook's 3rd voyage. Orig wash col.. Excellent. [2] £893 $1700

CARTE NOUVELLE DE L'AMERIQUE ANGLOISE CONTENANT TOUT CE QUE LES ANGLOIS POSSEDENT SUR LE CONTINENT DE L'AMERIQUE SEPTENTRIONALE SAVIOR LE CANADA, LA NOUVELLE ECOSSE OU ACADIE, LES TREIZE PROVINCES UNIES... [c. 1776] 60x50cm. (23½x19½") Full color. [15] £339 $645

[same title] [1778] 60x49cm. (23½x19½") Original color. Excellent. [22] £394 $750

MAPPE MONDE OU CARTE GENERALE DE L'UNIVERS ... [1782] 49x92cm. (19x36½") Original color. Some small surface marks. [31] £946 $1800

REGNUM HIBERNIA ... [c.1740] 58x48cm. (22½x19½") Original color. Excellent. [21] £355 $675

TABULA NOVISSIMA ACCURATISSIMA REGNORUM ANGLIAE, SCOTIAE HIBERNIAE [c. 1770] 56x49cm. (22x19½") Color. Very good. [23] £250 $476

LOTTERY MAGAZINE

A DRAUGHT OF THE HARBOUR OF HALIFAX IN NOVA SCOTIA BY AN OFFICER ON BOARD THE RAINBOW SR. GEO. COLLIER. [1777] 17x23cm. (7x9") Jolly LOT-4. Fine. [10] £202 $385

LUCAS

BARBADOES [1823] 28x24cm. (11x9½") Original color. Repaired margin tear. [31] £68 $130

CONNECTICUT [1823] 25x30cm. (9½x12") Broad outline color. Immaculate. [12] £97 $185

CUBA [1823] 30x44cm. (11½x17½") Original color. Very good. [31] £81 $155

DELAWARE [1816] 28x20cm. (11x8") Outline color. [6] £155 $295

DOMINICA [1823] 30x22cm. (11½x8½") Original color. Light spotting in margin. [31] £39 $75

FLORIDA [1823] 30x25cm. (11½x9½") Wide outline color. Fine. [12] £150 $285

GEORGIA [1823] 30x23cm. (11½x9") Wide outline col. Two trivial spots; else fine. [12] £131 $250

GRENADA [1823] 30x23cm. (12x9") Original color. Very good. [31] £58 $110

HAYTI OR SAINT DOMINGO [1823] 48x30cm. (19x12") Original color. Very good. [31] £68 $130

ILLINOIS [1823] 30x23cm. (12x9") Wide outline color. Fine. [12] £171 $325

JAMAICA [1823] 23x31cm. (9x12") Original color. Very good. [31] £66 $125

MARTINICO [1823] 24x31cm. (9½x12½") Orig color. Very good. [31] £66 $125

MARYLAND [1816] 20x28cm. (8x11") Drawn by S. Lewis; H.S. Tanner, sc. Outline col. [6] £155 $295

MARYLAND [1823] 28x50cm. (11x19½") Wide outline color. Light, even time-toning; centerfold end repaired; else excellent. [12] £184 $350

NEW YORK [1816] 20x28cm. (8x11") By S. Lewis; H.S. Tanner, sc. Outline color. [6] £155 $295

NTH CAROLINA [1823] 28x48cm. (11x19") Wide outline color. Slight offsetting; scattered light spots & foxing; o/w/ excellent. [12] £171 $325

ST. CHRISTOPHERS [1823] 22x31cm. (8½x12") Original color. Very good. [31] £66 $125

TENNESSEE [1823] 28x46cm. (11x18") Wide outline color. Repaired lower margin tears; some light offsetting. [12] £197 $375

TOBAGO [1823] 25x29cm. (10x11½") Original color. Very good. [31] £58 $110

TRINIDAD [1823] 24x29cm. (9½x11½") Original color. Light spotting in margin. [31] £50 $95

LUFFMAN

CHARLESTON HARBOUR ... ONE OF THE MOST COMMODIOUS PORTS IN N. AMERICA [1801] 18x13cm. (6½x5") [15] £39 $75

LUMSDEN

NORTH AMERICA [1755] 18x23cm. (7x8½") Color. [15] £58 $110

MacKENZIE

PART OF LONG ISLAND FROM SOUTH-UIST TO HARRIS... [1775] 107x104cm. (42x41") Browning, especially at centerfold; fold tears repaired without loss. [11] £70 $133

THE LEWIS, OR NORTH PART OF LONG ISLAND; ... [1775] 86x104cm. (33½x40½") Crease lines; fold tears and mostly marginal worming repaired. [11] £85 $162

THE NORTH-WEST COAST OF SCOTLAND, FROM RUREA IN ROSS SHIRE, TO CAPE WRATH IN STRATHNAVER ... [1776] 104x97cm. (40½x38") Brown spotting, one 8" long mark; repaired fold splits. [11] £70 $133

THE SOUTH COAST OF CARDIGAN BAY ... [1775] 51x142cm. (19½x56") Strumble Head to Borth. By Murdoch Mackenzie, Sr. Damp-marking on fold. [11] £110 $209

THE SOUTH PART OF LONG-ISLAND, FROM BARA HEAD TO BENBECULA I; ... [1775] 74x107cm. (28½x41½") Brown marks; repaired worming and fold splits. [11] £75 $143

THE SOUTH-WEST COAST OF WALES FROM TENBY TO CARDIGAN ... [1775] 74x104cm. (29x40½") Damp-marking at fold. [11] £110 $209

THE WEST COAST OF SCOTLAND FROM ARDNAMURCHAN TO THE ISLAND SKY ... [1776] 107x102cm. (41½x39½") Repaired fold tears; light damp-marking near centerfold. [11] £90 $171

MacKINLAY

MACKINLAY'S MAP OF THE PROVINCE OF NOVA SCOTIA, INCLUDING THE ISLAND OF CAPE BRETON [n.d.] 77x97cm. (30½x38") Linen-backed folding map in covers. Color. Backstrip torn and loose. Slight age-darkening and foxing; very good. [19] £71 $135

MAGINI *Try Ptolemy (1596-1621, Magini)*

MAIRE, N.

CARTE TOPOGRAPHIQUE DES ENVIRONS DE PARIS [1837] 64x91cm. (25x36") Linen-backed folding map. Very good+. [19] £250 $475

MALBY, T.

MALBY'S TERRESTRIAL GLOBE, ... MANUFACTURED AND PUBLISHED UNDER THE SUPERINTENDANCE OF THE SOCIETY FOR THE DIFFUSION OF USEFUL KNOWLEDGE, ... [1860] Diameter: 30 cm. (12") On original wooden stand with brass meridian and fittings. Original color. Minor chipping repaired; some discoloration; repairs to horizon ring. [22] £2627 $5000

MALLET

[MEDITERRANEAN SEA] [1685] 15x10cm. (5½x4") In three parts. [17] £47 $90

ABISSINIE [1683] 14x10cm. (5½x4") [10] £26 $50

ANCIEN CONTINENT [1683] 14x10cm. (5½x4") [10] £26 $50

ANCIEN CONTINENT AVEC PLUSIEURS ISLES [1683] 14x10cm. (5½x4") [10] £26 $50

ANCIEN CONTINENT AVEC PLUSIEURS ISLES, OCEANS ET MERS [1683] 14x10cm. (5½x4") [10] £26 $50

ANCIEN CONTINENT AVEC PLUSIEURS ISLES, OCEANS, MERS, GOLFES [1683] 14x10cm. (5½x4") [10] £26 $50
ANCIENNE REGION DES SINES [1683] 15x11cm. (6x4") [10] £16 $30
ASIE ANCIENNE [1683] 15x11cm. (6x4") [10] £26 $50
ASIE MINEURS [1683] 15x10cm. (6x4") [10] £13 $25
ASIE MODERNE [1683] 15x11cm. (6x4") [10] £18 $35
BRESIL [1683] 15x10cm. (5½x4") [10] £24 $45
CARTE GENERAL [Eastern Hemisphere] [1685] 15x10cm. (5½x4") Color. VG. [17] £53 $100
CONGO [1683] 14x10cm. (5½x4") Small oil stain. [10] £18 $35
CONTINENT ARCTIQUE [1683] 15x11cm. (6x4") [10] £39 $75
COSTAS D'ABEX D'AIAN ET DE ZANGUEBAR [1683] 15x10cm. (5½x4") [10] £18 $35
EMPIRE DES ABYSSINS [1683] 15x10cm. (5½x4") [10] £13 $25
EMPIRE DES ABYSSINS COMME IE EST PRESENTEMENT [1683] 14x10cm. (5½x4") [10] £13 $25
FLORIDE [1683] 15x13cm. (6x4½") Color. [15] £66 $125
GEORGIE, ARMENIE &C. [1683] 14x10cm. (5½x4") [10] £16 $30
GLOBE TERRESTRE [1685] 14x10cm. (5½x4") Globe on design device in town view. Color. [17] £42 $80
GUINEE [1683] 14x10cm. (5½x4") [10] £18 $35
ILE BOURBON [1683] 14x10cm. (5½x4") (Reunion Island) [10] £16 $30
INDE [1683] 14x10cm. (5½x4") [10] £13 $25
INDE ANCIENNE A L'OCCIDENT DU GANGE [1683] 15x10cm. (6x4") [10] £16 $30
INDE ANCIENNE A L'ORIENT DU GANGE [1683] 15x10cm. (6x4") [10] £16 $30
IS. DE CUBA ET DE JAMAICA [1683] 17x10cm. (6½x4") Bird's eye map. Color. [15] £47 $90
ISLE DE CAYENNE [1683] 14x10cm. (5½x4") Full color. [36] £42 $80
ISLE DE TERRE NEUVE [1683] 15x10cm. (6x4") Color. [15] £53 $100
ISLES DE SALOMON [1683] 15x10cm. (6x4") [10] £39 $75
ISLES DES LARRONS [1683] 15x10cm. (6x4") [10] £26 $50
[same title, date, dimensions] Color. [15] £26 $50
LA CHINE [1684] 15x10cm. (6x4") [10] £34 $65
MEXIQUE OU NOUVELLE ESPAGNE [1683] 15x10cm. (5½x4") Good. [30] £97 $185
NATOLIE [1683] 14x10cm. (5½x4") [10] £18 $35
NOUVEAU CONTINENT [c. 1683] 20x13cm. (8x5½") Insular California. Full color. [3] £158 $300
NOUVEAU CONTINENT AVEC PLUSIEURS ISLES ET MERS [c. 1687] 14x10cm. (5½x4") German edition. Later full color. [20] £158 $300
NOUVEAU CONTINENT OU AMERIQUE [1683] 15x10cm. (6x4") Insular California. [15] £63 $120
NOUVEAU MEXIQUE ET CALIFORNIE [1683] 14x10cm. (5½x4") [10] £171 $325
NOUVELLE GUINEE ET CARPENTARIE [1683] 15x11cm. (5½x4½") [10] £26 $50
NUBIE [1683] 15x10cm. (5½x4") [10] £16 $30
PARIS [c. 1685] 16x12cm. (6x4½") View. Full col. Old tape stain upper margin; o/w fine. [37] £34 $65
PARTIE DE LA TERRE FERME DE L'INDE OU L'EMPIRE DU MOGOL [1683] 14x10cm. (5½x4") [10] £18 $35
PARTIE ORIENTALE DE LA TERRE FIRME DE L'INDE MODERNE [1683] 15x10cm. (6x4") [10] £13 $25
PAYS DES NEGRES [1683] 15x10cm. (5½x4") [10] £18 $35
PLANISPHERE DE TURQUET / PLANISPHERE DE BERTIUS / PLANISPHERE D'ARZAEL [1685] 14x10cm. (5½x4") Color. [17] £53 $100
PRESQU ISLE DE L'INDE A L'ORIENT DU GOLFE DE BENGALA [1683] 14x10cm. (5½x4") [10] £16 $30
PRESQU-ISLE DE L'INDE DECA LA GOLFE DE BENGAL [1683] 14x10cm. (5½x4") [10] £18 $35
QUEBEC [1683] 15x10cm. (6x4") Color. [15] £58 $110
SOURCE DU NIL [1683] 15x10cm. (6x4") [10] £18 $35
SYRIE ANCIENNE [1683] 15x10cm. (6x4") [10] £16 $30
SYRIE MODERNE [1683] 14x10cm. (5½x4") [10] £18 $35
TURQUIE EN ASIE [1683] 14x10cm. (5½x4") [10] £16 $30

MALTE-BRUN

AMERIQUE SEPTENTRIONALE [1838] 23x30cm. (8½x12") Color. [15] £45 $85

MANSELL, F.

AMERICA [c. 1842] 23x15cm. (8½x5½") Color. [15] £24 $45

MARIETTE

CARTE GENERALE DES INDES ORIENTALES ... [1650] 38x48cm. (15x18½") Original outline color. Slight foxing; else excellent. [22] £657 $1250

MARSH, W. S.

CONNECTICUT [1819] 18x25cm. (7x10") From *A Gazetteer of the States of Connecticut and Rhode-Island* [6] £102 $195

MARSHALL

A MAP OF PART OF RHODE ISLAND SHEWING THE POSITIONS OF THE AMERICAN AND BRITISH ARMIES AT THE SIEGE OF NEWPORT, AND THE SUBSEQUENT ACTION ON THE 29TH OF AUGUST 1778 [1807] 43x25cm. (17½x10") By S. Lewis. Color. [15] £71 $135

A PLAN OF THE NORTHERN PART OF NEW JERSEY, SHEWING THE POSITIONS OF THE AMERICAN AND BRITISH ARMIES AFTER CROSSING THE NORTH RIVER IN 1776 [1806] 40x25cm. (16x10") By Lewis. Color. [15] £71 $135

MARZOLLA

CARTE GENERALE DELL' OCEANIA [1865] 42x51cm. (16½x20") Orig outline col. [10] £42 $80

MESSICO E STATI DELL' AMERICA CENTRALE [1854] 43x61cm. (17½x24") Published at Naples. Original outline color. Faint water stain upper left; good. [30] £97 $185

MAST, CROWELL

MAP OF KENTUCKY AND TENNESSEE [1889] 25x33cm. (10x13") Color. [15] £11 $20

MEARES

CARTE DE LA COTE N.O. D'AMERIQUE ET DE LA COTE N.E. D'ASIE RECONNUES EN 1778 ET 1779. PAR LE CAPITAINE COOK ET PLUS PARTICULIEREMENT ENCORE EN 1788. ET 89. PAR LE CAPNE. J. MEARES [1794] 42x61cm. (16½x24") [10] £131 $250

MEIJER

WERELD KAART VOLGENS DE LAATSTE ONTOEKKING DOOR E. BOWEN UITGEGEVEN 1768 [1768] 15x28cm. (6x11") Hemispheres. Color. [15] £129 $245

MELISH

FALLS OF OHIO [1815] 15x10cm. (6x4") Very good. [26] £50 $95

MAP OF THE SEAT OF WAR IN NORTH AMERICA [1817] 41x56cm. (15½x21½") Outline color. On heavy paper, with some splits and pinholes; o/w excellent. [12] £236 $450

SKETCH OF THE ACTION ON THE HEIGHTS OF CHARLESTOWN JUNE 17TH 1775 [1824] 33x51cm. (13x20") Engraved by Kneass, Young & Co. after Chapman's drawing based on De Berniere's contemporary sketch. Centerfold repair; fine. [27] £342 $650

UNITED STATES OF AMERICA [1820] 43x53cm. (17x21") Original color. VG. [31] £447 $850

[same title] [1821] 43x56cm. (17x22") Full color. [3] £223 $425

MENTELLE

MAPPE-MONDE SUIVANT LA PROJECTION DES CARTES REDUITES OU L'ON A TRACE LES ROUTES DE MR. DE BOUGAINVILLE, ET LES DEUX DERNIERU VOYAGES DU CAPTAINE COOK [1797-1801] 36x46cm. (14x18") Outline & soft wash color. Excellent. [26] £137 $260

MENZIES

A NEW AND ACCURATE MAP OF NORTH AMERICA FROM THE BEST AUTHORITIES [1794] 28x33cm. (11½x13") Edinburgh: T. Brown. Color. [15] £76 $145

MERCATOR (Folio) *Try Hondius, Jansson*

[TITLE PAGE] ATLAS OU REPRESENTATION DU MONDE UNIVERSEL ... [1633] 38x23cm. (14½x9½") Henry Hondius. Orig color finished in gold. Small marginal repairs; good. [30] £307 $585

AFRICA EX MAGNA ORBIS TERRE DESCRIPTIONE GERARDI MERCATORIS DESUMPTA, STUDIO ET INDUSTRIA G.M. IUNIORIS [1619] 38x47cm. (15x18½") Color. [40] £690 $1314

ALGESEY. WIGHT VECTIS OLIM. GARNESEY. IARSAY. [1595] 33x43cm. (12½x17") Original color. Toned; good. [21] £289 $550

AMERICA MERIDIONALIS [c. 1630] 36x49cm. (14x19½") Color. [40] £759 $1445

AMERICA SIVE INDIA NOVA AD MAGNAE GERARDI MERCATORIS AVI UNIVERSALIS IMITATIONEM IN COMPENDIUM REDACTA. PER MICHAELEM MERCATOREM DUYSBURGENSEM [(1595) 1633] 37x47cm. (14½x18½") Original color. Old lower centerfold repair; light browning. [5] £2150 $4091

[same title] [1595+] 37x46cm. (14½x18") Full original color. Centerfold rubbed with slight loss; reinforcement to few oxidized areas; good. [21] £2049 $3900

[same title] [1595, 1606+] 37x46cm. (14½x18") Full color. Mint. [37] £2207 $4200

ANGLESEY [on sheet with] WIGHT VECTIS [and] GARNESAY [and] IARSAY [1619] 32x43cm. (12½x17") Color. [40] £242 $460

ANGLIA, SCOTIA ET HIBERNIA [c.1609, 1628] 32x40cm. (12½x15½") Color. VG. [23] £450 $856

ARGOW. IN HAC TABULA LUCERNA, VREN, SWYTZ, UNDERWALD, GLARONA PAGI [c. 1630] 36x47cm. (14x18½") Color. Two small tears restored. [40] £179 $342

ASIA EX MAGNA ORBIS TERRE DESCRIPTIONE GERARDI MERCATORIS DESUMPTA, STUDIO ET INDUSTRIA G.M. IUNIORIS [(1595) c. 1620] 37x47cm. (15x18½") Color. Small invisible centerfold repair; o/w fine. [5] £650 $1237

[same title] [1619] 38x47cm. (15x18½") Old color. Small rust spot. [40] £621 $1182

AUSTRIA ARCHIDUCATUS [1613] 33x48cm. (12½x19½") Amsterdam: Hondius. Original color. Very good. [31] £236 $450

BELGII [1613] 36x46cm. (14x18") Amsterdam: Hondius. Orig color. Very good. [31] £289 $550

BELGII INFERIORIS DESCRIPTIO EMENDATA CUM CIRCUMIACENTIUM REGIONU CONFINIJS [1619] 36x46cm. (14x18") Color. [40] £207 $394

CANDIA CUM INSULIS ALIQUOT CIRCA GRAECIAM [1633] 34x48cm. (13½x18½") Map of Corfu, Zante, Milo, Nicsia, Santorini, Scarpanto Amsterdam: Hondius. Full color. VG. [22] £315 $600

CHAMPAGNE COMITATUS CAMPANIA [1595] 38x51cm. (15x19½") Original color. Lightly browned. [21] £197 $375

CHINA [1606 (1623)] 36x46cm. (13½x18") Amsterdam: Hondius. Full color. Small margins; repaired centerfold split; good+. [34] £499 $950

DANIAE REGNU [1619] 38x44cm. (15x17½") Color. [40] £242 $460

EMDEN & OLDENBORCH COMIT. [1619] 34x43cm. (13½x16½") Color. [40] £483 $919

FIONIA [1619] 36x40cm. (14x15½") Color. [40] £155 $296

HABES HIC NOVAM & ACCURATISSIMAM DESCRIPTIONEM TRACTUS ILLIUS FLANDRIAE ... [1619] 37x52cm. (14½x20½") By Kaerius. Color. [40] £204 $387

HOLSATIA DUCATUS [1619] 35x48cm. (14x19") Color. [40] £269 $512

HUNGARIA [1613] 37x44cm. (14½x17½") Amsterdam: Hondius. Orig color. VG. [31] £236 $450

[same title] [1619] 37x45cm. (14½x17½") Color. [40] £166 $315

IAPONIA [1606] 35x45cm. (13½x17½") Original color. Excellent. [38] £1944 $3700

[same title] [1606+] 34x44cm. (13½x17½") Full orig color. One stain; else VG. [22] £1576 $3000

INS. CEILAN [1613] 36x51cm. (13½x19½") Amsterdam: Hondius. Orig color. VG. [31] £368 $700

INS. CEILAN QUAE INCOLIS TENARISIN DICITUR [1619] 35x50cm. (13½x19½") Col. [40] £311 $591

IUTIA SEPTENTRIONALIS [1619] 29x40cm. (11½x15½") Color. [40] £131 $250

L'ISLE DE FRANCE. PARISIESIS AGRI DESCRIPTIO [c. 1630] 34x47cm. (13x18½") Color. [40] £135 $256

LA II TABLE D'IRLANDE ... ULTONIE, CONNACIE MEDIE, ET PARTIE DE LAGENIE [1619] 34x47cm. (13½x18½") Color. [40] £86 $164

LA SECONDE TABLE D'ECOSSE [c.1630] 35x45cm. (14x17½") Color. Centerfold repaired. [40] £145 $276

LEODIENSIS DIOECESIS TYPUS [1619] 34x49cm. (13x19") Color. [40] £190 $361

LITHUANIA [1613] 37x44cm. (14½x17") Amsterdam: Hondius. Original color. VG. [31] £197 $375

MACEDONIA EPIRUS ET ACHAIA [1589 (1623)] 36x43cm. (14x17") Outline col. Fine. [34] £131 $250

ORBIS TERRAE COMPENDIOSA DESCRIPTIO QUAM EX MAGNA UNIVERSALI GERARDI MERCATORIS ... [1587 (1623)] 29x52cm. (11x20½") Shirley 157. Full original color. Lower margin repair outside engraved area; o/w fine. [37] £2470 $4700

[same title] [1587 (1630)] 29x52cm. (11½x20½") Shirley 157. Full color. Minor stains in margin; else fine. [34] £2627 $5000

ORBIS TERRAE COMPENDIOSA DESCRIPTIO QUAM EX MAGNA UNIVERSALI GERARDI MERCATORIS ... [1595] 30x52cm. (11½x20½") First double hemisphere world map in an atlas. Shirley 157. Text below. Old color. Fold and two tears repaired. [40] £2761 $5254

PECHELI, XANSI, XANTUNG, HONAN, NANKING, IN PLAGA REGNI SINENSIS INTER SEPTENTRIONEM AC ORIENTEM CECIAM VERSUS SITAE PROVINCIAE [1658] 47x52cm. (18½x20½") Original color. Invisible mended slit; o/w excellent. [37] £250 $475

POLONIA ET SILESIA [1613] 34x46cm. (13½x18") Original color. Very good. [31] £250 $475

[same title] [1619] 35x46cm. (13½x18") Color. [40] £173 $328

QUERCY CADURCIUM [1619] 38x50cm. (15x19½") Color. [40] £76 $144

SALZBURG ARCHIEPISCOPATUS CUM DUCATU CARINTHIAE [1619] 34x48cm. (13½x19") Color. [40] £238 $453

SCLAVONIA, CROATIA, BOSNIA CUM DALMATIAE PARTE [1613] 36x46cm. (14x18½") Amsterdam: Hondius. Original color. Very good. [31] £184 $350

SCOTIA REGNUM [1619] 35x41cm. (14x16") Color. [40] £207 $394

SEPTENTRIONALIUM TERRARUM DESCRIPTIO. PER GERARDUM MERCATOREM CUM PRIVILEGIO [1595] 37x40cm. (14½x15½") Old col. Short lower fold tear restored. [40] £828 $1576

[same title] [(1595) 1633] 37x40cm. (14½x15½") Original color. Some browning; fine. [5] £685 $1304

[same title] [1602-1623] 41x36cm. (15½x14") Original color. Excellent. [21] £1156 $2200

SUCHUEN, ET XENSI, PROVINCIAE SEU PRAEFECTURAE REGNI SINENSIS. VERSUS CAURUM ID EST INTER OCCIDENTEM ET SEPTENTRIONEM SITAE [1658] 47x53cm. (18½x20½") Original color. Excellent. [37] £250 $475

TAURICA CHERSONESUS. NOSTRA AETATE PRZECOPSCA ET GAZARA DICTUR [c. 1630] 32x41cm. (12½x16") Color. [40] £131 $250

THE SECOND MAP OF IRELAND [and] THE THIRD MAP OF IRELAND [1636] 36x48cm. (13½x18½") Complementary map pair of Northern and Southern Ireland. English edition. Dimensions for each map. Full color. Excellent. [35] £236 $450

TRIER & LUTZENBURG [c.1620] 37x47cm. (14½x18½") Col. Waterstain in margin. [40] £311 $591

ULTONIAE ORIENTALIS PARS. [1619] 35x38cm. (14x15") Color. [40] £86 $164

VIRGINIAE ITEM ET FLORIDAE AMERICAE PROVINCIARUM, NOVA DESCRIPTIO [1606] 34x49cm. (13½x19") By Hondius. Some light offsetting; excellent. [1] £946 $1800

[same title] [1606 (1613)] 34x49cm. (13½x19") Color. Age toned; o/w VG. [34] £867 $1650

[same title] [c. 1635] 33x47cm. (13x18½") Old color. Slight waterstain lower area. [16] £587 $1116

MERCATOR (Small) *Try Purchas, Ptolemy (1578-1730)*

AMERICAE DESCRIPTIO [1628] 15x20cm. (6x8") Amsterdam: Jansson. Outline & wash col. [36] £223 $425

COMITATUS FLANDRIA [1628] 13x18cm. (5x7") Color. [36] £37 $70

CUBA INSUL / HISPANIOLA / HAVANA PORTUS / I.JAMAICA / I.S. IOANNIS / I.MARGARETA [1613] 15x18cm. (5½x7") 6 map on one sheet. French edition. Original color. [12] £92 $175

GRAECIA [c. 1610] 14x18cm. (5½x7") Narrow top margin; o/w very good. [18] £76 $145

HONDIUS HIS MAP OF FLORIDA - VIRGINIA ET FLORIDA [1635] 15x18cm. (6x7½") St. Augustine to Chesapeake. Color. [15] £129 $245

IAPONIA [1628] 14x19cm. (5½x7½") [36] £131 $250

INSULA CEILAN [1628] 15x18cm. (5½x7") Color. [36] £53 $100

INSULAE CUBA HISPANIOLA &C. [1628] 15x18cm. (6x7") Amsterdam: Jansson. Outline & wash color. [36] £79 $150

LITHUANIA [1628] 14x20cm. (5½x8") Outline & wash color. [36] £47 $90

MACEDONIA, EPIR. ET ACHAIA [c. 1610] 14x17cm. (5½x7") Very good. [18] £50 $95

NOVA HELVETIA TABULA [1628] 15x20cm. (5½x7½") Color. [36] £47 $90

NOVA VIRGINIAE TABULA [1630] 14x19cm. (5½x7½") By Pieter van den Keere; from French edition of Atlas Minor. Modern color. Fine. [12] £171 $325

[same title, date] 18x25cm. (7x10") Engraved by van den Keere. Color. Excellent. [35] £210 $400

PERIGRINATIO ISRAILITARU IN DESERT [1608] 15x18cm. (6x7½") [35] £63 $120

POLUS ARCTICUS CUM VICINIS REGIONIBUS [1635] 10x20cm. (4½x7½") Hondius. Col. [15] £123 $235

SEPTENTRIONALIUM TERRARUM DESCRIPTIO [1628] 15x20cm. (5½x8") Amsterdam: Jansson. Outline & wash color. [36] £105 $200

SICILIAE REGNUM [1628] 15x20cm. (5½x7½") Color. [36] £45 $85

TYPUS ORBIS TERRARUM [1628] 15x21cm. (6x8") Double hemisphere. Amsterdam: Jansson; A. Goos, sc. Insular California. Color. [36] £210 $400

MERIAN

MAGNA BRITANNIAE ET HIBERNIAE TABULA [c. 1638] 26x35cm. (10x14") VG. [23] £250 $476

NOVA TOTIUS TERRARUM ORBIS GEOGRAPHICA AC HYDROGRAPHICA TABULA [1646] 26x36cm. (10x14") Color. Fine. [15] £552 $1050

MERULA

TOTIUS ORBIS COGNITI UNIVERSALIS DESCRIPTIO [1605] 30x50cm. (11½x19½") Engraved by Van Doetecum. Shirley 254. Printer's wrinkle; ¼" burn mark & pin hole; o/w VG. [31] £1366 $2600

METELLUS

REGNUM CHINAE [c.1596] 15x21cm. (6x8½") With Botero. Published in Cologne. Fine. [5] £300 $571

MEYER

ALBANY IN NEW-YORK - VEREINIGTE STAATEN [1833] 10x16cm. (4x6") City viewed in distance. From *Meyer's Universum.* [16] £24 $46

ALBANY ON THE HUDSON [1859] (no dims.) General view from *Meyer's Universum.* [16] £48 $92

ALTON AM MISSISSIPPI (IN ILLINOIS) [1857] 11x16cm. (4½x6½") General view. [16] £48 $92

BALTIMORE [1859] 10x15cm. (4x6") Overall view from *Meyer's Universum.* [16] £90 $171

BAY OF NEWYORK FROM HOBOKEN [1857] 11x17cm. (4½x6½") View. [16] £97 $184

BUENOS AYRES [1847] View from river bank. From *Meyer's Universum.* [16] £62 $118

BURLINGTON AM MISSISSIPPI [1860] 11x16cm. (4½x6") View. [16] £35 $66

CHIHUAHUA IN NEW-MEXICO [1857] 11x16cm. (4½x6") Overall view. [16] £24 $46

DAVENPORT (IOWA) [1860] 11x16cm. (4x6") Overall view. [16] £35 $66

HAVANNAH [1841] 10x15cm. (4x6") Harbor view from *Meyer's Universum.* [16] £62 $118

JEFFERSON CITY (MISSOURI RIVER) [1852] 11x16cm. (4x6") View. [16] £35 $66

KARTE VON WISCONSIN NACH DEN NEUESTEN HULFSMITTEIN GEZEICHNET [1852] 38x33cm. (15x12½") By J. Graessl. Color. [15] £71 $135

LIMA [1841] 10x15cm. (4x6") View from river. From *Meyer's Universum.* [16] £35 $66

LOUISVILLE [1857] 10x16cm. (3½x6½") Main street view from *Meyer's Universum.* [16] £48 $92

MEXICO [1857] 11x16cm. (4½x6") View of cathedral. From *Meyer's Universum.* [16] £28 $53

MONTEREY [1857] 11x17cm. (4½x6½") General view from *Meyer's Universum.* [16] £48 $92

NEUESTE KARTE VOM NORD POL [1842] 30x30cm. (12x12") Color. [15] £34 $65

NEUESTE KARTE VON ARKANSAS MIT SEINEN CANAELEN STRASSEN & ENTFERNUNGEN DE HAUPTPUNKTE [1851] 38x30cm. (15x12") 47 counties. Color. [15] £71 $135

NEUESTE KARTE VON ILLINOIS MIT SEINEM STRASSEN ENTFEMUNG DER HAUPTPUNKTE [1846] 38x30cm. (15x12") Color. [15] £79 $150

NEUESTE KARTE VON MISSOURI NACH DEN BESTEN QUELLEN VERBESSERT [1845] 38x30cm. (15x12") 42 counties. Color. [15] £71 $135

NEUESTE KARTE VON NEW JERSEY ... [1846] 37x30cm. (14½x12") Outline col. Fine. [12] £66 $125

NEUESTE KARTE VON PENNSYLVANIA MIT SEINEN CANAELEN, EISENBAHNEN &C. [1845] 30x38cm. (12x14½") Color. [15] £66 $125

NEUESTE KARTE VON SUD CAROLINA [1845] 31x37cm. (12x14½") Color. [15] £66 $125

NEW-ORLEANS [1847] 10x15cm. (3½x5½") General view from the *Universum.* [16] £90 $171

NEW-YORK [1835] 10x16cm. (3½x6") View after Dupre from the *Universum.* [16] £166 $315

NEW YORK-BAY VON STATEN-ISLAND AUS GESEHEN [1857] 11x16cm. (4½x6½") View. [16] £131 $250

NIAGARA FALL (ALLEGEMEINE ANSICHT VOM CLIFTON HOUSE) [1860] 11x16cm. (4x6") View from *Meyer's Universum.* [16] £21 $39

NIAGARA FALL (HORSESHOE-FALL) [1860] 11x16cm. (4x6") View. [16] £21 $39

NORD-AMERICANISCHE FREISTAATEN [1845] 30x38cm. (12x14½") By C. Radefeld. Texas as a Republic. Color. [15] £87 $165

PANAMA [1852] 11x16cm. (4x6") City view from *Meyer's Universum.* [16] £35 $66

QUEBECK IN CANADA [1838] 11x17cm. (4x6½") Overall view from *Meyer's Universum.* [16] £24 $46

RIO JANEIRO [c. 1842] 10x15cm. (4x6") View from sea. From *Meyer's Universum.* [16] £35 $66

SACRAMENTO-CITY IN CALIFORNIEN [1852] 11x16cm. (4x6") Overall view. [16] £48 $92

SAN FRANCISCO [1850] 11x16cm. (4½x6½") View of crowded harbor. [16] £90 $171
SAN JUAN DE NICARAGUA [1852] 11x16cm. (4½x6") Overall view. [16] £41 $79
SAN LOUIS AM MISSISSIPPI [1857] 11x16cm. (4x6½") Overall view. [16] £76 $144
ST. ANTONIO (TEXAS) [1857] 11x16cm. (4½x6") Overall view. [16] £76 $144
STAATEN AM ATLANTISHCEN OCEAN [1868] 34x43cm. (13x17") From *Meyer's Hand-Atlas*. Outline color. [16] £41 $79

MIALHE

VISTA DE LA HABANA, PARTE DE ESTRAMURAS TOMADO DESDE LA ENTRADA DEL PUERTO [c. 1870] 23x28cm. (9x11") Havana: Marquier, lith. Bird's eye view. Aquatint. [15] £66 $125

MICHAULT

COSTES ET RIVIERES DE VIRGINIE, DE MARILAND ET DE NOUVELLE ANGLETERRE [1684] 19x25cm. (7½x9½") Excellent. [38] £315 $600

MIDDLETON

A PERSPECTIVE VIEW OF THE CITY OF DUBLIN FROM PHOENIX PARK [c. 1778] 25x26cm. (10x10") Very good. [24] £65 $124
THE CITY OF MALACCA IN THE EAST INDIES [1779] 16x27cm. (6x10½") [10] £39 $75

MILNE

MILNE'S PICTORIAL PLAN OF EDINBURGH [1845] 45x56cm. (17½x22") Linen-backed folding plan with self-backs in original slipcase with gold embossed picture. Color. Very good. [19] £131 $250

MITCHELL, JOHN *Try Le Rouge*

A MAP OF THE BRITISH AND FRENCH DOMINIONS IN NORTH AMERICA ... [1755] 69x48cm. (26½x19") Top center sheet; region of the four western Great Lakes. Col. Minor repair. [15] £460 $875

MITCHELL, S.A.

MAP OF MAINE, NEW HAMPSHIRE AND VERMONT [1834] 56x66cm. (22x26") Pocket map folded into original case. Full color. Partially rebacked. [3] £92 $175
MAP OF THE STATE OF TEXAS [1846] 28x20cm. (10½x8") From *School and Family Geography* with Mexican War notes. Original color. Very light spotting. [31] £92 $175
MITCHELL'S TRAVELERS GUIDE THROUGH THE UNITED STATES [1832] 44x54cm. (17x21") Pocket map on bank note paper in gold-lettered calf cover. Outline color. Age-toned; slight offsetting; cover corners rubbed/gnawed affecting index, not map; o/w very good. [7] £381 $725
[same title] [1837] 46x51cm. (18x20") Phila: Mitchell and Hinman. Pocket map in case, with 78 text pages. Noted as found on civil War battlefield. Full color. Map excellent; case VG. [3] £223 $425
No. 10. MITCHELL'S SERIES OF OUTLINE MAPS FOR THE USE OF ACADEMIES AND SCHOOLS [VIRGINIA & MARYLAND] [1841] 58x69cm. (23x27") Hartford: Mather, Case, Tiffany & Burnham. On linen. Fair condition: rough edges, browned. [6] £105 $200

MITCHELL, S.A. (Atlas Maps 1859 & Earlier)
Try DeSilver & Thomas, Cowperthwait

A NEW MAP OF ALABAMA WITH ITS ROADS AND DISTANCES FROM PLACE TO PLACE ALONG THE STEAMBOAT ROUTES [1847] 36x28cm. (14x11") Bright color. [36] £47 $90
[same title] [1850] 41x33cm. (16x13") Full color. Very good. [26] £37 $70
A NEW MAP OF ARKANSAS WITH ITS CANALS, ROADS AND DISTANCES [1848] 38x31cm. (15x12") 48 counties. Color. [15] £47 $90
[same title] [1850] 41x33cm. (16x13") Full color. [26] £32 $60
A NEW MAP OF GEORGIA WITH ITS ROADS AND DISTANCES [1847] 36x30cm. (14x11½") [36] £45 $85
[same title] [1850] 41x33cm. (16x13") Full color. Very good. [26] £37 $70
A NEW MAP OF ILLINOIS WITH ITS PROPOSED CANALS, ROADS AND DISTANCES FROM PLACE TO PLACE ALONG THE STEAMBOAT ROUTES [1847] 41x33cm. (16x13") Full color. [35] £42 $80
A NEW MAP OF INDIANA WITH ITS ROADS & DISTANCES [1847] 36x29cm. (14x11½") Color. [12] £45 $85
[same title] [1848] 36x29cm. (14x11½") With transient Richardville Co. [15] £58 $110
[same title] [1850] 41x33cm. (16x13") Full color. [26] £32 $60

A NEW MAP OF KENTUCKY WITH ITS ROADS AND DISTANCES FROM PLACE TO PLACE ALONG THE STAGE AND STEAMBOAT ROUTES [1846] 29x36cm. (11½x14") Phila: H. Burroughs. Color. [15] £76 $145

[same title] [1850] 33x41cm. (13x16") Full color. [26] £37 $70

A NEW MAP OF LOUISIANA [1850] 33x41cm. (13x16") Full color. [26] £37 $70

A NEW MAP OF MAINE [1850] 41x33cm. (16x13") Full color. [26] £37 $70

A NEW MAP OF MARYLAND AND DELAWARE [1850] 33x41cm. (13x16") Full col. VG. [26] £37 $70

A NEW MAP OF MICHIGAN WITH ITS CANALS, ROADS, AND DISTANCES [1847] 38x30cm. (15x12") Color. [15] £66 $125

[same title] [1850] 41x33cm. (16x13") Full color. [26] £42 $80

A NEW MAP OF MISSISSIPPI [1850] 41x33cm. (16x13") Full color. [26] £37 $70

A NEW MAP OF NTH. CAROLINA [1850] 33x41cm. (13x16") Full color. [26] £39 $75

A NEW MAP OF PENNSYLVANIA WITH ITS CANALS, RAILROADS, &C. [1848] 30x36cm. (11½x14½") Color. [15] £47 $90

A NEW MAP OF SOUTH CAROLINA [1850] 33x41cm. (13x16") Full color. [26] £37 $70

A NEW MAP OF TENNESSEE WITH ITS ROADS AND DISTANCES FROM PLACE TO PLACE ALONG THE STAGE AND STEAMBOAT ROUTES [1847] 29x39cm. (11½x15½") 2nd state of 1846 edition. Color. [15] £66 $125

[same title]) [1850] 33x41cm. (13x16") Full color. [26] £37 $70

CITY OF NEW YORK [1850] 41x33cm. (16x13") Full color. [26] £39 $75

CITY OF WASHINGTON [1850] 33x41cm. (13x16") Full color. [26] £37 $70

CONNECTICUT [1848] 33x38cm. (12½x15") Color. [15] £47 $90

[same title] [1850] 33x41cm. (13x16") Full color. [26] £37 $70

FLORIDA [1850] 41x33cm. (16x13") Full color. Very good. [26] £53 $100

IOWA [c. 1845] 41x33cm. (16x13") After Tanner; Carey & Hart, pub. Color. Light brown spots; else excellent. [12] £118 $225

[same title] [1847] 41x33cm. (16x13") Full color. [35] £58 $110

[same title] [1848] 41x33cm. (16x13") 31 counties. Color. [15] £71 $135

LENGTHS OF THE PRINCIPAL RIVERS IN THE WORLD ... [1846] 33x41cm. (13x16") And mountain heights. Full color. [3] £42 $80

MAP OF MISSOURI [1850] 41x33cm. (16x13") Full color. Very good. [26] £37 $70

MAP OF TEXAS FROM THE MOST RECENT AUTHORITIES [1850] 33x41cm. (13x16") Full color. Clean. [26] £189 $360

MAP OF THE STATE OF CALIFORNIA, THE TERRITORIES OF OREGON & UTAH, AND THE CHIEF PART OF NEW MEXICO. [1845 (1850)] 41x33cm. (15½x12½") Lacks publisher's name. Full color. Immaculate. [12] £158 $300

MASSACHUSETTS AND RHODE ISLAND [1850] 33x41cm. (13x16") Full color. VG. [26] £37 $70

OREGON AND UPPER CALIFORNIA [1847] 41x33cm. (15½x12½") (also dated 1845.) Full color. Immaculate. [12] £202 $385

[same title] [1847] 41x33cm. (16x13") Full bright color. Excellent. [26] £145 $275

OREGON, UPPER CALIFORNIA AND NEW MEXICO [1849] 41x33cm. (16½x13") H.N. Burroughs, 1845. Original wash color. Good. [29] £255 $485

[same title] [1850] 41x33cm. (16x13") Bright color. [26] £171 $325

PERU AND BOLIVIA [1847] 33x38cm. (12½x15") Color. [15] £24 $45

PHILADELPHIA [1848] 41x33cm. (15½x13") Color. [15] £47 $90

MITCHELL, S.A. (Atlas Maps 1860 & Later) *Try Bradley*

AFRICA. [1872] 20x28cm. (8½x11") Color. [15] £13 $25

CHICAGO [1872] 56x38cm. (22x14½") Color. [26] £37 $70

COLORADO [1878] 30x37cm. (12x15") Full color. Very good. [3] £47 $90

[same title] [1878] 30x38cm. (11½x15") Grape cluster border. Color. [12] £47 $90

[same title] [1885] 30x37cm. (12x15") Rapid western development. Full color. VG. [3] £42 $80

[same title] [1885] 28x38cm. (11x14½") Plain border. Color. [12] £45 $85

[same title] [1887] 30x36cm. (11½x14") Full color. [26] £45 $85

COUNTY AND TOWNSHIP MAP DAKOTA [1887] 38x30cm. (15x12") Full color. [26] £37 $70

COUNTY AND TOWNSHIP MAP OF ARIZONA AND NEW MEXICO [1881] 37x55cm. (15x22") Full color. Very good. [3] £37 $70

COUNTY AND TOWNSHIP MAP OF THE STATES OF KANSAS AND NEBRASKA [1878] 38x58cm. (15x23") Full color. Very good. [3] £42 $80

COUNTY AND TOWNSHIP MAP OF THE STATES OF NEW HAMPSHIRE AND VERMONT [c.1879] 48x30cm. (19x12") Color. [6] £26 $50

COUNTY AND TOWNSHIP OF MAP MONTANA, IDAHO AND WYOMING [1887] 38x56cm. (15x22") Full soft color. [26] £39 $75

COUNTY MAP OF CALIFORNIA [1863] 35x27cm. (14x11") Bright color. [3] £47 $90

[same title] [1867] 35x27cm. (14x11") Full color. [3] £47 $90

COUNTY MAP OF COLORADO, WYOMING, DAKOTA, MONTANA [1878] 50x37cm. (20x15") Full color. Very good. [3] £47 $90

COUNTY MAP OF GEORGIA AND ALABAMA [1860] 23x30cm. (9x12") Full col. Fine. [13] £32 $60

[same title] [1870] 23x30cm. (9½x12") Pastel coloring. Fine. [13] £24 $45

COUNTY MAP OF KENTUCKY & TENNESSEE [1873] 33x51cm. (13x20") Color. [6] £32 $60

COUNTY MAP OF OHIO AND INDIANA [1863] 28x36cm. (10½x13½") By W. Gamble. Col. [15] £21 $40

[same title] [1867] 30x36cm. (11½x14") Bright color. Very good. [14] £26 $50

COUNTY MAP OF TEXAS [1861] 30x36cm. (12x14") Full color. [3] £63 $120

[same title] [1867] 26x34cm. (10x13½") Color. [15] £58 $110

COUNTY MAP OF THE STATE OF CALIFORNIA [1875] 54x36cm. (21½x14½") Full col. [3] £47 $90

COUNTY MAP OF THE STATE OF ILLINOIS [1863] 38x30cm. (15x12") Full color. [26] £34 $65

[same title] [1875] 35x28cm. (14x11") [3] £37 $70

COUNTY MAP OF THE STATE OF NEW YORK [1874] 36x53cm. (14x21") Color. [15] £18 $35

COUNTY MAP OF THE STATE OF TEXAS, SHOWING ALSO PORTIONS OF ADJOINING TERRITORIES [1882] 37x54cm. (14½x21½") By W.H. Gambel. Color. [15] £50 $95

COUNTY MAP OF THE STATES OF GEORGIA AND ALABAMA [1880] 35x54cm. (14x21½") Full color. Fine. [13] £32 $60

COUNTY MAP OF THE STATES OF GEORGIA AND ALABAMA [1881] 36x56cm. (14x22") Color. [15] £29 $55

COUNTY MAP OF UTAH AND NEVADA [1879] 29x36cm. (11½x14") Color. [6] £42 $80

COUNTY MAP OF VIRGINIA AND WEST VIRGINIA [1863] 30x36cm. (12x14½") [15] £24 $45

INDIAN TERRITORY [1887] 30x43cm. (12x17") Light color. [26] £47 $90

INDIANA [1884] 36x28cm. (14x11") Full color. Very good. [14] £18 $35

MAP OF KANSAS, NEBRASKA AND COLORADO [1860 (1861)] 29x36cm. (11½x14") Full color. Some very light spots; trivial marginal dampstains; o/w fine. [12] £92 $175

[same title] [1861] 30x36cm. (12x14") Full color. Very good. [3] £47 $90

MAP OF OCEANA EXHIBITING ITS VARIOUS DEVISIONS ISLAND GROUPS [1863] 30x38cm. (11½x14½") Bright color. [26] £32 $60

MAP OF ONTARIO IN COUNTIES [1874] 28x36cm. (10½x13½") Color. [15] £16 $30

MAP OF OREGON, WASHINGTON, AND PART OF BRITISH COLUMBIA [1860 (1861-62)] 27x34cm. (10½x13½") Full color. Fine. [12] £58 $110

MAP OF OREGON, WASHINGTON, IDAHO, AND PART OF MONTANA [1866] 30x36cm. (11½x14") Full color. Very good. [26] £39 $75

MAP OF THE UNITED STATES AND TERRITORIES, TOGETHER WITH CANADA &C. [1860] 36x56cm. (13½x21½") Gigantic Idaho. [15] £58 $110

MINNESOTA AND DACOTAH [1860] 27x34cm. (10½x13½") 1st ed. Col. Pristine. [12] £66 $125

NORTHWESTERN AMERICA SHOWING THE TERRITORY CEDED BY RUSSIA TO THE UNITED STATES [1878] 30x37cm. (12x14½") Full bright color. [3] £32 $60

[same title] [1879] 30x36cm. (12x14") Color. [6] £39 $75

OKLAHOMA AND INDIAN TERRITORY [1890] 29x36cm. (11½x14½") Full color. [3] £63 $120

PLAN OF NEW ORLEANS [1871] 25x30cm. (9½x11½") Color. [15] £24 $45

PLAN OF PHILADELPHIA [1860] 28x33cm. (11x13") By W. Williams. Color. [15] £32 $60

PLAN OF THE CITY OF DETROIT [1881] 28x36cm. (11x14") [15] £24 $45

RAILROAD MAP OF THE UNITED STATES, SHOWING ... LINES OF COMMUNICATION FROM THE ATLANTIC TO THE PACIFIC ... [1880] 36x58cm. (14x22½") Color. [15] £32 $60

TERRITORY OF DAKOTA [c. 1879] 36x30cm. (14x12") Color. [6] £50 $95

TERRITORY OF IDAHO [1880] 37x27cm. (14½x10½") Color. Pristine. [12] £42 $80

TERRITORY OF MONTANA [1879] 27x36cm. (11x14½") Full color. [3] £39 $75

[same title, date] 33x41cm. (13x16") Adjoining territories not shown. Full color. [26] £42 $80

TERRITORY OF WYOMING [1879] 27x36cm. (11x14") Full color. [3] £39 $75

TEXAS [1873] 20x43cm. (8x17") Philadelphia: E. H. Butler. Color. [15] £26 $50

THE WORLD IN HEMISPHERES WITH OTHER PROJECTIONS &C. &C. [1863] 30x38cm. (11½x14½") Bright color. [26] £47 $90

UTAH AND NEVADA [1865] 29x35cm. (11½x14") First known edition. Color. [12] £58 $110

MOGG

A NEW TRAVELLING MAP OF ENGLAND, WALES AND SCOTLAND; DRAWN FROM ALL THE SURVEYS ... DESCRIBING THE DIRECT AND PRINCIPAL CROSS ROADS, CITIES, BOROUGHS, MARKET TOWNS AND VILLAGES ... [1812] 72x62cm. (28½x24") Linen-backed folding map with self-backs and original marbled slipcase with label. Color. Uniform age-darkening; slipcase scuffed; o/w very good. [19] £74 $140

MOGG'S TWENTY FOUR MILES ROUND LONDON [1817] Diameter: 54 cm. (21") Linen-backed folding map in original slipcase with label. Color. Small tear at end of a fold; small stain at edge; very good. [19] £315 $600

[same title] [1829] 62x58cm. (24x23") Linen-backed folding map. Diameter: 54 cm. (21"). Outline and wash color. Some age-soiling and darkening in margins; backing worn through at two fold intersections; good+. [19] £210 $400

MOGG'S TWENTY FOUR MILES ROUND LONDON & CRYSTAL PALACE EXCURSION MAP [c.1851] 68x53cm. (27x21") Folding map in self- folder. Diameter: 54 cm. (21") Color. Slight marginal staining; slight paper failure at fold intersections. [19] £142 $270

MOLL (Large)

A MAP OF THE EAST-INDIES AND THE ADJACENT COUNTRIES; WITH THE SETTLEMENTS, FACTORIES AND TERRITORIES, EXPLAINING WHAT BELONGS TO ENGLAND, SPAIN, FRANCE, HOLLAND, DENMARK, PORTUGAL &C. ... [c. 1730] 62x122cm. (24x48") Original color. Folds repaired on verso. [20] £499 $950

A NEW AND CORRECT MAP OF THE WHOLE WORLD SHEWING YE SITUATION OF ITS PRINCIPAL PARTS... [1719] 70x120cm. (27½x47") Outline color. Fold repairs with little loss. [1] £1971 $3750

A NEW AND CORRECT MAP OF THE WORLD, LAID DOWN ACCORDING TO THE NEWEST DISCOVERIES ... [c. 1730] 56x96cm. (22x38") Double hemispheres. Full color, partially early; folds reinforced, light staining; else very good. [22] £1156 $2200

A NEW AND EXACT MAP OF THE UNITED PROVINCES OR NETHERLANDS [c. 1715] 61x102cm. (23½x40") Outline color. Little margin; numerous repairs. [35] £197 $375

A NEW & EXACT MAP OF THE COASTS, COUNTRIES AND ISLANDS WITHIN YE LIMITS OF YE SOUTH SEA COMPANY, FROM YE RIVER ARANOCA TO TERRA DEL FUEGO, AND FROM THENCE THROUGH YE SOUTH SEA, TO YE NORTH PART OF CALIFORNIA &C. ... [c. 1711] 43x48cm. (17x19") dimensions for main map. Color. [15] £139 $265

[same title] [c. 1720] 65x49cm. (25½x19") Original outline color. Unobtrusive glue stain at junction of the two sheets; o/w fine. [12] £394 $750

SOUTH AMERICA, ACCORDING TO THE NEWEST AND MOST EXACT OBSERVATIONS... [1732-1735] 58x97cm. (23x38") Orig outline col. Minor restoration to upper and lower fold; o/w fine. [10] £145 $275

TO THE RIGHT HONORABLE CHARLES EARL OF SUNDERLAND AND BARON SPENCER OF WORMLEIGHTON ... THIS MAP OF SOUTH AMERICA ... [c. 1710-15] 58x97cm. (23x37½") Full original color. Slight centerfold reinforcement; o/w excellent. [21] £657 $1250

TO THE RIGHT HONOURABLE WILLIAM LORD COWPER, ... THIS MAP OF ASIA ACCORDING TO YE NEWEST AND MOST EXACT OBSERVATIONS ... [1716] 58x97cm. (22½x38") Full color. Reinforcement at one area of fold intersection; else excellent. [22] £788 $1500

MOLL (Small)

A DRAFT OF THE CITY OF JERUSALEM AS IT IS NOW, TAKEN FROM THE SOUTH EAST [1737] 13x23cm. (5x9") By C. Le Brun. Bird's eye view. [15] £32 $60

A GENERAL CHART OF THE SEA COAST OF EUROPE, AFRICA & AMERICA. ACCORDING TO E. WRIGHTS OR MERCATOR'S PROJECTION ... [1752] 35x28cm. (14x11") From Awnsham & Churchill's *Collection of Voyages and Travels* ... Fine. [12] £105 $200

A MAP OF INDEPENDENT TARTARY CONTAINING THE TERRITORIES OF USBECK, GASGAR, TIBET, LASSA &C [c. 1732] 18x25cm. (7x10") [36] £42 $80

A MAP OF MEXICO OR NEW SPAIN, FLORIDA NOW CALLED LOUISIANA AND PART OF CALIFORNIA &C. [1711-17] 18x25cm. (7x10") From *Atlas Geographicus*. Fine. [29] £202 $385

[same title]. [1732] 18x25cm. (7x10") Outline color. Excellent. [35] £145 $275

A MAP OF NEW FRANCE CONTAINING CANADA, LOUISIANA &C. IN NTH. AMERICA ACCORDING TO THE PATENT GRANTED GRANTED BY THE KING OF FRANCE TO MONSIEUR CROZAT DATED 14TH SEP. 1712, REGISTRED IN PARLIAMENT OF PARIS THE 24TH OF SAME MONTH [1712-17] 19x26cm. (7½x10") From *Atlas Geographicus*. Fine. [29] £208 $395

A MAP OF THE NORTH POLE ... [1727] 20x28cm. (8x11") Very good. [31] £97 $185

A MAP OF THE WEST INDIES &C. MEXICO OR NEW SPAIN. ALSO YE TRADE WINDS, AND YE SEVERAL TRACTS MADE BY YE GALLEONS AND YE FLOTA FROM PLACE TO PLACE [1732-1740] 20x26cm. (8x10½") Outline color. [36] £123 $235

A NEW MAP OF NORTH AMERICA ACCORDING TO THE NEWEST OBSERVATIONS. BY H. MOLL GEOGRAPHER [n.d.] 18x25cm. (7x10") California as an island. [3] £289 $550

[same title] [1711-17] 18x25cm. (7x10") From *Atlas Geographicus*. Fine. [29] £236 $450

A NEW MAP OF THE ISLAND OF BARBADOES, CONTAINING ALL YE PARISHES, AND PRINCIPAL PLANTATIONS; TOGETHER WITH YE FORTS, LINES, BATTERIES, ROADS, &C. [c. 1716] 18x25cm. (7x10") Color. [15] £123 $235

A NEW MAP OF THE WORLD ACCORDING TO THE NEW OBSERVATIONS BY H. MOLL GEOGRAPHER [c. 1700] 18x28cm. (7x11") Double hemisphere, with North polar map; insular California. [3] £250 $475

A NEW MAP OF THE WORLD ACCORDING TO THE NEW OBSERVATIONS ... [1752] 18x28cm. (7x11") Double hemispheres. From Awnsham & Churchill, ... Voy*ages and Travels* ... Fine. 12] £131 $250

A VIEW OF YE GENERAL & COASTING TRADE-WINDS, MONSOONS OR YE SHIFTING TRADE WINDS THROUGH YE WORLD ... BY H. MOLL GEOGRAPHER [1746] 18x52cm. (7x20½") Color. [15] £129 $245

[same title] [1752] 20x53cm. (7½x20½") From Awnsham & Churchill. Fine. [12] £118 $225

AFRICA, ACCORDING TO YE NEWEST AND MOST EXACT OBSERVATIONS [1746] 18x25cm. (7x10") Very good+. [18] £79 $150

AMERICA [c. 1720] 23x30cm. (9x12") Insular California. Full color. [3] £342 $650

ASIA ACCORDING TO YE NEWEST OBSERVATIONS [1712] 18x25cm. (7x10") [10] £16 $30

CANAAN PALESTINE OR THE HOLY LAND &C. DIVIDED INTO THE 12 TRIBES OF ISRAEL [1709] 23x18cm. (9x7") Laor 499. Color. [15] £50 $95

CHILE, MAGELLAN-LAND, AND TERRA DEL FUEGO &C. [c.1709] 16x18cm. (6½x7") Col. [15] £39 $75

FLORIDA CALL'D BY YE FRENCH LOUISIANA &C. [1729] 20x28cm. (8x11") Original outline color. [10] £92 $175

INDIA BEYOND GANGES [c. 1750] 26x20cm. (10x8") Southeast Asia. Splits into map joined. [10] £45 $85

IRELAND [c. 1695+] 18x17cm. (7x6½") Color. Very good. [24] £65 $124

NEWFOUNDLAND, ST. LAURENS BAY, THE FISHING BANKS, ACADIA, AND PART OF NEW SCOTLAND ... [1729] 20x27cm. (8x10½") Outline color. [10] £131 $250

SUISSE OR SWITZERLAND [1726] 23x25cm. (9x10") Outline color. Very good. [34] £53 $100

THE ENGLISH EMPIRE IN AMERICA, NEWFOUND-LAND. CANADA. HUDSONS BAY. &C. IN PLANO. HERMAN MOLL FECIT [1710] 22x18cm. (8½x7") Maritimes to Florida. London: Churchill. Text below and verso. Color. [15] £76 $145

THE ISLAND OF BARBADOES. DIVIDED INTO ITS PARISHES, WITH THE ROADS, PATHS, &C. ACCORDING TO AN ACTUAL AND ACCURATE SURVEY [1746] 29x36cm. (11½x14½") Fine. [17] £118 $225

THE ISLAND OF JAMAICA DIVIDED INTO ITS PRINCIPAL PARISHES WITH THE ROADS &C. [1746] 20x28cm. (8x11") [17] £105 $200

MONIN

BRESIL - PARAGUAY ET URUGUAY ... [c.1850] 45x31cm. (17½x12") Outline col. [16] £76 $144

MONK

MONK'S NEW AMERICAN MAP EXHIBITING ... NORTH AMERICA ... UNITED STATES AND TERRITORIES, MEXICO AND CENTRAL AMERICA, INCLUDING THE WEST INDIA ISLANDS, CANADAS, NEW BRUNSWICK AND NOVA SCOTIA [1856] 145x155cm. (57x61") Wall map. Color. Age toned; moderate wrinkling; small surface loss at side edges; one small separation; slight upper margin stain; good. [7] £242 $460

NEW MAP OF THAT PORTION OF NORTH AMERICA, EXHIBITING THE UNITED STATES AND TERRITORIES, THE CANADAS, NEW BRUNSWICK, NOVA SCOTIA AND MEXICO, CENTRAL AMERICA AND THE WEST INDIA ISLANDS [1853] 140x150cm. (55x59") Wall map. Color. Slight age-toning and wear at edges; whitening at slight wrinkles; very good. [7] £462 $880

MONTANUS *Try Ogilby*

[TITLE PAGE] DE NIEUWE EN ONBEKENDE WEERELD: OF BESCHRYVING VAN AMERICA [1671] 30x18cm. (11½x7") [15] £45 $85

DE STADT OSACCO [1669] 26x69cm. (10x27") Osaca panorama with Dutch key. Color. Signs of original vertical creases. [5] £350 $666

MEACO [(1669) 1670] 29x79cm. (11½x31") Kyoto panorama. From Ogilby, *Atlas Jappanensis*. Color. [5] £385 $733

PAGUS HISPANORUM IN FLORIDA [1671] 27x35cm. (10½x14") View. Color. [15] £236 $450

MONTRESOR

A MAP OF THE PROVINCE OF NEW YORK WITH PART OF PENSILVANIA, AND NEW ENGLAND, FROM AN ACTUAL SURVEY ... [1775 / 1777] 71x91cm. (28½x36") Four sheets in two, 53 x 36" if joined. Contemporary wash color. Excellent. [1] £1839 $3500

MORDEN

A NEW MAP OF CAROLINA [1700] 13x13cm. (5x5") From *Geography Rectified*. Col. [33] £240 $457

A NEW MAP OF NEW JERSEY AND PENSILVANIA BY ROBT. MORDEN [1688] 15x13cm. (5½x5") Old color. [15] £171 $325

AMERICA [c. 1700] 12x13cm. (5x5") Insular California. [3] £197 $375

ASIA [1695] 17x19cm. (7x7½") [10] £18 $35

CONGO [c. 1685] 10x12cm. (4x5") [10] £16 $30

CYPRI INSULA [1700] 15x13cm. (5½x5") From *Geography Rectified*. [33] £140 $266

DENBIGH SH. [n.d.] 9x6cm. (3½x2½") Playing card map: Four of Spades. 2nd ed. OL col. G. [32] £165 $314

GLOCESTER SH. [n.d.] 9x6cm. (3½x2½") Playing card map: Jack of Diamonds. 2nd edition. Outline color. Good. [32] £225 $428

HABESSINIA SEV ABASSIA AT ETHIOPIA [c. 1685] 14x12cm. (5½x5") [10] £21 $40

INSULA JAMAICAE ... [1700] 13x13cm. (4½x5") London: Cockerill. 12 parishes. Col. [15] £58 $110

JAPONAE AC TERRAE ESONIS NOVISSIMA DESCRIPTIO [(1680) 1684] 11x13cm. (4½x5") With accompanying English text. Fine. [5] £300 $571

[same title] [c. 1700] 11x13cm. (4½x5") Not first state; coordinates & plate number changed. Fine. [5] £295 $561

KENT [n.d.] 9x6cm. (3½x2½") Playing card map: Nine of Hearts. 2nd ed. OL col. G. [32] £240 $457

LANCASTER SH. [n.d.] 9x6cm. (3½x2½") Playing card map: 3 of Clubs. 2nd ed. OL col. G. [32] £225 $428

MALTHA ... [1700] 11x13cm. (4½x5") From *Geography Rectified*. [33] £120 $228

MIDDLESEX [n.d.] 9x6cm. (3½x2½") Playing card maps: King of Hearts. Charles II portrait. 2nd edition. Outline color. Good. [32] £240 $457

NEW MEXICO VEL NEW GRANATA ET MARATA ET CALIFORNIA ... [1700] 11x13cm. (4½x5") From *Geography Rectified*. Insular California. Color. [33] £320 $609

OXFORD SH. [n.d.] 9x6cm. (3½x2½") Playing card map: 2 of Diamonds. 2nd ed. OL col. G. [32] £225 $428

SURREY [n.d.] 9x6cm. (3½x2½") Playing card map: Ten of Hearts. 2nd edition. Outline color. Good; a little rubbed. [32] £200 $381

SUSSEX [n.d.] 9x6cm. (3½x2½") Playing card map: 4 of Diamonds. 2nd ed. OL col. G. [32] £240 $457

TERRA MAGELLANICA [1680] 13x11cm. (5x4½") Fine. [10] £32 $60

THE COAST OF ZANGUEBAR AND AIEN ... [c.1685] 12x10cm. (5x4") Orig outline col. [10] £26 $50

THE ISLAND OF BARBADOS [1700] 13x11cm. (5x4½") From *Geography Rectified*. [33] £180 $343

THE ISLES OF SONDA [1688] 10x14cm. (4x5½") Outline color. Fine. [38] £97 $185

THE KINGDOM OF IRELAND [c. 1695] 41x34cm. (16x13½") Color. Very good. [24] £180 $343

THE NORTH WEST PART OF AMERICA BY R. MORDEN AT YE ATLAS IN CORNHILL [1693] 11x14cm. (4½x5½") Color. [15] £79 $150

MORRIS

... ST. GEORGE' CHANNEL &C. SURVEYED UNDER THEIR LORDSHIP'S DIRECTION BY THE LATE LEWIS MORRIS ESQR. WHICH IS NOW EXTENDED BY AN ACTUAL SURVEY (...) FROM LIVERPOOL TO CARDIFF ... [1800] 91x91cm. (36x36") All of Wales. Blue backed. Short fold splits repaired. [11] £350 $666

A PLAN OF MILFORD HAVEN ... [Wales] [1748-1800] 18x23cm. (7x9") Wm. Morris' reissue of father's plans. Color. [11] £35 $67

A PLAN OF THE BAY & HARBOUR OF DUBLIN [1800] 18x33cm. (7½x12½") Wm. Morris reissue of father's plans. Color. [11] £40 $76

ABERAERON AND NEW KEY ... [Wales] [1748-1800] 18x23cm. (7x9") Wm. Morris' reissue of father's plans. Color. [11] £34 $65

ABERDARON ROAD ... [Wales] [1748-1800] 18x23cm. (7x9") Wm. Morris' reissue of father's plans. Color. [11] £32 $61

ABERDARON ROAD ON THE SOUTH SIDE OF BARDSEY SOUND ... [Wales] [1748] 18x24cm. (7x9½") Brown mark. [11] £36 $69

ABERDOVEY BAY, BAR & HARBOUR [Wales] [1748-1800] 18x23cm. (7x9") Wm. Morris' reissue of father's plans. [11] £35 $67

BARDSEY ISLE ... [Wales] [1748-1800] 18x23cm. (7x9") Wm. Morris' reissue. Color. [11] £34 $65

BARMOUTH BAY BARS & HARBOUR [Wales] [1748-1800] 18x23cm. (7x9") Wm. Morris' reissue of father's plans. [11] £34 $65

BURRY BAY, BAR AND HARBOUR [Wales] [1748-1800] 18x23cm. (7x9") Wm. Morris' reissue of father's plans. Color. [11] £34 $65

CAMLYN BAY & HARBOUR ... [Wales] [1748-1800] 18x23cm. (7x9") Wm. Morris' reissue of father's plans. [11] £32 $61

CARDIGAN BAY, BAR AND HARBOUR [Wales] [1748-1800] 18x23cm. (7x9") Wm. Morris' reissue of father's plans. Color. Repair at right edge. [11] £20 $38

CARMARTHEN, LOUGHARN, AND CYDWELY ... [Wales] [1748-1800] 18x23cm. (7x9") Wm. Morris' reissue of father's plans. Color. [11] £34 $65

DULAS BAY & HARBOUR [Wales] [1748-1800] 18x23cm. (7x9") Wm. Morris' reissue of father's plans. [11] £34 $65

FISCARD BAY AND HARBOUR [Wales] [1748] 18x24cm. (7x9½") [11] £45 $86

[same title] [1748-1800] 18x23cm. (7x9") Wm. Morris' reissue of father's plans. Col. [11] £32 $61

GOLDTOP ROAD IN ST. BRIDES BAY [Wales] [1748] 18x24cm. (7x9½") [11] £40 $76

[same title] [1748-1800] 18x23cm. (7x9") Wm. Morris' reissue of father's plans. Color. [11] £34 $65

NEWPORT BAY & HARBOUR ... [Wales] [1748] 18x24cm. (7x9½") Right margin has not printed. [11] £32 $61

[same title] [1748-1800] 18x23cm. (7x9") Wm. Morris' reissue of father's plans. Color. Lacks margin corner. [11] £34 $65

PORTHDINLLEYN & NEV YN BAY AND HARBOUR [Wales] [1748-1800] 18x23cm. (7x9") Wm. Morris' reissue of father's plans. [11] £34 $65

SOLVACH BAY & HARBOUR ... [Wales] [1748] 18x24cm. (7x9½") [11] £40 $76

[same title] [1748-1800] 18x23cm. (7x9") Wm. Morris' reissue of father's plans. Color. [11] £34 $65

ST. TUDSWALS ROAD AND KEIRIAD ROAD [Wales] [1748-1800] 18x23cm. (7x9") Wm. Morris' reissue of father's plans. Color. [11] £34 $65

TENBY HARBOUR & ROAD AND CALDY ROADS ... [Wales] [1748] 18x24cm. (7x9½") [11] £45 $86

THE NORTH ENTRANCE OF BARDSEY SOUND AND THE ROADS [Wales] [1748] 18x24cm. (7x9½") Mark, crease. [11] £30 $57

[same title] [1748-1800] 18x23cm. (7x9") Wm. Morris' reissue of father's plans. [11] £34 $65

THE ROADS IN RAMSEY SOUND ... [Wales] [1748] 18x24cm. (7x9½") [11] £40 $76

MORSE & BREESE

ALABAMA [1852] 30x38cm. (12x15") Color. [15] £47 $90

ARKANSAS [1842-44] 30x38cm. (12x15") 48 counties. Color. [15] £58 $110

CITY OF NEW YORK [1842] 38x30cm. (15x12") North to 32nd Street. Color. [15] £39 $75

GEORGIA [1845] 36x29cm. (14x11½") Printed col. Water stain in periphery; fine. [13] £58 $110
ILLINOIS [1844] 36x28cm. (14x11") Color. [15] £58 $110
INDIANA [1842] 36x28cm. (14x11") Printed color. Fine. [14] £45 $85
MEXICO [1846] 33x41cm. (13x16") Cerographic printed color. Fine. [12] £71 $135
MICHIGAN [1844] 33x38cm. (12½x15") Color. [15] £58 $110
SOUTH CAROLINA [1843] 33x38cm. (12½x15") Color. [15] £58 $110
TEXAS [1844 (1846)] 38x30cm. (15x12") Cerographic outline color. Fine. [12] £131 $250
WISCONSIN SOUTHERN PART [c. 1845] 33x41cm. (12½x15½") Color. [15] £50 $95

MORSE & GASTON

GEORGIA [1857] 15x13cm. (6x5") S.F. Baker, engraver. Full color. Fine. [13] £29 $55
INDIANA [1857] 15x13cm. (6x5") From *The World in Miniature American*. S.F. Baker, engraver Full color. Fine. [14] £21 $40

MORSE, J. *Try Stockdale*

A CHART OF THE NTH. WEST COAST OF AMERICA, & THE NTH. EAST COAST OF ASIA, ... [c. 1800] 18x28cm. (7x11") E. Gridley, sc. Left margin darkened with some of neat line absent; fold reinforced. [6] £79 $150
[same title] [1802] 18x30cm. (7x11½") [12] £84 $160
A CORRECT MAP OF THE GEORGIA WESTERN TERRITORY [1797] 18x15cm. (7x6") From *The American Gazetteer*. Wheat & Brun 618. Fold lines. [6] £155 $295
[same title, date, dimensions] Fine. [13] £105 $200
[same title, date, dimensions] Fine. [38] £158 $300
[same title] [1798] 18x15cm. (7x6") London issue. [18] £105 $200
A MAP OF GEORGIA, ALSO THE TWO FLORIDAS, FROM THE BEST AUTHORITIES [1796] 19x31cm. (7½x12") Folds reinforced; some loss at left neat line. [6] £118 $225
[same title, date, dimensions] By Doolittle. Very good. [13] £118 $225
A MAP OF MASSACHUSETTS, FROM THE BEST AUTHORITIES [1796] 19x25cm. (7½x10") By Denison. Reinforced at folds. [6] £102 $195
A MAP OF NEW HAMPSHIRE [1794] 23x18cm. (9x7") London: Stockdale. Col. Minor repair. [15] £58 $110
A MAP OF PENNSYLVANIA FROM THE BEST AUTHORITIES [1794] 18x23cm. (7x9") London: Stockdale. Color. [15] £66 $125
A MAP OF THE DISTRICT OF MAINE WITH NEW BRUNSWICK & NOVA SCOTIA [1796] 18x23cm. (7x9") Doolittle, sc. [6] £102 $195
A MAP OF THE NORTH WESTERN TERRITORY [1796] 19x24cm. (7½x9½") Hill, sc. Faint impression. [6] £102 $195
A MAP OF THE NORTHERN AND MIDDLE STATES; COMPREHENDING THE WESTERN TERRITORY AND THE BRITISH DOMINIONS IN NORTH AMERICA ... [1792] 31x39cm. (12½x15½") By Islington. London: Stockdale. Minor tear repaired; 3" of blank margin replaced. [10] £97 $185
A MAP OF THE STATE OF KENTUCKY AND THE TENNESSEE GOVERNMENT COMPILED FROM THE BEST AUTHORITIES BY CYRUS HARRIS [1796] 20x26cm. (8x10") From *The American Universal Geography*; Doolittle, engr. Rebacked with rice paper; minor loss at folds; narrow margin an inch at lower left. [6] £155 $295
A MAP OF THE STATES OF NEW HAMPSHIRE AND VERMONT BY J. DENISON [1796] 19x24cm. (7½x9½") Doolittle; sc. Reinforced at fold line. [6] £102 $195
A NEW MAP OF NOVA SCOTIA, NEW BRUNSWICK AND CAPE BRUNSWICK AND CAPE BRETON ... [1794] 18x22cm. (7x8½") By Stockdale. [10] £26 $50
MAP OF NORTH AND SOUTH CAROLINA [1796] 19x23cm. (7½x9") By J. Denison; Doolittle, sc. Fold line, minor separation to neat line. [6] £102 $195
MAP OF THE SOUTHERN PARTS OF THE UNITED STATES OF AMERICA ... [1797] 20x39cm. (8x15½") By Abraham Bradley. Fold lines. [6] £129 $245
[same title, date, dimensions]. Slightly trimmed at bottom. [31] £150 $285
MAP OF THE STATE OF NEW YORK [1796] 19x24cm. (7½x9½") By Denison; Doolittle, sc.. Reinforced at fold. [6] £102 $195
MAP OF THE STATES OF MARYLAND AND DELAWARE [1796] 18x25cm. (7x10") By J. Denison. Reinforced at fold. [6] £102 $195
NEW JERSEY [1796] 19x15cm. (7½x6") S. Hill, sc.. [6] £102 $195

PENNSYLVANIA DRAWN FROM THE BEST AUTHORITIES [1796] 20x33cm. (8x13") By Cyrus Harris; Doolittle, sc. [6] £102 $195

RHODE-ISLAND AND CONNECTICUT [1796] 19x33cm. (7½x13") By H. Harris in *The American Universal Geography* [6] £102 $195

VIRGINIA [1796] 16x20cm. (6x8") Hill, sc. [6] £92 $175

MORSE, S.

FLORIDA [c. 1840] 13x15cm. (5x5½") 20 counties. Color. [15] £18 $35

GREENLAND AND LABRADOR [1848] 28x33cm. (11x13") With Iceland. Minor foxing. [26] £32 $60

SIAM [1848] 30x25cm. (12x10") Modern color. [26] £32 $60

MORTIER *Try Jaillot*

[TITLE PAGE] NOUVEAU THEATRE D'ITALIE TOM I. [1704-5] 29x45cm. (11½x17½") From reissue of Blaeu's townbook of Italy. Color. Some small worm holes. [5] £120 $228

CARTA PARTICULIERE DES COSTES DE L'AFRIQUE QUI COMPRENT UNE PARTIE DE LA GUINEE ET PARTIE DE MINA ... [1700] 51x79cm. (20x31") Fine. [11] £150 $285

CARTE DES COSTES DE L'ASIE SUR L'OCEAN CONTENANT LES BANCS ISLES ET COSTES &C. [c. 1700] 58x86cm. (23x34") Full old col. Some wear & creasing; else VG to fine. [34] £657 $1250

CARTE NOUVELLE DE L'AMERIQUE ANGLOISE CONTENANT LA VIRGINIE, MARY-LAND, CAROLINE, PENSILVANIA NOUVELLE IORCK, N. IARSEY N: FRANCE, ET LES TERRES NOUVELLEMENT DECOUVERTE [1700] 60x91cm. (23½x36") After Sanson. Full original color. Very good. [22] £1314 $2500

[same title] [1700-1708] 60x91cm. (23½x36") Orig outline col. Lightly age-toned; VG. [20] £1209 $2300

CARTE PARTICULIERE DE L'AMERIQUE SEPTENTRIONALE OU SONT COMPRIS LE DESTROIT DE DAVIDS, LE DESTROIT DE HUDSON, &C. [1698] 58x84cm. (23x32½") Outline col. [15] £289 $550

PARTIE ORIENTALE DE L'AMERIQUE ANGLOISE [c.1693] 61x46cm. (24x18½") Col. [15] £460 $875

MOUNT & PAGE

[TITLE PAGE] THE ENGLISH PILOT, FOURTH BOOK DESCRIBING WEST-INDIA NAVIGATION [1758] 41x23cm. (15½x9") [15] £45 $85

A CHART OF THE BANKS AND HARBOURS OF NEWFOUNDLAND ... [1702-1713] 45x58cm. (17½x22½") From *The English Pilot. The Fourth Book.* [33] £500 $952

A CHART OF THE SEA COAST OF NEWFOUND LAND, NEW SCOTLAND, NEW ENGLAND, NEW YORK, NEW JERSEY, WITH VIRGINIA AND MARYLAND [1713 / c.1750] 45x58cm. (18x22½") Strong impression. Excellent. [1] £788 $1500

A GENERAL CHART OF THE WESTERN OCEAN ... [1715 (1730)] 46x58cm. (18x23") Slight creasing; small repairs at lower margin. [11] £320 $609

A LARGE CHART OF THE ISLAND ANTEGUA [1713] 42x42cm. (16½x16½") Unrecorded Thornton chart with rectangular title frame. From *The English Pilot. The Fourth Book.* [33] £800 $1522

A NEW AND CORRECT DRAUGHT OF THE BAY, OF MATANZAS, ON YE NORTH SIDE OF YE ISLAND CUBA, DONE FROM A SURVEY BY ROBT PEARSON ... [1789] 23x31cm. (9x12") Mount & Davidson; *The English Pilot, Fourth Book.* [10] £39 $75

BARBADOS [1789] 29x26cm. (11½x10") *The English Pilot, Fourth Book.* With text. [10] £116 $220

VIRGINIA, MARYLAND, PENNSILVANIA, EAST & WEST NEW JERSEY ... [1784] 51x79cm. (20x31") After Thornton. Light toning; fold repaired; o/w fine. [1] £2365 $4500

MOUZON

AN ACCURATE MAP OF NORTH AND SOUTH CAROLINA WITH THEIR INDIAN FRONTIERS ... [1775] 99x142cm. (39x55½") Four sheets, joined to form two, each about 20 x 55 inches. Original color. Trimmed, as often, at right margins with some loss, fully restored. [22] £3678 $7000

MOXON

ISRAELS PERIGRINATIONS OR THE FORTY YEARS TRAVEL OF THE CHILDREN OF ISRAEL OUT OF EGYPT ... INTO CANAAN [1671] 32x46cm. (12½x18½") Amsterdam: Visscher. Laor 519. Color. [15] £250 $475

MULLER

AMERICA MERIDIONALIS [1692] 7x8cm. (2½x3") [10] £53 $100

NOUVELLE CARTE DES DECOUVERTES FAITES PAR DES VAISSEAUX RUSSIENS AUX COTES INCONNUES DE L'AMERIQUE SEPTENTRIONALE ... [1754 (1773)] 46x64cm. (18x25") Color. Slight paper discoloration; else very good. [34] £788 $1500

MUNSTER

... GENERAL TAFEL ... [1540 (c. 1544)] 26x35cm. (10x13½") The World. State I. Shirley 77. Excellent. [38] £1682 $3200

[MONSTERS: SEA & LAND PREDATORS] [c. 1550] 26x35cm. (10½x13½") Many animals after Olaus Magnus 1539 map. Excellent. [38] £394 $750

AFRICA [c. 1590] 13x16cm. (5x6") From Cosmographia. [10] £32 $60

ALTERA GENERALIS TAB. SECUNDUM PTOL. [c. 1550] 26x35cm. (10½x13½") Shirley 76. Full color. Excellent. [21] £631 $1200

APHRICAE TABULA I [1542] 26x33cm. (10x13") Ptolemaic N.W. Africa. Age darkening, minor show-through; small stain in left margin & border; small centerfold repairs; small wormholes in bottom margin. [17] £81 $155

DAS ANDER BUCH [ALLEGORICAL EUROPE] [1545] 25x15cm. (10x6½") Europe in form of a monarch. Color. [1] £184 $350

DAS ERST GENERAL INHALTEND DIE BESCHREIBUNG UND DEN CIRCKEL DES GANTZEN ERDTRICHS UND MORE [c. 1550] 26x38cm. (10½x15") Munster's second world map. Shirley 92. Full color. Excellent. [21] £1051 $2000

[same title] [1550-1578] 26x38cm. (10½x15") Lightly soiled & worn; top marginal centerfold defect; repaired inconspicuous tear entering map; small pale stain; o/w good+. [20] £657 $1250

DER STAAT MEXICO SONSTEN. THEMISTITAN [c. 1588] 18x15cm. (7½x6½") [15] £87 $165

DER STATT ROM IN AFFER WELT BESANNE CONTRAFEHOUNG NACH JEZIGER GELEGENHEIT [c. 1555] 28x36cm. (11x14") View. Color. Lightly toned; fine. [37] £131 $250

DIE NEUWEN INSELN SO HINDER HISPANIEN GEGEN ORIENT BEY DEM LANDT INDIE GELEGEN.. [c. 1540] 25x36cm. (10x13½") Narrow North American "Verrazano Isthmus" at Carolina. Slight centerfold darkening; else fine. [34] £1708 $3250

[same title] [1540 / c.1550] 25x33cm. (10x13½") Excellent. [1] £1445 $2750

DIE NEWEN INSELN / SO HINDER HISPANIAM GEGEN ORIENT / BEY DEM LANDT INDIE GELEGEN .. [c. 1588] 33x36cm. (12½x14½") Excellent. [15] £867 $1650

EUROPA PRIMA NOVA TABULA [1540-1544] 27x33cm. (10½x13") South at top. [33] £420 $799

EUROPAE TABULA [c. 1550] 28x33cm. (10½x13½") South at top. Full color. Marginal repair; lightly toned; early hand notes on verso; else very good. [21] £447 $850

INDIA EXTREMA [Asia] [c. 1540] 26x35cm. (10x13½") Fine. [38] £394 $750

[same title] [c. 1550] 26x34cm. (10½x13½") Full col. Light centerfold stain; else excel. [21] £499 $950

LA DESCRIPTION D'AFFRICQUE ... [c.1566] 15x18cm. (5½x7") On page with text. Excel. [26] £74 $140

LA FIGURE DU MONDE UNIVERSEL [c. 1550] 25x38cm. (10½x15") Shirley 92. Second state. Light age toned, else very good. [2] £1366 $2600

LA TABLE DE LA REGION ORIENTALE ... [c. 1550] 25x34cm. (10x13½") Some text see-through; fine. [5] £385 $733

LA TABLE DES ISLES NEUSUES [1540 (c. 1552)] 26x34cm. (10x13½") Excel. [38] £1682 $3200

LA TABLE & DESCRIPTION UNIVERSELLE DE TOUTE L'AFRIQUE... [1540 (c. 1552)] 26x35cm. (10x13½") Excellent. [38] £342 $650

MOSCOVIE [c. 1555] 20x15cm. (8x6½") From *Cosmographia*. [15] £50 $95

NOVAE INSULAE XVII NOVA TABULA [1540+] 26x34cm. (10x13½") Early state, predating addition of "Die Nuw Welt" to South America. Centerfold reinforced, expertly rebacked, lightly age-toned. [20] £1261 $2400

NOVAE INSULAE XXVI NOVA TABULA [1552] 30x38cm. (11½x14½") Only issue with longitudinal and latitudinal grids. Wash color. Lower corners inconspicuously restored; VG. [21] £1445 $2750

PTOLEMEISCH GENERAL TAFEL / DIE HALBE KUGEL DER WELT BEGREIFFENDE [1550] 30x36cm. (12x14") Fine. [10] £394 $750

SARMATIA ASIE [1566] 25x18cm. (9½x6½") [36] £87 $165

SEPTENTRIONALES REGIONES XVIII NO. TAB. [1552] 28x36cm. (11x14") VG. [31] £578 $1100

TABULA ASIAE II [1552] 25x33cm. (10x13") From *Geographia*. Basel: Petri. VG. [31] £131 $250

TABULA ASIAE VII [1542] 25x34cm. (10x13½") Ptolemaic Central Asia. Slight age darkening along repaired centerfold split; a few minor wormholes. [17] £84 $160

TABULA ASIAE VII [1552] 25x34cm. (10x13") From *Geographia.* Basel: Petri. VG. [31] £131 $250

TABULA ASIAE VIII [1552] 25x33cm. (10x13") From *Geographia.* Basel: Petri. VG. [31] £210 $400

TABULA ASIAE IX [1552] 25x34cm. (10x13") From *Geographia.* Basel: Petri. VG. [31] £131 $250

TABULA ASIAE X [1552] 25x34cm. (10x13") From *Geographia.* Basel: Petri. VG. [31] £158 $300

TABULA ASIAE XI [1552] 25x34cm. (10x13") From *Geographia.* Basel: Petri. VG. [31] £210 $400

TABULA ASIAE XII [1552] 26x34cm. (10x13") From *Geographia.* Basel: Petri. VG. [31] £158 $300

TABULA EUROPAE IX [1542] 26x33cm. (10x13") Ptolemaic Balkans. Faint age darkening. [17] £210 $400

TABULA ORIENTALIS REGIONIS, ASIAE SCILICET EXTREMAS COMPLECTENS TERRAS & REGNA [1540, c.1550] 25x33cm. (10x13") Some light toning; very good. [1] £289 $550

TERRA SANCTA XXIII. NOVA TABULA [c. 1550] 25x34cm. (10x13½") Excellent. [36] £223 $425

[same title] [1552] 25x33cm. (10x13") From *Geographia.* Basel: Petri. Very good. [31] £420 $800

TYPUS ORBIS PTOL. DESCRIPTUS [(1540)-1552] 25x36cm. (10x13½") Shirley 76. VG. [31] £841 $1600

TYPUS ORBIS UNIVERSALIS [c. 1550] 26x38cm. (10x15") Shirley 92. Color. [5] £950 $1808

[same title, date] 27x38cm. (10½x15") 2nd state with modern Iceland. Shirley 92. Excel. [38] £1209 $2300

TYPUS UNIVERSALIS [1540-] 26x35cm. (10x13½") With "Verrazano Sea"; replaced in 1550. Shirley 77. [33] £1500 $2855

[same title] [1540 / c.1550] 26x35cm. (10½x14") 1st edition. Excellent. [1] £1314 $2500

[same title] [(1540)-1552] 26x37cm. (10½x15") Basel: Henri Petri. Shirley 92. [31] £1314 $2500

VENETIARUM AMPLISSIMA & MARITIMA URBS, SUM MULTIS CIRCUMACIENTIBUS INSULIS [c. 1555] 25x39cm. (9½x15") View. Full color. Close side margins; fine. [37] £184 $350

MURRAY, J.

A SKETCH OF THE ISLAND OF SINGPORE [1830] 18x33cm. (7x13") From *Memoir of the Life and Public Services of Sir Stamford Raffles.* [5] £260 $495

GENERAL MAP OF THE UNITED STATES SHOWING EXTENT OF FREE & SLAVE-HOLDING STATES AND TERRITORIES OF THE UNION [1857] 33x43cm. (13x16½") By H. Rogers. Color. [15] £34 $65

TABULA QUA GRAECIA SUPERIOR, QUALIS TEMPORE BELLI PELOPONNESIACI INEUNTIS FUIT [1830] 56x69cm. (22x27") By C. Odofredo Muller. Linen-backed folding map with ribbon edge. Outline color. Some slight age-soiling and wear at intersections; good. [19] £102 $195

VIEW OF SINGAPORE TOWN AND HARBOUR TAKEN FROM THE GOVERNMENT HILL [1830] 23x80cm. (9x31½") From *Memoir of the Life and Public Services of Sir Stamford Raffles.* Color. [5] £800 $1522

MYRITIUS

UNIVERSALIS ORBIS DESCRIPTIO [1590] 27x40cm. (10½x15½") Woodcut from *Opusculum Geographicum Rarum*, Ingolstadt. Shirley 175. Side borders added. [5] £2250 $4282

NATIONAL GEOGRAPHIC SOCIETY

THE NATIONAL GEOGRAPHIC MAP OF ALASKA [1914] 38x51cm. (15x20") Some color. Folded; minor loss at some corners. [26] £32 $60

NAVAL CHRONICLE

PORT ROYAL IN JAMAICA. [1809] 12x16cm. (4½x6½") Jolly NAV-22. Color. One close margin. [15] £24 $45

SKETCH OF THE POSITION OF THE BRITISH AND AMERICAN FORCES, DURING THE OPERATIONS AGAINST NEW ORLEANS, FROM 23D. DECR. 1814, TO 18TH. JANY 1815. [1815] 13x21cm. (5x8") Jolly NAV-55. [15] £66 $125

NEPTUNE FRANCOIS *Try Depot de la Marine, Jaillot, Mortier*

NEW YORK STATE DOCUMENTARY HISTORY

A MAP OF A TRACT OF LAND IN THE STATE OF NEW YORK CALLED MACOMB'S PURCHASE [1850] 33x38cm. (12½x15") By C. Brodhead. [15] £32 $60

A MAP OF THE GENESEE LANDS IN THE COUNTY OF ONTARIO AND STATE OF NEW YORK ... 1790 [1850] 33x20cm. (12½x8½") Color. [15] £26 $50

A MAP OF THE MANOR RENSELAERWICK ... 100 CHAINS TO AN INCH ... 1767 [1850] 38x53cm. (15x21") By J. Bleeker. Color. [15] £32 $60

MAP OF LIVINGSTON MANOR ANNO 1714 [1848] 23x28cm. (8½x10½") By Beatty. [15] £24 $45

PLAN OF THE CITY OF ALBANY ABOUT THE YEAR 1770 - FROM THE ORIGINAL SURVEY BY ROBT. YATES [1850] 20x30cm. (8x11½") First printing of MS plan. Color. [15] £39 $75

NEWTON & BERRY

NEW & IMPROVED TERRESTRIAL GLOBE [and] NEWTON'S IMPROVED POCKET CELESTIAL GLOBE [1820] Globe pair. Diameters: 7cm. (2¾") In modern wooden cases. [2] £3048 $5800

NEWTON'S NEW & IMPROVED TERRESTRIAL GLOBE PUBLISHED BY NEWTON SON & BERRY ... [and] NEWTON'S IMPROVED POCKET CELESTIAL GLOBE [c. 1838] Globe pair. Diameters: 8 cm. (3") With brass meridians, in shagreen cases. Astronomical charts inside top covers. Wooden display mounts. Vibrant original color. [22] £5,780 $11,000

NICOL

KERGUELEN'S LAND CALLED BY C. COOK ISLAND OF DESOLATION [1784] 25x28cm. (10x11") By Y. de Kerguelen. [15] £34 $65

ST. IAGO - SE LAGUES - NATAVIDAET [Mexico] [1806] 15x10cm. (6x4") By. Burney. [15] £32 $60

NOLIN

L'AMERIQUE OU LE NOUVEAU CONTINENT DRESSEE SUR LES MEMOIRES LES PLUS NOUVEAUX ... DEDIEE ET PRESENTEE A MONSIEGNEUR LAW ... [1742] 46x61cm. (17½x23½") Full color. Age toning, minor chipping at margin; else very good. [34] £946 $1800

L'AMERIQUE SEPTENTRIONALE, OU LA PARTIE SEPTENTRIONALE DU INDES OCCIDENTALES [1689] 45x59cm. (17½x23") Original color. Excellent. [38] £2733 $5200

LA VIRGINIE, PENNSILVANIE, NOUVELLE ANGLETERRE ET AUTRES PAYS ... PARTIE DES POSSESSIONS ANGLOISES ... [1781] 20x25cm. (8x10½") Color. [15] £139 $265

LE ROYAVME D'IRLANDE DIVISE EN PROVINCES SUBDIVISEES EN COMTEZ ET EN BARONIES ... [c. 1690] 46x61cm. (18x24") Orig outline col. Partly cropped upper neat line; o/w fine. [38] £355 $675

MAPPE MONDE ... [1759] 48x65cm. (19x25½") Ornate baroque decoration. Col. Fine. [5] £1300 $2474

PARTIE ORIENTALE DU CANADA OU DE LA NOUVELLE FRANCE ... AVEC LA NOUVELLE ANGLETERRE, LA NOUVELLE ECOSSE, LA NOUVELLE YORCK, ET LA VIRGINIE ... PAR LE P. CORONELLI ... A PARIS ... CHEZ I.B. NOLIN ... 1688 [1689] 45x60cm. (17½x23½") Second issue. Original outline color. Excellent. [1] £2102 $4000

ROUTE MARITIME DE BREST A SIAM, ET DE SIAM A BREST, FAITE EN 1685 ET 1686 ... PAR LE PERE CORONELLI ... [1687] 44x72cm. (17½x28") Col. Side borders trimmed; else fine. [37] £631 $1200

NORIE

A NEW CHART OF THE SKAGER RAK OR SLEEVE INCLUDING THE COASTS OF NORWAY AND SWEDEN, FROM THE NAZE TO CHRISTIANA & GOTHENBORG WITH PART OF THE COAST OF JUTLAND ... [1820 (1850)] 81x122cm. (32x48") Black linen backing and silk bound. Clean; good. [11] £200 $381

CHART OF THE VARIATIONS OF THE MAGNETIC NEEDLE FOR ALL THE KNOWN SEAS ... [1824] 53x142cm. (21x56") By T. Yeates; drawn by J. Walker. [15] £66 $125

NORMAN

PLAN OF THE TOWN OF BOSTON, WITH THE ATTACK ON BUNKERS-HILL [1781] 28x13cm. (11½x5½") Some minor wear. [31] £289 $550

NORRIS PETERS CO.

MAP OF PUBLIC LANDS IN PORTO RICO [1905] 20x36cm. (7½x14") Hand color. [15] £21 $40

NUREMBURG CHRONICLE *Try Schedel*

OGILBY *Try Montanus*

A NEW MAP OF ASIA [1673] 42x54cm. (16½x21½") [32] £800 $1522

BRASILIA [1671] 28x36cm. (11x14") Full color. [35] £118 $225

DE STADT ST. MARTIN [1671] 28x37cm. (11x14½") 1629 battle view. Color. [15] £202 $385

EGYPTISCHE PIRAMIDEN [1670] 25x36cm. (10x14") [35] £79 $150

GUINEA [1670] 25x36cm. (10½x14½") [36] £105 $200

INSULA S. LAURENTII VULGO MADAGASCAR [1671] 28x36cm. (11x14") Color. [15] £92 $175

NOVA HISPANIA, NOVA GALICIA, GUATIMALA [1671] 29x36cm. (11½x14") Col. [15] £360 $685

THE CITY CAIRAS [1670] 23x36cm. (9x13½") Cairo. [35] £87 $165

THE CITY OF ALEXANDRIA OR SCANDERIK [1670] 25x36cm. (10x13½") [35] £74 $140

THE ROAD FROM LONDON TO ABERISTWITH ... [1675] 31x44cm. (12x17½") Col. Fine. [5] £170 $324

YUCATAN CONVENTUS IURIDICI HISPANIA NOVAE PARS OCCIDENTALIS ET GUATIMALA CONVENTUS [1671] 28x36cm. (11½x14½") Color. [15] £302 $575

OLIVER & BOYD

OLIVER & BOYD'S NEW TRAVELLING MAP OF ENGLAND & WALES [19th c.] 69x56cm. (27x22") Linen-backed folding map in original marbled slipcase with label. Original color. Small smudges, minimal age-darkening; o/w very good. [19] £105 $200

OLNEY

MAP OF PART OF THE SOUTHERN STATES [1858] 28x46cm. (11x17½") By Sherman & Smith, "To Illustrate Olney's School Geography" Full color. Very good. [13] £32 $60

MAP OF THE CENTRAL STATES TO ILLUSTRATE OLNEY'S SCHOOL GEOGRAPHY [1858] 28x46cm. (10½x17½") By Sherman & Smith. Full col. Left margin & border repairs; good. [14] £32 $60

WESTERN TERRITORIES OF THE UNITED STATES [1847] 28x46cm. (10½x17½") Said to be first map to show Salt Lake City. Full color. [12] £97 $185

ORTELIUS (Folio)

[PORTRAIT] SPECTANDUM DEDIT ORTELIUS ... [1592] 21x32cm. (8½x12½") Engraved by Phillipe Galle, published by C. Planti Color. [5] £150 $285

[same title]. [c. 1595] 21x32cm. (8½x12½") Original color; heightened with gold. Laid down on light paper, but excellent. [5] £200 $381

[TITLE PAGE] THEATRUM ORBIS TERRARUM [1595] 37x24cm. (14½x9½") Original color; heightened with gold. Original ownership inscription and notes at bottom. [5] £200 $381

AFRICAE TABULA NOVA [1570+] 37x50cm. (14½x19½") Issued before crack in plate. Full color. Repair near centerfold bottom and top margin; o/w very good. [21] £631 $1200

AMERICAE SIVE NOVI ORBIS, NOVA DESCRIPTIO [1570+] 36x49cm. (14x19½") 1st edition. Full color. Excellent. [21] £2207 $4200

[same title] [c. 1572] 37x50cm. (14½x19½") Color. Excellent. [5] £2050 $3901

[same title] [1584] 36x50cm. (14x19½") First issue of second plate. Full col. Excel. [38] £2207 $4200

[same title] [1587] 36x49cm. (14x19½") South American bulge removed. Orig col. Excel. [1] £2365 $4500

[same title, date, dimensions] Full color. Mint. [37] £2365 $4500

[same title] [(1587) c. 1598] 36x48cm. (14x19") Third state. Original color. Fine. [5] £2000 $3806

ANGLIAE ET HIBERNIAE ACCURATA DESCRIPTION VETERIBUS ET RECENTIORIBUS [1606-1612] 43x58cm. (17x22½") Published by Vrients. Full color. Few stains, small repaired tear, close left margin; o/w very good to excellent. [22] £1708 $3250

ANGLIAE REGNI FLORENTISSIMI NOVA DESCRIPTIO, AUCTORE HUMFREDO LHUYD DENBYGIENSE [c. 1590] 36x46cm. (14x18") Color. Very good. [23] £450 $856

ANGLIAE, SCOTIAE, ET HIBERNIAE, SIVE BRITANNICAR: INSULARUM DESCRIPTIO [c. 1574] 34x49cm. (13½x19½") Color. Very good. [23] £450 $856

ASIAE NOVA DESCRIPTIO [(1570) c. 1595] 38x49cm. (15x19") Orig color; fine. [5] £775 $1475

[same title] [1570+] 37x49cm. (14½x19") Full color. Excellent. [22] £893 $1700

[same title] [1570 (1612)] 37x48cm. (14½x18½") Color. Centerfold wormholes & edge tears repaired; very good. [34] £657 $1250

CHINAE, OLIM SINARUM REGIONIS, NOVA DESCRIPTIO. AUCTORE LUDOVICO GEORGIO [(1584) 1598] 37x47cm. (14½x18½") Original color. Superb. [5] £1350 $2569

[same title] [1584-1603] 37x47cm. (14½x18½") Color. Very good. [2] £1524 $2900

CRETA IOUIS MAGNI, MEDIO IACET INSULA PONTO ... [1584-1612] 33x48cm. (13½x19½") With Corsica & Sardinia. Original color. Excellent. [22] £394 $750

CULIACANAE AMERICAE REGIONIS DESCRIPTIO ... [and] HISPANIOLAE, CUBAE, ALIARUMQUE INSULARUM CIRCUMIACENTIUM, DELINEATIO [1579] 36x50cm. (14x19½") Antilles, with western Mexico. Full color. Excellent. [38] £381 $725

DESCRIPTIO PEREGRINATIONIS D. PAULI APOSTOLI... [c. 1600] 38x52cm. (15x20½") Modern color; laid on fine tissue. [10] £63 $120

ERYN. HIBERNIAE, INSULAE, NOVA DESCRIPTIO. IRLANDT [1572+] 36x48cm. (14x19") Original color. Lightly toned; else very good. [22] £499 $950

EUROPAE [1570] 34x46cm. (13½x18") Full color. Very good. [21] £394 $750

[same title, date, dimensions] Full color. Fine. [38] £255 $485

FEZZAE ET MAROCCHI REGNA AFRICAE CELEBERRIMA [c. 1595] 38x51cm. (15x20") Old color. [15] £150 $285

[same title] [1595] 39x50cm. (15x19½") [34] £263 $500

GALLIAE REGNI POTENTISS. NOVA DESCRIPTIO, IOANNE IOLIVETO AUCTORE [1570 (1603)] 34x50cm. (13½x20") Color. Centerfold split repaired; else very good. [34] £315 $600

HIBERNIAE, BRITANNICAE INSULAE, NOVA DESCRIPTIO [c. 1574] 35x48cm. (14x19") Color. Very good. [24] £580 $1104

INDIAE ORIENTALIS INSULARUMQUE ADIACIENTIUM TYPUS [(1570) 1598] 35x50cm. (14x19½") Original color. Fine. [5] £1150 $2188

ISLANDIA [1585] 34x49cm. (13x19½") Full color. Excellent. [38] £1682 $3200

[same title] [(1585) c. 1598] 34x49cm. (13½x19") Color. Small invisible top margin repair; o/w excellent. [5] £1600 $3045

MARIS PACIFICI (QUOD VULGO MAR DEL ZUR), CUM REGIONIBUS CIRCUMIACENTIBUS, INSULISQUE IN CODEM PASSIM SPARSIS, NOVISSIMA DESCRIPTIO [1589] 35x50cm. (13½x19½") Color. Excellent. [37] £2470 $4700

[same title] [(1589) c. 1600] 34x50cm. (13½x19½") Color. Excellent. [5] £2580 $4910

PALESTINAE SIVE TOTIUS TERRAE PROMISSIONIS NOVA DESCRIPTIO AUCTORE TILEMANNO STELLA SIGENENS [1570-1571] 34x46cm. (13½x18½") Color. Centerfold reinforcement; else excellent. [21] £578 $1100

[same title] [1599] 33x46cm. (13½x18") State III. Laor 540B. Col. Creasing at centerfold; else VG. [34] £499 $950

PERUVIAE AURIFERAE REGIONIS TYPUS. DIDACO MENDEZIO AUCTORE [on sheet with] LA FLORIDA. AUCTORE HIERON. CHAVES [and] GUASTECAN REG. [1584+] 36x46cm. (14x18") Three map on one sheet. Full color. Marginal staining; else excellent. [22] £788 $1500

[same title] [1584-1608] 33x46cm. (13x18") 3 maps. Full orig col. Excel. [2] £893 $1700

PORTUGALLIAE QUE OLIM LUSITANIA, NOVISSIMA & EXACTISSIMA DESCRIPTIO [1570] 34x52cm. (13½x20½") Full color. Excellent. [38] £276 $525

REGNI NEAPOLITANI VERISSIMA SECUNDUM ANTIQUORUM ET RECENTORIUM TRADITIONEM DESCRIPTIO, PYRRHO LIGORIO AUCT. [1575] 37x50cm. (14½x19½") Full original color. Excellent. [37] £236 $450

TARTARIAE SIVE MAGNI CHAM, REGNI TYPUS [(1570) c. 1580] 35x47cm. (14x18½") Original color. Reinforced short lower centerfold split; o/w fine. [5] £680 $1294

TERRA SANCTA A PETRO LAICSTAIN PERLUSTRATA, ET AB EIUS ORE ET SCHEDIS A CHRISTIANO SCHROT IN TABULAM REDACTA [1584-1612] 37x50cm. (14½x19½") Full original color. Lightly toned; else excellent. [22] £788 $1500

TYPUS ORBIS TERRARUM [c. 1574-1579] 36x51cm. (13½x19½") With South American "bulge". Shirley 122. Full color. Centerfold reinforcement; else very good. [22] £2522 $4800

[same title] [1579] 34x50cm. (13x19½") Some early & modern color. [10] £1839 $3500

[same title] [1587] 36x48cm. (14x19½") Without South American "bulge". Shirley 158. Color. Minor centerfold reinforcement, light toning; very good. [22] £2102 $4000

ORTELIUS (Miniature)

AEGIIPTI RECENTIOR DESCRIPTIO [1588] 8x11cm. (3x4") Dark impression; few pencil marks. [18] £47 $90

ANDALUZIA [1588] 8x11cm. (3x4") Small pencil marks; deep impression; o/w fine. [18] £32 $60

ANGLIA [1595] 8x11cm. (3x4") Outline color. Fine. [37] £66 $125

BARBARIAE ET BILEDULGERID NOVA DESCRIPTIO [1588] 8x11cm. (3x4") Dark impression; few pencil marks. [18] £47 $90

CARTHAGINIS CELEBERRIM SINUS TYPUS PORTUS [1588] 8x11cm. (3x4") Deep impression. [18] £42 $80

GALLIA [1595] 8x11cm. (3x4½") Outline color. Excellent. [37] £24 $45

HIBERNIA [c. 1602] 7x10cm. (3x4") Color. Very good. [24] £125 $238

HISPANIA [1595] 8x11cm. (3x4½") Outline color. Excellent. [37] £45 $85

IAPONIA INSULA [(1598) c. 1600] 8x10cm. (3x4") Antwerp: Plantin. Minor worming and water stain at top margin. [5] £285 $542

NORMANDIA [1588] 8x11cm. (3x4") Minor pencil marks; o/w very good. [18] £39 $75

PRESBITERI IOHANNIS SIVE ABYSINORUM IMPERY DESCRIPTIO [1588] 8x11cm. (3x4½") Fine. [18] £79 $150

SCOTIA [1595] 8x11cm. (3x4½") Outline color. Fine. [37] £66 $125

SEPTENTRIONALIUM REGIONUM DESCRIP. [1588] 8x11cm. (3x4") Deep impression. [18] £131 $250

TARTARIAE SIVE MAGNI CHAMI REGNI TYPUS [1588] 8x11cm. (3x4½") Small pencil mark; o/w fine. [18] £131 $250

VALENTIA REGNUM [1588] 8x11cm. (3x4") Two small pencil marks; o/w fine. [18] £34 $65

OTTENS

[TITLE PAGE] [c. 1740] 27x44cm. (10½x17½") Frontispiece after Jacob Robyn's *Zee-Atlas*. Color. A few short marginal tears. [5] £140 $266

[TITLE PAGE] [c. 1740] 29x46cm. (11½x18") Frontispiece from composite atlas. Col. [5] £140 $266

ASIA [c. 1730] 100x240cm. (39½x94½") Cartouche with double hemisphere world map, animals & costum Six sheets joined and laid on modern canvas. Orig outline color. Good. [33] £2850 $5424

CARTE DE LA NOUVELLE FRANCE OU SE VOIT LE COURS DES GRANDES RIVIERES DE S. LAURENS & DE MISSISSIPI AUJOUR D'HUI S. LOUIS, AUX ENVIRONS DES QUELLES ... [c. 1730] 50x55cm. (19½x21½") Orig wash col. Narrow, adequate margins; o/w excel. [37] £1156 $2200

CARTE DES POSSESSIONS ANGLOISES & FRANCOISES DU CONTINENT DE L'AMERIQUE SEPTENTRIONALE [1755] 41x58cm. (16x22½") French & Dutch titles at top. Old body color a bit faded. Some foxing; else very good. [34] £631 $1200

CARTE NOUVELLE DE MOSCOVIE REPRESENTE LA PARTIE SEPTENTRIONALE [c. 1720] 41x56cm. (16½x22") Color. [15] £118 $225

PARTIE MERIDIONALE DE MOSCOVIE DRESSEE PAR G. DE L'ISLE [1720] 41x56cm. (16½x22") Color. [15] £92 $175

RECENTISSIMA NOVI ORBIS SIVE AMERICAE [c. 1725-50] 48x58cm. (19½x22½") Ottens reissue of uncertain attribution to Danckerts or De Wit. Full color. Minor centerfold reinforcement; else very good. [21] £1051 $2000

TABULA NOVISSIMA ATQUE ACCURATISSIMA CARAIBICARUM INSULARUM SIVE CANNIBALUM ... [c. 1740] 60x50cm. (23½x20") Full orig color. Excellent. [2] £250 $475

OVERTON

A NEW AND CORRECT MAP OF THIRTY MILES ROUND LONDON [c. 1720] 63x95cm. (25x37½") References at sides. Outline color. Very good. [23] £350 $666

A NEW AND EXACT MAP OF GREAT BRITAIN ... [1708] 94x56cm. (36½x22½") Full early color. Few small stains; else excellent. [21] £631 $1200

A NEW MAPP OF LINCOLN SHIRE WITH THE POST & CROSS ROADS, & OTHER REMARKS, ... [1712] 39x49cm. (15½x19½") Original color. Excellent. [38] £255 $485

PALAIRET

CARTE DES POSSESSIONS ANGLOISES & FRANCOISES DU CONTINENT DE L'AMERIQUE SEPTENTRIONALE [1755-63] 41x58cm. (16½x22½") Engraved by Kitchin for *Atlas Methodique*, London & Paris. Original wash color. Lower centerfold repair; fine. [27] £736 $1400

PARKER, N.H.

PARKER'S SECTIONAL AND GEOLOGICAL MAP OF IOWA INCLUDING IRON, LEAD, COPPER AND COAL AND OTHER GEOLOGICAL RESOURCES AND ALL RAILROADS ... [1856] 81x112cm. (32x44") Pocket map folding into red embossed case. Full color. Very good. [3] £118 $225

PAYNE

A NEW MAP OF CONNECTICUT FROM THE BEST AUTHORITIES [1799] 19x24cm. (7½x9½") Very good. [31] £58 $110

NORTH AMERICA WITH THE BOUNDARIES OF THE THIRTEEN UNITED STATES AS SETTLED BY THE TREATY OF 1783 [1791] 33x36cm. (13½x14½") Published at London. Color. [15] £139 $265

NORTH CAROLINA ... [1800] 18x33cm. (7½x12½") Very good. [31] £71 $135

RHODE ISLAND [1799] 24x19cm. (9½x7½") Very good. [31] £58 $110

SWITZERLAND, CONTAINING THE THIRTEEN CANTONS ... [1793] 20x28cm. (7½x11") Published at Dublin. Outline color. Very good. [34] £34 $65

THE PROVINCE OF MAINE ... [1799] 28x18cm. (10½x7") Narrow bottom margin. [31] £79 $150

THE STATE OF KENTUCKY WITH THE ADJOINING TERRITORIES, FROM THE BEST AUTHORITIES ... [1800] 19x22cm. (7½x8½") Invisibly reinforced thin spot; light glue spot; o/w excellent. [12] £97 $185

THE STATE OF MASSACHUSETTS FROM THE BEST INFORMATION [1799] 19x24cm. (7½x9½") Excellent. [12] £58 $110

THE STATE OF NEW YORK FROM THE BEST INFORMATION 1800 [1800] 19x22cm. (7½x8½") Narrow bottom margin. [31] £45 $85

THE WORLD FROM THE BEST AUTHORITIES [1798] 20x38cm. (7½x14½") NY: J. Low Color. [15] £74 $140

PECK, J.

GEOLOGICAL MAP OF THE MINING DISTRICTS IN THE STATE OF GEORGIA, WESTERN PARTS OF NORTH CAROLINA AND IN EAST TENNESSEE [1829] 30x36cm. (11½x14½") J.W. Barber, sc. Very good. [13] £158 $300

PELTON

PELTON'S OUTLINE MAP OF N. AMERICA [1852] 165x180cm. (65x70½") Wall map. Philadelphia: Sower & Barnes. Color. Minor wrinkling; stains in margin, chipping and some loss at left, small hole and separation at top; very good. [8] £328 $625

PENNSYLVANIA MAGAZINE

A NEW PLAN OF BOSTON HARBOUR FROM AN ACTUAL SURVEY [1775] 25x18cm. (10½x7½") By Robert Aitken. First depiction of Bunker Hill Battle. Very good. [31] £394 $750

EXACT PLAN OF GENERAL GAGE'S LINES ON BOSTON NECK IN AMERICA [1775] 30x23cm. (11½x9") By Robert Aitken. Very good. [31] £289 $550

MAP OF THE MARITIME PARTS OF VIRGINIA EXHIBITING THE SEAT OF WAR AND OF L. DUNMORE'S DEPREDATIONS IN THAT COLONY [1776] 25x28cm. (9½x11") First American map of Virginia. By Robert Aitken. Wheat & Brun 540. Light offsetting; loss from binding damage not affecting significant printed area. [38] £578 $1100

PEOPLE'S ATLAS

CITY OF MONTREAL [1895] 25x33cm. (9½x13½") Color. [15] £18 $35

DETROIT [1889] 25x30cm. (10x12") Color. [15] £16 $30

NEW YORK CITY, SOUTHERN PART [1895] 28x25cm. (11x9½") North to 61st Street. Color. [15] £16 $30

NORTH AMERICA [1873] 64x43cm. (25x17") Full color. [12] £47 $90

PERELLE

URBS WARSOVIA SEDES ORDINARIA REGUM POLONIAE [c. 1660] 25x64cm. (10x25") View after drawing by Dahlberg. Two sheets joined. Marginal repair; fine. [28] £394 $750

PETERMANN

ORIGINALKARTE DE CALIFORNISCHEN HALBINSEL ... FUR DIE LOWER CALIFORNIA COMPANY ... [1868] 36x23cm. (13½x9") Gotha: J. Perthes. Color. [15] £45 $85

ORIGINALKARTE DER URWOHNSITZE DER AZTEKEN UND VERWANDTEN PUEBLOS IN NEW MEXICO [1876] 25x20cm. (10x8") Some color. [26] £37 $70

SKIZZE DER ENTDECKUNGEN DER ENGLISCHEN POLAR-EXPEDITION UNTER NARES 1876 [1876] 25x15cm. (10x6½") Color. [15] £21 $40

VEREINIGTE STAATEN VON NORD-AMERIKA IN 6 BLATTERN, BL. 1 [1876] 36x41cm. (13½x16½") Pub. by Stieler. Northwestern U.S. sheet. Outline col. A little foxing. [36] £53 $100

PETRI *Try Munster*

PHARUS-VERLAG

GROSSER VERKEHRS-PLAN BERLIN UND SEINE VORORTE [1919] 87x118cm. (34½x46½") Folding paper plan and gazetteer. Bright printed color. Large tear at fold, small ones at junctures of plan; a repaired fold; gazetteer age-darkened, small tears at edges; good. [19] £66 $125

PHELPS & WATSON

PHELPS AND WATSON'S HISTORICAL AND MILITARY MAP OF THE BORDER & SOUTHERN STATES [1863] 60x87cm. (23½x34½") Folding map between paper covers with linen spine. Bright wash color. Minor wear at fold intersections, light color fade along folds; good+. [19] £158 $300

PHILIP, G.

ANTIQUA TO BRITAIN / GUADALOUPE TO FRANCE / MARIE GALLANTE TO FRANCE [1856] 51x61cm. (20x24") Three maps on one sheet. Full original color. [10] £21 $40

BRITISH COLUMBIA, ATHABASCA & ALBERTA WITH PARTS OF SASKATCHEWAN & ASSINIBOLA [Late 1890's] 51x56cm. (20x22") By William Shawe. Full color. VG. [26] £34 $65

BRITISH ISLES [19th c.] 62x51cm. (24x20") On cover. "Philips' Series of Maps for Travellers". Linen-backed folding map between original boards. Outline and wash color. Light age-soiling at folds, margin damp stain; slipcase worn; good+. [19] £39 $75

MANITOBA WITH PARTS OF SASKATCHEWAN, ASSINIBOLA, ONTARIO, & KEEWATIN [Late 1890's] 51x56cm. (20x22") By William Shawe. Full color. [26] £39 $75

NORTH AMERICA [1851] 51x61cm. (20x24") Color. [15] £71 $135

OROGRAPHICAL MAP OF NORTH AMERICA BY WILLIAM SHAWE, F.R.G.S. [c. 1898] 61x51cm. (24x20") Color indicates elevations and depths. [26] £37 $70

OROGRAPHICAL MAP OF SOUTH AMERICA BY WILLIAM SHAWE, F.R.G.S. [c. 1898] 61x51cm. (24x20") Color indicates elevations and depths. [26] £37 $70

PHILIP'S MAP OF IRELAND WITH DISTANCES FROM DUBLIN AND THE PRINCIPAL SEA PORTS SHEWING THE LINES OF RAILWAY, CANAL, &C. [1852] 77x61cm. (30x24") Linen-backed folding map between embossed board and self-back. Outline col. Light age-darkening at folds; o/w VG. [19] £210 $400

PHILIPS' NEW CLEAR-PRINT REFERENCE PLAN OF THE COUNTY OF LONDON [19th c.] 64x91cm. (25x35½") Linen-backed folding plan in self-backs. Printed color. Back worn at some folds, former owner's pencil marks; cover extremities worn; index guide lacking; good. [19] £37 $70

PHILIPS' NEW LARGE PRINT MAP OF THE COUNTY OF LONDON [19th c.] 94x138cm. (37x54") Linen-backed folding plan between original gilt stamped boards. Partial color. Top of spine slightly worn; very good. [19] £66 $125

PHILIPS' TAPE INDICATOR MAP OF LONDON DIVIDED INTO QUARTER MILE SQUARES FOR REFERENCE AND MEASURING DISTANCES [20th c.] 59x87cm. (23x34") Attached measuring tape. With 79 page index. Linen-backed folding plan between boards. Color. Index age-darkened; small tears at some fold edges. [19] £79 $150

ST. VINCENT TO BRITAIN [1852] 51x30cm. (20x11½") Color. [15] £45 $85

THE JAPANESE EMPIRE WITH CENTRAL AND SOUTHERN MANCHUKUO (MANCHURIA) [c. 1920-30] 64x86cm. (25x33½") Linen-backed folding map. Color. One self-back missing. Very good. [19] £39 $75

THE PACIFIC STATES, THE TERRITORIES AND A PORTION OF THE NORTH-WESTERN STATES [c. 1898] 51x56cm. (20x22") Full color. Excellent. [26] £39 $75

TOBAGO TO BRITAIN [1853] 25x30cm. (9½x11½") Color. [15] £39 $75

WESTERN HEMISPHERE [1856] Diameter: 52 cm. (20½") Orig outline & wash col. [10] £32 $60

PHILLIPS

CARIBBEE OR LEEWARD ISLAND [1820] 18x13cm. (7½x4½") By J.A. Walker. Color. [15] £32 $60

PIQUET

CARTE DES COTES DE BARBARE COMPRENANT LES ETATS DE MAROC, FEZ, ALGER, TUNIS ET TRIPOLI ... [1816] 62x92cm. (24x36") Paris: E. Collin. Linen-backed folding map with original label on backing in modern slipcase. Original color. Uniform age darkening. [19] £105 $200

PITT

A MAP OF THE NORTH POLE AND THE PARTS ADJOINING. ... MDCLXXX [1680] 46x58cm. (18x23") Original color. Minor centerfold reinforcement; else pristine. [22] £1576 $3000

[same title, date, dimensions] Extra folds near center; else fine. [37] £1156 $2200

PLANCIUS

ORBIS TERRARUM TYPUS DE INTEGRO MULTIS IN LOCIS EMENDATUS [1594] 41x57cm. (16x22½") Engraved by Van Doetecum. Shirely 187. Color. Slight trim to outer side borders, reinstated; o/w excellent. [5] £4450 $8468

[same title] [1594-1599] 41x57cm. (16x22½") Color. Good. [10] £3941 $7500

POIRSON

CARTE D'AMERIQUE ... [1808] 53x69cm. (20½x27") Separately issued (lacks centerfold). Original outline color. Foxed; margin repair to neat line; else good. [21] £250 $475

CARTE DE LA FRANCE DIVISEE EN PREFECTURES ET SOUS PREFECTURES, ARCHEVECHES ET EVECHES, ET EN 27 DIVISIONS MILITAIRES [1803] 77x92cm. (30x36") Linen-backed folding map with original chemise and marbled slipcase with embossed label. Outline color. Slight foxing and age-soiling at folds; very good. [19] £173 $330

CARTE DU MEXIQUE ET DES PAYS LIMITROPHES [1811] 43x74cm. (17x29") Minor margin repairs; fine. [30] £342 $650

POLITICAL MAGAZINE

A MAP AND CHART OF THOSE PARTS OF THE BAY OF CHESAPEAK YORK AND JAMES RIVERS WHICH ARE AT PRESENT THE SEAT OF WAR. [1781] 25x38cm. (10½x14½") By J. Lodge. Jolly POL-38. Color. [15] £150 $285

A NEW & ACCURATE MAP OF THE PROVINCE OF CANADA, IN NORTH AMERICA; FROM THE LATEST AND BEST AUTHORITIES [1782] 26x34cm. (10x13") London: John Bew. Jolly POL-57. Trimmed, with neat line partially shaved; map fine. [10] £116 $220

[same title, date, dimensions] Fine. [30] £202 $385

[same title, date, dimensions] Color. Excellent. [37] £184 $350

A NEW AND ACCURATE CHART OF THE HARBOUR OF BOSTON, IN NEW ENGLAND. IN NORTH AMERICA. [1782] 22x17cm. (9x6½") Jolly POL-63. Later wash color. Light offsetting top third. [18] £126 $240

A NEW AND ACCURATE MAP OF NORTH CAROLINA, AND PART OF SOUTH CAROLINA, WITH THE FIELD OF BATTLE BETWEEN EARL CORNWALLIS AND GENERAL GATES. [1780] 27x38cm. (11x15") Lodge, sc. Jolly POL-16. Fold line; close lower half right margin, ragged left margin, neat lines unaffected. [6] £208 $395

[same title, date, dimensions] Chip in one corner; a few repaired tears. [31] £171 $325

A NEW AND ACCURATE MAP OF VIRGINIA, AND PART OF MARYLAND AND PENNSYLVANIA. [1780] 27x37cm. (10½x14½") Jolly POL-17. Very good. [31] £171 $325

POPPLE

[MEXICO] [c. 1740] 48x66cm. (19x26") A few unobtrusive stains. [35] £184 $350

A MAP OF THE BRITISH EMPIRE IN AMERICA ... [Sheet 5: Wisconsin, Minnesota, Iowa, Dakota, part of Illinois] [1733] 51x66cm. (19½x26") Color. [15] £413 $785

A MAP OF THE BRITISH EMPIRE IN AMERICA WITH THE FRENCH AND SPANISH SETTLEMENTS ADJACENT THERETO. BY HENRY POPPLE [1733] 239x229cm. (94x90") Large folio; 21 map sheets (dimensions if joined); includes separate key map. Bound in contemporary marbled paper over worn and rebacked boards; excellent. [21] £12874 $24500

A PLAN OF THE HARBOUR OF PORT ANTONIO IN JAMAICA [1733] 15x15cm. (6x6") Kapp, Jam. 57. Color. [15] £45 $85

PORCACCHI

DESCRITTIONE DELL'ISOLA D'INGHILTERRA [1572-1590] 10x15cm. (4x5½") Engraved by Porro. [36] £105 $200

DESCRITTIONE DELLA GRAN CITTA & ISOLA DEL TEMISTITAN [1576] 15x18cm. (5½x6½") [15] £58 $110

MONDO NUOVO [1574] 10x15cm. (4x6") On 8 x 11" sheet with text. Reverse of text portion archivally backed; map excellent. [35] £184 $350

PORRO

[TITLE PAGE] LA SECONDA PARTA DELLA GEOGRAFIA DI CL. TOLOMEO [1620] 25x18cm. (10x7") Cosmographers flanking tower. [15] £39 $75

DESCRITTIONE DELL'AFRICA E QUELLE DELL ISOLE CHE A LEI S. ASPETTANO - AFRICA [1598] 18x18cm. (6½x7") [15] £92 $175

PORTER, T.

MAP OF THE UNITED STATES SHOWING THE PRINCIPAL BOTANICAL DIVISIONS [1873] 30x38cm. (12x15") Color keyed. [15] £24 $45

PREVOST D'EXILES *Try Bellin*

PLAN DE LA VILLE DE QUEBEC [c. 1754] 20x28cm. (8x11") Color. [15] £66 $125

PROBST

[AFRICA] [1748] 28x39cm. (11x15½") 1736 trip to Goa in portolan style, from *Reisach Missionari* Repaired tear; tissue back to reinforce folds. [32] £420 $799

PTOLEMY *Also try Munster*

PTOLEMY (1522-1541, Strassburg)

TABULA MODER. SICILI & SARDI [1535] 28x41cm. (11x16") Servetus, Lyon. Occasional spotting; else fine. [34] £184 $350

PTOLEMY (1548, Venice)

CALECUT NUOVA TAVOLA [1548] 13x17cm. (5x7") Centerfold somewhat age-darkened. [18] £97 $185

GERMANIA NOVA TABULA MDXXXXII [1548] 13x17cm. (5x6½") By Gastaldi. VG. [18] £95 $180

INDIA TERCERA NUOVA TAVOLA [1548] (no dims.) By Gastaldi. Mint. [37] £394 $750

NUEVA HISPANIA TABULA NOVA [1548] 13x17cm. (5x6½") By Gastaldi. Excel. [38] £1156 $2200

TABULA ASIAE X [SOUTH ASIA] [1548] 13x17cm. (5x7") By Gastaldi. Very good. [18] £97 $185

TIERRA NOVA [SOUTH AMERICA] [1548] 13x17cm. (5x6½") By Gastaldi. First printed map exclusively of the continent. [10] £210 $400

[same title, date] 13x18cm. (5x7") Excellent. [37] £342 $650

PTOLEMY (1561-1599, Venice)

AFRICA MINOR NUOVA TAVOLA [1574] 18x24cm. (7x9½") Ruscelli. Very good. [18] £47 $90

ANGLIA ET HIBERNIA NOVA [1574] 18x25cm. (7x10") By Ruscelli. Excellent. [37] £131 $250

[same title] [1599] 18x25cm. (7x10") By Ruscelli. Very good++. [18] £158 $300

ARABIA FELICE NUOVA TAVOLA [1561] 19x25cm. (7½x9½") Ruscelli. Excellent. [37] £53 $100

[same title] [1599] 18x25cm. (7½x9½") Ruscelli. Very good. [18] £53 $100

BRASIL NUOVA TABULA [1598] 19x26cm. (7½x10") By Ruscelli; vignettes added by Rosaccio. Excellent. [37] £92 $175

CALECUT NUOVA TAVOLA [1561] 18x24cm. (7x9½") Ruscelli. Age toned centerfold. [18] £53 $100

[same title] [(1561)-1574] 19x25cm. (7½x9½") By Ruscelli, after Gastaldi. Venice: Ziletti. Slight burn mark at side edges. [31] £76 $145

CARTA MARINA NUOVA TAVOLA [1561] 18x24cm. (7x9½") Ruscelli. Very pale centerfold darkening; very good. [20] £289 $550

CELCUT NUOVA TAVOLA [1598] 19x25cm. (7½x10") By Rosaccio, after Ruscelli. Excel. [37] £50 $95

DI HUNGARIA ET TRANSILVANIA. TAVOLA NOVISSIMA [1599] 15x20cm. (5½x8") Ruscelli. Show-through, light marginal soil. [18] £79 $150

EGITTO NUOVA TAVOLA [1561] 18x25cm. (7½x9½") By Ruscelli. Light stain lower margin; very good. [18] £53 $100

[same title, date, dimensions] Excellent. [37] £53 $100

[same title] [1562] 18x25cm. (7½x9½") Venice: Valgrisi. [15] £45 $85

EUROPAE TABULA V [DALMATIA] [1561] 19x25cm. (7½x10") Ruscelli. Excellent [37] £39 $75

EUROPAE TABULA IX [BALKANS] [1598] 19x25cm. (7½x10") By Rosaccio, after Ruscelli. Excellent. [37] £53 $100

EUROPAE TABULA X [GREECE] [1561] 19x25cm. (7½x9½") Ruscelli. Excellent [37] £79 $150

[same title] [1599] 19x25cm. (7½x10") By Rosaccio, after Ruscelli. Excellent. [37] £79 $150

GALLIA NOVA TABULA [1561] 19x25cm. (7½x9½") By Ruscelli. Excellent. [37] £39 $75

[same title] [1598] 19x25cm. (7½x9½") By Rosaccio. Excellent. [37] £39 $75

[same title] [1599] 19x25cm. (7½x9½") By Ruscelli. Slight text show-through; VG. [18] £45 $85

HISPANIA NOVA TABULA [1561] 19x25cm. (7½x10") Ruscelli. Excellent. [37] £79 $150

[same title, date, dimensions] Marginal age soil, centerfold darkening; o/w VG. [18] £79 $150

[same title] [1599] 19x25cm. (7½x10") By Rosaccio. Excellent. [37] £79 $150

ISOLA CUBA NOVA [1561] 19x25cm. (7½x9½") Ruscelli. Excellent. [37] £131 $250

ISOLA SPAGNOLA NOVA [1561] 19x25cm. (7½x9½") Ruscelli. Excellent. [37] £66 $125

MARMARICA NUOVA TAVOLA [1561] 18x25cm. (7x9½") By Ruscelli. Light centerfold age tone, minor soil in margin; o/w very good. [18] £32 $60

MOSCHOVIA TAVOLA NUOVA [1561] 19x24cm. (7½x9½") Ruscelli. Excellent. [37] £39 $75

[same title, date, dimensions] Minor worming bottom margin; very good. [18] £58 $110

NATOLIA NUOVA TAVOLA [1561] 18x25cm. (7½x10") Ruscelli. 1st edition. VG. [18] £53 $100

[same title] [1598] 19x25cm. (7½x10") By Rosaccio, after Ruscelli. Excellent. [37] £39 $75

NUEVA HISPANIA TABULA NOVA [1561] 23x18cm. (9½x6½") Venice: Valgrisi. By Ruscelli after Gastaldi. Small old hand note. [31] £289 $550

PERSIA NUOVA TAVOLA [1561] 18x25cm. (7x9½") By Ruscelli. Top margin trimmed to plate mark; very good. [18] £39 $75

POLONIA ET HUNGARIA NUOVA TAVOLA [1561] 19x25cm. (7½x10") Ruscelli. Excel. [37] £53 $100

[same title, date, dimensions] Some worming above map. [36] £79 $150

[same title] [1574] 19x25cm. (7½x10") Age toning, light soil & some show-through; VG. [18] £79 $150

[same title] [1598] 19x25cm. (7½x10") By Rosaccio, after Ruscelli. Excellent. [37] £53 $100

PTOLEMAEI TYPUS [1561] 16x26cm. (6x10") Ruscelli. Shirley 109. Excellent. [37] £131 $250

SEPTENTRIONALIUM PARTIUM NOVA TABULA [1561] 19x24cm. (7½x9½") The "Zeno" map. Ruscelli. Excellent. [37] £236 $450

TABULA APHRICAE II [NORTH AFRICA] [1561] 18x25cm. (7x9½") Ruscelli. Very minor show-through; very good. [18] £32 $60

TABULA ASIAE I [ASIA MINOR] [1598] 19x26cm. (7½x10") By Rosaccio, after Ruscelli. Exc. [37] £39 $75

[same title] [1599] 18x25cm. (7x9½") Ruscelli. Very good. [18] £53 $100

TABULA ASIAE II [CAUCASUS, ETC.] [1599] 18x25cm. (7x9½") By Ruscelli. Minor show-through; very good. [18] £34 $65

TABULA ASIAE III [ARMENIA, ETC.] [1561] 18x24cm. (7x9½") Ruscelli. VG. [18] £45 $85

[same title, date] 19x25cm. (7½x9½") Excellent. [37] £26 $50

[same title, date] 20x25cm. (8x10") Venice: Valgrisi. By Gastaldi. [15] £50 $95

TABULA ASIAE IIII [HOLY LAND] [1561] 19x25cm. (7½x9½") Ruscelli. Excel. [37] £184 $350

TABULA ASIAE V [PERSIA] [1561] 20x25cm. (7½x10") By Ruscelli. [35] £53 $100

[same title, date, dimensions] Excellent. [37] £26 $50

[same title] [1599] 18x25cm. (7x9½") By Ruscelli; pictorial details added by Rosaccio. Slight worming at top margin. [18] £29 $55

TABULA ASIAE VI [ARABIA] [1561] 19x25cm. (7½x9½") Ruscelli. Excellent. [37] £47 $90

[same title] 18x24cm. (7x9½") Minor text show-through, light ink tone; very good. [18] £53 $100

TABULA ASIAE VII [CENTRAL ASIA] [1574] 18x24cm. (7x9½") By Ruscelli. Show-through, age soil, stains at top margin, small wormhole. [18] £39 $75

TABULA ASIAE X [SOUTH ASIA] [1561] 19x25cm. (7½x9½") Ruscelli. Excellent. [37] £26 $50

[same title] [1574] 19x24cm. (7½x9½") Very good. [18] £53 $100

TABULA ASIAE XI [FAR EAST] [1561] 18x23cm. (7x9") Ruscelli. Excellent. [37] £79 $150

[same title, date, dimensions] Minor show-through, o/w very good. [18] £53 $100

TABULA ASIAE XII [CEYLON] [1561] 19x25cm. (7½x9½") Ruscelli. Excellent. [37] £79 $150

TABULA EUROPAE II [SPAIN & PORTUGAL] [1561] 19x25cm. (7½x10") Ruscelli. Exc. [37] £66 $125

[same title] [1599] 19x26cm. (7½x10") By Ruscelli. Pictorial details added by Rosaccio. Wormhole near top fold, o/w very good. [18] £79 $150

TABULA EUROPAE III [FRANCE] [1561] 18x24cm. (7x9½") Ruscelli. Slight age-toning & text show-through; very good. [18] £39 $75

[same title] [1574] 19x24cm. (7½x9½") Excellent. [37] £34 $65

TABULA EUROPAE IIII [GERMANY & DENMARK] [1574] 18x25cm. (7x9½") Ruscelli. Age toning, text show-through, o/w very good. [18] £53 $100

[same title, date, dimension] Excellent. [37] £79 $150

TABULA EUROPAE V [DALMATIA COAST] [1561] 18x25cm. (7x9½") Ruscelli. [36] £66 $125

TABULA EUROPAE VI [ITALY] [1561] 19x25cm. (7½x9½") Ruscelli. Excellent. [37] £92 $175
[same title] [1599] 19x25cm. (7½x9½") After Ruscelli by Rosaccio. Excellent. [37] £92 $175
TABULA EUROPAE VII [SICILY & SARDINIA] [1561] 19x25cm. (7½x10") Excel. [37] £53 $100
TABULA EUROPAE VIII [EASTERN EUROPE] [1561] 19x25cm. (7½x10") Ruscelli. Exc. [37] £39 $75
[same title, date, dimensions] Slight age toning; tiny centerfold slit; very good. [18] £50 $95
TABULA EUROPAE IX [BALKANS] [1561] 19x25cm. (7½x10") Ruscelli. Excellent. [37] £53 $100
[same title, date, dimensions] Very good. [18] £53 $100
[same title, date, dimensions] [35] £47 $90
TABULA EUROPAE X [GREECE] [1561] 19x25cm. (7½x9½") Ruscelli. [36] £79 $150
[same title, date. dimensions] Centerfold age toned; slight show through; very good. [18] £79 $150
TAVOLA NUOVA DELLA MARCA TRIVIGIANA [1561] 19x25cm. (7½x10") Ruscelli. Exc. [37] £53 $100
[same title] [1599] 19x25cm. (7½x10") After Ruscelli, by Rosaccio. Excellent. [37] £53 $100
TAVOLA NUOVA DI PIEMONTE [1561] 19x25cm. (7½x10") Ruscelli. Excellent. [37] £39 $75
TAVOLA NUOVA DI PRUSSIA ET DI LIVONIA [1561] 19x25cm. (7½x10") Ruscelli. Exc. [37] £53 $100
[same title, date, dimensions] Some worming above map; else excellent. [36] £71 $135
[same title] [1574] 19x25cm. (7½x10") By Ruscelli. Wormhole in title, o/w very good. [18] £39 $75
[same title] [1598] 19x25cm. (7½x10") By Rosaccio, after Ruscelli. Excellent. [37] £53 $100
TAVOLA NUOVA DI SARDIGNA ET DI SICILIA [1561] 19x25cm. (7½x9½") Ruscelli. Exc. [37] £53 $100
TAVOLA NUOVA DI SCHIAVONIA [1561] 19x25cm. (7½x9½") Ruscelli. Excellent. [37] £39 $75
[same title] [1574] 19x25cm. (7½x9½") Slight stain & age darkening; o/w very good. [18] £45 $85
TIERRA NOVA [1561 (1574)] 18x25cm. (7x9½") By Ruscelli, after Gastaldi; Ziletti, pub. Small stains at side edges. [31] £184 $350
TIERRA NUEVA [1561] 18x25cm. (7½x9½") Ruscelli. Light centerfold darkening; o/w VG. [20] £263 $500
TOSCANA NUOVA TAVOLA [1561] 18x26cm. (7x10") By Ruscelli. Excellent. [37] £53 $100

PTOLEMY (1578-1730, Mercator)

ASIAE VII TAB. MEDIUS MERIDIANES 114 [1698] 36x46cm. (14x18") Pub. Utrecht. Color. [15] £97 $185

PTOLEMY (1596-1621, Magini)

AMERICA [1596-1621] 13x17cm. (5x6½") On sheet, "Descrittione Dell' America ...", 28 x 20 cm. Very good. [20] £223 $425
HUNGARIA ET TRANSILVANIA [1598] 13x18cm. (5x7") With text, 11 x 8". Color. Slight text show-through; else very good. [34] £45 $85
PERSIAE REGNUM SIVE SOPHORUM IMPERIUM [1597-1598] 13x17cm. (5x7") Text below. [10] £39 $75
TABULA ASIAE II [1617] 12x17cm. (5x6½") Published by Jansson. [10] £21 $40
TABULA ASIAE III [1617] 12x17cm. (5x6½") Published by Jansson. [10] £26 $50
TABULA ASIAE VI [1597-1598] 12x17cm. (5x6½") Reverse: Tabula VII. Each with text below. [10] £45 $85
TABULA ASIAE VIII [1617] 12x17cm. (5x6½") Published by Jansson. [10] £21 $40
TABULA ASIAE XI [1617] 12x17cm. (5x6½") [10] £24 $45
TABULA ASIAE XII [1597-1598] 13x17cm. (5x6½") (Taprobana.) [10] £53 $100
TABULA EUROPAE IIII [1596] 13x17cm. (5x6½") Ptolemaic Germany & Denmark. Outline color. Fine [37] £34 $65
TABULA EUROPAE QUINTA [1596] 13x17cm. (5x6½") Ptolemaic Italy. Outline col. Exc. [37] £39 $75

PURCELL

A MAP OF THE STATES OF VIRGINIA, NORTH CAROLINA, SOUTH CAROLINA AND GEORGIA; COMPREHENDING THE SPANISH PROVINCES OF EAST AND WEST FLORIDA: ... BY JOSEPH PURCELL [c. 1792] 30x36cm. (12x14") Published by Vint & Anderson; like Morse map by Doolittle. [6] £260 $495

PURCHAS *Try Mercator (small)*

A GENERAL AND PARTICULAR DESCRIPTION OF AMERICA [1625] 20x20cm. (8x7½") [15] £171 $325

QUAD

[TITLE PAGE] EUROPAE TOTIUS ORBIS TERRARUM PARTIS ... [1594] 15x21cm. (6x8½") Color. [5] £75 $143

ANGLIAE REGNI FLORENTISSIMI NOVA AUCTORE HUMFREDO LHUYD DENBYGIENSE [1600] 18x27cm. (7x10½") Color. Excellent. [38] £210 $400

APHRICA [1600] 21x30cm. (8½x11½") Text at left. Some show-through at left. [18] £171 $325

HISPANIAE NOVAE SIVE MAGNAE VERA DESCRIPTIO [1608] 21x29cm. (8x11½") [10] £100 $190

ITALIA [c. 1600] 22x27cm. (8½x10½") Full color. Excellent. [37] £197 $375

NOVI ORBIS PARS BOREALIS, AMERICA SCILICET, COMPLECTENS FLORIDAM, BACCALAON, CANADAM, TERRAM CORTERIALEM, VIRGINIAM, NOROMBECAM... [c. 1600] 23x30cm. (9x11½") Excellent. [37] £1445 $2750

SEPTENTRIONALIUM REGIONUM SUETIAE GOTHIAE NORVEGIAE DANIAE &C [c. 1600] 22x30cm. (8½x12") Full color. Excellent. [37] £307 $585

TYPUS ORBIS TERRARUM, AD IMITATIONEM UNIVERSALIS GERHARDI MERCATORIS ... [1596] 22x32cm. (9x13") Substantial color. Four tiny wormholes top center; o/w VG. [3] £657 $1250

[same title, date, dimensions] Shirley 197. Full color. Remargined top & left, small loss to upper border. [37] £736 $1400

RADEFELD

NEUESTE KARTE VON AMERICA NACH DEN BESSTEN QUELLEN ENTWORF U. GEZEICH ... [1850] 38x30cm. (15x11½") Color. [15] £50 $95

RAILROAD COMPANY MAPS

[DENVER AND RIO GRANDE WESTERN RAILROAD SYSTEM] [c. 1885] 36x43cm. (14x17") Similar to 1883 Rand, McNally (Modelski, RR of Amer, #49). Small tape stains at neat lines and an inch into image at left center; narrow margins. [6] £79 $150

ATLANTA, BIRMINGHAM AND ATLANTIC RAILWAY [1916] 48x56cm. (18½x22") [26] £32 $60

BOSTON AND MAINE RAILROAD AND CONNECTIONS [c. 1900] 58x76cm. (23x30") Show New England. Rail line in red. [26] £32 $60

DENVER & RIO GRANDE RAILROAD SYSTEM [c. 1882] 38x46cm. (14½x17½") Colorado, with line to Santa Fe & Ogden. Colorful. [15] £76 $145

ESTES-ROCKY MOUNTAIN NATIONAL PARK, REACHED VIA UNION PACIFIC SYSTEM THE BIG THOMSON CANYON ROUTE [1917] 58x66cm. (23x26") Some color. [26] £32 $60

MAP ACCOMPANYING THE PROPOSAL OF THE LOS ANGELES, SAN DIEGO & YUMA RAILWAY CO. FOR A SITE FOR ... HARBOR DEFENSES AT SAN DIEGO [1891] 38x30cm. (15x12") By W.H. Carlson. Color. [15] £26 $50

MAP EXHIBITING THE ANDROSCOGGIN RAILROAD AND ITS CONNECTIONS [1851] 64x41cm. (25x15½") By B.W. Thayer, published by Harmon & Williams, Portland. Color. [15] £123 $235

MAP OF FLORIDA AND THE WEST INDIES PUBLISHED BY THE FLORIDA EAST COAST RAILWAY [1899] 20x23cm. (7½x9½") Norris-Peters Co. Color. [15] £16 $30

MAP OF THE ARKANSAS LAND GRANT OF THE ST. LOUIS, IRON MOUNTAIN & SOUTHERN RAILWAY CO. [c. 1890] 91x23cm. (36x9") Folding, double-sided. Minor flaws: misfolds, short splits, small marginal loss. [12] £92 $175

MAP OF THE CHICAGO, DANVILLE AND VINCENNES RAILROAD [1876] 30x23cm. (11½x8½") Slight folds as issued; very good. [26] £39 $75

MAP SHEWING THE ROUTE OF THE NORTH PENNSYLVANIA RAILROAD FROM PHILADELPHIA TO BETHLEHEM WITH BRANCHES TO DOYLESTOWN & FREEMANSBURG & CONNECTIONS WITH LEHIGH VALLEY [1857] 61x122cm. (24x48") By A. Easton; Phila: Duval Lith. Wall map, with 30 page report. Old color. Minor repair. [15] £118 $225

MAP SHOWING THE LOCATION OF THE LAND GRANT OF SANTA FE PACIFIC R.R. CO. IN NEW MEXICO [c. 1900] 86x64cm. (33½x25") Some color. [12] £197 $375

SOUTH WEST-VIRGINIA MINERAL RESOURCES & RAILWAY FACILITIES. C.R. BOYD C.E. 1882 [1883] 51x97cm. (20x38") From 2nd Annual Report of the Norfolk & Western Railroad. Philadelphia: Allen, Lane & Scott's Printing House. Color. [6] £131 $250

THE ATCHISON TOPEKA AND THE SANTA FE RAILWAY SYSTEM [1926] 43x89cm. (17x35") Color. [26] £47 $90

THE NORTH WESTERN LINE [1912] (no dims.) Wall map by Rand, McNally. Color. Water stain at upper margin causing title to run; tears at top repaired with tape; G to VG. [7] £71 $135

RAMUSIO

[LA NUOVA FRANCIA] [c. 1556] 27x37cm. (10½x14½") State II. Excellent. [2] £1025 $1950

MEXICO [1565] 28x18cm. (10½x7") Clean. [15] £202 $385

PRIMA TAVOLA [c. 1560] (no dims.) All of Africa with Atlantic islands; south at top. Sliver clipped at center from binding; else excellent. [38] £512 $975

SECONDA TAVOLA [c. 1560] 29x38cm. (11x15") Indian Ocean rim. Copperplate version. Excellent. [38] £184 $350

TERZA OSTRO TAVOLA [c. 1570] 28x38cm. (11x15") Inverted map from *Della Navigatione e Viaggi*. Some centerfold browning. [5] £850 $1618

UNIVERSALE DELLA PARTE DEL MONDO NUOVAMENTE RITROVATA [1556] 27x27cm. (11x11") From *Della Navigationi e Viaggi*. Excellent. [5] £985 $1874

RAND, McNALLY & CO.

[CALIFORNIA] [1892] 69x51cm. (26½x19½") 2 insets. Color. [15] £42 $80

[GEORGIA] [1882] 51x36cm. (20x14") Color. 6 index pages. [15] £32 $60

[NEW MEXICO] [1895] 30x23cm. (12x9") Color. [6] £34 $65

[WASHINGTON] [1895] 23x30cm. (9x12") Color. [6] £24 $45

BROOKLYN AND VICINITY [N.Y.] [1902] 48x69cm. (19x26½") Color. [15] £24 $45

CALIFORNIA RAILROADS [1895] 69x48cm. (27x19½") 2 insets. Color. [15] £42 $80

CLEVELAND [1904] 33x48cm. (13½x19") Color. [15] £26 $50

CONNECTICUT. RHODE ISLAND. RAILROADS [1904] 33x51cm. (12½x19½") Col. [15] £21 $40

DAKOTA [NORTHERN PORTION] [1882] 32x47cm. (12½x18½") Printed color. [12] £37 $70

FLORIDA [1898] 23x30cm. (9x12½") Color. [15] £11 $20

GENERAL MAP OF THE REPUBLIC OF MEXICO CONTRUCTED FROM BEST AUTHORITIES SHOWING RAILWAYS, STEAMSHIP ROUTES & TELEGRAPHIC COMMUNICATIONS [1882] 122x170cm. (48x67") 4 sheets dissected on linen in original slipcase. Immaculate. [15] £129 $245

GEORGIA [1888] 48x33cm. (18½x13") From *Indexed Atlas of the World*. Col. Fine. [13] £21 $40

[same title] [1898] 66x48cm. (26x19") Printed color. Fine. [13] £21 $40

ILLINOIS RAILROADS [1904] 66x44cm. (26x17") Color. [15] £26 $50

INDIAN TERRITORY [1882] 33x50cm. (13x19½") Printed outline. Fine. [12] £45 $85

INDIANA [1888] 64x46cm. (25½x18½") From *Indexed Atlas of the World*. With 6 pages of text. Printed color. Fine. [14] £21 $40

INDIANA RAILROADS [1895] 66x48cm. (26x19") Color. [15] £32 $60

INDIANAPOLIS & ENVIRONS [1902] 66x48cm. (26x19") Color. [15] £26 $50

LOUISIANA RAILROADS [1895] 48x69cm. (19½x27") Color. [15] £34 $65

MANITOBA RAILROADS [1895] 33x48cm. (13x19") Color. [15] £24 $45

MAP OF ALASKA [1895] 23x31cm. (9x12") Color. [6] £26 $50

MAP OF BRITISH COLUMBIA [1895] 23x33cm. (9x12½") Color. [15] £13 $25

MAP OF MAIN PORTION OF ST. PAUL [1895] 33x23cm. (12½x9½") Color. [15] £11 $20

MAP OF OKLAHOMA SHOWING RECENT ADDITIONS TO TERRITORY [c. 1890-91] 33x38cm. (12½x15") Color. [26] £47 $90

MINNESOTA RAILROADS [1895] 66x48cm. (26x19") Outline color. [15] £29 $55

NEW MEXICO [1877] 49x32cm. (19½x12½") Outline color. [35] £42 $80

NEW SECTIONAL AND TOWNSHIP MAP OF OHIO [1881] 33x51cm. (13x20") 2 sheets, dimensions for each. With 13 index pages. Color. [15] £29 $55

OCEANICA [1881] 33x48cm. (13x19") Color. [15] £21 $40

OKLAHOMA - INDIAN TERRITORY [1892 (1898)] 31x48cm. (12x19") 2 printed colors. [12] £39 $75

ONTARIO RAILROADS [1904] 48x69cm. (19x27") Color. [15] £21 $40

PENNSYLVANIA [1898] 23x30cm. (9½x12½") Color. [15] £11 $20

QUEBEC RAILROADS [1895] 48x66cm. (19x26") [15] £24 $45

RAND, MCNALLY & CO.'S INDEXED COUNTY AND TOWNSHIP MAP OF INDIANA [1882] 51x33cm. (19½x13") Pocket map with 52 pages of index and ads in paper covers. Printed color. Crayon markings on map; o/w very good. [14] £26 $50

RAND, MCNALLY & CO.'S INDIAN TERRITORY AND OKLAHOMA [1898] 30x48cm. (12x19") Railroads & boundaries overprinted in red. [6] £39 $75

RAND, MCNALLY'S POCKET MAP AND SHIPPER'S GUIDE OF IOWA [1899] (no dims.) 50 text pages and large folding map. Map loose; map and case very good. [3] £26 $50

RAND MCNALLY'S POCKET MAP AND SHIPPERS GUIDE OF NEW MEXICO [1901] 51x66cm. (20x26") Pocket map folding into cardboard case with 26 text pages. Very good. [3] £32 $60

SOUTH CAROLINA RAILROADS [1903] 51x66cm. (19½x26") Color. [15] £24 $45

SOUTH DAKOTA [1891] 38x58cm. (15x22½") Printed outline color. Fine. [12] £39 $75

THE RAND MCNALLY VEST POCKET MAP OF MONTANA [1904] 41x51cm. (16x20") Folds into cardboard case. Full color. [3] £24 $45

THE UNITED STATES [1901] 48x66cm. (19x26") Color. [15] £18 $35

TORONTO [1898] 30x48cm. (12½x19") Color. [15] £39 $75

UTAH [1895] 30x23cm. (12x9") Color. [6] £24 $45

VIRGINIA RAILROADS [1889] 51x69cm. (19½x27") Outline color. [15] £34 $65

WEST INDIES [1881] 25x33cm. (9½x13") Color. [15] £13 $25

WYOMING [1881] 25x33cm. (10x13") 7 counties. Outline color. [15] £34 $65

[same title] [1882] 25x33cm. (10x12½") Printed outline color. [12] £37 $70

RAPKIN *Try Tallis*

UNITED STATES [1861] 28x43cm. (10½x16½") "Federal", "Border Slaveholding" and "Confederate" states distinguished. Color. [15] £34 $65

RASPE

PLAN VON DEN OPERATINEN DER KOENIGLICHEN ARMEE [1777] 38x28cm. (15x10½") In Korn's *Geschichte der Kriege in und ausser Europa*. Original color. Very good. [31] £118 $225

RAVENSTEIN, F. G.

MAP OF THE SOUTH-WESTERN PORTION OF THE UNITED STATES SONORA & CHIHUAHUA [1870] 33x38cm. (12½x14½") London: J. Murray. Features W. A. Bell's explorations. Color. [15] £39 $75

REAL ESTATE AND PROMOTIONAL MAPS

LITTLE KAUKAUNA [Wisc.] [1898] 48x46cm. (19x18") 36 waterfront lot plan by W.S. Nearing; Norris Peters Co. Color. [15] £18 $35

MAP OF ABILENE [Texas] [c. 1890] 58x64cm. (23x25") By A.H. Kirby; published by Louis C. Wise & Co. Pristine. [12] £210 $400

MAP OF CHULA VISTA, SAN DIEGO COUNTY ... SUBDIVISION OF NATIONAL RANCHO [1892] 25x36cm. (9½x13½") San Diego Land & Town Co. Color. [15] £26 $50

MAP OF THE FALLS OF BEAVER RIVER AND VICINITY [1833] 15x30cm. (6½x11½") By Stealey. 16 x 14" broadside sheet. Molineux, engr. Folds; repaired marginal tears; o/w VG. [31] £236 $450

RECLUS

MEXICO AND ITS VALLEY [1872] 23x15cm. (8½x5½") London: Virtue. [15] £18 $35

REICHARD

AMERICA ENTVWORFEN VON C. G. REICHARD 1816 REVIDIRT UND NEU GESTOCHEN 1823 [1823] 38x28cm. (15x11½") Color. [15] £63 $120

REID

AN ACCURATE MAP OF THE UNITED STATES OF AMERICA ACCORDING TO THE TREATY OF PEACE OF 1783 [1796] 36x46cm. (14x18") Very good. [31] £197 $375

CONNECTICUT FROM THE BEST AUTHORITIES [1796] 36x43cm. (14x17½") VG. [31] £250 $475

GEORGIA FROM THE LATEST AUTHORITIES [1796] 23x38cm. (8½x15") To Mississippi River. Very good. [31] £315 $600

THE PROVINCE OF MAINE FROM THE BEST AUTHORITIES. 1795 [1796] 36x25cm. (14½x10") Very good. [31] £250 $475

THE STATE OF PENNSYLVANIA FROM THE LATEST SURVEYS [1796] 33x46cm. (12½x17½") Color wash. Very good. [31] £263 $500

THE STATE OF VIRGINIA FROM THE BEST AUTHORITIES [1796] 34x47cm. (13x18½") [6] £313 $595

[same title, date] 34x46cm. (13½x18") Very good. [31] £223 $425

RELAND

LE JAPON DEVISE EN SOISSANTE ET SIX PROVINCES [1715] 31x45cm. (12x17½") From Bernard, *Receuil de voyages au Nord*. After a Japanese map with kanji characters denoting provinces. Col. Fine. [5] £1400 $2664

RENARD

MAGNUM MARE DEL ZUR CUM INSULA CALIFORNIA [1715] 50x57cm. (19½x22½") Color. Mint. [37] £1314 $2500

TERRA NEUF, AN DE CUSTEN VAN NIEU VRANCKRYCK, NIEU ENGELAND, NIEU NEDERLAND, NIEU ANDALUSIA, GUIANA EN VENEZUELA ... / TERRA NOVA AC MARIS TRACTUS CIRCA NOVAM FRANCIA, ANGLIAM, BELGIUM, VENEZUELAM ... [1715] 48x56cm. (19x22") Color. Excellent. [37] £360 $685

[same title, date, dimensions] Color. Mint. [38] £394 $750

RENNELL, J.

A MAP SHEWING THE PROGRESS OF DISCOVERY & IMPROVEMENT IN THE GEOGRAPHY OF NORTH AFRICA [1798] 41x71cm. (16x28") Mungo Park's first journey. Mounted on linen. Some offsetting; else excellent. [35] £66 $125

THE ROUTE OF MR. MUNGO PARK [1798] 25x66cm. (10½x25½") Routes in color. [35] £47 $90

REYNOLDS, J.

BOOTH'S NEW PLAN OF LONDON; EXTENDING TO BLACKWALL, WITH THE ALTERATIONS AND IMPROVEMENTS ... [1846] 35x77cm. (13½x30½") Linen-backed folding plan between original boards with labels. Color. Wear just visible at some fold intersections; very good. [19] £158 $300

REYNOLDS' MAP OF LONDON WITH RECENT IMPROVEMENTS 1878. DIVIDED INTO QUARTER MILE SECTIONS FOR MEASURING DISTANCES [1878] 48x74cm. (19x29") Linen-backed folding plan between original boards embossed with gilt, with guide. Partial color. Water stains with slight affect along bottom section folds; guide detached; o/w good. [19] £145 $275

REYNOLDS'S MAP OF MODERN LONDON DIVIDED INTO QUARTER MILE SECTIONS [1859] 48x73cm. (19x28½") Linen-backed folding plan between boards. Partial color. Some age-soiling; only two pages of accompanying guide present; good+. [19] £105 $200

[same title] [(1862)] 48x73cm. (19x28½") Linen-backed folding plan in original embossed covers and marbled self-backs. Color. Some tears along fold lines; good+. [19] £139 $265

REYNOLDS'S NEW MAP OF LONDON AND ITS SUBURBS [1883] 65x101cm. (25½x39½") 44 page street guide. Linen-backed folding plan in boards. Outline & wash color. Boards & corner of plan stained; several quadrant corners slightly detached without damage; former owner's name present; good+. [19] £79 $150

[same title] [1884] 66x100cm. (26x39½") Linen-backed folding plan between original boards. Wash color. Small repair at a fold; good+. [19] £116 $220

REYNOLDS, R.

AN ACCURATE MAP OF AFRICA [c. 1780] 19x28cm. (7½x11") [10] £18 $35

RICE

RICE'S SECTIONAL MAP OF DAKOTA [1878] 76x66cm. (29½x26") Published by St. Paul Litho. and Engraving Co. Folding map with original case; notes by previous owner. [36] £92 $175

RICHARDSON

A TOPOGRAPHICAL PLAN OF MODERN ROME WITH THE NEW ADDITIONS BY MR. HARWOOD [1865] 54x65cm. (21x25½") Linen-backed folding plan. Partial color. Very good. [19] £158 $300

RICHARDSON'S MAP OF SOUTH EAST AND CENTRAL ENGLAND ... SHOWING BOROUGHS IN SEPARATE COLOURS, ROADS, RAILWAYS, & GOLF LINKS [20th c.] 118x94cm. (46½x37") On cover: "Bacon's map ..." Linen-backed folding map between boards. Original color. Boards soiled and backstrip torn at foot; very good. [19] £42 $80

RIZZI ZANNONI

CARTE DE LA PARTIE SEPTENTRIONALE DE L'EMPIRE OTOMAN ... [1774] 72x155cm. (28½x61") Linen-backed folding map. One section lacking in Balkan area; o/w VG. [19] £145 $275

ROBERT DE VAUGONDY *Try De Vaugondy*

ROBERTS, H.

A GENERAL CHART EXHIBITING THE DISCOVERIES MADE BY CAPT. JAMES COOK IN THIS AND HIS TWO PRECEEDING VOYAGES WITH THE TRACKS OF THE SHIPS UNDER HIS COMMAND [c.1785] 55x92cm. (21½x36") Some small splits & tears supported on back. [10] £84 $160

ROBINSON

A CHART OF THE NORTHWEST COAST OF AMERICA FROM CALIFORNIA TO COOK'S RIVER; AGREEABLE TO THE DISCOVERIES MADE IN THE YEARS 1786-1787 BY FRENCH FRIGATES BOUSSOLE & ASTROLABE [1798] 22x18cm. (8½x7") Color. [15] £42 $80

A CHART OF THE WESTERN & SOUTHERN OCEANS DESCRIBING THE COURSE OF SIR JOHN NARBROUGH'S VOYAGE TO THE SOUTH SEA. [1711] 28x25cm. (10½x10") Americas and part of Europe & Africa. Color. [15] £92 $175

CHART OF THE NORTHWEST COAST OF AMERICA EXPLORED BY THE BOUSSOLE AND ASTROLABE IN 1786 [1798] 36x48cm. (14½x19½") Clonard Bay to Mt. St. Elias. Color. [15] £89 $170

PLAN OF THE ENTRANCE OF THE PORT OF BUCARELLI ON THE NORTH WEST COAST OF AMERICA ... [1798] 38x49cm. (15x19½") By J. F. Quadra. Color. [15] £74 $140

ROBYN

NIEUW AERDSCH PLEYN [1696] 59x52cm. (23x20½") By Danckerts. Polar projection. Shirley 582. Full original color. Narrow right margin; else excellent. [38] £2522 $4800

ROCQUE

PLAN OF PART OF FORT GEORGE, WITH THE BARRACKS &C. ERECTED IN THE YEAR 1759 [1763] 13x18cm. (5x7") [6] £50 $95

ROLLOS

AN ACCURATE MAP OF NORTH AMERICA DRAWN FROM THE SIEUR ROBERT WITH IMPROVEMENTS [1762] 18x30cm. (7½x11½") Color. [15] £58 $110

ROMOLO BULLA

PLANTA GUIDA DELLA CITTA DI ROMA [1892 penned in] 53x64cm. (20½x24½") Bird's eye view. Age toned; slight surface loss along folds; good. [8] £47 $90

ROSACCIO *Try Ptolemy (1562-1599, Venice)*

ROSSI

[TITLE PAGE] MERCURIO GEOGRAPHICO ... [1689] 27x43cm. (10½x17") Some soiling; marginal tears and damage laid down on heavy paper. [5] £125 $238

IL REGNO DELLA CHINA ... [(1682) 1689] 112x140cm. (44x55") From *Mercurio Geographico*, Rome. Color. Fine. [5] £750 $1427

ROSSI, L.

INDIE OCCIDENTALI [1820] 20x30cm. (7½x12½") Milan: Batelli & Fanfani. Color. [15] £66 $125

ROUSSIN

CARTA GENERALE DELLE COSTE DEL BRASILE ... [1857] 76x48cm. (29½x18½") Two sheets: Rio de la Plata to Victoria. Repaired fold splits & edge tears; slight browning at folds. [11] £40 $76

ROWE

ROWE'S MAP OF THE COUNTRY TWENTY-ONE MILES ROUND LONDON [1825] Circular map. Diameter 51 cm. (20") Linen-backed folding map in original slipcase with label. Color. Offsetting in margin; owner's label present; good+. [19] £208 $395

ROYAL GEOGRAPHICAL SOCIETY

ICELAND. TO ILLUSTRATE THE PAPER BY DR. TH. THORODDSON ... [1899] 40x57cm. (15½x22½") Linen-backed folding map between original boards with label. Color. Very good. [19] £58 $110

SKETCH SHEWING THE ROUTE OF THE RECENT ARCTIC LAND EXPEDITION [1835] 18x23cm. (6½x9") Some color. Trivial offsetting; else fine. [12] £58 $110

RUGGLES

NEW-HAMPSHIRE, FROM LATE SURVEY ... [1817] 76x46cm. (30x18") O. T. Eddy, engr. Laid down on rice paper; darkened by original linen; few tiny surface losses; reasonably good. [2] £499 $950

RUSCELLI *Try Ptolemy (1561-1599, Venice)*

RUSSELL

AN ACCURATE MAP OF THE WEST INDIES WITH THE ADJACENT COAST OF AMERICA [1794] 35x51cm. (14x20") Very good. [3] £74 $140

BRITISH AMERICA COMPREHENDING CANADA, LABRADOR, NEW-FOUNDLAND, NOVA SCOTIA &C. [1808] 33x38cm. (13x15") London: Longman. Minor repair. [15] £87 $165

CHINA DIVIDED INTO PROVINCES DRAWN FROM THE BEST AUTHORITIES [1811] 39x45cm. (15½x18") Original outline color. [10] £26 $50

MAP OF THE MIDDLE STATES OF AMERICA, COMPREHENDS NEW-YORK, NEW-JERSEY, PENNSYLVANIA, DELAWARE, AND THE TERRITORY N.W. OF OHIO. BY J. RUSSELL [1794] 38x48cm. (15x19") Very Good. [3] £95 $180

[same title, date] 36x46cm. (14x18") London: H.D. Symonds. [6] £208 $395

STATES OF AMERICA, DRAWN FROM THE BEEST AUTHORITIES [1801] 41x46cm. (16½x18½") London: Mawman. Color. [15] £129 $245

UNITED STATES [c. 1798] 18x23cm. (7½x8½") Color. [15] £45 $85

S.D.U.K. *Try Society for the Diffusion of Useful Knowledge*

SANSON (Folio) *Try Jaillot, Mortier*

AMERIQUE SEPTENTRIONALE PAR N. SANSON D'ABBEVILLE GEOG. ORDRE. DU ROY... [1650] 41x56cm. (15½x22") California as immense island; Five Great Lakes. Paris: Mariette. 1st ed., 1st state. Original outline color. [15] £1393 $2650

[same title, date] 39x56cm. (15½x22") Original outline color. Fine. [37] £1682 $3200

JESU CHRISTI SALVATORIS NOSTRI ET APOSTOLORUM PETRI, ET PAULI MANSIONES, ITINERA PEREGRINIATIONES &C. [1665] 38x56cm. (15x22") Laor 697. Color. [15] £171 $325

L'AFRICA NUOUAMENTE CORRETTA ET ACCRESECUITA SECONDO LO RELATIONI PIU MODERNE ... [1677] 41x56cm. (16x21½") Rome: Rossi. Color. [15] £297 $565

L'ASIE ... [1669] 41x56cm. (16x22½") Original outline color. Excellent. [21] £289 $550

LA CHINE ROYAUME [1656 (1679)] 42x53cm. (16½x21") Attributed to Ricci. Col. Fine. [5] £500 $952

LE CANADA OU NOUVELLE FRANCE ... [1652] 40x54cm. (15½x21½") Original outline color. Mint. [37] £2207 $4200

[same title] [1656] 40x54cm. (16x21½") 1st edition. Orig color. Silk backing. VG. [2] £2365 $4500

[same title] [1656] 40x54cm. (15½x21½") Original outline color. Fine; trimmed and mounted on larger composite atlas sheet. [38] £1944 $3700

LE NOUVEAU MEXIQUE, ET LA FLORIDE; TIREE DE DIVERSES CARTES, ET RELATIONS, ... [1656] 31x55cm. (12x21½") Original outline color. Mint. [37] £2365 $4500

LE PARAGUAY TIRE DES RELATIONS LES PLUS RECENTES. [1668] 41x56cm. (16x21½") Color. [15] £202 $385

LES DEUX POLES ARCTICQUE OU SEPTENTRIONAL, ET ANTARCTICQUE OU MERIDIONAL, OU DESCRIPTION DES TERRES ARCTICQUES ET ANTARCTICQUES; ET DES PAYS CIRCOMVOISINS... [1675] 38x53cm. (15x21") Full original color. Excellent. [2] £788 $1500

SANSON (Small)

AUDIENCE DE GUADALAJARA, NOUVEAU MEXIQUE, CALIFORNIE, &C. PAR N. SANSON D'ABBEVILLE GEOGR ORDIN DU ROY [1657] 21x24cm. (8x9½") Insular California. Outline color. Excellent. [38] £402 $765

[same title] [1656 (c. 1690)] 20x33cm. (8x13") Original outline color. Excellent. [37] £355 $675

CEYLON ET LES MALDIVES [1683] 18x24cm. (7x9½") [10] £26 $50

DETROIT DE MAGELLAN, TERRE ET ISLES MAGELLANIQUES, &C. PAR N. SANSON D'ABBEVILLE, GEOGR ORDINAIRE DU ROY [1682] 19x24cm. (7½x9½") Outline & wash color. [35] £66 $125

FRANCE [1682] 18x23cm. (7x9½") Outline color. [36] £53 $100

ISLES BRITANNIQUES [c. 1682] 23x18cm. (9x7") [36] £71 $135

[same title] [c. 1700] 22x17cm. (8½x6½") Color. Very good. [23] £125 $238

LA FLORIDE [1657] 18x25cm. (7x10") Outline & wash color. [35] £223 $425

LE CANADA, OU NOUVELLE-FRANCE, &C. TIREE DE DIVERSES RELATIONS DES FRANCOIS, ANGLOIS, HOLLANDOIS, &C. ... [1657] 21x31cm. (8½x12") Outline col. Excel. [38] £250 $475

LE ZANGUEBAR / PARTIE DU ZANGUEBAR OU SONT LES COSTES D'AJAN ET D'ABEX [1683] 18x30cm. (7x11½") [10] £21 $40

LES ISLES DU IAPON [1651] 18x24cm. (7½x9½") 1st ed. Orig outline col. Excel. [21] £512 $975

LES ISLES MOLUCQUES, CELEBES, GILOLO, &C. [1792] 19x25cm. (7½x10") A little fragile. [10] £39 $75

MAPPE MONDE OU CARTE GENERALE DU GLOBE TERRESTRE [c. 1700] 13x18cm. (5x7") Insular California. [3] £250 $475

MER NOIRE OU MER MAIEVRE [c. 1682] 18x25cm. (7½x9½") Outline color. [36] £47 $90

PARTIE DE LA HAUTE AETHIOPIE OU SONT L'EMPIRE DES ABISSINS DES ET LA NUBIE &C. [1652] 30x23cm. (12x8½") Color. [15] £66 $125

PRESQU'ISLE DE L'INDE DECA LA GANGE [1683] 19x24cm. (7½x9½") [10] £21 $40

ROYAUME DE LA CHINE [1682] 24x19cm. (9½x7½") Outline & wash color. [35] £71 $135

[same title] [1683] 24x19cm. (9½x7½") Original outline color; gold highlights. [10] £39 $75

SCANDINAVIE OU SONT LES ESTATS DE DANEMARK DE SUEDE &C. [1682] 18x25cm. (7½x9½") Outline & wash color. Excellent. [36] £58 $110

SORIE ET DIARBECK [1683] 19x26cm. (7½x10") [10] £26 $50

'T GEBIEDT VAN MEXICO [c. 1705] 18x28cm. (6½x10½") Pristine. [12] £71 $135

TERRE FERME, NOUVEAU ROYME DE GRENADE, &C. ... [1682] 19x29cm. (7½x11½") Outline & wash color. Excellent. [35] £87 $165

TRYK VAN DEN GROOTEN MOGOL [1705] 19x24cm. (7½x9½") Original outline color; gold highlights. [10] £24 $45

ZANGUEBAR / T'GEDEELTE VAN ZANGUEBAR [1705] 18x30cm. (7x12") Full original color; gold highlights. [10] £34 $65

SANTINI

LA ROMELIE ET LES ENVIRONS DE CONSTANTINOPLE [1777] 43x56cm. (16½x21½") By Rizzi-Zannoni. Outline color. [36] £87 $165

PARTIE MERIDIONALE DE LA LOUISIANE, AVEC LA FLORIDE, LA CAROLINE ET LA VIRGINIE, PAR LE SR. D ANVILLE. A VENISE ... [1776] 48x57cm. (19x22½") Cartouche and outline color. [6] £313 $595

[same title] [1784] 48x57cm. (19x22½") Chez Remondini; republication of 1776 version. Original outline & cartouche color. Centerfold lower half thinned & stained. [6] £236 $450

SARTINE

PLAN DE LA BAIE ET DU HAVRE DE CASCO ET DES ILES ADJACENTES PAR LE CAPE. CYPRIAN SOUTHACK ... [1779] 41x58cm. (16x23") Faint waterstain; else excel. [22] £289 $550

SAUTHIER

A TOPOGRAPHICAL MAP OF HUDSONS RIVER [1776] 81x53cm. (32x21") London: Faden. Third state. Close cut to neat lines & text all around. Reinforced old folds & tears repaired; repaired 3/4" hole, bottom right quadrant. [31] £1261 $2400

SAYER *Try Jefferys*

A MAP EXHIBITING THE DARK SHADOW OF THE MOON OVER ENGLAND AND OTHER PARTS OF EUROPE ... [1787] 30x30cm. (12x12") Probably separately issued. Five 18 c. solar eclipse paths. Original wash color. Minor tear repaired; else excellent. [21] £788 $1500

A MAP OF SOUTH AMERICA CONTAINING TIERRA-FIRMA, GUAYANA, NEW GRENADA, AMAZONIA, BRASIL, PERU, PARAGUAY, CHACO, TUCUMAN, CHILI AND PATAGONIA. FROM MR. D'ANVILLE ... [1775] 102x119cm. (40x47") Two 20 x 47" sheets. Original outline color. Some faint offsetting. [31] £368 $700

A NEW MAP OF NORTH AMERICA ... ACCORDING TO THE DEFINITIVE TREATY, CONCLUDED AT PARIS ... [1763] 59x96cm. (23x37½") Orig outline col. Repaired fold & tear. [10] £447 $850

COURSE OF THE RIVER MISSISSIPPI, FROM THE BALISE TO FORT CHARTRES TAKEN ON AN EXPEDITION TO THE ILLINOIS IN THE LATTER END OF THE YEAR 1765 BY LIEUT. ROSS [1775] 114x36cm. (45x14") Original outline color. Minor repairs. [15] £657 $1250

[same title, date] 112x34cm. (44x13½") By Lieut. John Ross. Original outline color. Some faint staining, two small mended tears; o/w very good. [22] £788 $1500

PLAN OF THE STRAITS OF BANCA [1791] 48x33cm. (18½x13") After D'Apres de Mannevillette. [11] £75 $143

THE CATHOLIC NETHERLANDS ... [1783] 48x64cm. (18½x25½") Outline color. [35] £53 $100

THE RUSSIAN DISCOVERIES FROM THE MAP PUBLISHED BY THE IMPERIAL ACADEMY OF ST. PETERSBURG [1775] 48x66cm. (19x26") Northwest America & Northeast Asia. Some color. [3] £342 $650

SAYER & BENNETT *Try Jefferys*

A CHART OF DELAWARE BAY AND RIVER; CONTAINING A FULL AND EXACT DESCRIPTION OF THE SHORES, CREEKS, HARBOURS, SOUNDINGS, SHOALS, SANDS AND BEARINGS, OF THE MOST CONSIDERABLE LAND MARKS ... BY JOSHUA FISHER [1776] 48x69cm. (18½x27") Excellent. [1] £1576 $3000

A CHART OF THE CHINA SEA, AND PHILIPPINE ISLANDS, WITH THE ARCHIPELAGOS OF FELICIA AND SOLOO, SHEWING THE WHOLE TRACT COMPRIZED, BETWEEN CANTON AND BALAMBANGAN ... BY CAPT ROBERT CARR AND COMPARED WITH A MAP OF PEDRO MURILLO VELARDE[1778] 76x61cm. (30x24") Minor edge tears repaired; o/w VG. [11] £425 $809

A CHART OF THE COAST OF PEGU WITH THE ADJACENT COASTS OF ARAKAN AND TANASSERIAM [1778] 79x56cm. (31x22") Chips & tears at wide margin; some offsetting. [10] £92 $175

A CHART OF THE GULF OF ST. LAURENCE, COMPOSED FROM A GREAT NUMBER OF ACTUAL SURVEYS AND OTHER MATERIALS, REGULATED AND CORRECTED BY ASTRONOMICAL OBSERVATIONS ... [1775] 61x51cm. (24x19½") Color. [15] £202 $385

A CHART OF THE NORTHERN PART OF THE CHINA SEAS SHOWING THE PASSAGE FROM FORMOSA TO JAPAN WITH THE EASTERN COAST OF CHINA AND THE LEKEYO ISLANDS BY VAN KEULEN FROM THE MAPS DRAWN IN CHINA BY FATHER GAUBIL [1778] 56x56cm. (22x22") [5] £200 $381

A CHART OF THE NORTHERN PART OF THE INDIAN OCEAN CONTAINING A PART OF THE COAST OF AFRICA FROM MAGADASHO RIVER ... AND THE COAST OF ASIA ... TO THE MOUTH OF THE GANGES; WITH THE LAKEDIVAS, MALDIVAS AND CEYLON. [1778] 59x90cm. (23½x35½") By D'Apres de Mannevillette. Margins chipped and cracked; short tears without loss. [10] £66 $125

A CHART OF THE STRAITS OF MAGELLAN INLARGED FROM THE CHART PUBLISHED AT MADRID IN 1769, BY DON JUAN DE LA CRUZ CANO Y OLMEDILLA... [1775] 51x69cm. (20½x27") Original outline color. Some faint staining; else excellent. [22] £263 $500

[same title] [1775 (1778)] 52x69cm. (20½x27") By Jefferys. Orig outline col. Fine. [28] £289 $550

A CHART OF THE WEST COAST OF SUMATRA FROM THE EQUINOCTIAL LINE TO THE STRAITS OF SUNDA ... [1778] 67x49cm. (26½x19½") By D'Apres de Mannevillette. Chips and tears at wide margin. [10] £53 $100

A CHART OF THE WESTERN COAST OF SUMATRA FROM TOUROUMANE RIVER TO POINT INDRAPOUR ... [1778] 68x49cm. (26½x19½") After D'Apres de Mannevillette. Chips and tears at wide margin. [10] £53 $100

A GENERAL MAP OF THE NORTHERN BRITISH COLONIES IN AMERICA, WHICH COMPREHENDS THE PROVINCE OF QUEBEC, THE GOVERNMENT OF NEWFOUNDLAND, NOVA-SCOTIA, NEW-ENGLAND AND NEW-YORK [1776] 48x66cm. (19x26") Title over border: "The Seat of War, in the Northern Colonies", similar to The Military Pocket Atlas map, without folds. Orig outline col. Light toning; marginal mends & reinforcement at top centerfold; else VG. [21] £1051 $2000

A MAP OF PENNSYLVANIA EXHIBITING NOT ONLY THE IMPROVED PARTS OF THAT PROVINCE BUT ALSO ITS EXTENSIVE FRONTIERS ... CHIEFLY FROM THE LATE MAP OF W SCULL, PUBLISHED 1770 ... [1775] 68x134cm. (27x52½") Printed on 3 sheets. Original outline color. Marginal chipping and fraying not involving image; repairs on verso; some fold splitting without loss. [20] £2049 $3900

[same title, date, dimensions] Original outline color. Very good. [31] £1892 $3600

A NEW MAP OF IRELAND DIVIDED INTO PROVINCES, COUNTIES &C. [1777] 64x57cm. (25x22") By Kitchin. Linen-backed folding map in original marbled slipcase with label. Outline color. Very good. [19] £342 $650

A NEW MAP OF THE PROVINCE OF QUEBEC, ACCORDING TO THE ROYAL PROCLAMATION, OF THE 7TH OF OCTOBER 1763... [1776] 50x67cm. (19½x26½") Montreal & Quebec insets. Original outline and wash color. Slight offsetting; o/w excellent. [22] £736 $1400

A SURVEY OF LAKE CHAMPLAIN INCLUDING LAKE GEORGE, CROWN POINT AND ST. JOHN. SURVEYED BY ORDER OF HIS EXCELLENCY MAJOR GENERAL SR. JEFFERY AMHERST...LONDON, PRINTED FOR ROBT. SAYER & JNO. BENNETT, 1762 [1776] 66x46cm. (25½x18") By W. Brassier. 2nd state. Original color. Clean & crisp. [15] £709 $1350

A TOPOGRAPHICAL SURVEY OF THE COUNTRY, FROM THIRTY FIVE TO FORTY MILES, ROUND LONDON ... [1775] 50x55cm. (19½x21½") By M. Bowen. Linen-backed folding map. Outline color. Backing worn at places along folds; o/w good+. [19] £145 $275

CHART OF THE WEST COAST OF SUMATRA, FROM BENCOOLEN TO KEYSERS BAY [1778] 52x63cm. (20½x25") Several insets. By Huddart. Chips and tears at wide margins. [10] £47 $90

[same title, date] 53x64cm. (20½x24½") Some browning in margins. [11] £120 $228

NORTH AMERICA FROM THE FRENCH OF MR. D'ANVILLE IMPROVED WITH THE ENGLISH SURVEYS MADE SINCE THE PEACE [1775] 46x51cm. (18x20") Col. Excel. [22] £342 $650

THE COAST OF INDIA FROM GOA TO CAP COMORIN ... [1778] 61x61cm. (24x24") [11] £45 $86

THE PROVINCES OF NEW YORK AND NEW JERSEY, WITH PART OF PENSILVANIA, AND THE GOVERNMENTS OF TROIS RIVIERES, AND MONTREAL, DRAWN BY CAPT. HOLLAND [1776] 135x69cm. (53x26½") Original outline color. A few minor mends; else VG. [21] £998 $1900

THE SEAT OF ACTION, BETWEEN THE BRITISH AND AMERICAN FORCES, OR AN AUTHENTIC PLAN OF THE WESTERN PART OF LONG ISLAND, WITH THE ENGAGEMENT OF THE 27TH. AUGUST 1776 ... [1776] 43x38cm. (17½x15½") Published as a separate. Original outline color. Browned; some repaired wormholes; o/w good. [21] £1471 $2800

THE THEATRE OF WAR IN NORTH AMERICA ... [1776] 16x51cm. (6½x20") Separately issue broadsheet, with text below map. Orig outline col. Light surface spotting; o/w good. [33] £3200 $6090

SCHEDEL

[EUROPE: CENTRAL AND NORTHERN] [1493] 40x58cm. (15½x23") In *Nuremberg Chronicle*, by Hieronymous Munzer. Restoration to corners, some loss not affecting significant map areas. [38] £657 $1250

SECUNDA ETAS MUNDI [1493] 37x51cm. (14½x20") Shirley 19. Full color. Usual repaired thread holes; excellent. [21] £3941 $7500

SCHENK

[TITLE PAGE] ATLAS CONTRACTUS [c. 1700] 43x28cm. (17½x11") Neptune leans against globe. Original color, faded at upper left. Good. [30] £289 $550

NIEU AMSTERDAM, EEN STEDEKEN IN NOORD AMERIKAES NIEU HOLLANT, OP HET EILANT MANKATTAN: NAMAELS NIEU JORK GENAEMT, TOEN HET GERAEKTE IN 'T GEBIET DER ENGELSCHEN [1702] 22x26cm. (8½x10½") View. Original color. [1] £1839 $3500

PLANISPHAERIUM COELESTE [1705] 48x56cm. (19½x22") Full orig col. Excel. [2] £788 $1500

SCHERER

[TITLE PAGE: ALLEGORICAL EARTH] [c. 1700] 23x18cm. (9x7") Various peoples support globe of Western Hemisphere. Excellent. [37] £131 $250

AMERICA BOREALIS...1699 [1699] 23x36cm. (9x14") Fine. [12] £578 $1100

AMERICA BOREALIS MULTIS IN LOCIS DEI MATREM COLIT & HONORAT, ET HAEC SUIS CULTORIBUS MULTOS FAVORES & BENEFICIA PRAESTAT [1699] 23x36cm. (9x13½") Fine. [12] £578 $1100

ARCHIPELAGUS ATLANTICUS CUM SUIS INSULIS CANARIIS [1700] 23x34cm. (9x13½") Much of West Africa. [10] £39 $75

FONTES NILI FLUMINIS EORUMQUE SITUS [1700] 23x18cm. (9x7") [10] £26 $50

HISPANIA CUM FIMITIMIS REGIONIBUS NOVISSIME DELINEATA. ANNO MDCCIII [1703] 23x33cm. (9x13½") Heinrich, engr. Four tiny repaired worm holes at top center. [35] £76 $145

IDEA NATURALIS AMERICAE BOREALIS DIGITO DEI FORMATA GEOGRAPHICE PROPOSITA [1700] 23x36cm. (8½x13½") Fine. [12] £604 $1150

NOVA ET VERA EXHIBITIO GEOGRAPHICA INSULARUM MARIANARUM CUM INSULIS DE PAIS... [1700 (1710)] 23x34cm. (9x13½") Excellent. [37] £184 $350

PARADISI TERRESTRIS VERA ET SACRIS LITERIS CONFORMIS EXHIBITIO GEOGRAPHICA [1703] 23x36cm. (9x13½") [35] £118 $225

PROVINCIAE BOREALIS AMERICAE NON ITA PRIDEM DETECTAE AUT MAGIS AB EUROPAEIS EXCULTAE [c. 1700] 23x36cm. (9x13½") Fine. [12] £657 $1250

RELIGIONIS CATHOLICAE AUSTRALI AMERICAE IMPLANTATAE DESCRIPTIO GEOGRAPHICA [1703] 22x34cm. (8½x13½") [35] £118 $225

RELIGIONIS CATHOLICAE IN AMERICAE BOREALI DISSEMINATAE REPRAESENTATIO GEOGRAPHICA [c. 1700] 23x36cm. (8½x13½") Fine. [12] £617 $1175

REPRAESENTATIO AMERICAE BOREALIS CUIUS PROVINCIAE VERA FIDE ILLUMINATAE UMBRAM NON HABENT, RELIQUAE UMBRIS IMMERSAE SUNT [c. 1700] 25x36cm. (9½x14") Fine. [12] £657 $1250

[same title, date] 24x35cm. (9½x13½") Full color. Excellent. [37] £342 $650

TYPUS TOTIUS ORBIS TERRAQUEI GEOGRAPHICE DELINEATUS ... [c. 1700] 22x35cm. (8½x13½") World in a set of twelve gores. Shirley 633. Excellent. [38] £394 $750

SCHOOLCRAFT

MAP OF OREGON SHOWING THE LOCATION OF INDIAN TRIBES [1852] 21x25cm. (8x10") Outline color. [12] £66 $125

SOURCES OF THE MISSISSIPPI ... [1834] 20x20cm. (8x8") [15] £34 $65

SCHRAEMBL

[CENTRAL UNITED STATES & CANADA] [(1800)] 51x59cm. (20x23") Inset: Canadian north. Original outline color. Fine. [20] £368 $700

SCHREIBER

DIE CARIBISCHEN INSULN IN NORD AMERICA - GUADALOUPE, MARTINIQUE, MARIA GALANTA, DOMINIQUE U. DESIDERADE [1761] 20x25cm. (7½x10") Full color. One small rust spot; else fine. [12] £71 $135

SCHROPP & CO.

NEUESTE POST-KARTE DURCH GANZ DEUTSCHLAND UND FRANKREICH BIS PARIS, DURCH OBER-ITALIEN, OESTREICH, UNGARN, PREUSSEN, POHLEN UND DAENMARK ... [1818] 62x79cm. (24x31") French title in top margin. Linen-backed folding map with seller's label on back; separate chemise and slipcase. Outline color. Slipcase worn at corners; very good. [19] £171 $325

SCHROTER

DIE INSEL HISPANIOLA [1752] 18x30cm. (7x11½") After D'Anville. Color. [35] £39 $75

SCOTT

DELAWARE [1795] 18x15cm. (7x6") Color. [15] £118 $225

GEORGIA [1795] 15x19cm. (6x7½") With Western Territory. Small, dark paper inclusion lower border; else excellent. [12] £92 $175

[same title, date] 16x18cm. (6½x7½") Some transfer, wrinkles; good. [13] £184 $350

[same title] [1799] 18x20cm. (6½x7½") Close side margins; minor transference; clean. [26] £84 $160

MAINE [1799] 20x18cm. (7½x6½") Some transfer at vertical folds; minor tear repaired. [26] £47 $90

N.W. TERRITORY [1795] 18x15cm. (7x6") Fine. [12] £92 $175

NEW HAMPSHIRE [1795] 19x15cm. (7½x6") Green outline color. Some tiny dark spots; o/w excellent. [12] £53 $100

NORTH CAROLINA [1799] 18x20cm. (6½x7½") Rebacked. [26] £58 $110

RHODE ISLAND [1799] 20x18cm. (7½x6½") Very minor transfer; o/w very good. [26] £47 $90

S.W. TERRITORY [1795] 15x20cm. (6x7½") Tennessee and adjacent. Lower left margin close to neat line; map fine. [12] £131 $250

SOUTH CAROLINA [1795] 15x18cm. (6x7") Fine. [12] £71 $135

[same title] [1799] 18x20cm. (6½x7½") Very clean. [26] £58 $110

STATE OF VERMONT [1799] 19x17cm. (7½x6½") Very good. [26] £58 $110

VERMONT [1795] 20x15cm. (7½x6") Original outline color. Tiny spot; else fine. [12] £47 $90

SEALE

A MAP OF THE KINGDOM OF IRELAND [c. 1750] 48x39cm. (19x15½") Col. VG. [24] £150 $285

A NEW AND ACCURATE MAP OF NORTH AMERICA, DRAWN FROM THE FAMOUS MR. D'ANVILLE ... [1771] 47x51cm. (18½x20") By Peter Bell. Orig wash & outline col. Fine. [10] £499 $950

SELLER

A CHART OF THE CHANNEL [c. 1680] 43x56cm. (17x22") Old outline color. Hairline top and bottom margins; good. [34] £236 $450

A CHART OF THE SEA COASTS OF NEW ENGLAND, NEW JERSEY, VIRGINIA, MARYLAND, AND CAROLINA FROM CAPE COD TO CAPE HATTERAS [1675] 43x56cm. (17½x21½") Original color. Very good. [1] £10,247 $19,500

SENEX

A CHART OF THE ATLANTICK OCEAN FROM ORONOQUE RIVER TO THE RIVER MAY WITH THE CARIBBEE & BAHAMA IS. [1728] 51x117cm. (19½x45½") With J. Harris. East to Cape Verde Islands. Old color. [15] £255 $485

A GLOBULAR DRAUGHT FROM THE NORTH POLE TO THE LATITUDE OF 60 DEGREES [1728] 48x41cm. (19½x16") Color. Immaculate. [15] £197 $375

A MAP OF LOUISIANA AND OF THE RIVER MISSISSIPI BY IOHN SENEX [1721] 49x58cm. (19x22½") After De L'Isle. Original outline color. [31] £972 $1850

A MAP OF THE WORLD [1711] 59x107cm. (23x42") First edition with Maxwell. Hemispheres; insular California. Original outline color. [33] £1650 $3140

A NEW AND CORRECT CHART OF THE ATLANTIC OCEAN REDUCED, DESCRIBING PART OF THE COASTS OF EUROPE, AFRICA & AMERICA [1728] 51x58cm. (20½x23") [15] £171 $325

A NEW MAP OF INDIA & CHINA FROM THE LATEST OBSERVATIONS BY J. SENEX [c. 1720] 50x59cm. (19½x23") Original outline color. Some light browning; fine. [5] £450 $856

A NEW MAP OF THE CITY OF AMSTERDAM [1720] 48x58cm. (19½x23") S. Parker, sc. [36] £171 $325

A NEW MAP OF THE WORLD ... [1719] 42x54cm. (16½x21") Double hemisphere with decoration. Full original color. Excellent. [21] £946 $1800

NORTH AMERICA CORRECTED FROM THE OBSERVATIONS COMMUNICATED TO THE ROYAL SOCIETY AT LONDON, AND THE ROYAL ACADEMY AT PARIS. BY IOHN SENEX AND IOHN MAXWELL GEOGRAPHER [1710] 97x66cm. (37½x25½") Precursor of "Beaver Map". Original outline color. Excellent. [21] £1839 $3500

SOUTH AMERICA CORRECTED FROM OBSERVATIONS COMMUNICATED TO THE ROYAL SOCIETY ... [1710] 69x58cm. (27x23") Color. Minor repair. [15] £192 $365

SEUTTER (Large)

ACCURATA DELINEATIO CELEBERRIMAE REGIONIS LUDOVICIANAE VEL GALLICE LOUISANAE OT. CANADAE ET FLORIDAE ADPELLATIONE IN SEPTEMTRIONALI AMERICA DESCRIPAE QUOE HODI NOMINE FLUMINIS MISSIPPI...MATTHAEI SEUTTERI, CHALCOG. AUGUSTON. [c.1730] 49x56cm. (19½x22") Orig col. Bit of light staining; else exc. [22] £946 $1800

[same title] [c. 1740] 49x56cm. (19½x22") Original wash color. Fine. [37] £946 $1800

AFRICA JUXTA NAVIGATIONES ET OBSERVATIONES... [1730] 49x57cm. (19½x22½") Original wash color. Excellent. [1] £394 $750

DELINEATIO AC FINITIMA REGIO MAGNAE BRITTANIAE METROPOLEOS LONDINI ... [1734] 51x58cm. (19½x22½") Full original color. Excellent. [2] £263 $500

IMPERII MOSCOVITICI PARS AUSTRALIS IN LUCEM, EDITA PAR G. DE L'ISLE [1725] 51x58cm. (19½x23") Color. [15] £92 $175

LE PAYS DE PEROU ET CHILI [1730] 48x58cm. (19½x23") South America except eastern Brazil. Original wash color. 1 inch repaired tear; light stain in lower margin; o/w fine. [28] £289 $550

LONDINI [c. 1730] 49x57cm. (19½x22½") Color. Very good. [23] £480 $913

MADRITUM SIVE MANTUA CARPETANORUM CELEBERRIMA CASTILIAE NOVAE CIVITAS ... [pre-1760] 51x58cm. (19½x22½") Original color. Excellent. [21] £788 $1500

PLAN VON NEU EBENEZER ... [c. 1747] 51x56cm. (19½x22½") Full orig col. Exc. [2] £2049 $3900

RECENS EDITA TOTIUS NOVI BELGII, IN AMERICA SEPTENTRIONALI SITI, DELINEATIO CURA ET SUMTIBUS MATTHAEI SEUTTERI [1730] 50x58cm. (19½x22½") With "Restitutio View" of Manhattan. Original color. Excellent. [21] £1576 $3000

REGNI JAPONIAE NOVA MAPPA GEOGRAPHICA ... [1730] 49x56cm. (19½x22") After Kaempfer-Scheuchzer map without the kanji. Original color. Side margins cut to plate mark without loss. [5] £2250 $4282

SPHAERAE ARTIFICIALES ... [c. 1740] 48x58cm. (19x22½") Engraving of terrestrial, celestial & artificial spheres. Full color. Close top margin, no loss; excellent. [21] £736 $1400

SEUTTER (Small)

IMPERIUM RUSSIAE MAGNAE [1744] 19x26cm. (7½x10") Orig col. Slightly stained. [10] £39 $75

SHARPE

UNITED STATES - SOUTH WEST [1848] 43x30cm. (17x12") London: Chapman & Hall. Color. [15] £32 $60

SMITH, C.

A NEW MAP OF ENGLAND AND WALES, COMPREHENDING THE WHOLE OF THE TURNPIKE ROADS, WITH THE GREAT RIVERS, AND NAVIGABLE CANALS [1821] 57x46cm. (22½x18") Linen-backed folding map in marbled slipcase with label. Color. Light age-soiling, slipcase worn and torn; good+. [19] £105 $200

EXTENDED INDICATOR MAP OF LONDON DIVIDED INTO QUARTER MILE SQUARES FOR MEASURING DISTANCES [1896-97] 59x87cm. (23x34") Attached measuring tape, with guide. Linen-backed folding plan between boards. Worn; small loss at junctures. [19] £92 $175

INDICATOR MAP OF LONDON DIVIDED INTO QUARTER MILE SQUARES FOR MEASURING DISTANCES [c. 1902] 49x74cm. (19½x29") Attached measuring tape. Linen-backed folding plan between boards. Color. Some age darkening at folds; o/w good. [19] £92 $175

[same title] [1915] 57x87cm. (22½x34") Linen-backed folding plan with tape measure between boards; with index. Color. Map sharp and bright, separating from backing at some fold junctures; backstrip torn at head; very good. [19] £79 $150

NEW BRUNSWICK NOVA SCOTIA &C. [1836] 20x36cm. (8x14½") Col. Top margin restored. [15] £18 $35

NORTH AMERICA [c. 1826] 28x36cm. (11x14") Color. [15] £50 $95

SMITH'S MAP OF ENGLAND AND WALES, CONTAINING THE WHOLE OF THE TURNPIKE ROADS, RIVERS & CANALS; WITH THE DISTANCE FROM LONDON TO EVERY PRINCIPAL TOWN ... [1825] 77x61cm. (30½x24") Linen-backed folding map in marbled self-backs and original slipcase with label. Color. Some damping at folds; o/w very good. [19] £145 $275

SMITH'S MAP OF ENGLAND AND WALES, SHOWING ALL THE RAILWAYS, ROADS, RIVERS & CANALS [1849] 115x94cm. (45x37") Linen-backed folding map in original slipcase with label. Color. Slipcase damaged; slight offsetting; map very good. [19] £155 $295

SMITH'S NEW AND ACCURATE MAP OF THE LAKES, IN THE COUNTIES OF CUMBERLAND, WESTMORELAND AND LANCASTER [1802] 60x48cm. (23½x19") Linen-backed folding map. Original color. Backing worn at fold junctures and some ends, map not affected. [19] £131 $250

TRAVELLING MAP OF EUROPE, SHEWING THE LINES OF RAILWAY &C. [1890] 61x81cm. (24x32") Linen-backed folding map in boards. Orig col. Boards worn; map VG. [19] £63 $120

SMITH, J.

MEXICO AND WEST INDIES [c.1820] 38x58cm. (14½x23") London: J. Pickett, Col. [15] £71 $135

SMITH, JOHN

THE SUMMER ILS [BERMUDA] ... BY MR. NORWOOD ALL CONSTRUCTED INTO THIS ORDER BY CAPTAINE JOHN SMITH [1624] 28x36cm. (11x14") Repairs and restoration; some facsimile work. [10] £2233 $4250

SMITH, R.C.

MAP OF THE UNITED STATES ENGRAVED TO ACCOMPANY SMITH'S GEOGRAPHY FOR SCHOOLS [1853] 28x43cm. (11x17") Full color. Very good. [26] £34 $65

SMITH, W. H.

ENVIRONS OF LONDON [c. 1890] 72x83cm. (28½x32½") Linen-backed folding plan between boards. Color. Worn along folds, no paper loss; very good. [19] £105 $200

NEW PLAN OF LONDON [c. 1895] 57x82cm. (22½x32") By John Bartholomew. Linen-backed folding plan between cloth boards, with 37 page guide. Printed col. Cover worn & stained; VG. [19] £29 $55

SOCIETY FOR ANTI-GALLICIANS

A NEW AND ACCURATE MAP OF THE ENGLISH EMPIRE IN NORTH AMERICA ... [1755] 43x86cm. (17x33½") London: Herbert & Sayer. 7 map insets. Orig color. Good. [1] £2365 $4500

SOCIETY FOR THE DIFFUSION OF USEFUL KNOWLEDGE

Try Balwin & Cradock, Chapman & Hall, Cox, Knight, Stanford

[BALEARIC ISLANDS / MALTA / CORSICA / SARDINIA] [c. 1831] 30x36cm. (12x14") Outline color. Very good. [25] £25 $48

[NORTH AMERICA, EASTERN PART: Set of 15 maps including INDEX and NORTH AMERICA I through XIV] [1832-1834] 30x38cm. (12x15") Approximate dimensions; eight in vertical format. Canadian Maritimes to Florida to Louisiana to Lake Superior. Outline color. One sheet with a tear. [39] £235 $447

AFRICA [1844] 33x39cm. (13x15½") Outline color. [39] £31 $59

AMSTERDAM [1835] 33x38cm. (13x15") City plan. Old color. [39] £17 $33

ANCIENT SYRIA [1843] 39x33cm. (15½x13") Outline color. [39] £10 $20

ANTWERP. (ANTWERPEN.) (ANVERS.) [1832] 31x39cm. (12x15½") City plan. [39] £14 $26

ARABIA WITH EGYPT, NUBIA AND ABYSSINIA [1843] 31x39cm. (12x15½") Original outline color. [10] £16 $30

ASIA [1844] 33x40cm. (13x15½") Outline color. [39] £24 $46

AUSTRALIA IN 1839 [1840] 32x40cm. (12½x15½") Original outline color. [10] £21 $40

[same title, date, dimensions] (12½x15½") Original outline color. Very good. [31] £76 $145

BIRMINGHAM [1844] 34x40cm. (13½x15½") City plan. [39] £14 $26

BORDEAUX [1832] 31x38cm. (12x15") City plan. Old color. [39] £24 $46

BRITISH NORTH AMERICA [1834] 31x39cm. (12½x15½") Orig outline col. Fine. [12] £66 $125

[same title, date] 31x40cm. (12½x15½") Outline color. [39] £48 $92

CALCUTTA [1842] 32x40cm. (12½x16") Old color. Narrow side margins. [39] £21 $39

CIRCUMJACENT THE SOUTH POLE [1831] 27x28cm. (10½x11") Outline color. [39] £66 $125

CONSTANTINOPLE. STAMBOOL [1840] 32x39cm. (12½x15½") City plan [39] £62 $118

DENMARK AND PART OF NORWAY [1833] 40x31cm. (15½x12") Outline col. With foldout. [39] £24 $46

DUBLIN [1836] 30x38cm. (12x15") Some color. Very good. [34] £53 $100

[same title] [1844] 32x40cm. (12½x15½") Old color. Small tear at old fold. [39] £45 $85

[same title] [c. 1864] 31x39cm. (12x15½") Color. Very good. [24] £56 $107

EASTERN HEMISPHERE [1844] 34x34cm. (13x13½") Outline color. [39] £28 $53

EASTERN SIBERIA [1844] 34x39cm. (13½x15½") East of Yenesey River. Outline col. [39] £35 $66

EDINBURGH [1834] 31x39cm. (12x15½") City plan. Old color. [39] £31 $59

EGYPT [1831] 37x30cm. (14½x11½") Outline color. [39] £59 $112

EMPIRE OF JAPAN [1835] 40x32cm. (15½x12½") Outline color. [39] £131 $250

FLORENCE. FIRENZE [1835] 29x38cm. (11½x15") City plan. Old color. [39] £41 $79

FRANCE IN PROVINCES [1831] 30x30cm. (12x12") Outline color. [39] £14 $26

FRANKFORT (FRANKFURT AM MAYN) [1844] 31x38cm. (12x15") Old col. [39] £121 $230

HAMBURG [1841] 31x39cm. (12x15½") City plan. Old color. [39] £97 $184

IRELAND [1844] 60x47cm. (23½x18½") Two sheets joined. Outline color. [39] £41 $79

ISLANDS IN THE ATLANTIC [1836] 40x33cm. (15½x13") 16 small maps. Outline col. [39] £45 $85

LAKE SUPERIOR REDUCED FROM THE ADMIRALTY SURVEY [1842] 31x38cm. (12x15") By C. Knight. [15] £26 $50

LIVERPOOL [1836] 31x38cm. (12x15") City plan. [39] £17 $33

MADRID [1831] 31x37cm. (12x14½") City plan. Old color. [39] £14 $26

MARSEILLE [1840] 33x40cm. (13x15½") City plan. Old color. [39] £14 $26

MILAN (MILANO) [1832] 33x38cm. (13x15") City plan. [39] £10 $20

NEW SOUTH WALES [1833] 39x33cm. (15½x13") Original outline color. [10] £24 $45

NEW YORK [1852] 31x38cm. (12x15") Color. fine. [10] £50 $95

NORTH AMERICA [1844] 38x31cm. (15x12") Knight, pub. Outline color. [39] £55 $105

NORTH AMERICA SHEET I NOVA SCOTIA WITH PART OF NEW BRUNSWICK AND LOWER CANADA [1832] 41x33cm. (15½x12½") London: Chapman & Hall. Color. [15] £21 $40

NORTH AMERICA SHEET VI NEW-YORK, VERMONT, MAINE, NEW-HAMPSHIRE, MASSACHUSETTS, CONNECTICUT, RHODE-ISLAND, AND NEW-JERSEY [1832] 35x31cm. (13½x12") London: Baldwin & Cradock. [6] £26 $50

NORTH AMERICA SHEET VII PENNSYLVANIA, NEW JERSEY, MARYLAND, DELAWARE, COLUMBIA AND PART OF VIRGINIA [1833] 37x31cm. (14½x12½") Baldwin & Cradock. [6] £37 $70

NORTH AMERICA SHEET VIII OHIO, WITH PARTS OF KENTUCKY, VIRGINIA AND INDIANA [1833] 31x35cm. (12x14") London: Baldwin & Cradock. [6] £37 $70

[same title, date, dimensions] Outline color. Fine. [14] £37 $70

NORTH AMERICA SHEET IX PARTS OF MISSOURI, ILLINOIS, AND INDIANA [1833] 30x37cm. (12x14½") London: Baldwin & Cradock. [6] £26 $50

[same title, date, dimensions] Outline color. Fine. [14] £50 $95

NORTH AMERICA SHEET X PARTS OF MISSOURI, ILLINOIS, KENTUCKY, TENNESSEE, ALABAMA, MISSISSIPPI AND ARKANSAS [1842] 33x41cm. (13x15½") London: C. Knight. Color. [15] £24 $45

NORTH AMERICA SHEET XI PARTS OF NORTH AND SOUTH CAROLINA [1833] 38x33cm. (15x13") London: Baldwin & Cradock. [6] £26 $50

[same title, date, dimensions] Color. [15] £24 $45

NORTH AMERICA SHEET XII GEORGIA WITH PARTS OF NORTH & SOUTH CAROLINA, TENNESSEE, ALABAMA & FLORIDA [1833] 40x31cm. (15½x12") Outline col. Fine. [13] £47 $90

[same title, date, dimensions] London: Baldwin & Cradock. Date trimmed. [6] £26 $50

[same title] [c. 1850] 40x31cm. (15½x12") London: Chas. Knight. Outline col. Fine. [13] £47 $90

[same title] [1860] 40x31cm. (15½x12") London: Edward Stanford. Outline col. Fine. [13] £47 $90

NORTH AMERICA SHEET XIV FLORIDA [1834] 40x31cm. (15½x12") Narrow margins as published. [26] £84 $160

PALESTINE WITH THE HAURAN AND THE ADJACENT DISTRICTS [1843] 41x33cm. (16x12½") By Hughes. Laor 362. Color. [15] £21 $40

[same title, date, dimensions] Outline color. [39] £104 $197

PARIS [1852] 39x29cm. (15x11½") City plan on two sheets: "Western Division of Paris" and "Eastern Division of Paris"; approximate dimensions. [39] £14 $26

PHILADELPHIA [1844] 38x30cm. (15x12") City plan. Old color. [39] £41 $79

RUSSIA IN EUROPE PART VI [1835] 39x32cm. (15x12½") Central Russia and Ukraine. Outline color. [39] £17 $33

RUSSIA IN EUROPE PART IX [1835] 32x40cm. (12½x15½") Georgia, Armenia, Astrakan and Caucasus. Outline color. [39] £31 $59

RUSSIA IN EUROPE PART X [1840] 40x32cm. (15½x12½") Outline color. [39] £17 $33

SIBERIA AND CHINESE TARTARY [1844] 32x40cm. (12½x15½") Outline color. [39] £38 $72

SOUTH AMERICA [1844] 40x32cm. (15½x12½") Outline color. [39] £35 $66

SOUTH AMERICA SHEET IV LA PLATA AND CHILE [1840] 31x39cm. (12x15½") Outline color. [39] £17 $33

SPAIN (ESPANA) [1831] 25x34cm. (10x13½") Three sheets: "Northeast Spain", "Northwest Spain" and "Southern Spain"; approximate dimensions. Outline color. [39] £28 $53

STOCKHOLM [1838] 34x39cm. (13x15½") City plan. Old color. [39] £31 $59

SYRACUSE WITH THE REMAINING VESTIGES OF ITS FIVE CITIES [1839] 33x40cm. (13x15½") Plan. Old color. [39] £21 $39

SYRIA [1843] 40x31cm. (15½x12") Outline color. [39] £52 $99

THE BRITISH ISLES [1842] 40x33cm. (15½x13") Outline color. [39] £21 $39

THE ENVIRONS OF DUBLIN [c. 1844] 31x39cm. (12x15½") Color. Very good. [24] £19 $36

THE ENVIRONS OF EDINBURGH [1844] 31x40cm. (12x15½") Old color. [39] £21 $39

THE ENVIRONS OF PARIS [1840] 32x38cm. (12½x15") Outline color. [39] £21 $39

THE ISLANDS OF NEW ZEALAND [1833] 39x31cm. (15x12½") Orig outline col. [10] £16 $30

THE PACIFIC OCEAN [1840] 31x39cm. (12x15½") Original outline color. [10] £16 $30

[same title, date, dimensions] Outline color. [39] £41 $79

THE TURKISH EMPIRE IN EUROPE AND ASIA WITH THE KINGDOM OF GREECE [1844] 32x40cm. (12½x15½") Outline color. [39] £21 $39

THE WORLD AS KNOWN TO THE ANCIENTS [1844] 40x62cm. (15½x24½") From two plates. Outline color. Lower centerfold split; narrow top margin. [39] £10 $20

THE WORLD ON MERCATOR'S PROJECTION [1844] 39x62cm. (15½x24½") From two plates. Outline color. [39] £38 $72

TOULON [1840] 31x38cm. (12x15") City plan. Old color. [39] £21 $39

VENICE. VENEZIA. VENEDIG. [1838] 39x59cm. (15x23") On two sheets. Old col. [39] £69 $131
WESTERN HEMISPHERE [1844] 34x33cm. (13x13") Outline color. [39] £41 $79
WESTERN SIBERIA, INDEPENDENT TARTARY, KHIVA, BOKHORA [1838] 40x33cm. (15½x13") Outline color. [39] £21 $39

SOLINUS

[ASIA] [1538] 25x33cm. (9½x13") Attributed to Munster. Excellent. [38] £473 $900

SOTZMANN, D.H.

NEW YORK ... [1799] 49x63cm. (19x25") Hamburg: C.E. Bohn. W. Sander, sc. Old color. Narrow margin. [16] £759 $1445

SPANISH ADMIRALTY *Try Direccion de Hidrografia*

SPEED *Try Van den Keere*

[PORTRAIT] VIRI CLARISSIMI JOANNES SPEED ... [1631] 26x19cm. (10x7½") Published after 1631 by Savery & Humble. Trimmed to margins; small tear into image. [5] £150 $285
[TITLE PAGE] THE THEATRE OF THE EMPIRE OF GREAT BRITAINE ... [(1627) 1631] 38x24cm. (15x9½") Published by Humble. [5] £280 $533
[TITLE PAGE] THE THEATRE OF THE EMPIRE OF GREAT BRITAIN ... A PROSPECT OF THE MOST FAMOUS PARTS OF THE WORLD ... [1676] 38x24cm. (15x9½") Published by Bassett & Chiswell. Color. [5] £160 $304
A MAP OF NEW ENGLAND AND NEW YORK [1676] 38x51cm. (15x20") Color. Lower centerfold restoration. [5] £1050 $1998
[same title, date, dimensions] Full color. Very good. [22] £1576 $3000
A MAP OF VIRGINIA AND MARYLAND [1676] 38x50cm. (15x19½") State I. Outline color. Fine. [37] £1839 $3500
A NEW AND ACCURAT MAP OF THE WORLD [1626-1676] 41x53cm. (15½x20½") Double hemisphere, with small hemispheres. Shirley 317. Full color. Minor mend lower centerfold; else excellent. [21] £3153 $6000
A NEW MAPPE OF THE ROMANE EMPIRE NEWLY DESCRIBED BY JOHN SPEEDE [(1627) 1676] 40x51cm. (15½x20") Color. [5] £400 $761
AMERICA WITH THOSE KNOWN PARTS IN THAT UNKNOWNE WORLD BOTH PEOPLE AND MANNER OF BUILDINGS DISCRIBED AND INLARGED BY I.S. ANO 1626 [1676] 40x52cm. (15½x20½") "Carte a figures". Insular California. Color. [32] £2800 $5328
ASIA, WITH THE ISLANDS ADJOINING DESCRIBED, THE ATIRE OF THE PEOPLE, & TOWNES OF IMPORTANCE, ALL OF THEM NEWLY AUGMENTED BY JS. ANO. DOM. 1626 [1626] 39x52cm. (15½x20½") Panels at top and sides. Color. Good. [1] £1839 $3500
[same title] [1626-1676] 39x53cm. (15½x20½") Color. Excellent. [21] £1156 $2200
CHINA [1646] 9x12cm. (3½x5") Engraved by Kaerius. Outline col. Close lower margin; exc. [38] £118 $225
EUROP, AND THE CHIEFE CITIES CONTAYNED THEREIN ... [1626] 38x51cm. (15½x20") Top & side panels. Outline col. Age toned; centerfold tape residue top and bottom; else VG. [34] £447 $850
FRANCE, REVISED AND AUGMENTED, THE ATTIRES OF THE FRENCH ... [1627 (1676)] 40x52cm. (15½x20½") Vignettes of cities and dress. Trimmed close to neat line; laid on canvas; but fine. [38] £118 $225
ITALIA [c. 1676] 9x12cm. (3½x4½") Very good. [25] £125 $238
THE COUNTIE AND CITIE OF LYNCOLNE DESCRIBED WITH THE ARMES OF THEM THAT HAVE BENE EARLES THEREOF SINCE THE CONQUEST [1610] 38x51cm. (15x20") Full color. Trimmed close; repaired tear; o/w good. [21] £197 $375
THE COUNTIE PALLATINE OF LANCASTER DESCRIBED AND DIVIDED ... [1610-1612] 38x50cm. (15x19½") Border with portraits. Color. Small tear across a portrait. [32] £800 $1522
[same title] [(1611) 1631] 39x51cm. (15x20") Color. Fine. [5] £595 $1132
THE INVASIONS OF ENGLAND AND IRELAND [1676] (no dims.) Fine. [5] £550 $1047
THE KINGDOME OF CHINA ... [(1627) c. 1631] 39x51cm. (15½x20") Top and side panels. Color. Trimmed to lower outer border; centerfold reinforced. [5] £1550 $2950
THE KINGDOME OF DENMARKE [1627 (1676)] 40x52cm. (15½x20½") Orig col. VF. [38] £236 $450
THE KINGDOME OF IRLAND [1610] 38x51cm. (15½x20") Hondius, engraver. Full color. Excellent. [21] £788 $1500

SPROULE

A SKETCH OF THE ENVIRONS OF CHARLESTOWN IN SOUTH CAROLINA [1780] 51x71cm. (20½x28½") 2nd state. Prepared for *Atlantic Neptune*. Orig col. Light browning at left. [31] £1051 $2000

ST. LOUIS REPUBLICAN

MAP OF THE NEW LIMITS OF THE CITY OF ST. LOUIS AND WARD BOUNDARIES [1877] 53x28cm. (20½x11") On 21" x 16" supplement sheet. Folds; mended short margin tears; o/w excellent. [12] £66 $125

STACKHOUSE

RUSSIA IN EUROPE [1784] 38x36cm. (15x14½") Color. [15] £71 $135

WESTERN HEMISPHERE ENGRAVED BY S. NEELE [1792] 38x36cm. (15x14½") Col. [15] £97 $185

STANDARD ATLAS

[MARYLAND AND DELAWARE] [1898] 23x33cm. (9x13") [15] £11 $20

IDAHO [1888] 30x25cm. (12x9½") 15 counties. Color. [15] £21 $40

MINNESOTA [1887] 30x25cm. (12½x9½") Color. [15] £13 $25

OCEANICA [1888] 23x30cm. (9x11½") Color. [15] £13 $25

PENNSYLVANIA [1887] 30x41cm. (12x16") Color. [15] £16 $30

STANFORD *Try Society for the Diffusion of Useful Knowledge*

ASIATIC ARCHIPELAGO, ON MERCATOR'S PROJECTION [1903] 49x61cm. (19½x24") With color guide. 2" lower fold tear repaired. [10] £32 $60

AUSTRALIA EAST [1903] 61x50cm. (24x19½") Orig color. Repaired at fold split at margin. [10] £26 $50

BRITISH COLUMBIA, MANITOBA, AND THE NORTH WEST TERRITORIES [1903] 52x70cm. (20½x27½") Margin & lower fold repaired. [10] £79 $150

BRITISH COLUMBIA, VANCOUVER ISLAND &C. [1859] 30x38cm. (12x15") Full col. [26] £63 $120

BRITISH NEW GUINEA AND THE SOLOMAN, SANTA CRUZ & NEW HEBRIDES ISLANDS [1903] 51x62cm. (20x24½") Repair at lower fold margin. [10] £18 $35

BURMA AND ADJACENT COUNTRIES [1903] 72x51cm. (28x20") Color code. 1.5" lower fold tear repaired. [10] £24 $45

CHART OF THE NORTH POLAR SEA [c. 1874] 79x62cm. (31x24") Linen-backed folding map with self-backs and original labeled slipcase. Very slight foxing; very good. [19] £236 $450

COLLINS' STANDARD MAP OF LONDON [c. 1865] 62x84cm. (24x33") By Collins. With 23-page guide. Linen-backed folding plan between original boards with label. Partial color. Barely visible water stains on backing. [19] £89 $170

DAVIES'S NEW MAP OF THE BRITISH METROPOLIS. THE BOUNDARIES OF THE BOROUGHS, COUNTY COURT DISTRICTS, RAILWAYS, AND MODERN IMPROVMENTS [1877] 94x94cm. (37x37") On cover: "Davies Map of the British Metropolis with Extension to Crystal Palace ..." Linen-backed folding map between boards. Color. Covers somewhat sunned; VG. [19] £131 $250

EGYPTIAN SUDAN. THE NILE FROM METEMMA TO KHARTUM COMPILED IN THE INTELLEGENCE DIVISION, WAR OFFICE ... [c. 1898] 80x44cm. (31½x17") Linen-backed folding map between original cloth boards with label. Color. Worming and foxing, clean except one spot; some sections loose but present; Boards have water stain. [19] £79 $150

FRANCE [c. 1900] 61x51cm. (24x20") Linen-backed folding map between original boards with label. Color. Very good+. [19] £32 $60

GEOLOGICAL MAP OF ENGLAND & WALES [1877] 94x81cm. (37x32") By Andrew Ramsay. 4th edition. Linen-backed folding map in slip case. Orig col.. Slight uniform age darkening; VG. [19] £236 $450

GEOLOGICAL MAP OF THE BRITISH ISLES [1878] 140x129cm. (55x51") By Andrew Ramsay. Linen-backed folding map in original slip case with label. Color keyed. Small stains not affecting map; slipcase lacks bottom; very good. [19] £202 $385

INDO-CHINA [1903] 50x34cm. (19½x13½") Color code. 1½" lower fold tear repaired. [10] £34 $65

JAPAN [1903] 60x47cm. (23½x18½") Original color. Centerfold margin tear repaired. [10] £39 $75

MANITOBA [1903] 47x61cm. (18½x24") Marginal split repaired. [10] £74 $140

MAP OF THE SEAT OF WAR IN AMERICA [1862] 55x75cm. (21½x29½") London: Davies & Co. Linen-backed folding map with boards and label. Outline color. Very good+. [19] £512 $975

MAPS OF THE BOSPHORUS AND CONSTANTINOPLE, DARDANELLES AND THE TROAD [1877] 47x62cm. (18½x24½") 2 maps on one sheet. Linen-backed folding map between stained boards with label. Light age-staining; very good. [19] £63 $120

NATAL [South Africa] [1924] 46x59cm. (18x23") Linen-backed folding map. Color. Some pencil marks; very good. [19] £45 $85

NEW SOUTH WALES [1903] 51x65cm. (20x25½") Repaired tear at lower fold margin. [10] £18 $35

NEW ZEALAND [1903] 60x47cm. (23½x18½") Splits at binders folds repaired. [10] £18 $35

NEWFOUNDLAND [1903] 59x48cm. (23x19") Minor splits repaired. [10] £21 $40

QUEENSLAND [1903] 65x49cm. (25½x19½") Repair at fold margin. [10] £18 $35

SOUTH AUSTRALIA [AND NORTHERN TERRITORY] [1903] 48x66cm. (19x26") Minor repair at lower centerfold; o/w fine. [10] £18 $35

STANFORD'S GENERAL MAP OF THE UNITED STATES [1894] 70x110cm. (27½x43½") Linen-backed folding map with labeled cloth boards. Color. Slight corner foxing; covers worn and sunned on spine; very good. [19] £102 $195

STANFORD'S MAP OF BRITISH SOUTH AFRICA [1899] 54x70cm. (21½x27½") Linen-backed folding map between original boards with label. Printed color. Very good. [19] £79 $150

STANFORD'S MAP OF THE SEAT OF WAR IN AMERICA [1861] 130x106cm. (51x41½") Linen-backed folding map. Very good. [19] £504 $960

STANFORD'S NEW HAND MAP OF THE UNITED STATES WITH THE RESULT OF THE CENSUS OF 1860 ... [1861] 47x57cm. (18½x22½") Confederate states in red. Folding map with boards with labels. Color. Some small tears along folds and junctions; minor repairs. [19] £184 $350

STANFORD'S PORTABLE MAP OF ENGLAND & WALES WITH THE RAILWAYS CLEARLY DELINEATED, THE CITIES AND TOWNS DISTINGUISHED ACCORDING TO THEIR POPULATION &C. AND THE MOUNTAINS AND HILLS CAREFULLY REDUCED FROM THE ORDNANCE SURVEY [1881] 76x68cm. (30x27") Linen-backed folding map between boards. Pastel wash and bright outline color. Slight age-browning; covers fading; very good. [19] £39 $75

STANFORD'S SMALLER RAILWAY MAP OF THE UNITED STATES DISTINGUISHING THE UNSETTLED TERRITORIES; THE RAILWAYS; THE CITIES AND TOWNS ACCORDING TO POPULATION; ALSO THE STATE CAPITALS AND COUNTY TOWNS [1875] 40x70cm. (15½x27½") Linen-backed folding map between original boards with label. Color. Small stains at crossfolds; very good. [19] £145 $275

STANFORD'S TWO INCH MAP OF LONDON AND ITS ENVIRONS [after 1901] 67x109cm. (26½x43") Linen-backed folding plan between covers with label. Color. Early pencil marks; VG. [19] £39 $75

THE BAHAMAS [1903] 50x61cm. (19½x24") Color. Short lower fold tear repaired. [10] £131 $250

THE COUNTRIES AROUND THE MEDITERRANEAN [n.d.] 50x32cm. (19½x12½") One map in two parts. Linen-backed folding map between boards. Orig col. Uniform age darkening; o/w good. [19] £21 $40

THE FOUNDLING HOSPITAL ESTATE, LONDON. ... [1915] 64x87cm. (25x34½") Some small holes in backing at fold intersections; faint owners pencil marks; very good+. [19] £105 $200

THE ISLANDS OF NEW ZEALAND [1881] 40x32cm. (15½x12½") Orig outline col. [10] £16 $30

THE LEEWARD ISLANDS [1903] 47x60cm. (18½x23½") Original printed color. Lower fold tear repaired; o/w fine. [10] £92 $175

THE NETHERLANDS AND BELGIUM [n.d.] 62x51cm. (24½x20") Linen-backed folding map in original boards with label. Original color. Slight foxing in margin; very good. [19] £24 $45

THE PHILIPPINE ISLANDS [1903] 50x34cm. (19½x13") Original color. Fine. [10] £16 $30

THE UNITED STATES OF NORTH AMERICA (WESTERN PART) [1903] 65x50cm. (25½x19½") Color. Fold tear and 2" tear repaired. [10] £118 $225

THE YUKON DISTRICT [1903] 51x34cm. (20x13½") Printed color. Minor marginal repairs; o/w fine. [10] £131 $250

VICTORIA [1903] 34x53cm. (13½x21") [10] £18 $35

WESTERN AUSTRALIA [1903] 62x51cm. (24½x20") Some delineating color. Minor repair at fold split and margin tear. [10] £26 $50

WESTERN PART [CANADA] [1903] 61x49cm. (24x19") Color. Split repaired. [10] £21 $40

STARLING

MEXICO AND GUATEMALA [1820] 9x15cm. (3½x6") Color. [26] £26 $50

STEBBINS, H.

CENTRAL STATES [1868] 38x66cm. (14½x26") Color. [15] £18 $35

COLUMBUS, FRANKLIN CO. [Ohio] [1868] 38x28cm. (14½x11") By E.F. Bowen. Color. [15] £50 $95

DAYTON [Ohio] [1868] 36x43cm. (14x16½") By J.S. Binkerd. Color. [15] £50 $95

SPRINGFIELD, CLARKE CO. [Ohio] [c.1859] 28x36cm. (10½x14") By J. Moler. Color. [15] £50 $95

STEDMAN

A TOPOGRAPHICAL MAP OF THE NORTHN. PART OF NEW YORK ISLAND, EXHIBITING THE PLAN OF FORT WASHINGTON, NOW FORT KNYPHAUSEN, SHEWING THE SEVERAL ATTACKS OF THE ROYAL ARMY [1793] 46x26cm. (18½x10") Slight offsetting. Fine. [10] £155 $295

[same title] [1793 (1794)] 46x26cm. (18½x10") Fine. [12] £158 $300

[same title] [1794] 46x26cm. (18½x10") Repaired tear. [31] £131 $250

PLAN OF THE ATTACK OF THE FORTS CLINTON & MONTGOMERY UPON HUDSONS RIVER, WHICH WERE STORMED BY HIS MAJESTY'S FORCES UNDER THE COMMAND OF SIR HENRY CLINTON, K.B. ON THE 6TH OF OCTR. 1777 [1793] 65x51cm. (25½x20") Some foxing. [10] £250 $475

PLAN OF THE BATTLE FOUGHT NEAR CAMDEN, AUGUST 16TH 1780 [1794] 22x19cm. (8½x7½") Very good. [31] £79 $150

PLAN OF THE POSITION WHICH THE ARMY UNDER LT. GENL. BURGOINE TOOK AT SARATOGA ON THE 10TH OF SEPTEMBER 1777, AND IN WHICH IT REMAINED TILL THE CONVENTION WAS SIGNED [1793] 22x47cm. (8½x18½") Fine. [10] £79 $150

[same title] [1794] 22x47cm. (8½x18½") Very good. [31] £118 $225

PLAN OF THE SIEGE OF CHARLESTOWN IN SOUTH CAROLINA [1794] 25x30cm. (10x11½") Slight offsetting; o/w fine. [10] £145 $275

PLAN OF THE SIEGE OF SAVANNAH, WITH THE JOINT ATTACK OF THE FRENCH AND AMERICANS ON THE 9TH OCTOBER 1779, IN WHICH THEY WERE DEFEATED ... [1794] 41x57cm. (16x22½") Very good. [31] £342 $650

PLAN OF THE SIEGE OF YORK TOWN IN VIRGINIA [1794] 28x27cm. (11x10½") VG. [31] £131 $250

POSITION OF THE ENGLISH AND FRENCH FLEETS IMMEDIATELY PREVIOUS TO THE ACTION ON THE 5TH SEPR. 1781 [1794] 22x25cm. (8½x10") Color. [15] £76 $145

SKETCH OF GENERAL GRANTS POSITION ON LONG ISLAND [1794] 35x26cm. (13½x10½") 6" tear skillfully repaired; o/w fine. [10] £66 $125

[same title, date, dimensions] Very good. [31] £131 $250

SKETCH OF THE ACTION ON THE HEIGHTS OF CHARLESTOWN JUNE 17TH. 1775 [1794] 33x51cm. (13½x20") Some repaired tears. [31] £250 $475

SKETCH OF THE CATAWBA RIVER AT McCOWNS FORD [1794] 15x18cm. (6½x7") Very good. [31] £79 $150

STIELER *Try Petermann*

INDIEN & INNER ASIA [1881] 36x41cm. (13½x16") Some highlight color. [26] £39 $75

NORD AMERICA ENTWORFEN W. GEZEICHNET [1847] 33x38cm. (13x15½") By Stulpnagel. Color. [15] £66 $125

SUD-AMERICA IN ZWEI BLATTERN ... [1853] 33x40cm. (13x15½") Gotha: Perthes. Dimensions for each of two sheets. Outline color. Foxing and marginal waterstains. [16] £83 $158

SUD-POLAR KARTE [1864] 35x41cm. (13½x16") By Petermann. Printed color. [35] £37 $70

VEREINIGTE STAATEN VON NORD-AMERICA, IN 6 BLATTERN, BL. 5 [1876] 33x41cm. (13x16") Outline color. Immaculate. [12] £71 $135

STIGER & CO.

CHART OF THE ROAD OF THE SIMPLON BETWEEN BRIGG AND DOMO D'OSSOLA [n.d.] 24x51cm. (9½x20") Linen-backed folding map. Slight age-soiling; very good. [19] £92 $175

STOCKDALE *Try Morse*

A MAP OF THE NORTHERN AND MIDDLE STATES; COMPREHENDING THE WESTERN TERRITORY AND THE BRITISH DOMINIONS IN NORTH AMERICA [1792] 33x41cm. (13x16") From Morse, *American Geography* London edition. [26] £210 $400

[same title] [1792] 32x39cm. (12½x15½") Outline color. [36] £145 $275

A NEW MAP OF UPPER & LOWER CANADA [1798] 18x23cm. (7x9") Color. [15] £50 $95

A PLAN OF THE RIVER ST. LAURENCE FROM SILLERY TO THE FALL OF MONTMERENCI, WITH THE OPERATIONS OF THE SIEGE OF QUEBEC 5TH SEPT. 1759 [1812] 19x24cm. (7½x9½") Color. One margin restored. [15] £42 $80

AN EYE SKETCH OF THE FALLS OF NIAGARA [1798] 17x23cm. (6½x9") By I. Weld. Col. [15] £58 $110

MAP OF VIRGINIA, MARYLAND AND DELAWARE [1794] 25x48cm. (10x19") London: From Morse, *American Geography*. Excellent. [36] £105 $200

STOOPENDAAL

DE GELENGENTHEYT VAN'T PARADYS EN'T LANDT CANAAN [1702] 36x46cm. (13½x18") Laor 805. Wash color. Fine. [30] £460 $875

STRABO

ORBIS TERRAE COMPENDIOSA DESCRIPTIO ... [1587] 29x52cm. (11x20½") First issue of double hemisphere map from Geneva edition of *Geographia* without text below; later incorporated into Mercator atlas. Shirley 157. Mint. [38] £2995 $5700

STRADA

NOVUS XVII INFERIORIS GERMANIAE PROVINCIARUM [1653] 18x13cm. (7x5") Leo Belgicus map. Color. Excellent. [38] £236 $450

STRYPE

A MAPP OF THE PARISH OF ST. GILES IN THE FIELDS [1735] 30x38cm. (11½x14½") Reissue of Stow's Survey of London. [35] £66 $125

A MAPP OF THE PARISH OF ST. MARTIN'S IN THE FIELDS [1735] 30x36cm. (11½x14") Reissue of Stow's Survey of London. [35] £66 $125

A MAPP OF THE PARISHES OF ST. CLEMENT DANES AND ST. MAY SAVOY [1735] 36x30cm. (14x11½") Reissue of Stow's Survey of London. [35] £66 $125

A NEW PLAN OF THE CITY OF LONDON, WESTMINSTER AND SOUTHWARK [1721] 49x67cm. (19½x26½") Color. Fine. [5] £520 $990

[same title] [c. 1720] 49x66cm. (19½x26") Color. Very good. [23] £750 $1427

STUCCHI

AMERICA SETTENTIONRALE O COLOMBIA [1830] 56x74cm. (21½x28½") Italian edition of Malte-Brun; Milan: Maggi. Color. [15] £158 $300

STUMPF

FORM UND GESTALT HISPANIE [1548] 13x17cm. (5x6½") Non-Ptolemaic woodcut in *Schwyzer Chronick*. Excellent. [38] £76 $145

SWANSTON

ENLARGED MAP OF BRITISH COLUMBIA AND VANCOUVER'S ISLAND SHEWING THE FRASER RIVER GOLD FIELDS [c. 1858] 10x15cm. (4½x6½") Color. [15] £21 $40

OREGON AND CALIFORNIA [1849] 25x15cm. (9½x6") Color. [15] £42 $80

THE SOUTH EASTERN STATES COMPRISING MISSISSIPPI, ALABAMA, TENNESSEE, GEORGIA ... [1860] 41x51cm. (16x20") Edinburgh: Fullarton. Color. [15] £32 $60

UNITED STATES, NORTH AMERICA [1849] 43x53cm. (16½x20½") Color. [15] £50 $95

UNITED STATES, SOUTH CENTRAL COMPRISING TEXAS, LOUISIANA, ARKANSAS, WESTERN TERRITORY [1858] 51x41cm. (20x16") Edinburgh: A. Fullarton. Color. [15] £39 $75

UNITED STATES ... THE NORTH CENTRAL SECTION ... [c. 1860] 41x51cm. (16x20½") Edinburgh: Fullarton. Indiana to Nebraska. Outline color. Very good. [14] £79 $150

SWENY, M.A.

LIVERPOOL BAY [1892 (1893)] 124x147cm. (49x57½") Issued by Mersey Docks and Harbour Board. Dissected and laid down on linen folding in half calf cloth boards. Tinted wash. Chart fine; boards worn. [11] £300 $571

TALBOT

UNITED STATES OF AMERICA EXHIBITING THE SEAT OF WAR ON THE CANADIAN FRONTIER FROM 1812 TO 1815 [1816] 25x34cm. (10x13½") Color. [15] £76 $145

TALLIS

[TITLE PAGE] THE ILLUSTRATED ATLAS [c. 1850] 32x23cm. (12½x9") Soiled around margins; o/w good. [5] £45 $86

BOSTON [1851] 26x32cm. (10x13") Color. [10] £50 $95

BRITISH AMERICA [1850] 26x33cm. (10x13") Original outline color. [10] £74 $140

CENTRAL AMERICA [c. 1865] 26x33cm. (10x13") Color. [10] £24 $45

CHILI AND LA PLATA [1851] 34x25cm. (13½x10") [10] £18 $35

EAST CANADA AND NEW BRUNSWICK [1851] 25x33cm. (10x13") Full color. [15] £34 $65

FALKLAND ISLANDS AND PATAGONIA [c. 1850] 34x25cm. (13x9½") With text sheet. Outline & wash color. [36] £42 $80

MEXICO, CALIFORNIA AND TEXAS [1850] 25x33cm. (10x13") Original outline color; gold fields in yellow. [10] £84 $160

NORTHERN INDIA [1851] 24x32cm. (9½x12½") A little soiled. [10] £16 $30

PERSIA [1851] 36x25cm. (13½x10") Outline color. [35] £39 $75

SOUTHERN INDIA [c. 1851] 32x23cm. (12½x9") Orig outline col. Slightly soiled. [10] £13 $25

UNITED STATES [1850] 25x34 cm. (9½x13") Original outline color. Fine [10] £92 $175

[same title] [1851] 24x33cm. (9½x13") Outline color. Fine. [12] £118 $225

VENEZUELA, NEW GRANADA, EQUADOR, AND THE GUAYANAS [c. 1865] 25x33cm. (10x13") Third state. Outline color. [10] £24 $45

WEST CANADA [c. 1850] 25x33cm. (10x13") Original outline color. [10] £74 $140

TANNER

A MAP OF NORTH AMERICA [1822] 108x146cm. (42½x57½") Four joinable sheets. Original color. Some chips; slight discoloration at folds; a few scattered spots; very good. [31] £2496 $4750

A NEW MAP OF GEORGIA WITH ITS ROADS & DISTANCES [1836] 34x27cm. (13x10½") Pastel color. Fine. [13] £79 $150

[same title] [1839 (1844)] 28x33cm. (10½x13") Full col. Evenly time-toned; else fine. [12] £97 $185

A NEW MAP OF ILLINOIS WITH ITS PROPOSED CANALS, ROADS & DISTANCES FROM PLACE TO PLACE ALONG THE STAGE AND STEAM BOAT ROUTES [1841] 36x28cm. (14x11½") Color. [15] £87 $165

A NEW MAP OF INDIANA WITH ITS ROADS & DISTANCES [1836] 34x27cm. (13x10½") Full color. Fine. [14] £66 $125

[same title] [1846] 35x28cm. (14x11") Full color. Very fine. [14] £58 $110

A NEW MAP OF KENTUCKY WITH ITS ROADS & DISTANCES FROM PLACE TO PLACE ALONG THE STAGE & STEAM-BOAT ROUTES [1846] 36x41cm. (13½x16") Bright color. VG. [26] £63 $120

A NEW MAP OF MICHIGAN WITH ITS CANALS, ROADS & DISTANCES [1841] 38x30cm. (15x12") Full color. [3] £47 $90

A NEW MAP OF MISSISSIPPI WITH ITS ROADS AND DISTANCES [1836 (1845)] 36x30cm. (14x11½") Carey & Hart, pub. Color. [12] £79 $150

[same title] [1846] 41x36cm. (16x13½") Bright color. Very good. [26] £63 $120

A NEW MAP OF PENNSYLVANIA WITH ITS CANALS, RAIL-ROADS & DISTANCES FROM PLACE TO PLACE ALONG THE STAGE ROADS [1840] 28x33cm. (11x13½") 58 counties. Color. [15] £76 $145

A NEW MAP OF TENNESSEE WITH ITS ROADS & DISTANCES FROM PLACE TO PLACE ALONG THE STAGE & STEAM BOAT ROUTES [1836] 28x38cm. (11x15") Color. [15] £92 $175

[same title] [1846] 36x41cm. (13½x16") Color. Very good. [26] £63 $120

A NEW MAP OF VIRGINIA WITH ITS CANALS, ROADS & DISTANCES ... ALONG THE STAGE & STEAMBOAT ROUTES [1836] 28x33cm. (11x13") Color. [15] £84 $160

CITY OF WASHINGTON [1836 (1844)] 30x37cm. (11½x14½") Carey & Hart, pub. Color. [12] £105 $200

[same title] [1846] 33x41cm. (12½x15½") Philadelphia: S. A. Mitchell. [15] £76 $145

ILLINOIS AND MISSOURI [1823] 71x58cm. (28x23") From *A New American Atlas*. Color. [6] £260 $495

[same title] [1825] 74x58cm. (29x23") Full color. Very good. [3] £578 $1100

LOUISIANA AND MISSISSIPPI [1825] 74x58cm. (29x23") Full color. Excellent. [3] £420 $800

MAP OF NORTH CAROLINA AND SOUTH CAROLINA BY H.S. TANNER [1825] 58x74cm. (23x29") From folio *American Atlas*, 2nd edition. Full color. [3] £420 $800

MAP OF PENNSYLVANIA AND NEW JERSEY [1823] 53x71cm. (21x28") In *A New American Atlas*. Color. Centerfold stain. [6] £260 $495

MAP OF PENNSYLVANIA AND NEW JERSEY [1825] 58x74cm. (23x29") From *American Atlas*, 2nd edition. Full color. Excellent. [3] £342 $650

MAP OF THE STATES OF MAINE, NEW HAMPSHIRE, VERMONT, MASSACHUSETTS, CONNECTICUT, & RHODE ISLAND [1820 (1823)] 69x56cm. (27x22") From *A New American Atlas*. Wash color. Some centerfold stains. [6] £365 $695

MEXICO & GUATEMALA [1834 (1845)] 29x37cm. (11½x14½") Carey & Hart, pub. Full col. [12] £197 $375

NEW JERSEY REDUCED FROM T. GORDON'S MAP ... [1840] 38x31cm. (15x12") 19 counties. Color. [15] £76 $145

NEW YORK [1819 (1823)] 56x66cm. (22x26") From *A New American Atlas*. Wash color. Centerfold stain. [6] £260 $495

OCEANA OR PACIFIC OCEAN [1846] 33x41cm. (13x16") Inset: Wilkes discoveries. Color. [26] £42 $80

OHIO AND INDIANA [1819 (1823)] 53x66cm. (21x26") From *A New American Atlas*. Color. Centerfold stain. [6] £260 $495

PLAN OF THE CITY OF PHILADELPHIA [1836] 41x33cm. (16x13") Pocket map folding into 4.5 x 2.5" case. Full color. Very good crisp map; case excellent. [3] £118 $225

THE WORLD ON MERCATOR'S PROJECTION [1823] 58x74cm. (23x29") From *American Atlas*, 2nd edition. Full color. Clean; excellent. [3] £263 $500

VIRGINIA, MARYLAND AND DELAWARE [1820 (1823)] 52x73cm. (20½x29") Wash color. Browning at centerfold. [6] £365 $695

[same title] [1825] 58x73cm. (23x29") Full color. Excellent. [3] £420 $800

WISCONSIN [1846] 41x36cm. (16x13½") Full color. Very good. [26] £74 $140

TARDIEU

AMERIQUE SEPTENTRIONALE [1809] 28x23cm. (11x9") With "Orleans" Terr. Color. [15] £66 $125

CARTE DES ANTILLES [1797] 33x43cm. (13x17") Color. [15] £97 $185

CARTE DES DEUX AMERIQUES, AVEC LEURS NOUVELLES DIVISIONS POLITIQUES: DRESSEE D'APRES LES DECOUVERTES RECENTES; PAR HERISSON GEOG.HE ... [1827] 51x70cm. (20x27½") Color. [16] £656 $1248

CARTE DES ROUTES DE POSTES DE L'EMPIRE FRANCAIS, DU ROYAUME D'ITALIE, ET DE LA CONFEDERATION DU RHIN [1814] 3 of 4 parts. Various sizes: 57 x 59 cm; 81 x 58 cm; 58 x 79 Linen-backed folding maps in chemise and slipcase of leather with gilt border. VG; foxing, worming in one section; small paper loss at fold intersections; stout slipcase worn at extremities. [19] £197 $375

CARTE DU GOLFE DU MEXIQUE ... [1821] 41x56cm. (16x21½") Outline color. Centerfold wormhole; else fine. [34] £79 $150

CARTE GENERALE DES ETATS-UNIS DE L'AMERIQUE SEPTENTRIONALE, RENFERMANT AUSSI QUELQUES PROVINCES ANGLOISES ADJACENTES [c. 1792] 33x43cm. (13x17") Color. [15] £123 $235

TAUNTON

TAUNTON'S POCKET EDITION OF THE MERCHANT'S AND SHIPPER'S GUIDE TO THE PORT OF NEW YORK [1879] 66x46cm. (26x18") 14 text pages. 3-color lithography. Wraps rubbed; map detached, browned and separated along folds; good. [7] £32 $60

TAVERNIER

CARTE DES ISLES DU JAPON ... [1679] 22x33cm. (8½x13") Reduced from folio version of same year. Short repaired tear into left center; o/w fine. [5] £550 $1047

TAYLOR, T.

TAYLOR'S MAP OF LIVERPOOL AND ITS ENVIRONS, ... [1833] 35x48cm. (13½x19") Linen-backed folding map in slipcase. Some stains on backing, map unaffected; very good. [19] £37 $70

TEESDALE *Try Dower*

VAN DIEMANS LAND [c. 1850] 41x34cm. (16x13") Color coding. [10] £26 $50

THESAURUS GEOGRAPHICUS *Try Moll (Small)*

THOMAS, COWPERTHWAIT & CO. *Try Mitchell (Atlas Maps 1859 or Earlier)*

A NEW MAP OF GEORGIA WITH ITS ROADS AND DISTANCES [1850] 36x30cm. (14x11½") Color. Fine. [13] £50 $95

A NEW MAP OF INDIANA WITH ITS ROADS AND DISTANCES [1850] 33x25cm. (12½x10") Full color. Marginal browning; very good. [14] £45 $85

A NEW MAP OF MICHIGAN WITH ITS CANALS, ROADS, AND DISTANCES [1850] 38x29cm. (15x11½") Color. [15] £45 $85

[same title] [1854] 38x31cm. (15x12") Full color. [3] £39 $75

A NEW MAP OF MISSISSIPPI WITH ITS ROADS AND DISTANCES [1850] 36x30cm. (14½x11½") Color. [15] £45 $85

A NEW MAP OF NTH. CAROLINA WITH ITS CANALS, ROADS & DISTANCES FROM PLACE TO PLACE ALONG THE STAGE & STEAM BOAT ROUTES [1850] 30x36cm. (12x14½") Color. [15] £50 $95

A NEW MAP OF THE STATE OF CALIFORNIA, THE TERRITORIES OF OREGON, WASHINGTON, UTAH & NEW MEXICO [1850 (1853)] 41x33cm. (15½x12½") Full color. Immaculate. [12] £189 $360

A NEW MAP OF THE STATE OF CALIFORNIA, THE TERRITORIES OF OREGON & UTAH, AND THE CHIEF PART OF NEW MEXICO. [1850 (1852)] 41x33cm. (15½x12½") Full color. Immaculate. [12] £158 $300

A NEW MAP OF THE STATE OF ILLINOIS WITH ITS PROPOSED CANALS, ROADS AND DISTANCES FROM PLACE TO PLACE ALONG THE STEAMBOAT ROUTES [1854] 39x34cm. (15½x13½") Full color. [3] £42 $80

A NEW MAP OF THE STATE OF IOWA [1854] 34x41cm. (13½x16") Full color. [3] £34 $65

A NEW MAP OF THE STATE OF MISSOURI [1854] 36x41cm. (13½x16") Full color. [3] £42 $80

A NEW MAP OF THE STATE OF OHIO [1854] 40x34cm. (16x13½") Full color. [3] £32 $60

A NEW MAP OF VIRGINIA WITH ITS CANALS, ROADS & DISTANCES ... ALONG THE STAGE & STEAMBOAT ROUTES [1850] 30x36cm. (11½x14") Color. [15] £42 $80

MAP OF MINNESOTA TERRITORY [1850] 34x41cm. (13x16") 9 counties. Color. [15] £66 $125

[same title] [1854] 33x41cm. (13x16") Full color. [35] £79 $150

MAP OF NEW JERSEY REDUCED FROM T. GORDON'S MAP [1850] 39x32cm. (15x12½") 20 counties. Color. [15] £50 $95

MAP OF THE STATE OF MISSOURI [1851] 33x41cm. (13x16") Color. [15] £47 $90

PALESTINE & ADJACENT COUNTRIES [1850] 41x33cm. (16x12½") Color. [15] £21 $40

RUSSIA IN EUROPE [1850] 31x26cm. (12x10") Color. [15] £18 $35

THOMSON

ARABIA, EGYPT, ABYSSINIA, RED SEA, &C. [1814] 51x58cm. (20x23") Broad outline & wash color. [35] £79 $150

BRITISH INDIA, NORTHERN PART [1817] 51x61cm. (20x24") Three maps: largest 13 x 24"; with "Cabul" & "Nepaul". Color. [26] £131 $250

DENMARK [1817] 51x61cm. (20x24") Body color. Light stain upper centerfold; minor tranference; else fine. [34] £53 $100

HAITI, HISPANIOLA OR ST. DOMINGO [1815] 28x61cm. (11x24") Color. [15] £37 $70

IRELAND [c. 1815] 60x50cm. (23½x20") Color. Very good. [24] £45 $86

NORTH AMERICA [1812] 23x30cm. (9½x11½") By J. Wyld. Color. [15] £47 $90

[same title] [c. 1818] 23x30cm. (9x11½") By Wyld. Outline col. Pristine. [12] £97 $185

NORTHERN HEMISPHERE [1814] 53x51cm. (21½x20") North Pole to Equator. Col. [15] £63 $120

SOUTHERN PROVINCES OF THE UNITED STATES [1817] 51x58cm. (19½x23½") Color. Good. [28] £223 $425

SPANISH NORTH AMERICA [1814] 51x62cm. (20x24½") Includes present U.S. Southwest. Color. [15] £202 $385

THE COURSE OF THE RIVER ST. LAWRENCE, FROM LAKE ONTARIO TO MANICOUAGAN POINT [1816] 41x23cm. (16x9") Color. [15] £18 $35

UNITED STATES [1812] 23x30cm. (9x11½") By J. Wyld. Features "Franklinia". Color. [15] £66 $125

UNITED STATES OF AMERICA [and] THE COURSE OF THE RIVER ST. LAURENCE FROM LAKE ONTARIO TO MANICOUAGAN POINT [1817] 41x61cm. (16x24") Two maps on a sheet; main U.S. map: 16 x 15". Full color. Light offsetting; else fine. [12] £118 $225

WEST INDIES [1797] 18x23cm. (7½x8½") Published at Dublin. Color. [15] £39 $75

WESTERN HEMISPHERE [1815] 53x51cm. (21x20") Color. [15] £71 $135

THORNTON

PART OF NEW ENGLAND NEW YORK EAST NEW IARSEY AND LONG ILAND [1689] 43x51cm. (16½x20½") From *The English Pilot: The Fourth Book*. Toned; minor centerfold reinforcement; VG to excellent. [21] £4992 $9500

THROOP

MAP OF THE UNITED STATES TERRITORY OF OREGON WEST OF THE ROCKY MOUNTAINS EXHIBITING THE VARIOUS TRADING DEPOTS OR FORTS OCCUPIED BY THE BRITISH HUDSON BAY COMPANY CONNECTED WITH THE WESTERN AND NORTHWESTERN FUR TRADE. [1846] 28x43cm. (10½x16½") From W. Robertson's *History of Oregon*. Part of lower right margin extended; else excellent. [12] £184 $350

TILGMANN, F.

SUOMEN KASIKARTTA - HANDKARTA OFVER FINLAND [1905] 69x51cm. (27x20") Dissected, linen-backed folding map. Color. Age-toning; lightly soiled at edges; very good. [8] £24 $45

TIRINUS

CHOROGRAPHIA TERRAE SANCTE [1638 - c.1650] 33x83cm. (13x32½") Biblical objects illustrated on three sides. Laor 771. Trimmed; slight loss at right border. [32] £600 $1142

TIRION *Try Albrizzi*

DE REEDE EN HAVEN VAN VERA CRUZ [1766] 18x25cm. (7x10") Color. [15] £45 $85

GEZIGT VAN'T SPAANSCHE VLEK PENSACOLA, AAN DE BAAY ... IN DE GOLF VAN MEXIKO ... JAAR 1743 [1769] 16x26cm. (6½x10") View from seaward. Color. [15] £58 $110

GRONDVLAKTE VAN NIEUW ORLEANS, DE HOOFDSTAD VAN LOUISIANA [and] DE UITLOOP VAN DE RIVIER MISSISIPPI [and] DE OOSTELYKE INGANG VAN DE MISSISIPPI, MET EEN PLAN VAN HET FORT, 'T WELK HET KANAAL BEHEERSCHT [1769] 33x45cm. (13x17½") Fine. [12] £236 $450

KAART VAN DE LANDENGTE VAN PANAMA, VOLGENS DE SPAANSCHE AFTEKENINGE OPGEMAAKT [c. 1765] 27x30cm. (10½x12") Full color. Excellent. [36] £66 $125

KAART VAN GEHEEL GUAJANA OF DE WILDEN-KUST, EN DIE DER SPAANSCHE WESTINDIEN, OP HET NOORD-END VAN ZUID-AMERIKA. ... [1765] 33x40cm. (13x16") Outline & wash color. [36] £118 $225

NIEUWE KAART VAN AMERICA UITGEGEVEN TE AMSTERDAM BY ISAAK TIRION [1766] 28x32cm. (11x12½") Wash col. Unobtrusive margin corner replacement; o/w fine. [29] £255 $485

NIEUWE KAART VAN DE NOORD POOL ... [1735] 30x28cm. (12x11") North Pole to 35 deg. North. Insular California. Color. [15] £171 $325

NIEUWE KAART VAN HET WESTELYKSTE DEEL DE WEERELD [1754] 33x36cm. (13x14") Right margin extended; else mint. [12] £118 $225

NIEUWE KAART VAN KANADA, DE LANDEN AAN DE HUDSONS-BAAY EN DE NOORDWESTELIYKE DEELEN VAN NOORD-AMERIKA. TE AMSTERDAM BY ISAAK TIRION [1769] 31x44cm. (12x17") Color. [10] £97 $185

[same title, date, dimensions] Wash color. Excellent. [37] £202 $385

NUOVA CARTA DEL POLO ARTICO SECONDO L'ULTIME OSSERVAZIONE A AMSTERDAM [c.1738] 28x33cm. (11x12½") Italian edition, Venice. Color. [15] £118 $225

QUEBEK DE HOOFDSTAD VAN KANADA; AAN DE RIVIER VAN ST. LAURENS: DOOR DE ENGELSCHEN BELEGERD EN BY VERDRAG BEMAGTIGD, IN 'T JAAR 1759 [1769] 33x43cm. (13x17") Color. [15] £131 $250

TOMS

THIS PLAN OF THE HARBOUR, TOWN, AND FORTS, OF CARTAGENA ... [1740] 42x58cm. (16½x22½") Separately published, with price noted. Color. [33] £240 $457

TORNIELLO

SITUS PARTIUM PRAECIPUARUM TOTIUS ORBIS TERRARUM [1609] 20x38cm. (7½x15") Shirley 267. Some foxing, primarily in the margins, o/w good. [2] £998 $1900

TOUSSAINT

PARIS, DIVISE EN 12 ARONDISSEMENTS, ET 48 QUATIERS, DRESSE PAR TOUSSAINT, ARCHITECTE [c. 1820] 74x112cm. (29x44") Paris: Binet. Linen-backed folding plan. Partial color. Very good+. [19] £210 $400

TUNISON

TUNISON'S GEORGIA AND SOUTH CAROLINA [1883] 25x33cm. (10x12½") Full col. VG. [13] £16 $30

[same title] [c. 1892] 25x33cm. (10x12½") Color. [15] £16 $30

TUNISON'S GEORGIA, NORTH AND SOUTH CAROLINA [c. 1900] 25x36cm. (10x13½") Reverse: SD. Printed color. Fine. [13] £21 $40

U.S. *Try Duval, Fremont*

[MAP OF THE SANDY AND BEAVER CANAL IN OHIO] [1835] 30x28cm. (12x11") Canals in color. [6] £53 $100

A CHART OF THE SEA COAST OF THE STATE OF MISSISSIPPI EXECUTED BY AUTHORITY OF THE STATE 1839 [1840] 30x51cm. (11½x20½") By J. Wheeler. With 3 page report. [15] £66 $125

A MAP OF THE EXTREMITY OF CAPE COD INCLUDING THE TOWNSHIPS OF PROVINCETOWN & TRURO; WITH A CHART OF THEIR SEA COAST AND OF CAPE COD HARBOUR, STATE OF MASSACHUSETTS [1836] 73x88cm. (28½x34½") Four joinable sheets, each these dimensions. A number of chips and tears, some in image area, repaired on verso with no significant paper loss. [20] £473 $900

A PLAN OF A TRACT OF LAND ON BAYOU BOEUF SURVEYED BY SPANISH COMMISSION OF THE SURVEYOR GENERAL ... OCT. 1803 [1813] 30x41cm. (12x16") By S. Levi Wells. Color. [15] £45 $85

ANCHOR BAY, LAKE ST. CLAIR [1847] 64x58cm. (25x23") GLO. Plots 98 tracts. [15] £58 $110

ATLANTIC & PACIFIC JUNCTION, TOPOGRAPHICAL MAP, A PORTION OF THE ISTHMUS OF DARIEN, SITE OF PROPOSED INTER-OCEANIC NAVIGATION [1852] 36x51cm. (14x19½") By L. Gisborne. Color. [15] £45 $85

BOUNDARIES OF THE RESERVATION FOR WABASH SALINE. GENERAL LAND OFFICE. DEC. 10TH 1816 [c. 1816] 41x33cm. (16x13") By J. Meigs. Color. [15] £34 $65

BROAD RIVER AND ITS TRIBUTARIES, S.C. [1864] 30x18cm. (12x7") By Willenbucher. [15] £21 $40

CAMPAIGN OF THE ARMY OF WEST MISSISSIPPI, MAJ. GEN. E.R.S. CANBY, COMDG., IN SOUTHERN ALABAMA, MARCH & APRIL 1865. PLATE CX [1891-95] 41x69cm. (16½x27½") From *Atlas ... of the Union and Confederate Armies*. Col. Centerfold slightly browned; fine. [28] £97 $185

CHART OF THE COAST OF SOUTH CAROLINA SHOWING THE LOCATION OF THE NATURAL OYSTER BEDS FROM LONG ID. TO KIAWAH ID. [1890] 66x66cm. (26x25½") Lt. R. Platt; issued by Fishery Comm. [15] £32 $60

COBSCOOK BAY, MAINE SURVEYED IN 1836 ... [1838] 38x30cm. (14½x12") By Cooper & Donaldson. [15] £50 $95

DISTRICT OF KASKASKIA [1808] 36x23cm. (14x8½") By D.C. Robinson. [15] £58 $110

GENERAL MAP SHOWING THE COUNTRIES EXPLORED & SURVEYED BY THE UNITED STATES & MEXICAN BOUNDARY COMMISSION IN THE YEARS 1850, 51, 52 & 53 ... [1854] 41x51cm. (15½x19½") By John R. Bartlett. Repairs. [26] £137 $260

[same title] [1855] 41x51cm. (15½x19½") By J. R. Bartlett, in Soule. J. H. Colton, lith. Short mended tear to right border; o/w flawless. [12] £184 $350

GEOLOGICAL CHART OF PART OF IOWA, WISCONSIN & ILLINOIS [1844] 58x46cm. (23x18") By D. Owen. Strata in 9 colors. [15] £87 $165

GEOLOGICAL MAP OF ISLE ROYALE, LAKE SUPERIOR [1847 (1849)] 46x64cm. (17½x25") Color. Trivial offsetting; else fine. [12] £66 $125

GEOLOGICAL MAP OF THE VICINITY OF SAN FRANCISCO ... 1853 [1856] 18x23cm. (6½x9½") By W. Blake. Color key to strata. [15] £18 $35

GEOLOGICAL MAP OF WISCONSIN, IOWA & MINNESOTA; EXHIBITING COAL FIELDS INTO MISSOURI & ILL. [1851] 114x66cm. (44½x26½") By D. Owen. Multi-color key. [15] £139 $265

GRAND AND LESSER CAYMANS FROM A BRITISH SURVEY IN 1881 [1884] 64x79cm. (24½x30½") U.S. Hydrographic Office. Color. [15] £236 $450

HARBOR OF MICHIGAN CITY, INDIANA [1853] 30x48cm. (12x18½") By J. R. Bowes. Margin repairs. [15] £26 $50

LANDS ADJACENT TO LAKE SUPERIOR CEDED TO THE UNITED STATES BY TREATY OF 1842 WITH THE CHIPPEWAS [1845] 91x114cm. (35½x45") By Col. G. Talcott. Wall map. Outline color. [15] £92 $175

MAP EXHIBITING THE ROUTES BETWEEN FORT DALLES AND THE GREAT SALT LAKE BY BVT 2D LIEUT. JOSEPH DIXON ... 1859 [1861] 66x84cm. (26x33") Thin paper, some browning at folds. [6] £155 $295

MAP, NO. 2. SHOWING A CONTINUATION OF DETAILS OF FORT SMITH AND SANTA FE ROUTE FROM OLD FORT HOLMES TO MOUNDS NEAR 100 1/2 DEGREE OF LONGITUDE [1849 (1850)] 28x51cm. (11x19½") Light spots lower right; else good. [12] £66 $125

MAP OF A RECONNAISSANCE FROM CARROLL, MONTANA TER. TO THE YELLOWSTONE NATIONAL PARK AND RETURN [1875 (1876)] 64x48cm. (24½x19") Minor creases; else excellent. [12] £71 $135

MAP OF ALASKA [1898] 64x81cm. (25x32") By Harry King; DOI. Full color. Folds. [3] £47 $90

MAP OF ARKANSAS [1832] 53x58cm. (21x23") GLO. With 1825 Indian Boundaries. Col. [15] £39 $75

MAP OF CENTRAL AMERICA SHOWING THE PRETENDED BOUNDARIES OF THE MOSQUITO KINGDOM, TH ROUTE OF THE PROPOSED CANAL, ETC. [1849] 25x28cm. (10x11") By E. Squier. Color. [15] £32 $60

MAP OF MILL CREAK NEAR CINCINNATI SHOWING CONTEMPLATED IMPROVEMENTS [1862] 15x46cm. (6x18") Bowen, lith. Color. [15] £18 $35

MAP OF NICARAGUA [1850] 36x43cm. (14½x17") By E. Squier. Color. [15] £32 $60

MAP OF OREGON AND UPPER CALIFORNIA FROM THE SURVEYS OF JOHN CHARLES FREMONT AND OTHER AUTHORITIES [1850] 51x43cm. (20x17") Smaller reissue of large map. [3] £184 $350

MAP OF PART OF LOUISIANA NORTH OF THE BASE LINE [1835] 48x30cm. (19½x12½") Public Lands Dept. Color. [15] £34 $65

MAP OF THE BATTLEFIELD OF GETTYSBURG [1903] 122x84cm. (48x33") Commemorative issue. Substantial color. Very good. [3] £63 $120

MAP OF THE CITY OF AUGUSTA, GA [1889] 64x147cm. (25½x58") O.M. Carter & Geo. Brown, U.S. Engineer's Office. Wall map. Levee line in red. Fine. [13] £79 $150

MAP OF THE COMMON FIELD LANDS & LOW LAND COMMONS OF PRAIRIE DU ROCHER ... [1810] 25x38cm. (10x15") By W. Rector. [15] £32 $60

MAP OF THE COUNTRY UPON THE BRAZOS AND BIG WICHITA RIVERS EXPLORED IN 1854 ... EMBRACING THE LANDS APPROPRIATED BY THE STATE OF TEXAS FOR THE USE OF THE INDIANS. DRAWN BY CAPT. MARCY [1856] 64x79cm. (25x31") Wagner-Camp 278. With 48 page Senate document. Thin paper; minor browning. [6] £158 $300

MAP OF THE COUNTRY UPON UPPER RED-RIVER EXPLORED IN 1852...UNDER ORDERS FROM THE HEAD QUARTERS OF THE U.S. ARMY [c. 1852] (no dims.) Folding map between embossed boards. Some tears, one map separated from boards, no loss. [19] £63 $120

MAP OF THE FORMER TERRITORIAL LIMITS OF THE CHEROKEE "NATION OF" INDIANS EXHIBITING THE BOUNDARIES OF THE VARIOUS CESSIONS OF LAND MADE BY THEM TO THE COLONIES AND TO THE UNITED STATES [1884] 71x81cm. (28x31½") By C.C. Royce. Includes parts of VA, WV, NC, SC, KY, TN, AL, Color. Left margin partly extended; some folds reinforced; rice paper backing; o/w fine. [29] £202 $385

MAP OF THE MILITARY DEPARTMENT OF NEW MEXICO, ... 1864 [1892] 43x61cm. (16½x23½") From *Atlas ... of the Union and Confederate Armies, 1861-1865* Some color. Excel. [36] £92 $175

MAP OF THE MILITARY RESERVATION AT FORT YUMA, CALIFORNIA [1883] 41x61cm. (16x24") By Lt. Geo. Wheeler, 1869. Folded as issued; very good. [3] £42 $80

MAP OF THE NORTHERN PART OF THE STATE OF MAINE & ADJACENT BRITISH PROVINCES SHOWING THE PORTION OF WHICH BRITAIN LAYS CLAIM [1838] 43x38cm. (17x15") By S. Dashiell. With 7 page Kent boundary report. [15] £47 $90

MAP OF THE ROUTE PASSED OVER BY AN EXPEDITION INTO THE INDIAN COUNTRY IN 1832 TO THE SOURCE OF THE MISSISSIPPI, BY LIEUT. J. ALLEN, U.S. INF. [c. 1861] 38x47cm. (15x18½") [Early facsimile.] Invisibly mended short splits; o/w perfect. [12] £105 $200

MAP OF THE TERRITORY OF NEW MEXICO [c. 1889] 51x33cm. (20x13") 17 counties; 80 mining districts Color. [15] £34 $65

MAP OF THE TERRITORY OF NEW MEXICO MADE BY ORDER OF BRIG. GEN. S.W. KEARNY UNDER INSTRUCTIONS FROM LIEUT. W.H. EMORY, U.S.T.E. BY LIEUT'S J.W. ABERT AND W.G. PECK, U.S.T.E., ... [1846-47] 64x50cm. (25x19½") Good. [35] £145 $275

MAP OF THE UNITED STATES AND TERRITORIES WITH ADJACENT PARTS OF CANADA AND MEXICO ... [1894] 163x203cm. (64x80") Townships indicated. Linen-backed wall map. Outline color. Faint marginal stains; wrinkles where lifting from linen; small hole; rail & roller separating; fair to good. [7] £84 $160

MAP OF THE WABASH & ERIE CANAL LINE FROM THE MOUTH OF TIPPECANOE TO TERRE-HAUTE [1838-39] 33x25cm. (12½x10") Light offsetting. [12] £47 $90

MAP & PROFILES, OF THE PENNSYLVANIA AND OHIO CANAL, FROM AKRON ON THE OHIO CANAL BY THE VALLIES OF THE CUYAHOGA AND MAHONING ON THE SHENANGO [1835] 48x71cm. (19x28") Attached to 74 page Senate document. Thin folded paper; fold lines, minor foxing at left. [6] £53 $100

MAP SHOWING INDIAN RESERVATIONS WITHIN THE LIMITS OF THE UNITED STATES AND TERRITORIES ... [1890] 53x84cm. (21x33") Some color. Trimmed close at left; folded as issued; good. [26] £63 $120

MAP SHOWING POSITION OF SAN BERNARD RIVER & OTHER WATERWAYS ... CAPT. C. RICHE ... [1899] 71x51cm. (27½x20") By S. Wilcox. [15] £32 $60

MAP SHOWING ROUTES OF THE RIVER AND LAND PARTIES ENGAGED IN EXPLORING THE GRAND CANON OF THE COLORADO [1871 (1889)] 38x41cm. (15x16") Wheeler Survey, Geological Report, Vol. 1. Tinted. Pristine. [12] £92 $175

MAP SHOWING THE LINES OF COMMUNICATION BETWEEN SOUTHERN COLORADO AND NORTHERN NEW MEXICO ... [1876] 51x61cm. (20x24") By Lt. Ruffner. Folded as issued. Very good. [3] £42 $80

MAP SHOWING THE LOCATIONS OF THE INDIAN RESERVATIONS WITHIN THE LIMITS OF THE UNITED STATES AND TERRITORIES ... [1885] 53x84cm. (21x33") Some color. Slightly browned paper; repaired tear. [26] £47 $90

MAP SHOWING THE ROUTE OF E. F. BEALE FROM FORT SMITH, ARK. TO ALBUQUERQUE ... [1860] 18x124cm. (7x49") Short marginal tears repaired; o/w fine. [12] £92 $175

MAP SHOWING THE ROUTES TRAVELLED BY THE COMMAND OF MAJR. E. STEEN, U.S. DRAG'S AGAINST SNAKE INDIANS IN 1860 BY LIEUT JOSEPH DIXON ... [1861] 61x86cm. (24x34") Wagner-Camp 372a. Thin paper. Some browning at folds. [6] £158 $300

MEXICAN BOUNDARY B. EXTRACT FROM THE TREATY MAP OF DISTURNELL OF 1847 [1851 (1852)] 23x41cm. (9x15½") Excellent. [12] £66 $125

MICHIGAN CITY [INDIANA] [1839] 25x23cm. (9½x9½") By Tho. Jefferson Cram. [15] £45 $85

MONTANA TERRITORY [1879] 38x53cm. (15x21") By C. Roeser. [15] £50 $95

NORTH PART OF N.E. LAND DISTRICT OF ILLINOIS [1836] 18x15cm. (7x6") Philadelphia: Bowen, lith. Color. [15] £50 $95

NORTH WEST LAND DISTRICT OF ILLINOIS [1836] 33x28cm. (12½x10½") Philadelphia: Bowen, lith. Color. [15] £50 $95

OHIO RIVER BETWEEM MOUND CITY & CAIRO [1864] 38x56cm. (15x22") By F. H. Gerdes, U.S.N. With street plans. Slight browning at two folds. [6] £37 $70

[same title, date, dimensions] [15] £32 $60

OWLS HEAD HARBOR MAINE SURVEYED IN 1836 UNDER DIRECTION OF LT. COL. S.H. LONG [1838] 38x30cm. (15x12") By J. Cooper. [15] £50 $95

PART OF THE STATE OF ALABAMA SHOWING THE POSITION OF THE CHEROKEE LAND ... UNDER TREATY OF 29TH DEC. 1835 [c. 1838] 41x28cm. (16x10½") Color. [15] £37 $70

PLAN OF A TRACT OF LAND ON BAYOU BOEUF SURVEYED ... SUPPOSED CLAIM OF THE APPALACHIE INDIANS ... AT RAPIDES THIS 17TH JAN. 1804 [1813] 33x20cm. (13x8") By Levi Wells. [15] £32 $60

PLAN OF THE FRONT PART OF THE CITY OF NEW ORLEANS IN 1818 [1836] 20x56cm. (7½x22") By J. Pilie. [15] £21 $40

PLAN OF THE NAVY YARD IN THE HARBOUR OF MEMPHIS, TENN. [1844] 46x64cm. (17½x25") By Commissioner W.P.S. Sanger. Folds; minor repaired tears. [31] £79 $150

PLAN OF THE SETTLEMENT AT GREEN BAY FROM THE REPORT OF J. LEE ESQR. 1821 [1834] 38x46cm. (15x18") Locates 66 land owners. [15] £87 $165

PLAN OF THE SETTLEMENT AT PRAIRIE DES CHIENS 1820 [1834] 51x33cm. (19½x13") By J. Lee. Show 87 land grants. [15] £45 $85

PLAN OF THE UNITED STATE MARINE HOSPITAL LAND, CHELSEA, MASS. ... [1835] 64x48cm. (25x18½") By Alonzo Lewis. Shows surrounding features. [15] £71 $135

PLANO FIGURATIVO DE LOS TRENTA LEGUAS PLANAS DE TIERRAS, CON CEDIDAS A SENOR MARQUES DE MAISON ROUGE ... LUISIANA 1797 ... [1813] 30x18cm. (11½x7") General Land Office. Color. [15] £32 $60

PLAT OF THE COMMON FIELD AND TOWN TRACT OF KASKASKIA [c. 1818] 46x36cm. (18x14") By W. Rector. [15] £66 $125

PLAT OF THE MILWAUKEE AND ROCK RIVER CANAL [1838] 28x46cm. (11x18") Folds as issued; very good. [3] £32 $60

PROVISIONAL GEOLOGICAL MAP OF THE CHIPPEWAY LAND DISTRICT OF WISCONSIN WITH PART OF IOWA & MINNESOTA TERR. [1847] 86x64cm. (34x25½") By D. Owen. 12 color strata key. [15] £97 $185

SKETCH OF GENERAL RILEY'S ROUTE THROUGH THE MINING DISTRICTS JULY & AUG. 1849 ... FROM ORIGINAL SKETCH BY LT. DERBY ... BY J.M.C. HOLLINGSWORTH [1850] 53x50cm. (21x20") Folds as issued; very good. [3] £184 $350

[same title, date] 53x51cm. (21½x20") House Ex. Doc. 17, 31st Cong. 1st Sess. Repaired tear top right; rice paper backing; o/w good. [28] £255 $485

SKETCH OF PART ... LOUISIANA ACCOMPANYING A REPORT ... [1829] 48x58cm. (18½x22½") General Land Office. Eastern half of state; canals, locks. Color. [15] £39 $75

SKETCH OF THE DYEA AND SKAGUA TRAILS ... [1897] 25x20cm. (10x8") By C.B. Talbot; DOI. [3] £32 $60

SKETCH OF THE LEAD MINE DISTRICT IN WASHINGTON COUNTY MISSOURI TERRITORY [1816] 48x41cm. (18½x15½") General Land Office. By J. Meigs. Color. [15] £76 $145

SOIL MAP - CORPUS CHRISTI SHEET [1908] 48x76cm. (19x30") Eight color. Scattered foxed spots; o/w fine. [12] £24 $45

SOIL MAP - FARGO SHEET [NORTH DAKOTA] [1903] 33x94cm. (13x37") Ten lithographed colors. Invisible fold intersection pinhole mends; else fine. [12] £18 $35

SOIL MAP - GRAND ISLAND SHEET [NEBRASKA] [1903] 48x71cm. (18½x27½") Seven lithographed colors. Fine. [12] £18 $35

SOIL MAP - LOS ANGELES SHEET [1903] 89x76cm. (35x30") Color. Tiny fold intersection splits repaired. else superb. [12] £71 $135

SOIL MAP - PARKERSBURG AREA [WEST VIRGINIA] [1908] 81x132cm. (32x52") Multi-color lithography. [12] £26 $50

TERRITORY OF ARIZONA [1903] 51x40cm. (20x16") DOI. Full color. Folds as issued. [3] £37 $70

THE CONNECTED PLAN OF COMMON LANDS OF FORT CHARTRES OF PRAIRIE DU ROCHER ... JUNE 2ND 1809 [1810] 43x41cm. (16½x15½") General Land Office. By W. Rector. [15] £50 $95

THE STATE OF FLORIDA ... FROM THE BEST AUTHORITIES ... [1846] 109x99cm. (42½x39½") Bureau of Topographical Engineers; by J. Goldsborough Bruff. [15] £171 $325

THE WEST INDIES WITH THE GULF OF MEXICO AND CARIBBEAN SEA [c. 1910] 81x127cm. (32x50") U.S. Navy chart. Color. Large folds; chipping and soiling at edges. [26] £53 $100

TOPOGRAPHICAL MAP OF NORTH ISLAND [Washington] [1891] 61x41cm. (24x15½") By Miller & Briggs. Color. [15] £24 $45

U.S. COAST SURVEY

... LOS ANGELES BASE LINE AND ITS ... CONNECTION WITH THE MAIN TRIANGULATION [1889] 56x71cm. (22x28") By F. Westdahl. [15] £34 $65

BASE CHART OF THE UNITED STATES [1877] 58x71cm. (22½x28") Lines of Equal Magnetic Declination. By A. Lindenkohl. [15] £21 $40

CHART OF PORT ROYAL ENTRANCE, BEAUFORT BROAD AND CHECHESSEE RIVERS ... [1862] 84x56cm. (33x22") Minor repair. [15] £24 $45

CHINCOTEAGUE INLET AND SHOALS IN THE VICINITY, SEA COAST OF VIRGINIA [1852] 36x43cm. (14x17") By Lt. J. Almy. [15] £21 $40

CITY OF SAN FRANCISCO AND ITS VICINITY, CALIFORNIA [1859] 61x89cm. (23½x34½") North at right. Folded; sizable repair, lower left margin and neat line. [35] £87 $165

COAST CHART NO. 55 COAST OF SOUTH CAROLINA AND GEORGIA FROM HUNTING ISLAND TO OSSALAW ISLAND INCLUDING PORT ROYAL SOUND AND SAVANNAH RIVER [1873] 84x102cm. (33x40") Folding chart, with minor repair at intersections; very good. [13] £79 $150

DELAWARE AND CHESAPEAKE BAYS & SEA COAST FROM CAPE HENLOPEN TO CAPE CHARLES [1855] 79x64cm. (31x25") [15] £39 $75

ENTRANCE OF SAVANNAH RIVER GEORGIA [1851] 36x51cm. (14x19½") [15] £24 $45

ENTRANCE TO BRAZOS RIVER TEXAS [1858] 41x46cm. (15½x18") [15] £32 $60

HEMPSTEAD HARBOR LONG ISLAND [N.Y.] [1859] 46x38cm. (18x14½") By Blunt & Gerdes. Margin repair. [15] £26 $50

KENNEBEC AND SHEEPSCOT RIVERS MAINE [1862] 97x58cm. (38x23") [15] £39 $75

OREGON INLET, N. CAROLINA [1862] 41x46cm. (15½x17½") [15] £21 $40

PRELIMINARY CHART OF HUDSON RIVER ... FROM POUGHKEEPSIE TO GLASCO NEW YORK [1862] 102x33cm. (39½x12½") [15] £26 $50

PRELIMINARY CHART OF EASTPORT HARBOR, MAINE [1864] 52x43cm. (20½x17") Color. [15] £39 $75

PRELIMINARY CHART OF HATTERAS INLET NORTH CAROLINA [1862] 41x38cm. (16½x15") By T. Phelps. [15] £21 $40

PRELIMINARY CHART OF MONTEREY BAY CALIFORNIA [1857] 79x53cm. (31x20½") By R. D. Cutts. Minor fold repair. [15] £32 $60

PRELIMINARY CHART OF SAN LUIS PASS TEXAS [1853] 36x43cm. (14x17") [15] £26 $50

PRELIMINARY CHART OF ST. SIMONS SOUND AND BRUNSWICK HARBOR [1856] 46x61cm. (17½x24") By Lt. S. Trenchard. [15] £26 $50

PRELIMINARY CHART OF THE ST. JOHN'S RIVER FLORIDA FROM BROWN'S CREEK TO JACKSONVILLE [1856] 51x69cm. (19½x27") With Jacksonville street plan. By W. Schultz. [15] £39 $75

PRELIMINARY SKETCH OF GALVESTON BAY [1851] 48x41cm. (19x16") Folded as issued. One fold repaired. [3] £32 $60

PRELIMINARY SKETCH OF MOBILE BAY [1853] 41x30cm. (16x12") Folded as issued; a fold repaired. [3] £26 $50

PRELIMINARY SURVEY OF OCRACOKE INLET NORTH CAROLINA ... [1857] 45x37cm. (18x14½") [15] £21 $40

PRELIMINARY SURVEY OF POINT REYES & DRAKE'S BAY, CALIFORNIA [1855] 22x25cm. (8½x10") By Lt. Alden. [15] £26 $50

PROVINCETOWN HARBOR, MASSACHUSETTS [1857] 37x44cm. (14½x17") Pristine. [35] £32 $60

RECONNAISANCE OF NEW RIVER AND BAR NORTH CAROLINA [1852] 46x36cm. (17½x13½") By Lt. J. Maffitt. [15] £21 $40

RECONNOISSANCE OF THE WESTERN COAST OF THE UNITED STATES FROM MONTEREY TO THE COLUMBIA RIVER [1851] 51x46cm. (20x17½") Sheet 1 - Monterey to Cape Mendocino. [15] £32 $60

SAN DIEGO ENTRANCE AND APPROACHES [1851] 33x33cm. (13x13") [26] £37 $70

SAND ANTONIO CREEK, CALIFORNIA [1857] 36x48cm. (13½x19") With Oakland plan. Exc. [35] £34 $65

SKETCH MAP SHOWING DISTRIBUTION OF QUICKSILVER MINES IN CALIFORNIA [c. 1857] 25x18cm. (10x7") By G. Becker. Color. Small repair. [15] £18 $35

ST. CATHERINES SOUND GEORGIA [1869] 56x74cm. (22x29") Very good. [13] £45 $85

THE PACIFIC COAST FROM POINT PINOS TO BODEGA HEAD CALIFORNIA [1862] 99x71cm. (39x28") [15] £32 $60

U.S. EXPLORING EXPEDITION

MAP OF THE OREGON TERRITORY BY THE U.S. EX. EX., CHARLES WILKES ESQR. COMMANDER [1841] 58x86cm. (22½x34½") Repairs. [35] £131 $250

[same title] [1841] 56x89cm. (22x34½") Wheat, Trans-Mississippi West, 457. Partly remargined on left; rice paper backing; o/w good. [29] £447 $850

SAMOAN OR NAVIGATOR ISLANDS BY U.S. EX. EX. ... 1839 [1850] 20x30cm. (8x11½") By C. Wilkes. Phila: C. Sherman. [15] £34 $65

U.S. GEOLOGICAL SURVEY

ASPEN SPECIAL [1898] 46x38cm. (17½x15") From Geology of the Aspen Mining District. Lithographed color. [12] £66 $125

BATTLEMENT MESA FOREST RESERVE [Col.] [1898] 43x48cm. (17½x19") By G. B. Sudworth. Color. [15] £21 $40

LOCATION OF AREAS IRRIGATED ... [1889] 46x36cm. (18x13½") U.S. west of 97°. Col. [15] £18 $35

MAP SHOWING FOREST RESERVES & NATIONAL PARKS IN WESTERN UNITED STATES [1899] 46x38cm. (18x14½") U.S. west of 97 deg. Color. [15] £21 $40

WEST POINT NEW YORK [1883] 66x53cm. (26½x21") By H.D. Evans. [15] £32 $60

YELLOWSTONE NATIONAL PARK & FOREST RESERVE [c.1894] 51x51cm. (20x19½") Col. [15] £45 $85

YOSEMITE NATIONAL PARK CALIFORNIA [1910] 71x74cm. (27½x28½") By R. Marshall & A. Sylvester. Color. [15] £34 $65

U.S. PACIFIC R.R. SURVEY

EXPLORATIONS AND SURVEYS FOR A RAIL ROAD ROUTE ... NEAR THE 35TH PARALLEL FROM THE RIO GRANDE TO THE PACIFIC OCEAN ... [1855] 55x128cm. (22x50") By A.W. Whipple. Backed. [15] £123 $235

EXPLORATIONS AND SURVEYS FOR A RAIL ROAD ROUTE ... NEAR THE 47TH PARALLEL MILK R. TO THE CROSSING OF THE COLUMBIA R. [1855] 60x154cm. (23½x60½") By I. Stevens. Backed and clean. [15] £118 $225

FROM THE PIMA VILLAGES TO FORT FILLMORE ... 1854 AND 55 [1861] 76x102cm. (30x40") By Lieut. John G. Parke. Folded as issued; minor foxing; some small repairs. [26] £32 $60

GENERAL MAP OF THE EXPLORATIONS AND SURVEYS IN CALIFORNIA ... 1853 [1861] 64x51cm. (25x20") By Lieut. R.S. Williamson. Folded as issued; minor foxing; small repairs. [26] £32 $60

GEOLOGICAL MAP OF A PART OF THE STATE OF CALIFORNIA EXPLORED IN 1853 BY LIEUT R.S. WILLIAMSON U.S. TOP ENGR ... [1856] 56x41cm. (22x16") Color keyed. Good. [36] £53 $100

GEOLOGICAL MAP OF THE ROUTE EXPLORED BY CAPT. JN. POPE ... NEAR THE 32ND PARALLEL ... [1854] 25x61cm. (10x24") Red River to Rio Grande. Geological features colored. [3] £42 $80

MAP 2 FROM GREAT SALT LAKE TO THE HUMBOLDT MTS. ... [1855] 53x48cm. (21x18½") By Capt. E. Beckwith. Color. [15] £76 $145

MAP AND PROFILE OF THE TEJON PASS ... 1853 [1861] 64x102cm. (25x40") By Lieut. R. S. Williamson. Folded as issued; minor foxing; some small repairs. [26] £16 $30

MAP OF THE PASSES IN THE SIERRA NEVADA FROM WALKERS PASS TO THE COAST RANGE ... 1853 [1861] 51x64cm. (20x25") By Lieut. R. S. Williamson. Folded as issued; minor foxing; some small repairs. [26] £16 $30

PRELIMINARY SKETCH OF THE NORTHERN PACIFIC RAIL ROAD EXPLORATION AND SURVEY ... [1855] 56x76cm. (22x30") Ft. Union to Rocky Mts. First edition. Folds as issued; minor separation at corners. [3] £47 $90

SAN FRANCISCO BAY TO THE NORTHERN BOUNDARY OF CALIFORNIA ... 1853 [1861] 81x64cm. (32x25") By Lieut. R.S. Williamson. Folded as issued; minor foxing; small repairs. [26] £42 $80

SAN FRANCISCO BAY TO THE PLAINS OF LOS ANGELES ... 1854 AND 55 [1861] 76x102cm. (30x40") By Lieut. John G. Parke. Folded as issued; minor foxing; small repairs. [26] £37 $70

U.S. STATE SURVEYS

A DIAGRAM OF A PORTION OF OREGON TERRITORY [1851] 91x33cm. (36x13") Olympia to California line. Folded as issued. [3] £63 $120

A DIAGRAM OF OREGON [1861] 46x56cm. (18x22") Recent, soft green color. [26] £39 $75

A DIAGRAM OF THE PUBLIC SURVEYS IN OREGON [1862] 46x58cm. (18x23") Folded as issued. [3] £63 $120

A PLAT EXHIBITING THE STATE OF THE SURVEYS IN THE STATE OF FLORIDA WITH REFERENCES [1853] 56x64cm. (22x25") [6] £76 $145

ALASKA [1906] 71x97cm. (28x38") Full bright color. Folded as issued. [3] £63 $120

ARKANSAS [1856] 41x43cm. (15½x17") By H. Rector. With "Old Cherokee Line". [15] £26 $50

ARKANSAS. MAP OF THE ARKANSAS SURVEYING DISTRICT, SHEWING THE EXTENT OF PUBLIC SURVEYS [1841] 38x41cm. (14½x16") Color. [15] £32 $60

DIAGRAM OF THE PUBLIC SURVEYS IN IOWA [1866] 43x51cm. (17x20") Outline color. Light toning at folds, with archival tape reinforcement; o/w excellent. [12] £47 $90

DIAGRAM OF THE STATE OF ILLINOIS [1837] 61x36cm. (24x14") GLO. Color. [15] £50 $95

DIAGRAM OF THE SURVEYING DISTRICT SOUTH OF TENNESSEE. SURVEYOR'S OFFICE, JACKSON, MISS. 1843 [c.1843] 64x41cm. (25x16") Chocktaw boundaries. By A. Downing. [15] £58 $110

DIAGRAM OF THE SURVEYING DISTRICT SOUTH OF TENNESSEE. SURVEYOR'S OFFICE, JACKSON, MISS. [c.1847] 43x28cm. (17x11") Chocktaw & Chickasaw Cession bounds. By C. Bradford. [15] £34 $65

MAP OF LOUISIANA REPRESENTING THE SEVERAL LAND DISTRICTS ... DONALDSON, LA. OCT. 25th, 1851 [c. 1851] 56x43cm. (21½x17") [15] £26 $50

MAP OF PUBLIC SURVEYS IN CALIFORNIA ... 1860 [1861] 91x76cm. (36x30") 340 grants & 3 reservations listed. Thin folded paper; browning at folds. [6] £53 $100

[same title, date, dimensions] 411 grants & 3 reservations listed. Thin folded paper. [6] £53 $100

[same title] [1862] 102x76cm. (40x30") 430 Spanish land grants. Minimal flaws at folds [26] £63 $120

MAP OF PUBLIC SURVEYS IN CALIFORNIA & NEVADA ... [1866] 91x79cm. (36x30½") Little of Nevada. Outline color. Some light fold discoloration; repaired fold intersection pinholes; narrow left margin; o/w fine. [12] £197 $375

MAP OF PUBLIC SURVEYS IN NEVADA TERRITORY [1862] 76x51cm. (30x20") By E. Beale. Color. [15] £76 $145

MAP OF THAT PART OF THE WASHINGTON TERRITORY LYING WEST OF THE ROCKY MOUNTAINS ... [1858] 38x25cm. (15x9½") Folds. [3] £32 $60

MAP OF THE PUBLIC LANDS AND TERRITORIES [1864] 71x114cm. (28x45") By J. Hawes; D. McClelland, sc. Backed. [15] £192 $365

MAP OF THE PUBLIC SURVEY IN THE TERRITORY OF WASHINGTON FOR THE REPORT OF THE SURV: GENL: [1862] 41x91cm. (16x36") Folded as issued. [3] £63 $120

MAP OF THE STATE OF FLORIDA SHOWING THE PROGRESS OF THE SURVEYS [1866] 61x64cm. (23½x24½") Outline color. Part of left margin extended; else excellent. [12] £145 $275

MAP OF THE SURVEYED PART OF WISCONSIN TERRITORY COMPILED FROM PUBLIC SURVEYS [1835] 58x43cm. (22½x17") GLO. Inset of private claims at Green Bay. Color. [15] £50 $95

MAP OF THE TERRITORY OF HAWAII [1904] 56x79cm. (22x31") Full col. Folded as issued. [3] £39 $75

MAP SHOWING THE EXTENT OF SURVEYS IN THE TERRITORY OF UTAH [1856] 84x41cm. (32½x15½") Salt Lake region. Hannibal Hamlin's ex-lib stamp; left margin extended; excel. [12] £92 $175

OREGON [1866] 43x56cm. (17x22") Outline color. Age toning; tear past bottom neat line; 1" of lower margin missing to neat line. [6] £155 $295

PLAT OF THE ANCIENT POSSESSIONS OF UPPER PRAIRIE CONFIRMED BY THE GOVERNORS [1835] 30x23cm. (11½x9") General Land Office. Shows Vincennes, Indiana area. [15] £39 $75

SKETCH OF PUBLIC SURVEYS IN NEW MEXICO & ARIZONA ... [1866] 53x71cm. (20½x28") Issued by GLO. Outline color. Trivial fold intersections splits mended. [12] £236 $450

SKETCH OF PUBLIC SURVEYS IN THE TERRITORY OF MINNESOTA [1856] 56x53cm. (22x21") Shows western boundary of Feb. 1857. Minor repair. [15] £24 $45

SKETCH OF THE PUBLIC SURVEYS IN MICHIGAN [1847] 56x56cm. (21½x22") [15] £32 $60

SKETCH OF THE PUBLIC SURVEYS IN NEW MEXICO 1860 [1861] 58x81cm. (23x32") Thin folded paper; browning & minor tears at folds. [6] £92 $175

STATE OF ALABAMA [1866] 48x30cm. (18½x11½") Outline color. Pale browning at some folds; o/w fine. [12] £79 $150

STATE OF CALIFORNIA [1879] 97x84cm. (38½x33") By. C. Roeser. Two sheets. Color. [15] £123 $235

STATE OF IDAHO [1909] 107x69cm. (42x27") Full color. Folded as issued. [3] £47 $90

STATE OF INDIANA [1878] 81x56cm. (32x22") By Roeser; Julius Bien & Co. Original linen backing. Marginal stains; o/w very good. [14] £74 $140

STATE OF OREGON [1876] 61x81cm. (24x32") Folded as issued. [26] £63 $120

[same title] [1884] 61x71cm. (24x28") Substantial color. Folded as issued. Very good. [3] £74 $140

TERRITORY OF ARIZONA [1896] 52x43cm. (20½x17") Lithographed color. Immaculate. [12] £47 $90

[same title] [1907] 52x43cm. (20½x17") Lithographed color. Immaculate. [12] £45 $85

TERRITORY OF NEW MEXICO [1903] 71x51cm. (28x20") By Frank Bond. Full color. [3] £39 $75

WASHINGTON TERRITORY [1884] 56x71cm. (22x28") Color. Folds as issued. [26] £66 $125

[same title, date] 58x76cm. (23x30") Substantial color. Folds. [3] £74 $140

U.S. WAR DEPARTMENT

[CRAWFORD COUNTY, ARKANSAS] [1838] 15x28cm. (6x10½") Ft. Smith to Van Buren. [15] £24 $45

A SKETCH OF THE HARBOUR OF BRUNSWICK [1837] 28x33cm. (11x13") By Lt. J. Mansfield, U.S.T.E., with 5 page report. [15] £45 $85

ALBEMARLE AND CHESAPEAKE AND DISMAL SWAMP CANALS WITH THEIR CONNECTING WATERS [1879] 36x25cm. (14x9½") By F. W. Frost, U.S.A.E. [15] £16 $30

BAR AT THE NORTHWEST ENTRANCE TO KEY WEST HARBOR, FLA. ... [1899] 48x66cm. (19x26") By F. W. Bruce, U.S.A.E. [15] £18 $35

BISCAYNE BAY, FLORIDA [1903] 20x30cm. (8x12") Proposed canal from Miami to Atlantic. By Capt. F. Shunk, U.S.A.E. [15] £18 $35

BRAZOS SANTIAGO TEXAS ... MAJ. MANSFIELD [1882] 20x38cm. (8x15") U.S.A.E. By H.C. Ripley. [15] £18 $35

CHART OF DETROIT RIVER FROM LAKE ERIE TO LAKE ST. CLAIR, SURVEYED IN 1840, '41, & '42 ... [1844] 107x76cm. (42x30") By Lt. Macomb & Lt. Warner. Minor transference; o/w excel. [26] £74 $140

CHART OF ROMERLY MARCHES BETWEEN WASSAW AND OSSABAW SOUNDS, GA. ... [1880] 30x46cm. (12x18") By S. L. Fremont, U.S.A.E. [15] £18 $35

CHART OF THAT PORTION OF LAKE ERIE IN THE VICINITY OF BUFFALO & BLACK ROCK ... EXHIBITING A PLAN FOR AN EXTENSIVE OUTER HARBOR ... [1835] 61x94cm. (24½x37") By T.S. Brown, U.S.T.E. With 5 page report. [15] £66 $125

CHART OF THE SAVANNAH RIVER, GA. FROM SAVANNAH CITY TO TYBEE ROADS ... [1880] 36x66cm. (14x25½") By Col. Q. Gillmore, U.S.A.E. [15] £21 $40

CHART SHOWING LOCATION OF PROPOSED SHIP CANAL ACROSS CHARLESTON NECK [1880] 30x25cm. (12x10") By J. C. Post, U.S.A.E. [15] £16 $30

CLIFTON [Mich.] [1840] 20x20cm. (7½x8") By Lt. T. Webster, U.S.T.E. [15] £26 $50

CORONADO HEIGHTS SAND DIEGO COUNTY, CALIFORNIA [1891] 33x51cm. (13½x20") Color. [15] £50 $95

DELTA OF THE MISSISSIPPI ... [1839] 107x76cm. (42x30") By Lt. T. Lee, U.S.T.E. With 4 page report. [15] £76 $145

ENTRANCE TO BRAZOS RIVER TEXAS ... MAJ. S. MANSFEILD [1882] 43x41cm. (16½x16") By J. M. Picton. [15] £21 $40

FROM A MAP OF THE ENTIRE TERRITORIES OF WISKONSAN & IOWA ... LEGISLATIVE ASSEMBLY OF WISKONSAN 1838 [1840] 20x30cm. (8x11½") By U.S.T.E. [15] £32 $60

GALVESTON HARBOR TEXAS, CAPT. C. RICHE IN CHARGE [1899] 41x51cm. (16x19½") U.S.A.E. By E. Hartrick. [15] £21 $40

GEOLOGICAL MAP OF ... CALIFORNIA EXPLORED IN 1855 BY LIEUT. R. S. WILLIAMSON [1857] 56x41cm. (22½x16½") By W. Blake, U.S.T.E. Color key to strata. [15] £66 $125

HYDROGRAPHY IN FRONT OF EUREKA, CAL. SHOWING CONDITION OF CHANNEL ... [1905] 28x74cm. (11x28½") By H. L. Demeritt, U.S.A.E. [15] £18 $35

LAKE DRUMMOND, VA. SURVEYED ... 1879 [1896] 43x30cm. (16½x12") By Capt. C. Phillips, U.S.A.E. [15] £16 $30

LAKE SUPERIOR - MISSISSIPPI RIVER SURVEY. MAP SHOWING PROPOSED CANAL VIA ST. LOUIS RIVER [1896] 43x51cm. (16½x20") By. J. Krey, U.S.A.E. [15] £18 $35

MAP ILLUSTRATING THE SIEGE OF ATLANTA, GA. BY THE U.S. FORCES UNDER COMMAND OF MAJ. GENERAL SHERMAN FROM PASSAGE OF PEACH TREE CREEK, JULY 19, 1864 TO ... SOUTH OF ATLANTA, AUG. 26, 1864 [1866] 30x53cm. (12½x21") Earliest printed street plan of Atlanta. Color. [15] £139 $265

MAP NO. 3 SHOWING CONTINUATION OF DETAILS OF FORT SMITH & SANTA FE ROUTE FROM 100 1/2 DEG. W. TO TUCUMEARI CREEK [1849] 33x51cm. (12½x20") U.S.T.E. By J. Simpson. [15] £50 $95

MAP OF A PORTION OF ALABAMA SHOWING PROJECTED SYSTEM OF IMPROVEMENT OF MOBILE, TOMBIGBEE, WARRIOR & BLACK WARRIOR RIVERS [1902] 51x36cm. (20x14") To Birmingham; 20 locks. By Capt. S. Cosby, U.S.A.E. [15] £21 $40

MAP OF DUNKIRK HARBOR SHOWING WORKS ERECTED BY THE UNITED STATES [N.Y.] [1838] 33x61cm. (13x24") By I. H. Simpson, U.S.T.E. [15] £47 $90

MAP OF HILLSBORO BAY, FLA. [1898] 38x28cm. (15x10½") By Col. W. Benyaurd, U.S.A.E. [15] £18 $35

MAP OF PART OF THE SOUTH SHORE OF LAKE ERIE IN THE VICINITY OF THE TWENTY MILE CREEK, PENN. [1830] 30x38cm. (12x15") U.S.T.E., by T. Foster & J. Maurice. [15] £34 $65

MAP OF THE DEFENCES OF THE CITY OF MOBILE [1866] 28x38cm. (11x15") Lightly browned fold repaired. [12] £32 $60

MAP OF THE NEW MADRID & ST. FRANCIS RIVER SWAMP IN THE STATES MISSOURI & ARKANSAS [1844] 36x25cm. (13½x9½") By Capt. W.B. Guion, U.S.T.E. With 6 page report. Color. [15] £50 $95

MAP OF THE SEAT OF WAR IN FLORIDA, COMPILED BY ORDER OF BRIG. GEN. Z. TAYLOR ... BY CAPT. JOHN MACKAY AND LIEUT. J. E. BLAKE, ... [1839] 107x74cm. (42x29") Folded as issued. Very good. [26] £263 $500

MAP OF THE UNITED STATES AND THEIR TERRITORIES, BETWEEN THE MISSISSIPPI AND THE PACIFIC OCEAN AND PART OF MEXICO. COMPILED UNDER ORDER OF W. H. EMORY ... 1857-8 [1858] 52x58cm. (20½x23") U.S.T.E. By T. Jekyll. [15] £123 $235

MAP OF THE VALLEY OF THE ALLEGHANY RIVER [1838] 36x28cm. (14x11") By J. M. Berrien, U.S.T.E. [15] £45 $85

MAP OF THE VICINITY OF BUFFALO [1836] 28x41cm. (10½x16") By. W.G. Williams. [15] £42 $80

MAP OF THE YOSEMITE NATIONAL PARK ... FOR THE USE OF U.S. TROOPS [1896] 51x51cm. (20x20") By N.F. McClure, U.S.A.E. Special purpose variants were issued. [3] £32 $60

[same title, date] 41x51cm. (16½x20") By N.F. McClure. [15] £32 $60

MAP SHOWING LOCATION OF THE DISMAL SWAMP CANAL VIRGINIA & N. CAROLINA [1896] 33x94cm. (12½x36½") Capt. T.L. Casey, U.S.A.E. [15] £18 $35

MAP SHOWING ROUTE OF THE MARCHES OF THE ARMY OF GNL. W. T. SHERMAN FROM ATLANTA, GA. TO GOLDSBORO, N.C. [1866] 28x41cm. (11x16") Details Sherman's sweep. Color. [15] £71 $135

MAP SHOWING THE LINES OF COMMUNICATION BETWEEN SOUTHERN COLORADO AND NORTHERN NEW MEXICO COMPILED BY 1ST LIEUT. E.H. RUFFNER DRAWN BY ADO HUNNIUS, JAN. 1ST 1876 [1876] 37x47cm. (14½x18½") With 27 text pages. [12] £118 $225

MAP SHOWING THE MOUTH OF THE MIAMI RIVER BISCAYNE BAY, FLORIDA [1897] 48x33cm. (19x13") By. O. N. Bie, U.S.A.E. [15] £26 $50

MICHIGAN CITY [1839] 25x23cm. (9½x9") By Capt. Cram, U.S.T.E. Fine. [12] £24 $45

MOUTH OF DOUBLE BAYOU FROM SURVEY [1898] 33x28cm. (12½x11"). [15] £18 $35

NO. 1. MAP OF THE DES MOINES RAPIDS. OF THE MISSISSIPPI RIVER. ... [1837] 56x130cm. (22x51") Surveyed by Lt. Robert E. Lee. Thin folded paper; some foxing and tears at folds. [6] £155 $295

NO. 2. MAP OF THE ROCK ISLAND RAPIDS. OF THE MISSISSIPPI. [1837] 56x163cm. (22x64") Surveyed by Lt. Robert E. Lee. Thin folded paper; some foxing and tears at folds. [6] £155 $295

NORTHERN EXTREMITY OF LAKE WINNEBAGO [Mich.] [1840] 13x20cm. (4½x8") By Lt. T. Webster, U.S.T.E. [15] £26 $50

NORTHERN & NORTH-WESTERN LAKES SHOWING THE DIFFERENT LOCALITIES OF THE PUBLIC WORKS [1866] 23x48cm. (9x19½") With all Great Lakes. Molitor, lith. [15] £21 $40

OUTLINE MAP SHOWING A NEW ROUTE FROM TEXAS TO FT. YUMA, FOR CATTLE DROVES & TRAINS TO CALIFORNIA BY CAPT. OVERMAN [1869] 104x38cm. (40½x15") U.S.A.E. By C.W. Pressler. [15] £47 $90

OUTLINE MAP ... SOUTHERN CALIFORNIA & SOUTH-WESTERN NEVADA SHOWING THE RELATIVE AREAS OF DRAINAGE [1876] 41x48cm. (15½x19½") By Lt. G. Wheeler, U.S.A.E. San Diego to Monterey. Color. [15] £45 $85

PLAN AND SECTION OF THE NORTH CUT AT MILWAUKEE [1854] 43x33cm. (17x12½") By J. Kearney. [15] £26 $50

PLAN OF CHICAGO HARBOR ... [1839] 28x36cm. (11x14") By Capt. Cram, U.S.T.E. Trace of foxing; else fine. [12] £92 $175

PORTIONS OF GEORGIA AND SOUTH CAROLINA [c. 1864] 76x76cm. (30x30") Campaign map: Milledgeville to Savannah and north. Dissected, linen backed. [3] £210 $400

PRESIDIO, SAN FRANCISCO [1870] 20x18cm. (8x6½") 1" = 350 feet. With 14 text pages (some photocopied). [12] £45 $85

REBEL LINE OF WORKS AT BLAKELY CAPTURED BY THE ARMY OF WEST MISS. APL. 9, 1865 [1866] 25x38cm. (10x15") Color. [15] £39 $75

SAN DIEGO CAL. AND VICINITY SHOWING THE PLATS OF LAND OFFERED FOR THE SITE OF A MILITARY POST ... 1891 [c. 1891] 48x36cm. (18½x13½") Color. [15] £34 $65

SEIGE OPERATIONS AT SPANISH FORT MOBILE BAY BY U.S. FORCES UNDER MAJ. GENERAL CANBY. CAPTURED BY ARMY OF WEST MISS. ... APRIL 8 & 9 [1865] 33x43cm. (12½x16½") By Maj. H. McAlester. [15] £45 $85

SKETCH OF INDIAN RIVER & SOUTHERN PORTION OF MOSQUITO LAGOON, FLORIDA [1884] 41x25cm. (15½x9½") By Col. Q. Gillmore, U.S.A.E. [15] £18 $35

SKETCH OF ROANOKE ISLAND, N.C. [1863] 18x18cm. (7½x6½") By Gen. J. Foster. [15] £18 $35

SKETCH OF THE BATTLE GROUND AT RESACA DE LA PALMA, TEXAS MAY 8TH 1846 [1846] 28x20cm. (10½x8") From Gen. Taylor's report. Color. [15] £58 $110

SKETCH OF THE COUNTRY EMBRACING SEVERAL ROUTES FROM PORTSMOUTH OHIO, TO LINVILLE, N.C. AND EXHIBITING THE ... CONTEMPLATED ROAD ... BETWEEN THE ATLANTIC OCEAN AND THE NORTHERN LAKES [1836] 104x30cm. (41x12½") By Col. S.H. Long, U.S.T.E. [15] £76 $145

SKETCH OF THE ENTRANCE OF SODUS BAY CAYUGA COUNTY [N.Y.] [1854] 13x23cm. (5x9") By W. Turnbull, U.S.T.E. [15] £13 $25

SKETCH OF THE HARBOR OF BLACK RIVER [N.Y.] [1854] 20x41cm. (8½x15½") By H. Stansbury, U.S.T.E. [15] £13 $25

SKETCH OF THE MOUTH OF ELK CREEK [Penn.] [1838] 56x38cm. (22x15") U.S.T.E., by J. Kearney. With 3 page report. [15] £34 $65

SKETCH OF THE SABINE RIVER, LAKE AND PASS FROM CAMP SABINE TO THE GULF, ... [1838] 89x23cm. (34½x8½") By J.H. Eaton, U.S.T.E. With report. [15] £71 $135

SKETCH SHOWING ... SECTION FOR CURRENT OBSERVATIONS AT FORT YUMA CALIFORNIA [1876] 18x25cm. (6½x10") By Lt. Bergland, U.S.A.E. [15] £21 $40

SURVEY FOR THE OPENING OF STEAMBOAT COMMUNICATION FROM LAKE WINDER TO TOHOPOKELIGA LAKE [1881] 33x53cm. (13x21") By Col. Q. Gillmore, U.S.A.E. [15] £18 $35

SURVEY OF THE HARBOR OF WHITEHALL [N.Y.] [1837] 28x89cm. (10½x35") By C.M. Watson, U.S.T.E. With 3 page report. [15] £50 $95

SURVEY OF THE MOUTH OF GALIEN RIVER MICHIGAN [1835] 51x76cm. (20x29½") By Lt. J. Berrien, U.S.T.E. New Buffalo street plan. With 4 page report. [15] £84 $160

SURVEY OF THE NEENAH OR FOX RIVER, GRAND CHUTE [1840] 13x20cm. (4½x8") By Capt. T. Cram, U.S.T.E. Show Appleton City, Wis. [15] £32 $60

SURVEY OF THE WATER ROUTES FROM NORFOLK HARBOR TO ... CAPE FEAR RIVER, N.C. [1879] 56x38cm. (22x15") By F.W. Frost, U.S.A.E. [15] £21 $40

TOPOGRAPHICAL SKETCH SHOWING THE ... PRACTICABILITY OF A DIVISION OF THE COLORADO RIVER FOR ...IRRIGATION [1875] 41x48cm. (16x18½") By Lt. G. Wheeler, U.S.A.E. Colorado River to L.A. [15] £50 $95

TURTLE BAYOU TEXAS SHOWING CONNECTION TO TRINITY BAY ... [1899] 89x53cm. (35x20½") U.S.A.E. By F. Oppikofer. [15] £24 $45

UPPER GEYSER BASIN - DRAWN UNDER DIRECTION OF CAPT. W. LUDLOW [c. 1872] 23x38cm. (9x15") U.S.A.E. By C. Becker. [15] £26 $50

ULLOA

PLAN DE LA BAYE ET VILLE DE PORTOBELO EN 1736 [c.1749] 15x23cm. (5½x9") Col. [15] £37 $70

UNIVERSAL MAGAZINE

A NEW AND ACCURATE MAP OF THE PRESENT SEAT OF WAR IN NORTH AMERICA, COMPREHENDING NEW JERSEY, PHILADELPHIA, PENSYLVANIA, NEW-YORK &C. [1777] 37x29cm. (14½x11½") Jolly UNIV-178. Color. Minor repair. [15] £139 $265

A NEW AND ACCURATE MAP OF THE PROVINCE OF GEORGIA IN NORTH AMERICA [1779] 33x28cm. (12½x11") Jolly UNIV-179. Two short repairs at old folds; good. [28] £255 $485

A NEW AND ACCURATE MAP OF THE PROVINCE OF PENNSYLVANIA IN NORTH AMERICA, FROM THE BEST AUTHORITIES. [1780] 27x33cm. (11x13") Jolly UNIV-185. [6] £155 $295

A NEW MAP OF THE PROVINCE OF MARYLAND IN NORTH AMERICA. [1780] 28x33cm. (11x13") Jolly UNIV-184. With two text pages. A little offsetting; else fine. [12] £184 $350

[same title, date, dimensions] Color. [15] £171 $325

AN ACCURATE MAP OF NEW HAMPSHIRE IN NEW ENGLAND, FROM A LATE SURVEY. [1781] 32x28cm. (12½x11") Jolly UNIV-191. Color. Margin repair. [15] £139 $265

AN ACCURATE MAP OF NEW YORK IN NORTH AMERICA, FROM A LATE SURVEY. [1780] 34x27cm. (13x10½") Jolly UNIV-187. Color. [15] £118 $225

VALENTYN

[TITLE PAGE] BESCHRYVING VAN OUD EN NIEUUW OOST-INDIEN [1724] 18x28cm. (7x11") [5] £120 $228

KAART DER ZUYD-WESTER EYLANDEN VAN BANDA. ... [1724] 34x47cm. (13½x18½") Close top margin; else excellent. [38] £131 $250

KAART VAN HET EYLAND AMBOINA [1724, c. 1755] 30x41cm. (12½x16") Published by Van Keulen. [11] £150 $285

VALK

AMERICA AUREA PARS ALTERA MUNDI AUCTORIBUS [c. 1702] 48x60cm. (19x23½") Original color. Stain lower center crease; o/w good. [1] £841 $1600

ASIA QUA NULLA BEATIOR ORA; TRACTUS IN EOOS VERGENS MUNDIQUE TEPOREM [c.1690] 48x58cm. (19x23") Full original color. Some slight soiling. [1] £263 $500

IMPERIUM TURCICUM IN EUROPA, ASIA ET AFRICA ... [1690] 48x58cm. (19x23½") Full original color. Excellent. [2] £236 $450

MAPPE-MONDE GEO-HYDROGRAPHIQUE OU DESCRIPTION GENERALE DU GLOBE TERRESTRE ET AQUATIQUE EN DEUX-PLANS-HEMISPHERES ... [c. 1700] 48x58cm. (19x23") Hemispheres, with two polar hemispheres & lush surrounds. Full orig col. Excel. [1] £2365 $4500

SCANDINAVIA, VEL REGNA SEPTENTRIONALIS, SVECIA, DANIA, ET NORVEGIA, DIVISA IN EPISCOPATUS BERGARUM STAVANGRIAE, ET ANSOLAE, DUCATUS FINLANDIAE, LIVONIAE ... [c. 1690] 58x48cm. (23x19½") Original color. Small stain at top margin; o/w very good. [1] £210 $400

VALK & SCHENK

MONA INSULA VULGA ANGLESEY. MONA INSULA: VULGO THE ISLE OF MAN. VECTIS INSULA ANGLICE THE ISLE OF WIGHT [c. 1700] 43x53cm. (17½x21½") Original color. Excellent. [21] £263 $500

NOVA ET ACCURATA JAPONIAE TERRAE ESONIS AC INSULARUM ADJACENTIUM ... [c. 1700] 46x55cm. (18x21½") Reissue of Jansson map. Original color. Excellent. [5] £1750 $3330

VAN DEN KEERE

AMERICA [1646] 10x13cm. (3½x5") London: Wm. Humble. From "miniature Speed atlas". Wash color. Fine. [29] £202 $385

GREECE [1646] 8x13cm. (3½x5") From "miniature Speed atlas". Outline color. [36] £39 $75

IAPONIA [1628] 13x19cm. (5x7½") After Hondius 1606 map. Color. [5] £275 $523

LEO BELGICUS / ARRIFICIOSA & GEOGRAPHICA TABULA SUB LEONIS FIGURA A 17 INFERIORIS GERMANIAE PROVINCIAS ... [1617] 37x45cm. (14½x18") Lowlands as Lion. Original color. Excellent. [22] £8408 $16000

ORBIS TERRARUM TYPUS DE INTEGRO MULTIS IN LOCES EMENDATUS ... [1607] 40x57cm. (15½x22½") After Plancius. Shirley 244. Full original color. Reinforced tear into lower right corner; close margins with some loss at left reinstated. [5] £4850 $9230

VAN DER AA

BAY ET CHATEAU DE PORTO BELLO [c.1700] 23x30cm. (8½x12½") Leyden: Mortier. Col. [15] £74 $140

CANADA OU NOUVELLE FRANCE [and] LA FLORIDE [1708+] 53x38cm. (20½x15") Two maps, each 9 x 12", on one sheet. Minor wear at edges. [31] £946 $1800

CARTE NOUVELLE ET EXACTE DE LA GAULE CISALPINE ET SUR TOUT DE LA LIGURIE DE L'INSUBRIE ... [c. 1729] 33x41cm. (13½x16") Outline & wash color. [36] £105 $200

CARTE PARTICULIERE A TOUTE NOUVELLE DE MILIANOIS, AVEC TOUS SES CONFINS ... [c.1729] 36x43cm. (13½x17") Excellent. [36] £105 $200

CERCLE DE LA HAUTE SAXE [1729] 23x30cm. (9x12") Color. [36] £66 $125

D. BLEFKENIUS SCHEEPS-TOGT NA YSLAND EN GROENLAND ... [1706] 15x23cm. (6x9") Blefkenius' 1563 voyage. [32] £450 $856

L'AMERIQUE SELON LES NOUVELLES OBSERVATIONS DE MESSRS, DE L'ACADEMIE DES SCIENCE, ETC. ... [1700] 46x66cm. (18½x26") Excellent. [2] £2365 $4500

L'EUROPE SELON LES NOUVELLES OBSERVATIONS ... [1713] 48x66cm. (18½x26") Dark impression. [32] £500 $952

LA CHINE [1729] 23x30cm. (9x12") Full color. [36] £84 $160

LA GRANDE TARTARIE SUIVANT LES NOUVELLES OBSERVATIONS [1729] 23x30cm. (9x12") [15] £66 $125

LA RADE DE GAMMERON [1727] 20x15cm. (7½x6½") Strait of Ormuz. Outline & wash col. [35] £26 $50

LE DETROIT DE MALACCA, DRESSEE SUR LES MEMOIRES DES PLUS SAVANS VOYAGEURS MODERNS [1714] 26x16cm. (10x6½") Excellent. [38] £223 $425

MEXIQUE OU NOUVELLE ESPAGNE SUIVANT LES NOUVELLES OBSERVATIONS DE MESSRS. DE L'ACADEMIE ROYALE DES SCIENCES... [1729] 22x29cm. (9x11") Full color. Somewhat yellowed. [35] £145 $275

NICARAGUA EN DE KUSTEN DER ZUYD-ZEE BOORDWAARD VON PANAMA ... [1707] 15x23cm. (6x9") Color. [15] £129 $245

NOUVELLE CARTE DE L'AMERIQUE [1729] 43x53cm. (17x21") Good. [28] £867 $1650

PLANISPHERE TERRESTRE, SUIVANT LES NOUVELLES OBSERVATIONS DES ASTRONOMES. DRESSEE PRESENTE AU ROY TRES CHRETIEN PAR MR. CASSINI ... [c. 1713] 54x65cm. (21½x25½") North polar projection. Color. Some reinforcement at lower centerfold split and margins; good. [5] £2000 $3806

QUEBEC, VILLE D L'AMERIQUE SEPTENTRIONALE DANS LA NOUVELLE FRANCE [c. 1700] 20x28cm. (8x11") Color. [15] £236 $450

ROYAUMES DE CONGO ET ANGOLA [1727] 28x36cm. (11½x13½") Full color. [36] £92 $175

ST. FRANCISCO DE CAMPECHE PETITE VILLE DE L'AUDIENCE DE MEXIQUE [1729] 30x36cm. (11½x14") View. [15] £150 $285

WILLIAM ADAMS REYSTOGT NA OOST INDIEN ... [1707] 15x23cm. (6x9") Adams was first Englishman in Japan. Pristine. [5] £885 $1684

YUCATAN PARTIE DE LA NOUVELLE ESPAGNE ET GUATIMALA [1729] 28x36cm. (11x14") [35] £158 $300

VAN DER SCHLEY

CARTE DE LA COSTE ORIENTALE D'AFRIQUE DEPUIS LE CAP DE BONNE ESPERANCE JUSQU'AU CAP DEL GADA [c. 1747] 25x23cm. (10x9") Color. [15] £50 $95

VAN GEELKERKEN

NOVA TOTIUS ORBIS TERRARUM DESCRIPTIO [1619] 32x45cm. (12½x17½") Excel. [37] £1682 $3200

VAN KEULEN

CAART VAN HET EYLAND NOESSA-LAOET [and] CAART VAN HET EYLAND OMA [c. 1755] 46x28cm. (17½x11") After Valentyn. Two plans on one sheet. Clean; good. [11] £120 $228

CAART VAN HET EYLANDT MANIPA ... [and] CAART VAN HET EYLAND HONIMOA [c. 1755] 46x28cm. (18x11") After Valentyn. Two plans on a sheet. Clean; good. [11] £120 $228

DE LANDVOOGDY DER MOLUCCOS, MET DE AANGRENZENDE EYLANDEN [1724, c. 1755] 46x58cm. (18½x23") After Valentyn. Clean, good. [11] £425 $809

DE RIVIER TYNE OF NEW CASTLE ... [(1734)] 53x58cm. (20½x23") Sunderland to Blyth. [11] £260 $495

DE TALAUTSE EYLANDEN [c. 1755] 46x28cm. (18x11") After Valentyn. [11] £100 $190

HET EYLAND SANGIR [c. 1755] 46x28cm. (18x11½") After Valentyn, 1724. [11] £120 $228

KAART DER ZUYD_WESTER EYLANDEN VAN BANDA [c. 1755] 36x48cm. (13½x18½") After Valentyn, 1724. Fine. [11] £280 $533

NIEUWE GENERALE PASKAART VAN DE BOCHT VAN VRANKRYK BISCAIA EN GALLISSIA TUSSEN I. DE OUESSANT EN C. DE FINISTERRE [1734 (c. 1750)] 61x99cm. (23½x39½") New edition from Zee-Fakkel Part II. Slight damp-marking in lower margin. [11] £180 $343

NIEUWE PASCAART VOOR EEN ... VAN BARBARIA BEGINNENDE VAN C. RISATO TOT ALEXANDRIA [c. 1681] 51x58cm. (20x23") Color. Minor repair. [15] £171 $325

NIEUWE PASKAERT VAN D'OOST KUST VAN ENGELANDT VAN DOVER TOT DUNWICH... [1682] 50x58cm. (19½x23") Thames estuary. Bright early color. Short lower fold split repaired with no loss; o/w excellent. [11] £450 $856

NIEUWE PASKAERT VAN DE ZEE KUSTEN VAN PROVENCE EN ITALIAE ... T'EYLANDT CORSICA ... [1682] 51x58cm. (20x23") Full original color. Lower centerfold reinforcement. Double-thick paper; o/w excellent. [22] £788 $1500

NIEUWE PASKAERT VAN DE ZEE KUSTEN VAN'T EYLANDT SICILIA ... [1685] 51x58cm. (20x23") Full original color. Excellent. [2] £788 $1500

NIEUWE PLATTE PASKAART VAN DE STRAAT DAVIDS ... ALLES NAAWKEURIG AFGETECKENT DOOR SCHIPPER LAURENS FEYKES HAAN ... [1728] 58x99cm. (23x39") Full early color. Fold lines, light creasing; o/w excellent. [11] £720 $1370

NIEUWE ... WASSENDE GRAADEN PASKAART ... AARD BODEM OF WERELT [c. 1720] 58x99cm. (23x39") Two joined sheets. Color. Narrow margins as issued lightly reinforced. [5] £3625 $6898

PAS KAART VAN DE CARIBES TUSSCHEN I. BARBADOS EN I.S. MARTIN ... [c. 1682] 51x59cm. (20x23") Color. [15] £518 $985

[same title] [1685-1734] 51x58cm. (20x23") Full original color. Excellent. [2] £631 $1200

PAS-KAART VAN DE GOLFF DE GUANAIOS MET 'T CANAAL TUSSCHEN YUCATAN EN I. CUBA ... [c. 1681] 51x58cm. (20½x23") Early color. [15] £631 $1200

PAS KAART VAN DE GOLFF VAN MEXICO ... [1684] 51x58cm. (20½x23") First edition. Full original color. Excellent. [2] £2890 $5500

[same title, date, dimensions] By Vooght. Original color. Some toning; lower centerfold reinforced. [37] £1787 $3400

PAS KAART VAN DE NOORD KUST VAN ESPANIOLA MET D'EYLANDEN DOOR BENOORDEN DOOR VOOGT... [c. 1681] 51x59cm. (20x23½") Color. [15] £394 $750

PAS KAART VAN DE ZEE KUSTEN VAN VIRGINIA TUSSCHEN C HENRY EN T HOOGE LAND VAN RENSELAARS HOEK ... [1684] 51x58cm. (20½x23") By Vooght, after Augustine Hermann. Full original color, heightened in gold leaf. [37] £3205 $6100

[same title] [1685-1734] 50x58cm. (20x23") Full original color. Excellent. [2] £3416 $6500

PAS-KAART VANDE ZEE KUSTEN INDE BOGHT VAN NIEU ENGELAND ... [1684] 51x61cm. (20x23½") Full original color. Excellent. [1] £1971 $3750

PAS-KAART VANDE ZEE KUSTEN VAN NIEW NEDERLAND ANDERS GENAAMT NIEW YORK TUSSCHEN RENSELAARS HOEK EN DE STAATEN HOEK ... [1684] 51x58cm. (20x23") Hudson River detail. Original color. Excellent. [1] £2890 $5500

[same title] [1685] 51x56cm. (20½x22") Color. Excellent. [21] £2522 $4800

PASCAARTE VANDE ZEE CUSTEN VAN GUINEA, EN BRASILIA: VAN CABO DE VERDE, TOT C. DE BONA ESPERANCA: EN VAN R. DE AMAZONES TOT RIO DE LA PLATA... [1681] 51x58cm. (20½x23½") Full original color. Excellent. [2] £499 $950

PASCAERTE VAN WESTINDIEN BEGRYPENDE IN ZICH DE VASTE KUSTEN EN EYLANDEN, ALLES OP SYN WAERE LENGTE EN BREET OP WASSENDE GRADEN GELEGT [1684] 51x60cm. (20x23½") Full original color. Excellent. [2] £1839 $3500

PASCAERTE VANDE CARIBES, S. IUAN DE PORTO RICO, DE OOSTHOECK VAN I. ESPANGNOLA ALS MEDE DE VASTE CUST VAN NUEVA ANDALUSIA MET DE EYLANDEN DAER OMTRENT GHELEGEN, NIEULYCKX UYTGEGEVEN EN VAN VEEL FOUTEN VERBETERT [1681] 51x61cm. (20½x24½") Full original color. Some light staining lower section; o/w excellent. [2] £499 $950

PASKAART VAN DE BOGHT VAN FLORIDA MET DE CANAAL TUSSCHEN FLORIDA EN CUBA ... [1682] 51x58cm. (20½x23½") Full orig color heightened with gold. Pristine. [22] £2365 $4500

PASKAART VAN DE ZEE KUSTEN VAN'T EYLANDT SARDINIA ... BARBARIA ... [1685] 51x58cm. (20x23") Full original color. Excellent. [2] £631 $1200

PASKAERT WAER IN DE GRADEN DER BREEDDE OVER WEDER ZYDEN VANDE MIDDELLYN WASSENDE ... [1681] 53x61cm. (20½x23½") Full original color. Cut close at top margin; o/w excellent. [2] £460 $875

VAN LINSCHOTEN *Try Vrients*

[PORTRAIT] IOANNES HUGONIS A LINSCHOTEN ... [1619] 18x16cm. (7x6½") By Cloppenburgh. [5] £170 $324

[TITLE PAGE] IOHN HUIGHEN VAN LINSCHOTEN. HIS DISCOURS OF VOYAGES INTO YE EAST AND WEST INDIES [1598] 17x25cm. (6½x10") English edition. Trimmed to right margin with manuscript reinstatement. [5] £100 $190

[TITLE PAGE] ITINERARIO, VOYAGE OFTE SCHIPSVAERT / VAN JAN HUYGEN VAN LINSCHOTEN ... [1596] 28x19cm. (11x7½") Cut very close to right margin. [5] £110 $209

[TITLE PAGE] NAVIGATIO ACITINERARIUM IOHANNIS HUGONIS LINSCOTANI IN ORIENTALEM [1599] 28x18cm. (11x7") [15] £87 $165

[WORLD] [1598] 8x12cm. (3½x5") "Third Book", first English edition. W Rogers, sc. [10] £131 $250

DELINEATIO OMNIUM ORARUM TOTIUS AUSTRALIS PARTIS AMERICAE, DICTAE PERUVIANAE, A R. DE LA PLATA, BRASILIAM, PARIAM, & CASTELLAM ... [1596] 39x55cm. (15½x21½") Full color. [37] £1261 $2400

VAN LOCHOM

L'EUROPE NOUVELLEMENT TRACEE, ET RENDUE PLUS CLAIRE ... [c. 1660] 38x50cm. (15x19½") By Pierre van Lochom, probably from a Tavernier atlas. With inset and information panel. [33] £520 $990

NOVISSIMA DESCRIPTIO ANGLIAE SCOTIAE ET HIBERNIAE [1639-43] 38x50cm. (15x19½") After Hondius, in D'Avita's *Geography*; Henri Le Roy, engra Color. [5] £415 $790

PALESTINAE DELINEATIO AD GEOGRAPHICA CANONES REVOCATA [c. 1640] 39x54cm. (15½x21½") Not in Laor. Trimmed to lower border. [32] £480 $913

VAN LOON

IMPERII SINARUM NOVA DESCRIPTIO ... [1660-1700] 46x51cm. (18x20½") Full original color. One small stain, o/w excellent. [2] £499 $950

[same title] [1661-1668] 46x53cm. (18½x21") Outline color. Laid down; age-toned, slightly soiled and foxed, edge tears up to 3". [8] £150 $285

VAN ZOUTEVEEN

KAART VAN CALIFORNIE NAAR GOEDE BRONNEN BEWERKT [1872] 43x33cm. (17x13") Color. [15] £66 $125

VANCOUVER

A CHART SHEWING PART OF THE COAST OF N.W. AMERICA WITH THE TRACKS OF HIS MAJESTY'S SLOOP DISCOVERY AND ARMED TENDER CHATHAM COMMANDED BY GEORGE VANCOUVER [1798] 79x61cm. (30½x24") California to Alaska. Minor fold repairs. [15] £255 $485

A CHART SHEWING PART OF THE COAST OF N.W. AMERICA WITH THE TRACKS OF HIS MAJESTY'S SLOOP DISCOVERY & ARMED TENDER CHATHAM ... BY LT. JOSEPH BAKER [1798] 58x74cm. (22½x29") Minor repair. [15] £342 $650

[same title] [1801] 76x58cm. (30x23") Inset of Hawaiian Islands. Color. Slight wear at folds; else excellent. [21] £1156 $2200

CARTA DELLA PARTE DELLA COSTA NORD-OUEST DELL'AMERICAE ... RICONOSCIUTA DEL 1792 E 1794 [1820] 28x20cm. (10½x8½") Milan: L. Rossi. Color. [15] £47 $90

COTE NORD-OUEST DE L'AMERIQUE RECONNUE PAR LE CAPE. VANCOUVER. 2E PARTIE ... [c. 1799] 76x61cm. (30x24") Inset: Trinidad Bay. 1st French edition. [15] £255 $485

COTE NORD-OUEST DE L'AMERIQUE RECONNUE PAR LE CAPE. VANCOUVER. IVe PARTIE [1799] 76x61cm. (29½x24") 52Ø N. to 57Ø30' N. Excellent. [15] £302 $575

VANDERMAELEN

AMER. MERID. NO. 1 PARTIE DE LA COLOMBIE [1825] 47x56cm. (18½x22") Nicaragua to Panama. Color. [15] £87 $165

[same title, date] 46x56cm. (18x22") By H. Ghiesbreght. Color [15] £131 $250

AMER. SEP. NO. 2 DECOUVERTES BOREALES [1825] 48x58cm. (19x23") Color. [15] £76 $145

AMER. SEP. NO. 3 BAIE DE BAFFIN [1825] 51x58cm. (19½x22½") Color. [15] £76 $145

AMER. SEP. NO. 35 PARTIE DE LA NOUVELLE BRETAGNE [1825] 48x58cm. (18½x22½") Color. [15] £97 $185

AMER. SEP. NO. 39 PARTIE DES ETATS-UNIS [1827] 48x53cm. (19x21") Idaho, western Montana, etc. A single yellow boundary. Immaculate. [12] £150 $285

AMER. SEP. NO. 40 PARTIE DES ETATS-UNIS [1825] 47x51cm. (18½x20") Dakotas, Wyoming & E. Montana. Color. [15] £202 $385

AMER. SEP. NO. 41 PARTIE DES ETATS-UNIS [1825] 48x53cm. (18½x20½") Wisconsin & Minnesota. Color. [15] £184 $350

[same title] [1827] 48x53cm. (18½x20½") Wisconsin & Minnesota. Color. [15] £171 $325

AMER. SEP. NO. 44 NOUVELLE ECOSSE ET NOUVEAU BRUNSWICK [1825] 48x53cm. (18½x21") Color. [15] £123 $235

AMER. SEP. NO. 56 PARTIE DES ETATS UNIS [1825] 48x48cm. (18½x19½") Mississippi & Alabama, part of Louisiana & Arkansas. Color. [15] £171 $325

AMER. SEP. NO. 57 PARTIE DES ETATS UNIS [1827] 46x49cm. (18x19") Georgia, South Carolina, half of North Carolina. Color. Bright; very fine. [13] £236 $450

AMER. SEP. NO. 64 PARTIE DU MEXIQUE [1825] 46x53cm. (18½x21") Guadalajara & Lake Chapala. Color. [15] £84 $160

AMER. SEP. NO. 66 MERIDA [1825] 46x53cm. (18x21") Yucatan. Color. [15] £92 $175

VAUGONDY *Try De Vaugondy*

VELTEN

HISTORISCH-GEOGRAPHISCHE CARTE DER NORDAMERIKANISCHEN FREISTAATEN [1829] 51x66cm. (20x26") Text at sides. Color. [15] £58 $110

VILLEDIEU

NOUVEAU PLAN DE LA VILLE DE PARIS DIVISE EN DOUZE ARRONDISSEMENTS AVEC TOUS LES CHANGEMENS ET EDIFICES PUBLICS ... [1836] 59x79cm. (23x31") Folding plan between original marbled boards with label. Outline color. Few small holes at fold intersections, no loss; tape marks at corners; very good. [19] £158 $300

VINCENDON-DEMOULIN *Try Depot de la Marine*

VISSCHER *Try Schenk. Valk & Schenk*

ANGLIAE REGNUM TAM IN SEPTEM ANTIQUA ANGLO-SAXONUM REGNA ... [1694] 56x49cm. (22x19½") State I. Original color. Excellent. [38] £276 $525

CARTE DE L'AFRIQUE MERIDIONALE, OU PAYS ENTRE LA LIGNE & LE CAP DE BONNE ESPERANCE ET L'ISLE DE MADAGASCAR [c. 1710] 50x57cm. (19½x22½") Full original color. Excellent. [2] £631 $1200

DE GELEGENHEYT VAN T'PARADYS ENDE T'LANDT CANAAN, MITSGADERS DE EERST BEWOONDE LANDEN [1648] 30x48cm. (12x19") Laor 784. Color. [15] £197 $375

GEOGRAPHISCHE BESCHRYVINGLE VAN DE WANDELING DER APOSTELEN ENDE DE REYSEN PAULI [c. 1660] 33x48cm. (12½x18½") Travels of St. Paul. Laor 796. Outline color. Two short repaired tears at top; good. [30] £447 $850

HET BELOOFDE LANDT CANAAN DOOR WANDELT VAN ONSEN SALICHMAECKER JESU CHRISTO [1650] 32x47cm. (12½x18½") Laor 791. Color. [15] £255 $485

HET BELOOFIE LANDT CANAAN [c. 1700] 31x47cm. (12½x18½") Full color. Time toning; slight centerfold crease. [31] £197 $375

HIBERNIAE REGNUM TAM IN PRAECIPUAS ULTONIAE, CONNACIAE, LAGENIAE, ET MOMONIAE ... [1690] 56x48cm. (22x18½") Full original color. Excellent. [2] £657 $1250

INDIAE ORIENTALIS ... [c. 1680] 47x57cm. (18½x22½") Color. Trimmed close to neat line; restoration at lower right corner. [38] £250 $475

INDIAE ORIENTALIS NEC NON INSULARUM ADIACENTIUM NOVA DESCRIPTIO [c. 1680] 47x57cm. (18½x22½") Original color. Minor repair lower centerfold; o/w very good. [37] £460 $875

[same title] [c. 1690] 46x56cm. (18x22") Small facsimile restoration at lower left. [10] £342 $650

JAMAICA, AMERICAE SEPTENTRIONALIS AMPLA INSULA, A CHRISTOPHERO COLUMBO DETECTA ... [1680] 52x59cm. (20½x23½") Full original wash and outline color. Upper margin and border restored; o/w good. [10] £168 $320

LA SCANDIE. OU LES TROIS ROYAUMES DU NORD SUEDE, DANEMARC & NORVEGE ...LA VEUVE DE NICOLAS VISSCHER [1702] 58x74cm. (23x28½") By Elizabeth Visscher. Full color. Excellent. [22] £631 $1200

NOVA TABULA GEOGRAPHICA COMPLECTENS BOREALIOREM AMERICAE ... CANADA SIVE NOVA FRANCIA, NOVA SCOTIA, NOVA ANGLIA, NOVUM BELGIUM, PENSYLVANIA, VIRGINIA, CAROLINA ET TERRA NOVA, ... [and] CARTE NOUVELLE CONTENANT LA PARTIE D'AMERIQUE LA PLUS SEPTENTRIONALE [1680] 59x47cm. (23x18½") dimensions for each of a matching pair of maps. Full original color. Faintest trace of damp stain; Very good+ [20] £762 $1450

NOVA TABULA GEOGRAPHICA COMPLECTENS BOREALIOREM AMERICAE PARTEM: IN QUA EXACTE DELINEATAE SUNT CANADA SIVE NOVA FRANCIA, NOVA SCOTIA, NOVA ANGLIA, NOVUM BELGIUM, PENSYLVANIA, VIRGINIA, CAROLINA ET TERRA NOVA, ... A NICOLAO VISSCHER... [c. 1685-1695] 61x89cm. (23½x35½") 2 SHEETS joined. Original outline color. Excellent. [1] £1471 $2800

[same title] [c. 1685, 1712+] 47x59cm. (18½x23") Published by Schenk. Full orig col. Exc. [37] £736 $1400

[same title] [1695-1715] 59x47cm. (23x18½") Orig color. Lower blank margin restored. [10] £657 $1250

NOVI BELGII NOVAEQUE ANGLIAE NEC NON PARTIS VIRGINIAE TABULA MULTIS IN LOCIS EMENDATA A NICOLAO JOANNIS VISSCHERO [c. 1655] 46x55cm. (18½x21½") With view of New York. State IV. Original color. Excellent. [37] £2733 $5200

NOVISSIMA TOTIUS TERRARUM ORBIS TABULA [c. 1679] 43x52cm. (17x20½") Double hemisphere with decoration. Shirley 486. Full color. Minor centerfold reinforcement; few creases; else very good. [21] £1944 $3700

ORBIS TERRARUM NOVA ET ACCURATISSIMA TABULA ... [1658] 47x56cm. (18½x22") Shirley 410. Original body color with later additions. Tiny verdigris repair top center; old lower centerfold repair; browning at margins. [5] £2650 $5043

REGNUM HUNGARIAE ... [c. 1670] 48x58cm. (19x22½") Full orig color. Excellent. [2] £197 $375

VIVIEN

CARTE GENERALE DU MEXIQUE ET DES PROVINCES-UNIES DE L'AMERIQUE CENTRALE [1826] 30x41cm. (12½x16") Paris: Menard. Color. [15] £79 $150

VON EULER

MAPPA GEOGRAPHICA AMERICAE SEPTENTRIONALIS AD EMENDATIORA EXEMPLARIE ADHUC EDITA ... DESCRIPTA PARS 11 [1753] 36x36cm. (13½x14½") Color. [15] £210 $400

TAB: GEOG. AMERICAE AD EMENDATIORA [1753] 30x36cm. (12½x14½") Color. [15] £229 $435

VON KOTZEBUE

CHART OF BEHRING'S STRAIT UPON MERCATOR'S PROJECTION ... [1822] 20x20cm. (8x8") Color. [15] £45 $85

VON REILLY

GENERAL KARTE VON GROSSBRITANNIEN UND IRELAND [c. 1790] 28x22cm. (11x8½") Very good. [23] £125 $238

KARTE VON AMERIKA NACH D'ANVILLE UND POWNALL ... [1796] 58x76cm. (23x30") Old color. Fine. [15] £307 $585

VON SCHLIEBEN

DIE VEREINIGTEN STAATEN VON NORD AMERIKA. XIV GEBIET MICHIGAN. XV DAS NORDWESTLICHE GEBIET [1830] 20x25cm. (8x10½") Color. [15] £42 $80

VON STULPNAGEL

NORD AMERICA [1848] 33x38cm. (12½x15") Published by Stieler. Outline & wash col. Exc. [36] £79 $150

VEREIN-STAATEN VON NORD-AMERICA, MEXICO, YUCATAN U.A. [1853] 33x41cm. (13x16") Gotha: Stieler. Color. [15] £58 $110

VEREIN-STAATEN VON NORD-AMERICA MIT AUSNAHME FLORIDA'S UND DER WESTLICHEN TERR. [1866] 36x41cm. (13½x15½") Gotha: Perthes. Color. [15] £34 $65

VRIENTS

ORBIS TERRAE COMPENDIOSA DESCRIPTIO ... [1596] 40x57cm. (15½x22½") Shirley 192. After Plancius by Van Langeren, sc., for Van Linschoten's *Itinerario*. Small repair in left margin; fine. [5] £4850 $9230

VUILLEMIN

NOUVEAU PLAN ILLUSTRE DE LA VILLE DE PARIS AVEC LE SYSTEME COMPLET DE SES FORTIFICATIONS ET FORTS DETACHES ET DES COMMUNES DE LA BANLIEUE ... GRAVE SUR ACIER PAR BENARD [1845] 84x107cm. (33x42") Linen-backed folding plan in marbled slipcase. Uniform age-darkening; slipcase worn, edges bumped. [19] £197 $375

NOUVELLE CARTE ILLUSTREE DE L'OCIENIE ... [1858] 60x84cm. (23½x33") Engraved views at sides. [10] £236 $450

PLAN DE LA VILLE ET FAUBOURGS DE PARIS AVEC SES MONUMENTS. DIVISE PAR QUARTIERS ET ARRONDISSEMENTS [1814] 83x91cm. (32½x36") Paris. By J. Bonnisel. Folding plan between original boards with label. Outline color. Small tears at folds and junctures, repairs on back; no loss; good+. [19] £368 $700

PLANISPHERE ELEMENTAIRE ET ILLUSTRE ... [1856] 63x85cm. (25x33½") Original wash and outline color. [10] £255 $485

WAGHENAER

A CARDE OF THE BELDT, WITH ALL THE SEA COASTES, BOUNDS, AND SITE OF THE COUNTRIES CALLED LALAND, UNTO STEVENS HEAD [1588] 33x53cm. (13x20½") Narrow side margins; minor centerfold damage repaired. [11] £900 $1713

A DESCRIPTION OF THE SEA COASTES OF EYDER DITMERS & A PART OF JEUERLAND WITH THE RIVERS OF WESER, ELVE, EYDER, HEUER AND OTHER ENTREES SANDES AND SHOALDES, LIENGE ALONGEST THES SEA COASTE OF GERMANY [1588] 33x51cm. (13x19½") From *The Mariner's Mirror*. Repaired lower fold margin split; o/w very good. [11] £850 $1618

BESCHRIJVINGE VANDE NOORTCOSTEN VAN ENGELANT ENDE SCOTLANT, ENDE GHELEGENTHEIT VAN DIEN MITSGADERS DE MONDEN VANDE RIVIEREN, ENDE HAVENEN, ENDE WAER VOREN, MEN HEM MOET WACHTEN [1592 (c. 1602)] 19x55cm. (7½x21½") 2nd state. Narrow margins, almost to lower left neat line; clean, good. [11] £1650 $3140

BESCHRIJVINGE VANDE NOORTCOSTEN VAN ENGELANT, MITSGADERS DE WONDERLIJCKE SANDE ENDE BANCKEN VOOR DE RIVIERE VAN LONDON, HERWITS, FERMUDE ENDE LINT GELEGEN, HOMEN DE SELSDE MOET SCUWEN ENDE WACHTEN; ALL OP SYN MERCKEN ENDE STREKEN [1592, c. 1602] 19x55cm. (7½x21½") Close margins, within neat line in places; small repair at upper right just into engraved area; clean. [11] £1600 $3045

WAITE

BRITISH COLUMBIA [1894] 23x33cm. (9½x12½") Color. [15] £13 $25

CLEVELAND [1894] 25x30cm. (10x12") Color [15] £11 $20

CONNECTICUT [1896] 25x33cm. (10x13") Color. [15] £11 $20

MAP OF WASHINGTON [1896] 23x30cm. (9x11½") Color. [15] £16 $30

NEW JERSEY [1896] 33x25cm. (13x9½") Color. [15] £11 $20

NEW MEXICO [1892] 30x25cm. (12x10") 17 counties. Color. [15] £16 $30

WORLD SHOWING THE MOST IMPORTANT DISCOVERIES [1896] 30x46cm. (12x17½") Color. [15] £13 $25

WALCH

TABULA GEOGRAPHICA MAXIMAE PARTIS AMERICAE MEDIAE SIVE INDIAE OCCIDENTALIS / KARTE DES BETRAECHTLICHSTEN THEILS VON MITTEL=AMERICA ODER WESTINDIEN ENTWORFEN NACH DER GROSSEN KARTE DES D. EDWARDS ... [1820] 49x60cm. (19½x23½") Outline color. Wear at margins. [16] £269 $512

WALDSEEMULLER

TABULA MODERNA SECUNDA PORCIONIS APHRICE [1513] 37x51cm. (14½x20") Southern Africa. Stain at center above map. [38] £1471 $2800

WALES, W.

PORT PRAIJA AAN HET EILAND ST. JAGO [1777 (1795)] 18x15cm. (7½x6½") Allart & Van Cleef, pub. [11] £18 $34

WALKER & MILES

MAP OF THE CITY OF QUEBEC [1875] 33x38cm. (12½x15½") [15] £24 $45

TIMBERLANDS MAP QUEBEC, COMPILED IN THE CROWN TIMBERLANDS OFFICE [1875] 41x64cm. (16x24½") By J. Tache. [15] £21 $40

WALKER, G.

BOSTON HARBOR. [1897] 31x47cm. (12x18½") Bird's eye view. Folding map between original covers. Color. [19] £32 $60

MARTHA'S VINEYARD [1907] 51x71cm. (19½x28") Pocket map on linen. Color. [15] £37 $70

NEW MAP OF BOSTON GIVING ALL POINTS OF INTEREST [1883] 41x46cm. (16x18") Vest pocket map in cardboard case. Substantial color. Wear at folds; o/w very good. [3] £39 $75

WALKER, J. & C.

MAP OF THE EAST INDIA RAILWAY, SHEWING THE LINE PROPOSED TO BE CONSTRUCTED TO CONNECT CALCUTTA WITH THE NORTH WEST PROVINCES AND THE INTERMEDIATE CIVILIAN AND MILITARY STATIONS ... [1846] 110x106cm. (43x41½") Linen-backed folding map with marbled self-covers & original slipcase with label. Minimal age-darkening; VG. [19] £155 $295

WALLING

COLUMBUS, FRANKLIN CO. [Ohio] [1868] 30x28cm. (12x11") [26] £32 $60

CONNECTICUT WESTERN RESERVE, INCLUDING THE COUNTIES OF ASHTABULA. TRUMBULL, MAHONING, LAKE CEAUGA, PORTAGE, CAYAHOGA, SUMMIT, MEDINA, LORAIN, ERIE AND HURON [1868] 38x58cm. (15x23") [26] £37 $70

GEOLOGICAL MAP OF OHIO BY J.S. NEWBURY ... [1868] 58x38cm. (23x15") Col. [26] £32 $60

NORTHWESTERN AMERICA SHOWING THE TERRITORY CEDED BY RUSSIA TO THE UNITED STATES [1868] 33x41cm. (13x15½") Full color. Very good. [26] £34 $65

OHIO [1868] 38x58cm. (15x23") Color. [26] £32 $60

SOUTHERN STATES [1868] 38x58cm. (15x23") Full color. [26] £47 $90

THE CITY OF CINCINATTI [1868] 25x33cm. (10x13") Full color. Slight discoloration at top edge of outside border. [26] £32 $60

TOLEDO, LUCAS CO. [Ohio] [1868] 36x30cm. (13½x12") Full color. [26] £32 $60

WALLING & GRAY

CITY OF ALLENTOWN [1872] 28x38cm. (11x15") Color. [12] £39 $75

GEOLOGICAL MAP OF OHIO [1872] 38x28cm. (14½x10½") By J. S. Newberry. 13 colors. Excellent. [36] £32 $60

KANSAS AND THE TERRITORIES OF ARIZONA, COLORADO, NEW MEXICO, UTAH AND INDIAN TERRITORY [1872] 41x64cm. (16x25") From *Atlas of Ohio*. Full col. Fine. [36] £87 $165

MAP OF MARYLAND AND THE DISTRICT OF COLUMBIA, COLORED TO ILLUSTRATE THE GEOLOGICAL FORMATIONS [1873] 38x61cm. (14½x24") Pristine. [12] £84 $160

WALLIS

WALLIS'S PICTURESQUE ROUND GAME OF THE PRODUCE AND MANUFACTURE OF THE COUNTIES OF ENGLAND AND WALES [19th c.] 64x49cm. (25x19") County specialties depicted. Linen-backed folding map. Color. [19] £336 $640

WALLIS'S PLAN OF THE CITIES OF LONDON AND WESTMINSTER FOR 1800. TO WHICH ARE ADDED COACH FARES BY AUTHORITY OF THE COMMISSIONERS OF THE COACH OFFICE [1800] (no dims.) Linen-backed folding plan with original very worn labeled slipcase. Slight age darkening at folds; very good. [19] £145 $275

WALTON

A NEW PLAINE, AND EXACT MAP OF ASIA ... [c. 1660] 41x51cm. (16½x20½") Surround of panels. Age-toned; else fine. [34] £1051 $2000

A NEW, PLAINE & EXACT MAP OF EUROPE ... [c. 1660] 43x53cm. (16½x20½") Full color panels all around. Outline color. Small faint stain; small margin; else very good. [34] £788 $1500

WARNER & BEERS

COUNTIES OF COOK, DUPAGE, KANE, KENDALL AND WILL [Ill.] [1876] 43x36cm. (16½x14") Color. Marginal dampstaining; else good. [12] £47 $90

WARNER, B.

UNITED STATES OF AMERICA [1820] 43x66cm. (17x25½") From *General Atlas for Guthrie's Geography*. Wash color. On tissue-thin paper with rice paper backing; good. [29] £307 $585

WATSON

ATLAS MAP OF THE WORLD [1885] 30x46cm. (12x18") Color. [15] £18 $35

MICHIGAN & WISCONSIN [1885] 30x48cm. (12x19") Color. [15] £13 $25

WATSON'S NEW COUNTY, RAILROAD AND DISTANCE MAP OF MONTANA AND WYOMING [1875] 36x43cm. (14x16½") Color. [26] £74 $140

WEALE

WEALE'S MAP OF LONDON AND ITS VICINITY ... [1851] 50x94cm. (19½x37") Linen-backed folding plan in gold embossed board self-back. Partial color. Top detached; VG. [19] £102 $195

WEAVER, H.

MAP OF EUROPE COMPILED FROM THE MOST RECENT SURVEYS PUBLISHED FOR THE ELECTRIC & INTERNATIONAL TELEGRAPH COMPANY ... [1863] 80x96cm. (31½x37½") Linen-backed folding map between original boards. Color. Foxing, o/w VG. [19] £184 $350

WEEKLY DISPATCH *Try Ettling, Weller*

BRITISH COLUMBIA / VANCOUVER ISLAND [1858-59] 43x31cm. (17x12") By Weller. Outline color. Archival tape to flatten folds; else fine. [12] £47 $90

COAST OF CHINA FROM HIE CHE-CHIN BAY TO SAN MOON BAY [1858] 43x30cm. (17x12") By Weller. Chart in two sections. Tinted. Slight creasing. [11] £20 $38

VENICE [c. 1860] 30x43cm. (12x17") By T. Ettling. Wash color. [36] £37 $70

WEIGEL

FACIES POLI ARCTICA ADIACENTIUMQUE EI REGIONUM EX RECENTISSIMIS ITINERARIIS DELINEATA CURA [c. 1720] 33x36cm. (13x14½") North polar projection. Color. [15] £181 $345

WEIMAR GEOGRAPHISCHES INSTITUT

AMERICA [1851] 64x51cm. (25x20") By Kiepert. Outline color. Slight foxing. [16] £83 $158

[same title] [1857] 64x51cm. (25x20") By Kiepert, from *Hand-Atlas der Erde* ... Outline col. [16] £97 $184

AMERICA ... [1865] 44x35cm. (17x14") From Graf's Atlas. Outline color. Light browning; repaired marginal tear. [16] £83 $158

CARTE COMPARATIVE ET SYNCHRONIQUE DE L'ETENDUE TERRITORIALE DES TROIS GRANDES PUISSANCES FRANCE, ANGLETERRE, RUSSIE PENDANT LE DERNIER SIECLE, 1740-1840 [1853] 42x59cm. (16½x23") Original wash and outline color. Two tears just to printed surface. [10] £26 $50

CHARTE VON AMERICA NACH DEN NEUESTEN MATERIALIEN ... [1810] 59x47cm. (23x18½") Color. [16] £200 $381

CHARTE VON DEN VEREINIGTEN STAATEN VON NORD-AMERICA NEBST LOUISIANA UND FLORIDA ... VON F.L. GUSSEFELD, 1805 ... VON A.F. GOETZE [1812] 47x68cm. (18½x27") Outline color. Florida on separate portion imperfectly attached. [16] £407 $775

CHARTE VON NORD-AMERICA ... [1813] 59x53cm. (23x20½") By Reichard. Outline color. Minor marginal damage. [16] £200 $381

[same title] [1814] 43x30cm. (16½x12") Color. [15] £118 $225

CHARTE VON WEST INDIEN ... VON F.L. GUSSEFELD [1804] 44x61cm. (17x24") Outline color. [16] £166 $315

DIE VEREINIGTEN STAATEN VON NORDAMERICA ... [1865] 38x50cm. (15x19½") By Ohmann. Outline color. Light browning. [16] £76 $144

DIE VEREINIGTEN STAATEN VON NORDAMERICA NEBST CANADA ... [1851] 53x64cm. (20½x25") By Kiepert. Outline color. Marginal flaw at top. [16] £131 $250

[same title] [1857] 53x64cm. (21x25") By Kiepert, from *Hand-Atlas der Erde* ... Outline col. [16] £62 $118

DIE VEREINIGTEN STAATEN VON NORDAMERICA (OSTLICHER THEIL) [1857] 63x57cm. (25x22½") Northeastern U.S. Oval inset 18 cm. high of New York City area. Outline color. [16] £145 $276

MEXICO UND DIE REPUBLIKEN VON CENTRAL-AMERICA ... [1857] 56x65cm. (22x25½") By Graf. Outline color. [16] £131 $250

NORD AMERICA ... [1828] 59x54cm. (23x21½") By Wieland. 12 panels mounted on linen. Outline color. Trimmed to neat line. [16] £131 $250

NORD AMERICA MIT WESTINDIEN [1850] 60x51cm. (23½x20") By Kiepert. Outline color. Small repaired marginal tears. [16] £83 $158

[same title] [1857-1859] 60x51cm. (23½x20") By Kiepert, revised by Graf; from *Hand-Atlas der Erde* ... Outline color. [16] £97 $184

SUD AMERICA ... [1804] 70x52cm. (27½x20½") By Reichard. Outline color. Old fold wrinkle, tears, staining in lower margin; lower right corner lacking to neat line. [16] £97 $184

[same title] [1857] 56x46cm. (22x18") From *Hand Atlas der Erde* ... [16] £97 $184

WEST INDIEN ... [1844] 48x59cm. (19x23") By Weiland. Outline color. Lacks part of left margin without image loss. [16] £131 $250

WESTINDIEN CENTRAL-AMERICA UND DAS NORDLICHE UND NORDWESTLICHE SUD AMERICA - NUEVA GRANADA UND VENEZUELA [1854] 53x63cm. (21x24½") From *Hand-Atlas der Erde ...* Outline color. [16] £131 $250

WESTINDIEN CENTRAL-AMERICA UND DAS NORDWESTLICHE - SUD AMERICA [1866] 35x42cm. (13½x16½") From Graf's Atlas. Outline color. Slight browning. [16] £90 $171

WELD, I.

A PLAN OF THE CITY OF QUEBEC [1798] 18x25cm. (7x9½") From *Travels through the States of North America*. Color. [15] £66 $125

WELLER *Try Weekly Dispatch*

ISLANDS OF IMPORTANCE [1863] 43x30cm. (17x12") Includes Bermuda. [10] £26 $50

SEAT OF WAR IN VIRGINIA AND MARYLAND [1863] 45x31cm. (18x12") Three sheets, joinable in irregular format. Original outline color. [10] £150 $285

TASMANIA OR VAN DIEMENS LAND [1858] 43x30cm. (17x12") In "Supplement" to *Weekly Dispatch*. Original outline color. [10] £16 $30

VICTORIA [1858] 31x43cm. (12x17") In "Supplement" to *Weekly Dispatch*. Orig outline col. [10] £16 $30

WELLS

A NEW MAP OF SOUTH AMERICA SHEWING ITS GENERAL DIVISIONS, CHIEF CITIES & TOWNS, RIVERS, &C. [1700] 38x48cm. (14½x19½") Color. Minor repair. [15] £158 $300

A NEW MAP OF THE BRITISH ISLES ... [1700] 38x51cm. (15x20") Unobtrusive margin stain; center fold creasing; else very good. [34] £184 $350

A NEW MAP OF THE ISLANDS OF THE AEGEAN SEA TOGETHER WITH THE ISLAND OF CRETE AND THE ADJOINING ISLES [1700] 51x38cm. (19½x14½") Outline color. [36] £118 $225

A NEW MAP OF THE TERRAQUEOUS GLOBE ACCORDING TO THE LATEST DISCOVERIES AND MOST GENERAL DIVISIONS OF IT INTO CONTINENTS AND OCEANS [1700] 53x38cm. (21x14½") Shirley 609. Outline color; full color vignettes. Minor creasing; else VG. [34] £1051 $2000

ANTIQUAE ASIAE TABULA [1718] 10x16cm. (3½x6½") [10] £16 $30

HODIERNAE ASIAE TABULA [1709] 10x16cm. (3½x6½") [10] £21 $40

WETSTEIN

PLATTE KAART VEN DE GEHEELE WERELT [1730] 37x46cm. (14½x18") Full color. Adequate, but narrow margins; slight darkening lower centerfold margin; o/w very good+. [20] £604 $1150

WHITCHURCH, W.

CHART OF PART OF THE SOUTH SEAS SHEWING THE TRACTS & DISCOVERIES MADE BY HIS MAJESTY'S SHIPS ... [1777] 36x66cm. (14x26") London: W. Strahan. With Australia. Color. [15] £297 $565

WIGHTMAN, T.

A MAP OF THE ALLEGHANY, MONONGAHELA AND YOHIOGANY RIVERS [1805] 33x23cm. (13x9") From T.M. Harris, ... *Tour in the Territory Northwest of the Alleghany Mountains* ... Lower left margin extended; else fine. [12] £197 $375

WILKES

NORTH AMERICA [1798] 25x20cm. (9½x7½") Color. [15] £47 $90

WILKINSON

AN ACCURATE MAP OF THE WEST INDIES FROM THE LATEST IMPROVEMENTS [1794] 20x25cm. (7½x10") By W. Harrison. Color. [15] £42 $80

MERCATOR'S CHART [WORLD] [1825] 28x48cm. (11x18½") Outline col. & full tint. [12] £71 $135

NORTH AMERICA [1825] 30x23cm. (12x9") Full color. [3] £63 $120

THE AFFAIR OF BLADENSBURG AUGUST 24TH 1814 [1816] 15x18cm. (6½x7½") Col. [15] £63 $120

THE PURVEYORSHIPS IN THE REIGN OF SOLOMON [1798] 28x22cm. (11x8½") Original full wash color. Very good. [18] £58 $110

WILLDEY

AFRICA CORRECTED FROM OBSERVATIONS ... [1721] 66x97cm. (25½x37½") By Price & Senex. Original outline color. Reinforcement at fold; else excellent. [21] £788 $1500

EUROPE [1712] 62x90cm. (24x35½") Original outline color. Some reinforcement at folds; else clean. [21] £788 $1500

WILLIAMS, C.S.

N. & S. CAROLINA AND GEORGIA [1832] 18x25cm. (7½x9½") From *A New General Atlas*. Color. Fine. [13] £92 $175

WILLIAMS, W.

MAP OF THE CHIEF PART OF THE SOUTHERN STATES [1839] 28x43cm. (10½x16½") Phila: S.A. Mitchell. Color. [15] £34 $65

MAP OF THE SOUTHERN AND SOUTH-WESTERN STATES [1849] 30x46cm. (12½x17½") Carolinas to Florida to Louisiana. Color. [15] £21 $40

WILLYAMS, C.

MAP OF THE ISLAND OF MARTINIQUE FOR AN ACCOUNT OF THE EXPEDITION AGAINST THE FRENCH WEST INDIA ISLANDS [1796] 19x23cm. (7½x9") Privately printed. Fine. [10] £29 $55

WILMORE

STATE OF GEORGIA [1885] 15x15cm. (6x5½") Printed color. Good. [13] £13 $25

WILSON

A CHART OF THE COAST OF GUAYANA, &C. WITH ENGLARGED PLANS OF THE PRINCIPAL HARBOURS [1854 (1873)] 65x81cm. (25½x31½") Blueback. Clean; good. [11] £70 $133

A CHART OF THE EAST COAST OF ENGLAND FROM DUNGENESS TO NEWCASTLE INCLUDING THE ENTRANCES OF THE THAMES AND THE COAST OF FRANCE &C. FROM BOULOGNE TO FLUSHING... [1849 (1855)] 90x238cm. (35½x93½") Clean; good. [11] £220 $419

ST. GEORGE'S CHANNEL. ETC. [1855 (1867)] 86x178cm. (34x69½") Many insets. Blueback. Small margin chips; repaired 12" edge tear; o/w good. [11] £110 $209

THE CATTEGAT, THE SOUND, AND THE GREAT AND LITTLE BELTS ... [1852 (1864)] 81x221cm. (32x87") Many insets. Blueback. Edge repair without surface loss. [11] £160 $304

WINTERBOTHAM

PLAN OF FRANKLINVILLE, IN MASON COUNTY, KENTUCKY [1796] 18x13cm. (6½x4½") Wheat & Brun 648 [15] £45 $85

PLAN OF LYSTRA IN NELSON-COUNTY, KENTUCKY [1796] 18x13cm. (6½x4½") Wheat & Brun 649. [15] £45 $85

WISLIZENUS, A.

MAP OF A TOUR FROM INDEPENDENCE TO SANTA FE, CHIHUAHUA, MONTEREY & MATAMOROS IN 1846 & 1847 [1848] 51x41cm. (20x16") Balto: Weber Lith. Col. [15] £145 $275

WOODBRIDGE

PHYSICAL MAP OF THE UNITED STATES [1843] 30x41cm. (12x16") Some color. Minor wear at edge. [3] £63 $120

WYLD

A MAP OF PART OF THE WESTERN COAST OF AFRICA EXTENDING FROM THE ISLES DE LOSS TO SHERBORO ISLAND ... [1846] 65x92cm. (25½x36") Voyage tracks color coded. [10] £150 $285

A MAP OF THE PROVINCE OF UPPER CANADA, ... FROM QUEBEC TO LAKE HURON. ... [1846] 57x87cm. (22½x34½") Outline color. Fine. [10] £189 $360

A NEW MAP OF THE COUNTRY TWENTY FIVE MILES ROUND LONDON [c. 1850] 104x130cm. (41x51") Linen-backed folding map in original slipcase with labels. Partial color. Ink stains at right, some marginal soiling; slipcase damaged, bottom lacking; o/w very good. [19] £210 $400

A NEW MAP OF THE COUNTY OF DERBY DIVIDED INTO HUNDREDS AND THE PARLIAMENTARY DIVISIONS [1832] 51x45cm. (20x17½") Linen-backed folding map. Fragile; backing torn at some folds, some uniform age-darkening; all sections present and clear. [19] £26 $50

CHINA COMPILED FROM ORIGINAL SURVEYS & SKETCHES [1844] 61x80cm. (24x31½") Original outline color. [10] £92 $175

EXTENDED TAPE INDICATOR MAP OF LONDON AND VISITOR GUIDE [1891] 58x86cm. (22½x33½") Successor to G. Smith. Dissected, linen backed map folding into covers with 69 page guide. Color. Age-toned, small fold separations; guide worn, dirty, repaired; cover torn at spine, corners rubbed; o/w good. [8] £39 $75

MAP OF AMERICA [c. 1847] 52x59cm. (20½x23½") [10] £34 $65

MAP OF ASIA [1846-1850] 53x65cm. (21x25½") Original outline color. [10] £24 $45

MAP OF CENTRAL AMERICA, SHEWING THE DIFFERENT LINES OF ATLANTIC & PACIFIC COMMUNICATION [c. 1850] 58x81cm. (23x32") Color. One margin restored. [15] £123 $235

MAP OF CHINA COMPILED FROM ORIGINAL SURVEYS & SKETCHES [1840] 61x80cm. (24x31½") [10] £39 $75

MAP OF INDIA, CONSTRUCTED WITH GREAT CARE AND RESEARCH FROM ALL THE LATEST AUTHORITIES AND ... TO FACILITATE A REFERENCE TO THE CIVIL AND MILITARY STATIONS ... [c. 1852] 98x65cm. (38½x25½") Linen-backed folding map. Some age-soiling, pencil marks; o/w very good. [19] £210 $400

MAP OF NORTH AMERICA, EXHIBITING THE RECENT DISCOVERIES. GEOGRAPHICAL AND NAUTICAL ... [c. 1840] 46x36cm. (18x14½") On heavy paper. Outline color. [35] £118 $225

[same title] [1844] 48x36cm. (19x14½") Color. [15] £71 $135

MAP OF THE PENINSULA OF INDIA, FROM THE 19TH DEGREE OF NORTH LATITUDE TO CAPE CORMORIN [1844] 99x83cm. (39x32½") Two sheets. Original outline color. [10] £45 $85

MAP OF THE WEST INDIA & BAHAMA ISLANDS WITH THE ADJACENT COASTS OF YUCATAN, HONDURAS, CARACAS &C. [1825] 53x78cm. (20½x30½") Linen-backed folding map with marbled self-backs and original worn slipcase. Original color. Slight foxing at two places; VG. [19] £342 $650

MAP OF THE WEST INDIA ISLANDS [c. 1845] 23x28cm. (9x11") Color. [15] £42 $80

MEXICO AND GUATEMALA, SHEWING THE POSITION OF THE MINES [1850] 33x80cm. (13x31½") Yucatan to Panama. Color. [15] £97 $185

NEW SOUTH WALES [1847] 55x39cm. (21½x15½") [10] £18 $35

PLAN OF THE TOWN & HARBOUR OF BEIROUT, ANCIENT BERYTUS [1840] 21x27cm. (8½x10½") Linen-backed folding plan between boards. Very good. [19] £92 $175

SKETCH OF PART OF THE ISLAND OF STE. LUCIE. ... [1793-(1829)] 38x48cm. (15x19") Separately printed. Minor splits and tears repaired; fine. [10] £168 $320

TASMANIA OR VAN DIEMENS LAND [1847] 55x39cm. (21½x15½") [10] £16 $30

THE BASIN OF THE PACIFIC [1850] 57x84cm. (22x33") Outline color. Expert lower centerfold repair. [10] £145 $275

THE CRIMEA [1854] 47x64cm. (18½x25") Second edition. Linen-backed folding map. Outline color. Very good. [19] £39 $75

THE ISLANDS OF JAPAN [1868] 83x66cm. (32½x26") Linen-backed folding map with marbled self-backs and slipcase with label. Partial color. Small border ink blot; some light age-soil; o/w very good. [19] £328 $625

THE WORLD, DESIGNED TO SHOW THE LANGUAGES AND DIALECTS INTO WHICH THE BRITISH FOREIGN BIBLE SOCIETY HAS TRANSLATED THE SCRIPTURES OR AIDED IN THEIR DISTRIBUTION ... [n.d.] 88x131cm. (34½x51½") Linen-backed folding map. Color. Soiling, some age-darkening, some section corners separating, small holes at map corners; good+. [19] £171 $325

THE WORLD ON MERCATOR'S PROJECTION [1849] 64x93cm. (25x36½") There is a smaller Wyld map of the same title. Original outline color. Tear skillfully repaired. [10] £155 $295

WYLD'S MAP OF INDIA CONSTRUCTED WITH GREAT CARE AND RESEARCH FROM ALL THE LATEST AUTHORITIES ... TO FACILITATE A REFERENCE TO THE CIVIL AND MILITARY STATIONS [1857] 82x67cm. (32½x26") Linen-backed folding map between original boards lacking ties. Color. Light age-soil; very good. [19] £105 $200

WYLD'S MAP OF PARTS OF FRANCE AND PRUSSIA INCLUDING BELGIUM, & THE FRONTIER OF SOUTH GERMANY ... [1870] 54x81cm. (21½x32") Linen backing. Outline color. Very good. [19] £66 $125

WYLD'S NEW PLAN OF LONDON AND ITS VICINITY [1869] 73x108cm. (28½x42½") Linen-backed folding plan between original boards with label. Outline & wash col. Top board separating. [19] £145 $275

WYLD'S ROAD DIRECTORY THROUGH ENGLAND AND WALES BEING A NEW AND COMPREHENSIVE DISPLAY OF THE ROADS AND DISTANCES FROM TOWN TO TOWN AND OF EACH REMARKABLE PLACE FROM LONDON [1838] 52x61cm. (20½x24") Linen-backed folding map. Original color. Good. [19] £37 $70

WYLD'S ROAD DIRECTORY THROUGH ENGLAND AND WALES BEING A NEW AND COMPREHENSIVE DISPLAY OF THE ROADS AND DISTANCES FROM TOWN TO TOWN AND OF EACH REMARKABLE PLACE FROM LONDON [1859] 62x52cm. (24x20½") Linen-backed folding map between self-backs in original slipcase with label. Outline col. Very good. [19] £79 $150

WYTFLIET

CUBA INSULA ET IAMAICA [1597] 23x29cm. (9x11½") Excellent. [38] £447 $850

IUCATANA REGIO ET FONDURA [1597] 23x29cm. (9x11") Central America. Exc. [38] £302 $575

LIMES OCCIDENTALIS QUIVIRA ET ANIAN [1597] 23x29cm. (9x11½") Mint. [37] £946 $1800

NORUMBEGA ET VIRGINIA [1597] 23x30cm. (9x11½") Very good. [31] £841 $1600

[same title, date] 24x30cm. (9½x11½") State I. Remargined. [38] £1209 $2300

NOVA FRANCIA ET CANADA [1597] 24x30cm. (9½x11½") Excellent. [37] £946 $1800

PLATA AMERICAE PROVINCIA [1597-98?] 23x29cm. (9x11½") Fine. [10] £250 $475

YEAGER

KENTUCKY, WITH THE LATEST IMPROVEMENTS [c. 1828] 20x28cm. (8x10½") Philadelphia. By S. Atkinson. Color. [15] £118 $225

YOUNG, J.H. *Try Tanner, Mitchell*

THE TOURIST'S POCKET MAP OF THE STATE OF GEORGIA EXHIBITING ITS INTERNAL IMPROVEMENTS ROADS DISTANCES &C. [1836] 38x30cm. (15x12") Phila: S.A. Mitchell. Folding map. Marginal repair; very good. [13] £155 $295

[same title] [1837] 38x30cm. (15x12") Phila: Hinman & Dutton. Fine. [13] £184 $350

THE TOURIST'S POCKET MAP OF THE STATE OF INDIANA EXHIBITING ITS INTERNAL IMPROVEMENTS ROADS DISTANCES &C. [1836] 36x30cm. (14½x12") Phila: S.A. Mitchell. Folds into 5 x 3" gilt and blind-stamped red leather covers. Full color. Burn stains, loss at some folds, repaired and reinforced; fair. [14] £53 $100

ZATTA

[TITLE PAGE] ATLANTE NOVISSIMO [1779] 31x42cm. (12x16½") [5] £70 $133

IL CANADA, LE COLONIE INGLESI CON LA LUIGIANA E FLORIDA... [1778] 31x41cm. (12x16") Color. [15] £158 $300

IL MAPPAMONDO O SIA DESCRIZIONE GENERALE DEL GLOBO [1779] 29x40cm. (11x15½") Original outline color; figures in full color. Centerfold lightly age-darkened; o/w VG. [20] £342 $650

IL MARYLAND, IL JERSEY MERIDIONALE, LA DELAWARE, E LA PARTE ORIENTALE DELLA VIRGINIA, E CAROLINA SETTENTRIONALE [1788] 33x43cm. (12½x16½") Original outline color. Excellent. [1] £145 $275

IL PAESE DE SELVAGGI OUTAGAMIANI, MASCOUTENSI, ILLINESE, E PARTE DELLE VI NAZIONI [1778] 32x42cm. (13x16½") Original outline color. Trace of centerfold discoloration; o/w fine. [12] £197 $375

ISOLE FILIPPINE [1785] 40x31cm. (16x12") Original color. Some repaired worming at centerfold margin. [5] £225 $428

LA PENSILVANIA, LA NUOVA YORK, IL JERSEY SETTENTRIOLE: CON LA PARTIE OCCIDENTALE DEL CONNECTICUT, MASSACHUSETTS BAYE E L'IROCHESIA. FOGL. V. [1788] 33x43cm. (12½x16½") Original outline color. Excellent. [1] £145 $275

LI REGNI DI VALENZA E MURCIA CON L'ISOLE BALEARI, E PITIUSE [1775] 30x38cm. (11½x15½") Outline color; cartouche in full color. [36] £71 $135

LUIGIANA INGLESE, COLLA PARTE OCCIDENTALE DELLA FLORIDA, DELLA GIORGIA, E CAROLINA MERIDIONALE [1778] 32x42cm. (12½x16½") Outline color. Fine. [30] £276 $525

[same title, date, dimensions] Outline color. Fine. [34] £184 $350

MESSICO OVERO NUOVA SPAGNA CHE CONTIENE IL NUOVO MESSICO, LA CALIFORNIA, CON UNA PARTE DE' PAESI ADJACIENTI ... [1785] 32x40cm. (13x16") Outline col. [3] £355 $675

NUOVE SCOPERTE DE' RUSSI AL NORD DEL MARE DEL SUD SI NELL'ASIA, CHE NELL'AMERICA [1776] 30x40cm. (12x15½") Original color. [5] £220 $419

[same title, date] 31x40cm. (12x15½") Color. [15] £250 $475

[same title, date, dimensions] Orig color. Very light centerfold darkening; o/w VG+. [20] £394 $750

PARTE ORIENTALE DELLA FLORIDA, DELLA GEORGIA, E CAROLINA MERIDIONALE [1778] 32x42cm. (12½x16½") Color. [15] £118 $225

TITLE INDEX

[STANDING GLOBE]	ANONYMOUS	7 cm, diam
[STANDING GLOBES: TERRESTRIAL & CELESTIAL]	BARDIN	46 cm, diam
[SUMATRA, WEST COAST]	HERBERT	44 x 43 cm
[TERRESTRIAL GLOBE]	GUSSFIELD	10 cm, diam
[TITLE PAGE: ALLEGORICAL EARTH]	SCHERER	23 x 18 cm
[TITLE PAGE] ATLANTE NOVISSIMO	ZATTA	31 x 42 cm
[TITLE PAGE] ATLAS	OTTENS	27 x 44 cm
[TITLE PAGE] ATLAS COELESTIS ...	CELLARIUS	43 x 25 cm
[TITLE PAGE] ATLAS CONTRACTUS	SCHENK	43 x 28 cm
[TITLE PAGE] [ATLAS FRONTISPIECE]	DE WIT	48 x 25 cm
[TITLE PAGE] ATLAS MINOR OU BRIEVE AND VIVE DESCRIPTION DE TOUT ...	HONDIUS	16 x 21 cm
[TITLE PAGE] ATLAS NOVUS ...	HOMANN	48 x 28 cm
[TITLE PAGE] ATLAS NOVUS ... ATLAS FRANCOIS ...	COVENS & MORTIER	28 x 49 cm
[TITLE PAGE] ATLAS OU REPRESENTATION DU MONDE UNIVERSEL ...	MERCATOR (Folio)	38 x 23 cm
[TITLE PAGE] ATLAS UNIVERSEL	DE VAUGONDY	35 x 48 cm
[TITLE PAGE] BESCHRYVING VAN OUD EN NIEUUW OOST-INDIEN	VALENTYN	18 x 28 cm
[TITLE PAGE] BRITANNIA	CAMDEN	27 x 17 cm
[TITLE PAGE] COSMOGRAPHIE IN FOURE BOOKES ...	HEYLIN	19 x 30 cm
[TITLE PAGE] DE NIEUWE EN ONBEKENDE WEERELD: ...VAN AMERICA	MONTANUS	30 x 18 cm
[TITLE PAGE] DE PRAECIPIUS TOTIUS UNIVERSI URBIBUS LIBER SECUNDUS	BRAUN & HOGENBERG	35 x 22 cm
[TITLE PAGE] EUROPAE TOTIUS ORBIS TERRARUM PARTIS ...	QUAD	15 x 21 cm
[TITLE PAGE] IOHN HUIGHEN VAN LINSCHOTEN. HIS DISCOURS OF VOYAGES ...	VAN LINSCHOTEN	17 x 25 cm
[TITLE PAGE] ITINERARIO, VOYAGE OFTE SCHIPSVAERT / VAN JAN HUYGEN ...	VAN LINSCHOTEN	28 x 19 cm
[TITLE PAGE] L'ATLAS CURIEUX OU LE MONDE ...	DE FER (Large)	23 x 34 cm
[TITLE PAGE] L'HYDROGRAPHIE FRANCOIS ...	BELLIN (Large)	39 x 51 cm
[TITLE PAGE] LA SECONDA PARTA DELLA GEOGRAFIA DI CL. TOLOMEO	PORRO	25 x 18 cm
[TITLE PAGE] MERCURIO GEOGRAPHICO ...	ROSSI	27 x 43 cm
[TITLE PAGE] NAVIGATIO ACITINERARIUM ... LINSCOTANI IN ORIENTALEM	VAN LINSCHOTEN	28 x 18 cm
[TITLE PAGE] NEPTUNE FRANCOIS	DEPOT DE LA MARINE	51 x 36 cm
[TITLE PAGE] NOUVEAU THEATRE D'ITALIE TOM I.	MORTIER	29 x 45 cm
[TITLE PAGE] NOVUS ATLAS SINENSIS A MARTINO MARTINI	BLAEU	27 x 43 cm
[TITLE PAGE] REGNO DI NEGROPONTE ...	CORONELLI	23 x 39 cm
[TITLE PAGE] SECOND VOLUME DE L'ATLAS FRANCOIS	JAILLOT	29 x 45 cm
[TITLE PAGE] THE ENGLISH PILOT, FOURTH BOOK ... WEST-INDIA NAVIGATION	MOUNT & PAGE	41 x 23 cm
[TITLE PAGE] THE ILLUSTRATED ATLAS	TALLIS	32 x 23 cm
[TITLE PAGE] THE THEATRE OF THE EMPIRE OF GREAT BRITAINE ...	SPEED	38 x 24 cm
[TITLE PAGE] THEATRI PRAECIPUARUM TOTIUS MUNDI URBIUM LIBER SEXTUS	BRAUN & HOGENBERG	36 x 23 cm
[TITLE PAGE] THEATRUM ORBIS TERRARUM	ORTELIUS (Folio)	37 x 24 cm
[TITLE PAGE] THEATRUM ORBIS TERRARUM SIVE ATLAS NOVUS ...	BLAEU	25 x 40 cm
[UNITED STATES; BOUNDARY MAP]	DUVAL	33 x 56 cm
[WASHINGTON]	RAND, McNALLY	23 x 30 cm
[WEST INDIES, ETC.]	BORDONE	8 x 15 cm
[WESTERN PACIFIC]	LAPIE	41 x 56 cm
[WESTERN TERRITORY]	KINGSBURY	51 x 89 cm
[WORLD]	BORDONE	22 x 38 cm
[WORLD]	VAN LINSCHOTEN	8 x 12 cm
[WORLD & CONTINENTS; 5 MAPS] A' FOLD OT RESZEINEK LER AJZOLASA ...	ANONYMOUS	33 x 41 cm
... CHART OF FELICIA AND PLAN OF THE ISLAND BALAMBANGAN ...	DALRYMPLE	61 x 48 cm
... CHART OF THE ENGLISH CHANNEL ...	HEATHER	81 x 193 cm
... CONSISTORII WITTEBERGENSIS	HOMANN	49 x 56 cm
... GENERAL TAFEL ...	MUNSTER	26 x 35 cm
... LOS ANGELES BASE LINE AND ITS ... MAIN TRIANGULATION	U.S. COAST SURVEY	56 x 71 cm
... ST. GEORGE' CHANNEL &C. SURVEYED UNDER THEIR LORDSHIP'S DIR. ...	MORRIS	91 x 91 cm
6ME. CARTE PARTICULIERE DES COSTES DE BRETAGNE ...	BELLIN (Large)	58 x 81 cm
A CARDE OF THE BELDT, WITH ALL THE SEA COASTES, BOUNDS, ...	WAGHENAER	33 x 53 cm
A CHART OF CAPTN. CARTERET'S DISCOVERY AT NEW BRITAIN, ...	HOGG	15 x 36 cm
A CHART OF DELAWARE BAY AND RIVER; CONTAINING A FULL AND EXACT ...	SAYER & BENNETT	48 x 69 cm
A CHART OF DELAWARE BAY AND RIVER, FROM THE ORIGINAL BY MR. FISHER	GENTLEMAN'S MAG.	18 x 23 cm
A CHART OF PART OF NORTH AMERICA, ... CAPE HATTERAS TO CAPE CANSO	ARROWSMITH	51 x 79 cm
A CHART OF THE ATLANTICK OCEAN FROM ORONOQUE RIVER TO THE RIVER ...	SENEX	51 x 117 cm
A CHART OF THE BANKS AND HARBOURS OF NEWFOUNDLAND ...	MOUNT & PAGE	45 x 58 cm
A CHART OF THE CHANNEL	SELLER	43 x 56 cm
A CHART OF THE CHINA SEA, AND PHILIPPINE ISLANDS, ...	SAYER & BENNETT	76 x 61 cm
A CHART OF THE CHINA SEA INSCRIBED TO MONSR.	D'APRES DE MANVIL.	65 x 48 cm
A CHART OF THE COAST OF DEVONSHIRE FROM EXMOUTH TO RAME HEAD; ...	LAURIE & WHITTLE	64 x 79 cm
A CHART OF THE COAST OF GUAYANA, &C. WITH ENGLARGED PLANS ...	WILSON	65 x 81 cm

A CHART OF THE COAST OF PEGU WITH THE ADJACENT COASTS ...	SAYER & BENNETT	79 x 56 cm
A CHART OF THE COASTS OF CHINA FROM CAMBODIA TO NAMQUAM ...	HALLEY	50 x 60 cm
A CHART OF THE DOWNS ...	LAURIE & WHITTLE	53 x 71 cm
A CHART OF THE EAST COAST OF ENGLAND FROM DUNGENESS TO NEW. ...	WILSON	90 x 238 cm
A CHART OF THE ENTRANCE INTO ST. MARY'S RIVER ... CAPTN. W. FULLER ...	JEFFERYS	51 x 61 cm
A CHART OF THE ENTRANCE OF THE RED SEA ...	LAURIE & WHITTLE	58 x 66 cm
A CHART OF THE ETHIOPIC OR SOUTHERN OCEAN, & PART PACIFIC ...	FADEN	60 x 90 cm
A CHART OF THE GULF OF ST. LAURENCE, COMPOSED FROM ...	SAYER & BENNETT	61 x 51 cm
A CHART OF THE ISLAND OF BOURBON IN THE INDIAN OCEAN	HERBERT	55 x 70 cm
A CHART OF THE ISLANDS IN THE MIDDLE PART OF THE INDIAN OCEAN	HERBERT	50 x 74 cm
A CHART OF THE ISLANDS TO THE SOUTHWARD OF TCHU-SAN ...	DALRYMPLE	54 x 35 cm
A CHART OF THE MADERAS AND CANARY ISLANDS	LAURIE & WHITTLE	61 x 48 cm
A CHART OF THE MAHE AND ADMIRANTES ISLANDS WITH THEIR SHOALS ...	LAURIE & WHITTLE	43 x 58 cm
A CHART OF THE NORTHERN PART OF THE CHINA SEAS ...	SAYER & BENNETT	56 x 56 cm
A CHART OF THE NORTHERN PART OF THE INDIAN OCEAN ...	SAYER & BENNETT	59 x 90 cm
A CHART OF THE NORTHWEST COAST OF AMERICA FROM CALIFORNIA ...	ROBINSON	22 x 18 cm
A CHART OF THE NTH. WEST COAST OF AMERICA, & THE NTH. EAST COAST ...	MORSE, J.	18 x 30 cm
A CHART OF THE PACIFIC OCEAN FROM THE EQUINOCTIAL TO ... 39 1/2 ° N	ANSON	28 x 89 cm
A CHART OF THE SANDS AND CHANNELS FROM THE NORE TO MARGATE ...	LAURIE & WHITTLE	46 x 61 cm
A CHART OF THE SEA COAST OF NEWFOUND LAND, NEW SCOTLAND, ...	MOUNT & PAGE	45 x 58 cm
A CHART OF THE SEA COAST OF THE STATE OF MISSISSIPPI ...	U.S.	30 x 51 cm
A CHART OF THE SEA COASTS OF NEW ENGLAND, NEW JERSEY, VIRGINIA, ...	SELLER	43 x 56 cm
A CHART OF THE STRAITS OF MAGELLAN INLARGED FROM THE CHART ...	SAYER & BENNETT	51 x 69 cm
A CHART OF THE STREIGHTS OF DRNON, CONTAINING THOSE LANDS ...	HERBERT	45 x 108 cm
A CHART OF THE WEST COAST OF SUMATRA FROM THE EQUINOCTIAL ...	SAYER & BENNETT	67 x 49 cm
A CHART OF THE WESTERN COAST OF SUMATRA FROM TOUROUMANE	SAYER & BENNETT	68 x 49 cm
A CHART OF THE WESTERN & SOUTHERN OCEANS DESCRIBING THE COURSE ...	ROBINSON	28 x 25 cm
A CHART OF THE WORLD UPON MERCATOR'S PROJECTION ...	JEFFERYS	39 x 46 cm
A CHART SHEWING PART OF THE COAST OF N.W. AMERICA ...	VANCOUVER	76 x 58 cm
A CHART SHEWING THE TRACK OF THE CENTURIAN ROUND THE WORLD	ANSON	23 x 43 cm
A CHOROGRAPHICAL MAP OF THE PROVINCE OF NEW-YORK ...	FADEN	122 x 124 cm
A COMPLETE MAP OF THE SOUTHERN CONTINENT SURVEY'D BY ... TASMAN	BOWEN, E.	37 x 48 cm
A CORRECT CHART OF THE CHINA SEAS CONTAINING THE COASTS ...	HERBERT	60 x 77 cm
A CORRECT DRAUGHT OF THE NORTH POLE AND OF THE COUNTRIES ...	BOWEN, E.	39 x 43 cm
A CORRECT MAP OF THE GEORGIA WESTERN TERRITORY	MORSE, J.	18 x 15 cm
A CORRECT MAP OF VIRGINIA	CAREY	33 x 48 cm
A DESCRIPTION OF THE SEA COASTES OF EYDER DITMERS & A PART OF ...	WAGHENAER	33 x 51 cm
A DIAGRAM OF A PORTION OF OREGON TERRITORY	U.S. STATE SURVEYS	91 x 33 cm
A DIAGRAM OF OREGON	U.S. STATE SURVEYS	46 x 56 cm
A DIAGRAM OF THE PUBLIC SURVEYS IN OREGON	U.S. STATE SURVEYS	46 x 58 cm
A DRAFT OF THE CITY OF JERUSALEM AS IT IS NOW, TAKEN FROM THE [S.E.]	MOLL (Small)	13 x 23 cm
A DRAUGHT OF BONTHAIN BAY ...	HOGG	20 x 33 cm
A DRAUGHT OF THE HARBOUR OF HALIFAX IN NOVA SCOTIA ...	LOTTERY MAGAZINE	17 x 23 cm
A GENERAL AND PARTICULAR DESCRIPTION OF AMERICA	PURCHAS	20 x 20 cm
A GENERAL CHART EXHIBITING THE DISCOVERIES MADE BY CAPT. ... COOK ...	COOK	58 x 91 cm
A GENERAL CHART EXHIBITING THE DISCOVERIES MADE BY CAPT. ... COOK ...	ROBERTS, H.	55 x 92 cm
A GENERAL CHART OF THE SEA COAST OF EUROPE, AFRICA & AMERICA. ...	MOLL (Small)	35 x 28 cm
A GENERAL CHART OF THE WEST INDIA ISLANDS ...	FADEN	53 x 75 cm
A GENERAL CHART OF THE WESTERN OCEAN ...	MOUNT & PAGE	46 x 58 cm
A GENERAL MAP OF IRELAND TO ACCOMPANY THE REPORT OF THE RAIL. ...	HODGES & SMITH	195 x 162 cm
A GENERAL MAP OF NEW FRANCE COM, CALL'D CANADA	LA HONTAN	34 x 22 cm
A GENERAL MAP OF THE BRITISH MIDDLE COLONIES IN AMERICA ...	JEFFERYS	48 x 66 cm
A GENERAL MAP OF THE DISCOVERIES OF ADMIRAL DE FONTE & OTHERS, ...	GENTLEMAN'S MAG.	20 x 26 cm
A GENERAL MAP OF THE MIDDLE BRITISH COLONIES IN AMERICA ...	BOWLES	49 x 65 cm
A GENERAL MAP OF THE NORTHERN BRITISH COLONIES IN AMERICA, ...	SAYER & BENNETT	48 x 66 cm
A GENERAL MAP OF THE WORLD, OR TERRAQUEOUS GLOBE, ...	DUNN	105 x 123 cm
A GENERAL MAPP OF THE EAST INDIES, COMPREHENDING THE ESTATS ...	BLOME	40 x 34 cm
A GENERAL PLOTT AND DESCRIPTION OF THE FENNES AND SUROUNDED ...	HONDIUS	44 x 56 cm
A GENERALL CHART FOR THE WEST INDIES	GRIERSON	45 x 57 cm
A GENERALL MAP OF THE ISLES OF GREAT BRITAINE ... SANSON	BLOME	38 x 50 cm
A GENERALL MAPP OF ARABIA WITH THE RED SEA AND CIRCUMJACENT ...	BLOME	28 x 39 cm
A GENERALL MAPP OF ASIA ...	BLOME	39 x 55 cm
A GENERALL MAPP OF THE KINGDOM OF TARTARIA ...	BLOME	26 x 39 cm
A GLOBULAR DRAUGHT FROM THE NORTH POLE TO THE LATITUDE OF 60 ...	SENEX	48 x 41 cm
A LARGE CHART OF THE ISLAND ANTEGUA	MOUNT & PAGE	42 x 42 cm
A MAP AND CHART OF THOSE PARTS OF THE BAY OF CHESAPEAK YORK ...	POLITICAL MAG.	25 x 38 cm
A MAP EXHIBITING THE DARK SHADOW OF THE MOON OVER ENGLAND ...	SAYER	30 x 30 cm
A MAP OF 100 MILES ROUND BOSTON.	GENTLEMAN'S MAG.	23 x 25 cm

A MAP OF A TRACT OF LAND IN THE STATE OF NEW YORK ...	N.Y. STATE DOC. HIS.	33 x 38 cm
A MAP OF CONNECTICUT AND RHODE ISLAND, WITH LONG ISLAND SOUND	GENTLEMAN'S MAG.	17 x 23 cm
A MAP OF ENGLAND, WALES & SCOTLAND ...	FADEN	74 x 62 cm
A MAP OF GEORGIA, ALSO THE TWO FLORIDAS, FROM THE BEST AUTHORITIES	MORSE, J.	19 x 31 cm
A MAP OF HUDSON'S BAY AND STRAITS	JEFFERYS	15 x 21 cm
A MAP OF INDEPENDENT TARTARY CONTAINING ... USBECK, GASGAR, TIBET	MOLL (Small)	18 x 25 cm
A MAP OF INDIA ON THE WEST SIDE OF THE GANGES ...	BOWEN, E.	32 x 23 cm
A MAP OF IRELAND	CARY	51 x 42 cm
A MAP OF LOUISIANA AND OF THE RIVER MISSISSIPI BY IOHN SENEX	SENEX	49 x 58 cm
A MAP OF MASSACHUSETTS, FROM THE BEST AUTHORITIES	MORSE, J.	19 x 25 cm
A MAP OF MEXICO OR NEW SPAIN, FLORIDA NOW CALLED LOUISIANA ...	MOLL (Small)	18 x 25 cm
A MAP OF NEW ENGLAND AND NEW YORK	SPEED	38 x 51 cm
A MAP OF NEW FRANCE CONTAINING CANADA, LOUISIANA &C. ...	MOLL (Small)	19 x 26 cm
A MAP OF NEW HAMPSHIRE	MORSE, J.	23 x 18 cm
A MAP OF NORTH AMERICA	TANNER	108 x 146 cm
A MAP OF PARADISE ...	ANONYMOUS	28 x 36 cm
A MAP OF PART OF RHODE ISLAND SHEWING THE POSITIONS ...	MARSHALL	43 x 25 cm
A MAP OF PART OF THE WESTERN COAST OF AFRICA EXTENDING ...	WYLD	65 x 92 cm
A MAP OF PART OF WEST FLORIDA, FROM PENSACOLA TO THE MOUTH ...	GENTLEMAN'S MAG.	19 x 35 cm
A MAP OF PENNSYLVANIA EXHIBITING NOT ONLY THE IMPROVED PARTS ...	SAYER & BENNETT	68 x 133 cm
A MAP OF PENNSYLVANIA FROM THE BEST AUTHORITIES	MORSE, J.	18 x 23 cm
A MAP OF PHILADELPHIA AND PARTS ADJACENT, BY N. SCULL AND G. HEAP.	GENTLEMAN'S MAG.	34 x 29 cm
A MAP OF SCOTLAND DIVIDED INTO COUNTIES SHEWING THE PRINCIPAL ...	LEWIS, SAMUEL, CO.	63 x 131 cm
A MAP OF SOUTH AMERICA CONTAINING TIERRA-FIRMA, GUAYANA, ...	JEFFERYS	71 x 117 cm
A MAP OF SOUTH AMERICA CONTAINING TIERRA-FIRMA, GUAYANA, ...	SAYER	102 x 119 cm
A MAP OF THAT PART OF PENSYLVANIA NOW THE PRINCIPLE SEAT OF WAR	GENTLEMAN'S & LON.	38 x 29 cm
A MAP OF THE ALLEGHANY, MONONGAHELA AND YOHIOGANY RIVERS	WIGHTMAN, T.	33 x 23 cm
A MAP OF THE BRITISH AND FRENCH DOMINIONS IN NORTH AMERICA ...	MITCHELL, JOHN	69 x 48 cm
A MAP OF THE BRITISH AND FRENCH SETTLEMENTS IN NORTH AMERICA; ...	GEN. MAG. OF ARTS .	41 x 48 cm
A MAP OF THE BRITISH AND FRENCH SETTLEMENTS IN NORTH AMERICA.	GENTLEMAN'S MAG.	28 x 39 cm
A MAP OF THE BRITISH EMPIRE IN AMERICA ... [Sheet 5: Wisconsin, ...	POPPLE	51 x 66 cm
A MAP OF THE BRITISH EMPIRE IN AMERICA WITH THE FRENCH AND SPANISH ...	POPPLE	239 x 229 cm
A MAP OF THE BRITISH & FRENCH PLANTATIONS IN NORTH AMERICA	LONDON MAGAZINE	21 x 26 cm
A MAP OF THE COUNTREY AND CITTY OF PANAMA	ESQUEMELIN	17 x 28 cm
A MAP OF THE COUNTRY BETWEEN CROWN POINT AND FORT EDWARD.	GENTLEMAN'S MAG.	19 x 12 cm
A MAP OF THE COUNTRY ROUND PHILADELPHIA INCLUDING PART OF ...	GENTLEMAN'S MAG.	18 x 22 cm
A MAP OF THE DISTRICT OF MAINE WITH NEW BRUNSWICK & NOVA SCOTIA	MORSE, J.	18 x 23 cm
A MAP OF THE EAST-INDIES AND THE ADJACENT COUNTRIES; ...	MOLL (Large)	62 x 122 cm
A MAP OF THE EXTREMITY OF CAPE COD INCLUDING ... PROVINCETOWN ...	U.S.	73 x 88 cm
A MAP OF THE FIVE GREAT LAKES WITH PART OF PENSILVANIA, NEW YORK, ...	LONDON MAGAZINE	21 x 26 cm
A MAP OF THE FRENCH SETTLEMENTS IN NORTH AMERICA BY THOS. KITCHIN	LONDON MAGAZINE	17 x 18 cm
A MAP OF THE GENESEE LANDS IN THE COUNTY OF ONTARIO ...	N.Y. STATE DOC. HIS.	33 x 20 cm
A MAP OF THE GOLD COAST, FROM ISSIMI TO ALAMPI	D'ANVILLE	20 x 36 cm
A MAP OF THE ICY SEA IN WHICH THE SEVERAL COMMUNICATIONS ...	GENTLEMAN'S MAG.	20 x 20 cm
A MAP OF THE INHABITED PART OF CANADA FROM THE FRENCH SURVEYS; ...	FADEN	86 x 58 cm
A MAP OF THE ISLAND OF DOMINICA TAKEN FROM AN ACTUAL SURVEY; ...	BOWEN, T.	25 x 20 cm
A MAP OF THE ISLAND OF ORLEANS WITH THE ENVIRONS OF QUEBEC	GENTLEMAN'S MAG.	11 x 19 cm
A MAP OF THE ISLAND OF TOBAGO, DRAWN FROM AN ACTUAL SURVEY, ...	GENTLEMAN'S MAG.	19 x 24 cm
A MAP OF THE KINGDOM OF IRELAND	SEALE	48 x 39 cm
A MAP OF THE MANOR RENSELAERWICK ... 100 CHAINS TO AN INCH ... 1767	N.Y. STATE DOC. HIS.	38 x 53 cm
A MAP OF THE MIDDLE STATES OF AMERICA, ...	CONDER	30 x 46 cm
A MAP OF THE MOST INHABITED PART OF NEW ENGLAND, CONTAINING ...	JEFFERYS	53 x 99 cm
A MAP OF THE MOST INHABITED PART OF NEW ENGLAND, CONTAINING ...	LOTTER	102 x 97 cm
A MAP OF THE NORTH POLE ...	MOLL (Small)	20 x 28 cm
A MAP OF THE NORTH POLE AND THE PARTS ADJOINING. ... MDCLXXX	PITT	46 x 58 cm
A MAP OF THE NORTH WESTERN TERRITORY	MORSE, J.	19 x 24 cm
A MAP OF THE NORTHERN AND MIDDLE STATES; ... WESTERN TERRITORY ...	MORSE, J.	31 x 39 cm
A MAP OF THE NORTHERN AND MIDDLE STATES; ... WESTERN TERRITORY ...	STOCKDALE	33 x 41 cm
A MAP OF THE PROVINCE OF MEXICO IN NEW SPAIN	CARY	16 x 23 cm
A MAP OF THE PROVINCE OF NEW YORK WITH PART OF PENSILVANIA, ...	MONTRESOR	71 x 91 cm
A MAP OF THE PROVINCE OF PENSILVANIA DRAWN ... T. KITCHIN	LONDON MAGAZINE	17 x 22 cm
A MAP OF THE PROVINCE OF UPPER CANADA, ... FROM QUEBEC TO LAKE ...	WYLD	57 x 87 cm
A MAP OF THE PROVINCES OF NEW-YORK AND NEW-JERSEY, WITH A PART ...	LOTTER	38 x 57 cm
A MAP OF THE STATE OF KENTUCKY AND THE TENNESSEE GOVERNMENT ...	MORSE, J.	20 x 26 cm
A MAP OF THE STATE OF PENNSYLVANIA	HOWELL	56 x 86 cm
A MAP OF THE STATES OF NEW HAMPSHIRE AND VERMONT BY J. DENISON	MORSE, J.	19 x 24 cm
A MAP OF THE STATES OF VIRGINIA, NORTH CAROLINA, SOUTH CAROLINA ...	PURCELL	30 x 36 cm
A MAP OF THE UNITED STATES, ... WITH THE HEIGHTS OF MOUNTAINS	BOYNTON	69 x 61 cm

A MAP OF THE WEST INDIES &C. MEXICO OR NEW SPAIN. ...	MOLL (Small)	20 x 26 cm
A MAP OF THE WORLD	SENEX	59 x 107 cm
A MAP OF THE WORLD FROM THE BEST AUTHORITIES	CAREY	25 x 51 cm
A MAP OF THE WORLD FROM THE BEST AUTHORITIES ...	COWLEY	15 x 25 cm
A MAP OF THE WORLD, FROM THE LATEST AUTHORITIES	KITCHIN	25 x 51 cm
A MAP OF VIRGINIA AND MARYLAND	SPEED	38 x 50 cm
A MAP OF VIRGINIA, NORTH AND SOUTH CAROLINA, GEORGIA, MARYLAND ...	LONDON MAGAZINE	22 x 26 cm
A MAP SHEWING THE PROGRESS OF DISCOVERY & IMPROVEMENT IN THE ...	RENNELL, J.	41 x 71 cm
A MAPP OF THE EMPIRE OF THE SOPHIE OF PERSIA, ...	BLOME	27 x 39 cm
A MAPP OF THE ESTATES OF THE GREAT DUKE OF RUSSIA, ... OR MOSCOVIA	BLOME	(no dimens.)
A MAPP OF THE HIGHER AND LOWER AETHIOPIA COMPREHENDING YE SEVERAL	BLOME	30 x 41 cm
A MAPP OF THE KINGDOME OF IRELAND	BLOME	37 x 39 cm
A MAPP OF THE PARISH OF ST. GILES IN THE FIELDS	STRYPE	30 x 38 cm
A MAPP OF THE PARISH OF ST. MARTIN'S IN THE FIELDS	STRYPE	30 x 36 cm
A MAPP OF THE PARISHES OF ST. CLEMENT DANES AND ST. MAY SAVOY	STRYPE	36 x 30 cm
A MAPP OR GENERALL CARTE OF THE WORLD DESIGNED IN ... HEMISPHERES ...	BLOME	39 x 53 cm
A NAUTIC SURVEY OF MOUNTS BAY IN CORNWALL, WITH THE ADJACENT ...	LAURIE & WHITTLE	48 x 69 cm
A NEW & ACCURATE CHART OF THE WESTERN OR ATLANTIC OCEAN	BOWEN, E.	37 x 45 cm
A NEW & ACCURATE MAP OF CHINA, DRAWN FROM SURVEYS ...	BOWEN, E.	34 x 42 cm
A NEW & ACCURATE MAP OF NORTH AMERICA...	BOWEN, T.	27 x 44 cm
A NEW & ACCURATE MAP OF THE PROVINCE OF CANADA, IN NORTH ...	POLITICAL MAG.	26 x 34 cm
A NEW & ACCURATE MAP OF THE WHOLE RUSSIAN EMPIRE AS CONTAIN'D ...	BOWEN, E.	36 x 48 cm
A NEW ACCURATE TRAVELLING MAP OF SCOTLAND WITH THE DISTANCES ...	BROWN, T.	56 x 47 cm
A NEW AND ACCURAT MAP OF THE WORLD	SPEED	41 x 53 cm
A NEW AND ACCURATE CHART (FROM CAPTAIN HOLLAND'S SURVEYS) ...	LAURIE & WHITTLE	79 x 249 cm
A NEW AND ACCURATE CHART OF THE HARBOUR OF BOSTON, . .	POLITICAL MAG.	22 x 17 cm
A NEW AND ACCURATE CHART OF THE MOUTH OF THE THAMES ...	LAURIE & WHITTLE	69 x 102 cm
A NEW AND ACCURATE CHART OF THE WEST INDIES WITH THE ADJACENT ...	BOWEN, E.	37 x 45 cm
A NEW AND ACCURATE MAP OF AMERICA	BOWEN, E.	35 x 45 cm
A NEW AND ACCURATE MAP OF ANATOLIA OR ASIA MINOR WITH SYRIA ...	BOWEN, E.	35 x 43 cm
A NEW AND ACCURATE MAP OF EAST AND WEST FLORIDA, DRAWN ...	LONDON MAGAZINE	18 x 20 cm
A NEW AND ACCURATE MAP OF FRANCE WITH ITS ACQUISITIONS ...	BOWEN, E.	36 x 44 cm
A NEW AND ACCURATE MAP OF IRELAND	BOWEN, T.	29 x 19 cm
A NEW AND ACCURATE MAP OF ITALY	KITCHIN	43 x 39 cm
A NEW AND ACCURATE MAP OF LOUISIANA, WITH PART OF FLORIDA ...	BOWEN, E.	34 x 42 cm
A NEW AND ACCURATE MAP OF NORTH AMERICA, DRAWN FROM THE ...	BOWLES	47 x 51 cm
A NEW AND ACCURATE MAP OF NORTH AMERICA, DRAWN FROM THE ...	SEALE	47 x 51 cm
A NEW AND ACCURATE MAP OF NORTH AMERICA FROM THE BEST AUTH. ...	MENZIES	28 x 33 cm
A NEW AND ACCURATE MAP OF NORTH CAROLINA, AND PART OF SOUTH ...	POLITICAL MAG.	27 x 38 cm
A NEW AND ACCURATE MAP OF PERSIA WITH THE ADJACENT COUNTRIES ...	BOWEN, E.	35 x 42 cm
A NEW AND ACCURATE MAP OF POLAND, LITHUANIA &C. DIVIDED INTO ...	BOWEN, E.	35 x 43 cm
A NEW AND ACCURATE MAP OF SAVOY, PIEDMONT, AND MONTERRAT, ...	BOWEN, E.	35 x 43 cm
A NEW AND ACCURATE MAP OF THE EAST INDIA ISLANDS ...	BOWEN, E.	34 x 42 cm
A NEW AND ACCURATE MAP OF THE ENGLISH EMPIRE IN NORTH AMERICA ...	SOC. FOR ANTI-GALLIC	43 x 86 cm
A NEW AND ACCURATE MAP OF THE NORTHERN PARTS OF ITALY ...	BOWEN, E.	32 x 23 cm
A NEW AND ACCURATE MAP OF THE PRESENT SEAT OF WAR IN NORTH AMER.	UNIVERSAL MAG.	37 x 29 cm
A NEW AND ACCURATE MAP OF THE PROVINCE OF GEORGIA IN NORTH AMER. ...	UNIVERSAL MAG.	33 x 28 cm
A NEW AND ACCURATE MAP OF THE PROVINCE OF PENNSYLVANIA ...	UNIVERSAL MAG.	27 x 33 cm
A NEW AND ACCURATE MAP OF THE WORLD DRAWN FROM THE BEST ...	BOWEN, E.	29 x 55 cm
A NEW AND ACCURATE MAP OF TURKEY IN ASIA, ARABIA, &C. ...	BOWEN, E.	35 x 43 cm
A NEW AND ACCURATE MAP OF TURKEY IN EUROPE, WITH THE ADJACENT ...	BOWEN, E.	35 x 43 cm
A NEW AND ACCURATE MAP OF VIRGINIA, AND PART OF MARYLAND ...	POLITICAL MAG.	27 x 37 cm
A NEW AND ACCURATE MAP OF VIRGINIA & MARYLAND LAID DOWN ...	BOWEN, E.	33 x 23 cm
A NEW AND COMPLETE MAP OF THE WEST INDIES COMPREHENDING ALL ...	LAURIE & WHITTLE	46 x 59 cm
A NEW AND CORRECT CHART EXTENDING FROM LONDON BRIDGE TO ORFORD	LAURIE & WHITTLE	89 x 97 cm
A NEW AND CORRECT CHART OF ALL THE KNOWN WORLD LAID DOWN ...	BOWEN, E.	38 x 46 cm
A NEW AND CORRECT CHART OF THE ATLANTIC OCEAN REDUCED, ...	SENEX	51 x 58 cm
A NEW AND CORRECT CHART OF THE MEDITERRANEAN SEA	CUTLER	48 x 120 cm
A NEW AND CORRECT DRAUGHT OF THE BAY, OF MATANZAS, ON YE NORTH ...	MOUNT & PAGE	23 x 31 cm
A NEW AND CORRECT MAP OF THE BRITISH COLONIES IN NORTH AMERICA ...	LAURIE & WHITTLE	48 x 67 cm
A NEW AND CORRECT MAP OF THE COAST OF AFRICA	BOLTON	38 x 48 cm
A NEW AND CORRECT MAP OF THE PROVINCE OF CONNAUGHT	HOGG	29 x 21 cm
A NEW AND CORRECT MAP OF THE PROVINCE OF LEINSTER	HOGG	30 x 20 cm
A NEW AND CORRECT MAP OF THE PROVINCE OF MUNSTER	HOGG	22 x 32 cm
A NEW AND CORRECT MAP OF THE PROVINCE OF ULSTER	HOGG	20 x 32 cm
A NEW AND CORRECT MAP OF THE WHOLE WORLD SHEWING YE SITUATION ...	MOLL (Large)	70 x 120 cm
A NEW AND CORRECT MAP OF THE WORLD, LAID DOWN ACCORDING TO ...	MOLL (Large)	56 x 96 cm
A NEW AND CORRECT MAP OF THIRTY MILES ROUND LONDON	OVERTON	63 x 95 cm

A NEW AND CORRECT PLAN OF LONDON, WESTMINSTER AND SOUTHWARK ...	DODSLEY	36 x 66 cm
A NEW AND EXACT MAP OF AFRICA AND THE ILANDS ...	HOLLAR	37 x 48 cm
A NEW AND EXACT MAP OF GREAT BRITAIN ...	OVERTON	94 x 56 cm
A NEW AND EXACT MAP OF THE UNITED PROVINCES OR NETHERLANDS	MOLL (Large)	61 x 102 cm
A NEW CHART OF THE ISLAND OF GUERNSEY WITH THOSE OF SARK, ...	LAURIE & WHITTLE	51 x 71 cm
A NEW CHART OF THE ISLE OF WIGHT WITH THE ADJACENT COAST OF ...	LAURIE & WHITTLE	64 x 79 cm
A NEW CHART OF THE SKAGER RAK OR SLEEVE INCLUDING THE COASTS ...	NORIE	81 x 122 cm
A NEW CHART OF THE SOUTHERN COAST OF AFRICA FROM THE CAPE ...	LAURIE & WHITTLE	61 x 74 cm
A NEW & EXACT MAP OF THE COASTS ... WITHIN YE LIMITS OF YE SOUTH SEA	MOLL (Large)	43 x 48 cm
A NEW & EXACT MAPP OF YE ISLE OF JAMAICA ...	BLOME	29 x 33 cm
A NEW MAP OF ALABAMA	MITCHELL, S.A. (1859-)	41 x 33 cm
A NEW MAP OF ALABAMA WITH ITS ROADS AND DISTANCES ...	DESILVER	37 x 29 cm
A NEW MAP OF ALABAMA WITH ITS ROADS AND DISTANCES ...	MITCHELL, S.A. (1859-)	36 x 28 cm
A NEW MAP OF ARKANSAS	MITCHELL, S.A. (1859-)	41 x 33 cm
A NEW MAP OF ARKANSAS WITH ITS CANALS, ROADS AND DISTANCES	MITCHELL, S.A. (1859-)	38 x 31 cm
A NEW MAP OF ARKANSAS WITH ITS COUNTIES, TOWNS, POST OFFICES, &C.	DESILVER	41 x 36 cm
A NEW MAP OF ASIA	OGILBY	42 x 54 cm
A NEW MAP OF CANADA, ALSO THE NORTH PARTS OF NEW ENGLAND ...	ANONYMOUS	20 x 30 cm
A NEW MAP OF CAROLINA	MORDEN	13 x 13 cm
A NEW MAP OF CENTRAL AMERICA	DESILVER	36 x 41 cm
A NEW MAP OF CONNECTICUT FROM THE BEST AUTHORITIES	PAYNE	19 x 24 cm
A NEW MAP OF EGYPT, FROM THE LATEST AUTHORITIES	CARY	48 x 53 cm
A NEW MAP OF ENGLAND AND WALES, COMPREHENDING THE ... ROADS, ...	SMITH, C.	57 x 46 cm
A NEW MAP OF GEORGIA	MITCHELL, S.A. (1859-)	41 x 33 cm
A NEW MAP OF GEORGIA WITH ITS ROADS AND DISTANCES	MITCHELL, S.A. (1859-)	36 x 30 cm
A NEW MAP OF GEORGIA WITH ITS ROADS AND DISTANCES	THOMAS, COWPERTH.	36 x 30 cm
A NEW MAP OF GEORGIA WITH ITS ROADS & DISTANCES	TANNER	34 x 27 cm
A NEW MAP OF GEORGIA WITH PART OF CAROLINA, FLORIDA, AND LOUISIANA	BOWEN, E.	36 x 48 cm
A NEW MAP OF ILLINOIS WITH ITS PROPOSED CANALS, ROADS ...	MITCHELL, S.A. (1859-)	41 x 33 cm
A NEW MAP OF ILLINOIS WITH ITS PROPOSED CANALS, ROADS ...	TANNER	36 x 28 cm
A NEW MAP OF INDIA & CHINA FROM THE LATEST OBSERVATIONS ...	SENEX	50 x 59 cm
A NEW MAP OF INDIANA	MITCHELL, S.A. (1859-)	41 x 33 cm
A NEW MAP OF INDIANA EXHIBITING ITS INTERNAL IMPROVEMENTS ROADS ...	DESILVER	41 x 36 cm
A NEW MAP OF INDIANA WITH ITS ROADS AND DISTANCES	THOMAS, COWPERTH.	33 x 25 cm
A NEW MAP OF INDIANA WITH ITS ROADS & DISTANCES	DESILVER	36 x 29 cm
A NEW MAP OF INDIANA WITH ITS ROADS & DISTANCES	MITCHELL, S.A. (1859-)	36 x 29 cm
A NEW MAP OF INDIANA WITH ITS ROADS & DISTANCES	TANNER	35 x 28 cm
A NEW MAP OF IRELAND	KITCHIN	63 x 56 cm
A NEW MAP OF IRELAND DIVIDED INTO PROVINCES, COUNTIES &C.	SAYER & BENNETT	64 x 57 cm
A NEW MAP OF KENTUCKY	DESILVER	36 x 41 cm
A NEW MAP OF KENTUCKY	MITCHELL, S.A. (1859-)	33 x 41 cm
A NEW MAP OF KENTUCKY WITH ITS ROADS AND DISTANCES ...	MITCHELL, S.A. (1859-)	29 x 36 cm
A NEW MAP OF KENTUCKY WITH ITS ROADS & DISTANCES ...	TANNER	36 x 41 cm
A NEW MAP OF LOUISIANA	MITCHELL, S.A. (1859-)	33 x 41 cm
A NEW MAP OF LOUISIANA WITH ITS CANALS, ROADS & DISTANCES ...	DESILVER	30 x 38 cm
A NEW MAP OF MAINE	DESILVER	38 x 28 cm
A NEW MAP OF MAINE	MITCHELL, S.A. (1859-)	41 x 33 cm
A NEW MAP OF MARYLAND AND DELAWARE	MITCHELL, S.A. (1859-)	33 x 41 cm
A NEW MAP OF MARYLAND AND DELAWARE WITH THEIR CANALS, ROADS ...	DESILVER	30 x 38 cm
A NEW MAP OF MEXICO, CALIFORNIA & OREGON	JAMES, J.A. & U.P.	33 x 25 cm
A NEW MAP OF MICHIGAN WITH ITS CANALS, ROADS & DISTANCES	DESILVER	37 x 30 cm
A NEW MAP OF MICHIGAN WITH ITS CANALS, ROADS, AND DISTANCES	MITCHELL, S.A. (1859-)	38 x 30 cm
A NEW MAP OF MICHIGAN WITH ITS CANALS, ROADS & DISTANCES	TANNER	38 x 30 cm
A NEW MAP OF MICHIGAN WITH ITS CANALS, ROADS, AND DISTANCES	THOMAS, COWPERTH.	38 x 31 cm
A NEW MAP OF MICHIGAN, WITH ITS ROADS, CANALS & DISTANCES	MITCHELL, S.A. (1859-)	41 x 33 cm
A NEW MAP OF MISSISSIPPI	MITCHELL, S.A. (1859-)	41 x 33 cm
A NEW MAP OF MISSISSIPPI WITH ITS ROADS AND DISTANCES	DESILVER	36 x 30 cm
A NEW MAP OF MISSISSIPPI WITH ITS ROADS AND DISTANCES	TANNER	41 x 36 cm
A NEW MAP OF MISSISSIPPI WITH ITS ROADS AND DISTANCES	THOMAS, COWPERTH.	36 x 30 cm
A NEW MAP OF NEW JERSEY AND PENSILVANIA BY ROBT. MORDEN	MORDEN	15 x 13 cm
A NEW MAP OF NORTH AMERICA ACCORDING TO THE NEWEST OBSERV. ...	MOLL (Small)	18 x 25 cm
A NEW MAP OF NORTH AMERICA ... ACCORDING TO THE DEFINITIVE TREATY ...	SAYER	59 x 96 cm
A NEW MAP OF NORTH AMERICA WITH THE WEST INDIA ISLANDS ...	LAURIE & WHITTLE	100 x 116 cm
A NEW MAP OF NOVA SCOTIA, NEW BRUNSWICK AND CAPE BRUNSWICK ...	MORSE, J.	18 x 22 cm
A NEW MAP OF NOVA SCOTIA, NEWFOUNDLAND ETC. FROM THE LATEST ...	CARY	46 x 51 cm
A NEW MAP OF NTH. CAROLINA	MITCHELL, S.A. (1859-)	33 x 41 cm
A NEW MAP OF NTH. CAROLINA WITH ITS CANALS, ROADS & DISTANCES ...	DESILVER	30 x 38 cm
A NEW MAP OF NTH. CAROLINA WITH ITS CANALS, ROADS & DISTANCES ...	THOMAS, COWPERTH.	30 x 36 cm

A NEW MAP OF PENNSYLVANIA WITH ITS CANALS, RAIL-ROADS & DISTANCES ...	TANNER	28 x 33 cm
A NEW MAP OF PENNSYLVANIA WITH ITS CANALS, RAILROADS, &C.	MITCHELL, S.A. (1859-)	30 x 36 cm
A NEW MAP OF SCOTLAND	CARY	89 x 102 cm
A NEW MAP OF SCOTLAND COMPILED FROM ACTUAL SURVEYS ...	LAURIE & WHITTLE	63 x 49 cm
A NEW MAP OF SOUTH AMERICA SHEWING ITS GENERAL DIVISIONS, ...	WELLS	38 x 48 cm
A NEW MAP OF SOUTH CAROLINA	MITCHELL, S.A. (1859-)	33 x 41 cm
A NEW MAP OF SOUTH CAROLINA WITH ITS CANALS, ROADS & DISTANCES ...	DESILVER	30 x 36 cm
A NEW MAP OF SPAIN AND PORTUGAL, EXHIBITING THE CHAINS OF MOUNT. ...	FADEN	116 x 158 cm
A NEW MAP OF TENNESSEE	MITCHELL, S.A. (1859-)	33 x 41 cm
A NEW MAP OF TENNESSEE WITH ITS ROADS AND DISTANCES ...	MITCHELL, S.A. (1859-)	29 x 39 cm
A NEW MAP OF TENNESSEE WITH ITS ROADS & DISTANCES FROM PLACE ...	TANNER	36 x 41 cm
A NEW MAP OF THE BRITISH ISLES ...	WELLS	38 x 51 cm
A NEW MAP OF THE CIRCLE OF FRANCONIA ...	CARY	46 x 51 cm
A NEW MAP OF THE CIRCLE OF UPPER SAXONY WITH THE DUCHY OF SILESIA ...	CARY	46 x 53 cm
A NEW MAP OF THE CITY OF AMSTERDAM	SENEX	48 x 58 cm
A NEW MAP OF THE COUNTIES TEN MILES ROUND THE CITIES OF LONDON ...	COLE	24 x 29 cm
A NEW MAP OF THE COUNTRY TWENTY FIVE MILES ROUND LONDON	WYLD	104 x 130 cm
A NEW MAP OF THE COUNTY OF DERBY DIVIDED INTO HUNDREDS ...	WYLD	51 x 45 cm
A NEW MAP OF THE ISLAND OF BARBADOES, CONTAINING ALL YE PARISHES, ...	MOLL (Small)	18 x 25 cm
A NEW MAP OF THE ISLANDS OF THE AEGEAN SEA TOGETHER WITH THE IS. ...	WELLS	51 x 38 cm
A NEW MAP, OF THE ONLY USEFUL AND FREQUENTED PART OF NEW FOUND ...	LONDON MAGAZINE	18 x 24 cm
A NEW MAP OF THE PHILIPPINE ISLANDS, ...	KITCHIN	23 x 13 cm
A NEW MAP OF THE PROVINCE OF MARYLAND IN NORTH AMERICA.	UNIVERSAL MAG.	28 x 33 cm
A NEW MAP OF THE PROVINCE OF QUEBEC, ACCORDING TO THE ROYAL ...	SAYER & BENNETT	50 x 67 cm
A NEW MAP OF THE PROVINCE OF QUEBEC IN NORTH AMERICA; DRAWN ...	LONDON MAGAZINE	18 x 23 cm
A NEW MAP OF THE SEAT OF WAR, COMPREHENDING GERMANY; POLAND, ...	LAURIE & WHITTLE	74 x 81 cm
A NEW MAP OF THE STATE OF CALIFORNIA, THE TERRITORIES OF OREGON, ...	DESILVER	41 x 33 cm
A NEW MAP OF THE STATE OF CALIFORNIA, THE TERRITORIES OF OREGON, ...	THOMAS, COWPERTH.	41 x 33 cm
A NEW MAP OF THE STATE OF GEORGIA EXHIBITING IT'S INTERNAL IMPROV. ...	DESILVER	41 x 33 cm
A NEW MAP OF THE STATE OF ILLINOIS	DESILVER	41 x 36 cm
A NEW MAP OF THE STATE OF ILLINOIS WITH ITS PROPOSED CANALS, ...	THOMAS, COWPERTH.	39 x 34 cm
A NEW MAP OF THE STATE OF IOWA	DESILVER	34 x 41 cm
A NEW MAP OF THE STATE OF IOWA	THOMAS, COWPERTH.	34 x 41 cm
A NEW MAP OF THE STATE OF MISSOURI	DESILVER	36 x 41 cm
A NEW MAP OF THE STATE OF MISSOURI	THOMAS, COWPERTH.	36 x 41 cm
A NEW MAP OF THE STATE OF OHIO	DESILVER	41 x 33 cm
A NEW MAP OF THE STATE OF OHIO	THOMAS, COWPERTH.	40 x 34 cm
A NEW MAP OF THE STATE OF PENNSYLVANIA INCLUDING NEW JERSEY	DESILVER	41 x 69 cm
A NEW MAP OF THE STATE OF VIRGINIA EXHIBITING ITS INTERNAL IMPROV. ...	DESILVER	33 x 41 cm
A NEW MAP OF THE STATE OF WISCONSIN	DESILVER	41 x 34 cm
A NEW MAP OF THE TERRAQUEOUS GLOBE ACCORDING TO THE LATEST ...	WELLS	53 x 38 cm
A NEW MAP OF THE UNITED STATES OF AMERICA	DESILVER	40 x 66 cm
A NEW MAP OF THE WORLD ...	SENEX	42 x 54 cm
A NEW MAP OF THE WORLD ACCORDING TO THE NEW OBSERVATIONS ...	MOLL (Small)	18 x 28 cm
A NEW MAP OF UPPER & LOWER CANADA	STOCKDALE	18 x 23 cm
A NEW MAP OF VIRGINIA, FROM THE BEST AUTHORITIES: BY T. KITCHIN	LONDON MAGAZINE	18 x 23 cm
A NEW MAP OF VIRGINIA WITH ITS CANALS, ROADS & DISTANCES ...	TANNER	28 x 33 cm
A NEW MAP OF VIRGINIA WITH ITS CANALS, ROADS & DISTANCES ...	THOMAS, COWPERTH.	30 x 36 cm
A NEW MAPP OF AFRICA DESIGNED BY MOUNSIR. SANSON, ...	BLOME	39 x 54 cm
A NEW MAPP OF AMERICA SEPTENTRIONALE	BLOME	38 x 54 cm
A NEW MAPP OF LINCOLN SHIRE WITH THE POST & CROSS ROADS ...	OVERTON	39 x 49 cm
A NEW MAPP OF THE WORLD BY PHIL. LEA.	LEA	43 x 53 cm
A NEW MAPP OF YE EMPIRE OF CHINA WITH ITS SEVERALL PROVINCES ...	BLOME	30 x 39 cm
A NEW MAPPE OF THE ROMANE EMPIRE NEWLY DESCRIBED BY JOHN SPEEDE	SPEED	40 x 51 cm
A NEW PLAINE, AND EXACT MAP OF ASIA ...	WALTON	41 x 51 cm
A NEW, PLAINE & EXACT MAP OF EUROPE ...	WALTON	43 x 53 cm
A NEW PLAN OF BOSTON HARBOUR FROM AN ACTUAL SURVEY	PENNSYLVANIA MAG.	25 x 18 cm
A NEW PLAN OF GLASGOW WITH SUBURBS, FROM ORDNANCE ... SURVEYS, ...	BARTHOLOMEW	77 x 89 cm
A NEW PLAN OF THE CITY OF LONDON, WESTMINSTER AND SOUTHWARK	STRYPE	49 x 66 cm
A NEW POCKET PLAN OF THE CITIES OF LONDON & WESTMINSTER; ...	FADEN	45 x 89 cm
A NEW PROJECTION OF THE EASTERN HEMISPHERE OF THE EARTH ...	GENTLEMAN'S MAG.	23 x 21 cm
A NEW SURVEY OF THE COAST OF AFRICA FROM SENEGAL AND CAPE VERDE ...	LAURIE & WHITTLE	99 x 66 cm
A NEW TERRESTRIAL GLOBE ...	HILL, N.	6 cm, diam
A NEW TRAVELLING MAP OF ENGLAND, WALES AND SCOTLAND; ...	MOGG	72 x 62 cm
A PARTICULAR PLAN OF ACHEEN ROAD WITH THE ISLANDS ADJACENT	HERBERT	50 x 40 cm
A PERSPECTIVE VIEW OF THE CITY OF DUBLIN FROM PHOENIX PARK	MIDDLETON	25 x 26 cm
A PLAIN CHART OF THE CASPIAN SEA	GIBSON	36 x 56 cm
A PLAN OF A TRACT OF LAND ON BAYOU BOEUF SURVEYED BY SPANISH ...	U.S.	30 x 41 cm

A PLAN OF EFFINGHAM IN BERKLEY'S SOUND	BARCLAY	20 x 23 cm
A PLAN OF ENGLISH ROAD IN THE ISLAND OF ASCENSION ...	LAURIE & WHITTLE	28 x 43 cm
A PLAN OF JERUSALEM ACCORDING TO JOSEPHUS AND YE RABBIES	BLUNDELL	23 x 18 cm
A PLAN OF JUAN FERNANDES ISLAND IN THE SOUTH SEAS IN LAT. OF 33° 40'	ANSON	25 x 51 cm
A PLAN OF LONDON AND ITS ENVIRONS	LEWIS, SAMUEL & CO.	(no dimens.)
A PLAN OF MILFORD HAVEN IN PEMBROKE SHIRE, WITH THE FORTIFICATIONS ...	LAURIE & WHITTLE	51 x 69 cm
A PLAN OF MILFORD HAVEN ... [Wales]	MORRIS	18 x 23 cm
A PLAN OF TABLE BAY, WITH THE ROAD OF THE CAPE OF GOOD HOPE ...	LAURIE & WHITTLE	48 x 56 cm
A PLAN OF THE BAY & HARBOUR OF DUBLIN	MORRIS	18 x 33 cm
A PLAN OF THE CITY AND ENVIRONS OF PHILADELPHIA	LOTTER	58 x 46 cm
A PLAN OF THE CITY & HARBOUR OF LOUISBURG; SHEWING ...	GENTLEMAN'S MAG.	19 x 26 cm
A PLAN OF THE CITY OF CANTON ON THE RIVER TA HO	HARRIS	28 x 20 cm
A PLAN OF THE CITY OF QUEBEC	WELD, I.	18 x 25 cm
A PLAN OF THE COUNTRY FROM THE LANDING PLACE ... OF THE TROOPS ...	ANONYMOUS	11 x 19 cm
A PLAN OF THE HARBOUR AND TOWN OF LOUISBOURG IN THE ISLAND OF ...	ENTICK	18 x 25 cm
A PLAN OF THE HARBOUR OF PORT ANTONIO IN JAMAICA	POPPLE	15 x 15 cm
A PLAN OF THE HARBOUR OF RYE IN SUSSEX	LAURIE & WHITTLE	43 x 30 cm
A PLAN OF THE NORTHERN PART OF NEW JERSEY, SHEWING THE POSITIONS ...	MARSHALL	40 x 25 cm
A PLAN OF THE PRINCIPAL HARBOUR AND TOWN OF THE ISL. S. MARIES, ...	HERBERT	44 x 59 cm
A PLAN OF THE RAPIDS IN THE RIVER OHIO BY THOS. HUTCHINS	HUTCHINS	15 x 18 cm
A PLAN OF THE RIVER ST. LAURENCE FROM SILLERY TO THE FALL OF ...	STOCKDALE	19 x 24 cm
A PLAN OF THE SEAT OF WAR AT AND NEAR QUEBEC, WITH THE LINE ...	GRAND MAG. OF MAG.	11 x 19 cm
A PLAN OF THE STRAITS OF ST. MARY, AND MICHILIMAKINAC, TO SHEW ...	LONDON MAGAZINE	24 x 33 cm
A PLAN OF THE TOWN OF NEW HAVEN WITH ALL THE BUILDINGS IN 1748 ...	KENSETT	69 x 48 cm
A PLAT EXHIBITING THE STATE OF THE SURVEYS IN THE STATE OF FLORIDA ...	U.S. STATE SURVEYS	56 x 64 cm
A SKETCH OF THE ENVIRONS OF CHARLESTOWN IN SOUTH CAROLINA	SPROULE	51 x 71 cm
A SKETCH OF THE HARBOUR OF BRUNSWICK	U.S. WAR DEPT.	28 x 33 cm
A SKETCH OF THE ISLAND OF SINGPORE	MURRAY, J.	18 x 33 cm
A SURVEY OF LAKE CHAMPLAIN INCLUDING LAKE GEORGE, CROWN POINT ...	SAYER & BENNETT	66 x 46 cm
A SURVEY OF THE COASTS OF CORNWALL AND DEVONSHIRE...FROM ST. ...	ADMIRALTY	95 x 62 cm
A SURVEY OF THE SOUTH COAST OF ENGLAND FROM PLYMOUTH TO ...	ADMIRALTY	64 x 95 cm
A TOPOGRAPHICAL MAP OF HUDSONS RIVER	SAUTHIER	81 x 53 cm
A TOPOGRAPHICAL MAP OF THE COUNTRY TWENTY MILES ROUND LONDON, ...	FADEN	58 cm, diam
A TOPOGRAPHICAL MAP OF THE NORTHN. PART OF NEW YORK ISLAND, ...	FADEN	47 x 26 cm
A TOPOGRAPHICAL MAP OF THE NORTHN. PART OF NEW YORK ISLAND, ...	STEDMAN	46 x 26 cm
A TOPOGRAPHICAL PLAN OF MODERN ROME WITH THE NEW ADDITIONS ...	RICHARDSON	54 x 65 cm
A TOPOGRAPHICAL SURVEY OF THE COUNTRY, FROM THIRTY FIVE TO FORTY ...	SAYER & BENNETT	50 x 55 cm
A TRIGONOMETRICAL SURVEY OF THE BAY OF CORINGA	ADMIRALTY	36 x 60 cm
A VIEW OF YE GENERAL & COASTING TRADE-WINDS, MONSOONS OR YE ...	MOLL (Small)	18 x 52 cm
A VIEW ON THE HUDSON RIVER	APPLETON	23 x 71 cm
ABBILDUNG DER KEYSRL. FREYEN- REICHS- WAHL ... FRANCKFURT AM MAYNE	HOMANN	50 x 58 cm
ABERAERON AND NEW KEY ... [Wales]	MORRIS	18 x 23 cm
ABERDARON ROAD ON THE SOUTH SIDE OF BARDSEY SOUND ... [Wales]	MORRIS	18 x 24 cm
ABERDARON ROAD ... [Wales]	MORRIS	18 x 23 cm
ABERDOVEY BAY, BAR & HARBOUR [Wales]	MORRIS	18 x 23 cm
ABISSINIE	MALLET	14 x 10 cm
ACCURATA DELINEATIO CELEBERRIMAE REGIONIS LUDOVICIANAE VEL GALLICE	SEUTTER (Large)	49 x 56 cm
ACCURATE VORSTELLUNG DER BERUHMTEN MEER-ENGE ZWISCHEN DER NORD	HOMANN	50 x 60 cm
ACCURATER GRUNDRIS UND PROSPECT .... BRANDENB. BAYREUTHISCH.	HOMANN	50 x 59 cm
ACCURATISSIMA BRASILIAE TABULA	JANSSON	38 x 48 cm
ACCURATISSIMA EUROPAE TABULA MULTIS LOCIS ...	ALLARD	51 x 58 cm
ACCURATISSIMA TOTIUS ASIA TABULA RECENS EMENDATA PER ...	DANCKERTS	48 x 58 cm
ADEN AND ADJACENT BAYS	ADMIRALTY	64 x 89 cm
ADEN, ARABIA SOELICIS EMPORIUM CELEBERRIMI NOMINIS, QUO EX INDIA, ...	BRAUN & HOGENBERG	33 x 48 cm
AEGIIPTI RECENTIOR DESCRIPTIO	ORTELIUS (Miniature)	8 x 11 cm
AETHIOPIA INFERIOR VEL EXTERIOR	JANSSON	39 x 50 cm
AETHIOPIA SUPERIOR VEL INTERIOR; VULGO ABISSINORUM SIVE PRESBITERI ...	JANSSON	39 x 50 cm
AFBEELDINGE DER STAD JERUSALEM	BACHIENE	38 x 48 cm
AFRICA	ARROWSMITH	124 x 146 cm
AFRICA	BOTERO	18 x 25 cm
AFRICA ...	LOTTER	46 x 58 cm
AFRICA.	MITCHELL, S.A. (1860+)	20 x 28 cm
AFRICA	MUNSTER	13 x 16 cm
AFRICA	S.D.U.K.	33 x 39 cm
AFRICA, ACCORDING TO YE NEWEST AND MOST EXACT OBSERVATIONS	MOLL (Small)	18 x 25 cm
AFRICA CORRECTED FROM OBSERVATIONS ...	WILLDEY	66 x 97 cm
AFRICA EX MAGNA ORBIS TERRE DESCRIPTIONE GERARDI MERCATORIS ...	MERCATOR (Folio)	38 x 47 cm
AFRICA JUXTA NAVIGATIONES ET OBSERVATIONES...	SEUTTER (Large)	49 x 57 cm

AFRICA MINOR NUOVA TAVOLA	PTOLEMY (1561-1599)	18 x 24 cm
AFRICA OR LIBIA ULTERIOUR WHERE ARE THE COUNTRIES OF SAARA ...	BLOME	29 x 40 cm
AFRICA SECUNDUM LEGITIMAS PROJECTIONIS STEREOGRAPHICAE REGULAS	HOMANN	49 x 58 cm
AFRICA TERTIA PARS TERRAE	BUNTING	28 x 36 cm
AFRICAE NOVA DESCRIPTIO	BLAEU	41 x 55 cm
AFRICAE PARS MERIDIONALIS CUM PROMONTORIO BONAE SPEI...	LOTTER	46 x 56 cm
AFRICAE TABULA NOVA	ORTELIUS (Folio)	37 x 50 cm
AGRI PARISIENSIS TABULA PARTICULARIS, QUA MAXIMA PARS INSULAE ...	HOMANN	59 x 49 cm
AL MOLTO MAGCO SIGOR MARCO DEL SOLE SIGOR MIC OSSER.MO ...	LAFRERI SCHOOL	25 x 36 cm
ALABAMA	BARTHOLOMEW	38 x 28 cm
ALABAMA	BRADFORD	36 x 29 cm
ALABAMA	COLTON	38 x 30 cm
ALABAMA	CRAM	56 x 43 cm
ALABAMA	MORSE & BREESE	30 x 38 cm
ALABAMA, GEORGIA, SUD CAROLINA UND FLORIDA	LANGE	33 x 28 cm
ALASKA	CRAM	43 x 56 cm
ALASKA	U.S. STATE SURVEYS	71 x 97 cm
ALBANY IN NEW-YORK - VEREINIGTE STAATEN	MEYER	10 x 16 cm
ALBANY ON THE HUDSON	MEYER	(no dimens.)
ALBEMARLE AND CHESAPEAKE AND DISMAL SWAMP CANALS ...	U.S. WAR DEPT.	36 x 25 cm
ALEXANDRIA, VETUSTISSUMUM AEGYPTI EMPORIUM ...	BRAUN & HOGENBERG	37 x 49 cm
ALGESEY. WIGHT VECTIS OLIM. GARNESEY. IARSAY.	MERCATOR (Folio)	33 x 43 cm
ALGOA BAY	ADMIRALTY	61 x 97 cm
ALTERA GENERALIS TAB. SECUNDUM PTOL.	MUNSTER	26 x 35 cm
ALTON AM MISSISSIPPI (IN ILLINOIS)	MEYER	11 x 16 cm
AMACAO	DE BRY	26 x 33 cm
AMAZONIA TERRA FIRMA, PART BRASIL & PERU, REVISED BY MR. BOLTON	D'ANVILLE	43 x 76 cm
AMER. MERID. NO. 1 PARTIE DE LA COLOMBIE	VANDERMAELEN	47 x 56 cm
AMER. MERID. NO. 1 PARTIE DE LA COLOMBIE	VANDERMAELEN	46 x 56 cm
AMER. SEP. NO. 2 DECOUVERTES BOREALES	VANDERMAELEN	48 x 58 cm
AMER. SEP. NO. 3 BAIE DE BAFFIN	VANDERMAELEN	51 x 58 cm
AMER. SEP. NO. 35 PARTIE DE LA NOUVELLE BRETAGNE	VANDERMAELEN	48 x 58 cm
AMER. SEP. NO. 39 PARTIE DES ETATS-UNIS	VANDERMAELEN	48 x 53 cm
AMER. SEP. NO. 40 PARTIE DES ETATS-UNIS	VANDERMAELEN	47 x 51 cm
AMER. SEP. NO. 41 PARTIE DES ETATS-UNIS	VANDERMAELEN	48 x 53 cm
AMER. SEP. NO. 44 NOUVELLE ECOSSE ET NOUVEAU BRUNSWICK	VANDERMAELEN	48 x 53 cm
AMER. SEP. NO. 56 PARTIE DES ETATS UNIS	VANDERMAELEN	48 x 48 cm
AMER. SEP. NO. 57 PARTIE DES ETATS UNIS	VANDERMAELEN	46 x 49 cm
AMER. SEP. NO. 64 PARTIE DU MEXIQUE	VANDERMAELEN	46 x 53 cm
AMER. SEP. NO. 66 MERIDA	VANDERMAELEN	46 x 53 cm
AMERICA	ARROWSMITH	60 x 48 cm
AMERICA	CLUVER	20 x 26 cm
AMERICA	HONDIUS	38 x 51 cm
AMERICA	MANSELL, F.	23 x 15 cm
AMERICA	MOLL (Small)	23 x 30 cm
AMERICA	MORDEN	12 x 13 cm
AMERICA	PTOLEMY (1596-1621)	13 x 17 cm
AMERICA	VAN DEN KEERE	10 x 13 cm
AMERICA ...	WEIMAR GEOGRAPH.	44 x 35 cm
AMERICA	WEIMAR GEOGRAPH.	64 x 51 cm
AMERICA AUREA PARS ALTERA MUNDI AUCTORIBUS	VALK	48 x 60 cm
AMERICA BOREALIS...1699	SCHERER	23 x 36 cm
AMERICA BOREALIS MULTIS IN LOCIS DEI MATREM COLIT & HONORAT, ...	SCHERER	23 x 36 cm
AMERICA DAS SUDLICHE	GEBAUERS, J.	33 x 43 cm
AMERICA ENTVWORFEN VON C. G. REICHARD 1816 REVIDIRT UND NEU ...	REICHARD	38 x 28 cm
AMERICA MERIDIONALIS	HONDIUS	46 x 56 cm
AMERICA MERIDIONALIS	MERCATOR (Folio)	36 x 49 cm
AMERICA MERIDIONALIS	MULLER	7 x 8 cm
AMERICA MERIDIONALIS CONCINNATA JUXTA OBSERVATIONES ...	LOTTER	46 x 57 cm
AMERICA NOVA TABULA	BLAEU	41 x 53 cm
AMERICA NOVITER DELINEATA	HONDIUS	38 x 50 cm
AMERICA NOVITER DELINEATA	JANSSON	38 x 50 cm
AMERICA SEPTENTRIONAL	LOPEZ	18 x 32 cm
AMERICA SEPTENTRIONALIS	JANSSON	47 x 55 cm
AMERICA SEPTENTRIONALIS A DOMINO D'ANVILLE IN GALLIIS EDITA NUNC IN ...	HOMANN	46 x 51 cm
AMERICA SEPTENTRIONALIS, CONCINNATA JUXTA OBSERVATIONES ...	LOTTER	18 x 23 cm
AMERICA SETTENTIONRALE O COLOMBIA	STUCCHI	56 x 74 cm
AMERICA SIVE INDIA NOVA AD MAGNAE GERARDI MERCATORIS ...	MERCATOR (Folio)	37 x 46 cm

AMERICA WITH THOSE KNOWN PARTS IN THAT UNKNOWNE WORLD ...	SPEED	40 x 52 cm
AMERICAE DESCRIPTIO	MERCATOR (Small)	15 x 20 cm
AMERICAE MAPPA GENERALIS	HOMANN	48 x 55 cm
AMERICAE MAPPA GENERALIS SECUNDUM LEGITIMAS PROJECTIONIS ...	HOMANN	46 x 53 cm
AMERICAE NOVA TABULA	BLAEU	41 x 55 cm
AMERICAE NOVA TABULA. AUCT: GUILJELMO BLAEU	BLAEU	41 x 55 cm
AMERICAE PARS MERIDIONALIS	JANSSON	46 x 53 cm
AMERICAE RETECTIO	GALLE	22 x 26 cm
AMERICAE SIVE NOVI ORBIS, NOVA DESCRIPTIO	ORTELIUS (Folio)	36 x 50 cm
AMERIQUE CENTRALE	DUFOUR	25 x 33 cm
AMERIQUE DU NORD	LEVI	23 x 30 cm
AMERIQUE MERIDIONALE	LEVASSEUR	28 x 32 cm
AMERIQUE MERIDIONALE, DRESSEE, SUR LES MEMOIRES LES PLUS RECENTS ...	DE VAUGONDY	48 x 59 cm
AMERIQUE SEPTENTRIONALE	FILLOEUL	25 x 41 cm
AMERIQUE SEPTENTRIONALE	LEVASSEUR	30 x 43 cm
AMERIQUE SEPTENTRIONALE	LORRAIN	28 x 38 cm
AMERIQUE SEPTENTRIONALE	MALTE-BRUN	23 x 30 cm
AMERIQUE SEPTENTRIONALE	TARDIEU	28 x 23 cm
AMERIQUE SEPTENTRIONALE DIVISEE EN SES PRINCIPALES PARTIES ...	JAILLOT	56 x 89 cm
AMERIQUE SEPTENTRIONALE DRESSEE D'APRES LES DECOUVERTES DU CAP. ...	DELAMARCHE	20 x 23 cm
AMERIQUE SEPTENTRIONALE DRESSEE SUR LES RELATIONS LES PLUS MOD. ...	DE VAUGONDY	48 x 59 cm
AMERIQUE SEPTENTRIONALE ET MERIDIONALE, POUR SERVIR AUX LECONS ...	GAULTIER	43 x 36 cm
AMERIQUE SEPTENTRIONALE, OU SE REMARQUENT LES ETATS UNIS	BRION DE LA TOUR	51 x 73 cm
AMERIQUE SEPTENTRIONALE PAR N. SANSON D'ABBEVILLE GEOG. ORDRE. ...	SANSON (Folio)	39 x 56 cm
AMERIQUE SUIVANT LE R. P. CHARLEVOIX J. TE MR. DE LA CONDAMINE ...	LE ROUGE	48 x 64 cm
AMPLISSIMAE REGIONIS MISSISSIPPI SEU PROVINCIAE LUDOVICIANAE ...	HOMANN	48 x 58 cm
AMSTELREDAMUM, NOBILE INFERIORIS GERMANIAE OPPIDUM ...	BRAUN & HOGENBERG	34 x 48 cm
AMSTERDAM	S.D.U.K.	33 x 38 cm
AN ACCURATE MAP OF AFRICA	REYNOLDS, R.	19 x 28 cm
AN ACCURATE MAP OF IRELAND	BOWEN, E.	17 x 22 cm
AN ACCURATE MAP OF NEW HAMPSHIRE IN NEW ENGLAND, ...	UNIVERSAL MAG.	32 x 28 cm
AN ACCURATE MAP OF NEW YORK IN NORTH AMERICA, FROM A LATE SURVEY.	UNIVERSAL MAG.	34 x 27 cm
AN ACCURATE MAP OF NORTH AMERICA DESCRIBING AND DISTINGUISHING ...	BOWEN, E.	101 x 117 cm
AN ACCURATE MAP OF NORTH AMERICA DRAWN FROM THE SIEUR ROBERT ...	ROLLOS	18 x 30 cm
AN ACCURATE MAP OF NORTH AND SOUTH CAROLINA WITH THEIR INDIAN ...	MOUZON	99 x 142 cm
AN ACCURATE MAP OF THE BRITISH EMPIRE IN NTH. AMERICA AS SETTLED ...	GENTLEMAN'S MAG.	21 x 25 cm
AN ACCURATE MAP OF THE EAST INDIES EXHIBITING THE COURSE OF THE ...	BOWEN, E.	37 x 45 cm
AN ACCURATE MAP OF THE HOLY LAND WITH ADJACENT COUNTRIES	BOWEN, T.	28 x 18 cm
AN ACCURATE MAP OF THE UNITED STATES OF AMERICA ACCORDING TO ...	REID	36 x 46 cm
AN ACCURATE MAP OF THE WEST INDIES. DRAWN FROM THE BEST AUTH. ...	BOWEN, E.	35 x 42 cm
AN ACCURATE MAP OF THE WEST INDIES. EXHIBITING NOT ONLY ALL THE ...	GENTLEMAN'S MAG.	30 x 39 cm
AN ACCURATE MAP OF THE WEST INDIES FROM THE LATEST IMPROVEMENTS	WILKINSON	20 x 25 cm
AN ACCURATE MAP OF THE WEST INDIES WITH THE ADJACENT COAST	RUSSELL	35 x 51 cm
AN ANCIENT OR BIBLE MAP, DESIGNED FOR THE USE OF BIBLE CLASSES, ...	ANDRUS & JUDD	30 x 51 cm
AN AUTHENTIC PLAN OF THE RIVER ST. LAURENCE, FROM SILLERY TO THE ...	GIBSON	18 x 18 cm
AN AUTHENTIC PLAN OF THE TOWN & HARBOUR OF CAP-FRANCOIS ...	JEFFERYS	33 x 48 cm
AN EXACT CHART OF THE RIVER ST. LAURENCE, FROM FORT FRONTENAC ...	JEFFERYS	60 x 94 cm
AN EXACT DRAUGHT OF THE CASTLE OF SAN LORENZO YE VILLAGE & RIVER ...	GENTLEMAN'S MAG.	14 x 17 cm
AN EXACT MAP OF THE FIVE GREAT LAKES WITH PART OF PENSILVANIA, ...	LODGE	23 x 25 cm
AN EYE SKETCH OF THE ENTRANCE OF YEALME RIVER WITH THE DEPTHS ...	LAURIE & WHITTLE	48 x 36 cm
AN EYE SKETCH OF THE FALLS OF NIAGARA	STOCKDALE	17 x 23 cm
AN INDEX MAP TO THE FOLLOWING SIXTEEN SHEETS, BEING A COMPLEAT ...	JEFFERYS	41 x 66 cm
AN OUTLINE TO SHEW THE CONNECTED DISCOVERIES OF CAPTAINS ROSS ...	FRANKLIN	38 x 46 cm
ANCHOR BAY, LAKE ST. CLAIR	U.S.	64 x 58 cm
ANCIEN CONTINENT	MALLET	14 x 10 cm
ANCIEN CONTINENT AVEC PLUSIEURS ISLES	MALLET	14 x 10 cm
ANCIEN CONTINENT AVEC PLUSIEURS ISLES, OCEANS ET MERS	MALLET	14 x 10 cm
ANCIEN CONTINENT AVEC PLUSIEURS ISLES, OCEANS, MERS, GOLFES	MALLET	14 x 10 cm
ANCIENNE REGION DES SINES	MALLET	15 x 11 cm
ANCIENT SYRIA	S.D.U.K.	39 x 33 cm
ANDALUZIA	ORTELIUS (Miniature)	8 x 11 cm
ANDALUZIA CONTINENS SEVILLAM ET CORDUBAM	BLAEU	37 x 50 cm
ANGLESEY [on sheet with] WIGHT VECTIS [and] GARNESAY [and] IARSAY	MERCATOR (Folio)	32 x 43 cm
ANGLIA	ORTELIUS (Miniature)	8 x 11 cm
ANGLIA ET HIBERNIA NOVA	PTOLEMY (1561-1599)	18 x 25 cm
ANGLIA REGNUM	BLAEU	38 x 49 cm
ANGLIA REGNUM	JANSSON	38 x 49 cm
ANGLIA, SCOTIA ET HIBERNIA	MERCATOR (Folio)	32 x 40 cm

ANGLIAE ET HIBERNIAE ACCURATA DESCRIPTION VETERIBUS ET RECENT. ...	ORTELIUS (Folio)	43 x 58 cm
ANGLIAE REGNI FLORENTISSIMI NOVA AUCTORE HUMFREDO LHUYD ...	QUAD	18 x 27 cm
ANGLIAE REGNI FLORENTISSIMI NOVA DESCRIPTIO, AUCTORE HUMFREDO ...	ORTELIUS (Folio)	36 x 46 cm
ANGLIAE REGNUM TAM IN SEPTEM ANTIQUA ANGLO-SAXONUM REGNA ...	VISSCHER	56 x 49 cm
ANGLIAE, SCOTIAE, ET HIBERNIAE, SIVE BRITANNICAR: INSULARUM DESCRIPTIO	ORTELIUS (Folio)	34 x 49 cm
ANGLORUM IN VIRGINIAM ADVENTUS	DE BRY	16 x 23 cm
ANTIENT MEXICO	HARRIS	21 x 33 cm
ANTIQUA TO BRITAIN / GUADALOUPE TO FRANCE / MARIE GALLANTE ...	PHILIP, G.	51 x 61 cm
ANTIQUAE ASIAE TABULA	WELLS	10 x 16 cm
ANTIQUOR ? IMPERISSUM TABULA ...	DE VAUGONDY	47 x 62 cm
ANTWERP. (ANTWERPEN.) (ANVERS.)	S.D.U.K.	31 x 39 cm
APHRICA	QUAD	21 x 30 cm
APHRICAE TABULA I	MUNSTER	26 x 33 cm
API POINT TO THE RIVER SARAWAK	ADMIRALTY	46 x 64 cm
APPROACHES TO STORNOWAY	ADMIRALTY	50 x 65 cm
ARABIA	BLAEU	43 x 53 cm
ARABIA, EGYPT, ABYSSINIA, RED SEA, &C.	THOMSON	51 x 58 cm
ARABIA FELICE NUOVA TAVOLA	PTOLEMY (1561-1599)	18 x 25 cm
ARABIA WITH EGYPT, NUBIA AND ABYSSINIA	S.D.U.K.	31 x 39 cm
ARCHIDUCATUS AUSTRIAE INFERIORIS	HOMANN	49 x 59 cm
ARCHIDUCATUS AUSTRIAE SUPERIORIS	HOMANN	49 x 59 cm
ARCHIEPISCOPATUS ET ELECTORATUS COLONIENSIS UT ET...JULIACENSIS...	HOMANN	49 x 58 cm
ARCHIEPISCOPATUS TREVIRENSIS DESCRIPTIO NOVA	JANSSON	41 x 48 cm
ARCHIPELAGUE DU MEXIQUE, OU SONT LES ISLES DE CUBA, ESPAGNOLE, ...	COVENS & MORTIER	61 x 99 cm
ARCHIPELAGUS ATLANTICUS CUM SUIS INSULIS CANARIIS	SCHERER	23 x 34 cm
ARCIPELAGO COLOMBIANO CIOE LE ISOLE LUCAJE LE GRANDE E PICCOLE ...	LE SAGE	36 x 48 cm
ARGOW. IN HAC TABULA LUCERNA, VREN, SWYTZ, UNDERWALD, GLARONA ...	MERCATOR (Folio)	36 x 47 cm
ARIZONA	CRAM	30 x 23 cm
ARIZONA AND NEW MEXICO	BRADLEY	38 x 56 cm
ARKANSAS	BRADFORD	29 x 37 cm
ARKANSAS	BURR	28 x 30 cm
ARKANSAS	CENTURY ATLAS	28 x 38 cm
ARKANSAS	COLTON	33 x 41 cm
ARKANSAS	GRAY	42 x 62 cm
ARKANSAS	GREENLEAF	28 x 33 cm
ARKANSAS	MORSE & BREESE	30 x 38 cm
ARKANSAS	U.S. STATE SURVEYS	41 x 43 cm
ARKANSAS AND PORTION OF INDIAN TERRITORY	ASHER & ADAMS	41 x 57 cm
ARKANSAS. MAP OF THE ARKANSAS SURVEYING DISTRICT, SHEWING ...	U.S. STATE SURVEYS	38 x 41 cm
ARRAGONIA REGNUM	JANSSON	42 x 52 cm
ASHER & ADAMS' DAKOTA	ASHER & ADAMS	58 x 41 cm
ASHER & ADAMS' IDAHO. MONTANA WESTERN PORTION	ASHER & ADAMS	58 x 41 cm
ASHER & ADAMS' INDIAN TERRITORY AND TEXAS NORTH WEST PORTION	ASHER & ADAMS	41 x 58 cm
ASHER & ADAMS' MONTANA EASTERN PORTION	ASHER & ADAMS	41 x 58 cm
ASHER & ADAMS' NEW MEXICO	ASHER & ADAMS	43 x 58 cm
ASHER & ADAMS' OREGON	ASHER & ADAMS	41 x 58 cm
ASHER & ADAMS' UTAH	ASHER & ADAMS	41 x 58 cm
ASHER & ADAMS' WASHINGTON	ASHER & ADAMS	41 x 58 cm
ASIA ...	DE WIT	44 x 55 cm
ASIA	MORDEN	17 x 19 cm
ASIA	OTTENS	100 x 240 cm
ASIA	S.D.U.K.	33 x 40 cm
ASIA ACCORDING TO YE NEWEST OBSERVATIONS	MOLL (Small)	18 x 25 cm
ASIA AND ITS SEVERAL ISLANDS AND REGIONS ...	KITCHIN	43 x 56 cm
ASIA EX MAGNA ORBIS TERRE DESCRIPTIONE GERARDI MERCATORIS ...	MERCATOR (Folio)	38 x 47 cm
ASIA NOVITER DELINEATA	BLAEU	41 x 56 cm
ASIA, PLATE II, JAPAN, KOREA, THE MOGULS AND PART OF CHINA	BOLTON	53 x 36 cm
ASIA, PLATE III, THE PHILIPPINES, CAROLINES, MOLUCCAS AND SPICE ISLANDS	BOLTON	48 x 36 cm
ASIA QUA NULLA BEATIOR ORA; TRACTUS IN EOOS VERGENS MUNDIQUE ...	VALK	48 x 58 cm
ASIA RECENS SUMMA CURA DELINEATA	JANSSON	41 x 51 cm
ASIA RECENS SUMMA CURA DELINEATA. AUCT: JUD: HONDIO	HONDIUS	38 x 50 cm
ASIA SECUNDA PARS TERRAE IN FORMA PEGASI	BUNTING	28 x 36 cm
ASIA SECUNDUM LEGITIMAS PROJECTIONIS STEREOGRAPHICAE	HOMANN	41 x 58 cm
ASIA VULGO MINOR DICTA ANTIQUA ET NOVA CUM INSULIS ADJACENTIBUS	CRAMER, J.A.	61 x 95 cm
ASIA, WITH THE ISLANDS ADJOINING DESCRIBED, THE ATIRE OF THE PEOPLE, ...	SPEED	39 x 52 cm
ASIAE	D'EXPILLY	15 x 18 cm
ASIAE MINORIS VETERIS ET NOVAE, ITEMQUE PONTI EUXINI ET PALUDIS ...	HOMANN	51 x 59 cm
ASIAE NOVA DESCRIPTIO	ORTELIUS (Folio)	37 x 49 cm

ASIAE VII TAB. MEDIUS MERIDIANES 114	PTOLEMY (1578-1730)	36 x 46 cm
ASIATIC ARCHIPELAGO, ON MERCATOR'S PROJECTION	STANFORD	49 x 61 cm
ASIE	DE FER (Small)	13 x 16 cm
ASIE ANCIENNE	MALLET	15 x 11 cm
ASIE MINEURS	MALLET	15 x 10 cm
ASIE MODERNE	MALLET	15 x 11 cm
ASIE PAR N. DE FER	DE FER (Small)	14 x 16 cm
ASPEN SPECIAL	U.S. GEOL. SURVEY	46 x 38 cm
ASTRONOMIA COMPARATIVA	DOPPELMAYR	48 x 58 cm
ATAQUE DE QUEBEC	LA HONTAN	10 x 18 cm
ATLANTA	CRAM	30 x 25 cm
ATLANTA, BIRMINGHAM AND ATLANTIC RAILWAY	RAILROAD COMPANY	48 x 56 cm
ATLANTIC & PACIFIC JUNCTION, TOPOGRAPHICAL MAP, A PORTION OF ...	U.S.	36 x 51 cm
ATLAS MAP OF THE WORLD	WATSON	30 x 46 cm
AUDIENCE DE GUADALAJARA, NOUVEAU MEXIQUE, CALIFORNIE, &C. ...	SANSON (Small)	21 x 24 cm
AUSFUHRLICHE GEOGRAPHISCHE VORSTELLUNG DER GEGEND UM LONDON ...	HOMANN	50 x 57 cm
AUSTRALASIA	LEWIS & ARROWSMITH	20 x 25 cm
AUSTRALIA	BLACK	41 x 55 cm
AUSTRALIA	JOHNSTON	51 x 61 cm
AUSTRALIA EAST	STANFORD	61 x 50 cm
AUSTRALIA IN 1839	S.D.U.K.	32 x 40 cm
AUSTRIA ARCHIDUCATUS	MERCATOR (Folio)	33 x 48 cm
AZORES OR WESTERN ISLES	ADMIRALTY	48 x 64 cm
BACON'S BIRD'S-EYE VIEW OF SOUTH AFRICA	BACON	61 x 96 cm
BACON'S EXCELSIOR MAP OF WALES AND MONMOUTHSHIRE. ... RAILWAYS, ...	BACON	120 x 94 cm
BACON'S LARGE-PRINT MAP OF LONDON AND SUBURBS WITH GUIDE	BACON	69 x 90 cm
BACON'S NEW MAP OF LONDON DIVIDED INTO HALF MILE SQUARES ...	BACON	66 x 97 cm
BACON'S NEW MAP OF LONDON DIVIDED INTO HALF MILE SQUARES ...	BACON	61 x 82 cm
BACON'S WAR-MAP OF EGYPT INCLUDING SUDAN AND ABYSSINIA	BACON	62 x 43 cm
BAHIA HONDA. CHART NO. 382	DIRECCION DE HIDRO.	18 x 27 cm
BALTIMORE	BRADFORD	29 x 36 cm
BALTIMORE	MEYER	10 x 15 cm
BAR AT THE NORTHWEST ENTRANCE TO KEY WEST HARBOR, FLA. ...	U.S. WAR DEPT.	48 x 66 cm
BARBADOES	LUCAS	28 x 24 cm
BARBADOS	MOUNT & PAGE	29 x 26 cm
BARBARIAE ET BILEDULGERID NOVA DESCRIPTIO	ORTELIUS (Miniature)	8 x 11 cm
BARDSEY ISLE ... [Wales]	MORRIS	18 x 23 cm
BARMOUTH BAY BARS & HARBOUR [Wales]	MORRIS	18 x 23 cm
BARNES DRIVING MAP OF PHILADELPHIA	BARNES	76 x 76 cm
BARTHOLOMEW'S REDUCED SURVEY MAP OF SOUTH AFRICA COLOURED ...	BARTHOLOMEW	59 x 84 cm
BASE CHART OF THE UNITED STATES	U.S. COAST SURVEY	58 x 71 cm
BASS STRAIT	ADMIRALTY	97 x 66 cm
BATTLEMENT MESA FOREST RESERVE [Col.]	U.S. GEOL. SURVEY	43 x 48 cm
BAVARIAE CIRCULUS ET ELECTORAT	HOMANN	58 x 49 cm
BAVARIAE PARS INFERIOR	HOMANN	49 x 59 cm
BAVARIAE PARS SUPERIOR	HOMANN	59 x 50 cm
BAY ET CHATEAU DE PORTO BELLO	VAN DER AA	23 x 30 cm
BAY OF CHEDABUCTO - LENOR OR PETIT PASSAGE [Nova Scotia]	DES BARRES	53 x 64 cm
BAY OF NEWYORK FROM HOBOKEN	MEYER	11 x 17 cm
BAYES D'HUDSON ET DE BAFFINS, ET TERRE DE LABRADOR	DE VAUGONDY	16 x 16 cm
BELGII	MERCATOR (Folio)	36 x 46 cm
BELGII INFERIORIS DESCRIPTIO EMENDATA CUM CIRCUMIACENTIUM ...	MERCATOR (Folio)	36 x 46 cm
BELGII NOVI, ANGLIAE NOVAE, ET PARTIS VIRGINIAE NOVISSIMA DELINEATIO	JANSSON	43 x 51 cm
BELGII PARS SEPTENTRIONALIS VULGO HOLLANDIA	HOMANN	48 x 56 cm
BEQUIA OR BECOUYA, THE NORTHERNMOST OF THE GRANADILLES	LAURIE & WHITTLE	33 x 46 cm
BESCHREIBUNG DES HEILIGEN LANDES	BUNTING	27 x 38 cm
BESCHRIJVINGE VANDE NOORTCOSTEN VAN ENGELANT ENDE SCOTLANT, ...	WAGHENAER	19 x 55 cm
BESCHRIJVINGE VANDE NOORTCOSTEN VAN ENGELANT, MITSGADERS DE ...	WAGHENAER	19 x 55 cm
BESONDERE LAND KARTE DES HERZOGTH. OD CHURKREISES SACHSEN ...	HOMANN	70 x 96 cm
BETTS'S NEW MAP OF ENGLAND AND WALES, ...	BETTS	75 x 64 cm
BETTS'S TOUR THROUGH ENGLAND & WALES	BETTS	66 x 60 cm
BIRD'S EYE VIEW OF BOSTON HARBOR ALONG THE SOUTH SHORE ...	FINN	51 x 61 cm
BIRD'S EYE VIEW OF CLINTON, MASS.	BAILEY & CO.	48 x 69 cm
BIRD'S EYE VIEW OF PHILADELPHIA	HARPER BROS.	53 x 76 cm
BIRDS-EYE VIEW OF THE CITY AND COUNTY OF NEW-YORK WITH ENVIRONS.	LANGE & KRONFELD	13 x 20 cm
BIRMINGHAM	S.D.U.K.	34 x 40 cm
BISCAIA ET GUIPUSCOA CANTABRIAE VETERIS PARS	BLAEU	38 x 50 cm
BISCAIA ET GUIPUSCOA CANTABRIAE VETERIS PARS. AMSTELODAMI ...	JANSSON	38 x 50 cm

BISCAYNE BAY, FLORIDA	U.S. WAR DEPT.	20 x 30 cm
BOLONIA & GUINES COMITATUS	HONDIUS	38 x 50 cm
BONACCA ISLAND [Honduras]	ADMIRALTY	46 x 64 cm
BOOTH'S NEW PLAN OF LONDON; EXTENDING TO BLACKWALL, ...	REYNOLDS, J.	35 x 77 cm
BORDEAUX	S.D.U.K.	31 x 38 cm
BORNEO INSULA	DE BRY	14 x 20 cm
BORUSSIAE OCCIDENTALIS TABULA	HOMANN	58 x 45 cm
BOSTON	TALLIS	26 x 32 cm
BOSTON AND MAINE RAILROAD AND CONNECTIONS	RAILROAD COMPANY	58 x 76 cm
BOSTON HARBOR.	WALKER, G.	31 x 47 cm
BOUNDARIES OF THE RESERVATION FOR WABASH SALINE. GENERAL LAND ...	U.S.	41 x 33 cm
BOURBONOIS BORBONIUM DUCATUS	HONDIUS	38 x 50 cm
BOWLE'S DRAUGHT OF THE RIVER THAMES, FROM IT'S SPRING ...	BOWLES	20 x 88 cm
BOWLES' NEW MAP OF NORTH AMERICA AND THE WEST INDIES ...	BOWLES	101 x 115 cm
BOWLES'S NEW ONE-SHEET MAP OF ASIA DIVIDED INTO ITS EMPIRES, ...	BOWLES	48 x 56 cm
BOWLES'S NEW POCKET MAP OF THE MOST INHABITED PART OF NEW ENG. ...	BOWLES	64 x 51 cm
BOWLES'S NEW TRAVELLING MAP OF ENGLAND AND WALES EXHIBITING ...	BOWLES	59 x 52 cm
BRASIL NUOVA TABULA	PTOLEMY (1561-1599)	19 x 26 cm
BRASILIA	BERTIUS	9 x 13 cm
BRASILIA	OGILBY	28 x 36 cm
BRAZOS SANTIAGO TEXAS ... MAJ. MANSFIELD	U.S. WAR DEPT.	20 x 38 cm
BRESIL	MALLET	15 x 10 cm
BRESIL - PARAGUAY ET URUGUAY ...	MONIN	45 x 31 cm
BRITANNIA PROUT DIVISA FUIT TEMPORIBUS ANGLO-SAXONUM PRAESERTIM ...	BLAEU	42 x 53 cm
BRITISH AMERICA	TALLIS	26 x 33 cm
BRITISH AMERICA COMPREHENDING CANADA, LABRADOR, NEW-FOUNDLAND, ...	RUSSELL	33 x 38 cm
BRITISH COLUMBIA	CRAM	36 x 51 cm
BRITISH COLUMBIA	WAITE	23 x 33 cm
BRITISH COLUMBIA, ATHABASCA & ALBERTA WITH PARTS OF SASKATCH. ...	PHILIP, G.	51 x 56 cm
BRITISH COLUMBIA, MANITOBA, AND THE NORTH WEST TERRITORIES	STANFORD	52 x 70 cm
BRITISH COLUMBIA / VANCOUVER ISLAND	WEEKLY DISPATCH	43 x 31 cm
BRITISH COLUMBIA, VANCOUVER ISLAND &C.	STANFORD	30 x 38 cm
BRITISH DOMINIONS IN AMERICA AGREEABLE TO THE TREATY OF 1763; ...	KITCHIN	43 x 53 cm
BRITISH INDIA, NORTHERN PART	THOMSON	51 x 61 cm
BRITISH ISLES	PHILIP, G.	62 x 51 cm
BRITISH NEW GUINEA AND THE SOLOMAN, SANTA CRUZ & NEW HEBRIDES ...	STANFORD	51 x 62 cm
BRITISH NORTH AMERICA	S.D.U.K.	31 x 40 cm
BRITISH POSSESSIONS IN THE INDIAN SEAS	FULLARTON	47 x 31 cm
BRITISH POSSESSIONS ON THE NORTH WEST COAST OF SOUTH AMERICA	FULLARTON	47 x 31 cm
BRITTANIA DUCATUS ...	BLAEU	33 x 38 cm
BROAD HAVEN BAY	ADMIRALTY	61 x 97 cm
BROAD RIVER AND ITS TRIBUTARIES, S.C.	U.S.	30 x 18 cm
BROOKE'S TRAVELLING COMPANION THROUGH ENGLAND AND WALES	DARTON	58 x 49 cm
BROOKLYN AND VICINITY [N.Y.]	RAND, McNALLY	48 x 69 cm
BUENOS AYRES	MEYER	(no dimens.)
BUFFALO	LADIES REPOSITORY	(no dimens.)
BURLINGTON AM MISSISSIPPI	MEYER	11 x 16 cm
BURMA AND ADJACENT COUNTRIES	STANFORD	72 x 51 cm
BURRY BAY, BAR AND HARBOUR [Wales]	MORRIS	18 x 23 cm
CAART VAN HET EYLAND NOESSA-LAOET [&] CAART VAN HET EYLAND OMA	VAN KEULEN	46 x 28 cm
CAART VAN HET EYLANDT MANIPA ... [&] CAART VAN HET EYLAND HONIMOA	VAN KEULEN	46 x 28 cm
CALCUTTA	S.D.U.K.	32 x 40 cm
CALECUT NUOVA TAVOLA	PTOLEMY (1548 Venice)	13 x 17 cm
CALECUT NUOVA TAVOLA	PTOLEMY (1561-1599)	19 x 25 cm
CALIFORNIA	COLTON	38 x 31 cm
CALIFORNIA	COLTON	33 x 25 cm
CALIFORNIA	CRAM	48 x 30 cm
CALIFORNIA, MEXICO, GUATIMALA &C.	DOWER	21 x 26 cm
CALIFORNIA & NEVADA	CRAM	28 x 23 cm
CALIFORNIA & NEVADA	GRAY	66 x 40 cm
CALIFORNIA RAILROADS	RAND, McNALLY	69 x 48 cm
CAMBAIA	BERTIUS	9 x 13 cm
CAMLYN BAY & HARBOUR ... [Wales]	MORRIS	18 x 23 cm
CAMPAIGN OF THE ARMY OF WEST MISSISSIPPI, MAJ. GEN. E.R.S. CANBY, ...	U.S.	41 x 69 cm
CANAAN PALESTINE OR THE HOLY LAND &C. DIVIDED INTO THE 12 TRIBES ...	MOLL (Small)	23 x 18 cm
CANADA	FINLEY	20 x 28 cm
CANADA EAST FORMERLY LOWER CANADA	DESILVER	33 x 41 cm
CANADA EAST OR LOWER CANADA AND NEW BRUNSWICK	COLTON	36 x 43 cm

CANADA, LOUISIANE ET TERRES ANGLOISES	D'ANVILLE	48 x 56 cm
CANADA, NEW BRUNSWICK AND NOVA SCOTIA	HALL	43 x 51 cm
CANADA ORIENTALE NELL'AMERICA SETTENTRIONALI DESCRITTA ...	CORONELLI	45 x 60 cm
CANADA OU NOUVELLE FRANCE [and] LA FLORIDE	VAN DER AA	53 x 38 cm
CANADA WEST OR UPPER CANADA	COLTON	33 x 41 cm
CANDIA CUM INSULIS ALIQUOT CIRCA GRAECIAM	MERCATOR (Folio)	34 x 48 cm
CANDIA OLIM CRETA	JANSSON	38 x 53 cm
CANTABRIGIENSIS COMITATUS; CAMBRIDGE SHIRE	BLAEU	42 x 53 cm
CANTON FREIBURG SIVE PAGUS HELVETIA FRIBURGENSIS	HOMANN	49 x 58 cm
CAPE ANN HARBOUR SURVEYED BY THE REV. C. FETCH & W. MALBONE ...	BLUNT	20 x 20 cm
CAPE OF GOOD HOPE AND ADJACENT COASTS FROM HONDEKLIP BAY ...	ADMIRALTY	64 x 97 cm
CARDIGAN BAY, BAR AND HARBOUR [Wales]	MORRIS	18 x 23 cm
CARIBBEE OR LEEWARD ISLAND	PHILLIPS	18 x 13 cm
CARMARTHEN, LOUGHARN, AND CYDWELY ... [Wales]	MORRIS	18 x 23 cm
CAROLINAE FLORIDAE NEC NON INSULARUM BAHAMENSIUM. ...	CATESBY	(no dimens.)
CARTA COSMOGRAPHICA, CON LOS NOMBRES, PROPRIEDAD, Y VIRTUD ...	APIANUS	19 x 28 cm
CARTA DE LA ISLA DE SAN CHRISTOVAL REDUCIDA Y GRAVADA POR ...	LOPEZ	37 x 39 cm
CARTA DE LOS CANALES BAHAMA, PROVIDENCIA Y SANTAREN, ... LA FLORIDA	DIRECCION DE HIDRO.	56 x 87 cm
CARTA DELLA PARTE DELLA COSTA NORD-OUEST DELL'AMERICAE ...	VANCOUVER	28 x 20 cm
CARTA ESFERICA DE LA COSTA ORIENTAL DE CHINA...	DIRECCION DE HIDRO.	61 x 94 cm
CARTA ESFERICA DE LA COSTA ORIENTAL DE CHINA DESDE EL RIO NGAU-KEANG	DIRECCION DE HIDRO.	94 x 61 cm
CARTA ESFERICA QUE COMPRENDE PARTE DE LAS ISLAS DE STO. DOMINGO, ...	DIRECCION DE HIDRO.	91 x 61 cm
CARTA GENERALE DELLE COSTE DEL BRASILE ...	ROUSSIN	76 x 48 cm
CARTA MARINA NOVA TABULA	GASTALDI	14 x 17 cm
CARTA MARINA NUOVA TAVOLA	PTOLEMY (1561-1599)	18 x 24 cm
CARTA PARTICOLARE CHE MOSTRA IL CAPO BUONA SPERANZA CON IL MARE	DUDLEY	46 x 76 cm
CARTA PARTICOLARE DEL MARE DEL SUR CHE COMINCIA CON L'ISOLE DI SAL.	DUDLEY	48 x 75 cm
CARTA PARTICOLARE DEL' MARE DEL' ZUR CHE COMINCIA CON IL CAPO S. FR.	DUDLEY	48 x 76 cm
CARTA PARTICOLARE DELL'ISOLE DI ISLANDIA E FRISLANDIA, CON L'ISOLETTE	DUDLEY	48 x 76 cm
CARTA PARTICOLARE DELLA BRASILIA AUSTRALE CHE COMINCIA DEAL' PORO:	DUDLEY	48 x 38 cm
CARTA PARTICOLARE DELLA COSTA DEL' PERU PARTE AUSTRALE CON PARTE .	DUDLEY	48 x 36 cm
CARTA PARTICOLARE DELLA COSTA DI NUOVA ZEMBLA	DUDLEY	48 x 74 cm
CARTA PARTICULIERE DES COSTES DE L'AFRIQUE QUI COMPRENT UNE PARTIE	MORTIER	51 x 79 cm
CARTA PRIMA GENERALE D'AMERICA DELL'INDIA OCCIDENTALE E MARE DEL	DUDLEY	48 x 70 cm
CARTA RAPPRESENTANTE I CINQUE LAGHI DEL CANADA	GAZETTIERE AMER.	25 x 18 cm
CARTA RAPPRESENTANTE IL GOLFO DEL FIUME S. LORENZO	GAZETTIERE AMER.	25 x 19 cm
CARTA SECONDA GENERALE DEL'AMERICA	DUDLEY	44 x 37 cm
CARTE ADMINISTRATIVE PHYSIQUE ET ROUTIERE DE LA FRANCE INDIQUANT ...	DUFOUR	53 x 96 cm
CARTE COMPARATIVE ET SYNCHRONIQUE DE L'ETENDUE TERRITORIALE ...	WEIMAR GEOGRAPH.	42 x 59 cm
CARTE CONTENANT LE ROYAUME DU MEXIQUE ET LA FLORIDE	CHATELAIN	40 x 53 cm
CARTE D'AFRIQUE	DE L'ISLE	53 x 74 cm
CARTE D'AFRIQUE	DUFOUR	56 x 74 cm
CARTE D'AMERIQUE ...	POIRSON	53 x 69 cm
CARTE D'ARTOIS ET DES ENVIRONS	HOMANN	48 x 56 cm
CARTE D'ASIE	DE L'ISLE	50 x 64 cm
CARTE D'UN TRES GRAND PAIS NOUVELLEMENT DECOUVERT DANS L'AMER. ...	HENNEPIN	38 x 44 cm
CARTE D'UNE PARTIE DE L'AMERIQUE POUR LA NAVIGATION DES ISLES ...	BUACHE	51 x 94 cm
CARTE DE L'ACADIE, ISLE ROYALE ET PAIS VOISINS	BELLIN (Small)	21 x 33 cm
CARTE DE L'AFRIQUE FRANCOISE OU DU SENEGAL	DE L'ISLE	48 x 61 cm
CARTE DE L'AFRIQUE MERIDIONALE, OU PAYS ENTRE LA LIGNE & LE CAP ...	VISSCHER	50 x 57 cm
CARTE DE L'AMERIQUE ET DES MERS VOISINES ... 1763	BELLIN (Small)	46 x 31 cm
CARTE DE L'AMERIQUE SEPTENTRIONALE	BRUE	36 x 51 cm
CARTE DE L'AMERIQUE SEPTENTRIONALE POUR SERVIR A L'HISTOIRE ...	BELLIN (Small)	28 x 36 cm
CARTE DE L'ARABIE, DU GOLFE PERSIQUE, ET DE LA MER ROUGE, ...	BONNE	21 x 31 cm
CARTE DE L'ASIE DRESSE SUR LES RELATIONS LES PLUS NOUVELLES ...	DE VAUGONDY	47 x 53 cm
CARTE DE L'EMPIRE CHINOIS ET DU JAPON	LAPIE	41 x 53 cm
CARTE DE L'EMPIRE DE LA CHINE, DE LA TARTARIE CHINOISE, ET DU ROYAUME	BONNE	32 x 21 cm
CARTE DE L'EMPIRE DE TURQUIE EN EUROPE ET EN ASIE	HERISSON	52 x 77 cm
CARTE DE L'EMPIRE FRANCOIS AVEC SES ETABLISSEMENTS POLITIQUES, ...	DEPOT GEN. GUERRE	65 x 103 cm
CARTE DE L'ENTREE DE LA TAMISE AVEC LES BANCS, PASSES, ISLES ...	JAILLOT	46 x 91 cm
CARTE DE L'ENTREE DE NORTON ET DU DETROIT DE BHERING OU L'ON VOIT ...	COOK	28 x 38 cm
CARTE DE L'ENTREE DU GOLFE DE LA MER ROUGE	D'APRES DE MANNEVIL.	34 x 49 cm
CARTE DE L'ENTREE DU RIO NUNEZ ...	DEPOT DE LA MARINE	89 x 61 cm
CARTE DE L'HEMISPHERE AUSTRAL ...	BELLIN (Large)	54 x 54 cm
CARTE DE L'HEMISPHERE AUSTRALE MONTRANT LES ROUTES DES NAVIGAT ...	LA HARPE	53 x 53 cm
CARTE DE L'ILE DE LA JAMAIQUE EXTRAITE DES CARTES TOPOGRAPHIQUES ...	DEPOT DE LA MARINE	58 x 86 cm
CARTE DE L'ILE DE MARTHA'S VINEYARD ...	DE CREVECOEUR	23 x 25 cm
CARTE DE L'ILE DE NANTUCKET POUR LES LETTRES D'UN CULTIVATEUR AMER. ...	DE CREVECOEUR	20 x 28 cm

CARTE DE L'INDE ... DE SIAM, DE TUNQUIN, PEGU, AVA, ARACAN ETC ...	BELLIN (Small)	28 x 28 cm
CARTE DE L'INDE DRESSEE POUR LA COMPAGNIE DES INDES PAR LE SR. ...	D'ANVILLE	89 x 107 cm
CARTE DE L'ISLE D'ORLEANS ET DU PASSAGE DE LA TRAVERSE DANS LE ...	BELLIN (Small)	19 x 28 cm
CARTE DE L'ISLE DE CEYLON ...	BELLIN (Small)	26 x 25 cm
CARTE DE L'ISLE DE JAVA ...	CHATELAIN	38 x 87 cm
CARTE DE L'ISLE DE LA GRENADE ...	BELLIN (Large)	89 x 56 cm
CARTE DE L'ISLE DE LA JAMAIQUE	BELLIN (Small)	20 x 31 cm
CARTE DE L'ISLE DE LA JAMAIQUE	BONNE	23 x 36 cm
CARTE DE L'ISLE DE LA MARTINIQUE, COLONIE FRANCOISE DANS LES ISLES...	BONNE	36 x 23 cm
CARTE DE L'ISLE DE LA MARTINIQUE COLONIE FRANCOISE DE L'UNE DES ISLES	BUACHE	47 x 61 cm
CARTE DE L'ISLE DE LA MARTINIQUE DRESSEE PAR MR. BELLIN ...	HOMANN	48 x 56 cm
CARTE DE L'ISLE DE PORTSEY, ET HAVRE DE PORTSMOUTH	BELLIN (Small)	21 x 15 cm
CARTE DE L'ISLE DE SAINTE LUCIE ...	BELLIN (Large)	89 x 57 cm
CARTE DE L'ISLE DE ST. DOMINGUE UNE DES GRANDES ANTILLES, COLONIE...	BONNE	23 x 36 cm
CARTE DE L'ISLE ST. CHRISTOPHE ...	BELLIN (Small)	19 x 31 cm
CARTE DE L'ISTHME DE DARIEN ET DU GOLFE DE PANAMA	DAMPIER	18 x 15 cm
CARTE DE L'ITALIE	DE VAUGONDY	47 x 53 cm
CARTE DE L'OCEAN PACIFIQUE AU NORD DE L'EQUATEUR, ET DES COTES ...	LOTTER	46 x 51 cm
CARTE DE L'OCEANIE COMPRENANT L'AUSTRALIE, LA POLYNESIE ...	HERISSON	53 x 76 cm
CARTE DE LA BAIE DE CHESAPEAKE ...	DEPOT DE LA MARINE	58 x 86 cm
CARTE DE LA BAIE DE HUDSON	BELLIN (Small)	22 x 30 cm
CARTE DE LA BARBARIE DE LA NIGRITIE ET DE LA GUINEE	DE L'ISLE	48 x 64 cm
CARTE DE LA BAYE DE CAMPECHE	DAMPIER	15 x 27 cm
CARTE DE LA BAYE DE CHESAPEACK; ...	BELLIN (Small)	19 x 29 cm
CARTE DE LA BAYE DE CHESAPEAK ET PAYS VOISINS	BELLIN (Small)	28 x 38 cm
CARTE DE LA BAYE DE HUDSON	BELLIN (Small)	23 x 30 cm
CARTE DE LA BAYE DE MOSAMBIQUE	BELLIN (Small)	21 x 16 cm
CARTE DE LA CALIFORNIA SUIVANT I. CARTE MANUSCRIT 1604; II. SANSON ...	DE VAUGONDY	28 x 38 cm
CARTE DE LA CALIFORNIE ET DES PAYS NORD-OUEST SEPARE'S DE L'ASIE ...	DE VAUGONDY	28 x 36 cm
CARTE DE LA CAROLINE ET GEORGIE	BELLIN (Small)	18 x 29 cm
CARTE DE LA CAYQUE DE L'OUEST, ET PARTIE DE CELLE DU NORD	BELLIN (Small)	(no dimens.)
CARTE DE LA COSTE D'ARABIE, MER ROUGE, ET GOLFE DE PERSE	BELLIN (Small)	22 x 25 cm
CARTE DE LA COSTE ORIENTALE D'AFRIQUE DEPUIS LE CAP DE BONNE ESPER.	VAN DER SCHLEY	25 x 23 cm
CARTE DE LA COTE N.O. D'AMERIQUE ET DE LA COTE N.E. D'ASIE ...	MEARES	42 x 61 cm
CARTE DE LA COTE N.O. DE L'AMERIQUE ET DE LA COTE N.E. DE L'ASIE, ...	BENARD	39 x 66 cm
CARTE DE LA COTE OCCIDENTALE DE L'ISLE SUMATRA DEPUIS LA LIGNE EQUI.	D'APRES DE MANNEVIL.	66 x 48 cm
CARTE DE LA FLORIDE DE LA LOUISIANE	BELLIN (Small)	22 x 30 cm
CARTE DE LA FLORIDE, DE LA LOUISIANE ET PAYS VOISINS. POUR SERVIR ...	BELLIN (Small)	25 x 33 cm
CARTE DE LA FRANCE DIVISEE EN PREFECTURES ET SOUS PREFECTURES, ...	POIRSON	77 x 92 cm
CARTE DE LA LOUISIANE ET DE LA FLORIDE	BONNE	41 x 23 cm
CARTE DE LA LOUISIANE ET DE LA FLORIDE	BONNE	33 x 23 cm
CARTE DE LA LOUISIANE ET PAYS VOISINS ...	BELLIN (Small)	22 x 30 cm
CARTE DE LA NOUVELLE ANGLETERRE, NOUVELLE YORCK ET PENSILVANIE	BELLIN (Small)	21 x 30 cm
CARTE DE LA NOUVELLE FRANCE OU SE VOIT LE COURS DES GRANDE RIVIERES	ANONYMOUS	50 x 550 cm
CARTE DE LA NOUVELLE FRANCE OU SE VOIT LE COURS DES GRANDES RIV. ...	OTTENS	50 x 55 cm
CARTE DE LA NOUVELLE GEORGIE	BELLIN (Small)	21 x 15 cm
CARTE DE LA PALESTINE SOUS LA DOMINATION ROMAINE ...	BRUE	51 x 36 cm
CARTE DE LA PARTIE INFERIEURE DE L'INDE	BONNE	21 x 32 cm
CARTE DE LA PARTIE NORD, DES ETATS UNIS, DE L'AMERIQUE SEPTENTRIONALE	BONNE	20 x 36 cm
CARTE DE LA PARTIE OCCIDENTALE D'INAGUE ...	BELLIN (Small)	(no dimens.)
CARTE DE LA PARTIE SEPTENTRIONALE DE L'EMPIRE OTOMAN ...	RIZZI ZANNONI	72 x 155 cm
CARTE DE LA PARTIE SUD DES ETATS UNIS DE L'AMERIQUE SEPTENTRIONALE	BONNE	23 x 41 cm
CARTE DE LA RIVIERE DE COOK, DANS LA PARTIE N.O. DE L'AMERIQUE	COOK	23 x 30 cm
CARTE DE LA SIBERIE ET DES PAYS VOISINS	BELLIN (Small)	30 x 46 cm
CARTE DE LA TARTARIE INDEPENDANTE QUI COMPREND LE PAYS DES ...	BONNE	30 x 46 cm
CARTE DE LA VIRGINIE	DU VAL (Small)	10 x 13 cm
CARTE DE LA VIRGINIE ET DU MARYLAND DRESSEE SUR LA GRANDE CARTE ...	DE VAUGONDY	48 x 64 cm
CARTE DE LA VIRGINIE MARI-LAND &A. TIREE DES MEILLEURES CARTES ANG. ...	BELLIN (Small)	8 x 12 cm
CARTE DE LAC DE MEXICO ET DE SES ENVIRONS LORS DE LA CONQUETE	BELLIN (Small)	23 x 15 cm
CARTE DE MOSCOVIE...	DE L'ISLE	99 x 66 cm
CARTE DE PHASES DE L'ECLIPSE DU 1 AVRIL 1764 ET DE TOUS LES PAYS ...	ANONYMOUS	33 x 33 cm
CARTE DE TARTARIE DRESSEE SUR LES RELATIONS DE PLUSIERS VOYAGEURS ...	DE L'ISLE	48 x 64 cm
CARTE DES ANTILLES	TARDIEU	33 x 43 cm
CARTE DES ANTILLES FRANCOISES ET DES ISLES VOISINES DRESSEE SUR ...	CHATELAIN	48 x 33 cm
CARTE DES BAYES DU MESLE DES FLAMANDS ET DE CAVAILLON ...	BELLIN (Small)	23 x 36 cm
CARTE DES BAYES, RADES ET PORT DE PLAISANCE DANS L'ISLE DE TERRE	BELLIN (Small)	20 x 29 cm
CARTE DES COSTES DE L'ASIE SUR L'OCEAN CONTENANT LES BANCS ...	MORTIER	58 x 86 cm
CARTE DES COSTES DE LA FLORIDE FRANCOISE ...	BELLIN (Small)	21 x 14 cm

CARTE DES COTES DE BARBARE COMPRENANT LES ETATS DE MAROC, FEZ, ...	PIQUET	62 x 92 cm
CARTE DES DEBOUQUEMENS DE ST. DOMINGUE	BELLIN (Small)	(no dimens.)
CARTE DES DECOUVERTES ... LA MER PACIFIQUE ... PAR LE CAPTAINE COOK	LA HARPE	36 x 46 cm
CARTE DES DEUX AMERIQUES, AVEC LEURS NOUVELLES DIVISIONS ...	TARDIEU	51 x 70 cm
CARTE DES EMBOUCHURES DU MISSISSIPI ... PAR N.B. INGR. DE LA MARINE ...	BELLIN (Small)	20 x 29 cm
CARTE DES ETATS-UNIS D'AMERIQUE ...	LAPIE	51 x 76 cm
CARTE DES ETATS-UNIS D'AMERIQUE COMPRENANT UNE PARTIE DES DIST. ...	ANDRIVEAU-GOUJON	38 x 51 cm
CARTE DES ETATS-UNIS DU MEXIQUE	LAPIE	55 x 40 cm
CARTE DES FONDS BLANCS ET RESCIF ENTRE LA PETITE CAYQUE ET FRANC- ...	BELLIN (Small)	(no dimens.)
CARTE DES GOUVERNMENTS D'ANJOU ET DE SAUMUROIS, DE LA TOURRAINE ...	LATTRE	41 x 30 cm
CARTE DES GOUVERNMENTS DE BOURGOGNE, DE FRANCHE COMTE ET DE ...	LATTRE	41 x 30 cm
CARTE DES ISLES A L'EST DES ISLES TURQUES	BELLIN (Small)	(no dimens.)
CARTE DES ISLES ANTILLES ET DU GOLFE DU MEXIQUE; ...	BONNE	66 x 145 cm
CARTE DES ISLES CANARIES	BELLIN (Small)	20 x 28 cm
CARTE DES ISLES CAP VERD	BELLIN (Small)	21 x 28 cm
CARTE DES ISLES D'AKLIN DE LA FORTUNE DE KROO-KED	BELLIN (Small)	(no dimens.)
CARTE DES ISLES DE JAVA, SUMATRA, BORNEO &C. ...	BELLIN (Small)	25 x 29 cm
CARTE DES ISLES DE LA SOCIETE	BONNE	23 x 36 cm
CARTE DES ISLES DU CAP VERD	BELLIN (Small)	21 x 28 cm
CARTE DES ISLES DU JAPON ...	TAVERNIER	22 x 33 cm
CARTE DES ISLES ET DANGERS SITUES AU NORD-EST DE L'ISLE MADAGASCAR...	D'APRES DE MANNEVIL.	34 x 50 cm
CARTE DES ISLES KOURILES ...	BELLIN (Small)	24 x 26 cm
CARTE DES ISLES KOURILES D'APRES LA CARTE RUSSE	LA HARPE	24 x 27 cm
CARTE DES ISLES NICOBAR ...	D'APRES DE MANNEVIL.	46 x 30 cm
CARTE DES ISLES PHILIPPINES	BELLIN (Small)	21 x 30 cm
CARTE DES ISLES TURQUES	BELLIN (Small)	(no dimens.)
CARTE DES LACS DU CANADA...	BELLIN (Small)	20 x 29 cm
CARTE DES LACS DU CANADA ... SUR LE JOURNAL DU RP. DE CHARLEVOIX	BELLIN (Large)	30 x 46 cm
CARTE DES LIEUX ON LES DIFFERENT LONGEURS DE PENDULE / CARTE DU ...	BUACHE	51 x 66 cm
CARTE DES OBSERVATIONS ... SUR LA CAYE D'ARGENT	BELLIN (Small)	(no dimens.)
CARTE DES PARTIES DU NORD-OUEST DE L'AMERIQUE SUIVANT LES VOYAGES ...	BELLIN (Small)	21 x 27 cm
CARTE DES PARTIES NORD ET OUEST DE L'AMERIQUE DRESSE D'APRES LES ...	DE VAUGONDY	30 x 38 cm
CARTE DES POSSESSIONS ANGLOISES & FRANCOISES DU CONTINENT ...	OTTENS	41 x 58 cm
CARTE DES POSSESSIONS ANGLOISES & FRANCOISES DU CONTINENT ...	PALAIRET	41 x 58 cm
CARTE DES ROUTES DE POSTES DE L'EMPIRE FRANCAIS, DU ROYAUME D'ITAL. ...	TARDIEU	(various dim.)
CARTE DES TROUBLES DE L'AMERIQUE LEVEE PAR ORDRE DU CHEVALIER ...	LE ROUGE	71 x 51 cm
CARTE DES VARIATIONS DE LA BOUSSOLE ET DES VENTS GENERAUX ...	BELLIN (Large)	56 x 86 cm
CARTE DES VOYAGES DE MR. TAVERNIER, DANS LES INDES, ...	DESBRUSLINS	22 x 30 cm
CARTE DES VOYAGES DE NOTRE SEIGNEUR ET CEUX DES APOSTRES ST. PIERRE	DE VAUGONDY	46 x 58 cm
CARTE DU BRESIL PREM. PARTIE DEPUIS LA RIVIERE DES AMAZONES JUSQU'A ...	BELLIN (Small)	24 x 32 cm
CARTE DU CANADA, DE LA LOUISIANE ...	D'ANVILLE	48 x 66 cm
CARTE DU CANADA OU DE LA NOUVELLE FRANCE, & DES DECOUVERTES ...	CHATELAIN	40 x 52 cm
CARTE DU CANADA OU DE LA NOUVELLE FRANCE ET DES DECOUVERTES ...	DE L'ISLE	50 x 65 cm
CARTE DU COURS DE FLEUVE DE ST. LAURENT DEPUIS QUEBEC ... LAC ONT. ...	BELLIN (Small)	19 x 28 cm
CARTE DU COURS DU FLEUVE DE ST. LAURENT DEPUIS SON EMBOUCHURE ...	BELLIN (Small)	19 x 29 cm
CARTE DU COURS FLEUVE DE SAINT LAURENT...	BELLIN (Large)	57 x 86 cm
CARTE DU DEBOUQUEMENT DE KROO-KED-ISLAND	BELLIN (Small)	(no dimens.)
CARTE DU GOLFE DU MEXIQUE ...	TARDIEU	41 x 56 cm
CARTE DU GOLFE PERSIQUE DEPUIS BASSORA JUSQU'AU CAP RASALGATE	D'APRES DE MANNEVIL.	49 x 67 cm
CARTE DU GOLPHE DE ST. LAURENT ET PAYS VOISINS ...	BELLIN (Small)	22 x 37 cm
CARTE DU GOLPHE DU MEXIQUE ET DES ISLES DE L'AMERIQUE	BELLIN (Small)	27 x 37 cm
CARTE DU GRAND DUCHE DE LITUANIAE ...	HOMANN	48 x 53 cm
CARTE DU JAPON ET DE LA COREE	LE ROUGE	20 x 28 cm
CARTE DU MEXIQUE	BELLIN (Small)	20 x 29 cm
CARTE DU MEXIQUE ET DE LA FLORIDE DES TERRES ANGLOISES ET DES ISLES ...	DE L'ISLE	20 x 24 cm
CARTE DU MEXIQUE ET DES PAYS LIMITROPHES	POIRSON	43 x 74 cm
CARTE DU PARAGUAY DU CHILI DU DETROIT DE MAGELLAN &C. ...	DE L'ISLE	51 x 64 cm
CARTE DU PARAGUAY ET DES PAYS VOISINS	BELLIN (Small)	20 x 31 cm
CARTE DU PLACET DES CAYQUES	BELLIN (Small)	(no dimens.)
CARTE DU PLAN DU VENISE, L'ETAT DE SA NOBLESSE, ...	CHATELAIN	38 x 48 cm
CARTE DU SPITS-BERG	BELLIN (Small)	22 x 30 cm
CARTE DU TERRITOIRE D'ARKANSAS ET DES AUTRES TERRITOIRES ...	BUCHON	48 x 61 cm
CARTE GENERAL [Eastern Hemisphere]	MALLET	15 x 10 cm
CARTE GENERALE D L'ASIE	BRUE	36 x 51 cm
CARTE GENERALE DE LA CHINE	D'ANVILLE	61 x 51 cm
CARTE GENERALE DE LA MARTINIQUE POUR LA TOPOGRAPHIE ...	DEPOT DE LA MARINE	91 x 64 cm
CARTE GENERALE DE TOUTES LES PARTIES CONNUES DE LA SURFACE ...	BONNE	25 x 36 cm
CARTE GENERALE DELL' OCEANIA	MARZOLLA	42 x 51 cm

CARTE GENERALE DES COSTES D'IRELANDE ET DES COSTES OCCIDENTALES ...	BELLIN (Large)	61 x 88 cm
CARTE GENERALE DES ETATS DE VIRGINIE, MARYLAND, DELAWARE, ...	DE CREVECOEUR	48 x 65 cm
CARTE GENERALE DES ETATS-UNIS DE L'AMERIQUE SEPTENTRIONALE, ...	TARDIEU	33 x 43 cm
CARTE GENERALE DES ILES ANTILLES DES ISLES ET BANCS DE BAHAMA, ...	BRUE	64 x 94 cm
CARTE GENERALE DES INDES EN-DECA ET AU-DELA DE GANGE	BRUE	36 x 51 cm
CARTE GENERALE DES INDES ORIENTALES ...	MARIETTE	38 x 48 cm
CARTE GENERALE DES ROYAUMES D'ESPAGNE & DE PORTUGAL AVEC LEUR ...	HUSSON	48 x 56 cm
CARTE GENERALE DU CANADA EN PETIT POINT	LA HONTAN	10 x 15 cm
CARTE GENERALE DU MEXIQUE ET DES PROVINCES-UNIES DE L'AMERIQUE CENT.	VIVIEN	30 x 41 cm
CARTE GEOGRAPHIQUE, STATISTIQUE ET HISTORIQUE DE L'AMERIQUE	BUCHON	48 x 64 cm
CARTE GEOGRAPHIQUE, STATISTIQUE ET HISTORIQUE DE L'INDIANA	BUCHON	28 x 23 cm
CARTE GEOGRAPHIQUE, STATISTIQUE ET HISTORIQUE DE LA JAMAIQUE	BUCHON	46 x 61 cm
CARTE GEOGRAPHIQUE, STATISTIQUE ET HISTORIQUE DE LA MARTINIQUE	BUCHON	47 x 61 cm
CARTE GEOGRAPHIQUE, STATISTIQUE ET HISTORIQUE DU KENTUCKY	BUCHON	28 x 46 cm
CARTE GEOGRAPHIQUE, STATISTIQUE ET HISTORIQUE DU NEW-YORK	BUCHON	47 x 62 cm
CARTE GEOGRAPHIQUE, STATISTIQUE ET HISTORIQUE DU VERMONT	BUCHON	46 x 61 cm
CARTE HYDROGRAPHIQUE & CHOROGRAPHIQUE DES ISLES PHILIPPINES	HOMANN	97 x 55 cm
CARTE HYDROGRAPHIQUE DE LA RIVIERE DE LA PLATA ...	BELLIN (Small)	41 x 56 cm
CARTE HYDROGRAPHIQUE DES PARTIES CONNUES DU GLOBE, ENTRE LE ...	BEAUTEMPS-BEAUPRE	38 x 76 cm
CARTE NOUVELLE DE L'AMERIQUE ANGLOISE CONTENANT LA VIRGINIE, ...	MORTIER	60 x 91 cm
CARTE NOUVELLE DE L'AMERIQUE ANGLOISE CONTENANT TOUT CE QUE ...	LOTTER	60 x 49 cm
CARTE NOUVELLE DE LA GRANDE TARTARIE OU DE L'EMPIRE DU GRAND CHAM	CHATELAIN	41 x 51 cm
CARTE NOUVELLE DE MOSCOVIE REPRESENTE LA PARTIE SEPTENTRIONALE	OTTENS	41 x 56 cm
CARTE NOUVELLE ET EXACTE DE LA GAULE CISALPINE ET SUR TOUT DE LA ...	VAN DER AA	33 x 41 cm
CARTE PARTICULIERE A TOUTE NOUVELLE DE MILIANOIS, AVEC TOUS ...	VAN DER AA	36 x 43 cm
CARTE PARTICULIERE DE CANAL DE BRISTOL ...	DEPOT DE LA MARINE	57 x 89 cm
CARTE PARTICULIERE DE L'AMERIQUE SEPTENTRIONALE OU SONT COMPRIS ...	MORTIER	58 x 84 cm
CARTE PARTICULIERE DE LA COTE DU NORD-OUEST DE L'AMERIQUE RECONNUE	LA PEROUSE	51 x 69 cm
CARTE PARTICULIERE DU FLEUVE SAINT LOUIS ...	CHATELAIN	28 x 33 cm
CARTE PHYSIQUE ET ROUTIERE DE L'ITALIE INDIQUANT LES DISTANCES ...	ANDRIVEAU-GOUJON	121 x 96 cm
CARTE PLATE QUI COMPREND L'ISLE DE CEYLON ET UNE PARTIE DES COTES ...	D'APRES DE MANNEVIL.	48 x 67 cm
CARTE POUR ALLER DU DETROIT DE LA SONDE OU DE BATAVIA AU DETROIT ...	D'APRES DE MANNEVIL.	69 x 51 cm
CARTE REDUITE D'UNE PARTIE DES COSTES OCCIDENTALES ET ... DE L'AFRIQUE	BELLIN (Large)	89 x 55 cm
CARTE REDUITE DE L'ISLE DE SAINT DOMINGUE ET DE SES DEBOUQUEMENTS...	BELLIN (Large)	56 x 90 cm
CARTE REDUITE DE L'OCEAN MERIDIONALE...	DEPOT DE LA MARINE	62 x 78 cm
CARTE REDUITE DE L'OCEAN MERIDIONALE ... LES COSTES DE L'AMERIQUE ...	DEPOT DE LA MARINE	55 x 88 cm
CARTE REDUITE DE L'OCEAN ORIENTAL OU MER DES INDES ...	BELLIN (Large)	61 x 79 cm
CARTE REDUITE DES COSTES OCCIDENTALES D'AFRIQUE	BELLIN (Large)	89 x 55 cm
CARTE REDUITE DES COSTES ORIENTALES DE L'AMERIQUE SEPTENTRIONALE. ...	BELLIN (Large)	51 x 84 cm
CARTE REDUITE DES COTES ET DU GOLFE DE CALIFORNIE DEPUIS LE CAP ...	DEPOT DE LA MARINE	84 x 57 cm
CARTE REDUITE DES COTES ORIENTALES DE L'AMERIQUE SEPTENTRIONALE ...	DEPOT DE LA MARINE	61 x 86 cm
CARTE REDUITE DES DEBOUQUEMENS DE ST. DOMINGUE DRESSEE POUR ...	BELLIN (Large)	58 x 91 cm
CARTE REDUITE DES ISLES ANTILLES ...	BELLIN (Large)	89 x 57 cm
CARTE REDUITE DES ISLES PHILIPPINES ...	BELLIN (Large)	55 x 88 cm
CARTE REDUITE DES MERS DU NORD	BELLIN (Small)	33 x 44 cm
CARTE REDUITE DES PARTIES SEPTENTRIONALES DU GLOBE, SITUEES ENTRE ...	BELLIN (Small)	21 x 34 cm
CARTE REDUITE DES TERRES ET DES MERS DU GLOBE TERRESTRE	BONNE	23 x 33 cm
CARTE REDUITE DU GOLPHE DU MEXIQUE ET DES ISLES DE L'AMERIQUE	BELLIN (Small)	20 x 30 cm
CARTE TOPOGRAPHIQUE DES ENVIRONS DE PARIS	MAIRE, N.	64 x 91 cm
CARTES POUR SERVIR A L'HISTOIRE DE LA NOUVELLE FRANCE OU DU CANADA ...	DUSSIEUX	20 x 30 cm
CARTHAGINIS CELEBERRIM SINUS TYPUS PORTUS	ORTELIUS (Miniature)	8 x 11 cm
CARY'S NEW TERRESTRIAL GLOBE, ... [and] CELESTIAL GLOBE ...	CARY	30 cm, diam
CARY'S REDUCTION OF HIS LARGE MAP OF ENGLAND AND WALES, ...	CARY	75 x 62 cm
CELCUT NUOVA TAVOLA	PTOLEMY (1561-1599)	19 x 25 cm
CENTRAL AMERICA	TALLIS	26 x 33 cm
CENTRAL ASIA; COMPRISING BOKHARA, CABOOL, PERSIA. THE RIVER INDUS ...	ARROWSMITH	48 x 72 cm
CENTRAL STATES	STEBBINS, H.	38 x 66 cm
CERCLE DE LA HAUTE SAXE	VAN DER AA	23 x 30 cm
CETTE CARTE DE CALIFORNIE ET DU NOUVEAU MEXIQUE EST TIREE ...	DE FER (Small)	23 x 34 cm
CEYLON ET LES MALDIVES	SANSON (Small)	18 x 24 cm
CHAMPAGNE COMITATUS CAMPANIA	HONDIUS	38 x 50 cm
CHAMPAGNE COMITATUS CAMPANIA	MERCATOR (Folio)	38 x 51 cm
CHAPMAN'S NEW SECTIONAL MAP OF MINNESOTA	CHAPMAN	81 x 64 cm
CHAPMAN'S SECTIONAL MAP OF THE STATE OF IOWA	CHAPMAN	69 x 107 cm
CHARLESTON	LADIES REPOSITORY	13 x 20 cm
CHARLESTON HARBOUR	BLUNT	18 x 10 cm
CHARLESTON HARBOUR ... ONE OF THE MOST COMMODIOUS PORTS ...	LUFFMAN	18 x 13 cm
CHART FOR THE JOURNAL OF MR. LE MARQUIS DE CHASTELLUX ...	DE CHASTELLUX	18 x 25 cm

CHART OF BEHRING'S STRAIT UPON MERCATOR'S PROJECTION ...	VON KOTZEBUE	20 x 20 cm
CHART OF BOSTON HARBOR AND MASSACHUSETTS BAY. WITH MAP OF ...	DUTTON & CO.	63 x 49 cm
CHART OF COOKS RIVER IN THE N.W. PART OF AMERICA	COOK	25 x 41 cm
CHART OF DETROIT RIVER FROM LAKE ERIE TO LAKE ST. CLAIR, SURVEYED ...	U.S. WAR DEPT.	107 x 76 cm
CHART OF ISOTHERMAL LINES SHEWING THE MEAN ANNUAL TEMP. ...	BLACK	28 x 38 cm
CHART OF NECKER ISLAND	LA PEROUSE	39 x 50 cm
CHART OF NORTON SOUND AND OF BHERINGS STRAIT MADE BY THE EAST ...	COOK	30 x 41 cm
CHART OF NORTON SOUND AND OF BHERINGS STRAIT MADE BY THE EAST ...	HOGG	20 x 33 cm
CHART OF PART OF THE NORTH WEST COAST OF AMERICA EXPLORED BY ...	LA PEROUSE	51 x 38 cm
CHART OF PART OF THE SOUTH SEAS SHEWING THE TRACTS & DISCOVERIES ...	WHITCHURCH, W.	36 x 66 cm
CHART OF PORT ROYAL ENTRANCE, BEAUFORT BROAD AND CHECHESSEE ...	U.S. COAST SURVEY	84 x 56 cm
CHART OF ROMERLY MARCHES BETWEEN WASSAW AND OSSABAW SOUNDS ...	U.S. WAR DEPT.	30 x 46 cm
CHART OF SOME ISLANDS BETWEEN BORNEO AND BANCA ...	GREGORY	59 x 36 cm
CHART OF THAT PORTION OF LAKE ERIE IN THE VICINITY OF BUFFALO & ...	U.S. WAR DEPT.	61 x 94 cm
CHART OF THE ARCHIPELAGO OF NAVIGATORS DISCOVERED BY MR. ...	LA PEROUSE	39 x 49 cm
CHART OF THE COAST OF HAMPSHIRE FROM PORTSMOUTH TO SOUTHAMP. ...	FADEN	64 x 54 cm
CHART OF THE COAST OF SOUTH CAROLINA SHOWING THE LOCATION ...	U.S.	66 x 66 cm
CHART OF THE COASTS OF AMERICA & ASIA FROM CALIFORNIA TO MACAO ...	LA PEROUSE	38 x 49 cm
CHART OF THE DISCOVERIES MADE IN 1787 IN THE SEAS OF CHINA AND ...	LA PEROUSE	36 x 49 cm
CHART OF THE EAST INDIA ISLANDS, EXHIBITING THE SEVERAL PASSAGES ...	ARROWSMITH	125 x 188 cm
CHART OF THE GREAT PACIFIC OCEAN OR SOUTH SEA, TO ILLUSTRATE ...	LA PEROUSE	35 x 49 cm
CHART OF THE N.W. COAST OF AMERICA AND THE N.E. COAST OF ASIA, ...	FADEN	40 x 68 cm
CHART OF THE NORTH POLAR SEA	STANFORD	79 x 62 cm
CHART OF THE NORTH WEST COAST OF AMERICA EXPLORED BY THE BOUSSOLE	LA PEROUSE	38 x 49 cm
CHART OF THE NORTHWEST COAST OF AMERICA EXPLORED BY THE BOUSSOLE	ROBINSON	36 x 48 cm
CHART OF THE ROAD OF THE SIMPLON BETWEEN BRIGG AND DOMO D'OSSOLA	STIGER & CO.	24 x 51 cm
CHART OF THE SAVANNAH RIVER, GA. FROM SAVANNAH CITY TO TYBEE ...	U.S. WAR DEPT.	36 x 66 cm
CHART OF THE SOCIETY ISLES DISCOVERED BY LIEUT J. COOK 1769	COOK	30 x 43 cm
CHART OF THE TRACK OF THE DOLPHIN, TAMAR, SWALLOW & ENDEAVOR, ...	GENTLEMAN'S MAG.	26 x 64 cm
CHART OF THE VARIATIONS OF THE MAGNETIC NEEDLE FOR ALL THE KNOWN ...	NORIE	53 x 142 cm
CHART OF THE WEST COAST OF SUMATRA, FROM BENCOOLEN TO KEYSERS	SAYER & BENNETT	53 x 64 cm
CHART OF THE WEST INDIES AND SPANISH DOMINIONS IN NORTH AMERICA. ...	ARROWSMITH	61 x 143 cm
CHART OF VAN DIEMANS LAND	COOK	23 x 36 cm
CHART SHOWING LOCATION OF PROPOSED SHIP CANAL ACROSS CHARLESTON	U.S. WAR DEPT.	30 x 25 cm
CHARTE VOM HERZOGTHUM CLEVE WORAUF ZUGLEICH DAS FURSTENTHUM ...	HOMANN	45 x 56 cm
CHARTE VON AMERICA NACH DEN NEUESTEN MATERIALIEN ...	WEIMAR GEOGRAPH.	59 x 47 cm
CHARTE VON DEN VEREINIGTEN STAATEN VON NORD-AMERICA NEBST LOUIS. ...	WEIMAR GEOGRAPH.	47 x 68 cm
CHARTE VON NORD-AMERICA ...	WEIMAR GEOGRAPH.	59 x 53 cm
CHARTE VON NORD-AMERICA ...	WEIMAR GEOGRAPH.	43 x 30 cm
CHARTE VON RUSSISCH LITAUEN, WELCHE DIE VON POLEN AN RUSSLAND ...	HOMANN	56 x 46 cm
CHARTE VON WEST INDIEN ... VON F.L. GUSSEFELD	WEIMAR GEOGRAPH.	44 x 61 cm
CHERSONESI QUAE HODIE NATOLIA	CLUVER	20 x 26 cm
CHICAGO	GRAY	41 x 33 cm
CHICAGO	LADIES REPOSITORY	15 x 20 cm
CHICAGO	MITCHELL, S.A. (1860+)	56 x 38 cm
CHIHUAHUA IN NEW-MEXICO	MEYER	11 x 16 cm
CHILE, MAGELLAN-LAND, AND TERRA DEL FUEGO &C.	MOLL (Small)	16 x 18 cm
CHILE, MAITENCILLO TO HERRADURA	ADMIRALTY	62 x 47 cm
CHILI	HONDIUS	37 x 48 cm
CHILI	JANSSON	37 x 48 cm
CHILI AND LA PLATA	TALLIS	34 x 25 cm
CHINA	ARROWSMITH	52 x 68 cm
CHINA	DESILVER	36 x 41 cm
CHINA	HONDIUS	34 x 46 cm
CHINA	MERCATOR (Folio)	36 x 46 cm
CHINA	SPEED	9 x 12 cm
CHINA COMPILED FROM ORIGINAL SURVEYS & SKETCHES	WYLD	61 x 80 cm
CHINA DIVIDED INTO PROVINCES DRAWN FROM THE BEST AUTHORITIES	RUSSELL	39 x 45 cm
CHINA ... HIESHAN ISLES TO THE YANG-TSE-KIANG INCLUDING THE CHUSAN ...	ADMIRALTY	97 x 64 cm
CHINA REG-NUM	DE JODE	36 x 45 cm
CHINA VETERIBUS SINARUM REGIO	BLAEU	41 x 50 cm
CHINA VETERIBUS SINARUM REGIO (****)	JANSSON	41 x 50 cm
CHINA VETERIBUS SINARUM REGIO NUNC INCOLIS TAME DICTA	JANSSON	41 x 50 cm
CHINAE, OLIM SINARUM REGIONIS, NOVA DESCRIPTIO. AUCTORE ...	ORTELIUS (Folio)	37 x 47 cm
CHINCOTEAGUE INLET AND SHOALS IN THE VICINITY, SEA COAST OF VIR. ...	U.S. COAST SURVEY	36 x 43 cm
CHIRIQUI LAGOON	ADMIRALTY	64 x 94 cm
CHOROGRAPHIA TERRAE SANCTE	TIRINUS	33 x 83 cm
CHOROGRAPHIA TERRITORII NAUMBURGOCITIENSIS	HOMANN	49 x 58 cm

CHOROGRAPHIE DU CERCLE DE SOUABE	DE PRETOT	25 x 33 cm
CIRCULI FRANCONIAE PARS ORIENTALIS ET POTIOR ...	HOMANN	59 x 50 cm
CIRCULI SUEVIAE	HOMANN	52 x 58 cm
CIRCULI WESTPHALIAE	HOMANN	59 x 49 cm
CIRCULUS SAXONIAE INFERIORIS	HOMANN	49 x 58 cm
CIRCULUS SAXONIAE SUPERIORIS IN QUO DUCATUS & ELECTORATUS SAXONIAE	HOMANN	49 x 58 cm
CIRCULUS WESTPHALICUS, SIVE GERMANIAE INFERIORIS	JANSSON	41 x 54 cm
CIRCUMJACENT THE SOUTH POLE	S.D.U.K.	27 x 28 cm
CITY OF ALLENTOWN	WALLING & GRAY	28 x 38 cm
CITY OF CINCINNATI	GRAY	41 x 64 cm
CITY OF MONTREAL	PEOPLE'S ATLAS	25 x 33 cm
CITY OF NEW YORK	MITCHELL, S.A. (1859-)	41 x 33 cm
CITY OF NEW YORK	MORSE & BREESE	38 x 30 cm
CITY OF SAN FRANCISCO AND ITS VICINITY, CALIFORNIA	U.S. COAST SURVEY	61 x 89 cm
CITY OF SANTA FE	ANONYMOUS	13 x 25 cm
CITY OF SUPERIOR, WIS.	CRAM	33 x 48 cm
CITY OF WASHINGTON	MITCHELL, S.A. (1859-)	33 x 41 cm
CITY OF WASHINGTON	TANNER	33 x 41 cm
CIVITAS EXONIAE (VULGO EXCESTER) URBS PRIMARIA IN COMITATU DEVONIAE	BRAUN & HOGENBERG	33 x 36 cm
CLASON'S GUIDE MAP OF DENVER COLORADO	CLASON MAP CO.	48 x 61 cm
CLEVELAND	RAND, McNALLY	33 x 48 cm
CLEVELAND	WAITE	25 x 30 cm
CLIFTON [Mich.]	U.S. WAR DEPT.	20 x 20 cm
CLIMATOLOGICAL MAP OF OHIO SHOWING THE MEAN ANNUAL TEMP. ...	LLOYD	36 x 30 cm
CLIVIA DUCATUS ET RAVESTEIN DOMINIUM	JANSSON	38 x 50 cm
COAST CHART NO. 55 COAST OF SOUTH CAROLINA AND GEORGIA ...	U.S. COAST SURVEY	84 x 102 cm
COAST OF CHINA FROM HIE CHE-CHIN BAY TO SAN MOON BAY	WEEKLY DISPATCH	43 x 30 cm
COBSCOOK BAY, MAINE SURVEYED IN 1836 ...	U.S.	38 x 30 cm
COLLINS' STANDARD MAP OF LONDON	STANFORD	62 x 84 cm
COLONIENSIS ARCHIEPISCOPATUS	JANSSON	38 x 49 cm
COLONY OF NEW SOUTH WALES AND AUSTRALIA FELIX	JOHNSTON	51 x 64 cm
COLORADO	BRADLEY	43 x 56 cm
COLORADO	CENTURY ATLAS	28 x 38 cm
COLORADO	CRAM	23 x 30 cm
COLORADO	CRAM	36 x 51 cm
COLORADO	CRAM	43 x 56 cm
COLORADO	GRAY	33 x 41 cm
COLORADO	MITCHELL, S.A. (1860+)	30 x 37 cm
COLTON'S CALIFORNIA AND NEVADA	COLTON	74 x 43 cm
COLTON'S DELAWARE AND MARYLAND	COLTON	33 x 41 cm
COLTON'S INDIAN TERRITORY	COLTON	33 x 41 cm
COLTON'S INDIANA	COLTON	36 x 28 cm
COLTON'S KANSAS	COLTON	43 x 61 cm
COLTON'S KANSAS AND NEBRASKA	COLTON	43 x 66 cm
COLTON'S KENTUCKY AND TENNESSEE	COLTON	36 x 64 cm
COLTON'S LAKE SUPERIOR AND UPPER PENINSULA OF MICHIGAN	COLTON	43 x 64 cm
COLTON'S MAINE	COLTON	38 x 33 cm
COLTON'S MAP OF LAKE SUPERIOR AND THE UPPER PENINSULA OF MICH. ...	COLTON	43 x 64 cm
COLTON'S MAP OF NEW YORK	COLTON	51 x 51 cm
COLTON'S MAP OF PENNSYLVANIA	COLTON	36 x 46 cm
COLTON'S MAP OF THE TERRITORY OF ALASKA (RUSSIAN AMERICA) ...	COLTON	41 x 51 cm
COLTON'S MAP OF THE UNITED STATES OF AMERICA	COLTON	38 x 66 cm
COLTON'S MISSISSIPPI	COLTON	40 x 33 cm
COLTON'S NEBRASKA	COLTON	43 x 61 cm
COLTON'S NEW JERSEY	COLTON	51 x 36 cm
COLTON'S NEW MAP OF THE CITY AND COUNTRY OF NEW YORK ...	COLTON	69 x 134 cm
COLTON'S NEW MEXICO AND ARIZONA	COLTON	43 x 64 cm
COLTON'S NEW SECTIONAL MAP OF THE STATE OF ILLINOIS, COMPILED ...	COLTON	91 x 61 cm
COLTON'S OREGON, WASHINGTON AND IDAHO	COLTON	43 x 61 cm
COLTON'S PENNSYLVANIA	COLTON	33 x 41 cm
COLTON'S RAILROAD & TOWNSHIP MAP OF OHIO	COLTON	51 x 61 cm
COLTON'S TOWNSHIP MAP OF THE STATE OF IOWA	COLTON	41 x 56 cm
COLTON'S VERMONT	COLTON	40 x 33 cm
COLUMBIA, OR THE WESTERN HEMISPHERE	LAURIE & WHITTLE	60 cm, diam
COLUMBUS DER ERSTE ERFINDER DER NEWEN WELT	DE BRY	15 x 20 cm
COLUMBUS, FRANKLIN CO. [Ohio]	STEBBINS, H.	38 x 28 cm
COLUMBUS, FRANKLIN CO. [Ohio]	WALLING	30 x 28 cm
COMITATUS BENTHEIM ET STEINFURT	JANSSON	38 x 50 cm

COMITATUS FLANDRIA	MERCATOR (Small)	13 x 18 cm
COMITATUS FLANDRIAE	HOMANN	49 x 59 cm
COMITATUS LAGENIAE. THE COUNTIE OF LEINSTER	JANSSON	38 x 49 cm
COMITATUS LIMPURGENSIS	HOMANN	46 x 54 cm
COMITATUS MANSFELD	HOMANN	49 x 56 cm
COMITATUS MANSFELDIA	HONDIUS	39 x 51 cm
COMITATUS NAMUR	HOMANN	51 x 58 cm
COMITATUS PRINCIPALIS TIROLIS IN QUO EPISC. TRIDENTIN ET BRIXENSIS, ...	HOMANN	49 x 59 cm
COMITATUS SCHOENBURGENSIS	HOMANN	47 x 46 cm
COMITATUS WERTHEIMICI FINITIMARUMQUE REGIONUM NOVA ET EXACTA ...	JANSSON	38 x 50 cm
COMITATUUM OLDENBURG ET DELMENHORST	HOMANN	50 x 51 cm
CONGO	MALLET	14 x 10 cm
CONGO	MORDEN	10 x 12 cm
CONNECTICUT	CAREY	14 x 20 cm
CONNECTICUT	FINLEY	22 x 28 cm
CONNECTICUT	LEWIS & ARROWSMITH	20 x 25 cm
CONNECTICUT	LUCAS	25 x 30 cm
CONNECTICUT	MARSH, W. S.	18 x 25 cm
CONNECTICUT	MITCHELL, S.A. (1859-)	33 x 41 cm
CONNECTICUT	WAITE	25 x 33 cm
CONNECTICUT FROM THE BEST AUTHORITIES	REID	36 x 43 cm
CONNECTICUT. RHODE ISLAND. RAILROADS	RAND, McNALLY	33 x 51 cm
CONNECTICUT WESTERN RESERVE, INCLUDING THE COUNTIES OF ASHTABULA ...	WALLING	38 x 58 cm
CONSTANTINOPLE. STAMBOOL	S.D.U.K.	32 x 39 cm
CONTINENT ARCTIQUE	MALLET	15 x 11 cm
CONWAY HARBOUR - PORT AYLESBURY [Nova Scotia]	DES BARRES	53 x 69 cm
COQUET ROAD AND CHANNEL	ADMIRALTY	94 x 61 cm
CORONADO HEIGHTS SAND DIEGO COUNTY, CALIFORNIA	U.S. WAR DEPT.	33 x 51 cm
COSTAS D'ABEX D'AIAN ET DE ZANGUEBAR	MALLET	15 x 10 cm
COSTES ET RIVIERES DE VIRGINIE, DE MARILAND ET DE NOUVELLE ANGLETERRE	MICHAULT	19 x 25 cm
COTE NORD-OUEST DE L'AMERIQUE RECONNUE PAR LE CAPE. VANCOUVER. ...	VANCOUVER	76 x 61 cm
COTE ORIENTALE D'ANGLETERRE DEPUIS SOUTH FORELAND, JUSQU'A ...	DEPOT DE LA MARINE	60 x 91 cm
COTE ORIENTALE DE MADAGASCAR DEPUIS LA RIVIERE D'IVONDROU ...	D'APRES DE MANNEVIL.	48 x 33 cm
COUNTIES OF COOK, DUPAGE, KANE, KENDALL AND WILL [Ill.]	WARNER & BEERS	43 x 36 cm
COUNTY AND TOWNSHIP MAP DAKOTA	MITCHELL, S.A. (1860+)	38 x 30 cm
COUNTY AND TOWNSHIP MAP OF ARIZONA AND NEW MEXICO	MITCHELL, S.A. (1860+)	37 x 55 cm
COUNTY AND TOWNSHIP MAP OF THE STATES OF KANSAS AND NEBRASKA	MITCHELL, S.A. (1860+)	38 x 58 cm
COUNTY AND TOWNSHIP MAP OF THE STATES OF NEW HAMPSHIRE AND VER.	MITCHELL, S.A. (1860+)	48 x 30 cm
COUNTY AND TOWNSHIP OF MAP MONTANA, IDAHO AND WYOMING	MITCHELL, S.A. (1860+)	38 x 56 cm
COUNTY MAP OF CALIFORNIA	MITCHELL, S.A. (1860+)	35 x 27 cm
COUNTY MAP OF COLORADO, UTAH, NEW MEXICO, AND ARIZONA	LLOYD	41 x 36 cm
COUNTY MAP OF COLORADO, WYOMING, DAKOTA, MONTANA	MITCHELL, S.A. (1860+)	50 x 37 cm
COUNTY MAP OF GEORGIA AND ALABAMA	MITCHELL, S.A. (1860+)	23 x 30 cm
COUNTY MAP OF KANSAS, NEBRASKA, DAKOTA, AND MINNESOTA	LLOYD	43 x 36 cm
COUNTY MAP OF KENTUCKY & TENNESSEE	MITCHELL, S.A. (1860+)	33 x 51 cm
COUNTY MAP OF OHIO AND INDIANA	MITCHELL, S.A. (1860+)	30 x 36 cm
COUNTY MAP OF TEXAS	MITCHELL, S.A. (1860+)	30 x 36 cm
COUNTY MAP OF TEXAS	MITCHELL, S.A. (1860+)	26 x 34 cm
COUNTY MAP OF THE STATE OF CALIFORNIA	MITCHELL, S.A. (1860+)	54 x 36 cm
COUNTY MAP OF THE STATE OF ILLINOIS	MITCHELL, S.A. (1860+)	35 x 28 cm
COUNTY MAP OF THE STATE OF NEW YORK	MITCHELL, S.A. (1860+)	36 x 53 cm
COUNTY MAP OF THE STATE OF TEXAS, SHOWING ALSO PORTIONS OF ...	MITCHELL, S.A. (1860+)	37 x 54 cm
COUNTY MAP OF THE STATES OF GEORGIA AND ALABAMA	BRADLEY	30 x 53 cm
COUNTY MAP OF THE STATES OF GEORGIA AND ALABAMA	MITCHELL, S.A. (1860+)	35 x 54 cm
COUNTY MAP OF UTAH AND NEVADA	MITCHELL, S.A. (1860+)	29 x 36 cm
COUNTY MAP OF VIRGINIA AND WEST VIRGINIA	MITCHELL, S.A. (1860+)	30 x 36 cm
COUNTY, TOWNSHIP AND RAILROAD MAP OF THE STATE OF PENNSYLVANIA	BARNES	84 x 124 cm
COURS DU MISSISSIPI ET LA LOUISIANE	DE VAUGONDY	22 x 16 cm
COURSE OF THE RIVER MISSISSIPPI, FROM THE BALISE TO FORT CHARTRES; ...	SAYER	112 x 34 cm
COX'S TERRESTRIAL GLOBE [and] CELESTIAL GLOBE	COX	6 cm, diam
CRAM'S NEW SECTION MAP OF THE STATE OF MINNESOTA	CRAM	97 x 79 cm
CRETA IOUIS MAGNI, MEDIO IACET INSULA PONTO ...	ORTELIUS (Folio)	33 x 48 cm
CROSS'S LONDON GUIDE	CROSS, J.	43 x 68 cm
CRUCHLEY'S ENVIRONS OF LONDON EXTENDING THIRTY MILES ...	CRUCHLEY	88 x 90 cm
CRUCHLEY'S IMPROVED ENVIRONS OF LONDON	CRUCHLEY	57 x 57 cm
CRUCHLEY'S NEW PLAN OF LONDON SHEWING ALL THE NEW ...	CRUCHLEY	42 x 60 cm
CRUCHLEY'S NEW TRAVELLING MAP AND ITINERARY COMPRISING ...	CRUCHLEY	63 x 50 cm
CUBA	LUCAS	30 x 44 cm

CUBA INSUL / HISPANIOLA / HAVANA PORTUS / I.JAMAICA / I.S. IOANNIS / ...	MERCATOR (Small)	15 x 18 cm
CUBA INSULA ET IAMAICA	WYTFLIET	23 x 29 cm
CULIACANAE AMERICAE REGIONIS DESCRIPTIO ... [and] HISPANIOLAE, CUBAE, ...	ORTELIUS (Folio)	36 x 50 cm
CYPRI INSULA	MORDEN	15 x 13 cm
CYPRUS INS.	HONDIUS	35 x 49 cm
D.B. COOKE & CO.'S RAILWAY MAP OF THE UNITED STATES AND ...	COOKE	81 x 112 cm
D. BLEFKENIUS SCHEEPS-TOGT NA YSLAND EN GROENLAND ...	VAN DER AA	15 x 23 cm
DAKOTA	COLTON	40 x 32 cm
DAKOTA	GRAY	38 x 33 cm
DAKOTA AND WYOMING	COLTON	34 x 42 cm
DAKOTA [NORTHERN PORTION]	RAND, McNALLY	32 x 47 cm
DAMASCUS	BRAUN & HOGENBERG	33 x 36 cm
DAN	FULLER	24 x 31 cm
DANIAE, FRISIAE, GRONINGAE ET ORIENTALIS FRISIAE LITTORA	DE WIT	49 x 57 cm
DANIAE REGNU	MERCATOR (Folio)	38 x 44 cm
DANUBII FLUMINIS ... PARS INFIMA IN QUA TRANSYLVANIA, ...	HOMANN	48 x 58 cm
DARBY'S LONDON GUIDE	DARTON & CLARK	42 x 64 cm
DARIEN	ARROWSMITH	23 x 31 cm
DAS ANDER BUCH [ALLEGORICAL EUROPE]	MUNSTER	25 x 15 cm
DAS ERST GENERAL INHALTEND ... CIRCKEL DES GANTZEN ERDTRICH	MUNSTER	26 x 38 cm
DAVENPORT (IOWA)	MEYER	11 x 16 cm
DAVIES'S NEW MAP OF THE BRITISH METROPOLIS. THE BOUNDARIES ...	STANFORD	94 x 94 cm
DAYTON [Ohio]	STEBBINS, H.	36 x 43 cm
DE CUSTE VAN NOORWEGEN TUSSCHEN SCHAERSONDT EN ...	COLOM	38 x 53 cm
DE CUSTE VAN NOORWEGEN VAN BERGEN TOT STEMMESHEST ...	COLOM	38 x 52 cm
DE CUSTEN VAN ENGELANT TUSSCHEN DE TWEEN POINTEN VAN ...	JACOBSZ	43 x 53 cm
DE GELEGENHEYT VAN T'PARADYS ENDE T'LANDT CANAAN, ...	VISSCHER	30 x 48 cm
DE GELENGENTHEYT VAN'T PARADYS EN'T LANDT CANAAN	STOOPENDAAL	36 x 46 cm
DE LANDVOOGDY DER MOLUCCOS, MET DE AANGRENZENDE EYLANDEN	VAN KEULEN	46 x 58 cm
DE REEDE EN HAVEN VAN VERA CRUZ	TIRION	18 x 25 cm
DE RIVIER TYNE OF NEW CASTLE ...	VAN KEULEN	53 x 58 cm
DE-SCRIPTIO CHORO-GRAPHICA REG-NI CHI-NE	DE BRY	29 x 34 cm
DE STADT OSACCO	MONTANUS	26 x 69 cm
DE STADT ST. MARTIN	OGILBY	28 x 37 cm
DE TALAUTSE EYLANDEN	VAN KEULEN	46 x 28 cm
DELAWARE	BRADFORD	36 x 30 cm
DELAWARE	CAREY	19 x 14 cm
DELAWARE	FINLEY	29 x 22 cm
DELAWARE	LEWIS & ARROWSMITH	25 x 20 cm
DELAWARE	LUCAS	28 x 20 cm
DELAWARE	SCOTT	18 x 15 cm
DELAWARE AND CHESAPEAKE BAYS & SEA COAST FROM CAPE ...	U.S. COAST SURVEY	79 x 64 cm
DELAWARE AND MARY-LAND	BURR	28 x 33 cm
DELAWARE AND MARYLAND	COLTON	12 x 15 cm
DELAWARE, FROM THE BEST AUTHORITIES	CAREY	41 x 23 cm
DELINEATIO AC FINITIMA REGIO MAGNAE BRITTANIAE ... LONDINI ...	SEUTTER (Large)	51 x 58 cm
DELINEATIO CARTAE TRIUM NAVIGATIONUM PER BATAVOS, ...	DE BRY	38 x 28 cm
DELINEATIO GEOGRAPHICA GENERALIS, COMPREHENDENS VI. FOLIIS ...	HOMANN	45 x 54 cm
DELINEATIO GEOGRAPHICA ... VOGTLANDIAE	HOMANN	51 x 58 cm
DELINEATIO OMNIUM ORARUM TOTIUS AUSTRALIS PARTIS AMER. ...	VAN LINSCHOTEN	39 x 55 cm
DELTA OF THE MISSISSIPPI ...	U.S. WAR DEPT.	107 x 76 cm
DENBIGH SH.	MORDEN	9 x 6 cm
DENMARK	THOMSON	51 x 61 cm
DENMARK AND PART OF NORWAY	S.D.U.K.	40 x 31 cm
DENVER & RIO GRANDE RAILROAD SYSTEM	RAILROAD COMPANY	38 x 46 cm
DER RHEIN DIE MAASS UND MOSEL MIT DEN ANLIEGENDEN LANDERN ...	HOMANN	62 x 50 cm
DER STAAT MEXICO SONSTEN. THEMISTITAN	MUNSTER	18 x 15 cm
DER STATT ROM IN AFFER WELT BESANNE CONTRAFEHOUNG NACH ...	MUNSTER	28 x 36 cm
DES POSSESSIONS FRANCOISES AUJOURD-HUI SOUS ... ANGLOISES ...	CLOUET	33 x 56 cm
DESCRIPCION DE LAS YNDIAS DE MEDIODIA	DE HERRERA	22 x 29 cm
DESCRIPCION DE LAS YNDIAS OCCIDENTALIS	DE HERRERA	23 x 32 cm
DESCRIPCION DEL AUDIENCIA DE LOS CHARCAS	DE HERRERA	15 x 18 cm
DESCRIPCION DEL AUDIENCIA DE PANAMA	DE HERRERA	22 x 29 cm
DESCRIPCION DEL DESTIETO DEL AUDIENCA DE LIMA 11	DE BRY	15 x 23 cm
DESCRIPCION DEL DESTRICTO DE AUDIENCIA DE LA NEUEVA GALICIA	DE HERRERA	20 x 29 cm
DESCRIPTIO CHOROGRAPHICA REFNU CHINAE	DE BRY	29 x 34 cm
DESCRIPTIO CORSICAE INSULAE	JANSSON	34 x 23 cm
DESCRIPTIO PEREGRINATIONIS D. PAULI APOSTOLI...	ORTELIUS (Folio)	38 x 52 cm

DESCRIPTIO SARDINIAE INSULAE	JANSSON	35 x 23 cm
DESCRIPTIO SEU ICHNOGRAPHIA VETERIS URBIS HIERUSALEM ...	JOLY, J.	36 x 46 cm
DESCRIPTION DE LA COSTE SETENTRIONALE DE NOVA GUINEA ...	LE MAIRE	15 x 27 cm
DESCRIPTION DE SARDAIGNE	BERTIUS	9 x 13 cm
DESCRIPTION DEL DESTRICTO DEL AUDIENCIA DE NUEVA ESPANA 4	DE BRY	18 x 28 cm
DESCRIPTION DEL DESTRICTO DEL AUDIENCIA NUEVA ESPANA	DE HERRERA	15 x 28 cm
DESCRIPTION DU GOUVERNEMENT DE LA CAPPELLE	JANSSON	37 x 50 cm
DESCRITTIONE DELL'AFRICA E QUELLE DELL ISOLE CHE A LEI S. ASP. ...	PORRO	18 x 18 cm
DESCRITTIONE DELL'ISOLA D'INGHILTERRA	PORCACCHI	10 x 15 cm
DESCRITTIONE DELLA GRAN CITTA & ISOLA DEL TEMISTITAN	PORCACCHI	15 x 18 cm
DETROIT	PEOPLE'S ATLAS	25 x 30 cm
DETROIT DE MAGELLAN, TERRE ET ISLES MAGELLANIQUES, &C. ...	SANSON (Small)	19 x 24 cm
DI HUNGARIA ET TRANSILVANIA. TAVOLA NOVISSIMA	PTOLEMY (1561-1599)	15 x 20 cm
DIAGRAM OF THE PUBLIC SURVEYS IN IOWA	U.S. STATE SURVEYS	43 x 51 cm
DIAGRAM OF THE STATE OF ILLINOIS	U.S. STATE SURVEYS	61 x 36 cm
DIAGRAM OF THE SURVEYING DISTRICT SOUTH OF TENNESSEE. ...	U.S. STATE SURVEYS	64 x 41 cm
DIAGRAM OF THE SURVEYING DISTRICT SOUTH OF TENNESSEE. ...	U.S. STATE SURVEYS	43 x 28 cm
DIE AMERIKANISCHE STAATS-DOMANE (NATIONAL PARK) IM ... YELLOWSTONE	HAYDEN, F.	25 x 43 cm
DIE CARIBISCHEN INSULN IN NORD AMERICA - GUADALOUPE, MARTINIQUE ...	SCHREIBER	20 x 25 cm
DIE ENGLISCHE COLONIE-LAENDER AUF DEN INSULN VON AMERICA	HOMANN	50 x 59 cm
DIE GANTZE WELT IN EIN KLEBERBLAT BELCHES IST DER STADT HANNOVER / ...	BUNTING	25 x 36 cm
DIE GANTZE WELT IN EIN KLEBERBLAT / WELCHES IST DER STADT HANNOVER ...	BUNTING	26 x 36 cm
DIE GEGEND UM PRAG ODER DER ALTE PRAGER KREYS, ...	HOMANN	53 x 61 cm
DIE GRAFSCHAFT PYRMONT MIT DEN ... HANOVERISCHEN, BRAUNSCHWEIG ...	HOMANN	47 x 57 cm
DIE GROS-BRITANNISCHE COLONIE-LAENDER, IN NORD-AMERICA	HOMANN	51 x 56 cm
DIE INSEL HISPANIOLA	SCHROTER	18 x 30 cm
DIE NEUWEN INSELN ...	MUNSTER	25 x 36 cm
DIE NEWEN INSELN / SO HINDER HISPANIAM GEGEN ORIENT / BEY DEM LANDT ...	MUNSTER	33 x 36 cm
DIE NEWEN INSELN SO HINDER HISPANIEN GEGEN ORIENT BEY DEM LANDT INDIE	MUNSTER	25 x 33 cm
DIE STADT U. VESTUNG LUXEMBURG	HOMANN	52 x 60 cm
DIE VEREINIGTEN STAATEN VON NORD AMERIKA. XIV GEBIET MICHIGAN. ...	VON SCHLIEBEN	20 x 25 cm
DIE VEREINIGTEN STAATEN VON NORDAMERICA ...	WEIMAR GEOGRAPH.	38 x 50 cm
DIE VEREINIGTEN STAATEN VON NORDAMERICA NEBST CANADA ...	WEIMAR GEOGRAPH.	53 x 64 cm
DIE VEREINIGTEN STAATEN VON NORDAMERICA (OSTLICHER THEIL)	WEIMAR GEOGRAPH.	63 x 57 cm
DIEFERT SITUS ORBIS HYDROGRAPHORUM AB EO QUEM PTOLOMEUS POSIT	FRIES	29 x 46 cm
DISTRICT OF COLUMBIA	BRADFORD	25 x 19 cm
DISTRICT OF KASKASKIA	U.S.	36 x 23 cm
DOMINICA	LUCAS	30 x 22 cm
DOMINICA FROM AN ACTUAL SURVEY COMPLEATED IN THE YEAR 1773	JEFFERYS	64 x 48 cm
DREW'S NEW AND CORRECT PLAN OF THE CITIES OF LONDON AND WESTMIN. ...	DREW, J.	41 x 53 cm
DUBLIN	S.D.U.K.	32 x 40 cm
DUCATUS BRUNSUICENSIS	HONDIUS	40 x 50 cm
DUCATUS HOLSATIAE NOVA TABULA	JANSSON	38 x 51 cm
DUCATUS IULIACI & BERGENSIS TABULA GEOGRAPHICA, ... CLIVIAE & MEURSIAE	HOMANN	57 x 49 cm
DUCATUS LUNEBURGICI ET COMITATUS DANNEBERGENSIS	HOMANN	50 x 59 cm
DUCATUS LUXEMBURGI	HOMANN	49 x 59 cm
DUCATUS MEKLENBURGICI TABULA GENERALIS CONTINENS DUC. VANDALIAE ...	HOMANN	50 x 58 cm
DUCATUS SABAUDIAE PRINCIPATUS PEDEMONTIUM ET ... MONTISFERRATI	HOMANN	50 x 58 cm
DUCATUS SILESIAE GLOGANI VERA DELINEATIO	JANSSON	42 x 53 cm
DUCATUS SILESIAE GROTGANUS CUM DISTRICTU EPISCOPALI NISSENSI	JANSSON	40 x 51 cm
DUCATUS SILESIAE LIGNICIENSIS	HONDIUS	39 x 49 cm
DUCATUS SILESIAE TABULA GEOGRAPHICA GENERALIS	HOMANN	48 x 55 cm
DUCATUS STIRIAE	HOMANN	50 x 59 cm
DUCATUS WESTPHALIAE	HOMANN	48 x 57 cm
DUCATUS WURTEMBERGICI CUM...CIRCULI SUEVICI...MARCHIONATU BADNSI...	HOMANN	59 x 49 cm
DULAS BAY & HARBOUR [Wales]	MORRIS	18 x 23 cm
EAST CANADA AND NEW BRUNSWICK	TALLIS	25 x 33 cm
EAST COAST OF SOUTH AMERICA SHEET VI FROM THE RIO DE LA PLATA ...	ADMIRALTY	47 x 62 cm
EAST INDIA ARCHIPELAGO [Eastern Passages to China & Japan]	IMRAY	104 x 130 cm
EAST INDIA ARCHIPELAGO [Western route to China]	IMRAY	104 x 130 cm
EAST LOCH TARBERT	ADMIRALTY	66 x 94 cm
EASTER ISLAND, LATITUDE 27 Deg. 5' SO.	COOK	23 x 20 cm
EASTERN HEMISPHERE	S.D.U.K.	34 x 34 cm
EASTERN SIBERIA	S.D.U.K.	34 x 39 cm
EDENBURGUM, SCOTIAE METROPOLIS	BRAUN & HOGENBERG	34 x 45 cm
EDENIS SEU PARADISI TERRESTRIS SITUS	BOCHARTI	30 x 20 cm
EDINBURGH	S.D.U.K.	31 x 39 cm
EGITTO NUOVA TAVOLA	PTOLEMY (1561-1599)	18 x 25 cm

EGMONT HARBOR	DES BARRES	81 x 61 cm
EGYPT	S.D.U.K.	37 x 30 cm
EGYPTIAN SUDAN. THE NILE FROM METEMMA TO KHARTUM COMPILED ...	STANFORD	80 x 44 cm
EGYPTISCHE PIRAMIDEN	OGILBY	25 x 36 cm
EMBOUCHURES DU FLEUVE ST. LOUIS OU MISSISSIPPI 1763	BELLIN (Small)	23 x 18 cm
EMDEN & OLDENBORCH COMIT.	MERCATOR (Folio)	34 x 43 cm
EMISFERO TERRESTRE SETTENTRIONALE [with] EMISFERO ... MERIDIONALE	CASSINI	34 x 46 cm
EMPIRE D'ALLEMAGNE	DE FER (Small)	13 x 16 cm
EMPIRE DES ABYSSINS	MALLET	15 x 10 cm
EMPIRE DES ABYSSINS COMME IE EST PRESENTEMENT	MALLET	14 x 10 cm
EMPIRE OF JAPAN	S.D.U.K.	40 x 32 cm
ENGLAND AND WALES RAILWAY MAP	CHAPMAN & HALL	61 x 43 cm
ENGLAND, WALES, AND THE SOUTHERN PART OF SCOTLAND	COOPER, J.	78 x 63 cm
ENGLAND WEST COAST SHEET II PADSTOW TO THE BRISTOL CHANNEL	ADMIRALTY	64 x 46 cm
ENGLAND WEST COAST SHEET VI WALES NEW QUAY TO BARDSEY	ADMIRALTY	64 x 46 cm
ENGLAND WEST COAST SHEET VII WALES BARDSEY ISLAND TO POINT LYNUS	ADMIRALTY	64 x 46 cm
ENLARGED MAP OF BRITISH COLUMBIA AND VANCOUVER'S ISLAND ...	SWANSTON	10 x 15 cm
ENTRANCE OF SAVANNAH RIVER GEORGIA	U.S. COAST SURVEY	36 x 51 cm
ENTRANCE TO BRAZOS RIVER TEXAS	U.S. COAST SURVEY	41 x 46 cm
ENTRANCE TO BRAZOS RIVER TEXAS ... MAJ. S. MANSFEILD	U.S. WAR DEPT.	43 x 41 cm
ENTRANCE TO THE CHESAPEAKE BAY REDUCED FROM SURVEYS ...	BLUNT	19 x 21 cm
ENTRANCE TO THE RIVER HUMBER	ADMIRALTY	66 x 94 cm
ENTREE DE LA RIVIERE D'HUDSON ...	LE ROUGE	66 x 51 cm
ENVIRONS OF LONDON	SMITH, W. H.	72 x 83 cm
EPHRIAM VITULA EST EDOCTA AMANS TRITURARE	FULLER	28 x 34 cm
EPISCOPATUS HILDESIENSIS DESCRIPTIO NOVISSIMA AUTHORE IOANNE ...	JANSSON	41 x 45 cm
EPISCOPATUS PADERBORN NEC NON ABBATIAE CORVEI ... COMITATIBUS LIPPE...	HOMANN	46 x 48 cm
EPISCOPATUS PADERBORNENSIS DESCRIPTIO NOVA	JANSSON	38 x 49 cm
ERYN. HIBERNIAE, INSULAE, NOVA DESCRIPTIO. IRLANDT	ORTELIUS (Folio)	36 x 48 cm
ESPAGNE PAR N. DE FER	DE FER (Small)	14 x 16 cm
ESQUISSE D'UNE CARTE GEOLOGIQUE D'ITALIE	ANDRIVEAU-GOUJON	82 x 60 cm
ESQUISSE DES RIVIERES MUSKINGHUM ET GRAND CASTOR QUE J'AI TIREE DU ...	DE CREVECOEUR	25 x 53 cm
ESSAY D'UNE CARTE REDUITE CONTENANT LES PARTIES CONNUEES DU GLOBE	BELLIN (Large)	50 x 69 cm
ESTADOS UNIDOS D'AMERICA, TERRA NOVA, CANADA, LUIZIANA E FLORIDA	LOPEZ	24 x 21 cm
ESTATS DE LA COURONNE DE POLOGNE	DE FER (Small)	14 x 16 cm
ESTES-ROCKY MOUNTAIN NATIONAL PARK, REACHED VIA UNION PACIFIC ...	RAILROAD COMPANY	58 x 66 cm
ETATS UNIS DE L'AMERIQUE	BLONDEAU	18 x 20 cm
ETATS-UNIS DE L'AMERIQUE SEPTENTRIONALE ...	LAPIE	23 x 30 cm
ETATS-UNIS ET MEXIQUE	DUVOTENAY	36 x 43 cm
ETHNOLOGICAL MAP OF THE INDIAN TRIBES OF THE UNITED STATES ...	EASTMAN	23 x 30 cm
EUROP, AND THE CHIEFE CITIES CONTAYNED THEREIN ...	SPEED	38 x 51 cm
EUROPA. CARTA QUINTA. SECOA	DUDLEY	44 x 72 cm
EUROPA PRIMA NOVA TABULA	MUNSTER	27 x 33 cm
EUROPA PRIMA PARS TERRAE IN FORMA VIRGINIS	BUNTING	24 x 35 cm
EUROPA, SECUNDUM LEGITIMAS PROJECTIONIS ...	HOMANN	49 x 57 cm
EUROPAE	ORTELIUS (Folio)	34 x 46 cm
EUROPAE	ORTELIUS (Folio)	34 x 46 cm
EUROPAE TABULA	MUNSTER	28 x 33 cm
EUROPAE TABULA V	PTOLEMY (1561-1599)	19 x 25 cm
EUROPAE TABULA IX	PTOLEMY (1561-1599)	19 x 25 cm
EUROPAE TABULA X	PTOLEMY (1561-1599)	19 x 25 cm
EUROPE	WILLDEY	62 x 90 cm
EXACT PLAN OF GENERAL GAGE'S LINES ON BOSTON NECK IN AMERICA	PENNSYLVANIA MAG.	30 x 23 cm
EXACTISSIMA ASIAE DELINEATIO ...	ALLARD	51 x 58 cm
EXACTISSIMA PALATINUS AD RHENUM ... WORMACIENSIS ET SPIRENSIS	HOMANN	49 x 58 cm
EXPLORATIONS AND SURVEYS FOR A RAIL ROAD ROUTE ... 35TH PARALLEL ...	U.S. PACIFIC R.R.	55 x 128 cm
EXPLORATIONS AND SURVEYS FOR A RAIL ROAD ROUTE ... 47TH PARALLEL ...	U.S. PACIFIC R.R.	60 x 154 cm
EXTENDED INDICATOR MAP OF LONDON DIVIDED INTO QUARTER MILE ...	SMITH, C.	59 x 87 cm
EXTENDED TAPE INDICATOR MAP OF LONDON AND VISITOR GUIDE	WYLD	58 x 86 cm
FACIES POLI ARCTICA ADIACENTIUMQUE EI REGIONUM EX RECENTISSIMIS ...	WEIGEL	33 x 36 cm
FALKLAND ISLANDS AND PATAGONIA	TALLIS	34 x 25 cm
FALLS OF OHIO	MELISH	15 x 10 cm
FALMOUTH & ENGLISH HARBOURS [Antigua]	ADMIRALTY	61 x 46 cm
FESSAE ET MAROCCHI ... (****)	ORTELIUS (Folio)	39 x 50 cm
FEZZAE ET MAROCCHI REGNA AFRICAE CELEBERRIMA ...	JANSSON	39 x 50 cm
FEZZAE ET MAROCCHI REGNA AFRICAE CELEBERRIMA	ORTELIUS (Folio)	38 x 51 cm
FINAL PLANS OF THE PANAMA CANAL	HAMMOND	25 x 48 cm
FIONIA	MERCATOR (Folio)	36 x 40 cm

FISCARD BAY AND HARBOUR [Wales]	MORRIS	18 x 24 cm
FLORENCE. FIRENZE	S.D.U.K.	29 x 38 cm
FLORIDA	BRADFORD	36 x 33 cm
FLORIDA	CRAM	58 x 43 cm
FLORIDA	GASKELL	33 x 23 cm
FLORIDA	GRAY	43 x 66 cm
FLORIDA	LUCAS	30 x 25 cm
FLORIDA	MITCHELL, S.A. (1859-)	41 x 33 cm
FLORIDA	MORSE, S.	13 x 15 cm
FLORIDA	RAND, McNALLY	23 x 30 cm
FLORIDA CALL'D BY YE FRENCH LOUISIANA &C.	MOLL (Small)	20 x 28 cm
FLORIDA ET REGIONES VICINAE	DE LAET	28 x 36 cm
FLORIDE	MALLET	15 x 13 cm
FONTES NILI FLUMINIS EORUMQUE SITUS	SCHERER	23 x 18 cm
FORM UND GESTALT HISPANIE	STUMPF	13 x 17 cm
FRANCE	SANSON (Small)	18 x 23 cm
FRANCE	STANFORD	61 x 51 cm
FRANCE IN PROVINCES	S.D.U.K.	30 x 30 cm
FRANCE, REVISED AND AUGMENTED, THE ATTIRES OF THE FRENCH ...	SPEED	40 x 52 cm
FRANCISCUS DRACO CARTHAGENAM CIVITATEM EXPUGNAT	DE BRY	15 x 21 cm
FRANCONIAE NOVA DESCRIPTIO	JANSSON	42 x 54 cm
FRANKFORT (FRANKFURT AM MAYN)	S.D.U.K.	31 x 38 cm
FRETI MAGELLANICI AC NOVI FRETI VULGO LE MAIRE EXACTISSIMA DELIN. ...	JANSSON	38 x 49 cm
FRETUM MAGELLANICUM	BERTIUS	9 x 13 cm
FROM A MAP OF THE ENTIRE TERRITORIES OF WISKONSAN & IOWA ...	U.S. WAR DEPT.	20 x 30 cm
FROM THE PIMA VILLAGES TO FORT FILLMORE ... 1854 AND 55	U.S. PACIFIC R.R.	76 x 102 cm
GAD ...	FULLER	28 x 34 cm
GALIGNANI'S PLAN OF PARIS	GALIGNANI	38 x 49 cm
GALLIA	ORTELIUS (Miniature)	8 x 11 cm
GALLIA NOVA TABULA	PTOLEMY (1561-1599)	19 x 25 cm
GALLIAE REGNI POTENTISS. NOVA DESCRIPTIO, IOANNE IOLIVETO AUCTORE	ORTELIUS (Folio)	34 x 50 cm
GALVESTON HARBOR TEXAS, CAPT. C. RICHE IN CHARGE	U.S. WAR DEPT.	41 x 51 cm
GASPAR STRAIT	ADMIRALTY	99 x 66 cm
GENERAL-CARTE VON CANADA	HAPPEL	10 x 15 cm
GENERAL CHARTE VOM KONIGREICH DAENEMARK NEBST DEM HERZOGTHUM ...	HOMANN	50 x 58 cm
GENERAL KARTE VON GROSSBRITANNIEN UND IRELAND	VON REILLY	28 x 22 cm
GENERAL MAP OF THE EXPLORATIONS AND SURVEYS IN CALIFORNIA ...	U.S. PACIFIC R.R.	64 x 51 cm
GENERAL MAP OF THE REPUBLIC OF MEXICO CONTRUCTED FROM BEST ...	RAND, McNALLY	122 x 170 cm
GENERAL MAP OF THE UNITED STATES SHOWING EXTENT OF FREE & SLAVE- ...	MURRAY, J.	33 x 43 cm
GENERAL MAP SHOWING THE COUNTRIES EXPLORED & SURVEYED BY THE	U.S.	41 x 51 cm
GENERAL VIEW OF THE CITY OF NASHVILLE, TENN.	HARPER'S WEEKLY	23 x 36 cm
GENUA	BRAUN & HOGENBERG	15 x 48 cm
GEOGRAPHIA SACRA	JANSSON	36 x 48 cm
GEOGRAPHICA DESCRIPTIO MONTANI CUIUSDAM DISTRICTUS IN FRANCONIA ...	HOMANN	50 x 57 cm
GEOGRAPHICAL AND STATISTICAL MAP OF ENGLAND	LAVOISNE	38 x 33 cm
GEOGRAPHICAL, HISTORICAL AND STATISTICAL MAP OF AMERICA	LAVOISNE	41 x 51 cm
GEOGRAPHICAL, STATISTICAL, AND HISTORICAL MAP OF ALABAMA	CAREY & LEA	31 x 23 cm
GEOGRAPHICAL, STATISTICAL, AND HISTORICAL MAP OF AMERICA	CAREY & LEA	43 x 53 cm
GEOGRAPHICAL, STATISTICAL, AND HISTORICAL MAP OF ARKANSAS TERR. ...	CAREY & LEA	37 x 38 cm
GEOGRAPHICAL, STATISTICAL, AND HISTORICAL MAP OF GEORGIA	CAREY & LEA	30 x 38 cm
GEOGRAPHICAL, STATISTICAL, AND HISTORICAL MAP OF ILLINOIS	CAREY & LEA	30 x 22 cm
GEOGRAPHICAL, STATISTICAL AND HISTORICAL MAP OF INDIANA	CAREY & LEA	37 x 29 cm
GEOGRAPHICAL, STATISTICAL AND HISTORICAL MAP OF KENTUCKY	CAREY & LEA	30 x 47 cm
GEOGRAPHICAL, STATISTICAL, AND HISTORICAL MAP OF MEXICO	CAREY & LEA	39 x 37 cm
GEOGRAPHICAL, STATISTICAL, AND HISTORICAL MAP OF MISSISSIPPI	CAREY & LEA	32 x 24 cm
GEOGRAPHICAL, STATISTICAL AND HISTORICAL MAP OF NEW JERSEY	CAREY & LEA	43 x 53 cm
GEOGRAPHICAL, STATISTICAL, AND HISTORICAL MAP OF NORTH AMERICA	CAREY & LEA	36 x 33 cm
GEOGRAPHICAL, STATISTICAL AND HISTORICAL MAP OF RHODE ISLAND	CAREY & LEA	29 x 21 cm
GEOGRAPHICAL, STATISTICAL AND HISTORICAL MAP OF UPPER AND LOWER ...	CAREY & LEA	43 x 53 cm
GEOGRAPHICAL, STATISTICAL AND HISTORICAL MAP OF VERMONT	CAREY & LEA	31 x 24 cm
GEOGRAPHISCH-STATISTISCHE POST UND REISEKARTE ZU...RHEIN- UND MAIN-...	BAUERKELLER	50 x 38 cm
GEOGRAPHISCHE BESCHRYVINGLE VAN DE WANDELING DER APOSTELEN ...	VISSCHER	33 x 48 cm
GEOGRAPHISCHE LAGE DER SUDLICHEN BRAUNSCHWEIGISCHEN ...	HOMANN	52 x 57 cm
GEOLOGICAL CHART OF MISSISSIPPI	LOCAL & STATE	36 x 25 cm
GEOLOGICAL CHART OF PART OF IOWA, WISCONSIN & ILLINOIS	U.S.	58 x 46 cm
GEOLOGICAL MAP OF A PART OF THE STATE OF CALIFORNIA EXPLORED ...	U.S. PACIFIC R.R.	56 x 41 cm
GEOLOGICAL MAP OF ... CALIFORNIA EXPLORED IN 1855 BY LIEUT. ...	U.S. WAR DEPT.	56 x 41 cm
GEOLOGICAL MAP OF COLORADO	HAYDEN, F.	76 x 94 cm

GEOLOGICAL MAP OF ENGLAND & WALES	STANFORD	94 x 81 cm
GEOLOGICAL MAP OF ISLE ROYALE, LAKE SUPERIOR	U.S.	46 x 64 cm
GEOLOGICAL MAP OF OHIO	WALLING & GRAY	38 x 28 cm
GEOLOGICAL MAP OF OHIO BY J.S. NEWBURY, ...	WALLING	58 x 38 cm
GEOLOGICAL MAP OF THE BRITISH ISLES	STANFORD	140 x 129 cm
GEOLOGICAL MAP OF THE MINING DISTRICTS IN THE STATE OF GEORGIA, ...	PECK, J.	30 x 36 cm
GEOLOGICAL MAP OF THE ROUTE EXPLORED BY CAPT. JN. POPE ... 32ND PARA.	U.S. PACIFIC R.R.	25 x 61 cm
GEOLOGICAL MAP OF THE VICINITY OF SAN FRANCISCO ... 1853	U.S.	18 x 23 cm
GEOLOGICAL MAP OF WISCONSIN, IOWA & MINNESOTA; EXHIBITING COAL ...	U.S.	114 x 66 cm
GEORGIA	BRADFORD	25 x 20 cm
GEORGIA	BRADFORD & GOODRICH	36 x 30 cm
GEORGIA	CAREY	20 x 15 cm
GEORGIA	COLTON	36 x 28 cm
GEORGIA	CRAM	30 x 25 cm
GEORGIA	FINLEY	29 x 22 cm
GEORGIA	LEWIS & ARROWSMITH	20 x 25 cm
GEORGIA	LUCAS	30 x 23 cm
GEORGIA	MORSE & BREESE	36 x 29 cm
GEORGIA	MORSE & GASTON	15 x 13 cm
GEORGIA	RAND, McNALLY	66 x 48 cm
GEORGIA	RAND, McNALLY	48 x 33 cm
GEORGIA	SCOTT	16 x 18 cm
GEORGIA	SCOTT	15 x 19 cm
GEORGIA, ALABAMA AND FLORIDA	COLTON	33 x 25 cm
GEORGIA FROM THE LATEST AUTHORITIES	CAREY	23 x 41 cm
GEORGIA FROM THE LATEST AUTHORITIES	REID	23 x 38 cm
GEORGIE, ARMENIE &C.	MALLET	14 x 10 cm
GERMANIA NOVA TABULA MDXXXXII	PTOLEMY (1548 Venice)	13 x 17 cm
GERMANIAE NOVA ET ACCURATA DELINEATIO	JANSSON	35 x 48 cm
GERMANIAE VETERIS ...	JANSSON	48 x 38 cm
GERMANIAE VETERIS NOVA DESCRIPTIO	JANSSON	38 x 48 cm
GEZIGT VAN'T SPAANSCHE VLEK PENSACOLA, AAN DE BAAY ...	TIRION	16 x 26 cm
GLI STATI UNITI DELL'AMERICA ... PRIMO FOGLIO (Great Lakes) [etc.]	CASSINI	35 x 48 cm
GLOBE TERRESTRE	MALLET	14 x 10 cm
GLOBE TERRESTRE DRESSEE SUR LES RELATIONS LES PLUS NOUVELLES ...	DESNOS	23 cm, diam
GLOBE TERRESTRE / GLOBE CELESTE / SPHERE ARTIFICIELLE ...	DE FER (Small)	23 x 33 cm
GLOCESTER SH.	MORDEN	9 x 6 cm
GOLD BELT MAP OF COLORADO	COMPANY MAPS	25 x 36 cm
GOLDTOP ROAD IN BRIDES BAY [Wales]	MORRIS	18 x 24 cm
GOLDTOP ROAD IN ST. BRIDE'S BAY ... [Wales]	MORRIS	18 x 23 cm
GOLFE DE ST. LAURENT, ISLE ET BANCS DE TERRE NEUVE	DE VAUGONDY	17 x 18 cm
GORDA SOUND	ADMIRALTY	48 x 64 cm
GOTHIA	JANSSON	39 x 49 cm
GRAECIA	BLAEU	41 x 52 cm
GRAECIA	MERCATOR (Small)	14 x 18 cm
GRAECIAE ANTIQUAE SPECIMEN GEOGRAPHICUM	D'ANVILLE	53 x 50 cm
GRANADA	BRAUN & HOGENBERG	33 x 51 cm
GRANATA ET MURCIA REGNA	JANSSON	38 x 49 cm
GRAND AND LESSER CAYMANS FROM A BRITISH SURVEY IN 1881	U.S.	64 x 79 cm
GRAND PLAN DE PARIS ILLUSTRE	GARNIER	60 x 91 cm
GRANDE TARTARIE	DE FER (Small)	14 x 16 cm
GRAY'S ATLAS CLIMATOLOGICAL MAP OF THE UNITED STATES ...	GRAY	41 x 66 cm
GRAY'S ATLAS MAP OF INDIANA	GRAY	38 x 30 cm
GRAY'S GEOLOGICAL MAP OF THE UNITED STATES, BY ... HITCHCOCK ...	GRAY	43 x 69 cm
GRAY'S MAP OF THE CITY OF PROVIDENCE	GRAY	38 x 33 cm
GRAY'S NEW MAP OF DAKOTA WITH PART OF MANITOBA, ETC.	GRAY	66 x 43 cm
GRAY'S NEW MAP OF GEORGIA	GRAY	64 x 41 cm
GRAY'S NEW MAP OF INDIANA	GRAY	64 x 41 cm
GRAY'S NEW MAP OF KANSAS	GRAY	43 x 69 cm
GRAY'S NEW MAP OF NORTH CAROLINA AND SOUTH CAROLINA	GRAY	41 x 69 cm
GRAY'S NEW MAP OF TEXAS AND THE INDIAN TERRITORY	GRAY	43 x 66 cm
GREECE	VAN DEN KEERE	8 x 13 cm
GREECE AND THE IONIAN ISLANDS	ARROWSMITH	61 x 49 cm
GREECE, ARCHIPELAGO AND PART OF ANADOLI	FADEN	53 x 76 cm
GREENLAND AND LABRADOR	MORSE, S.	28 x 33 cm
GRENADA	LUCAS	30 x 23 cm
GRENADA DIVIDED INTO ITS PARISHES...	JEFFERYS	46 x 62 cm
GRONDVLAKTE VAN NIEUW ORLEANS, DE HOOFDSTAD VAN LOUISIANA [and] ...	TIRION	33 x 45 cm

GROOM'S POCKET MAP OF LONDON	FOSTER GROOM	47 x 71 cm
GROSSER VERKEHRS-PLAN BERLIN UND SEINE VORORTE	PHARUS-VERLAG	87 x 118 cm
GRUNDRISS DE STADT JERSALEM	ANONYMOUS	28 x 30 cm
GRUNDRISS ... ST. PETERSBURG	ANONYMOUS	48 x 69 cm
GUAYANE, TERRE FERME, ISLES ANTILLES, ET NLLE. ESPAGNE	BRION DE LA TOUR	28 x 48 cm
GUIANA SIVE AMAZONUM REGIO	JANSSON	37 x 49 cm
GUIDE THROUGH OHIO, MICHIGAN, INDIANA, ILLINOIS, MISSOURI, WISC. ...	COLTON	47 x 57 cm
GUINEA	OGILBY	25 x 36 cm
GUINEE	MALLET	14 x 10 cm
GULF OF ST. LAWRENCE, MINGAN ISLANDS. EASTERN SHEET ...	ADMIRALTY	46 x 62 cm
GULF OF ST. LAWRENCE, MINGAN ISLANDS. WESTERN SHEET ...	ADMIRALTY	46 x 63 cm
HABES HIC NOVAM & ACCURATISSIMAM DESCRIPTIONEM ... FLANDRIAE ...	MERCATOR (Folio)	37 x 52 cm
HABESSINIA SEV ABASSIA AT ETHIOPIA	MORDEN	14 x 12 cm
HAEC EST NOBILIS, & FLORENS ILLA NEAPOLIS ...	BRAUN & HOGENBERG	33 x 48 cm
HAITI, HISPANIOLA OR ST. DOMINGO	THOMSON	28 x 61 cm
HALIFAX HARBOUR	IMRAY	25 x 15 cm
HAMBURG	S.D.U.K.	31 x 39 cm
HARBOR OF MICHIGAN CITY, INDIANA	U.S.	30 x 48 cm
HARWICH HARBOUR	ADMIRALTY	66 x 127 cm
HASSIA LANDGRAVIATUS	JANSSON	44 x 56 cm
HASSIAE SUPERIORIS ET WETTERAU	HOMANN	48 x 57 cm
HAUPT UND RESIDENZ STADT LONDON	HOMANN	48 x 58 cm
HAVANNAH	MEYER	10 x 15 cm
HAYTI OR SAINT DOMINGO	LUCAS	48 x 30 cm
HELVETIA TREDECIM STATIBUS LIBERIS QUOS CANTONES VOCANT ...	HOMANN	45 x 57 cm
HEMISPHAERIUM COELI AUSTRALE IN QUO FIXARUM LOCA SECUNDUM ...	DOPPELMAYR	48 x 58 cm
HEMISPHAERIUM STELLATUM BOREALE ANTIQUUM	CELLARIUS	43 x 51 cm
HEMISPHERE OCCIDENTAL OU DU NOUVEAU MONDE ...	D'ANVILLE	66 x 61 cm
HEMISPHERE SEPTENTRIONAL POUR VOIR ... LES TERRES ARCTIQUES	DE L'ISLE	46 x 46 cm
HEMPSTEAD HARBOR LONG ISLAND [N.Y.]	U.S. COAST SURVEY	46 x 38 cm
HET BELOOFIE LANDT CANAAN ...	VISSCHER	31 x 47 cm
HET CANAAL TUSSCHEN ENGELAND EN VRANCRIICK ...	GOOS	43 x 55 cm
HET EYLAND SANGIR	VAN KEULEN	46 x 28 cm
HIBERNIA	ORTELIUS (Miniature)	7 x 10 cm
HIBERNIA REGNUM	HOMANN	57 x 48 cm
HIBERNIAE	HOLE	26 x 33 cm
HIBERNIAE, BRITANNICAE INSULAE, NOVA DESCRIPTIO	ORTELIUS (Folio)	35 x 48 cm
HIBERNIAE REGNUM TAM IN PRAECIPUAS ULTONIAE, CONNACIAE, LAGENIAE, ...	VISSCHER	56 x 48 cm
HIEROSOLYMA CLARISSIMA TOTIUS ORIENTIS CIVITAS IUDAEE METROPOLIS	BRAUN & HOGENBERG	33 x 49 cm
HIERUSALEM	LAFRERI SCHOOL	30 x 43 cm
HISPANIA	ORTELIUS (Miniature)	8 x 11 cm
HISPANIA CUM FIMITIMIS REGIONIBUS NOVISSIME DELINEATA. ...	SCHERER	23 x 33 cm
HISPANIA NOVA TABULA	PTOLEMY (1561-1599)	18 x 25 cm
HISPANIAE NOVAE SIVE MAGNAE, RECENS ET VERA DESCRIPTIO. 1595	DE BRY	33 x 44 cm
HISPANIAE NOVAE SIVE MAGNAE VERA DESCRIPTIO	QUAD	21 x 29 cm
HISTORISCH-GEOGRAPHISCHE CARTE DER NORDAMERIKANISCHEN FREI. ...	VELTEN	51 x 66 cm
HODIERNAE ASIAE TABULA	WELLS	10 x 16 cm
HOLLANDIAE CATTORUM REGIONIS TYPUS	GUICCIARDINI	24 x 32 cm
HOLSATIA DUCATUS	MERCATOR (Folio)	35 x 48 cm
HOLY ILAND / GARNSEY / FARNE / JARSEY	JANSSON	51 x 41 cm
HONDIUS HIS MAP OF FLORIDA - VIRGINIA ET FLORIDA	MERCATOR (Small)	15 x 18 cm
HUNGARIA	MERCATOR (Folio)	37 x 45 cm
HUNGARIA ET TRANSILVANIA	PTOLEMY (1596-1621)	13 x 18 cm
HUNGARIAE	HOMANN	51 x 62 cm
HYDROGRAPHY IN FRONT OF EUREKA, CAL. SHOWING CONDITION ...	U.S. WAR DEPT.	28 x 74 cm
I. LADRONES	DE BRY	14 x 19 cm
IAPAN I.	HONDIUS	13 x 17 cm
IAPONIA	HONDIUS	34 x 45 cm
IAPONIA	MERCATOR (Folio)	35 x 45 cm
IAPONIA	MERCATOR (Small)	14 x 19 cm
IAPONIA	VAN DEN KEERE	13 x 19 cm
IAPONIA ET TERRA ESONIS	JANSSON	15 x 19 cm
IAPONIA INSULA	ORTELIUS (Miniature)	8 x 10 cm
IAPONIA REGNUM	BLAEU	42 x 57 cm
IAPONIAE NOVA DESCRIPTIO	JANSSON	34 x 45 cm
ICELAND. TO ILLUSTRATE THE PAPER BY DR. TH. THORODDSON ...	ROYAL GEOG. SOCIETY	40 x 57 cm
IDAHO	CRAM	30 x 25 cm
IDAHO	STANDARD ATLAS	30 x 25 cm

IDEA NATURALIS AMERICAE BOREALIS DIGITO DEI FORMATA GEOGRAPHICE ...	SCHERER	23 x 36 cm
IL CANADA, LE COLONIE INGLESI CON LA LUIGIANA E FLORIDA...	ZATTA	31 x 41 cm
IL DESSEGNO DELLA TERZA PARTE DELL'ASIA ...	GASTALDI	64 x 74 cm
IL DISEGNO DELLA TERZA PARTE DELL' ASIA. DI GIACOPO DI GASTALDI ...	LAFRERI SCHOOL	41 x 36 cm
IL MAPPAMONDO O SIA DESCRIZIONE GENERALE DEL GLOBO	ZATTA	29 x 40 cm
IL MARYLAND, IL JERSEY MERIDIONALE, LA DELAWARE, E LA PARTE ...	ZATTA	33 x 43 cm
IL PAESE DE SELVAGGI OUTAGAMIANI, MASCOUTENSI, ILLINESE, E PARTE ...	ZATTA	32 x 42 cm
IL REGNO DELLA CHINA ...	ROSSI	112 x 140 cm
ILE BOURBON	MALLET	14 x 10 cm
ILLINOIS	BURR	33 x 27 cm
ILLINOIS	COLTON	41 x 36 cm
ILLINOIS	FINLEY	29 x 22 cm
ILLINOIS	JOHNSON	42 x 32 cm
ILLINOIS	LUCAS	30 x 23 cm
ILLINOIS	MORSE & BREESE	36 x 28 cm
ILLINOIS AND MISSOURI	TANNER	71 x 58 cm
ILLINOIS RAILROADS	RAND, McNALLY	66 x 44 cm
IMP. CAES. CAROLO VI. ... PROVINCIA BRISGOIA	HOMANN	59 x 50 cm
IMPERII MOSCOVITICI PARS AUSTRALIS IN LUCEM, EDITA PAR G. DE L'ISLE	SEUTTER (Large)	51 x 58 cm
IMPERII RUSSICI ET TATARIAE UNIVERSAE TAM MAJORIS ET ASIATICAE	HOMANN	47 x 55 cm
IMPERII SINARUM NOVA DESCRIPTIO	BLAEU	47 x 60 cm
IMPERII SINARUM NOVA DESCRIPTIO	DU VAL (Small)	12 x 12 cm
IMPERII SINARUM NOVA DESCRIPTIO ...	VAN LOON	46 x 53 cm
IMPERIUM JAPONICUM	KAEMPFER	46 x 53 cm
IMPERIUM RUSSIAE MAGNAE	SEUTTER (Small)	19 x 26 cm
IMPERIUM TURCICUM IN EUROPA, ASIA ET AFRICA	HOMANN	50 x 58 cm
IMPERIUM TURCICUM IN EUROPA, ASIA ET AFRICA ...	VALK	48 x 58 cm
INDE	MALLET	14 x 10 cm
INDE ANCIENNE A L'OCCIDENT DU GANGE	MALLET	15 x 10 cm
INDE ANCIENNE A L'ORIENT DU GANGE	MALLET	15 x 10 cm
INDEXED RAILROAD AND TOWNSHIP MAP OF MISSOURI	CRAM	64 x 51 cm
INDIA, AS DESCRIBED BY ALL AUTHORS BEFORE THE FIFTH CENTURY	HARRIS	22 x 31 cm
INDIA BEYOND GANGES	MOLL (Small)	26 x 20 cm
INDIA EXTREMA	MUNSTER	26 x 34 cm
INDIA INTRA GANGEM	DU VAL (Small)	10 x 13 cm
INDIA ON BOTH SIDES OF THE GANGES	GIBSON	6 x 9 cm
INDIA QUAE ORIENTALIS DICITUR, ET INSULAE ADIACENTES	BLAEU	41 x 50 cm
INDIA QUAE ORIENTALIS DICITUR, ET INSULAE ADIACENTES	HONDIUS	39 x 49 cm
INDIA TERCERA NUOVA TAVOLA	PTOLEMY (1548 Venice)	(no dimens.)
INDIAE ORIENTALIS ...	VISSCHER	47 x 57 cm
INDIAE ORIENTALIS INSULARUMQUE ADIACIENTIUM TYPUS	ORTELIUS (Folio)	35 x 50 cm
INDIAE ORIENTALIS NEC NON INSULARUM ADIACENTIUM NOVA DESCRIPTIO	VISSCHER	47 x 57 cm
INDIAE ORIENTALIS NOVA DESCRIPTIO	JANSSON	39 x 50 cm
INDIAN ARCHIPELAGO ...	FULLARTON	41 x 51 cm
INDIAN TERRITORY	BRADLEY	33 x 43 cm
INDIAN TERRITORY	MITCHELL, S.A. (1860+)	30 x 43 cm
INDIAN TERRITORY	RAND, McNALLY	33 x 50 cm
INDIANA	BRADFORD	36 x 28 cm
INDIANA	BRADFORD & GOODRICH	36 x 30 cm
INDIANA	BRADLEY	36 x 30 cm
INDIANA	BURR	34 x 27 cm
INDIANA	COLTON	36 x 28 cm
INDIANA	CRAM	30 x 23 cm
INDIANA	CRAM	56 x 38 cm
INDIANA	FINLEY	28 x 23 cm
INDIANA	GRAY	64 x 39 cm
INDIANA	GREENLEAF	32 x 27 cm
INDIANA	MITCHELL, S.A. (1860+)	36 x 28 cm
INDIANA	MORSE & BREESE	36 x 28 cm
INDIANA	MORSE & GASTON	15 x 13 cm
INDIANA	RAND, McNALLY	64 x 46 cm
INDIANA & OHIO	BRADFORD	20 x 25 cm
INDIANA RAILROADS	RAND, McNALLY	66 x 48 cm
INDIANAPOLIS [and] LOUISVILLE	GRAY	38 x 30 cm
INDIANAPOLIS & ENVIRONS	RAND, McNALLY	66 x 48 cm
INDICATOR MAP OF LONDON DIVIDED INTO QUARTER MILE SQUARES ...	SMITH, C.	57 x 87 cm
INDICATOR MAP OF LONDON DIVIDED INTO QUARTER MILE SQUARES ...	SMITH, C.	49 x 74 cm
INDIE OCCIDENTALI	ROSSI, L.	20 x 30 cm

INDIEN & INNER ASIA	STIELER	36 x 41 cm
INDO-CHINA	STANFORD	50 x 34 cm
INS. CEILAN	MERCATOR (Folio)	36 x 51 cm
INS. CEILAN QUAE INCOLIS TENARISIN DICITUR	MERCATOR (Folio)	35 x 50 cm
INSULA CEILAN	MERCATOR (Small)	15 x 18 cm
INSULA ET PRINCIPATUS RUGIAE	HOMANN	49 x 58 cm
INSULA JAMAICAE ...	MORDEN	13 x 13 cm
INSULA MADAGASCAR DICTA ST. LAURENS NUNC INSULA DAUPHINE	DU VAL (Small)	10 x 13 cm
INSULA S. JUAN DE PUERTO RICO CARIBES; VEL CANIBALUM INSULAE	HONDIUS	41 x 51 cm
INSULA S. LAURENTII VULGO MADAGASCAR	OGILBY	28 x 36 cm
INSULAE AMERICANAE IN OCEANO SEPTENTRIONALI, CUM TERRIS ...	BLAEU	38 x 53 cm
INSULAE AMERICANAE IN OCEANO SEPTENTRIONALI, CUM TERRIS ...	JANSSON	38 x 52 cm
INSULAE AMERICANAE NEMPE: CUBA, HISPANIOLA, IAMAICA, PTO RICO, ...	DANCKERTS	51 x 58 cm
INSULAE CUBA HISPANIOLA &C.	MERCATOR (Small)	15 x 18 cm
INSULAE DANICAE ... ZEELANDIA, FIONIA, LANGELANDIA, LALANDIA FALSTRIA, ...	HOMANN	50 x 59 cm
INSULAE INDIAE ORIENTALIS	HONDIUS	14 x 20 cm
INSULAE INDIAE ORIENTALIS PRAECIPUAE, IN QUIBUS MOLUCCAE ...	HONDIUS	35 x 48 cm
INSULAE IOHANNIS MAYEN CUM UNIVERSO SITU SINUUM ET PROMONTORIUM	JANSSON	41 x 52 cm
INSULAE PHILIPPINAE	LANGENES	9 x 13 cm
INSULARUM MOLUCCARUM NOVA DESCRIPTIO. AMSTELOMI ...	JANSSON	38 x 50 cm
IOWA	COLTON	33 x 41 cm
IOWA	COLTON	33 x 41 cm
IOWA	MITCHELL, S.A. (1859-)	41 x 33 cm
IOWA & NEBRASKA	JOHNSON	43 x 60 cm
IRELAND	JEFFERYS	18 x 19 cm
IRELAND	JOHNSTON	60 x 49 cm
IRELAND	MOLL (Small)	18 x 17 cm
IRELAND	S.D.U.K.	60 x 47 cm
IRELAND	THOMSON	60 x 50 cm
IS. DE CUBA ET DE JAMAICA	MALLET	17 x 10 cm
ISLA DE CUBA ... [and] ... ISLA DE CUBA. MEDIAS HOJAS EXTREMAS ORIENTAL ...	COELLO	74 x 102 cm
ISLA DE CUBA. COSTA MERIDIONAL. PLANO DEL PUERTO DE CASILDA MASIO, ...	DIRECCION DE HIDRO.	31 x 47 cm
ISLA DE CUBA. PLANO DEL PUERTO DE BAITIQUERI LEVANTADO EN 1861 ...	DIRECCION DE HIDRO.	30 x 45 cm
ISLA DE CUBA. PLANO DEL PUERTO DE MATA LEVANTADO EN 1860 ...	DIRECCION DE HIDRO.	30 x 45 cm
ISLAND OF JAMAICA	FULLARTON	15 x 23 cm
ISLAND OF MADERA / THE DRAGON TREE	ASTLEY MAGAZINE	23 x 15 cm
ISLANDIA	ORTELIUS (Folio)	34 x 49 cm
ISLANDS IN THE ATLANTIC	S.D.U.K.	40 x 33 cm
ISLANDS OF IMPORTANCE	WELLER	43 x 30 cm
ISLE DE CAYENNE	MALLET	14 x 10 cm
ISLE DE LA GUADELOUPE SCITUEE A 16 DEGRES DE LAT. SEPTENTRIONALE	LABAT	13 x 20 cm
ISLE DE ST. DOMINGUE ...	LE ROUGE	20 x 28 cm
ISLE DE TERRE NEUVE	MALLET	15 x 10 cm
ISLES BRITANIQUES OU SONT LES ROYAUMES D'ANGLETERRE D'ESCOSSE ...	DE FER (Small)	13 x 16 cm
ISLES BRITANNIQUES	SANSON (Small)	22 x 17 cm
ISLES D'AMERIQUE DITES CARIBES OU CANNIBALES ET DE BARLOVENTO	DU VAL (Small)	34 x 26 cm
ISLES DE SALOMON	MALLET	15 x 10 cm
ISLES DES LARRONS	MALLET	15 x 10 cm
ISLES MAYORQUE, MINORQUE ET YVICE	BONNE	23 x 36 cm
ISOLA CEILON	ALBRIZZI	28 x 36 cm
ISOLA CUBA NOVA	PTOLEMY (1561-1599)	19 x 25 cm
ISOLA D'ISLAND	CORONELLI	23 x 31 cm
ISOLA DE IAMES, A GIAMAICA, POSSEDUTTA DAL RE BRITANNICO DIVISA ...	CORONELLI	22 x 29 cm
ISOLA DEL GIAPONE E PENISOLA DI COREA...DAL P.M. CORONELLI...	CORONELLI	46 x 61 cm
ISOLA DI CORFU	BERTELLI	21 x 16 cm
ISOLA DI MARIA GALANTE NELLE ANTILLI POSSEDUTA DA S. M. CRISTIANISSIMA	CORONELLI	23 x 30 cm
ISOLA SPAGNOLA NOVA	PTOLEMY (1561-1599)	19 x 25 cm
ISOLE DELL' INDIA CIOE LE MOLUCCHE LE FILIPPINE E DELLA SONDA ...	CANTELLI DA VIGNOLA	46 x 58 cm
ISOLE DELL'INDIE, DIVISE IN FILIPPINE, MOLUCCHE, E DELLA SONDA ...	CORONELLI	45 x 61 cm
ISOLE FILIPPINE	ZATTA	40 x 31 cm
ISOLE NEL MARE DI SUR SCOPERTE NEL 1617 ...	DUDLEY	48 x 74 cm
ISRAELS PERIGRINATIONS OR THE FORTY YEARS TRAVEL OF THE CHILDREN ...	MOXON	32 x 46 cm
ITALIA	QUAD	22 x 27 cm
ITALIA	SPEED	9 x 12 cm
ITALIA NUOUAMENTE PIU PERFETTA CHE MAI PER INANZI POSTA IN LUCE ...	HONDIUS	38 x 51 cm
IUCATANA REGIO ET FONDURA	WYTFLIET	23 x 29 cm
IUDAEA SEU PALAESTINA ... HODIE DICTA TERRA SANCTA PROUT OLIM ...	HOMANN	50 x 58 cm
IUDAEA, SEU TERRA SANCTA QUAE ISRAELITARUM IN SUAS DUODECIM ...	JAILLOT	51 x 81 cm

IULIACENSIS ET MONTENSIS DUCATUS. DE HERTOGHDOMEN GULICK EN ...	JANSSON	38 x 50 cm
IUTIA SEPTENTRIONALIS	MERCATOR (Folio)	29 x 40 cm
JAMAICA	LUCAS	23 x 31 cm
JAMAICA, AMERICAE SEPTENTRIONALIS AMPLA INSULA, A CHRISTOPHERO...	VISSCHER	52 x 59 cm
JAPAN	LEWIS & ARROWSMITH	20 x 25 cm
JAPAN	STANFORD	60 x 47 cm
JAPONAE AC TERRAE ESONIS NOVISSIMA DESCRIPTIO	MORDEN	11 x 13 cm
JAPONIA	HONDIUS	34 x 45 cm
JEFFERSON CITY (MISSOURI RIVER)	MEYER	11 x 16 cm
JERUSALEM NIEWLICKS UYTE DE SCHRIFTEN IOSEPHUS AFGEBEELD	COCCETUS, J.	33 x 41 cm
JESU CHRISTI SALVATORIS NOSTRI ET APOSTOLORUM PETRI, ET PAULI ...	SANSON (Folio)	38 x 56 cm
JOHNSON'S CALIFORNIA. TERRITORIES OF NEW MEXICO AND UTAH	JOHNSON	43 x 62 cm
JOHNSON'S CALIFORNIA, TERRITORIES OF NEW MEXICO, ARIZONA, COLO. ...	JOHNSON	43 x 61 cm
JOHNSON'S CENTRAL AMERICA	JOHNSON	31 x 40 cm
JOHNSON'S DELAWARE AND MARYLAND	JOHNSON	32 x 41 cm
JOHNSON'S GEORGIA AND ALABAMA	JOHNSON	41 x 57 cm
JOHNSON'S ILLINOIS	JOHNSON	58 x 43 cm
JOHNSON'S INDIANA	JOHNSON	56 x 41 cm
JOHNSON'S IOWA AND NEBRASKA	JOHNSON	43 x 58 cm
JOHNSON'S LOWER CANADA AND NEW BRUNSWICK [on sheet with] UPPER CAN.	JOHNSON	56 x 36 cm
JOHNSON'S MICHIGAN & WISCONSIN	JOHNSON	46 x 61 cm
JOHNSON'S MINNESOTA	JOHNSON	61 x 43 cm
JOHNSON'S MINNESOTA AND DAKOTA	JOHNSON	33 x 41 cm
JOHNSON'S NEBRASKA, DAKOTA, COLORADO, IDAHO AND KANSAS	JOHNSON	33 x 41 cm
JOHNSON'S NEBRASKA, DAKOTA, IDAHO AND MONTANA	JOHNSON	48 x 61 cm
JOHNSON'S NEW BRUNSWICK, NOVA SCOTIA, NEWFOUNDLAND, AND ...	JOHNSON	32 x 40 cm
JOHNSON'S NEW ILLUSTRATED ... COUNTY MAP OF THE REP. OF N. AMER.	JOHNSON	166 x 178 cm
JOHNSON'S NEW JERSEY	JOHNSON	38 x 33 cm
JOHNSON'S NEW MAP OF THE STATE OF TEXAS	JOHNSON	43 x 62 cm
JOHNSON'S NEW MILITARY MAP OF THE UNITED STATES SHOWING THE FORTS	JOHNSON	44 x 59 cm
JOHNSON'S OHIO AND INDIANA	JOHNSON	40 x 58 cm
JOHNSON'S OREGON AND WASHINGTON	JOHNSON	46 x 33 cm
JOHNSON'S OREGON AND WASHINGTON [with] JOHNSON'S MINNESOTA	JOHNSON	38 x 56 cm
JOHNSON'S VIRGINIA, DELAWARE, MARYLAND & WEST VIRGINIA	JOHNSON	43 x 60 cm
JOHNSON'S WASHINGTON AND OREGON	JOHNSON	33 x 41 cm
JOHNSON'S WASHINGTON, OREGON AND IDAHO	JOHNSON	33 x 41 cm
JOHNSON'S WISCONSIN AND MICHIGAN	JOHNSON	43 x 59 cm
JOHNSON'S WORLD ON MERCATOR'S PROJECTION	JOHNSON	42 x 58 cm
JOHNSTONS' PLAN OF THE SEIGE OF SEVASTOPOL SHOWING THE POSITIONS ...	JOHNSTON	48 x 63 cm
KAART DER ZUYD-WESTER EYLANDEN VAN BANDA. ...	VALENTYN	34 x 47 cm
KAART DER ZUYD_WESTER EYLANDEN VAN BANDA	VAN KEULEN	36 x 48 cm
KAART VAN CALIFORNIE NAAR GOEDE BRONNEN BEWERKT	VAN ZOUTEVEEN	43 x 33 cm
KAART VAN DE AWATSKA-BAAI, OP DE OOST KUST VAN KAMTSCHATKA	COOK	25 x 20 cm
KAART VAN DE GEHEELE WERELD NA DE ALDERLACTSTE ONDEKKINGEN ...	GRAVIUS	18 x 30 cm
KAART VAN DE LAND-ENGTE VAN PANAMA EN PROVINTIEN VAN VERAGUA, ...	BELLIN (Small)	20 x 28 cm
KAART VAN DE LANDENGTE VAN PANAMA, VOLGENS DE SPAANSCHE ...	TIRION	27 x 30 cm
KAART VAN DE NOORD-WEST KUST VAN AMERIKA EN DE NOORD-OOST KUST ...	COOK	38 x 64 cm
KAART VAN DE ONTDEKKINGEN IN DE STILLE ZUID-ZEE, VAN KAPITEIN COOK ...	COOK	36 x 46 cm
KAART VAN GEHEEL GUAJANA OF DE WILDEN-KUST, EN DIE DER SPAANSCHE ...	TIRION	33 x 40 cm
KAART VAN HET EILAND JAMAIKA	BACHIENE	23 x 30 cm
KAART VAN HET EYLAND AMBOINA	VALENTYN	30 x 41 cm
KAART VAN HET Z.O. GEDEELTE VAN HE VUURLAND DE STRAAT LE MAIRE ...	COOK	30 x 33 cm
KANSAS	COLTON	42 x 61 cm
KANSAS AND THE TERRITORIES OF ARIZONA, COLORADO, NEW MEXICO, UTAH	WALLING & GRAY	41 x 64 cm
KARTA K' ISTORII NARODOV' OBITAVSHICH' V' SREDNEI AZIL V' DREVNIJA ...	ANONYMOUS	64 x 145 cm
KARTA OFVER BELAGENHETEN OMKRING STOCKHOLM	CARPELAN	33 x 55 cm
KARTE DER QUELLGEBIETE DER FLUSSE WITCHITA, BRAZOS, COLORADO ...	ANONYMOUS	18 x 20 cm
KARTE DES NORDENS VON AMERICA, ZUR BEURTHEILUNG DE ...	FORSTER, G.	51 x 66 cm
KARTE VON AMERIKA NACH D'ANVILLE UND POWNALL ...	VON REILLY	58 x 76 cm
KARTE VON CAROLINA UND GEORGIEN ZUR ALLGEMEINEN ...	BELLIN (Small)	18 x 25 cm
KARTE VON DEM EYLANDE TERRE-NEUVE ENTWORFEN VON N. B. ... 1744	BELLIN (Small)	28 x 36 cm
KARTE VON DEM MEXICANISHEN MEERBUSEN UND DEM INSELN VON AMER.	BELLIN (Small)	28 x 38 cm
KARTE VON DEN AN DEN MOLUCKEN ...	BELLIN (Small)	20 x 29 cm
KARTE VON DER GEGEND UM MUNCHEN	HOMANN	50 x 59 cm
KARTE VON DER HUDSONS BAY AND STRASSE ZUR ALLGEMEINEN HISTORIE	BELLIN (Small)	20 x 30 cm
KARTE VON DER HUDSONS BAY DURCH N. BELLIN 1744	BELLIN (Small)	23 x 28 cm
KARTE VON DER INSEL CELEBES ODER MACASSAR	BELLIN (Small)	21 x 15 cm
KARTE VON DEUTSCHLAND, HOLLAND, BELGIEN, DER SCHWEIZ, NORD-ITALIEN ...	GROSS, R.	67 x 87 cm

KARTE VON WISCONSIN NACH DEN NEUESTEN HULFSMITTEIN GEZEICHNET	MEYER	38 x 33 cm
KARTE VON YUCATAN NACH DER HANDSCHRIFTLICHEN KARTE ...	HELLER, C.	48 x 34 cm
KATTEGAT	IMRAY	124 x 102 cm
KELLER'S LITHOGRAPHIERTE REISEKARTE DER SCHWEIZ	KELLER	45 x 65 cm
KENNEBEC AND SHEEPSCOT RIVERS MAINE	U.S. COAST SURVEY	97 x 58 cm
KENT	MORDEN	9 x 6 cm
KENTUCKEY	CAREY	15 x 20 cm
KENTUCKY	FINLEY	22 x 28 cm
KENTUCKY	LEWIS & ARROWSMITH	20 x 25 cm
KENTUCKY AND TENNESSEE	BLACK	28 x 33 cm
KENTUCKY AND TENNESSEE	BURR	28 x 33 cm
KENTUCKY - TENNESSEE	CRAM	41 x 56 cm
KENTUCKY, WITH THE LATEST IMPROVEMENTS	YEAGER	20 x 28 cm
KERGUELEN'S LAND CALLED BY C. COOK ISLAND OF DESOLATION	NICOL	25 x 28 cm
L'AFRICA NUOUAMENTE CORRETTA ET ACCRESECUITA SECONDO LO ...	SANSON (Folio)	41 x 56 cm
L'AFRIQUE ...	DE L'ISLE	44 x 58 cm
L'AMERIQUE MERIDIONALE	JAILLOT	47 x 61 cm
L'AMERIQUE MERIDIONALE DRESSEE SUR LES OBSERVATIONS DE MRS.	DE L'ISLE	46 x 60 cm
L'AMERIQUE MERIDIONALE, ET SEPTENTRIONALE ...	DE FER (Large)	47 x 60 cm
L'AMERIQUE, MERIDIONALE ET SEPTENTRIONALE ...	DE FER (Small)	22 x 33 cm
L'AMERIQUE OU LE NOUVEAU CONTINENT DRESSEE SUR LES MEMOIRES ...	NOLIN	46 x 61 cm
L'AMERIQUE PAR LE S. ROBERT DE VAUGONDY ...	DE VAUGONDY	25 x 23 cm
L'AMERIQUE SELON LES NOUVELLES OBSERVATIONS DE MESSRS, ...	VAN DER AA	46 x 66 cm
L'AMERIQUE SEPTENTRIONALE DIVISEE EN SES PRINCIPAUX ETATS	JANVIER	31 x 45 cm
L'AMERIQUE SEPTENTRIONALE DIVISEE EN SES PRINCIPAUX ETATS	LAPORTE	18 x 23 cm
L'AMERIQUE SEPTENTRIONALE. DRESSEE SUR LES OBSERVATIONS ...	DE L'ISLE	45 x 58 cm
L'AMERIQUE SEPTENTRIONALE, OU LA PARTIE SEPTENTRIONALE DU INDES OCC.	NOLIN	45 x 59 cm
L'AMERIQUE SUIVANT LES DERNIERS RELATIONS ... AVEC LES ROUTES ...	DU VAL (Large)	41 x 55 cm
L'ANCIEN ET LE NOUVEAU MEXIQUE, AVEC LA FLORIDE ET LA BASSE LOUSIANE	BONNE	36 x 23 cm
L'ANCIEN MONDE ET LE NOUVEAU EN DEUX HEMISPHERES	BONNE	21 x 41 cm
L'ARCHEVESCHE DE CAMBRAY	HONDIUS	37 x 50 cm
L'ASIE ...	DE L'ISLE	46 x 58 cm
L'ASIE	DE LA FEUILLE	13 x 18 cm
L'ASIE ...	SANSON (Folio)	41 x 56 cm
L'ASIE AVEC LES NOUVELLES DECOUVERTES	LE ROUGE	22 x 27 cm
L'ASIE DRESSEE SELON LES OBSERVATIONS MRS. DE L'ACADEMIE ROYALE ...	CHIQUET	16 x 22 cm
L'EMPIRE DE JAPON TIRE DES CARTES DES JAPONNAIS	CHATELAIN	36 x 44 cm
L'EMPIRE DE LA CHINE	BELLIN (Small)	29 x 40 cm
L'EUROPE NOUVELLEMENT TRACEE, ET RENDUE PLUS CLAIRE ...	VAN LOCHOM	38 x 50 cm
L'EUROPE PAR N. DE FER	DE FER (Small)	13 x 16 cm
L'EUROPE SELON LES NOUVELLES OBSERVATIONS ...	VAN DER AA	48 x 66 cm
L'HEMISPHERE SEPTENTRIONAL POUR VOIR ... LES TERRES ARCTIQUES PAR	COVENS & MORTIER	46 x 51 cm
L'IRLANDE	DE VAUGONDY	24 x 22 cm
L'IRLANDE DIVISEE PAR PROVINCES CIVILES ET ECCLESIATIQUES	BRION DE LA TOUR	27 x 31 cm
L'ISLE DE FRANCE. PARISIESIS AGRI DESCRIPTIO	MERCATOR (Folio)	34 x 47 cm
L'ISLE DE LA DOMINIQUE PAR M. J. M. ANGLOIS ... CHEZ LATTRE	LATTRE	61 x 48 cm
L'ISLE DE TERRE-NEUVE, L'ACADIE, OU LA NOUVELLE ECOSSE, L'ISLE ST JEAN ...	BONNE	23 x 36 cm
L'ISLE ST. DOMINGUE PAR FILS DE MR. ROBERT ...	DE VAUGONDY	15 x 23 cm
L'ITALIE	DE FER (Small)	22 x 33 cm
L'ITALIE	DE L'ISLE	49 x 62 cm
LA CALIFORNIE OU NOUVELLE CAROLINE, TEATRO DE LOS TRABAJOS, ...	DE FER (Large)	45 x 65 cm
LA CHINE	MALLET	15 x 10 cm
LA CHINE	VAN DER AA	23 x 30 cm
LA CHINE ROYAUME	SANSON (Folio)	42 x 53 cm
LA DESCRIPTION D'AFFRICQUE ...	MUNSTER	15 x 18 cm
LA FIGURE DU MONDE UNIVERSEL	MUNSTER	25 x 38 cm
LA FLORIDE	SANSON (Small)	18 x 25 cm
LA FLORIDE DIVISEE EN FLORIDE ET CAROLINE	DE VAUGONDY	17 x 18 cm
LA FRANCE ET SES AEQUISITIONS JUSQU'A LA TREVE DE 1684	DE FER (Small)	14 x 16 cm
LA GRANDE TARTARIE SUIVANT LES NOUVELLES OBSERVATIONS	VAN DER AA	23 x 30 cm
LA GUADELOUPE DEDIEE A MGR. CHARLES PHILIPPE D'ALBERT DUC DE LUYNES ...	LE ROUGE	48 x 55 cm
LA II TABLE D'IRLANDE ... ULTONIE, CONNACIE MEDIE, ET PARTIE DE LAGENIE	MERCATOR (Folio)	34 x 47 cm
LA PARTE ORIENTALE DELL'ANTICO, E NUOVO MESSICO CON LA FLORIDA ...	CASSINI	48 x 35 cm
LA PENSILVANIA, LA NUOVA YORK, IL JERSEY SETTENTRIOLE: ...	ZATTA	33 x 43 cm
LA RADE DE GAMMERON	VAN DER AA	20 x 15 cm
LA ROMELIE ET LES ENVIRONS DE CONSTANTINOPLE	SANTINI	43 x 56 cm
LA RUSSIE ASIATIQUE TIREE DE LA CARTE DONNEE PAR ORDRE DU FEU CZAR	ANONYMOUS	41 x 53 cm
LA SCANDIE. OU LES TROIS ROYAUMES DU NORD SUEDE, DANEMARC & NORV.	VISSCHER	58 x 74 cm

LA SECONDE TABLE D'ECOSSE	MERCATOR (Folio)	35 x 45 cm
LA SPAGNUOLA DESCRITTA DAL P. COSMOGRAFO CORONELLI, E DEDICATA ...	CORONELLI	24 x 30 cm
LA SUISSE DIVISEE EN SES TREZE CANTONS, SES ALLIEZ & SES SUJETS ...	JAILLOT	48 x 61 cm
LA TABLE DE LA REGION ORIENTALE ...	MUNSTER	25 x 34 cm
LA TABLE DES ISLES NEUSUES	MUNSTER	26 x 34 cm
LA TABLE & DESCRIPTION UNIVERSELLE DE TOUTE L'AFRIQUE...	MUNSTER	26 x 35 cm
LA VERA-CRUZ, VILLE DU MEXIQUE	BELLIN (Small)	22 x 17 cm
LA VIRGINIE, PENNSILVANIE, NOUVELLE ANGLETERRE ET AUTRES PAYS ...	NOLIN	20 x 25 cm
LACUS LAMANNI ...	BLAEU	51 x 41 cm
LAKE DRUMMOND, VA. SURVEYED ... 1879	U.S. WAR DEPT.	43 x 30 cm
LAKE SUPERIOR AND THE NORTHERN PART OF MICHIGAN	COLTON	30 x 38 cm
LAKE SUPERIOR - MISSISSIPPI RIVER SURVEY. MAP SHOWING PROPOSED CANAL	U.S. WAR DEPT.	43 x 51 cm
LAKE SUPERIOR REDUCED FROM THE ADMIRALTY SURVEY	S.D.U.K.	31 x 38 cm
LALANDIAE ET FALSTRIAE ACCURATA DESCRIPTIO	JANSSON	41 x 53 cm
LANCASTER SH.	MORDEN	9 x 6 cm
LANDGRAVIAT THURINGIAE TABULA GENERALIS	HOMANN	49 x 57 cm
LANDS ADJACENT TO LAKE SUPERIOR CEDED TO THE UNITED STATES ...	U.S.	91 x 114 cm
LATIUM CUM OMNIBUS SUIS CELEBRIORIBUS UIIS QUOAD ANTIQUUM & NOV.	HOMANN	51 x 59 cm
LAURIE & WHITTLE'S NEW MAP OF LONDON WITH ITS ENVIRONS	LAURIE & WHITTLE	59 x 78 cm
LE BRIXA / SETTENIL	BRAUN & HOGENBERG	33 x 41 cm
LE CANADA FAICT PAR LE SR. DE CHAMPLAIN, OU SONT LA NOUVELLE FRANCE	DU VAL (Large)	35 x 55 cm
LE CANADA OU NOUVELLE FRANCE ...	SANSON (Folio)	40 x 54 cm
LE CANADA, OU NOUVELLE-FRANCE, &C. TIREE DE DIVERSES RELATIONS ...	SANSON (Small)	21 x 31 cm
LE CANADA, OU NOUVELLE FRANCE, LA FLORIDE, LA VIRGINIE, PENSILVANIE, ...	DE FER (Small)	24 x 34 cm
LE COSTE NORD OUEST DELL'AMERICA E NORD EST DELL'ASIA	CASSINI	35 x 49 cm
LE COURS DU DANUBE DES SA SOURCE JUSQU'A SES EMBOUCHURES ...	HOMANN	49 x 56 cm
LE DETROIT DE MALACCA, DRESSEE SUR LES MEMOIRES DES PLUS SAVANS ...	VAN DER AA	26 x 16 cm
LE DIOCESE DE SARLAT DIOCCESIS SARLATENSIS	HONDIUS	37 x 48 cm
LE GRAN ROYAUME DE HONGRIE OU PARTIE SEPTENTRIONALE DE LA TURQUIE ...	DE FER (Small)	14 x 16 cm
LE JAPON DEVISE EN SOISSANTE ET SIX PROVINCES	RELAND	31 x 45 cm
LE NOUVEAU MEXIQUE	BONNE	21 x 31 cm
LE NOUVEAU MEXIQUE, AVEC LA PARTIE SEPTENTRIONALE DE L'ANCIEN, ...	BONNE	21 x 32 cm
LE NOUVEAU MEXIQUE, ET LA FLORIDE; TIREE DE DIVERSES CARTES, ...	SANSON (Folio)	31 x 55 cm
LE NUOVE EBRIDI Y LA NOUOVA CALEDONIA DELINEATE DEL CAP. COOK	CASSINI	48 x 36 cm
LE PARAGUAY TIRE DES RELATIONS LES PLUS RECENTES.	SANSON (Folio)	41 x 56 cm
LE PAYS DE PEROU ET CHILI	SEUTTER (Large)	48 x 58 cm
LE PAYS DES HOTTENTOTS AUX ENVIRONS DU CAP DE BONNE ESPERANCE	BELLIN (Small)	24 x 35 cm
LE PORT MARIANNE ...	BELLIN (Small)	23 x 17 cm
LE ROYAUME DE NAPLES	DE FER (Small)	22 x 33 cm
LE ROYAVME D'IRLANDE DIVISE EN PROVINCES SUBDIVISEES EN COMTEZ ..	NOLIN	46 x 61 cm
LE VIEUX MEXIQUE OU NOUVELLE ESPAGNE AVEC LES COSTES DE LA FLORIDE ...	DE FER (Small)	23 x 33 cm
LE ZANGUEBAR / PARTIE DU ZANGUEBAR OU SONT LES COSTES D'AJAN ...	SANSON (Small)	18 x 30 cm
LEGIONIS REGNUM ET ASTURIARUM PRINCIPATUS	JANSSON	38 x 48 cm
LEIGH'S NEW ROAD MAP OF ENGLAND, WALES AND SCOTLAND, DRAWN ...	HALL	100 x 75 cm
LENGTHS OF THE PRINCIPAL RIVERS IN THE WORLD ...	MITCHELL, S.A. (1859-)	33 x 41 cm
LEO BELGICUS / ARRIFICIOSA & GEOGRAPHICA TABULA SUB LEONIS FIGURA ...	VAN DEN KEERE	37 x 45 cm
LEODIENSIS DIOECESIS TYPUS	MERCATOR (Folio)	34 x 49 cm
LES COSTES AUX ENVIRONS DE LA RIVIERE DE MISISIPI. DECOUVERTES PAR ...	DE FER (Small)	22 x 33 cm
LES COTES DE LA GRECE ET L'ARCHIPEL	D'ANVILLE	54 x 71 cm
LES DEUX POLES ARCTICQUE OU SEPTENTRIONAL, ET ANTARCTICQUE ...	SANSON (Folio)	38 x 53 cm
LES ETATS UNIS DE L'AMERIQUE SEPTENTRIONALE, CONTENANT EN OUTRE, ...	BONNE	33 x 23 cm
LES ISLES BRITANNIQUES ...	DE L'ISLE	44 x 56 cm
LES ISLES BRITANNIQUES; QUI CONTIENNENT LES ROYAUMES D'ANGLETERRE ...	JAILLOT	53 x 85 cm
LES ISLES DE L'AMERIQUE CONNUES SOUS LE NOM D'ANTILLES ...	DE FER (Small)	22 x 33 cm
LES ISLES DE LA GUADELOUPE, DE MARIE GALANTE, DE LA DESIRADE, ...	BONNE	21 x 32 cm
LES ISLES DU IAPON	SANSON (Small)	18 x 24 cm
LES ISLES MOLUCQUES, CELEBES, GILOLO, &C.	SANSON (Small)	19 x 25 cm
LES ISLES PHILIPPINES, CELLE DE FORMOSE, LE SUD DE LA CHINE, ...	BONNE	22 x 32 cm
LES PAYS BAS OU SONT REMARQUEES LES AQUISITIONS DE LA FRANCE ...	BOWEN, E.	14 x 16 cm
LI REGNI DI VALENZA E MURCIA CON L'ISOLE BALEARI, E PITIUSE	ZATTA	30 x 38 cm
LIBANUS ET EJUS VICINIA	FULLER	28 x 33 cm
LIMA	MEYER	10 x 15 cm
LIMES OCCIDENTALIS QUIVIRA ET ANIAN	WYTFLIET	23 x 29 cm
LITHUANIA	MERCATOR (Folio)	37 x 44 cm
LITHUANIA	MERCATOR (Small)	14 x 20 cm
LITTLE EGG HARBOR [N.J.]	BLUNT	13 x 20 cm
LITTLE KAUKAUNA [Wisc.]	REAL ESTATE	48 x 46 cm
LIVERPOOL	S.D.U.K.	31 x 38 cm

Title	Mapmaker	Size
LIVERPOOL BAY	SWENY, M.A.	124 x 147 cm
LLOYD'S NEW MAP OF THE UNITED STATES, THE CANADAS AND NEW BRUNS. ...	LLOYD	96 x 127 cm
LLOYD'S RAILROAD, TELEGRAPH & EXPRESS MAP OF THE EASTERN STATES ...	LLOYD	97 x 66 cm
LOCATION OF AREAS IRRIGATED IN 1889	U.S. GEOL. SURVEY	46 x 36 cm
LONDINI	SEUTTER (Large)	49 x 57 cm
LONDINUM FERACISSIMI ANGLIAE REGNI METROPOLIS ...	DE BELLEFOREST	31 x 48 cm
LONDON AND WESTMINSTER IN THE REIGN OF QUEEN ELIZABETH, ...	ANONYMOUS	20 x 54 cm
LOUISIANA	BURR	27 x 32 cm
LOUISIANA	CAREY	41 x 43 cm
LOUISIANA	CAREY	15 x 20 cm
LOUISIANA	CENTURY ATLAS	28 x 38 cm
LOUISIANA	CRAM	30 x 30 cm
LOUISIANA	EHRMANN	22 x 17 cm
LOUISIANA	FINLEY	22 x 28 cm
LOUISIANA AND MISSISSIPPI	ASHER & ADAMS	58 x 43 cm
LOUISIANA AND MISSISSIPPI	TANNER	74 x 58 cm
LOUISIANA AND PART OF ARKANSAS	BRADFORD	25 x 20 cm
LOUISIANA, AS FORMERLY CLAIMED BY FRANCE, NOW CONTAINING ...	LONDON MAGAZINE	18 x 23 cm
LOUISIANA BY DE RIVER MISSISIPPI	LAW	19 x 16 cm
LOUISIANA DRAWN BY S. LEWIS	LEWIS & ARROWSMITH	25 x 20 cm
LOUISIANA RAILROADS	RAND, McNALLY	48 x 69 cm
LOUISVILLE	CRAM	25 x 33 cm
LOUISVILLE	MEYER	10 x 16 cm
LOWER CANADA	BURR	28 x 33 cm
LOWER CANADA AND NEW BRUNSWICK	BRADFORD	28 x 36 cm
LOWER CANADA NEW BRUNSWICK NOVA SCOTIA PRINCE EDWARDS ID. ...	ARROWSMITH	61 x 48 cm
LUIGIANA INGLESE, COLLA PARTE OCCIDENTALE DELLA FLORIDA, DELLA ...	ZATTA	32 x 42 cm
LUSATIA SUPERIOR	JANSSON	38 x 50 cm
LUSATIAE SUPERIORIS TABULA	HOMANN	46 x 57 cm
LUTETIA, VULGARI NOMINE PARIS, URBS GALLIA MAXIMA ...	BRAUN & HOGENBERG	36 x 48 cm
MACEDONIA, EPIR. ET ACHAIA	MERCATOR (Small)	14 x 17 cm
MACEDONIA EPIRUS ET ACHAIA	MERCATOR (Folio)	36 x 43 cm
MACKINLAY'S MAP OF THE PROVINCE OF NOVA SCOTIA, INCLUDING ...	MacKINLAY	77 x 97 cm
MADRID	S.D.U.K.	31 x 37 cm
MADRITUM SIVE MANTUA CARPETANORUM CELEBERRIMA CASTILIAE ...	SEUTTER (Large)	51 x 58 cm
MAGN. DUCATUS LITUANIAE	HOMANN	50 x 58 cm
MAGNA BRITANNIA COMPLECTENS ANGLIAE, SCOTIAE ET HIBERNIAE REGNA	HOMANN	48 x 56 cm
MAGNA BRITANNIAE ET HIBERNIAE TABULA	MERIAN	26 x 35 cm
MAGNAE BRITANNIAE ET HIBERNIAE NOVA DESCRIPTIO	JANSSON	42 x 53 cm
MAGNAE BRITANNIAE ET HIBERNIAE TABULA	HONDIUS	38 x 51 cm
MAGNAE BRITTANIAE ET HIBERNIAE TABULA	BLAEU	38 x 49 cm
MAGNI MOGOLIS IMPERIUM	JANSSON	37 x 50 cm
MAGNUM MARE DEL ZUR CUM INSULA CALIFORNIA	RENARD	50 x 57 cm
MAINE	BURR	32 x 27 cm
MAINE	CAREY	20 x 15 cm
MAINE	FINLEY	28 x 23 cm
MAINE	LEWIS & ARROWSMITH	20 x 25 cm
MAINE	SCOTT	20 x 18 cm
MAJICO SIMA GROUP	ADMIRALTY	48 x 62 cm
MALACCA	BERTIUS	9 x 14 cm
MALACCA	LANGENES	9 x 13 cm
MALBY'S TERRESTRIAL GLOBE, ... MANUFACTURED AND PUBLISHED ...	MALBY, T.	30 cm, diam
MALTHA ...	MORDEN	11 x 13 cm
MANASSE TRANS-JORDANICAM	FULLER	27 x 32 cm
MANITOBA	STANFORD	47 x 61 cm
MANITOBA, BRITISH COLUMBIA AND THE NORTHWEST TERRITORIES	CENTURY ATLAS	28 x 38 cm
MANITOBA RAILROADS	RAND, McNALLY	33 x 48 cm
MANITOBA WITH PARTS OF SASKATCHEWAN, ASSINIBOLA, ONTARIO, & ...	PHILIP, G.	51 x 56 cm
MANTUA DUCATUS	JANSSON	35 x 47 cm
MAP 2 FROM GREAT SALT LAKE TO THE HUMBOLDT MTS. ...	U.S. PACIFIC R.R.	53 x 48 cm
MAP ACCOMPANYING THE PROPOSAL OF THE LOS ANGELES, SAN DIEGO & ...	RAILROAD COMPANY	38 x 30 cm
MAP AND PROFILE OF THE TEJON PASS ... 1853	U.S. PACIFIC R.R.	64 x 102 cm
MAP EXHIBITING THE ANDROSCOGGIN RAILROAD AND ITS CONNECTIONS	RAILROAD COMPANY	64 x 41 cm
MAP EXHIBITING THE ROUTES BETWEEN FORT DALLES AND THE GREAT SALT ...	U.S.	66 x 84 cm
MAP ILLUSTRATING THE SIEGE OF ATLANTA, GA. BY THE U.S. FORCES ...	U.S. WAR DEPT.	30 x 53 cm
MAP, NO. 2. SHOWING A CONTINUATION OF DETAILS OF FORT SMITH ...	U.S.	28 x 51 cm
MAP NO. 3 SHOWING CONTINUATION OF DETAILS OF FORT SMITH & SANTA FE	U.S. WAR DEPT.	33 x 51 cm
MAP OF A PORTION OF ALABAMA SHOWING ... IMPROVEMENT OF MOBILE, ...	U.S. WAR DEPT.	51 x 36 cm

MAP OF A RECONNAISSANCE FROM CARROLL, MONTANA TER. TO. ...	U.S.	64 x 48 cm
MAP OF A TOUR FROM INDEPENDENCE TO SANTA FE, CHIHUAHUA, MONTEREY	WISLIZENUS, A.	51 x 41 cm
MAP OF ABILENE [Texas]	REAL ESTATE	58 x 64 cm
MAP OF ALABAMA	DOWER	36 x 23 cm
MAP OF ALABAMA	HARPER'S WEEKLY	28 x 23 cm
MAP OF ALASKA	RAND, McNALLY	23 x 31 cm
MAP OF ALASKA	U.S.	64 x 81 cm
MAP OF AMERICA	WYLD	52 x 59 cm
MAP OF ARKANSAS	U.S.	53 x 58 cm
MAP OF ASIA	WYLD	53 x 65 cm
MAP OF ASIA MINOR TO ILLUSTRATE THE JOURNEYS OF W. I. HAMILTON ...	ARROWSMITH	48 x 64 cm
MAP OF BRITISH COLUMBIA	RAND, McNALLY	23 x 33 cm
MAP OF CANON CITY COLORADO	LOCAL & STATE	71 x 51 cm
MAP OF CENTRAL AMERICA, SHEWING THE DIFFERENT LINES OF ATLANTIC ...	WYLD	58 x 81 cm
MAP OF CENTRAL AMERICA SHOWING THE PRETENDED BOUNDARIES OF ...	U.S.	25 x 28 cm
MAP OF CHINA COMPILED FROM ORIGINAL SURVEYS & SKETCHES	WYLD	61 x 80 cm
MAP OF CHULA VISTA, SAN DIEGO COUNTY ... NATIONAL RANCHO	REAL ESTATE MAPS	25 x 36 cm
MAP OF CONNECTICUT	DESILVER	32 x 37 cm
MAP OF DAKOTA AND NEBRASKA	GRAY	38 x 30 cm
MAP OF DUNKIRK HARBOR SHOWING WORKS ERECTED BY THE ... [N.Y.]	U.S. WAR DEPT.	33 x 61 cm
MAP OF EUROPE COMPILED FROM THE MOST RECENT SURVEYS PUBLISHED ...	WEAVER, H.	80 x 96 cm
MAP OF FLORIDA AND THE WEST INDIES PUBLISHED BY THE FLORIDA EAST ...	RAILROAD COMPANY	20 x 23 cm
MAP OF GEORGIA	HARDESTY	51 x 36 cm
MAP OF GEORGIA	HARPER'S WEEKLY	28 x 23 cm
MAP OF GEORGIA CENTRAL R.R. AND CONNECTIONS	COLTON	25 x 36 cm
MAP OF HILLSBORO BAY, FLA.	U.S. WAR DEPT.	38 x 28 cm
MAP OF HUDSON'S RIVER, WITH THE ADJACENT COUNTRY.	GENTLEMAN'S MAG.	29 x 21 cm
MAP OF ILLINOIS	COLTON	36 x 28 cm
MAP OF INDIA, CONSTRUCTED WITH GREAT CARE AND RESEARCH ...	WYLD	98 x 65 cm
MAP OF INDIAN TERRITORY	GRAY	30 x 38 cm
MAP OF INDIAN TERRITORY	HARDESTY	33 x 51 cm
MAP OF IOWA	COLTON	33 x 38 cm
MAP OF KANSAS, NEBRASKA AND COLORADO	MITCHELL, S.A. (1860+)	30 x 36 cm
MAP OF KENTUCKY AND TENNESSEE	MAST, CROWELL	25 x 33 cm
MAP OF LIVINGSTON MANOR ANNO 1714	N.Y. STATE DOC. HIS.	23 x 28 cm
MAP OF LOUISIANA REPRESENTING THE SEVERAL LAND DISTRICTS ...	U.S. STATE SURVEYS	56 x 43 cm
MAP OF MAIN PORTION OF ST. PAUL	RAND, McNALLY	33 x 23 cm
MAP OF MAINE, NEW HAMPSHIRE AND VERMONT	HINTON	36 x 25 cm
MAP OF MAINE, NEW HAMPSHIRE AND VERMONT	MITCHELL, S.A.	56 x 66 cm
MAP OF MAJ. GEN. ROSS'S ROUTE, WITH THE BRITISH COLUMN, ...	JAMES, W.	36 x 41 cm
MAP OF MARYLAND AND THE DISTRICT OF COLUMBIA, COLORED TO ILLUS. ...	WALLING & GRAY	38 x 61 cm
MAP OF MASSACHUSETTS CONNECTICUT & RHODE ISLAND CONSTRUCTED ...	FINLEY	43 x 56 cm
MAP OF MASSACHUSETTS, RHODE ISLAND AND CONNECICUT ...	ENSIGN	64 x 86 cm
MAP OF MASSACHUSETTS, RHODE-ISLAND & CONNECTICUT COMPILED ...	ENSIGN & THAYER	66 x 84 cm
MAP OF MILL CREAK NEAR CINCINNATI SHOWING CONTEMPLATED IMPROV. ...	U.S.	15 x 46 cm
MAP OF MINNESOTA TERRITORY	THOMAS, COWPERTH.	33 x 41 cm
MAP OF MISSISSIPPI	HARPER'S WEEKLY	28 x 23 cm
MAP OF MISSOURI	MITCHELL, S.A. (1859-)	41 x 33 cm
MAP OF MONTANA	CRAM	36 x 51 cm
MAP OF NEW JERSEY COMPILED FROM THE LATEST AUTHORITIES	DESILVER	38 x 33 cm
MAP OF NEW JERSEY REDUCED FROM T. GORDON'S MAP	THOMAS, COWPERTH.	39 x 32 cm
MAP OF NICARAGUA	U.S.	36 x 43 cm
MAP OF NORTH AMERICA	BURGESS	27 x 21 cm
MAP OF NORTH AMERICA	GALL & INGLIS	46 x 64 cm
MAP OF NORTH AMERICA, EXHIBITING THE RECENT DISCOVERIES. GEOG. ...	WYLD	46 x 36 cm
MAP OF NORTH AND SOUTH CAROLINA	MORSE, J.	19 x 23 cm
MAP OF NORTH CAROLINA AND SOUTH CAROLINA BY H.S. TANNER	TANNER	58 x 74 cm
MAP OF OCEANA EXHIBITING ITS VARIOUS DEVISIONS ISLAND GROUPS	MITCHELL, S.A. (1860+)	30 x 38 cm
MAP OF OKLAHOMA SHOWING RECENT ADDITIONS TO TERRITORY	RAND, McNALLY	33 x 38 cm
MAP OF ONTARIO IN COUNTIES	MITCHELL, S.A. (1860+)	28 x 36 cm
MAP OF OREGON AND UPPER CALIFORNIA FROM THE SURVEYS OF...FREMONT...	FREMONT	48 x 43 cm
MAP OF OREGON AND UPPER CALIFORNIA FROM THE SURVEYS OF...FREMONT...	U.S.	51 x 43 cm
MAP OF OREGON SHOWING THE LOCATION OF INDIAN TRIBES	SCHOOLCRAFT	21 x 25 cm
MAP OF OREGON, WASHINGTON, AND PART OF BRITISH COLUMBIA	MITCHELL, S.A. (1860+)	27 x 34 cm
MAP OF OREGON, WASHINGTON, IDAHO, AND PART OF MONTANA	MITCHELL, S.A. (1860+)	30 x 36 cm
MAP OF PARKERSBURG WEST VIRGINIA AND VICINITY	CRAM	33 x 25 cm
MAP OF PART OF LOUISIANA NORTH OF THE BASE LINE	U.S.	48 x 30 cm
MAP OF PART OF THE SOUTH SHORE OF LAKE ERIE ... TWENTY MILE CREEK	U.S. WAR DEPT.	30 x 38 cm

MAP OF PART OF THE SOUTHERN STATES	OLNEY	28 x 46 cm
MAP OF PENNSYLVANIA AND NEW JERSEY	TANNER	58 x 74 cm
MAP OF PORTO RICO	CRAM	33 x 51 cm
MAP OF PUBLIC LANDS IN PORTO RICO	NORRIS PETERS CO.	20 x 36 cm
MAP OF PUBLIC SURVEYS IN CALIFORNIA ...	U.S. STATE SURVEYS	102 x 76 cm
MAP OF PUBLIC SURVEYS IN CALIFORNIA & NEVADA ...	U.S. STATE SURVEYS	91 x 79 cm
MAP OF PUBLIC SURVEYS IN NEVADA TERRITORY	U.S. STATE SURVEYS	76 x 51 cm
MAP OF RHODE ISLAND AND PROVIDENCE PLANTATIONS; CORRECTED ...	LOCKWOOD	25 x 18 cm
MAP OF SOUTH ITALY AND ADJACENT COASTS	ARROWSMITH	131 x 164 cm
MAP OF SYRIA ... 1818, BY CAPTN. ARMAR L. CORRY R.N. ...	ARROWSMITH	83 x 135 cm
MAP OF TEXAS FROM THE MOST RECENT AUTHORITIES	MITCHELL, S.A. (1859-)	33 x 41 cm
MAP OF THAT PART OF THE WASHINGTON TERRITORY LYING WEST ...	U.S. STATE SURVEYS	38 x 25 cm
MAP OF THE ALPINE COUNTRY IN THE SOUTH OF EUROPE. ...	ARROWSMITH	126 x 151 cm
MAP OF THE ARKANSAS LAND GRANT OF THE ST. LOUIS, IRON MOUNTAIN ...	RAILROAD COMPANY	91 x 23 cm
MAP OF THE BATTLEFIELD OF GETTYSBURG	U.S.	122 x 84 cm
MAP OF THE BRITISH SETTLEMENTS, AND THE UNITED STATES OF NORTH AM.	LAMBERT, J.	38 x 38 cm
MAP OF THE CENTRAL STATES TO ILLUSTRATE OLNEY'S SCHOOL GEOG.	OLNEY	28 x 46 cm
MAP OF THE CHICAGO, DANVILLE AND VINCENNES RAILROAD	RAILROAD COMPANY	30 x 23 cm
MAP OF THE CHIEF PART OF THE SOUTHERN STATES	WILLIAMS, W.	28 x 43 cm
MAP OF THE CITY AND COUNTY OF NEW YORK WITH THE ADJACENT COUNTRY	BURR	51 x 127 cm
MAP OF THE CITY OF AUGUSTA, GA	U.S.	64 x 147 cm
MAP OF THE CITY OF INDIANAPOLIS	CRAM	36 x 51 cm
MAP OF THE CITY OF OAKLAND BERKELEY AND ALAMEDA	CRAM	33 x 51 cm
MAP OF THE CITY OF QUEBEC	WALKER & MILES	33 x 38 cm
MAP OF THE CITY OF SACRAMENTO THE CAPITAL OF CALIFORNIA	GRAY	30 x 38 cm
MAP OF THE CLANS OF SCOTLAND WITH THE POSSESSIONS OF THE HIGHLAND	JOHNSTON	75 x 57 cm
MAP OF THE COMMON FIELD LANDS & ... COMMONS OF PRAIRIE DU ROCHER ...	U.S.	25 x 38 cm
MAP OF THE COUNTRY BETWEEN THE YAMPA & WHITE RIVERS	HAYDEN, F.	41 x 97 cm
MAP OF THE COUNTRY BETWEEN WILLS CREEK AND FORT DU QUESNE.	GRAND MAG. OF MAG.	19 x 12 cm
MAP OF THE COUNTRY THIRTY THREE MILES AROUND THE CITY OF NEW YORK	COLTON	64 x 61 cm
MAP OF THE COUNTRY UPON THE BRAZOS AND BIG WICHITA RIVERS ...	U.S.	64 x 79 cm
MAP OF THE COUNTRY UPON UPPER RED-RIVER EXPLORED IN 1852 ...	U.S.	(no dimens.)
MAP OF THE DEFENCES OF THE CITY OF MOBILE	U.S. WAR DEPT.	28 x 38 cm
MAP OF THE EAST INDIA RAILWAY, SHEWING THE LINE PROPOSED ...	WALKER, J. & C.	110 x 106 cm
MAP OF THE EUROPEAN SETTLEMENTS IN SOUTH AMERICA AND ...	KITCHIN	33 x 45 cm
MAP OF THE FALLS OF BEAVER RIVER AND VICINITY	REAL ESTATE	15 x 30 cm
MAP OF THE FORMER TERRITORIAL LIMITS OF THE CHEROKEE "NATION OF" ...	U.S.	71 x 81 cm
MAP OF THE FRONTIERS OF THE NORTHERN COLONIES WITH THE BOUNDARY ...	GAVIT & DUTHIE	28 x 43 cm
MAP OF THE HAWAIIAN ISLANDS	CRAM	28 x 43 cm
MAP OF THE ISLAND OF MARTINIQUE FOR AN ACCOUNT OF THE EXPEDITION ...	WILLYAMS, C.	19 x 23 cm
MAP OF THE ISLAND OF TOBAGO FOR THE HISTORY OF THE WEST INDIES ...	EDWARDS	18 x 24 cm
MAP OF THE MARITIME PARTS OF VIRGINIA EXHIBITING THE SEAT OF WAR ...	PENNSYLVANIA MAG.	25 x 28 cm
MAP OF THE MIDDLE STATES OF AMERICA, COMPREHENDS NEW-YORK, ...	RUSSELL	38 x 48 cm
MAP OF THE MILITARY DEPARTMENT OF NEW MEXICO, ... 1864	U.S.	43 x 61 cm
MAP OF THE MILITARY RESERVATION AT FORT YUMA, CALIFORNIA	U.S.	41 x 61 cm
MAP OF THE NEW LIMITS OF THE CITY OF ST. LOUIS AND WARD BOUNDARIES	ST. LOUIS REPUBLICAN	53 x 28 cm
MAP OF THE NEW MADRID & ST. FRANCIS RIVER SWAMP IN THE STATES ...	U.S. WAR DEPT.	36 x 25 cm
MAP OF THE NORTH PART OF AMERICA ON WHICH IS LAID DOWN MacKENZIE'S	COOPER, H.	20 x 25 cm
MAP OF THE NORTHERN PART OF THE STATE OF MAINE & ADJACENT BRITISH	U.S.	43 x 38 cm
MAP OF THE OREGON TERRITORY BY THE U.S. EX. EX., CHARLES WILKES	U.S. EXPL. EXPED.	58 x 86 cm
MAP OF THE PASSES IN THE SIERRA NEVADA FROM WALKERS PASS ...	U.S. PACIFIC R.R.	51 x 64 cm
MAP OF THE PENINSULA OF INDIA, FROM THE 19TH DEGREE OF NORTH LAT. ...	WYLD	99 x 83 cm
MAP OF THE PUBLIC LANDS AND TERRITORIES	U.S. STATE SURVEYS	71 x 114 cm
MAP OF THE PUBLIC SURVEY IN THE TERRITORY OF WASHINGTON	U.S. STATE SURVEYS	41 x 91 cm
MAP OF THE RICHMOND AND LOUISVILLE R.R. CONNECTING THE RAILROADS ...	COLTON	76 x 102 cm
MAP OF THE RICHMOND AND LOUISVILLE R.R. CONNECTING THE RAILROADS ...	COLTON	64 x 127 cm
MAP OF THE ROADS OF PORTUGAL	ARROWSMITH	56 x 130 cm
MAP OF THE ROADS OF PORTUGAL	ARROWSMITH	58 x 128 cm
MAP OF THE ROUTE PASSED OVER BY AN EXPEDITION INTO THE INDIAN ...	U.S.	38 x 47 cm
MAP OF THE SEAT OF WAR IN AMERICA	STANFORD	55 x 75 cm
MAP OF THE SEAT OF WAR IN FLORIDA, ... BY ORDER OF BRIG. GEN. Z. TAYLOR	U.S. WAR DEPT.	107 x 74 cm
MAP OF THE SEAT OF WAR IN NORTH AMERICA	MELISH	41 x 56 cm
MAP OF THE SEAT OF WAR IN VIRGINIA	ILLUS. LONDON NEWS	35 x 24 cm
MAP OF THE SOUTH-WESTERN PORTION OF THE UNITED STATES SONORA ...	RAVENSTEIN, F. G.	33 x 38 cm
MAP OF THE SOUTHERN AND SOUTH-WESTERN STATES	WILLIAMS, W.	30 x 46 cm
MAP OF THE SOUTHERN PARTS OF THE UNITED STATES OF AMERICA ...	MORSE, J.	20 x 39 cm
MAP OF THE SOUTHWESTERN PART OF NEW MEXICO COMPILED FROM ...	EASTMAN	20 x 30 cm
MAP OF THE STATE OF ALABAMA	BURR	33 x 28 cm

MAP OF THE STATE OF CALIFORNIA, THE TERRITORIES OF OREGON & UTAH, ...	MITCHELL, S.A. (1859-)	41 x 33 cm
MAP OF THE STATE OF FLORIDA SHOWING THE PROGRESS OF THE SURVEYS	U.S. STATE SURVEYS	61 x 64 cm
MAP OF THE STATE OF MAINE	COLBY	84 x 64 cm
MAP OF THE STATE OF MISSOURI	THOMAS, COWPERTH.	33 x 41 cm
MAP OF THE STATE OF NEW YORK	FINLEY	43 x 53 cm
MAP OF THE STATE OF NEW YORK	MORSE, J.	19 x 24 cm
MAP OF THE STATE OF NEW YORK AND THE SURROUNDING COUNTRY	BURR	50 x 63 cm
MAP OF THE STATE OF NEW YORK COMPILED FROM THE LATEST AUTHORITIES	DESILVER	41 x 66 cm
MAP OF THE STATE OF NEW YORK SHOWING THE BOUNDARIES OF COUNTIES ...	DISTURNELL	48 x 61 cm
MAP OF THE STATE OF TEXAS	MITCHELL, S.A.	28 x 20 cm
MAP OF THE STATE OF TEXAS FROM THE LATEST AUTHORITIES BY J.H. YOUNG	DESILVER	32 x 40 cm
MAP OF THE STATE OF VERMONT	JEWETT & CO.	28 x 15 cm
MAP OF THE STATES OF INDIANA AND OHIO, WITH PART OF MICHIGAN TERR.	HINTON	25 x 40 cm
MAP OF THE STATES OF MAINE, NEW HAMPSHIRE, VERMONT, MASS. ...	TANNER	69 x 56 cm
MAP OF THE STATES OF MARYLAND AND DELAWARE	MORSE, J.	18 x 25 cm
MAP OF THE STATES OF NORTH & SOUTH CAROLINA	HINTON	25 x 41 cm
MAP OF THE SURVEYED PART OF WISCONSIN TERRITORY COMPILED FROM...	U.S. STATE SURVEYS	58 x 43 cm
MAP OF THE TERRITORY OF ALASKA, (RUSSIAN AMERICA) CEDED BY RUSSIA ...	COLTON	33 x 41 cm
MAP OF THE TERRITORY OF ALASKA (RUSSIAN AMERICA) CEDED BY RUSSIA ...	GRAY	30 x 43 cm
MAP OF THE TERRITORY OF FLORIDA	BURR	33 x 28 cm
MAP OF THE TERRITORY OF HAWAII	U.S. STATE SURVEYS	56 x 79 cm
MAP OF THE TERRITORY OF NEW MEXICO	U.S.	51 x 33 cm
MAP OF THE TERRITORY OF NEW MEXICO MADE BY ORDER OF ... S.W. KEARNY	U.S.	64 x 50 cm
MAP OF THE UNITED STATES	GALL & INGLIS	53 x 43 cm
MAP OF THE UNITED STATES AND CANADA SHEWING CAPT. HALL'S ROUTE ...	LIZARS	33 x 28 cm
MAP OF THE UNITED STATES AND TERRITORIES, TOGETHER WITH CANADA &C.	MITCHELL, S.A. (1860+)	36 x 56 cm
MAP OF THE UNITED STATES AND TERRITORIES WITH ADJACENT PARTS OF ...	U.S.	163 x 203 cm
MAP OF THE UNITED STATES AND THEIR TERRITORIES, BETWEEN THE MISS. ...	U.S. WAR DEPT.	52 x 58 cm
MAP OF THE UNITED STATES ENGRAVED TO ACCOMPANY SMITH'S GEOG. ...	SMITH, R.C.	28 x 43 cm
MAP OF THE UNITED STATES OF AMERICA, THE BRITISH PROVINCES, MEXICO ...	COLTON	91 x 117 cm
MAP OF THE UNITED STATES OF NORTH AMERICA, UPPER & LOWER CANADA, ...	ETTLING	69 x 94 cm
MAP OF THE UNITED STATES SHOWING THE PRINCIPAL BOTANICAL DIVISIONS	PORTER, T.	30 x 38 cm
MAP OF THE UNITED STATES TERRITORY OF OREGON WEST OF THE ROCKY ...	THROOP	28 x 43 cm
MAP OF THE VALLEY OF THE ALLEGHANY RIVER	U.S. WAR DEPT.	36 x 28 cm
MAP OF THE VALLEYS OF THE RIO GRANDE AND RIO GILA	EMORY	20 x 25 cm
MAP OF THE VICINITY OF BUFFALO	U.S. WAR DEPT.	28 x 41 cm
MAP OF THE VIRGIN ISLANDS, FOR THE HISTORY OF THE WEST INDIES ...	EDWARDS	17 x 23 cm
MAP OF THE WABASH & ERIE CANAL LINE FROM THE MOUTH OF TIPPECANOE ...	U.S.	33 x 25 cm
MAP OF THE WEST INDIA & BAHAMA ISLANDS WITH ... COASTS OF YUCATAN ...	WYLD	53 x 78 cm
MAP OF THE WEST INDIA ISLANDS	WYLD	23 x 28 cm
MAP OF THE WEST INDIES	GALL & INGLIS	46 x 58 cm
MAP OF THE YOSEMITE NATIONAL PARK ... FOR THE USE OF U.S. TROOPS	U.S. WAR DEPT.	51 x 51 cm
MAP OF THE YOSEMITE NATIONAL PARK ... FOR USE OF U.S. TROOPS	U.S. WAR DEPT.	41 x 51 cm
MAP OF VERMONT	COLTON	36 x 28 cm
MAP OF VIRGINIA, MARYLAND AND DELAWARE	STOCKDALE	25 x 48 cm
MAP OF WASHINGTON	WAITE	23 x 30 cm
MAP & PROFILES, OF THE PENNSYLVANIA AND OHIO CANAL, FROM AKRON ...	U.S.	48 x 71 cm
MAP SHEWING THE ROUTE OF THE NORTH PENNSYLVANIA RAILROAD ...	RAILROAD COMPANY	61 x 122 cm
MAP SHOWING FOREST RESERVES & NATIONAL PARKS IN WESTERN ...	U.S. GEOL. SURVEY	46 x 38 cm
MAP SHOWING INDIAN RESERVATIONS WITHIN THE LIMITS ...	U.S.	53 x 84 cm
MAP SHOWING LOCATION OF THE DISMAL SWAMP CANAL VIRGINIA & ...	U.S. WAR DEPT.	33 x 94 cm
MAP SHOWING POSITION OF SAN BERNARD RIVER & OTHER WATERWAYS ...	U.S.	71 x 51 cm
MAP SHOWING PRIVATE LAND CLAIMS, PATENTED OR UNPATENTED, ...	DONALDSON, T.	33 x 46 cm
MAP SHOWING ROUTE OF THE MARCHES OF ... SHERMAN FROM ATLANTA,	U.S. WAR DEPT.	28 x 41 cm
MAP SHOWING ROUTES OF THE RIVER AND LAND PARTIES ... GRAND CANON ...	U.S.	38 x 41 cm
MAP SHOWING THE EXTENT OF SURVEYS IN THE TERRITORY OF UTAH	U.S. STATE SURVEYS	84 x 41 cm
MAP SHOWING THE LINES OF COMMUNICATION BETWEEN SOUTHERN COLO. ...	U.S.	51 x 61 cm
MAP SHOWING THE LINES OF COMMUNICATION BETWEEN SOUTHERN COLO. ...	U.S. WAR DEPT.	37 x 47 cm
MAP SHOWING THE LOCATION OF THE LAND GRANT OF SANTA FE PACIFIC	RAILROAD COMPANY	86 x 64 cm
MAP SHOWING THE LOCATIONS OF THE INDIAN RESERVATIONS WITHIN ...	U.S.	53 x 84 cm
MAP SHOWING THE MOUTH OF THE MIAMI RIVER BISCAYNE BAY, FLORIDA	U.S. WAR DEPT.	48 x 33 cm
MAP SHOWING THE ROUTE OF E. F. BEALE FROM FORT SMITH, ARK. TO ALBU. ...	U.S.	18 x 124 cm
MAP SHOWING THE ROUTES TRAVELLED BY ... MAJR. E. STEEN, ...	U.S.	61 x 86 cm
MAPPA AESTIVARUM INSULARUM, ALIAS BARMUDAS DICTARUM ...	BLAEU	40 x 53 cm
MAPPA AESTIVARUM INSULARUM, ALIAS BARMUDAS DICTARUM...	JANSSON	39 x 52 cm
MAPPA AESTIVARUM INSULARUM, ALIAS BERMUDAS, DICTARUM...	HONDIUS	39 x 52 cm
MAPPA FLUXUS ET REFLUXUS RATIONES IN ISTHMO AMERICAE ...	KIRCHER	34 x 41 cm
MAPPA GEOGRAPHICA AMERICAE SEPTENTRIONALIS AD EMENDATIORA ...	VON EULER	36 x 36 cm

MAPPA GEOGRAPHICA, COMPLECTENS INDIAE OCCIDENTALIS PARTEM MEDIAM	HOMANN	61 x 48 cm
MAPPA GEOGRAPHICA REGNI POLONIAE	HOMANN	50 x 59 cm
MAPPE DIESER LANDTSCHAFFT ODER INSEL CELON	DE BRY	28 x 19 cm
MAPPE MONDE ...	NOLIN	48 x 65 cm
MAPPE MONDE DU GLOBE TERRESTRE	CLOUET	43 x 64 cm
MAPPE-MONDE GEO-HYDROGRAPHIQUE, OU DESCRIPTION GENERALE DU GLOBE	JAILLOT	46 x 64 cm
MAPPE-MONDE GEO-HYDROGRAPHIQUE OU DESCRIPTION GENERALE DU GLOBE	VALK	48 x 58 cm
MAPPE MONDE OU CARTE GENERALE DE L'UNIVERS ...	LOTTER	49 x 92 cm
MAPPE-MONDE OU CARTE GENERALE DE LA TERRE ...	DE FER (Large)	44 x 70 cm
MAPPE-MONDE, OU CARTE GENERALE DE LA TERRE, DIVISEE EN DEUX HEMI. ...	DE FER (Large)	44 x 70 cm
MAPPE MONDE OU CARTE GENERALE DU GLOBE TERRESTRE	SANSON (Small)	13 x 18 cm
MAPPE MONDE OU DESCRIPTION DU GLOBE TERRESTRE VU EN CONCAVE ...	DE LETH	46 x 66 cm
MAPPE-MONDE SUIVANT LA PROJECTION DES CARTES REDUITES OU L'ON A ...	MENTELLE	36 x 46 cm
MAPS OF THE BOSPHORUS AND CONSTANTINOPLE, DARDANELLES AND ...	STANFORD	47 x 62 cm
MAR DEL NORT	JANSSON	43 x 56 cm
MAR DEL ZUR HISPANIS MARE PACIFICUM	JANSSON	44 x 54 cm
MAR DI INDIA	JANSSON	44 x 55 cm
MARCHIONATUS BRANDENBURGICUS	JANSSON	48 x 55 cm
MARCHIONATUS MISNIAE UNA CUM VOITLANDIA	JANSSON	42 x 52 cm
MARCHIONATUS MORAVIAE CIRCULI ZNOYMENSIS ET INGLAVIENSIS	HOMANN	49 x 59 cm
MARCHIONATUS MORAVIAE CIRCULUS BRUNNENSIS...	HOMANN	51 x 61 cm
MARCHIONATUS MORAVIAE CIRCULUS OLOMUCENSIS	HOMANN	50 x 58 cm
MARE DEL NORD AUTTORE IL P.M. CORONELLI...	CORONELLI	45 x 60 cm
MARE DEL SUD, DETTO ALTRIMENTI MARE PACIFICO AUTTORE ...	CORONELLI	45 x 60 cm
MARIS PACIFICI	ORTELIUS (Folio)	34 x 50 cm
MARIS PACIFICI (QUOD VULGO MAR DEL ZUR), CUM REGIONIBUS CIRCUM. ...	ORTELIUS (Folio)	35 x 50 cm
MARMARICA NUOVA TAVOLA	PTOLEMY (1561-1599)	18 x 25 cm
MARSEILLE	S.D.U.K.	33 x 40 cm
MARTHA'S VINEYARD	WALKER, G.	51 x 71 cm
MARTINICO	LUCAS	24 x 31 cm
MARYLAND	BRADFORD	29 x 36 cm
MARYLAND	LUCAS	20 x 28 cm
MARYLAND	LUCAS	28 x 50 cm
MARYLAND AND DELAWARE	CENTURY ATLAS	28 x 38 cm
MASSACHUSETTS	CAREY	15 x 19 cm
MASSACHUSETTS	FINLEY	23 x 28 cm
MASSACHUSETTS	LEWIS & ARROWSMITH	20 x 25 cm
MASSACHUSETTS AND RHODE ISLAND	MITCHELL, S.A. (1859-)	33 x 41 cm
MASSACHUSETTS, RHODE ISLAND AND CONNECTICUT	BURR	28 x 33 cm
MEACO	MONTANUS	29 x 79 cm
MECHLINIA ...	BLAEU	51 x 41 cm
MEKLENBURG DUCATUS	JANSSON	37 x 48 cm
MEMPHIS	CRAM	33 x 25 cm
MER NOIRE OU MER MAIEVRE	SANSON (Small)	18 x 25 cm
MERCATOR'S CHART [WORLD]	WILKINSON	28 x 48 cm
MESSICO E STATI DELL' AMERICA CENTRALE	MARZOLLA	43 x 61 cm
MESSICO OVERO NUOVA SPAGNA CHE CONTIENE IL NUOVO MESSICO, LA ...	ZATTA	32 x 40 cm
MEXICAN BOUNDARY B. EXTRACT FROM THE TREATY MAP OF DISTURNELL ...	U.S.	23 x 41 cm
MEXICO	ARROWSMITH	23 x 30 cm
MEXICO	HALL	26 x 36 cm
MEXICO	HAMILTON, ADAMS	25 x 28 cm
MEXICO	MEYER	11 x 16 cm
MEXICO	MORSE & BREESE	33 x 41 cm
MEXICO	RAMUSIO	28 x 18 cm
MEXICO AND GUATEMALA	STARLING	9 x 15 cm
MEXICO AND GUATEMALA, SHEWING THE POSITION OF THE MINES	WYLD	33 x 80 cm
MEXICO AND ITS VALLEY	RECLUS	23 x 15 cm
MEXICO AND WEST INDIES	SMITH, J.	38 x 58 cm
MEXICO, CALIFORNIA AND TEXAS	TALLIS	25 x 33 cm
MEXICO [CITY]	DE BRY	15 x 18 cm
MEXICO & GUATEMALA	KELLY	20 x 25 cm
MEXICO & GUATEMALA	TANNER	29 x 37 cm
MEXICO, GUATEMALA AND THE WEST INDIES	BRADFORD	20 x 28 cm
MEXICO & GUATIMALA	DOWER	21 x 26 cm
MEXICO & TEXAS	ARCHER	24 x 28 cm
MEXICO UND DIE REPUBLIKEN VON CENTRAL-AMERICA ...	WEIMAR GEOGRAPH.	56 x 65 cm
MEXIQUE	DUVOTENAY	30 x 23 cm
MEXIQUE OU NOUVELLE ESPAGNE	MALLET	15 x 10 cm

MEXIQUE OU NOUVELLE ESPAGNE SUIVANT LES NOUVELLES OBSERVATIONS ...	VAN DER AA	22 x 29 cm
MICHIGAN	BURR	33 x 28 cm
MICHIGAN	COLTON	40 x 32 cm
MICHIGAN	LANGE	23 x 28 cm
MICHIGAN	MORSE & BREESE	33 x 38 cm
MICHIGAN AND WISCONSIN	JOHNSON	43 x 61 cm
MICHIGAN CITY	U.S. WAR DEPT.	25 x 23 cm
MICHIGAN CITY [INDIANA]	U.S.	25 x 23 cm
MICHIGAN SOUTHERN PART	CENTURY ATLAS	38 x 28 cm
MICHIGAN & WISCONSIN	WATSON	30 x 48 cm
MICHIGAN, WISCONSIN AND MINNESOTA	LLOYD	30 x 41 cm
MIDDLE BASS ISLAND [Ohio]	HARDESTY	33 x 43 cm
MIDDLESEX	MORDEN	9 x 6 cm
MILAN (MILANO)	S.D.U.K.	33 x 38 cm
MILFORD HAVEN	ADMIRALTY	48 x 61 cm
MILFORD HAVEN AND THE ISLANDS ADJACENT	COLLINS, G.	44 x 56 cm
MILNE'S PICTORIAL PLAN OF EDINBURGH	MILNE	45 x 56 cm
MINNESOTA	ASHER & ADAMS	56 x 41 cm
MINNESOTA	COLTON	33 x 41 cm
MINNESOTA	CRAM	30 x 23 cm
MINNESOTA	JOHNSON	58 x 43 cm
MINNESOTA	STANDARD ATLAS	30 x 25 cm
MINNESOTA AND DACOTAH	MITCHELL, S.A. (1860+)	27 x 34 cm
MINNESOTA RAILROADS	RAND, McNALLY	66 x 48 cm
MISSISSIPPI	BRADFORD	25 x 20 cm
MISSISSIPPI	CENTURY ATLAS	38 x 28 cm
MISSISSIPPI	COLTON	40 x 33 cm
MISSISSIPPI	CRAM	30 x 25 cm
MISSISSIPPI	GREENLEAF	33 x 28 cm
MISSISSIPPI TERRITORY	CAREY	15 x 20 cm
MISSISSIPPI TERRITORY	LEWIS & ARROWSMITH	20 x 25 cm
MISSISSIPPI TERRITORY AND GEORGIA	CAREY	15 x 20 cm
MISSOURI	BURR	28 x 33 cm
MISSOURI	COLTON	41 x 33 cm
MISSOURI	FINLEY	28 x 23 cm
MISSOURI	GREENLEAF	28 x 33 cm
MISSOURI AND KANSAS	JOHNSON	44 x 60 cm
MISSOURI TERRITORY	CAREY	30 x 36 cm
MITCHELL'S TRAVELERS GUIDE THROUGH THE UNITED STATES	MITCHELL, S.A.	46 x 51 cm
MOBILE - THE GULF CITY	HARPER'S WEEKLY	23 x 33 cm
MOGG'S TWENTY FOUR MILES ROUND LONDON	MOGG	62 x 58 cm
MOGG'S TWENTY FOUR MILES ROUND LONDON & CRYSTAL PALACE ...	MOGG	68 x 53 cm
MOLUCCAE INSULAE CELEBERRIMAE	BLAEU	37 x 49 cm
MONA INSULA VULGA ANGLESEY. MONA INSULA: VULGO THE ISLE OF MAN. ...	VALK & SCHENK	43 x 53 cm
MONASTERIENSIS EPISCOPATUS	JANSSON	37 x 49 cm
MONDO NUOVO	PORCACCHI	10 x 15 cm
MONK'S NEW AMERICAN MAP EXHIBITING ... NORTH AMERICA ...	MONK	145 x 155 cm
MONTANA	CENTURY ATLAS	28 x 38 cm
MONTANA, IDAHO & WYOMING	COLTON	43 x 64 cm
MONTANA TERRITORY	U.S.	38 x 53 cm
MONTEREY	MEYER	11 x 17 cm
MONTREAL	CRAM	25 x 33 cm
MOSCHOVIA TAVOLA NUOVA	PTOLEMY (1561-1599)	19 x 24 cm
MOSCOVIAE PARS AUSTRALIS AUCTORE ISACCO MASSA	JANSSON	38 x 50 cm
MOSCOVIE	MUNSTER	20 x 15 cm
MOSELLAE FLUMINIS TABULA SPECIALIS IN QUA ... TREVIRENSIS	HOMANN	49 x 58 cm
MOUTH OF DOUBLE BAYOU FROM SURVEY	U.S. WAR DEPT.	33 x 28 cm
N. & S. CAROLINA AND GEORGIA	WILLIAMS, C.S.	18 x 25 cm
N.W. TERRITORY	SCOTT	18 x 15 cm
NASHVILLE	CRAM	33 x 25 cm
NASSOVIA COMITATUS	JANSSON	38 x 50 cm
NATAL [South Africa]	STANFORD	46 x 59 cm
NATOLIA NUOVA TAVOLA	PTOLEMY (1561-1599)	18 x 25 cm
NATOLIE	MALLET	14 x 10 cm
NEBRASKA	CRAM	25 x 33 cm
NEBRASKA AND KANSAS	COLTON	33 x 41 cm
NEBRASKA, DAKOTA, IDAHO AND MONTANA	JOHNSON	43 x 59 cm
NEU UND VERBESSERTER PLAN DER ST. U. HAFENS HAVANA AUF DER INS. ...	HOMANN	49 x 30 cm

NEUESTE KARTE VOM NORD POL	MEYER	30 x 30 cm
NEUESTE KARTE VON AMERICA NACH DEN BESSTEN QUELLEN ENTWORF ...	RADEFELD	38 x 30 cm
NEUESTE KARTE VON ARKANSAS MIT SEINEN CANAELEN STRASSEN ...	MEYER	38 x 30 cm
NEUESTE KARTE VON ILLINOIS MIT SEINEM STRASSEN ENTFEMUNG ...	MEYER	38 x 30 cm
NEUESTE KARTE VON MISSOURI NACH DEN BESTEN QUELLEN VERBESSERT	MEYER	38 x 30 cm
NEUESTE KARTE VON NEW JERSEY ...	MEYER	37 x 30 cm
NEUESTE KARTE VON PENNSYLVANIA MIT SEINEN CANAELEN, EISENBAHNEN ..	MEYER	30 x 38 cm
NEUESTE KARTE VON SUD CAROLINA	MEYER	31 x 37 cm
NEUESTE POST-KARTE DURCH GANZ DEUTSCHLAND UND FRANKREICH ...	SCHROPP & CO.	62 x 79 cm
NEUESTER PLAN DER HAUPT- UND RESIDENZSTADT WIEN ... L	ARTARIA & CO.	60 x 74 cm
NEVADA	CRAM	51 x 36 cm
NEW BRUNSWICK - BAY OF FUNDY - L'ETANG HARBOUR ...	ADMIRALTY	48 x 63 cm
NEW BRUNSWICK NOVA SCOTIA &C.	SMITH, C.	20 x 36 cm
NEW BRUNSWICK, NOVA SCOTIA, NEWFOUNDLAND AND PRINCE EDWARD ID.	COLTON	33 x 41 cm
NEW HAMPSHIRE	BRADFORD	38 x 28 cm
NEW HAMPSHIRE	CAREY	20 x 15 cm
NEW HAMPSHIRE	SCOTT	19 x 15 cm
NEW-HAMPSHIRE, FROM LATE SURVEY ...	RUGGLES	76 x 46 cm
NEW HAMPSHIRE & VERMONT	BRADFORD	25 x 19 cm
NEW HAMPSHIRE, VERMONT, MASSACHUSETTS, RHODE IS. & CONN.	ASHER & ADAMS	43 x 58 cm
NEW & IMPROVED TERRESTRIAL GLOBE [and] NEWTON'S...CELESTIAL GLOBE	NEWTON & BERRY	7 cm, diam
NEW JERSEY	BURR	33 x 25 cm
NEW JERSEY	FINLEY	28 x 22 cm
NEW JERSEY	LEWIS & ARROWSMITH	25 x 20 cm
NEW JERSEY	MORSE, J.	19 x 15 cm
NEW JERSEY	WAITE	33 x 25 cm
NEW JERSEY REDUCED FROM T. GORDON'S MAP ...	TANNER	38 x 31 cm
NEW MAP OF BOSTON GIVING ALL POINTS OF INTEREST	WALKER, G.	41 x 46 cm
NEW MAP OF THAT PORTION OF NORTH AMERICA, EXHIBITING THE [U.S.] ...	MONK	140 x 150 cm
NEW MEXICO	RAND, McNALLY	49 x 32 cm
NEW MEXICO	WAITE	30 x 25 cm
NEW MEXICO FROM THE LATEST FEDERAL, STATE AND TRANSPORTATION ...	CRAM	36 x 28 cm
NEW MEXICO VEL NEW GRANATA ET MARATA ET CALIFORNIA ...	MORDEN	11 x 13 cm
NEW-ORLEANS	MEYER	10 x 15 cm
NEW ORLEANS - THE CRESCENT CITY - LAKE PONTCHARTRAIN IN THE DISTANCE	HARPER'S WEEKLY	51 x 76 cm
NEW PLAN OF LONDON	SMITH, W. H.	57 x 82 cm
NEW RAIL ROAD AND COUNTY MAP OF NEBRASKA	CRAM	23 x 33 cm
NEW RAIL ROAD MAP OF THE STATE OF OHIO	GRAY	43 x 61 cm
NEW RAILROAD AND COUNTY MAP OF THE STATES OF OREGON, CALIFORNIA ...	GRAY	66 x 38 cm
NEW RAILROAD MAP OF INDIANA OHIO AND PART OF ILLINOIS	COLTON	41 x 71 cm
NEW RAILROAD MAP OF THE UNITED STATES AND DOMINION OF CANADA	BELDEN	43 x 66 cm
NEW SECTIONAL AND TOWNSHIP MAP OF OHIO	RAND, McNALLY	33 x 51 cm
NEW SECTIONAL MAP OF IOWA	CRAM	61 x 71 cm
NEW SOUTH WALES	S.D.U.K.	39 x 33 cm
NEW SOUTH WALES	STANFORD	51 x 65 cm
NEW SOUTH WALES	WYLD	55 x 39 cm
NEW WARD AND INDEX MAP OF ST. LOUIS, MISSOURI	FLAMM	66 x 89 cm
NEW YORK	CAREY	14 x 22 cm
NEW YORK	COLTON	28 x 36 cm
NEW YORK	GREENLEAF	28 x 33 cm
NEW YORK	LEWIS & ARROWSMITH	20 x 25 cm
NEW YORK	LUCAS	20 x 28 cm
NEW-YORK	MEYER	10 x 16 cm
NEW YORK	S.D.U.K.	31 x 38 cm
NEW YORK ...	SOTZMANN, D.H.	49 x 63 cm
NEW YORK	TANNER	56 x 66 cm
NEW YORK AND ADJACENT CITIES	COLTON	42 x 63 cm
NEW YORK AND PENSILVANIA	GIBSON	8 x 10 cm
NEW YORK-BAY VON STATEN-ISLAND AUS GESEHEN	MEYER	11 x 16 cm
NEW YORK CITY, SOUTHERN PART	PEOPLE'S ATLAS	28 x 25 cm
NEW ZEALAND	STANFORD	60 x 47 cm
NEWFOUNDLAND	STANFORD	59 x 48 cm
NEWFOUNDLAND, NEW BRUNSWICK, NOVA SCOTIA, PRINCE EDWARD ISLAND ...	FULLARTON	41 x 53 cm
NEWFOUNDLAND, NOVA SCOTIA AND NEW BRUNSWICK	BURR	28 x 33 cm
NEWFOUNDLAND, ST. LAURENS BAY, THE FISHING BANKS, ACADIA, AND ...	MOLL (Small)	20 x 27 cm
NEWPORT BAY & HARBOUR ... [Wales]	MORRIS	18 x 23 cm
NEWTON'S NEW & IMPROVED TERRESTRIAL GLOBE PUBLISHED BY ...	NEWTON & BERRY	8 cm, diam
NIAGARA FALL (ALLEGEMEINE ANSICHT VOM CLIFTON HOUSE)	MEYER	11 x 16 cm

NIAGARA FALL (HORSESHOE-FALL)	MEYER	11 x 16 cm
NICARAGUA EN DE KUSTEN DER ZUYD-ZEE BOORDWAARD VON PANAMA ...	VAN DER AA	15 x 23 cm
NIEU AMSTERDAM, EEN STEDEKEN IN NOORD AMERIKAES NIEU HOLLANT, ...	SCHENK	22 x 26 cm
NIEUW AERDSCH PLEYN	ROBYN	59 x 52 cm
NIEUWE GENERALE PASKAART VAN DE BOCHT VAN VRANKRYK BISCAIA ...	VAN KEULEN	61 x 99 cm
NIEUWE KAART VAN AMERICA UITGEGEVEN TE AMSTERDAM BY ...	TIRION	28 x 32 cm
NIEUWE KAART VAN DE NOORD POOL ...	TIRION	30 x 28 cm
NIEUWE KAART VAN HET WESTELYKSTE DEEL DE WEERELD	TIRION	33 x 36 cm
NIEUWE KAART VAN KANADA, DE LANDEN AAN DE HUDSONS-BAAY ...	TIRION	31 x 44 cm
NIEUWE PASCAART VOOR EEN ... VAN BARBARIA BEGINNENDE VAN C. RISATO	VAN KEULEN	51 x 58 cm
NIEUWE PASCAERT VAN'T SUYDERLYCKSTEDEEL VAN SUYT AMERICA ...	DE WIT	48 x 56 cm
NIEUWE PASKAERT VAN D'OOST KUST VAN ENGELANDT VAN DOVER TOT ...	VAN KEULEN	50 x 58 cm
NIEUWE PASKAERT VAN DE ZEE KUSTEN VAN PROVENCE EN ITALIAE...CORSICA	VAN KEULEN	51 x 58 cm
NIEUWE PASKAERT VAN DE ZEE KUSTEN VAN'T EYLANDT SICILIA ...	VAN KEULEN	51 x 58 cm
NIEUWE PLATTE PASKAART VAN DE STRAAT DAVIDS ...	VAN KEULEN	58 x 99 cm
NIEUWE ... WASSENDE GRAADEN PASKAART ... AARD BODEM OF WERELT	VAN KEULEN	58 x 99 cm
NO. 1 INDEX TO RECORDED FIELD NOTES INDIANA	DUVAL	38 x 28 cm
NO. 1. MAP OF THE DES MOINES RAPIDS. OF THE MISSISSIPPI RIVER. ...	U.S. WAR DEPT.	56 x 130 cm
No. 10. MITCHELL'S SERIES OF OUTLINE MAPS FOR THE USE OF ACADEMIES ...	MITCHELL, S.A.	58 x 69 cm
NO. 2. MAP OF THE ROCK ISLAND RAPIDS. OF THE MISSISSIPPI.	U.S. WAR DEPT.	56 x 163 cm
NORD-AMERICA	KIEPERT	42 x 54 cm
NORD AMERICA	VON STULPNAGEL	33 x 38 cm
NORD AMERICA ...	WEIMAR GEOGRAPH.	59 x 54 cm
NORD AMERICA ENTWORFEN W. GEZEICHNET	STIELER	33 x 38 cm
NORD AMERICA MIT WESTINDIEN	WEIMAR GEOGRAPH.	60 x 51 cm
NORD-AMERICANISCHE FREISTAATEN	MEYER	30 x 38 cm
NORMANDIA	ORTELIUS (Miniature)	8 x 11 cm
NORMANNIA GALLIAE CELEBRIS PROVINCIA	HOMANN	49 x 58 cm
NORTH AMERICA	ARROWSMITH	23 x 30 cm
NORTH AMERICA	BLACK	41 x 30 cm
NORTH AMERICA	BURR	33 x 28 cm
NORTH AMERICA	COLTON	40 x 33 cm
NORTH AMERICA	CUMMINGS & HILLIARD	23 x 28 cm
NORTH AMERICA	FINLEY	29 x 22 cm
NORTH AMERICA	JEFFERYS	18 x 23 cm
NORTH AMERICA	JOHNSON	56 x 43 cm
NORTH AMERICA	JOHNSTON	61 x 51 cm
NORTH AMERICA	LEWIS & ARROWSMITH	25 x 20 cm
NORTH AMERICA	LUMSDEN	18 x 23 cm
NORTH AMERICA	PEOPLE'S ATLAS	64 x 43 cm
NORTH AMERICA	PHILIP, G.	51 x 61 cm
NORTH AMERICA	S.D.U.K.	38 x 31 cm
NORTH AMERICA	SMITH, C.	28 x 36 cm
NORTH AMERICA	THOMSON	23 x 30 cm
NORTH AMERICA	THOMSON	23 x 30 cm
NORTH AMERICA	WILKES	25 x 20 cm
NORTH AMERICA	WILKINSON	30 x 23 cm
NORTH AMERICA CORRECTED FROM THE OBSERVATIONS COMMUNICATED ...	SENEX	97 x 66 cm
NORTH AMERICA DRAWN FROM THE LATEST AND BEST AUTHORITIES	KITCHIN	36 x 41 cm
NORTH AMERICA EAST COAST SHEET III BANKS OFF NEWFOUNDLAND	ADMIRALTY	48 x 62 cm
NORTH AMERICA EAST COAST ... SHEET IV [NOVA SCOTIA AND GULF OF ...	ADMIRALTY	47 x 62 cm
NORTH AMERICA EAST COAST ... SHEET VII [Georgia to North Carolina]	ADMIRALTY	48 x 62 cm
NORTH AMERICA FROM THE BEST AUTHORITIES	BARLOW	20 x 23 cm
NORTH AMERICA FROM THE FRENCH OF MR. D'ANVILLE IMPROVED ...	SAYER & BENNETT	46 x 51 cm
NORTH AMERICA SHEET I NOVA SCOTIA WITH PART OF NEW BRUNSWICK ...	S.D.U.K.	41 x 33 cm
NORTH AMERICA SHEET V THE NORTH WEST AND MICHIGAN TERRITORIES	S.D.U.K.	30 x 38 cm
NORTH AMERICA SHEET VI NEW-YORK, VERMONT, MAINE, NEW-HAMPSHIRE ...	S.D.U.K.	35 x 31 cm
NORTH AMERICA SHEET VII PENNSYLVANIA, NEW JERSEY, MARYLAND, ...	S.D.U.K.	37 x 31 cm
NORTH AMERICA SHEET VIII OHIO, WITH PARTS OF KENTUCKY, VIRGINIA ...	S.D.U.K.	31 x 35 cm
NORTH AMERICA SHEET IX PARTS OF MISSOURI, ILLINOIS, AND INDIANA	S.D.U.K.	30 x 37 cm
NORTH AMERICA SHEET X PARTS OF MISSOURI, ILLINOIS, KENTUCKY, ...	S.D.U.K.	33 x 41 cm
NORTH AMERICA SHEET XI PARTS OF NORTH AND SOUTH CAROLINA	S.D.U.K.	38 x 33 cm
NORTH AMERICA SHEET XII GEORGIA WITH PARTS OF NORTH & SOUTH ...	S.D.U.K.	40 x 31 cm
NORTH AMERICA SHEET XIV FLORIDA	S.D.U.K.	40 x 31 cm
NORTH AMERICA WITH THE BOUNDARIES OF THE THIRTEEN UNITED STATES ...	PAYNE	33 x 36 cm
NORTH AND SOUTH CAROLINA	BURR	27 x 32 cm
NORTH AND SOUTH CAROLINA	JOHNSON	42 x 59 cm
NORTH AND SOUTH DAKOTA	BRADLEY	53 x 43 cm

Title	Publisher	Size
NORTH BASS ISLAND [Ohio]	HARDESTY	41 x 33 cm
NORTH CAROLINA	BRADFORD	20 x 28 cm
NORTH CAROLINA	BRADFORD	29 x 36 cm
NORTH CAROLINA	CAREY	15 x 20 cm
NORTH CAROLINA	COLTON	33 x 41 cm
NORTH CAROLINA	FINLEY	22 x 29 cm
NORTH CAROLINA	LEWIS & ARROWSMITH	20 x 25 cm
NORTH CAROLINA ...	PAYNE	18 x 33 cm
NORTH CAROLINA	SCOTT	18 x 20 cm
NORTH CAROLINA FROM THE LATEST SURVEYS, BY SAMUEL LEWIS	CAREY	28 x 48 cm
NORTH CAROLINA, SOUTH CAROLINA AND GEORGIA	BRADFORD	20 x 26 cm
NORTH DAKOTA	CRAM	41 x 56 cm
NORTH PART OF N.E. LAND DISTRICT OF ILLINOIS	U.S.	18 x 15 cm
NORTH & SOUTH CAROLINA	BLACK	28 x 41 cm
NORTH WEST LAND DISTRICT OF ILLINOIS	U.S.	33 x 28 cm
NORTHERN AFRICA	BRADFORD	20 x 25 cm
NORTHERN AMERICA, BRITISH, RUSSIAN AND DANISH	COLTON	(no dimens.)
NORTHERN EXTREMITY OF LAKE WINNEBAGO [Mich.]	U.S. WAR DEPT.	13 x 20 cm
NORTHERN HEMISPHERE	THOMSON	53 x 51 cm
NORTHERN INDIA	TALLIS	24 x 32 cm
NORTHERN & NORTH-WESTERN LAKES SHOWING THE DIFFERENT LOCALITIES ...	U.S. WAR DEPT.	23 x 48 cm
NORTHERN PORTS & HARBOURS IN THE UNITED STATES	FULLARTON	43 x 29 cm
NORTHERN REGIONS	COLTON	41 x 33 cm
NORTHWESTERN AMERICA SHOWING THE TERRITORY CEDED BY RUSSIA ...	MITCHELL, S.A. (1860+)	30 x 37 cm
NORTHWESTERN AMERICA SHOWING THE TERRITORY CEDED BY RUSSIA ...	WALLING	33 x 41 cm
NORUMBEGA ET VIRGINIA	WYTFLIET	24 x 30 cm
NOUVAUX MAPPEMONDE OU GLOBE TERRESTRE ...	CHATELAIN	46 x 66 cm
NOUVEAU CONTINENT	MALLET	20 x 13 cm
NOUVEAU CONTINENT AVEC PLUSIEURS ISLES ET MERS	MALLET	14 x 10 cm
NOUVEAU CONTINENT OU AMERIQUE	MALLET	15 x 10 cm
NOUVEAU MEXIQUE ET CALIFORNIE	MALLET	14 x 10 cm
NOUVEAU PARIS OU GUIDE DES ETRANGERS DANS LES 20 ARRONDISSEMENTS	LALLEMAND	46 x 62 cm
NOUVEAU PLAN DE LA VILLE DE PARIS DIVISE EN DOUZE ARRONDISSEMENTS ...	VILLEDIEU	59 x 79 cm
NOUVEAU PLAN DE PARIS AVEC SES AUGMENTATIONS TANT FINIES QUE ...	BRION DE LA TOUR	57 x 81 cm
NOUVEAU PLAN DE PARIS DIVISE EN 20 ARRONDISSEMENTS	LOGEROT	69 x 102 cm
NOUVEAU PLAN ILLUSTRE DE LA VILLE DE PARIS AVEC LE SYSTEME COMPLET ...	VUILLEMIN	84 x 107 cm
NOUVEAU PLAN ROUTIER DE LA VILLE ET FAUBOURGS DE PARIS DIVISE EN ...	JOURNEAUX L'AINE	55 x 77 cm
NOUVELLE CARTE D'ANGLETERRE D'ECOSSE ET D'IRLANDE	CHATELAIN	47 x 63 cm
NOUVELLE CARTE DE BELGIQUE, A L'ECHELLE DE 1/300000 ...	ETAB. GEOG. DE BRUX.	75 x 87 cm
NOUVELLE CARTE DE L'AMERIQUE	VAN DER AA	43 x 53 cm
NOUVELLE CARTE DE LA PETITE TARTARIE OU TAURIE, MONTRANT LES ...	ELWE	51 x 61 cm
NOUVELLE CARTE DES DECOUVERTES FAITES PAR DES VAISSEAUX RUSSIENS ...	MULLER	46 x 64 cm
NOUVELLE CARTE DU MEXIQUE ET D'UNE PARTIE DES PROVINCES UNIES ...	BRUE	94 x 64 cm
NOUVELLE CARTE ILLUSTREE DE L'OCIENIE ...	VUILLEMIN	60 x 84 cm
NOUVELLE ESPAGNE NOUVEAU MEXIQUE ISLES ANTILLES ...	DELAMARCHE	25 x 38 cm
NOUVELLE ESPAGNE, NOUVEAU MEXIQUE, ISLES ANTILLES CORRIGES ...	DE VAUGONDY	24 x 31 cm
NOUVELLE GUINEE ET CARPENTARIE	MALLET	15 x 11 cm
NOUVELLE ORLEANS	GARNERAY	41 x 51 cm
NOVA AFRICAE TABULA	HONDIUS	38 x 50 cm
NOVA ALBION	DE BRY	13 x 18 cm
NOVA ALEMANNIAE SIVE SUEVIAE SUPERIORIS TABULA	JANSSON	39 x 49 cm
NOVA ANGLIA NOVUM BELGIUM ET VIRGINIA	JANSSON	39 x 50 cm
NOVA ANGLIA SEPTENTRIONALI AMERICAE IMPLANTATA ...	HOMANN	49 x 58 cm
NOVA BARBARIAE DESCRIPTIO	JANSSON	35 x 52 cm
NOVA BELGICA ET ANGLIA NOVA	BLAEU	39 x 50 cm
NOVA BELGICA ET ANGLIA NOVA	JANSSON	39 x 50 cm
NOVA COMITATUS PAPPENHEIMENSIS	HOMANN	50 x 59 cm
NOVA ET ACCURATA CARINTHIAE DUCATUS	HOMANN	50 x 59 cm
NOVA ET ACCURATA DESCRIPTIO DELPHINATUS VULGO DAUPHINE	JANSSON	38 x 51 cm
NOVA ET ACCURATA JAPONIAE TERRAE ESONIS AC INSULARUM ADJACENTIUM	JANSSON	46 x 55 cm
NOVA ET ACCURATA JAPONIAE TERRAE ESONIS AC INSULARUM ADJACENTIUM	VALK & SCHENK	46 x 55 cm
NOVA ET ACCURATA REGNI HUNGARIAE ...	COVENS & MORTIER	46 x 56 cm
NOVA ET ACCURATA TABULA EPISCOPATUUM STAVANGRIENSIS, BERGENSIS...	JANSSON	41 x 50 cm
NOVA ET VERA EXHIBITIO GEOGRAPHICA INSULARUM MARIANARUM ...	SCHERER	23 x 34 cm
NOVA EUROPAE DESCRIPTIO	HONDIUS	38 x 51 cm
NOVA FRANCIA ET CANADA	WYTFLIET	24 x 30 cm
NOVA FRANCIA ET REGIONES ADIACENTES	DE LAET	28 x 36 cm
NOVA HELVETIA TABULA	MERCATOR (Small)	15 x 20 cm

NOVA HISPANIA, ET NOVA GALICIA	JANSSON	35 x 48 cm
NOVA HISPANIA, NOVA GALICIA, GUATIMALA	OGILBY	29 x 36 cm
NOVA MARIS CASPII ET REGIONIS USBECK	HOMANN	50 x 60 cm
NOVA ORBIS TABULA, IN LUCEM EDITA, A. F. DE WIT [with] AFRICA [etc]	DE WIT	48 x 56 cm
NOVA SCOTIA AND NEW BRUNSWICK	CRAM	23 x 30 cm
NOVA SCOTIA, DRAWN FROM SURVEYS BY T KITCHIN GR.	LONDON MAGAZINE	11 x 17 cm
NOVA TABULA GEOGRAPHICA COMPLECTENS BOREALIOREM AMERICAE ...	VISSCHER	59 x 47 cm
NOVA TABULA GEOGRAPHICA COMPLECTENS BOREALIOREM AMERICAE ...	VISSCHER	61 x 89 cm
NOVA TABULA INDIA ORIENTALIS ...	ALLARD	46 x 56 cm
NOVA TABULA SCANIAE, QUAE EST GOTHIA AUSTRALIS PROVINCIAS SCANIAM	HOMANN	50 x 59 cm
NOVA TERRITORII ERFORDIEN	HOMANN	49 x 59 cm
NOVA TOTIUS GERMANIAE DESCRIPTIO	BLAEU	48 x 38 cm
NOVA TOTIUS LIVONIAE ACCURATA DESCRIPTIO	JANSSON	39 x 51 cm
NOVA TOTIUS ORBIS TERRARUM DESCRIPTIO	VAN GEELKERKEN	32 x 45 cm
NOVA TOTIUS TERRARUM ORBIS GEOGRAPHICA AC HYDROGRAPHICA TABULA	BLAEU	41 x 54 cm
NOVA TOTIUS TERRARUM ORBIS GEOGRAPHICA AC HYDROGRAPHICA TABULA	CAVAZZA	35 x 46 cm
NOVA TOTIUS TERRARUM ORBIS GEOGRAPHICA AC HYDROGRAPHICA TABULA	HONDIUS	38 x 54 cm
NOVA TOTIUS TERRARUM ORBIS GEOGRAPHICA AC HYDROGRAPHICA TABULA	MERIAN	26 x 36 cm
NOVA TOTIUS TERRARUM ORBIS TABULA ...	DANCKERTS	48 x 55 cm
NOVA TOTIUS TERRARUM ORBIS TABULA EX OFFICINA F. DE WIT ...	DE WIT	48 x 56 cm
NOVA VIRGINIAE TABULA	BLAEU	37 x 48 cm
NOVA VIRGINIAE TABULA	HONDIUS	38 x 50 cm
NOVA VIRGINIAE TABULA	MERCATOR (Small)	18 x 25 cm
NOVAE INSULAE XVII NOVA TABULA	MUNSTER	26 x 34 cm
NOVAE INSULAE XXVI NOVA TABULA	MUNSTER	30 x 38 cm
NOVI BELGII NOVAEQUE ANGLIAE NEC NON PARTIS VIRGINIAE TABULA MULTIS	VISSCHER	46 x 55 cm
NOVI BELGII NOVAEQUE ANGLIAE NEC NON PENNSYLVANIAE ET PARTIS ...	DANCKERTS	47 x 55 cm
NOVI ORBIS PARS BOREALIS, AMERICA SCILICET, COMPLECTENS FLORIDAM, ...	QUAD	23 x 30 cm
NOVISSIMA DESCRIPTIO ANGLIAE SCOTIAE ET HIBERNIAE	VAN LOCHOM	38 x 50 cm
NOVISSIMA ET ACCURATISSIMA TOTIUS ITALIAE CORSICAE ET SARDINIAE, ...	DE WIT	49 x 56 cm
NOVISSIMA ET PERFECTISSIMA AFRICAE ...	ALLARD	51 x 58 cm
NOVISSIMA RUSSIAE TABULA	JANSSON	47 x 55 cm
NOVISSIMA TOTIUS TERRARUM ORBIS TABULA	VISSCHER	43 x 52 cm
NOVUS BRASILIA TYPUS	BLAEU	38 x 49 cm
NOVUS XVII INFERIORIS GERMANIAE PROVINCIARUM	STRADA	18 x 13 cm
NTH CAROLINA	LUCAS	28 x 48 cm
NUBIA AND ABYSSINIA	JOHNSTON	48 x 61 cm
NUBIE	MALLET	15 x 10 cm
NUEVA HISPANIA TABULA NOVA	PTOLEMY (1548 Venice)	13 x 17 cm
NUEVA HISPANIA TABULA NOVA	PTOLEMY (1561-1599)	23 x 18 cm
NUOVA CARTA DEL POLO ARTICO	ALBRIZZI	28 x 33 cm
NUOVA CARTA DEL POLO ARTICO SECONDO L'ULTIME OSSERVAZIONE ...	TIRION	28 x 33 cm
NUOVA CARTA DELL'IMPERIO DEL GIAPPONE	ANONYMOUS	35 x 41 cm
NUOVA ED ESTATTA CARTA DEL MONDO TRATTA DA AUTHENTICHE ...	BOWEN, E.	38 x 48 cm
NUOVE SCOPERTE DE' RUSSI AL NORD DEL MARE DEL SUD SI NELL'ASIA, ...	ZATTA	31 x 40 cm
OAK HARBOR [Ohio]	HARDESTY	41 x 33 cm
OBSIDIUM HAFFNIENSE A. 1658	DAHLBERG	29 x 105 cm
OCCIDENTALIS AMERICAE PARTIS, VEL, EARUM REGIONUM QUAS ...	DE BRY	33 x 43 cm
OCEANA OR PACIFIC OCEAN	TANNER	33 x 41 cm
OCEANICA	RAND, McNALLY	33 x 48 cm
OCEANICA	STANDARD ATLAS	23 x 30 cm
OCEANICA OR OCEANIA	BRADFORD	20 x 25 cm
OFFICIAL MAP OF SACRAMENTO CAL.	CRAM	23 x 33 cm
OHIO	BURR	27 x 31 cm
OHIO	CAREY	14 x 21 cm
OHIO	FINLEY	29 x 22 cm
OHIO	LEWIS & ARROWSMITH	25 x 20 cm
OHIO	WALLING	38 x 58 cm
OHIO AND INDIANA	TANNER	53 x 66 cm
OHIO RIVER BETWEEM MOUND CITY & CAIRO	U.S.	38 x 56 cm
OKLAHOMA AND INDIAN TERRITORY	MITCHELL, S.A. (1860+)	29 x 36 cm
OKLAHOMA AND INDIAN TERS.	CRAM	36 x 51 cm
OKLAHOMA - INDIAN TERRITORY	RAND, McNALLY	31 x 48 cm
OLDENBURG COMITATUS	JANSSON	38 x 49 cm
OLIVER & BOYD'S NEW TRAVELLING MAP OF ENGLAND & WALES	OLIVER & BOYD	69 x 56 cm
ONTARIO RAILROADS	RAND, McNALLY	48 x 69 cm
ORBIS ROMANI PARS OCCIDENTALIS ...	D'ANVILLE	69 x 56 cm
ORBIS ROMANI PARS ORIENTALIS AUSPICIIS SERENISSIMI PRINCIPIS ...	D'ANVILLE	59 x 56 cm

Title	Mapmaker	Size
ORBIS TERRAE COMPENDIOSA DESCRIPTIO ...	STRABO	29 x 52 cm
ORBIS TERRAE COMPENDIOSA DESCRIPTIO ...	VRIENTS	40 x 57 cm
ORBIS TERRAE COMPENDIOSA DESCRIPTIO QUAM EX MAGNA UNIVERSALI ...	MERCATOR (Folio)	30 x 52 cm
ORBIS TERRARUM NOVA ET ACCURATISSIMA TABULA ...	VISSCHER	47 x 56 cm
ORBIS TERRARUM TYPUS	CLUVER	15 x 23 cm
ORBIS TERRARUM TYPUS DE INTEGRO MULTIS IN LOCES EMENDATUS ...	VAN DEN KEERE	40 x 57 cm
ORBIS TERRARUM TYPUS DE INTEGRO MULTIS IN LOCIS EMENDATUS	PLANCIUS	41 x 57 cm
ORBIS VETERIBUS NOTUS AUSPICIIS SERENISSIMI PRINCIPIS ...	D'ANVILLE	54 x 76 cm
OREGON	CRAM	23 x 30 cm
OREGON	U.S. STATE SURVEYS	43 x 56 cm
OREGON AND CALIFORNIA	SWANSTON	25 x 15 cm
OREGON AND UPPER CALIFORNIA	MITCHELL, S.A. (1859-)	41 x 33 cm
OREGON INLET, N. CAROLINA	U.S. COAST SURVEY	41 x 46 cm
OREGON TERRITORY	BURR	28 x 33 cm
OREGON, UPPER CALIFORNIA AND NEW MEXICO	MITCHELL, S.A. (1859-)	41 x 33 cm
OREGON, WASHINGTON AND IDAHO	COLTON	43 x 64 cm
ORIENTALIORA INDIARUM ORIENTALIUM CUM INSULIS ADJACENTIBUS A ...	DE WIT	44 x 54 cm
ORIGINALKARTE DE CALIFORNISCHEN HALBINSEL ... FUR DIE LOWER CALIF. ...	PETERMANN	36 x 23 cm
ORIGINALKARTE DER URWOHNSITZE DER AZTEKEN UND VERWANDTEN PUEBLOS	PETERMANN	25 x 20 cm
OROGRAPHICAL MAP OF SOUTH AMERICA BY WILLIAM SHAWE, F.R.G.S.	PHILIP, G.	61 x 51 cm
OSTIA	BRAUN & HOGENBERG	30 x 48 cm
OSTLICHES NORDAMERICA	KIEPERT	51 x 44 cm
OUTLINE MAP SHOWING A NEW ROUTE FROM TEXAS TO FT. YUMA, ...	U.S. WAR DEPT.	104 x 38 cm
OUTLINE MAP ... SOUTHERN CALIFORNIA & SOUTH-WESTERN NEVADA ...	U.S. WAR DEPT.	41 x 48 cm
OUTLINES OF THE PHYSICAL AND POLITICAL DIVISIONS OF SOUTH AMERICA	ARROWSMITH	200 x 240 cm
OWLS HEAD HARBOR MAINE SURVEYED IN 1836 UNDER DIRECTION OF...LONG	U.S.	38 x 30 cm
OXFORD SH.	MORDEN	9 x 6 cm
PAGUS HISPANORUM IN FLORIDA	MONTANUS	27 x 35 cm
PALAESTINA	D'ANVILLE	40 x 44 cm
PALAESTINA IN XII TRIBUS DIVISA, CUM TERRIS ADIACENTIBUS DENUO REVISA...	HOMANN	48 x 53 cm
PALATINATUS BAVARIAE	JANSSON	37 x 50 cm
PALEONTOLOGICAL MAP OF THE BRITISH ISLANDS	JOHNSTON	46 x 28 cm
PALERMO	BRAUN & HOGENBERG	13 x 48 cm
PALESTINAE DELINEATIO AD GEOGRAPHICA CANONES REVOCATA	VAN LOCHOM	39 x 54 cm
PALESTINAE SIVE TOTIUS TERRAE PROMISSIONIS NOVA DESCRIPTIO ...	ORTELIUS (Folio)	33 x 46 cm
PALESTINE	JOHNSTON	60 x 50 cm
PALESTINE & ADJACENT COUNTRIES	THOMAS, COWPERTH.	41 x 33 cm
PALESTINE OF THE HOLY LAND	KINCAID, A.	20 x 15 cm
PALESTINE OR THE HOLY LAND OR LAND OF CANAAN	BURR	33 x 25 cm
PALESTINE WITH THE HAURAN ...	S.D.U.K.	41 x 33 cm
PANAMA	MEYER	11 x 16 cm
PANORAMIC VIEW FROM BUNKER HILL MONUMENT	CROSMAN & MALLORY	17 x 120 cm
PARADISI TERRESTRIS VERA ET SACRIS LITERIS CONFORMIS EXHIBITIO GEOG. ...	SCHERER	23 x 36 cm
PARAGUAY	JANSSON	37 x 48 cm
PARAGUAY, O PROV. DE RIO DE LA PLATA CUM REGIONIBUS ADJACENTIBUS ...	BLAEU	37 x 48 cm
PARAGUAY, O PROV. DE RIO DE LA PLATA CUM REGIONIBUS ADIACENTIBUS ...	JANSSON	37 x 48 cm
PARIS	MALLET	16 x 12 cm
PARIS	S.D.U.K.	39 x 29 cm
PARIS, DIVISE EN 12 ARONDISSEMENTS, ET 48 QUATIERS, DRESSE PAR ...	TOUSSAINT	74 x 112 cm
PARIS ILLUSTRE ET SES FORTIFICATIONS	LOGEROT	52 x 72 cm
PARKER'S SECTIONAL AND GEOLOGICAL MAP OF IOWA INCLUDING IRON, ...	PARKER, N.H.	81 x 112 cm
PARS VEDEROVIAE PLURIMAS DITIONES PRINC. ET COM. NASSOVICOR. ...	HOMANN	49 x 58 cm
PART OF LONG ISLAND FROM SOUTH-UIST TO HARRIS...	MacKENZIE	107 x 104 cm
PART OF NEW ENGLAND NEW YORK EAST NEW IARSEY AND LONG ILAND	THORNTON	43 x 51 cm
PART OF NORTH AMERICA, CONTAINING CANADA, THE NORTH PARTS OF ...	FIELDING	21 x 28 cm
PART OF THE GREAT PACIFIC OCEAN SHEWING THE ROUTE OF THE SPANISH ...	LA PEROUSE	24 x 38 cm
PART OF THE PACIFIC OCEAN BETWEEN CALIFORNIA AND THE PHILIPPINE ...	LA PEROUSE	35 x 48 cm
PART OF THE STATE OF ALABAMA SHOWING THE POSITION OF THE CHEROKEE	U.S.	41 x 28 cm
PARTE OCCIDENTALE DELLA CHINA ... [and] PARTE ORIENTALE DELLA CHINA ...	CORONELLI	61 x 89 cm
PARTE ORIENTALE DELLA CHINA ... [and] PARTE OCCIDENTALE DELLA CHINA ...	CORONELLI	61 x 89 cm
PARTE ORIENTALE DELLA FLORIDA, DELLA GEORGIA, E CAROLINA MERIDIONALE	ZATTA	32 x 42 cm
PARTICULAR PLANS OF ISLANDS, ROCKS AND SHOALS IN THE INDIAN OCEAN	LAURIE & WHITTLE	53 x 53 cm
PARTIE DE L'AMERIQUE SEPTENTRIONALE, QUI COMPREND LA NOUVELLE FRANCE	DE VAUGONDY	48 x 61 cm
PARTIE DE LA COSTE DE LA LOUISIANE ET DE LA FLORIDE DEPUIS LE MISSISSIPI	BELLIN (Small)	20 x 44 cm
PARTIE DE LA HAUTE AETHIOPIE OU SONT L'EMPIRE DES ABISSINS DES ET ...	SANSON (Small)	30 x 23 cm
PARTIE DE LA MER DU NORD, OU SE TROUVENT LES GRANDES ET LES PETITES...	DE VAUGONDY	48 x 59 cm
PARTIE DE LA TERRE FERME DE L'INDE OU L'EMPIRE DU MOGOL	MALLET	14 x 10 cm
PARTIE DU CANADA OU SE TROUVENT LE FLEUVE ST. LAURENT ET LA ...	DE VAUGONDY	17 x 22 cm

PARTIE DU MEXIQUE OU DE LA NOUV'LE ESPAGNE OU ... GUADALAJARA	DE VAUGONDY	16 x 20 cm
PARTIE MERIDIONALE D'AFRIQUE OU SE TROUVENT LE BASSEE GUINEE ...	DE FER (Small)	20 x 33 cm
PARTIE MERIDIONALE DE LA LOUISIANE, AVEC LA FLORIDE, LA CAROLINE ET ...	SANTINI	48 x 57 cm
PARTIE MERIDIONALE DE MOSCOVIE DRESSEE PAR G. DE L'ISLE	OTTENS	41 x 56 cm
PARTIE OCCIDENTAL DE L'EMPIRE DE RUSSIE ... PARTIE ORIENTALE ...	LATTRE	43 x 61 cm
PARTIE OCCIDENTALE DE LA NOUVELLE FRANCE ET DU CANADA ...	BELLIN (Large)	48 x 61 cm
PARTIE OCCIDENTALE DE LA NOUVELLE FRANCE OU DU CANADA ...	HOMANN	44 x 54 cm
PARTIE OCCIDENTALE DU CANADA, CONTENANT LES CINQ GRAND LACS, ...	BONNE	21 x 31 cm
PARTIE ORIENTALE DE L'AMERIQUE ANGLOISE	MORTIER	61 x 46 cm
PARTIE ORIENTALE DE LA NOUVELLE FRANCE OU DU CANADA. ...	BELLIN (Large)	47 x 61 cm
PARTIE ORIENTALE DE LA NOUVELLE FRANCE OU DU CANADA. PAR MR. BELLIN	HOMANN	45 x 55 cm
PARTIE ORIENTALE DE LA TERRE FIRME DE L'INDE MODERNE	MALLET	15 x 10 cm
PARTIE ORIENTALE DU CANADA OU DE LA NOUVELLE FRANCE ...	NOLIN	45 x 60 cm
PARTIE ORIENTALE DU GOLFE DE FINNLAND	HOMANN	50 x 44 cm
PAS-CAART VAN GUINEA EN DE CUSTEN DAER AER GELEGEN VAN CABO VERDE	GOOS	44 x 54 cm
PAS-CAART VANT CANAAL VERTOONENDE IN 'T GHEHEEL ENGELANDT, ...	GOOS	45 x 55 cm
PAS CAERT VAN'T IN KOMEN VAN DE CANAEL ...	DONCKER	43 x 53 cm
PAS CAERTE VAN NIEU NEDERLANDT EN DE ENGELSCHE VIRGINIES VAN CABO ...	GOOS	44 x 54 cm
PAS CAERTE VAN NIEU NEDERLANDT EN DE ENGELSCHE VIRGINIES VAN CABO ...	GOOS	44 x 54 cm
PAS KAART VAN DE CARIBES TUSSCHEN I. BARBADOS EN I.S. MARTIN ...	VAN KEULEN	51 x 58 cm
PAS-KAART VAN DE GOLFF DE GUANAIOS MET 'T CANAAL TUSSCHEN YUCATAN	VAN KEULEN	51 x 58 cm
PAS KAART VAN DE GOLFF VAN MEXICO ...	VAN KEULEN	51 x 58 cm
PAS KAART VAN DE NOORD KUST VAN ESPANIOLA MET D'EYLANDEN DOOR ...	VAN KEULEN	51 x 59 cm
PAS KAART VAN DE ZEE KUSTEN VAN VIRGINIA TUSSCHEN C HENRY EN ...	VAN KEULEN	51 x 58 cm
PAS-KAART VANDE ZEE KUSTEN INDE BOGHT VAN NIEU ENGELAND ...	VAN KEULEN	51 x 61 cm
PAS-KAART VANDE ZEE KUSTEN VAN NIEW NEDERLAND ANDERS GENAAMT ...	VAN KEULEN	51 x 56 cm
PASCAART VANT CANAAL ...	JANSSON	43 x 55 cm
PASCAARTE VAN ENGELANT VAN T' VOORLANDT TOT AEN BLAKENEY ...	GOOS	43 x 54 cm
PASCAARTE VANDE ZEE CUSTEN VAN GUINEA, EN BRASILIA: VAN CABO DE ...	VAN KEULEN	51 x 58 cm
PASCAERT VANDE CARIBES EYLANDEN	GOOS	44 x 54 cm
PASCAERTE VAN WESTINDIEN BEGRYPENDE IN ZICH DE VASTE KUSTEN EN ...	VAN KEULEN	51 x 60 cm
PASCAERTE VANDE CARIBES, S. IUAN DE PORTO RICO, DE OOSTHOECK ...	VAN KEULEN	51 x 61 cm
PASCAERTE VANDE VLAEMSCHE, SOUTE, EN CARIBESCHE EYLANDEN, ...	GOOS	45 x 54 cm
PASCAERTE VANDE ZUYD-ZEE TUSSCHE CALIFORNIA, EN ILHAS DE LADRONES ...	GOOS	45 x 55 cm
PASKAART VAN DE BOGHT VAN FLORIDA MET DE CANAAL TUSSCHEN FLORIDA	VAN KEULEN	51 x 58 cm
PASKAART VAN DE ZEE KUSTEN VAN'T EYLANDT SARDINIA ... BARBARIA ...	VAN KEULEN	51 x 58 cm
PASKAART VAN GUINEA VAN C. VERDE TOT R. DE GALION	DONCKER	43 x 53 cm
PASKAARTE OM ACHTER YRLANDT OM TE ZEYLEN VAN HITLANT TOT AEN ...	GOOS	44 x 55 cm
PASKAERT WAER IN DE GRADEN DER BREEDDE OVER WEDER ZYDEN VANDE ...	VAN KEULEN	53 x 61 cm
PASKAERTE VAN DE ZUYDT EN NOORDT REVIER IN NIEU NEDERLANT ...	GOOS	51 x 60 cm
PASKAERTE VAN NOVA GRANADA, EN T'EYLANDT CALIFORNIA	GOOS	45 x 55 cm
PASKAERTE VAN'T IN COMEN VAN'T CANAAL ...	GOOS	44 x 53 cm
PASKAERTE ZYNDE T'OOSTERDEEL VAN OOST INDIEN MET ALLES DE EYLANDEN	GOOS	46 x 55 cm
PAYS DES NEGRES	MALLET	15 x 10 cm
PECHELI, XANSI, XANTUNG, HONAN, NANKING, IN PLAGA REGNI SINENSIS ...	MERCATOR (Folio)	47 x 52 cm
PELTON'S OUTLINE MAP OF N. AMERICA	PELTON	165 x 180 cm
PENINSOLA DELL INDIA DI LA DAL GANGE DIVISA NE I REGNI CHE IN ESSASI...	CANTELLI DA VIGNOLA	53 x 41 cm
PENINSULA INDIAE CITRA GANGEM, HOC EST, ORAE CELEBERRIMAE MALABAR...	HOMANN	57 x 50 cm
PENNSYLVANIA	BRADFORD	29 x 36 cm
PENNSYLVANIA	BURR	27 x 31 cm
PENNSYLVANIA	CAREY	15 x 20 cm
PENNSYLVANIA	CAREY	30 x 46 cm
PENNSYLVANIA	CRAM	30 x 41 cm
PENNSYLVANIA	FINLEY	23 x 33 cm
PENNSYLVANIA	LEWIS & ARROWSMITH	18 x 20 cm
PENNSYLVANIA	RAND, McNALLY	23 x 30 cm
PENNSYLVANIA	STANDARD ATLAS	30 x 41 cm
PENNSYLVANIA BY DAVID H. BURR NEW YORK	BURR	28 x 33 cm
PENNSYLVANIA DRAWN FROM THE BEST AUTHORITIES	MORSE, J.	20 x 33 cm
PEREGRINATIE OFTE VEERTICH-IARIGE REYSE DER KINDEREN ISRAELS ...	KEUR	30 x 46 cm
PERIGRINATIO ISRAILITARU IN DESERT	MERCATOR (Small)	15 x 18 cm
PERSE PAR N. DE FER.	DE FER (Small)	14 x 16 cm
PERSIA	TALLIS	36 x 25 cm
PERSIA NUOVA TAVOLA	PTOLEMY (1561-1599)	18 x 25 cm
PERSIAE REGNUM SIVE SOPHORUM IMPERIUM	PTOLEMY (1596-1621)	13 x 17 cm
PERU	JANSSON	38 x 49 cm
PERU AND BOLIVIA	MITCHELL, S.A. (1859-)	33 x 38 cm
PERU CAPE LOBOS TO PESCADORES POINT	ADMIRALTY	48 x 62 cm

PERUVIAE AURIFERAE REGIONIS TYPUS. DIDACO MENDEZIO ... / LA FLORIDA. ...	ORTELIUS (Folio)	36 x 46 cm
PHELPS AND ENSIGN'S TRAVEL GUIDE AND MAP OF THE UNITED STATES ...	ENSIGN	43 x 97 cm
PHELPS AND WATSON'S HISTORICAL AND MILITARY MAP OF THE BORDER & ...	PHELPS & WATSON	60 x 87 cm
PHENOMENA OF VOLCANIC ACTION SHOWING THE REGION VISITED BY EARTH...	JOHNSTON	20 x 28 cm
PHILADELPHIA	COLTON	41 x 36 cm
PHILADELPHIA	MITCHELL, S.A. (1859-)	41 x 33 cm
PHILADELPHIA	S.D.U.K.	38 x 30 cm
PHILIP'S MAP OF IRELAND WITH DISTANCES FROM DUBLIN AND THE PRINCIPAL	PHILIP, G.	77 x 61 cm
PHILIPS' NEW CLEAR-PRINT REFERENCE PLAN OF THE COUNTY OF LONDON	PHILIP, G.	64 x 91 cm
PHILIPS' NEW LARGE PRINT MAP OF THE COUNTY OF LONDON	PHILIP, G.	94 x 138 cm
PHILIPS' TAPE INDICATOR MAP OF LONDON DIVIDED INTO QUARTER MILE...	PHILIP, G.	59 x 87 cm
PHYSICAL GEOGRAPHY, HUMBOLDT'S DISTRIBUTION OF PLANTS IN EQUI. ...	BLACK	28 x 38 cm
PHYSICAL MAP OF THE UNITED STATES	WOODBRIDGE	30 x 41 cm
PIANO DELLA CITTA DI QUEBEC	GAZETTIERE AMER.	25 x 23 cm
PIANTA TOPOGRAFICA DELLA CITTA' DI ROMA COLL' AGGIUNTA DELLE	CUCCIONI	54 x 65 cm
PLAN AND SECTION OF THE NORTH CUT AT MILWAUKEE	U.S. WAR DEPT.	43 x 33 cm
PLAN D'UNE PARTIE DE L'ILE DE WIGHT ET DE LA COTE DE HAMPSHIRE ...	DEPOT DE LA MARINE	94 x 61 cm
PLAN DE L'ANCE A L'EAU DANS LA CAYQUE DU NORD	BELLIN (Small)	(no dimens.)
PLAN DE L'ANCE AU CANOT DANS LA CAYQUE DU NORD	BELLIN (Small)	(no dimens.)
PLAN DE L'ARCHIPEL DE MERGUY [and] PLAN DE L'ISLE JUNKSEILON ET DE ...	D'APRES DE MANNEVIL.	33 x 48 cm
PLAN DE L'ENTREE DE NOOTKA	COOK	28 x 20 cm
PLAN DE L'ISLE D'INAGUE	BELLIN (Small)	(no dimens.)
PLAN DE L'ISLE DE MOGANE	BELLIN (Small)	(no dimens.)
PLAN DE L'ISLE DE SAMANA ...	BELLIN (Small)	(no dimens.)
PLAN DE LA BAIE DE TCHINKITANE (LA BAIA DE GUADALUPA DES ESPAGNOLS ...	CLARET DE FLEURIEU	22 x 17 cm
PLAN DE LA BAIE ET DU HAVRE DE CASCO ET DES ILES ADJACENTES PAR LE ...	SARTINE	41 x 58 cm
PLAN DE LA BASSE OU ROCHES DE ST. PHILIPPE ...	BELLIN (Small)	(no dimens.)
PLAN DE LA BAYE DE CHEDABOUCTOU AUJOURD'HUI HAVRE DE MILFORT ...	BELLIN (Small)	20 x 28 cm
PLAN DE LA BAYE DE PENSACOLA	BELLIN (Small)	20 x 28 cm
PLAN DE LA BAYE DE PENSACOLA DANS LA FLORIDE	BELLIN (Small)	21 x 17 cm
PLAN DE LA BAYE ET VILLE DE PORTOBELO EN 1736	ULLOA	15 x 23 cm
PLAN DE LA BAYE SAINT LOUIS ...	BELLIN (Small)	23 x 36 cm
PLAN DE LA CAYQUE DE L'OUEST OU LA PETITE CAYQUE	BELLIN (Small)	(no dimens.)
PLAN DE LA COTE MERIDIONALE D'ANGLETERRE DEPUIS ABBOTSBURY ...	DEPOT DE LA MARINE	62 x 94 cm
PLAN DE LA COTE MERIDIONALE D'ANGLETERRE DEPUIS ST. ALBAN HEAD ...	DEPOT DE LA MARINE	64 x 93 cm
PLAN DE LA GRANDE SALINE L'UNE DES ISLES TURQUES	BELLIN (Small)	(no dimens.)
PLAN DE LA NOUVELLE ORLEANS	BELLIN (Small)	19 x 28 cm
PLAN DE LA PARTIE DES ILES OU ARCHIPEL DE COREE	LA PEROUSE	50 x 69 cm
PLAN DE LA PETITE SALINE LA SECONDE DES ISLES TURQUES	BELLIN (Small)	(no dimens.)
PLAN DE LA RADE ET VILLE DU PETIT GOAVE ...	BELLIN (Small)	23 x 36 cm
PLAN DE LA VILLE DE BORDEAUX	BERO, D.	55 x 72 cm
PLAN DE LA VILLE DE BOSTON ET SES ENVIRONS	ANONYMOUS	18 x 20 cm
PLAN DE LA VILLE DE BOSTON ET SES ENVIRONS	BELLIN (Small)	16 x 27 cm
PLAN DE LA VILLE DE DUBLIN	BELLIN (Small)	21 x 28 cm
PLAN DE LA VILLE DE QUEBEC	BELLIN (Small)	20 x 28 cm
PLAN DE LA VILLE DE QUEBEC	PREVOST D'EXILES	20 x 28 cm
PLAN DE LA VILLE ET FAUBOURGS DE PARIS AVEC SES MONUMENTS. ...	VUILLEMIN	83 x 91 cm
PLAN DE MOUILLAGE DE L'ISLE DE KROO-KED	BELLIN (Small)	(no dimens.)
PLAN DE PORT DE MILFORD ...	BELLIN (Large)	51 x 66 cm
PLAN DE PORT-ROYAL ET DES ENVIRONS DANS LA BAYE DE CAMPECHE	BELLIN (Small)	18 x 14 cm
PLAN DES ISLES PLATES ...	BELLIN (Small)	(no dimens.)
PLAN DES VILLES, FORTS, PORT, RADE ET ENVIRONS DE CARTAGENE...	DE FER (Small)	23 x 32 cm
PLAN DU BASSIN DE QUEBEC ET DE SES ENVIRONS	BELLIN (Small)	20 x 28 cm
PLAN DU CUL DE SAC DES ROSEAUX DANS L'ISLE DE STE. LUCIE 1763	BELLIN (Small)	23 x 18 cm
PLAN DU DETROIT DE BANCA ...	D'APRES DE MANNEVIL.	48 x 33 cm
PLAN DU MOUILLAGE DE LA PARTIE DE L'OUEST DE L'ISLE	BELLIN (Small)	(no dimens.)
PLAN DU PORT D'ACAPULCO SUR LA COTE DU MEXIQUE DANS LA MER DU SUD	BELLIN (Small)	19 x 15 cm
PLAN DU PORT DAUPHIN ET DE SA RADE AVEC L'ENTREE DE LABRADOR ...	BELLIN (Small)	20 x 28 cm
PLAN DU PORT DE ST. AUGUSTIN DANS LA FLORIDE	BELLIN (Small)	21 x 16 cm
PLAN DU PORT DE ST. DIEGO EN CALIFORNIE ... [and] PLAN DU PORT ...	LA PEROUSE	51 x 33 cm
PLAN DU PORT ET VILLE DE LOUISBOURG DANS L'ISLE ROYALE	BELLIN (Small)	20 x 28 cm
PLAN OF A TRACT OF LAND ON BAYOU BOEUF SURVEYED ... SUPPOSED CLAIM	U.S.	33 x 20 cm
PLAN OF ADVENTURE BAY ON VAN DIEMANS LAND	COOK	23 x 15 cm
PLAN OF BOSTON CORRECTED UNDER THE DIRECTION OF COMMITTEE ON...	CRAFTS, H.	71 x 99 cm
PLAN OF CHICAGO HARBOR ...	U.S. WAR DEPT.	28 x 36 cm
PLAN OF CINCINATTI	DANBY, T.	33 x 25 cm
PLAN OF COUNCIL BLUFFS	ANDREAS	33 x 43 cm
PLAN OF EASTER ISLAND TAKEN IN APRIL 1786 / PLAN OF COOK'S BAY	LA PEROUSE	37 x 49 cm

PLAN OF FORT DU QUESNE BEFORE IT WAS DESTROY'D, 1758.	GRAND MAG. OF MAG.	19 x 11 cm
PLAN OF FRANKLINVILLE, IN MASON COUNTY, KENTUCKY	WINTERBOTHAM	18 x 13 cm
PLAN OF KURILE ISLANDS AND LANDS LITTLE KNOWN ...	LA PEROUSE	49 x 38 cm
PLAN OF LYSTRA IN NELSON-COUNTY, KENTUCKY	WINTERBOTHAM	18 x 13 cm
PLAN OF MALTA FROM THE SURVEY BY LIEUTT, WORSLEY R.E. ...	BRITISH GOVERNMENT	60 x 59 cm
PLAN OF MATHURIN BAY, ON THE NORTH SIDE OF THE ISLAND OF DIEGO ...	LAURIE & WHITTLE	51 x 64 cm
PLAN OF NEW ORLEANS	MITCHELL, S.A. (1860+)	25 x 30 cm
PLAN OF NEW ORLEANS THE CAPITAL OF LOUISIANA.	LONDON MAGAZINE	17 x 23 cm
PLAN OF PART OF FORT GEORGE, WITH THE BARRACKS &C. ERECTED IN ...	ROCQUE	13 x 18 cm
PLAN OF PART OF THE ISLANDS OF MAOUNA / PLAN OF MASSACRE COVE	LA PEROUSE	37 x 24 cm
PLAN OF PART OF THE ISLANDS OR ARCHIPELLAGO OF COREA	LA PEROUSE	38 x 49 cm
PLAN OF PHILADELPHIA	MITCHELL, S.A. (1860+)	28 x 33 cm
PLAN OF PORT DES FRANCAIS ON THE NORTH WEST COAST OF AMERICA	LA PEROUSE	57 x 49 cm
PLAN OF ST PETERSBURG; WITH IT'S FORTIFICATIONS, BUILT BY PETER ...	GENTLEMAN'S MAG.	19 x 24 cm
PLAN OF STAMFORD [Conn.]	BEERS, ELLIS & SOULE	53 x 64 cm
PLAN OF THE ATTACK OF THE FORTS CLINTON & MONTGOMERY UPON ...	STEDMAN	65 x 51 cm
PLAN OF THE BATTLE FOUGHT NEAR CAMDEN, AUGUST 16TH 1780	STEDMAN	22 x 19 cm
PLAN OF THE BAY AND HARBOUR OF RIO-JANEIRO ...	LAURIE & WHITTLE	48 x 30 cm
PLAN OF THE BAY OF CONCEPTION IN CHILI	LA PEROUSE	25 x 37 cm
PLAN OF THE CITY AND HARBOUR OF HAVANNA.	GENTLEMAN'S MAG.	11 x 19 cm
PLAN OF THE CITY OF ALBANY ABOUT THE YEAR 1770 - FROM THE ORIGINAL. ...	N.Y. STATE DOC. HIS.	20 x 30 cm
PLAN OF THE CITY OF DETROIT	MITCHELL, S.A. (1860+)	28 x 36 cm
PLAN OF THE CITY OF HAVANAH.	GENTLEMAN'S MAG.	10 x 10 cm
PLAN OF THE CITY OF NEW YORK.	LONGWORTH, D.	38 x 53 cm
PLAN OF THE CITY OF PHILADELPHIA	TANNER	41 x 33 cm
PLAN OF THE CITY OF WASHINGTON, IN THE TERRITORY OF COLUMBIA, CEDED	ELLICOTT	53 x 71 cm
PLAN OF THE DIFFERENT CHANNELS, LEADING FROM KINGSTON TO LAKE ...	BOUCHETTE	22 x 25 cm
PLAN OF THE ENTRANCE OF THE PORT OF BUCARELLI ON THE NORTH WEST ...	LA PEROUSE	38 x 49 cm
PLAN OF THE ENTRANCE OF THE PORT OF BUCARELLI ON THE NORTH WEST ...	ROBINSON	38 x 49 cm
PLAN OF THE FORTS ONTARIO AND OSWEGO, WITH PART OF THE RIVER ...	GENTLEMAN'S MAG.	20 x 10 cm
PLAN OF THE FRONT PART OF THE CITY OF NEW ORLEANS IN 1818	U.S.	20 x 56 cm
PLAN OF THE HARBOUR OF CADIZ SURVEYED BY BRIGADIER ...	FADEN	56 x 87 cm
PLAN OF THE HARBOUR OF SAN FERNANDO DE OMOA	JEFFERYS	21 x 28 cm
PLAN OF THE NAVY YARD IN THE HARBOUR OF MEMPHIS, TENN.	U.S.	46 x 64 cm
PLAN OF THE OPERATIONS OF THE BRITISH & AMERICAN FORCES BELOW NEW...	JAMES, W.	51 x 20 cm
PLAN OF THE POSITION WHICH THE ARMY UNDER LT. GENL. BURGOINE TOOK ...	STEDMAN	22 x 47 cm
PLAN OF THE ROAD AND PORT OF LA VERA CRUZ	JEFFERYS	20 x 31 cm
PLAN OF THE SETTLEMENT AT GREEN BAY FROM THE REPORT OF J. LEE ...	U.S.	38 x 46 cm
PLAN OF THE SETTLEMENT AT PRAIRIE DES CHIENS 1820	U.S.	51 x 33 cm
PLAN OF THE SIEGE OF CHARLESTOWN IN SOUTH CAROLINA	STEDMAN	25 x 30 cm
PLAN OF THE SIEGE OF SAVANNAH, WITH THE JOINT ATTACK OF THE FRENCH...	STEDMAN	41 x 57 cm
PLAN OF THE SIEGE OF YORK TOWN IN VIRGINIA	STEDMAN	28 x 27 cm
PLAN OF THE STRAITS OF BANCA	SAYER	48 x 33 cm
PLAN OF THE TOWN AND FORT OF GRENADA BY MR. DE CAYLUS ENGINEER ...	JEFFERYS	30 x 23 cm
PLAN OF THE TOWN AND FORTIFICATIONS OF MONTREAL OR VILLE MARIE ...	JEFFERYS	33 x 51 cm
PLAN OF THE TOWN & HARBOUR OF BEIROUT, ANCIENT BERYTUS	WYLD	21 x 27 cm
PLAN OF THE TOWN OF BOSTON, WITH THE ATTACK ON BUNKERS-HILL	NORMAN	28 x 13 cm
PLAN OF THE TOWN OF PITTSBOURG	COLLOT	20 x 28 cm
PLAN OF THE TOWN OF WILLIAM HENRY	BOUCHETTE	24 x 22 cm
PLAN OF THE UNITED STATE MARINE HOSPITAL LAND, CHELSEA, MASS. ...	U.S.	64 x 48 cm
PLAN PANORAMA DE PARIS FORTIFIE AVEC ILLUSTRATION. PLAN GARANTI ...	LALLEMAND	59 x 86 cm
PLAN ROUTIER DE LA VILLE ET FAUBOURGS DE PARIS DIVISE EN 12 MAIRIES	JEAN	57 x 85 cm
PLAN SCENOGRAPHIQUE DE LA CITE DES ROIS OU LIMA CAPITALE DU ...	BELLIN (Small)	19 x 32 cm
PLAN TOPOGRAPHIQUE DE LA VILLE PORT, ET BAYE DE GIBRALTAR ...	DHEULLAND	63 x 47 cm
PLAN VON DEN OPERATINEN DER KOENIGLICHEN ARMEE	RASPE	38 x 28 cm
PLAN VON NEU EBENEZER ...	SEUTTER (Large)	51 x 56 cm
PLANIGLOBII TERRESTRIS CUM UTROQ HEMISPHAERIO CAELESTI ...	HOMANN	48 x 53 cm
PLANIGLOBII TERRESTRIS MAPPA UNIVERSALIS ...	HOMANN	48 x 56 cm
PLANISFERO DEL MONDO NUOVO, DESCRITTO DAL P. CORONELLI, ...	CORONELLI	46 x 61 cm
PLANISPHAERIUM COELESTE	SCHENK	48 x 56 cm
PLANISPHAERIUM TERRESTRE, SIVE TERRARUM ORBIS, ...	ALLARD	51 x 61 cm
PLANISPHERE	LEVASSEUR	30 x 41 cm
PLANISPHERE CELESTE SUR LE QUEL LES ETOILLES SIXE SONT PLACEES ...	BION	15 x 25 cm
PLANISPHERE DE TURQUET / PLANISPHERE DE BERTIUS / PLANISPHERE D'ARZAEL	MALLET	14 x 10 cm
PLANISPHERE ELEMENTAIRE ET ILLUSTRE ...	VUILLEMIN	63 x 85 cm
PLANISPHERE PHYSIQUE OU L'ON VOIT DU POLE SEPTENTRIONALE CE QUE ...	BUACHE	36 x 46 cm
PLANISPHERE TERRESTRE, SUIVANT LES NOUVELLES OBSERVATIONS ...	VAN DER AA	54 x 65 cm
PLANISPHERIO CELESTE	DE AEFFERDEN	14 x 27 cm

PLANO DE LA BOCA DEL PUERTO DE CABANES EN LA COSTA NORTE DE LA ISLA	DIRECCION DE HIDRO.	22 x 32 cm
PLANO FIGURATIVO DE LOS TRENTA LEGUAS PLANAS DE TIERRAS, ...	U.S.	30 x 18 cm
PLANS OF PORTS IN WALES ...	ADMIRALTY	48 x 61 cm
PLANTA GUIDA DELLA CITTA DI ROMA	ROMOLO BULLA	53 x 64 cm
PLAT OF THE ANCIENT POSSESSIONS OF UPPER PRAIRIE CONFIRMED BY ...	U.S. STATE SURVEYS	30 x 23 cm
PLAT OF THE COMMON FIELD AND TOWN TRACT OF KASKASKIA	U.S.	46 x 36 cm
PLAT OF THE MILWAUKEE AND ROCK RIVER CANAL	U.S.	28 x 46 cm
PLAT OF THE SEVEN RANGES OF TOWNSHIPS BEING PART OF THE TERRITORY...	CAREY	61 x 34 cm
PLATA AMERICAE PROVINCIA	WYTFLIET	23 x 29 cm
PLATTE KAART VEN DE GEHEELE WERELT	WETSTEIN	37 x 46 cm
PLYMOUTH SOUND, HAMOAZE AND CATWATER WITH THE LEADING MARKS ...	LAURIE & WHITTLE	94 x 66 cm
POLAR REGIONS	LIZARS	41 x 38 cm
POLONIA ET HUNGARIA NUOVA TAVOLA	PTOLEMY (1561-1599)	19 x 25 cm
POLONIA ET SILESIA	MERCATOR (Folio)	35 x 46 cm
POLUS ARCTICUS CUM VICINIS REGIONIBUS	MERCATOR (Small)	10 x 20 cm
PORT MILLS, PORT MANSFIELD, GAMBIER HARBOR [Nova Scotia]	DES BARRES	73 x 209 cm
PORT PRAIJA AAN HET EILAND ST. JAGO	WALES, W.	18 x 15 cm
PORT ROYAL IN JAMAICA.	NAVAL CHRONICLE	12 x 16 cm
PORT SETUBAL	ADMIRALTY	45 x 60 cm
PORTHDINLLEYN & NEV YN BAY AND HARBOUR [Wales]	MORRIS	18 x 23 cm
PORTIONS OF GEORGIA AND SOUTH CAROLINA	U.S. WAR DEPT.	76 x 76 cm
PORTO BELLO AND ADJACENT COAST FROM A SPANISH M.S. ...	ADMIRALTY	61 x 46 cm
PORTS AND HARBOURS ON THE SOUTH EAST COAST OF ENGLAND	FULLARTON	46 x 30 cm
PORTS & HARBOURS ON THE NORTH WEST COAST OF ENGLAND	FULLARTON	48 x 30 cm
PORTS & HARBOURS ON THE SOUTH WEST COAST OF ENGLAND AND WALES	BARTHOLOMEW	43 x 30 cm
PORTUGALLIA ET ALGARBIA QUAE OLIM LUSITANIA. AUCTORE ...	JANSSON	38 x 49 cm
PORTUGALLIAE QUE OLIM LUSITANIA, NOVISSIMA & EXACTISSIMA DESCRIPTIO	ORTELIUS (Folio)	34 x 52 cm
POSITION OF THE DETACHMENT UNDER ... AT WALMSCOCK NEAR BENNINGTON	FADEN	28 x 36 cm
POSITION OF THE ENGLISH AND FRENCH FLEETS IMMEDIATELY PREVIOUS ...	STEDMAN	22 x 25 cm
POST OFFICE LONDON DIRECTORY	KELLY	68 x 90 cm
POSTKARTE DES GROSSHERZOGTHUMS BADEN UND ... WURTEMBERG ...	ANONYMOUS	45 x 44 cm
PRAEFECTURAE PARANAMBUCAE PARS BOREALIS	BLAEU	41 x 53 cm
PRELIMINARY CHART OF HUDSON RIVER ... FROM POUGHKEEPSIE TO GLASCO ...	U.S. COAST SURVEY	102 x 33 cm
PRELIMINARY CHART OF EASTPORT HARBOR, MAINE	U.S. COAST SURVEY	52 x 43 cm
PRELIMINARY CHART OF HATTERAS INLET NORTH CAROLINA	U.S. COAST SURVEY	41 x 38 cm
PRELIMINARY CHART OF MONTEREY BAY CALIFORNIA	U.S. COAST SURVEY	79 x 53 cm
PRELIMINARY CHART OF SAN LUIS PASS TEXAS	U.S. COAST SURVEY	36 x 43 cm
PRELIMINARY CHART OF ST. SIMONS SOUND AND BRUNSWICK HARBOR	U.S. COAST SURVEY	46 x 61 cm
PRELIMINARY CHART OF THE ST. JOHN'S RIVER FLORIDA FROM BROWN'S ...	U.S. COAST SURVEY	51 x 69 cm
PRELIMINARY SKETCH OF GALVESTON BAY	U.S. COAST SURVEY	48 x 41 cm
PRELIMINARY SKETCH OF MOBILE BAY	U.S. COAST SURVEY	41 x 30 cm
PRELIMINARY SKETCH OF THE NORTHERN PACIFIC RAIL ROAD EXPLORATION ...	U.S. PACIFIC R.R.	56 x 76 cm
PRELIMINARY SURVEY OF OCRACOKE INLET NORTH CAROLINA ...	U.S. COAST SURVEY	45 x 37 cm
PRELIMINARY SURVEY OF POINT REYES & DRAKE'S BAY, CALIFORNIA	U.S. COAST SURVEY	22 x 25 cm
PRESBITERI IOHANNIS SIVE ABYSINORUM IMPERY DESCRIPTIO	ORTELIUS (Miniature)	8 x 11 cm
PRESIDIO, SAN FRANCISCO	U.S. WAR DEPT.	20 x 18 cm
PRESQU ISLE DE L'INDE A L'ORIENT DU GOLFE DE BENGALA	MALLET	14 x 10 cm
PRESQU-ISLE DE L'INDE DECA LA GOLFE DE BENGAL	MALLET	14 x 10 cm
PRESQU'ISLE DE L'INDE DE CA LE GOLFE DU GANGE / PRESQU'ISLE DE L'INDE ...	DE FER (Small)	14 x 16 cm
PRESQU'ISLE DE L'INDE DECA LA GANGE	SANSON (Small)	19 x 24 cm
PRIMA PARS BRABANTIAE ...	JANSSON	51 x 41 cm
PRIMA TAVOLA	RAMUSIO	(no dimens.)
PRINCIPATUS BRANDENBURGICO-CULMBACENSIS VEL BARUTHINUS TABULA ...	HOMANN	50 x 57 cm
PRINCIPATUS ISENACENSIS	HOMANN	50 x 57 cm
PRINCIPATUS TRANSILVANIAE	HOMANN	50 x 59 cm
PROSPECT UND GRUNRIS DER KEISERL. FREYEN REICHS ... STADT BREMEN ...	HOMANN	49 x 58 cm
PROTOPARCHIAE MINDELHEMENSIS NOVA TABULA GEOGRAPHICA	HOMANN	49 x 59 cm
PROVINCETOWN HARBOR, MASSACHUSETTS	U.S. COAST SURVEY	37 x 44 cm
PROVINCIA. LA PROVENCE	HONDIUS	38 x 50 cm
PROVINCIAE BOREALIS AMERICAE NON ITA PRIDEM DETECTAE AUT MAGIS ...	SCHERER	23 x 36 cm
PROVISIONAL GEOLOGICAL MAP OF THE CHIPPEWAY LAND DISTRICT ...	U.S.	86 x 64 cm
PRUSSIA ACCURATE DESCRIPTA	JANSSON	38 x 49 cm
PTOLEMAEI TYPUS	PTOLEMY (1561-1599)	16 x 26 cm
PTOLEMEISCH GENERAL TAFEL / DIE HALBE KUGEL DER WELT BEGREIFFENDE	MUNSTER	30 x 36 cm
PUERTO DEL MARIEL. CHART NO. 380	DIRECCION DE HIDRO.	18 x 27 cm
PUERTO ESCONDIDO. CHART NO. 386	DIRECCION DE HIDRO.	18 x 23 cm
QUANTUNG E FOKIEN ...	CORONELLI	46 x 61 cm
QUEBEC	MALLET	15 x 10 cm

Title	Mapmaker	Size
QUEBEC RAILROADS	RAND, McNALLY	48 x 66 cm
QUEBEC, VILLE D L'AMERIQUE SEPTENTRIONALE DANS LA NOUVELLE FRANCE	VAN DER AA	20 x 28 cm
QUEBEC, VILLE DE L'AMERIQUE SEPTENTRIONALE DANS LA NOUVELLE FRANCE	DE FER (Small)	20 x 30 cm
QUEBECK IN CANADA	MEYER	11 x 17 cm
QUEBEK DE HOOFDSTAD VAN KANADA; AAN DE RIVIER VAN ST. LAURENS: ...	TIRION	33 x 43 cm
QUEENSLAND	STANFORD	65 x 49 cm
QUERCY CADURCIUM	MERCATOR (Folio)	38 x 50 cm
RAIL ROAD MAP OF NEW ENGLAND AND EASTERN NEW YORK	GOLDTHWAIT	(no dimens.)
RAILROAD AND COUNTY MAP OF DAKOTA & MANITOBA	CRAM	56 x 43 cm
RAILROAD AND COUNTY MAP OF GEORGIA	GRANT, A.	58 x 41 cm
RAILROAD AND COUNTY MAP OF INDIAN TER.	CRAM	43 x 58 cm
RAILROAD AND COUNTY MAP OF LOUISIANA	GRANT, A.	58 x 41 cm
RAILROAD AND COUNTY MAP OF MANITOBA	GRANT, A.	41 x 53 cm
RAILROAD AND COUNTY MAP OF MISSISSIPPI	GRANT, A.	58 x 41 cm
RAILROAD AND COUNTY MAP OF MONTANA	CRAM	43 x 58 cm
RAILROAD AND COUNTY MAP OF NEVADA	CRAM	58 x 43 cm
RAILROAD AND COUNTY MAP OF NEW MEXICO	CRAM	57 x 41 cm
RAILROAD AND COUNTY MAP OF OHIO	CRAM	43 x 58 cm
RAILROAD AND COUNTY MAP OF VIRGINIA, WEST VIRGINIA	CRAM	43 x 58 cm
RAILROAD & COUNTY MAP OF TEXAS	CRAM	41 x 56 cm
RAILROAD MAP OF NEW ENGLAND & EASTERN NEW YORK COMPILED FROM ...	GOLDTHWAIT	64 x 48 cm
RAILROAD MAP OF OHIO	LOCAL & STATE	74 x 81 cm
RAILROAD MAP OF THE UNITED STATES, SHOWING ... LINES OF ...	MITCHELL, S.A. (1860+)	36 x 58 cm
RAILROAD & SECTIONAL MAP OF WISCONSIN	HARRISON & WARNER	66 x 64 cm
RAMA	DE BRUYN	21 x 62 cm
RAND, McNALLY & CO.'S INDEXED COUNTY AND TOWNSHIP MAP OF INDIANA	RAND, McNALLY	51 x 33 cm
RAND, McNALLY & CO.'S INDIAN TERRITORY AND OKLAHOMA	RAND, McNALLY	30 x 48 cm
RAND, McNALLY'S POCKET MAP AND SHIPPER'S GUIDE OF IOWA	RAND, McNALLY	(no dimens.)
RAND McNALLY'S POCKET MAP AND SHIPPERS GUIDE OF NEW MEXICO	RAND, McNALLY	51 x 66 cm
RANGAOUNOU OR AWANUI RIVER	ADMIRALTY	65 x 48 cm
REBEL LINE OF WORKS AT BLAKELY CAPTURED BY THE ARMY OF WEST MISS.	U.S. WAR DEPT.	25 x 38 cm
RECENS EDITA TOTIUS NOVI BELGII, IN AMERICA SEPTENTRIONALI SITI, ...	SEUTTER (Large)	50 x 58 cm
RECENTISSIMA NOVI ORBIS SIVE AMERICAE	OTTENS	48 x 58 cm
RECONNAISANCE OF NEW RIVER AND BAR NORTH CAROLINA	U.S. COAST SURVEY	46 x 36 cm
RECONNOISSANCE OF THE WESTERN COAST OF THE [U.S.] FROM MONTEREY	U.S. COAST SURVEY	51 x 46 cm
REGNI BOHEMIAE CIRCULUS PILSNENSIS	HOMANN	49 x 55 cm
REGNI GALLIAE SEU FRANCIAE ET NAVARRAE TABULA GEOGRAPHICA	HOMANN	52 x 58 cm
REGNI JAPONIAE NOVA MAPPA GEOGRAPHICA ...	SEUTTER (Large)	49 x 56 cm
REGNI MEXICANI SEU NOVAE HISPANIAE LUDOVICIANAE, N. ANGLIAE, ...	HOMANN	48 x 57 cm
REGNI NEAPOLITANI VERISSIMA SECUNDUM ANTIQUORUM ET RECENTORIUM...	ORTELIUS (Folio)	37 x 50 cm
REGNI NORVEGIAE ACCURATA TABULA IN QUA PRAEFECTURAE QUINQUE ...	HOMANN	59 x 50 cm
REGNO DI NAPOLI	BLAEU	38 x 51 cm
REGNORUM MAGNAE BRITANNIAE ET HIBERNIAE ...	HOMANN	52 x 56 cm
REGNORUM MAGNAE BRITTANIAE, SIVE ANGLIAE SCOTIAE NEC NON HIBERNIA...	ALLARD	51 x 58 cm
REGNUM ANGLIAE	HOMANN	56 x 47 cm
REGNUM BORUSSIAE	HOMANN	50 x 59 cm
REGNUM CHINAE	METELLUS	15 x 21 cm
REGNUM HIBERNIA ...	LOTTER	58 x 48 cm
REGNUM HUNGARIAE ...	VISSCHER	48 x 58 cm
REGNUM NEAPOLIS ...	DE WIT	58 x 48 cm
REGNUM SALOMONICUM SEU TABULA DIGESTA AD LIBROS JUDICUM REGNUM	DE LA RUE	41 x 53 cm
RELIGIONIS CATHOLICAE AUSTRALI AMERICAE IMPLANTATAE DESCRIPTIO ...	SCHERER	22 x 34 cm
RELIGIONIS CATHOLICAE IN AMERICAE BOREALI DISSEMINATAE REPRAESENT. ...	SCHERER	23 x 36 cm
REPRAESENTATIO AMERICAE BOREALIS CUIUS PROVINCIAE VERA FIDE ...	SCHERER	24 x 35 cm
REYNOLDS' MAP OF LONDON WITH RECENT IMPROVEMENTS 1878. DIVIDED...	REYNOLDS, J.	48 x 74 cm
REYNOLDS'S MAP OF MODERN LONDON DIVIDED INTO QUARTER MILE ...	REYNOLDS, J.	48 x 73 cm
REYNOLDS'S NEW MAP OF LONDON AND ITS SUBURBS	REYNOLDS, J.	66 x 100 cm
RHEIN-PANORAMA COLN BIS MAINZ	FOPPEN	187 x 18 cm
RHENUS FLUVIORUM EUROPAE CELEBERRIMUS, CUM MOSA, MOSELLA, ET ...	JANSSON	42 x 94 cm
RHODE ISLAND	CAREY	20 x 15 cm
RHODE ISLAND	FINLEY	28 x 22 cm
RHODE ISLAND	PAYNE	24 x 19 cm
RHODE ISLAND	SCOTT	20 x 18 cm
RHODE-ISLAND AND CONNECTICUT	MORSE, J.	19 x 33 cm
RICE PORTS OF INDIA	IMRAY	127 x 102 cm
RICE'S SECTIONAL MAP OF DAKOTA	RICE	76 x 66 cm
RICHARDSON'S MAP OF SOUTH EAST AND CENTRAL ENGLAND ... SHOWING ...	RICHARDSON	118 x 94 cm
RIO JANEIRO	MEYER	10 x 15 cm

RIO JANERO	DE BRY	15 x 18 cm
RIVER HOOGHLY. CALCUTTA TO SAUGOR POINT	ADMIRALTY	97 x 64 cm
RIVER ST. LAWRENCE, LONG POINT TO LACHINE RAPIDS INCLUDING MONTREAL	ADMIRALTY	97 x 64 cm
RIVER TAY	ADMIRALTY	64 x 99 cm
RIVER THAMES SHEET 2 N. FORELAND TO THE NORE	ADMIRALTY	61 x 69 cm
ROMA	BRAUN & HOGENBERG	33 x 48 cm
ROME & ITS ENVIRONS, FROM A TRIGONOMETRICAL SURVEY	GELL, W.	72 x 98 cm
ROUTE MARITIME DE BREST A SIAM, ET DE SIAM A BREST, FAITE EN 1685 ET ...	NOLIN	44 x 72 cm
ROUTE OF THE EXPEDITION FROM ISLE A LA CROSSE TO FORT PROVIDENCE ...	FRANKLIN	51 x 24 cm
ROWE'S MAP OF THE COUNTRY TWENTY-ONE MILES ROUND LONDON	ROWE	51 cm, diam
ROYAUME D'IRLANDE	JAILLOT	89 x 62 cm
ROYAUME DE LA CHINE	SANSON (Small)	24 x 19 cm
ROYAUMES DE CONGO ET ANGOLA	VAN DER AA	28 x 36 cm
RUATAN OR RATTAN SURVEYED BY ... BARNSLEY WITH IMPROVEMENTS ...	JEFFERYS	46 x 61 cm
RUSSIA	CLARK	23 x 18 cm
RUSSIA	JOHNSON	41 x 33 cm
RUSSIA IN EUROPE	STACKHOUSE	38 x 36 cm
RUSSIA IN EUROPE	THOMAS, COWPERTH.	31 x 26 cm
RUSSIA IN EUROPE PART IX	S.D.U.K.	32 x 40 cm
RUSSIA IN EUROPE PART VI	S.D.U.K.	39 x 32 cm
RUSSIA IN EUROPE PART X	S.D.U.K.	40 x 32 cm
RUSSIAE, VULGO MOSCOVIA DICTAE, PARTES SEPTENTRIONALIS ET ORIENT.	JANSSON	42 x 54 cm
RUSSIE BLANCHE OR MOSCOVIE	DE FER (Small)	14 x 16 cm
S. CAROLINA	GASKELL	25 x 30 cm
S.R.I. CIRCULAS RHENANUS INFERIOR SIVE ELECTORATUM RHENI ...	HOMANN	60 x 50 cm
S.R.I. CIRCULUS RHENANUS SUPERIOR...LANDGRAVIATUS HASSO-CASSELENSIS	HOMANN	50 x 59 cm
S.R.I. PRINCIPATUS & EPISCOPATUS EISTETTENSIS	HOMANN	50 x 59 cm
S.R.I. PRINCIPATUS ET ARCHIEPISCOPATUS SALISBURGENSIS	HOMANN	49 x 59 cm
S.R.I. PRINCIPATUS FULDENSIS IN BUCHONIA	HOMANN	49 x 58 cm
S.R.IMP. COMITATUS HANAU ... ET COMITATUS SOLMS BUDINGEN ET NIDDA ...	HOMANN	50 x 58 cm
S.W. TERRITORY	SCOTT	15 x 20 cm
SAC. RO. IMPERII PRINCIPATUS & EPISCOPATUS BAMBERGENSIS NOVA TABULA	HOMANN	50 x 58 cm
SACRAMENTO-CITY IN CALIFORNIEN	MEYER	11 x 16 cm
SACRAMENTO IN CALIFORNIEN	HESSE, J.	23 x 36 cm
SALT LAKE CITY	HARPER'S WEEKLY	23 x 36 cm
SALZBURG ARCHIEPISCOPATUS CUM DUCATU CARINTHIAE	MERCATOR (Folio)	34 x 48 cm
SAMOAN OR NAVIGATOR ISLANDS BY U.S. EX. EX. ... 1839	U.S. EXPLOR. EXPED.	20 x 30 cm
SAN DIEGO CAL. AND VICINITY SHOWING THE PLATS OF LAND OFFERED FOR ...	U.S. WAR DEPT.	48 x 36 cm
SAN DIEGO ENTRANCE AND APPROACHES	U.S. COAST SURVEY	33 x 33 cm
SAN FRANCISCO	MEYER	11 x 16 cm
SAN FRANCISCO BAY TO THE NORTHERN BOUNDARY OF CALIFORNIA ...	U.S. PACIFIC R.R.	81 x 64 cm
SAN FRANCISCO BAY TO THE PLAINS OF LOS ANGELES ... 1854 AND 55	U.S. PACIFIC R.R.	76 x 102 cm
SAN JUAN DE NICARAGUA	MEYER	11 x 16 cm
SAN LOUIS AM MISSISSIPPI	MEYER	11 x 16 cm
SAND ANTONIO CREEK, CALIFORNIA	U.S. COAST SURVEY	36 x 48 cm
SARMATIA ASIE	MUNSTER	25 x 18 cm
SARMATIA ET SCYTHIA RUSSIA ET TARTARIA EUROPAEA	CLUVER	23 x 25 cm
SAVANNAH, GA.	APPLETON	18 x 23 cm
SAXONIA INFERIOR	JANSSON	38 x 46 cm
SAXONIAE TRACTUS DUCATUM MAGDEBURGENSEM CUM SUO CIRCULO ...	HOMANN	49 x 54 cm
SCANDIA OR SCANDINAVIA COMPREHENDING THE KINGDOM OF SWEDEN ...	FADEN	72 x 50 cm
SCANDINAVIA, VEL REGNA SEPTENTRIONALIS, SVECIA, DANIA, ET NORVEGIA, ...	VALK	58 x 48 cm
SCANDINAVIE OU SONT LES ESTATS DE DANEMARK DE SUEDE &C.	SANSON (Small)	18 x 25 cm
SCENOGRAPHIA PORTUS PULCHRI EX PROTOTYPO LONDINENSI VECUSA	HOMANN	23 x 28 cm
SCIENTIA TERRARUM ET COELORUM, OR THE HEAVENS AND EARTH ...	DUNN	103 x 123 cm
SCLAVONIA, CROATIA, BOSNIA CUM DALMATIAE PARTE	MERCATOR (Folio)	36 x 46 cm
SCOTIA	ORTELIUS (Miniature)	8 x 11 cm
SCOTIA REGNUM	MERCATOR (Folio)	35 x 41 cm
SEAHAM HARBOUR	ADMIRALTY	61 x 48 cm
SEAT OF WAR IN VIRGINIA AND MARYLAND	WELLER	45 x 31 cm
SECONDA TAVOLA	RAMUSIO	29 x 38 cm
SECTIO INFERIOR, DUCATUM VINARIENSEM	HOMANN	37 x 48 cm
SECTIONAL MAP OF THE SURVEYED PORTION OF MINNESOTA AND THE ...	HILL, A.J.	84 x 64 cm
SECUNDA ETAS MUNDI	SCHEDEL	37 x 51 cm
SEIGE OPERATIONS AT SPANISH FORT MOBILE BAY BY U.S. FORCES ...	U.S. WAR DEPT.	33 x 43 cm
SEPTEM PROVINCIAE SEU BELGIUM FOEDERATUM...GENERALITER HOLLANDIA...	HOMANN	48 x 52 cm
SEPTENTRIONALES REGIONES XVIII NO. TAB.	MUNSTER	28 x 36 cm
SEPTENTRIONALIUM PARTIUM NOVA TABULA	PTOLEMY (1561-1599)	19 x 24 cm

SEPTENTRIONALIUM REGIONUM DESCRIP.	ORTELIUS (Miniature)	8 x 11 cm
SEPTENTRIONALIUM REGIONUM SUETIAE GOTHIAE NORVEGIAE DANIAE &C	QUAD	22 x 30 cm
SEPTENTRIONALIUM TERRARUM DESCRIPTIO	MERCATOR (Small)	15 x 20 cm
SEPTENTRIONALIUM TERRARUM DESCRIPTIO. PER GERARDUM MERCATOREM	MERCATOR (Folio)	37 x 40 cm
SEPTENTRIONALUM REGIONU DESCRIP.	BERTIUS	8 x 12 cm
SEVILLA	BRAUN & HOGENBERG	36 x 48 cm
SHEET 1 POINT DE MONTS TO BERSIMIS RIVER [St. Laurence River]	ADMIRALTY	46 x 64 cm
SHEET 3 GREEN ISLAND TO THE PILGRIMS [St. Laurence River]	ADMIRALTY	46 x 64 cm
SIAM	MORSE, S.	30 x 25 cm
SIBERIA AND CHINESE TARTARY	S.D.U.K.	32 x 40 cm
SICILIAE REGNUM	JANSSON	34 x 48 cm
SICILIAE REGNUM	MERCATOR (Small)	15 x 20 cm
SIGNORIA DI VERCELLI	JANSSON	39 x 50 cm
SILESIA INFERIOR	JANSSON	42 x 52 cm
SIMEON	FULLER	27 x 33 cm
SITUS PARTIUM PRAECIPUARUM TOTIUS ORBIS TERRARUM	TORNIELLO	20 x 38 cm
SKETCH BY COMPASS OF PORT MULGRAVE LAT 59 deg. 33' N.	DIXON	41 x 28 cm
SKETCH MAP SHOWING DISTRIBUTION OF QUICKSILVER MINES IN CALIFORNIA	U.S. COAST SURVEY	25 x 18 cm
SKETCH OF GENERAL GRANTS POSITION ON LONG ISLAND	STEDMAN	35 x 26 cm
SKETCH OF GENERAL RILEY'S ROUTE THROUGH THE MINING DISTRICTS ..	U.S.	53 x 50 cm
SKETCH OF INDIAN RIVER & SOUTHERN PORTION OF MOSQUITO LAGOON FL.	U.S. WAR DEPT.	41 x 25 cm
SKETCH OF NEW SOUTH SHETLAND ...	ADMIRALTY	18 x 23 cm
SKETCH OF PART ... LOUISIANA ACCOMPANYING A REPORT ...	U.S.	48 x 58 cm
SKETCH OF PART OF THE ISLAND OF STE. LUCIE. ...	WYLD	38 x 48 cm
SKETCH OF PUBLIC SURVEYS IN NEW MEXICO & ARIZONA ...	U.S. STATE SURVEYS	53 x 71 cm
SKETCH OF PUBLIC SURVEYS IN THE TERRITORY OF MINNESOTA	U.S. STATE SURVEYS	56 x 53 cm
SKETCH OF ROANOKE ISLAND, N.C.	U.S. WAR DEPT.	18 x 18 cm
SKETCH OF THE ACTION ON THE HEIGHTS OF CHARLESTOWN JUNE 17TH ...	MELISH	33 x 51 cm
SKETCH OF THE ACTION ON THE HEIGHTS OF CHARLESTOWN JUNE 17TH. ...	STEDMAN	33 x 51 cm
SKETCH OF THE BATTLE GROUND AT RESACA DE LA PALMA, TEXAS MAY 8TH	U.S. WAR DEPT.	28 x 20 cm
SKETCH OF THE CATAWBA RIVER AT McCOWNS FORD	STEDMAN	15 x 18 cm
SKETCH OF THE COUNTRY EMBRACING SEVERAL ROUTES FROM PORTSMOUTH	U.S. WAR DEPT.	104 x 30 cm
SKETCH OF THE COUNTRY ILLUSTRATING THE LATE ENGAGEMENT IN LONG I.	GENTLEMAN'S MAG.	20 x 31 cm
SKETCH OF THE DYEA AND SKAGUA TRAILS ...	U.S.	25 x 20 cm
SKETCH OF THE ENTRANCE OF SODUS BAY CAYUGA COUNTY [N.Y.]	U.S. WAR DEPT.	13 x 23 cm
SKETCH OF THE HARBOR OF BLACK RIVER [N.Y.]	U.S. WAR DEPT.	20 x 41 cm
SKETCH OF THE HARBOUR OF SAMGANOODA, ON THE ISLAND OF OONALASKA	COOK	21 x 33 cm
SKETCH OF THE LEAD MINE DISTRICT IN WASHINGTON COUNTY MISSOURI ...	U.S.	48 x 41 cm
SKETCH OF THE MARQUESAS DE MENDOCA	COOK	20 x 15 cm
SKETCH OF THE MOUTH OF ELK CREEK [Penn.]	U.S. WAR DEPT.	56 x 38 cm
SKETCH OF THE POSITION OF THE BRITISH AND AMERICAN FORCES, DURING ...	NAVAL CHRONICLE	13 x 21 cm
SKETCH OF THE PUBLIC SURVEYS IN MICHIGAN	U.S. STATE SURVEYS	56 x 56 cm
SKETCH OF THE PUBLIC SURVEYS IN NEW MEXICO 1860	U.S. STATE SURVEYS	58 x 81 cm
SKETCH OF THE SABINE RIVER, LAKE AND PASS FROM CAMP SABINE TO ...	U.S. WAR DEPT.	89 x 23 cm
SKETCH OF THE STRAITS OF GASPAR ...	LAURIE & WHITTLE	64 x 48 cm
SKETCH SHEWING THE ROUTE OF THE RECENT ARCTIC LAND EXPEDITION	ROYAL GEOG. SOC.	18 x 23 cm
SKETCH SHOWING ... SECTION FOR CURRENT OBSERVATIONS AT FORT YUMA ...	U.S. WAR DEPT.	18 x 25 cm
SKIZZE DER ENTDECKUNGEN DER ENGLISCHEN POLAR-EXPEDITION UNTER NARES	PETERMANN	25 x 15 cm
SMITH'S MAP OF ENGLAND AND WALES, CONTAINING THE WHOLE OF THE ...	SMITH, C.	77 x 61 cm
SMITH'S MAP OF ENGLAND AND WALES, SHOWING ALL THE RAILWAYS, ...	SMITH, C.	115 x 94 cm
SMITH'S NEW AND ACCURATE MAP OF THE LAKES, IN THE COUNTIES OF ...	SMITH, C.	60 x 48 cm
SOIL MAP - CORPUS CHRISTI SHEET	U.S.	48 x 76 cm
SOIL MAP - FARGO SHEET [NORTH DAKOTA]	U.S.	33 x 94 cm
SOIL MAP - GRAND ISLAND SHEET [NEBRASKA]	U.S.	48 x 71 cm
SOIL MAP - LOS ANGELES SHEET	U.S.	89 x 76 cm
SOIL MAP - PARKERSBURG AREA [WEST VIRGINIA]	U.S.	81 x 132 cm
SOLVACH BAY & HARBOUR ... [Wales]	MORRIS	18 x 23 cm
SORIE ET DIARBECK	SANSON (Small)	19 x 26 cm
SOURCE DU NIL	MALLET	15 x 10 cm
SOURCES OF THE MISSISSIPPI ...	SCHOOLCRAFT	20 x 20 cm
SOURIE OU TERRE SAINCTE MODERNE	DE LA RUE	39 x 53 cm
SOUTH AFRICA	BLACK	42 x 56 cm
SOUTH AFRICA COMPILED FROM THE MS MAPS IN THE COLONIAL OFFICE	BALDWIN & CRADOCK	33 x 41 cm
SOUTH AFRICA FROM OFFICIAL & OTHER AUTHENTIC AUTHORITIES	FULLARTON	42 x 53 cm
SOUTH AMERICA	S.D.U.K.	40 x 32 cm
SOUTH AMERICA, ACCORDING TO THE NEWEST AND MOST EXACT OBSERV. ...	MOLL (Large)	58 x 97 cm
SOUTH AMERICA COAST OF CHILE ...	ADMIRALTY	27 x 28 cm
SOUTH AMERICA CORRECTED FROM OBSERVATIONS COMMUNICATED TO ...	SENEX	69 x 58 cm

SOUTH AMERICA SHEET IV LA PLATA AND CHILE	S.D.U.K.	31 x 39 cm
SOUTH AMERICAN STATES. NEW GRANADA & VENEZUELA ...	FULLARTON	41 x 53 cm
SOUTH AND EAST COASTS OF AUSTRALIA [IN FOUR CHARTS]. CHART NO.1 ...	IMRAY	101 x 128 cm
SOUTH ATLANTIC	IMRAY	101 x 158 cm
SOUTH AUSTRALIA [AND NORTHERN TERRITORY]	STANFORD	48 x 66 cm
SOUTH CAROLINA	BRADFORD	30 x 38 cm
SOUTH CAROLINA	CAREY	15 x 20 cm
SOUTH CAROLINA	CENTURY ATLAS	28 x 38 cm
SOUTH CAROLINA	COLTON	33 x 41 cm
SOUTH CAROLINA	FINLEY	22 x 29 cm
SOUTH CAROLINA	MORSE & BREESE	33 x 38 cm
SOUTH CAROLINA	SCOTT	18 x 20 cm
SOUTH CAROLINA RAILROADS	RAND, McNALLY	51 x 66 cm
SOUTH DAKOTA	CRAM	36 x 51 cm
SOUTH DAKOTA	CRAM	43 x 56 cm
SOUTH DAKOTA	RAND, McNALLY	38 x 58 cm
SOUTH WEST-VIRGINIA MINERAL RESOURCES & RAILWAY FACILITIES. ...	RAILROAD COMPANY	51 x 97 cm
SOUTHERN INDIA	TALLIS	32 x 23 cm
SOUTHERN PORTS & HARBOURS IN THE UNITED STATES	FULLARTON	41 x 30 cm
SOUTHERN PROVINCES OF THE UNITED STATES	THOMSON	51 x 58 cm
SOUTHERN REGIONS	COLTON	41 x 33 cm
SOUTHERN STATES	WALLING	38 x 58 cm
SPAIN (ESPANA)	S.D.U.K.	25 x 34 cm
SPANISH NORTH AMERICA	LIZARS	23 x 28 cm
SPANISH NORTH AMERICA	THOMSON	51 x 62 cm
SPHAERAE ARTIFICIALES ...	SEUTTER (Large)	48 x 58 cm
SPRINGFIELD, CLARKE CO. [Ohio]	STEBBINS, H.	28 x 36 cm
ST. ANTONIO (TEXAS)	MEYER	11 x 16 cm
ST. CATHERINES SOUND GEORGIA	U.S. COAST SURVEY	56 x 74 cm
ST. CHRISTOPHERS	LUCAS	22 x 31 cm
ST. FRANCISCO DE CAMPECHE PETITE VILLE DE L'AUDIENCE DE MEXIQUE	VAN DER AA	30 x 36 cm
ST. GEORGE'S CHANNEL. ETC.	WILSON	86 x 178 cm
ST. IAGO - SE LAGUES - NATAVIDAET [MEXICO]	NICOL	15 x 10 cm
ST. LOUIS	LADIES REPOSITORY	15 x 20 cm
ST. LOUIS, MISSOURI	HARPER'S WEEKLY	23 x 33 cm
ST. PETERSBURG	HALL	28 x 38 cm
ST. TUDSWALS ROAD AND KEIRIAD ROAD [Wales]	MORRIS	18 x 23 cm
ST. VINCENT TO BRITAIN	PHILIP, G.	51 x 30 cm
STAATEN AM ATLANTISHCEN OCEAN	MEYER	34 x 43 cm
STANFORD'S GENERAL MAP OF THE UNITED STATES	STANFORD	70 x 110 cm
STANFORD'S MAP OF BRITISH SOUTH AFRICA	STANFORD	54 x 70 cm
STANFORD'S MAP OF THE SEAT OF WAR IN AMERICA	STANFORD	130 x 106 cm
STANFORD'S NEW HAND MAP OF THE UNITED STATES WITH THE RESULT ...	STANFORD	47 x 57 cm
STANFORD'S PORTABLE MAP OF ENGLAND & WALES WITH THE RAILWAYS ...	STANFORD	76 x 68 cm
STANFORD'S SMALLER RAILWAY MAP OF THE UNITED STATES DISTINGUISHING	STANFORD	40 x 70 cm
STANFORD'S TWO INCH MAP OF LONDON AND ITS ENVIRONS	STANFORD	67 x 109 cm
STATE OF ALABAMA	U.S. STATE SURVEYS	48 x 30 cm
STATE OF CALIFORNIA	U.S. STATE SURVEYS	97 x 84 cm
STATE OF GEORGIA	WILMORE	15 x 15 cm
STATE OF IDAHO	U.S. STATE SURVEYS	107 x 69 cm
STATE OF INDIANA	U.S. STATE SURVEYS	81 x 56 cm
STATE OF OREGON	U.S. STATE SURVEYS	61 x 71 cm
STATE OF OREGON	U.S. STATE SURVEYS	61 x 81 cm
STATE OF RHODE ISLAND	EVERTS & RICHARDS	99 x 76 cm
STATE OF VERMONT	SCOTT	19 x 17 cm
STATES OF AMERICA	FISHER, H.	18 x 22 cm
STATES OF AMERICA, DRAWN FROM THE BEEST AUTHORITIES	RUSSELL	41 x 46 cm
STATUS ECCLESIASTICI NEC NON MAGNI DUCATUS TOSCANAE NOVA TABULA	HOMANN	49 x 57 cm
STIRIA	JANSSON	31 x 42 cm
STOCKHOLM	S.D.U.K.	34 x 39 cm
STRAIT OF MALACCA	ADMIRALTY	64 x 97 cm
SUCHUEN, ET XENSI, PROVINCIAE SEU PRAEFECTURAE REGNI SINENSIS. ...	MERCATOR (Folio)	47 x 53 cm
SUCHUEN IMPERII SINARUM PROVINCIA SEXTA	BLAEU	40 x 48 cm
SUD AMERICA ...	WEIMAR GEOGRAPH.	56 x 46 cm
SUD AMERICA ...	WEIMAR GEOGRAPH.	70 x 52 cm
SUD-AMERICA IN ZWEI BLATTERN ...	STIELER	33 x 40 cm
SUD-POLAR KARTE	STIELER	35 x 41 cm
SUD SEITS DES LANDTS TERSA DEL FUOCO	DE BRY	15 x 17 cm

SUECIAE, NORVEGIAE, ET DANIAE, NOVA TABULA	JANSSON	48 x 56 cm
SUIRAH OR MOGADOR HARBOUR	ADMIRALTY	46 x 61 cm
SUISSE OR SWITZERLAND	MOLL (Small)	23 x 25 cm
SUITE DE LA CARTE REDUITE DU GOLPHE DE ST. LAURENT CONTENANT ...	DEPOT DE LA MARINE	90 x 56 cm
SUITE DE PEROU AUDIENCE DE CHARCAS	D'ANVILLE	23 x 30 cm
SUITE DU BRESIL ...	BELLIN (Small)	23 x 17 cm
SUITE DU BRESIL, DEPUIS LA BAIE DE TOUS LE SAINTS JUSQU'A ST. PAUL	BELLIN (Small)	23 x 17 cm
SUITE DU BRESIL, DEPUIS LA BAYE DE TOUS LES SAINTS JUSQU'A ST. PAUL	BELLIN (Small)	23 x 17 cm
SUITE DU COURS DE FLEUVE DE ST. LAURENT DEPUIS QUEBEC ... LAC ONTARIO	BELLIN (Small)	22 x 34 cm
SUITE DU PEROU AUDIENCE DE CHARCAS ...	BELLIN (Small)	22 x 30 cm
SUITE DU PEROU AUDIENCE DE LIMA ...	BELLIN (Small)	21 x 29 cm
SUOMEN KASIKARTTA - HANDKARTA OFVER FINLAND	TILGMANN, F.	69 x 51 cm
SURREY	MORDEN	9 x 6 cm
SURVEY FOR THE OPENING OF STEAMBOAT COMMUNICATION FROM LAKE ...	U.S. WAR DEPT.	33 x 53 cm
SURVEY OF THE HARBOR OF WHITEHALL [N.Y.]	U.S. WAR DEPT.	28 x 89 cm
SURVEY OF THE MOUTH OF GALIEN RIVER MICHIGAN	U.S. WAR DEPT.	51 x 76 cm
SURVEY OF THE NEENAH OR FOX RIVER, GRAND CHUTE	U.S. WAR DEPT.	13 x 20 cm
SURVEY OF THE WATER ROUTES FROM NORFOLK HARBOR TO ... CAPE FEAR ...	U.S. WAR DEPT.	56 x 38 cm
SUSSEX	MORDEN	9 x 6 cm
SWITZERLAND, CONTAINING THE THIRTEEN CANTONS ...	PAYNE	20 x 28 cm
SYRACUSE WITH THE REMAINING VESTIGES OF ITS FIVE CITIES	S.D.U.K.	33 x 40 cm
SYRIA	S.D.U.K.	40 x 31 cm
SYRIE ANCIENNE	MALLET	15 x 10 cm
SYRIE MODERNE	MALLET	14 x 10 cm
'T GEBIEDT VAN MEXICO	SANSON (Small)	18 x 28 cm
TAB: GEOG. AMERICAE AD EMENDATIORA	VON EULER	30 x 36 cm
TABLE BAY	ADMIRALTY	94 x 61 cm
TABU. NOVA ORBIS	FRIES	28 x 46 cm
TABULA APHRICAE II [NORTH AFRICA]	PTOLEMY (1561-1599)	18 x 25 cm
TABULA AQUITANIA COMPLECTENS GUBERNATIONEM GUINNAE ET VASCONIAE	HOMANN	48 x 58 cm
TABULA ASIAE I [ASIA MINOR]	PTOLEMY (1561-1599)	18 x 25 cm
TABULA ASIAE II	MUNSTER	25 x 33 cm
TABULA ASIAE II [CAUCASUS, ETC.]	PTOLEMY (1561-1599)	18 x 25 cm
TABULA ASIAE III	PTOLEMY (1596-1621)	12 x 17 cm
TABULA ASIAE III [ARMENIA, ETC.]	PTOLEMY (1561-1599)	18 x 24 cm
TABULA ASIAE IIII	PTOLEMY (1561-1599)	19 x 25 cm
TABULA ASIAE V [PERSIA]	PTOLEMY (1561-1599)	18 x 25 cm
TABULA ASIAE VI	PTOLEMY (1596-1621)	12 x 17 cm
TABULA ASIAE VI [ARABIA]	PTOLEMY (1561-1599)	18 x 24 cm
TABULA ASIAE VII	MUNSTER	25 x 34 cm
TABULA ASIAE VII [CENTRAL ASIA]	PTOLEMY (1561-1599)	18 x 24 cm
TABULA ASIAE VIII	MUNSTER	25 x 33 cm
TABULA ASIAE VIII	PTOLEMY (1596-1621)	12 x 17 cm
TABULA ASIAE IX	MUNSTER	25 x 34 cm
TABULA ASIAE X	MUNSTER	25 x 34 cm
TABULA ASIAE X [SOUTH ASIA]	PTOLEMY (1548 Venice)	13 x 17 cm
TABULA ASIAE X [SOUTH ASIA]	PTOLEMY (1561-1599)	19 x 24 cm
TABULA ASIAE XI	MUNSTER	25 x 34 cm
TABULA ASIAE XI	PTOLEMY (1596-1621)	12 x 17 cm
TABULA ASIAE XI [FAR EAST]	PTOLEMY (1561-1599)	18 x 22 cm
TABULA ASIAE XII	MUNSTER	26 x 34 cm
TABULA ASIAE XII	PTOLEMY (1561-1599)	19 x 25 cm
TABULA ASIAE XII	PTOLEMY (1596-1621)	13 x 17 cm
TABULA EUROPAE II [SPAIN & PORTUGAL]	PTOLEMY (1561-1599)	19 x 26 cm
TABULA EUROPAE III [FRANCE]	PTOLEMY (1561-1599)	18 x 24 cm
TABULA EUROPAE IIII	PTOLEMY (1596-1621)	13 x 17 cm
TABULA EUROPAE IIII [GERMANY]	PTOLEMY (1561-1599)	18 x 25 cm
TABULA EUROPAE QUINTA	PTOLEMY (1596-1621)	13 x 17 cm
TABULA EUROPAE V [DALMATIA COAST]	PTOLEMY (1561-1599)	18 x 25 cm
TABULA EUROPAE VI	PTOLEMY (1561-1599)	19 x 25 cm
TABULA EUROPAE VII	PTOLEMY (1561-1599)	19 x 25 cm
TABULA EUROPAE VIII [EASTERN EUROPE]	PTOLEMY (1561-1599)	19 x 25 cm
TABULA EUROPAE IX	MUNSTER	26 x 33 cm
TABULA EUROPAE IX [BALKANS]	PTOLEMY (1561-1599)	18 x 25 cm
TABULA EUROPAE X [GREECE]	PTOLEMY (1561-1599)	19 x 25 cm
TABULA FRISIAE ORIENTALIS	HOMANN	50 x 59 cm
TABULA GENERALIS MARCHIONATUS MORAVIAE	HOMANN	49 x 59 cm
TABULA GEOGRA. REGNI CONGO	DE BRY	31 x 38 cm

TABULA GEOGRAPHICA EXHIBENS REGNUM SCLAVONIAE CUM SYRMII DUCATU	HOMANN	50 x 58 cm
TABULA GEOGRAPHICA IN QUA...PRINCIPATUS GOTHA, COBURG ET ALTERBURG	HOMANN	49 x 56 cm
TABULA GEOGRAPHICA MAXIMAE PARTIS AMERICAE MEDIAE SIVE INDIAE OCC.	WALCH	49 x 60 cm
TABULA INDIAE ORIENTALIS	DE WIT	46 x 57 cm
TABULA ISLANDIAE AUCTORE GEORGIO CAROLO FLANDRO	JANSSON	38 x 49 cm
TABULA ITALIAE ANTIQUAE GEOGRAPHICA QUAM EXCELLENTISSIMUS ...	D'ANVILLE	64 x 50 cm
TABULA MARCHIONATUS BRANDENBURGICI ET DUCATUS POMERANIAE	HOMANN	49 x 56 cm
TABULA MODER. SICILI & SARDI	PTOLEMY (1522-1541)	28 x 41 cm
TABULA MODERNA SECUNDA PORCIONIS APHRICE	WALDSEEMULLER	37 x 51 cm
TABULA NOVA INDIAE ORIENTALIS & MERIDIONALIS	FRIES	28 x 43 cm
TABULA NOVISSIMA ACCURATISSIMA REGNORUM ANGLIAE, SCOTIAE HIBERNIAE	LOTTER	56 x 49 cm
TABULA NOVISSIMA ATQUE ACCURATISSIMA CARAIBICARUM INSULARUM ...	OTTENS	60 x 50 cm
TABULA ORIENTALIS REGIONIS, ASIAE SCILICET EXTREMAS COMPLECTENS ...	MUNSTER	25 x 33 cm
TABULA QUA GRAECIA SUPERIOR, QUALIS TEMPORE BELLI PELOPONNESIACI ...	MURRAY, J.	56 x 69 cm
TABULA TERRA PROMISSAE AB AUCTORE COMMENTARII JOSUE DELINEATA ...	CALMET	46 x 23 cm
TABULA TERRAE NOVAE	FRIES	29 x 38 cm
TABULAM HANC AEGYPTI, SI AEQUUS AC DILIGENS LECTOR, CUM ALYS, ...	DE BRY	55 x 40 cm
TAFFEL DER LENDER DARIN DER APOSTEL PAULUS GEPREDIGET HAT	BUNTING	30 x 38 cm
TAFFEL DES HEILIGEN LANDES ZU DEM NEWEN TESTAMENT DIENLICH	BUNTING	28 x 20 cm
TANGIER BAY	ADMIRALTY	48 x 65 cm
TARTARIA SIVE MAGNI CHAMI IMPERIUM	JANSSON	38 x 51 cm
TARTARIAE SIVE MAGNI CHAM, REGNI TYPUS	ORTELIUS (Folio)	35 x 47 cm
TARTARIAE SIVE MAGNI CHAMI REGNI TYPUS	ORTELIUS (Miniature)	8 x 11 cm
TASMANIA OR VAN DIEMENS LAND	WELLER	43 x 30 cm
TASMANIA OR VAN DIEMENS LAND	WYLD	55 x 39 cm
TAUNTON'S POCKET EDITION OF THE MERCHANT'S AND SHIPPER'S GUIDE ...	TAUNTON	66 x 46 cm
TAURICA CHERSONESUS NOSTRA AETATE PRZECOPSCA ET GAZARA DICITUR	BLAEU	38 x 50 cm
TAURICA CHERSONESUS. NOSTRA AETATE PRZECOPSCA ET GAZARA DICTUR	MERCATOR (Folio)	32 x 41 cm
TAVOLA NUOVA DELLA MARCA TRIVIGIANA	PTOLEMY (1561-1599)	19 x 25 cm
TAVOLA NUOVA DI PIEMONTE	PTOLEMY (1561-1599)	19 x 25 cm
TAVOLA NUOVA DI PRUSSIA ET DI LIVONIA	PTOLEMY (1561-1599)	18 x 25 cm
TAVOLA NUOVA DI SARDIGNA ET DI SICILIA	PTOLEMY (1561-1599)	19 x 25 cm
TAVOLA NUOVA DI SCHIAVONIA	PTOLEMY (1561-1599)	19 x 25 cm
TAYLOR'S MAP OF LIVERPOOL AND ITS ENVIRONS, ...	TAYLOR, T.	35 x 48 cm
TENBY HARBOUR & ROAD AND CALDY ROADS ... [Wales]	MORRIS	18 x 24 cm
TENNESSEE	BRADFORD	20 x 25 cm
TENNESSEE	LEWIS & ARROWSMITH	20 x 25 cm
TENNESSEE	LUCAS	28 x 46 cm
TENNESSEE, WESTERN PART - EASTERN PART	CENTURY ATLAS	20 x 56 cm
TERRA MAGELLANICA	MORDEN	13 x 11 cm
TERRA NEUF, AN DE CUSTEN VAN NIEU VRANCKRYCK, NIEU ENGELAND, ...	RENARD	48 x 56 cm
TERRA NEUF, EN DE CUSTEN VAN NIEU VRANCKRYCK, NIEU ENGELAND, ...	DE WIT	48 x 56 cm
TERRA NOVA	BERTIUS	9 x 12 cm
TERRA SANCTA	HOMANN	48 x 56 cm
TERRA SANCTA	HONDIUS	36 x 49 cm
TERRA SANCTA A PETRO LAICSTAIN PERLUSTRATA, ET AB EIUS ORE ...	ORTELIUS (Folio)	37 x 50 cm
TERRA SANCTA SIVE PROMISSIONIS, OLIM PALESTINA RECENS DELINEATA	DE WIT	46 x 55 cm
TERRA SANCTA XXIII. NOVA TABULA	MUNSTER	25 x 34 cm
TERRE ARTICHE ...	CORONELLI	46 x 61 cm
TERRE FERME, NOUVEAU ROYME DE GRENADE, &C. ...	SANSON (Small)	19 x 29 cm
TERRITORII NOVOFORENSIS IN SUPERIORE PALATINATU ACCURATA DESCRIPTIO	JANSSON	51 x 52 cm
TERRITORIUM ABBATIAE HERESFELDENSIS. 'T STIFT HIRSSFELD	JANSSON	38 x 49 cm
TERRITORIUM NORIMBERGENSE	JANSSON	36 x 47 cm
TERRITORY OF ARIZONA	U.S.	51 x 40 cm
TERRITORY OF ARIZONA	U.S. STATE SURVEYS	52 x 43 cm
TERRITORY OF DAKOTA	MITCHELL, S.A. (1860+)	36 x 30 cm
TERRITORY OF IDAHO	MITCHELL, S.A. (1860+)	37 x 27 cm
TERRITORY OF MONTANA	MITCHELL, S.A. (1860+)	27 x 36 cm
TERRITORY OF MONTANA	MITCHELL, S.A. (1860+)	33 x 41 cm
TERRITORY OF NEW MEXICO	U.S. STATE SURVEYS	71 x 51 cm
TERRITORY OF WYOMING	MITCHELL, S.A. (1860+)	27 x 36 cm
TERZA OSTRO TAVOLA	RAMUSIO	28 x 38 cm
TEXAS	BRADLEY	43 x 58 cm
TEXAS	COLTON	43 x 58 cm
TEXAS	COLTON	33 x 41 cm
TEXAS	COLTON	33 x 28 cm
TEXAS	MITCHELL, S.A. (1860+)	20 x 43 cm
TEXAS	MORSE & BREESE	38 x 30 cm

TEXAS EASTERN PORTION	ASHER & ADAMS	58 x 41 cm
TEXAS WESTERN PORTION	ASHER & ADAMS	56 x 41 cm
THE AFFAIR OF BLADENSBURG AUGUST 24TH 1814	WILKINSON	15 x 18 cm
THE ALPINE CLUB MAP OF SWITZERLAND WITH PARTS OF THE NEIGHBORING ...	JOHNSTON	104 x 146 cm
THE ARCTIC REGIONS, SHOWING THE NORTH-WEST PASSAGE AS DETERMINED	FULLARTON	25 x 25 cm
THE ATCHISON TOPEKA AND THE SANTA FE RAILWAY SYSTEM	RAILROAD COMPANY	43 x 89 cm
THE BAHAMAS	STANFORD	50 x 61 cm
THE BASIN OF THE PACIFIC	WYLD	57 x 84 cm
THE BAY OF ALGOA ... [&] PLAN OF MOSSEL BAY ... [&] PLAN OF FLESH BAY ...	LAURIE & WHITTLE	58 x 25 cm
THE BRITISH ISLES	S.D.U.K.	40 x 33 cm
THE BRITISH POSSESSIONS IN NORTH AMERICA FROM THE BEST AUTHORITIES	CAREY	38 x 44 cm
THE CAPE OF GOOD HOPE AND FALSE BAY	ADMIRALTY	99 x 64 cm
THE CAPE VERD ISLANDS ...	LAURIE & WHITTLE	53 x 28 cm
THE CATHOLIC NETHERLANDS ...	SAYER	48 x 64 cm
THE CATTEGAT, THE SOUND, AND THE GREAT AND LITTLE BELTS ...	WILSON	81 x 221 cm
THE CENTENNIAL NAVAL PARADE IN THE UPPER BAY – THE U.S.S. 'DESPATCH'...	HARPER'S WEEKLY	36 x 112 cm
THE CIRCUIT OF THE LAKES, IN THE COUNTIES OF CUMBERLAND, ...	DARTON	59 x 49 cm
THE CIRCUITEER. A SERIES OF DISTANCE MAPS FOR ALL THE PRINCIPAL TOWNS	FRIEDERICHS, J.	49 x 69 cm
THE CITY AND HARBOR OF SAVANNAH, GA.	HARPER'S WEEKLY	23 x 36 cm
THE CITY CAIRAS	OGILBY	23 x 36 cm
THE CITY OF ALEXANDRIA OR SCANDERIK	OGILBY	25 x 36 cm
THE CITY OF CHARLESTON, S.C.	HARPER'S WEEKLY	25 x 36 cm
THE CITY OF CINCINATTI	WALLING	25 x 33 cm
THE CITY OF MALACCA IN THE EAST INDIES	MIDDLETON	16 x 27 cm
THE CITY OF NEW YORK	GALT & HOY	188 x 102 cm
THE CITY OF SAVANNAH, GEORGIA [and] THE CITY OF CHARLESTON, ...	COLTON	28 x 36 cm
THE COAST OF INDIA FROM GOA TO CAP COMORIN ...	SAYER & BENNETT	61 x 61 cm
THE COAST OF NOVA SCOTIA, NEW ENGLAND - NEW YORK, JERSEY, THE GULF	DES BARRES	81 x 119 cm
THE COAST OF ZANGUEBAR AND AIEN ...	MORDEN	12 x 10 cm
THE CONNECTED PLAN OF COMMON LANDS OF FORT CHARTRES OF PRAIRIE...	U.S.	43 x 41 cm
THE COUNTIE AND CITIE OF LYNCOLNE DESCRIBED WITH THE ARMES OF THEM	SPEED	38 x 51 cm
THE COUNTRIES AROUND THE MEDITERRANEAN	STANFORD	50 x 32 cm
THE COUNTRY BETWEEN CROWN POINT AND ALBANY BEING THE GREAT PASS	GRAND MAG. OF MAG.	19 x 11 cm
THE COUNTYE PALLATINE OF LANCASTER DESCRIBED AND DIVIDED INTO ...	SPEED	39 x 51 cm
THE COURSE OF THE RIVER ST. LAWRENCE, FROM LAKE ONTARIO TO MANI. PT.	THOMSON	41 x 23 cm
THE CRIMEA	WYLD	47 x 64 cm
THE EMPIRE CITY. MAP OF NEW YORK CITY AND DIRECTORY	HAASIS & LUBRECHT	69 x 91 cm
THE EMPIRE OF JAPAN	LAURIE & WHITTLE	46 x 64 cm
THE ENGLISH EMPIRE IN AMERICA, NEWFOUND-LAND. CANADA. HUDSONS BAY	MOLL (Small)	22 x 18 cm
THE ENTRANCE TO THE RIVER TAGUS	ADMIRALTY	65 x 94 cm
THE ENVIRONS OF DUBLIN	S.D.U.K.	31 x 39 cm
THE ENVIRONS OF EDINBURGH	S.D.U.K.	31 x 40 cm
THE ENVIRONS OF PARIS	S.D.U.K.	32 x 38 cm
THE EUROPEAN PART OF THE RUSSIAN [EMPIRE] & THE ASIATIC PARTS ...	LAURIE & WHITTLE	48 x 127 cm
THE FALKLAND ISLANDS	ADMIRALTY	64 x 94 cm
THE FOUNDLING HOSPITAL ESTATE, LONDON. ...	STANFORD	64 x 87 cm
THE GALLAPAGOS ISLANDS DISCOVERED AND DESCRIBED BY CAPT. COWLEY	BOWEN, E.	32 x 20 cm
THE GALLAPAGOS ISLANDS DISCOVERED AND DESCRIBED BY CAPT. COWLEY	HARRIS	32 x 20 cm
THE GRAHAM SHOAL AND OTHER VOLCANIC PATCHES ON THE ADVENTURE ...	ADMIRALTY	47 x 64 cm
THE GREAT SALT LAKE OF THE MORMONS, LOOKING WEST ...	ILLUS. LONDON NEWS	23 x 36 cm
THE HUDSON BY DAYLIGHT. MAP FROM NEW YORK BAY TO THE HEAD OF TIDE	BRYANT UNION	14 x 254 cm
THE INLAND NAVIGATION, RAIL ROADS, GEOLOGY AND MINERALS OF ENGLAND	ARROWSMITH	61 x 49 cm
THE INVASIONS OF ENGLAND AND IRELAND	SPEED	(no dimens.)
THE IRISH OR ST. GEORGE'S CHANNEL ...	IMRAY	102 x 191 cm
THE ISLAND OF BARBADOES. DIVIDED INTO ITS PARISHES, WITH THE ROADS, ...	MOLL (Small)	29 x 36 cm
THE ISLAND OF BARBADOS	MORDEN	13 x 11 cm
THE ISLAND OF BARBUDA ...	ADMIRALTY	29 x 20 cm
THE ISLAND OF CUBA WITH PART OF THE BAHAMA BANKS & THE MARTYRS	JEFFERYS	49 x 63 cm
THE ISLAND OF JAMAICA DIVIDED INTO ITS PRINCIPAL PARISHES WITH THE ...	MOLL (Small)	20 x 28 cm
THE ISLAND OF NAVASSA; BETWEEN ST. DOMINGO & JAMAICA	ADMIRALTY	28 x 23 cm
THE ISLANDS OF JAPAN	WYLD	83 x 66 cm
THE ISLANDS OF NEW ZEALAND	S.D.U.K.	39 x 31 cm
THE ISLANDS OF NEW ZEALAND	STANFORD	40 x 32 cm
THE ISLES OF SONDA	MORDEN	10 x 14 cm
THE JAPANESE EMPIRE WITH CENTRAL AND SOUTHERN MANCHUKUO ...	PHILIP, G.	64 x 86 cm
THE KINGDOM OF IRELAND	MORDEN	41 x 34 cm
THE KINGDOME OF CHINA ...	SPEED	39 x 51 cm
THE KINGDOME OF DENMARKE	SPEED	40 x 52 cm

THE KINGDOME OF IRLAND	SPEED	38 x 51 cm
THE KINGDOME OF POLAND WITH ITS SEVERAL DUKEDOMS & PROVINCES ...	LEA	42 x 54 cm
THE LEEWARD ISLANDS	STANFORD	47 x 60 cm
THE LEWIS, OR NORTH PART OF LONG ISLAND; ...	MacKENZIE	86 x 104 cm
THE MIDDLE STATES AND WESTERN TERRITORIES OF THE UNITED STATES ...	ANONYMOUS	20 x 25 cm
THE NATIONAL GEOGRAPHIC MAP OF ALASKA	NATIONAL GEOG. SOC.	38 x 51 cm
THE NETHERLANDS AND BELGIUM	STANFORD	62 x 51 cm
THE NORTH ENTRANCE OF BARDSEY SOUND ... [Wales]	MORRIS	18 x 23 cm
THE NORTH-WEST COAST OF SCOTLAND, FROM RUREA IN ROSS SHIRE, TO ...	MacKENZIE	104 x 97 cm
THE NORTH WEST PART OF AMERICA BY R. MORDEN AT YE ATLAS IN CORNHILL	MORDEN	11 x 14 cm
THE NORTH WEST PROVINCES AND OUDH FOR MURRAY'S HANDBOOK TO ...	ANONYMOUS	42 x 48 cm
THE NORTH WESTERN LINE	RAILROAD COMPANY	(no dimens.)
THE NORTHERN HEMISPHERE	CONDER	25 x 25 cm
THE PACIFIC COAST FROM POINT PINOS TO BODEGA HEAD CALIFORNIA	U.S. COAST SURVEY	99 x 71 cm
THE PACIFIC OCEAN	S.D.U.K.	31 x 39 cm
THE PACIFIC OCEAN INCLUDING OCEANA WITH ITS SEVERAL DIVISIONS, ...	DESILVER	36 x 41 cm
THE PACIFIC STATES, THE TERRITORIES AND A PORTION OF THE [N.W] STATES	PHILIP, G.	51 x 56 cm
THE PHILIPPINE ISLANDS	STANFORD	50 x 34 cm
THE PORT OF VERACRUZ, AND ANCHORAGE OF ANTON LIZARDO ...	ADMIRALTY	60 x 79 cm
THE PROVINCE OF MAINE ...	PAYNE	28 x 18 cm
THE PROVINCE OF MAINE FROM THE BEST AUTHORITIES. 1795	REID	36 x 25 cm
THE PROVINCE OF NEW JERSEY, DIVIDED INTO EAST AND WEST ...	FADEN	79 x 56 cm
THE PROVINCES OF NEW YORK AND NEW JERSEY, WITH PART OF PENSILVANIA	SAYER & BENNETT	135 x 69 cm
THE PURVEYORSHIPS IN THE REIGN OF SOLOMON	WILKINSON	28 x 22 cm
THE RAILROAD COMMISSIONER'S MAP OF ILLINOIS	CRAM	122 x 71 cm
THE RAND McNALLY VEST POCKET MAP OF MONTANA	RAND, McNALLY	41 x 51 cm
THE ROAD FROM LONDON TO ABERISTWITH ...	OGILBY	31 x 44 cm
THE ROAD OF PALLEACATE ... [and] THE ROAD OF TENGEPATNAM ...	LAURIE & WHITTLE	53 x 23 cm
THE ROADS IN RAMSEY SOUND ... [Wales]	MORRIS	18 x 24 cm
THE ROUTE OF MR. MUNGO PARK	RENNELL, J.	25 x 66 cm
THE RUSSIAN DISCOVERIES FROM THE MAP PUBLISHED BY THE IMPERIAL ACAD.	SAYER	48 x 66 cm
THE SEAT OF ACTION, BETWEEN THE BRITISH AND AMERICAN FORCES, ...	SAYER & BENNETT	43 x 38 cm
THE SECOND MAP OF IRELAND [and] THE THIRD MAP OF IRELAND	MERCATOR (Folio)	36 x 48 cm
THE SIEGE OF RHODE ISLAND, TAKEN FROM MR. BRINDLEY'S HOUSE, ...	GENTLEMAN'S MAG.	13 x 23 cm
THE SOUTH COAST OF CARDIGAN BAY ...	MacKENZIE	51 x 142 cm
THE SOUTH EASTERN STATES COMPRISING MISSISSIPPI, ALABAMA, ...	SWANSTON	41 x 51 cm
THE SOUTH PART OF LONG-ISLAND, FROM BARA HEAD TO BENBECULA I; ...	MacKENZIE	74 x 107 cm
THE SOUTH-WEST COAST OF WALES FROM TENBY TO CARDIGAN ...	MacKENZIE	74 x 104 cm
THE STATE OF FLORIDA ... FROM THE BEST AUTHORITIES ...	U.S.	109 x 99 cm
THE STATE OF KENTUCKY WITH THE ADJOINING TERRITORIES, FROM ...	PAYNE	19 x 22 cm
THE STATE OF MARYLAND, FROM THE BEST AUTHORITIES. BY SAMUEL LEWIS	CAREY	28 x 41 cm
THE STATE OF MASSACHUSETTS FROM THE BEST INFORMATION	PAYNE	19 x 24 cm
THE STATE OF NEW HAMPSHIRE COMPILED CHIEFLY FROM ACTUAL SURVEYS	CAREY	45 x 28 cm
THE STATE OF NEW JERSEY, COMPILED FROM THE MOST AUTHENTIC ...	CAREY	47 x 31 cm
THE STATE OF NEW YORK FROM THE BEST INFORMATION 1800	PAYNE	19 x 22 cm
THE STATE OF PENNSYLVANIA FROM THE LATEST SURVEYS	REID	33 x 46 cm
THE STATE OF RHODE-ISLAND; COMPILED, FROM THE SURVEYS AND OBSERV.	CAREY	34 x 24 cm
THE STATE OF VIRGINIA FROM THE BEST AUTHORITIES	REID	34 x 47 cm
THE STATE OF VIRGINIA FROM THE BEST AUTHORITIES, BY SAMUEL LEWIS. ...	CAREY	35 x 51 cm
THE STATES OF PENNSYLVANIA NEW JERSEY AND DELAWARE FROM THE ...	BENTON	41 x 53 cm
THE SUMMER ILS [BERMUDA] ... BY MR. NORWOOD ALL CONSTRUCTED ...	SMITH, JOHN	28 x 36 cm
THE TERRITORIES OF WASHINGTON AND OREGON	COLTON	32 x 41 cm
THE THEATRE OF WAR IN NORTH AMERICA ...	SAYER & BENNETT	16 x 51 cm
THE TOURIST'S POCKET MAP OF THE STATE OF GEORGIA EXHIBITING ITS ...	YOUNG, J.H.	38 x 30 cm
THE TOURIST'S POCKET MAP OF THE STATE OF INDIANA EXHIBITING ITS ...	YOUNG, J.H.	36 x 30 cm
THE TURKISH EMPIRE IN EUROPE AND ASIA WITH THE KINGDOM OF GREECE	S.D.U.K.	32 x 40 cm
THE UNITED KINGDOM OF GREAT BRITAIN & IRELAND, WITH THE ADJACENT ...	ENOUY, J.	71 x 61 cm
THE UNITED STATES	RAND, McNALLY	48 x 66 cm
THE UNITED STATES OF AMERICA	COLTON	38 x 64 cm
THE UNITED STATES OF MEXICO, DRAWN AND PUBLISHED BY DAVID H. BURR	BURR	31 x 26 cm
THE UNITED STATES OF NORTH AMERICA. ATLANTIC STATES AND VALLEY ...	BLACKIE & SON	51 x 69 cm
THE UNITED STATES OF NORTH AMERICA (WESTERN PART)	STANFORD	65 x 50 cm
THE UPPER TERRITORIES OF THE UNITED STATES	CAREY	43 x 32 cm
THE WASH SKEGNESS TO BALKENEY	ADMIRALTY	64 x 97 cm
THE WEST COAST OF SCOTLAND FROM ARDNAMURCHAN TO THE ISLAND SKY	MacKENZIE	107 x 102 cm
THE WEST INDIES WITH THE GULF OF MEXICO AND CARIBBEAN SEA	U.S.	81 x 127 cm
THE WESTERN HEMISPHERE OR NEW WORLD	DARTON	25 x 23 cm
THE WORLD	CRUCHLEY	53 x 65 cm

THE WORLD AS KNOWN TO THE ANCIENTS	S.D.U.K.	40 x 62 cm
THE WORLD, DESIGNED TO SHOW THE LANGUAGES AND DIALECTS ...	WYLD	88 x 131 cm
THE WORLD FROM THE BEST AUTHORITIES	PAYNE	20 x 38 cm
THE WORLD IN HEMISPHERES, WITH COMPARATIVE VIEWS OF THE HEIGHTS ...	JOHNSTON	53 x 61 cm
THE WORLD IN HEMISPHERES WITH OTHER PROJECTIONS &C. &C.	MITCHELL, S.A. (1860+)	30 x 38 cm
THE WORLD ON MERCATOR'S PROJECTION	ARROWSMITH	25 x 41 cm
THE WORLD ON MERCATOR'S PROJECTION	BETTS	44 x 76 cm
THE WORLD ON MERCATOR'S PROJECTION	S.D.U.K.	39 x 62 cm
THE WORLD ON MERCATOR'S PROJECTION	TANNER	58 x 74 cm
THE WORLD ON MERCATOR'S PROJECTION	WYLD	64 x 93 cm
THE WORLD WITH THE LATEST DISCOVERIES	BYRNE, P.	25 x 48 cm
THE WORLD'S INDUSTRIAL AND COTTON ... EXPOSITION, NEW ORLEANS, LA ...	ANONYMOUS	69 x 94 cm
THE YUKON DISTRICT	STANFORD	51 x 34 cm
THEATRUM BELLI INTER IMPERAT. CAROL VI. ET SULT. ACHMET IV. ...	HOMANN	54 x 114 cm
THEORIAN LUNAE	DOPPELMAYR	48 x 58 cm
THIS PLAN OF THE HARBOUR, TOWN AND FORTS OF PORTO BELLO ...	DURELL	42 x 58 cm
THIS PLAN OF THE HARBOUR, TOWN, AND FORTS, OF CARTAGENA ...	TOMS	42 x 58 cm
TIERRA NOVA	PTOLEMY (1561-1599)	18 x 25 cm
TIERRA NOVA [SOUTH AMERICA]	PTOLEMY (1548 Venice)	13 x 18 cm
TIERRA NUEVA	PTOLEMY (1561-1599)	18 x 25 cm
TIMBERLANDS MAP QUEBEC, COMPILED IN THE CROWN TIMBERLANDS OFFICE	WALKER & MILES	41 x 64 cm
TO MY WORTHY ... TWO ATTEMPTS TO ARRIVE AT THE SOURCE OF THE NILE	BRUCE, J.	51 x 30 cm
TO THE OFFICERS IN THE HONOURABLE EAST INDIA COMPANY'S SERVICE ...	HEATHER	66 x 119 cm
TO THE RIGHT HONORABLE CHARLES EARL OF SUNDERLAND AND BARON ...	MOLL (Large)	58 x 97 cm
TO THE RIGHT HONORABLE THE LORDS ... CHART OF THE NORTH WEST COAST	DIXON	61 x 89 cm
TO THE RIGHT HONORABLE...MAP SHEWING THE TRACT OF SOLOMAN'S FLEET	BRUCE, J.	69 x 30 cm
TO THE RIGHT HONOURABLE WILLIAM LORD COWPER, ... THIS MAP OF ASIA ...	MOLL (Large)	58 x 97 cm
TOBAGO	LUCAS	25 x 29 cm
TOBAGO TO BRITAIN	PHILIP, G.	25 x 30 cm
TOLEDO, LUCAS CO.	LLOYD	38 x 30 cm
TOLEDO, LUCAS CO. [Ohio]	WALLING	36 x 30 cm
TOPOGRAPHICAL MAP FOR COMMERCE OF CHATTANOOGA, TENNESSEE	FLAMM	64 x 86 cm
TOPOGRAPHICAL MAP OF NORTH ISLAND [Washington]	U.S.	61 x 41 cm
TOPOGRAPHICAL MAP OF THE ROAD FROM MISSOURI TO OREGON SECTION 2	FREMONT	38 x 61 cm
TOPOGRAPHICAL SKETCH SHOWING THE ... A DIVISION OF THE COLORADO	U.S. WAR DEPT.	41 x 48 cm
TORONTO	RAND, McNALLY	30 x 48 cm
TOSCANA NUOVA TAVOLA	PTOLEMY (1561-1599)	18 x 26 cm
TOTIUS AFRICAE ACCURITISSIMA TABULA	DANCKERTS	48 x 58 cm
TOTIUS AMERICAE SEPTENTRIONALIS ET MERIDIONALIS NOVISSIMA ...	HOMANN	48 x 57 cm
TOTIUS DANUBII CUM ADJACENTIBUS REGNIS NEC NON TOTIUS GRAECIAE ...	HOMANN	47 x 56 cm
TOTIUS HISPANIAE NOVA DESCRIPTIO. ANNO 1633	JANSSON	38 x 52 cm
TOTIUS ORBIS COGNITI UNIVERSALIS DESCRIPTIO	MERULA	30 x 50 cm
TOTIUS SUEVIAE NOVISSIMA TABULA	JANSSON	39 x 49 cm
TOULON	S.D.U.K.	31 x 38 cm
TOULON AND THE ADJACENT COAST	ADMIRALTY	46 x 61 cm
TOWN OF DANBURY [Conn.]	BEERS, ELLIS & SOULE	41 x 33 cm
TOWN OF NORWALK [Conn.]	BEERS, ELLIS & SOULE	43 x 58 cm
TOWN OF WESTPORT [Conn.]	BEERS, ELLIS & SOULE	41 x 33 cm
TOWNSHIP MAP OF THE STATE OF NEW YORK PUBLISHED BY J.H. COLTON	COLTON	61 x 76 cm
TOWNSHIP MAP OF THE STATE OF NEW-YORK WITH PARTS OF THE ADJOINING	COLTON	56 x 61 cm
TRACTUS AUSTRALIOR AMERICAE MERIDIONALIS, A RIO DE LA PLATA ...	DE WIT	48 x 55 cm
TRACTUS EICHSFELDIAE ... NEC NON TERRITORII MVHLHVSANI CHOROGRAPHIA	HOMANN	42 x 52 cm
TRACTUS LITTORALES GUINEAE A PROMONTORIO VERDE USQUE AD SINUM ...	DE WIT	49 x 56 cm
TRACTUS NORVEGIAE SUECICUS PRAEFECTURAM BAHUSIAE ...	HOMANN	48 x 55 cm
TRANSYLVANIA, SIBENBURGEN	JANSSON	34 x 43 cm
TRAVELLING MAP OF EUROPE, SHEWING THE LINES OF RAILWAY &C.	SMITH, C.	61 x 81 cm
TRIER & LUTZENBURG	MERCATOR (Folio)	37 x 47 cm
TRIGONOMETRICAL SURVEY OF THE FALLS OF NIAGARA	HAINES, W.	23 x 41 cm
TRINIDAD	LUCAS	24 x 29 cm
TRUGILLO	DE LAET	28 x 36 cm
TRYK VAN DEN GROOTEN MOGOL	SANSON (Small)	19 x 24 cm
TUCSON, SONORA [Arizona]	BARTLETT, J. R.	13 x 18 cm
TUNETIS URBIS, AC NOVAE EIUS ARCIS, ET GULETAE, ...	BRAUN & HOGENBERG	33 x 42 cm
TUNISON'S GEORGIA AND SOUTH CAROLINA	TUNISON	25 x 33 cm
TUNISON'S GEORGIA, NORTH AND SOUTH CAROLINA	TUNISON	25 x 36 cm
TURCICI IMPERII IMAGO	HONDIUS	36 x 48 cm
TURQUIE EN ASIE	DE FER (Small)	14 x 16 cm
TURQUIE EN ASIE	MALLET	14 x 10 cm

TURTLE BAYOU TEXAS SHOWING CONNECTION TO TRINITY BAY ...	U.S. WAR DEPT.	89 x 53 cm
TYPUS GEOGRAPHICUS CHILI PARAGUAY FRETI MAGELLANICI	HOMANN	49 x 57 cm
TYPUS GEOGRAPHICUS DUCAT. LAUENBURGICI	HOMANN	56 x 48 cm
TYPUS ORBIS PTOL. DESCRIPTUS	MUNSTER	25 x 36 cm
TYPUS ORBIS TERRARUM	HONDIUS	14 x 20 cm
TYPUS ORBIS TERRARUM	LANGENES	9 x 13 cm
TYPUS ORBIS TERRARUM	MERCATOR (Small)	15 x 21 cm
TYPUS ORBIS TERRARUM	ORTELIUS (Folio)	36 x 48 cm
TYPUS ORBIS TERRARUM, AD IMITATIONEM UNIVERSALIS GERHARDI MER. ...	QUAD	22 x 32 cm
TYPUS ORBIS TERRARUM DESCRIPTION DE LA TERRE UNIVERSELLE	BOISSEAU	13 x 20 cm
TYPUS ORBIS UNIVERSALIS	MUNSTER	27 x 38 cm
TYPUS TOTIUS ORBIS TERRAQUEI GEOGRAPHICE DELINEATUS ...	SCHERER	22 x 35 cm
TYPUS UNIVERSALIS	MUNSTER	26 x 35 cm
TYPUS UNIVERSALIS	MUNSTER	26 x 35 cm
ULTONIAE ORIENTALIS PARS.	MERCATOR (Folio)	35 x 38 cm
ULTRAIECTINI DOMINII TABULA	DE WIT	46 x 56 cm
UNITED STATES	ARROWSMITH	61 x 48 cm
UNITED STATES	ARROWSMITH	23 x 30 cm
UNITED STATES ...	BURR	27 x 32 cm
UNITED STATES	CORNELL	32 x 52 cm
UNITED STATES	FINDLAY	20 x 24 cm
UNITED STATES	GREENLEAF	29 x 33 cm
UNITED STATES	HALL	43 x 53 cm
UNITED STATES	KELLY	19 x 24 cm
UNITED STATES	LEWIS & ARROWSMITH	20 x 25 cm
UNITED STATES	LIZARS	18 x 23 cm
UNITED STATES	LONDON PRINT & PUB.	25 x 43 cm
UNITED STATES	RAPKIN	28 x 43 cm
UNITED STATES	RUSSELL	18 x 23 cm
UNITED STATES	TALLIS	24 x 33 cm
UNITED STATES	THOMSON	23 x 30 cm
UNITED STATES AND TEXAS	JOHNSTON	51 x 61 cm
UNITED STATES, CANADA & NEW BRUNSWICK	BETTS	30 x 38 cm
UNITED STATES, NORTH AMERICA	SWANSTON	43 x 53 cm
UNITED STATES OF AMERICA	CAREY & LEA	43 x 54 cm
UNITED STATES OF AMERICA	MELISH	43 x 56 cm
UNITED STATES OF AMERICA	WARNER, B.	43 x 66 cm
UNITED STATES OF AMERICA [and] THE COURSE OF THE RIVER ST. LAURENCE ...	THOMSON	41 x 61 cm
UNITED STATES OF AMERICA EXHIBITING THE SEAT OF WAR ON THE CANADIAN	TALBOT	25 x 34 cm
UNITED STATES, SOUTH CENTRAL COMPRISING TEXAS, LOUISIANA, ...	SWANSTON	51 x 41 cm
UNITED STATES - SOUTH WEST	SHARPE	43 x 30 cm
UNITED STATES ... THE NORTH CENTRAL SECTION ...	SWANSTON	41 x 51 cm
UNIVERSALE DELLA PARTE DEL MONDO NUOVAMENTE RITROVATA	GASTALDI	27 cm, diam
UNIVERSALE DELLA PARTE DEL MONDO NUOVAMENTE RITROVATA	RAMUSIO	27 x 27 cm
UNIVERSALIS COSMOGRAPHIA. TIGURI IVE MDXLVI	HONTER	12 x 16 cm
UNIVERSALIS ORBIS DESCRIPTIO	MYRITIUS	27 x 40 cm
UNIVERSELE OF WAERELD KAART VOLGENS DE LAATSTE ONTDEKKINGEN ...	ELWE	15 x 20 cm
UPPER CANADA	BRADFORD	29 x 36 cm
UPPER CANADA	BURR	28 x 33 cm
UPPER GEYSER BASIN - DRAWN UNDER DIRECTION OF CAPT. W. LUDLOW	U.S. WAR DEPT.	23 x 38 cm
UPPER TERRITORIES OF THE UNITED STATES	CAREY	20 x 15 cm
URBS WARSOVIA SEDES ORDINARIA REGUM POLONIAE	PERELLE	25 x 64 cm
UTAH	RAND, McNALLY	30 x 23 cm
UTAH AND NEVADA	MITCHELL, S.A. (1860+)	29 x 35 cm
UTRIUSQUAE ALSATIAE SUPERIORIS AC INFERIORIS NOVA TABULA	JANSSON	39 x 55 cm
VALENTIA REGNUM	ORTELIUS (Miniature)	8 x 11 cm
VALENTIA REGNUM. COTESTINI. PTOL. EDENTANI PLIN.	JANSSON	36 x 48 cm
VAN DIEMANS LAND	TEESDALE	41 x 34 cm
VENETIARUM AMPLISSIMA & MARITIMA URBS, SUM MULTIS ...	MUNSTER	25 x 39 cm
VENEZUELA, CUM PARTE AUSTRALI NOVAE ANDALUSIAE	JANSSON	38 x 49 cm
VENEZUELA, NEW GRANADA, EQUADOR, AND THE GUAYANAS	TALLIS	25 x 33 cm
VENICE	WEEKLY DISPATCH	30 x 43 cm
VENICE. VENEZIA. VENEDIG.	S.D.U.K.	39 x 59 cm
VEREIN-STAATEN VON NORD-AMERICA, MEXICO, YUCATAN U.A.	VON STULPNAGEL	33 x 41 cm
VEREIN-STAATEN VON NORD-AMERICA MIT AUSNAHME FLORIDA'S ...	VON STULPNAGEL	36 x 41 cm
VEREINIGTE STAATEN VON NORD-AMERICA, IN 6 BLATTERN, BL. 5	STIELER	33 x 41 cm
VEREINIGTE STAATEN VON NORD-AMERIKA IN 6 BLATTERN, BL. 1	PETERMANN	36 x 41 cm
VEREINIGTE STAATEN VON NORDAMERIKA	HANDTKE	53 x 71 cm

VERMONT	BRADFORD	36 x 27 cm
VERMONT	CAREY	20 x 15 cm
VERMONT	FINLEY	27 x 22 cm
VERMONT	LEWIS & ARROWSMITH	24 x 20 cm
VERMONT	SCOTT	20 x 15 cm
VERMONT AND NEW HAMPSHIRE	GREENLEAF	32 x 26 cm
VERMONT FROM ACTUAL SURVEY	CAREY	39 x 31 cm
VICTORIA	STANFORD	34 x 53 cm
VICTORIA	WELLER	31 x 43 cm
VICTORIA [Australia]	LOCAL & STATE	56 x 84 cm
VIEW OF BUCKSPORT, ME.	EMERY	41 x 74 cm
VIEW OF GUILFORD, CONNECTICUT	BAILEY & CO.	48 x 64 cm
VIEW OF ... JAMES' ISLAND ONE OF THE GALAPAGOS - CHATHAM ISLAND ...	COLNETT	18 x 28 cm
VIEW OF SINGAPORE TOWN AND HARBOUR TAKEN FROM THE GOVERNMENT ...	MURRAY, J.	23 x 80 cm
VIEW OF THE ISLAND OF ST. CATHERINE	LA PEROUSE	20 x 30 cm
VIEW OF THE TOWN AND CASTLE OF MACAO	HARRIS	20 x 31 cm
VILLE DE MANATHE OU NOUVELLE-YORC	BELLIN (Small)	23 x 18 cm
VILNA LITVANIAE METROPOLIS	BRAUN & HOGENBERG	36 x 51 cm
VIRGINIA	BURR	27 x 32 cm
VIRGINIA	CAREY	15 x 20 cm
VIRGINIA	CENTURY ATLAS	25 x 41 cm
VIRGINIA	LEWIS & ARROWSMITH	20 x 25 cm
VIRGINIA	MORSE, J.	16 x 20 cm
VIRGINIA ITEM ET FLORIDAE AMERICAE PROVINCIARUM NOVA DESCRIPTIO	CLOPPENBURGH	19 x 26 cm
VIRGINIA, MARYLAND AND DELAWARE	TANNER	58 x 73 cm
VIRGINIA, MARYLAND, PENNSILVANIA, EAST & WEST NEW JERSEY ...	MOUNT & PAGE	51 x 79 cm
VIRGINIA, MARYLANDIA ET CAROLINA IN AMERICA SEPTENTRIONALI	HOMANN	49 x 59 cm
VIRGINIA PARTIS AUSTRALIS, ET FLORIDAE PARTIS ORIENTALIS ...	BLAEU	38 x 51 cm
VIRGINIA RAILROADS	RAND, McNALLY	51 x 69 cm
VIRGINIA UND MARYLAND	HOMANN	28 x 20 cm
VIRGINIAE ITEM ET FLORIDAE ...	HONDIUS	34 x 48 cm
VIRGINIAE ITEM ET FLORIDAE AMERICAE PROVINCIARUM NOVA DESCRIPTIO	HONDIUS	34 x 48 cm
VIRGINIAE ITEM ET FLORIDAE AMERICAE PROVINCIARUM, NOVA DESCRIPTIO	MERCATOR (Folio)	34 x 49 cm
VIRGINIE, MARYLAND EN 2 FEUILLES PAR FRY ET JEFFERSON ...	LE ROUGE	67 x 98 cm
VISTA DE LA HABANA, PARTE DE ESTRAMURAS TOMADO DESDE LA ENTRADA	MIALHE	23 x 28 cm
VOIES DE COMMUNICATION DES ETATS-UNIS - CARTE GENERAL DES ETATS-UNIS	CHEVALIER	61 x 64 cm
VORSTELLUNG DER LINIE U. INONDATION VON BRUCHSAHL BIS KETSCH, ...	HOMANN	34 x 69 cm
VORSTELLUNG DES CAMPEMENTS DER KAYSERL. ... ARMEE ZU BRUCHSAL	HOMANN	27 x 90 cm
VUE DE LA VILLE DU MEXIQUE PRIS DU COTE DU LAC	DAUMONT	25 x 38 cm
VUE DE NEW YORK. PRISE DE WEAHAWK - A VIEW OF NEW YORK, ...	GARNERAY	38 x 46 cm
VUE DU ALGERS, EN BARBARIE, SUR LA MER MEDITERRANEE	HAFFNER, J.C.	32 x 41 cm
VUE DU CANAL DE L'ISTHME DE SUEZ	DEROY	30 x 48 cm
W. INDIES	ARROWSMITH	24 x 31 cm
WAGVISARE I STOCKHOLM. GUIDE ET MANUEL DU VOYAGEUR A STOCKHOLM	ANONYMOUS	50 x 45 cm
WALACHIA SERVIA, BULGARIA, ROMANIA	JANSSON	34 x 47 cm
WALDECK COMITATUS	JANSSON	38 x 51 cm
WALES NORTH COAST SHEET VIII POINT LYNUS TO ABERGELE	ADMIRALTY	48 x 64 cm
WALKER'S TOUR THROUGH ENGLAND AND WALES, A NEW PASTIME	DARTON	51 x 43 cm
WALLIS'S PICTURESQUE ROUND GAME OF THE PRODUCE AND MANUFACTURE	WALLIS	64 x 49 cm
WALLIS'S PLAN OF THE CITIES OF LONDON AND WESTMINSTER FOR 1800.	WALLIS	(no dimens.)
WASHINGTON	CRAM	25 x 38 cm
WASHINGTON	CRAM	36 x 51 cm
WASHINGTON TERRITORY	U.S. STATE SURVEYS	56 x 71 cm
WATSON'S NEW COUNTY, RAILROAD AND DISTANCE MAP OF MONTANA AND	WATSON	36 x 43 cm
WEALE'S MAP OF LONDON AND ITS VICINITY ...	WEALE	50 x 94 cm
WERELD KAART VOLGENS DE LAATSTE ONTOEKKING DOOR E. BOWEN ...	MEIJER	15 x 28 cm
WEST CANADA	TALLIS	25 x 33 cm
WEST CHAZY, N.Y.	BURLEIGH LITH.	38 x 61 cm
WEST COAST OF NORTH AMERICA FROM SAN BLAS TO SAN FRANCISCO	IMRAY	130 x 102 cm
WEST COAST OF SOUTH AMERICA, PERU AND BOLIVIA ... QUILCA TO COBIJA ...	BERGHAUS, H.	55 x 36 cm
WEST INDIEN ...	WEIMAR GEOGRAPH.	48 x 59 cm
WEST INDIES	ARROWSMITH	48 x 62 cm
WEST INDIES	BLACK	26 x 39 cm
WEST INDIES	BURR	28 x 33 cm
WEST INDIES	DESILVER	28 x 41 cm
WEST INDIES	RAND, McNALLY	25 x 33 cm
WEST INDIES	THOMSON	18 x 23 cm
WEST INDIES BONACCA ISLAND ...	ADMIRALTY	47 x 63 cm

WEST INDIES SHEET XI FROM CAYOS RATIONES TO SAN JUAN DE NICARAGUA	ADMIRALTY	48 x 61 cm
WEST POINT NEW YORK	U.S. GEOL. SURVEY	66 x 53 cm
WESTERN AUSTRALIA	STANFORD	62 x 51 cm
WESTERN HEMISPHERE	FINLEY	23 x 23 cm
WESTERN HEMISPHERE	PHILIP, G.	52 cm, diam
WESTERN HEMISPHERE	S.D.U.K..	34 x 33 cm
WESTERN HEMISPHERE	THOMSON	53 x 51 cm
WESTERN HEMISPHERE - EASTERN HEMISPHERE	FADEN	36 x 71 cm
WESTERN HEMISPHERE ENGRAVED BY S. NEELE	STACKHOUSE	38 x 36 cm
WESTERN PART [CANADA]	STANFORD	61 x 49 cm
WESTERN SIBERIA, INDEPENDENT TARTARY, KHIVA, BOKHORA	S.D.U.K.	40 x 33 cm
WESTERN STATES	LINCOLN & EDMANDS	15 x 18 cm
WESTERN STATES INCLUDING CALIFORNIA, OREGON, UTAH, WASHINGTON, ...	BLACK	43 x 56 cm
WESTERN TERRITORIES OF THE UNITED STATES	OLNEY	28 x 46 cm
WESTINDIEN CENTRAL-AMERICA UND DAS NORDLICHE UND NORDWESTLICHE	KIEPERT	53 x 64 cm
WESTINDIEN CENTRAL-AMERICA UND DAS NORDLICHE UND NORDWESTLICHE	WEIMAR GEOGRAPH.	53 x 63 cm
WESTINDIEN CENTRAL-AMERICA UND DAS NORDWESTLICHE - SUD AMERICA	WEIMAR GEOGRAPH.	35 x 42 cm
WESTLICHES - NORDAMERICA	KIEPERT	55 x 44 cm
WILLIAM ADAMS REYSTOGT NA OOST INDIEN ...	VAN DER AA	15 x 23 cm
WIRTENBERG DUCATUS	JANSSON	37 x 45 cm
WISCONSIN	CENTURY ATLAS	38 x 28 cm
WISCONSIN	COLTON	43 x 33 cm
WISCONSIN	COLTON	41 x 33 cm
WISCONSIN	TANNER	41 x 36 cm
WISCONSIN SOUTHERN PART	MORSE & BREESE	33 x 41 cm
WORLD ON MERCATOR'S PROJECTION	ARROWSMITH	25 x 30 cm
WORLD SHOWING THE MOST IMPORTANT DISCOVERIES	WAITE	30 x 46 cm
WYLD'S MAP OF INDIA CONSTRUCTED WITH GREAT CARE AND RESEARCH ...	WYLD	82 x 67 cm
WYLD'S MAP OF PARTS OF FRANCE AND PRUSSIA INCLUDING BELGIUM, & ...	WYLD	54 x 81 cm
WYLD'S NEW PLAN OF LONDON AND ITS VICINITY	WYLD	73 x 108 cm
WYLD'S ROAD DIRECTORY THROUGH ENGLAND AND WALES BEING A NEW ...	WYLD	52 x 61 cm
WYOMING	ASHER & ADAMS	41 x 58 cm
WYOMING	CRAM	36 x 51 cm
WYOMING	RAND, McNALLY	25 x 33 cm
WYOMING, COLORADO AND UTAH	COLTON	43 x 64 cm
YARMOUTH AND THE SANDS ABOUT IT ...	COLLINS, G.	46 x 57 cm
YELLOWSTONE NATIONAL PARK & FOREST RESERVE	U.S. GEOL. SURVEY	51 x 51 cm
YOSEMITE NATIONAL PARK CALIFORNIA	U.S. GEOL. SURVEY	71 x 74 cm
YUCATAN CONVENTUS IURIDICI HISPANIA NOVAE PARS OCCIDENTALIS ET ...	OGILBY	28 x 36 cm
YUCATAN PARTIE DE LA NOUVELLE ESPAGNE ET GUATIMALA	VAN DER AA	28 x 36 cm
ZANGUEBAR / T'GEDEELTE VAN ZANGUEBAR	SANSON (Small)	18 x 30 cm
ZELANDIAE TYPUS	GUICCIARDINI	24 x 31 cm
ZURYCH	BRAUN & HOGENBERG	38 x 48 cm

GEOGRAPHICAL INDEX

The world has been divided into hemispheres, continents, oceans, and a few miscellaneous categories. Each item is listed in only one location. Where there is more than one item by a particular map-maker, the number of items is indicated in square brackets.

The Geographical Index has been revised with this edition, although the categories used in previous editions are unchanged. The embracing concept is to start with the *general* and end with the *particular*. Accordingly, the first heading is the **World**. Next comes **Hemispheres**; then the **Continents** in alphabetical order, and within North America there is further subdivision into Canada, Mexico and Central America, the United States, and the West Indies. The **Oceans** are next, in alphabetical order. And finally, **Miscellaneous**.

Maps of what is now the United States are listed under the main heading of *North America* if before about 1770, and under *United States* if after about 1770. An exception is in the case of a single colony which became a state -- Pennsylvania, for example -- which would appear under *United States*. Generally when a U.S. map shows two states, it is listed under the one occurring first alphabetically. Maps of portions of the United States showing unusual features, such as the state of "Franklin", are listed under that feature. Maps of the Americas -- North and South America together -- are listed under *Western Hemisphere*. Many maps showing the northwest coast of North America are listed under *Pacific Ocean, North*. Major geographical features such as Chesapeake Bay or the Gulf of Mexico may be under *North America* rather than *United States*. North American cities are listed under their respective countries and states, regardless of age, rather than under North America.

To help locate items, the order of the major headings is listed below:

WORLD: World & continents, sets of continents, sets of globe gores, globes

HEMISPHERES of the WORLD: The Americas, the Arctic Sea, Antarctica

AFRICA

ASIA: includes the Holy Land, Persian Gulf, and the East Indies

AUSTRALIA

EUROPE: includes the Mediterranean

NORTH AMERICA: The whole continent and U.S. regions before Independence

- **CANADA**
- **MEXICO and CENTRAL AMERICA**
- **UNITED STATES**: Cities from all periods
- **WEST INDIES**

SOUTH AMERICA

OCEANS -

- **ATLANTIC**
- **INDIAN**: includes Red Sea
- **PACIFIC**

MISCELLANEOUS: includes allegorical, celestial, oddities, portraits, title pages, etc.

WORLD

ANCIENT WORLD: D'Anville; S.D.U.K.
GLOBE GORES, TERRESTRIAL: Coronelli [2]
GLOBES, including Terrestrial & Celestial: Anonymous; Bardin; Cary; Cox; Desnos; Gussfield; Hill, N.; Malby, T.; Newton & Berry [2]
MODERN WORLD: Allard; Anson; Apianus; Arrowsmith [2]; Beautemps-Beaupre; Bellin (Large) [2]; Betts; Black; Blaeu [2]; Blome [2]; Boisseau; Bonne [3]; Bordone; Bowen, E. [4]; Buache; Bunting; Byrne, P.; Carey; Cavazza; Chatelain; Clouet; Cluver; Cook; Cowley; Cruchley; Danckerts; De Fer (Large) [3]; De Leth; De Wit; Dunn [3]; Elwe; Faden; Fries [3]; Gastaldi; Gentleman's Magazine; Gravius; Heather; Homann [3]; Hondius [3]; Honter; Jaillot; Jefferys; Johnson; Johnston [3]; Kitchin; Langenes; Lea; Levasseur; Lotter; Mallet [2]; Meijer; Mentelle; Mercator (Folio) [3]; Mercator (Small); Merian; Merula; Mitchell, S.A. (Atlas Maps 1860 & Later); Moll (Large) [2]; Moll (Small) [4]; Munster [9]; Myritius; Nolin; Norie; Ortelius (Folio) [3]; Payne; Plancius [2]; Ptolemy (1561-99 Venice); Quad [2]; Roberts, H.; Robyn; Sanson (Folio); Sanson (Small); Scherer; Senex [2]; S.D.U.K.; Speed; Strabo; Tanner; Torniello; Valk; Van Den Keere; Van Der Aa; Van Geelkerken; Van Keulen; Van Linschoten; Visscher [2]; Vrients; Vuillemin; Waite; Watson; Weimar Geographisches Institut; Wells; Wetstein; Wilkinson; Wyld [2]; Zatta
PTOLEMAIC WORLD: Munster [3]; Ptolemy (1561-99 Venice); Schedel
WORLD & 4 CONTINENTS: Anonymous; Cassini; De Wit
WORLD & CELESTIAL: De Fer (Small)

HEMISPHERES of the WORLD

EASTERN: Gentleman's Magazine; Mallet [5]; Nolin; S.D.U.K.
NORTHERN and ARCTIC SEA: Albrizzi; Bowen, E.; Buache; Colton; Conder [2]; Coronelli; Covens & Mortier; De Bry; De L'isle [2]; Fullarton; Gentleman's Magazine [2]; Lizars; Mallet; Mercator (Folio) [3]; Mercator (Small) [2]; Meyer; Moll (Small); Petermann; Pitt [2]; Senex; Stanford; Thomson; Tirion [2]; Weigel
SOUTHERN and ANTARCTICA: Bellin (Large); Colton; La Harpe; S.D.U.K.; Stieler
WESTERN; The AMERICAS: Anonymous; Arrowsmith [2]; Bellin (Small); Blaeu [7]; Bowen, E.; Buchon; Carey & Lea [2]; Cluver [2]; Coronelli [2]; D'Anville; Darton; De Fer (Large); De Fer (Small) [2]; De Herrera; De Vaugondy; Du Val (Large); Finley; Fries; Gastaldi [2]; Gaultier; Homann [5]; Hondius [3]; Jansson; Kircher; Lafreri School; Laurie & Whittle; Lavoisne; Le Rouge; Mallet [3]; Mansell, F.; Mercator (Folio) [3]; Mercator (Small); Moll (Large) [2]; Moll (Small); Morden; Munster [6]; Nolin; Ortelius (Folio) [6]; Ottens; Philip, G.; Poirson; Ptolemy (1596-1621 Magini); Purchas; Radefeld; Ramusio; Reichard; Robinson; S.D.U.K.; Speed; Stackhouse; Tardieu; Thomson; Tirion [2]; Valk; Van Den Keere; Van Der Aa [2]; Von Euler; Von Reilly; Weimar Geographisches Institut [3]; Wyld

AFRICA

AFRICA (ALL): Allard; Arrowsmith; Blaeu; Blome; Botero; Bunting; Danckerts; De Bry; De L'isle [2]; Dufour; Hollar; Homann; Hondius; Lotter; Mercator (Folio); Mitchell, S.A. (Atlas Maps 1860 & Later); Moll (Small); Munster [3]; Ortelius (Folio); Ortelius (Miniature); Porro; Probst; Quad; Ramusio; Reynolds, R.; Sanson (Folio); Seutter (Large); S.D.U.K.; Willdey
— **(EAST):** Blome; Bruce, J.; Mallet [2]; Morden [2]; Sanson (Small) [2]
— **(NORTH):** Blome; Bradford; Ptolemy (1561-99 Venice) [2]; Rennell, J.
— **(NORTHEAST):** Bacon; S.D.U.K.; Van Keulen
— **(SOUTH):** Admiralty; Baldwin & Cradock; Bartholomew; Bellin (Large); Bellin (Small) [2]; Black; De Bry; De Fer (Small); Dudley; Fullarton; Jansson; Lotter; Stanford; Van Der Schley; Visscher; Waldseemuller
— **(WEST):** Bellin (Large); Bolton; D'Anville; De L'isle; Doncker; Laurie & Whittle; Mallet; Rennell, J.; Scherer
ABYSSINIA: Jansson; Johnston; Mallet [2]
ALGIERS: Haffner, J.C.
BARBARY: Jansson; Ortelius (Miniature); Piquet
CONGO: De Bry; Mallet; Morden; Van Der Aa

EGYPT: Braun & Hogenberg; Cary; Deroy; Ogilby [3]; Ortelius (Miniature); Ptolemy (1561-99 Venice) [3]; S.D.U.K.
ETHIOPIA: Sanson (Small)
GUINEA: De Wit; Depot De La Marine; Goos; Mallet; Mortier; Ogilby
LIBYA: Ptolemy (1561-99 Venice)
MADAGASCAR: Du Val (Small); Herbert; Ogilby
MAURITANIA: Munster
MOROCCO: Admiralty; Jansson [2]; Ortelius (Folio) [2]
MOZAMBIQUE: Bellin (Small)
NILE RIVER: Bruce, J.; Mallet; Scherer; Stanford
NUBIA: Mallet
SENEGAL: De L'isle
SIERRA LEONE: Wyld
SOUTH AFRICA: Admiralty [3]; Bacon; Laurie & Whittle [3]; Stanford
TANGIER: Admiralty
TUNIS: Braun & Hogenberg; Ortelius (Miniature)

ASIA

ASIA (ALL): Allard; Blaeu [2]; Blome; Bowles; Brue; Chiquet; D'Expilly; Danckerts; De Fer (Small) [2]; De L'isle [2]; De La Feuille; De Vaugondy; De Wit; Homann; Hondius; Jansson; Kitchin; Lafreri School; Le Rouge; Mallet [2]; Mercator (Folio) [2]; Moll (Large); Moll (Small); Morden; Munster [4]; Ogilby; Ortelius (Folio) [3]; Ottens; Sanson (Folio); S.D.U.K.; Solinus; Speed [2]; Valk; Walton; Wells [2]; Wyld
— **(CENTRAL):** Anonymous; Arrowsmith; Moll (Small); Munster [3]; Ptolemy (1561-99 Venice) [2]; Ptolemy (1578-1730 Mercator)
— **(EAST):** Bonne; De Wit; Mallet
— **(MIDDLE EAST):** Andrus & Judd; Bonne; Bowen, E.; D'Anville; De Fer (Small); De Vaugondy; Mallet; Sanson (Small); Stoopendaal; Visscher; Wyld
— **(MISCELLANEOUS):** Fullarton
— **(SOUTH):** Bellin (Small); Ptolemy (1548 Venice); Ptolemy (1561-99 Venice)
— **(SOUTHEAST & EAST INDIES):** Blaeu [2]; Mariette; Moll (Large); Ortelius (Folio); Ramusio
— **(SOUTHEAST):** Blome; Brue; Cantelli Da Vignola; De Fer (Small); Desbruslins; Fries; Gastaldi; Gibson; Moll (Small); Mortier; Munster; Ptolemy (1548 Venice); Ptolemy (1561-99 Venice); Senex; Stanford; Visscher [2]
ARABIA: Blaeu; Blome; Braun & Hogenberg; Ptolemy (1561-99 Venice) [3]; Thomson
ARMENIA: Mallet; Munster; Ptolemy (1561-99 Venice); S.D.U.K.
BLACK SEA & CRIMEA: Johnston; Sanson (Small); Wyld
BURMA: Herbert; Imray; Sayer & Bennett
CASPIAN SEA: Gibson; Homann
CEYLON: Albrizzi; Bellin (Small); D'Apres De Mannevillette; De Bry [2]; Herbert; Mercator (Folio) [2]; Mercator (Small); Munster; Sanson (Small)
CHINA: Admiralty; Arrowsmith; Bellin (Small); Blaeu [2]; Bowen, E.; Coronelli [3]; D'Anville; Dalrymple; De Bry [2]; De Jode; Desilver; Direccion De Hidrografia [2]; Halley; Harris; Jansson [2]; La Perouse; Mallet [2]; Mercator (Folio) [3]; Metellus; Ortelius (Folio) [2]; Russell; Sanson (Small) [2]; Sayer & Bennett; Speed; Van Der Aa; Van Loon; Weekly Dispatch; Wyld [2]
— **MACAO:** De Bry; Harris
CHINA & JAPAN: Blaeu; Blome [3]; Bolton; De Jode; Du Val (Small); Hondius [4]; Jansson; Lapie; Rossi; Sanson (Folio); Speed
CHINA & KOREA: Van Loon
CYPRUS: Hondius; Morden
EAST INDIES (ALL): Arrowsmith; Bolton; Bowen, E. [2]; Cantelli Da Vignola; Coronelli [2]; De Wit; Fullarton; Goos; Hondius [3]; Jansson; Stanford [2]; Van Keulen; Visscher
— **(MISCELLANEOUS):** Bonne; Gregory; Herbert; Imray [2]
— **AMBOINA:** Valentyn
— **BANCA STRAIT:** D'Apres De Mannevillette; Sayer
— **BORNEO:** Admiralty; De Bry
— **CELEBES:** Bellin (Small); Hogg; Van Keulen
— **INDONESIA:** Admiralty; Bellin (Small); D'Apres De Mannevillette; Laurie & Whittle; Morden; Valentyn; Van Keulen [2]

EAST INDIES: JAVA: Chatelain
—— **MALAYA:** Bertius; Dalrymple; Langenes; Middleton
—— **MOLUCCAS:** Bellin (Small); Blaeu; Jansson; Sanson (Small); Van Keulen [2]
—— **NEW GUINEA:** Le Maire; Mallet; Stanford
—— **SINGAPORE:** Murray, J. [2]
—— **STRAIT OF MALACCA:** Admiralty; Van Der Aa
—— **SUMATRA:** D'Apres De Mannevillette; Herbert [2]; Sayer & Bennett [4]
HOLY LAND: Bowen, T.; Brue; Bunting [2]; Burr; Calmet; Coccetus, J.; D'Anville; De Bruyn; De La Rue [2]; De Vaugondy; De Wit [2]; Fuller [6]; Homann [5]; Hondius; Jaillot; Jansson; Johnston; Joly, J.; Keur; Kincaid, A.; Mercator (Small); Moll (Small); Moxon; Munster [2]; Ortelius (Folio) [3]; Sanson (Folio); S.D.U.K. [2]; Thomas, Cowperthwait & Co.; Tirinus; Van Lochom; Visscher [2]; Wilkinson
—— **JERUSALEM:** Anonymous; Bachiene; Blundell; Braun & Hogenberg [2]; Lafreri School; Moll (Small)
INDIA: Admiralty [2]; Anonymous; Bertius; Bonne; Bowen, E.; D'Anville; Du Val (Small); Harris; Homann; Jansson; Laurie & Whittle; Mallet [5]; Munster; Ptolemy (1548 Venice); Ptolemy (1561-99 Venice) [3]; Ramusio; Sanson (Small) [2]; Sayer & Bennett; S.D.U.K.; Tallis [2]; Thomson; Walker, J. & C.; Wyld [3]
JAPAN: Admiralty; Anonymous; Blaeu; Chatelain; Coronelli; Hondius [3]; Jansson [4]; Kaempfer; Lewis & Arrowsmith; Mercator (Folio) [2]; Mercator (Small); Montanus [2]; Morden [2]; Ortelius (Miniature); Reland; Sanson (Small); Seutter (Large); S.D.U.K.; Stanford; Tavernier; Valk & Schenk; Van Der Aa; Wyld
JAPAN & KOREA: La Perouse; Laurie & Whittle; Le Rouge; Philip, G.; Van Den Keere
KOREA: La Perouse
OTTOMAN EMPIRE: Herisson; Homann; S.D.U.K.
PERSIA: Blome; Bowen, E.; De Fer (Small); Ptolemy (1561-99 Venice) [3]; Ptolemy (1596-1621 Magini); Tallis
PERSIAN GULF: D'Apres De Mannevillette; Van Der Aa
PTOLEMAIC: Munster [2]; Ptolemy (1561-99 Venice) [8]; Ptolemy (1596-1621 Magini) [6]
RUSSIA: Seutter (Small)
—— **(EAST):** Anonymous
—— **(ENTIRE & MISCELLANEOUS):** Bellin (Small); Blome [2]; Bowen, E.; De L'isle; Homann; Lattre; Laurie & Whittle; S.D.U.K.
—— **(WEST):** Thomas, Cowperthwait & Co.
—— **KAMTCHATKA:** Cook
—— **KURILE ISLANDS:** Bellin (Small); La Harpe
—— **SIBERIA:** S.D.U.K. [2]
SYRIA: Arrowsmith; Braun & Hogenberg; Mallet [2]; S.D.U.K. [2]
TARTARY: Blome; Bonne; Chatelain; De Fer (Small); Jansson; Ortelius (Folio); Ortelius (Miniature); Ptolemy (1561-99 Venice); S.D.U.K.; Van Der Aa
THAILAND: D'Apres De Mannevillette; Mallet; Morse, S.
TIBET: Stieler
TURKEY: Arrowsmith; Bowen, E.; Cluver; Cramer, J.A.; Homann; Hondius; Mallet [2]; Ptolemy (1561-99 Venice) [3]; Rizzi Zannoni; Valk
—— **CONSTANTINOPLE:** S.D.U.K.; Stanford
YEMEN: Admiralty

AUSTRALIA

AUSTRALIA (ALL): Admiralty; Black; Bowen, E.; Johnston; S.D.U.K. [2]; Stanford
—— **(MISCELLANEOUS):** Coronelli; Imray
—— **& NEW ZEALAND:** Lewis & Arrowsmith
NEW SOUTH WALES: Johnston; S.D.U.K.; Stanford; Wyld
QUEENSLAND: Stanford
SOUTH AUSTRALIA: Stanford
TASMANIA: Cook [2]; Teesdale; Weller; Wyld
VICTORIA: Local And State Government Maps; Stanford; Weller
WESTERN AUSTRALIA: Stanford

EUROPE

EUROPE (ALL): Allard; De Fer (Small); Homann [2]; Hondius; Munster [2]; Ortelius (Folio) [2]; Smith, C.; Speed [2]; Van Der Aa; Van Lochom; Walton; Weaver, H.; Willdey
— **(CENTRAL):** Gross, R.; Laurie & Whittle; Schedel; Schropp & Co.
— **(MISCELLANEOUS):** Arrowsmith; Tardieu
— **(SOUTHEAST):** Homann
— **(WEST):** Wyld
AUSTRIA: Homann [5]; Jansson; Mercator (Folio) [2]
— **TIROL:** Homann
— **VIENNA:** Artaria & Co.
BALKANS: Bowen, E.; De Fer (Small); Homann [3]; Mercator (Folio); Mercator (Small); Munster; Ptolemy (1561-99 Venice) [5]
BALTIC STATES: Jansson
BELGIUM: Etablissement Geographique De Bruxelles; Homann; Sayer
— **ANTWERP:** S.D.U.K.
— **BRABANT:** Jansson
— **FLANDERS:** Homann; Mercator (Folio); Mercator (Small)
— **LIEGE:** Mercator (Folio)
— **MECHLIN:** Blaeu
— **NAMUR:** Homann
BOHEMIA: Homann
— **PRAGUE:** Homann
BRITISH ISLES (ALL): Allard; Blaeu [3] Blome; Chatelain; De Fer (Small); De L'isle; Enouy, J.; Faden [2]; Goos; Hall; Homann [2]; Hondius; Jaillot [2]; Jansson [2]; Johnston; Lotter; Mercator (Folio); Merian; Ortelius (Folio) [3]; Philip, G.; Porcacchi; Ptolemy (1561-99 Venice) [2]; Sanson (Small) [2]; S.D.U.K.; Speed; Stanford; Van Lochom; Von Reilly; Wells
— **IRISH SEA:** Collins, G.; Imray; Wilson
BYELORUS: Homann
DANUBE RIVER: Homann
DENMARK: Homann [2]; Imray; Jansson; Mercator (Folio); S.D.U.K.; Speed; Thomson; Waghenaer; Wilson
— **COPENHAGEN:** Dahlberg; Homann
— **FUNEN:** Mercator (Folio)
— **JUTLAND:** Mercator (Folio)
ENGLAND (ALL): Blaeu; Cruchley [2]; Jansson; Lavoisne; Ortelius (Miniature); Quad; Richardson
— **(MISCELLANEOUS):** Admiralty [2]; Bartholomew; Braun & Hogenberg; Collins, G.; Darton; Fullarton [2]; Hondius; Smith, C.; S.D.U.K. [2]; Waghenaer [2]; Wilson
— **(MISCELLANEOUS ISLANDS):** Jansson; Laurie & Whittle; Valk & Schenk
— **BRISTOL CHANNEL:** Depot De La Marine
— **CAMBRIDGESHIRE:** Blaeu
— **CHANNEL ISLANDS:** Mercator (Folio) [2]
— **CORNWALL:** Admiralty [2]; Collins, G. [2]; Laurie & Whittle
— **DERBYSHIRE:** Wyld
— **DEVONSHIRE:** Admiralty; Collins, G.; Jacobsz; Laurie & Whittle [3]
— **DORSETSHIRE:** Depot De La Marine [2]
— **DURHAM:** Admiralty; Van Keulen
— **HAMPSHIRE:** Bellin (Small); Depot De La Marine; Faden
— **ISLE OF MAN:** Collins, G.
— **ISLE OF WIGHT:** Laurie & Whittle
— **KENT:** Admiralty; Laurie & Whittle [2]
— **LANCASHIRE:** Speed [2]; Sweny, M.A.; Taylor, T.
— **LINCOLNSHIRE:** Admiralty; Overton; Speed
— **LONDON:** Anonymous; Bacon [3]; Cole; Cross, J.; Cruchley [4]; Darton & Clark; De Belleforest; Dodsley; Drew, J.; Faden [2]; Family Times; Foster Groom; Friederichs, J.; Homann [3]; Kelly; Laurie & Whittle; Lewis, Samuel & Co.; Mogg [3]; Overton; Philip, G. [3]; Reynolds, J. [6]; Rowe; Sayer & Bennett; Seutter (Large) [2]; Smith, C. [3]; Smith, W. H. [2]; Stanford [4]; Strype [5]; Wallis; Weale; Wyld [3]

NETHERLANDS: ZEELAND: Guicciardini
NETHERLANDS & BELGIUM: Homann; Mercator (Folio)
NORTH SEA: De Wit
NORWAY: Colom [2]; Homann; Jansson
— **SPITZBERGEN:** Bellin (Small)
POLAND: De Fer (Small); Homann; Mercator (Folio) [2]; Ptolemy (1561-99 Venice) [4]
— **WARSAW:** Perelle
POLAND & LITHUANIA: Bowen, E.; Lea
PORTUGAL: Admiralty [2]; Arrowsmith [2]; Jansson; Ortelius (Folio)
PTOLEMAIC: Ptolemy (1561-99 Venice) [12]; Ptolemy (1596-1621 Magini) [2]
RHINE RIVER: Foppen; Homann; Jansson
RUSSIA: Blaeu; Clark; Cluver; De Fer (Small); De L'isle; Dudley; Jansson [3]; Johnson; Munster; Ottens [2]; Ptolemy (1561-99 Venice) [2]; Seutter (Large); S.D.U.K.; Stackhouse
— **ST. PETERSBURG:** Anonymous; Gentleman's Magazine; Hall
SCANDINAVIA (ALL): Faden; Jansson; Munster; Sanson (Small); Valk; Visscher
— **(MISCELLANEOUS):** Norie
SCOTLAND (ALL): Brown, T.; Cary; Johnston; Laurie & Whittle; Lewis, Samuel & Co.; Mercator (Folio); Ortelius (Miniature)
— **(ISLANDS):** Mackenzie
— **(MISCELLANEOUS):** Admiralty [3]; Bartholomew; Mackenzie; Mercator (Folio)
— **ABERDEEN SHIRE:** Admiralty
— **EDINBURGH:** Milne
— **EDINBURGHSHIRE:** Braun & Hogenberg; S.D.U.K. [2]
— **HEBRIDES:** Mackenzie [3]
SPAIN (ALL): Braun & Hogenberg [2]; Jansson; S.D.U.K. [2]
— **(MISCELLANEOUS):** Blaeu; Braun & Hogenberg [2]; De Bry; Faden; Jansson
— **ANDALUSIA:** Blaeu; Ortelius (Miniature)
— **ARAGON:** Jansson
— **ASTURIA:** Jansson
— **BALEARIC ISLANDS:** Bonne; Zatta
— **BAY OF BISCAY:** Van Keulen
— **GIBRALTAR:** Dheulland
— **GRANADA:** Jansson
— **MADRID:** Seutter (Large)
— **PALOS:** De Bry [2]
— **VALENCIA:** Jansson; Ortelius (Miniature)
SPAIN & PORTUGAL: De Fer (Small); Faden; Husson; Moll (Large); Ortelius (Miniature); Ptolemy (1561-99 Venice) [4]; Scherer; Stumpf
SWEDEN: Homann [2]; Jansson; S.D.U.K.
— **STOCKHOLM:** Anonymous; Carpelan
SWITZERLAND: Blaeu; Braun & Hogenberg; Homann [2]; Jaillot; Johnston; Keller; Mercator (Folio); Mercator (Small); Moll (Small); Payne; Stiger & Co.
TRANSYLVANIA: Homann; Jansson
TURKEY IN EUROPE: Santini
UKRAINE: Elwe; Mercator (Folio); Ptolemy (1561-99 Venice)
WALES (ALL): Bacon; Morris
— **(MISCELLANEOUS):** Admiralty [3]; Collins, G.; Morris [26]
— **ANGLESEY:** Admiralty
— **CARDIGANSHIRE:** Mackenzie [2]
— **PEMBROKESHIRE:** Admiralty [3]; Bellin (Large); Laurie & Whittle
WALLACHIA: Jansson

NORTH AMERICA: GENERAL & Pre-Independence U.S.

NORTH AMERICA (ALL): Arrowsmith; Barlow; Bellin (Small); Black; Blome; Bowen, E. [2]; Bowen, T. [2]; Bowles; Brion De La Tour; Brue; Burgess; Burr [2]; Carey & Lea; Colton [2]; Cummings & Hilliard; D'Anville; De L'isle; De Vaugondy [3]; Delamarche; Filloeul; Finley; Gall & Inglis; Hennepin; Homann; Jaillot [3]; Jansson [3]; Janvier; Jefferys; Johnson [3]; Johnston [2]; Kiepert; Kitchin; Laporte; Laurie & Whittle; Levasseur [2]; Levi; Lewis & Arrowsmith [2]; Lopez; Lorrain; Lotter; Lumsden; Malte-Brun; Menzies; Moll (Small) [2]; Nolin; Payne; Pelton; People's Atlas; Philip, G. [2]; Popple; Porcacchi; Quad; Rollos; Sanson (Folio) [2]; Sayer; Scherer [6]; Smith, C.; S.D.U.K.; Stieler; Stucchi; Tanner; Tardieu; Thomson [2]; Velten; Von Stulpnagel; Weimar Geographisches Institut [8]; Wilkes; Wilkinson; Wyld [2]

— **(CENTRAL):** Gibson; Homann [2]; La Hontan; Le Rouge; Lodge; Mitchell, John; Popple; Schraembl; Seutter (Large) [2]; U.S. War Department; Zatta

— **(EAST COAST):** Depot De La Marine; Des Barres; Dudley; Mount & Page; Seller; Van Keulen

— **(EAST):** Anonymous; Bowles; De Fer (Small); De Wit; Du Val (Large); Fielding; General Magazine Of Arts & Sciences; Jansson; Kiepert [2]; Kitchin; Le Rouge; Lotter [2]; Melish; Moll (Small); Mortier [3]; Nolin; Ottens; Palairet; Sayer & Bennett [2]; Seale; Senex; Society For Anti-Gallicians; S.D.U.K.; Thomson; Visscher [4]; Von Euler; Wytfliet [2]; Zatta

— **(NORTH):** Forster, G.; Franklin

— **(NORTHEAST):** Anonymous; Arrowsmith; Bellin (Large); Bonne; Lambert, J.; Michault; Ptolemy (1561-99 Venice)

— **NORTHWEST):** Cook [3]; De Vaugondy; Dixon; La Perouse [7]; Mitchell, S.A. (Atlas Maps 1860 & Later); Robinson [3]; Vancouver [4]; Wytfliet

— **(SOUTH):** Bonne; Bradford; Moll (Small) [2]

— **(SOUTHEAST):** Cloppenburgh; Santini [2]; Zatta

— **(SOUTHWEST):** Bonne; Brue; Morden; Ptolemy (1548 Venice); Ravenstein, F. G.; Tallis; Vancouver [2]; Wislizenus, A.

— **(UNITED STATES, PRE-INDEPENDENCE):** Nolin; Scherer

— **(WEST COAST):** Imray

— **& WEST INDIES:** Homann [2]; Monk [2]

ARCTIC: De Vaugondy

CALIFORNIA: De Bry; De Fer (Large); De Fer (Small); De Vaugondy; Dudley; Goos; La Perouse; Sanson (Small) [2]

CALIFORNIA & NEW MEXICO: Mallet

CAROLINA: Bellin (Small); De Bry; Morden; Mouzon

CAROLINA & FLORIDA: Catesby

CAROLINA & GEORGIA: Bellin (Small) [2]

CAROLINA, MARYLAND & VIRGINIA: Homann [5]

CHESAPEAKE BAY: Blunt; Depot De La Marine; Mount & Page; Stedman

DELAWARE BAY: Gentleman's Magazine; Sayer & Bennett

ENGLISH POSSESSIONS: Gentleman's Magazine [3]; Homann; Laurie & Whittle; Sayer & Bennett

ENGLISH & FRENCH POSSESSIONS: Gentleman's Magazine; London Magazine [2]

FLORIDA: Bellin (Small); De Laet; De Vaugondy; Gentleman's Magazine [2]; Jefferys; London Magazine; Mallet; Moll (Small); Montanus; Ortelius (Folio) [2]; Van Keulen

FLORIDA & LOUISIANA: Bellin (Small) [3]; Bonne [2]; Cassini; Sanson (Small)

FLORIDA & MEXICO: Chatelain; De L'isle

FLORIDA & VIRGINIA: Blaeu [3]; Hondius [3]; Mercator (Folio) [3]; Mercator (Small)

FRENCH POSSESSIONS: London Magazine

GEORGIA: Bellin (Small); Bowen, E.; Seutter (Large); Universal Magazine

GREAT LAKES: Bellin (Small); Bonne; Chatelain; Colton; Gazzettiere Americano; London Magazine [3]; S.D.U.K.

GULF COAST: Bellin (Small) [3]; De Fer (Small)

GULF OF MEXICO: Tardieu; Van Keulen [2]

LOUISIANA: Bellin (Small) [2]; Bowen, E.; Law; Le Page Du Pratz; London Magazine [2]; Senex; Tirion; Zatta [2]

MARYLAND & VIRGINIA: Bellin (Small) [3]; Bowen, E.; De Chastellux; De Vaugondy [2]; Homann; Speed

MIDDLE BRITISH COLONIES: Bellin (Small) [2]; Bowles; Du Val (Small); Jefferys; Morden; Sayer & Bennett

MISSISSIPPI RIVER: De Vaugondy [2]; Sayer [2]

NEW ENGLAND: Bellin (Small) [3]; Blaeu [4]; Danckerts [2]; Des Barres; Goos [3]; Homann [2]; Jansson; Jefferys; Lotter; Seutter (Large); Speed [2]; Visscher

NEW FRANCE: Bellin (Large) [2]; Bellin (Small); Chatelain; D'Anville; De Laet [3]; De Vaugondy [2]; Dussieux; Happel; La Hontan; Moll (Small); Ottens; Ramusio; Sanson (Folio) [3]; Sanson (Small); Wytfliet

NEW MEXICO: Anonymous; Bonne [2]

NEW YORK: Grand Magazine Of Magazines; Gentleman's Magazine [3]; Lotter; Rocque; Van Keulen [2]; Universal Magazine

NORTH CAROLINA: Political Magazine [2]

NORTHERN BRITISH COLONIES: Anonymous; Jansson [2]; Le Rouge; Thornton

PENNSYLVANIA: Gentleman's & London Magazine; London Magazine; Universal Magazine

PENNSYLVANIA, FORT DU QUESNE: Grand Magazine Of Magazines [2]

VIRGINIA: Blaeu [3]; De Bry; Hondius [2]; London Magazine [3]; Mercator (Small) [2]; Political Magazine; Van Keulen [2]

NORTH AMERICA: CANADA

CANADA (ALL): Carey; Carey & Lea; Colton; Cooper, H.; De L'isle; Faden; Hall; S.D.U.K. [2]; Stockdale; Tallis; Tirion [2]; Van Der Aa; Zatta

— **(CENTRAL):** Bellin (Large); Homann; Stanford; Wyld

— **(EAST):** Bellin (Small); Bonne; Cary; Coronelli; Desilver; Finley; Homann [2]; Johnson; Political Magazine [3]; Russell; Tallis; Vandermaelen [2]

— **(LOWER):** Arrowsmith; Bradford; Burr; Colton

— **(NORTH):** Franklin; Mortier; Royal Geographical Society; Vandermaelen

— **(UPPER):** Bradford [2]; Burr [2]; Colton

— **(WEST):** Century Atlas; Homann; Philip, G. [2]; Stanford; Tallis

BAFFIN BAY: Vandermaelen

BAY OF FUNDY: Admiralty

BRITISH COLUMBIA: Barclay; Cook; Cram; Rand, Mcnally & Co.; Stanford; Swanston; Waite; Weekly Dispatch

CAPE BRETON ISLAND, LOUISBURG: Bellin (Small); Entick; Gentleman's Magazine

DAVIS STRAIT: Van Keulen

HUDSON BAY: Bellin (Small) [4]; Jefferys; Morden

LABRADOR: Bellin (Small)

MANITOBA: Grant, A.; Rand, Mcnally & Co.; Stanford

MARITIME PROVINCES: Anonymous; Burr; Colton; Cram; De Vaugondy; Fullarton; Johnson; Morse, J.; Smith, C.

NEWFOUNDLAND: Bellin (Small) [2]; Bertius; Mallet; Moll (Small); Mount & Page; London Magazine [2]; Stanford

NOVA SCOTIA: Admiralty; Bellin (Small); Des Barres [5]; Mackinlay; London Magazine [2]; S.D.U.K.

— **HALIFAX:** Imray; Lottery Magazine

ONTARIO: Bouchette; Mitchell, S.A. (Atlas Maps 1860 & Later); Rand, Mcnally & Co.

— **TORONTO:** Rand, Mcnally & Co.

QUEBEC: Bellin (Small); Bouchette; Gibson; London Magazine; Rand, Mcnally & Co.; Sayer & Bennett; Stockdale; Walker & Miles

— **MONTREAL:** Cram; Jefferys; People's Atlas

— **QUEBEC CITY:** Bellin (Small); De Fer (Small); Gazzettiere Americano; Gentleman's Magazine; Grand Magazine Of Magazines; La Hontan; Mallet; Meyer; Prevost D'Exiles; Tirion; Van Der Aa; Walker & Miles; Weld, I.

ST. LAWRENCE GULF: Admiralty [2]; Bellin (Small) [3]; Depot De La Marine; Gazzettiere Americano; Sayer & Bennett

ST. LAWRENCE RIVER: Admiralty [3]; Bellin (Large); Bellin (Small) [4]; Jefferys [2]; Thomson

YUKON: Stanford

NORTH AMERICA: MEXICO and CENTRAL AMERICA

CENTRAL AMERICA (ALL): Desilver; Dufour; Johnson; Tallis; Wyld; Wytfliet
— **(MISCELLANEOUS):** Admiralty; Jefferys; U.S.
GUATEMALA: Vandermaelen
HONDURAS: Admiralty [2]; De Laet; Jefferys
MEXICO: Admiralty; Archer; Arrowsmith; Bellin (Small) [3]; Burr; Carey & Lea; Cary; Dampier; Daumont; De Bry [2]; De Fer (Small); De Herrera [2]; De Vaugondy [3]; Depot De La Marine; Hall; Hamilton, Adams & Co.; Homann; Jansson [2]; Kelly; Lapie; Lizars; Mallet; Nicol; Ogilby; Petermann; Popple; Porcacchi; Ptolemy (1561-99 Venice); Quad; Rand, Mcnally & Co.; Reclus; Sanson (Small); Thomson; Van Der Aa [2]; Vandermaelen [2]; Vivien; Zatta
— **MEXICO CITY:** Bellin (Small); De Bry; Harris [2]; Meyer; Munster; Ramusio
— **VERA CRUZ:** Bellin (Small); Jefferys; Tirion
MEXICO & CENTRAL AMERICA: Marzolla; Ogilby; Weimar Geographisches Institut
MEXICO & GUATEMALA: Dower; Wyld
MEXICO & WEST INDIES: Delamarche; Homann; Smith, J.; Van Keulen
NICARAGUA: Meyer; U.S.; Van Der Aa
PANAMA: Admiralty [2]; Arrowsmith; Bellin (Small); Dampier; De Herrera; Esquemelin; Hammond; Meyer [2]; Tirion; U.S.
— **CHAGRE:** Gentleman's Magazine
— **PORTO BELLO:** Durell; Homann; Ulloa; Van Der Aa
YUCATAN: Heller, C.; Van Der Aa

NORTH AMERICA: UNITED STATES

UNITED STATES (ALL): Andriveau-Goujon; Arrowsmith; Blackie & Son; Bonne; Burr; Carey & Lea; Cassini; Chevalier; Clouet; Colton [2]; Cornell; Desilver; Duval; Eastman; Ensign; Ettling [2]; Findlay [2]; Gall & Inglis; Gray [3]; Greenleaf; Hall; Handtke; Johnson; Johnston; Kelly; Lapie [3]; Lizars; London Printing And Publishing; Melish [2]; Meyer; Mitchell, S.A.; Mitchell, S.A. (Atlas Maps 1860 & Later) [2]; Murray, J.; Porter, T.; Rand, Mcnally & Co.; Rapkin; Russell [2]; Smith, R.C.; Stanford [3]; Stieler; Swanston; Talbot; Tallis [2]; Tardieu; U.S. [3]; U.S. Coast Survey; U.S. State Surveys; Von Stulpnagel; Warner, B.; Weimar Geographisches Institut; Woodbridge
— **(CENTRAL):** Buchon; Lloyd; Stanford; Stebbins, H.; Swanston
— **(CITIES, MISCELLANEOUS):** Colton; Fullarton [2]; Gray
— **(EAST COAST):** Laurie & Whittle
— **(EAST):** Arrowsmith; Blondeau; Cooke; De Crevecoeur; Fisher, H.; Johnson; Lewis & Arrowsmith; Lloyd; Lopez; Meyer; Mitchell, S.A.; Reid; Russell [2]; S.D.U.K.; Stanford [2]; Tanner [2]; U.S. War Department; Weimar Geographisches Institut
UNITED STATES (MIDWEST): Carey [2]; Colton; Johnson; Lincoln & Edmands; Lloyd; Mitchell, S.A. (Atlas Maps 1860 & Later); S.D.U.K. [2]; Swanston; U.S. [2]; Von Schlieben
— **(NEW ENGLAND):** Asher & Adams; Bowles; Goldthwait; Railroad Company Maps
— **(NORTHEAST):** Anonymous; Bonne; Conder; Gavit & Duthie; Lloyd; Morse, J.; Olney; Stockdale [2]; Tanner; Universal Magazine; Weimar Geographisches Institut; Zatta
— **(NORTHWEST):** Colton; Johnson; Mitchell, S.A. (Atlas Maps 1860 & Later); Petermann
— **(SOUTH):** Bradford; Phelps & Watson; Sharpe; S.D.U.K.; Swanston; Thomson; Vandermaelen; Walling; Williams, W. [2]
— **(SOUTHEAST):** Bonne; Colton [2]; Morse, J. [8]; Olney; Purcell; Reid; U.S.; Vandermaelen; Williams, C.S.
— **(SOUTHWEST):** Lloyd; U.S. Pacific R.R. Survey; U.S. War Department
— **(SOUTHWEST & MEXICO):** Dower; Duvotenay; Morse & Breese; Sanson (Folio); Starling; Tanner; U.S. [3]
— **(WEST):** Black; Carey [2]; Colton [3]; Desilver; Fremont; James, J.A. & U.P.; Johnson [8]; Kingsbury; Lewis & Arrowsmith; Mitchell, S.A. (Atlas Maps 1859 & Earlier) [5]; Mitchell, S.A. (Atlas Maps 1860 & Later) [5]; Olney; Philip, G.; Railroad Company Maps [4]; Thomas, Cowperthwait & Co. [2]; U.S. [2]; U.S. Geological Survey [2]; U.S. Pacific R.R. Survey; U.S. War Department; Walling & Gray; Watson
— **& CANADA:** Belden; Betts; Lizars; Weimar Geographisches Institut [2]
— **& MEXICO:** Duvotenay; Poirson; Von Stulpnagel

ALABAMA: Bartholomew; Bradford; Burr [2]; Carey & Lea; Colton; Cram; Desilver; Dower; Harper's Weekly [2]; Mitchell, S.A. (Atlas Maps 1859 & Earlier) [2]; Morse & Breese; U.S. [2]; U.S. Coast Survey; U.S. State Surveys; U.S. War Department [4]

ALABAMA & GEORGIA: Bradley; Johnson [5]; Mitchell, S.A. (Atlas Maps 1860 & Later) [4]; Railroad Company Maps

ALABAMA & MISSISSIPPI: Lewis & Arrowsmith [2]

ALASKA: Claret De Fleurieu; Colton [2]; Cook [2]; Cram; Gray; Hogg; Mitchell, S.A. (Atlas Maps 1860 & Later); Morse, J. [2]; National Geographic Society; Rand, Mcnally & Co.; U.S. [2]; U.S. State Surveys; Walling

ARIZONA: Bartlett, J. R.; Cram; U.S. [2]; U.S. State Surveys [2]; U.S. War Department

ARIZONA & NEW MEXICO: Bradley; Colton; Donaldson, T.; Eastman; Emory; Mitchell, S.A. (Atlas Maps 1860 & Later); U.S. State Surveys [2]

ARKANSAS: Asher & Adams; Bradford; Burr [3]; Carey & Lea; Century Atlas; Colton [2]; Desilver; Gray; Greenleaf [2]; Meyer; Mitchell, S.A. (Atlas Maps 1859 & Earlier) [2]; Morse & Breese; Railroad Company Maps; U.S.; U.S. State Surveys [2]; U.S. War Department

ARKANSAS & MISSOURI: U.S. War Department

CALIFORNIA: Colton [2]; Cram [3]; Gray; Hesse, J.; Meyer [2]; Mitchell, S.A. (Atlas Maps 1860 & Later) [3]; Railroad Company Maps; Rand, Mcnally & Co. [2]; Real Estate And Promotional Maps; U.S. [4]; U.S. Coast Survey [8]; U.S. Geological Survey; U.S. Pacific R.R. Survey [8]; U.S. State Surveys [4]; U.S. War Department [7]; Van Zouteveen

CALIFORNIA, SAN FRANCISCO: Meyer; U.S.; U.S. Coast Survey; U.S. War Department

CALIFORNIA & NEVADA: Colton; Cram; Gray; U.S. State Surveys; U.S. War Department

CALIFORNIA & OREGON: Fremont; Swanston; U.S.

CALIFORNIA, NEVADA & OREGON: Gray

COLORADO: Bradley; Century Atlas; Clason Map Co.; Company Maps; Cram [3]; Gray [2]; Hayden, F. [3]; Local And State Government Maps; Mitchell, S.A. (Atlas Maps 1860 & Later) [5]; Railroad Company Maps; U.S.; U.S. Geological Survey [2]; U.S. War Department

CONNECTICUT: Bailey & Co.; Beers, Ellis & Soule [4]; Carey; Desilver; Finley; Gentleman's Magazine; Kensett; Lewis & Arrowsmith; Lucas; Mitchell, S.A. (Atlas Maps 1859 & Earlier) [2]; Payne; Reid; Waite

CONNECTICUT & RHODE ISLAND: Marsh, W. S.; Morse, J.; Rand, Mcnally & Co.

DAKOTA TERRITORY: Asher & Adams; Colton [3]; Cram; Gray [3]; Mitchell, S.A. (Atlas Maps 1860 & Later); Rice; Vandermaelen

DELAWARE: Bradford; Carey [2]; Finley [2]; Lewis & Arrowsmith; Lucas; Scott

DELAWARE & MARYLAND: Burr [2]; Century Atlas; Colton [2]; Desilver; Johnson; Mitchell, S.A. (Atlas Maps 1859 & Earlier); Morse, J.; Standard Atlas

DISTRICT OF COLUMBIA: Bradford; Ellicott; Mitchell, S.A. (Atlas Maps 1859 & Earlier); Tanner [2]; Waite

FLORIDA: Bradford; Burr; Colton; Cram; Gaskell; Gray; Lange; Lucas; Mitchell, S.A. (Atlas Maps 1859 & Earlier); Morse, S.; Railroad Company Maps; Rand, Mcnally & Co.; S.D.U.K.; U.S.; U.S. Coast Survey; U.S. State Surveys [2]; U.S. War Department [7]

— **PENSACOLA:** Bellin (Small) [2]; Tirion

— **ST. AUGUSTINE:** Bellin (Small)

FRANKLIN: Thomson

GEORGIA: Appleton; Bradford; Bradford & Goodrich; Carey; Carey & Lea; Colton; Cram [3]; Desilver; Finley; Grant, A.; Gray; Hardesty; Harper's Weekly [2]; Lewis & Arrowsmith [2]; Lucas; Mitchell, S.A. (Atlas Maps 1859 & Earlier) [2]; Morse & Breese; Morse & Gaston; Peck, J.; Rand, Mcnally & Co. [3]; S.D.U.K. [4]; Stedman; Tanner [2]; Thomas, Cowperthwait & Co.; Tunison; U.S.; U.S. Coast Survey [2]; U.S. War Department [3]; Wilmore; Young, J.H. [2]

GEORGIA & SOUTH CAROLINA: Tunison [2]; U.S. Coast Survey [2]; U.S. War Department [3]

GEORGIA, WITH WESTERN TERRITORY: Carey [2]; Scott [3]

HAWAII: Cram; U.S. State Surveys

IDAHO: Cram; Mitchell, S.A. (Atlas Maps 1860 & Later); Standard Atlas; U.S. State Surveys

IDAHO & MONTANA: Asher & Adams; U.S. Pacific R.R. Survey; Vandermaelen

IDAHO, MONTANA & WYOMING: Colton [2]

ILLINOIS: Burr; Carey & Lea; Colton [3]; Cram; Desilver [2]; Finley; Johnson [4]; Lucas; Meyer [2]; Mitchell, S.A. (Atlas Maps 1859 & Earlier); Mitchell, S.A. (Atlas Maps 1860 & Later) [2]; Morse & Breese; Railroad Company Maps; Rand, Mcnally & Co.; Tanner; Thomas, Cowperthwait & Co.; U.S. [9]; U.S. State Surveys

ILLINOIS: CHICAGO: Gray; Ladies Repository; Mitchell, S.A. (Atlas Maps 1860 & Later); U.S. War Department; Warner & Beers

ILLINOIS & MISSOURI: Tanner [2]

INDIAN TERRITORY: Colton; Gray; Mitchell, S.A. (Atlas Maps 1860 & Later)

INDIANA: Bradford [4]; Bradford & Goodrich; Bradley; Buchon [2]; Burr; Carey & Lea; Colton [4]; Cram [4]; Desilver [2]; Duval; Finley [3]; Gray [3]; Greenleaf; Johnson; Mitchell, S.A. (Atlas Maps 1859 & Earlier) [3]; Mitchell, S.A. (Atlas Maps 1860 & Later); Morse & Breese; Morse & Gaston; Rand, Mcnally & Co. [3]; Tanner [2]; Thomas, Cowperthwait & Co.; U.S. [3]; U.S. State Surveys [2]; U.S. War Department; Young, J.H.

INDIANA & OHIO: Bradford; Colton; Hinton [2]; Johnson; Mitchell, S.A. (Atlas Maps 1860 & Later) [2]; Tanner

IOWA: Andreas; Chapman; Colton [4]; Cram; Desilver; Meyer [2]; Mitchell, S.A. (Atlas Maps 1859 & Earlier) [3]; Parker, N.H.; Rand, Mcnally & Co.; Thomas, Cowperthwait & Co.; U.S. State Surveys

IOWA & NEBRASKA: Johnson [2]

IOWA & WISCONSIN: U.S. War Department

KANSAS: Colton [2]; Gray; Rand, Mcnally & Co.

KANSAS & NEBRASKA: Colton [5]; Mitchell, S.A. (Atlas Maps 1860 & Later)

KENTUCKY: Buchon; Carey; Carey & Lea [2]; Cram; Desilver; Finley; Hutchins; Lewis & Arrowsmith; Meyer; Mitchell, S.A. (Atlas Maps 1859 & Earlier) [2]; Payne; Tanner; Winterbotham [2]; Yeager

KENTUCKY & TENNESSEE: Black; Burr [2]; Colton; Cram; Mast, Crowell; Mitchell, S.A. (Atlas Maps 1860 & Later); Morse, J.

LOUISIANA: Bradford; Burr; Carey [2]; Century Atlas; Cram; Desilver; Ehrmann; Finley; Grant, A.; James, W.; Mitchell, S.A. (Atlas Maps 1859 & Earlier); Rand, Mcnally & Co.; U.S. [5]; U.S. State Surveys; U.S. War Department

— **NEW ORLEANS:** Anonymous; Bellin (Small) [3]; Garneray; Harper's Weekly;.London Magazine;. Meyer; Mitchell, S.A. (Atlas Maps 1860 & Later); Naval Chronicle; U.S.

LOUISIANA & MISSISSIPPI: Asher & Adams; Tanner

MAINE: Burr [2]; Carey; Colby; Colton; Des Barres [4]; Desilver [2]; Emery; Finley; Lewis & Arrowsmith [2]; Mitchell, S.A. (Atlas Maps 1859 & Earlier); Morse, J.; Payne; Railroad Company Maps; Reid; Sartine; Scott; U.S. [3]; U.S. Coast Survey [2]

MARYLAND: Bradford; Carey; James, W.; Lucas [2]; Meyer; Universal Magazine [2]; Walling & Gray; Wilkinson

MARYLAND, BALTIMORE: Bradford [2]

MARYLAND & VIRGINIA: Mitchell, S.A.; U.S. Coast Survey

MASSACHUSETTS: Bailey & Co.; Blunt; Carey; De Crevecoeur [3]; Des Barres [4]; Finley; Finn; Lewis & Arrowsmith; Morse, J.; Payne; U.S.; U.S. Coast Survey; Walker, G.

— **BOSTON:** Anonymous; Bellin (Small); Crafts, H.; Crosman & Mallory; Dutton & Co.; Gentleman's Magazine [3]; Melish; Norman; Pennsylvania Magazine [2]; Political Magazine; Stedman; Tallis; U.S.; Walker, G. [2]

MASSACHUSETTS & RHODE ISLAND: Mitchell, S.A. (Atlas Maps 1859 & Earlier)

MASSACHUSETTS, CONNECTICUT & RHODE ISLAND: Burr [2]; Ensign; Ensign & Thayer; Finley

MICHIGAN: Burr [3]; Century Atlas; Colton [4]; Desilver; Lange; Mitchell, S.A. (Atlas Maps 1859 & Earlier) [2]; Mitchell, S.A. (Atlas Maps 1860 & Later); Morse & Breese; People's Atlas; Tanner; Thomas, Cowperthwait & Co. [2]; U.S. [2]; U.S. State Surveys; U.S. War Department [4]

MICHIGAN & WISCONSIN: Johnson [3]; Watson

MINNESOTA: Asher & Adams; Chapman; Colton [3]; Cram [2]; Hill, A.J.; Johnson [3]; Mitchell, S.A. (Atlas Maps 1860 & Later); Rand, Mcnally & Co. [2]; Standard Atlas; Thomas, Cowperthwait & Co. [2]; U.S.; U.S. State Surveys; U.S. War Department

MINNESOTA & WISCONSIN: U.S.; Vandermaelen [2]

MISSISSIPPI: Bradford; Carey & Lea; Century Atlas; Colton [2]; Cram; Desilver; Grant, A.; Greenleaf; Harper's Weekly; Local And State Government Maps; Mitchell, S.A. (Atlas Maps 1859 & Earlier); Tanner [2]; Thomas, Cowperthwait & Co.; U.S.; U.S. State Surveys [2]

MISSISSIPPI RIVER: Schoolcraft; U.S. War Department [2]

MISSISSIPPI TERRITORY: Carey

MISSOURI: Burr; Colton; Cram; Desilver [2]; Finley; Greenleaf; Johnson [2]; Meyer [2]; Mitchell, S.A. (Atlas Maps 1859 & Earlier); Thomas, Cowperthwait & Co. [2]

— **ST. LOUIS:** Flamm; Harper's Weekly; Ladies Repository; Meyer; St. Louis Republican

MISSOURI TERRITORY: U.S.

SOUTH CAROLINA, CHARLESTON: Harper's Weekly; Luffman; Sproule; Stedman; U.S. War Department

SOUTH DAKOTA: Cram [2]; Rand, Mcnally & Co.

TENNESSEE: Bradford; Century Atlas; Cram [2]; Flamm; Harper's Weekly; Lewis & Arrowsmith; Lucas; Mitchell, S.A. (Atlas Maps 1859 & Earlier) [2]; Scott; Tanner [2]; U.S.

TEXAS: Anonymous; Asher & Adams [2]; Bradley; Colton [3]; Cram [2]; Desilver; Gray; Johnson; Meyer; Mitchell, S.A.; Mitchell, S.A. (Atlas Maps 1859 & Earlier); Mitchell, S.A. (Atlas Maps 1860 & Later) [4]; Morse & Breese; Real Estate And Promotional Maps; U.S. [4]; U.S. Coast Survey [3]; U.S. War Department [8]

UTAH: Asher & Adams; Harper's Weekly; Illustrated London News; Rand, Mcnally & Co.; U.S. State Surveys

VERMONT: Bradford; Buchon; Carey [3]; Carey & Lea; Colton [3]; Faden; Finley [2]; Jewett & Co.; Lewis & Arrowsmith; Scott [2]

VIRGINIA: Burr [2]; Carey [3]; Century Atlas; Colton [2]; Desilver; Illustrated London News; Le Rouge [2]; Lewis & Arrowsmith; Morse, J.; Pennsylvania Magazine; Political Magazine; Railroad Company Maps; Rand, Mcnally & Co.; Reid [2]; Stedman; Tanner; Thomas, Cowperthwait & Co.; U.S. Coast Survey; U.S. War Department; Weller

VIRGINIA & WEST VIRGINIA: Cram; Mitchell, S.A. (Atlas Maps 1860 & Later)

VIRGINIA, MARYLAND & DELAWARE: Stockdale

WASHINGTON: Asher & Adams; Cram [2]; Rand, Mcnally & Co.; U.S.; U.S. State Surveys [4]

WEST VIRGINIA: Cram; U.S.

WISCONSIN: Century Atlas; Colton [3]; Cram; Desilver [2]; Harrison & Warner; Meyer; Morse & Breese; Real Estate And Promotional Maps; Tanner; U.S. [4]; U.S. State Surveys; U.S. War Department [2]

WYOMING: Asher & Adams; Cram [2]; Hayden, F.; Mitchell, S.A. (Atlas Maps 1860 & Later); Rand, Mcnally & Co. [2]; U.S. Geological Survey; U.S. War Department

NORTH AMERICA: WEST INDIES

WEST INDIES (ALL): Arrowsmith [3]; Bellin (Small) [3]; Black; Blaeu; Bonne; Bordone; Bowen, E. [2]; Brion De La Tour; Brue; Buache; Burr; Covens & Mortier; Danckerts; De Bry [3]; De Fer (Small) [2]; Desilver; Direccion De Hidrografia; Faden; Gall & Inglis; Gentleman's Magazine; Grierson; Homann [2]; Jansson [3]; Jefferys; Kiepert; Laurie & Whittle; Le Sage; Moll (Small); Ortelius (Folio); Rand, Mcnally & Co.; Rossi, L.; Russell; Thomson; U.S.; Van Keulen; Walch; Weimar Geographisches Institut [4]; Wilkinson; Wyld [2]

— **(MISCELLANEOUS):** Admiralty; De Bry; Homann; Laurie & Whittle; Mercator (Small)

ANTIGUA: Admiralty; Mount & Page

BAHAMA CHANNEL: Direccion De Hidrografia

BAHAMAS: Bellin (Small) [9]; Stanford

BARBADOS: Lucas; Moll (Small) [2]; Morden; Mount & Page

BARBUDA: Admiralty

CARIBBEE ISLANDS: Hondius; Phillips; Van Keulen

CAYMAN ISLANDS: U.S.

CUBA: Bellin (Small); Coello; Direccion De Hidrografia [7]; Jefferys; Lucas; Mount & Page; Wytfliet

— **HAVANA:** Gentleman's Magazine [2]; Homann; Meyer; Mialhe

CUBA & JAMAICA: Mallet; Ptolemy (1561-99 Venice)

DOMINICA: Bowen, T.; Jefferys; Lattre; Lucas

FRENCH ANTILLES: Chatelain

GREATER ANTILLES: Mercator (Small)

GRENADA: Bellin (Large); Jefferys [2]; Lucas

GUADELOUPE: Bonne; Labat; Le Rouge

HISPANIOLA: Bellin (Large) [2]; Bellin (Small) [4]; Bonne; Coronelli; De Vaugondy; Jefferys; Le Rouge; Lucas; Ptolemy (1561-99 Venice); Schroter; Thomson; Van Keulen

JAMAICA: Bachiene; Bellin (Small); Blome; Bonne; Buchon; Coronelli; Depot De La Marine; Fullarton; Lucas; Moll (Small); Morden; Popple; Visscher

JAMAICA, PORT ROYAL: Naval Chronicle

LESSER ANTILLES: Bellin (Large); De Vaugondy; Du Val (Small); Goos; Ottens; Philip, G.; Schreiber; Tardieu; Van Keulen [2]

MARIE GALANTE: Coronelli

MARTINIQUE: Bonne [2]; Buache; Buchon; Depot De La Marine; Homann; Lucas; Willyams, C.
PUERTO RICO: Cram; Norris Peters Co.
ST. KITTS: Bellin (Small); Lopez; Lucas
ST. LUCIA: Bellin (Large); Bellin (Small) [2]; Wyld
ST. MARTIN: **Ogilby**
ST. VINCENT: Philip, G.
TOBAGO: Edwards; Gentleman's Magazine; Lucas; Philip, G.
TRINIDAD: Lucas
TURKS & CAICOS ISLANDS: Bellin (Small) [12]
VIRGIN ISLANDS: Admiralty; Edwards; Stanford

SOUTH AMERICA

SOUTH AMERICA (ALL): Arrowsmith; De Herrera; De L'isle; De Vaugondy; Gebauers, J.; Hondius; Jaillot; Jansson; Jefferys; Levasseur; Lotter; Mercator (Folio); Moll (Large) [2]; Muller; Philip, G.; Ptolemy (1548 Venice) [2]; Ptolemy (1561-99 Venice); Sayer; Scherer; Senex; Seutter (Large); S.D.U.K.; Stieler; Van Linschoten; Wells
— **(NORTH):** D'Anville; Sanson (Small)
— **(SOUTH):** Blaeu; De L'isle [2]; De Wit [2]; Homann
ARGENTINA: Admiralty; Bellin (Small); Meyer; S.D.U.K.; Wytfliet
BOLIVIA: De Herrera
BOLIVIA & PERU: Berghaus, H.; D'Anville; Mitchell, S.A. (Atlas Maps 1859 & Earlier)
BRAZIL: Bellin (Small) [5]; Bertius; Blaeu [2]; De Bry; Dudley; Jansson; La Perouse; Laurie & Whittle; Mallet; Meyer; Monin; Ogilby; Ptolemy (1561-99 Venice); Roussin
BRITISH GUYANA: Fullarton
CHILE: Admiralty [2]; Hondius; Jansson; La Perouse; Tallis
COLOMBIA: Vandermaelen
— **CARTAGENA:** De Bry; De Fer (Small); Toms
FALKLAND ISLANDS: Admiralty
GUIANA: Jansson; Mallet; Tirion; Wilson
MAGELLAN STRAITS & TIERRA DEL FUEGO: Bertius; Cook; De Bry; Jansson; Moll (Small); Morden; Sanson (Small); Sayer & Bennett [2]
PARAGUAY: Bellin (Small); Blaeu; Jansson [2]; Sanson (Folio)
PERU: Admiralty; Bellin (Small) [2]; De Bry; Dudley; Jansson; Meyer
— **LIMA:** Bellin (Small)
VENEZUELA: Fullarton; Jansson [2]; Tallis

OCEANS: ATLANTIC

ATLANTIC OCEAN (ALL): Bowen, E.; Coronelli; Jansson; Moll (Small); Senex; Van Keulen
— **(MISCELLANEOUS):** Astley Magazine; Jansson; S.D.U.K.
— **(NORTH):** Bellin (Small); Bertius; Dudley; Mount & Page; Ortelius (Miniature); Ptolemy (1561-99 Venice); Quad
— **(SOUTH):** Depot De La Marine [2]; Faden; Imray; Van Keulen
— **(WEST):** Goos; Kitchin; Renard [2]; Senex
ASCENSION ISLAND: Laurie & Whittle
AZORES: Admiralty
BERMUDA: Blaeu; Hondius; Jansson; Smith, John
CANARY ISLANDS: Bellin (Small); Laurie & Whittle
CAPE VERDE ISLANDS: Bellin (Small) [2]; Laurie & Whittle; Wales, W.
FALKLAND ISLANDS: Tallis
GREENLAND: Morse, S.
ICELAND: Coronelli; Jansson; Ortelius (Folio) [2]; Royal Geographical Society; Van Der Aa
SOUTH SHETLAND ISLANDS: Admiralty

OCEANS: INDIAN

INDIAN OCEAN (ENTIRE, ISLANDS & MISCELLANEOUS): Allard; Bellin (Large) [2]; D'Apres De Mannevillette [2]; Herbert [2]; Jansson; Laurie & Whittle [2]; Sayer & Bennett
BAY OF BENGAL: Herbert
GULF OF ADEN: Herbert
NICOBAR ISLANDS: D'Apres De Mannevillette
RED SEA: Bellin (Small); D'Apres De Mannevillette; Laurie & Whittle
REUNION ISLAND: Herbert; Mallet
SEYCHELLES: Laurie & Whittle

OCEANS: PACIFIC

PACIFIC OCEAN (ALL): Anson; Bradford; Coronelli [2]; Desilver; Dudley; Goos; Jansson [2]; La Perouse [2]; Marzolla; Mitchell, S.A. (Atlas Maps 1860 & Later); Ortelius (Folio) [2]; Rand, Mcnally & Co.; Renard; S.D.U.K. [2]; Standard Atlas; Tanner; Vuillemin; Wyld
— **(EAST):** Dudley
— **(ISLANDS):** Cassini; Cook; La Perouse; Nicol
— **(MISCELLANEOUS):** Anson; Bellin (Small); Dudley; Hogg; La Harpe; La Perouse
— **(NORTH):** Benard; Cassini; Cook [3]; Dixon; Faden [3]; Von Kotzebue; La Perouse; Lotter; Meares; Muller; Sayer; Zatta [3]
— **(NORTHERN):** Gentleman's Magazine
— **SOUTH):** Whitchurch, W.
— **(WEST):** Herisson; La Perouse; Lapie; Scherer
CHINA SEA: D'Apres De Mannevillette; Herbert
EASTER ISLAND: Cook; La Perouse
GALAPAGOS ISLANDS: Bowen, E.; Colnett; Harris
GUAM: De Bry
HAWAIIAN ISLANDS: La Perouse
MARIANAS ISLANDS: Mallet [2]
MARQUESAS ISLANDS: Cook
NEW ZEALAND: Admiralty; S.D.U.K.; Stanford [2]
PHILIPPINES: Bellin (Large); Bellin (Small) [2]; Bonne; Homann; Kitchin; Langenes; Sayer & Bennett; Stanford; Zatta
SAMOA: La Perouse [2]; U.S. Exploring Expedition
SOCIETY ISLANDS: Cook
SOLOMON ISLANDS: Mallet

MISCELLANEOUS

ALLEGORICAL: Munster
CELESTIAL: Cellarius; De Aefferden; Doppelmayr [3]; Jamieson, A.; Schenk
— **ECLIPSE TRACK:** Sayer
— **SPHERES:** Bion; Seutter (Large)
ISLANDS: Weller
MOUNTAINS & RIVERS: Mitchell, S.A. (Atlas Maps 1859 & Earlier)
ODDITIES: Boynton [2]; Bunting [3]
PARADISE: Anonymous; Bocharti; Scherer
PLAYING CARDS: Morden [8]
PORTRAIT: De Bry; Hondius; La Perouse; Ortelius (Folio) [2]; Speed; Van Linschoten
TITLE PAGE: Bellin (Large); Blaeu [2]; Braun & Hogenberg [2]; Camden; Cellarius; Coronelli; Covens & Mortier; De Fer (Large); De Vaugondy; De Wit; Depot De La Marine; Heylin; Homann; Hondius; Jaillot; Mercator (Folio); Montanus; Mortier; Mount & Page; Ortelius (Folio); Ottens [2]; Porro; Quad; Rossi; Schenk; Scherer; Speed [2]; Tallis; Valentyn; Van Linschoten [3]; Zatta
UNCLASSIFIED: Black; Bunting; Galle; Munster

ORDERING INFORMATION

The *Price Record* and the books described on the next page may be ordered directly from Kimmel Publications. The price of a single copy is **$36.00**, plus shipping (and sales tax in Massachusetts). Libraries and non-profit institutions may deduct ten percent on *prepaid* orders only. Payment by VISA or MasterCard for *single copies only*, may be made through Amherst Antiquarian Maps, P.O. Box 12, Amherst, MA 01004, USA; Fax (413) 256-6291.

Price Record Quantity Discount Schedule

2 copies, 10% discount; **3 or 4 copies,** 25% discount; **5 or more copies**, 30%.

Purchasers may place a standing order: subscribers will receive a 15% discount if payment is made within 30 days of receipt. Special terms are available to dealers who offer the *Price Record* for sale in their catalogs.

Shipping Charges for All Books

	Book Post/Surface Mail		**First Class/Air Mail**	
	First copy	Each additional copy	First copy	Each additional copy
U.S.	$2.00	$1.00	$3.50	$2.00
Canada	3.00	1.00	5.00	2.00
Western Hemisphere	3.00	1.50	7.00	5.00
Europe	3.00	1.50	10.00	9.00
Asia, Africa & Pacific Rim	3.00	1.50	14.00	12.00

United Parcel Service (U.S. only) is $5.00 for first copy and $0.50 for each additional copy. Delivery must be to a street address, not a P.O. box.

Massachusetts residents should add 5% to the merchandise total for Sales Tax.

Available Volumes of *Antique Map Price Record & Handbook*

Volumes 1 through 10, (1983) through (1992), are all o*ut of print*

Volume 11 (1993) ISBN 0-9638100-0-6 *(Current Volume)* $36.00

Order from: **KIMMEL PUBLICATIONS, P.O Box 12, Amherst, MA 01004, USA**
For inquiries: Telephone **(413) 256-8900**, Fax **(413) 256-6291**

Payment should accompany order. Make check payable to *Kimmel Publications*.

Foreign customers should pay by check in U.S. Dollars, payable at a U.S. bank, or postal money order in U.S. dollars. Prices and shipping charges are effective until August 31, 1994.

MAILING LISTS AVAILABLE

Five mailing lists are available from the publisher. These lists do *not* include the names of individuals who have written to order this book. Those names are treated as confidential to protect the privacy of individual customers. The U.S. entries are zip-sorted. The lists are furnished for *one time use* on peelable, self-adhesive labels. One simply peels them off the wax-paper backing and presses them on the envelope. The printing is very high quality, laser printer output.

List 1. ***North American Map Dealers.*** This contains about 300 North American dealers. This list is useful for dealers sending price lists, for publishers selling books, and for collectors offering material for sale. It saves much boring typing, and is kept current. **$40.**

List 2. ***North American Libraries and Institutions with Collections of Early Maps.*** Most of the approximately 900 entries on this list specifically mention the map librarian or the rare book/map department. This list is ideal for publishers selling books on early maps who wish their literature to reach the right person, and is also useful for dealers mailing catalogs. **$85.**

List 3. ***Overseas Map Dealers.*** This contains about 400 names. **$40.**

List 4. ***United Kingdom Libraries and Institutions with Collections of Early Maps.*** Approximately 400 entries. **$45.**

List 5. ***Worldwide Libraries and Institutions with Collections of Early Maps.*** This excludes regions covered by Lists 2 and 4, and includes mostly continental Europe, along with Latin America, Asia, Australia, and Africa. About 250 names. **$30.**

Lists 1 & 3, **World-wide Dealers** (over 700 names) may be ordered together for **$75.00**

List 2, 4 & 5, **World-wide Institutions** (over 1550 names) may be for **$140.00**

All five lists (over 2,250 names) ordered together are **$200.00**.

Prices include postage, first class to the U.S. and Canada, or airmail overseas.

Prices are effective until August 31, 1994.

Order from: **KIMMEL PUBLICATIONS, P.O. Box 12, Amherst, MA 01004**

Payment should accompany order. Make checks payable to Kimmel Publications.

Note for *foreign* customers:Payment should be by check in U.S. dollars, payable at a U.S. bank, or postal money order in U.S. dollars. Unless otherwise requested, "USA" will be added to the United States labels. Other country names are in English.

CUMULATIVE ERRATA

In the 1984 edition:

Cassini, *l'Amerique* . . . , $2200 should read *l'America* . . . , $220.
Gentleman's Magazine, *A Map of the British and French Settlements in North America* . . . should have been listed under General Magazine of Arts & Sciences.

In the 1985 edition:

de Fer, *Le Detroit de Magellan* . . . , $855 should be $85.

In the 1989 edition:

Ellis, *North America* should be *United States*.
The Monthly Itelligence item should appear under Grand Magazine of Magazines.

Before 1992:

London Gazette items should be listed under Gentleman's Magazine.
Monthly Chronologer & Monthly Intelligencer items should be listed under London Magazine.

In the interests of uniformity, some names have been changed.

Old Name	New Name	Date Changed
Reilly	von Reilly	1984
Linschoten	van Linschoten	1986
Chabert	de Chabert	1987
Charlevoix	de Charlevoix	1987
Condamine	de la Condamine	1987
Crevecoeur	de Crevecoeur	1987
Freycinet	de Freycinet	1987
Humboldt	von Humboldt	1987
Schley	van der Schley	1987
Staehlin	von Staehlin	1987
Stulpnagel	von Stulpnagel	1987
Herrera	de Herrera	1988

If errors are noted in any edition, especially in prices, please contact the publisher:

Kimmel Publications, P.O. Box 12, Amherst, MA 01004, USA
Tel. (413) 256-8900 Fax. (413) 256-6291

WARNING!

Users of this work are warned that typographical errors may be present, and that prices for some items may not reflect the price that would be set by a majority of dealers. The publisher disclaims responsibility for any consequences of such errors and anomalies. Price information is given as an approximate guide to market values, and should be used with caution. An expert should always be consulted before making purchases or sales.

CURRENCY CONVERSION TABLE

These exchange rates were in effect at **mid-year 1993**, and were used in the compilation of the price listing.

Country (Unit)	*Value in U.S. Dollars*	*Number per U.S. Dollar*	*Percent change since 1992 edition*
Argentina *(Peso)*	**1.010**	**0.9900**	(new)
Australia *(Dollar)*	**0.7465**	**1.339**	- 2.6
Austria *(Schilling)*	**0.0933**	**10.72**	18.8
Belgium *(Franc)*	**0.0318**	**31.43**	18.6
Brazil *(Cruziero)*	**0.0003**	**3296.**	- 90.9
Canada *(Dollar)*	**0.8335**	**1.200**	- 4.8
Denmark *(Krone)*	**0.1710**	**5.848**	19.3
Europe *(ECU)*	**1.347**	**0.7425**	18.7
Finland *(Mark)*	**0.2410**	**4.149**	3.6
France *(Franc)*	**0.19555**	**5.114**	19.9
Germany *(Mark)**	**0.6568**	**1.523**	19.9
Great Britain *(Pound)**	**1.903**	**0.5254**	18.2
Greece *(Drachma)*	**0.00534**	**185.2**	8.0
Hong Kong *(Dollar)*	**0.1294**	**7.729**	4.0
Ireland *(Punt)*	**1.751**	**0.5712**	20.0
Israel *(Shekel)*	**0.4173**	**2.3964**	- 2.4
Italy *(Lira)*	**0.000868**	**1147.**	17.2
Japan *(Yen)*	**0.00797**	**125.5**	9.9
Mexico *(Peso)*	**0.000320**	**3122.**	- 3.3
Netherlands *(Guilder)*	**0.5833**	**1.714**	19.0
New Zealand *(Dollar)*	**0.5438**	**1.839**	-5.4
Norway *(Krone)*	**0.1679**	**5.960**	18.3
Portugal *(Escudo)*	**0.00789**	**126.8**	24.6
Saudi Arabia *(Riyal)*	**0.2667**	**3.750**	0.0
Singapore *(Dollar)*	**0.6185**	**1.617**	9.5
South Africa *(Rand)*	**0.3618**	**2.764**	4.5
Spain *(Peseta)*	**0.0104**	**96.1**	18.6
Sweden *(Krona)*	**0.1820**	**5.496**	18.8
Switzerland *(Franc)*	**0.7292**	**1.372**	13.7
Venezuela *(Bolivar)*	**0.0150**	**66.5**	- 16.4

* During 1992 the British pound (£) ranged against the U.S. dollar from a high of about $1.93 to a low of $1.51 at years end, or from 2% above down to 21% below the mid-year exchange rate reference level. Accordingly, adjustments should be made in prices converted to sterling or prices that were originally quoted in British pounds. Similarly, the Deutsche Mark ranged from a high of 1.39 down to 1.69 per dollar, or 11% above, to 10% below the mid-year reference point.

CATALOGUE CODES

The numbers below in square brackets correspond to the dealer codes in the main "Price Listing". See the "Directory of Dealers" for a general listing of antiquarian map dealers.

Richard B. Arkway, Inc., 538 Madison Avenue, New York, NY 10022, U.S.A.

[1] Catalogue XXXIX; Fine Antique Maps.

[2] Catalogue XL; Fine Antique Maps and Globes.

Art Source International, 1237 Pearl Street, Boulder, CO 80302

[3] Catalog Number 22; December 1991 Christmas Catalogue; A Selection of Old Maps and Books.

David Bannister, 26 Kings Road, Cheltenham GL5 26B, England

[4] Maps by Jacques Nicolas Bellin [1703-1772]. (prices in sterling)

Roderick M. Barron, 21 Bayham Road, Sevenoaks, Kent TN13 3XD, England

[5] Catalogue 20; Columbus; Autumn-Winter 1992. (prices in sterling)

Cartographic Arts, Luke and Patricia Vavra, P.O. Box 2202, Petersburg, VA 23804

[6] Catalog 6; State and Regional Maps of the United States and Canada.

Cartographics of Vermont, P.O. Box 145, East Middlebury, VT 05740

[7] Occasional List No.11; Americana.

[8] Occasional List No.12; Miscellany.

[9] Occasional List No.15; Vermontiana.

W. J. Faupel, 3 Halsford Lane, East Grinstead, West Sussex RH19 1NY, England

[10] Catalogue 101.

Susanna Fisher, Early Sea Charts, Spencer, Upham, Southampton SO3 1JD, England

[11] Early Sea Charts; List No. 66. (prices in sterling)

Richard Fitch, Old Maps & Prints & Books, 2324 Calle Halcon, Santa Fe, NM 87505

[12] Americana; Catalogue 51; 1992.

Murray Hudson, 109 S. Church St., P.O. Box 163, Halls, TN 38040

[13] Maps of Georgia; September 1992.

[14] Maps of Indiana; October 1992.

Capt. K. S. Kapp, Antiquarian Maps, P.O. Box 64, Osprey, FL 34229, U.S.A.

[15] Catalogue XXVII; The Americas, &c., Maps & Prints.

Antiquariat Kiepert GmbH, Knesebeckstr. 20, 1000 Berlin 12, Germany

[16] America - Graphik und Bucher - August 1992. (prices in Deutsche Mark)

G.B. Manasek, Inc., P. O. Box 1204, Norwich VT, 05055

[17] Mappings 20; Unusual Antique Maps.
[18] Mappings 22; Small and Old.
[19] Mappings; Special Issue, Antique Folding Maps.
[20] Mappings 24; Americas and the World.

Martayan Lan, 48 East 57th Street, New York, NY 10022

[21] Catalogue 7; Fine Antique Maps and Atlases.
[22] Catalogue 10; Fine Antique Maps, Atlases & Globes.

Avril Noble, 2 Southampton St., London WC2E 7HA, England

[23] British Isles: England/Wales: London (prices in sterling)
[24] Ireland. (prices in sterling)
[25] Italy-Sardinia. (prices in sterling)

The Old Map Gallery, Paul F. Mahoney, 1746 Blake Street, Denver, CO 80202

[26] Catalogue #4; Antique Maps and Books; August 1992.

The Old Print Gallery, 1220 31st St. N.W., Washington, DC 20007

[27] Showcase; Vol. XVIII, Number 4, December 1991.
[28] Showcase; Vol. XIX, Number 1, April 1992.
[29] Showcase; Vol. XIX, Number 2, June 1992.
[30] Showcase; Vol. XIX, Number 3, September 1992.

The Philadelphia Print Shop, Ltd., 8441 Germantown Avenue, Philadelphia, PA 19118

[31] Catalogue 1-92; Maps of the World.

Jonathan Potter Ltd., 125 New Bond Street, London W1Y 9AF, England

[32] A Selection of Recent Acquisitions. (prices in sterling)
[33] Choice items from stock. (prices in sterling)

George Ritzlin, Maps & Books, 469 Roger Williams Avenue, Highland Park, IL 60035

[34] Catalog 10.

G. Robinson Old Prints and Maps, 124-D Bent St., Taos, NM 87571

[35] Catalogue #50 - Winter 1991-'92.
[36] Catalogue #53 - Fall, 1992..

Thomas & Ahngsana Suarez, 1146 Irving St., Valley Stream, NY 11580

[37] ESOTERICARTOGRAPHICUM 1992, A Selection of Maps, 1491-1840.
[38] Summer nineteen ninety two.

H. TH. Wenner, Buch- und Kunstantiquariat, Heger Strasse 2 - 3, 4500 Osnabrück, Germany

[39] Stadtansichten Und Landkarten 382. (prices in Deutsche Mark)
[40] Stadtansichten Und Landkarten 384. (prices in Deutsche Mark)